Paul and Mark

Beihefte zur Zeitschrift für die neutestamentliche Wissenschaft

Edited by
James D. G. Dunn, Carl R. Holladay,
Matthias Konradt, Hermann Lichtenberger,
Jens Schröter and Gregory E. Sterling

Volume 198

Paul and Mark

Comparative Essays Part I
Two Authors at the Beginnings of Christianity

Edited by
Oda Wischmeyer, David C. Sim and Ian J. Elmer

DE GRUYTER

ISBN 978-3-11-055267-6
e-ISBN 978-3-11-027282-6
ISSN 0171-6441

Library of Congress Cataloging-in-Publication Data
A CIP catalog record for this book has been applied for at the Library of Congress.

Bibliographic Information published by the Deutsche Nationalbibliothek
The Deutsche Nationalbibliothek lists this publication in the Deutsche Nationalbibliografie; detailed bibliographic data are available in the Internet at http://dnb.dnb.de.

© 2017 Walter de Gruyter GmbH, Berlin/Boston
This volume is text- and page-identical with the hardback published in 2014.
Printing: Hubert & Co. GmbH & Co. KG, Göttingen
♾ Printed on acid-free paper
Printed in Germany

www.degruyter.com

Vorwort / Preface

David Sim und ich wollten eine *klassische Frage der neutestamentlichen Exegese* neu aufnehmen: die These Ferdinand Christian Baurs von einem *markinischen Paulinismus*. Um dies Thema ist es seit Martin Werners Monographie still geworden, gegenwärtig wird die „Paulus – Markus – Beziehung" aber von Exegeten wie Joel Marcus wieder für wichtig und vielversprechend gehalten[1]. Zu diesem Thema legen wir hier eine zweisprachige Sammlung von Aufsätzen vor, die deutschsprachige Beiträge mit englischsprachigen Aufsätzen aus der australischen neutestamentlichen Wissenschaft und mit zwei skandinavischen Beiträgen[2] verbindet und zugleich Beiträge und Sichtweisen älterer und jüngerer Autorinnen und Autoren präsentiert. Ergebnis ist der Band: „Paul and Mark. Comparative Essays Part I: Two Authors at the Beginnings of Christianity." David Sim konnte Ian Elmer als Mitherausgeber gewinnen und so die Bedeutung der Beiträge australischer Exegetinnen und Exegeten unterstreichen. Zusammen mit der Aufsatzsammlung vorwiegend skandinavischer Exegetinnen und Exegeten: „Mark and Paul. Comparative Essays Part II: For and Against Pauline Influence on Mark" findet damit die alte Frage der Tendenzkritik nach der Verbindung frühchristlicher Typen von Theologie mit führenden Gestalten der frühen Gemeinden und nach frühchristlichen „Parteien" eine Fortsetzung unter neuen methodischen und sachlichen Bedingungen und Fragestellungen.

Band I bemüht sich *wissenschaftspolitisch*, angelsächsische und deutschsprachige Sichtweisen und exegetische Literatur miteinander zu vermitteln. Hier besteht ein großer Bedarf an Austausch. Trotz vieler Verbindungen laufen teilweise thematisch ähnliche Untersuchungen unverbunden nebeneinander her. So werden augenblicklich Fragestellungen der Tübinger Schule ganz überwiegend von der angelsächsischen Exegese aufgenommen, ohne dass diese Option von der deutschsprachigen Exegese unter Berücksichtigung der bekannten wissenschaftsgeschichtlichen Kontexte der Werke von Baur und seinen Kollegen angemessen diskutiert wird. Hier ist ein neuer Dialog notwendig[3]. Neutestamentliche Wissenschaft ist seit langem international, und der verlässliche und aktuelle Austausch auch nur zwischen angelsächsischen und deutschsprachigen Forschungsperspektiven und Ergebnissen muss ständig intensiviert werden, zumal das Feld sehr groß ist, die Menge der Beiträge sich nicht leicht bewältigen lässt und

---

[1] Vgl. den Beitrag von J. Marcus in Bd. II.
[2] E.-M. Becker, Aarhus, und J. Svartvik, Lund.
[3] Vgl. jetzt die Beiträge in: Ferdinand Christian Baur und die Geschichte des frühen Christentums, hg. von M. Bauspieß, Ch. Landmesser und D. Lincicum (WUNT), Tübingen 2014.

bestimmte Perspektiven bestimmten Forscher-*communities* näher liegen als andere, ohne dass diese Optionen methodisch offengelegt werden[4]. Band I will mit seiner konsequenten Zweisprachigkeit ein praktisches Modell bieten, wie ein wichtiges Thema der neutestamentlichen Wissenschaft in einer internationalen Dimension behandelt werden kann.

Am Schluss steht der *Dank:* Wir als Herausgebergremium des Bandes freuen uns, nun das Ergebnis unserer Bemühungen vorzulegen. Wir danken allen Autorinnen und Autoren für ihr Interesse an unserm Publikationsprojekt und für ihre Beiträge. Wir danken dem Herausgebergremium von BZNW dafür, dass wir in dieser Reihe publizieren können. Wir danken dem Verlag de Gruyter, vertreten durch Herrn Dr. Albrecht Döhnert, für die stets freundschaftliche Zusammenarbeit. Wir danken Frau Sabina Dabrowski, Frau Sophie Wagenhofer und Herrn Stefan Selbmann für die ebenso professionelle wie freundliche Betreuung der Drucklegung. Die Register für die deutschsprachigen Beiträge hat freundlicherweise Frau cand. phil. et theol. Michaela Durst, Universität Erlangen, erstellt.

Oda Wischmeyer, David C. Sim, Ian J. Elmer   Erlangen, 20.12.2013

---

[4] Das gilt natürlich in viel höherem Maß für die romanischen Sprachen. Hier leistet der Beitrag von Th. Söding wichtige Transferarbeit.

Inhalt / Table of Contents

Vorwort / Preface — V

Oda Wischmeyer
Einführung / Introduction — 1

Teil 1 / Part 1: Forschungsgeschichte / History of Research

Johannes Wischmeyer
Universalismus als Tendenz und Entwicklungsmoment. Die Frage nach Markus und Paulus in der historisch-kritischen Geschichtsschreibung des Urchristentums von 1850 bis 1910 — 19

Teil 2 / Part 2: Historische Fragen / Historical Considerations

Michael P. Theophilos
The Roman Connection: Paul and Mark — 45

David C. Sim
The Family of Jesus and the Disciples of Jesus in Paul and Mark: Taking Sides in the Early Church's Factional Dispute — 73

Teil 3 / Part 3: Theologische Heuristik / Theological Considerations

Nina Irrgang
„Judentum" im Markusevangelium und in den Paulusbriefen. Begriffe, Konzepte und Narrationen — 103

Jesper Svartvik
"East is East and West is West:" The Concept of Torah in Paul and Mark — 157

Florian Wilk
„Die Schriften" bei Markus und Paulus — 189

Elizabeth V. Dowling
"Do this in Remembrance": Last Supper Traditions in Paul and Mark —— 221

Michael Theobald
Die Passion Jesu bei Paulus und Markus —— 243

Udo Schnelle
Paulinische und markinische Christologie im Vergleich —— 283

Andreas Lindemann
Das Evangelium bei Paulus und im Markusevangelium —— 313

Oda Wischmeyer
Konzepte von Zeit bei Paulus und im Markusevangelium —— 361

Eve-Marie Becker
Die Konstruktion von ‚Geschichte'. Paulus und Markus im Vergleich —— 393

William Loader
The Concept of Faith in Paul and Mark —— 423

Thomas Söding
Das Liebesgebot bei Markus und Paulus. Ein literarischer und theologischer Vergleich —— 465

Lorenzo Scornaienchi
Die Relativierung des Unreinen. Der Einfluss des Paulus auf „Markus" in Bezug auf die Reinheit —— 505

John Painter
Mark and the Pauline Mission —— 527

Teil 4 / Part 4: Rezeptionsgeschichte / Reception-History

Alan H. Cadwallader
The Struggle for Paul in the Context of Empire: Mark as a Deutero-Pauline Text —— 557

David C. Sim
The Reception of Paul and Mark in the Gospel of Matthew —— 589

Lukas Bormann
Die Paulusbriefe und das Markusevangelium in der Perspektive des Lukasevangeliums und der Apostelgeschichte —— 617

Wilhelm Pratscher
Die Rezeption von Paulus und Markus bei Johannes —— 647

Ian J. Elmer
Robbing Paul to Pay Peter: The Papias Notice on Mark —— 671

Beiträger und Beiträgerinnen/ List of Contributors —— 699

Autorenregister/Index of Modern Authors —— 701

Sachregister —— 707

Index of Subjects —— 709

Oda Wischmeyer
Einführung / Introduction

1 Paulus und Markus

Mit Paulus und „Markus" stehen zwei Gestalten am Anfang des frühen Christentums, die die folgende frühchristliche Theologie und Literatur entscheidend geprägt haben: Sie waren es, die dem entstehenden Christentum die literarischen und theologischen Grundimpulse gaben und jene theologisch-literarische Dynamik auslösten, die zur Entstehung der deutero- und tritopaulinischen Briefe und der großen synoptischen Evangelien führte. Vergleichende Studien zu Paulus und Markus sind daher zunächst ein Beitrag zur *Geschichte* der Anfänge des Christentums in Gestalt seiner frühen Gemeinden und ihrer Leiter. Gleichzeitig liefern sie Einsichten in die Grundbedingungen frühchristlicher *Literatur* und in die Grundlinien einer neuen Weltinterpretation, die die Basis aller späteren christlichen *Theologie* darstellt.

Wenn der Vergleich zwischen Paulus und Markus gegenwärtig nicht zu den Standardthemen der neutestamentlichen Wissenschaft gehört[1], dann liegt das mindestens zum Teil an Martin Werners Monographie: *Der Einfluß paulinischer Theologie im Markusevangelium (Gießen Töpelmann, 1923)*[2]. Nach Werners Verdikt hat sich so etwas wie ein stillschweigender wissenschaftlicher Konsens darüber hergestellt, dass dies Thema nicht weiterführe[3]. Die Konstruktion eines „Paulinismus", wie sie Ferdinand Christian Baur erarbeitet hatte[4], sowie die Bestreitung eines markinischen „Paulinismus" durch Werner ist differenzierteren Erklärungsmodellen gewichen, die nicht mehr primär von durch „Einflussnahmen" gebildeten theologischen Gruppierungen oder „Parteien" und deren „Einflüssen" ausgehen und damit letzten Endes das von gegensätzlichen Strebungen und theologischen Grundkonflikten geprägte Geschichtsmodell Baurs zugrunde legen, sondern eher das sich in vielfältigen positiven und negativen Beziehungen entwickelnde Netzwerk frühchristlicher Traditionen und Texte, ihrer Autoren, Adressaten und ihres Umfeldes in den Blick nehmen.

---

1 Das Paulus Handbuch, hg. von F.W. Horn, Tübingen 2013, widmet dem Thema eine halbe Seite (M. Konradt, S. 554).
2 Vgl. dazu den Beitrag von H. Omerzu in Bd. II.
3 Das dokumentieren auch die sehr knappen Ausführungen von M. Konradt zum gegenwärtigen Stand der Frage: „Antipaulinismus und Paulinismus im neutestamentlichen Schrifttum", in: Paulus Handbuch, 552–557.
4 Vgl. dazu den Beitrag von J. Wischmeyer im vorliegenden Band.

Nun haben sich in den letzten Jahren zwei unterschiedliche Forschergruppierungen wieder dem Thema „Paulus und Markus" zugewendet. Ihre Untersuchungen erscheinen in zwei Bänden: *Paul and Mark. Comparative Essays Part I: Two Authors at the Beginnings of Christianity (BZNW 198)*, und: *Mark and Paul. Comparative Essays Part II: For and Against Pauline Influence on Mark (BZNW 199)*. Den Ausgangspunkt bildet die Wiederaufnahme der Frage nach dem Paulinismus des Markusevangeliums und damit die Frage nach einem der wichtigsten Stränge der frühesten christlichen Theologie: Wirkte Paulus auf „Markus"? Wo finden wir Spuren dieser Wirkung? Wie sollen wir uns diese Wirkung vorstellen – direkt oder indirekt durch Personen vermittelt, lokal oder traditionsgeschichtlich weitergegeben oder durch eine „Schule" begründet? Gab es eine direkte Kontinuität zwischen den literarisch und theologisch produktiven Vertretern der ersten und zweiten Generation frühchristlicher Gemeindeleiter und Theologen? Wie weit reichten der „Einfluss" oder die „Wirkung" des Paulus? Und umgekehrt: War „Markus" nicht nur in bezug auf die literarische Gattung, sondern auch in seiner Theologie ein Neuanfang?

Der hier vorgelegte Band I geht auf eine Initiative von David Sim zurück, der aufgrund seiner Studien zu Matthäus und Paulus das Thema „Paulus und Markus" in Auseinandersetzung mit Martin Werner neu aufgreifen wollte und mich von der Notwendigkeit einer vertieften Beschäftigung mit dieser Fragestellung *post Werner* überzeugte. David Sim, der selbst zahlreiche Beiträge zur Gemeinde- und Theologiegeschichte des 1. Jahrhunderts verfasst hat[5], geht von der Arbeitshypothese aus, dass zwischen Paulus und „Markus" ein Zusammenhang bestehe, der historisch und thematisch-theologisch neu zu kartographieren sei. Dazu passte, dass in dem von mir in Zusammenarbeit mit Lorenzo Scornaienchi herausgegebenen Band zur frühchristlichen Polemik[6] zu dieser Frage bereits verschiedene Ergebnisse vor allem aus der Perspektive literarischer Polemik vorgelegt worden sind. Damit sind wichtige Voraussetzungen für das Zustandekommen von *Paul and Mark. Comparative Essays Part I.* genannt: Es geht um die Gewinnung neuer Fragestellungen und Ergebnisse zu einem klassischen Thema der frühesten christlichen Gemeinde- und Theologiegeschichte.

Der zweite Band: *Mark and Paul. Comparative Essays Part II: For and Against Pauline Influence on Mark*[7] ist das Ergebnis zweier Konferenzen der Universitäten

---

5 Vgl. die bibliographischen Angaben in Sims Beiträgen im vorliegenden Band. Vgl. besonders seinen Beitrag über „Polemical Strategies in the Gospel of Matthew", in: Polemik in der frühchristlichen Literatur. Texte und Kontexte, herausgegeben von O. Wischmeyer/L. Scornaienchi (BZNW 170), Berlin 2011, 491–515.
6 S.o. Anm. 5.
7 Ed. by E.-M. Becker, T. Engberg-Pedersen and M. Müller (BZNW 199), Berlin/Boston 2014.

von Aarhus und Kopenhagen zu demselben Thema. Die dänischen Neutestamentler/innen kamen ebenfalls zu dem Urteil, die Paulus-Markus-Verbindung müsse neu diskutiert werden. Hier sind Beiträge aus der skandinavischen Welt, den Vereinigten Staaten und Deutschland zusammengestellt, wieder im Zusammenspiel erfahrener Exegeten mit jungen Wissenschaftlerinnen und Wissenschaftlern. Den Ausgangspunkt für Band II bildete die Frage nach dem „Gospel – Letter – Divide" und der Weiterentwicklung und möglichen Überwindung einer bloßen Dichotomie der Genres: „*Beyond* the Gospel – Letter Divide". Daher stehen in Band II literaturwissenschaftliche, motivgeschichtliche und exegetische Untersuchungen im Vordergrund.

Beide Bände wurden unabhängig voneinander konzipiert[8] und haben unterschiedliche Schwerpunkte. Teils ergänzen sich die Perspektiven, teils führen thematisch ähnliche Beiträge zu sehr unterschiedlichen Lösungen[9]. Ihre gleichzeitige Entstehung nehmen wir als ein Zeichen dafür, dass unsere Fragestellung „an der Zeit ist". Gemeinsam gelesen, können beide Bände die gegenwärtigen methodischen und thematischen Zugänge zu einer klassischen Fragestellung der neutestamentlichen Wissenschaft dokumentieren und neue Möglichkeiten der Beschäftigung mit den Anfangsschriften des frühesten Christentums eröffnen.

2 Einführung in Band I

Der vorliegende Band beginnt nach der Forschungsgeschichte (Teil I) mit den vergleichenden historischen, d.h. gemeindegeschichtlichen Beiträgen (Teil II). Dabei wird auf Ansätze von F.Ch. Baur zur Differenzierung der frühchristlichen Gemeindetypen zurückgegriffen. Im Zentrum des Bandes (Teil III) steht dann der Vergleich der Theologien, die auf ihre Eigenart sowie ihre möglichen Interdependenzen befragt werden. Den Abschluss (Teil IV) bilden die wieder stärker historisch fokussierten Beiträge zur innerneutestamentlichen Rezeptionsgeschichte sowie zu Papias. Band I arbeitet also mit einer Verbindung gemeindegeschichtlicher, theologischer und rezeptionsgeschichtlicher Fragestellungen. Verschiedene analoge Untersuchungen zur Aufhellung des Beziehungsgeflechts zwischen Personen, Gemeinden, Schriften und theologischen Linien sind in den letzten Jahren erschienen[10]. So findet die Interpretation des Matthäusevangeliums

---

[8] E.-M. Becker und ich haben an der Kopenhagen-Konferenz teilgenommen und Beiträge für beide Bände verfasst.
[9] Vgl. die Beiträge von A. Lindemann in Bd. I und G. Theissen in Bd. II zu *euaggélion*.
[10] Vgl. nur: Mark and Matthew I, Comparative Readings: Understanding the Earliest Gospels in their First-Century Settings, ed. by E.-M. Becker/A. Runesson (WUNT 271), Tübingen 2011; Mark

seit langem im Fadenkreuz der Interpretation von Paulus einerseits – hier geht es um die klassischen Begriffe von ‚Paulinismus' und ‚Antipaulinismus' – und dem Markusevangelium andererseits – unter der kontrovers diskutierten Fragestellung „What was Mark for Matthew?"[11] – statt. Von der anderen Seite her stellt sich immer wieder die Frage, wie das Verhältnis des Paulus zu den synoptischen Evangelien und den in ihnen aufbewahrten und bearbeiteten Jesusüberlieferungen zu bestimmen sei[12].

Besondere Aufmerksamkeit wird im vorliegenden ersten Band den Grundlinien dessen, was später als christliche Theologie bezeichnet werden sollte, entgegengebracht. Diese Theologie entstand in der doppelten Anfangsgestalt narrativer und argumentativer Auslegung des *euaggélion Jesou Christou im kairós* für die Zeitgenossen. Dabei wird in der Literatur allgemein das Evangelium als zentrales Konzept bei Paulus und im Markusevangelium genannt[13]. Der Vergleich zwischen dem Verständnis des *euaggélion Jesou Christou* bei Paulus und bei Markus stellt daher auch einen zentralen Aspekt des vorliegenden Bandes dar[14], denn in den beiden unterschiedlichen Konzeptionen von *euaggélion* ist die ganze Breite der Möglichkeiten späterer christlicher Rede von Jesus Christus, d. h. die Christologie zwischen Jesuserzählung und Lehre von der Gottessohnschaft, ebenso angelegt wie das gemeinsame Fundament der späteren Theologien benannt. Der Vergleich der theologischen Konzepte entspricht der Eigenart der Paulusbriefe und des Markusevangeliums, sachlich die Verkündigung des *euaggélion* in den Mittelpunkt zu stellen. Der theologische Vergleich wird in vier Ansätzen unternommen: *erstens* von den Grundlagen beider zu vergleichender Theologien aus: dem „Judentum" (*ioudaismós*), der Tora und den „Schriften", *zweitens* im Vergleich der Christologien, *drittens* im Vergleich der zentralen theologischen Konzepte, die sich bei Paulus *und* „Markus" finden: Evangelium, Zeit, Geschichte, Glaube, Liebe, sowie *viertens* für zwei Themen, die Paulus und

---

and Matthew II, Comparative Readings: Reception History, Cultural Hermeneutics, and Theology, ed. by E.-M. Becker/A. Runesson (WUNT 304), Tübingen, 2013.
11 So der Titel von: J.A. Doole, What Was Mark for Matthew? (WUNT 2.R. 344), Tübingen 2013.
12 Dazu zuletzt: E.K.C. Wong, Evangelien im Dialog mit Paulus. Eine intertextuelle Studie zu den Synoptikern (NTOA/SUNT 89), Göttingen/Oakville CT, 2012.
13 Bei Konradt, Paulus Handbuch, 554, fehlt dieser Begriff. Er nennt dagegen den Tod Jesu (s. im vorliegenden Band den Beitrag von M. Theobald), den Reinheitstopos (s. im vorliegenden Band den Beitrag von L. Scornaienchi), die Heidenmission (s. im vorliegenden Band den Beitrag von J. Painter) sowie die Zeichnung der Rolle von Jesu Familie und die Stellung der Jünger (s. im vorliegenden Band den Beitrag von D. Sim).
14 S. den Beitrag von A. Lindemann im vorliegenden Band. Vgl. auch den Beitrag von G. Theissen in Bd. II, der zu deutlich anderen Ergebnissen kommt.

der Verfasser des Markusevangeliums gleichermaßen für ebenso neu wie notwendig halten: ein neues Reinheitsverständnis und die sog. Heidenmission.

3 Der *Vergleich:* Ergebnisse und neue Aufgaben

Den Rahmen der genannten Einzeluntersuchungen bilden die Paulusbriefe und das Markusevangelium *im Vergleich*. Was aber soll verglichen werden, und *wie* soll verglichen werden? Die Antworten, die in Band I gegeben werden, sind kontrovers. In einem nicht geringen Teil der Beiträge dieses Bandes wird die historische Frage nach „Abhängigkeiten" und „Einflüssen" in ihren Ergebnissen bezweifelt. Welche Ergebnisse lassen sich dann dem Vergleich entnehmen? Im Folgenden fasse ich zunächst einige wichtige Ergebnisse der Beiträge von Band I zusammen und werde daran Überlegungen zu Fragestellungen „Beyond Paul und Mark", die sich aus beiden vorliegenden Bänden ergeben, anschließen.

3.1 Ergebnisse

Die Aufsätze setzen unterschiedliche Akzente. Während die englischsprachigen Beiträge überwiegend die teils als kompetitiv, teils als antagonistisch interpretierte Welt frühchristlicher Gemeinden und Führungsgestalten und ihrer Theologien *post Baur et Werner* neu rekonstruieren und die bleibende Notwendigkeit der historischen Frage für den Übergang von der ersten zur zweiten frühchristlichen Generation und ihrer leitenden Personen und Theologien demonstrieren, bleiben die deutschsprachigen Aufsätze demgegenüber großenteils skeptisch und öffnen stattdessen den Blick für literarische und theologische Strukturvergleiche. Beide Sichtweisen sind notwendig und ergänzen einander, denn die Theologien der Paulusbriefe und des Markusevangeliums sind Teil der Erfahrungen ihrer Autoren mit den Gemeinden, in denen sie lebten und die sie leiteten oder deren Führungsmitglieder sie waren, und nicht ohne diese Gemeindebezüge vorstellbar.

In der Einführung in die Forschungsgeschichte zwischen Baur und Werner stellt zunächst Johannes Wischmeyer die große Breite der Möglichkeiten historistisch geprägter Fragestellungen und Voten der führenden deutschsprachigen Exegeten aus der 2. Hälfte des 19. Jahrhunderts zum Thema dar. Der Beitrag ruft ins – teilweise sehr kurze – exegetische Gedächtnis, dass die Fragestellung beider Bände zu Paulus und „Markus" nicht erst mit Martin Werner beginnt, sondern Werner selbst auf eine lange Forschungsgeschichte zurückblickt, in der bereits alle historischen Lösungsmöglichkeiten durchgespielt wurden, so dass nur methodische Neuansätze zu neuen Lösungen führen konnten und können. Das Ende des tendenzkritischen Modells um ca. 1900 lässt sich als Voraussetzung von Werners Monographie verstehen, die *post festum* einen vorläufigen Schlussstrich unter die Fragestellung „Paulus und Markus" zog[15].

Zwei einschlägige gemeindegeschichtliche Fragestellungen eröffnen dann die thematische Agenda des Bandes: die Beziehungen von Paulus und „Markus" zu Rom (M.P. Theophilos) und die Sicht von Paulus und „Markus" auf die Familie Jesu und auf seine Jünger (D.C. Sim). Michael Theophilos findet eine Reihe wichtiger Analogien zwischen dem Römerbrief und dem Markusevangelium und bescheinigt dem Evangelium „a distinctive Pauline perspective" – mit Ausnahme der Rolle der Jüngerschaft. Dort sieht er „radical discontinuity between Romans and Mark". Eben Letzteres behandelt David Sim und kommt für diesen Punkt zu einem anders gewichtenden Ergebnis. Er findet bei Berücksichtigung der unterschiedlichen historischen Situationen des „Markus" gegenüber Paulus doch „a significant agreement between Mark and Paul in terms of the depictions of Jesus' family and his disciples" und verortet von daher „Markus" deutlich in der theologischen Nachfolge des Paulus.

Die folgenden drei Beiträge nähern sich mit sehr unterschiedlichen Fragestellungen dem Thema „Judentum" bei Paulus und „Markus". Nina Irrgang interpretiert das Markusevangelium als religiöse Erzählung und wählt ihren Zugang von der Erzähltheorie her. Sie zeichnet die „große Erzählung vom Judentum" nach, in die „Markus" seinen Protagonisten Jesus stellt. Paulus dagegen zeichnet sich selbst in die Erzählung vom Judentum ein und verändert diese gleichzeitig von seinen Erfahrungen her anthropologisch. Das führt nach Irrgang zu einem neuen theologisch-anthropologischen Verständnis von Israel und dem Judentum jenseits bloßer ethnischer Zugehörigkeit. Jesper Svartvik setzt bei dem wichtigsten und exegetisch heiß umstrittenen jüdischen Theologumenon an, wenn er die Position von Paulus und „Markus" zum „Gesetz" vergleicht. Er kommt zu folgendem Ergebnis: „We have shown that the relationship between Jews and Gentiles is a key issue for both Paul and Mark. We are inclined to argue that both Paul and Mark believed that the Torah continued to be relevant to Jews, at the same time as it remained a non-option for Gentiles. Both also believed that Gentile Christians should remain what they are and not adhere to Jewish *halakhah* – not because *halakhah* would be wrong for everyone, but simply because it is right for Jews". Florian Wilk fragt in einer detaillierten Dokumentation nach dem Umgang von Paulus und „Markus" mit der „Schrift". Während Svartvik und Irrgang den strukturellen Vergleich bevorzugen, d. h. von unterschiedlichen Themen her die gemeinsame jüdische Grundlage beider Autoren ausleuchten, kommt Wilk zu

---

15 Vgl. H. Omerzu in Bd. II.

einem historisch grundierten Fazit, wenn er eine gemeinsame syrische Tradition hinter dem Schriftgebrauch beider Autoren vermutet.

Drei Beiträge gelten den christologischen Konzepten beider Autoren. Elizabeth Dowling untersucht die Abendmahlsberichte bei Paulus und „Markus" und kommt zu einem vorsichtigen traditionsgeschichtlichen Urteil: „While the differences between the two Last Supper rituals raise doubts about Mark's direct use of Paul, it would seem that Mark is at least familiar with a similar Last Supper tradition to that used by Paul." Michael Theobalds gründlicher Vergleich von paulinischem und markinischem Passionsbericht führt zu einem eher noch zurückhaltenderen Ergebnis. Dass Paulus eine Vorform der markinischen Passionserzählung gekannt habe, lässt sich nach Theobald nicht wahrscheinlich machen. Wichtiger ist ihm folgende Überlegung: „Grundsätzlich bieten die hier gebotenen Überlegungen ein Lehrstück für die Frage, wie sich die *narrative* Überlieferung und die der *Glaubensformeln* samt ihrer theologischen Entfaltung – zwei recht unterschiedliche Gestalten frühchristlicher Traditionsbildung – zueinander verhalten. Dass die Passions- und Ostererzählung das „Credo" von 1Kor 15,3b–5a nicht einfach narrativ entfaltet, sollte hier deutlich geworden sein." Udo Schnelle führt durch alle wichtigen Aspekte der paulinischen und markinischen Christologie und formuliert abschließend: „Auch wenn eine direkte Bezugnahme auf paulinische Briefe durch Markus nicht nachzuweisen ist, legt sich aus den genannten Übereinstimmungen eine Kenntnis und eigenständige Verarbeitung paulinischer Gedanken durch den ältesten Evangelisten nahe. Sie könnte in Rom erfolgt sein, wo beide mit einem nicht allzu großen zeitlichen Abstand wirkten und Markus seine Kenntnis paulinischer Theologie wahrscheinlich erwarb."

Die fünf Beiträge zu theologischen Konzepten, die bei Paulus und „Markus" deutlich hervortreten, setzen unterschiedliche Schwerpunkte. Andreas Lindemann legt den Fokus auf eine eingehende semantische Analyse: *euaggélion* hat bei Paulus und „Markus" eine vergleichbare Bedeutung, während der Bezugsradius differiert. Eine direkte literarische Abhängigkeit möchte Lindemann nicht annehmen. Die Zeit erweist sich im Anschluss an *euaggélion* als eine der großen theologischen vergleichenden Erschließungskategorien. Den differierenden Bezugsrahmen für das *euaggélion*, nämlich einerseits die Zeit seit Jesu Auferweckung und andererseits die Zeit der Wirksamkeit Jesu bis zu seinem Tod, zeichnet Oda Wischmeyer nach. Gerade in der Zeitinterpretation werden die Unterschiede in den theologischen Interessen und den christologischen Schwerpunkten zwischen Paulus und „Markus" deutlich. Erst „Markus" interpretiert die Zeit des Wirkens Jesu über dessen bloßes „Gekommensein" hinaus als Zeit des *euaggélion* und erschließt damit die Jesustradition als inhaltlichen Teil des *euaggélions*. Der Unterschied liegt nicht einfach in den *genres*, sondern die neue Gattung des Evangeliums ist Ausdruck eines neuen christologischen Zeitverständnisses bei „Markus". Eve-Marie Becker behandelt das verwandte, konkretere Thema der Geschichte. Sie findet einerseits nicht erst bei „Markus", sondern schon bei Paulus eine theologisch-historische Dimension: „Beide erzählen über Vergangenes deutend". Andererseits unterscheiden sich „die paulinische und die markinische Geschichtskonstruktion ... im Blick auf den Gegenstandsbereich und die Personenbindung der Erzählung" – ein Ergebnis, dass den Beitrag zur Zeit bestätigt und literarisch und theologisch vertieft.

William Loader betont einerseits die enge thematische Verbindung und den ähnlichen Stellenwert von *pístis* bei Paulus und „Markus" und ihre Beziehung zu den Fragen nach der Bedeutung des Gesetzes in heidenchristlichen Gemeinden, kommt aber andererseits zu dem Urteil: „Mark cannot be seen as simply a more radical Paulinist. The common ground suggests a Christian group within the diverse mix of evolving Christian communities, which had also needed to deal with inclusion of Gentiles by addressing issues of Law, but in its self-understanding and primitive concept of faith was much more closely aligned with what appears to have been the message and mission of the historical Jesus, which it therefore seeks to re-present." Thomas Söding entwirft ein ebenfalls sehr differenziertes Bild von „Liebe" bei Paulus und Markus. Während er bei „Markus" keine direkte literarische Abhängigkeit von Paulus sehen kann, betont er doch die große grundsätzliche Nähe der beiden frühesten christlichen Autoren in Bezug auf die zentrale Rolle des Liebesgebotes und macht deutlich, dass diese Option für die *agápe* nicht selbstverständlich ist, sondern Ausdruck der „große(n) Übereinstimmung zwischen der paulinischen und der markinischen Ethik". Für Söding „vertieft sich [dadurch] der Eindruck, dass das Neue Testament eine – in sich vielschichtige – Einheit darstellt".

Lorenzo Scornaienchi fragt nach dem Konzept von Reinheit bei Paulus und „Markus" und zieht ein vorsichtiges Fazit: „Man kann ... feststellen, dass die Position des Markus durchaus ihren Platz auf der Geraden zwischen Paulus und dem Autor des Titusbriefes, dessen späterem Schüler, findet". Einen direkten „Paulinismus" sieht Scornaienchi in Mk 7 nicht. Er schlägt vielmehr eine traditionsgeschichtliche Lösung vor, wenn er vermutet, „dass Paulus *dieselbe Tradition* verwendet, die in Mk 7 dokumentiert ist", d. h. sich auf ein Jesuslogion bezieht, ohne es zu nennen. John Painter widmet sich der historischen Frage nach der Heidenmission bei Paulus und „Markus". Sein Interesse liegt bei der Nachzeichnung der komplizierten Verhältnisse in den frühen Gemeinden. Sein Interesse ist, „only to show that Mark was both shaped by and provided a basis for the Pauline mission to the nations." Dabei musste „Markus" das Verhalten Jesu berücksichtigen: „[He] has retained the perspective of the mission of the historical Jesus to Israel in a restoration and renewal movement. At the same time, there are aspects of the Marcan account that press in a direction that seems to lessen the shock of the Pauline Law-free mission to the nations".

Die historische Frage wird unter dem Stichwort „Rezeptionsgeschichte" in den fünf abschließenden Beiträgen wieder aufgenommen. Allan Cadwalladar setzt bei der augusteischen Familienpolitik an und vergleicht die gegenüber Paulus restaurative Haustafelethik des Kolosserbriefs mit „Markus". Er kommt zu dem Ergebnis, dass die konservative Ethik des Kolosserbriefs der Gefährdung der jungen Christengemeinden und -haushalte durch das *imperium* Rechnung trägt und analog zu den herrschenden Vorstellungen der frühen Kaiserzeit patriarchale Züge entwickelt, während das Markusevangelium die nicht-patriarchale paulinische Familienmetaphorik weiterführt: „Mark could not extract the household code from its imperial hold. Accordingly Paul's references to community and his metaphorical use of familial language became, in the second Gospel, the warrant for a major critique of the household code, part of the apparatus of an empire against which the early followers of Jesus (and Paul) were pitted." David Sim sieht auf Paulus und „Markus" aus der Perspektive des „Matthäus" zurück. Sein Ergebnis: „Matthew's reception of Paul and Mark is ... characterised by mutual hostility towards these texts. Standing within the Christian Jewish and Law-observant tradition of the Jerusalem church, Matthew viewed the Pauline gospel and epistles and the Pauline-influenced Gospel of Mark, as requiring substantial correction and critique. The Gospel of Matthew therefore stands as a clearly anti-Pauline document, not simply criticising Paul and his errant theology but also critiquing and emending the original Gospel that was so closely tied in with Paul's Law-free theology". Lukas Bormann untersucht beide Autoren aus der lukanischen Perspektive. Er versteht Lukas als eigenständigen Theologen und Schriftsteller, der – erstaunlich genug für den Verfasser einer ersten Missionsbiographie, in deren zweitem Teil Paulus im Mittelpunkt steht – seinen eigenen Weg jenseits paulinischer Theologie und antipaulinischen Standpunkten ging und den „weder die narrative Theologie des Markusevangeliums noch die begrifflich dialektische Theologie des Paulus ... erkennbar beeinflusst [haben]. Da Lukas aber wohl doch mit beiden vertraut war, wird man schließen können, dass ihn weder die Theologie des Markus noch die des Paulus überzeugen konnte". Für die johanneische Literatur kommt Wilhelm Pratscher nach detaillierter Einzelanalyse zu folgendem Urteil: „Zwischen Paulus und Markus einerseits und Johannes andererseits bestehen enge sachliche Parallelen. Die Relation von Gemeinsamkeiten und Differenziertheit ist aber dergestalt, dass eine literarische Benützung nicht nachweisbar ist. Die Beziehungen sind am ehesten durch die Annahme sekundärer Oralität zu erklären".

Der Band wird mit dem Beitrag von Ian Elmer zu Papias abgeschlossen. Elmer verortet Papias in der judenchristlichen Tradition und vermutet folgende Gründe hinter der Zuschreibung des Markusevangeliums zur petrinischen Tradition: „The ascription of Mark to Peter served not only to defend Mark against accusation of inadequate order and inept style *via* an appeal to apostolic authority, but also to provide a literary bolster to the legacy of Peter as a bulwark against the increasingly dominant *Paulusbild* of the second century". Damit hätte Papias 1900 Jahre vor Werner schon einmal vergeblich versucht, das Kapitel „Paulus und Markus" zu beenden.

Im Rückblick wird das Spektrum möglicher Verstehens- und Erklärungsmodelle deutlich, mit denen die Autorinnen und Autoren das Thema „Paulus und Markus" behandelt haben. Die historische Rekonstruktion divergierender persönlicher Beziehungen und theologischer Strömungen bzw. Optionen steht neben dem Vergleich theologischer Konzepte oder *frames* (L. Bormann). Der Blick kann eher auf die Texte selbst, ihre Argumentation und ihre literarische Struktur gerichtet werden oder auf die theologischen Überzeugungen und historischen Gegebenheiten hinter den Texten. Alle Beiträge aber gehen von einer besonderen sachlichen Nähe zwischen wichtigen Aspekten bei Paulus und „Markus" aus, und alle Beiträge kommen durch konsequent durchgeführte Vergleiche zu neuen Ergebnissen für die einzelnen Paulustexte und das Markusevangelium.

Ob hier dann Paulinismus oder Antipaulinismus diagnostiziert wird, hängt von den methodischen Rahmenbedingungen ab, die die einzelnen Autorinnen und Autoren wählen, sowie von dem Grad historischer Konkretion und Eindeutigkeit, die die Exegeten erzielen wollen. Dass es in der ersten und zweiten frühchristlichen Generation verschiedene Richtungen gab, ist angesichts der Paulusbriefe evident. Dass Paulus diese als Parteien verstand und kritisierte, ist nach dem 1. Korintherbrief ebenfalls unstrittig. Dort fällt auch sein eigener Name im Sinne einer Parteidevise. 1Kor 1,12 könnte die Textbasis für so etwas wie eine Pauluspartei, aus der ein „Paulinismus" hervorgegangen wäre, abgeben. Hier ist aber alles umstritten, und die Tatsache, dass außer im Galaterbrief auch keine Jakobuspartei greifbar wird, lässt es fraglich erscheinen, ob „Paulinismus und „Antipaulinismus" adäquate Begriffe für Positionen darstellen, die von Jakobus und anderen Gemeindeführern und ihren Gesandten vertreten wurden. Der Begriff „Paulinismus" selbst begegnet nicht – anders als *ioudaismós*, auch nicht im Jakobusbrief. Im Sinne eines strukturellen Vergleichs theologischer Positionen kann er sich aber auch ohne die Hegelsche Geschichtsphilosophie, der Baur verpflichtet ist, in wichtigen Beiträgen dieses Bandes behaupten.

3.2 Perspektiven

(1) Den Ausgangspunkt für Untersuchungen zu „Paulus und Markus" stellt das historische, biographische und theologische Interesse an den *beiden ersten literarisch tätigen Gestalten des entstehenden Christentums* in ihrer faszinierenden Unähnlichkeit dar: hier der uns autobiographisch und biographisch sehr präsente *Paulos*, der nach den Informationen der Apostelgeschichte ursprünglich den gräzisierten jüdischen Königsnamen *Saulos* trug, dort der für uns vielleicht namenlose, vielleicht *Markos* heißende Verfasser des Markusevangeliums, dessen Profil wir nur in einigen Grundzügen, und auch das nur sehr kontrovers, aus seinem Buch rekonstruieren können. Über die historische Beziehung beider Männer zueinander – sei sie persönlich gewesen oder als spätere Kenntnis- und Bezugnahme von „Markus" vorzustellen – wissen wir nichts: Im Markusevangelium finden die Jünger, nicht aber Paulus Erwähnung. Das gilt dann auch für die späteren Evangelien – und das, obgleich mindestens Lukas auf der Nahtstelle zwischen seinem Evangelium und der Apostelgeschichte Paulus noch in die „Ostergeschichten" hätte einführen können. Sein ganz anderes Erzählkonzept zeigt, dass Paulus nicht nur nicht von „Markus", sondern nicht einmal von „Lukas" als dem Schriftsteller, der eine Art Missionsbiographie über ihn schreibt, in Verbindung mit den Evangelien, und das heißt: mit den Aposteln als Jesu Jüngern, gebracht wird. Dem entspricht die spätere Rubrizierung der Schriften des Neuen Testaments in die beiden Abteilungen: „der *kyrios*" und „der *apóstolos*". Die Evangelien als Jesusbücher sind den Briefen als – bloßen – Apostelschreiben vorgeordnet, wobei aber Paulus innerhalb des Briefteils seine dominierende Stellung behält. Aber: auch die Kirchenschriftsteller schweigen über mögliche Beziehungen zwischen Paulus und Markus – im Gegenteil: Seit Papias ist Petrus, nicht Paulus, mit dem Markusevangelium verbunden[16]. Es gibt also keinen Weg von Paulus zu „Markus" oder „Markus" zu Paulus über die Quellen im historischen Sinn. Wir wissen nichts darüber, ob und was „Markus" über Paulus wusste und ob und wie Paulus auf „Markus" wirkte. Und außerdem wissen wir nicht, ob es einen Markus als Verfasser des Markusevangeliums gegeben hat und, wenn es so gewesen wäre, wer dieser Markus war.

So führt der Weg über das Evangelium und die Briefe, also über die Texte und ihre Autoren. Bei Paulus und „Markus" handelt es sich um Autoren, und zwar die ersten Autoren der neuen christusgläubigen Gemeinden zwischen Jerusalem und Rom. Beide schreiben Griechisch, beide stammen aus städtischem Milieu und lassen sich – ebenso wie ihre Adressatenschaft – in der östlichen, Griechisch

---

16 Vgl. den Beitrag von I. Elmer im vorliegenden Band.

sprechenden Hälfte des *imperium Romanum* im 1. Jahrhundert n. Chr. verorten[17]. Beide gehen von der jüdischen Rechts-, Staats- und Religionsurkunde, der Heiligen Schrift des „Gesetzes", aus, die sie in Gestalt der Septuaginta benutzen. Beide verstehen den Kosmos und die Menschheit von dem einen Gott, dem Gott Israels, her, dessen Handeln an den Menschen sie im Lichte des Evangeliums von Jesus Christus, dem Sohn Gottes[18], neu interpretieren[19]. Paulus ist ethnisch und religiös Jude und setzt sich ausführlich mit seiner Zugehörigkeit zum Judentum auseinander. Über die Frage, ob „Markus" Juden- oder Heidenchrist[20] gewesen sei, wissen wir nichts Genaues. Immerhin verwendet er die Septuaginta so sicher und klug, dass wir mindestens eine große Nähe zum Judentum bei ihm voraussetzen müssen. Beide Schriftsteller haben nicht nur raschen, sondern auch anhaltenden Erfolg bei ihren Gemeinden. Sonst wären ihre Schriften, die trotz ihrer grundlegenden Bedeutung den Charakter des Neuen, Situationsbezogenen, Skizzenhaften und Unfertigen tragen, nicht neben den späteren, stärker durchgearbeiteten Schüler- und Nachfolgerschriften der Deutero- und Tritopaulinen und der späteren „großen" Evangelien erhalten geblieben[21]. Wichtige theologische Grundimpulse – in diesem Band als „theologische Konzepte" bezeichnet – werden in den Folgeschriften verändert, abgeschwächt oder auch fallengelassen. Diese Veränderungsprozesse sichern den Anfangsschriften, den Paulusbriefen und dem Markusevangelium, ihre historisch wie theologisch grundlegende und bleibende Bedeutung. Gerade die hier gesammelten Studien zu den *theologischen Konzepten* zeigen, dass zentrale paulinische und markinische Theologumena nicht in die späteren frühchristlichen Schriften aufgenommen wurden. Sie waren bereits in der Anfangsliteratur formuliert und entfalteten von dorther ihre Wirkung.

Für die Autoren gilt: Während Paulus ein hohes Selbstbewusstsein und eine fast analogielose Vorstellung von der Bedeutung seiner Person hat, die ungeachtet eigener, neuer Interpretationen grundsätzlich von seinen Schülern übernommen wurde[22], hält Markus seine Person vollständig verborgen. Über eine Schule des

---

17 Rom ist hier als die Stadt mit den lebhaftesten Beziehungen zur östlichen, griechischsprachigen Reichshälfte eingeschlossen.
18 Röm 1,1–4 und Mk 1,1. Vgl. dazu den Beitrag von O. Wischmeyer in Bd. II.
19 Hier liegt nach wie vor das theologische Fundament eines Vergleichs zwischen Paulus und Markus.
20 Die Nützlichkeit dieser Unterscheidung ist zweifelhaft.
21 Darauf weist – gegenüber prononcierten Ersetzungstheorien (D. Sim) – für „Markus" vor allem Doole, What was Mark for Matthew?, hin.
22 Zum Begriff der Paulusschule vgl. die ausgewogene Skizze von J. Herzer: Die Paulusschule und die theologische Entwicklung in den deuteropaulinischen Briefen, in: Paulus Handbuch, 520–523.

„Markus" wissen wir nichts. Sicher waren die Autoren des Matthäus- und des Lukasevangeliums keine Markusschüler[23].

Analoges gilt für das Missverhältnis zwischen dem lebendigen historischen und sozialgeschichtlichen Bild, das wir von den Gemeinden, mit denen Paulus verbunden war, haben, und der völligen Ungewissheit über eine spezielle Gemeindezugehörigkeit oder auch nur eine Beziehung zu einer oder mehreren Gemeinden bei „Markus" – was das Markusevangelium mit dem Lukasevangelium verbindet[24]. Trotzdem bringt gerade hier ein Vergleich wichtige Einsichten: Paulus und „Markus" schreiben für griechischsprachige Mitglieder christusgläubiger Gemeinden zwischen Jerusalem und Rom. Es ist die theologische Leistung – oder vielleicht auch nur Absicht – des Paulus, eine einheitliche Gemeindetheologie und -ethik für die neu entstehende christusgläubige Welt der Gemeinden im *imperium Romanum* zu schaffen. Und es ist die – historisch gesehen modernere – theologisch-literarische Leistung des Markus, diesen Gemeinden ein Jesusbuch zu geben. Weder Paulus noch Markus entwerfen Theologie argumentativen und narrativen Formats lediglich für bestimmte Gemeinden[25]. Das Matthäus- und das Johannesevangelium haben dagegen eine deutlichere Beziehung zu „ihren" spezifischen Gemeinden – wie auch immer diese im Einzelnen in der exegetischen Forschung rekonstruiert werden. Trotzdem hat gerade die eher kurze erzählende Schrift, die wir als „Markusevangelium" kennen, theologisch und literarisch wohl den wichtigsten Impuls für die Entstehung der christlichen Anfangsliteratur gegeben, indem hier Jesu Wirken und Lebensende als Teil der Verkündigung verstanden und erzählt wird.

(2) Der Vergleich gilt *zweitens* den *Anfängen der christlichen Literatur*, der Gattung des (halb-)öffentlichen Briefes und der Gattung des Evangeliums[26]. Beide Gattungen entstehen als literarische Kommunikationsträger des *euaggélion* von Jesus Christus im Zeitraum zwischen 50 und 70 n. Chr., beide fügen sich bis zu einem gewissen Grade in die Gattungen der zeitgenössischen Literatur ein, andererseits stehen beide auch quer zur zeitgenössischen Literatur und lassen sich als neue hybride Gattungen verstehen, die ihrerseits aber sehr schnell schulbildend wirken und Nachfolger finden. Insofern sind beide Autoren – sicher ohne eine derartige eigene Intention – zu Initiatoren christlicher *literary activity* ge-

---

23 Das machen die Beiträge von D. Sim und L. Bormann deutlich.
24 Weder die Rom- noch die Antiochiathese hat sich durchsetzen können. Ein Konsens ist nicht in Sicht.
25 Paulus schreibt nicht nur an „seine" – sehr unterschiedlichen – Gemeinden, sondern sein wichtigstes Schreiben geht gerade nicht an eine eigene Gemeinde.
26 Dazu in Bd. I besonders den Beitrag von N. Irrgang, weiter die Beiträge in Bd. II.

worden[27]. Entscheidende Aufschlüsse gibt die literatursoziologische Verortung dieser Literatur: Sie gehört weder der hellenistisch-römischen Bildungsliteratur an, noch lässt sie sich einfach als Teil der frühjüdischen kanonischen (Septuaginta) und außerkanonischen griechischsprachigen Literatur beschreiben. Paulus und Markus sind keine griechischen Schriftsteller in dem Sinn, dass sie Teil des griechisch-römischen Literaturbetriebes ihrer Zeit wären – von diesem werden sie nicht wahrgenommen. Ebenso wenig wollen sie als jüdische religiöse Schriftsteller verstanden werden – sie werden auch weder vom zeitgenössischen noch vom späteren Judentum rezipiert –, obgleich sie aus hellenistisch-römischer Sicht durchaus als solche gewirkt haben können. Andererseits hat Paulus nicht als Beauftragter seiner Gemeinden geschrieben, sondern im Gegenteil als Apostel, also als autoritatives Gegenüber seiner Gemeinden. Und auch dem Markusevangelium lässt sich nichts entnehmen, das darauf hindeuten könnte, „Markus" sei der Beauftrage einer Gemeinde gewesen[28]. Über die Motive beider Autoren, literarisch tätig zu werden, können wir nur spekulieren. Deutlich ist ihre literarische Begabung, undeutlich ihr Bildungsprofil, offensichtlich ihr Erfolg. *Sie* sind es, die die in ihren Texten die Basis christlicher Weltinterpretation gelegt haben, nicht die „Säulen" Petrus, Jakobus und Johannes.

Damit ergibt sich folgende weiterführende Perspektive: Auf der Grundlage der vergleichenden Beiträge beider Bände muss die Frage vertieft bearbeitet werden, wieweit *Literatur mit theologischen Ansprüchen* an den Anfängen des Christentums steht, in welchem Umfang Briefliteratur und narrative Darstellung (und in der dritten Generation apokalyptische Dichtung) zu den Ursprüngen christlicher Theologie gehört und wie aus Narration, Vision[29], Argumentation und Paränese theologische Weltdeutungen entwickelt werden. Letzteres ist besonders wichtig, wenn wir Paulus und „Markus" als theologische Anfangsliteratur lesen. Über die Konzepte von Epistolographie und Narrativität hinaus[30] stellt sich die Aufgabe, die christliche Anfangsliteratur gleichermaßen von ihrer autoren- und gemeindebezogenen, ihrer theologischen und ihrer literarischen Seite aus zu verstehen und als Anfangsliteratur einer neuen religiösen Gruppierung im frühkaiserzeitlichen *imperium Romanum* zu interpretieren[31]. Wir werden dann, an diesem Punkt eher in

---

27 Vgl. dazu den Beitrag von E.-M. Becker in Bd. II.
28 Vgl. meine Überlegungen dazu: O. Wischmeyer, Forming Identity through Literature. The Impact of Mark for the Building of Christ-Believing Communities in the Second Half of the First Century C.E., in: Mark and Matthew I, 355–378.
29 Vgl. Texte wie Mk 13 einerseits und 1Kor 15; 2Kor 5; Röm 8 andererseits.
30 Siehe das Konzept von Bd. II.
31 Damit beziehe ich mich auf das Selbstverständnis beider Autoren, die sich in den Begriffen „Jesus der Christus", „neu" und „Evangelium" zusammenfassen lässt. Vgl. dazu besonders

Übereinstimmung mit Martin Werner, bei „Markus" nicht nur bestimmte Züge einer „paulinistischen" Theologie im Gegensatz zu anderen Typen wie der johanneischen Theologie oder den theologischen Überzeugungen des Jakobusbriefes finden, sondern einerseits die Umsetzung frühchristlicher Christologie in Narration und andererseits die selbständige Einarbeitung entscheidender theologischer Konzepte, die wir schon bei Paulus finden, in eben die markinische Jesuserzählung, die sehr verschieden von der paulinischen Christologie ist. So verstanden erweist sich die Methode des Vergleichs zwischen den historischen (Gemeinden und Städte wie Rom oder Antiochia, Führungspersonen wie Paulus, Petrus und Jakobus), literarischen (Autor, Gattungen, Leserschaften) und theologischen (Heidenmission, ethisches Reinheitskonzept u. a.) Konzepten bei Paulus und „Markus" als äußerst erhellend. Die Heuristik der Christologie und der theologischen Konzepte beider Schriftsteller eröffnet neue Einsichten in die Grundbausteine frühchristlicher Weltdeutung.

---

meinen Beitrag im vorliegenden Band. Dass diese neue religiöse Gruppierung aus dem zeitgenössischen Judentum hervorging, muss nicht eigens betont werden Vgl. dazu besonders die Beiträge von J. Svartvik und N. Irrgang und die dort verarbeitete umfangreiche und multiperspektivische bis kontroverse Lit.

Teil 1 / Part 1: **Forschungsgeschichte /
History of Research**

Johannes Wischmeyer
Universalismus als Tendenz und Entwicklungsmoment. Die Frage nach Markus und Paulus in der historisch-kritischen Geschichtsschreibung des Urchristentums von 1850 bis 1910

Das Verständnis der Entstehung des Neuen Testaments und seiner Einzelschriften wandelte sich im Verlauf des 19. Jahrhunderts durch die Leistung einiger protestantischer Exegeten in grundlegender Weise. Sie ließen sich von einer allgemeinen ideengeschichtlichen Dynamik leiten, die im Gefolge romantischer und idealistischer Diskurse den Begriff der *Geschichte* zu einer zentralen Erschließungskategorie wissenschaftlicher Erkenntnis befördert hatte. In der interdisziplinären Diskussion während der ersten Hälfte des 19. Jahrhunderts erfuhr der Begriff der Geschichte dabei eine Pluralität von Auslegungen, die auf den ersten Blick verwirren mag. Einerseits betonte man das Eigenrecht bzw. die Individualität allen vergangenen Geschehens und legte damit dem Historiker eine einfühlsame und von Rationalisierungen oder anderen ideenpolitischen Vereinnahmungen freie hermeneutische Grundhaltung ans Herz. Andererseits gewann die Vergangenheit große Bedeutung als sinn- und identitätsstiftende Instanz für die Selbstvergewisserungsprozesse der zeitgenössischen Gesellschaft. Geschichte bot einen Rahmen, innerhalb dessen das Verhältnis von Institutionen wie der Nation, ebenso aber auch der christlichen Kirche oder des Protestantismus zu ihren Ursprüngen und Referenzpunkten als kontinuierliches Werden thematisiert werden konnte[1].

Diese Ambivalenz von Abstand und gleichzeitiger Kontinuität der Gegenwart zu ihren Gründungsgeschichten kennzeichnet den frühen Historismus oder die ‚Schwellenzeit' im deutschsprachigen Geschichtsdiskurs zwischen 1800 und 1850

---

[1] Vgl. G. Scholtz, Art. Geschichte, Historie IV, in: HWPh 3 (1974), 361-371; J. Mehlhausen, Art. Geschichte/Geschichtsschreibung/Geschichtsphilosophie VII/2. 19.–20. Jahrhundert, in: TRE 12 (1984), 642-658; H. W. Blanke, Aufklärungshistorie und Historismus: Bruch und Kontinuität, in: Historismus in den Kulturwissenschaften. Geschichtskonzepte, historische Einschätzungen, Grundlagenprobleme, hg. von O.G. Oexle und J. Rüsen, Köln-Weimar-Wien 1996, 69-97; J. Nordalm, Historismus im 19. Jahrhundert. Zur Fortdauer einer Epoche des geschichtlichen Denkens, in: Historismus im 19. Jahrhundert. Geschichtsschreibung von Niebuhr bis Meinecke, hg. von J. Nordalm, Stuttgart 2006, 7-46.

– eine Epoche, die sich charakteristisch ebenso vom Pragmatismus der Spätaufklärung wie von der betonten Subjektivität und (zumindest behaupteten) Theorieabstinenz des nachfolgenden ‚klassischen Historismus' unterschied[2]. Die theologischen Disziplinen erschlossen sich die historistischen Fragestellungen nur mit einer gewissen Verzögerung und in unterschiedlicher Form und Intensität; dennoch prägte das neue Interesse an einer als normativ verstandenen Geschichtlichkeit der christlichen Überlieferung die Theologieproduktion positionenübergreifend vom liberalen bis ins konfessionalistische Lager[3].

In der neutestamentlichen Exegese führte der historistische Ansatz im Verlauf des 19. Jahrhunderts zur Etablierung weitgreifender und raffinierter Interpretationsverfahren, mit deren Hilfe man dem aus der Aufklärung überkommenen Anliegen der Quellenkritik auf einem neuen Niveau gerecht werden wollte. Als Interpretationsgrundlage dienten nicht länger eine ahistorische Universalanthropologie oder kausale Rekonstruktionen im Sinne einer Alltagslogik. Vielmehr wurden anspruchsvolle, meist nach dialektischen oder organologischen Mustern konstruierte Modelle diskutiert, mit deren Hilfe die Entwicklungstendenzen vergangener Epochen untersucht werden sollten. Am innovativsten erwiesen sich hier Vertreter des dogmatisch und kirchenpolitisch freisinnigen bzw. liberalen Spektrums – beinahe alle im Folgenden näher vorgestellten Exegeten sind diesem zuzurechnen. Kristallisationspunkt der Richtung, die herkömmlich in der alt- und neutestamentlichen Wissenschaft als ‚historisch-kritische' bezeichnet wird, die aber nach dem bisher Gesagten womöglich auch als Bestandteil der pluralen (früh-)historistischen Bewegung in der Historiographie des 19. Jahrhunderts gesehen werden kann, war die sogenannte jüngere Tübinger Schule Ferdinand Christian Baurs.

Auch die Frage nach dem Verhältnis zwischen dem Markusevangelium und der paulinischen Überlieferung wurde vor allem von Exegeten aus Baurs Umfeld aufgegriffen: Hatte zuvor die Diskussion an den frühchristlichen Traditionen angesetzt, die eine persönlich Beziehung des Johannes Markus zum Apostel Paulus nahelegten, so bildeten jetzt hypothetische Rekonstruktionen der Theo-

---

[2] Vgl. St. Jordan, Zwischen Aufklärung und Historismus. Deutschsprachige Geschichtstheorie in der ersten Hälfte des 19. Jahrhunderts, in: Sitzungsberichte der Leibniz-Sozietät 48, Heft 5 (2001), 5-20. – Der folgende Beitrag kommentiert das Thema aus theologiegeschichtlicher Perspektive, ohne die deutlichen kirchenpolitischen Positionierungen der hier besprochenen Theologen im Einzelnen darstellen zu können.
[3] Vgl. zu einem Exponenten des lutherischen Neukonfessionalismus J. Wischmeyer, Heilsgeschichte im Zeitalter des Historismus. Das geschichtstheologische Programm Johann Christian Konrad Hofmanns, in: Heil und Geschichte. Die Geschichtsbezogenheit des Heils und das Problem der Heilsgeschichte in der biblischen Tradition und in der theologischen Deutung, hg. von J. Frey u.a. (WUNT 248), Tübingen 2009, 633-646.

logiegeschichte des Urchristentums die Basis für einen neuen Diskurs. In methodischer Hinsicht kam die sogenannte ‚Tendenzkritik' ins Spiel[4]. Baur hatte darauf hingewiesen, dass die Frage nach der historischen Wahrheit biblischer Texte bei den Motiven und Zielen ansetzen müsse, die die jeweiligen Verfasser in ihrem zeitgenössischen Kontext zu ihrem literarischen Unternehmen motivierten. Eine zentrale theologische Tendenz im Urchristentum, so waren sich die meisten Anhänger Baurs mit ihrem Schulhaupt einig, war die paulinische Verkündigung im Sinne einer gesetzesfreien Heidenmission. Was das Markusevangelium betraf, konnte man nun gezielt untersuchen, inwieweit es (unter anderem) ein Produkt dieses ‚Paulinismus' war.

Gleichzeitig rückte die Frage nach der Beziehung der für authentisch erachteten paulinischen Briefe und des Markusevangeliums in die Nähe der heiß diskutierten synoptischen Frage: Man musste sich, um Klarheit über die Originalität der markinischen Überlieferung und ihren zeitlichen Abstand zu den bereits relativ genau datierten Paulinen zu gewinnen, an eines der gängigen Synoptikermodelle anschließen. Dies machte gleichzeitig eine Verhältnisbestimmung zu den anderen Evangelien notwendig, ebenso eine hypothetische Gesamtchronologie der neutestamentlichen Schriften.

1 Adolf Hilgenfeld und Ferdinand Christian Baur

Der erste bedeutende Entwurf, der unter diesen Prämissen – wenn auch nur im Vorübergehen – das Problem ‚Markus und Paulus' in den Blick nahm, stammte von dem theologisch freisinnigen Jenaer Exegeten Adolf Hilgenfeld (1823-1907). Für Hilgenfeld befindet sich der ‚Ur-Markus' – der später im Zuge der Kanonisierung einer Redaktion unterzogen worden sei – seiner theologischen Tendenz nach zwischen dem deutlich ‚judaisierenden' Matthäusevangelium und dem ‚heidenchristlichen' Lukasevangelium. Der Verfasser habe die judaistische Tendenz des ersten Evangeliums planmäßig gemildert. Der Autor des Lukasevangeliums wiederum habe den Ur-Markus wegen dessen relativ ausgeprägter Nähe zu seiner eigenen Theologie umstandslos als Vorlage verwenden können[5].

---

4 Vgl. O. Pfleiderer, Die Entwicklung der protestantischen Theologie in Deutschland und in Großbritannien seit 1825, Freiburg 1891, 252-313; U. Köpf, Die theologischen Tübinger Schulen, in: Historisch-kritische Geschichtsbetrachtung. Ferdinand Christian Baur und seine Schüler; 8. Blaubeurer Symposion, hg. von U. Köpf (Contubernium 40), Sigmaringen 1994, 10-51.
5 A. Hilgenfeld, Das Markus-Evangelium, nach seiner Composition, seiner Stellung in der Evangelien-Literatur, seinem Ursprung und Charakter, Leipzig 1850, 127. 129.

Die im Vergleich zum Autor des Matthäusevangeliums ‚liberalere' Tendenz des Ur-Markus bringt Hilgenfeld auf die Formel des ‚Universalismus'. Dieser ziehe sich wie ein Leitmotiv durch das Evangelium (vgl. nur Mk 16,20; 11,17) – die Beobachtung, so setzt er hinzu, müsse aber in keinem Fall bedeuten, dass der Evangelist paulinische Einflüsse aufgenommen habe[6]. Hilgenfeld zufolge handelt es sich eher um den Universalismus von sich allmählich emanzipierenden Judenchristen[7], die jüdische Gesetzlichkeit und die damit verbundene Absonderung ablehnten, aber an Grundthemen jüdischer Theologie wie einem strikten Monotheismus und der Liebe als ethischer Pflicht und gleichzeitig Gottesattribut festhielten – er postuliert eine inhaltliche Verwandtschaft mit den Pseudo-Clementinen. Auch die Wichtigkeit des persönlichen Glaubens und die hohen moralischen Ansprüche im Markusevangelium scheinen Hilgenfeld in diese Richtung zu weisen. Dies bedeutet übrigens auch eine implizite Kritik an Albrecht Ritschl, der alle synoptischen Stellen, die den Begriff des Glaubens hervorheben, für paulinisch beeinflusst hielt[8].

Ferdinand Christian Baur (1792-1860) schloss sich in seinem Markuskommentar Hilgenfeld insoweit an, als er die theologische Originalität des Evangelisten nun höher bewertete als in seinen früheren Publikationen. Zwar mochte er nach wie vor nicht einmal eine Priorität des Markus vor dem Lukasevangelium zugestehen.[9] Markus bleibt in Baurs Analyse ein Eklektiker „sekundären Charakters"[10] und ohne ein „durchgreifenderes dogmatisches Interesse"[11]. Doch für die auffälligen Unterschiede gegenüber dem Matthäusevangelium – etwa das Fehlen der Bergpredigt oder die deutlich selteneren alttestamentlichen Zitate – erkennt er jetzt „dogmatische Gründe" an, die mit einer „freieren Stellung zum Alten Testament, zum Judenthum und Judaismus" zusammenhingen[12]. Zwar sei dem Autor der ‚paulinische Universalismus' fremd geblieben, doch nehme sein Evangelium nicht nur in formaler, sondern eben auch in dogmatischer Hinsicht eine „mittlere Stellung" zwischen den beiden anderen Synoptikern ein, allerdings mit einer stärker ausgeprägten Nähe zum judenchristlichen Matthäusevangelium. Es fällt Baur erkennbar schwer, die leitende Idee des Markusevangeliums auf eine

---

6 Ebd., 123.
7 „[D]er Geist eines zwar nicht paulinischen, aber freieren, tieferen judaistischen Christenthums" (ebd., 126).
8 Ebd., 125.
9 F. Ch. Baur, Das Markusevangelium nach seinem Ursprung und Charakter. Nebst einem Anhang über das Evangelium Marcion's, Tübingen 1831 [i.e.: 1851]), 153-176.
10 Ebd., 152.
11 Ebd., 150.
12 Ebd., 148.

Formel zu bringen, ohne die seinem historistischen Interpretationsmuster zufolge doch kein Autor eines literarischen Werkes in seiner historischen Individualität verstanden werden kann. Doch nimmt er den Verfasser des Markusevangeliums als Historiker ernst, wenn er ihm attestiert, dieser habe sich zur Aufgabe gemacht, das ‚objectiv Thatsächliche' darzustellen; in Baurs von Dichotomien geprägter geschichtsmethodologischer Nomenklatur bedeutet dies die „Kunst, mit welcher er das einzelne auszumalen und dadurch seiner Darstellung Leben und Farbe zu geben weiß"[13]. Lob für die Anschaulichkeit verbindet sich mit Kritik daran, dass der Verfasser nicht vermocht habe, in geschärfter Reflexion seinen Subjektivismus zu überwinden. Seine eigene literarische Leistung beschränke sich vor allem darauf, vordergründige Motivationen für den Gang der Ereignisse gefunden zu haben, sich in die „Empfindungen und Gemüthsaffektionen" der handelnden Personen hineinzuversetzen und die Vorgänge „mit einer gewissen Aufregung und mit Geräusch" darzustellen[14].

2 Gustav Volkmar

Für Baur und seinen engeren Schülerkreis stellte sich die Frage nach dem Charakter der Beziehung zwischen dem Markusevangelium und den paulinischen Schriften, wie gesehen, nur am Rande. Ungleich drängender wurde sie für diejenigen, die im Gefolge der beiden Pioniere Chr. G. Wilke (1786-1854) und Ch. H. Weisse (1804-1866) die Hypothese der Markuspriorität akzeptierten. Doch auch unter dieser Bedingung ergab sich keineswegs ein zwingendes Interesse an der Fragestellung; über die Tübinger Schule hinaus blieben viele Exegeten bei der Suche nach ‚paulinischen' Spuren in den Synoptikern auf das Lukasevangelium fixiert[15]. Es war vor allem der Zürcher Neutestamentler Gustav Volkmar (1809-1893), der die Konsequenz aus der zeitlichen Priorisierung des Markusevangeliums zog und es als ein Dokument des expliziten Paulinismus deutete[16]. Dies geschah zuerst 1857 im Rahmen einer populärwissenschaftlichen Darstellung des Urchristentums, mit der Volkmar eine Summe aus seinen bisherigen Forschungen zog.

---

13 Ebd., 150.
14 Ebd., 151.
15 Vgl. nur ebd., 221-225.
16 Vgl. den beachtlichen und nach wie vor lesenswerten Beitrag von B. Wildemann, Das Evangelium als Lehrpoesie. Leben und Werk Gustav Volkmars, in: Kontexte 1, Frankfurt a. M. u. a. 1983, hier 252-255.

Selbstbewusst weist der Zürcher Exeget dort auf die Bedeutung seiner „geschichtlichen Erklärung der ältesten Evangelien überhaupt" hin: Das Gesamtbild werde in Zukunft durch den wissenschaftlichen Fortschritt zwar sicher noch im Detail modifiziert werden, doch ist Volkmar gewiss, dass „in das Ganze dieser Erzählung keine Änderung mehr eingreifen wird"[17]. Er resümiert seine Auseinandersetzungen mit Neutestamentlern aller theologischen Positionen. Zwar wusste er sich am ehesten Baurs Tübinger Schule verbunden[18]. Ganz im Einklang mit ihr strebte Volkmar danach, die „lebendige geschichtliche Entwicklung" des Urchristentums und seine ‚innerlichen Prinzipien' zu ergründen[19], ohne das methodische *Caveat* zu vernachlässigen, dass die verfügbaren literarischen Quellen nicht naiv als historische Tatsachenberichte gelesen werden können, sondern in ihrem jeweiligen Entstehungskontext als Träger bestimmter Interessen dienten[20]. Doch in der Frage nach dem Verhältnis von Markus und Paulus habe er stets eine eigene Interpretation vertreten, die inzwischen auch der engere Kreis der Tübinger Schule anerkennen müsse. Neben dem Tübinger Einfluss wirkte auch Bruno Bauers (1809-1882) These eines ohne Bezug auf vorhergehende Tradition dogmatisch schöpferischen Urevangelisten prägend auf Volkmar; er markierte allerdings stets bei sachlicher Anerkennung von Bauers Kritik seinen Abstand gegenüber dessen ‚negativ'-christentumsfeindlicher Einstellung[21].

Volkmars zwar historisch-kritischer, doch im Vergleich zu Baur deutlich weniger differenzierter Geschichtsbegriff zielt darauf, dass der Wahrheitsanspruch der Historie nicht aufgegeben werden dürfe, auch wenn die historischen Quellen eine allegorische Dimension besitzen. Die historische Wahrheit des Markusevangeliums sieht er dementsprechend darin begründet, dass es „die Darstellung vom wahren Wesen Jesu Christi" sei, das ebenso wie in dessen irdischer Wirksamkeit auch seit der Auferstehung und im Wirken der Apostel zum Ausdruck gekommen sei: „Das Evangelium hat volle geschichtliche Wahrheit, aber welt-

---

17 G. Volkmar, Die Religion Jesu und ihre erste Entwicklung nach dem gegenwärtigen Stande der Wissenschaft, Leipzig 1857, XV.
18 Wildemann, Das Evangelium, 242-251.
19 G. Volkmar, Ueber das Lukas-Evangelium nach seinem Verhältniss zu Marcion und seinem dogmatischen Charakter, mit besonderer Beziehung auf die kritischen Untersuchungen F. Ch. Baur's und A. Ritschl's, in: ThJB (T) (1850), 110-138; 185-235, hier 115.
20 Das Markusevangelium gilt Volkmar als „Tendenzschrift" und keineswegs als „eine Biographie Jesu im prosaischen Sinne des Wortes": Volkmar, Die Religion Jesu, 263.
21 G. Volkmar, Die Evangelien oder Marcus und die Synopsis der kanonischen und außerkanonischen Evangelien nach dem ältesten Text mit historisch-exegetischem Commentar, Leipzig 1870, VII; ders., Die Religion Jesu, 552; vgl. Wildemann, Das Evangelium, 256-267. Von Bauer übernimmt Volkmar auch sein Modell der Evangelienentstehung: Volkmar, Die Religion Jesu, 542.

geschichtliche, in der auch das individuelle Geschichtliche mit inbegriffen ist, nur ohne ausdrückliche Unterscheidung. Es ist eine kostbare Quelle für das Leben Jesu, aber auch eine solche für das Leben des Paulus und der Christenheit nach ihm"[22]. Aus dem literarischen Programm des Verfassers, das ‚wahre Wesen Christi' darzustellen, leitet Volkmar die konkrete hermeneutische Folgerung ab, dass auch die gesamte Darstellung von Jesu irdischem Wirken bereits im Lichte seines Wirkens als erhöhter Menschensohn zu interpretieren sei[23]. Diese knappen konzeptionellen Ausführungen sind wohl als das Alternativprogramm zu Baurs spekulativem bzw. hypothesengeleitetem Verfahren gemeint, das Volkmar als schwankend und letzten Ende ergebnislos empfand. Volkmar selbst redet dem „geraden, nach jeder Seite hin rücksichtslosen Einhalten der rein geschichtlichen Tendenz" das Wort, was beispielsweise auch bedeuten müsse, dass philologische und chronologische Evidenzen schwerer zu gewichten seien als postulierte theologische Tendenzen[24].

Inhaltlich weicht Volkmars Rekonstruktion der theologiegeschichtlichen Epochenfolge innerhalb des Urchristentums deutlich von anderen Tübinger Konstruktionen ab[25]. Er entwickelt ein Schema, das dem zeitgenössischen Modell einer Kausalbeziehung von Revolution, Reaktion und Regeneration folgt: Das gesetzesfreie paulinische Evangelium, dessen Lehre „in ihrer ganzen Schärfe für ein judenchristliches Herz unerträglich" war[26], sieht er als „eine neue Offenbarung Jesu, eine Revolution gegen die erste, jüdisch beschränkte Fassung des neuen Weltprincips"[27]. Nach dem Tod des Paulus folgte eine judenchristliche „Reaction", die sich tatsächlich auch mit einem „höchsten Geistesaufschwung" verband und ihren literarischen Gipfel in der Johannesoffenbarung erreichte[28]. Erst als deutlich wurde, dass die apokalyptischen Vorhersagen über den bevorstehenden Untergang des Römischen Reiches nicht eintrafen und das „Bedürfniß, die Parusie Christi in gegenwärtiger Herrlichkeit zu schauen", wuchs, gewann die paulinische Richtung wieder an Einfluss[29]. Ihr literarisches ‚Manifest' war das Ur-Markus-

---

[22] Ebd., 269.
[23] Ebd.
[24] Ebd., 552.
[25] Zur Distanznahme gegenüber der Tübinger Schule vgl. ebd., 552.
[26] Ebd., 193.
[27] Ebd., 194.
[28] Ebd.
[29] Ebd., 202; vgl. Wildemann, Das Evangelium, 314-335, der darauf hinweist, dass das von Volkmar durchgehend zugrunde gelegte Verständnis des ‚Paulinismus' inhaltlich stark auf die Topoi Glaubensgewissheit, Universalismus und präsentische Eschatologie zentriert bleibt (ebd., 314 f.); hier kommt m.E. Volkmars häufige, freisinnig motivierte Hervorhebung der paulinischen Gesetzeskritik etwas zu kurz.

evangelium, gegen 80 n.Chr. in Rom verfasst[30] und bis auf den unechten Schluss und geringfügige Interpolationen mit dem überlieferten Markusevangelium identisch. Es identifiziert Jesus als den Sohn Gottes (und nicht wie in der judenchristlichen Sicht als Davidssohn) mit dem ‚Geistesmessias', dem Christus für die Heidenwelt, der in seiner irdischen Wirksamkeit real gelitten hat[31]. Als „Epos von der ersten Parusie Christi" spiritualisiert das Markusevangelium in Volkmars Sichtweise die christliche Hoffnung auf die zweite Parusie, indem es im Modus der Innerlichkeit beschreibt, wie Christus während seiner irdischen Wirksamkeit diese Parusie bereits bewährte[32]. Demgegenüber, so Volkmar, identifizierten die Judenchristen Christus weiterhin bruchlos mit dem Messias der alttestamentlichen Überlieferung. Als Zeugnis dieser Richtung sei das Ur-Matthäusevangelium entstanden. Eine Antwort hierauf habe wiederum das paulinische Lukasevangelium geboten; auf dessen Grundlage sei das endgültige, überlieferte Matthäusevangelium von ‚freisinnigeren Judenchristen' redigiert worden, die sich ihren paganen Mitbrüdern gegenüber geöffnet hätten[33]. Im Vergleich zum Verfasser des Markusevangeliums bezeichnet Volkmar den Autor des Lukasevangeliums als den „gereiztern Pauliner"[34].

Das Markusevangelium definiert Volkmar als „Darstellung echt christlichen Sinnes paulinischer Lehre in erzählender Form, nach einer durchgreifenden Sachdisposition"[35]. Ganz folgerichtig markiere es den Ursprung eines eigenen literarischen Genus, denn der neue Geist des Christentums habe auch eine neue Form verlangt[36]. Auf der syntaktischen Ebene, so Volkmar, sei der Autor allerdings durchaus der Tradition der „hebräischen Poesie" mit ihrem *parallelismus membrorum* verpflichtet[37]. Eigenständig sei demgegenüber die Darstellung im Medium des Sinnbildes, das sich zur „Einkleidung oder Abbild des geistigen Gehalts"[38] vor allem alttestamentlicher Typologien bedient. Der allegorische Stil sei nicht nur zur Erbauung und als intellektuelle Herausforderung der heidenchristlichen Rezipienten gedacht, sondern ebenso als eine „geistige Schule" für die in ihrer sinnli-

---

30 Volkmar, Die Religion Jesu, 203; vorsichtiger in Bezug auf den Abfassungsort ders., Die Evangelien, 646.
31 Volkmar, Die Religion Jesu, 236-240; 262 f.
32 Ebd., 203.
33 Vgl. hierzu auch H. J. Holtzmann, Die synoptischen Evangelien. Ihr Ursprung und geschichtlicher Charakter, Leipzig 1863, 41 f.
34 Volkmar, Die Religion Jesu, 307.
35 Ebd., 203 f.; Mk 4,33 wird als Schlüsselstelle zum Verständnis hervorgehoben.
36 Ebd., 223.
37 Ebd., 215.
38 Ebd., 268.

chen Anschauungsform befangene judenchristliche Mehrheit[39] bzw. die „blöde Menge", die „keine directe Vertheidigung paulinischen Wesens ertrug"[40]. Den literarischen Gesamtcharakter des Markusevangeliums bringt Volkmar auf die Formel des ‚Menschheitsepos' und der ‚Lehrpoesie' – es sei „ganz geschichtlich und ganz Poesie, Beides in Einem"[41].

Inhaltlich und seiner übergreifenden Struktur nach sei das ganze Evangelium als eine durchgehende, zwar implizite, jedoch nachdrückliche Rechtfertigung der Theologie des Paulus gedacht und erkennbar als Gegenstück zur Johannesoffenbarung angelegt[42]. Indem es Gehalte aus der urchristlichen Überlieferung mit solchen aus der Frömmigkeit der paulinischen Gemeinden kombiniere, gebe es „das wahre Christenthum selbst" zu verstehen[43]. Ganz wie Paulus sehe der Verfasser Form und Geist des Christentums durch die Theologumena von Gotteinigkeit, Sündenvergebung und Öffnung gegenüber der Heidenwelt sowie in einer spiritualisierten Ethik repräsentiert. Im gesamten Aufriss des Evangeliums entdeckt Volkmar wohlkomponierte „Fingerzeige" auf den jeweils geistigen Sinn der Narrationen[44]: Die systematische Umsetzung des paulinischen Evangeliums von Glaube, Liebe und Hoffnung konzentriert sich etwa im Bericht von Jesu Leidensweg in Mk 15[45]. Dem Apostel Paulus selbst wird in Volkmars Deutung vor allem am Schluss des Evangeliums ein besonderer Platz eingeräumt, indem ihn der Verfasser zu den zwölf Aposteln zählt und im – von Volkmar der Urschrift zugerechneten – Schlussabschnitt Mk 16 die in den paulinischen Briefen nur angedeutete, ‚unsagbare' Offenbarungsvision (1Kor 15,6; 2Kor 12,2) in Worte fasst (Mk 16,15 f.)[46]. Doch bereits von Beginn des Evangeliums an, etwa in den Anspielungen auf Elias Wirken unter den Heiden, sind nach Volkmars Interpretation sinnbildliche Hinweise auf den Heidenapostel zu finden[47].

---

39 Ebd., 242 f.
40 Ebd., 275.
41 Ebd., 276.
42 Ebd., 207; einen Kurzüberblick über die „Disposition" der Gesamtschrift gibt Volkmar ebd., 264-268; noch deutlicher systematisiert in Volkmar, Die Evangelien, 643 f.
43 Volkmar, Die Religion Jesu, 206.
44 Ebd., 243.
45 Ebd., 243.
46 Ebd., 258 f.
47 Ebd., 303 f.; vgl. auch ders., Die Evangelien, 645 f. Dort werden explizit genannt: Jesu Verteidigung der Heidenmission, die Erwählung eines Jüngerkreises jenseits der Zwölf, Jesu Wirken jenseits der jüdische Grenzen, direkte Parallelisierungen von Jesu Wirken und der paulinischen Mission (Wanderung ἐν κύκλῳ; Meeresüberschreitung; Überwindung des Meersturmes; Sturz der Götzengeister ins Meer; Heidenmahl; Verfolgung in Jerusalem; außerdem, kaum nachvollziehbar, die Verklärungsvision). Besondere literarische Parallelen bemerkt Volk-

Gut sichtbar wird Volkmars Interpretationsverfahren an seiner Erklärung von Mk 10,1-16, wo Jesus das Gesetz als nur vorläufig wegen der Verhärtung des Volkes verhängt bezeichnet: „Auf das sinnigste hat der Pauliner in seinem Bestreben, paulinisches Wesen durchzuführen, in der evangelischen Form und doch nicht beim Judenchristen allzu sehr anzustoßen, das Schibboleth der Partei, das Gesetz, ob es gelte oder nicht, zur Seite gelassen, vermieden es auszusprechen. Aber er zeigt um so eindringlicher factisch die Ueberwindung des Moses an einem Punkt und Beispiel, an welchem der Judenchrist selbst längst über das mosaische Gesetz hinausgedrungen war, in Betreff der so willkürlichen Ehescheidung [...] Hier mußte also der Judenchrist zugeben, das Gesetz des Mose kann nur transitorische Bedeutung haben, und man hat darüber hinaus, d.h. zurückzugehen auf ein höheres allgemeines Gesetz Gottes, wie es schon in seiner ganzen Schöpfung liegt"[48].

In seiner zuerst 1870 publizierten Gesamtdarstellung der kanonischen Synoptiker bekräftigt Volkmar den Rang des Verfassers des Markusevangeliums: Er sei „einer der geistvollsten und einflussreichsten Schriftsteller, die es nach Paulus gegeben hat"[49]. In der Zweitauflage des Werkes schlägt er noch höhere Töne an: Um den „großen christlichen Lehrdichter, der Alles überragt", zu würdigen, müsse man sich vor Augen führen, dass dieser „den vollen Umsturz der hergebrachten Anschauungen, Wünsche und Hoffnungen zu ertragen und in sich zu einer neuen Position zu bringen" hatte[50]. Die Abfassung des „echt und antik Paulinischen Lehrbuches des wahren Christenthums", als die das Markusevangelium gelten müsse, sei eine ‚nach Sinn und Kunst geradezu geniale' Leistung[51]. Auch in dem als eine Art Summe seiner Forschungen gedachten Leben Jesu, das Volkmar mit

---

mar zwischen Apg 28,1-10 und Mk 1,21-39: der Lukas vorliegende Reisebericht von einer Fieberheilung des Paulus auf Malta könnte dem Verfasser des Mk bekannt gewesen sein; „dann wird es möglich bleiben, dass er dies Walten des Apostels auf das Haupt, das ihn ausrüstete, übertrug" (ebd., 98); außerdem zwischen Apg 20,11-15 und Mk 6,45-52: die „Ueberwindung der Meerschranke" nach dem Typus von 2 Kön 2,8,14 orientiere sich an einer erinnerten Begebenheit aus dem Leben des Paulus, als dieser nach Predigt und Abendmahl seinen eingeschifften Begleitern ein Stück Weges an Land vorausging (ebd., 377).

48 Volkmar, Die Religion Jesu, 246; weitere Beispiele für die ‚ideale' Darstellungsform eines ‚universalen' Gehalts von ‚höherer Bedeutung' in narrativen Einzelstücken bringt Volkmar ebd., 269-273 (ebd., 270 f., etwa die Deutung von Jesu Auftreten in Kapernaum Mk 1,12 ff. als ein „Programm für das ganze Paulinische Evangelium").
49 Volkmar, Die Evangelien, 647.
50 G. Volkmar, Die kanonischen Synoptiker in Uebersicht mit Randglossen und Register und das Geschichtliche vom Leben Jesu. Separat-Abdruck aus der neuen erweiterten Ausgabe der „Evangelien", Zürich 1876, IX; zusammenfassend zum Markusevangelium ebd., 681-688.
51 Ebd., 688; 683.

einer Ausgabe des Markustextes nach dem *Codex Vaticanus* sowie den Notizen des Josephus über Jesus in deutscher Übersetzung verband, bleibt er bei seinem Urteil: Er bringt hier den Verfasser des Markusevangeliums mit der Tradition in die Nähe des aus der Apostelgeschichte und den Paulinen bekannten Johannes Markus. Dieser sei, gerade weil er im 1. Petrusbrief als Petrusjünger gerühmt werde, de facto als „ein Pauliner vermittelnder Art" anzusehen[52].

Adolf Hilgenfeld nahm kurz nach Erscheinen der Volkmarschen Markusdeutung erneut Stellung. Er kritisiert Volkmars Chronologie und sein Konzept der tendenziellen Dynamiken im 1. Jahrhundert von Grund auf: Volkmar habe sich trotz seiner These von der Integrität des Markusevangeliums in Wirklichkeit „ein kurzes, ächt paulinisches Urevangelium in dem Markus-Evangelium zurechtgelegt"[53]. Die These von einem abermaligen Vorherrschen und erneuten Rückschlag des ‚Judaismus' bis zur Abfassung des Lukasevangeliums sei ganz unplausibel; außerdem müsse Volkmar eingestehen, dass er implizit sogar einen von essenischen Einflüssen noch freien ‚Ur-Matthäus' annehmen müsse. Die Vorstellung, dass das Matthäusevangelium als das jüngste synoptische Evangelium eine populäre Vermittlung von judenchristlichen und paulinischen Ideen geleistet habe, quittiert Hilgenfeld mit Spott[54]. Es macht ihm spürbar zu schaffen, dass Volkmar die von den Tübingern angenommene Aufwärtsentwicklung infrage stellt, als deren Zielpunkt sie „das reine paulinische Evangelium des Lukas" erkannt hatten, und stattdessen „ein stetiges Sinken des ursprünglichen Aufschwungs der Evangelienbildung" unterstellen muss, an deren Ende sich „eine wiederholte kräftige Erhebung des Paulinismus allmählig in den Sand verläuft"[55]. In Hilgenfelds Augen überspannt Volkmar den tendenzkritischen Ansatz, indem er den Paulinismus als Leitgedanken und Abfassungszweck in das Markusevangelium hineinliest – Baurs traditionskritisches Argument, dass das Evangelium nicht, wie die kirchliche Tradition es wolle, in enger Beziehung zu petrinischer Überlieferung stehe, sei nachvollziehbar, doch nicht Volkmars Stilisierung des Markusevangeliums als „antipetrinische Tendenzschrift des Paulinismus"[56]. Hilgenfeld weist Volkmars Interpretation der Stellen zurück, in denen dieser implizite Hinweise auf das Wirken des Heidenapostels gefunden hatte – dies sei „poetische Phantasie"[57].

---

52 G. Volkmar, Jesus Nazarenus und die erste christliche Zeit mit den beiden ersten Erzählern, Zürich 1882, 173.
53 A. Hilgenfeld, Die Evangelienfrage und ihre neuesten Behandlungen von Weiss, Volkmar und Meyer, in: ThJB (T) (1857), 381-440, hier 390.
54 Ebd., 391 f.
55 Ebd., 394.
56 Ebd., 421.
57 Ebd., 427.

In einem gewissen Gegensatz zu Baur betont er, dass sich an Stellen wie Mk 1,29 durchaus petrinische Traditionen fänden[58]. Der dem Paulinismus ganz fremde Verfasser habe keineswegs eine generell antijüdische Einstellung vertreten, sondern die Polemik Jesu richte sich stets gegen „das Judenthum der Schriftgelehrten und Pharisäer"[59]. Mit seinem willkürlichen Verfahren könne Volkmar „jede beliebige Schrift des christlichen Alterthums zu einer paulinischen stempeln"[60]. Dies alles geschieht im Rahmen einer angestrengten Zurückweisung der Markuspriorität. Hilgenfeld erkennt allerdings an, dass das Markusevangelium „in dogmatischer Hinsicht eine lichtvolle Urkunde der immer freiern Entwicklung ist, zu welcher der christliche Judaismus durch die geistige Macht des Paulinismus gedrängt ward"[61].

Viele zeitgenössische Exegeten verweigerten sich dem tendenzkritischen Ansatz ganz. Für sie konnte die Frage nach dem Verhältnis von Markus und Paulus nur begrenzt interessant sein. Stellvertretend für die große Zahl dogmatisch-‚positiver' und neukonfessionalistischer Theologen sei die knappe Stellungnahme erwähnt, die sich in der Erstauflage von Herzogs weitverbreiteter ‚Real-Encyklopädie', der ersten modernen protestantisch-theologischen Großenzyklopädie findet: Der Berner Neutestamentler Eduard Güder (1817-1882) konstatiert als Grundproblem der historisch-kritischen Forschung zum Thema, dass sich das von der Mehrheit der Forscher als neutral – weder dem exklusiven Juden- noch dem exklusiven Heidenchristentum verpflichtet – betrachtete Markusevangelium nur schwer in ein Modell der Parteigegensätze des Urchristentums einpassen lasse[62].

3 Heinrich Julius Holtzmann

Die zunehmende Akzeptanz der Zwei-Quellen-Theorie hatte bereits während der geschilderten Auseinandersetzungen im Tübinger Kreis die Parameter der Markus-Interpretation verschoben: Die Hypothese einer selbständigen Logienquelle als Sammlung urchristlicher Lehrgehalte hatte implizit zur Folge, dass man die Gattung der Evangelien von ihrer Funktion als Träger der Lehrüberlieferung entlastete. Kohärent ausgearbeitet wurde ein entsprechender Ansatz zunächst vor allem durch Heinrich Julius Holtzmann (1832-1910). Der gemäßigt liberale Rothe-Schüler

---

58 Ebd., 439 u.ö.
59 Ebd., 423.
60 Ebd., 425.
61 Ebd., 439 f.
62 [Eduard] Güder, Art. Marcus, Evangelist, in: RE 1. Aufl. Bd. 9 (1858), 44-51, hier 49.

und Heidelberger Neutestamentler prägte die Synoptikerforschung beinahe 50 Jahre lang mit[63].

Holtzmann zufolge hat Markus das Urevangelium ('A') für seine Gemeinde redigiert, um als Ergänzung zur ihm ebenfalls vorliegenden Logienquelle (Λ), die den Christen in seiner Umgebung bereits vertraut war, ein Erzählwerk zu schaffen. Im Anschluss an Ferdinand Hitzig (1807-1875) folgert Holtzmann, der Verfasser habe im Evangelium auf Lehrgehalte weitgehend verzichtet, um seine Hörer zu Nachfragen anzuregen[64]. Er geht davon aus, dass der Verfasser dem Judenchristentum entstammt, aber gegenüber dem Judaismus eine eigenständige Haltung entwickelt habe; das Zielpublikum seien Heidenchristen gewesen.

Die Vorstellung Hilgenfelds und auch Volkmars – letzterer wird als der „üppigste Schößling der Tendenzkritik" mit leichtem Spott bedacht, das Mk enthalte ‚paulinistische' Vorstellungen oder sei sogar als Manifest einer paulinischen Partei zu verstehen, weist Holtzmann zurück: Hier sei „[u]ebertriebener Scharfsinn" am Werk[65]. Gegenüber dem tendenzkritischen Ansatz verhält sich Holtzmann allgemein sehr reserviert. Ebenso wie die hypothetisch rekonstruierten Quellen A und Λ repräsentieren Holtzmann zufolge auch die überlieferten Evangelien ganz unterschiedliche theologische Tendenzen. Die Basisquellen haben seiner Ansicht nach eher durch ihre literarische Form die nachfolgenden Schriften beeinflusst – die epische Form des Markusevangeliums, die von der Tübinger Schule durchweg verkannt worden sei, verdanke sich klar dem Vorbild des Urevangeliums und schließe als solche gerade jede forcierte theologische Parteinahme aus[66].

Eine allgemein ‚universalistische' Grundtendenz findet er allerdings durchaus im Markusevangelium. Sie dient ihm auch als Argument zur Widerlegung der Matthäus-Priorität im Sinne einer Redaktionshypothese, auf der, wie gesehen, die älteren Tübinger beharrten: Zwar setzt er die kanonische Endgestalt des Matthäusevangeliums zeitlich vor den Abschluss von Markus und Lukas. Doch dass der Verfasser des Markusevangeliums das Matthäusevangelium oder gar Matthäus und Lukas gekannt habe, ist Holtzmann zufolge unvorstellbar. Aus welchem

---

63 E. Dinkler, Art. Holtzmann, Heinrich, in: NDB 9 (1972), 560-561; É. Trocmé, L'oeuvre scientifique de Heinrich Julius Holtzmann, in: Société de l'Histoire du Protestantisme Français: Bulletin de la Société de l'Histoire du Protestantisme Français 136 (1990), 55-64.
64 Holtzmann, Die synoptischen Evangelien, 385.
65 Ebd., 386. Umgekehrt ist Holtzmann zufolge eine Bekanntschaft des Paulus mit dem Urevangelium A zwar chronologisch möglich, aber unwahrscheinlich. Die These, 2 Kor 8,18 f. stelle einen Bezug zu dem traditionell genannten Verfasser Johannes Marcus her, wurde u.a. von F. Hitzig ausgearbeitet: F. Hitzig, Über Johannes Marcus und seine Schriften, oder: welcher Johannes hat die Offenbarung verfaßt? Eine Abhandlung in drei Büchern, Zürich 1843, 167-173.
66 Holtzmann, Die synoptischen Evangelien, 387. Ebd., 388, würdigt Holtzmann jedoch Baurs allmählichen Erkenntnisfortschritt.

Grund hätte er das gesamte dort zu findende ‚universalistische' Material, das seine eigene Haltung unterstützt hätte, in seiner Darstellung weglassen sollen?[67]

In seiner eine Generation später erschienenen ‚Neutestamentlichen Theologie' urteilt Holtzmann konzilianter[68]. Zunächst diskutiert er, eingehender als zuvor, die von der Tradition und auch von manchen Zeitgenossen wie Hilgenfeld behauptete Nähe des Markusevangeliums zur petrinischen Tradition. Die zahlreichen Petrusepisoden im zweiten Evangelium gehören seiner Meinung nach jedoch allesamt der Traditionsschicht des Urevangeliums A an. In diesem Rahmen können sie „ungezwungen auf Mittheilungen des Pt zurückgeführt werden", ohne dass dies Aufschluss über die Stellung des Verfassers des Markusevangeliums zu Petrus gibt[69]. Demgegenüber nehme das Markusevangelium im Gegensatz zu den beiden anderen Synoptikern durchaus eine „positive Stellung" zum Paulinismus ein. Vorausgesetzt – so die methodische Absicherung –, man erkenne „die Unbefangenheit und relative Geschichtlichkeit der Erzählung an sich" an, könne man die „paulin. Begriffswelt" als ein Medium betrachten, „durch welches gewisse, die Wirklichkeit übersteigende, aus dogmatischen oder ästhetischen Motiven zu begreifende Elemente hindurchgegangen sind"[70]. Das Evangelium insgesamt könne durchaus als „die richtige geschichtliche Illustration zu der paulin. Predigt vom gekreuzigten Christus und ihrem Losungswort ‚Durch Tod zum Leben'" gelten[71]. Bereits die summarische Formel der Predigt Jesu, so Holtzmann im Anschluss an Volkmar, entspreche den paulinischen Formeln, die Evangelium und Glauben in Beziehung setzen. Im Einzelnen sieht er die „deterministische Teleologie" der für die Ungläubigen bestimmten Gleichnisrede Mk 4,10-12 nach Vorbildstellen im Röm (Röm 9,18-29; 10,16-21; 11,8.10) und besonders parallel zu 1Kor 14,21 f. angelegt. Auch die Verklärungsgeschichte Mk 9,2-8 verdankt sich in seiner (von Neutestamentlern wie Otto Pfleiderer, Carl Heinrich Weizsäcker oder Hans von Soden geteilten) Sicht eindeutig dem „Midrasch vom Erglänzen des vom Sinai herabkommenden Moses" 2Kor 3,7-4,6[72]. Parallelen werden auch für den Abbaruf Mk 14,36

---

67 Ebd., 389.
68 H.J. Holtzmann, Lehrbuch der neutestamentlichen Theologie, Bd. 1, Freiburg i.Br/Leipzig 1897, 419.
69 Ebd., 422. Vgl. zeitgenössisch E. Scharfe, Die petrinische Strömung der neutestamentlichen Literatur. Untersuchungen über die schriftstellerische Eigentümlichkeit des ersten Petrusbriefs, des Marcusevangeliums und der petrinischen Reden der Apostelgeschichte, Berlin 1893, 173 f.
70 Holtzmann, Lehrbuch der neutestamentlichen Theologie, 423.
71 Ebd., 424.
72 Ebd., 424 Anm. 1 m. Nachw.

(vgl. Röm 8,15; Gal 4,6) sowie für einige „paulinisirende Zuspitzung[en] der Gedankens Jesu" gesehen[73].

4 Karl Holsten

Einen äußerst eigenständigen Ansatz verfolgte der Heidelberger Neutestamentler Karl Holsten (1825-1897), ein Freisinniger, der ähnlich wie Volkmar aufgrund seiner persönlichen theologischen und exegetischen Entwicklung von sich aus eine prinzipiell affirmative Stellung zur Tübinger Schule Baurs aufgenommen hatte; sein Werk kreiste in erster Linie um die paulinische Theologie[74]. In einigen darüber hinausgreifenden Beiträgen entwarf er das Modell dreier selbständiger Verkündigungsstränge im apostolischen Zeitalter, wie er es aus dem authentischen Corpus Paulinum rekonstruieren zu können meinte: des gesetzesfreien Evangeliums des Paulus, der gemäßigt judenchristlichen Verkündigung des Petrus sowie der streng judenchristlichen des Jakobus. Die drei jeweils mit Ausschließlichkeitsanspruch auftretenden und sich „bis zur Vernichtung" bekämpfenden Formen des Evangeliums setzten je auf eigene Weise die idealen Ideen der Gerechtigkeit, des Gottesreiches und des Messias als „Formprincipien" ein, „unter deren Herrschaft das geschichtliche Leben Jesu von Nazareth als das Messiasleben des Heilsbringers von den heilverlangenden Gemütern gestaltet wurde" – literarisches Endprodukt dieses Vorgangs waren die drei synoptischen Evangelien[75].

Holsten zufolge kann die synoptische Frage also nur auf der Basis einer Rekonstruktion der ‚dogmatisch-religiösen Gegensätze' angegangen werden, welche das Urchristentum in der ersten Phase mündlicher Traditionsweitergabe prägten. Mit diesem Leitbegriff, der sich eng an Baurs mit Antithesen operierende Tendenzkritik anlehnt, operierend, verficht Holsten die Matthäuspriorität im Sinne einer Benutzungshypothese: Das streng judenchristliche und antipaulinische Matthäusevangelium sei anschließend – mangels einer eigenen Jesusüberlieferung der Paulusgemeinden – von dem klar paulinisch gesonnenen Verfasser des Markusevangeliums redigiert worden, der „die Lehre Jesu als das Vorbild und den

---

[73] Ebd., 425; ebd. aber auch der Verweis auf das Fehlen einer zentralen Semantik wie δίκαιος usw. – Ebenso positiv in puncto eines paulinischen Einflusses auf das Mk äußert sich Holtzmann gegen neue Infragestellungen zehn Jahre später in seinem hochinteressanten Forschungsüberblick: H.J. Holtzmann, Die Marcus-Kontroverse in ihrer heutigen Gestalt, in: Archiv für Religionswissenschaft 10 (1907), 18-40; 161-200, hier 37-40.
[74] R. Knopf, Art. Holsten, Karl Christian Johann, in: ADB 50 (1905), 450-455.
[75] K. Holsten, Die drei ursprünglichen, noch ungeschriebenen Evangelien. Zur synoptischen Frage (Karlsruhe/Leipzig) 1883, 55.

Inhalt der Lehre des Paulus aufgestellt und damit das Recht des Apostels und seines Evangeliums begründet" habe[76]. Für den Verfasser des Lukasevangeliums sei demgegenüber das paulinische Evangelium bereits eine Tatsache gewesen, die er an den meisten Stellen nicht mehr hinterfragt habe; er wird deswegen von Holsten mit einer der zeitgenössischen Kirchenpolitik entlehnten Semantik als ‚Unionspauliner' bezeichnet.

Ausgangspunkt der markinischen Redaktion seien die inneren Widersprüche des Matthäusevangeliums gewesen: Während der Verfasser des Markusevangeliums die judaistischen Elemente dieses ersten Evangeliums ablehnen musste, konnte er sich mit der petrinischen Messiasanschauung identifizieren, die Jesus als „den todesleidenden, den gekreuzigten Christus, den sündensünenden und schon auf erden sündenvergebenden erlöser" [sic] sah, der sich frei gegenüber dem mosaischen Gesetz verhielt, seine Vollmacht gegenüber den Dämonen ausübte, dem jüdischen Volk wegen seiner Herzensverhärtung die Verstoßung, sein Evangelium aber für die gesamte Völkerwelt verkündete[77]. Die religionsgeschichtliche Leistung des Verfassers sei nichts weniger gewesen, als den Paulinismus in die „Urquelle" des christlichen Bewußtseins zurückzuleiten, nämlich „das geschichtliche leben und die geschichtliche offenbarung Jesu Christi", und ihn dadurch dauerhaft lebensfähig zu machen[78]. Neben der ‚dogmatisch-religiösen Umformung' des Matthäusevangeliums habe der Verfasser des Markusevangeliums, so Holsten, an hunderten von Einzelstellen Unklarheiten und Widersprüche im Text des ihm vorliegenden ersten Evangeliums korrigiert[79].

Der Verfasser des Markusevangeliums hebt Holsten zufolge durchweg mit literarischen Mitteln hervor, „was in der Verkündigung Jesu gleiches mit der Verkündigung des Paulus gegeben war, und den gleichen Hass der Volksgenossen wider die Neuheit der Lehre beider"[80]. Jesus werde immer wieder als ‚Typus' des

---

[76] Ebd., 70; vgl. K. Holsten, Die synoptischen evangelien nach der form ihres inhaltes. Für das studium der synoptischen frage dargestellt und erläutert, Heidelberg 1885, 180.

[77] Ebd., 179 f. Die These resümierend das für Holstens Verständnis von Geschichtlichkeit charakteristische Zitat: „Wir dürfen nur im geiste eines pauliners etwa ums jar 80 das matthaeusevangelium lesen, um beides zu begreifen, dass dieser pauliner grade auf grund des matthaeusevangeliums das geschichtliche bild Jesu im matthaeusevangelium als ein judaistisch getrübtes erkannte, und dass dieser pauliner grade auf grund des matthaeusevangeliums sich dazu gedrängt fülte, aus dem matthaeusevangelium jene judaistischen züge auszulöschen, die petrinischen kräftiger hervorzuheben, um das für ihn geschichtlich ware, das paulinische Mesiasbild herzustellen" (ebd., 180).

[78] Holsten, Die synoptischen evangelien, 180.

[79] Zu Holstens exegetischer Rekonstruktion im einzelnen ebd., 94-102; 183-207.

[80] Holsten, Die drei ... Evangelien, 70; zum Motiv des Hasses auf Paulus ebd., 72; ders. 1885, 182; 201.

Paulus dargestellt[81]. Deswegen lasse der Verfasser vor allem in charakteristischer Weise die matthäische Bergpredigt sowie die messianische Vorgeschichte aus, um die paulinischen Konzepte von Glaubensgerechtigkeit und hoher Christologie nicht zu kompromittieren[82]. Als Schlüssel zum Verständnis der theologischen Tendenz im Markusevangelium betrachtet Holsten die zweite Leidensankündigung Mk 9,32: Sie setze das bereits in Mk 1,21-28 angelegte „Messiasprogramm" mit dem paulinischen Evangelium gleich, das die dämonenüberwindende Macht der Verkündigung Jesu und seinen Kreuzestod als notwendig zur Herstellung universaler Gerechtigkeit verstehe[83]. Nichtverstehen und Verstockung der Hörer Jesu im Markusevangelium seien als Anspielung darauf zu verstehen, wie die Judenchristen auf die neue Lehre des Paulus reagierten[84]. Aber auch viele kleine Anspielungen stellten literarisch die Verbindung zum Corpus Paulinum her, etwa der nur im Markusevangelium zu findende Vorwurf, Jesus habe einen unreinen Geist (Mk 3,30), der mit der entsprechenden Klage über Paulus 1Thess 2,3 korreliert sei[85].

Den Einwand, solche subtilen Parallelen könne das zeitgenössische Zielpublikum kaum verstanden haben, nimmt Holsten vorweg: Tatsächlich seien die paulinischen „Schlagworte", wie etwa die Rede vom Auflösen des Gesetzes, in aller Munde gewesen und beim Hören des Markusevangeliums sofort als paulinisch erkannt worden[86]. Dagegen urteilt Holtzmann in einer summarischen Fußnote: „Eine solche Kenntniss der Finessen des Paulinismus, wie sie Holsten bei seiner Erklärung des 2. Evglms durchweg dem Mc zutraut, besass kein Mann des apostol. und nachapostol Zeitalters"[87].

5 Otto Pfleiderer

Otto Pfleiderer (1893-1908), ein Epigone der Tübinger Schule, entwickelte nach 1870 eine Konzeption der Theologiegeschichte des Urchristentums, die einerseits von Baurs Modellbildung deutlich abweicht, andererseits aber auch Albrecht Ritschl (1822-1889) und seinen Schülern, vor allem Adolf Harnack, widerspricht: Er möchte den Gegensatz zwischen ‚Paulinismus' und Judenchristentum als Triebfeder theologischer Auseinandersetzungen auf die apostolische Zeit beschränken.

---

81 Ebd., 197.
82 Holsten, Die drei ... Evangelien, 71; ders., Die synoptischen evangelien, 184 f.
83 Holsten, Die drei ... Evangelien, 67 f.; Zitat 67.
84 Ebd. 66.
85 Holsten, Die synoptischen evangelien, 182.
86 Holsten, Die drei ... Evangelien, 70.
87 Holtzmann, Lehrbuch, 424, Anm. 2

Die heidenchristliche Kirche habe demgegenüber von Beginn an – und nicht erst durch den Einbruch des Gnostizismus – „auf dem Boden des Hellenismus, welcher ausser jenem Gegensatze lag, sich gebildet und entwickelt"[88]. Das Heidenchristentum habe sich als ein Amalgam von Christusverkündigung und Elementen des pagan beeinflussten hellenistischen Denkens entwickelt – bereits den paulinischen Schriften sei der Hellenismus nicht fremd gewesen, und die zeitlich anschließende urchristliche Literatur gebe davon in vielen unterschiedlichen Ausprägungen kund[89].

Das Markusevangelium als zeitlich ältestes Evangelium zeichnet sich Pfleiderer zufolge durch die Ursprünglichkeit seiner Überlieferung und die Klarheit seiner literarischen Anlage aus – die beiden anderen Synoptiker wirkten ihm gegenüber oft sekundär[90]. Pfleiderer betont einerseits diesen authentischen Charakter der markinischen Geschichtsdarstellung. Doch gleichzeitig habe den Verfasser in vielen seiner Auffassungen „der bestimmende Einfluss des grossen Lehrers Paulus", dessen persönlicher Schüler er wahrscheinlich gewesen sei, geprägt[91]. Wenig spricht laut Pfleiderer gegen die traditionelle Identifizierung mit dem Paulusvertrauten Johannes Marcus[92]. Ziel seiner literarischen Arbeit sei gewesen, „das Evangelium von Jesus als dem Christus, welches Paulus als theologische Lehre verkündigt hatte, in der erzählenden Form einer Geschichte des Lebens und Leidens Jesu darzustellen"[93]. Obgleich Pfleiderer, wie gleich zu sehen ist, zu ähnlichen Ergebnissen wie Volkmar und Holsten gelangt, setzt er sich methodisch deutlich von ihnen ab: Das Vorgehen des Verfassers dürfe keineswegs als bloß symbolische Einkleidung idealer Lehrinhalte verstanden werden[94]. Vielmehr habe er in einzelnen Passagen des Markusevangeliums, auf authentischer Jüngerüberlieferung fußend, mit literarischen Mitteln „den sinnbildlichen Ausdruck der paulinischen Idee" gestaltet. Gleich zu Beginn des Evangeliums ist die Geisttaufe Jesu, als Illustration der paulinischen Christologie in Röm 1,4, ein Beispiel hierfür[95]. Auch den Inhalt der Jesusverkündigung – Glaubensforderung und Glaubensgehorsam – schildere der Autor des Markusevangeliums in dersel-

---

[88] O. Pfleiderer, Das Urchristenthum, seine Schriften und Lehren in geschichtlichem Zusammenhang, Berlin 1887, IV.
[89] Ebd., V.
[90] Ebd., 359 u.ö; für das Postulat eines Ur-Markus besteht Pfleiderer zufolge kein Anlass.
[91] Ebd., 360.
[92] Ebd., 415.
[93] Ebd.
[94] Ebd., 364.
[95] Ebd., 361.

ben Form wie Paulus, besonders ausgeprägt bei der Jüngerberufung Mk 1,14 f.[96]. Ebenfalls bei der Theorie der Gleichnisrede Mk 4,10-12 nimmt Pfleiderer, wie Holtzmann, eine paulinische Prägung an. Seine Idee einer prinzipiellen historischen Authentie der markinischen Darstellung lässt ihn allerdings darüber hinaus folgen, der Verfasser habe mit seiner Deutung den Sinn der ursprünglichen Jesusäußerung ins Gegenteil verkehrt[97]. Die doppelte Orientierung des Verfassers des Markusevangeliums an ursprünglicher Jesusüberlieferung und paulinischem Evangelium bringt Pfleiderer auf die Formel, dass viele der Jesuslogien „zwar den freien Geist des Paulinismus athmen, aber von der Form der paulinischen Theologie sehr weit verschieden sind"; sie könnten weder aus der Paulustradition noch aus dem Judenchristentum abgeleitet werden, sondern seien „eben echte Worte des originalen religiösen Genius Jesus selbst"[98]. Die ausdrücklichen Leidensweissagungen etwa, die Pfleiderer als historisch unwahrscheinlich einschätzt, seien demgegenüber Produkt der dogmatischen Reflexion des paulinischen Verfassers[99].

---

[96] Ebd., 362, Verweis auf charakteristische paulinische Formeln; zu weiteren direkten Paulinismen ebd., 384; 390 zur Verklärungsgeschichte („eine allegorische Dichtung des Evangelisten [...], welche paulinische Gedanken in den durch die heilige Sage gegebenen Bildern zu veanschaulichen gegeben ist"); 394 f.; 400; 408; 413.
[97] Ebd., 371.
[98] Ebd., 380; ebenso zur Kindersegung ebd., 393.
[99] Ebd, 383 f.; ebd. die Parallelsetzung von Mk 8,34 und Gal 2,19; 6,14. In der zweiten Auflage seines Werks reagiert Pfleiderer mit einer grundlegenden Neubearbeitung vor allem der Passagen zur Christologie des Mk auf die aktuelle exegetische Diskussion; dort wird die Quelle der Leidensweissagungen in der Tradition „der ältesten christlichen Apologetik" ausgemacht, also nicht mehr direkt als Produkt des Evangelisten gesehen. Gleichzeitig verstärkt Pfleiderer seiner Sicht, die apokalyptischen Sprüche im Umfeld der Leidensankündigungen (Mk 8,34-37) gehörten zu den echten Jesuslogien, sie seien in ihrer sprachlichen Form aber „durchweg durch paulinische Sprache beeinflusst": O. Pfleiderer, Das Urchristentum, seine Schriften und Lehren in geschichtlichem Zusammenhang, Berlin ²1902, Bd. 1, 360-363; Zitat: 362. Die Idee der Lebenshingabe als Aufgabe des Messias Mk 10:45 verdanke sich dagegen rein der paulinischen Dogmatik, sie habe Jesus ebenso ferngelegen wie die Identifikation mit dem apokalyptischen Menschensohn: „beide stammen aus dem durch Paulus beeinflussten Glaubensbewusstsein der Gemeinde, nicht aus dem ursprünglichen Selbstbewusstsein Jesu" (ebd., 372). Abschließend bekräftigt Pfleiderer nochmals die auf „unzweideutigen Indizien" beruhende These vom direkten paulinischen Einfluß auf das Mk (ebd., 403).

6 Religionsgeschichtliche Schule

Seit den 1880er Jahren veränderten sich die intellektuellen Rahmenbedingungen der deutschsprachigen protestantischen Theologie im Allgemeinen ebenso wie die der neutestamentlichen Exegese deutlich. Die Theologie des Göttinger Dogmatikers und Dogmenhistorikers Albrecht Ritschl – ursprünglich der Baurschule angehörig – brach allmählich das Feld der bis dahin gegeneinander stehenden Positionen von vermittelnd-positiver Theologie, lutherischem Neukonfessionalismus und Freisinnig-Liberalen auf. Die mit Ritschl in enger Beziehung stehende sogenannte religionsgeschichtliche Schule propagierte in der Evangelienforschung neue Methoden; vor allem der formgeschichtliche Ansatz verlagerte dabei das Interesse deutlich von der theologischen Interpretation der literarischen Endprodukte hin zur Untersuchung der einzelnen Überlieferungselemente und ihrer ursprünglichen religiösen Funktion. Viele jüngere Exegeten stellten einen selbständigen theologischen Gestaltungswillen der Evangelisten infrage. Die Frage nach dem Verhältnis zwischen dem Markusevangelium und dem Corpus Paulinum blieb zwar in der Diskussion präsent, doch nahm das Interesse am Thema allmählich lagerübergreifend ab.

Charakteristisch für die Situation um die Jahrhundertwende ist das Urteil Paul Wernles (1872-1939), die dialektische Interpretation der Urchristentumsgeschichte mit den beiden Polen des Judenchristentums und des Paulinismus, wie sie die Tübinger Schule vertreten habe, sei „ganz allgemein aufgegeben"[100]. Keineswegs müsse das Evangelium als Parteischrift betrachtet werden, der Evangelist „als Mann der zweiten Generation" habe vielmehr seine eigenen, vom früheren Parteigegensatz weit entfernten Gedanken einfließen lassen[101]. Zwar sei dem Markusevangelium der Judaismus fremd; andererseits stehe es aber auch dem Paulinismus vollkommen fern, ja, es sei „unbegreiflich, wie diese Thatsache hat verkannt werden können"[102]. Seine „vollständig untheologische Haltung" sei vielmehr eng an der laienhaften, der rabbinischen Theologie gegenüber feindlichen Frömmigkeit des Petrus orientiert[103]. Die Christologie des Markusevangeliums sei den paulinischen Ideen von himmlischer Präexistenz und Versöhnungstod demgegenüber geradezu entgegengesetzt, ebenso die Soteriologie: „Die Unmöglichkeit der Gesetzerfüllung und die Rettung allein aus Gnaden ist ein dem

---

[100] P. Wernle, Die synoptische Frage, Freiburg i. Br./Leipzig/Tübingen 1899, 198.
[101] Ebd.
[102] Ebd., 199.
[103] Eine eigenwillige und stark psychologisierende Charakterisierung dieser Frömmigkeit ebd., 200 f.; Zitat: ebd., 203.

Mr ganz fremder Gedanke"[104]. Der Leser, so Wernle, könne das Markusevangelium überhaupt nur verstehen, insofern er bei der Lektüre den Paulinismus vergesse.

Im Vorwort zu seiner Monographie hatte Wernle angegeben, er besitze nur eine eingeschränkte Kenntnis der Forschungsdiskussion[105], und tatsächlich begleitet keinerlei konkreter Literaturverweis seine dezidierte Absage an die Tendenzkritik. Es war in der Ritschlschule durchaus typisch, den Bezug auf theologische Vorgängergenerationen zu verschleiern oder in jovialem Ton deren Leistungen zu relativieren. Ein solches Vorgehen ist auch bei dem Breslauer Neutestamentler William Wrede (1859-1906) zu beobachten, als er 1901 in seiner Monographie über das Messiasgeheimnis auf sein Verhältnis zu Volkmar zu sprechen kommt: Zwar sei diesem Allegorismus und Symbolismus vorzuwerfen, doch bleibe das Hauptwerk von 1870/76 „das geistreichste und scharfsinnigste und m. E. überhaupt das bedeutendste, das wir über Markus besitzen"[106]. Nähere Andeutungen zu Volkmars Ergebnissen bleiben allerdings auf ein einziges Zitat beschränkt, da Wrede darauf besteht, seine Konzeption ohne jede Kenntnis von Volkmars Publikationen entwickelt zu haben. Volkmar sei immerhin „der Erste gewesen [...], der die Verbote Jesu mit dem Gedanken an die Auferstehung interpretiert hat" – doch er blieb, so darf der Leser folgern, ohne klares Bewusstsein seiner eigenen Innovationsleistung und konnte daher auch nicht den Schluss ziehen, dass der irdische Jesus seine Messianität absichtlich verhüllt habe[107].

Johannes Weiß (1863-1914), ein Wegbereiter der Formgeschichte, lehnt den engen Bezug zwischen Paulus und dem Markusevangelium, wie ihn Volkmar, Holsten und in eingeschränkter Form auch noch Holtzmann postuliert hatten, ebenso ab wie Baurs „These von der blassen Neutralität des Markus"[108]. Durchaus spiegeln sich Weiß zufolge die „Ideen und Interessen des Paulinischen Kreises" im Markusevangelium. Weiß begründet dies in erster Linie über die von ihm postulierte Verfasserschaft des Johannes Markus, die auch gewisse Parallelen zum 1. Petrusbrief erkläre[109]. Das Verhältnis von paulinischer und petrinischer Überlieferung auf das Markusevangelium sei so zu denken, „dass der gewaltige Theologe in formeller Weise auf unsren Evangelisten gewirkt hat, während ihm von Petrus

---

[104] Ebd., 200.
[105] Ebd., VII.
[106] W. Wrede, Das Messiasgeheimnis in den Evangelien. Zugleich ein Beitrag zum Verständnis des Markusevangeliums, Göttingen 1901, 283.
[107] Ebd.
[108] J. Weiß, Das älteste Evangelium. Ein Beitrag zum Verständnis des Markus-Evangeliums und der ältesten evangelischen Überlieferung, Göttingen 1903, 95; wie gezeigt, verzeichnet dies Baurs Einschätzung.
[109] Ebd, 96.

die breite Fülle des Stoffes zugekommen ist"[110]. Eine solche formale Nähe stelle etwa die unmittelbare Deutung eines Gleichnisses dar (Mk 2,17), die erst für die apostolische Zeit charakteristisch sei. Nur bei wenigen charakteristischen Ideen wie der Johannestaufe Mk 1,4 oder dem Geistwort Mk 14,38 sieht Weiß direkte inhaltliche Bezüge[111]. Er akzeptiert zwar grundsätzlich Volkmars These, dass das Evangelium nicht als Biographie, sondern als „eine Lehr- und Erbauungsschrift in erzählender Form" zu verstehen sei[112]. Doch habe der Zürcher Neutestamentler diesen Gedanken bis zur Karikatur übertrieben. Sogar aus einer stärker an der literarischen Leistung des Verfassers interessierten Perspektive wirke dies schädlich: „Die symbolische Erklärung zerstört die Poesie und Kraft dieser Darstellungen", die Jesu Wirken eher als allgemeinen Typus in seiner prinzipiellen Vorbildhaftigkeit für jedes christliche Handeln vorführen wollten[113]. Seinem formgeschichtlichen Ansatz entsprechend, sieht Weiß den Verfasser des Evangeliums insgesamt „bei weitem mehr als Vermittler einer Überlieferung, denn als Schöpfer einer Christusbildes und einer Christuslehre"[114].

Zum selben Zeitpunkt kam auch der Volkmar persönlich nahestehende, nicht zur religionsgeschichtlichen Schule gehörige Adolf Jülicher (1857-1938) zu dem Schluss, dass der tendenzkritische Absatz überholt sei. Alle Versuche, das Markusevangelium als „Parteievangelium" zu verstehen oder „ihm eine besondere theologische Tendenz anzudichten", seien gescheitert[115]. Jülicher unterstellt dem Verfasser, der als „religiöser Agitator" aufgetreten sei, literarische Selbständigkeit, weist aber Volkmars These zur ‚Lehrpoesie'-Gattung zurück[116]. Ziel des Verfassers sei schlicht gewesen, „jedem der lesen wollte, die Geschichte Jesu objektiv, ohne dogmatischen Kommentar und ohne erbauliche Reflexion darzubieten"[117]. Dies sei wunderbar gelungen: Die Abgewogenheit des Evangeliums, die Konzentration auf das Wesentliche und der „Mut, das Evangelium sich ganz durch sich allein verteidigen zu lassen", hebe den Verfasser über seine Lehrer Petrus und Paulus hinaus „zu einer weltgeschichtlichen Größe".

Theologisch konservativeren Exegeten wie dem Wiener Neutestamentler Paul Feine (1859-1933) kam solche Kritik an der Tübinger Schule gelegen. Ähnlich wie der theologisch ganz anders positionierte Wernle kommt er zu dem Schluss, dass

---

110 Ebd, 95.
111 Ebd.
112 Ebd. 99; 103 f.
113 Ebd., 102
114 Ebd., 105.
115 [Adolf] Jülicher, Art. Marcus im NT, in: RE 3. Aufl. Bd. 12 (1903), 288-297, hier 293.
116 Ebd., 294.
117 Ebd., 295.

das Markusevangelium ohne jeden direkten Einfluss aus dem Corpus Paulinum geblieben sei[118]. Feine klagt über die willkürlichen Ergebnisse der tendenzkritischen Evangelienauslegung, die sich im Effekt als „nicht viel besser als die Allegorese der Alten Kirche" erwiesen habe[119]. Volkmar und Holsten gegenüber zieht er einen Umkehrschluss: Die inhaltlichen Berührungsflächen zwischen Passagen des Markusevangeliums und der paulinischen Verkündigung sprächen nicht dafür, „dass Markus die Erzählungen bevorzugt habe, in denen sich die Verbindungsfäden zwischen Jesus und Paulus aufzeigen lassen, oder dass er die zutreffende geschichtliche Illustration zu der paulinischen Predigt […] biete, sondern schon der Überlieferungsstoff des ältesten Evangeliums zeigt, dass Paulus die Bedeutung des Wirkens Jesu richtig erfasst hat"[120]. Auf den Feldern von Christologie und Ethik sieht Feine tiefe sachliche Differenzen; der Heilsuniversalismus des Markusevangeliums spiegele nicht mehr als das ganz allgemeine „Bewusstsein der damaligen Heidenkirche"[121]. Bei der Interpretation der soteriologischen Zentralstellen Mk 8,31 etc. schließlich argumentiert Feine polemisch, dass es sich hierbei um authentische Jesuslogien handeln müsse – denn erwiesen sich die Leidensweissagungen als eine Bildung der paulinischen Gemeinde, so müsse auch Paulus als „der eigentliche Schöpfer des Christentums" gelten, „des Gedankens, dass es durch Tod zum Leben, durch selbstloses Dienen zur Grösse im Reiche Gottes gehe, dass der Kreuzestod die Höhe der heilsmittlerischen Leistung Christi war"[122]. Damit müsse man dann aber konsequenterweise das Christusbild der Kirche über Bord werfen und ein ‚historisches' an seine Stelle setzen[123]. Sein Fazit lautet daher: „Das Markusevangelium steht somit nicht unter dem Einflusse der paulinischen Theologie"[124].

7 Schluss

Der Diskurs über Paulinismus im Markusevangelium – verstanden als bewusst im Zuge der Redaktion durch den Verfasser gesetzte Bezüge auf Theologumena des Corpus Paulinum – war nach zirka fünfzig Jahren exegetischer Diskussion an ein

---

118 Ebd., 149.
119 P. Feine, Jesus Christus und Paulus, Leipzig 1902, 135-149, hier 137.
120 Ebd., 138. Sogar die Verklärungsgeschichte 2 Kor 3,10-14 beruhe auf authentischer Überlieferung (ebd., 149).
121 Ebd., 140.
122 Ebd., 146.
123 Ebd.
124 Ebd., 149.

vorläufiges Ende gekommen. Alle Argumentionen für die Paulinismusthese hatten in der einen oder anderen Weise einen tendenzkritischen Ansatz vorausgesetzt, mitsamt der Festlegung auf die Existenz einer paulinischen Richtung oder Partei als prägender Komponente in der Urchristentumsgeschichte des Ersten Jahrhunderts. Diese Voraussetzungen schienen um 1900 endgültig überholt. Das Verebben des Paulinismusdiskurses stellt sich in einer wissenschaftstheoretischen Perspektive allerdings eher als Folge eines Paradigmenwechsels dar, nicht als die Widerlegung einer zwischenzeitlich mit erheblichem exegetischem Aufwand unterfütterten und im Zuge lebhafter Diskussionen modifizierten Hypothese. Wie gesehen, setzten sich die Gegner der These mit den differenzierten Argumentationen ihrer Verfechter kaum mehr detailliert auseinander. Es ist davon auszugehen, dass eine große Zahl exegetischer Beobachtungen, die im Zuge des hier nachgezeichneten Diskurses gemacht wurden, in der Fachdiskussion nach 1900 nicht mehr weiterverfolgt wurden.

Neben der zu engen Bindung an die Tendenzkritik, die der Paulinismusthese trotz aller Modifikationen anhaftete, stellte wohl der oft nur vage Bezug auf das sich verändernde Bild der Theologie des Paulus eine intrinsische Schwäche dar. Pfleiderers Synthese, die als eine letzte große Untermauerung von Baurs Idee einer paulinischen Partei als aktiver Größe im Urchristentum gedacht war[125], wurde nur verhalten rezipiert. Um 1900 hatte sich die Fragestellung zu den strittigen Belegstellen bereits deutlich gewandelt, ein neuer Diskurs, jetzt zum Thema ‚Jesus und Paulus', formierte sich[126]. In ideengeschichtlicher Hinsicht bleibt interessant, welche Energien liberale protestantische Exegeten in die Vorstellung investierten, im zeitlich ersten Evangelienbericht theologische Spuren des paulinischen Freiheitschristentums auffinden zu können. Ihr Anliegen war, einer möglichst authentischen Jesusüberlieferung jene Tendenz einzuschreiben, die man im Sinne einer historistischen Entwicklungsidee als das Ferment protestantischer Religion in ihrer langfristigen geschichtlichen Anlage betrachtete.

---

125 O. Pfleiderer, Der Paulinismus. Ein Beitrag zur Geschichte der urchristlichen Theologie, Leipzig 1873 [²1890].
126 Vgl. hierzu A. Lindemann, Paulus und die Jesustradition, in: ders. (Hrsg.), Glauben, Handeln, Verstehen. Studien zur Auslegung des Neuen Testaments, Bd. II (WUNT 282), Tübingen 2011, 73-115.

Teil 2 / Part 2: **Historische Fragen /
Historical Considerations**

Michael P. Theophilos
The Roman Connection: Paul and Mark

1 Introduction

The last decade of Marcan scholarship has witnessed a resurging, if incremental, awareness of Pauline influence on the Marcan narrative. Despite its main twentieth century detractor, that is, Martin Werner,[1] several have argued, in various levels of depth and complexity, that Mark was influenced by, or was drawing upon, Pauline material. Perhaps the most confident appraisal of such influence is expressed in Albert C. Outler's suggestion that "Romans was Mark's 'Q' - obviously not in the same sense as Holtzmann's postulation of a common *Quelle* for Matthew and Luke, but in the more important sense that Paul's *soteriology* and Mark's 'memoirs' support each other."[2] With obvious hyperbole, Outler highlights a feature of the debate that is often neglected, namely, the extent to which both theological *and* historical considerations must be taken into consideration when assessing the literary and contextual influence of Pauline material on the Marcan composition. This paper will argue that there are strong theological overtones within a plausible Roman historical context to suggest that the author of Mark's Gospel knew and drew upon the Pauline Roman connection.

2 Assumptions and Definitions: Romans

The general consensus of Pauline scholarship holds that the epistle to the Roman church was composed in the mid 50s CE and was sent from Corinth with the letter carrier identified as the deaconess Phoebe, διάκονον τῆς ἐκκλησίας τῆς ἐν Κεγχρεαῖς (16:1).[3] Although other locations for composition are possi-

---

[1] Martin Werner, *Der Einfluss paulinischer Theologie im Markusevangelium: eine Studie zur neutestamentlichen Theologie* (Giessen: Töpelmann, 1923).
[2] Albert C. Outler, "The Gospel According to St. Mark." *Perkins School of Theology Journal* 33-34 (1980): 3-9 at 7.
[3] Dieter Georgi, *Die Geschichte der Kollekte des Paulus für Jerusalem* (Hamburg: Herbert Reich, 1965), 95-96; Charles K. Barrett, *A Commentary on the Epistle to the Romans* (London: A & C Black, 1971), 3-4; Günther Bornkamm, *Paul* (London: Hodder & Stoughton, 1971), xii; Robert Jewett, *Dating Paul's Life* (London: SCM, 1979); and Helmut Koester, *Introduction to the New Testament*, vol. 2 (Philadelphia, Pa.: Fortress Press, 1982), 138.

ble (Athens, Ephesus, Philippi, Thessalonica, and Macedonia),⁴ several manuscripts include a postscript, πρὸς Ῥωμαίους ἐγράφη ἀπὸ Κορίνθου (B03 [4th century, Codex Vaticanus corrected reading], and D06 [6th century, Codex Claromontanus corrected reading]) or variations thereof identifying Corinth as the place of composition (049 218 489 927 999 1243 1244 1245 1628 1720 1874 1876 1877 1881). Although some commentators have suggested that precision regarding provenance and date bear no immediate consequence on interpretation,⁵ this study will attempt to demonstrate that a date in the mid 50s CE has important implications for both interpretation and the relationship of the Roman epistle with the Gospel of Mark.

What then can be said of the occasion and purpose of the letter? It is certainly true that the discernable purpose of Romans is far less conspicuous than any other of the Pauline corpus.⁶ This is amply demonstrated by the sheer variety of scholarly proposals regarding the epistle's purpose and function.⁷ Writing in the late nineteenth century, Frédéric L. Godet suggested that Romans consisted of "the apostle's dogmatic and moral catechism,"⁸ and similarly Günther Bornkamm, who states that Romans "summarizes and develops the most important themes and thoughts of the Pauline message...[and] elevates his theology above the moment of definite situations and conflicts into the sphere of the eternally and universally valid, this letter to the Romans is the last will and testament of the Apostle Paul."⁹ Despite some obvious lacunae (ecclesiology [1Cor 12-14], Eucharist [cf. 1Cor 11:17-34], resurrection and eschatology [cf. 1Cor 15; 1Thess 4:13 - 5:11]),¹⁰ understanding Romans as a doctrinal encapsulation of Pauline theology was a common approach throughout the medieval and later periods as demonstrated by the history of the epistle's interpretation.¹¹

---

4 Cited with support in Joseph A. Fitzmyer, *Romans*, AB 33 (New York, N.Y.: Doubleday, 1993), 85.
5 James D.G. Dunn, *Romans 1-8*, WBC 38A (Dallas, Tex.: Word Books, 1988), xliii.
6 L. Ann Jervis, *The Purpose of Romans: A Comparative Letter Structure Investigation*, JSNTSup 55 (Sheffield: JSOT Press), 11.
7 Fenton J. A. Hort, *Prolegomena to St. Paul's Epistles to the Romans and the Ephesians* (London: Macmillian, 1895), 5.
8 Cited in Fitzmyer, *Romans*, 74.
9 Günther Bornkamm, "The Letter to the Romans as Paul's Last Will and Testament." *ABR* 11 (1963-64): 2-14 at 14.
10 Karli Kuula, *The Law, The Covenant and God's Plan* (Göttingen: Vandenhoeck & Ruprecht, 2003), 37.
11 Karl P. Donfried, ed., *The Romans Debate* (Minneapolis, Minn.: Augsburg Press, 1977); see further Jervis, *Romans*, 11-28, for an overview of the history of interpretation.

This dominant interpretive trajectory came under serious scrutiny and critique by Ferdinand Christian Baur whose starting point was the ad hoc nature of epistolary correspondence.[12] Baur argued that the letter must be interpreted according to its historical circumstances, and not as a comprehensive theoretical theological treatise. As noted by Baur, the occasional genre of Romans is of no consequential difference when compared to Galatians or Corinthians, and thus must be interpreted in light of its concrete historical reality.

Internal evidence suggests that Paul's occasion for writing Romans was a combination of at least seven distinct elements. First, Romans is distinct among the Pauline epistles, for it does not presuppose a relationship with its recipients. Indeed, it is the only extant Pauline letter where he cannot rely on either his status as founder or any discernable prior relationship with its community[13] Second, in what is a relatively distinctive occurrence in the Pauline corpus, Romans is sent by Paul without any mention of a co-sender or a literary collaborator (cf. Sosthenes [1Cor 1:1]; Timothy [2Cor 1:1; Phil 1:1; Col 1:1; Phlm 1:1]; all the brothers [Gal 1:2]; Silvanus and Timothy [1Thess 1:1; 2Thess 1:1]). This scenario is perhaps even more notable given the mention of Timothy as συνεργός in Romans 16:21. Third, the opening of the epistle includes a clear emphasis on Paul's divinely sanctioned apostleship. In 1:1 Paul self-identifies as κλητὸς ἀπόστολος, and further provides an inclusio in vv. 4-5, by reaffirming the source of his apostolic authority, Ἰησοῦ Χριστοῦ τοῦ κυρίου ἡμῶν, δι᾽ οὗ ἐλάβομεν...ἀποστολήν. This theme is also apparent in 1:8-9, where God himself is invoked as a witness to Pauline jurisdiction.[14] This feature is even more striking given that it occurs in a context where, in both first century Greco-Roman letters and other Pauline correspondence, the sender typically prays for the wellbeing and health of recipients. In deviating from this expected norm, Paul emphatically accentuates his apostolic position.[15] Fourth, there is no hint in the letter that Paul writes to address specific erroneous doctrinal issues. Rather, Paul presents the gospel in terms that he anticipates his readers will share (1:3-4.8-9), as indeed evidenced by Paul's acknowledgement of their maturity (1:6; 15:14-15; 16:17-20). The emphasis on this shared, rather than distinct, understanding of the gospel, can be understood as a means of reinforcing his close connection with the recipients. Fifth, Paul indicates that the recipients fall under his apostolic responsibility

---

12 Ferdinand Christian Baur, "Über Zweck und Veranlassung des Römerbriefs und der damit zusammenhängenden Verhältnisse der römischen Gemeinde." *TZT* 9 (1836): 59-178.
13 Brendan Byrne, *Romans*, SP 6 (Collegeville, Pa.: Liturgical Press, 1996), 1.
14 See further Robert Jewett, *Romans: A Commentary*, Hermeneia (Minneapolis, Minn.: Fortress Press, 2007), 120.
15 Jervis, *Romans*, 158.

and includes a note of divine sanction in support (1:5-6). Indeed, the scope of Paul's missionary calling is nothing less than ἐν πᾶσιν τοῖς ἔθνεσιν (1:5).[16] Sixth, Paul evidences an enduring and sincere desire to visit the Christian community in Rome. His eagerness to do so is expressed in the hitherto unattested combination in Hellenistic Greek of εἴ πως (if perhaps [Phil 3:11; Acts 27:13]) with ἤδηποτὲ (now at last [Phil 4:10]) in Rom 1:10.[17] Although one may question whether Paul's desire to visit Rome in his early ministry occupied such pressing urgency,[18] the reference to a visit in v. 10, which is then reiterated in v. 11, presents a strong case for his passionate desire of an imminent visit. Paul provides an enigmatic explanation for the mitigating factors which has thus far prevented him from coming to Rome, καὶ ἐκωλύθην ἄχριτοῦ δεῦρο (but have been prevented so far). Paul describes his attempts as πολλάκις (many times, often, frequently), a term commonly employed by orators such as Demosthenes, Isocrates and Lysias.[19] This theme reappears toward the end of the epistle (15:22.25.31-32), and is combined with a request from Paul for their prayerful support during his upcoming journey to Jerusalem, in effect inviting their participation in his apostolic duties.[20] Finally, as 15:22-24 expressly indicates, Rome suited Paul as a platform for his mission to Spain.[21] Yet, Ernst Käsemann aptly notes that "Paul must avoid the suspicion that he wants to make the world capital his own domain, and he does not want to say brusquely that he regards it merely as a bridgehead."[22]

Taking several of these aspects into consideration, Romans can be understood as Paul's letter of introduction, "since he was by no means *persona grata* in certain Christian circles, he could not be altogether sure of a welcome."[23] Further to this, it was specifically Paul's mission to the Gentile world that he was attempting to justify and expound.[24] However, some have objected that this hardly provides the impetus for such a full and detailed explanation of the Pau-

---

16 Jewett, *Romans*, 111.
17 Jewett, *Romans*, 123.
18 Charles E. B. Cranfield, *The Epistle to the Romans*, vol. 1, ICC (Edinburgh: T & T Clark, 1994), 77.
19 Jewett, *Romans*, 129.
20 Jervis, *Romans*, 160.
21 David Aune, *The New Testament in its Literary Environment* (Philadelphia, Pa.: Westminster Press, 1987), 219.
22 Ernst Käsemann, *Commentary on Romans*, trans. Geoffrey W. Bromiley (Grand Rapids, Mich.: Eerdmans, 1980), 397.
23 Charles H. Dodd, *The Epistle of Paul to the Romans* (London: Hodder and Stoughton, 1932), xxv.
24 Jervis, *Romans*, 158.

line gospel in Romans.²⁵ One potential solution would be to see Paul motivated by his desire to provide clarification, before embarking on his journey to Spain via Rome, to those who had undoubtedly heard rumours of his former life as a Pharisee and persecutor of the Christian church.

Is there, however, something more specific that can be deduced in light of Baur's observation regarding the ad hoc occasion of epistolary correspondence? The question that naturally arises is whether a concrete historical circumstance can account for the particulars of Paul's presentation of material, especially in light of the climactic nature of chapters 9-11? A hypothesis proposed by Willi Marxsen in 1968 explored the implications of an edict issued by the Emperor Claudius in 49 CE.²⁶ Writing in the third decade of the second century (c. 120 CE), Suetonius records in his *Vita Claudii* 25.4 that Claudius "Judaeos impulsore Chresto assidue tumultuantis" (expelled from Rome Jews who were causing continual disturbances at the instigation of Chrestus). Despite the ambiguity of the instigation and the reference to Chrestus, which one assumes was an iotacistic error for Χριστός, Claudius' solution to Jewish unrest is certainly in keeping with imperial precedence, as evidenced, for example of Emperor Tiberius (Tac. *Ann.* 11.8.5, Suet. *Tib.* 36), and also echoes Claudius' own practice in resolving Jewish unrest in Alexandria in 41 CE (*P.Lond* VI.1912).²⁷ With respect to *Vita Claudii* 25.4 and the edict of 49 CE, Fitzmyer argues that Suetonius' statement refers to circumstances brought about by overzealous intrusions of Christian elements in the Jewish congregations of Rome,²⁸ or as Marxsen notes, "the Gospel of Christ which had called forth the ferment among the Jews of Rome."²⁹ It is indeed of interest that there is a historical glimpse of just this circumstance preserved in records of Paul's interactions with Aquila and Priscilla, after travelling from Athens to Corinth, Acts 18:2; "There he found a Jew named Aquila, a native of Pontus, who had recently come from Italy with his wife Priscilla, because Claudius had ordered all Jews to leave Rome." Whether Claudius' edict affected all Jews, or only their leaders is unknown,³⁰ however with the death of Claudius in 54 CE, the edict would almost certainly have been relaxed, if not completely

---

25 Fitzmyer, *Romans*, 75.
26 Willi Marxsen, *Introduction to the New Testament: An Approach to its Problems*, trans. George Buswell (Oxford: Blackwell, 1968), 98-101.
27 Graeme W. Clarke, "The Origins and Spread of Christianity." In *The Cambridge Ancient History,* Volume X: *The Augustan Empire 43 B.C.-A.D. 69,* eds Alan K. Bowman, Edward Champlin, and Andrew Lintott (Cambridge: Cambridge University Press, 1996), 848-72 at 869.
28 Fitzmyer, *Romans*, 77.
29 Marxsen, *Introduction*, 99.
30 Ernst Haenchen, *Die Apostelgeschichte* (Göttingen: Vandenhoeck & Ruprecht, 1959).

disregarded by Nero, whose wife Poppea Sabina was known to display Jewish sympathies. The net result of this would include a Jewish and Jewish Christian influx into Rome after 54 CE, returning to a Christian community that had evolved in a predominantly Gentile environment. This scenario provides the historical framework for a) Paul's emphasis on Israel's story in chapters 9-11, that is, to address the question of Jewish rejection of the gospel if, in fact, it is the legitimate fulfilment of God's *Heilsgeschichte*, and b) Paul's guidelines on adherence to dietary and calendric customs regarding the "weak" (those of Jewish background) and "strong" (those of Gentile background) within the community (Rom 14-15).

3 Assumptions and Definitions: Mark

Early testimony and Patristic tradition place the writing of Mark's gospel in Rome in the mid to late 60s CE.[31] Clement of Alexandria (Eusebius *H.E.* 6.14.5-6), Irenaeus (*Adv. Haer.* 3.1.1), and the Anti-Marcionite prologue attest to the Gospel's composition in Rome or the regions around Italy.[32] Furthermore, several dimensions of internal evidence also point towards Rome as the provenance of the Gospel.

First, of the 18 occurrences of Latinisms in the New Testament, 10 are found in Mark,[33] a frequency which is higher than any other Greek literary text of the period.[34] Add to this that several of the Latinisms are unattested in any Greek

---

[31] This testimony however, is not unanimous as John Chrysostom claims Mark was written in Egypt (*Homily on Matthew* 1.7). However, others have noted that Chrysostom's attribution of Mark to an Egyptian provenance may be due to his misinterpretation of Eusebius' comments in *H.E.* 2.16; see Henry B. Swete, *Commentary on Mark: The Greek Text with Introduction, Notes and Indexes* (Grand Rapids, Mich.: Kregel, 1977), xxxix.

[32] Helmut Koester, *Ancient Christian Gospels: Their History and Development* (London: SCM, 1990), 243 notes that the Anti-Marcionite prologues were "originally composed in Greek [and] appear in several dozen Latin Bible manuscripts...a date in the second half of the 4th century is likely for...Mark."

[33] δηνάριον (=*denarius* in 12:15); κεντυρίων (=*centurio* in 15:39.44.45); κῆνσος (=*census* in 12:14); κοδράντης (=*quadrans* in 12:42); λεγιών (=*legio* in 5:9.15); μόδιος (=*modius* in 4:21); ξέστης (=*sextarius* in 7:4); πραιτώριον (=*praetorium* in 15:16); σπεκουλάτωρ (=*speculator* in 6:27); φραγελλόω (=*flagellum* in 15:15).

[34] Martin Hengel, *Studies in the Gospel of Mark* (London: SCM, 1985), 29. See further Archibald T. Robertson, *A Grammar of the Greek New Testament in Light of Historical Research* (London: Hodder & Stoughton, 3rd edn 1919), 108-11; Friedrich Blass, Albert Debrunner, and F. Rehkopf, *Grammatik des neutestamentlichen Griechisch* (Göttingen: Vandenhoeck & Ruprecht, 14th edn 1975), 6-9.

texts prior to the first century, a portion of which appear uniquely within Mark or sources that have clearly used Mark as a literary source (κῆνσος, ξέστης, πραιτώριον, σπεκουλάτωρ, τίτλος, φραγελλόω),[35] and one may legitimately question Morna Hooker's bold claim that the connection between Mark and Rome based on Latinisms "has no substance."[36] Although James Keenan et al. have suggested that "penetration of Latin terms into everyday Egyptian Greek was limited, artificial, and superficial,"[37] Brian J. Incigneri argues, upon investigating several higher order linguistic features including word construction and syntax, that "the most likely place for Latinisms to predominate is in the city of Rome, where the Latin and Greek languages were closely intermingled as nowhere else at that time."[38]

Second, Hengel points to the story of the Syrophoenician woman in Mark 7:24-30 as additional evidence of a Roman provenance for the Gospel. Mark 7:26 refers to the woman as Ἑλληνίς, Συροφοινίκισσα τῷ γένει (Greekspeaking, Syrophoenician born). Hengel regards the addition of Συρο to Φοινίκισσα as redundant, and argues that it would seem nonsensical, if indeed the Gospel came from Syria/Palestine.[39] A Roman provenance however would necessitate the need to distinguish between Συροφοινίκισσα (Syrophoenician) and Λιβυφοινίκες (Carthaginian), as is the case in several occurrences in literature of the period (Lucilius 15.fr.496ff.; Juvenal 8.159ff.; Pliny *Natural History* 7.201).[40]

With respect to the dating, two early testimonies (Anti-Marcionite prologue and Irenaeus, *Adv. Haer.* 3.1.1) attribute the date of composition to after Peter's death in c. 65 CE. However, Clement of Alexandria (Eusebius, *H.E.* 6.14.5-6) intimates that the Gospel was written within Peter's lifetime. Modern scholarly debate typically concentrates on whether the Gospel was written in the years lead-

---

[35] See the helpful table in Allan Millard, *Reading and Writing in the Time of Jesus* (Sheffield: Sheffield Academic Press, 2000), 150.
[36] Morna D. Hooker, *The Gospel According to St. Mark*, (London: A & C Black, 1991), 7; also contra Adela Yarbro Collins, *Mark: A Commentary*, Hermeneia (Minneapolis, Minn.: Fortress Press, 2007), 9-10.
[37] James G. Keenan, "Review of *Il lessico latino nel Greco d'Egitto* (Barcelona: Institut de Teologia Fondamental, Seminario de Papirologia, 2ndedn, 1991) by S. Daris." *BASP* 29 (1992): 219-20.
[38] Brian J. Incigneri, *The Gospel to the Romans* (Leiden: Brill, 2003), 102. See further Peter Dschulnigg, *Sprache, Redaktion und Intention des Markus-Evangeliums: Eigentümlichkeiten der Sprache des Markus-Evangeliums und ihre Bedeutung für die Redaktionskritik* (Stuttgart: Katholisches Bibelwerk, 1986), 276-78; and Adam Winn, *The Purpose of Mark's Gospel* (Tübingen: Mohr Siebeck, 2008), 82-83.
[39] Hengel, *Studies*, 29.
[40] Cited in Hengel, *Studies*, 29.

ing up to the temple's destruction⁴¹ in August of 70 CE, or in the aftermath of that tragic event.⁴²The suggestion by several commentators that the parable of the wicked tenants (Mark 12:1-11), and in particular, the phraseology in v. 9, τί οὖν ποιήσει ὁ κύριοςτοῦ ἀμπελῶνος; ἐλεύσεται καὶ ἀπολέσει τοὺς γεωργοὺς καὶ δώσειτὸν ἀμπελῶνα ἄλλοις, indicates a post 70 CE date is not convincing. There were other prophetic figures who are recorded as prophesying the ruin of the temple during a time of peace, Jesus ben Ananias in 62 CE (Josephus, *War* 6.300-309) being one example. Commentators typically rely on the so-called "eschatological discourse" in Mark 13 to ascertain which elements delimit a *terminus ad quem* of the discourse. We find the analysis of Martin Hengel convincing in this regard,⁴³ and have adopted a date in the late 60s CE as the most probable for the composition of the Gospel. Hengel's evaluation of the relevance of Mark 13:2 (βλέπεις ταύτας τὰς μεγάλας οἰκοδομάς; οὐ μὴ ἀφεθῇ ὧδε λίθος ἐπὶ λίθονὃςοὐ μὴ καταλυθῇ) is particularly helpful, as is his pointing out that "the threat of the destruction of the temple had a long prehistory,"⁴⁴ as is evident from a variety of Jewish texts (Ps 74; Jer 7:12-14; 26:6, 9, 18; 2Kgs 25:9; 2Chron 36:19; Dan 8:11; 2Macc 14:33).

If then, on the basis of external and internal evidence, it is most plausible to hold that Mark originated in Rome toward the end of the 60s, one might expect to find certain theological points of contact or continuity between it and the earlier Pauline epistle to the Romans. Although Paul did not found the Christian community in Rome, he was certainly well connected to Christians in the city, as evidenced from his extended greetings in chapter 16. The specifics of the historical context will be detailed and explored at length in section 5 below. We will also note the later development in circumstances which accounts for a potentially significant point of discontinuity between Romans and Mark.

---

41 See Charles E. B. Cranfield, *The Gospel According to St. Mark* (Cambridge: Cambridge University Press, 1959), 8; William L. Lane, *The Gospel According to Mark: The English Text with Introduction, Exposition and Notes* (Grand Rapids, Mich.: Eerdmans, 1974), 17-21; Dennis E. Nineham, *The Gospel of St. Mark* (Baltimore, Md: Penguin Books, 1969), 42; and Eduard Schweizer, *The Good News According to Mark* (Atlanta, Ga.: John Knox Press, 1970), 25.
42 Joachim Gnilka, *Das Evangelium nach Markus*, vol. 1 (Zurich: Benziger, 3rd edn 1989), 35; Walter Grundmann, *Das Evangelium nach Markus* (Berlin: Evangelische Verlagsanstalt, 1959), 25; Incigneri, *Gospel*, 116-55; John S. Kloppenborg, "*Evocatio deorum* and the Date of Mark." *JBL* (2005): 419-50; and Dieter Lührmann, *Das Markusevangelium* (Tübingen: Mohr Siebeck, 1987), 6.
43 Hengel, *Studies*, 14-28.
44 Hengel, *Studies*, 15.

4 The Connection Between Romans and Mark

Since the publication of Martin Werner's 1923 monograph,[45] discernable theological points of continuity between Romans and Mark were predominantly regarded as superficial similarities common to a general expression of Christianity in the early era. Although there were a handful of early detractors,[46] the general consensus which endured well into the late twentieth century held that there is no specific connection between Paul and Mark, and *a fortiori* between Romans and Mark. Joel Marcus' recent article,[47] however, notes the changing tide of scholarly opinion.[48] What has been lacking in this evolving debate is attention to the influence of Romans on Mark within the particular historical parameters sketched above. It is to this context that we seek to demonstrate Pauline influence on Mark. This is not to suggest that the two writers must or should display unreserved theological correspondence,[49] but that a reasonable case can be made that there is a sustained connection between the two.

A distinct and prominent feature common to Mark's Gospel and the epistle to the Romans is the frequency and importance of the term εὐαγγέλιον. Mark uses the noun (unattested in Luke and John) to describe his literary account of Jesus's life and death (Mark 1:1, Ἀρχὴ τοῦ εὐαγγελίου Ἰησοῦ Χριστοῦ), as well as a description of the content of Jesus' teaching (Mark 1:14, ὁ Ἰησοῦς εἰς τὴν Γαλιλαίαν κηρύσσων τὸ εὐαγγέλιον τοῦ θεοῦ). It is significant to note that Paul too, commences Romans with reference to the εὐαγγέλιον in relation to

---

45 Werner, *Einfluss*.
46 Benjamin W. Bacon, *The Gospel of Mark: Its Composition and Date* (Oxford: Oxford University Press, 1925); John C. Fenton, "Paul and Mark." In *Studies in the Gospels: Essays in Memory of R. H. Lightfoot*, ed. Dennis E. Nineham (Oxford: Blackwell, 1957), 89-112.
47 Joel Marcus, "Mark – Interpreter of Paul." *NTS* 46 (2000): 473-87.
48 Michael D. Goulder, "Those Outside (Mk 4:10-12)." *NovT* 33 (1991): 289-302; John R. Donahue, "The Quest for the Community of Mark's Gospel." In *The Four Gospels 1992: Festschrift Frans Neirynck*, vol. 2, eds. Frans Van Segbroeck et al., BETL 100 (Leuven: Leuven University Press, 1992), 817-38; Wolfgang Schenk, "Sekundäre Jesuanisierungen von primären Paulus-Aussagen bei Markus." In Van Segbroeck et al, *The Four Gospels*, 877-904; John R. Donahue, "Windows and Mirrors: The Setting of Mark's Gospel." *CBQ* 57 (1995): 1-26; and Heikki Räisänen, "Jesus and the Food Laws: Reflections on Mark 7.15." In *Jesus, Paul and Torah: Collected Essays*, JSNTSup 43 (Sheffield: Sheffield Academic Press, 1992), 127-47. Also see David Seeley, "Rulership and Service in Mark 10:41-45." *NovT* 35 (1993): 234-50; William R. Telford, *The Theology of the Gospel of Mark* (Cambridge: Cambridge University Press, 1999), 164-69; and Michael D. Goulder, "Jesus' Resurrection and Christian Origins: A Response to N.T.Wright." *JSHJ* 3 (2005): 187-95.
49 This criticism, which seeks absolute correspondence between Paul and Mark, is commonly found in Martin Dibelius, "Evangelienkritik und Christologie." In *Zur Formgeschichte des Evangeliums*, ed. Ferdinand Hahn (Darmstadt: Wissenschaftliche Buchgesellschaft, 1935), 53-54.

the Χριστός (Rom 1:1), and uses the relatively rare and distinctive phrase, εὐαγγέλιον θεοῦ in 1:1 and 15:16 to refer to the content of the account of Jesus as well as oral proclamation.[50] Furthermore, Willi Marxsen notes that in all cases (aside from the previously mentioned Mark 1:1.14), Mark consistently employs the noun εὐαγγέλιον in its absolute form without any genitive modifiers,[51] such as Matthew's εὐαγγέλιον τῆς βασιλείας (Matt 4:23; 9:35; 24:14) or εὐαγγέλιον τοῦτο (Matt 26:13). The similar absolute use in the Pauline corpus is striking, so much so that Marxsen concludes that, "this fact indicates the proximity of Markan to Pauline usage."[52]

The connection between Mark and Paul is also strengthened in light of the shared theological vision for the role of Gentiles in the evangelistic mission. Jesus' encounter with the Syro-Phoenician woman (Mk 7:24-30) forms the initial story in the triplet of a section devoted to the mission of Jesus extending to neighbouring people (7:24-30, Syro-Phoenician Woman; 7:31-37, a healing in the Decapolis; 8:1-10, feeding of the four thousand). One common conception amongst interpreters is that the story of the Syro-Phoenician woman (7:24-30) portrays Israel very positively and Gentiles very negatively. Jesus' stern response to the woman's request for help is seen as indicative; "Let the children be fed first, for it is not fair to take the children's food and throw it to the dogs" (7:27). Typical in this regard is Christopher S. Mann who states that "this is one of the strongest assertions on Jesus' lips in our sources defining his mission as being primarily, if not exclusively to Israel."[53] While one may be inclined to accept a tempered version of this statement, it remains clear that given that the immediately preceding story involves serious disputations between Jesus and the "Pharisees and some of the scribes" (7:1), and that he ἐκεῖθεν δὲ ἀναστὰς (got up and went away from there, 7:24), this pericope functions as a strong polemic against the Jewish leaders of 7:1 and following. In this regard, Francis J. Moloney concludes that "in the face of a negative reception, Jesus has risen from his place in Israel and walked away."[54] The broader context of the passage sheds crucial interpretive light on Marcan structure. The pericope that immediately follows (after a second story on the Jesus' activity in the Gentile region

---

[50] Bar one exception (1Pet 4:17), "gospel of God" is a unique phrase within the Pauline corpus (Rom 1:1; 15:16; 2Cor 11:7; 1Thess 2:2.8-9) and Mark (1:1).
[51] Willi Marxsen, *Mark the Evangelist*, trans. James Boyse (Nashville. Tenn.: Abingdon Press, 1969), 127.
[52] Marxsen, *Mark*, 127.
[53] Christopher S. Mann, *Mark: A New Translation with Introduction and Commentary*, AB 27 (New York. N.Y.: Doubleday, 1986), 321.
[54] Francis J. Moloney, *The Gospel of Mark* (Peabody, Mass.: Hendrickson, 2002), 146.

of the Decapolis) is the feeding of the four thousand (8:1-11), which also includes mention of a superfluous crumb (ἄρτος and κλάσμα in Mark 8:4.8; ἄρτος and ψιχίον in Mark 7:27-28). The two stories are mutually interpretive in that, if the Gentiles are permitted to eat only the leftover crumbs, "Yes, Lord, but even the dogs under the table feed on the children's crumbs" (7:28), then the abundant amount of leftovers in the subsequent feeding story (8:8) has important implications for demonstrating the inclusion of Gentiles into the mission of the church. This is highlighted by Cranfield's statement regarding the interrelationship; "she does not want to diminish Israel's privileges, but desires a superfluous crumb."[55] However, rather than a leftover crumb, the subsequent pericope offers seven baskets full of bread. This interpretation is also confirmed by the close proximity of the earlier Marcan feeding story, namely the feeding of the five thousand (Mark 6:30-44).[56]

Kelly R. Iverson notes the key role played by the reference to πρῶτον (first) in the respective feeding of Jews and Gentiles in Mark 7:27 ("Let the children be fed first [πρῶτον], for it is not fair to take the children's food and throw it to the dogs"), in that "the children [Israel] are to be satisfied *first*. That is the Jewish people are given priority in the ministry of Jesus, a ministry that up until this point has been focused ostensibly on Israel."[57] Adela Yarbro Collins similarly notes that the reference to πρῶτον implies "the chronological and qualitative priority of the Jews in the history of salvation."[58] This is precisely the emphasis

---

55 Cranfield, *Mark*, 249.
56 A feature which contributes to this imagery is the respective number of leftover baskets; twelve in the feeding of the five thousand (6:43) and seven in the feeding of the four thousand (8:8). The suggestion that the number of baskets in 6:43 simply refers to the practical result of having twelve in charge of the distribution and collection does not take into account the parallel story in 8:1-10, which is similarly organised but mentions only seven baskets. Quentin Quesnell suggests that the "probable significance of the number of baskets" is that "twelve and seven... [are] representative respectively of Judaism and Gentility;" Quentin Quesnell, *The Mind of Mark: Interpretation and Method Through the Exegesis of Mark 6:52* (Rome: Pontifical Biblical Institute, 1969), 229. In support of this is the association of the number twelve and Israel within Mark's account of Jesus' selection of twelve disciples to carry on his work of healing and restoration (Mark 3:14.16). The representative nature of the number seven for the Gentile world is less specific but nonetheless discernable from various usages in the LXX and New Testament. Commentators have been inclined to find support for this idea in Acts 6:1-6, where seven men are chosen to aid in the daily distribution of food to the Hellenists' widows. That the seven corresponds to a definitive group is evident from Acts 21:8. Greater specificity in this regard is seen in Deut 7:1, where there is mention of seven nations.
57 Kelly R. Iverson, *Gentiles in the Gospel of Mark:"Even the Dogs Under the Table Eat the Dog's Crumbs"*, LNTS 339 (London: T & T Clark International, 2007), 45.
58 Collins, *Mark*, 367.

Paul expounds in Romans 1:16-17 ("I am not ashamed of the gospel, because it is the power of God for the salvation of everyone who believes: first for the Jew, then for the Gentile, for in it the righteousness of God is revealed"). The correlative syntactical construction τε...καὶ serves to indicate Paul's interest in chronologically prioritising the status of the Jew in God's mission.[59] Paul adheres to this principle both theologically (Rom 1:16-17; 9-11), and in his practical missionary *modus operandi* (Acts 17:1.10; 19:8-9). It is precisely this emphasis we see in Mark's Jesus, and thus is suggestive of a discernable connection between the two authors.[60]

The abrogation of food laws is further distinctive evidence of a relationship between Mark and Romans. Although there were continued debates concerning elements of the *halakhah*,[61] in particular, stricter or more moderate applications of the law, the summative statements in Mark 7:19b and Romans 14:14.20 are similar enough to suggest a homologous trajectory.

Rom 14:20 πάντα [βρώματα] μὲν καθαρά
Cleansing all the foods
Mk 7:19b καθαρίζων πάντα τὰ βρώματα
Thus he declared all foods clean.

David J. Rudolph notes that both pericopes include the term ἀκοινός, whose root occurs three times in Rom 14:14 and seven times in Mark 7 (vv. 2.5.15.18.20.23). Rudolph concludes that, "while direct influence cannot be proven, the textual affinity and Roman audience make it a reasonable hypothesis that Mark has taken Pauline halakhah (specifically for Gentile Christians) and rooted it in Mark 7."[62] Jesper Svartvik, in his analysis, goes as far to postulate that the Gospel of Mark functions as a Pauline Gospel,[63] however, stops short, accurately in our opinion, of suggesting an "historical-genetic connection between the historical

---

[59] Fitzmyer, *Romans*, 257.
[60] Several commentators note the Pauline and Marcan connection at this point; see further Hooker, *Mark*, 183; John R. Donahue and Daniel J. Harrington, *The Gospel of Mark*, SP 2 (Collegeville, Pa.: Liturgical Press, 2002), 233; Joel Marcus, *Mark 1-8*, AB 27 (New York, N.Y.: Doubleday, 2000), 466; and John Painter, *Mark's Gospel* (London: Routledge, 1997), 4-6.
[61] Gerd Theissen, *The Sociology of Palestinian Christianity* (Philadelphia, Pa.: Fortress Press, 1978), and 75-79; Markus Bockmuehl, *Jewish Law in Gentile Churches: Halakah and the Beginning of Christian Public Ethics* (Edinburgh: T & T Clark, 2000), 10.
[62] David J. Rudolph, "Jesus and the Food Laws: A Reassessment of Mark 7:19b." *EQ* 74 (2002): 304-08 at 305.
[63] Jesper Svartvik, *Mark and Mission: Mk 7:1-23 in its Narrative and Historical Contexts*, CBNTS 32 (Stockholm: Almqvist & Wiksell, 2000), 344-47

Paul and the real author of Mk."[64] James G. Crossley objects to the correlation of Rom 14 and Mark 7, by noting other potential sources for this material, such as Peter's vision in Acts 10:9-17.[65] Yet this, on closer inspection, does not eliminate Pauline influence.[66] Peter's vision in Acts 10 is bereft of any injunction regarding the abrogation of food laws. Rather, as is evident from vv. 34-35, the visionary experience is interpreted as a parable of God's impartiality; "God shows no partiality, but in every nation anyone who fears him and does what is right is acceptable to him," a theme further developed in the story of the Gentiles receiving the Holy Spirit (Acts 10: 44-48).

The correlation between Mark and Romans is also strengthened on the basis of an analysis of the use of the Old Testament in quotation and allusion. Kazimierz Romaniuk's discussion of the Pauline influence on Mark, while noting the comparable themes of μυστήριον in the pericope on the explanation of the purpose of parables in Mark 4:10-12 and related Pauline passages,[67] fails to make any mention of Isa 6:9-10, a text which is explicitly cited by both Mark and Paul. Joel Marcus notes in passing the parallel themes of the "new mode of seeing that God grants to his elect people while condemning outsiders to blindness (Mark 4:10-12; Rom 11:7-10),"[68] yet again, the explicit Isaianic citation is not addressed.

Several commentators have suggested that the underlying question which Paul seeks to address in his discussion of national Israel's rejection of Jesus (Rom 9-11) is the issue of the trustworthiness of the gospel, that is "just how trustworthy is this gospel if the very people whose history and covenant it fulfills reject it?"[69] James D. G. Dunn succinctly summarises this concern as, "has God's word failed?"[70] Paul's initial response to this question is characteristic, μὴ γέν-

---

64 Svartvik, *Mark*, 344. See further David Wenham, "Paul's Use of the Jesus Tradition: Three Samples." In *Gospel Perspectives: The Jesus Tradition Outside the Gospels*, ed. David Wenham (Sheffield: JSOT Press, 1984), 15; Richard T. France, *The Gospel of Mark* (Grand Rapids, Mich.: Eerdmans, 2002), 278; and Leander E. Keck, *Romans* (Nashville, Tenn.: Abingdon Press, 2005), 344-45.
65 James G. Crossley, "Mark, Paul and the Question of Influences." In *Paul and the Gospels: Christologies, Conflicts and Convergences*, eds. Michael F. Bird and Joel Willits, LNTS 411 (London: T & T Clark International, 2011), 10-29.
66 See further Michael F. Bird, "Mark: Interpreter of Peter and Disciple of Paul." In Bird and Willitts, *Paul and the Gospels*, 30-61 at 50-52.
67 Kazimierz Romaniuk, "Le problème des Paulinismes dans l'Évangile de Marc." *NTS* 23 (1976-1977): 266-74 at 273-74.
68 Marcus, "Mark," 475.
69 Rikk E. Watts, *Isaiah's New Exodus in Mark* (Tübingen: Mohr Siebeck, 1997), 387.
70 James D. G. Dunn, *Romans 9-16*, WBC 38B (Dallas, Tex.: Word Books, 1988), 518.

οιτο (Rom 9:14b), and begins his theological response by noting that not every individual Israelite is part of true Israel (9:1-29). Paul then develops the idea that Israel's pursuit of righteousness was misplaced (9:30-10:4), that Christ supersedes the giving of the Torah (10:5-10) and that lack of reception of Christ is due to Israel's resistance, rather than God's obfuscation (10:11-21). Finally, Paul argues that God has not abandoned his promise to save a remnant (11:1-10), and Israel's priority still stands (11:11-24).[71]

Throughout these sections Paul weaves quotations of the Old Testament in a midrashic fashion,[72] to address the problem of national Israel's rejection. At a high point in the argument, Paul opens with his traditional formula καθὼς γέγραπται (Rom 11:8), and alludes to Isa 6:10 in modifying Deuteronomy 29:3 (omitting the negative particle οὐκ from the phrase οὐκ ἔδωκεν in an ironic application) and pairing it with Isa 29:10, to formulate his pastiche, "God gave them...eyes that would not see and ears that would not hear" (Rom 11:8).[73] The context of the Isaianic condemnation of divinely sanctioned blindness (Isa 6) is a consistent theme throughout Isaiah's prophetic oracles,[74] and is a judgement of the rebellion detailed in the previous chapters. Isaiah 1-5 reads like a catalogue of legal complaint against Yahweh's people, including rebellion (1:2), corruption (1:4), hypocrisy (1:12-15), murder (1:21), bribery (1:23), covenantal infidelity (1:28), and many similar acts of wrongdoing. Particular emphasis is laid upon the leaders' failure to understand and their reliance on their own wisdom (1:10-15.23-26; 3:12; 5:18-24). Therefore, the prophetic oracle in Isa 6:9-13 is to be understood as, "ironic judgement upon the self-reliant wisdom of those who have rejected...[Yahweh's] word."[75] This broader Isaianic context coheres remarkably well with the issues Paul attempts to address in Rom 9-11.

---

71 For this structural analysis I am indebted to Rikk E. Watts, *A Reader's Guide to Romans 9-11* (Vancouver: Regent College, 2012), 3.
72 Dunn, *Romans 9-16*, 518; Richard Hays, *Echoes of Scripture in the Letters of Paul* (New Haven, Conn.: Yale University Press, 1989); and James W. Aageson, "Scripture and Structure in the Development of the Argument in Romans 9-11." *CBQ* 48 (1986): 265-89.
73 Charles E. B. Cranfield, *The Epistle to the Romans*, vol. 2, ICC (Edinburgh: T & T Clark, 1994), 550; Craig A. Evans, *To See and Not Perceive: Isaiah 6:9-10 in Early Jewish and Christian Interpretation* (Sheffield: JSOT Press, 1989), 81-89; E. Earle Ellis, *Paul's Use of the Old Testament* (Grand Rapids, Mich.: Baker, 1957), 84; Barnabas Lindars, *New Testament Apologetic* (Philadelphia, Pa.: Westminster Press, 1961), 159, 161, 164; Paul E. Dinter, "Paul and the Prophet Isaiah." *BTB* 13 (1983): 48-52; and Johannes Munck, *Christ and Israel: An Interpretation of Romans 9-11* (Philadelphia, Pa. Fortress Press, 1967), 114.
74 Gerhard von Rad, *Old Testament Theology*, vol. 2, trans. David M. G. Stalker (London: SCM, 1975), 154.
75 Watts, *Isaiah*, 194.

Significantly, Mark 4:12 quotes precisely the same Isaianic text in description of Israel's obduracy in rejecting Jesus' message of the kingdom. It too introduces the oracle of blindness after a period of condemning Israel's leaders for self-reliant wisdom and failure to recognise Yahweh at work in their midst (Mark 1-4). So much so that the telic force of the introductory ἵνα in Mark 4:12 can be allowed its full purposive weight. In this light, the connection of Mark and Romans is noted by Benjamin W. Bacon who observes the following; "So singular combination of Old Testament [Isa 6:9-10] quotation with current logia [Mk 4:11] in the interest of a particular form of anti-Jewish polemic apologetic is difficult to account for unless we suppose the evangelist to have been familiar with the parallel argument of Paul, which employs the same quotations in the same interest."[76]

Christology provides several points of comparison to further strengthen the link between Romans and Mark. Although Martin Werner attempted to drive a wedge between the Christology of Mark and that of Paul in general and Romans in particular,[77] his analysis displays several serious methodological drawbacks. Werner maintains the distinction between the strong πνεῦμα (Marcan [Mark 1:23-26; 1:30-31; 1:40-42 et al.]) and weak σάρξ (Pauline [Rom 8:3]) of Jesus' humanity, only by ignoring the second half of Mark's Gospel, including the passion narrative which is replete with references to Jesus' weakness and suffering. Positively however, one may note the following similar Christological themes in Mark and Romans: power over demonic realm (Rom 8:38-39; Mark 1:23-26; 5:1-15; 9:14-29); Son of David (Rom 1:3; Mark 12:37); eschatological age of prophetic hope as per the message of the prophets (Rom 3:21-22; Mark 1:1-15); and the centrality and importance of the resurrection (Rom 1:3-4; Mark 8:31; 9:9, 31; 10:34). Joel Marcus also provides further indications of the Christological symmetry between Mark and Romans on the basis of New Adam typology (Rom 5:12-21; Mark 1:11-12),[78] as well as comparative elements in the theology of the cross. We will find cause to assess, and nuance this comparison below (see section 5), and at greater length.

Tacitus (*Annals* 13.50-51) notes that in 58 CE Nero attempted to address the continued unrest in Rome over the exorbitant indirect taxes extracted by the *publican* (tax collectors), by proposing to repeal all such taxes, "and so confer

---

76 Bacon, *Mark*, 263.
77 Werner, *Einfluss*, 51-60.
78 Marcus, "Mark," 475; see further David Lincicum, "Genesis in Paul." In *Genesis in the New Testament*, ed. Steve Moyise and Maarten J. J. Menken (London: T & T Clark International, 2012), 99-116; and Otfried Hofius, "The Adam-Christ Antithesis and the Law: Reflections on Romans 5:12-21." In *Paul and the Mosaic Law*, ed. James D. G. Dunn (Grand Rapids, Mich.: Eerdmans, 2001), 165-206.

a most splendid gift on the human race." The senators, although providing initial support for Nero's gesture, eventually retracted their approval in fear of the consequent "dissolution of the empire" when, they assumed, there would be a "demand for the abolition of the direct taxes." The political turmoil regarding taxes during this period resulted in an edict regulating "the cupidity of the revenue collectors, that they might not by new oppressions bring into odium what for so many years had been endured without a complaint." Although Paul may have been writing before this time, he may well have been aware of the turbulent political feeling regarding taxation during this period, and as a result advocated that the his readers accept the Roman authorities as authoritative in matters of taxation and governance. Paul presents these dual themes in Rom 13:6-7 as a two-step chiasmus (see below). Having clarified for his readers their political and economic responsibilities toward the State, Paul follows his discussion on taxation with a short discourse on the commandments. He sums up his abbreviated list of the Decalogue by asserting that "love is the fulfillment of the Law" (Rom 13:10).

> A (13:6a) For the same reason you also pay taxes,
>   B (13:6b) for the authorities are God's servants, busy with this very thing.
> A' (13:7) Pay to all what is due them, taxes to whom taxes are due, revenue to whom revenue is due,
>   B' (13:7b) respect to whom respect is due, honour to whom honour is due.

This passage is intriguing for the Marcan connection on two levels. First, many commentators have noted the connection of Romans 13:6-7 with the Marcan passage regarding paying tribute to Caesar (12:12-17), in particular v. 17 when Jesus is recorded as declaring; "Give to the emperor the things that are the emperor's, and to God the things that are God's."[79] David Wenham suggests an echo,[80] while Charles E. B. Cranfield argues that the connection is extremely likely and that a stronger connection can be assumed based on, not only the "common reference to the subject of paying taxes...[but] the use of ἀπόδοτε in both, and the similarity of idea between τὰς ὀφειλάς and τὰ τοῦ..."[81] Second, and perhaps of greater importance for the connection between Mark and Romans, is the similarity of the following pericope in each case. As in Romans (noted above),

---

[79] Justin Martyr, *First Apology*, finds support in this reference that Christians should be willing to pay taxes and give their obedience to the government. Tertullian, *On Idolatry* 15, similarly interprets the passage to mean money is to be given to Caesar, but one's body, made in the image of God, should be given to God.
[80] Wenham, "Tradition," 15.
[81] Cranfield, *Romans*, 2:669.

Mark's pericope is, after a brief interlude regarding resurrection, followed by a debate over the greatest commandment, the second of which is, "You shall love your neighbour as yourself" (12:31).[82] The close proximity of subject matter, vocabulary and arrangement suggest a connection between the two authors.

Several commentators have suggested an intriguing, yet elusive, connection between Romans and Mark in the mention of the name Rufus in Romans 16:13 and Mark 15:21.[83] With respect to Mark 15:21, James R. Edwards states "Rufus was a member of the church in Rome in the mid-fifties...who is probably the same Rufus mentioned here."[84] Other commentators, including Adela Yarbro Collins, are more dubious, claiming that Rufus was "probably not the same person...since the latter was Jewish."[85] It is however, questionable if anything can be said of the nationality of Rufus, Jewish or otherwise. "Rufus" was originally a Latin name but was common among Greeks and Jews. Ludwig Edelstein and Vivian Nutton note that there was a Greek physician by the same name residing in Ephesus in the second half of the first century.[86] Thus all that can be said with any degree of certainty, with reference to Mark, is that the Rufus (and Alexander) were "presumably known to Mark's readers (by name if not in person)."[87] Without further evidence however, one cannot claim any certainty with respect to this identity with the Rufus referred to as Paul's acquaintance. It does however, remain a possibility if new evidence is unearthed.

5 Theological Continuity and Discontinuity in Mark and Romans

The centrality of the cross in Christian theology is ubiquitous, and indeed apparent in all discernable forms of first century Christianity.[88] There are, however,

---

82 Wenham, "Tradition," 15.
83 William Sanday and Arthur C. Headlam, *The Epistle to the Romans* (Edinburgh: T & T Clark, 1902), 426-27; Fitzmyer, *Romans*, 645; Peter Lampe, "Rufus." In *Anchor Bible Dictionary*, vol. 5, ed. David Noel Freedman (New York, N.Y.: Doubleday, 1990), 839.
84 James R. Edwards, *The Gospel According to Mark* (Leicester: Apollos, 2002), 470.
85 Collins, *Mark*, 737.
86 Ludwig Edelstein and Vivian Nutton, "Rufus of Ephesus." In *The Oxford Classical Dictionary*, eds. Simon Hornblower, and Anthony Spawforth (Oxford: Oxford University Press, 2003), 1337.
87 Hooker, *Mark*, 372.
88 Evidenced, for example in the abundant references in varied streams of literature (Acts 2:23-26; 4:10; 10:39; 13:28; 20:28; 1Pet 1:2.19; 2:21-23; 3:18; 4:1; Heb 9:11-28; 10:19, 29; 12:24; 13:12, 20). See Bird, "Mark," 39.

several distinctive theological kerygmatic elements shared between Romans and Mark which suggest some measure of dependence or direct relationship. Conversely, however, there is one significant point of dissimilarity between Romans and Mark, that is, Mark's emphasis on suffering discipleship. We will suggest that the theological elements of continuity, in regard to the "theology of the cross," strengthen the current hypothesis of connection between Romans and Mark, and that the one significant point of discontinuity does not detract from it, but uses it is a foundation for addressing the contemporary Roman context.

The most recent detailed analysis of comparative Marcan and Pauline Christology, particularly in regard to the significance of Jesus' death, is that of Joel Marcus,[89] wherein he cites voluminous evidence in support of the Marcan and Pauline connection on this point. We need not rehearse the minutiae of Marcus' arguments here, except to note that the connection may, in light of our subsequent discussion, reveal deeper and stronger Marcan connections with Romans than previously acknowledged.

The concepts and terminology of atonement and redemption in Romans are compellingly echoed in Mark's presentation of the soteriological significance of Jesus' death. At the conclusion of the Marcan pericope on Jesus' instruction concerning leadership (Mark 10:35-45), and the related request of James and John to sit εἷς σου ἐκ δεξιῶνκαὶ εἷς ἐξ ἀριστερῶν (v. 37), the logion in v. 45 acts as a "warrant and model for the teaching [previously] expressed."[90] Mark 10:45 concludes, καὶ γὰρ ὁ υἱὸς τοῦ ἀνθρώπου οὐκ ἦλθεν διακονηθῆναι ἀλλὰ διακονῆσαι καὶ δοῦναι τὴν ψυχὴν αὐτοῦ λύτρον ἀντὶ πολλῶν. In the LXX, the term λύτρον (ransom) [91], most commonly occurs in Leviticus, typically translates one of three Hebrew terms (פדה, גאל, and כפר), and characteristically refers to the redemption of a human life or the cancellation of a debt.[92] Evidence from the papyri also confirms that the term was commonly used in connection with the manumission of slaves in the mid to late first century. P.Oxy 1.48, dated to 86 C.E. refers (line 6) to a certain slave by the name of Euphrosyne who had been manumitted under Zeus, Earth, Sun, for a ransom (λύτροι[ς]). Similarly, Adolf Deissmann[93] notes the epigraphic evidence from Köres (Asia Minor) which attests the less

---

89 Marcus, "Mark," 473-87
90 Collins, *Mark*, 499.
91 The plural form of λύτρον is most common, with the singular occurring only at Lev 27:31 and Prov 6:35; 13:8.
92 Frederick Büchsel, "λύω." In *Theological Dictionary of the New Testament*, vol. 4, trans. Geoffrey W. Bromiley, ed. Gerhard Kittel (Grand Rapids, Mich.: Eerdmans, 1967), 340-49.
93 Adolf Deissmann, *Light from the Ancient East*, trans. Lionel R. M. Strachen (New York, N.Y.: Harper & Brothers, 1923), 322.

common singular form of the noun, with reference to Asclepias releasing himself from a vow, Γαλλικῷ Ἀσκληπιάς κώμη Κερυζέων παιδίσχη Διογένου λύτρον (To Gallicus, Asclepias, from the village of Ceryza, maidservant of Liogenes, presents this ransom).

In Romans, Paul uses the related compound term, ἀπολύτρωσις (redemption), both eschatologically, "while we wait for adoption, the redemption (ἀπολύτρωσιν) of our bodies" (Rom 8:23), and soteriologically, in reference to the atonement that Jesus wrought by his sacrificial death; "they are now justified by his grace as a gift, through the redemption (ἀπολυτρώσεως) that is in Christ Jesus," (Rom 3:24; cf. Col 1:14; Eph 1:7; 1Cor 1:30). Coupled together with the observation that Jesus' death acted as an apocalyptic "turning point of the ages,"[94] is presented as an ironic Roman triumph (Mark 14-15; Rom 8:37; cf. Col 2:15),[95] and was "not for the righteous but sinners" (Mark 2:17; Rom 5:19), and one has a strong sense that Mark was drawing on the Pauline kerygma in his theology of the cross. These variegated points of contact, noted here and above strengthen the connection between the epistle to the Romans and the Gospel of Mark.[96]

Yet, despite these similarities, there is but one conspicuous lacuna in Paul's Roman correspondence when compared with the Gospel of Mark, that is, the theme of suffering discipleship. The first hint of this in Mark is revealed not only in the joint plot of the Herodians and Pharisees to kill Jesus in 3:6 (cf. 2:20), but also in the murder of John the Baptist in 6:14-29. John's death raises the acute question of the fate of those willing to announce the message of the kingdom under and amid hostile political powers.[97] The three Marcan passion predictions regarding the suffering of the Son of Man (8:31; 9:31; 10:33-34) provide the context for Jesus' teaching on the nature of discipleship: self denial (8:34); willingness to "lose their life for my sake" (8:35); boldness in the face of persecution (8:38); one not obsessed with status and privilege, but servitude and humility (9:33-37); and above all the willingness to drink the same cup that Jesus drinks (10:39). Discipleship in Mark is defined by suffering and the real threat

---

[94] Marcus, "Mark," 475.
[95] Thomas E. Schmidt, "Mark 15:16-32: The Crucifixion Narrative and the Roman Triumphal Procession." NTS 41 (1995): 1-18; and Craig A. Evans, Mark 8:27-16:20, WBC 34B (Nashville, Tenn.: Thomas Nelson, 2001), lxxv-lxxxix.
[96] See further Rudolf Bultmann, History of Synoptic Tradition, trans. John Marsh (New York: Harper & Row, 1963), 370-371; and Marxsen, Mark, 147.
[97] Bird, "Mark," 40.

of imminent physical harm, arrest, betrayal and potential execution (13:9-13).⁹⁸ So much so, that when Peter challenges Jesus on the subject of Messianic suffering, he is sternly rebuked in an uncharacteristic manner; "Get behind me Satan" (8:33). Ironically, however, the phrase is introduced with ὕπαγε ὀπίσω μου, which could also be translated, "come behind me", and is thus reminiscent of the initial call narrative in 1:17, δεῦτε ὀπίσω μου. In this sense, Morna Hooker suggests 8:33 could be rendered, "Get back into line."⁹⁹

In contradistinction to this emphasis on suffering discipleship in Mark, L. Ann Jervis has cogently argued that discipleship in Paul's epistle to the Romans is characterised by encouraging the believer to achieve "likeness to God."¹⁰⁰ Jervis finds comparative material in the Greek tradition (Aristotle, *Nicomachean Ethics* 1178b 20-23; Socrates, *Epistle* 6.4), and the Jewish context (Philo, *De Somniis* 1:60; *1 En.* 38:4; 1QS 1; Josephus, *Antiquities* 1:23), which similarly has an emphasis on resembling the character of the gods or God. Emphasis is placed on being "in Christ" (Rom 8:1), through whom "the righteousness of God is revealed" (1:17). This δικαιοσύνη is probably best understood as a polyvalent concept, which in 1:17 refers to God's equitable fairness or "distributive justice" in making the εὐαγγέλιον (1:16) available to all, irrespective of gender, race, or socio-economic standing.¹⁰¹

Several commentators have noted the possibility that the motifs and themes of the Gospel of Mark fall under the ominous shadow of a persecuted Roman church.¹⁰² We propose therefore, in light of our discussion above, that the historical circumstances which engendered such different emphases on discipleship in Romans (c. 55 CE) contra Mark (c. 69 CE) can be attributed to a radical shift in political and social realities facing Christians in Rome, namely, the Neronian persecution (64 CE).

Tacitus' *Annals* 15:38-44 reports that the great conflagration of Rome during the reign of Nero, which broke out in July 64 CE, began in the Circus Maximus and spread to engulf or badly damage eleven of the fourteen divisions of the

---

98 See Richard A. Horsley, "Jesus Movements and the Renewal of Israel." In *Christian Origins*, ed. Richard A. Horsely (Minneapolis, Minn.: Fortress Press, 2005), 23-46 at 42-43.
99 Hooker, *Mark*, 207.
100 L. Ann Jervis, "Becoming like God through Christ: Discipleship in Romans." In *Patterns of Discipleship in the New Testament*, ed. Richard N. Longenecker (Grand Rapids, Mich.: Eerdmans, 1996), 143-62; cf. Brendan Byrne, "Living Out the Righteousness of God: The Contribution of Rom 6:1-8:13 to an Understanding of Paul's Ethical Presuppositions." *CBQ* 43 (1981): 557-81.
101 Frank Thielman, "God's Righteousness as God's Fairness in Rom 1:17: An Ancient Perspective on a Significant Phrase." *JETS* 54 (2011): 35-48.
102 Incigneri, *Gospel*, 115; Donahue, "Windows," 1-26; and Donald Senior, "The Gospel of Mark in Context." *TBT* 34 (1996): 215-21.

city. Tacitus presents a mixture of both a positive and negative portrayal of Nero's role in these events. Admiration for Nero is evident in Tacitus' portrayal of him as one who provided practical measures both in the immediate wake of the crisis (*Annals* 15.39.2), and the longer term project of the city's architectural and economic recovery (15.43.1-5). These positive elements, however, are significantly tempered with rumors of Nero's responsibility for the fire (*Annals* 15.38.1; 44.2), and reported grumbling (*Annals* 15.41.1; 43.5). At one point Tacitus notes the sustained criticism over Nero's luxurious "golden house" (*Annals* 15.42.1-2). Other contemporary sources are entirely critical. Suetonius (*Nero* 38.1) and Dio Cassius (62.16.2) explicitly denounce Nero on the charge that the fire was a solution for Nero's dilemma of urban expansion and the limited land resources for Nero's new palace. Tacitus also makes reference to perceived selfish motivation in noting that it was Nero's palace that was first repaired and rebuilt (15.42). In response to these sinister suspicions, Tacitus notes the manner in which Nero attempted to divert attention, that is, by fixing blame on the Christians.[103] The resulting events are revealing and vividly illustrate the extreme repercussions on the local Christian community in Rome. The well known passage from *Annals* 15.44.2-5 relates in detail the horrendous measures meted out to Christians who were "substituted as culprits" for the fire in Rome (§2). Christianity is referred to as *exitiabilis superstitio* (the pernicious superstition, §3), and refers to Christians punished in the most barbarous measures; "covered with wild beasts' skins and torn to death by dogs; or they were fastened on crosses, and, when daylight failed were burned to serve as lamps by night" (§4). Tacitus records that Nero exhibited these spectacles at his garden parties as entertainment for his dinner guests (§5). So intense was the persecution that Tacitus notes "there arose a sentiment of pity, due to the impression that they were being sacrificed not for the welfare of the state but to the ferocity of a single man" (§5).

Graeme W. Clarke suggests that Tacitus' reference to the *multitude ingens* (vast numbers) that Tacitus records as being affected by the Neronian persecution may have been a rhetorical enhancement of the numbers "in order to highlight Nero's monstrosities."[104] However, Marta Sordie's study implies that "a few hundred victims" would merit this description.[105] Irrespective of the precise

---

[103] Graeme W. Clarke notes that "the wording [*subditreos*] implies they [Christians] were not, in Tacitus' view, in fact responsible for the fire," Clarke, "Origins," 869.
[104] Clarke, "Origins," 870.
[105] Marta Sordie, *The Christians and the Roman Empire*, trans. Annabel Bedini (London: Croom Helm, 1986), 31. William H. C. Frend suggests that initially "Nero tried to make the Jews scapegoats and the latter diverted the odium onto the upstart synagogue of the Christians." See William H. C. Frend, "Martyrdom and Political Oppression." In *The Early Christian World*, vol. 2,

numbers, what is apparent is that the Neronian persecution was local to Rome, and that it was not an empire wide enactment against Christianity.[106]

In this light, Mark's emphasis on discipleship, as defined by willingness to take up one's cross and lose one's life (if necessary) for the sake of Jesus (Mark 8:34-35), coheres remarkably well within the context of the Neronian persecution. Adam Winn further notes a possible connection between Mark 13:12, καὶ παραδώσει ἀδελφὸς ἀδελφὸν εἰς θάνατονκαὶ πατὴρτέκνον, καὶ ἐπαναστήσονται τέκνα ἐπὶ γονεῖς καὶ θανατώσουσιν αὐτούς (Brother will betray brother to death, and a father his child, and children will rise against parents and have them put to death), and the betrayal implicit in *Annals* 15.44.4; "First, then, those who confessed were arrested; next, on their disclosures, vast numbers were convicted."[107]

6 Conclusions

Throughout this study we have sought to identify a distinctive Pauline perspective in the Marcan text. The arguments put forward in our present discussion for a comparable Roman context, yet distinct historical period for both documents (Romans in the mid 50s CE, and Mark in the late 60s CE), allowed a fruitful comparison of the continuity and discontinuity of theological motifs. Strong comparative points of influence between Romans and Mark were seen in: 1) the frequency, importance and meaning of the soteriological term εὐαγγέλιον; 2) the shared theological vision of the inclusion of the Gentiles in the evangelistic mission of the church; 3) Israel's chronological priority in the divine *Heilsgeschichte*;

---

ed. Philip F. Esler (London: Routledge, 2000), 820. However, James McLaren, nuances this argument by suggesting that although the identity of the potential informers is speculative, "there is good reason to support the view that it was members of the Jewish community residing in Rome," not necessarily motivated by an anti-Christian punitive measure, but as a "concern to protect their own position in Rome"; James McLaren, "The Fire in Rome in 64 CE: A Key Moment in Early Jewish-Christian Relations?", paper delivered to the *Society for the Study of Early Christianity* conference, hosted by Macquarie University Department of Ancient History, May 4, 2013.

106 Clarke, "Origins," 870. John Behr similar notes that in the Neronian persecution, "Christians were not subject to any wholesale attempt at repression, but they were subjected to occasional persecution;" John Beer, "Social and historical Setting." In *The Cambridge History of Early Christian Literature*, eds Frances Young, Lewis Ayres, and Andrew Louth (Cambridge: Cambridge University Press, 2004), 55-70 at 58.

107 Winn, *Purpose*, 82-83, who also connects "haters of the human race" (*Annals* 15.44.4) with "will be hated by all" (Mark 13:13).

4) the emphasis on the abrogation of food laws; 5) the distinctive hermeneutical employment of the Hebrew Bible in condemnation of continued Jewish obduracy; 6) similar Christological outlook; 7) economic responsibility to the state; 8) the potential, yet elusive, personal ecclesiastical connection with Rufus; and 9) the similar kerygmatic elements of the theological meaning of the cross. The one significant point of radical discontinuity between Romans and Mark (that of discipleship), rather than detracting from the connection between the two documents, is best understood as a reapplication of the theological motifs in Romans, which are then expanded and brought to full realisation in light of the Neronian persecution in Mark.

Bibliography

Aageson, James W. "Scripture and Structure in the Development of the Argument in Romans 9-11." *CBQ* 48 (1986): 265-89.
Aune, David. *The New Testament in its Literary Environment*. Philadelphia, Pa.: Westminster Press, 1987.
Bacon, Benjamin W. *The Gospel of Mark: Its Composition and Date*. Oxford: Oxford University Press, 1925.
Barrett, Charles K. *A Commentary on the Epistle to the Romans*. London: A & C Black, 1971.
Baur, Ferdinand C. "Über Zweck und Veranlassung des Römerbriefs und der damit zusammenhängenden Verhältnisse der römischen Gemeinde." *TZT* 9 (1836): 59-178.
Beer, John. "Social and historical Setting," in: *The Cambridge History of Early Christian Literature*, eds. Frances Young, Lewis Ayres, and Andrew Louth, 55-70. Cambridge: Cambridge University Press, 2004.
Bird, Michael F. "Mark: Interpreter of Peter and Disciple of Paul," in: *Paul and the Gospels: Christologies, Conflicts and Convergences*, eds. Michael F. Bird and Joel Willits, 30-61. LNTS 411. London: T & T Clark International, 2011.
Blass, Friedrich, Albert Debrunner, and Friedrich Rehkopf, *Grammatik des neutestamentlichen Griechisch*. Göttingen: Vandenhoeck & Ruprecht, 14th edn 1975.
Bockmuehl, Markus. *Jewish Law in Gentile Churches: Halakah and the Beginning of Christian Public Ethics*. Edinburgh: T & T Clark, 2000.
Bornkamm, Günther. "The Letter to the Romans as Paul's Last Will and Testament." *ABR* 11 (1963-64): 2-14.
—, *Paul*. London: Hodder & Stoughton, 1971.
Büchsel, Friedrich. "λύω," in: *Theological Dictionary of the New Testament*, vol. 4, trans. Geoffrey W. Bromiley. ed. Gerhard Kittel, 328-56. Grand Rapids: Mich., Eerdmans, 1967.
Bultmann, Rudolf. *History of Synoptic Tradition*, trans. John Marsh. New York, N.Y: Harper & Row, 1963.
Byrne, Brendan. "Living Out the Righteousness of God: The Contribution of Rom 6:1-8:13
—, *Romans*. SP 6. Collegeville, Pa.: Liturgical Press, 1996.
Clarke, Graeme W. "The Origins and Spread of Christianity," in: *The Cambridge Ancient History, Volume X: The Augustan Empire 43 B.C.-A.D. 69*, eds. Alan K. Bowman, Edward Champlin, and Andrew Lintott, 848-72. Cambridge: Cambridge University Press, 1996.
Collins, Adela Yarbro *Mark: A Commentary*. Hermeneia. Minneapolis, Minn.: Fortress Press, 2007.
Cranfield, Charles E. B. *The Gospel According to St. Mark*. Cambridge: Cambridge University Press, 1959.
—, *The Epistle to the Romans*, vol. 1. ICC. Edinburgh: T & T Clark, 1994.
—, *The Epistle to the Romans*, vol. 2. ICC. Edinburgh: T & T Clark, 1994.
Crossley, James G. "Mark, Paul and the Question of Influences," in: *Paul and the Gospels: Christologies, Conflicts and Convergences*, eds. Michael F. Bird and Joel Willits, 10-29. LNTS 411. London: T & T Clark International, 2011.
Deissmann, Adolf. *Light from the Ancient East*. trans. Lionel R. M. Strachen. New York, N.Y.: Harper & Brothers, 1923.

Dibelius, Martin. "Evangelienkritik und Christologie," in: *Zur Formgeschichte des Evangeliums*, ed. Ferdinand Hahn, 46-67. Darmstadt: Wissenschaftliche Buchgesellschaft, 1935.
Dinter, Paul E. "Paul and the Prophet Isaiah." *BTB* 13 (1983): 48-52.
Dodd, Charles H. *The Epistle of Paul to the Romans*. London: Hodder and Stoughton, 1932.
Donahue, John R. "The Quest for the Community of Mark's Gospel," in: *The Four Gospels 1992: Festschrift Frans Neirynck*, vol. 2, eds. Frans Van Segbroeck et al., 817-38. BETL 100. Leuven: Leuven University Press, 1992.
—, "Windows and Mirrors: The Setting of Mark's Gospel." *CBQ* 57 (1995): 1-26.
Donahue, John R. and Daniel J. Harrington, *The Gospel of Mark*. SP 2. Collegeville, Pa.: Liturgical Press, 2002.
Donfried, Karl P, ed. *The Romans Debate*. Minneapolis, Minn.: Augsburg Press, 1977.
Dschulnigg, Peter. *Sprache, Redaktion und Intention des Markus-Evangeliums: Eigentümlichkeiten der Sprache des Markus-Evangeliums und ihre Bedeutung für die Redaktionskritik*. Stuttgart: Katholisches Bibelwerk, 1986.
Dunn, James D. G. *Romans 1-8*. WBC 38A. Dallas, Tex.: Word Books, 1988.
—, *Romans 9-16*. WBC 38B. Dallas, Tex.: Word Books, 1988.
Edelstein, Ludwig, and Vivian Nutton, "Rufus of Ephesus," in: *The Oxford Classical Dictionary*, eds. Simon Hornblower and Anthony Spawforth, 1337. Oxford: Oxford University Press, 2003.
Edwards, James R. *The Gospel According to Mark*. Leicester: Apollos, 2002.
Ellis, E. Earle. *Paul's Use of the Old Testament*. Grand Rapids, Mich.: Baker, 1957.
Evans, Craig A. *To See and Not Perceive: Isaiah 6:9-10 in Early Jewish and Christian Interpretation*. Sheffield: JSOT Press, 1989.
—, *Mark 8:27-16:20*. WBC 34B. Nashville, Tenn.: Thomas Nelson, 2001.
Fenton, John C. "Paul and Mark," in: *Studies in the Gospels: Essays in Memory of R. H. Lightfoot*, ed. Dennis E. Nineham, 89-112. Oxford: Blackwell, 1957.
Fitzmyer, Joseph A. *Romans*. AB 33. New York. N.Y.: Doubleday, 1993.
France, Richard T. *The Gospel of Mark*. Grand Rapids, Mich.: Eerdmans, 2002.
Frend, William H. C. "Martyrdom and Political Oppression," in: *The Early Christian World*, vol. 2, ed. Philip F. Esler, 815-39. London: Routledge, 2000.
Georgi, Dieter. *Die Geschichte der Kollekte des Paulus für Jerusalem*. Hamburg: Herbert Reich, 1965.
Gnilka, Joachim. *Das Evangelium nach Markus*, vol. 1. Zurich: Benziger, 3rd edn 1989.
Goulder, Michael D. "Those Outside (Mk 4:10-12)." *NovT* 33 (1991): 289-302.
—, "Jesus' Resurrection and Christian Origins: A Response to N.T. Wright." *JSHJ* 3 (2005): 187-95.
Grundmann, Walter. *Das Evangelium nach Markus*. Berlin: Evangelische Verlagsanstalt, 1959.
Haenchen, Ernst. *Die Apostelgeschichte*. Göttingen: Vandenhoeck & Ruprecht, 1959.
Hays, Richard. *Echoes of Scripture in the Letters of Paul*. New Haven, Conn.: Yale University Press, 1989.
Hengel, Martin. *Studies in the Gospel of Mark*. London: SCM, 1985.
Hofius, Otfried. "The Adam-Christ Antithesis and the Law: Reflections on Romans 5:12-21," in: *Paul and the Mosaic Law*, ed. James D. G. Dunn, 165-206. Grand Rapids, Mich.: Eerdmans, 2001.
Hooker, Morna D. *The Gospel According to St. Mark*. London: A & C Black, 1991.

Horsley, Richard. A. "Jesus Movements and the Renewal of Israel," in: *Christian Origins*, ed. Richard A. Horsley, 23-46. Minneapolis, Minn.: Fortress Press, 2005.
Hort, Fenton J. A. *Prolegomena to St. Paul's Epistles to the Romans and the Ephesians*. London: Macmillian, 1895.
Incigneri, Brian J. *The Gospel to the Romans*. Leiden: Brill, 2003.
Iverson, Kelly R. *Gentiles in the Gospel of Mark: "Even the Dogs Under the Table Eat the Dog's Crumbs"*. LNTS 339. London: T & T Clark International, 2007.
Jervis, L. Ann. *The Purpose of Romans: A Comparative Letter Structure Investigation*.
—, "Becoming like God through Christ: Discipleship in Romans," in: *Patterns of Discipleship in the New Testament*, ed. Richard N. Longenecker, 143-62. Grand Rapids, Mich.: Eerdmans, 1996.
Jewett, Robert. *Dating Paul's Life*. London: SCM, 1979.
—, *Romans: A Commentary*. Hermeneia. Minneapolis, Minn.: Fortress Press, 2007.
Käsemann, Ernst. *Commentary on Romans*, trans. Geoffrey W. Bromiley. Grand Rapids, Mich.: Eerdmans, 1980.
Keck, Leander E. *Romans*. Nashville, Tenn.: Abingdon Press, 2005.
Keenan, James G. "Review of *Il lessico latino nel Greco d'Egitto* (Barcelona: Institut de Teologia Fondamental, Seminario de Papirologia, 2nd edn, 1991) by S. Daris." *BASP* 29 (1992): 219-20.
Kloppenborg, John S. "*Evocatio deorum* and the Date of Mark." *JBL* (2005): 419-50.
Koester, Helmut. *Introduction to the New Testament*, vol. 2. Philadelphia, Pa.: Fortress Press, 1982.
—, *Ancient Christian Gospels: Their History and Development*. London: SCM, 1990.
Kuula, Karli. *The Law, The Covenant and God's Plan*. Göttingen: Vandenhoeck & Ruprecht, 2003.
Lampe, Peter. "Rufus," in: *Anchor Bible Dictionary*, vol. 5, ed. David Noel Freedman, 839. New York, N.Y.: Doubleday, 1990.
Lane, William L. *The Gospel According to Mark: The English Text with Introduction, Exposition and Notes*. Grand Rapids, Mich.: Eerdmans, 1974.
Lincicum, David. "Genesis in Paul," in: *Genesis in the New Testament*, ed. Steve Moyise and
Lindars, Barnabas. *New Testament Apologetic*. Philadelphia, Pa.: Westminster Press, 1961.
Lührmann, Dieter. *Das Markusevangelium*. Tübingen: Mohr Siebeck, 1987.
Mann, Christopher S. *Mark: A New Translation with Introduction and Commentary*, AB 27. New York, N.Y.: Doubleday, 1986.
Marcus, Joel. *Mark 1-8*. AB 27. New York, N.Y.: Doubleday, 1999.
—, "Mark – Interpreter of Paul." *NTS* 46 (2000): 473-87.
Marxsen, Willi. *Introduction to the New Testament: An Approach to its Problems*, trans. George Buswell. Oxford: Blackwell, 1968.
—, *Mark the Evangelist*, trans. James Boyse. Nashville, Tenn.: Abingdon Press, 1969.
McLaren, James. "The Fire in Rome in 64 C.E.: A Key Moment in Early Jewish-Christian Relations?" Paper delivered to the *Society for the Study of Early Christianity* conference, hosted by Macquarie University Department of Ancient History, May 4, 2013.
Millard, Allan. *Reading and Writing in the Time of Jesus*. Sheffield: Sheffield Academic Press, 2000.
Moloney, Francis J. *The Gospel of Mark*. Peabody, Mass.: Hendrickson, 2002.
Munck, Johannes. *Christ and Israel: An Interpretation of Romans 9-11*. Philadelphia, Pa.: Fortress Press, 1967.

Nineham, Dennis E. *The Gospel of St.Mark*. Baltimore, Md.: Penguin Books, 1969.
Outler, Albert C. "The Gospel According to St. Mark." *Perkins School of Theology Journal* 33-34 (1980): 3-9.
Painter, John. *Mark's Gospel*. London: Routledge, 1997.
Quesnell, Quentin. *The Mind of Mark: Interpretation and Method Through the Exegesis of Mark 6:52*. Rome: Pontifical Biblical Institute, 1969.
Rad, Gerhard von. *Old Testament Theology*, vol. 2, trans. David M. G. Stalker. London: SCM, 1975.
Räisänen, Heikki. "Jesus and the Food Laws: Reflections on Mark 7.15," in: *Jesus, Paul and Torah: Collected Essays*, ed. Heikki Räisänen, 127-47. JSNTSup 43. Sheffield: Sheffield Academic Press, 1992.
Robertson, Archibald T. *A Grammar of the Greek New Testament in Light of Historical Research*. London: Hodder & Stoughton, 3rd edn 1919.
Romaniuk, Kazimierz. "Le problème des Paulinismes dans l'Évangile de Marc." *NTS* 23 (1976-1977): 266-74.
Rudolph, David J. "Jesus and the Food Laws: A Reassessment of Mark 7:19b." *EQ* 74 (2002): 304-08.
Sanday, William, and Arthur C. Headlam, *The Epistle to the Romans*. Edinburgh: T & T Clark, 1902.
Schenk, Wolfgang. "Sekundäre Jesuanisierungen von primären Paulus-Aussagen bei Markus," in: *The Four Gospels 1992: Festschrift Frans Neirynck*, vol. 2, eds. Frans Van Segbroeck et al., 877-904. BETL 100. Leuven: Leuven University Press, 1992.
Schmidt, Thomas E. "Mark 15:16-32: The Crucifixion Narrative and the Roman Triumphal Procession." *NTS* 41 (1995): 1-18.
Schweizer, Eduard. *The Good News According to Mark*. Atlanta, Ga.: John Knox Press, 1970.
Seeley, David. "Rulership and Service in Mark 10:41-45." *NovT* 35 (1993): 234-50.
Senior, Donald. "The Gospel of Mark in Context." *TBT* 34 (1996), 215-21.
Sordie, Marta. *The Christians and the Roman Empire*. trans. Annabel Bedini. London: Croom Helm, 1986.
Svartvik, Jesper. *Mark and Mission: Mk 7:1-23 in its Narrative and Historical Contexts*. CBNTS 32. Stockholm: Almqvist &Wiksell, 2000.
Swete, Henry B. *Commentary on Mark: The Greek Text with Introduction, Notes and Indexes*. Grand Rapids, Mich.: Kregel, 1977.
Telford, William R. *The Theology of the Gospel of Mark*. Cambridge: Cambridge University Press, 1999.
Theissen, Gerd. *The Sociology of Palestinian Christianity*. Philadeliphia, Pa.: Fortress Press, 1978.
Thielman, Frank. "God's Righteousness as God's Fairness in Rom 1:17: An Ancient Perspective on a Significant Phrase." *JETS* 54 (2011): 35-48.
Watts, Rikk E. *Isaiah's New Exodus in Mark*. Tübingen: Mohr Siebeck, 1997.
—, *A Reader's Guide to Romans 9-11*. Vancouver: Regent College, 2012.
Wenham, David. "Paul's Use of the Jesus Tradition: Three Samples," in: *Gospel Perspectives: The Jesus Tradition Outside the Gospels*, ed. David Wenham, 7-37. Sheffield: JSOT Press, 1985.
Werner, Martin. *Der Einfluss paulinischer Theologie im Markusevangelium: eine Studie zur neutestamentlichen Theologie*. Giessen: Töpelmann, 1923.
Winn, Adam. *The Purpose of Mark's Gospel*. Tübingen: Mohr Siebeck, 2008.

David C. Sim
The Family of Jesus and the Disciples of Jesus in Paul and Mark: Taking Sides in the Early Church's Factional Dispute

1 Introduction

The proposition that the early Christian movement was factionalised has a long history. Its first major statement came in the works of Ferdinand Christian Baur,[1] and was later restated and reinforced by later members of the so-called Tübingen school.[2] The theory essentially involves the thesis that the Christian movement was divided into two major factions that were in conflict with one another over the issue of the Torah and its role in the movement associated with Jesus of Nazareth. One group comprised Jewish Christians (or Christian Jews) who argued that all followers of Jesus, both Jew and Gentile, were required to observe the traditional Mosaic Law. The alternative group, which included the Hellenists and later Paul, were of the view that in the light of the Christ event the Torah was no longer necessary; the Law, which had previously distinguished Jews from Gentiles, had become redundant, since all that was required now was faith in Christ alone.

Not surprisingly, Baur's controversial thesis found plenty of critics, and its acceptance has waxed and waned in the 180 years since it was first proposed. In recent scholarship, there are still those who agree in broad terms with Baur's general depiction of early Christian factionalism, though of course they might disagree with Baur over certain points and there are even disagreements amongst themselves. One point of dissension concerns the involvement (or the extent of the involvement) of the Jerusalem church in this factional dispute. For some scholars Paul was in direct conflict with the leaders of the mother church, while others accept that the apostle was opposed by Christian Jews

---

[1] See Ferdinand Christian Baur, "Die Christuspartei in der korinthischen Gemeinde, der Gegensatz des paulinischen und petrinischen Christentums in der ältesten Kirche, der Apostel Petrus in Rom." *TZT* 4 (1831): 61-206. Baur restated and refined his position in later publications. See especially Ferdinand Christian Baur, *Paulus, der Apostel Jesus Christi. Sein Leben und Wirken, seine Briefe und seine Lehre* (2 vols; Stuttgart: Becher und Müller, 1845).
[2] For a detailed history of the Tübingen school, see Horton Harris, *The Tübingen School: A Historical and Theological Investigation of the School of F. C. Baur* (Grand Rapids, Mich.: Baker Academic, 1990).

who were either unaffiliated with the Jerusalem Christian community or at best had a loose connection with it. This complex issue cannot be dealt with here in any detail. I have, however, argued elsewhere that this factional debate initially involved the Law-observant Hebrews and the Law-free Hellenists in Jerusalem, and then later it concerned the Jerusalem church, led by the family and disciples of Jesus, and the apostle Paul.[3] The thesis presented there was refined, developed and expanded in a more recent study of Paul's opponents in Galatia by Ian J. Elmer.[4] It should be noted as well that the thesis of a factional conflict within the early church in its first few decades has been championed by Michael D. Goulder,[5] J. Louis Martyn,[6] and it largely informs the mammoth study of the first generation of the Christian movement by James D. G. Dunn.[7]

The dispute between the two major strands of the Christian tradition was not simply confined to the first Christian generation. Many later texts continue the Pauline battle against the Torah and "judaising" tendencies; examples are the Pastoral Epistles, the letter to the Colossians and sections of the epistles of Ignatius of Antioch.[8] On the other side, we find that the Law-observant and anti-Pauline tradition of the Jerusalem church, despite the destruction of that Christian Jewish community in the year 70 CE, is also found in certain canonical texts, notably the Gospel of Matthew and the epistle of James, and in later Christian Jewish documents and groups.[9] It is not surprising, therefore, that Mark also can be included within this factional divide. As other scholars have argued in recent studies and in this volume, Mark stands either in or very close to the Pauline

---

[3] See David C. Sim, *The Gospel of Matthew and Christian Judaism: The History and Social Setting of the Matthean Community*, SNTW (Edinburgh: T & T Clark, 1998), 12-27, 63-107.

[4] Ian J. Elmer, *Paul, Jerusalem and the Judaisers: The Galatian Crisis in its Broadest Historical Context*, WUNT 2.258 (Tübingen: Mohr Siebeck, 2009).

[5] Michael D. Goulder, *A Tale of Two Missions* (London: SCM, 1994); and id, *Paul and the Competing Mission in Corinth* (Peabody, Mass.: Hendrickson, 2001).

[6] J. Louis Martyn, *Theological Issues in the Letters of Paul*, SNTW (Edinburgh: T & T Clark, 1997), 7-36. The factional conflict in the early church also underpins Martyn's important commentary on Galatians. See J. Louis Martyn, *Galatians: A New Translation with Introduction and Commentary*, AB 33A (New York, N.Y.: Doubleday, 1997).

[7] James D. G. Dunn, *Christianity in the Making*, vol. 2, *Beginning from Jerusalem* (Grand Rapids, Mich.: Eerdmans, 2009).

[8] See Sim, *Matthew and Christian Judaism*, 172-77, 260-82.

[9] See Sim, *Matthew and Christian Judaism*, 177-211. The major study of anti-Paulinism in Christian Jewish texts, tradtions and groups is still Gerd Lüdemann, *Opposition to Paul in Jewish Christianity* (Minneapolis, Minn.: Fortress Press, 1989). Lüdemann examines the evidence from the time of Paul through to the third century but overlooks the importance of the Gospel of Matthew in his otherwise fine study. Matthew's anti-Paulinism will be discussed in much more detail in my chapter, "The Reception of Paul and Mark in the Gospel of Matthew," in this volume.

theological tradition.[10] It will be argued in this chapter that this view of Mark is strengthened by examining the evangelist's treatment of Paul's major opponents, the leaders of the Jerusalem church. Writing an account of Jesus' mission afforded Mark the opportunity to refer to both the family of Jesus and the disciples of Jesus, and in his narrative both of these groups are depicted in very negative terms. This is precisely what we would expect from a Gospel that demonstrates pro-Pauline tendencies in other ways.

2 The Jerusalem Church's View of Paul

While there is a mass of evidence as to Paul's view of the Jerusalem church, which will be dealt with shortly, it is perhaps best to begin with the Jerusalem community's attitude towards Paul. Needless to say, when we venture into this topic we are moving into an area of some speculation. We have no documents directly produced by the Jerusalem church and its leading members. What we do possess are texts that were written in the name of some of the church's leaders a generation or so after their deaths, notably the epistle of James and the two epistles of Peter, but how much accurate information they convey about these men is questionable and very much open to debate. But even if we have no texts written by the Jerusalem church or its leaders, we are not completely in the dark.

One text that is often overlooked in this respect is 1Cor 15:3-8, which strongly suggests that Paul was never included in the official list of resurrection witnesses compiled by the church in Jerusalem. The apostle refers to this list in 1Cor 15:3-7 when he reminds the Corinthians of his original preaching to them of a tradition that he had himself received. Given that all the events included in this tradition occurred in Jerusalem or were associated with members of the Christian community in that city, it is probable that Paul received it when he visited Jerusalem some three years after his conversion around the year 36 CE (Gal 1:18-19). This tradition attests that Christ died for our sins in accordance with the Scriptures, that he was buried and then raised in accordance with the Scriptures, and it then lists in order those who received personal appearances from the risen Christ. The resurrected Jesus appeared first to Cephas and then to the twelve (disciples). He next appeared to a group of more than five hundred, then to his brother James, and then he appeared to all the apostles. Scholars have expended

---

10 The most detailed statement in recent times is Joel Marcus, "Mark – Interpreter of Paul." *NTS* 46 (2000): 473-87.

much time and energy attempting to define the precise tradition Paul received and passed on and what additions he may have made to it. Many of them have argued that the original creedal formula extended from vv. 3-5a ("Christ died for our sins" to "he appeared to Cephas") or from vv. 3-5b (which would include the appearance to the twelve).[11] While there can be little doubt that in the list of later appearances Paul has added material,[12] it is equally clear that the references to the appearances to the 500, James and all the apostles also stem from very early tradition. Whether this material was joined to the early creedal formula in vv. 3-5 or whether it was originally independent and brought together by Paul, the important point is that in either case Paul in 15:3-7 is citing very early material from the church in Jerusalem.[13] The pre-Pauline tradition and the list of resurrection witnesses ends at that point, and Paul then adds his own encounter with the risen Christ as the next and final resurrection appearance (15:8). There is nothing to suggest that Paul is relating the traditional formula at this point, and every reason to believe that the apostle is appending his own experience to the official list.[14]

There are three interesting aspects to this material. The first is that the authorities in Jerusalem did not include Paul in the official list of resurrection witnesses. This might be explained away by the fact that the formula was fixed very early on and Paul's experience happened some years later, but such a response is not very plausible. As noted above, Paul visited the Jerusalem church some three years after his conversion experience, and the existing formula could easily have been updated to accommodate this extra appearance. The fact that it was not demonstrates that there was at least some suspicion in the mother church over Paul's claim to have received a visitation of the resurrected Jesus. Secondly, it is significant that the formula cited by Paul states that Jesus appeared to *all* the apostles. If that is the case, then the tradition makes the remarkable claim that the office of apostle was effectively closed prior to the appearance to Paul. By implication at least, any later claimant to the role of apostle was to all intents and purposes denied such inclusion, and this obviously included Paul, the

---

[11] The latter is more likely, since it is only here that Paul uses the term "the twelve." See Charles K. Barrett, *A Commentary on the First Epistle to the Corinthians* (London: A & C Black, 2nd edn 1971), 341-42. That the original creedal material ran to the end of v. 5 is accepted also by Raymond F. Collins, *First Corinthians*, SP 7 (Collegeville, Pa.: Liturgical Press, 1999), 529-31. On the other hand, Joseph A. Fitzmyer maintains that the creed ran from vv. 3b-5a and did not include the twelve; Joseph A. Fitzmyer, *First Corinthians: A New Translation with Introduction and Commentary*, AYB 32 (New Haven, Conn.: Yale University Press, 2008), 541-42.
[12] For example, the qualification that many of the 500 are still alive is clearly from his hand.
[13] In agreement with Fitzmyer, *First Corinthians*, 542.
[14] Fitzmyer, *First Corinthians*, 551.

self-styled apostle to the Gentiles.[15] Needless to say, Paul was well aware of the implications of this part of the tradition, and he tries to explain his omission from the official apostolic witnesses on the grounds that he is the least of the apostles and unfit to be called an apostle because of his prior persecution of the church, but is an apostle nonetheless through the grace of God (15:9-10).[16] Whether convincing or not, Paul here tries to defend his own apostolic status, while conceding that the Jerusalem formula appeared to omit him from that role. The third factor to note here is that Paul emphasises that the risen Christ's appearance to him was the last of all. The significance of this piece of information has not been fully appreciated by scholars, but what Paul accomplishes by this insertion is that the revelation of the risen Christ to him was basically the last word. No-one could contradict the claims of Paul by stating that they were later visited by Jesus who communicated a message that differed from that of the apostle. Conversely, Paul could claim that the message and commission given to him were entirely valid, even if they were not consistent with earlier revelations delivered to Peter or James, because they were later and thus more up to date.[17] In arguing in this way, Paul attempted to block or dismiss the arguments of his critics regarding the validity of his apostolic status and the legitimacy of his message.

The significance of Paul's omission from the list of accepted resurrection witnesses should not be underestimated. It reveals that Paul was not considered to be an apostle by the Jerusalem church, and it attests that there was substantial doubt or even disbelief that Paul had had an encounter with the risen Christ.[18] Given that Paul's mission to preach to the Gentiles and his Law-free version of the gospel were integrally connected with that encounter (Gal 1:11-12.16-17), it must have been the case that there was widespread suspicion in Jerusalem over the validity of his mission and the particular gospel he preached. When

---

15 So correctly Barrett, *First Epistle to the Corinthians*, 343; and Lüdemann, *Opposition to Paul*, 73. Some scholars maintain that Paul himself added the word "all" (πᾶσιν) in this sentence. So Collins, *First Corinthians*, 537; and Fitzmyer, *First Corinthians*, 551. But given the difficulty this word causes Paul, this is hardly likely.

16 See Lüdemann, *Opposition to Paul*, 73. Cf. too David C. Sim, "The Defensibility of Christian Judaism." In *Prayer and Spirituality in the Early Church*, vol. 3, *Liturgy and Life*, eds. Bronwen Neil, Geoffrey D. Dunn and Lawrence Cross (Sydney: St Pauls, 2003), 57-72 at 68-69.

17 For full discussion of the issue that the messages of the risen Jesus to Peter and James on the one hand, and to Paul on the other hand, were not consistent with one another, see David C. Sim, "The Appearances of the Risen Christ to Paul: Identifying their Implications and Complications." *ABR* 54 (2006): 1-12. Had they been consistent, then many of the problems that arose in the early Christian movement would never have arisen.

18 Lüdemann, *Opposition to Paul*, 73.

we examine these issues from Paul's perspective, we find that this was indeed the case.

3 Paul's Relationship with the Jerusalem Church

Paul's relationship with the Jerusalem church is best attested in the epistle to the Galatians. It seems clear that certain people had entered the Pauline communities in Galatia, and were preaching an alternative gospel to that taught by Paul (1:6-9). In direct contrast to the Pauline message, this gospel specified that following Jesus involved both faith in Christ and observance of the Jewish Law.[19] That it involved obedience to the Torah is clear from a number of passages that contrast justification by faith and justification by the Law (2:16-21; 3:2, 10-14; 21-25; cf. 4:21), and Paul specifically focuses on circumcision (5:2-12. 6:12; cf. 2:3, 12) and the rules concerning the Jewish holy days (4:10). An integral part of their message that Gentile believers in Jesus should obey the Law seemingly concerns the figure of Abraham who, as the prototypical Gentile, obeyed the command of God and circumcised himself and his household (cf. Gen 17:9-27). Paul's response to their version of the gospel, including his doctrine of faith alone and not by works of the Law, the futility and even soteriological dangers of circumcision, and his re-interpretation of the Abraham tradition (cf. 3:6-29; 4:21-31), are well known and need not be repeated here. What is of more importance for our purposes is how these outsiders depicted Paul himself.

In addition to their own preaching of faith in Christ married to observance of the Torah, a further strategy on their part was to discredit Paul and his understanding of the gospel.[20] There seems to have been a number of components to this plan.[21] First, these people claimed that Paul was not a legitimate apostle. Secondly, they argued that Paul came under the direct authority of the Jerusalem church and was answerable to it. Thirdly, these opponents seem to have circulated a version of the apostolic council according to which Paul was breaking the

---

19 For a sympathetic summary of the message of Paul's opponents in Galatia, see Martyn, *Galatians*, 120-26. A more detailed account can be found in Elmer, *Paul*, 131-62. Cf. too Martinus C. de Boer, *Galatians: A Commentary*, NTL (Louisville, Ky.: Westminster John Knox Press, 2011), 50-61.
20 Philip F. Esler correctly notes that in the highly competitive ancient Mediterranean culture an attack on a rival message went hand in hand with an attack on the person who communicated that message. A personal on Paul was thus inevitable. See Philip F. Esler, *Galatians*, NTR (London: Routledge, 1998), 71.
21 Dunn, *Beginning from Jerusalem*, 726-30.

terms of the agreement by continuing his Law-free mission to the Gentiles. Paul responds to these three charges in the initial section of his letter. He defends his apostleship in the very first sentence (Gal 1:1) by stating that he is an apostle through Jesus and God alone and not commissioned by men, and he reinforces this point a little later on when referring to his conversion (1:11-12.15-16). Paul counteracts the second argument that he came under the authority of Jerusalem by emphasising that he had no contact with the church there until three years after his conversion experience (1:16-24). As for the third accusation, Paul recounts his own version of the apostolic council in which he states that the three Pillars accepted his gospel and his commission to preach it, and that the only opposition he encountered was from some nebulous group which he calls "the false brothers" (2:1-10). Paul makes the point that none of these charges is valid. He is an apostle through the direct commission of Christ; he is independent of the Jerusalem church; and he has not broken the agreement reached in Jerusalem.

In responding to their attacks upon him, Paul fights fire with fire. He states that these people trouble the Galatians (1:6; 5:10) and have even bewitched them (3:1). They preach a contrary gospel which perverts the gospel of Christ (1:6-7), and are therefore accursed (1:8-9). In an extreme moment of polemical attack, Paul even wishes that those who unsettle his converts would mutilate themselves (5:12). There is no question that Paul vents his anger against these Christian Jewish missionaries, but an important question still remains. What was the relationship between these intruders and the Jerusalem church? The most plausible answer is that they were agents of the Jerusalem community and were acting under its direct instructions. This is indicated on first inspection by the fact that both groups questioned Paul's status as an apostle. But over and above this, Paul makes it very clear that his anger in this epistle is directed not just towards the troublemakers in Galatia, but also towards the Jerusalem church and its leadership, and this suggests that there were close relations between them.[22]

That Jerusalem was behind the mission of these outsiders explains why Paul spends so much time in the early part of the letter spelling out his own relationship with the original Christian community. He states that after his conversion experience when his commission and gospel were revealed to him, he did not immediately go to Jerusalem to visit those who were apostles before him (Gal 1:16-17). Then after a three year gap he went to Jerusalem for two weeks where he met with Peter and James the brother of Jesus (1:18-20). Paul does not spell

---

[22] For an overview, see Martyn, *Galatians*, 459-66, though I would disagree with his analysis at certain points.

out the nature of these discussions, but it is safe to assume that they did not talk about the Law-free mission to the Gentiles that Paul earlier in the letter said had been revealed to him.[23] The reason for this conclusion is that Paul says that it was only when he visited Jerusalem the next time did he set out the gospel he preached to the Gentiles (2:2). The implication is that this matter had not been raised previously with Peter and James.[24]

That second visit to Jerusalem, known as the apostolic council, is of more importance. Paul states that after a fourteen year period (in Antioch), he went up to Jerusalem because of a revelation (2:2) and took Barnabas and Titus with him. More trustworthy in this case is the alternative tradition in Acts. According to Acts 15:1-2, certain men came from Judea (Jerusalem?) to Antioch and told the Gentile Christians that they could not be saved unless they were circumcised and adopted the whole Mosaic Law. Paul and Barnabas debated with these men, and it was decided that they and some others should go to Jerusalem to discuss this matter with the leading apostles. Paul covers up the embarrassing truth that the Antiochene community was forced to defend its Gentile mission before the leaders of the Jerusalem church, since this would have compromised his argument that he was independent of the Jerusalem leadership. In any event Paul then offers his account of the meeting that took place. He and his companions had a private meeting with James the brother of Jesus and the disciples Peter and John, and it was only then that he set before them the Law-free gospel he preached to the Gentiles (2:2). Then false brothers came into the meeting, but Paul opposed them (2:3-5) and finally won the day. The Pillar apostles accepted that Paul had been charged with the mission to the Gentiles just as Peter had been commissioned to evangelise the Jewish world, and they gave him the right hand of friendship. The only condition was that Paul and the others would remember the poor, to which Paul willingly agreed (2:6-10).

There are substantial difficulties accepting Paul's version of the apostolic council,[25] but there is no need for our purposes to enter into detail on this. Whatever happened in Jerusalem, whether or not an agreement was reached, the same issue broke out again soon after in Antioch. Paul describes this incident immediately after in Gal 2:11-14. He states that when Peter came to Antioch, he was happy to associate with the Gentile Christians there, and he did so until certain

---

23 Contra Lüdemann, *Opposition to Paul*, 43-44; Martyn, *Galatians*, 172; and Jerome Murphy-O'Connor, *Paul: A Critical Life* (Oxford: Oxford University Press, 1996), 93.
24 So correctly Dunn, *Beginning from Jerusalem*, 369 nn. 214, 215. Dunn suggests the more likely alternative that during this visit Paul got to know Peter who informed him of the pre-passion mission of Jesus.
25 See Sim, *Matthew and Christian Judaism*, 82-88; and Elmer, *Paul*, 90-104.

men came from James in Jerusalem. After they came and fearing "those of the circumcision," he withdrew from table-fellowship with the Gentiles, taking with him Barnabas and the other Jews in the Antiochene church. Paul then openly opposed and publicly accused Peter of outright hypocrisy. How could Peter live like a Gentile and not like a Jew and then later compel the Gentiles to live like Jews? It is clear even from Paul's brief description as to what took place. For reasons unknown Peter visited Antioch and openly ate with Gentile Christians. James heard of this and sent messengers to put a stop to this practice. But more than this, the messengers of James told the Gentile Christians that they needed to observe the Law and be circumcised. This is evident not simply from the mention of "those of the circumcision," but also from Paul's sarcastic retort to Peter. After the message from James, Gentiles were to be compelled to live like Jews, and it is precisely because total Law-observance is at issue that Paul immediately launches into a defence of justification by faith rather than justification by works of the Law (2:15-17).[26]

In short what James and then Peter attempted to do in Antioch, to introduce circumcision and the whole Torah to the Gentile community there, was precisely what Paul's opponents in Galatia were doing. We have to infer from this evidence that these Christian Jewish missionaries who came to Galatia came at the behest of James in Jerusalem.[27] In fact James shows a clear pattern of intervention whereby he sent on a number of occasions messengers to Law-free churches with the message that Gentile Christians needed to be circumcised and to observe the Torah. The initial intervention was in Antioch which initiated the apostolic council, and this was followed by a second intervention in the same city after the council which resulted in the incident that ended in a public brawl between Peter and Paul. Then we have a further intervention in Galatia. Francis Watson has argued that in Gal 1:9 Paul seems to have expected the arrival of another gospel in Galatia,[28] and if this is correct then it confirms the suspicion that James' strategy of intervention by way of envoys was well-known to Paul. This scenario coheres precisely with Paul's attempt to represent himself as the champion of the Law-free gospel at every intervention, be it in Jerusalem, Antioch or now in Galatia. Confirmation that the Jerusalem church was behind the Galatian

---

[26] For detailed defences of this view, see Sim, *Matthew and Christian Judaism*, 92-100; Elmer, *Paul*, 104-14; Esler, *Galatians*, 135-38; and de Boer, *Galatians*, 130-38.
[27] So Esler, *Galatians*, 137-38; Elmer, *Paul*, 155-62; and James D. G. Dunn, *The Epistle to the Galatians* (London: A & C Black, 1993), 12-15. Slightly less certain of a definitive connection is Martyn, *Galatians*, 126.
[28] Francis Watson, *Paul, Judaism and the Gentiles: Beyond the New Perspective* (Grand Rapids, Mich.: Eerdmans, rev. and exp. edn 2007), 113-14.

crisis comes from Paul's less than flattering and even bitter description of those who belonged to that church.

Let us begin with the three Pillars who are identified as James, Peter and John (Gal 2:9). Even though Paul recounts that the Pillars ultimately sided with him, he refers to them in a manner that undermines their status and authority. In describing them as "those who were of repute" (2:2), "those who are reputed to be something but what they are makes no difference to me" (2:6), and "those who are reputed to be Pillars" (2:9), there is a clear attempt to accept on the one hand that these people enjoy authority but on the other to question or undermine it.[29] In addition to these descriptors, he implies that James broke the agreement reached in Jerusalem when later sending another group of envoys[30] and he accuses Peter of blatant hypocrisy. Apart from the three Pillars, Paul calls others "false brothers" (2:4) who tried to spy on Paul and his colleagues, and "those of the circumcision" (2:12). Moreover, in the allegory of Sarah and Hagar in 4:21-31, the two women represent two covenants. Hagar represents the Sinai covenant and is the mother who bears children for slavery, and she corresponds to the present Jerusalem. This enslaved Jerusalem is then contrasted with the free Jerusalem above, who Paul claims is his mother. He and the (Law-free Gentile) Galatians are like Isaac and so are the sons of promise. Moreover, just as the son of the slave persecuted the son of the free woman, so now do those born according to the flesh persecute those who are born according to the Spirit. I concur with the reading of this text by J. Louis Martyn, who argues that Paul is using and responding to the language of his opponents. They use "Jerusalem" as a shorthand reference to the Jerusalem church and they refer to it as their mother. Paul counters this in his allegory by suggesting that their mother, Jerusalem (or the Jerusalem church), actually enslaves people (cf. 2:4) by their attachment to the Torah.[31] It is here that Paul is at his most vitriolic, and he makes the explicit point now that the relationship between his church and the founding church in Jerusalem is one of persecution.[32] Paul could only speak of persecution if the situation in Galatia formed part of a pattern of interference, and it was noted above that James had intervened a number of times by sending messengers to Law-free churches with the Law-observant gospel.

---

29 See Dunn, *Galatians*, 92-93, 102-03.
30 Esler, *Galatians*, 136-37. For the view that Paul does not implicitly accuse James of failing to uphold the earlier agreement, see Watson, *Paul*, 107.
31 Martyn, *Galatians*, 462-66. So too de Boer, *Galatians*, 300-02.
32 Martyn, *Galatians*, 444-45. Other scholars confine the reference to persecution to the situation in Galatia; the Christian Jewish missionaries are persecuting the Gentile Galatians with their alternative preaching. Cf. de Boer, *Galatians*, 306-07.

The epistle to the Galatians provides clear evidence that in the late 40s and the early 50s Paul's relationship with the Jerusalem authorities, especially James and Peter, was one of bitter conflict. On a number of occasions James sent missionaries to more liberal Christian churches with the demand that Gentiles in the Christian movement were to observe the Torah, and part of that strategy was to cast doubt on Paul's status as an apostle and the validity of his Law-free gospel. Paul responded to these incursions with powerful polemic, defending his experience of the risen Christ and his commission to be the apostle to the Gentiles, and denigrating the leaders of the Jerusalem church who were at the root of his problems. But we need to ask a further question; what happened in later years? Did this situation continue or was it the case that Paul and his opponents in Jerusalem managed to sort out their problems and attain reconciliation with one another? The evidence that exists tends to support the first of these possibilities. That is to say that the interventions into Paul's Gentiles churches continued unabated in the following years. The Corinthian correspondence also reveals interference in Corinth by the mother church, and the same issues that we find in Galatians, notably Law-observance and the validity of Paul's apostleship, are again prominent in these two letters.[33] Moreover, there is evidence in Philippians as well that similar hostilities were either being played out in Philippi or at least were expected in the near future.[34] Limitations of space preclude a detailed analysis of these texts, but this is not problematic for the purpose at hand. That the fractured relationship between Paul and the Jerusalem church was never repaired can be inferred from the fate of the collection that Paul took to Jerusalem on his final and fateful journey to the holy city.

Paul relates in Gal 2:10 that as part of the negotiations at the Jerusalem council, the Pillars required the Gentile churches to remember the poor.[35] Perhaps as part of a strategy to repair relations with James, Paul continued to collect funds from the Gentile churches. Originally his plan was that representatives of each church were to take the collection to Jerusalem (1Cor 16:3), though he left open the possibility that he might do this task himself (1Cor 16:4), and when the time arrived Paul decided to scrap the original plan and implement the latter option (Rom 15:25).

---

33 See the recent discussion of Elmer, *Paul*, 165-88. Cf. Goulder, *Paul and the Competing Missions*, passim.
34 Elmer, *Paul*, 188-96; and Watson, *Paul*, 137-46.
35 The literature on the collection is enormous. The most detailed recent study is David J. Downs, *The Offering of the Gentiles: Paul's Collection for Jerusalem in Its Chronological, Cultural and Cultic Contexts*, WUNT 2.248 (Tübingen: Mohr Siebeck, 2008).

The reason for this is that it is likely that the collection had not been as successful as Paul had hoped. In Rom 15:26 he mentions that only the churches of Macedonia and Achaia (Corinth?) had contributed funds. Some years earlier Paul had referred to the collection of the Galatian communities (1Cor 16:2), but their omission in Romans suggests that in the intervening period Paul had lost their financial support. In addition, there is good evidence that certain problems had arisen over the collection in the Corinthian churches. In the first letter Paul instructs his readers to contribute weekly what they could afford (1Cor 16:2), but in the following epistle he sees the need to cajole the Corinthians to exceed the generosity of the Macedonian churches (2Cor 8:1-5; cf. 9:1-15). The later reluctance of the Corinthians can be attributed to a view that emerged after the first letter that Paul had not been administering the funds properly (2Cor 8:20; cf. 7:2). The meagre amount of monies collected from the Gentile churches was of such great concern to Paul that he asked the Romans to pray that the Jerusalem church would find the collection acceptable (Rom 15:30-31). These dual factors, the lack of success of the collection and the unpredictable response of the Jerusalem authorities, convinced Paul that he had to take the monies personally to try to convince the Jerusalem church to accept them.

While we have no definitive evidence as to the fate of the collection, it is more likely than not that Paul's worst fears were realised and the Jerusalem church rejected the donations from the Gentile churches.[36] It is significant that Luke, who devotes a large amount of space to Paul's final visit to Jerusalem (Acts 21:15-23:30), never mentions the collection at all. Had it been accepted then we would expect him to have mentioned it, since a good part of his agenda in Acts was to demonstrate the basic unity of the different Christian groups he describes. His complete silence on the very reason for Paul's visit to Jerusalem is more than likely an attempt to suppress the real story that Paul offered the Gentile monies to the authorities in Jerusalem and that they were refused. It should be noted that in Luke's sources, there is a reference to Paul bringing gifts to the poor (Acts 24:17), and this strengthens the case that Luke knew but then suppressed the information he had about the collection and its rejection.[37]

If this reading of the fate of the collection is correct, then the conflict between Paul and the Jerusalem church was never resolved. Although the details are sketchy, Paul was presumably arrested in Jerusalem and subsequently sent

---

36 See Lüdemann, *Opposition to Paul*, 59-62; Elmer, *Paul*, 206-12; and Dunn, *Beginning from Jerusalem*, 970-72.
37 This is rejected by Downs, *Offering of the Gentiles*, 60-69, who offers a different interpretation. Downs concludes that we cannot be certain that Luke even knew about the collection (*Offering of the Gentiles*, 69-70), but this is hardly feasible.

to Rome where, according to tradition, he died a martyr's death. Other early traditions relate that both Peter and James died as martyrs at around the same time. Because the conflict between Paul and the Jerusalem authorities was never resolved, later Christians and Christian authors had to decide where they stood in terms of this factional divide, and we noted above that the affiliations of many authors can be easily identified. Yet another text that shows its stance in this dispute is the Gospel of Mark, and it is to this Gospel that we now turn.

4 Mark and the Family of Jesus

Of special importance in terms of our particular topic is the general date of Mark's Gospel. Most scholars would date it to the years either during the Jewish revolt (66-70 CE) or very shortly afterwards. While most exegetes have focused on the Jewish war as a major context for the writing of Mark, what has not been sufficiently appreciated is that it was written in the years immediately following the deaths of Paul, Peter and James in the early 60s. This was a period of major upheaval in the Christian movement when its different factions had lost their leaders. Needless to say the Jewish war was a major crisis for the Jerusalem church, but the Gentile Pauline churches, despite being well away from the conflict and not directly involved in it, must have also found themselves in a situation of despair and turmoil with the loss of their leader and no apparent successor to replace him.[38] It is within this critical historical context that Mark was written.

If it was the case that Mark stood either in or near the Pauline camp, as many scholars have suggested recently, then we should expect two things in his account of Jesus' mission. First of all, we should expect that Mark introduced Pauline theological concepts into his portrayal of Jesus, and a number of studies in this volume have argued in favour of that proposal. But on the other side, we should expect that a Pauline Mark would discredit the major opponents of Paul, the family of Jesus and the disciples of Jesus, who formed the power *bloc* in the Jerusalem church. A careful and critical reading of Mark confirms that this is precisely what he does. He too has a very negative attitude towards James and the family of Jesus, and his portrayal of Peter and the other disciples is also less than flattering. Some scholars have noted, albeit more in passing than in detail, that there is a close connection between the apostle and the evangelist in this re-

---

38 Sim, *Matthew and Christian Judaism*, 169-70.

spect.³⁹ Unlike Paul, however, who tends to see both groups as a single *bloc*, Mark never connects the two in his narrative of Jesus' mission. There are traditions that describe the family of Jesus and their relationship with Jesus, and other narratives that portray Jesus' interactions with the disciples. This tendency of Mark to keep these groups apart has led many scholars to examine their respective depictions in the Gospel separately, and we find studies devoted either to Mark's depiction of the family of Jesus or to his presentation of Jesus' disciples. However, this practice tends to divide the evidence and lessen the impact of Mark's views of the two closely-related groups that led the later Christian movement. A better approach is to assess these two groups together in the Gospel account.⁴⁰ These common views deserve further examination and some sort of explanation. We shall begin our analysis with the evangelist's presentation of Jesus' natural family and then investigate his depiction of the disciples.

The Gospel of Mark has only two passages that refer to the relatives of Jesus, but they are of vital importance since in both these family members are treated extremely harshly. We are first introduced to these people in 3:19b-35. In the material that precedes this tradition, Jesus has proclaimed the kingdom of God and performed many healings and exorcisms. Then after he returns home, his family went out to seize him for they said that he was out of his senses or demon-possessed (v. 21; ἔλεγον γὰρ ὅτι ἐξέστη). That this is the meaning of v. 21 requires some further discussion and justification. First, the identity of those who attempt to seize Jesus is best understood as his relatives or kinfolk. The Greek οἱ παρ' αὐτοῦ can have a variety of senses, including close family members, but this particular meaning is demanded by the immediate context for a number of reasons. The mother and brothers of Jesus are specifically mentioned later in 3:31-35 and their appearance at that point is rather sudden and unexpected unless they had been referred to earlier in the narrative.⁴¹ Furthermore, 3:19-35 is a typical "Marcan sandwich;" it begins with the family of Jesus (οἱ παρ' αὐτοῦ) and concludes with his mother and brothers, which points to the same identity for both groups.⁴² That the relatives of Jesus believe him to be possessed by a demon

---

39 So, for example, William R. Telford, *The Theology of the Gospel of Mark* (Cambridge: Cambridge University Press, 1999), 164-65; and Joel Marcus, *Mark 1-8*, AB 27 (New York, N.Y.: Doubleday, 1999), 74.
40 As does Étienne Trocmé, *The Formation of the Gospel according to Mark* (London: SPCK, 1975), 120-37.
41 Trocmé, *Formation*, 134; and Adela Yarbro Collins, *Mark: A Commentary*, Hermeneia (Minneapolis, Minn.: Fortress Press, 2007), 226-27.
42 Marcus, *Mark 1-8*, 270. So too John D. Crossan, "Mark and the Relatives of Jesus." *NovT* 15 (1973): 81-113 at 85-86; and Raymond E. Brown, Karl P. Donfried et al, *Mary in the New Testament* (London: Geoffrey Chapman, 1978), 55-56.

is evident from the presence of ἐχέστε, which literally means "to stand outside (one's senses)," but in the ancient world insanity was often associated with demon-possession (cf. the close connection in John 10:20), and the charge of demonic influence almost certainly underlies this tradition.[43] The material that follows immediately after, the Beelzebul controversy, to which we shall return shortly, also concerns possession, and this strengthens the case that v. 21 also refers to this theme. It should be noted that many English translations have attempted to soften the implications of 3:21 by rendering ἔλεγον in an impersonal way; "for people were saying he is beside himself." On this reading of the text, the family of Jesus attempts to seize Jesus to protect him from the unfair accusations of third parties.[44] But this translation is extremely dubious and is no doubt designed to protect the relatives of Jesus from criticism. Not only is it problematic linguistically, but it masks the true intentions of Mark which was to indict Jesus' kinfolk. The evangelist wanted his readers to understand that the family of Jesus believed he was possessed by a demon, and so they attempted to seize him to conceal him from public view.

This episode is then followed by the Beelzebul controversy in 3:22-30, which continues and expands the theme of Jesus and demonic possession. In this pericope certain scribes who have travelled from Jerusalem accuse Jesus of being possessed by Beelzebul, the prince of demons, and it is this association that enables Jesus to perform successful exorcisms (v. 22). Jesus responds to this charge by highlighting its inherent illogicality. He asks "How can Satan cast out Satan?," which means effectively "Why would Satan cast out Satan?" He points out that a divided kingdom cannot stand and a divided household cannot stand, so if Satan is now divided and opposing himself, he will not be able to stand (vv. 23-26). Then Jesus turns the topic to himself. He contends that no-one can enter a strong man's house and plunder his goods unless he first binds the strong man. The meaning here is clear. Jesus has bound and controlled Satan or Beelzebul, and it is his power over the prince of demons that enables him to plunder his house and exorcise his demonic underlings (v. 27).

Having made this point and defended himself against these charges, Jesus next spells out the consequences for those who made the accusations (vv. 28-30). All sins and blasphemies can be forgiven with the sole exception of blasphemies against the Holy Spirit; this is an eternal sin for which there can be no for-

---

43 Marcus, *Mark 1-8*, 271; and Brown, Donfried et al, *Mary*, 56-57.
44 A slightly different view is presented by John Painter. Painter argues that the crowd believes Jesus to be possessed, but that it is the disciples and not the family of Jesus who try to seize Jesus. See John Painter, *Just James: The Brother of Jesus in History and Tradition* (Columbia, S.C.: University of South Carolina Press, 1997), 21-28.

giveness. Mark concludes this short section with the authorial comment "for they said he has an unclean spirit." From the perspective of the evangelist, any charge that Jesus is possessed by a demonic entity amounts to blasphemy against the Holy Spirit. Mark had made the point at the baptism of Jesus by John the Baptist that Jesus was in fact filled with or even possessed by the Spirit which descended from heaven upon him (1:9-11). To accuse Jesus of demon-possession rather than possession by the Holy Spirit therefore entails blasphemy against the latter.[45] An important question now presents itself. Just who, according to Mark, has committed this blasphemy and thus committed the single sin for which there is no forgiveness? There is no doubt that the scribes from Jerusalem are identified as such blasphemers since they had unambiguously stated that Jesus was possessed by Beelzebul. But it is also certain that Mark identifies the relatives of Jesus as those who have also committed this unforgiveable sin. They too had accused Jesus of being out of his mind or demon-possessed so what applies to the Jerusalem scribes would necessarily have to apply to them as well.[46] That the evangelist intends the family of Jesus to be so identified in this way is confirmed by the following pericope in 3:31-35.

Mark relates that Jesus' mother and brothers came and stood outside the house he was in, and then they sent to him and called him. A group around Jesus informs him that his family members are outside and are calling for him. He then replies, "Who are my mother and my brothers?," and looking at those around him he answers his own question by stating, "Here are my mother and my brothers. Whoever does the will of God is my brother, and sister and mother." The Marcan Jesus here clearly rejects his blood relations; they no longer qualify as his mother, brothers or sisters on account of their blasphemous and unforgiveable beliefs and are replaced by those who listen to Jesus and who do the will of God.[47] This account of Jesus' family is astonishing to say the least, and we shall return to its significance shortly.

In the meantime it is necessary to examine the other Marcan passage that mentions the close relations of Jesus, Mark 6:1-6, which continues the negative portrayal of 3:19-35. Jesus visits Nazareth and teaches in the synagogue on the Sabbath. Those who listen to his words are astonished and ask where Jesus received his wisdom and his miraculous powers. Knowing Jesus and his family well, they ask among themselves, "Is this not the carpenter, the Son of Mary

---

45 Marcus, *Mark 1-8*, 284.
46 So correctly Trocmé, *Formation*, 135-36; and Crossan, "Relatives of Jesus," 95-96.
47 So, with varying nuances, Crossan, "Relatives of Jesus," 96-97; Brown, Donfried et al, *Mary*, 58-59; Painter, *Just James*, 29-30; Marcus, *Mark 1-8*, 285-86; and Robert H. Gundry, *Mark: A Commentary on His Apology for the Cross* (Grand Rapids, Mich.: Eerdmans, 1993), 177-79.

and brother of James and Joses and Judas and Simon, and are not his sisters here with us?" In the end, however, they take offence that someone who is so familiar to them could speak and act with such wisdom and authority. Jesus then defends himself and replies to them; "a prophet is not without honour, except in his own country, and among his own kin, and in his own house" (v. 4), and he marveled at their unbelief (v. 6). While Jesus' criticism is doubtless aimed at the townspeople who demonstrate a lack of belief and understanding, it is also true that the family of Jesus who live in Nazareth as well are included in the charge. Jesus laments that even though he is a prophet, he has no honour among his kinfolk and in his own house. The unbelief and misunderstanding that his relatives displayed earlier is reinforced in this passage.[48] It is significant that on this occasion the Marcan Jesus identifies the family members in question. They include Jesus' mother Mary, his four brothers (James, Joses, Judas and Simon), as well as a number of unnamed sisters.

These two texts provide a rather damning picture of the relatives of Jesus in the Marcan narrative. His family, including his mother and brothers, show no understanding of Jesus and his mission, and their views are tantamount to blasphemy. For his part Jesus sees fit to reject his blood relations and replace them with those who believe in him and who do the will of God. Even though Mark's negative depiction of Jesus' relatives is set at the time of Jesus' ministry, it has important repercussions for the later history of the Christian movement. The brothers of Jesus who played leading roles in the early Jerusalem Church, have committed blasphemy and are guilty of a sin for which there can be no redemption or atonement. This means that their guilt remains during the period of the church, and it applies in particular to James, the brother of Jesus, who led the Jerusalem church in its dispute with Paul. The evangelist makes it very clear that the siblings of Jesus, and James in particular, had no right to lead the primitive movement initiated by their brother. They did not believe in Jesus and Jesus in turn rejected them. But more than this. In accusing Jesus of being in league with Satan, they blasphemed against the Holy Spirit and this is an unpardonable sin. People who are guilty of this crime stand condemned forever and clearly have no right to assume leadership roles in the movement initiated by Jesus.[49] In historical terms, this is an outright and vitriolic attack upon James.

It can easily be argued from this evidence that Mark has taken up the cause of Paul in attempting to discredit the character of James (and Jesus' other sib-

---

48 Crossan, "Relatives of Jesus," 103-04; Trocmé, *Formation*, 131; Brown, Donfried et al, *Mary*, 59-60; and Marcus, *Mark 1-8*, 376, 379. Painter, *Just James*, 31-33, notes but does not emphasise the anti-family tone of this tradition.
49 Trocmé, *Formation*, 136-37

lings),⁵⁰ but his critique of James goes much further than that of the apostle. While Paul was content to criticise James for breaking his word at the apostolic council and for undermining the Pauline Gentile mission by constantly intervening in the Law-free churches, he never accused James of eternal sins; the fact that he was to take the collection to Jerusalem himself suggests that he still entertained some hope that James could be brought around to Paul's way of thinking. Mark was much more aggressive by comparison, and this was no doubt due to his retrospective perspective. When Paul wrote the brother of Jesus was still alive and the possibility existed for him to change his mind, but Mark wrote after the death of James and he knew that James met his death while still vehemently opposed to Paul. It was necessary for Mark, if he was to support the theology and mission of Paul, to condemn and discredit James completely, and he accomplishes this task in his Gospel narrative.

5 Mark and the Disciples of Jesus

When we turn our attention to the Marcan portrayal of the disciples, we find again that the evangelist has a rather negative opinion of them. It must be said at the outset that not all the traditions in Mark are critical of the disciples; some are favourable, especially at the beginning of the narrative, and their presence in the Gospel should not be overlooked. The disciples are called by Jesus and they immediately leave their occupations to follow him (1:16-20; 2:13-14). This decision means that they leave everything, including their families, to follow Jesus, and he promises that those who make such a commitment will receive eternal rewards and eternal life in the age to come (10:28-31). The disciples support the decision of Jesus to eat with tax-collectors and sinners (2.15), and in turn Jesus defends his disciples against the charges that they do not fast properly (3:18-22) and that they break the Sabbath commandment (2:23-38). Jesus appoints twelve disciples who are named with Simon Peter heading the list; these are sent out to preach and to perform exorcisms (3:13-19a). A little later in the narrative, the disciples are sent out in pairs to preach repentance and to exorcise and heal (6:7-13), and upon their successful completion of their mission Jesus commands that they move to an isolated position to rest (6:30-31). The special position of the disciples is made clear when Jesus explains to them that they alone are given the

---

50 Crossan, "Relatives of Jesus," 112-13; and Goulder, *A Tale of Two Missions*, 11. Painter, *Just James*, 30-31 also raises the prospect that Mark rejects the natural family of Jesus because of his Pauline leanings.

secrets of the kingdom of God, while those outside the inner circle are excluded (4:10-12, 35). These early traditions paint the disciples in a favourable light, but as the narrative unfolds Mark's depiction of the disciples takes a severe turn for the worse. While there are some negative indications even in the early chapters, they increase dramatically during the course of the narrative.

In the episode of the stilling of the storm, they demonstrate a distinct lack of faith (4:35-51), and their lack of faith and prayer affects their ability to cast out an evil spirit (9:18-19.28-29). They are criticised by Jesus for keeping the children away from him (10:13-16) and for complaining about a non-disciple performing exorcisms in his name (9:38-41). Perhaps the most serious failing of the disciples in the Gospel of Mark is their failure to understand the teaching of Jesus and the nature of his mission. This runs right through the Marcan story. The disciples ask Jesus about his parables (4:10) and Jesus questions whether they will ever understand the parables he teaches (4:13). They also fail to comprehend the significance of the two miraculous feedings (6:51-52). More importantly, the disciples never understand the suffering nature of Jesus' messianic mission, despite Jesus' constant teaching on this issue. The passion predictions make this point with the utmost clarity. At Caesarea Philippi Peter correctly identifies Jesus as the messiah (10:29). Jesus then teaches the disciples that his messianic mission involves suffering, being killed and then being raised from the dead (v. 31). Peter refuses to accept this and rebukes Jesus (v. 32), and Jesus responds by associating Peter with Satan; "Get behind me Satan. For you are not on the side of God, but of men" (v. 33). He then explains to all the disciples and others that following him involves self-denial and the real possibility of death (v. 34). In the second passion prediction in 9:31-32, Jesus again teaches the disciples that he must suffer, die and be raised, but again they did not understand and were afraid to ask him about it. The disciples in fact condemn themselves all the more by discussing who was the greatest among them while Jesus was instructing them on his ultimate fate (9:33-37). Jesus explains for the third time the necessity of his suffering, death and resurrection, but his teaching only evokes a response by James and John that they be placed either side of him when he enters his glory (10:35-45). A further passage of interest in this regard is 9:9-10. In this episode Jesus comes down the mountain after the transfiguration accompanied by Peter, James and John, and instructs them to tell no-one what they witnessed until the Son of Man has been raised from the dead. They keep the matter to themselves but question what was meant by the resurrection from the dead. These texts in particular are extremely damning of the disciples, especially those two who formed part of the later Jerusalem church's triumvirate.[51] They refuse to accept the teaching of Jesus of the necessity of his suffering and death, and they have no understanding at all as to what his resurrection might mean.

In the passion narrative, Jesus prophesies that one of the disciples will betray him (14:17-21), that the rest of the disciples will desert him (14:27-28) and that Peter will deny him on three occasions (14:29-31). In the garden of Gethsemane Peter, James and John (again note the prominence of Peter and John) sleep for a sustained period while Jesus agonises over his imminent arrest and death (14.32-42). In accordance with the prophecies of Jesus, Judas betrays him (14:43-49; cf. 14:10-11), all the disciples flee as Jesus is arrested (14:50) and Peter denies him three times (14:66-72). These acts of betrayal, cowardice and denial conclude the activities of the male disciples in the Gospel of Mark. Certain female followers of Jesus then enter the story. Mary Magdalene, Mary the mother of James the younger and Joses, and Salome, as well as other women witness the crucifixion (15:40-41), and the three named women discover the empty tomb and are told of his resurrection by the angel (16:1-8). The angel conveys a message to the women that mentions Peter and the remaining disciples. He instructs them to tell the disciples that Jesus is going before them to Galilee where they will see him (cf. 14:28). But the Gospel ends with the women fleeing from the tomb in terror and saying nothing to anyone (16:8).

Mark's critical depiction of the disciples has long attracted the interest of scholars, and various interpretations of the evangelist's intentions have been presented.[52] In the view of many scholars, the intentions of the evangelist were purely pastoral. One version of this view argues that Mark uses the disciples' weaknesses and failure to comprehend as a foil to introduce a significant teaching of Jesus.[53] Another version contends that Mark's purpose was to make his readers identify with the disciples; they would either gain encouragement by noting the failures of Jesus' own followers or see their own shortcom-

---

51 It is interesting to note that on a number of occasions Mark uses the three-fold "Peter, James and John" (e.g. 5:37; 9:2, 14:33), the same names that comprise the triumvirate to which Paul refers in his account of the apostolic council. While it is tempting to see in these texts references to the later leadership of the Jerusalem church, any such conclusion would be mistaken. Mark takes care to distinguish the disciple James from the brother of Jesus who shares his name. The brother of Jesus is named in 6:3, while the disciple James is specifically described as the brother of John and the son of Zebedee (3:17; 5:37; 10:35).
52 See the recent study of C. Clifton Black, *The Disciples according to Mark: Markan Redaction in Current Debate* (Grand Rapids, Mich.: Eerdmans, 2nd edn 2012).
53 This view is most closely associated with Ernest Best. See his "The Role of the Disciples in Mark." NTS 23 (1976-77): 377-401; and id, "Mark's Use of the Twelve." ZNW 69 (1978): 11-35.

ings and come to repentance.⁵⁴ But the problem with these sorts of explanations is that the disciples are not simply fictional characters in a fictional story. They were real people who would have been familiar, at least by reputation, to the intended readers of Mark's narrative. It is thus unlikely that the evangelist would have depicted these significant figures in the early church in this critical way simply for pastoral concerns. A much more likely scenario is that he criticises the disciples of Jesus for the same reason as he criticises the family of Jesus. Standing in the Pauline tradition, Mark sees fit to discredit as much as he can the major opposition to Paul, which included both the family of Jesus and his disciples.⁵⁵

The strange conclusion to Mark's Gospel needs to be fully appreciated in this respect. Even though the angel states that Jesus will go to Galilee to meet with the disciples, there is no indication in the narrative that this meeting ever takes place. In fact the opposite is implied in so far as the women who run from the tomb say nothing of their experience or the angelic message; the implication is that the disciples never receive this instruction to return to Galilee and so never meet the risen Christ. This means that the disciples who misunderstood the teaching and mission of Jesus, and who deserted and denied him, are never rehabilitated in this Gospel. There is no indication at all that their prior misunderstanding of Jesus' messiahship is ever rectified, and since they receive no visitation from the risen Christ, they are still ignorant as to what the rising from the dead might mean (cf. 9:9). This abrupt conclusion to the Gospel in which the disciples are not rehabilitated is at odds with the other Gospels. In all the other three narratives the risen Christ appears to the disciples, and they are explicitly or implicitly forgiven for their earlier foibles and are prepared for their future work. The Matthean Jesus appears to the eleven disciples in Galilee and sends them on a world-wide mission (Matt 28:16-20), while the Johannine Jesus similarly sends out the disciples after giving them the Holy Spirit (John 20:19-23; cf. 21:15-19). In the Lucan writings Jesus explains the scriptural necessity of his death and resurrection which his disciples, after the event, now fully comprehend (Luke 24:13-45), and they too are commanded to missionise the world

---

54 See Robert Tannehill, "The Disciples in Mark: The Function of a Narrative Role." In *The Interpretation of Mark*, ed. William R. Telford (London: SPCK, 1985), 134-57; and Pheme Perkins, *Peter: Apostle for the Whole Church* (Columbia, S.C.: University of South Carolina Press, 1994), 57-66.
55 So Joseph B. Tyson, "The Blindness of the Disciples in Mark." In *The Messianic Secret*, ed. Christopher Tuckett (London: SPCK, 1983), 35-43. Similar views are presented by Trocmé, 120-30; Telford, *Theology of Mark*, 127-37; Goulder, *A Tale of Two Missions*, 11; and John Painter, *Mark's Gospel*, NTR (London: Routledge, 1997), 212-14, 216-17.

once they have received the Spirit (Acts 1:8). But the Marcan narrative knows nothing of these matters and we should not read Mark through the lens of these later texts. At the Gospel's end the male disciples stand condemned as cowards, deniers and as ones who never grasped the nature of Jesus' mission or the significance of his resurrection. They are never given any leadership roles or directives in terms of the mission of the early church.[56]

It also needs to be emphasised that the lack of comprehension of the disciples at the time of Jesus' mission covers concrete issues that played a role into the period of the church. The Marcan Jesus conducts missions to both Jews and Gentiles (cf. 4:35-5:21; 6:45-53; 7:24-8:10; 8:13-9:30),[57] but the disciples fail to understand the significance of the latter mission (cf. 8:14-21). Jesus also critiques the Jewish Law (cf. 7:19),[58] but the disciples fail to realise its implications. Mark therefore makes the point that the disciples in the time of the church did not follow the example of Jesus (as presented by Mark) because they never really grasped the content of his teaching. They opposed the Gentile mission and continued to observe the Torah. By contrast, it was Paul who did understand the teachings and actions Jesus by conducting the mission to the Gentiles and by stating that the (ritual) requirements of the Torah were now no longer necessary in the light of the Christ event.[59] One might even speculate that for Mark it was Paul who, having been visited by the risen Christ, fully understood and appreciated the significance of Jesus' resurrection.

---

[56] Telford, *Theology of Mark*, 137-43, 149-50. Painter goes further than this by suggesting that Mark criticises the historical disciples for not going to Galilee as Jesus had told them to do (14:28), but for remaining in Jerusalem. The disobedience of the disciples at the end of the Gospel constitutes their final failure. See Painter, *Mark*, 213-14.

[57] See Eric K. Wefald, "The Separate Gentile Mission in Mark: A Narrative Explanation of the Markan Geography, the Two Feeding Accounts, and Exorcisms." *JSNT* 60 (1995): 3-26 for a convincing argument that Mark presents two parallel missions in his narrative. Cf. too Elizabeth Struthers Malbon, *Narrative Space and Mythic Meaning in Mark* (Sheffield: JSOT Press, 1991), 40-43. For the most recent discussion of Gentiles and the Gentile mission in Mark, see Kelly R. Iverson, *Gentiles in the Gospel of Mark: "Even the Dogs under the Table Eat the Children's Crumbs"*, LNTS 339 (London: T & T Clark International, 2007).

[58] For full-scale discussions of the Torah in Mark's Gospel, see William R. G. Loader, *Jesus' Attitude Towards the Law*, WUNT 2.97 (Tübingen: Mohr Siebeck, 1997), 9-136; and more recently, Boris Repschinski, *Nicht aufzulösen, sondern zu erfüllen: Das jüdische Gesetz in den synoptischen Jesuserzählungen*, FzB 120 (Würzburg: Echter, 2009), 143-216.

[59] Painter, *Mark*, 216-17.

6 Conclusions

It has been argued in this chapter that there is a significant agreement between Mark and Paul in terms of the depictions of Jesus' family and his disciples. Paul accepted that these groups, especially James the brother of Jesus and Peter the disciple, were authoritative figures in the early church who had received visitations from the risen Lord (1Cor. 15:3-7). But Paul was intensely critical of these people, especially James and Peter, for their denial of his independent apostleship, their rejection of his Law-free gospel and most importantly their interference in his own Gentile churches. The opposition to the Pauline mission and gospel, which continued throughout the 50s, seemingly was never resolved. Despite Paul's wish that the Jerusalem church would accept the collection from the Gentile churches, the evidence suggests that this was not to be, and there was no reconciliation between Paul and the Pillars in Jerusalem.

Writing perhaps just a few years after the death of Paul (and Peter and James), Mark adopts an even more critical stance. He defends to some extent Paul's Law-free gospel in his presentation of Jesus' teaching, and does his best to discredit the later leaders of the Jerusalem church when referring to them in the context of Jesus' earthly mission. Whatever other traditions about these figures were circulating throughout the early Christian churches, Mark wanted his readers to share his understanding of the family and the disciples of Jesus, the two groups that formed the power *bloc* in the primitive Christian movement and which provided Paul with so much opposition. In his own account of the mission of Jesus, presumably the first to appear in narrative form, he depicts the later leaders of the early Christian movement in mostly negative terms. The family of Jesus, notably James the brother of Jesus who ultimately led the Jerusalem church, had rejected Jesus and had been in turn rejected by him. Moreover, and more seriously, James had blasphemed against the Holy Spirit and had thus committed an unforgiveable sin. From Mark's point of view, this eternal sin made James and any member of Jesus' family completely ineligible to run the early Christian movement. The disciples of Jesus, including Peter and John who formed with James the authoritative triumvirate in Jerusalem, fared a little better. The evangelist acknowledged that Jesus had chosen the disciples and that they had responded to his call, and in so doing had made considerable personal sacrifices. If Mark 10:28-31 is to be taken seriously, Mark accepted that the disciples had earned eschatological rewards and eternal life. They are therefore treated much better than the relatives of Jesus in this respect. But even so, the evangelist calls into question the competence of the disciples to lead the primitive Christian movement after the resurrection event. The disciples did not understand the teaching of Jesus, they misinterpreted the nature of his messianic mission, they had no understanding of the resurrection, and Mark implies strongly that the disciples were never rehabilitated because they were not privileged to receive a visitation from the risen Christ. Despite their service to Jesus during his earthly mission, these people too were ineligible to lead the early church.

Although Mark, unlike Luke, does not write a history of the church, it is reasonable to conclude that he would have viewed Paul, who was the recipient of a visitation from the risen Christ, as the one who did understand Jesus and who was the true heir to the mission of Jesus. And if Mark's intended readers were similarly sympathetic to Paul, as is likely, then they had more ammunition in the critical period when Mark wrote that Paul had been right and that the Jerusalem leaders had been wrong to oppose him.

It is interesting to observe that Paul's criticisms of Jesus' family members and his disciples are restricted to their activities in the time of the Christian movement and specifically in relation to their dealings with Paul himself. The apostle says nothing, either positive or negative, about any of these people during the time of Jesus' historical mission. There is no mention of Jesus' rejection by his family or the disciples' failure to comprehend the nature of Jesus' mission and their misunderstanding of Jesus' teachings. This can of course be explained by the fact that Paul had a general lack of interest in the mission and teaching of the historical Jesus, but it is surprising nonetheless. If Mark had access to accurate information, Paul could easily have discredited the leaders of the Jerusalem church by recalling those traditions circulating around the Christian communities that were unfavourable to his opponents. The fact that he did not do so should perhaps make modern exegetes pause and question the depiction of these people in Mark and in other sources.[60] But it might also be the case that Paul was more concerned to judge people, not by their actions during the mission of the historical Jesus, but by their actions in the period of the church and their attitudes towards him. We need to recall that Paul's own track record was not without blemish. He had on his own admission been a persecutor of the fledgling Christian community. What was most important to him were the present realities and dangers posed by the Jerusalem authorities, and Paul was clearly of the view that these immediate problems needed to be addressed by other

---

60 I have argued elsewhere that, despite Matthew's dependence on Mark, on some issues the depiction of the teachings and actions of the historical Jesus are better represented by Matthew. Two clear examples are Matthew's portrayal of Jesus as upholding the Torah and not being involved in a Gentile mission. See David C. Sim, "Matthew and Jesus of Nazareth." In *Matthew and His Christian Contemporaries*, eds. David C. Sim and Boris Repschinski, LNTS 333 (London: T & T Clark International, 2008), 155-72.

means, including his insistence on his visitation by the risen Christ, the legitimacy of his apostleship and his version of the gospel.

By composing an account of Jesus' mission, Mark was forced to adopt a completely new strategy. He obviously could not defend Paul and criticise the actions of the Jerusalem leadership during the time of the church, so he did what he could to question the leadership credentials of the disciples and the family of Jesus by emphasising their many shortcomings during the mission of the historical Jesus. In writing or perhaps rewriting many aspects of the history of Jesus' ministry, Mark betrays his impeccable Pauline credentials.

Bibliography

Barrett, Charles K. *A Commentary on the First Epistle to the Corinthians*. London: A & C Black, 2nd edn 1971.

Baur, Ferdinand Christian. "Die Christuspartei in der korinthischen Gemeinde, der Gegensatz des paulinischen und petrinischen Christentums in der ältesten Kirche, der Apostel Petrus in Rom." *TZT* 4 (1831): 61-206.

—, *Paulus, der Apostel Jesus Christi. Sein Leben und Wirken, seine Briefe und seine Lehre.* 2 vols. Stuttgart: Becher und Müller, 1845.

Best, Ernest. "The Role of the Disciples in Mark." *NTS* 23 (1976-77): 377-401.

—, "Mark's Use of the Twelve." *ZNW* 69 (1978): 11-35.

Black, C. Clifton. *The Disciples according to Mark: Markan Redaction in Current Debate*. Grand Rapids, Mich.: Eerdmans, 2nd edn 2012.

Brown, Raymond E., Donfried, Karl P. et al. *Mary in the New Testament*. London: Geoffrey Chapman, 1978.

Collins, Adela Yarbro. *Mark: A Commentary*. Hermeneia. Minneapolis, Minn.: Fortress Press, 2007.

Collins, Raymond F. *First Corinthians*. SP 7. Collegeville, Pa.: Liturgical Press, 1999.

Crossan, John D. "Mark and the Relatives of Jesus." *NovT* 15 (1973): 81-113.

de Boer, Martinus. *Galatians: A Commentary*. NTL. Louisville, Ky.: Westminster John Knox Press, 2011.

Downs, David J. *The Offering of the Gentiles: Paul's Collection for Jerusalem in Its Chronological, Cultural and Cultic Contexts*. WUNT 2.248. Tübingen: Mohr Siebeck, 2008.

Dunn, James D. G. *The Epistle to the Galatians*. London: A & C Black, 1993.

—, *Christianity in the Making*, vol. 2, *Beginning from Jerusalem*. Grand Rapids, Mich.: Eerdmans, 2009.

Elmer, Ian J. *Paul, Jerusalem and the Judaisers: The Galatian Crisis in its Broadest Historical Context*. WUNT 2.258. Tübingen: Mohr Siebeck, 2009.

Esler, Philip F. *Galatians*. NTR. London: Routledge, 1998.

Fitzmyer, Joseph A. *First Corinthians: A New Translation with Introduction and Commentary*. AYB 32. New Haven, Conn.: Yale University Press, 2008.

Goulder, Michael D. *A Tale of Two Missions*. London: SCM, 1994.

—, *Paul and the Competing Mission in Corinth*. Peabody, Mass.: Hendrickson, 2001.

Gundry, Robert H. *Mark: A Commentary on His Apology for the Cross*. Grand Rapids, Mich.: Eerdmans, 1993.

Harris, Horton. *The Tübingen School: A Historical and Theological Investigation of the School of F. C. Baur*. Grand Rapids, Mich.: Baker Academic, 1990.

Iverson, Kelly R. *Gentiles in the Gospel of Mark: "Even the Dogs under the Table Eat the Children's Crumbs"*. LNTS 339. London: T & T Clark International, 2007.

Loader, William R. G. *Jesus' Attitude Towards the Law*. WUNT 2.97. Tübingen: Mohr Siebeck, 1997.

Lüdemann, Gerd. *Opposition to Paul in Jewish Christianity*. Minneapolis, Minn.: Fortress Press, 1989.

Malbon, E. Struthers. *Narrative Space and Mythic Meaning in Mark*. Sheffield: JSOT Press, 1991.

Marcus, Joel, *Mark 1-8*. AB 27. New York, N.Y.: Doubleday, 1999.

—, "Mark – Interpreter of Paul." *NTS* 46 (2000): 473-87.
Martyn, J. Louis. *Theological Issues in the Letters of Paul*. SNTW. Edinburgh: T & T Clark, 1997.
—, *Galatians: A New Translation with Introduction and Commentary*. AB 33A. New York, N.Y.: Doubleday, 1997.
Murphy-O'Connor, Jerome. *Paul: A Critical Life*. Oxford: Oxford University Press, 1996.
Painter, John. *Just James: The Brother of Jesus in History and Tradition*. Columbia, S.C.: University of South Carolina Press, 1997.
—, *Mark's Gospel*. NTR. London: Routledge, 1997.
Perkins, Pheme. *Peter: Apostle for the Whole Church*. Columbia, S.C.: University of South Carolina Press, 1994.
Repschinski, Boris. *Nicht aufzulösen, sondern zu erfüllen: Das jüdische Gesetz in den synoptischen Jesuserzählungen*. FzB 120. Würzburg: Echter, 2009.
Sim, David C. *The Gospel of Matthew and Christian Judaism: The History and Social Setting of the Matthean Community*. SNTW. Edinburgh: T & T Clark, 1998.
—, "The Defensibility of Christian Judaism," in: *Prayer and Spirituality in the Early Church*, vol. 3, *Liturgy and Life*, eds. Bronwen Neil, Geoffrey D. Dunn and Lawrence Cross, 57-72. Sydney: St Pauls, 2003.
—, "The Appearances of the Risen Christ to Paul: Identifying their Implications and Complications." *ABR* 54 (2006): 1-12.
—, "Matthew and Jesus of Nazareth," in: *Matthew and His Christian Contemporaries*, eds. David C. Sim and Boris Repschinski, 155-72. LNTS 333. London: T & T Clark International, 2008.
Tannehill, Robert, "The Disciples in Mark: The Function of a Narrative Role," in: *The Interpretation of Mark*, ed. William R. Telford, 134-57. London: SPCK, 1985.
Telford, William R. *The Theology of the Gospel of Mark*. Cambridge: Cambridge University Press, 1999.
Trocmé, Étienne. *The Formation of the Gospel according to Mark*. London: SPCK, 1975.
Tyson, Joseph B. "The Blindness of the Disciples in Mark," in: *The Messianic Secret*, ed. Christopher Tuckett, 35-43. London: SPCK, 1983.
Watson, Francis. *Paul, Judaism and the Gentiles: Beyond the New Perspective*. Grand Rapids, Mich.: Eerdmans, rev. and exp. edn 2007.
Wefald, Eric K. "The Separate Gentile Mission in Mark: A Narrative Explanation of the Markan Geography, the Two Feeding Accounts, and Exorcisms." *JSNT* 60 (1995): 3-26.

Teil 3 / Part 3: **Theologische Heuristik / Theological Considerations**

Nina Irrgang
„Judentum" im Markusevangelium und in den Paulusbriefen. Begriffe, Konzepte und Narrationen

1 Vorbemerkungen

Eine Untersuchung aus dem Bereich der neutestamentlichen Wissenschaft, die den Terminus *Judentum* im Titel führt und diesen darüber hinaus in Anführungs- und Schlusszeichen setzt, bedarf einiger Vorüberlegungen: Zum einen wurden in den vergangenen Jahrzehnten gerade um das „Judentum" des Paulus heftige Debatten geführt, die teils ins Leere liefen, teils notwendige Korrekturen brachten[1]. Zum anderen wurde – wiederum im Zusammenhang dieser *New Perspective on Paul* – vor allem im englischsprachigen Raum eine Diskussion über Wesen, Eigenarten und vor allem Einheit des Judentums in hellenistisch-römischer Zeit begonnen, die in die Frage mündete, ob die identitätsstiftenden Momente des Bekenntnisses zum Bundesgedanken und der Tora stark genug wirkten, um jenseits aller Spannungen die Gemeinschaft des Judentums aufrechtzuerhalten (*common Judaism*) oder ob man vielmehr von einer Vereinzelung in ganz unterschiedliche Strömungen – von den Pharisäern bis zur Qumran-Gemeinde – ausgehen müsse, die von „Judentum" sachgemäß nur im Plural sprechen lasse (*Judaisms*)[2]. Diese Fragestellung wiederum hat auf die Jesus-Forschung

---

[1] So das ausgeglichene Urteil bei: J.-C. Maschmeier, Rechtfertigung bei Paulus. Eine Kritik alter und neuer Paulusperspektiven (BWANT 189), Stuttgart 2010, 11–19; 285–287 – hier ist auch die Literatur zur *New Perspective on Paul* gesammelt, die an dieser Stelle nicht nochmals zitiert zu werden braucht. Einen Überblick zum „Judentum des Paulus", der die wissenschaftlichen Diskussionen der vergangenen Jahrzehnte aufnimmt und bündelt, gibt: J. Frey, Das Judentum des Paulus, in: Paulus. Leben – Umwelt – Werk – Briefe, hg. von O. Wischmeyer (UTB 2767), Tübingen/Basel ²2012, 25–65.

[2] Hier stehen vor allem die Positionen E.P. Sanders' und J. Neusners gegeneinander. Sanders entwirft sein Modell eines vor allem auf dem Bundesgedanken basierenden „common Judaism" in: E.P. Sanders, Paulus und das palästinische Judentum. Ein Vergleich zweier Religionsstrukturen (StUNT 17), Göttingen 1985, hier: 397–406. Vgl. dagegen: J. Neusner, From Judaism to Judaisms. My Approach to the History of Judaism, in: J. Neusner, Ancient Judaism. Debates and Disputes. Second Series, Atlanta 1990, 181–221. – Eine konzise Zusammenfassung der Diskussion bietet: G. Stemberger, Was there a „mainstream Judaism" in the late Second Temple Period?, in: ders., Judaica Minora. Teil 1: Biblische Traditionen im rabbinischen Judentum (TSAJ 133), Tübingen 2010, 395–410.

zurückgewirkt, die sich der Einordnung (oder: Nicht-Einordnung) seiner Person in ein „palästinisches", „judäisches" oder doch „galiläisches Judentum" neu widmen musste[3]. Parallel dazu liefen und laufen Überlegungen, ob das antike Judentum denn sachgemäß unter die modernen Beschreibungskategorien von „Religion", „Ethnie", „Nation" und/oder „Kultur" zu fassen sei[4].

Der vorliegende Beitrag möchte sich an keiner der genannten Debatten beteiligen. Stattdessen mag der Begriff „Judentum" hier – deshalb in Anführungszeichen – in größtmöglicher Offenheit und ohne feste Definition gebraucht werden. Aufgabe des Beitrags ist, die Texte der Paulusbriefe und des Markusevangeliums auf die *unterschiedlichsten* Äußerungen von „Judentum" hin zu sichten: im technischen Sinne im Hinblick auf die in den Texten genannten Personen(-gruppen), Institutionen und Orte des antiken Judentums sowie die Realien einer jüdischen Lebenswelt, aber auch abseits dieser Konkreta im Hinblick auf die in den Texten sichtbar werdenden Traditionen, Themen und Konzepte jüdischer Religiosität. Bei all dem will der vorliegende Beitrag keine Wortstatistik abarbeiten[5], sondern einige zentrale *Begriffe*, Traditionen und *Konzepte* in Auswahl benennen und kommentieren[6], in welchen Paulus und der Verfasser des

---

[3] Diesen Teil der Debatte um den *Third Quest for the Historical Jesus* fasst forschungsgeschichtlich zusammen: R. Deines, Galiläa und Jesus. Anfragen zur Funktion der Herkunftsbezeichnung „Galiläa" in der neueren Jesusforschung, in: Jesus und die Archäologie Galiläas, hg. von C. Claußen/J. Frey (BThS 87), Neukirchen-Vluyn 2008, 271–320. – Dass die Frage nach dem „historischen Jesus" – selbstverständlich! – längst nicht abschließend beantwortet ist, zeigen die neueren Veröffentlichungen zu diesem großem Forschungskomplex, z. B.: Jesus – Gestaltung und Gestaltungen. Rezeptionen des Galiläers in Wissenschaft, Kirche und Gesellschaft, Festschrift für G. Theißen zum 70. Geburtstag, hg. von P. von Gemünden/D.G. Horrell/M. Küchler (NTOA 100), Göttingen 2013, und: Handbook for the Study of the Historical Jesus, ed. by T. Holmén/S.E. Porter, Leiden/Boston 2011.

[4] Der wohl wichtigste Beitrag hierzu: S. Mason, Jews, Judeans, Judaizing, Judaism. Problems of Categorization, in: Journal for the Study of Judaism 38 (2007), 457–512. Mason votiert für ein ethnisches Verständnis und schließt sich damit der römischen Perspektive an .– Eine sozusagen „zeitgenössische Stellungnahme", die für ein römisches Lesepublikum bestimmt ist, gibt Flavius Josephus in der Schrift Contra Apionem; dazu: Flavius Josephus. Translation and Commentary, ed. by S. Mason, Volume 10: Against Apion, Translation and Commentary by J.M.G. Barclay, Leiden/Boston 2007, hier: LV–LXI.

[5] In dieser Hinsicht sind die Texte über die üblichen Hilfsmittel der Exegese bereits hinreichend erschlossen, vor allem durch die Konkordanzen (hier: K. Aland, K. (Hg.), Vollständige Konkordanz zum griechischen Neuen Testament, Berlin/New York 1983), das Theologische Wörterbuch zum Neuen Testament sowie: R. Morgenthaler, Statistik des neutestamentlichen Wortschatzes, Zürich 1958.

[6] Diese Zusammenstellung muss schon deshalb „Auswahl" bleiben, weil die beiden großen Konzepte jüdischer Religiosität, „Gesetz" und „Schrift", in diesem Beitrag nicht näher behandelt

Markusevangeliums Erscheinungsformen und Ausprägungen jüdischen Lebens und jüdischer Religiosität beschreiben. Ziel dieses Vorgehens ist es, eine Heuristik aufzustellen, die es vermag, die Strategien offenzulegen, mittels derer Paulus einerseits und der Verfasser des Markusevangeliums andererseits diese Bezeichnungen, Begriffe und Phänomene von „Judentum" für ihre Texte in argumentativer und/oder narrativer Entfaltung nutzbar machen. Da sich dabei nun Paulus selbst als durchaus führender Vertreter des pharisäischen Diasporajudentums vorstellt[7], die (religiöse) Identität des Verfassers des Markusevangeliums im Gegensatz dazu aber völlig unbekannt bleibt, haben die Einleitungswissenschaften den beiden „Protagonisten" ganz divergierende biographisch-religiöse Hintergründe und Motive zugewiesen. Den bereits in Fülle vorhandenen Hypothesen darüber will der vorliegende Beitrag keine neuen hinzufügen. Wenn im Folgenden einige für das Markusevangelium und die Paulusbriefe bedeutsamen *Begriffe*, Traditionen und *Konzepte* jüdischer Religiosität vorgestellt werden, dann nicht mit dem primären Ziel der historischen Rückfrage. Besonders für das Markusevangelium sei gesagt: Im Mittelpunkt der Untersuchung steht hier nicht die Frage nach der (religiösen und damit möglicherweise *jüdischen*) Herkunft des Verfassers[8]. Es ist hier ebenfalls nicht zu diskutieren, ob die (intendierte) Leserschaft seines Evangeliums eher als „*juden-*" oder „heidenchristlich" zu definieren ist[9], und es

---

werden. Ein „Gesamtbild" kann sich nur in der Zusammenschau mit den entsprechenden Beiträgen von Jesper Svartvik und Florian Wilk im vorliegenden Band ergeben.
7 Dies vor allem in den „autobiographische" Passagen der Briefe, vgl. unten: 3.1.
8 Zur Frage der Herkunft des Verfasser des Markusevangeliums vgl. die gängigen Einleitungen und neueren Kommentare, zuvorderst D. Stökl Ben Ezra, Art. Markusevangelium, in: RAC 24 (2010), 173–207, und A. Yarbro Collins, Mark (Hermeneia), Minneapolis 2007, sowie die Zusammenfassung der Diskussionen bei: J. Dewey, The Historical Jesus in the Gospel of Mark, in: Handbook for the Study of the Historical Jesus, ed. by T. Holmén/S.E. Porter, Volume 3: The Historical Jesus, Leiden/Boston 2011, 1821–1852, hier: 1842ff. – Die Zuschreibungen schwanken hier zwischen dem „gebürtigen Jerusalemer" (vgl. M. Hengel, Die vier Evangelien und das Evangelium von Jesus Christus. Studien zu ihrer Sammlung und Entstehung (WUNT 224), Tübingen 2008, 141–184) und dem „Judenchristen aus der Diaspora" (D. Stökl Ben Ezra). Dazu auch: M. Meiser, Reinheitsfragen und Begräbnissitten. Der Evangelist Markus als Zeuge der jüdischen Alltagskultur, in: Neues Testament und hellenistisch-jüdische Alltagskultur, hg. von R. Deines/J. Herzer/K.-W. Niebuhr (WUNT 274),Tübingen 2011, 443–460, hier: 457ff.
9 Wie weit die Forschungsmeinungen dazu auseinandergehen, zeigen exemplarisch die Einschätzungen von P. Vielhauer, Geschichte der urchristlichen Literatur. Einleitung in das Neue Testament, die Apokryphen und die Apostolischen Väter, Berlin 1975, 345: „Es steht außer Zweifel, daß Mk sein Buch für hellenistisch-heidenchristliche Leser verfasst hat", und Stökl Ben-Ezra, 186: „Wie Sprache, Vorstellungswelt und Theologie erkennen lassen, ist das M[arkusevangelium] ein jüdisches Ev[angelium], das für Leser geschrieben wurde, die mit jüd[ischen] Traditionen u[nd] Institutionen vertraut waren".

wird auch nicht erörtert, inwiefern sich das Markusevangelium als „christlicher Text" zum *Judentum* positioniert. An dieser Stelle soll anderes geleistet werden: nämlich die Rekonstruktion einer Art *Erzählung vom Judentum*[10], wie sie sich auf Grund der der Textebene unmittelbar zu entnehmenden *Begriffe,* Traditionen und *Konzepte* jüdischer Religiosität für das Markusevangelium und die Paulusbriefe jeweils ergibt.

2 Die „Erzählung vom Judentum" innerhalb des Markusevangeliums

Der heuristische Entwurf, der dem vorliegenden Beitrag zu Grunde liegt, ist also von der Idee bestimmt, dass ausgehend von den im Markusevangelium und in den Paulusbriefen jeweils verwendeten Begrifflichkeiten und Konzepten jüdischer Religion eine je eigenständige *Narration vom Judentum* nachvollzogen werden kann. Damit übernimmt die vorliegende Untersuchung Beschreibungskategorien aus Erzähltheorie und Erzähltextanalyse und soll deshalb zunächst an demjenigen der beiden zu untersuchenden Textbereiche erprobt werden, dessen Struktur eindeutig narrativ angelegt ist: dem Markusevangelium[11].

2.1 „Synagoge", „Sabbat", „Pharisäer und Schriftgelehrte". Die jüdische Umwelt Jesu als Träger der Erzählsituation des Markusevangeliums

Die Lebenswelt des historischen Jesus, namentlich das Galiläa der frühen römischen Kaiserzeit, ist – trotz der komplexen Geschichte und den vielfältigen kulturellen Einflüssen, die auf den Landstrich wirkten[12] – als grundsätzlich jüdisch

---

[10] Zu dem erweiterten, eher kultur- als streng literaturwissenschaftlich profilierten Begriff von „Erzählung", der hier zu Grunde liegt, vgl. die Beiträge bei: A. Strohmaier (Hg.), Kultur – Wissen – Narration. Perspektiven transdisziplinärer Erzählforschung für die Kulturwissenschaften, Bielefeld 2013.
[11] Dazu: C. Rose, Theologie als Erzählung im Markusevangelium (WUNT II 236), Tübingen 2007, sowie: D. Rhoads/J. Dewey/D. Michie, Mark as Story: An Introduction to the Narrative of a Gospel, Minneapolis 1999, und: K.R. Iverson/C.W. Skinner (eds.), Mark as Story: Retrospect and Prospect (SBL Resources for Biblical Study 65), Atlanta 2011.
[12] Diese betont etwa: J. Zangenberg, Jesus – Galiläa – Archäologie. Neue Forschungen zu einer Region im Wandel, in: Jesus und die Archäologie Galiläas, hg. von C. Claußen/J. Frey (BThS 87), Neukirchen-Vluyn 2008, 7–38, hier: 14–38, sowie: M. Moreland, The Inhabitants of Galilee in

geprägt zu beschreiben[13]. Wer sich vornimmt, um die Gestalt Jesu von Nazareth herum eine biographisch orientierte Erzählung[14] zu gestalten, kommt also gar nicht umhin, den Protagonisten vor einer Kulisse zu präsentieren, die in ihren wesentlichsten Eigenschaften von der Kultur, der Tradition, den Institutionen und Gebräuchen des antiken Judentums gekennzeichnet ist. Dem Verfasser des Markusevangeliums sind damit einige Grundentscheidungen bezüglich der Gestaltung der allgemeinen Erzählsituation bereits abgenommen[15]: *Ort, Zeit und Akteure der Handlung*, mithin also die drei Parameter, die jede Erzählung konstituieren, haben die Gegebenheiten der jüdischen Umwelt, in der die Gestalt Jesu zu verorten ist, für den Leser erkennbar abzubilden. Die Ausgestaltung des *plots* in Mk 1,1– 9,50, des Teils der Erzählung also, der sich vor dem Hintergrund der Landschaft Galiläas abspielt, trägt diesem erzähltechnischen Grundprinzip mustergültig Rechnung. Ort, Zeit und Akteure der Handlung scheinen wie in Koordinatenform

---

the Hellenistic and Early Roman Periods. Probes in the Archaeological and Literary Evidence, in: Religion, Ethnicity, and Identity in Ancient Galilee. A Region in Transition, ed. by J. Zangenberg/ H.W. Attridge/D.B. Martin (WUNT 210), Tübingen 2007, 133–159.
13 Darauf weisen entschieden hin: J.H. Charlesworth/M. Aviam, Überlegungen zur Erforschung Galiläas im ersten Jahrhundert, in: Jesus und die Archäologie Galiläas, hg. von C. Claußen/J. Frey (BThS 87), Neukirchen-Vluyn 2008, 93–127, hier: 121 f., sowie: J. Schröter, Jesus aus Galiläa. Die Herkunft Jesu und ihre Bedeutung für das Verständnis seiner Wirksamkeit, in: Jesus und die Archäologie Galiläas, hg. von C. Claußen/J. Frey (BThS 87), Neukirchen-Vluyn 2008, 245–270, hier: 251–262, sowie: E.P. Sanders, Jesus' Galilee, in: Fair Play. Diversity and Conflicts in Early Christianity. Essays in Honour of Heikki Räisänen, ed. by I. Dunderberg/C. Tuckett/K. Syreeni, Leiden/Boston/Köln 2002, 3–41. Die Forschungsgeschichte fasst zusammen: H. Moxnes, When did Jesus become a Galilean. Revisiting the Historical Jesus debate of the Nineteenth Century, in: Jesus – Gestaltung und Gestaltungen. Rezeptionen des Galiläers in Wissenschaft, Kirche und Gesellschaft, Festschrift für G. Theißen zum 70. Geburtstag, hg. von P. von Gemünden/D.G. Horrell/M. Küchler (NTOA 100), Göttingen 2013, 391–409. – Der Frage nach den sozialen, politischen, und religiösen Bedingungen, die Jesus in Galiläa vorfand, und den Spuren, die sie in seiner Botschaft hinterließen, widmet der *Third Quest on the Historical Jesus* besondere Aufmerksamkeit (vgl. Anm. 3). Galiläa als Landschaft rückte damit seit den zahlreichen Arbeiten Sean Freynes in den Blickpunkt des Interesses. Einen Überblick gibt die Aufsatzsammlung: S. Freyne, Galilee and Gospel. Collected Essays (WUNT 125), Tübingen 2000, über die sich die zahlreichen Publikationen Freynes zum Thema leicht erschließen lassen. Eine Neubewertung der Situation Galiläas aus archäologischer Sicht begann mit: E.M. Meyers, Galilean Regionalism as a Factor in Historical Reconstruction, in: BASOR 221 (1976), 93–101.
14 Zur „Gattungsdiskussion" um das Markusevangelium vgl. beispielsweise den Forschungsüberblick bei: C. Rose, Theologie als Erzählung, 70–77.
15 Die Bedeutsamkeit des *settings* „Galiläa" für die Erzählkonstruktion des Markusevangeliums arbeitet auch heraus: S. Freyne, Galilee, Jesus, and the Gospels. Literary Approaches and Historical Investigations, Philadelphia 1988, 34–50.

konzentriert[16]. Zentralster Ort des Wirkens Jesu ist die *Synagoge* (ἐν τῇ συναγωγῇ; vgl. Mk 1,21[17].39; 3,1), brisantester Zeitpunkt dieses Wirkens der *Sabbat* (τοῖς σάββασιν; vgl. Mk 1,21; 2,23 f.; 3,2), und die Akteure, mit denen die Hauptfigur Jesus die schwerwiegendsten Konflikte auszutragen hat, sind die *Schriftgelehrten und Pharisäer*[18] (οἱ Φαρισαῖοι καὶ οἱ γραμματεῖς; Mk 1,22; 2,16.18.24; 3,6.22; 7,1.3.5; 8,11; 9,11). In dieser Fokussierung setzt der Verfasser des Markusevangeliums drei unübersehbare *marker*, die das *setting* der Erzählung als unverkennbar „jüdisch" kennzeichnen. Mit dem Ort der Synagoge und dem geheiligten Zeitraum des Sabbat ruft er zudem zwei Identitätsmarker des (Diaspora-)Judentums in hellenistisch-römischer Zeit auf: Das Halten der Sabbatruhe gilt seit der Periode des babylonischen Exils – auch in der Wahrnehmung durch Nichtjuden![19] – als Spezifikum jüdischer Lebensführung und religiöser Ausgestaltung des Alltags (Ex 31,13)[20]. Verletzungen des Gebots wurden rigoros bestraft (Ex 31,14). Auch in nachexilischer Zeit blieb der Sabbat die wichtigste Bestimmung des mosaischen Gesetzes, zu der man eine Vielzahl kasuistischer Einzelregelungen entwickelte[21].

---

16 Vgl. die ganz ähnliche Textwahrnehmung bei: G. Lüderitz, Rhetorik, Poetik, Kompositionstechnik im Markusevangelium, in: Markus-Philologie. Historische, literaturgeschichtliche und stilistische Untersuchungen zum zweiten Evangelium, hg. von H. Cancik (WUNT 33), Tübingen 1984, 165–203, hier: 188 f.
17 Bereits der erste öffentliche „Auftritt" Jesu findet in einer Synagoge statt, vgl. S. Freyne, Gospels, 42!
18 Obwohl im Markusevangelium die „Schriftgelehrten" (οἱ γραμματεῖς) häufiger genannt werden (21mal) als die Gruppe der „Pharisäer" (12mal) bzw. einmal die Junktur „Schriftgelehrte der Pharisäer" erscheint (οἱ γραμματεῖς τῶν Φαρισαίων: vgl. Mk 2,16), erscheinen wenigstens in Galiläa die „Pharisäer" als die wesentlichen Opponenten Jesu (vgl. Mk 3,6), zumal sich die Konflikte um typische „pharisäische Themen" bzw. halachische Fragen entspannen, vgl. R. Deines, Die Pharisäer und das Volk im Neuen Testament und bei Josephus, in: Josephus und das Neue Testament, hg. von C. Böttrich und J. Herzer unter Mitarbeit von T. Reiprich (WUNT 209), Tübingen 2007, 147–180, hier: 170 ff., unter Rückgriff auf: D. Lührmann, Pharisäer und Schriftgelehrte im Markusevangelium, in: ZNW 78 (1987), 169–185, hier: 181 f. Die jüdischen Religionsparteien werden neuerlich vorgestellt bei: E. Nodet, Pharisees, Sadducees, Essenes, Herodians, in: Handbook for the Study of the Historical Jesus, ed. by T. Holmén/S.E. Porter, Volume 2: The Study of Jesus, Leiden/Boston 2011, 1495–1523.
19 Vgl. Josephus, *Contra Apionem* 2,282; *Bellum Iudaicum* 7,45; 2,560.
20 Vgl. L. Doering, Art. Sabbat, II. Judentum, in: RGG⁴ 7 (2004), 713 f.; D.K. Falk, Art. Sabbath, in: The Eerdmans Dictionary of Early Judaism, ed. by J.J. Collins/D.C. Harlow, Grand Rapids/Cambridge 2010, 1174–1176, sowie: K. Grünwaldt, Exil und Identität. Beschneidung, Passa und Sabbat in der Priesterschrift, Frankfurt am Main 1992, 120–219; 222–228, und: H. Weiss, A Day of Gladness. The Sabbath among Jews and Christians in Antiquity, Columbia 2003.
21 Eine bündige Zusammenfassung, die vor allem Elemente praktischer Religionsausübung am Sabbat betont, bei: E.P. Sanders, Judaism. Practice and Belief 63BCE – 66CE, London/Philadelphia 1992, 208–211.

Die pharisäische Sabbat-Halakha ist im Einzelnen kaum zu rekonstruieren[22]. Da die Laienbewegung der Pharisäer aber sicher eine prägende (wenn auch nicht die einzige![23]) „intellektuelle und religiöse Kraft"[24] innerhalb des palästinischen Judentums des ersten Jahrhunderts darstellte, ist davon auszugehen, dass ihre Vorstellungen bezüglich einer strikten Observanz gegenüber dem Sabbatgebot in weiten Bevölkerungskreisen einflussreich war. Unabhängig von der umstrittenen Frage, welche Bedeutung der pharisäischen Gruppierung innerhalb der Gesellschaft der römischen Provinz Syria vor 70 n. Chr. im Detail zukam, ist festzuhalten: Die Pharisäer sind in der Wahrnehmung der maßgeblichen Quellen für die gesellschaftliche Situation des Landstrichs im ersten Jahrhundert – namentlich des Flavius Josephus und der frühchristlichen Autoren – die prominenteste Strömung innerhalb des palästinischen Judentums[25]. Mit ihrer Idee der konsequenten Bewahrung jüdischer Identität durch eine beständige Heiligung des Alltags fügen sie sich in ihrer dezidiert anti-hellenistischen Ausrichtung auf das Beste in das Bild der unmittelbaren Lebenswelt Jesu, wie es der Schilderung des Markusevangeliums zu entnehmen ist: Auch wenn die Pharisäer zahlenmäßig nicht die Mehrheit der jüdischen Gemeinschaft hinter sich vereinen konnten, stehen sie mit ihren Inhalten – und dies wiederum auch in der Wahrnehmung von Nichtjuden! – vielleicht doch näher an einem „allgemeinen Judentum" bzw. genauer: einem nach außen erkennbaren jüdischen Ethos, als alle übrigen Strömungen[26].

---

22 Dazu: L. Doering, Schabbat. Sabbathalacha und -praxis im antiken Judentum und Urchristentum (TSAJ 78), Tübingen 1999, 508–536.
23 Auf die Kontroverse um den tatsächlichen Einfluss der Pharisäer in Palästina bis 70 n.Chr. weisen hin: A.I. Baumgarten, Art. Pharisäer, in: RGG⁴ 6 (2003), 1262f., hier: 1263, sowie: R. Deines, Art. Pharisees, in: The Eerdmans Dictionary of Early Judaism, ed. by J.J. Collins/D.C. Harlow, Grand Rapids/Cambridge 2010, 1061–1063. Exemplarisch für die Einschätzung, dass die Pharisäer entgegen der Darstellung des Flavius Josephus (Antiquitates XVIII,15; dazu: P. Schäfer, Der vorrabbinische Pharisäismus, in: Paulus und das antike Judentum, hg. von M. Hengel/U. Heckel, Tübingen 1991, 125–175, hier: 166f.) nicht die einflussreichste religiöse Partei darstellten, sondern nur eine von mehreren wettstreitenden Gruppen repräsentierten, steht: M. Smith, Palestinian Judaism in the First Century, in: Israel. Its Role in Civilization, ed. by M. Davis, New York 1956, 67–81.
24 M. Tilly/W. Zwickel, Religionsgeschichte Israels. Von der Vorzeit bis zu den Anfängen des Christentums, Darmstadt 2011, 146.
25 Das zeigt allein die Häufigkeit der Nennung in beiden Textcorpora im Vergleich zu den anderen bekannten Gruppierungen, vgl. R. Deines, Art. Pharisees, 1061.
26 Ich schließe hier an die Einschätzung R. Deines' an, der den Pharisäismus als die „normierende" Instanz des palästinischen Judentums zwischen 150 v.Chr. und 70 n.Chr. bezeichnet, vgl. R. Deines, The Pharisees Between „Judaisms" and the „Common Judaism", in: Jusitfication and Variegated Nomism. Volume I: The Complexities of Second Temple Judaism, ed. by D.A. Carson/P.T. O'Brien/M.A. Seifrid (WUNT II.140), Göttingen 2001, 443–504, hier: 503: „Pharisaism

In ihrem – an mancher Stelle sicher polemisch überzeichneten – bedingungslosen Eintreten für Reinheitsvorschriften und weitere kultische Bestimmungen des Religionsgesetzes repräsentieren sie auf der Erzählebene des Markusevangeliums eben diese distinkten Merkmale jüdischer Religiosität in einer plakativen Bestimmtheit (und vielleicht historischen Undifferenziertheit der Darstellung), die auch sie zu einem *marker* der Erzählstruktur des Textes werden lässt – zum einen wird ihnen konsequent die Funktion der Antagonisten zugeordnet[27], zum anderen weisen sie darauf hin, dass nicht nur der topographische, sondern auch der soziale Handlungsraum des Protagonisten Jesus ganz von „Judentum", in diesem Fall von einem distinkt jüdischen Ethos, gekennzeichnet ist[28]. Der prädestinierte Ort dieses sozialen Handelns ist auf der Textebene des Markusevangeliums die Synagoge. Unabhängig davon, ob der Verfasser des Markusevangeliums in der Annahme, die Dörfer und Städte Galiläas seien in großer Zahl mit Synagogengebäuden ausgestattet gewesen[29], die historische Si-

---

can be called *normative, because whatever was integrated and thus legitimated* by its recognized representatives (generally probably its scribes and priests) over time became the possession of all of Israel. In the consciousness of the majority of the people, the Pharisees were the religious group that determined the boundaries of what was still and what was no longer Jewish." Mit demselben Gedanken schließt auch: ders., Die Pharisäer. Ihr Verständnis im Spiegel der christlichen und jüdischen Forschung seit Wellhausen und Graetz (WUNT 101), Tübingen 1997, 554f. – Auch das positive Bild, das Josephus wenigstens in den *Antiquitates* von den Pharisäern gezeichnet hat, mag beim literarischen Publikum eine gewisse Wirkung hinterlassen haben. P. Schäfer, Pharisäismus, 168, paraphrasiert dessen tendenziöse Einschätzung wie folgt: „Die altehrwürdige Partei der Pharisäer, die mit ihren Wurzeln weit in die jüdische Geschichte zurückreicht, verkörpert in Leben und Lehre die besten Seiten des jüdischen Volkes."
27 Dies übrigens mit Ausnahme der Diskussion um das Liebesgebot Mk 12,28–34.
28 Dazu passt, dass Interaktion mit nichtjüdischen Personen kaum stattfindet: Das soziale Handeln Jesu ist neben der Konfrontation mit Pharisäern und Schriftgelehrten beschränkt auf die Familie (Mk 3,21.35), die Jünger (z.B. Mk 8,14.21.32f.) und die Anhänger des Johannes. Wird vom Kontakt mit Nichtjuden doch berichtet, bedarf dies der (überhöhenden) Interpretation (vgl. Mk 7,24.30; 11,17; 13,10) – dennoch kann sich Jesus wie selbstverständlich in heidnischen Gebieten aufhalten und bewegen, vgl. Mk 5,1–2; 6,53; 7,24.31; 8,27; S. Freyne, Gospels, bringt diesen Aspekt der Erzählung mit der „kulturellen Durchlässigkeit" Galiläas in Verbindung. – Die Feststellung, dass die Pharisäer in den besprochenen Erzählsituationen als Antagonisten fungieren, ist wesentlich: Damit steht Jesus auf der Textebene nicht einfach in Konfrontation zum „Judentum insgesamt" – hier geht es in erster Linie um die Differenzen zu einem als „allgemeingültig" empfundenen jüdischen Ethos! Zur Mehrzahl der jüdischen Bevölkerung, ὄχλος, wird der Protagonist Jesus keineswegs durchgängig in Kontrast gesetzt, vgl. Mk 1,32; 2,12f.; 3,7.9; 4,1; 5,31; 6,31ff.; 8,1; dazu: S. Freyne, Gospels, 49f.
29 Vgl. Mk 1,39; dazu: S. Freyne, Gospels, 35.

tuation des ersten Jahrhunderts abbildet oder abbilden wollte[30], gilt wiederum das für die Erzählparameter „Sabbat" und „Pharisäer" Herausgearbeitete: Die Nennung des Ortes, an dem sich das erzählte Geschehen zuträgt, konturiert – wie die Angabe, wann sich das Erzählte ereignet und welche Personen die Handlung tragen – die Erzählung. Wenn das Markusevangelium den Ort der συναγωγή auf der Erzählebene so wesentlich erscheinen lässt, dann wiederum mit dem Effekt, den – diesmal primär sozialen – Ort des Geschehens als ganz und gar „jüdisch geprägt" erkennbar werden zu lassen. Denn ungeachtet der Frage, ob im Markusevangelium tatsächlich mehrheitlich von der συναγωγή als Gebäudetypus oder eher – wie Carsten Claußen vorschlägt – von einem nicht an eine architektonische Struktur gebundenen, einfachen „Versammlungsort für Juden"[31] die Rede ist, bleibt die Feststellung: Wenn Jesus in oder vor der συναγωγή auftritt, tritt er in jedem Fall vor einem ganz und gar jüdischen Auditorium auf[32].

Die Szenerie ist damit vollständig gesetzt und erreicht ihren dramatischen Höhepunkt in der Doppelperikope vom Ährenraufen und der Heilung am Sabbat (Mk 2,23–28; Mk 3,1–6)[33]: Die Koordinaten von Ort, Zeit und Akteuren definieren hier – gleich dem Aufriss eines klassischen Dramas – *den* einen Punkt, an dem der dramatische Knoten endgültig geschürzt ist: Am Sabbat – also zu dem wöchentlich wiederkehrenden Zeitpunkt, an dem jüdisches Ethos sich auf das Stärkste in

---

30 Der archäologische Befund bezüglich des Vorhandenseins solcher „Synagogengebäude" im Syrien-Palästina des ersten Jahrhunderts bleibt bekanntlich weiter unklar: J.H. Charlesworth/M. Aviam, Überlegungen, 110–112, halten mindestens für Gamla, das Herodium und Masada „Synagogenarchitektur" für nachweisbar. – Gerade für Kapernaum und Nazareth allerdings (vgl. Mk 1,21ff; 6,1f.), sind Synagogengebäude aus dem ersten Jahrhundert archäologisch in keiner Weise nachweisbar, dazu: C. Claußen, Jesus und die Versammlungen Galiläas. Zur Frage nach der Bedeutung von ἡ συναγωγή, in: Jesus und die Archäologie Galiläas, hg. von C. Claußen/J. Frey (BThS 87), Neukirchen-Vluyn 2008, 226–244, hier: 236–239.
31 Vgl. C. Claußen, Jesus, 228f.
32 H.A. McKay, Sabbath and Synagogue. The Question of Sabbath Worship in Ancient Judaism, Leiden 1994, 249, bemerkt dazu: „What is more, the gospel stories set in the ‚synagogues' are not told for the purpose of giving a description of what happened there; it is to make persuasive arguments about the value of Jesus in reforming the Jewish religion"; vgl. A.J. Mayer-Haas, „Geschenk aus Gottes Schatzkammer" (bSchab 10b). Jesus und der Sabbat im Spiegel der neutestamentlichen Schriften (NTA NS 43), Münster 2003, 136–258; sowie – besonders zur Synagoge als einem bedeutsamen „sozialen Ort": L.I. Levine, Art. Synagogues, in: The Eerdmans Dictionary of Early Judaism, ed. by J.J. Collins/D.C. Harlow, Grand Rapids/Cambridge 2010, 1260–1271, hier: 1270.
33 Die Bedeutsamkeit der Perikope für den erzählerischen Aufriss des Markusevangeliums insgesamt betont auch: A. Lindemann, Jesus und der Sabbat. Zum literarischen Charakter der Erzählung Mk 3,1–6, in: Text und Geschichte. Facetten theologischen Arbeitens aus dem Freundes- und Schülerkreis. D. Lührmann zum 60. Geburtstag, hg.v. S. Maser/E. Schlarb, Marburg 1999, 122–135.

der täglichen Lebensgestaltung manifestiert – gerät der Protagonist Jesus in der Synagoge – also an dem Ort, an dem jüdische Gemeinschaft sich am wirkungsvollsten konstituiert – mit den Pharisäern – also der Personengruppe, die ein allgemein verbindliches, distinkt jüdisches Ethos mit dem größten Nachdruck repräsentiert – in eine halachische Diskussion just über die rechte Ausgestaltung des Sabbat als des wesentlichsten Propriums eines solch jüdischen Ethos[34]. Tatsächlich ist es eine ethische Frage im Sinne des Wortes – also eine Frage nach dem Guten –, die diesen schärfsten innerjüdischen Konflikt zwischen Jesus und Pharisäern hervorruft[35]. Sie wird in Mk 3,4 pointiert gestellt: ἔξεστιν τοῖς σάββασιν ἀγαθὸν ποιῆσαι ἢ κακοποιῆσαι, ψυχὴν σῶσαι ἢ ἀποκτεῖναι; Dem Leser steht hier also eine literarisierte, gleichsam „ideale Szene"[36] vor Augen, die die Grundbedingungen der momentanen Erzählsituation auf das Schärfste konturiert, zugleich aber dem Weg des Protagonisten die entscheidende Wendung gibt; endet die Perikope doch in der düsteren Ankündigung, die Pharisäer würden mit den Herodianern darüber beraten, „wie sie ihn umbrächten". Jesu weiteres Agieren im jüdischen Umfeld Galiläas und besonders alle nachfolgend erzählten Konflikte mit den Pharisäern vom Streit über rituelle Reinheit und rechte Toraoberservanz (Mk 7,1–13) und der Diskussion nach der Brotvermehrung (Mk 8,11ff.) über die Frage nach der Ehescheidung (Mk 10,1–9) bis hin zur Frage nach den Steuern für den Kaiser (Mk 12,13–17) stehen unter dem Verdikt dieser Ankündigung[37].

Auf der Erzählebene kann der Protagonist damit längst nicht mehr aus dem Konflikt heraustreten – die Zuspitzung der Ereignisse ist unwiderruflich angelegt und überdies in den „Leidensankündigungen" (Mk 8,31; 9,31; 10,32f.) zur theologischen Ausdeutung vorbereitet. Die Erzählsituation hat diese Zuspitzung nachzuvollziehen, und sie tut dies im Weg „hinauf nach Jerusalem" in einer einfachen Steigerung der zuvor aufgerufenen Erzählparameter: War der Zeitpunkt,

---

[34] Dies alles tatsächlich zunächst ausschließlich im Referenzrahmen des Erzähltextes! L. Doering, Much Ado about Nothing? Jesus' Sabbath Healings and their Halakhic Implications Revisited, in: Judaistik und neutestamentliche Wissenschaft. Standorte – Grenzen – Beziehungen, hg. von L. Doering/H.-G. Waubke/F. Wilk (FRLANT 226), Göttingen 2008, 217–241, hebt hervor, dass offen bleiben muss, wie sich eventuelle Krankenheilungen Jesu im Sabbat tatsächlich zur im ersten Jahrhundert praktizierten Sabbath-Halachah verhielten.
[35] Vgl. M. Wyschogrod, On the Christian Critique on the Jewish Sabbath, in: Sabbath. Idea – History – Reality, ed. by G.J. Blidstein, Beer Sheva 2004, 43–56.
[36] Vgl. F. Wilk, Die synoptischen Evangelien als Quellen für die Geschichte der Pharisäer, in: Judaistik und neutestamentliche Wissenschaft. Standorte – Grenzen – Beziehungen, hg. von L. Doering/H.-G. Waubke/F. Wilk (FRLANT 226), Göttingen 2008, 85–107, hier: 104.
[37] Dazu: G. Stemberger, Pharisäer, Sadduzäer, Essener (SBS 144), Stuttgart 1991, 24–26, sowie überblicksartig: E.P. Sanders, Sohn Gottes. Eine historische Biographie Jesu, Stuttgart 1996, 303–347.

auf den sich die Erzählung in ihrem ersten Teil konzentrierte, der wöchentlich wiederkehrende Sabbat, ist es nun das jährliche *Pessachfest* (τὸ πάσχα, Mk 14,12) [38]. Als Feier zur Erinnerung an die Exodus-Ereignisse gibt es der Urerfahrung des Volkes Israel mit seinem Gott eine ritualisierte Form und wird in der Zeit des Zweiten Tempels zum Wallfahrtsfest, das Pilger in großer Zahl nach Jerusalem führte[39]: Wenigstens einmal jährlich hat die Gemeinschaft des Judentums hier die Möglichkeit, sich unter der Situation der Diaspora zu finden und die überdauernde Wirkkraft der gemeinsamen heilsgeschichtlichen Erfahrung zu beschwören. Die Szene vom „Einzug in Jerusalem" (Mk 11,1–11) lässt diese Gemeinschaft des Judentums, wie sie zur Zeit des Pessachfestes in der Stadt erlebt werden konnte, auch vor den Augen des Lesers sichtbar werden. Die Menge der Pilger (Mk 11,8: πολλοί) begleitet Jesus nicht nur (Mk 11,9: καὶ οἱ προάγοντες καὶ οἱ ἀκολουθοῦντες) [40] – sie nimmt ihn in die Mitte ihrer religiösen Gemeinschaft, ihrer Interpretationsgemeinschaft sogar, denn seine Begrüßung als mit dem Hosianna-Ruf und der Allusion zu Ps 117,26a LXX sowie die offensichtlich frei gewählte Formel: εὐλογημένη ἡ ἐρχομένη βασιλεία τοῦ πατρὸς ἡμῶν Δαυίδ wären für einen gedachten (nichtjüdischen) Beobachter auf der Textebene und sind für den Leser ohne die Kenntnis der alttestamentlichen Tradition ebenso wenig zu verstehen wie die gesamte messianisch-eschatologische Stilisierung der Szenerie: Jesus erreicht die Stadt vom Ölberg her, also von dem Ort aus, an dem der Prophet Sacharja die Endereignisse beginnen lässt (Sach 14,4). Frühjüdische Traditionen bringen überdies damit das Kommen des Messias aus Richtung Osten in Verbindung[41]. Weiterhin legt Jesus die letzte Wegstrecke auf einem Esel reitend zurück; analog dazu erwartet wiederum Sacharja die Ankunft des messianischen Friedenskönigs

---

38 E. Otto, Art. Feste/Feiern, II. Altes Testament, in: RGG⁴ 3 (2000), 87–89, hier: 87. Weitere Literatur: R. Schmitt, Exodus und Passah. Ihr Zusammenhang im Alten Testament, Göttingen ²1997; J.B. Segal, Hebrew Passover. From the Earliest Times to A.D. 70 (London Oriental Series 12), London 1963; S. Safrai, Religion in Everyday Life, in: The Jewish People in the First Century, ed. by S. Safrai/M. Stern, Philadelphia 1976, 793–833, hier: 808–810, und: ders., The Temple, in: The Jewish People in the First Century, ed. by S. Safrai/M. Stern, Philadelphia 1976, 865–907, hier: 891ff.
39 Dazu: G. Veltri, Art. Feste/Feiern, III. Judentum, in: RGG⁴ 3 (2000), 90–93, hier: 90, sowie: S. Safrai, Die Wallfahrt im Zeitalter des Zweiten Tempels (FJCD 3), Stuttgart 1981 – vgl. Flavius Josephus, *Bellum Iudaicum* 2,280.
40 Anders J. Gnilka, Das Evangelium nach Markus. 2. Teilband: Mk 8,27–16,20 (EKK II/2), 3. durchgesehene Auflage, Zürich/Braunschweig/Neukirchen-Vluyn 1989, 119, der meint, der Einzug Jesu spiele sich nur vor den Augen seiner Anhängerschaft ab. Schwer verständlich bleibt dann aber die Mengenbezeichnung „πολλοί" in Mk 11,8.
41 Vgl. dazu die Berichte über einen ägyptischen Messiasprätendenten bei Flavius Josephus, Bellum Iudaicum 2,13,5.

auf dem Fohlen einer Eselin (Sach 9,9). Die endgültige Identifikation dessen, der dort die Stadt erreicht, mit dem messianischen König oder dem „Davidssohn" wird zwar noch nicht vorgenommen, ist in der Allusion zu 2Kön 9,13 aber zumindest angelegt[42]. Als Bild bleibt: Das „Volk Israel", das sich zur Zeit des Pessachfestes – in höchstem Maße anachronistisch im Blick auf seine historische Situation – zur Einheit sammelt, sieht im Moment des Einzugs Jesu in die Stadt seine größte Hoffnung in Erfüllung begriffen.

Der maximalen theologischen Aufladung, die hier in der Wahl der Handlungszeit – des Pessachfestes als eines Zeitraumes höchster Sakralität – und in der interpretatorischen Ausdeutung des Erzählten – durch die messianisch-apokalyptische Färbung der Erzählszene – geschieht, entspricht die Wahl des Handlungsortes, der nun neu in den Mittelpunkt rückt: Statt der Synagoge in Galiläa ist dies jetzt der *Tempel in Jerusalem* (τὸ ἱερὸν, Mk 11,11), das *eine* kultische Zentrum der jüdischen Gemeinschaft und Gemeinde[43]. Es gehört zum schriftstellerischen Stil des Verfassers des Markusevangeliums, auf wort- und detailreiche Schilderungen der Tempelarchitektur, wie sie etwa bei Josephus zu finden sind[44], zu verzichten. Es gehört aber wohl ebenso zu seinem Stil, das bare Erstaunen des Betrachters über die Mächtigkeit des Baus mit all der mythischen Überhöhung, die in ihm angelegt war[45], ebenso schlicht wie eindrücklich in die ungläubige Bemerkung eines Jüngers zu kleiden: ἴδε ποταποὶ λίθοι καὶ ποταπαὶ οἰκοδομαί[46]. Die übermächtigen „Steine und Bauten" des Tempels geben nicht nur den Ort für die Jerusalemer Ereignisse vor, auf sie hin ist das gesamte Jesus-Geschehen in der

---

42 Vgl. J. Gnilka, Evangelium II, 115–119.
43 Vgl. J. Maier, Tempel und Tempelkult, in: Literatur und Religion des Frühjudentums, hg. von J. Maier/J. Schreiner, Würzburg 1973, 371–390.
44 Vgl. Flavius Josephus, Bellum Iudaicum 1,401; Antiquitates Iudaicae 15, 380–423.
45 Die Literatur dazu ist zahlreich, vgl. M. Tilly, Jerusalem – Nabel der Welt. Überlieferung und Funktion von Heiligtumstraditionen im antiken Judentum, Stuttgart 2002; M. Barker, The Gate of Heaven. The History and Symbolism of the Temple in Jerusalem, London 1991, sowie: L.I. Levine (Hg.), Jerusalem. Its Sanctity and Centrality to Judaism, Christianity and Islam, New York 1999, und: M. Poorthuis/C. Safrai (eds.), The Centrality of Jerusalem. Historical Perspectives, Kampen 1996.
46 Dazu: J. Ådna, Jerusalemer Tempel und Tempelmarkt im 1. Jahrhundert n.Chr. (ADPV 25), Wiesbaden 1999, 33–35. – die eindrückliche Wirkung des Gebäudekomplexes dürfte sich durch die umfangreichen Baumaßnahmen unter Herodes noch verstärkt haben, vgl. R. Riesner, Herodianische Architektur im Neuen Testament, in: Neues Testament und hellenistisch-jüdische Alltagskultur, hg. von R. Deines/J. Herzer/K.-W. Niebuhr (WUNT 274), Tübingen 2011, 165–196, hier: 180 f., sowie: A. Lichtenberger, „Sieh, was für Steine und was für Bauten!". Zur Rezeption herodianischer Architektur im Neuen Testament, in: Zeichen aus Text und Stein. Studien auf dem Weg zu einer Archäologie des Neuen Testaments, hg. von S. Alkier/J. Zangenberg (TANZ 42), Tübingen 2003, 209–221.

Stadt örtlich zentriert: Zum Ende der Einzugsszene wird der Weg Jesu in die Stadt mit dem Weg zum Tempel gleichgesetzt (Mk 11,11). Jesu „eigentliche" Geschichte in Jerusalem beginnt also dort, und auch der erste erzählerische Blick im Moment nach dem Tod Jesu – am vorläufigen Ende der Jesus-Geschichte – geht wiederum zum Tempel – in das Allerheiligste diesmal (Mk 15,38): Der „verhüllende Vorhang" (Ex 35,12;40,21; Num 4,5)[47], der nach der Exodus-Überlieferung die Bundeslade „verdeckte" (Ex 30,6; 40,3), reißt auf, wie es zuvor bereits der Himmel bei der Taufe Jesu getan hatte (Mk 1,10), und enthüllt die bis dahin im kultischen Zentrum des Judentums verborgene Präsenz Gottes[48]. Die Gemeinschaft des Judentums, vor der sich das Geschehen abspielt, ist damit – das Bild mag hier übernommen werden – in ihrem Innersten von den Jesus-Ereignissen berührt; von Ereignissen eschatologischer Qualität, denn das Bild des „Zerreißens" und damit „Enthüllens" von vormals der menschlichen Wahrnehmung Verborgenem gehört mit Jes 63,19b nicht nur zum Wortschatz der Theophanieschilderungen und rahmt im Markusevangelium die Jesus-Geschichte von der Taufe bis zum Tod am Kreuz. Auch die „Spaltung des Ölbergs", mit der nach Sach 14,4 LXX die dort geschilderten Endereignisse beginnen, wird analog zu Mk 1,10 und Mk 15,38 mit einer Form der griechischen Vokabel σχίζω beschrieben. Im Zerreißen des Vorhangs im Tempel nach dem Tod Jesu geschieht „Apokalypse" – so mag man auflösen – im ganz wörtlichen Sinne. Wie schon die Szene vom Einzug Jesu in Jerusalem im Vorfeld des Pessachfestes auf die Vorstellungswelt der alttestamentlichen Prophetie hinsichtlich der letzten Geschehnisse am Ende der Zeit Bezug genommen hatte, so werden auch hier die Jesus-Ereignisse in die Perspektive einer brisanten Zeitangabe gesetzt – was hier geschieht, ist darauf angelegt, „im ἔσχατον" zu geschehen.

Das Empfinden, dass im Auftreten Jesu die grundsätzlichsten religiösen, ja letzten Konzepte ihrer Glaubensgemeinschaft tangiert werden, vertreten auf der Textebene des Markusevangelium auch diejenigen „Gegenspieler" Jesu, die ihm erst in Jerusalem begegnen, stark mit dem neuen Handlungsort – also dem Tempel – assoziiert werden und deshalb höchste kultische Autorität besitzen: die gesamte

---

47 Dazu: J. Gnilka, Evangelium II, 324, sowie – deutlich ausführlicher: A. Yarbro Collins, Mark, 759–764. Collins wertet die Diskussion darüber, welcher der beiden Vorhänge im Tempel wohl gemeint ist, treffend aus: „Furthermore, the presentation of the event in Mark seems to have little interest in the effect of the tearing of the veil on the characters in the narrative. It is the audience of Mark who are expected to reflect on its significance" (760). Für den Erzähler des Evangeliums geht es hier um die Dramaturgie des Erzählganzen und ihre Wirkung auf den Leser: Der äußere Vorhang im Tempel hat keine herausgehobene kultische und damit symbolische Bedeutung. „Markus" wäre ein schlechter Literat, wenn er an dieser Stelle ein so schwaches Symbol in den Text setzte: Natürlich ist der innere Vorhang mit all seiner hochkarätigen kultischen Bedeutung gemeint!

48 Vgl. A. Yarbro Collins, Mark, 763f.

Tempelpriesterschaft, mithin die Mitglieder des Synhedriums, bestehend aus drei Gruppen: den Hohenpriestern (ἀρχιερεῖς), den Ältesten (πρεσβύτεροι) und den Schriftgelehrten (γραμματεῖς), sowie die Religionspartei der Sadduzäer (Σαδδουκαῖοι Mk 12,18). Sie alle treten, herausgefordert durch die „Tempelaktion" (Mk 11,15–19), mit der scharfen Frage nach der ἐξουσία seines Tuns an Jesus heran (bereits in Mk 1,22; 2,1–12; dann wieder aufgenommen in Mk 11,27–29). Dass Jesus außerdem mit den Sadduzäern über die Frage nach der Auferstehung der Toten in Streit gerät (Mk 12,18–27), scheint angesichts dieses Konflikts eher zweitrangig, zumal die Leugnung der Totenauferstehung von den Zeitgenossen offensichtlich als Proprium ihrer Lehre verstanden wurde[49].

Neben die Konfrontation mit den kultischen Autoritäten tritt in Jerusalem erstmals auch die mit der politischen Sphäre[50]. Die Gruppierung der Herodianer (Ἡρῳδιανοί), die bereits in Mk 3,6 im Zusammenhang mit dem Tötungsbeschluss der Pharisäer erwähnt wurde, erscheint in Mk 12,13 erneut – diesmal tatsächlich im Zusammenhang einer politischen Frage, nämlich der nach der kaiserlichen Steuer, wohingegen eine direkte Begegnung mit Herodes Antipas, dem galiläischen Landesherrn Jesu, ausbleibt; im Schicksal Johannes des Täufers ist sie in einer Art erzählerischen Prolepse bereits vorweggenommen.

Die Synagoge als der Ort, an dem sich die Gemeinschaft des Judentums als soziale Gruppierung konstituiert, der Sabbat als die Zeit, zur der sich das spezifische Ethos dieser Gemeinschaft nach außen präsentiert, und die Pharisäer und Schriftgelehrten als die Akteure, die für dieses spezifische Ethos nachdrücklich eintreten – das waren die Erzählparameter, in die hinein der Protagonist Jesus im ersten Teil der Erzählung gestellt wurde. Die Bedingungen der jüdischen Umwelt Jesu werden dabei kaum je „auserzählt", wie es etwa Josephus tut[51]. Sie werden schlicht gesetzt und stecken gerade dadurch den Handlungsraum, in dem die Gestalt Jesu agiert, exakt ab und definieren ihn präzise – als durch und durch „jüdisch" geprägt. Auf dem Weg, den der Erzählgang in Richtung Jerusalem zurücklegt, verdichtet sich dieser Handlungsraum der jüdischen Umwelt Jesu zusehends. Die Erzählparameter von Zeit, Ort und Akteuren der Handlung, die nun

---

[49] Vgl. B. Schröder, Art. Sadduzäer, in: RGG⁴ 7 (2004), 732f.
[50] Vor der Kulisse der gern so beschriebenen „ländlichen Idylle" Galiläas war diese kaum spürbar, vgl. dazu: S. Freyne, Gospels, 40 f.
[51] Vgl. die Beobachtungen bei: J. Schröter, Jesus aus Galiläa, 262f., und: S. Freyne, Gospels, 35, sowie bei: G. Lüderitz, Rhetorik, Poetik, Kompositionstechnik, 188f.; an gleicher Stelle nennt Lüderitz jedoch Passagen (besonders die Schilderung des Todes Johannes' des Täufers in Mk 6), die von einer anderen Stilistik geprägt sind. – Dieser Gesamteindruck bleibt, auch wenn, wie M. Meiser, Reinheitsfragen, für Mk 7,1–23 und Mk 15,42–47 zeigt, einzelne Elemente jüdischer Alltagskultur durchaus sorgfältig erläutert werden.

neu besetzt werden, ahmen dies nach: Zur Zeit des Pessachfestes, in dem das Bekenntnis des ganzen Volkes Israel als einer kultischen Gemeinschaft zur Heilsgeschichte mit seinem Gott Jahwe seinen feierlichsten Ausdruck findet, gerät der Protagonist Jesus im Umfeld des Jerusalemer Tempels, in dessen Allerheiligstem die kultische Präsenz dieses einen Gottes Jahwe maximal erfahrbar wird, in Auseinandersetzung mit der Tempelpriesterschaft, die im Hinblick auf die Deutung dieser göttlichen Präsenz die höchste kultische Autorität für sich in Anspruch nimmt.

Wenn der Verfasser im ersten Teil des Evangeliums das Judentum als eine vorwiegend ethisch bestimmte Gemeinschaft vorgestellt hat, in deren zentrale Orte, soziale Gruppierungen, Werte und Normen er den Protagonisten Jesus manchmal in Konfrontation, manchmal in Übereinstimmung einfügt, zeigt er das Judentum im zweiten Teil konsequent als kultische oder im engeren Sinne religiöse Gemeinschaft, die sich durch gemeinsame Konzepte der Welt- und Geschichtsdeutung verbunden weiß und insofern andere Qualität besitzt als eine bloße „Wertegemeinschaft"[52]. Der Stil der Erzählung verändert sich damit einhergehend in zweifacher Hinsicht: Es findet eine deutliche Intensivierung der Erzählsituation statt, die sich ab Mk 14,1 in immer exakter werdenden, kleinschrittigen Angaben von Ort, Zeit und Person zeigt[53]. Überdies hält ein neuer Ton Einzug. Statt der kargen (aber deshalb nicht effektlosen) Schilderungen der Situation Galiläas bedient der Autor sich nun in stetigen Anklängen der Sprache der Apokalyptik, deren Bildgewalt in der frühjüdischen Literatur ohne Vergleich blieb. Wie oben gezeigt, rahmen diese Anklänge die „Jesus-in-Jerusalem-Geschichte" von seinem Einzug in die Stadt bis zum ersten Augenblick nach dem Tod Jesu und münden in die größte Redekomposition des gesamten Textes: Mk 13.

Der eschatologische, näherhin apokalyptische Deutehorizont, der hier im erzählerischen *setting* angelegt ist, scheint auch die literarische Kulisse, die die Erzählung in ihrem zweiten Teil gänzlich umfängt, in besonderer Weise durchlässig werden zu lassen. Diese Kulisse – das ist die Stadt Jerusalem, zwischen deren heilsgeschichtlichen Fixpunkten, dem Ölberg und dem Tempel, sich die Jesus-Ereignisse zutragen. Der Ausdruck „Kulisse" ist dabei denkbar schwach gewählt, denn tatsächlich erscheint Jerusalem hier als ein τόπος von höchster Gültigkeit. Die Jesus-Erzählung des Markusevangeliums kulminiert nicht bloß im

---

52 Vgl. analog die theoretischen Überlegungen G. Theissens zu einer „Soziologie der Jesusbewegung"; dazu: ders., Die Jesusbewegung. Sozialgeschichte einer Revolution der Werte, Gütersloh 2004, 14–18.
53 Vgl. die Beobachtungen im Beitrag von Oda Wischmeyer im vorliegenden Band.

„erfahrbaren religiösen Zentrum des Judentums"[54]; sie kulminiert im (gedachten) Mittelpunkt dieser Gemeinschaft und ihrer Weltdeutung[55]. Nicht nur deshalb aber ist Jerusalem „*der* Ort des Judentums" schlechthin. Jerusalem ist auch und vor allem der Ort, auf den sich die Endzeitszenarien, die Imaginationen vom End- und Zielpunkt der Heilsgeschichte, die die Gemeinschaft des Judentums in großer literarischer Kreativität und Produktivität hervorgebracht hat, konzentrieren. „Erzählungen vom Judentum", die Jerusalem als τόπος wählen, stehen in dieser Tradition und bergen das literarische Potenzial, eine „Erzählung vom ἔσχατον" vorzulegen[56].

Der Erzähler des Markusevangeliums hält dieses Potenzial in der Komposition des Gesamttextes konsequent offen. Seine „Erzählung vom Judentum" beginnt jedoch zunächst damit, die spezifischen Zeiträume (*Sabbat* und *Pessach*), Orte (*Synagoge* und *Tempel*) und Personen (*Religionsparteien* und *Tempelpriesterschaft*) dieser Binnenerzählung – auf das engste verwoben mit der Makroerzählung des Evangeliums, deren grundsätzliche Erzählsituation sie ebenso bestimmen – vorzustellen und so den weiteren Erzählgang zur Interpretation aufzubereiten.

2.2 „Johannes der Täufer", „Elia", „David". Gestalten der jüdischen Tradition als Stützen der „biographischen Einordnung" der Person Jesu

Den weiteren Erzählgang mit interpretierenden Vorzeichen zu versehen – das ist auf anderer Ebene für beide Erzählungen längst geschehen: für die Jesus-Erzählung insgesamt mit dem programmatischen Auftakt in Mk 1,1, der über die Parallelisierung mit Hos 1,2 sofort den gattungsmäßigen Konnex zur prophetischen Literatur Israels herstellt und andererseits den Begriff εὐαγγέλιον als „Über-Begriff" der sich herausbildenden Gemeinschaft des Christentums etabliert[57]; und

---

54 M. Tilly, Jerusalem, 23; dazu auch: M. Hengel, Jerusalem als jüdische und hellenistische Stadt, in: Hellenismus, hg. von B. Funck, Tübingen 1996, 269–306, hier: 277.
55 Vgl. J.M. Lundquist, The Temple. Meeting Place of Heaven and Earth, London 1993, 84f., sowie: M.A. Fishbane, The Sacred Center, in: Texts and Responses. FS N.N. Glatzer, ed. by M.A. Fishbane/P.R. Flohr, Leiden 1975, 6–27. Die soziologischen Aspekte solcher „Mittelpunktskonstruktionen" stellt dar: E. Shils, Das Zentrum des Kosmos und das Zentrum der Gesellschaft, in: Sehnsucht nach dem Ursprung. FS M. Eliade, hg. von H.P. Duerr, Frankfurt am Main 1983, 538–557.
56 Vgl. die Gattungsbeschreibung bei A. Yarbro Collins, Mark, 42–44.
57 Ob dieser am besten als „Buchüberschrift" oder Teil eines „Prologs" bzw. „Prooemiums" zu bezeichnen ist, wurde vielfach diskutiert, ist für die hier zu behandelnde Fragestellung aber

für die dieser übergeordneten Erzählung inhärente „Erzählung vom Judentum" spätestens in Mk 1,4 durch die Einführung einer Gestalt der „jüdischen Zeitgeschichte Jesu"[58], die in ihrer Erscheinung zugleich den Bezug zu den prophetischen Gestalten der alttestamentlich-jüdischen Tradition gewährleistet: durch die Einführung der Gestalt *Johannes' des Täufers*. Zudem teilen die beiden Erzählanfänge, von denen eben die Rede war, einen gemeinsamen intertextuellen Bezugsrahmen, der den Rekurs auf die Prophetie Israels fast überdeutlich zu explizieren sucht: ein in Mk 1,2 als solches ausgewiesenes und in Mk 1,3 wörtlich ausgeführtes Zitat von Jes 40,3, in komplexer Verschränkung mit Allusionen auf Ex 23,20 und Mal 3,1[59]. Unabhängig von der Zuordnung der syntaktischen Perioden bis Mk 1,4 im Einzelnen, die in der Exegese umstritten ist[60], steht das Zitat wenigstens auf der Textoberfläche ἀπὸ κοινοῦ genau zwischen den Anfängen beider Erzählungen und verbindet und kommentiert beide gleichermaßen: Johannes und später Jesus treten zu einem distinkten Zeitpunkt in die hier zu erzählende Geschichte des Volkes Israel ein – zu dem Zeitpunkt nämlich, an dem die heilsame Ankunft Jahwes, die Jesajas Prophezeiung in Aussicht stellt, unmittelbar bevor steht[61].

Der „Auftritt" des in der Tracht der Propheten Israels[62] gekleideten Johannes wird in seiner exzentrischen Anmutung dem pagan-antiken, hellenistisch gebil-

---

nicht von Interesse. Die wissenschaftliche Diskussion ist zusammengefasst bei: E.-M. Becker, Mark 1:1 and the Debate on a ‚Markan Prologue', in: Filologia Neotestamentaria 22 (2009), 91– 106, sowie kommentiert bei: O. Wischmeyer, Romans 1:1–7 and Mark 1:1–3 in Comparison. Two Opening Texts at the Beginning of Early Christian Literature, in: Mark and Paul. Comparative Essays Part II: For and Against Pauline Influence on Mark, ed. by E.-M. Becker/M. Müller/T. Engberg-Pedersen, (BZNW 199), Berlin/Boston 2014, 121–146.
58 Vgl. die Überlieferung der Logienquelle (Q3,2–7,35) sowie: Flavius Josephus, *Antiquitates Iudaicae* 18,5,2. Zur Einordnung Johannes des Täufers in die Geschichte des Judentums im 1. Jahrhundert: J.E. Taylor, The Immerser. John the Baptist within Second Temple Judaism, Grand Rapids 1997, sowie: K. Backhaus, Echoes from the Wilderness. The Historical John the Baptist, in: Handbook for the Study of the Historical Jesus, ed. by T. Holmén/S.E. Porter, Volume 2: The Study of Jesus, Leiden/Boston 2011, 1747–1785.
59 Dazu sowie zur intertextuellen Verschränkung der Passage mit Ex 23,20 und Mal 3,1 vgl. ausführlich: O. Wischmeyer, Zitat und Allusion als literarische Eröffnung des Markusevangeliums, in: Im Namen des Anderen. Die Ethik des Zitierens, hg. von J. Jacob/M. Mayer (Ethik – Text – Kultur 3), München 2010, 175–186, hier: 178–181.
60 Die wichtigsten Vorschläge dazu präsentiert übersichtlich: O. Wischmeyer, Romans 1:1–7.
61 Dazu: J. Marcus, The Way of the Lord. Christological Exegesis of the Old Testament in the Gospel of Mark, Louisville/Edinburgh 1992, 18–29, und: K.R. Snodgrass, Streams of Tradition Emerging from Isaiah 40:1–5 and Their Adaption in the New Testament, in: JSNT 8 (1980), 24– 45.
62 Vgl. 1Kön 19,13.19; 2Kön 2,8.13 f.; Sach 13,4 (Mantel) und 2Kön 1,8 LXX (Gürtel).

deten ebenso wie dem neuzeitlichen Leser im Gedächtnis haften. Er verschafft dem Text damit einen über die Zeiten wirkungsvollen, effektvollen Einstieg. Mit der Gestalt des Johannes, einer Figur, die nicht nur, wie oben bemerkt, zur Zeitgeschichte des Protagonisten Jesus gehört, sondern auch zu der des Evangelisten, ist aber zugleich – und das ist die eigentliche Leistung des Erzählers an dieser Stelle – eine eindrucksvolle Personifikation der Zeitstimmung gefunden, wie sie zumindest in einigen Gruppen des hellenistischen Judentums präsent gewesen sein dürfte: Johannes begegnet als der ideale Vertreter der apokalyptischen Bewegungen, die als Reaktion auf die vielfältigen krisenhaften Geschichtserfahrungen, die das Volk Israel seit der Exilszeit zu deuten hatte, entstanden sind[63]. In der Wahrnehmung dieser Bewegungen war die Diskrepanz zwischen den Heilsweisungen der Prophetie und der erfahrbaren, in höchstem Maße „un-heilvollen" geschichtlichen Wirklichkeit so groß geworden, dass nur mehr auf ein radikales Ende der Geschichte und ein nicht minder radikales Eingreifen Gottes zur Rettung der Gerechten zu hoffen war. Im Kontext dieses imaginierten göttlichen Gerichts steht der Aufruf des Johannes zur μετάνοια, zur neuen Hinwendung zu Gott (Mk 1,4), die durch die Symbolhandlung der Taufe sichtbar gemacht wird (Mk 1,8). Die Botschaft des Johannes behält ein Spannungsverhältnis zu den prophetischen Trostworten Jesajas, die den Text eröffnet hatten, umgekehrt ergänzen diese aber seine Gerichtsankündigung durch eine Haltung des hoffnungsvollen Erwartens. Die durchaus kunstvolle biographische Einlage zu Johannes endet in Mk 1,14. Der Leser weiß bereits hier, dass Johannes den Feinden ausgeliefert wurde, auch wenn Mk 6,17–29 dies noch nachträgt. Sowie die Johannes-Einlage sozusagen „im Nebensatz" (der Genauigkeit halber: im Griechischen durch eine Konstruktion mit substantiviertem Infinitiv) abgeschlossen wurde, beginnt im Hauptsatz desselben Verses die Darstellung der öffentlichen Wirksamkeit Jesu. Durch den Textauftakt über das Jesajazitat einerseits und die Einführung der Figur des Johannes andererseits wird dieses öffentliche Wirken auf einer übergeordneten Ebene der Textinterpretation von Beginn an konsequent mit den leistungsfähigsten Instrumenten der Welt-, Geschichts- und Zukunftsdeutung des antiken Judentums in Verbindung gebracht: der Prophetie und der Apokalyptik[64]. Unmittelbar auf der Textebene bietet die Johannes-Einlage den Verlauf der Jesus-Erzählung, die doch

---

63 Zur knappen Einführung: M. Tilly, Apokalyptik (UTB 3651), Tübingen 2012, 36–46. Unterschiedliche Beiträge zum Thema sammeln: B. McGinn/J.J. Collins/S.J. Stein (eds.), The Encyclopedia of Apocalypticism, London/New York 2000–2003, sowie (grundlegend auch für die Klärung der Begrifflichkeiten „Apokalyptik" und „Apokalypse"): D. Hellholm (ed.), Apocalypticism in the Mediterranean World and the Near East, Tübingen 1989.
64 Dazu: J.E. Taylor, Art. John the Baptist, in: The Eerdmans Dictionary of Early Judaism, ed. by J.J. Collins/D.C. Harlow, Grand Rapids/Cambridge 2010, 819–821, hier: 820.

eben erst beginnen soll, proleptisch bereits vollständig dar⁶⁵. Beide Gestalten werden ihrem Schicksal nach – vom Beginn ihres öffentlichen Wirkens mit dem Aufruf zur Umkehr bis zu ihrem gewaltsamen Tod – deutlich parallelisiert⁶⁶. Die Gestalt des Johannes gibt nicht allein den Deutungsrahmen für die Gestalt Jesu vor. Auch Johannes selbst wird in der Darstellung des Markusevangeliums mit einer weiteren Figur aus der jüdischen Tradition überblendet: Er wird mit Zügen der *Elia-Gestalt* ausgestattet (Mk 6,15) – eine Allusion, die über die Verschränkung des Jesajazitates mit Mal 3,1 noch stärker akzentuiert wird, da dort erstmals die Tradition, Elia werde als „der eschatologische Vorläufer der Gottesherrschaft"⁶⁷ die Stämme Israels sammeln und den Beginn der Endereignisse anzeigen, begegnet⁶⁸. Explizit macht der Erzähler die mögliche Identifikation des Johannes als *Elia redivivus* in Mk 6,15, wo er der Volksmenge die Vermutung, Johannes sei der wieder gekommene Elia, in den Mund legt. Gleiches vermutet man in Mk 8,28 von Jesus selbst, bis Elia schließlich im Rahmen der Verklärungsperikope (Mk 9,2–13) tatsächlich im Erzählgang „erscheint": Gemeinsam mit Mose, dessen Wiederkommen in den Ereignissen der letzten Tage das antike Judentum ebenso erwartete wie das Elias⁶⁹, begleitet er das in mehrfacher Hinsicht parallel zu Ex 24 gestaltete Theophaniegeschehen⁷⁰. War die Gestalt Jesu bis zu diesem Punkt der Erzählung im Verbund mit Johannes dem Täufer vorwiegend als apokalyptischer Prediger, wenn man so will als Phänomen der Zeitgeschichte zu sehen, wird hier – im gemeinsamen Auftreten mit Elia und Mose als den Boten der Endzeit – seine Identität als eschatologische Gestalt, als prominente Figur der Heilsgeschichte, enthüllt: Noch in Mk 1,11 wurde allein Jesus als „Gottessohn" direkt angesprochen;

---

65 Vgl. H.-J. Klauck, Vorspiel im Himmel? Erzähltechnik und Theologie im Markusprolog (BThS 32), Neukirchen-Vluyn 1997, 94.
66 Vgl. U.B. Müller, Johannes der Täufer. Jüdischer Prophet und Wegbereiter Jesu (Biblische Gestalten 6), Leipzig 2002, 112f., sowie die sorgfältige Analyse bei: H.-J. Klauck, Vorspiel, 21–27. Dem Beginn des Markusevangeliums als „Fundament einer narrativen Meisterleistung" schenkt auch C. Rose, Theologie, *passim*, besondere Aufmerksamkeit.
67 Eine wichtige Unterscheidung ist hier zu treffen: Elia ist – wie gesagt – in den alttestamentlichen Belegen Vorbote der Gottesherrschaft. Als Vorgänger des Messias oder gar als Gestalt, die selbst messianische Züge trägt, gilt Elia erst im späteren jüdischen Schrifttum bzw. im Neuen Testament, vgl. M. Öhler, Elia im Neuen Testament (BZNW 88), Berlin/New York, 1997, 289–291, hier: 291, der „Markus" als „den Interpreten der Eliaerwartung" bezeichnet, „der sie zu einer christlichen Elia-Lehre umformt".
68 Vgl. Mal 3,23f., Sir 48,1–11 und 4Q558, 4–5; dazu: M. Öhler, Elia, 2–12, und: G. Necker, Art. Elia, II. Judentum, in: RGG⁴ 2 (1999), 1211f., hier: 1211.
69 Vgl. E. Lohmeyer, Die Verklärung Jesu, in: ZNW 21 (1922), 185–215; H.M. Teeple, The Mosaic Eschatological Prophet, in: JBLMS 10 (1957), 49–73, sowie: A. Yarbro Collins, Mark, 422–424.
70 Dazu M. Öhler, Elia, 130, mit dem Hinweis auf das Motiv der Wolke aus der Wüstenzeit, die auch für die Endereignisse wieder erwartet wird; vgl. Jes 4,5; 2Makk 2,8.

niemand sonst erhielt – auf der Textebene! – diese Information. Erst in Mk 9,7 wird diese Identität wenigstens für eine kleine Gruppe der Jünger „öffentlich". Die Spekulation über das Wesen Jesu erreicht in der Verklärungsperikope eine neue Stufe: Der Evangelist mag sich bis zu diesem Punkt der Erzählung an Mustern der Eliatraditionen der Königsbücher bedient haben, um „die Geschichte vom verfolgten und umher reisenden Jesus [...], vom Rabbi mit seinen Schülern, vom Wundertäter" und „vom Beter" zu erzählen, wie Johannes Majoros-Danowskis Untersuchung zum Elia-Bild des Markusevangeliums zeigt[71]. Mit der Verklärungsszene jedoch ist der Protagonist des Textes nicht mehr länger „bloß" der Prophet, der ungehört bleibt, der Rabbi, der lehrt, oder der Wundertäter, der die Menge erstaunt. Von dem Punkt der Erzählung an, zu dem der Protagonist Jesus mit den eschatologischen Gestalten Mose und Elia gemeinsam auftritt, erzählt der Evangelist zumindest auch die Geschichte vom „Boten Gottes", der der Elia-Typologie folgend dessen Kommen am Ende der Zeit ankündigt[72]. Spekulation über das Wesen Jesu ist also zugleich Spekulation über die Geschehnisse im ἔσχατον. Zu den komplexen literarischen Szenarien religiöser Spekulation, die das Frühjudentum dafür bereit hielt, gehört neben der bereits erwähnten erwarteten Wiederkunft Elias unter anderem auch die Idee der Auferstehung der Toten[73]. In der unmittelbar auf das Verklärungsgeschehen folgenden Perikope (Mk 9,9–13) vollziehen die anwesenden Jünger eben diese Spekulationen nach: Die Anweisung Jesu, über das Gesehene zu schweigen, ὅταν ὁ υἱὸς τοῦ ἀνθρώπου ἐκ νεκρῶν ἀναστῇ (Mk 9,9), irritiert sie – denn sieht das Zeugnis der Schrift nicht vor, dass „zuerst", also zu Beginn der Endereignisse, auf die der Hinweis Jesu doch anzuspielen scheint, „Elia wiederkommen müsse"? Jesus bestätigt diese Erwartung zunächst – fügt dann aber hinzu, dass es sich längst nicht mehr um eine „Erwartung" handelte: Ἠλίας ἐλήλυθεν. Für die Jünger – wie für den Leser – dürfte dieser Ausspruch wenig Klärung bringen: Meint Jesus damit nun sich selbst oder Johannes den Täufer?[74] Die markinische Darstellung, die das Gespräch zwischen

---

[71] J. Majoros-Danowski, Elija im Markusevangelium. Ein Buch im Kontext des Judentums (BWANT 180), Stuttgart 2008, 242.
[72] Vgl. dazu: J. Majoros-Danowski, Elija, 199–219.
[73] Dazu: G.W.E. Nickelsburg, Art. Resurrection (Early Judaism and Christianity), in: ADB 5, 684–691.
[74] Dies ist gegenüber den zahlreichen exegetischen Erwägungen, die die eindeutige Identifizierung des Johannes vornehmen wollen, doch zu betonen, vgl. ebenso: E.-M., Becker, Elija redivivus im Markus-Evangelium? Zur Typologisierung von Wiederkehr-Vorstellungen, in: Deuterocanonical und Cognate Literature. Yearbook 2008: Biblical Figures in Deuterocanonical and Cognate Literature, ed. by H. Lichtenberger/U. Mittmann-Richert, Berlin/New York 2009, 587–625; anders: M. Öhler, Elia, 46.

Jesus und den Jüngern an dieser Stelle verlässt, leistet es sich[75], im Spekulativen zu bleiben. Die matthäische Redaktion dagegen löst wie im Handstreich auf: τότε συνῆκαν οἱ μαθηταὶ ὅτι περὶ Ἰωάννου τοῦ βαπτιστοῦ εἶπεν αὐτοῖς (Mt 17,13). Auch wenn der Evangelist des markinischen Textes auf eine solche eindeutige Identifikation verzichtet – der sorgfältige Rekurs auf die Traditionen von Elia als dem endzeitlich wiederkehrenden Boten Gottes, sei es in der Gestalt des Johannes, sei es in der Gestalt Jesu, unterstützt, was schon das *setting* der Erzählung in Jerusalem als dem Ort der Endereignisse angelegt hatte. Mit den Worten: „Elia ist gekommen", die der Evangelist dem Protagonisten in den Mund legt – denn wen könnte er sie nachdrücklicher aussprechen lassen? –, kommentiert er zugleich das eigene literarische Vorhaben und charakterisiert es als eine „Erzählung vom ἔσχατον", die beinahe weniger mit ihrer „erzählten Zeit", also der zeitlichen Erstreckung der erzählten Ereignisse, beschäftigt scheint, als mit der konzisen Festlegung „ihres erzählten Zeit-Punktes" – denn dieser liegt, darauf verweist die Elia-Typologie, gerade im Beginn des ἔσχατον.

Neben die Figur des Elia, die die Deutung der Gestalt Jesu über die gesamte Erzählung des Markusevangeliums hinweg begleitet, tritt im zweiten Teil der Handlung, nämlich mit ihrem Eintritt nach Jerusalem, eben die Person der Geschichte des Alten Israel, die mit dieser Stadt in einmaliger Weise verbunden ist: *David*. So wird Jesus schon auf dem Weg nach Jerusalem von einem blinder Bettler bei Jericho als υἱὸς Δαυίδ begrüßt (Mk 10,48), und die Menschenmenge, die seinen Einzug in die Stadt begleitet, kommentiert diesen in der Erwartung der anbrechenden endzeitlichen Königsherrschaft Davids (Mk 11,10). Wie im Erzählgang aber immer wieder auf eine eindeutige Identifikation Jesu mit der Gestalt Elias verzichtet wird, so nimmt die knappe Perikope Mk 12,35 – 37 auch eine vorschnelle Gleichsetzung Jesu mit dem „Davidssohn" zurück: War die Einführung Davids in der Sabbatperikope Mk 2,23 – 28 noch als Hinweis auf die besondere Autorität des Handelns Jesu als des messianischen „Menschensohns" zu lesen[76], lässt der Evangelist hier Jesus selbst die Frage stellen, wie die Lehre von der Davidssohnschaft des Messias, die in der alttestamentlichen Überlieferung fest verankert ist (1Sam 7,12ff., Jes 11,1 und Ez 34,23[77]) und für die Zeit Jesu in den Qumranschriften neuerlich festgehalten wurde (1Qflor 1,11 und 1QPB[78]), mit den Kyriosprädikationen aus Ps 110,1 in Übereinstimmung zu bringen sei. Es wäre ein Leichtes für den Evangelisten, die alttestamentlich-jüdische Überlieferung beim Wort zu nehmen und Jesus spätestens an dieser Stelle der Erzählung mit dem messianischen Da-

---

75 Wie übrigens auch am Ende der Erzählung!
76 Vgl. A. Yarbro Collins, Mark, 581.
77 Für weitere Verweise vgl. J. Gnilka, Evangelium II, 170.
78 Dazu wiederum: J. Gnilka, Evangelium II, 170.

vidssohn zu identifizieren. Er unterlässt aber einmal mehr eine eindeutige Zuschreibung, sondern lässt vielmehr den Protagonisten selbst die Einordnung seiner Person problematisieren.

Johannes der Täufer als Person der Zeitgeschichte Jesu, dessen Botschaft die apokalyptisch-eschatologischen Strömungen des Judentums in der Zeit des Zweiten Tempels repräsentiert, Elia, die prophetische Gestalt aus der Königszeit, die zum Boten der Endzeit stilisiert wird, und David als der große politisch wirksame Akteur der Geschichte Israel, der den Hoffnungen auf die endzeitliche Wiederkehr einer rettenden Messiasgestalt einen Grund gab – alle drei tragen in unterschiedlicher Art und Weise zur Interpretation der Person Jesu, von der der Evangelist erzählen will, bei. Konsequent durchgeführt wird dabei keine der Titulierungen, die sich aus den Allusionen ergeben könnte: Jesus *ist nicht* einfach „Elia", Jesus *ist nicht* einfach „der Davidssohn". Die Spekulationen um das Wesen Jesu, die den Erzählgang des Markusevangeliums bekanntermaßen entscheidend prägen[79], finden ihr Ende erst unter dem Kreuz: Die Gestalten Johannes' des Täufers, Elias und Davids mögen den zu erzählenden Weg Jesu von Galiläa bis Jerusalem begleiten und in vielerlei Aspekten zur Deutung der Person Jesu beitragen – das Kreuzesgeschehen unterbricht aber alle bis dahin vorgetragenen literarischen Szenarien und religiösen Spekulationen. Hier wird das Wesen Jesu im Bekenntnis des römischen Hauptmannes endgültig enthüllt: ἀληθῶς οὗτος ὁ ἄνθρωπος υἱὸς θεοῦ ἦν (Mk 15,39).

υἱὸς θεοῦ – „Gottes Sohn" und damit „der Messias" – das ist Jesus in der Erzählung des Markusevangeliums[80]. Der Evangelist bewegt sich, was die „biographische Einordnung" seines Protagonisten angeht, ganz auf dem Boden antikjüdischer (Zeit-)Geschichte, Kultur und Religion. Er bettet nicht nur die Erzählung selbst, sondern auch die zentrale Person jener Erzählung sorgfältig in dieses Bezugssystem ein. Der Titel des „Gottessohnes", der alle möglichen Identifikationen mit einem apokalyptischen Prediger, Elia oder dem „Davidssohn" weit übersteigt, gehört mitten in dieses Bezugsystem hinein, oder besser: Er steht wiederum – wie bereits für die konstitutiven Parameter der Erzählung gezeigt wurde – „im ἔσχατον" dieses Bezugsystems. Denn auch die Gestalt des „Got-

---

[79] Dies erzählerische Vorgehen wird seit der Arbeit William Wredes als „Messiasgeheimnis" bezeichnet, vgl. W. Wrede, Das Messiasgeheimnis in den Evangelien (1901), Göttingen ⁴1969; dazu einleitend: U. Schnelle, Einleitung in das Neue Testament (UTB 1830), Göttingen ⁶2007, 252–257.
[80] Vgl. D. du Toit, Der abwesende Herr. Strategien im Markusevangelium zur Bewältigung der Abwesenheit des Auferstandenen (WMANT 111), Neukirchen-Vluyn 2006, 6: „Das Markusevangelium erzählt nämlich die Geschichte Jesu als eine Geschichte der Gegenwart des Gottessohnes in Israel, die sich zwischen den beiden Polen seiner Einsetzung zum Gottessohn und seinem Tod als Gottessohn [...] abspielt".

tessohnes", mit der Jesus vom Evangelisten nachdrücklich identifiziert wird, hat ihren Ort, vor allem gemäß der Überlieferung von Qumran, in den Ereignissen des ἔσχατον[81]. 4Q246 etwa belegt den „König der Endzeit" mit genau diesem Titel[82]: „‚Sohn Gottes' wird er genannt und ‚Sohn des Höchsten' wird man ihn rufen [...]"[83].

2.3 „Reich Gottes", „Menschensohn", „Messias". Konzepte jüdischer Religiosität als zentrale Interpretamente der Jesus-Erzählung

Das verdichtete Szenario einer endzeitlichen Königsherrschaft Gottes, das in dem knappen Text von 4Q246 enthalten ist, zeugt exemplarisch davon, dass die vielfältigen Spekulationen über das Ende der Zeit, die die jüdische Welt zur Zeit Jesu beschäftigen, in der Religion, Kultur und Gesellschaft des Frühjudentums das Amalgam einer apokalyptisch-eschatologischen Zeitstimmung erzeugten, die sich literarisch – vor allem in der Literaturgattung der Apokalypsen – ungeheuer produktiv niederschlug[84]. Dies Amalgam, diese spekulative Vorstellungswelt rund um das scheinbare „Ende der Zeit", besteht zum einen aus der gewaltigen Bilderwelt, die in der apokalyptischen Literatur Israels und des antiken Judentums tradiert ist; zum anderen setzt es sich zusammen aus mehreren Konzepten jüdischer Religiosität, die zur Interpretation der imaginierten Endereignisse fruchtbar gemacht werden sollen.

Nach der Darstellung des Markusevangeliums – die hier wohl tatsächlich die tragende Botschaft des historischen Jesus aufgreift[85] – bildet eines dieser Konzepte auch den Kern der Verkündigung Jesu: das *Konzept vom „Reich Gottes"*, der

---

81 Vgl. den Überblick bei: G.G. Xeravits, Art. Son of God, in: The Eerdmans Dictionary of Early Judaism, ed. by J.J. Collins/D.C. Harlow, Grand Rapids/Cambridge 2010, 1248–1249, sowie ausführlich: A. Yarbro Collins/J.J. Collins, King and Messiah as Son of God. Divine, Human, and Angelic Messianic Figures in Biblical and Related Literatur, Grand Rapids/Cambridge 2008, 65–74.
82 Dazu: A.M. Schwemer, Gott als König und seine Königsherrschaft in den Sabbatliedern aus Qumran, in: Königsherrschaft Gottes und himmlischer Kult im Judentum, Urchristentum und in der hellenistischen Welt, hg. von M. Hengel/A.M. Schwemer (WUNT 55), Tübingen 1991, 45–118.
83 Hier wiedergegeben nach: Maier, J., Die Qumran-Essener: Die Texte vom Toten Meer. Band II: Die Texte der Höhle 4 (UTB 1863), München/Basel 1995, 190 Anm. 278.
84 Einen ersten Überblick über die vielfältigen eschatologischen Spekulationen des antiken Judentums gibt: H.P. Müller, Art. Eschatologie, II. Altes Testament, in: RGG⁴ 2 (1999), 1546–1553.
85 Dazu ausführlich: Theißen, G./Merz, A., Der historische Jesus. Ein Lehrbuch, Göttingen ⁴2011, 221–253.

βασιλεία τοῦ θεοῦ[86]. Die Idee einer eschatologischen Heilszeit, in der Gott seine „Königsherrschaft" errichten wird, nimmt ihren Ausgang im alttestamentlichen Bild der „Königsherrschaft Gottes" (Ps 103,19; 145,13), das in der Reihe der „Jahwe-Königspsalmen" (Ps 47; 93; 96–99) auch dichterisch verarbeitet wurde[87]. Dies Bild wiederum verarbeitet Erfahrungen der unmittelbaren Lebenswelt, indem es das hoheitliche Handeln Gottes mit der Herrschaftsausübung der altorientalischen Könige vergleicht. Es handelt sich zwar weder um einen feststehenden „Begriff"[88] noch um ein „Hauptthema der frühjüdischen Literatur"[89], doch wo das Konzept genutzt wird, scheint es bekannt und nicht erklärungsbedürftig und verfügt, wie Friedrich Avemarie betont, über „theol[ogisches] Gewicht"[90]. Aus der bloßen Metapher vom „königlichen Handeln" Gottes, die vor allem der Zyklus der Sabbatlieder aus Qumran poetisch eindrucksvoll umsetzt[91], wird über die Propheten der exilischen[92] und nachexilischen Zeit (Sach 14,9.16f.)[93] eine eschatologische Spekulation, die in Dan 2 und Dan 7 prominent ausformuliert wird[94]. Alle menschliche Macht und alle Reiche der Geschichte werden – so künden die Visionen des Danielbuches – in Zukunft überwunden von einer „anderen Art der Herrschaftsausübung" (Dan 2,44: βασιλείαν ἄλλην). Der „Gott des Himmels" (wiederum Dan 2,44: ὁ θεὸς τοῦ οὐρανοῦ) wird dann seine Macht durchsetzen und sich dazu eines „himmlischen Agenten"[95] bedienen, der in Dan 7,13 als υἱὸς ἀνθρώπου vorgestellt wird.

---

[86] Einführend zu diesem Syntagma: G. von Rad/K.G. Kuhn, Art. βασιλεία τοῦ θεοῦ, in: ThWNT I (1933), 563–573; M. Buber, Königtum Gottes, Heidelberg ³1956, sowie – mit verschiedenen Beiträgen zum Thema: M. Hengel/A.M. Schwemer, Königsherrschaft. Für weiterführende Literaturhinweise vgl. ebenfalls: M. Hengel/A.M. Schwemer, Königsherrschaft, sowie – für neuere Literatur aus dem englischsprachigen Raum: D.C. Allison, Art. Kingdom of God, in: The Eerdmans Dictionary of Early Judaism, ed. by J.J. Collins/D.C. Harlow, Grand Rapids/Cambridge 2010, 860f.
[87] Zur Verknüpfung dieses Konzepts von der „Königsherrschaft Jahwes" mit dem Sabbat vgl. J. Schröter, Jesus, 195.
[88] Vgl. O. Camponovo, Königtum, Königsherrschaft und Reich Gottes in den frühjüdischen Schriften (Orbis biblicus et orientalis 58), Göttingen und Freiburg/Schweiz 1984, 437–439.
[89] Vgl. O. Camponovo, Königtum, 437; vgl. auch: J.J. Collins, Seers, Sibyls and Sages in Hellenistic-Roman Judaism, Boston/Leiden 2001, 99–114.
[90] F. Avemarie, Art. Reich Gottes, II. Antikes Judentum, in: RGG⁴ 7 (2004), 203f., hier: 203.
[91] Vgl. wiederum die detailgenaue Untersuchung bei: A.M. Schwemer, Gott.
[92] Hier ist vor allem Deuterojesaja zu nennen; vgl. Jes 52,7.
[93] Vgl. H. Merklein, Jesu Botschaft von der Gottesherrschaft. Eine Skizze (SBS 111), Stuttgart 1983, 24f. und 39–44.
[94] Collins untersucht weiter die sibyllinischen Orakel, das Testament Mose, die Psalmen Salomos, das Testament der zwölf Patriarchen und natürlich die apokalyptische Literatur.
[95] J. Schröter, Art. Reich Gottes, III. Neues Testament, in: RGG⁴ 7 (2004), 204–210, hier: 207.

Was die Visionen des Danielbuches noch als zukünftige Ereignisse in Aussicht gestellt haben, scheint in der „Zeitansage Jesu"[96], mit der der Evangelist des Markusevangeliums die Verkündigung Jesu beginnen lässt, mit einem Mal gegenwärtig zu sein: πεπλήρωται ὁ καιρὸς καὶ *ἤγγικεν ἡ βασιλεία τοῦ θεοῦ* (Mk 1,15)! In der Situationsbeschreibung, die der Evangelist den Protagonisten zu Beginn der Erzählhandlung geben lässt, *„ist"* die βασιλεία τοῦ θεοῦ also bereits *„herbeigekommen"*, wie es die perfektive Verbform ἤγγικεν beschreibt[97]. Die Feststellung ist zentral, denn sie trifft alle Modelle der Welt- und Geschichtsdeutung des Alten Israel ins Mark. Innerhalb wie außerhalb der Textebene müssen mit ihr heftige religiöse Erwartungen und profunde theologische Überlegungen einhergehen – Erwartungen und Überlegungen dahingehend nämlich, dass „von nun an" mit dem Erleben eines fundamentalen Eingreifens Gottes in die Geschichte im Allgemeinen und in die Geschichte des Volkes Israel im Besonderen zu rechnen sei. In narratologischer Hinsicht wird die von nun an als präsent postulierte βασιλεία τοῦ θεοῦ zum „Erzählraum" für das Folgende. Innerhalb und außerhalb der Textebene kann der Mensch diesen Erzählraum wahrnehmen (Mk 9,1 ἴδωσιν τὴν βασιλείαν τοῦ θεοῦ ἐληλυθυῖαν) und sich in ihn hineinbegeben (Mk 9,47: εἰσελθεῖν εἰς τὴν βασιλείαν τοῦ θεοῦ; Mk 10,23 ff.: εἰς τὴν βασιλείαν τοῦ θεοῦ εἰσελεύσονται) [98]. Affektiv und kognitiv erfahrbar wird sie – so stellt es das Markusevangelium und mit ihm die gesamte synoptische Überlieferung dar – zum einen in der Verkündigung Jesu, besonders in den Gleichnissen, sowie in seinem wundertätigen Handeln, das – so legen es die Synoptiker Jesus selbst immer wieder in den Mund – von besonderer ἐξουσία getragen ist[99]. Fundamental erfahrbar wird die βασιλεία τοῦ θεοῦ innerhalb und außerhalb der Textebene des Markusevangeliums aber natürlich auch und in erster Linie im und durch das Auftreten der Person Jesu selbst: Seine Gestalt „vermittelt" die *conditio* der βασιλεία τοῦ θεοῦ in wörtlichen Sinn, denn nur ihn lässt der Evangelist – Mk 15,43 ausgenommen – von der βασιλεία τοῦ θεοῦ sprechen[100]. Und mehr noch: Die Gestalt Jesu „vermittelt" das „Gekommensein" der βασιλεία τοῦ θεοῦ in ihrem Selbstverständnis, mithin nämlich in der *Selbstbezeichnung als „Menschensohn"*, als ὁ υἱὸς τοῦ ἀνθρώπου[101],

---

96 H.-J. Klauck, Vorspiel, 23.
97 So auch H.-J. Klauck, Vorspiel, 97, und: F. Hahn, Theologie des Neuen Testaments. Band I: Die Vielfalt des Neuen Testaments, Theologiegeschichte des Urchristentums, Tübingen 2002, 496.
98 Vgl. H. Merklein, Botschaft, 19.
99 Vgl. H. Merklein, Botschaft, 59–72.
100 Dazu: H. Merklein, Botschaft, 19.
101 Vgl. dazu den Überblick: M. Karrer, Jesus Christus im Neuen Testament (GNT 11), Göttingen 1998, 287–306, sowie: M. Müller, Art. Menschensohn im Neuen Testament, in: RGG⁴ 5 (2002), 1098–1100, und: G.W.E. Nickelsburg, Art. Son of Man, in: The Eerdmans Dictionary of Early Judaism, ed. by J.J. Collins/D.C. Harlow, Grand Rapids/Cambridge 2010, 1249–1251.

die wiederum auf die bereits erwähnten Danielsvisionen rekurriert und dort in einer eschatologisch ausgerichteten Lesart einen „Repräsentant[en] Gottes"[102] bezeichnet, der das Kommen der βασιλεία τοῦ θεοῦ begleitet und schließlich als Herrscher über die Welt eingesetzt wird (Dan 7,13 f.)[103]. Allerdings hat die neutestamentliche Forschung immer wieder erstens darauf hingewiesen, dass der Jesus der synoptischen Tradition nie eine Selbstprädikation als ὁ υἱὸς τοῦ ἀνθρώπου vornimmt und das „Ich" Jesu manchmal ganz klar von ὁ υἱὸς τοῦ ἀνθρώπου zu unterscheiden ist (Mk 8,38), und dass zweitens die Besetzung des Syntagmas durch den historischen Jesus ganz zweifelhaft bleibt[104]. Trotzdem geht man wohl nicht fehl, wenn man zumindest für den Verfasser des Markusevangeliums annimmt, dass er der Jesus-Gestalt seiner Erzählung die Selbstprädikation als ὁ υἱὸς τοῦ ἀνθρώπου zuordnet – Mk 13,26 f. legt dies ebenso nahe wie der bereits für die Rede von der βασιλεία τοῦ θεοῦ getätigte Befund: Auch die Worte vom „Menschensohn" führt im Markusevangelium allein der Protagonist im Mund. Mit der im Griechischen schwerfälligen und vielleicht deshalb in der Übertragung aus dem Aramäischen so schillernden Wendung lässt der Evangelist die Jesus-Gestalt das eigene Wirken und Schicksal gleichsam kommentieren – und dies in zweifacher Hinsicht[105]. Die „Menschensohnworte" erläutern das vollmächtige Handeln Jesu (Mk 2,10.28) und nehmen gleichzeitig schon früh im Erzählgang, in den Leidensankündigungen (Mk 8,31; 9,31; 10,33), das Geschick Jesu vorweg[106]. In dieser narratologischen Funktion erscheint die Rede vom „Menschensohn" als gekonnt gesetztes, die Dramatik der Erzählhandlung formendes, „literarisches Element"[107], sie trägt aber natürlich – wie es für die die Rede von der

---

102 J. Schröter, Schröter, J., Art. Reich Gottes, III. Neues Testament, in: RGG⁴ 7 (2004), 204–210, hier: 207.
103 Dazu: K. Koch, Die Bedeutung der Apokalyptik für die Interpretation der Schrift, in: ders., Die Reiche der Welt und der kommende Menschensohn. Studien zum Danielbuch, Gesammelte Aufsätze, Band 2, hg. von M. Rösel, Neukirchen-Vluyn 1995, 16–45, sowie – unter Zusammenfassung der wissenschaftlichen Diskussion und der dazugehörigen Literatur: J.J. Collins, Daniel (Hermeneia), Minneapolis 1993, 304–311, und: A. Yarbro Collins, The Influence of Daniel on the New Testament, in: J.J. Collins, Daniel, 90–105, hier: 92–98.
104 Vgl. nochmals: M. Karrer, Jesus Christus, 287–306, sowie: A. Lindemann, Art. Eschatologie, III. Neues Testament, in: RGG⁴ 2 (1999), 1553–1560, hier: 1553 f., und: A. Yarbro Collins, Mark, 187–189.
105 Vgl. J. Schröter, Jesus, 249.
106 Vgl. M. Karrer, Jesus Christus, 298, sowie: J. Adam, „Der Anfang vom Ende" oder „das Ende des Anfangs". Perspektiven der markinischen Eschatologie anhand der Leidensankündigungen Jesu, in: Eschatologie – Eschatology. The Sixth Durham-Tübingen Research Symposium: Eschatology in Old Testament, Ancient Judaism and Early Christianity (Tübingen, September, 2009), hg. von H.J. Eckstein/C. Landmesser/H. Lichtenberger (WUNT 272), Tübingen 2011, 91–124.
107 So auch: M. Karrer, Jesus Christus, 293.

βασιλεία τοῦ θεοῦ bereits festgestellt werden konnte – nicht nur eine literarische, sondern auch eine theologische Linie in den Text ein: Wie bereits angedeutet, ist auch die Bildrede vom „Menschensohn" Teil der eschatologischen Szenarien des antiken Judentums. Sie bezeichneten einen von Gott gesandten endzeitlichen Akteur, der – dies dokumentieren die Qumranschriften, das Henoch- und das Vierte Esrabuch gleichermaßen – mit unterschiedlichen Titeln belegt werden konnte. In der Henochtradition etwa kann er „Menschensohn" ebenso genannt werden wie „der Gerechte" oder „der Messias" (Hen 4,2.10; 52,1–9)[108]. Diese Prädikation sticht wohl auf Grund ihrer besonderen Wirkungsgeschichte nicht erst für den modernen Leser aus der Reihe der möglichen Titulaturen für den oben genannten endzeitlichen Repräsentanten der Gottesherrschaft hervor. Durch einen erzählerischen Kunstgriff, der die Benennung mit dem Nimbus des Unaussprechlichen und Unantastbaren versieht und der seit William Wrede die Markus-Forschung als „Messiasgeheimnis" beschäftigt[109], kommt der Prädikation auch innerhalb der Komposition des Markusevangeliums besondere Bedeutung zu. Die Identität Jesu mit der endzeitlichen Messiasgestalt tritt für den Leser bereits im „Petrusbekenntnis" zu Tage, soll im Rahmen der Erzählhandlung dem Schweigegebot Jesu entsprechend aber noch nicht offen kommuniziert werden. Auf dieser Ebene wird sie erst im „Bekenntnis" Jesu gegenüber Pilatus: ἐγώ εἰμι (Mk 14,62) endgültig bestätigt. Die teils abenteuerlichen Berichte des Flavius Josephus über eine Reihe von Messiasprätendenten, die im Palästina um die Zeitenwende für Aufsehen sorgten[110], dokumentieren, dass die Erwartung, die sich aus den Prophezeiungen über das davidische Königshaus aus 2Sam 7 speiste, die ersehnte „Messias-Gestalt" möge das Volk Israel endlich erreichen, die Zeitstimmung innerhalb der jüdischen Welt des ersten vor- und nachchristlichen Jahrhunderts angesichts der bedrückenden politischen Situation der römischen Fremdherrschaft maßgeblich prägte. Das Markusevangelium scheint diese Tendenzen ebenso aufzugreifen, wie es sich in die literarische Tradition zur Messiashoffnung einträgt, die vor allem von der Qumranliteratur repräsentiert wird. Jesus ist der

---

108 Vgl. auch: 4Esr 13; dazu neuerdings: J.J. Collins, The Son of Man in Ancient Judaism, in: Handbook for the Study of the Historical Jesus, ed. by T. Holmén/S.E. Porter, Volume 2: The Study of Jesus, Leiden/Boston 2011, 1545–1568. – Im Markusevangelium selbst wird dieser Zusammenhang durch den Titel des „Gottessohnes" noch erweitert, vgl. oben 2.2; dazu: S. Kim, „The ‚Son of Man'" as the Son of God (WUNT 30), Tübingen 1983.
109 Vgl. Anm. 79.
110 Dazu knapp: J.J. Collins, Seers, Sibyls and Sages, 110 f., und ausführlicher: R.A. Horsley/J. Hanson, Bandits, Prophets and Messiahs, Minneapolis 1986.

Christus, der Sohn Gottes, der Menschensohn – in dieser Trias gipfeln die Überlegungen des Markusevangelisten zur Identität seiner Hauptgestalt[111].

Die drei wesentlichen religiösen Konzepte – die Lehre vom Reich Gottes, die Idee von der Gestalt des „Menschensohnes" und die Hoffnung auf das Kommen des Messias –, die der Markus-Evangelist zur Deutung des Jesus-Geschehens heranzieht, entstammen also allesamt dem großen Bereich eschatologischer Spekulation im Judentum um die Zeitenwende[112]. Gebündelt werden alle diese für die Jesus-Erzählung des Evangelisten wesentlichen Überlegungen in der bereits zitierten Formel, mit der er die Verkündigung Jesu beginnen lässt: πεπλήρωται ὁ καιρὸς καὶ ἤγγικεν ἡ βασιλεία τοῦ θεοῦ (Mk 1,15).

2.4 Die „Erzählung vom Judentum" innerhalb des Markusevangeliums. Erzählen von einer Kultur im καιρός

Die Darstellung der Verkündigung Jesu setzt unverzüglich mit ihrem „Spitzensatz" ein. Die Ankündigung, das Reich Gottes sei nun herbeigekommen, die allein schon hinreichend Durchschlagskraft besitzen sollte, da sie doch mit Nachdruck herausstellen möchte, dass die Hoffnungen des Volkes Israel auf den Anbruch der eschatologischen Heilszeit nun in Erfüllung begriffen seien, wird eindringlich durch eine „Zeitangabe" präzisiert: πεπλήρωται ὁ καιρός. „Erfüllt ist die Zeit!", möchte man mit den gängigen deutschsprachigen Versionen als Übersetzung vorschlagen[113] – und geht damit nicht fehl, denn die Wörterbücher geben für καιρός auch die Bedeutung von „Zeitraum" oder „zeitlicher Erstreckung" an[114]. Der spezifische Sinngehalt der Vokabel geht darüber jedoch verloren. Denn dem

---

111 Vgl. C.A. Evans, Prophet, Sage, Healer, Messiah, and Martyr. Types and Identities of Jesus, in: Handbook for the Study of the Historical Jesus, ed. by T. Holmén/S.E. Porter, Volume 2: The Study of Jesus, Leiden/Boston 2011, 1217–1243, hier: 1243: „to deny Jesus as the Messiah is to deny the faith [...]."
112 Dazu: K. Scholtissek, Der Sohn Gottes für das Reich Gottes. Zur Verbindung von Christologie und Eschatologie bei Markus, in: Der Evangelist als Theologe. Studien zum Markusevangelium, hg. von T. Söding (SBS 163), Stuttgart 1995, 63–90, sowie: G.G. Xeravits, King, Priest, Prophet. Positive Eschatological Protagonists of the Qumran Library, Leiden 2003.
113 Vgl. die Übersetzungen der Lutherbibel in der revidierten Fassung von 1984, der Zürcher Bibel sowie der Einheitsübersetzung; vgl. dazu bei Bemerkungen bei: R. Feldmeier, Gott und die Zeit, in: Heil und Geschichte. Die Geschichtsbezogenheit des Heils und das Problem der Heilsgeschichte in der biblischen Tradition und in der theologischen Deutung, hg. von J. Frey/S. Krauter/H. Lichtenberger (WUNT 248), Tübingen 2009, 287–305, hier: 293–298.
114 Vgl. die jeweiligen Einträge bei: H.G. Liddell/R. Scott/H.S. Jones, A Greek-English Lexicon, Oxford 1968.

"Zeitlauf" liegt im Griechischen doch χρόνος näher. καιρός hingegen ist ein distinkter „Zeitpunkt", genauer: „der richtige Zeitpunkt", der zum Handeln auf- und herausfordert[115]. Der Sprachgebrauch des hellenistischen Judentums übernimmt diese Unterscheidung, differenziert καιρός aber weiter zu einem einmaligen „Moment" in der „Chronologie" des „Zeitlaufes" aus[116]: Der eine καιρός „teilt die Linie der Zeit und bildet insofern ihre formale Mitte"[117], wie Gerhard Delling erläutert. Er trennt damit den gegenwärtigen „Olam", den gegenwärtigen αἰών, vom ἔσχατον[118], setzt also weniger das „Ende der Zeit" oder gar das Ende der „Zeitgebundenheit" menschlicher Existenz fest, wie sie die griechische Welt ersehnte[119], sondern eben nur das „Ende der Jetzt-Zeit". ἔσχατον ist deshalb, so schlägt Delling vor, das „Hernach" [120], also der neue Olam, der neue αἰών, der seinen Anfang im καιρός nimmt. Formal übernimmt Mk 1,15 damit, wie Delling weiter ausführt, ganz unmittelbar das griechische Verständnis von καιρός – „aber das Wort hat einen völlig neuen Inhalt bekommen: [...] es ist der Kairos des Reiches, der sich erfüllt hat"[121]. Der „für das Handeln entscheidende Punkt" ist nun mehr der Punkt des maximalen, des absoluten Handelns Gottes innerhalb eines Zeitlaufes, der – nun ebenfalls ganz auf Gott bezogen – nicht mehr bloß Zeitlauf, sondern Heilsgeschichte ist.

Diesen καιρός, diesen einen Zeitpunkt, der zunächst einmal Ergebnis einer grundlegenden theologischen Aussage ist – es geht um den Wendepunkt der Heilsgeschichte, den „major eschatological turning point"[122] –, gestaltet der Evangelist des Markusevangeliums literarisch aus. Er stellt seine Jesus-Erzählung konsequent in den Rahmen der religiösen Symbolwelt des Frühjudentums hinein.

---

115 Die antike Ikonographie bildet diesen Sinngehalt einmal mehr treffend ab: καιρός wird als Jüngling mit wehendem Haarschopf dargestellt – ihn gilt es zu ergreifen wie eine „günstige Gelegenheit"; dazu: G. Delling, Das Zeitverständnis des Neuen Testaments, Gütersloh 1940, 83. – Vgl. dazu weiterhin die Beobachtungen zum Wortgebrauch im Beitrag von Oda Wischmeyer im vorliegenden Band, sowie: H. Weder, Gegenwart und Gottesherrschaft (BThS 20), Neukirchen-Vluyn 1993, 61.
116 G. Delling, Zeitverständnis, 83.
117 G. Delling, Zeitverständnis, 28 Anm. 10; so auch: O. Cullmann, Christus und die Zeit. Die urchristliche Zeit- und Geschichtsauffassung, durchgesehene Auflage, mit einem „Rückblick auf die Wirkung des Buches in der Theologie der Nachkriegszeit", Zürich 1962, hier: 84–94 und 117–159.
118 Vgl. Syr Bar 85,10; dazu nochmals: G. Delling, Zeitverständnis, 41–48.
119 Dazu: G. Delling, Zeitverständnis, 5–39.
120 G. Delling, Zeitverständnis, 44.
121 G. Delling, Zeitverständnis, 88.
122 A. Yarbro Collins, Mark, 70. Genau diesem „turning point" sind auch die weiteren Belegstellen für καιρός innerhalb des Markusevangeliums zuzuordnen, vgl. Mk 10,30; 11,13; 12,2 und 13,33; dazu: J. Adam, „Der Anfang vom Ende", 113.

Am Anfang steht die – nach Aristoteles ganz literarisch gedachte[123] – Frage: „Was könnte passieren, wenn...?" – Der Autor des Markusevangeliums fragt: „Wie lässt sich darstellen, dass *der* distinkte Zeitpunkt, den sich die kulturelle und religiöse Gemeinschaft des Judentums als *den entscheidenden Zeitpunkt ihrer Geschichte* denkt, tatsächlich eintritt oder *eingetreten ist?*" In seinem Versuch, sich dieser Anfrage *literarisch* zu nähern, ruft der Autor das Personal und die Konzepte frühjüdischer eschatologischer Szenarien auf. Die literarische Wirkkraft dieser Szenarien scheint ihn zu faszinieren, und er arbeitet mit all ihren Versionen. Die jüdische Welt, in die das Markusevangelium den Protagonisten Jesus stellt, erhält dadurch für einen nichtjüdischen Leser etwas geradezu „Magisches"[124], sei es im „theatralischen" Auftritt Johannes des Täufers, dem merkwürdigen Erscheinen der Elia-Gestalt, den geheimnisvollen Menschensohnworten oder der kräftigen Ankündigung der „apokalyptischen Wehen"[125] und ihrer Vernichtungsphantasien.

Diesen literarischen Gestaltungen des καιρός steht eine weitere Frage gegenüber: Wie lässt sich literarisch gestalten, dass Jesus von Nazareth, die *historische* Person, von dessen öffentlicher Wirksamkeit es zu erzählen gilt, mitten in dieses ganz und gar *eschatologische* Szenario hinein gehört? Der Evangelist kleidet die Antworten auf alle diese Anfragen in eine eigene literarische Form, die Adela Yarbro Collins „eschatological historical monograph"[126] nennt. Die *eine* Antwort aber, in der alle Fragen in eins fallen, überführt er in eine theologische Aussage und ein religiöses Bekenntnis zugleich. Die Antwort lautet: Ἰησοῦς Χριστὸς υἱὸς θεοῦ (Mk 1,1). Als theologische Aussage und als religiöses Bekenntnis liegt diese eine Antwort in der Makroerzählung des Evangeliums, in der Erzählung von Jesus Christus, begründet. Sie entbehrte aber jeder Referenz, wäre sie nicht rückgebunden an die „Erzählung vom Judentum", die sich aus dem Markustext ebenfalls rekonstruieren lässt. Leistung dieser Erzählung ist es zum einen – wie bereits gesagt, den Referenzrahmen der Jesus-Erzählung zu geben, die sonst in ihrer Rede vom „Reich Gottes", von „Menschensohn" und „Messias" ganz unverständlich bliebe. Die ganz eigene Leistung dieser Erzählung ist es aber auch, die theologische Vorstellungswelt des Frühjudentums und deren Spekulationen über eine ewige „Leerstelle" des Erzählens, über das einmalige Geschehen im καιρός

---

123 Aristoteles, *Poetik* 1451a 36–1451b 7.
124 Vgl. die sensiblen Textbeobachtungen bei: G. Zuntz, Ein Heide las das Markusevangelium, in: Markus-Philologie. Historische, literargeschichtliche und stilistische Untersuchungen zum zweiten Evangelium (WUNT 33), Tübingen 1984, 205–222.
125 Dazu: J. Adam, „Der Anfang vom Ende", 118 ff., sowie: E.E. Shively, Apocalyptic Imagination in the Gospel of Mark. The Literary and Theological Role of Mark 3,22:30 (BZNW 189), Berlin/Boston 2012.
126 A. Yarbro Collins, Mark, 42–44.

nämlich, ernst zu nehmen und in ihrer Tragkraft auszuloten. Der Autor tut dies, indem er sich in die Bilderwelt eschatologischer Spekulation hineinbegibt und sie in Beziehung zu dem kulturellen Kontext, dem sie zugeordnet ist, also den spezifischen Gegebenheiten einer „jüdischen Lebenswelt", setzt. Die Darstellung dieser Lebenswelt mag in ihrer Betonung jüdischer Indentitätsmarker theologisch verkürzend und historisch ungenau wirken, sie ist aber vor allem *konzentriert*: konzentriert auf den καιρός, dessen Einmaligkeit[127] und dessen Verortung im Zeitkonzept des Judentums, das ein solches Zeitkonzept immer nur als „Heilsgeschichte" kennt. Die „Erzählung", die das Markusevangelium vom Judentum gibt, ist so mitnichten eine Erzählung vom „Ende der jüdischen Religion"[128], sondern eine Erzählung vom wichtigsten Augenblick der Geschichte Gottes mit dem Volk Israel und damit gerade die Erzählung vom Beginn einer neuen Zeit, eines neuen Abschnitts der Heilsgeschichte[129].

3 Eine „Erzählung vom Judentum" in den Paulusbriefen?

Die Rekonstruktion einer „Erzählung vom Judentum" aus dem narrativ angelegten Text des Markusevangeliums ist – der Grundstruktur des Textes folgend – über die Betrachtung der grundlegenden Erzählparameter, einiger zentraler Personenkonstellationen sowie einiger in die Erzählung integrierter Angebote zur Interpretation des Erzählten erfolgt. Die Paulusbriefe hingegen sind in ihrer grund-

---

127 Vgl. G. Delling, Zeitverständnis, 88: „in der Gegenwart Jesu erfüllt sich Gottes zielvolles Handeln in höchster Verdichtung und Geschlossenheit. Es ist in völliger Sammlung auf einen Punkt gerichtet [...], auf ein einmaliges Geschehen, das weiterstrahlt in die ganze Weite der Schöpfung und der Geschichte".
128 W. Schmithals, Das Evangelium nach Markus. Kapitel 1–9,1 (ÖTK 2,1), Gütersloh ²1986, 46.
129 Vgl. zur Betonung der Dimension „Zeit" im Denken von Frühjudentum und beginnendem Christentum G. Delling, Zeit und Endzeit. Zwei Vorlesungen zur Theologie des Neuen Testaments, Neukirchen-Vluyn 1970, 11f.: „Bestimmt wird diese Bedeutsamkeit jedoch nicht von dem geographischen Raum an sich, sondern dadurch, daß in Palästina das jüdische Volk seine Mitte hat, daß es das heilige, von Gott ihm zugewiesene Land war, und daß insbesondere Jerusalem als die Stadt des Tempels des einen Gottes das Zentrum des jüdischen Volkes schlechthin darstellte – genauer: die Bedeutsamkeit des Wirkens Jesu im jüdischen Land gründet in dem geschichtlichen Handeln Gottes am jüdischen Volk. Weil dieses Volk durch Gottes Geschichte mit ihm der Träger der Verheißungen Gottes war, deshalb ging nach urchristlicher Auffassung der Heilbringer aus ihm hervor, ereignete sich in seiner Mitte das endgültige Heilshandeln Gottes [...]. *Nicht der Raum ist [...] für das biblische, insbesondere für das neutestamentliche Denken bestimmend, sondern die Zeit.*"

sätzlichen Ausrichtung argumentierende Texte. Sie verfügen nicht über einen „Erzählgang", an dem die Untersuchung entlang gehen könnte. Argumentierende Texte – und die Paulusbriefe zumal – erhalten ihr Grundgerüst durch Begrifflichkeiten, durch ein distinktes Vokabular. Im Mittelpunkt dieses zweiten Teils der Untersuchung stehen deshalb nun die unterschiedlichen Bezeichnungen und Begrifflichkeiten, mit denen Paulus des Phänomen „Judentum" zu erfassen sucht[130].

3.1 Ἰουδαῖος, ἰουδαΐζω, ἰουδαϊσμός – Paulinisches Vokabular zur Beschreibung des ἔθνος der Juden

Als Bürger des *imperium Romanum* mag Paulus seine soziale Bezugsgruppe, „die Juden", in einer ersten Perspektive als politische Größe im antiken Sinne des Wortes, als ἔθνος, wahrgenommen haben[131]. In den hellenistischen Städten der Diaspora lebten sie als Volksgruppe (πολίτευμα) mit eigenen Rechten und Privilegien[132], die sowohl unter hellenistischer als auch römischer Herrschaft zum Teil zwar ein Alltagsleben in Übereinstimmung mit dem jüdischen Religionsgesetz gewährleisteten, aber doch nie dauerhaft vor staatlichen Übergriffen und gesellschaftlicher Ausgrenzung schützten[133]. Reflexe auf die ambivalenten politischen Grundgegebenheiten, denen das ἔθνος der Juden innerhalb des *imperium Romanum* ausgesetzt war, finden sich in den Paulusbriefen wenige. Dass Paulus sie als Lebensrealitäten aber natürlich wahrgenommen hat, belegen nicht nur die Äußerungen aus Röm 13,1–7 exemplarisch[134]. Auch die paulinische Verwendung

---

130 Grundlegend dazu: M. Konradt, „Mein Wandel einst im ‚Ioudaismos'" (Gal 1,13). Paulus als Jude und das Bild des Judentums beim Apostel Paulus, in: Fremdbilder – Selbstbilder. Imaginationen des Judentums von der Antike bis in die Neuzeit, hg. von R. Bloch/S. Haeberli/R.C. Schwinges, Basel 2010, 25–67.
131 Zum Römischen Reich als dem „politischen Raum", in dem Paulus sich bewegte: A. Mehl, Der politische Raum des Paulus: Das Römische Reich, in: Paulus. Leben – Umwelt – Werk – Briefe, hg. von O. Wischmeyer (UTB 2767), Tübingen/Basel ²2012, 5–24.
132 Vgl. Josephus, Bellum Iudaicum 7,110 und Antiquitates 12,119–124; dazu: M. Pucci Ben Zeev, Jews Among Greeks and Romans, in: The Eerdmans Dictionary of Early Judaism, ed. by J.J. Collins/D.C. Harlow, Grand Rapids/Cambridge 2010, 237–255, sowie dies., Jewish Rights in the Roman World (TSAJ 74), Tübingen 1998, besonders: 374–377.
133 Vgl. dazu den Überblick bei: E.S. Gruen, Judaism in the Diaspora, in: The Eerdmans Dictionary of Early Judaism, ed. by J.J. Collins/D.C. Harlow, Grand Rapids/Cambridge 2010, 77–96.
134 Vgl. O. Wischmeyer, Staat und Christen nach Römer 13,1–7. Ein neuer hermeneutischer Zugang, in: dies., Von Ben Sira zu Paulus. Gesammelte Aufsätze zu Texten, Theologie und Hermeneutik des Frühjudentums und des Neuen Testaments, hg. von E.-M. Becker (WUNT 173), Tübingen 2004, 229–242, hier: 229.

von Lexemen aus dem Wortfeld „Ἰουδαῖος" legt dies nahe. Mit beinahe 200 Nennungen gehört der Begriff ohnehin „zu den am häufigsten im N[euen] T[estament] vertretenen Nomina"[135]. Bemerkenswert ist dabei allerdings die ganz ungleichmäßige Verteilung der Belegstellen: 79 bzw. 71 Belege entfallen allein auf die Apostelgeschichte und das Johannesevangelium, während dem Lexem im Markusevangelium keine signifikante Bedeutung zuzukommen scheint. Jedenfalls ist die Vokabel dort nur siebenmal zu finden – davon fünfmal in der Wendung βασιλεύς τῶν Ἰουδαίων, also im Zusammenhang der Passionsgeschichte und als ein in diesem Rahmen allein der Figur Jesu vorbehaltener Titel (Mk 15,2.9.12.26). Ob der Verfasser des Markusevangeliums, wie Gudrun Guttenberger vermutet, tatsächlich eine „eigenartige Distanz zu [diesem] Lexem" verspürte[136] und es deshalb in seiner Beschreibung des Phänomens „Judentum" beinahe gänzlich zurück tritt, mag dahingestellt bleiben. Auffällig ist aber, dass eben dieses Phänomen „Judentum" im Markusevangelium kaum in seiner Ganzheit als solches erfasst, sondern immer schon in seine Repräsentanten, Rituale und Gewohnheiten untergliedert beschrieben wird: Der Verfasser des Markusevangeliums spricht kaum einmal von „πάντες οἱ Ἰουδαῖοι" (dies ausnahmsweise in Mk 7,3!), sondern – wie oben gezeigt – von „οἱ Φαρισαῖοι καὶ οἱ γραμματεῖς", „οἱ Σαδδουκαῖοι" oder „οἱ Ἡρῳδιανοί". In den Paulusbriefen ist die Vokabel deutlich häufiger zu finden: Hier entfallen von 26 Belegen 11 auf den Römerbrief, acht auf den Ersten Korinther- und vier auf den Galaterbrief. Im Zweiten Korinther- und Ersten Thessalonicherbrief erscheint das Lexem je einmal. Paulus hat also sehr wohl das Phänomen „Judentum" in der Gesamtheit seiner Mitglieder als soziale Gruppierung im Blick: Wie die Diasporajuden insgesamt übernimmt auch er die (manchmal offensichtlich abwertend gebrauchte!) Benennung οἱ Ἰουδαῖοι, mit der man seit dem Ende der Exilszeit die Mitglieder des ἔθνος der Juden belegte, als Selbstbezeichnung[137], und zwar in zweifacher Hinsicht: zur Beschreibung einer ethnischen Gruppierung einerseits und einer kulturell-religiösen Gemeinschaft andererseits[138]. So wie die Juden der Diaspora – anders als die Mitglieder des palästinischen Judentums – diese Fremdbezeichnung internalisieren, spiegeln sie doch die damit verbunde-

---

135 H. Kuhli, Art. Ἰουδαῖος, in: EWNT² 2 (1981), 472–482, hier: 474.
136 Vgl. G. Guttenberger, Ethnizität im Markusevangelium, in: Jesus – Gestaltung und Gestaltungen. Rezeptionen des Galiläers in Wissenschaft, Kirche und Gesellschaft, Festschrift für G. Theißen zum 70. Geburtstag, hg. von P. von Gemünden/D.G. Horrell/M. Küchler (NTOA 100), Göttingen 2013, 125–152, hier: 141.
137 Dazu ausführlich: K.G. Kuhn, Art. Ἰσραήλ κτλ. B. Ἰσραήλ, Ἰουδαῖος, Ἑβραῖος in der nach-at.lichen jüdischen Literatur, in: ThWNT 3 (1938), 360–370, hier: 361–366.
138 Vgl. Josephus, Antiquitates 11,173, sowie 2Makk 6,6; 9,17; dazu: S.J.D. Cohen, Art. Ioudaios, in: The Eerdmans Dictionary of Early Judaism, ed. by J.J. Collins/D.C. Harlow, Grand Rapids/Cambridge 2010, 769.

nen Abgrenzungsmechanismen der nichtjüdischen Umwelt zugleich zurück, wenn sie ihrerseits – in Kontinuität mit der Antithese von „Israel" und „den Völkern" – die Gesamtheit der οἰκουμένη als Gegenüber von „Juden und Nichtjuden" verstehen[139]. Auch Paulus scheint seine Umwelt ganz grundsätzlich unter der Perspektive der Dichotomie εἴτε Ἰουδαῖοι εἴτε Ἕλληνες (1Kor 12,13; auch 1Kor 1,22 f.; 10,32; Röm 1,16; 2,9 f.; 3,9.29; 9,24; 10,12; Gal 3,28) erlebt zu haben. Seine eigene Positionierung innerhalb dieser sozialen Realitäten ist ebenso deutlich: καὶ ἐγενόμην τοῖς Ἰουδαίοις ὡς Ἰουδαῖος (1Kor 9,20), wie die Abgrenzung nach außen mitunter harsch ausfallen kann: ἡμεῖς φύσει Ἰουδαῖοι καὶ οὐκ ἐξ ἐθνῶν ἁμαρτωλοί (Gal 2,15)[140]. Der sozialen Gruppe der Ἰουδαῖοι wird hier – neben der gemeinsamen Herkunft – ein gemeinsamer Lebensstil, ein gemeinsames Ethos zugeordnet, das diese Gemeinschaft fundamental von der sozialen Umwelt unterscheidet. Manifestiert haben wird sich dieses spezifische Ethos nach außen besonders in der Sabbatobservanz und der Sitte der Beschneidung, also den beiden Gebräuchen, die seit der Exilszeit zu *den* großen Identitätsmarkern des Judentums geworden waren, sowie dem Einhalten der Speisegebote[141]. Die soziale Gruppierung, das ἔθνος der Juden, lässt sich also in der Wahrnehmung des Paulus offensichtlich auch als kulturelle Gemeinschaft identifizieren: Wer Mitglied des ἔθνος der Juden ist, „lebt jüdisch"[142]. Das in Gal 2,14 zur Beschreibung dieses Sachverhaltes gebrauchte Verbum ἰουδαΐζειν[143] folgt einer im Griechischen gebräuchlichen Wortbildung, die einen recht deutlich bestimmbaren semantischen Horizont vorgibt:

---

[139] Nicht nur das – einige der Vorwürfe, die an die jüdischen Gruppierungen in den Städten des hellenistischen Ostens bzw. später des *imperium Romanum* herangetragen worden sind, wird man gar internalisiert haben. Auch dafür steht Paulus, wenn er in 1Thess 2,15 äußert, Juden seien „πᾶσιν ἀνθρώποις ἐναντίων". Die Unterstellung der Menschenfeindlichkeit, die zumeist mit dem Vorwurf der „Gottlosigkeit", d. h. im paganen Sinn mit der Verweigerung dem Polytheismus gegenüber (vgl. Diodorus Siculus 34,1,1, sowie Josephus, Contra Apionem 1,309 f.; 2,148), verschränkt ist, gehört, wie Tacitus (*Historien* 5,5,1: „sed adversus omnes alios hostile odium") und Juvenal (Satiren 14,103 f.) belegen, zu den üblichen antijüdischen Stereotypen (vgl. wiederum Josephus, Contra Apionem 1,309 f.; 2,121 f.; dazu: R. Bloch, Art. Misanthropia, in: RAC 24 (2012), 840–842.
[140] Vgl. H. Koester, Art. φύσις κτλ., in: ThWNT 9 (1973), 265.
[141] Vgl. H. Merklein, Der erste Brief an die Korinther. Kapitel 5,1–11,1 (ÖTKNT 7/2), Gütersloh 2000, 229–231, sowie M. Konradt, „Die aus Glauben, diese sind Abrahams Kinder" (Gal 3,7). Erwägungen zum galatischen Konflikt im Lichte frühjüdischer Abrahamstraditionen, in: Kontexte der Schrift. Band 1: Text, Ethik, Judentum und Christentum, Gesellschaft. E.W. Stegemann zum 60. Geburtstag, hg. von G. Gelardini, Stuttgart 2005, 25–48, hier: 35 zu 1Kor 9,20.
[142] Dazu: O. Betz, Art. ioudaizo, Ioudaikws, Ioudaismos, ou, o, in: EWNT² 2 (1981), 470–472; vgl. Ἰουδαϊκῶς ζῇς (Gal 1,14).
[143] Dazu: S.J.D. Cohen, Art. Judaizing, in: The Eerdmans Dictionary of Early Judaism, ed. by J.J. Collins/D.C. Harlow, Grand Rapids/Cambridge 2010, 847 f.

Wer solches ἰουδαΐζειν betreibt, ist entweder politischer Unterstützer dieser Volksgruppe, hat deren Sitten in den eigenen Lebensstil integriert und/oder beherrscht deren Sprache. Während Bildungen wie ἑλληνίζειν durchaus häufig zu belegen sind[144], erscheint ἰουδαΐζειν in nicht-christlichen Texten nur fünfmal[145], entfaltet aber von Paulus ausgehend eine breite Wirkungsgeschichte in der Auseinandersetzung des beginnenden Christentums mit dem Judentum. Das Moment der Eigenständigkeit in der ethnischen, kulturellen und nicht zuletzt ethischen Identität scheint in dem ἰουδαΐζειν entsprechenden Substantiv noch stärker akzentuiert: Nur einmal in der uns erhaltenen Briefkorrespondenz spricht Paulus dezidiert vom ἰουδαϊσμός als einem unverkennbar jüdischen Lebenswandel, und zwar im Galaterbrief, in der polemischen Auseinandersetzung mit judenchristlichen Gruppierungen, die die Beschneidung nachdrücklich auch für Heidenchristen fordern (Gal 1,13 f.)[146]. Dass Paulus in der scharfen Auseinandersetzung eben auf diese einen jüdischen Lebensstil geradezu maximal definierende Vokabel rekurriert, passt zu deren Geschichte: Die Rede vom ἰουδαϊσμός etabliert sich in der Makkabäerzeit – die Wortbildung dient hier als „Kampfbegriff" gegen den Ἑλληνισμός (2Makk 4,13) der griechischen Eroberer[147]. Und als eine Art Kampfbegriff funktioniert sie zunächst auch in der Argumentation des Galaterbriefs: Wie beinahe immer in den autobiographischen Passagen seiner Briefe (2Kor 11,22; Phil 3,5: Röm 11,1) stellt Paulus auch hier zunächst die Untadeligkeit seiner jüdischen Lebensführung heraus. In diesem Sinne umfasst ἰουδαϊσμός, wie Oda Wischmeyer zusammenfasst, eine „besonders gute und traditionelle Ausbildung", eine „hervorragende Stellung im praktischen Lebensvollzug", „besondere[n] Eifer um die praktische Durchsetzung dieses Lebensvollzugs" und „im Zusammenhang damit

---

144 Vgl. Liddell-Scott zum Lemma.
145 Vgl. Plutarch, Cicero 7,6; Esth LXX 8,17; Gal 2,14; Josephus, Bellum Iudaicum 2,454 und 562. – Entsprechend gebildet ist das bei Josephus, Bellum Iudaicum 6,96 erscheinende ἑβραΐζειν.
146 Einführend: J. Frey, Galaterbrief, in: Paulus. Leben – Umwelt – Werk – Briefe, hg. von O. Wischmeyer, O. (UTB 2767), Tübingen/Basel ²2012, 232–256, sowie: D. Sänger, Literarische Strategien der Polemik im Galaterbrief, in: Polemik in der frühchristlichen Literatur. Texte und Kontexte, hg. von O. Wischmeyer/L. Scornaienchi (BZNW 170), Berlin/New York 2011, 155–181.
147 Vgl. dazu: K.-W. Niebuhr, Heidenapostel aus Israel. Die jüdische Identität des Paulus nach ihrer Darstellung in seinen Briefen (WUNT 62), Tübingen 1992, 21–24. – Wie das Substantiv in Gal 1,13 f. neutestamentliches Hapaxlegomenon bleibt, so sind auch die Belege außerhalb des Neuen Testaments spärlich: 2Makk 2,21; 8,1; 14,38; 4Makk 4,26; alle genannten Stellen betonen aber wiederum das Sich-Abgrenzen von der hellenistischen Kultur der οἰκουμένη bzw. die Eigenständigkeit und Unverwechselbarkeit eines jüdischen Lebensstils.

[die] aktive Bekämpfung der abweichenden Gruppe der ἐκκλησία τοῦ θεοῦ, d.h. der Christengemeinden"[148].

Paulus beruft sich damit auf die Grundeinsichten eines pharisäisch geprägten Judentums: Untadelig jüdisch lebt, wer ὑπὸ νόμον lebt (1Kor 9,20), also in Gesetzeskonformität. Aber: ἰουδαϊσμός, also eine durch und durch jüdische Existenzweise, scheint für Paulus eine weitere Dimension zu besitzen – ebenso wie sich das präpositionale ὑπὸ νόμον aus 1Kor 9,20 vielleicht in einem erweiterten Sinn verstehen lässt. Zu bemerken ist dabei zunächst, dass das Griechische weder eine unserem Religionsbegriff adäquate Vokabel noch einen Ausdruck, der die römisch gedachte Situation der *religio* abzubilden vermag, kennt. Vielmehr stellt die griechische Sprache zur Beschreibung unterschiedlicher Aspekte religiösen Handelns und Erlebens eine ganze Reihe von Begrifflichkeiten zur Verfügung, so etwa θεῶν τιμή, εὐσέβεια, λατρεία oder θρησκεία[149]. Auch νόμος gehört in diese Reihe und dient darin der Benennung einer umfassender gedachten „religiösgesetzlich Ordnung"[150]. Will man diesen Bedeutungsgehalt auch für den Präpositionalausdruck aus 1Kor 9,20 anlegen, dann bedeutete ein „Wandel im ἰουδαϊσμός" mit einem Mal mehr als die Orientierung an den Einzelgeboten der Tora – ἰουδαϊσμός wäre dann nicht weniger als eine Existenzweise, die sich bedingungslos an eine von Gott eingerichtete Welt- und Lebensordnung im umfassenden Sinn zurückgebunden weiß. Paulus scheint von dieser erweiterten Perspektivierung ganz eingenommen, wenn er in Röm 9,4f. seine soziale Bezugsgruppe, seine ἀδελφοί, in Kategorien beschreibt, die sich doch deutlich von den bisher genannten ethnischen, kulturellen und ethischen Attribuierungen unterscheiden und über diese hinausgehen: οἵτινές εἰσιν Ἰσραηλῖται, ὧν ἡ υἱοθεσία καὶ ἡ δόξα καὶ αἱ διαθῆκαι καὶ ἡ νομοθεσία καὶ ἡ λατρεία καὶ αἱ ἐπαγγελίαι, ὧν οἱ πατέρες καὶ ἐξ ὧν ὁ Χριστὸς τὸ κατὰ σάρκα[151]. Die neun Begriffe, die dieser Reihe unterliegen – „Israeliten" (Ἰσραηλῖται), „Sohnschaft" (υἱοθεσία), „Herrlichkeit" (δόξα), „Bundesordnungen" (διαθῆκαι), „Gesetzgebung" (νομοθεσία), „Gottesdienst" (λατρεία), „Verheißungen" (ἐπαγγελίαι), „Väter" (πατέρες), „Jesus als

---

148 O. Wischmeyer, Die Religion des Paulus. Eine Problemanzeige, in: dies., Von Ben Sira zu Paulus. Gesammelte Aufsätze zu Texten, Theologie und Hermeneutik des Frühjudentums und des Neuen Testaments, hg. von E.-M. Becker (WUNT 173), Tübingen 2004, 311–328, hier: 319; ähnlich: K.-W. Niebuhr, Heidenapostel, 23f.; eine detaillierte wortgeschichtliche Untersuchung bietet weiterhin: Y. Amir, Der Begriff ἰουδαϊσμός. Zum Selbstverständnis des hellenistischen Judentums, in: ders., Studien zum antiken Judentum (BEAT 2), Frankfurt am Main 1985, 101–113.
149 Vgl. U. Dierse u.a., Art. Religion, in: HWPh 8 (1992), 632–713, hier: 632, und: O. Wischmeyer, Die Religion des Paulus, hier: 316 Anm. 23.
150 U. Dierse, Art. Religion, 632.
151 Dazu: O. Wischmeyer, Religion, 320.

Jude" (Χριστός)¹⁵² –, lassen sich, wie bereits Walter Schmithals vorschlug, in Dreiergruppen zusammenstellen¹⁵³. Folgt man diesem Vorschlag, können wiederum drei Überbegriffe aus der Reihe herausgelöst werden, die die triadischen Wortgruppen anführen: „Israeliten", „Bundesordnungen", „Verheißungen". In der sprachlich knappest möglichen Form und trotzdem im theologischen Gehalt maximal pointiert umreißen diese drei Überbegriffe die umfassende Lebensordnung, die durch Gottes νόμος eingerichtet ist: Sie legen das „Israelit-Sein" als Grundbedingung „jüdischer" Existenz fest und sehen diese *conditio* wesentlich geprägt von den in Vergangenheit und Gegenwart wirksamen „Bundesordnungen" einerseits und den sich aus diesen „Bundesordnungen" für Gegenwart und Zukunft ergebenden „Verheißungshoffnungen" andererseits. Die beiden Begrifflichkeiten wiederum, die diesen Überbegriffen jeweils zugeordnet sind, entfalten nun diese grundsätzlichen Bestimmungen weiter, und zwar als Beziehungsgeschehen zwischen Gott und Mensch: Das „Israelit-Sein" des Menschen ergibt sich zum einen aus der δόξα des Gottes Israels als einer, wie Klaus Haacker es nennt, abstrakt bleibenden „Größe im Beziehungsfeld Gottes"¹⁵⁴ zu seinem Volk, es manifestiert sich aber zum anderen in der „Sohneswürde" Israels, die in der alttestamentlichen Überlieferung vielfältig betont wird¹⁵⁵. Besonders deutlich wird die Reziprozität des hier entfalteten „Beziehungsgeschehens" im Zusammenhang der Erläuterung des Überbegriffs der „Bundesordnungen": Von Seiten Gottes ist ihm die „Gesetzgebung", von Seiten des Menschen λατρεία, also der „Gottesdienst" als Ausdruck des „Verhältnis[ses] der Gemeinde zu Gott"¹⁵⁶ zugeordnet. Der dritte Überbegriff schließlich, „Verheißungen", rekurriert auf die „Väter" als ihre gewissermaßen „menschlichen Träger" und ihre Erfüllung durch die göttliche Offenbarung in Jesus Christus. „Jüdisch sein" bedeutet damit in der Perspektive des Paulus weit mehr als „unter dem Gesetz sein" im Sinne von korrekter Observanz und ethischer Lebensführung. ὑπὸ νόμον – und damit im ἰουδαϊσμός – lebt, wer sich in der göttlichen Ordnung, konstituiert durch die Erwählung der „Israeliten" und aufrechterhalten durch „Bundesordnungen" und „Verheißungen", aufgehoben weiß. „Judentum" ist so viel mehr als eine politische Größe, eine soziale und religiöse Bezugsgruppe oder Wertegemeinschaft: „Jüdisch" leben mit einem Mal all diejenigen, die ὑπὸ νόμον im umfassendsten Sinn leben, also all diejenigen, die ihre Existenz auf Gott gründen, die – modern ge-

---

152 Zu den Begriffen im Einzelnen vgl. R. Jewett, Romans. A Commentary (Hermeneia), Minneapolis 2007, 561–566.
153 Vgl. W. Schmithals, Der Römerbrief. Ein Kommentar, Gütersloh 1988, 330–333.
154 K. Haacker, Der Brief des Paulus an die Römer (ThHKNT 6), Leipzig 1999, 184.
155 Vgl. Ex 4,22; Jer 31,9.20; Hos 11,1; dazu: K. Haacker, 184.
156 M. Vahrenhorst, Kultische Sprache in den Paulusbriefen (WUNT 230), Tübingen 2008, 240.

sprochen – "eine Religion haben". Die Trennlinie verläuft nicht zwischen ethnischen Gruppierungen, nicht zwischen Ἰουδαῖοι und Ἕλληνες – sie verläuft zwischen denjenigen, die ἐν τῷ Ἰουδαϊσμῷ (Gal 1,13) als "Menschen vor Gott" leben, und denen, „die Gott nicht kennen" (1Thess 4,5: τὰ ἔθνη τὰ μὴ εἰδότα τὸν θεόν). In dieser existenziellen Bestimmtheit wird aus der ethnischen Größe der Ἰουδαῖοι eine Gemeinschaft von besonderer, von religiöser Qualität, die fundamental bestimmt ist von ihrem „Auf-Gott-Bezogen-Sein" – nur in dieser „Beziehung" konstituiert sich „Judentum" in Gänze![157]

3.2 „Israelit", „Benjaminit", „Hebräer von Hebräern" – Paulinisches Vokabular im Erzählen über den Juden Paulus

Wer Jude ist, so erkärt es Paulus in der definitorischen Begriffsreihung aus Röm 9,3f., sieht sich selbst existenziell abhängig vom Gott Israels. Er ist damit im Wesenskern seiner Existenz mehr als das Mitglied einer sozialen Gruppe. In seiner ethnischen Zugehörigkeit mag er als Ἰουδαῖος zu bezeichnen sein – im Vollsinn seiner Existenz ist er „Mensch vor Gott", oder genauer: ein Mitglied des erwählten Volkes Israel im Angesicht seines Gottes[158]. Zu dieser Beobachtung passt, dass Paulus von sich selbst kaum einmal als Ἰουδαῖος spricht[159]. sondern eine Selbstbezeichnung wählt, die mehr beschreibt als die ethnische Zugehörigkeit: An prominenten Stellen seiner Briefkorrespondenz stellt Paulus sich als Ἰσραηλίτης (Röm 11,1; 2Kor 11,22) vor. Diese Attribuierung übersteigt jede „Nationalitätsbezeichnung"![160] „Israel" ist ein von Grund auf sakraler Begriff [161], der schon bald mehr umfasst als den Zwölf-Stämme-Bund, dessen Gründung Jos 24 erzählt. „Israel" – das ist die „Ganzheit der von Jahwe Erwählten und der zum Jahwekultus

---

157 Und nur aus dieser „Beziehung" lässt sich die „politisch" anmutende Forderung (vgl. H.D. Betz, Der Galaterbrief. Ein Kommentar zum Brief des Apostels Paulus an die Gemeinden in Galatien. Ein Hermeneia-Kommentar, München 1988, 333–339), die Paulus in Gal 3,28 erhebt, ableiten: οὐκ ἔνι Ἰουδαῖος οὐδὲ Ἕλλην, οὐκ ἔνι δοῦλος οὐδὲ ἐλεύθερος, οὐκ ἔνι ἄρσεν καὶ θῆλυ·πάντες γὰρ ὑμεῖς εἷς ἐστε ἐν Χριστῷ Ἰησοῦ. Denn nur aus diesem „Auf-Gott-Bezogen-Sein" kann eine neue, die sozialen Verhältnisse übersteigende Realität entstehen.
158 Zu dieser grundsätzlichen Dimension paulinischer Anthropologie vgl. O. Wischmeyer, Neues Testament, in: Menschsein. Perspektiven des Alten und Neuen Testaments, hg. von C. Frevel/O. Wischmeyer (Die Neue Echter Bibel – Themen 11), Würzburg 2003, 105f.
159 Vgl. A. Lindemann, Der Erste Korintherbrief (HNT 9/1), Tübingen 2000, 212; Ausnahmen sind etwa Gal 2,15 und 1Kor 9,20.
160 K. Haacker, Brief des Paulus, 183.
161 Dazu: G. von Rad, Art. Ἰσραήλ κτλ. A. Israel, Juda, Hebräer im AT, in: ThWNT 3 (1938), 356–359, hier: 356.

Vereinten"¹⁶². Anders als „Juda" ist „Israel" nie nur ein „profaner Stammesname"¹⁶³, sondern bleibt auch nach dem Untergang der beiden Königreiche als wirkmächtige Idee erhalten, die sowohl alle Glaubensinhalte des erwählten Volkes in sich trägt, als auch weiterhin „Gegenstand der Hoffnung auf eine eschatologische Heilstat Gottes"¹⁶⁴ ist. Wenn Paulus in der Auseinandersetzung mit gegnerischen Wanderaposteln in 2Kor 11,22 die Selbstbezeichnung Ἰσραηλίτης wählt, bringt er damit, wie Karl-Wilhelm Niebuhr formuliert, „bekenntnishaft zum Ausdruck, daß die in der Vergangenheit des Gottesvolkes diesem von Gott verheißenen und eingestifteten Heilsgüter [...] die den Träger dieses Namens auch gegenwärtig in seinem religiösen Selbstverständnis bestimmenden Werte sind"¹⁶⁵. Der Stolz auf die besondere Erwählung des Gottesvolkes übersteht alle Krisen der Geschichte Israels: Das Bekenntnis zum Bund mit Gott, dessen sichtbares Zeichen die Beschneidung ist (vgl. Gen 17,13 bzw. im Neuen Testament: Röm 3,1; 4,11; Apg 7,8), verbindet die Mitglieder des Volkes Israel ebenso bleibend miteinander wie der Bezug auf die gemeinsame Abstammung vom „national-religiösen Heros¹⁶⁶ dieses Volkes: Abraham!¹⁶⁷ Auch sie nimmt Paulus für sich in Anspruch und übernimmt damit vielleicht eine Wendung der von ihm kritisierten „Pseudoapostel"¹⁶⁸. Entgegen dem Vorwurf der Gegner betont er entschlossen seine Blutsverwandtschaft mit dem wichtigsten Empfänger der Verheißungen Gottes und dem vorbildlichen Träger des Bundes (Gen 11ff.), der noch in der frühjüdischen (Philo, De Abrahamo 184) und frühchristlichen (Hebr 11,4–12) Literatur als Beispiel von Frömmigkeit und Glaubensstärke gilt¹⁶⁹. Auch Paulus selbst nutzt die Identifikationsfigur Abraham mehrmals zur theologischen Argumentation, nämlich als Vorbild für „Rechtfertigung aus dem Glauben" (Röm 4,1; Gal 3,6). Wenn Paulus hier in der Selbstvorstellung aber von seiner eigenen Abrahamskindschaft

---

162 G. von Rad, Art. Ἰσραήλ κτλ., 357.
163 Ebd.
164 G. von Rad, Art. Ἰσραήλ κτλ., 358.
165 K.-W. Niebuhr, Heidenapostel, 131. Vgl. auch: J. Gnilka, Der Philipperbrief (HthK X/3), Freiburg 1968, 189, sowie: C. Wolff, Der zweite Brief des Paulus an die Korinther (ThHK VIII), Berlin 1989, 230 f.
166 J. Jeremias, Art. Ἀβραάμ, in: THWNT 1 (1933), 7–9, hier: 7.
167 PsSal 9,17; 3Makk 6,3 u.ö.; vgl. Jeremias, 8 Anm. 4.
168 Vgl. E. Grässer, Der zweite Brief an die Korinther. Kapitel 8,1–13,13 (ÖTK 8/2), Gütersloh 2005, 159.
169 Zur ungebrochenen Betonung der Abrahamskindschaft im Neuen Testament vgl. O. Wischmeyer, Abraham unser Vater. Aspekte der Abrahamsgestalt im Neuen Testament, in: Deuterocanonical und Cognate Literature. Yearbook 2008: Biblical Figures in Deuterocanonical and Cognate Literature, ed. by H. Lichtenberger/U. Mittmann-Richert, Berlin/New York 2009, 567–585.

spricht, dann betont er dabei wieder, was schon die Selbstbezeichnung als Ἰσραηλίτης herausstellt: Paulus ist durch die Verwandtschaft mit Abraham und ihr körperliches Zeichen, die Beschneidung (Phil 3,5!), hineingenommen in die ältesten Verheißungen des Gottesvolkes, er hat Anteil an der Heilsgeschichte des Volkes Israel mit seinem Gott[170].

Wie Abraham als Stammvater des Volkes aber zugleich den Bezug zur ältesten Geschichte Israels herstellt, so stiftet in der Argumentation von 2Kor 11,22 der Verweis auf die Herkunft des Paulus als Ἑβραῖος (vgl. wiederum Phil 3,5) diesen Bezug[171]. Der Verweis ist als Statement eines Diasporajuden zu lesen, der sich nicht von den Traditionen des Mutterlands losgesagt hat, sondern sich zur „religiöse[n] und kulturelle[n] Eigenart des Judentums" bekennt, „die sich u. a. in der Kenntnis der hebräischen bzw. aramäischen Sprache äußert"[172]. Paulus betont damit seine „Zugehörigkeit zum Gottesvolk der alten Zeit"[173], eine Zugehörigkeit, die sich nicht nur, wie das Motiv der Abrahamskindschaft, auf Genealogie und Abstammung bezieht, sondern diesmal auf konkreten kulturellen Kompetenzen, mithin der Kenntnis der hebräischen Sprache, beruht.

Beide Momente bringt Paulus schließlich in Phil 3,5 in Anschlag, wenn er zudem von seiner Herkunft aus dem *Stamm Benjamin* spricht[174]. Er zeigt damit nicht nur, dass er aus einer traditionsreichen Familie stammt[175], die ihre Geschichte bis in die Vorzeit zurückverfolgen kann. Paulus stellt mit dieser Information auch sein eigenes Geschichtsbewusstsein heraus und zeigt, dass er dem Erbe seines nach dem jüngsten Sohn Jakobs (Gen 35,18) benannten Stammes, der trotz der bescheidenen Größe seines Gebietes mehrere Male in der Geschichte Israels bedeutsam wurde, verpflichtet ist.

Wie Paulus in Röm 9,3f. die Grundkonstituenten des ἰουδαϊσμός in eine Reihe von neun Begrifflichkeiten gefasst hatte, so fasst er in 2Kor 11,22 und Phil 3,5 seine eigene Existenz wiederum in knappen, von disktinkten Begrifflichkeiten getragenen Reihungen zusammen:

---

170 Vgl. K.-W. Niebuhr, Heidenapostel, 132, sowie: E. Grässer, Korinther, 160.
171 Vgl. J. Wanke, Art. Ἑβραῖος, ου, ὁ, in: EWNT² 1 (1980), 892ff., sowie: K. Koch, Art. Hebräer, in: RGG⁴ 3 (2000), 1493f.
172 C. Wolff, Korinther, 230, ähnlich: K.-W. Niebuhr, Heidenapostel, 106f., sowie: E. Grässer, Korinther,159.
173 M. Wolter, Paulus, 441.
174 Vgl. K.-D., Schunck, Art. Benjamin, in: ABD 1 (1992), 671–673; zum Stamm Benjamin in der alttestamentlichen Überlieferung vgl. 1Sam 9,1–2.21; 10,20f.; 2Sam 21,14; Jer 1,1; Jos 18,26; Neh 3,15.19.
175 Vgl. Hengel, M., Der vorchristliche Paulus, in: ders./Heckel, U. (Hgg.), Paulus und das antike Judentum, WUNT 58, Tübingen 1991, 177–293. 222.

περιτομῇ ὀκταήμερος, ἐκ γένους Ἰσραήλ, φυλῆς Βενιαμίν, Ἑβραῖος ἐξ Ἑβραίων, κατὰ νόμον Φαρισαῖος (Phil 3,5).
Ἑβραῖοί εἰσιν; κἀγώ. Ἰσραηλῖταί εἰσιν; κἀγώ. σπέρμα Ἀβραάμ εἰσιν; κἀγώ (1Kor 11,22).

Beide Äußerungen stehen in polemischem Kontext und mögen zunächst – wie bereits unter 3.1 für die Untadeligkeit der Lebensführung des Paulus im Sinne des ἰουδαϊσμός herausgestellt – „seine makellose jüdische Herkunft und Abstammung"[176] und so weiterhin seine unbestreitbare genealogische, kulturelle und religiöse Zugehörigkeit zum Judentum darstellen. Paulus ist sich seiner „jüdischen" Existenz gewiss. Dies demonstriert er durch die Hinweise auf

(1) seine Abkunft – er gehört dem Volk Israel, genauer: dem Stamm Benjamin, an, kann sich selbst zu den Nachkommen Abrahams zählen und ist beschnitten,

(2) seine kulturelle Prägung – er hat über die Kenntnis der hebräischen Sprache Zugang zu den ältesten Überlieferung seines Volkes und bekennt sich auch in der Situation der Diaspora zu ihnen,

(3) seine religiös-ethische Orientierung – als Pharisäer repräsentiert er jüdische Lebenspraxis mustergültig.

Bei all dem lässt er sich zunächst auf die verkürzte Perspektive, die er den Gegnern in ihrer Definition von „Judentum" offensichtlich unterstellt, ein. Wenn sich für sie „Judentum" über Abkunft, Sozialisation und Ethos konstituiert, dann kann Paulus – wie er in 2Kor 11,22 rhetorisch entschlossen belegt – jede dieser Kategorien mustergültig erfüllen. Und doch kommt es darauf nicht an! Die Erschließungsgrößen, die Paulus zur Vorstellung seiner selbst wählt, beziehen sich allesamt auf eine Wirklichkeit, die jenseits aller ethnischen, sozialen oder kulturellen Zuordnung liegt. Sie alle sind Dimensionen des „Israelit-Seins", das als Formel für eine Art „jüdische *conditio humana*" schon die Begriffsreihe in Röm 9,3 eröffnet hatte, und münden so wiederum in die grundsätzlichste anthropologische Perspektive des Paulus. Wenn er über sich selbst als „Jude" spricht, dann geschieht das in einer tiefen „religiöse[n] Selbstaussage"[177] vom „Menschen vor Gott", der durch die Abrahamskindschaft und die Beschneidung in die Heilsgeschichte mit hineingenommen ist. In dieser Selbstaussage ist allerdings bereits die Überzeugung enthalten, dass „Judentum", ἰουδαϊσμός, eine *allgemeine* anthropologische Möglichkeit ist, die Wirklichkeiten jenseits aller ethnischen, politischen und sozialen Realitäten erschließt. Alle Identitätszuschreibungen, die auf diese Realitäten beschränkt bleiben, greifen für Paulus zu kurz, wie er in Bezug auf

---

[176] K.-W. Niebuhr, Heidenapostel, 105–107, hier: 105, sowie – zu Phil 3,5: W. Gutbrod, Art. Ἰσραήλ, in: ThWNT 3 (1938), 357–394, 393, mit: J.B. Lightfoot, Saint Paul's Epistle to the Philippians, 1903, zur Stelle.
[177] K.G. Kuhn, ThWNT 3, 361.

ein wesentliches, gewöhnlich körperliches Merkmal des „Israelit-Seins" herausstellt: οὐ γὰρ ὁ ἐν τῷ φανερῷ Ἰουδαῖός ἐστιν οὐδὲ ἡ ἐν τῷ φανερῷ ἐν σαρκὶ περιτομή, 29 ἀλλ' ὁ ἐν τῷ κρυπτῷ Ἰουδαῖος, καὶ περιτομὴ καρδίας ἐν πνεύματι οὐ γράμματι, οὗ ὁ ἔπαινος οὐκ ἐξ ἀνθρώπων ἀλλ' ἐκ τοῦ θεοῦ (Röm 2,28)[178].

3.3 Der Mensch, Israel und Christus – paulinisches Vokabular zur Beschreibung der Heilswirklichkeit Gottes

Die Überlegungen des Paulus zum ἰουδαϊσμός als einer allgemeinmenschlichen Möglichkeit von Existenz vor Gott werden im Römerbrief weiter intensiviert. Dass sein theologisches Nachdenken im Übrigen tatsächlich ganz von der Perspektive „der Mensch vor Gott" geprägt ist, zeigt ein Blick auf die Wortstatistik zum Römerbrief exemplarisch: Die in diesem längsten Schreiben des Apostels am häufigsten verwendeten Nomina sind: θεός und ἐγώ[179]. Dieses ἐγώ ist dabei ebenso generisch wie die Anreden im Römerbrief überhaupt: ὦ ἄνθρωπε (Röm 2,1; 9,20), Ἰουδαῖος (Röm 2,17), σύ (Röm 11,17–24). Zu dieser Kommunikationssituation passt die theologische Grundeinsicht, die hier formuliert wird: Nach Röm 1,16f. kann das Evangelium seine soteriologische Kraft an allen Menschen entfalten[180]. Der Zug zum Universellen, der sich in der paulinischen Haltung zu den ethnischen Kategorisierungen der ihn umgebenden sozialen Wirklichkeit bereits abzeichnete (Gal 3,28), setzt sich hier konsequent fort: Die Trennlinie verläuft nun endgültig, wie bereits skizziert, nicht mehr zwischen Juden und Nichtjuden. „Neuer Oberbegriff" ist der Mensch als πιστεύων, also wiederum „der Mensch vor Gott"[181]. So ist es nur folgerichtig, dass endgültig eine Ausweitung des Bundesnomismus auf Nichtjuden stattfindet, und zwar sowohl im Hinblick auf die Gesetzeserfüllung als auch die Beschneidung (Röm 2,11–16; 2,17–24). Damit können sich nun auch Nichtjuden auf die Abrahamskindschaft berufen (Röm 4,1.12; 9,7f.; Gal 3,7.9.29; 4,22ff.)[182]. Abraham ist der „Vater vieler Völker" (Röm 4,18) – über die Verwandtschaft mit ihm werden auch Nichtjuden Mitglieder des erwählten λαὸς θεοῦ.

---

178 So ist wohl auch Gal 6,16 zu verstehen.
179 Vgl. O. Wischmeyer, Römerbrief, in: Paulus. Leben – Umwelt – Werk – Briefe, hg. von O. Wischmeyer (UTB 2767), Tübingen/Basel ²2012, 281–314, hier: 290 Anm. 26: Innerhalb des Römerbriefes gibt es 153 Belege für Formen von θεός und 90 für ἐγώ; dieser Befund deckt sich mit dem für das Corpus Paulinum insgesamt: θεός ist auch insgesamt mit 548 Belegen das am häufigsten gebrauchte Nomen, ἐγώ und ἡμεῖς folgen mit 397 Belegen an zweiter Stelle.
180 Vgl. O. Wischmeyer, Römerbrief, 299.
181 O. Wischmeyer, Römerbrief, 300.
182 Dazu: M. Konradt, „Die aus Glauben, diese sind Abrahams Kinder", 25–48.

Auch Nichtjuden ist es also möglich, die eigene Existenz so an Gott zurückzubinden, wie es dem ἰουδαϊσμός entspricht: Dem Vorbild Abrahams folgend können sie ihr Dasein ganz als κατέναντι θεοῦ (Röm 4,17), ganz als Dasein des „Menschen vor Gott" deuten. Auch Nichtjuden erhalten also Anteil an den bleibenden Heilsgütern des Gottesvolkes, die in der Begriffsreihung von Röm 9,3 genannt wurden: Zuerst werden sie Ἰσραηλῖται, d. h. sie sind nun ganz hineingenommen in das Beziehungsgeschehen zwischen Gott und Mensch, das die Begriffsreihe aus Röm 9,3–5 – wie oben gezeigt – entfaltet. So wie den Nichtjuden aber das „Israelit-Sein" als Möglichkeit einer menschlichen Existenz vor Gott abseits der Bundeszeichen von Gesetzeserfüllung und Beschneidung offen steht, eröffnet sich zugleich eine neue Heilsmöglichkeit, die in der Reihe der Heilsgüter Israel bereits genannt ist, ja sie sogar beschließt und damit in besonderer Weise mit dem „Israelit-Sein" als Existenzform des religiösen Menschen, das in der Reihe der Heilsgüter an erster Stelle steht, korrespondiert: der Glaube an Jesus Christus (Röm 3,22; 9,5).

ἰουδαϊσμός wurde im Laufe der vorliegenden Überlegungen als eine „religiöse Existenzform" bestimmt, als die Deutung des eigenen Daseins als eines „Menschen vor Gott". Verändert nun – so fragt letztlich auch Paulus in Röm 11,1 – Jesus Christus als neue Heilsmöglichkeit die *conditio* dieser Existenzform? Wenn es stimmt, dass die paulinischen Überlegungen zum Wesen von ἰουδαϊσμός von einer grundsätzlichen Perspektivierung, nämlich der Perspektive des „Menschen vor Gott", geprägt werden, dann lässt sich das paulinische Bekenntnis: πᾶς Ἰσραὴλ σωθήσεται (Röm 11,26), folgendermaßen lesen[183]: „Natürlich" wird ganz Israel gerettet, denn die Existenzform des „Israelit-Seins" beschreibt als primäres Heilsgut des Gottesvolkes Israel genau dieses Versprechen: Wer „Israelit" ist – wer sich also selbst zutiefst als „Mensch vor Gott" sieht! –, bleibt in die transzendente Wirklichkeit, die im Gott des Volkes Israel gründet, hineingenommen – auch wenn sich diese transzendente Wirklichkeit „in Christus" neu gestaltet (vgl. Gal 6,15; Röm 2,29; 2Kor 11,17; Gal 5,6). Für den Menschen, der den ἰουδαϊσμός als Existenzform ernst nimmt, bleibt die Rückbindung an diese Heilswirklichkeit selbstverständlich ununterbrochen: ἐγὼ Ἰσραηλίτης εἰμί, ἐκ σπέρματος Ἀβραάμ – so spricht am Ende nicht „der Jude Paulus" – so spricht ein „Mensch vor Gott"[184].

---

[183] Die zahlreiche Literatur dazu bei: M. Wolter, Das Israelproblem nach Gal 4,21–23 und Röm 9–11, in: ZThK 107 (2010), 1–30. Die Diskussion im Einzelnen kann hier nicht wiederholt werden. Dazu auch: E.W. Stegemann, Zur „apokalyptischen" Rekonstruktion einer kollektiven Identität bei Paulus, in: ders., Der Römerbrief: Brennpunkte der Rezeption, ausgewählt und hg. von C. Tuor und P. Wick, Zürich 2012, 89–120.
[184] Vgl. R. Jewett, Romans, zur Stelle: „Paul's concern is with Israel's identity as determined by God, not with Jewish identity by contrast with the identity of other nations".

3.4 Erzählen vom Judentum in den Paulusbriefen? – „Erzählen vom Menschen vor Gott"

Man kann dem Briefschriftsteller Paulus für zahlreiche Passagen seiner Schreiben ein autodiegetisches Konzept im Sinne Gérard Genettes zuordnen[185]: Denn Autodiegese liegt nach Genette vor, wenn der Erzähler selbst die beherrschende Figur der Erzählung ist. Dies gilt zumal für die oben besprochenen autobiographischen Passagen, in denen Paulus natürlich Aspekte seiner Biographie thematisiert: Paulus erzählt vom „Juden Paulus", der sich seiner sozialen Bezugsgruppe verbunden weiß, der deren Werte teilt und der sich kompetent innerhalb dieser sozialen Bezugsgruppe bewegen kann. Aber: Das „Ich" des Erzählers, das diese Texte trägt, behält trotz der biographischen Grundierung immer einen Zug zum Generischen.

Gewissermaßen „ex negativo" ist dies für die Röm 7,7–13[186] und die dort vorliegende drastische Beschreibung der Situation des Menschen unter dem Gesetz festzustellen: In fast „dramatischer" Art und Weise „schreit" hier ein generisches Ich sein der Sünde und dem Tod Verfallen-Sein heraus. – Es ist das generische Ich, das sich in Röm 11,11, als Erbe der Verheißung und als Nachkomme Abrahams ganz in das „Volk Gottes" und seine Heilswirklichkeit aufgenommen weiß: καὶ γὰρ ἐγὼ Ἰσραηλίτης εἰμί, ἐκ σπέρματος Ἀβραάμ.

„Erzählen vom Menschen im ἰουδαϊσμός" – das bedeutet für die Paulusbriefe zweierlei: Der Mensch, der hier von seiner religiösen Situation in der Ich-Form erzählt, ist natürlich Paulus, und damit ist sein „Erzählen vom Judentum" ganz unmittelbar ein „Erzählen über den Juden Paulus". Und trotzdem erschöpft sich seine Narration darin nicht: Dadurch, dass Paulus, der Ἰσραηλίτης, sich selbst ausschließlich im Gegenüber zu seinem Gott, dem Gott Israels, positioniert, wie es diese Selbstbeschreibung ganz bedingungslos verlangt, dieses „Israelit-Sein" für ihn aber zugleich eine grundsätzliche religiöse Situation, eine allgemein-

---

[185] Vgl. G. Genette, Die Erzählung (UTB 8083), München 1998², hier: 176 ff., dazu: O. Wischmeyer, Paulus als Ich-Erzähler. Ein Beitrag zu seiner Person, seiner Biographie und seiner Theologie, in: Biographie und Persönlichkeit des Paulus, hg. von E.-M. Becker und P. Pilhofer (WUNT 187), Tübingen 2005, 88–105, hier: 103.

[186] Vgl. dazu jetzt J. Schröter, Der Mensch zwischen Wollen und Tun. Erwägungen zu Römer 7 im Licht der „New Perspective on Paul", in: Paulus – Werk und Wirkung. FS für Andreas Lindemann zum 70. Geburtstag. Hg. von P.-G. Klumbies und D.S. du Toit, Tübingen 2013, 195–223 (Lit. zur Forschungsgeschichte und zum Forschungsstand). Schröter spricht im Anschluss an O. Hofius und K. Haacker von einem „der schwierigsten [Texte] des Briefes und vielleicht der Theologie des Paulus überhaupt" (S. 198). – Im vorliegenden Beitrag wird Röm 7 vom *literarischen* Aspekt her wahrgenommen. Ein Beitrag zur theologischen Einordnung soll nicht geleistet werden.

menschliche Möglichkeit des „Sich-auf-Gott-Beziehens" beinhaltet, können seine Beobachtungen zu den Grundstrukturen von ἰουδαϊσμός mehr werden als „religiöse Selstbetrachtung". Paulus erzählt von dem „Judentum", das er erlebt und von dem er überzeugt ist, als einer Möglichkeit und Bedingung des Menschseins zugleich: Er erzählt vom „Menschen vor Gott".

4 „Erzählen vom Judentum" im Markusevangelium und in den Paulusbriefen – „Heilsgeschichte Erzählen"

Wollte man abschließend nun doch eine „Erzählung vom Judentum" aus den Begrifflichkeiten, in denen Paulus das Phänomen „Judentum" in seinen argumentierenden Texten zu erfassen sucht, herausarbeiten, wäre der Protagonist dieser „Erzählung" deutlich zu bestimmen: Es ist „der Mensch" unter den spezifischen Bedingungen seiner Existenz, dem das Nachdenken des Paulus gilt. Oder genauer: Protagonist einer solchen Erzählung ist der Mensch ἐν τῷ Ἰουδαϊσμῷ, der sich selbst – losgelöst von ethnischen, kulturellen oder sozialen Zuschreibungen – als „Mensch vor Gott" versteht. Diese radikale Konzentration entbindet ihn aber natürlich nicht von den Lebensrealitäten, die zumindest den Ort dieser Erzählung vorgeben: Es ist dies die οἰκουμένη des östlichen Mittelmeerraums, es sind dies die Städte in den östlichen Provinzen des *imperium Romanum*, in denen Paulus als Jude in der Diaspora, als Mitglied des ἔθνος der Juden lebt und wirkt. Trotzdem: Diese Situierung bleibt blass. Der Skopus der Erzählung liegt so stark auf deren Protagonisten, nämlich dem „Menschen vor Gott", dass andere Verortungen, etwa im Hinblick auf ethnische Zugehörigkeiten und kulturelle oder ethisch-moralische Prägungen, dahinter deutlich zurücktreten müssen. Dies gilt ebenso für den dritten konstituierenden Parameter einer Erzählung: die Zeit. Paulus kann in seiner Erzählung vom Judentum die Weite der Vergangenheit von der Schöpfung über die Zeit Abrahams im Blick haben, aber auch ganz fokussiert sein auf das νῦν der gegenwärtigen Heilszeit, die durch das Kommen Jesu Christi begonnen hat (vgl. Gal 4,4). Für die paulinische Erzählung vom Judentum wirklich relevant ist dabei nur eine Bestimmung: „Zeit ist immer Gottes Zeit mit den Menschen"[187].

Die „Erzählung vom Judentum", die sich aus der Makroerzählung des Markusevangeliums heraus rekonstruieren lässt, erscheint in ihren Realien in gewisser Weise komplementär zur „Erzählsituation" der Paulusbriefe: Steht hier der

---

187 Vgl. den Beitrag von Oda Wischmeyer im vorliegenden Band.

„Mensch", exemplifiziert am Juden Paulus, als Protagonist im Mittelpunkt der Erzählung, ist der Akteur dort „das Judentum" als ethnische, kulturelle und ethische Gemeinschaft, repräsentiert durch seine gesellschaftlichen und religiösen Gruppierungen. Hat die „Erzählung vom Judentum" bei Paulus ihren Ort in der Diaspora mit den spezifischen Herausforderungen, die sich daraus ergeben, so erzählt das Markusevangelium vom Judentum in seinem Mutterland, einer durch und durch jüdisch geprägten Landschaft. Wo Paulus die ganze Weite der „Menschheitsgeschichte", von Adam bis zum Kommen Christi in den Blick nehmen kann, ist die „Erzählung vom Judentum" im Markusevangelium ganz konzentriert auf den einen Moment in der Zeit, den καιρός.

Gerade an dieser Stelle wird deutlich, inwiefern die beiden „Erzählungen vom Judentum", die hier nachvollzogen werden sollten, nicht nur komplementär sind, sondern grundlegende Gemeinsamkeiten haben. Beide Erzählungen können Faktisches darbieten, können, wie es oben genannt wurde, „Realien der Erzählsituation" benennen oder zumindest auf Realien rückschließen lassen. Beide Erzählungen rechnen aber konsequent auch mit einer transzendenten Wirklichkeit, die das Erzählte trägt und jederzeit verändern kann. Mehr noch: Der Skopus beider Erzählungen liegt immer auf dieser transzendenten Wirklichkeit – und er ließe sich zwischen beiden Erzählungen austauschen. Mit dem Geschehen im καιρός, dem die „Erzählung vom Judentum", wie sie im Markusevangelium begegnet, gewidmet ist, rechnet auch Paulus jederzeit – auch er sieht – wie der Verfasser des Markusevangeliums – „die Zeit" als „erfüllt": ὅτε δὲ ἦλθεν τὸ πλήρωμα τοῦ χρόνου, ἐξαπέστειλεν ὁ θεὸς τὸν υἱὸν αὐτοῦ (Gal 4,4; vgl. Mk 1,15: πεπλήρωται ὁ καιρός). Der Verfasser des Markusevangeliums wiederum könnte jederzeit die Perspektive, unter der die gesamte „Erzählung vom Judentum", wie sie sich aus den Paulusbriefen wiedergeben lässt, steht, teilen: „Der Mensch vor Gott" – das ist doch die Situation „im καιρός", also die Situation des maximalen Eingreifens Gottes in die Geschichte.

Letztlich wiederholen Paulus und der Verfasser des Markusevangeliums, wenn sie vom Judentum erzählen, die *eine* große Erzählung des Judentums: Sie erzählen von der Heilsgeschichte des Gottesvolkes – einmal, indem der *eine* Moment der Heilsgeschichte, der καιρός, literarisch gestaltet wird, einmal, indem das Heilshandeln Gottes am Menschen exemplarisch dargeboten wird.

Literatur

Adam, J., „Der Anfang vom Ende" oder „das Ende des Anfangs". Perspektiven der markinischen Eschatologie anhand der Leidensankündigungen Jesu, in: Eschatologie – Eschatology. The Sixth Durham-Tübingen Research Symposium: Eschatology in Old Testament, Ancient Judaism and Early Christianity (Tübingen, September, 2009), hg. von H.J. Eckstein/C. Landmesser/H. Lichtenberger (WUNT 272), Tübingen 2011, 91–124.
Ådna, J., Jerusalemer Tempel und Tempelmarkt im 1. Jahrhundert n.Chr. (ADPV 25), Wiesbaden 1999.
Aland, K. (Hg.), Vollständige Konkordanz zum griechischen Neuen Testament, Berlin/New York 1983
Allison, D.C., Art. Kingdom of God, in: The Eerdmans Dictionary of Early Judaism, ed. by J.J. Collins/D.C. Harlow, Grand Rapids/Cambridge 2010, 860 f.
Amir, Y., Der Begriff Ιουδαϊσμός. Zum Selbstverständnis des hellenistischen Judentums, in: ders., Studien zum antiken Judentum (BEAT 2), Frankfurt am Main 1985, 101–113.
Avemarie, F., Art. Reich Gottes, II. Antikes Judentum, in: RGG⁴ 7 (2004), 203 f.
Backhaus, K., Echoes from the Wilderness. The Historical John the Baptist, in: Handbook for the Study of the Historical Jesus, ed. by T. Holmén/S.E. Porter, Volume 2: The Study of Jesus, Leiden/Boston 2011, 1747–1785.
Barker, M., The Gate of Heaven. The History and Symbolism of the Temple in Jerusalem, London 1991.
Baumgarten, A.I., Art. Pharisäer, in: RGG⁴ 6 (2003), 1262 f.
Becker, E.-M., Elija redivivus im Markus-Evangelium? Zur Typologisierung von Wiederkehr-Vorstellungen, in: Deuterocanonical und Cognate Literature. Yearbook 2008: Biblical Figures in Deuterocanonical and Cognate Literature, ed. by H. Lichtenberger/U. Mittmann-Richert, Berlin/New York 2009, 587–625.
—, Mark 1:1 and the Debate on a ‚Markan Prologue', in: Filologia Neotestamentaria 22 (2009), 91–106.
Betz, O., Art. ioudaizo, Ioudaikws, Ioudaismos, ou, o, in: EWNT² 2 (1981), 470–472
Bloch, R., Art. Misanthropia, in: RAC 24 (2012), 840–842.
Buber, M., Königtum Gottes, Heidelberg ³1956.
Camponovo, O., Königtum, Königsherrschaft und Reich Gottes in den frühjüdischen Schriften (Orbis biblicus et orientalis 58), Göttingen/Freiburg, Schweiz 1984.
Charlesworth, J.H./Aviam, M., Überlegungen zur Erforschung Galiläas im ersten Jahrhundert, in: Jesus und die Archäologie Galiläas, hg. von C. Claußen/J. Frey (BThS 87), Neukirchen-Vluyn 2008, 93–127.
Claußen, C., Jesus und die Versammlungen Galiläas. Zur Frage nach der Bedeutung von ἡ συναγωγή, in: Jesus und die Archäologie Galiläas, hg. von C. Claußen/J. Frey (BThS 87), Neukirchen-Vluyn 2008, 226–244.
Cohen, S.J.D., Art. Ioudaios, in: The Eerdmans Dictionary of Early Judaism, ed. by J.J. Collins/D.C. Harlow, Grand Rapids/Cambridge 2010, 769.
—, Art. Judaizing, in: The Eerdmans Dictionary of Early Judaism, ed. by J.J. Collins/D.C. Harlow, Grand Rapids/Cambridge 2010, 847 f.
Collins, J.J., Daniel (Hermeneia), Minneapolis 1993.
—, Seers, Sibyls and Sages in Hellenistic-Roman Judaism, Boston/Leiden 2001.

—, The Son of Man in Ancient Judaism, in: Handbook for the Study of the Historical Jesus, ed. by T. Holmén/S.E. Porter, Volume 2: The Study of Jesus, Leiden/Boston 2011, 1545–1568.
Collins Yarbro, A., Mark (Hermeneia), Minneapolis 2007.
—, The Influence of Daniel on the New Testament, in: J.J. Collins, Daniel, 90–105.
—, /Collins, J.J., King and Messiah as Son of God. Divine, Human, and Angelic Messianic Figures in Biblical and Related Literatur, Grand Rapids/Cambridge 2008.
Cullmann, O., Christus und die Zeit. Die urchristliche Zeit- und Geschichtsauffassung, durchgesehene Auflage, mit einem „Rückblick auf die Wirkung des Buches in der Theologie der Nachkriegszeit", Zürich 1962.
Deines, R., Art. Pharisees, in: The Eerdmans Dictionary of Early Judaism, ed. by J.J. Collins/D.C. Harlow, Grand Rapids/Cambridge 2010, 1061–1063.
—, Die Pharisäer und das Volk im Neuen Testament und bei Josephus, in: Josephus und das Neue Testament, hg. von C. Böttrich und J. Herzer unter Mitarbeit von T. Reiprich (WUNT 209), Tübingen 2007, 147–180.
—, Die Pharisäer. Ihr Verständnis im Spiegel der christlichen und jüdischen Forschung seit Wellhausen und Graetz (WUNT 101), Tübingen 1997.
—, Galiläa und Jesus. Anfragen zur Funktion der Herkunftsbezeichnung „Galiläa" in der neueren Jesusforschung, in: Jesus und die Archäologie Galiläas, hg. von C. Claußen/J. Frey (BThS 87), Neukirchen-Vluyn 2008, 271–320.
—, The Pharisees Between „Judaisms" and the „Common Judaism", in: Jusitfication and Variegated Nomism. Volume I: The Complexities of Second Temple Judaism, ed. by D.A. Carson/P.T. O'Brien/M.A. Seifrid (WUNT II.140), Göttingen 2001, 443–504.
Delling, G., Das Zeitverständnis des Neuen Testaments, Gütersloh 1940.
—, Zeit und Endzeit. Zwei Vorlesungen zur Theologie des Neuen Testaments, Neukirchen-Vluyn 1970.
Dewey, D., The Historical Jesus in the Gospel of Mark, in: Handbook for the Study of the Historical Jesus, ed. by T. Holmén/S.E. Porter, Volume 3: The Historical Jesus, Leiden/Boston 2011, 1821–1852.
Dierse, U. u. a., Art. Religion, in: HWPh 8 (1992), 632–713.
Doering, L., Art. Sabbat, II. Judentum, in: RGG^4 7 (2004), 713f.
—, Much Ado about Nothing? Jesus' Sabbath Healings and their Halakhic Implications Revisited, in: Judaistik und neutestamentliche Wissenschaft. Standorte – Grenzen – Beziehungen, hg. von L. Doering/H.-G. Waubke/F. Wilk (FRLANT 226), Göttingen 2008, 217–241.
—, Schabbat. Sabbathalacha und -praxis im antiken Judentum und Urchristentum (TSAJ 78), Tübingen 1999.
Du Toit, D., Der abwesende Herr. Strategien im Markusevangelium zur Bewältigung der Abwesenheit des Auferstandenen (WMANT 111), Neukirchen-Vluyn 2006.
Evans, C.A., Prophet, Sage, Healer, Messiah, and Martyr. Types and Identities of Jesus, in: Handbook for the Study of the Historical Jesus, ed. by T. Holmén/S.E. Porter, Volume 2: The Study of Jesus, Leiden/Boston 2011, 1217–1243.
Falk, D.K., Art. Sabbath, in: The Eerdmans Dictionary of Early Judaism, ed. by J.J. Collins/D.C. Harlow, Grand Rapids/Cambridge 2010, 1174–1176.
Feldmeier, R., Gott und die Zeit, in: Heil und Geschichte. Die Geschichtsbezogenheit des Heils und das Problem der Heilsgeschichte in der biblischen Tradition und in der theologischen

Deutung, hg. von J. Frey/S. Krauter/H. Lichtenberger (WUNT 248), Tübingen 2009, 287–305.
Fishbane, M.A., The Sacred Center, in: Texts and Responses. FS N.N. Glatzer, ed. by M.A. Fishbane/P.R. Flohr, Leiden 1975, 6–27.
Frey, J., Das Judentum des Paulus, in: Paulus. Leben – Umwelt – Werk – Briefe, hg. von O. Wischmeyer (UTB 2767), Tübingen/Basel ²2012, 25–65.
—, Galaterbrief, in: Paulus. Leben – Umwelt – Werk – Briefe, hg. von O. Wischmeyer, O. (UTB 2767), Tübingen/Basel ²2012, 232–256.
Freyne, S., Galilee and Gospel. Collected Essays (WUNT 125), Tübingen 2000.
—, Galilee, Jesus, and the Gospels. Literary Approaches and Historical Investigations, Philadelphia 1988.
Gemünden, P. von /Horrell, D.G./Küchler, M. (Hg.), Jesus – Gestaltung und Gestaltungen. Rezeptionen des Galiläers in Wissenschaft, Kirche und Gesellschaft, Festschrift für G. Theißen zum 70. Geburtstag, (NTOA 100), Göttingen 2013.
Gnilka, J., Das Evangelium nach Markus. 2. Teilband: Mk 8,27–16,20 (EKK II/2), 3. durchgesehene Auflage, Zürich/Braunschweig/Neukirchen-Vluyn 1989.
—, Der Philipperbrief (HthK X/3), Freiburg 1968.
Grässer, E., Der zweite Brief an die Korinther. Kapitel 8,1–13,13 (ÖTK 8/2), Gütersloh 2005.
Gruen, E.S., Judaism in the Diaspora, in: The Eerdmans Dictionary of Early Judaism, ed. by J.J. Collins/D.C. Harlow, Grand Rapids/Cambridge 2010, 77–96.
Grünwaldt, K., Exil und Identität. Beschneidung, Passa und Sabbat in der Priesterschrift, Frankfurt am Main 1992.
Gutbrod, W., Art. Ἰσραήλ, in: ThWNT 3 (1938), 357–394.
Guttenberger, G., Ethnizität im Markusevangelium, in: Jesus – Gestaltung und Gestaltungen. Rezeptionen des Galiläers in Wissenschaft, Kirche und Gesellschaft, Festschrift für G. Theißen zum 70. Geburtstag, hg. von P. von Gemünden/D.G. Horrell/M. Küchler (NTOA 100), Göttingen 2013, 125–152.
Haacker, K., Der Brief des Paulus an die Römer (ThHKNT 6), Leipzig 1999.
Hahn, F., Theologie des Neuen Testaments. Band I: Die Vielfalt des Neuen Testaments, Theologiegeschichte des Urchristentums, Tübingen 2002.
Hellholm, D. (ed.), Apocalypticism in the Mediterranean World and the Near East, Tübingen 1989.
Hengel, M., Die vier Evangelien und das Evangelium von Jesus Christus. Studien zu ihrer Sammlung und Entstehung (WUNT 224), Tübingen 2008.
—, Jerusalem als jüdische und hellenistische Stadt, in: Hellenismus, hg. von B. Funck, Tübingen 1996, 269–306.
Holmén, T./Porter, S.E. (eds.), Handbook for the Study of the Historical Jesus, Leiden/Boston 2011.
Horsley, R.A./ Hanson, J., Bandits, Prophets and Messiahs, Minneapolis 1986.
Iverson, K.R./Skinner C.W. (eds.), Mark as Story: Retrospect and Prospect (SBL Resources for Biblical Study 65), Atlanta 2011.
Jeremias, J., Art. Ἀβραάμ, in: THWNT 1 (1933), 7–9.
Jewett, R., Romans. A Commentary (Hermeneia), Minneapolis 2007.
Karrer, M., Jesus Christus im Neuen Testament (GNT 11), Göttingen 1998.
Klauck, H.-J., Vorspiel im Himmel? Erzähltechnik und Theologie im Markusprolog (BThS 32), Neukirchen-Vluyn 1997.
Koch, K., Art. Hebräer, in: RGG⁴ 3 (2000), 1493f.

—, Die Bedeutung der Apokalyptik für die Interpretation der Schrift, in: ders., Die Reiche der Welt und der kommende Menschensohn. Studien zum Danielbuch, Gesammelte Aufsätze, Band 2, hg. von M. Rösel, Neukirchen-Vluyn 1995, 16 – 45.
Koester, H., Art. φύσις κτλ., in: ThWNT 9 (1973), 265.
Konradt, M., „Die aus Glauben, diese sind Abrahams Kinder" (Gal 3,7). Erwägungen zum galatischen Konflikt im Lichte frühjüdischer Abrahamstraditionen, in: Kontexte der Schrift. Band 1: Text, Ethik, Judentum und Christentum, Gesellschaft. E.W. Stegemann zum 60. Geburtstag, hg. von G. Gelardini, Stuttgart 2005, 25 – 48.
—, „Mein Wandel einst im ‚Ioudaismos'" (Gal 1,13). Paulus als Jude und das Bild des Judentums beim Apostel Paulus, in: Fremdbilder – Selbstbilder. Imaginationen des Judentums von der Antike bis in die Neuzeit, hg. von R. Bloch/S. Haeberli/R.C. Schwinges, Basel 2010, 25 – 67.
Kuhli, H., Art. Ἰουδαῖος, in: EWNT² 2 (1981), 472 – 482.
Kuhn, K.G., Art. Ἰσραήλ κτλ. B. Ἰσραήλ, Ἰουδαῖος, Ἑβραῖος in der nach-at.lichen jüdischen Literatur, in: ThWNT 3 (1938), 360 – 370.
Levine, L.I. (Hg.), Jerusalem. Its Sanctity and Centrality to Judaism, Christianity and Islam, New York 1999.
—, Art. Synagogues, in: The Eerdmans Dictionary of Early Judaism, ed. by J.J. Collins/D.C. Harlow, Grand Rapids/Cambridge 2010, 1260 – 1271.
Lichtenberger, A., „Sieh, was für Steine und was für Bauten!". Zur Rezeption herodianischer Architektur im Neuen Testament, in: Zeichen aus Text und Stein. Studien auf dem Weg zu einer Archäologie des Neuen Testaments, hg. von S. Alkier/J. Zangenberg (TANZ 42), Tübingen 2003, 209 – 221.
Liddell, H.G./ Scott, R./ Jones, H.S., A Greek-English Lexicon, Oxford 1968.
Lightfoot, J.B., Saint Paul's Epistle to the Philippians, London 1903.
Lindemann, A., Der Erste Korintherbrief (HNT 9/1), Tübingen 2000.
—, Jesus und der Sabbat. Zum literarischen Charakter der Erzählung Mk 3,1 – 6, in: Text und Geschichte. Facetten theologischen Arbeitens aus dem Freundes- und Schülerkreis. D. Lührmann zum 60. Geburtstag, hg.v. S. Maser/E. Schlarb, Marburg 1999, 122 – 135.
—, Art. Eschatologie, III. Neues Testament, in: RGG⁴ 2 (1999), 1553 – 1560.
Lohmeyer, E., Die Verklärung Jesu, in: ZNW 21 (1922), 185 – 215.
Lüderitz, G., Rhetorik, Poetik, Kompositionstechnik im Markusevangelium, in: Markus-Philologie. Historische, literaturgeschichtliche und stilistische Untersuchungen zum zweiten Evangelium, hg. von H. Cancik (WUNT 33), Tübingen 1984, 165 – 203.
Lührmann, D., Pharisäer und Schriftgelehrte im Markusevangelium, in: ZNW 78 (1987), 169 – 185.
Lundquist, J.M., The Temple. Meeting Place of Heaven and Earth, London 1993.
Maier, J., Tempel und Tempelkult, in: Literatur und Religion des Frühjudentums, hg. von J. Maier/J. Schreiner, Würzburg 1973, 371 – 390.
Majoros-Danowski, J., Elija im Markusevangelium. Ein Buch im Kontext des Judentums (BWANT 180), Stuttgart 2008.
Marcus, J., The Way of the Lord. Christological Exegesis of the Old Testament in the Gospel of Mark, Louisville/Edinburgh 1992.
Maschmeier, J.-C., Rechtfertigung bei Paulus. Eine Kritik alter und neuer Paulusperspektiven (BWANT 189), Stuttgart 2010.
Mason, S. (ed.), Flavius Josephus. Translation and Commentary, Volume 10: Against Apion, Translation and Commentary by J.M.G. Barclay, Leiden/Boston 2007.

—, Jews, Judeans, Judaizing, Judaism. Problems of Categorization, in: Journal for the Study of Judaism 38 (2007), 457–512.
Mayer-Haas, A.J., „Geschenk aus Gottes Schatzkammer" (bSchab 10b). Jesus und der Sabbat im Spiegel der neutestamentlichen Schriften (NTA NS 43), Münster 2003.
McGinn, B./Collins, J.J./Stein, S.J. (eds.), The Encyclopedia of Apocalypticism, London/New York 2000–2003.
McKay, H.A., Sabbath and Synagogue. The Question of Sabbath Worship in Ancient Judaism, Leiden 1994.
Mehl, A., Der politische Raum des Paulus: Das Römische Reich, in: Paulus. Leben – Umwelt – Werk – Briefe, hg. von O. Wischmeyer (UTB 2767), Tübingen/Basel ²2012, 5–24.
Meiser, M., Reinheitsfragen und Begräbnissitten. Der Evangelist Markus als Zeuge der jüdischen Alltagskultur, in: Neues Testament und hellenistisch-jüdische Alltagskultur, hg. von R. Deines/J. Herzer/K.-W. Niebuhr (WUNT 274),Tübingen 2011, 443–460.
Merklein, H., Der erste Brief an die Korinther. Kapitel 5,1–11,1 (ÖTKNT 7/2), Gütersloh 2000.
—, Jesu Botschaft von der Gottesherrschaft. Eine Skizze (SBS 111), Stuttgart 1983.
Meyers, E.M., Galilean Regionalism as a Factor in Historical Reconstruction, in: BASOR 221 (1976), 93–101.
Moreland, M., The Inhabitants of Galilee in the Hellenistic and Early Roman Periods. Probes in the Archaeological and Literary Evidence, in: Religion, Ethnicity, and Identity in Ancient Galilee. A Region in Transition, ed. by J. Zangenberg/H.W. Attridge/D.B. Martin (WUNT 210), Tübingen 2007, 133–159.
Morgenthaler, R., Statistik des neutestamentlichen Wortschatzes, Zürich 1958.
Moxnes, H., When did Jesus become a Galilean. Revisiting the Historical Jesus debate of the Nineteenth Century, in: Jesus – Gestaltung und Gestaltungen. Rezeptionen des Galiläers in Wissenschaft, Kirche und Gesellschaft, Festschrift für G. Theißen zum 70. Geburtstag, hg. von P. von Gemünden/D.G. Horrell/M. Küchler (NTOA 100), Göttingen 2013, 391–409.
Müller, H.P., Art. Eschatologie, II. Altes Testament, in: RGG⁴ 2 (1999), 1546–1553.
Müller, M., Art. Menschensohn im Neuen Testament, in: RGG⁴ 5 (2002), 1098–1100.
Müller, U.B., Johannes der Täufer. Jüdischer Prophet und Wegbereiter Jesu (Biblische Gestalten 6), Leipzig 2002.
Necker, G., Art. Elia, II. Judentum, in: RGG⁴ 2 (1999), 1211f.
Neusner, J., From Judaism to Judaisms. My Approach to the History of Judaism, in: J. Neusner, Ancient Judaism. Debates and Disputes. Second Series, Atlanta 1990, 181–221.
Nickelsburg, G.W.E., Art. Resurrection (Early Judaism and Christianity), in: ADB 5, 684–691.
—, Art. Son of Man, in: The Eerdmans Dictionary of Early Judaism, ed. by J.J. Collins/D.C. Harlow, Grand Rapids/Cambridge 2010, 1249–1251.
Niebuhr, K.-W., Heidenapostel aus Israel. Die jüdische Identität des Paulus nach ihrer Darstellung in seinen Briefen (WUNT 62), Tübingen 1992.
Nodet, E., Pharisees, Sadducees, Essenes, Herodians, in: Handbook for the Study of the Historical Jesus, ed. by T. Holmén/S.E. Porter, Volume 2: The Study of Jesus, Leiden/Boston 2011, 1495–1523.
Öhler, M., Elia im Neuen Testament (BZNW 88), Berlin/New York, 1997.
Otto, E., Art. Feste/Feiern, II. Altes Testament, in: RGG⁴ 3 (2000), 87–89.
Poorthuis, M./Safrai, C. (eds.), The Centrality of Jerusalem. Historical Perspectives, Kampen 1996.
Pucci Ben Zeev, M., Jewish Rights in the Roman World (TSAJ 74), Tübingen 1998.

—, Jews Among Greeks and Romans, in: The Eerdmans Dictionary of Early Judaism, ed. by J.J. Collins/D.C. Harlow, Grand Rapids/Cambridge 2010, 237–255
Rad, G. von, Art. Ἰσραὴλ κτλ. A. Israel, Juda, Hebräer im AT, in: ThWNT 3 (1938), 356–359.
Rad, G. von/Kuhn, K.G., Art. βασιλεία τοῦ θεοῦ, in: ThWNT I (1933), 563–573.
Rhoads, D./Dewey, J./Michie, D., Mark as Story: An Introduction to the Narrative of a Gospel, Minneapolis 1999.
Riesner, R., Herodianische Architektur im Neuen Testament, in: Neues Testament und hellenistisch-jüdische Alltagskultur, hg. von R. Deines/J. Herzer/K.-W. Niebuhr (WUNT 274), Tübingen 2011, 165–196.
Rose, C., Theologie als Erzählung im Markusevangelium (WUNT II 236), Tübingen 2007.
Safrai, S., Die Wallfahrt im Zeitalter des Zweiten Tempels (FJCD 3), Stuttgart 1981.
—, Religion in Everyday Life, in: The Jewish People in the First Century, ed. by S. Safrai/M. Stern, Philadelphia 1976, 793–833.
—, The Temple, in: The Jewish People in the First Century, ed. by S. Safrai/M. Stern, Philadelphia 1976, 865–907.
Sanders, E.P., Jesus' Galilee, in: Fair Play. Diversity and Conflicts in Early Christianity. Essays in Honour of Heikki Räisänen, ed. by I. Dunderberg/C. Tuckett/K. Syreeni, Leiden/Boston/Köln 2002, 3–41.
—, Judaism. Practice and Belief 63BCE – 66CE, London/Philadelphia 1992.
—, Paulus und das palästinische Judentum. Ein Vergleich zweier Religionsstrukturen (StUNT 17), Göttingen 1985.
—, Sohn Gottes. Eine historische Biographie Jesu, Stuttgart 1996.
Sänger, D., Literarische Strategien der Polemik im Galaterbrief, in: Polemik in der frühchristlichen Literatur. Texte und Kontexte, hg. von O. Wischmeyer/L. Scornaienchi (BZNW 170), Berlin/New York 2011, 155–181.
Schäfer, P., Der vorrabbinische Pharisäismus, in: Paulus und das antike Judentum, hg. von M. Hengel/U. Heckel, Tübingen 1991, 125–175.
Schmithals, W., Das Evangelium nach Markus. Kapitel 1–9,1 (ÖTK 2,1), Gütersloh ²1986.
—, Der Römerbrief. Ein Kommentar, Gütersloh 1988.
Schmitt, R., Exodus und Passah. Ihr Zusammenhang im Alten Testament, Göttingen ²1997.
Schnelle, U., Einleitung in das Neue Testament (UTB 1830), Göttingen ⁶2007.
Scholtissek, K., Der Sohn Gottes für das Reich Gottes. Zur Verbindung von Christologie und Eschatologie bei Markus, in: Der Evangelist als Theologe. Studien zum Markusevangelium, hg. von T. Söding (SBS 163), Stuttgart 1995, 63–90.
Schröder, B., Art. Sadduzäer, in: RGG⁴ 7 (2004), 732f.
Schröter, J., Art. Reich Gottes, III. Neues Testament, in: RGG⁴ 7 (2004), 204–210.
—, Jesus aus Galiläa. Die Herkunft Jesu und ihre Bedeutung für das Verständnis seiner Wirksamkeit, in: Jesus und die Archäologie Galiläas, hg. von C. Claußen/J. Frey (BThS 87), Neukirchen-Vluyn 2008, 245–270.
Schunck, K.-D., Art. Benjamin, in: ABD 1 (1992), 671–673.
Schwemer, A.M., Gott als König und seine Königsherrschaft in den Sabbatliedern aus Qumran, in: Königsherrschaft Gottes und himmlischer Kult im Judentum, Urchristentum und in der hellenistischen Welt, hg. von M. Hengel/A.M. Schwemer (WUNT 55), Tübingen 1991, 45–118.
Segal, J.B., Hebrew Passover. From the Earliest Times to A.D. 70 (London Oriental Series 12), London 1963.

Shils, E., Das Zentrum des Kosmos und das Zentrum der Gesellschaft, in: Sehnsucht nach dem Ursprung. FS M. Eliade, hg. von H.P. Duerr, Frankfurt am Main 1983, 538–557.
Shively, E.E., Apocalyptic Imagination in the Gospel of Mark. The Literary and Theological Role of Mark 3,22:30 (BZNW 189), Berlin/Boston 2012.
Smith, M., Palestinian Judaism in the First Century, in: Israel. Its Role in Civilization, ed. by M. Davis, New York 1956, 67–81.
Snodgrass, K.R., Streams of Tradition Emerging from Isaiah 40:1–5 and Their Adaption in the New Testament, in: JSNT 8 (1980), 24–45.
Stegemann, E.W., Zur „apokalyptischen" Rekonstruktion einer kollektiven Identität bei Paulus, in: ders., Der Römerbrief, Brennpunkte der Rezeption, ausgewählt und hg. von C. Tuor und P. Wick, Zürich 2012, 89–120.
Stemberger, G., Pharisäer, Sadduzäer, Essener (SBS 144), Stuttgart 1991.
—, Was there a „mainstream Judaism" in the late Second Temple Period?, in: ders., Judaica Minora. Teil 1: Biblische Traditionen im rabbinischen Judentum (TSAJ 133), Tübingen 2010, 395–410.
Stökl Ben Ezra, D., Art. Markusevangelium, in: RAC 24 (2010), 173–207.
Strohmaier (Hg.), S., Kultur – Wissen – Narration. Perspektiven transdisziplinärer Erzählforschung für die Kulturwissenschaften, Bielefeld 2013.
Taylor, J.E., Art. John the Baptist, in: The Eerdmans Dictionary of Early Judaism, ed. by J.J. Collins/D.C. Harlow, Grand Rapids/Cambridge 2010, 819–821.
—, The Immerser. John the Baptist within Second Temple Judaism, Grand Rapids 1997.
Teeple, H.M., The Mosaic Eschatological Prophet, in: JBLMS 10 (1957), 49–73
Theissen, G., Die Jesusbewegung. Sozialgeschichte einer Revolution der Werte, Gütersloh 2004.
Tilly, M., Apokalyptik (UTB 3651), Tübingen 2012.
—, Jerusalem – Nabel der Welt. Überlieferung und Funktion von Heiligtumstraditionen im antiken Judentum, Stuttgart 2002.
Tilly, M./Zwickel, W., Religionsgeschichte Israels. Von der Vorzeit bis zu den Anfängen des Christentums, Darmstadt 2011.
Vahrenhorst, M., Kultische Sprache in den Paulusbriefen (WUNT 230), Tübingen 2008.
Veltri, G., Art. Feste/Feiern, III. Judentum, in: RGG[4] 3 (2000), 90–93.
Vielhauer, P., Geschichte der urchristlichen Literatur. Einleitung in das Neue Testament, die Apokryphen und die Apostolischen Väter, Berlin 1975.
Wanke, J., Art. Ἑβραῖος, ου, ὁ, in: EWNT[2] 1 (1980), 892ff.
Weiss, H., A Day of Gladness. The Sabbath among Jews and Christians in Antiquity, Columbia 2003.
Wilk, F., Die synoptischen Evangelien als Quellen für die Geschichte der Pharisäer, in: Judaistik und neutestamentliche Wissenschaft. Standorte – Grenzen – Beziehungen, hg. von L. Doering/H.-G. Waubke/F. Wilk (FRLANT 226), Göttingen 2008, 85–107.
Wischmeyer, O., Romans 1:1–7 and Mark 1:1–3 in Comparison. Two Opening Texts at the Beginning of Early Christian Literature, in: Mark and Paul. Comparative Essays Part II: For and Against Pauline Influence on Mark, ed. by E.-M. Becker/M. Müller/T. Engberg-Pedersen, (BZNW 199), Berlin/Boston 2014, 121–146.
—, Abraham unser Vater. Aspekte der Abrahamsgestalt im Neuen Testament, in: Deuterocanonical und Cognate Literature. Yearbook 2008: Biblical Figures in Deuterocanonical and Cognate Literature, ed. by H. Lichtenberger/U. Mittmann-Richert, Berlin/New York 2009, 567–585.

—, Die Religion des Paulus. Eine Problemanzeige, in: dies., Von Ben Sira zu Paulus. Gesammelte Aufsätze zu Texten, Theologie und Hermeneutik des Frühjudentums und des Neuen Testaments, hg. von E.-M. Becker (WUNT 173), Tübingen 2004, 311–328.

—, Neues Testament, in: Menschsein. Perspektiven des Alten und Neuen Testaments, hg. von C. Frevel/O. Wischmeyer (Die Neue Echter Bibel – Themen 11), Würzburg 2003.

—, Römerbrief, in: Paulus. Leben – Umwelt – Werk – Briefe, hg. von O. Wischmeyer (UTB 2767), Tübingen/Basel ²2012, 281–314.

—, Staat und Christen nach Römer 13,1–7. Ein neuer hermeneutischer Zugang, in: dies., Von Ben Sira zu Paulus. Gesammelte Aufsätze zu Texten, Theologie und Hermeneutik des Frühjudentums und des Neuen Testaments, hg. von E.-M. Becker (WUNT 173), Tübingen 2004, 229–242.

—, Zitat und Allusion als literarische Eröffnung des Markusevangeliums, in: Im Namen des Anderen. Die Ethik des Zitierens, hg. von J. Jacob/M. Mayer (Ethik – Text – Kultur 3), München 2010, 175–186.

Wolff, C., Der zweite Brief des Paulus an die Korinther (ThHK VIII), Berlin 1989.

Wolter, M., Das Israelproblem nach Gal 4,21–23 und Röm 9–11, in: ZThK 107 (2010), 1–30.

Wrede, W., Das Messiasgeheimnis in den Evangelien (1901), Göttingen ⁴1969.

Wyschogrod, M., On the Christian Critique on the Jewish Sabbath, in: Sabbath. Idea – History – Reality, ed. by G.J. Blidstein, Beer Sheva 2004, 43–56.

Xeravits, G.G., Art. Son of God, in: The Eerdmans Dictionary of Early Judaism, ed. by J.J. Collins/D.C. Harlow, Grand Rapids/Cambridge 2010, 1248–1249,

—, King, Priest, Prophet. Positive Eschatological Protagonists of the Qumran Library, Leiden 2003.

Zangenberg, J., Jesus – Galiläa – Archäologie. Neue Forschungen zu einer Region im Wandel, in: Jesus und die Archäologie Galiläas, hg. von C. Claußen/J. Frey (BThS 87), Neukirchen-Vluyn 2008, 7–38.

Zuntz, G., Ein Heide las das Markusevangelium, in: Markus-Philologie. Historische, literargeschichtliche und stilistische Untersuchungen zum zweiten Evangelium (WUNT 33), Tübingen 1984, 205–222.

Jesper Svartvik
"East is East and West is West:"
The Concept of Torah in Paul and Mark

Two questions in New Testament scholarship are more fundamental and lingering than most other queries: First, *why did Paul write the Epistle to the Romans*, i. e. what was the purpose and context of his longest and most systematic treatise? Second, *why did Mark write his Gospel*, i.e. what are the prehistory and circumstances of the earliest narrative account of the life and work of Jesus of Nazareth? One might even suggest that all New Testament studies hang on these two questions; the rest is commentary.[1] This is what we want to discuss in this chapter, which not only addresses these two fundamental questions, but also – and particularly – seeks to explore the interplay between the Pauline and Marcan theologies of the Torah. In Pauline scholarship, both the *new* perspective (e.g. proposed by James D. G. Dunn, George Howard *et alii*) and what we could call the *newer* perspective (e.g. Paula Fredriksen, John G. Gager, Mark D. Nanos *et alii*) reject the idea that the *Torah* primarily was a personal problem in Pauls' life and theology. What the proponents of the newer perspective maintain is that Paul was convinced that Christ-believing pagans were not to become Jews. His focus was always on the Gentile mission, which is why he describes himself as a messenger to the Gentiles (e.g. Rom 11:13 and Gal 2:8). We will argue that, while embracing universalism, Paul nevertheless seeks to maintain Jewish particularism, as we are convinced that this line of thought sheds new light on the texts and theology of Paul.[2]

Furthermore, as a growing number of scholars (e.g. Joel Marcus, John Painter, David C. Sim, Jesper Svartvik *et alii*) argue for a Pauline-Marcan connection, Paul's and Mark's importance for early Christian perceptions of the Torah and

---

[1] Cf. Hillel's advice to a Gentile in *b. Shabbat* 31a. Is there a pun in this story that the Gentile seeks the essence while standing "on one foot" (Hebrew: *al regel achat*), that Shammai chases him away with "a stick" (Latin: *regula*), and that Hillel gives him the love commandment as "a rule" (Latin: *regula*)? For further comments, see Raphael Jospe, "Hillel's Rule." *JQR* 81 (1990): 45–57. One is also reminded of Alfred North Whitehead's remark that the history of Western philosophy is but a footnote to Plato's works.
[2] On Paul and universalism, see e.g. Daniel Boyarin, *A Radical Jew: Paul and the Politics of Identity* (Berkeley, Ca.: University of California Press, 1994), 52: " what motivated Paul ultimately was a profound concern for the one-ness of humanity."

the development of Jewish-Christian relations cannot be overstated.³ Indeed, the purpose of this entire collection of essays is to highlight why it is essential to explore the Pauline-Marcan affiliation and relationship.

In this chapter it will be argued that there is a cloud of misunderstanding of the entire research area of "Paul and the Law" that obscures the theological similarities between Paul and Mark. Once we understand Pauline theology better, we also see the similarities between the two influential theologians Paul and Mark. Now, the question of establishing a genetic relationship (asserting that Paul necessarily had access to a proto-Marcan text or that Mark must have read some of the Pauline epistles) is never raised in this chapter, but rather the question of whether the similarities between the Pauline epistles and the Marcan narrative are so conspicuous that placing them together furthers the investigation of the history of earliest Christianity. We commence this examination by exploring the role of the Torah in the Pauline epistles, before continuing with a study of the Marcan narrative. In a nutshell, what are the consequences of the new and newer perspectives on Paul for Marcan studies, especially in terms of how to interpret the role of the Torah in the early Christian movement?

1 Paul and the Torah

This can be but a brief outline of one of the most debated topics in New Testament scholarship of the last decades, not only in terms of the sheer number of scholarly articles and books (which, indeed, is vast), but also because of the doctrinal consequences for many Christians of this shift of emphasis in Pauline studies. The assertion that the critique of the Law is not only the focal point in Paul's theology, but also his personal pain and theological headache, has been the foundation stone of much of Christian theology. When using the rock metaphor,

---

3 A small selection of examples of scholarship in favour of a Pauline-Marcan connection: David C. Sim, *The Gospel of Matthew and Christian Judaism: The History and Social Setting of the Matthean Community*, SNTW (Edinburgh: T & T Clark, 1998), 198; Joel Marcus, "Mark – Interpreter of Paul," *NTS* 46 (2000): 473–87; John Painter, *Mark's Gospel* (London: Routledge, 1997), 4–6, 213; and Walter Brueggemann, *The Bible Makes Sense: Revised Edition with a New Introduction* (Louisville, Ky.: Westminster John Knox Press, 2001), 46. See also Jesper Svartvik, *Mark and Mission: Mk 7:1-23 in Its Narrative and Historical Contexts* (Stockholm: Almqvist & Wiksell, 2000), 344–47; id, "The Markan Interpretation of the Pentateuchal Food Laws." In *Biblical Interpretation in Early Christian Gospels. Volume I: The Gospel of Mark*, ed. Thomas R. Hatina (London: T & T Clark International, 2006), 169-81; and also id, "Matthew and Mark." In *Matthew and His Christian Contemporaries*, eds. David C. Sim and Boris Repschinski (London: T & T Clark International, 2008), 27-49.

one is reminded of Stephen Westerholm's statement that Aurelius Augustine of Hippo, Martin Luther of Wittenberg, and John Wesley of Aldersgate all had "eyes for the mountain" (suggesting that they may have misunderstood some minor details, but nevertheless clearly saw what one cannot avoid setting eyes on when reading the Pauline epistles).[4] However, the location and magnitude of this "Westerholmean" mountain, and even its sheer existence have been questioned in recent Pauline scholarship. Given the revolutionary nature of Pauline studies during the last few decades, the following discussion makes no claim to exhaust the topic. Its modest purpose is simply to highlight a few traits of particular importance to the issues that are discussed in this chapter: the Torah as a *burden*, as a set of *boundaries* and, using the Hebrew word for "covenant," as *berit*.

1.1 The Torah as a Burden: An Apostle Weighed Down with Guilt

To previous generations of scholars, especially among those who identified themselves with the Lutheran tradition, it was a given that the pre-Christian Paul was burdened with guilt. Since New Testament scholars at times tend to overlook the importance of the Pauline epistles in pre-modern Biblical interpretation, we may need to draw attention to the fact that Philipp Melanchthon called the epistle to the Galatians *Christianae religionis compendium* ("a summary of the Christian faith") and that Martin Luther wrote that he treasured it as highly as Katherine von Bora, i.e. to him it was as adorable and indispensable as his own wife. Luther's scriptural hermeneutics centred much on the principle of *was Christum treibet*, which never was Christology in general, but always referred to a particular type of forensic Christology, namely that the death of Jesus absolves humanity from the demands of the Law. Humans are justified by faith in Christ and not by their deeds. Hence, keeping the *mitswot* is thus the opposite of Christian faith; Judaism is therefore often understood as the exact opposite of Christian faith.[5] In other words, a Torah-centered Judaism is bad Christianity, and the road Christians are always tempted to choose, but are never supposed to take. Halakhic Judaism becomes the prototype for the kind of Christian faith that is *undeveloped* (as it is still concerned with the

---

[4] Stephen Westerholm, *Israel's Law and the Church's Faith: Paul and His Recent Interpreters* (Grand Rapids, Mich.: Eerdmans, 1988), 222.
[5] Needless to say, Lutheran tradition has never been opposed to Christians keeping the Ten Commandments. It is the so-called *ritual* commandments that are being discussed.

Law), *ungrateful* (because it does not realise what Christ has done and has to proffer), and maybe even *uncouth* (because it rejects the Christian gospel). At times, one gets the impression that a "Jew" is everyone who is self-sufficient, a person who needs neither God nor God's grace; and "to judaise" is what Christians do when they keep the covenantal commandments and have too positive an understanding of Judaism. One is reminded of Ignatius of Antioch who states that "it is out of place to talk about Jesus Christ and [at the same time] to Judaise" (*Magn.* 10.3). In short, Judaism is an expression of theological insubordination; it is the epitome of religious rebelliousness. In Pamela Eisenbaum's words, Judaism is presented as "the ultimate paradigm of bad religion."[6]

Since the Torah is so central in Judaism, it is only natural that one of the most comprehensive and profound discussions of the current New Testament research is the quest to understand Paul's attitude toward just the Torah. If those who claim that Paul's mission was antinomistic (i.e. against the Torah) are right, we cannot perceive Pauline theology as anything but a struggle against the emerging Rabbinic Judaism. In other and conspicuously blunt words, the existence of Judaism *post Christum* is a theological misfortune. Although it is a matter of fact that the hitherto most influential Pauline interpreter is Martin Luther, it is nevertheless remarkable that the Lutheran interpretation of Pauline theology is still widely held, since its problems are so numerous and extensive that it cannot be maintained.

Therefore, a giant leap for New Testament studies was taken when scholars began to agree that *Paul was not a Lutheran theologian*, in the sense that the Law was not a primarily existential problem in his life. Krister Stendahl's influential essay on Paul and the introspective conscience of the West was ground-breaking and is still a must read for all those who wish to acquaint themselves with Pauline theology.[7] We now realise that numerous articles and books on Paul's epistles are suspiciously Lutheran in their scope and conclusions, in the sense that the Law is presented as constituting the major theological predicament, to which the gospel is the answer. Many scholars have pointed out that the consequence is that Christianity, understood in this way, is presented as the solution to the problem that a Torah-centric Judaism constitutes. In a nutshell, Torah and Christ – like Law and Grace – are essentially incompatible and each others' radical opposites.

---

[6] Pamela Eisenbaum, *Paul Was Not a Christian: The Original Message of a Misunderstood Apostle* (San Francisco, Ca.: HarperOne, 2009), 244.
[7] Krister Stendahl, "The Apostle Paul and the Introspective Conscience of the West." *HTR* 56 (1963): 199–215.

As the conventional line of thought goes, Paul ultimately realised that human inadequacies made it impossible to keep the commandments. As soon as an interpreter of the Pauline epistles emphasises that the Law makes people boast and become triumphalistic, that it fosters an attitude of pride, then we are reminded of the Lutheran legacy, i.e. that justification by faith alone (*sola fide*) is presented not only as the centre of Paul's theology, but also of the rest of the New Testament, and, indeed, of the entire Christian faith. In other words, this chapter touches on the foundation of Protestant theology.

As antinomian readings of the Pauline epistles have been the *fons et origo* of much New Testament study, there has been no end to what has been stated about the characteristics of *Spätjudentum*: Paul Billerbeck, seemingly unconstrainedly, stated that it was "eine Religion völligster Selbsterlösung."[8] In more recent times Robert Hamerton-Kelly has suggested that the Law in Paul's theology is "a metonymy for the Jewish way of life characterized by exclusionism and violence;" to its adherents the Law is "a manifestation of the love of God," but Paul identified it as "an instrument of violence."[9] Needless to say, these statements are extreme. However, numerous interpreters still take for granted that the Torah constitutes a major problem for humanity. The assertion that it promotes legalistic works-righteousness can still be found in Biblical scholarship and Christian theology. According to this scheme, "Judaism" by definition *has* to be bad for Paul's gospel to be truly "the good news" (τὸ εὐαγγέλιον). This entire discourse amounts to a teaching of contempt, and it is not difficult to see who is paying the price for it.[10]

The way out of this conundrum is to recognise that there is little to suggest that Paul was burdened with guilt. As Alan F. Segal points out, it was quite the opposite: "[Paul] obviously thought of himself to be guilty of no infraction of Torah before he became a Christian."[11] To invoke Stendahl's renowned expression: Paul had "a rather 'robust' conscience."[12] What role, then, does the

---

[8] Hermann L. Strack and Paul Billerbeck, *Kommentar zum Neuen Testament aus Talmud und Midrasch*, 6 vols (Munich: Beck, 1922–28), 4:1, 6.
[9] Robert G. Hamerton-Kelly, *Sacred Violence: Paul's Hermeneutics of the Cross* (Minneapolis, Minn.: Fortress Press, 1992), 141. See also his study on Mark, in which he argues that "Jesus died as a result of a conflict with the temple," Robert G. Hamerton-Kelly, *The Gospel and the Sacred: Poetics of Violence in Mark* (Minneapolis, Minn.: Fortress Press, 1994), 1.
[10] Cf. the title of Jules Isaac's influential book: *The Teaching of Contempt: The Christian Roots of Anti-Semitism*, trans. Helen Weaver (New York: Holt, Rinehart & Winston, 1964).
[11] Alan F. Segal, *Paul the Convert: The Apostolate and Apostasy of Saul the Pharisee* (New Haven, Conn.: Yale University Press, 1990), 20.
[12] Stendahl, "The Apostle Paul and the Introspective Conscience of the West", 200.

Torah play in Pauline theology? It is time to make room for the new perspective on Paul.

1.2 The Torah as Boundaries: The New Perspective on Paul

In his book *Paul and the Jewish Law*, Peter J. Tomson presents three assumptions which he considers are taken for granted in traditional scholarship on Paul: (a) First, *the centre of Paul's thought is a polemic against the Law*. If this assertion were correct, we would find antinomian texts everywhere in *Corpus Paulinum*. Since this, as a matter of fact, is not the case, it cannot be argued that antinomianism was Paul's central concern, let alone his only interest. (b) Second, *the Law no longer had a practical meaning for Paul*. There is much that suggests that he devoted the rest of his life contemplating the relation between the given, i.e. the Scriptures, and the new, that is, his Christ kerygma. (c) Third, *ancient Jewish literature is no source for explaining his letters*. But from a methodological point of view it is strenuous to reconstruct first-century Jewish beliefs solely, or even primarily, from the Pauline epistles. Strictly speaking, what Paul writes represents his own beliefs, and – at least not without a major methodological discussion – cannot be representative of first-century Judaism in general.[13] One does not have to read many pages of Rabbinic literature to realise that the Torah is the most cherished of all words in Jewish tradition. Hence, the "Law" in Jewish thought cannot be set against the "gospel", because the Law *is* the gospel! As soon as one questions at least one of these three suppositions, one has moved from the traditional to a new perspective. In his book Tomson convincingly shows that these statements are unfounded.

Therefore, it was only to be expected that eventually a growing number of scholars would seek to do justice to first-century Judaism, and not merely present it as the rhetoric and gloomy background to early Christianity. "The new perspective" of James D. G. Dunn *et alii* was therefore due to come and was a most welcome correction of much of what previously had been written in Pauline scholarship.[14] It is a great advantage that the Torah is nowadays less often described as a juggernaut that crushes people beneath. Today most Pauline scholars are aware of the apologetic concerns that characterised, constrained and constricted earlier scholarship. However, as Pauline scholarship of previous

---

[13] Peter J. Tomson, *Paul and the Jewish Law: Halakha in the Letters of the Apostle to the Gentiles* (Assen: Van Gorcum, 1990), 1.
[14] James D. G. Dunn, "The New Perspective on Paul." *BJRL* 65 (1983): 94-122.

generations had portrayed Paul as a *Vorlage* to Martin Luther's tower experience, one could also compare the new perspective to another phenomenon, thus also highlighting some of the deficiencies of this new perspective. The supporters of the new perspective focus on the Torah as a set of identity markers (circumcision, *kashrut*, etc.) which thereby become a theological obstacle because they lead to exclusivism. *Halakhah* is wrong not because it constitutes a burden (*ut supra*), but because it creates boundaries between people. Hence, according to this line of thought, by breaking down barriers and crossing boundaries, Paul establishes a religious society which is characterised by boundlessness.

Some readers may think that, according to the new perspective, Pauline theology is similar to Reform Judaism. Is he not like someone who wants to modernise Judaism, and to bring it out of the constraints of traditional *halakhah*? Hence, is this not a good way to describe Paul's yearning, i.e. an *inner-Jewish* struggle for his own version of Judaism? Is it not true that numerous Pauline scholars emphasise that Paul was and remained a Jew?

However, what could be called the Reform Jewish hermeneutics is rather to be detected in the life and work of Jesus of Nazareth, a fact that has been recognised by Claude Montefiore, who did not find his own "profound attachment to Liberal Judaism inconsistent with a...high appreciation of the character and teaching of Jesus."[15] But we have to ask ourselves if, after all, there is a fundamental difference between Jesus of Nazareth and Paul of Tarsus. Whereas Jesus was clearly operating in an inner-Jewish environment (similar to what Jews who identify themselves with the Reform movement do), Paul explicitly described himself as an apostle to the Gentiles (which seems to be something entirely different, i.e. an "extra-Jewish" issue).

Although this line of thought – that Paul could and should be understood as someone who wished to reform the Jewish tradition from within – may seem seductive, the differences between Paul and Reform Judaism are nevertheless so vast that this comparison does not further our understanding of Pauline theology. Early Reform Judaism wanted to reform *Judaism*, not to undermine the Jewishness of Judaism (which, as a matter of fact, is the way in which Pauline theology far too often is presented). Furthermore, there is also a vast difference between Paul, the first-century Jew in the Mediterranean area, and Reform Judaism in Germany and the United States of the nineteenth century. Whereas the impetus of early Reform Judaism was that this was the *beginning* of a new era, a glorious future waiting ahead, the rational for much of Paul's theology was

---

15 Claude G. Montefiore, *The Synoptic Gospels. Edited with an Introduction and a Commentary.* Volume One (London: MacMillan, 2nd edn 1927), ix.

that the *end* was near.¹⁶ Hence, we see that on several issues Paul was arguing in the very opposite direction compared to Reform Judaism.

In other words, the emphasis on Torah as a set of identity markers, providing Israel with social boundaries is certainly not incorrect, but we are inclined to argue that it is incomplete. If it were true that Paul wanted to break down barriers between Jews and Gentiles (which we soon will contest, see below), we have to keep in mind that he most certainly reinstated exclusiveness, albeit in a new form.¹⁷

All this is to say that we need a third perspective, which in this chapter will be called the *newer* or *renewed* perspective on Paul – as it is grateful to the promoters of the new perspective, but nevertheless seeks to formulate Pauline theology in an alternative way, a way which furthers our understanding of first-century Judaism and earliest Christianity. The Torah to Paul is not a *burden*, nor is it primarily a *boundary*, but something else; it is an expression of covenantal particularity and a sign of the covenant, the *berit*.

1.3 The Torah as *Berit*: A Renewed Perspective on Covenantal Particularity

In his groundbreaking scholarship on Paul, Stendahl stressed that Paul's self-understanding must be the cornerstone of modern attempts to reconstruct Pauline theology. An important component of Stendahl's reconstruction is, first, that Paul describes himself in his letters as "apostle of the Gentiles" (ἐθνῶν ἀπόστολος, Rom 11:13) and sent "to the nations" (εἰς τὰ ἔθνη, Gal 2:8). Second, Stendahl emphasises that Paul, when describing his experience on the way to Damascus, uses a terminology from the prophetic texts in the Scriptures. Hence, his experience should be classified as a vocation rather than a conversion. Someone who converts changes religious system, but the one who is called receives a special

---

16 For a presentation of the early history of Reform Judaism, see e.g. Michael Meyer, *Response to Modernity: A History of the Reform Movement in Judaism* (Oxford: Oxford University Press, 1988).

17 For this argument, see, e.g. Francis Watson, *Paul, Judaism and the Gentiles: A Sociological Approach* (Cambridge: Cambridge University Press, 1986), 21-22.: "If in one sense it is true that Paul sought to break down the barrier between Jew and Gentile, he nevertheless did so only to reestablish exclusiveness in a new form." For important reflections on universalism, see Krister Stendahl, *Final Account: Paul's Letter to the Romans. Foreword by Jaroslav Pelikan* (Minneapolis, Minn.: Fortress Press, 1995), 43-44.: "But universalism is always the root of imperialism...[T]he Jewish scholar David Hartman has written a new model of theology in which he says: salvation is the recognition of limits."

assignment – and Paul seems to have been convinced that his mission was to carry the message of Christ to the nations. This means that the relationship between people and peoples, i.e. between the people of Israel and the nations of the world, is of central importance. Third, if we are looking for a centre in his epistle to the Romans, it is not to be found in the first chapters, but rather in chapters 9-11: "I am convinced that Pauline theology has its organizing center in Paul's apostolic perception of his mission to the Gentiles."[18] In other words, according to Stendahl, Paul is first and foremost a theologian who reflects on the relations between the people and the peoples: If the Torah is given to Israel and to Israel only, and if the Torah constitutes and defines Jewish life with its commands and prohibitions, what then is the meaning of Christ offering the nations covenantal embracing by the God of Israel? The discourse of justification by faith in the Pauline epistles cannot be isolated from his mission and work. Pagans are offered a relationship with God, not defined by the Jewish Law, but through faith in Christ. Stendahl quite correctly points out that the Law is not associated with a discourse of conscience and guilt, but with covenantal theology. In sum, Torah is not to be described as a *burden* to the *halakhic* person, nor primarily as *boundaries* (even if this is a more relevant question to pose), but rather as the Hebrew concept *berit*, i.e. covenant.

Hence, what is argued here is that it would be fundamentally wrong to assume that it is possible to reconstruct Second Temple Judaism with the help of a few passages in the Pauline epistles. The problem is that Jews would not recognise themselves in these descriptions. Ed Parish Sanders, for one, acknowledges the need for New Testament scholars to familiarise themselves with Jewish covenantal theology in order to understand the concept Torah and what it denotes. He therefore adopts a phenomenological perspective, in the sense that he seeks to understand each religious tradition on its own terms. The sub-heading of *Paul and Palestinian Judaism*, arguably his most influential book, is *A Comparison of Patterns of Religion*. He believes that one cannot simply compare words, phrases and concepts in Rabbinic texts and in the Pauline epistles. It is therefore meaningless to ask what Judaism thinks of "works righteousness" and *Selbsterlösung*. It is even less relevant to ask what Jews think of Jesus of Nazareth.[19] Instead, one must compare what Jews and Christians say about (or, in this case, rather what Jewish and Christian texts express), first, how one be-

---

18 Stendahl, *Final Account*, ix.
19 Cf. Norman Solomon, *Judaism: A Very Short Introduction* (Oxford: Oxford University Press, 2000 [1996]), 1: "If you find yourself asking questions like, 'What do Jews believe about Jesus?', or 'What is more important in Judaism, faith or works?', you have got off on the wrong footing; you are approaching Judaism with cultural baggage imported from Christianity."

comes a part of the covenant and, second, how one remains in the covenant. Israel never merited inclusion in the covenant; it was God who brought the people out of Egypt "on eagles' wings" (Exod 19:4) and brought them to Mount Sinai, where they received the tablets of the covenant. Now, the first "commandment" of the Jewish division is "I am the Lord your God, who brought you out of the land of Egypt, out of the house of slavery" (Exod 20:2). It is quite correct to say that this is not a "commandment", but rather serves as an introduction to a covenantal lifestyle. Jewish tradition refers to the ten statements as *'aseret ha-dibrot* ("the ten words"), hence emphasising that it is not a matter of commandments without a context. The other nine "words" could more properly be called "commandments", as they are Israel's way to respond to this divine initiative.[20] In short, observing the commandments is not a desperate attempt to please God; it is a way to respond to a gracious God. Sanders calls it "covenantal nomism," perhaps more than anyone else, he has surveyed and refuted the long and influential tradition in the New Testament studies that continually describes Judaism as a self-righteous religion characterised by *Selbsterlösung*.[21] His critique of this misrepresentation of Judaism in antiquity is a lasting contribution to Pauline studies that no one can afford to ignore, even if one need not be convinced that his own reconstruction best describes Paul's thought.

1.4 Three Assertions

Another way to move ahead is to present a set of statements that forms the basis for our further investigations:

(a) We always have to remind ourselves that, generally speaking, the word Torah in Jewish theology does not stand for a problem to be solved, but a life to be lived. Torah is basically an inherently positive concept. When one reads what some New Testament scholars have written about the Law, one cannot help but wonder how it is possible for Jews to have misunderstood the Torah so fundamentally. Indeed, it seems more or less impossible to bring together

---

[20] See, e.g., Göran Larsson, *Bound for Freedom: The Book of Exodus in Jewish and Christian Traditions* (Peabody, Mass.: Hendrickson, 1999), 129.

[21] Ed Parish Sanders, *Paul and Palestinian Judaism: A Comparison of Patterns of Religion* (Philadelphia, Pa.: Fortress Press, 1977), 422-23. See also his chapter "Comparing Judaism and Christianity: An Academic Autobiography." In *Redefining First-Century Jewish and Christian Identities: Essays in Honor of Ed Parish Sanders*, eds. Fabian E. Udoh with Susannah Heschel, Mark Chancey and Gregory Tatum (Notre Dame, Ind.: University of Notre Dame Press, 2008), 11-41.

what Jews and some Pauline scholars say that Judaism is. Whereas numerous New Testament scholars have argued, at some length, that the Law fosters an attitude of pride, the vast majority of religious Jews seem to take for granted that it is quite the opposite, i.e. that it cultivates people to become better persons.[22] One need only consult how Rabbinic commentaries elaborate verses such as Num 12:3: "Now the man Moses was very humble (*'anaw meod*), more so than anyone else on the face of the earth."

(b) Second, we need to consider the eschatological framework of the Pauline *Weltanschauung*. He was quite convinced that the end was near. From his letters we see that, if not a question of years, it was certainly not a matter of more than a few decades.[23] This is recognised by scholars who discuss issues such as slavery in Pauline and other early Christian texts.[24] Those who discuss the concept of Torah also need to take this into consideration.

(c) The third assertion may be the most controversial and arguably also the most important. *The only thing more obvious than the belief that the covenantal commandments in the Torah address Israel is the notion that these commandments do not address Gentiles.* If New Testament scholars fail to acknowledge this, then, unfortunately, their methods are inadequate and eventually their conclusions fail to convince. In other words, the line of thought we wish to explore in this study is that Paul consequently and coherently argued in favour of the assertion that Gentiles should remain Gentiles. Indubitably, this may seem to be a truism in New Testament scholarship, but we are inclined to argue that too many scholars have been paying lip-service to this statement. What we wish to do now is to see in what ways Paul actually *upholds* the distinction between Jews and Gentiles by emphasising the particularity of the commandments in the Torah, as in Rom 3:31: "Do we then overthrow (καταργοῦμεν) the Law by this faith? By no means! On the contrary, we uphold (ἱστάνομεν) the Law."[25] How can such a bold statement be combined with antinomian interpretations of other passages in the Pauline epistles?

---

22 See e.g. the chapter "The Law Fosters an Attitude of Pride" in Veronica Koperski, *What Are They Saying About Paul and the Law?* (New York, N.Y.: Paulist Press, 2001), 7-18.
23 See e.g. Rom 13:11-12; Phil 4.5, and 1Thess 4:14-7. For additional references and an extensive discussion of 1Cor 15:3-56, see Joseph Plevnik, *What Are They Saying About Paul and the End Time?* (New York, N.Y.: Paulist Press, 2009).
24 See e.g. Allen D. Callahan, Richard A. Horsley and Abraham Smith, eds., *Slavery in Text and Interpretation* (Atlanta, Ga.: SBL, 1998) and Jennifer A. Glancy, *Slavery in Early Christianity* (Oxford: Oxford University Press, 2002).
25 Another example is Rom 3:29 where it is emphasised that God is the God "also of the Gentiles", not "instead of the Jews," as it so often is being presented.

1.5 A Theological Duality

John G. Gager has pointed out that there are what he calls "pro-Israel" and "anti-Israel" statements in the Pauline epistles.²⁶ How are we to understand this duality? He argues, quite simply, that the Jewish people are a theological entity also *post Christum*, and it is only when we recognise this that the Pauline duality makes sense. If there are no differences between Jews and Gentiles, we have to conclude that Paul's contentions are murky. In other words, the seeming inconsistency is the result of a duality in Paul's theology; his conclusions depend on whether he addresses the issue of the people of Israel or the nations of the world.

Many Biblical scholars fail to see that Paul seeks to maintain Jewish particularism while embracing universalism. This is the rationale for his resistance to circumcising Gentiles; he actually wanted to *reinforce* the distinction between Jews and Gentiles. Theoretically, there could be (at least) two reasons for Paul to be against circumcision of Gentiles: either because it was *wrong for both Jews and Gentiles* or because it would be *wrong for Gentiles only*. Whereas the supporters of traditional interpretations (and, I would argue, also the adherents of the new perspective) are in favour of, or sometimes simply take for granted, the first alternative, a growing number of scholars are now in favour of the latter. We, too, are inclined towards Paul's argument that non-Jews were not to become Jews, not because being Jewish is wrong, but precisely the opposite, because it was perfectly right – but only for the Jewish people. Paul's sometimes harsh language has nothing to do with living a *halakhic* life *per se* (as if this would be erroneous!) but all the more to do with his vision of the inclusion of the Gentiles (reading between the lines, he seems to be asking: "why can my antagonists not see that now the nations of the world, *quae gentes*, are being welcomed into covenantal community?").

Hence, the best way to understand these statements is simply to recognise that the differences between Jews and non-Jews remained in force, as did the differences between men and women, and between slaves and free men. We would contend that this is the correct way to understand Gal 3:28. Few interpretations of other Pauline statements are characterised by a similar amount of utopian and wishful thinking. This often-quoted statement in Galatians quite simply was not a cry for equality in the Roman society in which Paul lived. It did not abolish

---

26 John G. Gager, "Paul, the Apostle of Judaism." In *Jesus, Judaism, and Christian Anti-Judaism: Reading the New Testament after the Holocaust*, eds. Paula Fredriksen and Adele Reinhartz (Louisville, Ky.: Westminster John Knox Press, 2002), 56-76 at 68-69.

differences. The differences remained, for better or for worse; for slaves it was certainly for the worse. Indeed, when using slavery metaphors, it might even be the case that he actually reinforces slavery.[27] One is reminded of 1Cor 7:17-24, in which he suggests that everyone should remain in the state in which they were before being called. This is certainly not an a-nomism; it is a recognition of *status quo*, especially v. 24 ("in whatever state each was called there let him remain with God"). Pauline scholars agree that Paul's mission was not to promote a Law-free gospel in the sense that there would be no rules or regulations whatsoever for Christ believers. Of course there was to be a set of laws for Christians. Why else would he write in 1Cor 7:19 that what really matters is "keeping the commandments of God"? In other words, the fundamental question is *which commandments are eligible for Gentiles?* The commandment to love one's neighbour as oneself is in the Torah (Rom 13:8 and Gal 5:14; cf. Lev 19:18); the sexual regulations that he discusses in the Corinthian correspondence can be found in the Torah (1Cor 5:1-13; cf. Lev 18:8), etc. If we said that the Torah played no role at all in Pauline theology, we would severely misrepresent Paul and his mission.

1.6 Is It a "Law-Free" Gospel?

Paula Fredriksen suggests that we ought to do away with the entire notion that Paul wished to present a "Law-free Gospel,"[28] What Paul actually wanted to promote was that *non-Jewish members of the Pauline communities were not to become Jews* (and that was the rationale for them not to undergo circumcision), but were to live as if they were "eschatological pagans."[29] In this way, the nations

---

27 Rom 1:1; Gal 1:10 and Phil 1:1. For additional comments, see e.g. Jesper Svartvik, "How Noah, Jesus and Paul Became Captivating Figures: The Side Effects of the Canonization of Slavery Metaphors in Jewish and Christians Texts." *Journal of Greco-Roman Christianity and Judaism* 2 (2005): 168-227 and a monograph (in Swedish); Jesper Svartvik, *Bibeltolkningens bakgator: Synen på judar, slavar och homosexuella i historia och nutid* (Stockholm: Verbum, 2006), 196–212.
28 Paula Fredriksen, "Judaizing the Nations: The Ritual Demands of Paul's Gospel." *NTS* 56 (2010): 232-52 at 252. See also Mark D. Nanos, "The Myth of the 'Law-Free' Paul Standing between Christians and Jews." *SCJR* 4 (2009): 1-21. He argues (see p. 9) that Paul did *not* leave Judaism, he was *not* Law-free, and he did *not* teach a Law-free gospel.
29 Fredriksen, "Judaizing the Nations," 242. See also Nanos, "The Myth of the 'Law-Free' Paul,", who on p. 8 calls them "members of a certain Judaism, of a Jewish subgroup" and describes it as "an amorphous identity." Cf. Gal 6:16 where Paul obviously wishes peace upon *two* groups: "them" (αὐτοὺς) and "the Israel of God," (For peace greetings, see e.g. Ps 125:5 and 128:6). There are no reasons to refer to this verse in order to seek to demonstrate that the church is the new

would join *with* Israel, but they would not join Israel; according to this line of thought, Gentiles are not grafted into Israel's family, but into God's family.[30] Paul's vision and mission may be described in the following way: he draws a new covenantal circle, larger than the former, but one that does not abrogate it. If we fail to perceive this, then Paul's grand plan of *Gentile inclusion* (i.e. the nations worshipping the God of Israel together with the people of Israel) is distorted into one of *Jewish exclusion* (i.e. that *post Christum* the concept "Israel" no longer has anything to do with Israel, but with another faith community instead).[31]

One example of how important scriptural discourse is to Paul is how he uses the temple metaphor. So central is the temple service to Paul that he likens it to his own Gentile mission.[32] In other words, reaching out to the Gentiles is "as if" (*ke-ilu* is the well-known Rabbinic expression for this way of thinking)[33] it were the temple service. Fredriksen states that the prohibition that there must be no *latreia* to native gods was not an ethical demand as much as a ritual demand. It was a judaising demand. In a nutshell, she argues that the last way we should describe Paul's gospel to the Gentiles is to say that it was "Law-free."[34]

Mark D. Nanos points out that "Paul insisted that non-Jews must remain non-Jews, and thus not come under Torah on the same terms as Jews."[35] In other words, he, too, detects a covenantal duality in Paul's theology: what is indispensable for Jews is not required of non-Jews; what is required of Jews is not always required of Gentiles. To a large extent, this particularistic perspective has been missing in previous Pauline scholarship.

Paul's decree that the non-Jew who undergoes circumcision is obligated to keep the entire Torah (Gal 5:3) is, as a matter of fact, a statement that underlines the continuing validity of the Torah, not an argument in favour of its disparagement, denigration and delegitimisation. That is the reason why Gentile Christ-followers had to be proselyte-conversion free. Nanos writes that "Paul is engaged in

---

Israel, when Paul actually maintains the distinction between those who belong to Israel and those who do not.

30 Fredriksen, "Judaizing the Nations," 243-44.
31 See e.g. Segal, *Paul the Convert*, 278: "The purpose of Paul's argument is not to eliminate Israel; rather, the problem continues to be what it always was during his life – the inclusion of the gentiles into the community."
32 See e.g. Rom 15:16. See also Fredriksen, "Judaizing the Nations," 248.
33 See e.g. *b. Sotah* 5b.
34 Fredriksen, "Judaizing the Nations," 251-52.
35 Nanos, "The Myth of the 'Law-Free' Paul," 7. See also his books *The Mystery of Romans: The Jewish Context of Paul's Letter* (Minneapolis, Minn.: Fortress Press, 1996) and *The Irony of Galatians: Paul's Letter in First-Century Context* (Minneapolis, Minn: Fortress Press, 2002).

intra-Jewish polemic about precisely how to interpret Torah and not in disparagement of Torah."[36] Nanos suggests that "it is useful to add 'for Christ-following non-Jews' to virtually all of his statements of instruction to non-Jews; otherwise, the universalizing of Paul's comments about circumcision and Torah-observance will appear to be inclusive of Jews, of everyone, and thereby miss his ethnically nuanced points."[37] Eisenbaum correctly concludes that "Paul's point is that God does not require the same things of all people at all times."[38]

Hence, Paul insisted that non-Jews remain non-Jews, and thus not come under Torah on the same terms as Jews, because it would compromise the propositional truth of the gospel of Christ that the end of the ages has dawned. We have already mentioned that it is important to recognise the eschatological framework in Paul's theology; In Nanos's words, "the awaited 'age to come' had dawned in Christ."[39]

1.7 Is Paul Indifferent, Deceitful or Rhetorical?

But what about the passages that are often referred to as evidence that Paul was indifferent to the Torah? One paragraph in the Pauline epistles that immediately comes to mind is 1Cor 9:19-22, in which he declares that to win Jews he is "like a Jew" (ὡς Ἰουδαῖος), to win those under the Law, he is "like one under the Law" (ὡς ὑπὸ νόμον), and to win the lawless, he becomes "like a lawless [person]" (ὡς ἄνομος).[40] Interesting as it may be, we have to leave aside the question of whether we can discern references to the three categories in this paragraph ([a] Jews, [b] God-fearers and/or proselytes and [c] pagans) in order to focus on the key issue: is this statement not proof that he was indifferent to the commandments in the Torah? If indifferent is too strong a word, should we not at least call him

---

36 Nanos, "The Myth of the 'Law-Free' Paul," 5.
37 Mark D. Nanos, "Paul and Judaism." In *The Jewish Annotated New Testament. New Revised Standard Version Bible Translation*, eds. Amy-Jill Levine and Marc Zvi Brettler (Oxford: Oxford University Press, 2011), 551-54 at 553. See also Eisenbaum, *Paul Was Not a Christian*, 216: "Paul's audience is made up of Gentiles, so everything he says about law applies to Gentiles, unless specified otherwise."
38 Eisenbaum, *Paul Was Not a Christian*, 62.
39 Nanos, "The Myth of the 'Law-Free' Paul," 12.
40 Limitation of space does not allow us to discuss at appropriate length other intriguing passages in the Pauline epistles, e.g. Phil 3:5-9. Suffice it to suggest that this entire passage in Phil 3 should be read in the light of Rom 9:4-5 where Paul does not devalue these aspects of Jewish life.

deceitful? Hence, we have to ask whether Paul intentionally was deceptive. Obviously, this is quite a challenge to many a reader of the New Testament.

How, then, are we to understand this passage? Nanos does not consider this a matter of "lifestyle adaptability," i.e. it is not a description of a person who changes his behaviour depending on the context, which would be intentionally deceptive. Instead, Nanos asserts that it is a matter of "rhetorical adaptability,"[41] and that Paul is referring to his rhetorical strategy to convince his conversation partner. He begins with the premises of those whom he seeks to persuade, in a way similar to the account in Acts 17:16-34 of Paul in Athens, in which the Lucan Paul refers to the concept of "the Unknown God." This hardly means that the speaker himself meant that God was unknown, only that, in this specific context, he became like those for whom this concept was important.

According to Nanos's line of thought, Torah – i.e. Jewish faith and life – for Paul is not adiaphorous; the key issue is that he argues in different ways in different contexts. His "becoming like" signifies not *behaving like* but rather *arguing like* or reasoning like. In short, he employs a strategy of rhetorical adaptability, not being intentionally deceptive, but using the discourse of his audience in order to reach out with his message. Nanos states that New Testament scholars for some time have recognised that indifference to Torah was not the norm either for Jesus or for James, and they now need to acknowledge that this is a valid conclusion to make in the case of Paul as well.[42]

1.8 Conclusions: The Pauline Inclusion of the Gentiles

In an article on Paul and his relation to Judaism, Gager is quite forthright, but not off the mark:

> There has been more nonsense written about Paul's conversion than on just about any other topic I can think of. The standard view is that Paul converted from Judaism to Christianity, that he abandoned Torah for Christ, and that he created the rejection-replacement view that characterizes Christian anti-Judaism.[43]

The first part of this article has presented three interpretations of the role Torah plays in Pauline theology. Although the first interpretation, which essentially presents the Torah as a *burden*, is time-honored and influential, this reading can-

---

41 Nanos, "The Myth of the 'Law-Free' Paul," 17-18.
42 Nanos, "The Myth of the 'Law-Free' Paul," 21.
43 Gager, "Paul, the Apostle of Judaism," 64.

not be sustained. The second understanding, which focuses on the *Torah* as a set of *boundaries*, rightly draws our attention to key issues that were discussed in earliest Christianity. However, whereas the questions posed are correct, the answers that are suggested seem less likely so. In this study we therefore adhere to a third explanation, an interpretation that seeks to do justice to the fundamental distinction in Paul's theology between the people of Israel and the nations of the world. We have argued that a distinct and coercive universalism has governed Pauline studies for a long time. This article seeks to uncover the particularity in the Pauline epistles, the starting-point of which is that Paul implicitly understands and explicitly describes himself as an apostle to the nations (Rom 11:13). He was convinced that he was entrusted with the gospel to the uncircumcised (Gal 2:7), and he vehemently defended the rights of the uncircumcised to be covenantally included through Jesus Christ. He firmly believed and forcefully argued that, in order to become full members of the church, Gentile Christians should not become Jews.[44] However, he also saw the risk that Gentile Christians might boast of superior advantages at the expense of Israel. As Nils A. Dahl pointed out, this is also what happened in subsequent generations.[45] In short, while Paul was in favour of *Gentile inclusion*, post-Pauline readers saw a call for *Jewish exclusion* in his texts.

2 Paul and Mark: Similarities and Dissimilarities

Before examining the role of the Torah in the Marcan narrative, we need to take a few moments to ponder, in general, some of the similarities and differences between the Pauline and Marcan texts. Since the Pauline-Marcan relationship is the meta-question of this entire volume, we will keep this topic to a minimum, solely focusing on a few aspects of particular relevance to our subject. At least three similarities ought to be mentioned:

First, neither Paul nor Mark emphasises the importance of *the twelve disciples*. For obvious reasons, Paul needed a *raison d'être* for his claim to be an apostle to the Gentiles although he had never met Jesus. It is more noteworthy that

---

44 Cf. Segal, *Paul the Convert*, 132: "He was defending a gentile minority against a majority opinion in Christianity that they all must become Jews before they could be accepted as Christians." Whereas we agree with what Segal writes on p. 123 (that it is on account of Christ's salvific death that the gentiles can be adopted into Abrahamic faith by the process of conversion), we have to disagree with his statement on p. 181, that Gentile Christians are "the true [sic] children of Abraham," if by true is meant being the *only* inheritor.
45 Nils A. Dahl, referred to in Segal, *Paul the Convert*, 282.

Mark does not portray the first disciples in a favourable light: he presents them in such a way that leads the reader to perceive that they are flawed in several ways, Judas's betrayal and Peter's denial being but two examples of these. Especially in comparison to Matthew, one perceives quite clearly how close Paul and Mark are to each other in this respect.[46]

A second example of agreements between Paul and Mark is the emphasis on *Gentiles*, an observation of particular importance to the present investigation. Paul describes himself as the apostle to the Gentiles; one of the tasks in the rest of this chapter is to uncover the Gentile mission motif in the Marcan narrative. Hence, we will return to this topic below. Suffice it now simply to state that the focus in Paul's theology is the Gentile mission. Chronologically, Pauline insights from missionary experiences precede by one or two decades the writing down of the final redaction of the Gospel of Mark. Mark intended his narrative account to be read in a community, mainly consisting of Gentile Christians.[47] In other words, we should not be surprised to detect similarities between the two theologians in this respect, but try to detect and to discuss them.

Before we do that, we must address the third topic, i.e. the distinct emphasis on *the cross* in both the Pauline and Marcan texts. Many interpreters have recognised that the cross event plays a similar role in both the Pauline and Marcan theologies. The cross event seems to be understood in a way that renders the teaching of Jesus less important. This feature becomes manifest when the Marcan narrative is compared to the Matthean and Lucan – not to speak of the Johannine – accounts. The other three Gospels in the New Testament contain a considerable number of speeches attributed to Jesus.

Hence, both Paul (who wrote the oldest surviving Christian texts) and Mark (who authored the first account of the life and death of Jesus) emphasise the importance of the death of Jesus. To take it one step further, not only did they presuppose that the death of Jesus *had happened* but they also reasoned that it *had to happen*. Or, to put it differently, due to both historical necessity and theological preferences there is a strong emphasis on *causality* in their theologies, but this causality is expressed remarkably differently by the two theologians, probably because they use two different genres. Being a narrator, Mark emphasises *causality*; this is not equally important to Paul, who stresses the *finality*. The question "Why did Jesus die?" is answered quite differently by Mark and Paul. Paul emphasises the "whereto?" (i.e. the *finality* of the gospel kerygma) and

---

[46] For further comments, see Svartvik, "Matthew and Mark," 43-45.
[47] The validity of Dennis E. Nineham's statement still stands: "of all the places suggested Rome has been by far the most popular, and, so far as the evidence permits of any conclusion, it is perhaps the most likely." See Dennis E. Nineham, *Saint Mark* (London: Penguin, 1968), 42.

Mark the "whence?" (i.e. the *causality* of the Gospel narrative).[48] The most obvious difference between Paul and Mark, therefore, is what is emphasised in their texts: either *finality* or *causality*.[49] We will return to this important observation in our concluding remarks. It is now time to ponder the role of the Torah in the Marcan narrative.

3 Mark and the Torah

It is quite astonishing that generations of commentators on the earliest narrative account of the life and death of Jesus of Nazareth, generally speaking, have not called attention to what is quite obvious in this text. In Mark's Gospel we encounter a pious Jew who regularly attends synagogue services (e.g., 1:21.39; 6:2); who instructs a cleansed leper to make the appropriate sacrifice in accordance with the regulations in the Torah (1:44);[50] who teaches regularly in the temple when in Jerusalem (14:49); and who celebrates a Passover *seder* with his disciples, ending with the *hallel*, i.e., Psalms 113-118 (14:26). Since this religious Jew is executed by the Romans on a Friday afternoon, it is only on Sunday, i.e. after *shabbat*, that some of his female followers come to the grave to anoint his body. Hence, the implicit and informed reader takes for granted that on *shabbat* the disciples of this religious leader rested according to the Biblical commandment (which, as a matter of fact, is explicitly stated in Luke 23:56).

Needless to say, there are some passages in Mark's Gospel which seem to point in another direction, but they should not conceal what is quite obvious: Jesus is presented as a Jew among Jews, as a Jew who lived a religious life and died as a pious Jew, who quoted the Psalms in his hour of death while being crucified by the Romans who called him "the King of the Jews" (15:26). We agree with Robert McFarlane who concludes that the Marcan Jesus is " a fig-

---

48 Krister Stendahl, *Holy Week Preaching* (Philadelphia, Pa.: Fortress Press, 1985), 23. For the classical presentation of the importance of causality in plots, see Edward Morgan Forster, *Aspects of the Novel edited by Oliver Stallybrass* (London: Penguin, 1990 [1927]), 87.
49 For additional comments on finality and causality, see Jesper Svartvik, "Forging an Incarnational Theology: Two Score Years after *Nostra Aetate*." In *Plural voices: Intradisciplinary Perspectives on Interreligious Issues*, eds. Patrik Fridlund, Lucie Kaennel and Catharina Stenqvist (Leuven: Peeters, 2009), 203-20 at 206-09.
50 He is not described as being "healed," but "cleansed," which is in accordance with the taxonomy in the Torah.

ure more representative of, than disjunctive with, elements within the rich tapestry of contemporary Judaism."[51]

But, what about those episodes in the Marcan narrative that may give the impression that this would be an incorrect description of the life and teachings of the Nazarene? When we turn to the most known pericopes, i.e. 2:23-28 and 3:1-5, we note that what is being discussed is the implementation of the *shabbat* commandment. While it has long been conventional to present what is happening in these two texts as violations of the *shabbat* regulations, a growing number of scholars argue that the key concern is not whether *halakhah* is mandatory for a religious first-century Jewish life, but in what way it is to be put into practice.

3.1 The Issue of *Kashrut* in the Gospel of Mark

In fact, only one text in the entire Gospel of Mark could be considered a conspicuous impediment to a religious Jewish everyday life, and that is Mark 7:1-23, given that it is interpreted according to the mainstream interpretation, which can be summarised in three points: (a) an emphasis is put on the fifteenth verse, and it interprets it as v. 19 seems to indicate, i.e. as an abrogation of *kashrut*; (b) it sees no reason to doubt the authenticity of the parabolic and rather elusive statement in v. 15; and (c) the conclusion of the two previous points is that the teaching of the historical Jesus was both anti-tradition (critical of the developing early Rabbinic interpretation of the Torah) and anti-nomistic (against the written Torah).[52] In a nutshell, according to the mainstream interpretation, the historical Jesus abolished *kashrut*, i.e. the Jewish food laws.[53]

During the last few decades, however, historical Jesus scholarship has come to question this interpretation. Unsurprisingly, it is difficult to summarise in a few sentences anything that stems from the *Leben Jesu Forschung*, especially those areas that touch upon his relation to contemporary Judaism, as so much has been refined and even refuted by previous generations of scholarship. What most scholars agree upon, however, is that whereas Mark in 7:19 seems

---

51 "Interpretive supremacy," to use McFarlane's term, should not be confused with supersessionism and lack of interest and/or knowledge in *halakhah*. See Robert McFarlane, "The Gospel of Mark and Judaism" (www.jcrelations.net/The+Gospel+of+Mark+and+Judaism.2208.0.html?L=3; accessed March 11, 2012), 3.
52 See Svartvik, *Mark and Mission*, 3-4.
53 For examples of statements issued by mainstream interpreters, see Svartvik, *Mark and Mission*, 3 n. 9.

to portray a protagonist who is in conflict with *halakhah*, the Matthean parallel (Matt 15:20) certainly presents a protagonist who argues within the boundaries of *halakhah* (whether *netilat yadayim* is required or not, a matter of dispute at the time).

It should be pointed out that Daniel Boyarin recently has suggested that also the Marcan text can be read as an inner-*halakhic* debate.[54] In the following discussion, however, we will assume that the Marcan text is less consistent with *halakhic* observance than the teachings and way of life of the historical Jesus of Nazareth. In short, we are inclined to argue that Mark 7:1-23 is a pericope that commences with an inner-*halakhic* discussion on *netilat yadayim*, but continues with what seems to be an editorial comment in v. 19, which moves the focus from hand-washing (which was a matter of discussion in the first century) to *kashrut* (which was not questioned *on the whole* in first-century Judaism): "[thereby] cleansing all foods" (καθαρίζων πάντα τὰ βρώματα). In order to further our understanding of the editor's agenda and concerns, we have to study the somewhat wider textual context around the seventh chapter.

3.2 Mark as Novelist and the Gospel of Mark as Story

In *The Charles Eliot Norton Lectures*, given in 1977–78, Frank Kermode deplores the "lingering obsession with historicity" in the study of Biblical texts.[55] However, some narrative analyses of the New Testament Gospels were presented in the late 70s and early 80s. Robert C. Tannehill's influential article, published in 1977, on the Marcan characterisation of the disciples was followed by Werner H. Kelber's book *Mark's Story of Jesus*, published in 1979; and *Mark as Story*, published in 1982 by David Rhoads and Donald Michie.[56]

---

[54] Daniel Boyarin, *Jewish Gospels: The Story of the Jewish Christ* (New York, N.Y.: New Press, 2012), 102-28. See also the discussion of *b. Avodah Zarah* 16b-17a in Ray A. Pritz, *Nazarene Jewish Christianity: From the End of the New Testament Period until Its Disappearance in the Fourth Century* (Jerusalem: Magnes Press, 1992 [1988]), 96-7. According to this Talmudic text, Jesus of Nazareth taught that an offering to the high priest obtained from immoral earnings was of no more value than human waste and its place was down the toilet. There are interesting features here: the offering motif, Jesus' earthy language, the denigration of something as human waste, and also the sewer motif.
[55] Frank Kermode, *The Genesis of Secrecy: On the Interpretation of Narrative* (Cambridge, Mass.: Harvard University Press, 1979), 130.
[56] Robert C. Tannehill, "The Characterization of the Disciples in Mark." *JR* 57 (1977): 386-405; Werner H. Kelber, *Mark's Story of Jesus* (Philadelphia, Pa.: Fortress Press, 1979); and David

One of the greatest merits and grandest achievements of narrative analyses of the Gospel of Mark is that we realise that it is not an uncomplicated, exclusively historical source given to the scholarly community in order to reconstruct the life of the historical Jesus or the earliest Christian communities. We agree with Mary-Ann Tolbert that the Gospel of Mark is "a mysterious, opaque, and peculiar story."[57] Like many a text, the Gospel of Mark is as unruly and disruptive as the sea. It is time to turn our eyes towards the Sea of Galilee, which Elizabeth Struthers Malbon calls "the geographical focal point for the first half of the Gospel of Mark, the center of the Marcan Jesus' movement in space."[58]

3.3 The Sea of Galilee: "East is East, and West is West"[59]

New Testament scholars have spent considerable time pondering the north-south axis in the Marcan narrative. Can we detect a Galilean-Judaean antithesis in the text? Although put forward by numerous scholars (e.g. Elizabeth Struthers Malbon, Bas van Iersel, Sean Freyne, Willard M. Swartley *et alii*), we have to regard the literary antithesis of Galilee and Judaea with scepticism. I have argued elsewhere that the east-west axis is far more central to the narrative than the north-south axis.[60] The hypothesis that Galilee might be *terra Christiana* should not overshadow what is more obvious, namely, the importance of the western and eastern shores of the Sea of Galilee. In a few words, *the Sea of Galilee is even more important than the soil of Galilee.*[61]

Rhoads and Donald Michie, *Mark as Story: An Introduction to the Narrative of a Gospel* (Philadelphia, Pa.: Fortress Press, 1982). For further comments, see Svartvik, *Mark and Mission*, 25-61.
57 Mary Ann Tolbert, *Sowing the Gospel: Mark's World in Literary-Historical Perspective* (Minneapolis, Minn: Fortress Press, 1989), 1. See also her definition of genre on p. 49: "a prior agreement between authors and readers...a set of shared expectations...a consensus of 'fore-understandings exterior to a text which enable us to follow that text'." The quotation is from Kermode, *The Genesis of Secrecy*, 163.
58 Elizabeth Struthers Malbon, "The Jesus of Mark and the Sea of Galilee." *JBL* 103 (1984): 363-77 at 363.
59 Rudyard Kipling, "The Ballad of East and West", first published in *Pioneer* (December 2, 1889).
60 Svartvik, *Mark and Mission*, 229-40.
61 Furthermore, we may have to point out that negative texts about Jerusalem should not lead us into the temptation of thinking that it would constitute a breach with Judaism. The Qumran community, one of the most well-known Jewish groups of late Second Temple Judaism, chose not to have anything to do with the religious elite in Jerusalem. How many scholars think of the Qumran community as an essentially non-Jewish or an anti-Jewish group?

In Mark 5-8 the distinct Greek expression πέραν ("on the other side") is used when Jesus and/or his disciples cross the Sea of Galilee. The Marcan setting reveals that this is not only a matter of trans-portation but, to a considerable extent, also a trans-national enterprise. On the east side of the Sea of Galilee, the disciples and the reader are met by Gentiles, non-Jewish paraphernalia (e. g. "a great herd of swine;" 5:11) and the reference to the plethora of Greek cities known as Decapolis (5:20). When Jesus crosses the Sea of Galilee again, the reader is immediately confronted with another set of properties; instead of swine and Greek cities, the reader hears about the synagogue leader Jairus. On his way to the home of this Jairus, Jesus meets a woman who touches his cloak (5:27). We have every reason to assume that the ἱμάτιον had fringes, (Gr. κράσπεδα; Heb. *tsitsiyot*), as this is stated explicitly in Mark 6:56. The Matthean and Lucan versions of the pericope have added that she touches the κράσπεδον, the fringe of the cloak.[62] Hence, the Jewishness of Jesus is underlined as he encounters individuals on the western shore. Similarly, when Jesus in 6:2 teaches on *shabbat* in the synagogue, both time and space accentuate Jesus as a Jew.

In sum, the spatial setting of 4:35-6:6 can certainly be outlined as a dichotomy between the *Jewish* west side of the sea and the *Gentile* east side of the sea. It appears that almost everything occurring on the west side of the sea throughout the Gospel is connected with Jews. It is there that Jesus teaches the disciples and the crowds and discusses Scripture and traditions with Pharisees and scribes. On the other side of the sea, no synagogues are visited, no temporal references to the *shabbat* are found, and no homilies are preached. We agree with Mark Allan Powell when he states that "[t]he Sea of Galilee serves as a 'boundary' between the homeland and the foreign lands."[63] We have reason to believe that there are sufficient indications to enable us to understand the western side of the sea as Jewish lands (with synagogues and *tsitsiyot*) and the eastern side of it as Gentile lands (with swine herds and Greek cities). Needless to say, we should not plead guilty to the referential fallacy, i.e. that everything mentioned in a story refers to the world outside the story, "the lingering obsession with historicity," that Kermode bemoaned. At this moment we need not concern ourselves with the historicity, i.e. whether there were only Gentiles living on the east-

---

[62] See Matt 9:20 and Luke 8:44. See also Matt 23:5, a discussion about the extent but by no means the existence of fringes. See also Jodi Magness, *Stone and Dung, Oil and Spit: Jewish Daily Life in the Time of Jesus* (Grand Rapids, Mich.: Eerdmans, 2011), 117: "Despite the lack of archaeological evidence, literary sources indicate that *tefillin* and *tzitzit* were a familiar sight in Palestine in the late Second Temple period and must have been worn regularly by some Jews."
[63] Mark Allan Powell, *What Is Narrative Criticism? A New Approach to the Bible* (London: SPCK, 1993 [1990]), 76.

ern shore of the Sea of Galilee. It suffices to conclude that the east shore carries Gentile connotations. One is reminded of Rudyard Kipling's famous words: "East is east, and west is west" – will the twain never meet?[64]

3.4 Let the Reader Understand the Two Bread Miracles

Biblical scholars constantly run the risk of overemphasising details in the Biblical texts, but every so often the readers are actually encouraged *by the text itself* to reflect on the importance of the details, lest they, like the disciples in the Marcan account, may be accused of not understanding the significance of what is being described in the narrative (Mark 8:19-21):

> "When I broke the five loaves for the five thousand, how many baskets [κοφι/νους] full of broken pieces did you collect?" They said to him, "Twelve." "And the seven for the four thousand, how many baskets [σπυί/δων] full of broken pieces did you collect?" And they said to him, "Seven." Then he said to them, "Do you not yet understand?"

In other words, to choose *not* to pay heed to this "passage" (both the passage in the Marcan text and the passage by boat over the Sea of Galilee) is not to take the narrator's directive seriously.

How, then, are we to interpret this key passage, in which Jesus reproaches his disciples for not understanding the significance of the two bread miracles? Three clues are given us: (a) first, the observation that the narrator uses two different words for "basket," κόφινος (6:43 and 8:19) and σπυρίς (8:8 and 8:20); (b) second, the Marcan protagonist emphasises the significance of the number of baskets filled with bread after each of the miracles; and (c) third, the simple fact that there are two bread miracles in the Marcan narrative.

(a) How are we to explain that two words are used for "baskets," both in the story about the bread miracles and then also in the following "debriefing" with the disciples? It is often pointed out that while κόφινος is used in agricultural contexts, σπυρίς is part of the fisherman's equipment.[65] However, a reading that furthers our understanding of the Marcan narrative is that the narrator de-

---

[64] This is not the place for a discussion on issues of colonialism in Kipling's poem. A relevant article on colonial readings of Biblical texts is Yvonne Sherwood, "'Colonizing the Old Testament' or 'Representing Christian Interests Abroad': Jewish-Christian Relations Across Old Testament Territory." In *Christian-Jewish Relations through the Centuries*, eds. Stanley E. Porter and Brook W. R. Pearson (London: T & T Clark International, 2004), 255-81.

[65] For additional comments, see Svartvik, *Mark and Mission*, 299.

liberately uses two different words in order to arouse associations and to make the reader aware of two different target groups in the two narratives, one Jewish and one Gentile.

(b) Then, what about the number of baskets with left-over bread? The most obvious conclusion is to see the twelve baskets of the first miracle as a reference to the twelve tribes; similarly, the seven baskets of the second miracle can easily be correlated to abundance (cf. "Not [only] seven times, but I tell you, seventy-seven times;" Matt 18:22) and also to the seventy nations of the world, i.e. the Gentiles.[66] Is it likely that the number "seven" refers to the ingathering of the nations of the world?

(c) What about the duality *per se*? Why two bread miracles? The seventh chapter is sandwiched between the two bread miracles in chapters six and eight. When interpreting the text, we will most probably be rewarded if we consider what is being sandwiched i.e., the Marcan protagonist's discussion on *Jewish* hand-washing and food regulations (7:1-23) and also his meeting with the Syro-Phoenician, i.e. *Gentile*, woman (7:24-30). We are inclined to argue that the first bread-miracle is presented in such a way as to be understood as Jesus satisfying the *Jewish* crowds, and the second miracle as Jesus reaching out to the *Gentiles* as well.

There are several indications that a Jew-Gentile matrix can be found in the Marcan bread cycle: *the choice of words*, (the remarkable reluctance of Jesus in 7:24-30), *the significance of numbers* and *the geopolitical setting* in Mark. Hence, by key-words, effects of surprise, numbers and geography, the narrator gives the reader a wider frame of interpretations than the text at first sight may seem to supply. In short, we have strong reasons to believe that the bread cycle most probably deals with the relations between Jews and Gentiles. Keeping in mind that Mark himself emphasises that these two miracles point beyond themselves ("Do you not yet understand?;" 8:21), we draw the conclusion that chapters 6-8 may be understood as a narrative presentation of the rationale for Gentile mission. *What Paul had argued for in his epistles some fifteen to twenty years earlier, Mark now presents in his narrative account.*

---

[66] Seventy nations are mentioned in Gen 10, excluding Nimrod, who is an individual, see Nahum M. Sarna, *Genesis: The Traditional Text with the New JPS Translation* (Philadelphia, Pa.: Jewish Publication Society, 1989), 69.

3.5 Reading Mark 7:1–23 in Its Narrative Context

We have already noted that in terms of Jesus' relation to *halakhah*, the tone and tenor are quite different in Mark 7:1-23, especially in v. 19, compared to the rest of the narrative.[67] How are we to recognise and also comprehend this discrepancy? As Gager does in his discussion on Pauline theology (arguing that there are pro-Israel and anti-Israel statements in the *Corpus Paulinum*), we are inclined to do something similar when studying the Gospel of Mark. There are inner-*halakhic* pericopes in this text, of which one could be read as a questioning *halakhah* in a surprising way. The general impression we get when reading the Marcan narrative is that the protagonist is an observant Jew, who often visits synagogues, who fervently discusses how to implement the *shabbat* commandment, and who keenly celebrates the Passover *seder* in Jerusalem together with his disciples.

In this article we have argued that chapters 6-8 are best interpreted allegorically, pointing beyond themselves to the major theological issue at that time, i. e. Gentile mission.[68] When reading 8:21 ("Do you not yet understand"), one is reminded of Mark's famous hint to the reader in 13:14 ("let the reader understand").[69] In chapters 6-8 Mark uses what we might want to call "a bread discourse" in order to convey his message that what Jesus has to offer suffices for Jews and Gentiles alike. If these texts in some way and to some extent constitute a window to the Marcan community, we are inclined to draw the conclusion that the issue of Gentiles played a significant role in his community.

We are reminded of a similar Lucan account, which will shed light on the Marcan narrative. In Acts 10.11 Peter sees something like a large sheet with all kinds of four-footed creatures, reptiles and birds of the air. When commanded to eat, he protests: "By no means, Lord, for I have never eaten anything that is profane or unclean" (10.14). It is only in v. 28 that the *nimshal* is presented: "God has shown me that I should not call anyone [NB not "anything," but "any-

---

67 See, however, Boyarin, *The Jewish Gospels*, 102-28. He proposes that also 7:19 be interpreted as an inner-*halakhic* statement, see e.g. 112.
68 On allegories in the Bible and in Biblical interpretation, see e.g. John F. A. Sawyer, *A Concise Dictionary of the Bible and Its Reception* (Louisville, Ky.: Westminster John Knox Press, 2009), 8-10. He refers to Ezek 17:2; 24:3 and Eccl 12:1-7 when giving examples of allegories in the Bible. Most New Testament scholars would say that Mark's fourth chapter is best described as an allegory, in which the details in the story of the sower (4:1-9) are explained afterwards (4:13-20).
69 Robert M. Fowler describes the Gospel of Mark as an "audience-oriented narrative" which favours the narratee at the expense of the characters; see Robert M. Fowler, *Let the Reader Understand: Reader-Response Criticism and the Gospel of Mark* (Minneapolis, Minn.: Fortress Press, 1991), 52 and 219.

one:" ἄνθρωπον] profane or unclean."[70] Quite obviously, Luke uses a vision of *non-kosher foods* in order to convince Peter that an outreach to *non-Jews* is theologically endorsed.

The present reader might think that we are reading things into Mark 6-8, which clearly are not there, at least not on the surface. Yes, we are emphasising the symbolism of the shores; and yes, we are suggesting that the text points in the direction of the inclusion of the Gentiles. In what way is this reading different from other readings? The answer is that we read Mark as a Pauline text; since Paul describes himself as the apostle to the Gentiles, we ask ourselves whether there is a "to the Jew first, and also to the Gentiles" paradigm in the Marcan account?[71] In short, we are inclined to discern and recognise Mark's contribution to first-century discussions about Gentile mission.

4 Conclusions: The Pauline and Marcan Understanding of Torah

This chapter has addressed two of the most central questions in New Testament studies: *Why did Paul write the Epistle to the Romans? Why did Mark write his Gospel?* We have suggested that the answer to these two questions is to be found, to a large extent, in their understanding of the relation between Jews and Gentiles. The key question in this chapter is whether Paul influenced Mark on the issue of the Torah. We have argued that a cloud of misunderstanding obscures their theological affinity. Once we understand Pauline theology better, we also see the similarities between these two theological authors at the beginning of Christianity.

We have emphasised that it is fundamentally flawed to present the role of the Torah in Pauline theology as a *burden*. It is also argued that it is insufficient to think of it principally as a set of *boundaries* that has to be overcome in order to pave the way for Gentile inclusion. The commandments of the Torah remain, also in Pauline theology, visible signs of the invisible *berit*, i.e. the covenant between God and Israel.

We have then turned to the Marcan account, and argued that we may detect a similar particularistic perspective in this narrative presentation of the life and

---

[70] David Stern defines *nimshal* as "the so-called explanation or application accompanying the narrative;" see his *Parables in Midrash: Narrative and Exegesis in Rabbinic Literature* (Cambridge, Mass.: Harvard University Press, 1991), 13.
[71] Cf. Rom 1:16 and 3:29.

works of Jesus of Nazareth. Scholars interested in the life and teaching of the historical Jesus have benefitted tremendously from the Gospel of Mark, being the first narrative account of Jesus of Nazareth. Having said this, however, we need to keep in mind that this was evidently not Mark's purpose. Mark was a skilled writer, who certainly has often been misunderstood or misrepresented as naïve and unsophisticated, but during the last decades we have seen a renewed interest in him as a novelist. There is certainly more in the Marcan narrative than first meets the eye.

It has been pointed out that Jesus is presented as a religious Jew. There is, however, one paragraph in his text that could be considered a conspicuous impediment to a religious Jewish everyday life, and that is Mark 7:1-23. We have argued in this article that this passage should not be interpreted in splendid isolation from the context. In a way which is conspicuously similar to the Lucan strategy in Acts 10, the cleansing of forbidden foods is used as a *carte blanche* for the Gentile mission: both Mark and Luke use foods in order to argue in favour of the Gentile mission. In Mark 8:21 the reader is encouraged to find the meaning of the two bread narratives ("Do you not yet understand?"). We could say that the editorial comment in 7:19 (καθαρίζων πάντα τὰ βρώματα) is followed up in 8:21, using the Lucan statement in Acts 10.28: "Do you not understand that God has shown that you should not call anyone profane or unclean?"

Finally, we have suggested that Mark attributes considerable symbolism to the shores of the Sea of Galilee. To express it in the Kiplingean manner: yes, "east is east, and west is west", i.e. the covenantal identity of the people of Israel remains. Now, according to Paul and Mark the twain actually do meet: the Gentiles are invited to covenantal community, but this is through the Christ event, not because of the abrogation of the Torah.

We have suggested that the Marcan emphasis on *causality* has to do with the narrative literary genre *per se*, and that Paul's stress on *finality* is to be understood as an outcome of his belief that he has been called to be the apostle to the Gentiles. By way of conclusion, we now need to reflect on a few more aspects of causality and finality.

Mark famously introduces his Gospel by stating that this is "the beginning of the gospel" (1:1; ἀρχὴ τοῦ εὐαγγελίου). Innumerable readers have read this, but not everyone has reflected on how long this beginning is. Where does ἡ ἀρχή end? We would argue that his entire narrative, all its sixteen chapters, constitute the beginning. By the time of his writing his narrative account, everyone knew the end – the death of Jesus on the cross and the inclusion of the Gentiles – but the question that he wishes to give a lengthy answer to is how it all began. That is why Mark describes his narrative as "the beginning of the gospel." Paul had already explained and emphasised the end and the ending of the Gospel, i.e. how it ended and the τέλος. He famously wrote that Christ was the τέλος νόμου, which we interpret as the culmination of the Torah, not as the one who brings an end to the Torah. We constantly have to keep in mind that the Pauline Gentile mission had been going on for some twenty years when Mark wrote his narrative presentation of the life and works of Jesus of Nazareth. That is the *Sitz im Leben* of the Gospel of Mark.

We have shown that the relationship between Jews and Gentiles is a key issue for both Paul and Mark. We are inclined to argue that both Paul and Mark believed that the Torah continued to be relevant to Jews, at the same time as it remained a non-option for Gentiles. Both also believed that Gentile Christians should remain what they are and not adhere to Jewish *halakhah* – not because *halakhah* would be wrong for everyone, but simply because it is right for Jews.

In other words, for the students of earliest Christianity it is absolutely essential to discern and recognise the Pauline-Marcan affiliation and the related interpretations of the Torah. That is why this collection of essays is imperative for all readers of the New Testament.

Bibliography

Boyarin Daniel. *A Radical Jew: Paul and the Politics of Identity.* Berkeley, Ca.: University of California Press, 1994.

—, *Jewish Gospels: The Story of the Jewish Christ.* New York, N.Y.: New Press, 2012.

Brueggemann, Walter. *The Bible Makes Sense: Revised Edition with a New Introduction.* Louisville, Ky.: Westminster John Knox Press, 2001.

Callahan, Allen D., Richard A. Horsley and Abraham Smith, eds. *Slavery in Text and Interpretation.* Atlanta, Ga.: SBL, 1998.

Dunn, James D. G. "The New Perspective on Paul." *BJRL* 65 (1983): 94-122.

Eisenbaum, Pamela. *Paul Was Not a Christian: The Original Message of a Misunderstood Apostle.* San Francisco, Ca.: HarperOne, 2009.

Forster, Edward Morgan. *Aspects of the Novel edited by Oliver Stallybrass.* London: Penguin, 1990 [1927].

Fowler, Robert M. *Let the Reader Understand: Reader-Response Criticism and the Gospel of Mark.* Minneapolis, Minn.: Fortress Press, 1991.

Fredriksen, Paula. "Judaizing the Nations: The Ritual Demands of Paul's Gospel." *NTS* 56 (2010): 232-252.

Gager, John G. "Paul, the Apostle of Judaism," in: *Jesus, Judaism, and Christian Anti-Judaism: Reading the New Testament after the Holocaust,* eds. Paula Fredriksen and Adele Reinhartz, 56-76. Louisville, Ky.: Westminster John Knox Press, 2002.

Glancy, Jennifer A. *Slavery in Early Christianity.* Oxford: Oxford University Press, 2002.

Hamerton-Kelly, Robert G. *Sacred Violence: Paul's Hermeneutics of the Cross.* Minneapolis, Minn.: Fortress Press, 1992.

—, Robert G. *The Gospel and the Sacred: Poetics of Violence in Mark.* Minneapolis, Minn.: Fortress Press, 1994.

Isaac, Jules. *The Teaching of Contempt: The Christian Roots of Anti-Semitism,* trans. Helen Weaver. New York: Holt, Rinehart & Winston, 1964.

Jospe, Raphael. "Hillel's Rule." *JQR* 81 (1990): 45-57.

Kelber, Werner H. *Mark's Story of Jesus.* Philadelphia, Pa.: Fortress Press, 1979.

Kermode, Frank. *The Genesis of Secrecy: On the Interpretation of Narrative.* Cambridge, Mass.: Harvard University Press, 1979.

Kipling, Rudyard. "The Ballad of East and West." *Pioneer* (December 2, 1889).

Koperski, Veronica. *What Are They Saying About Paul and the Law?* (New York, N.Y.: Paulist Press, 2001).

Larsson, Göran. *Bound for Freedom: The Book of Exodus in Jewish and Christian Traditions.* Peabody, Mass.: Hendrickson, 1999.

Magness, Jodi. *Stone and Dung, Oil and Spit: Jewish Daily Life in the Time of Jesus.* Grand Rapids, Mich.: Eerdmans, 2011.

Malbon, Elizabeth Struthers. "The Jesus of Mark and the Sea of Galilee." *JBL* 103 (1984): 363-77.

Marcus, Joel. "Mark – Interpreter of Paul." *NTS* 46 (2000): 473-87.

McFarlane, Robert. "The Gospel of Mark and Judaism" (www.jcrelations.net/The+Gospel+of+Mark+and+Judaism.2208.0.html?L=3; accessed March 11, 2012).

Meyer, Michael. *Response to Modernity: A History of the Reform Movement in Judaism.* Oxford: Oxford University Press, 1988.

Montefiore, Claude G. *The Synoptic Gospels. Edited with an Introduction and a Commentary.* Volume One. London: MacMillan, 2nd edn 1927.

Nanos, Mark, D. *The Mystery of Romans: The Jewish Context of Paul's Letter.* Minneapolis, Minn.: Fortress Press, 1996.

—, *The Irony of Galatians: Paul's Letter in First-Century Context.* Minneapolis. Minn.: Fortress Press, 2002.

—, "The Myth of the 'Law-Free' Paul Standing between Christians and Jews." *SCJR* 4 (2009): 1-21.

—, "Paul and Judaism," in *The Jewish Annotated New Testament. New Revised Standard Version Bible Translation*, eds. Amy-Jill Levine and Marc Zvi Brettler, 551-4. Oxford: Oxford University Press, 2011.

Nineham, Dennis E. *Saint Mark.* London: Penguin, 1968.

Painter, John. *Mark's Gospel.* London: Routledge, 1997.

Plevnik, Joseph. *What Are They Saying About Paul and the End Time?* New York, N.Y.: Paulist Press, 2009.

Powell, Mark Allan. *What Is Narrative Criticism? A New Approach to the Bible.* London: SPCK, 1993 [1990].

Pritz, Ray A. *Nazarene Jewish Christianity: From the End of the New Testament Period until Its Disappearance in the Fourth Century.* Jerusalem: Magnes Press, 1992 [1988].

Rhoads, David, and Donald Michie. *Mark as Story: An Introduction to the Narrative of a Gospel.* Philadelphia, Pa.: Fortress Press, 1982.

Sanders, Ed Parish. *Paul and Palestinian Judaism: A Comparison of Patterns of Religion.* Philadelphia, Pa.: Fortress Press, 1977.

—, "Comparing Judaism and Christianity: An Academic Autobiography," in: *Redefining First-Century Jewish and Christian Identities: Essays in Honor of Ed Parish Sanders*, eds. Fabian E. Udoh with Susannah Heschel, Mark Chancey and Gregory Tatum, 11-41. Notre Dame, Ind.: University of Notre Dame Press, 2008.

Sarna, Nahum M. *Genesis: The Traditional Text with the New JPS Translation.* Philadelphia, Pa.: Jewish Publication Society, 1989.

Sawyer, John F. A. *A Concise Dictionary of the Bible and Its Reception.* Louisville, Ky.: Westminster John Knox Press, 2009.

Segal, Alan F. *Paul the Convert: The Apostolate and Apostasy of Saul the Pharisee.* New Haven, Conn.: Yale University Press, 1990.

Sherwood, Yvonne. "'Colonizing the Old Testament' or 'Representing Christian Interests Abroad': Jewish-Christian Relations Across Old Testament Territory," in: *Christian-Jewish Relations through the Centuries*, eds. Stanley E. Porter and Brook W. R. Pearson, 255-81. London: T & T Clark International, 2004.

Sim, David C. *The Gospel of Matthew and Christian Judaism: The History and Social Setting of the Matthean Community.* SNTW. Edinburgh: T & T Clark, 1998.

Solomon, Norman. *Judaism: A Very Short Introduction.* Oxford: Oxford University Press, 2000 [1996].

Stendahl, Krister. "The Apostle Paul and the Introspective Conscience of the West." *HTR* 56 (1963): 199-215.

—, *Holy Week Preaching.* Philadelphia, Pa.: Fortress Press, 1985.

—, *Final Account: Paul's Letter to the Romans.* Foreword by Jaroslav Pelikan. Minneapolis, Minn.: Fortress Press, 1995.

Stern, David. *Parables in Midrash: Narrative and Exegesis in Rabbinic Literature.* Cambridge, Mass.: Harvard University Press, 1991.

Strack, Hermann L., and Paul Billerbeck. *Kommentar zum Neuen Testament aus Talmud und Midrasch.* 6 vols. Munich: Beck, 1922-28.

Svartvik, Jesper. *Mark and Mission: Mk 7:1-23 in its Narrative and Historical Contexts.* Stockholm: Almqvist & Wiksell, 2000.

—, "How Noah, Jesus and Paul Became Captivating Figures: The Side Effects of the Canonization of Slavery Metaphors in Jewish and Christians Texts." *Journal of Greco-Roman Christianity and Judaism* 2 (2005), 168-227.

—, "The Markan Interpretation of the Pentateuchal Food Laws," in: *Biblical Interpretation in Early Christian Gospels. Volume I: The Gospel of Mark*, ed. Thomas R. Hatina, 169-181. London: T & T Clark International, 2006.

—, *Bibeltolkningens bakgator: Synen på judar, slavar och homosexuella i historia och nutid.* Stockholm: Verbum, 2006.

—, "Matthew and Mark," in: *Matthew and His Christian Contemporaries*, eds. David C. Sim and Boris Repschinski, 27-49. London: T & T Clark International, 2008.

—, "Forging an Incarnational Theology: Two Score Years after *Nostra Aetate*," in: *Plural voices: Intradisciplinary Perspectives on Interreligious Issues*, eds. Patrik Fridlund, Lucie Kaennel and Catharina Stenqvist, 203-20. Leuven: Peeters, 2009.

Tannehill, Robert C. "The Characterization of the Disciples in Mark." *JR* 57 (1977): 386-405.

Tolbert, Mary Ann. *Sowing the Gospel: Mark's World in Literary-Historical Perspective.* Minneapolis, Pa.: Fortress Press, 1989.

Tomson, Peter J. *Paul and the Jewish Law: Halakha in the Letters of the Apostle to the Gentiles.* Assen: Van Gorcum, 1990.

Watson, Francis. *Paul, Judaism and the Gentiles: A Sociological Approach.* Cambridge: Cambridge University Press, 1986.

Westerholm, Stephen. *Israel's Law and the Church's Faith: Paul and His Recent Interpreters.* Grand Rapids, Mich.: Eerdmans, 1988.

Florian Wilk
„Die Schriften" bei Markus und Paulus[1]

1 Einführung

Sowohl im Evangelium nach Markus als auch in den Briefen des Apostels Paulus werden diverse biblische Aussagen zitiert, wörtlich übernommen, paraphrasiert oder in Form von Anspielungen rezipiert; und hier wie dort spielen solche Bezüge auf „die Schriften"[2] eine beträchtliche Rolle[3].

Wie aber soll man die Befunde zueinander in Beziehung setzen? Ein *Vergleich*, der das Verständnis der Verwendung und Interpretation der „Schriften" durch Markus und Paulus fördern könnte, bedürfte eines plausiblen Bezugsrahmens – doch der ist nicht leicht zu bestimmen. Erschwert wird solch eine Bestimmung vor allem dadurch, dass der intendierte Vergleich grundverschiedene literarische Dokumente beträfe: Stellt das Evangelium nach Markus eine episodische Erzählung vom öffentlichen Auftreten Jesu, zumal in Galiläa und Jerusalem, dar, deren Autor ebenso anonym bleibt wie deren Adressaten, so werden in den Briefen des Paulus drängende Fragen, Sorgen und Probleme in der Beziehung zwischen dem Apostel und konkreten Christengemeinden teils belehrend, teils ermahnend erörtert. Gewiss sind sowohl die Paulusbriefe als auch das Markusevangelium durch das Bekenntnis zu Jesus als dem Christus und Gottessohn geprägt[4]. Diese Prägung vollzieht sich jedoch hier und dort auf ganz eigene Weise: Markus schildert Jesu Wirken und Geschick in Israel als „Grundlage" und „Anfang" des in aller Welt verkündigten „Evangeliums von Jesus Christus"[5]; Paulus entfaltet im Dialog mit den Adressaten seiner Briefe argumentativ die Implikationen jener Heilsbotschaft für Glauben und Lebensgestaltung. Es stehen sich also Schriften gegenüber, die

---
[1] Gewidmet dem Gedenken an Friedrich Avemarie, den geschätzten und vertrauten Kollegen, der am 13. Oktober 2012 – während meiner Arbeit an diesem Beitrag – verstarb.
[2] So Mk 12,24; 14,49; Röm 15,4; 1Kor 15,3f., ähnlich Röm 1,2: „heilige Schriften", und Röm 4,3; 9,17; 10,11; 11,2; Gal 3,8.22; 4,30: „die Schrift".
[3] Vgl. H.C. Kee, The Function of Scriptural Quotations and Allusions in Mark 11–16, in: Jesus und Paulus. Festschrift für Werner Georg Kümmel zum 70. Geburtstag, hg. von E.E. Ellis/E. Gräßer, Göttingen 1975, 165–188, hier: 173.175–177; Th.R. Hatina, In Search of a Context. The Function of Scripture in Mark's Narrative (JSNT.S 232), Sheffield 2002, passim, sowie D.-A. Koch, Die Schrift als Zeuge des Evangeliums. Untersuchungen zur Verwendung und zum Verständnis der Schrift bei Paulus (BHTh 69), Tübingen 1986, 257–285.
[4] Vgl. einerseits Mk 1,1.11; 14,61f. u.ö., andererseits Röm 1,3f.; 1Kor 1,9 u.ö.
[5] Vgl. Mk 1,1 sowie 13,10 und dazu H. Merklein, Die Jesusgeschichte – synoptisch gelesen (SBS 156), Stuttgart 1994, 10.192.

verschiedenen Gattungen zugehören und verschiedene Inhalte aufweisen. Auch ein gemeinsames Umfeld ist nur ansatzweise erkennbar. Natürlich ist das Markusevangelium in einem geographischen Raum entstanden, der von der paulinischen Völkermission zumindest berührt worden ist – ganz gleich, ob man es in Syrien oder Rom lokalisiert[6]. Aber zum einen ist die Intensität jener Berührung gerade unklar; zum andern liegen, je nach Datierung der einzelnen Texte, mindestens fünf, wahrscheinlich eher zwölf bis 15 ereignisreiche Jahre zwischen der Abfassung des letzten Paulusbriefs und der des Markusevangeliums[7]. Ein Vergleich des paulinischen und des markinischen Schriftgebrauchs erscheint angesichts derart tief greifender formaler, sachlicher und situativer Unterschiede wenig sinnvoll.

Die Problematik solch eines Vergleichs tritt schon an dem Sachverhalt zutage, dass – bis auf eine Ausnahme (Mk 1,2f.) – alle expliziten Schriftzitate und -paraphrasen im Markusevangelium (s.u. 2.1) innerhalb von Dialogen Jesu mit Gegnern, Kritikern, Ratsuchenden, Zuhörern oder Jüngern begegnen. Aus diesem Sachverhalt erwächst nämlich nicht nur die oft genug kaum zu klärende Frage, inwieweit solche Schriftbezüge Markus bereits in den von ihm gesammelten Traditionen vorgegeben waren. Er nötigt insbesondere zu der Einsicht, dass der Evangelist sich bei der Auswahl, Gestaltung und literarischen Einbindung expliziter Schriftbezüge im Munde der Protagonisten seiner Jesuserzählung in engen, durch deren Stoffe und Verlauf gesetzten Grenzen bewegte. Ein Vergleich dieses Schriftgebrauchs mit der auktorialen, durch Sachfragen gesteuerten und sonst weitgehend selbstbestimmten Verwendung von Schriftzitaten und -paraphrasen in den Briefen des Paulus verspricht daher kaum weiterführende Erkenntnisse.

Die mit dem Titel dieses Beitrags gestellte Aufgabe muss also auf anderem Wege bearbeitet werden. Die erwähnte geographische Nähe zwischen dem Entstehungsort des Markusevangeliums und dem Wirkungsfeld des Paulus legt es

---

[6] Vgl. einerseits I. Broer, Einleitung in das Neue Testament. Studienausgabe, Würzburg 2006, 86–88, andererseits M. Ebner, Das Markusevangelium, in: Einleitung in das Neue Testament, hg. von M. Ebner/S. Schreiber, Stuttgart 2008, 154–183, hier: 171f.

[7] Das Markusevangelium ist, wie etliche Hinweise in Mk 13 belegen, wahrscheinlich während des Jüdischen Krieges (66–74 n.Chr.) entstanden; ob die Zerstörung des Jerusalemer Tempels in diesem Text bereits vorausgesetzt wird, ist in der Forschung strittig (vgl. in Kürze G. Theißen, Die Entstehung des Neuen Testaments als literaturgeschichtliches Problem [SHAW.PH 40], Heidelberg 2007, 78 [pro], und J. Roloff, Einführung in das Neue Testament, Stuttgart 1995, 153 [contra]). Die Serie der erhaltenen Paulusbriefe wiederum endete wohl mit dem im Jahr 56 n.Chr. verfassten Römerbrief (zu dieser Datierung vgl. S. Schreiber, Chronologie: Lebensdaten des Paulus, in: Einleitung in das Neue Testament, hg. von M. Ebner/S. Schreiber, Stuttgart 2008, 265–276) – wenn nicht der Philipper- und/oder der Philemonbrief in die römische Gefangenschaft des Paulus gehören (so etwa U. Schnelle, Paulus. Leben und Denken, Berlin 2003, 406–411.421).

nahe, nach *genetischen Zusammenhängen* zu fragen. Gewiss ist a priori unklar, wie eng man sich jene Nähe vorstellen darf. Es steht aber außer Zweifel, dass die markinische Konzeption des „Evangeliums" große Ähnlichkeiten mit paulinischen Aussagen aufweist[8] und daher nicht unabhängig davon entwickelt worden sein dürfte. Das Evangelium aber wird bei Paulus wie bei Markus programmatisch in der Schrift verankert[9]. Zugleich bezeichnet der Völkerapostel es gerade in seinem Schriftbezug als Traditionsgut (1Kor 15,3–5). Es gilt demnach zu prüfen, ob Einwirkungen vor-markinischer Überlieferungen auf den Schriftgebrauch des Paulus oder von ihm ausgehende Einflüsse auf den des Markus vorliegen – oder Abhängigkeiten beider Autoren von einer gemeinsamen Tradition. Eine solche Analyse der Verwendung der Schrift im Markusevangelium im Hinblick auf Berührungspunkte mit den Schriftbezügen innerhalb der Paulusbriefe verspricht, nähere Aufschlüsse über die methodische und hermeneutische Eigenart des markinischen Umgangs mit den „Schriften"[10] sowie über den Charakter der Beziehung des Evangelisten zum Werk des Paulus zu geben.

2 Analyse

Angesichts der erwähnten Unterschiede zwischen Markusevangelium und Paulusbriefen wird die Suche nach genetischen Zusammenhängen im Umgang mit der Schrift auf dessen materiale, technische und hermeneutische Aspekte zu konzentrieren sein. Innerhalb der Grenzen des vorliegenden Beitrags muss ich mich dabei auf solche Schriftbezüge beschränken, die explizit ausgewiesen oder aufgrund ihrer syntaktisch hervorgehobenen Stellung klar identifizierbar sind.

---

[8] Markus zufolge wird Jesus Christus nach Ostern in dem an alle Weltvölker zu verkündigenden Evangelium (Mk 13,10, vgl. 14,9), das auf seinen Tod als Heilsgeschehen konzentriert ist (vgl. 10,45; 14,7–9.24), gleichsam mit seinem eigenen Wort präsent (vgl. 8,35b.38a; 10,29 und zum Ganzen F. Wilk, Jesus und die Völker in der Sicht der Synoptiker [BZNW 109], Berlin 2002, 42.73f.). Das erinnert an Röm 1,1.4b–5 (εὐαγγέλιον θεοῦ ... ἐν πᾶσιν τοῖς ἔθνεσιν); Gal 2,2 (τὸ εὐαγγέλιον ὃ κηρύσσω ἐν τοῖς ἔθνεσιν) u.ö., 2Kor 13,3 (τοῦ ἐν ἐμοὶ λαλοῦντος Χριστοῦ) u.ö., Röm 15,8 (λέγω ... Χριστὸν διάκονον γεγενῆσθαι) sowie Gal 1,3f. (Ἰησοῦ Χριστοῦ τοῦ δόντος ἑαυτὸν ὑπὲρ τῶν ἁμαρτιῶν ἡμῶν) u.ö.
[9] Vgl. Röm 1,1–4 (und dazu F. Wilk, Paulus als Interpret der prophetischen Schriften, in: KuD 45 [1999], 284–306, hier 287) sowie Mk 1,1–4 (und dazu F. Wilk, Wer bereitet wem den Weg? Überlegungen eines Neutestamentlers zum Verhältnis zwischen Septuaginta und Neuem Testament anhand von Mk 1,2f., in: Die Göttinger Septuaginta – ein editorisches Jahrhundertprojekt, hg. von R.G. Kratz/B. Neuschäfer [AAWG. Neue Folge 22], Berlin 2013, 185–223).
[10] Wie die Forschungsgeschichte zeigt (vgl. den Überblick über die Jahre 1961–1997 bei Th.R. Hatina, Search, 8–48), besteht diesbezüglich kein wissenschaftlicher Konsens.

2.1 Zur Auswahl der Quelltexte

Bei explizit ausgewiesenen Schriftbezügen im Markusevangelium werden die biblischen Bücher wie folgt genutzt:

Quelltext bei atl. Zitaten		Zusatztext bei Mischzitaten	Quelltext bei atl. Paraphrasen/Verweisen		Mk-Text
Ex	3,6				Mk 12,26
Ex	20,12–16 / Dtn 5,16–20	Sir 4,1 / Dtn 24,14			Mk 10,19
Ex	21,16[17]				Mk 7,10c–d
			Lev	14,1–32	Mk 1,44c
			Lev	18,16 / 20,21	Mk 6,18
Lev	19,18				Mk 12,31
			Lev	24,9	Mk 2,26b
Dtn	5,16 / Ex 20,12				Mk 7,10a–b
Dtn	6,4–5				Mk 12,29–30
			Dtn	24,1–3	Mk 10,3–5
		Gen 38,8	Dtn	25,5–6	Mk 12,19
			1Sam	21,1–7	Mk 2,25–26
Ps	109[110],1	Ps 8,7			Mk 12,36
Ps	117[118],22–23				Mk 12,10–11
Sach	13,7				Mk 14,27
Mal	3,1	Ex 23,20			Mk 1,2
Jes	29,13				Mk 7,6–7
Jes	40,3				Mk 1,3
Jes	56,7				Mk 11,17b
			Dan	9,27 / 11,31 / 12,11	Mk 13,14[11]

Hinzu kommen einige summarische Verweise auf die Schrift: An drei Stellen rekurriert Jesus darauf, dass vom „Menschensohn" geschrieben sei, er werde „viel leiden und verachtet werden" (Mk 9,12c) bzw. in den Tod gehen (14,21a), oder dass in seiner Verhaftung als eines Räubers „die Schriften erfüllt" würden (14,48 f.); einmal hält er fest, das willkürliche Tun der Zeitgenossen an dem erneut ge-

---

[11] Die Parenthese „Der Lesende soll verstehen!" (Mk 13,14b) ist kaum als „Aufmerksamkeitsappell" gemeint (so W. Eckey, Das Markusevangelium. Orientierung am Weg Jesu. Ein Kommentar, Neukirchen-Vluyn 1998, 258). Da ἀναγινώσκω andernorts bei Markus stets auf das Lesen eines Schriftwortes verweist, das Jesus seine jeweiligen Gesprächspartner zu bedenken anhält (2,25; 12,10.26), wird er an dieser Stelle den Jüngern eine verständige Lektüre der Aussagen Daniels zum „Gräuel der Verwüstung" (13,14a) nahe legen, welche deren aktuellen Geschichtsbezug aufdeckt. Demnach liegt auch hier ein expliziter Schriftbezug vor.

kommenen Elija entspreche dem, was „über ihn geschrieben ist" (9,13b–c). Man kann nur mutmaßen, welches Schriftwort jeweils im Blick ist; Sprachgestalt und Sachgehalt der betreffenden Aussagen lassen es nicht zu, konkrete Bezüge zu identifizieren[12].

Ähnliches gilt für die Hinweise auf Äußerungen der „Schriftgelehrten" in Mk 9,11; 12,35. Dass „Elija zuerst (sc. vor der Auferstehung der Toten, vgl. 9,10)[13] kommen" müsse und „der Christus ein Sohn Davids" sei, ist natürlich aus der Schrift erschlossen[14]. Klare Schriftbezüge bietet aber hier wie dort erst der jeweilige Kommentar Jesu (in 9,12b [s.u.] und 12,36f.).

Mehrdeutig ist das δεῖ in der ersten Ankündigung von Passion, Tod und Auferstehung Jesu (Mk 8,31). Infolge ihrer Konvergenz mit 9,12c dürfte es sein Leiden summarisch als schriftgemäß ausweisen; im Blick auf Jesu Auferstehung wird es jedoch eher eine – wohl aus der Schrift abgeleitete (vgl. 9,11b) – Einsicht in Gottes Geschichtsplan (vgl. 13,7.10) bezeichnen[15]. Dafür sprechen das Fehlen eines expliziten Schriftbezugs bei sonstigen Aussagen zur Auferstehung Jesu und die Verarbeitung des Drei-Tage-Motivs in den auf den Schriftzitaten 11,17; 12,10f. und der Prophetie 13,2 basierenden Aussagen über einen Tempelbau Jesu (14,57f.; 15,29f.).

Schließlich sind diejenigen Stellen zu bedenken, an denen die Zulässigkeit (ἔξεστιν) bestimmter Verhaltensweisen diskutiert wird[16]: des Ährenrupfens (Mk 2,23b–24) sowie des Tuns von Gutem oder Bösen bzw. der Lebensrettung oder Tötung am Sabbat (3,4), der Entlassung einer Ehefrau (10,2) und der Zahlung der Kaiser-Steuer (12,14). Ohne Zweifel sind jeweils Schriftworte im Blick: das Gebot der Sabbatruhe (Ex 16,23–30; 20,10; 31,12–17; 34,21; 35,2 u.ö.), die Weisung zur Ehescheidung (Dtn 24,1–4) und das Gebot der ausschließlichen Ehrung Gottes (Ex 20,3; Jes 45,5f. u.ö.). Stets aber beruht das in Rede stehende konkrete Verbot auf einer halachischen Entscheidung, die nicht ohne weiteres aus der Schrift

---

[12] Vgl. M.D. Hooker, Isaiah in Mark's Gospel, in: Isaiah in the New Testament, eds. S. Moyise/M. J.J. Menken, London 2005, 35–49, hier 47; anders R.E. Watts, Isaiah's New Exodus and Mark (WUNT II/88), Tübingen 1997, 259–265: Mk 9,12c verweise auf Jes 53.
[13] Gegen H.-J. Steichele, Der leidende Sohn Gottes. Eine Untersuchung einiger alttestamentlicher Motive in der Christologie des Markusevangeliums (BU 14), Regensburg 1980, 97: Im Blick sei das Geschick des Menschensohns (Mk 8,31; 9,9).
[14] Vgl. einerseits mSot 9,15 (und dazu Mal 4,1–6 [3,19–24] u.ö.), andererseits PsSal 17,21 (und dazu 2Regn [2Sam] 7,12–16; Jer 23,5 u.ö.).
[15] Vgl. H. Anderson, The Old Testament in Mark's Gospel, in: The Use of the Old Testament in the New and Other Essays. Studies in Honor of William Franklin Stinespring, ed. J.M. Efird, Durham 1972, 280–306, hier 298f. und zum Folgenden F. Wilk, Jesus, 43–50.
[16] Die Diskutierbarkeit der betreffenden Regelungen unterscheidet diese von den als solchen unstrittigen, mit οὐκ ἔξεστιν bezeichneten Verboten, auf die Mk 2,26b und 6,18 verweisen.

abgeleitet werden kann[17]. Solche Verbote lassen sich deshalb nicht einfach als explizite Schriftbezüge werten.

Die Liste der explizit angeführten Schriftworte weist mit der entsprechenden Liste paulinischer Schriftbezüge[18] kaum Übereinstimmungen auf. Immerhin hat das Zitat aus Lev 19,18 in Mk 12,31 exakte Parallelen in Gal 5,14; Röm 13,9. Dabei findet auch die Aussage, das Nächstenliebegebot werde – im Konnex mit dem „Sch^{e}ma" (Dtn 6,4f.) – von keinem anderen Gebot an Bedeutung übertroffen (Mk 12,31c), eine Analogie in den paulinischen Äußerungen, in diesem Gebot sei „das ganze Gesetz erfüllt" (Gal 5,14a) und würden die auf „Leib und Gut" bezogenen Thoragebote „zusammengefasst" (Röm 13,9)[19]. Allerdings ist die Analogie begrenzt; während Paulus das Liebesgebot als ethische Leitlinie für das Zusammenleben präsentiert und demgemäß durch weitere Sozialgebote (13,9) oder Weisungen (Gal 5,15–26) konkretisiert, erscheint es bei Markus als Hauptgebot, dem die Gebote zum Opferkult nachgeordnet werden (Mk 12,33). Zudem gehörte das Lev-Zitat wohl schon in der vor-markinischen Überlieferung mit dem Gebot der Gottesliebe zusammen, das in den Paulustexten fehlt[20]. Es ist daher unwahrscheinlich, dass die Anführung des Nächstenliebegebots in Mk 12,31 auf paulinischen Einfluss zurückgeht. Andererseits ist die Kongruenz in der expliziten Zitation aus der Schrift bemerkenswert – zumal, da Jak 2,8 dazu eine weitere Parallele bietet[21], während entsprechende Belege in zeitgenössischen jüdischen Quellen fehlen[22]. So steht zu vermuten, dass alle drei neutestamentlichen Zitate

---

[17] Zur grundsätzlichen Problematik vgl. K. Müller, Anmerkungen zum Verhältnis von Tora und Halacha im Frühjudentum, in: Die Tora als Kanon für Juden und Christen, hg. von E. Zenger (HBS 10), Freiburg 1996, 257–291.

[18] Siehe u. Anhang 1 und vgl. dazu D.-A. Koch, Schrift, 21f.; F. Wilk, Schriftbezüge im Werk des Paulus, in: Paulus Handbuch, hg. von F.W. Horn, Tübingen 2013, 479–490, hier 482–484.

[19] Zur Deutung von Röm 13,9 vgl. Chr. Burchard, Die Summe der Gebote (Röm 13,7–10), das ganze Gesetz (Gal 5,13–15) und das Christusgesetz (Gal 6,2; Röm 15,1–6; 1Kor 9,21), in: Chr. Burchard, Studien zur Theologie, Sprache und Umwelt des Neuen Testaments, hg. von D. Sänger (WUNT 107), Tübingen 1998, 151–183, hier 163f.

[20] Vgl. die von Mk 12,28–34 literarisch unabhängige Überlieferung, die Lk 10,25–28 sowie – in Teilen – Mt 22,34–40 zugrunde liegt, und dazu F. Bovon, Das Evangelium nach Lukas. 2. Teilband: Lk 9,51–14,35 (EKK III/2), Zürich/Neukirchen-Vluyn 1996, 84.

[21] Dort erscheint Lev 19,18 als „Lesehilfe ... für das sachgerechte Verstehen des Gesetzes" und als „Maßstab", an dem zu prüfen ist, ob die Adressaten „das Gesetz ... ‚erfüllen'" (H. Frankemölle, Der Brief des Jakobus. Kapitel 2–5 [ÖTBK 17/2], Gütersloh/Würzburg 1994, 402). – Weitere, wohl redaktionelle Referenzen bietet das Matthäusevangelium in Mt 5,43 (vgl. 5,43–46 mit Lk 6,27f.32.35) und 19,19 (vgl. Mk 10,19 und Lk 18,20).

[22] Der früheste Beleg ist m.W. Sifra, Qedoschim 4,12, wo Rabbi Aqiba folgender Kommentar zu Lev 19,18 zugeschrieben wird: „Dies ist etwas Allgemeines, Großes in der Thora."

ihre Basis in der frühen Jesusüberlieferung haben[23]. Zu notieren ist ferner die Konvergenz zwischen Mk 10,19 und Röm 13,9 bei der Anführung dreier Dekaloggebote (Ex 20,13–15 / Dtn 5,17–19). Freilich werden diese hier und dort auf je andere Weise angeordnet und durch weitere Gebote ergänzt[24]; eine Abhängigkeit des Markus von Paulus oder des Paulus von einer vor-markinischen Tradition wird an dieser Stelle daher nicht vorliegen.

Fragt man nach weiteren Kontakten zwischen paulinischen und markinischen Zitaten oder Paraphrasen, so ist der positive Befund wiederum schmal: Eng benachbart sind die Schriftworte, die in 1Kor 9,9 (Dtn 25,4) und Mk 12,19 (Dtn 25,5f.) sowie 1Kor 1,19 (Jes 29,14)[25] und Mk 7,6f. (Jes 29,13) verwendet sind; aus demselben Kapitel (Lev 18) stammen die Anführungen in Mk 6,18 und Röm 10,5; Gal 3,12. Die Kontexte, in denen die Schriftbezüge jeweils auftauchen, sind jedoch so verschieden, dass sich ein genetischer Zusammenhang zwischen den Markus- und den Paulus-Stellen nicht plausibel machen lässt.

Eine signifikante Differenz besteht bei den summarischen Verweisen auf die Schrift[26]: Während diese bei Markus stets das Leidens- und Todesgeschick Jesu an sich betreffen (Mk 9,12; 14,21.48, vgl. 8,31), geht es in 1Kor 15,3 um die Heilsbedeutung des Todes Christi, in Röm 1,1–4 um seine durch Davidssohnschaft und Auferstehung definierte Identität als Gottessohn. Näher stehen einander das Bekenntnis, Christus sei „den Schriften gemäß am dritten Tage auferweckt worden" (1Kor 15,4), und die Ansage, der Menschensohn „müsse ... nach drei Tagen auferstehen" (Mk 8,31). Die Formulierungen fallen sehr unterschiedlich aus, doch scheinen alle sachverwandten Stellen im Neuen Testament von diesen beiden Aussagen abhängig zu sein[27]. Dies lässt darauf schließen, dass bei Markus und

---

23 Vgl. J.D.G. Dunn, Jesus Remembered. Christianity in the Making, Vol. 1, Grand Rapids 2003, 584f. – Für Mk 12,29–31 gilt dabei: Wenn der Primat des Doppelgebots der Liebe unter allen Geboten festgestellt wird, dann ist vorausgesetzt, dass man Lev 19,18 als das Zentrum der Thora für den zwischenmenschlichen Bereich identifiziert hat.
24 Mk 10,19 folgt dem MT von Ex 20,13–15 / Dtn 5,17–19 (vgl. die Korrekturen, die an beiden Stellen in A und weiteren LXX-Handschriften erfolgt sind) und ergänzt die Reihe durch Ex 20,16 / Dtn 5,20; Sir 4,1 sowie Ex 20,12 / Dtn 5,16 (jeweils in Kurzform). In Röm 13,9 jedoch, wo die Abfolge dem ältesten LXX-Text (B V etc.) von Dtn 5,17–19 (diff. Ex 20,13–15!) entspricht, fügt Paulus noch den Auftakt zu Dtn 5,21 / Ex 20,17 und den Hinweis auf mögliche weitere Gebote an, um dann Lev 19,18 als Zusammenfassung zu präsentieren.
25 Vgl. zudem den Rekurs auf Jes 29,10 in Röm 11,8 (und dazu F. Wilk, Die Bedeutung des Jesajabuches für Paulus [FRLANT 179], Göttingen 1998, 53f.).
26 Solche finden sich bei Paulus in 1Kor 15,3f. und Röm 1,1–4, ferner – innerhalb paränetischer Ausführungen – mit ethischem Akzent in 1Kor 4,6 und Röm 15,4.
27 Vgl. 1Kor 15,4 (ἐγήγερται τῇ ἡμέρᾳ τῇ τρίτῃ) mit Mt 16,21; 17,23; 20,19; Lk 9,22 und Apg 10,40 (Aktiv), Mk 8,31 (μετὰ τρεῖς ἡμέρας ἀναστῆναι) mit 9,31; 10,34 sowie Mt 12,40. Mischformen bieten Mt 27,63 (μετὰ τρεῖς ἡμέρας ἐγείρομαι) und Lk 24,7 (τῇ τρίτῃ ἡμέρᾳ ἀναστῆναι, ähnlich

Paulus jeweils eigenständige Ausformungen einer besonderen Deutung des Ostergeschehens im Bezug auf die Schrift vorliegen.

Beachtliche Gemeinsamkeiten zwischen beiden Autoren zeigen sich zudem bei der Nutzung bestimmter biblischer Bücher[28]: Markus führt überwiegend Worte aus Levitikus, Deuteronomium (je viermal), Exodus, Jesaja (je dreimal), den Psalmen und dem Dodekapropheton (je zweimal) an; Paulus bevorzugt Jesaja, Genesis (je 21-mal)[29], Exodus, Deuteronomium (je zwölfmal), die Psalmen (elfmal), Levitikus, Numeri (je fünfmal) und das Dodekapropheton (viermal)[30]. Demnach stammen Zitate und Paraphrasen hier wie dort überwiegend aus denselben sechs Büchern (Ex, Lev, Dtn, Pss, XII, Jes), bei Paulus zudem aus Genesis und Numeri. Allerdings sind in weiteren frühchristlichen und antik-jüdischen Texten ähnliche Vorlieben dokumentiert[31]; und ihre Schwerpunkte setzen Markus und Paulus je anders. Auf der Basis der expliziten Schriftbezüge kann man daher einen spezifischen Zusammenhang zwischen der markinischen und der paulinischen Schriftnutzung zwar vermuten, nicht aber aufweisen.

Nimmt man daraufhin die evidenten Anspielungen in den Blick, ergibt sich für Markus folgendes Bild:

Quelltext bei atl. Anspielungen		Zusatztext(e) bei vermischten Anspielungen	alternativer Quelltext	Mk-Text
Gen	1,27c		Gen 5,2	Mk 10,6
Gen	1,31			Mk 7,37b
Gen	2,24			Mk 10,7–8a

24,46 und 18,33). Andere Wendungen finden sich nur in den Tempelworten Mk 14,58 / Mt 26,61; Mk 15,29 / Mt 27,40 und Joh 2,19 f.

28 Die bei Mischzitaten ergänzend beigezogenen Texte sind im Folgenden nicht mitgezählt.
29 Vgl. Röm 2,24; 9,27f.29.33; 10,11.15.16.20.21; 11,26f.; 14,11; 15,12.21; 1Kor 1,19; 2,9; 14,21; 15,54; 2Kor 6,2.17a–c.d; Gal 4,27 (zu Jes), Röm 4,3.9 – 11.17.18 – 21.22f.; 5,12; 9,7.9.10 – 12; 1Kor 6,16; 11,8 – 12; 15,21.38 – 41.45; 2Kor 4,6; 11,3; Gal 3,6.8.16; 4,22f.29f. (zu Gen).
30 Vgl. Röm 9,15.17; 1Kor 10,1.1.3.4.7.18; 2Kor 3,7.13.16; 8,15 (zu Ex), Röm 7,7; 10,6.7.8; 10,19; 11,8; 12,19; 13,9a–d; 15,10; 1Kor 9,9; Gal 3,10.13 (zu Dtn) und Röm 3,4.10 – 18; 4,7f.; 8,36; 11,9f.; 15,3.9.11; 1Kor 3,20; 2Kor 4,13; 9,9 (zu Pss), ferner Röm 10,5; 13,9 g; 2Kor 6,16; Gal 3,12; 5,14 (zu Lev), 1Kor 10,5.6.8.9.10 (zu Num) und Röm 1,17; 9,13.25f.; 1Kor 15,55 (zu Hos-Mal [XII]). Vgl. daneben noch 2Kor 6,18 (2Sam); Röm 11,3.4 (1Kön); 1Kor 3,19 (Hi) und 1,31 (Jer).
31 Vgl. etwa Mt (und dazu M.J.J. Menken, Matthew's Bible. The Old Testament Text of the Evangelist [BEThL 173], Leuven 2004) und Lk-Apg (und dazu D. Rusam, Das Alte Testament bei Lukas [BZNW 112], Berlin 2003) sowie den Bestand an biblischen Handschriften (vgl. J.C. VanderKam, Einführung in die Qumranforschung. Geschichte und Bedeutung der Schriften vom Toten Meer, übers. v. M. Müller, Göttingen 1998, 50) und Schriftzitaten (vgl. D.L. Washburn, A Catalog of Biblical Passages in the Dead Sea Scrolls [Text-critical Studies 2], Atlanta 2002) in den Texten aus Qumran.

Quelltext bei atl. Anspielungen		Zusatztext(e) bei vermischten Anspielungen	alternativer Quelltext	Mk-Text
Ex	24,8	Lev 4,7 u. ö.; Jes 53,11 f.		Mk 14,24b
Lev	19,18	1Sam 15,22		Mk 12,33
Dtn	6,4–5	Jes 45,21		Mk 12,32–33
2Chr	18,16		Num 27,17	Mk 6,34b
Ps	2,7	Jes 42,1		Mk 1,11
Ps	2,7	Dtn 18,15		Mk 9,7
Ps	21[22],2			Mk 15,34
Ps	21[22],19			Mk 15,24
Ps	117[118],25–26			Mk 11,9
Mi	7,6			Mk 13,12b
Sach	2,6[10]	Dtn 30,4		Mk 13,27
Mal	4,4–5 [3,23–24]			Mk 9,12b
Jes	5,1–2			Mk 12,1
Jes	6,9–10			Mk 4,12
Jes	13,10			Mk 13,24
Jes	34,4			Mk 13,25
Jes	35,5–6			Mk 7,37c
Jes	66,24			Mk 9,48
Jer	5,21		Ez 12,2	Mk 8,18
Jer	7,11			Mk 11,17c
Ez	17,23	Ps 103[104],12		Mk 4,32
Dan	2,28–29.45			Mk 13,7c
Dan	7,13			Mk 13,26
Dan	7,13	Ps 109[110],1		Mk 14,62
Dan	12,1	Ex 9,18 u. ö.		Mk 13,19

Die Zahl übereinstimmender Schriftbezüge im Markusevangelium und in den Paulusbriefen bleibt selbst bei Einbeziehung der evidenten Anspielungen[32] gering: Zu den bereits genannten Stellen kommen lediglich Gen 2,24 (1Kor 6,16; Mk 10,7f.), Dtn 6,4f. (1Kor 8,3–6; Mk 12,29–33) und – verbunden mit Ps 8,7 – Ps 109[110],1 (1Kor 15,25.27; Mk 12,36) hinzu[33]. All diese Schriftworte aber sind im antiken Judentum sowie im frühen Christentum breit rezipiert und dabei ganz

---

32 Zu den paulinischen Anspielungen s.u. Anhang 2.
33 Ein Bezug auf das Verstockungswort Jes 6,9f. – das in Mk 4,12 angeführt wird – lässt sich vom Wortlaut her weder für 2Kor 3,14 noch für Röm 11,8 wahrscheinlich machen (gegen J.R. Wagner, Heralds of the Good News. Isaiah and Paul „In Concert" in the Letter to the Romans [NT. S 101], Leiden 2002, 244–251, der von Mk 8,17–21 und Joh 12,39–41 ausgehend vermutet, der Formulierung in Röm 11,8e liege eine andere griechische Übersetzung von Jes 6,9f. zugrunde).

unterschiedlich akzentuiert worden³⁴. So verwundert es nicht, dass auch die markinischen und die paulinischen Belege in Wiedergabe und Deutung des jeweiligen Quelltextes erheblich voneinander abweichen³⁵. Dass diese von jenen oder jene von diesen beeinflusst sind, ist deshalb unwahrscheinlich.

Die weiteren Kontakte bei der Nutzung der Schrift werden unter Berücksichtigung von Anspielungen ebenfalls nicht wesentlich vermehrt: Eng beieinander stehen die Quelltexte, die in 1Kor 11,7a und Mk 10,6 (Gen 1,27a–b und c), in 1Kor 11,8f.12 und Mk 10,7f. (Gen 2,18.21–23 und 24) sowie in Mk 13,7c und 1Kor 14,25 (Dan 2,28f.45 und 46f.) rezipiert sind; auf weitere Züge der Schöpfungsgeschichte (vgl. noch Mk 7,37b) geht Paulus in 1Kor 15,38–41.45.47 und 2Kor 4,6 ein; je aus denselben Kapiteln stammen die Anführungen in Mk 7,6f. und Röm 9,20 (Jes 29), in Mk 1,3 und Röm 9,6; 11,34; 1Kor 2,16 (Jes 40) sowie in Röm 13,11 und Mk 11,17 (Jes 56). Wiederum handelt es sich zumeist um Stellen und Passagen, die in diversen antik-jüdischen und frühchristlichen Texten aufgenommen wurden³⁶; und erneut sind die Schriftbezüge bei Markus und bei Paulus der Sache nach je anders ausgerichtet. Insofern spricht auch an diesen Stellen nichts für die Annahme spezifischer Zusammenhänge.

Was nun die Nutzung der biblischen Bücher angeht, so verschieben sich im markinischen Schriftgebrauch bei Hinzunahme der Anspielungen die Gewichte –

---

34 Vgl. die Zusammenstellung wichtiger Belege bei G. Dautzenberg, Φεύγετε τὴν πορνείαν. Eine Fallstudie zur paulinischen Sexualethik in ihrem Verhältnis zur Sexualethik des Frühjudentums, in: G. Dautzenberg, Studien zur paulinischen Theologie und zur frühchristlichen Rezeption des Alten Testaments, hg. von D. Sänger (Gießener Schriften zur Theologie und Religionspädagogik 13), Gießen 1999, 142–168, hier 147–154; K. Berger, Die Gesetzesauslegung Jesu. Ihr historischer Hintergrund im Judentum und im Alten Testament. Teil I: Markus und Parallelen (WMANT 40), Neukirchen-Vluyn 1972, 56–80, und D.M. Hay, Glory at the Right Hand. Psalm 110 in Early Christianity (SBL.MS 18), Nashville 1973.
35 Anders als Markus führt Paulus die genannten Schriftworte nur fragmentarisch an, und anders als Markus bezieht er Gen 2,24 generell auf den Geschlechtsverkehr (statt auf die Unauflöslichkeit der Ehe), Dtn 6,4f. auf den im Kontext vielfältiger paganer Gottesdienste notwendigen Zusammenhang von Gottesliebe und Gotteserkenntnis (statt auf das Verhältnis zu anderen Thorageboten) und Ps 109[110],1 auf die Bestimmung der Herrschaft des auferstandenen Christus, mit der künftigen Vernichtung des Todes die endgültige und alles umfassende Herrschaft Gottes selbst einzuleiten (statt auf das Verhältnis zur Davidssohnschaft des Christus).
36 Zu Gen 1–2 vgl. die Sammlung der Belege bei J.B. Schaller, Gen.1.2 im antiken Judentum. Untersuchungen über Verwendung und Deutung der Schöpfungsaussagen von Gen.1.2 im antiken Judentum, Diss. theol. Göttingen 1961, ergänzt von H. Lichtenberger, Schöpfung und Ehe in Texten aus Qumran sowie Essenerberichten und die Bedeutung für das Neue Testament, in: Judaistik und neutestamentliche Wissenschaft. Standorte – Grenzen – Beziehungen, hg. von L. Doering/H.-G. Waubke/F. Wilk (FRLANT 226), Göttingen 2008, 279–288; zu Dan 2 vgl. nur die Anspielungen in Lk 20,18 und Apk 1,1.19; 4,1; 22,6, zu Jes 40 die Zitate in 1QS VIII,14; 4Q176a I,4–9 sowie Joh 1,23 und 1Petr 1,24f.

zumal zugunsten Jesajas und der Psalmen –, während zusätzlich die Genesis relevant wird. Auch in den Briefen des Paulus gewinnen vor allem Jesaja und die Psalmen an Bedeutung, während die Sprüche neues Gewicht erhalten. Alles in allem ergibt sich hinsichtlich der Zahl der Schriftbezüge folgendes Bild:

	Markus		Paulus		Röm	1Kor	2Kor	Gal	Phil	1Th	1Kor–1Th
	Anzahl	%	Anzahl	%	jeweilige Anzahl						%
Jes	9 (3+6)	18,8	Jes	45 (21+24)	28,3	23	8	6	3	2	3	24,2
			Gen	24 (21+ 3)	15,1	9	7	2	5	1		16,5
Pss	7 (2+5)	14,6	Pss	22 (11+11)	13,8	13	6	2	1			9,9
Lev	5 (4+1)	10,4				9	5	1	3			9,9
Dtn	5 (4+1)	10,4	Dtn	18 (12+ 6)	11,3							
XII	5 (2+3)	10,4										
Dan	5 (1+4)	10,4										
Ex	4 (3+1)	8,3	Ex	14 (12+2)	8,8	2	6	5	1			13,2
Gen	3 (0+3)	6,3										
			XII	7 (4+3)	4,4	4	1	1	1			3,3
Jer	2 (0+2)	4,2	Num	7 (5+2)	4,4	1	6					6,6
			Lev	5 (5+0)	3,1	2		1	2			3,3
			Spr	5 (0+5)	3,1	3		2				2,2
1Sam	1 (1+0)	2,1	Hi	4 (1+3)	2,5	2			1		1	4,4
2Chr	1 (0+1)	2,1	Jer	3 (1+2)	1,9	1	1				1	3,3
Ez	1 (0+1)	2,1	1Kön	2 (2+0)	1,3	2						
			2Sam	1 (1+0)	0,6		1					1,1
			Ez	1 (0+1)	0,6						1	1,1
			Dan	1 (0+1)	0,6	1						1,1
AT	48 (20 + 28)		AT	159 (96 + 63)		68	43	22	16	4	6	

In der Gegenüberstellung treten Gemeinsamkeiten und Unterschiede deutlich zutage. Was Erstere angeht, so bestätigt sich zunächst weitgehend der bei den Zitaten erhobene Befund: Hier wie dort stellen Genesis, Exodus, Levitikus, Deuteronomium, Psalmen, Dodekapropheton und Jesaja die meisten – knapp 80 % (bei Markus) bzw. 85 % (bei Paulus) – aller Quelltexte. Damit entsprechen beide Autoren dem bereits erwähnten zeitgenössischen Trend. Es fällt aber darüber hinaus auf, dass sich die Bezüge auf jene sieben Bücher in fast gleicher Weise der Thora, den Propheten und den Psalmen[37] zuordnen:

---

[37] Diese Gruppierung war im 1. Jh. n.Chr. gängig, wie 4Q397 14–21 10 und Lk 24,44 sowie Philo, *De vita contemplativa*, 25; Josephus, *Contra Apionem*, 38–40 belegen; gegen C.A. Evans, The Beginning of the Good News and the Fulfillment of Scripture in the Gospel of Mark, in: Hearing

Summe der Bezüge auf die 7 Bücher	Thora (ohne Num)		Propheten (Jes + XII)		Psalmen	
	Anzahl	%	Anzahl	%	Anzahl	%
Markus	38	17	44,7	14	36,8	7	18,4
Paulus	135	61	45,2	52	38,5	22	16,3

Bemerkenswert ist ferner die Vorliebe beider Autoren für Jesaja, Psalmen, Deuteronomium und Exodus – und zwar in dieser Folge[38]. Solch doppelte Konvergenz legt die Annahme eines genetischen Zusammenhangs nahe. Allerdings kann man sich diesen kaum als Einwirkung des paulinischen Schriftgebrauchs auf das Markusevangelium vorstellen. Dort wären dann ja zwei Spezifika des Paulus – die enorme Bevorzugung des Jesajabuchs (nicht erst im Römerbrief!) und die intensive Rezeption der Erzählungen von den Erzvätern und dem Auszug aus Ägypten – erheblich reduziert beziehungsweise nahezu getilgt[39] worden; und dafür gäbe es keine plausible Erklärung. Andererseits stellen die vor-markinischen Traditionen keine Einheit dar, der sich ein derart profilierter Zugriff auf die heiligen Schriften zuschreiben ließe; eine Abhängigkeit des Paulus von ihnen ist deshalb unwahrscheinlich. So steht zu vermuten, dass Markus und Paulus durch ein und dieselbe traditionelle Umgangsweise mit der Schrift geprägt worden sind. Die vorhandenen Unterschiede bei der Gewichtung einzelner Bücher (wie Genesis, Levitikus und Dodekapropheton, ferner Numeri und Daniel) sind dann zwanglos darauf zurückzuführen, dass beide Autoren in ihren Werken ein je eigenes Profil der Schriftnutzung ausgebildet haben.

Überschaut man den gesamten Befund zur Auswahl der im Rahmen von Zitaten, Paraphrasen oder evidenten Anspielungen beigezogenen Quelltexte bei Markus und Paulus, so bietet er
- etliche Indizien für die Teilhabe beider an einer im antiken Judentum oder frühen Christentum verbreiteten Bevorzugung bestimmter Bücher (Gen, Ex,

---

the Old Testament in the New Testament, ed. by S.E. Porter (McMaster New Testament Studies), Grand Rapids 2006, 83–103, hier 84.

38 Der Vorrang Jesajas vor den Psalmen etwa steht im Kontrast zu den Befunden im Matthäusevangelium, im Doppelwerk des Lukas und bei den biblischen Manuskripten aus Qumran. – Von einer klaren Bevorzugung prophetischer und eschatologisch gedeuteter Passagen der Schrift (so H.C. Kee, Function, 173) lässt sich bei ca. 45 % Thora-Bezügen aber kaum sprechen.

39 Bei Markus begegnen die Erzväter nur in dem ihm wohl schon vorgegebenen Passus Mk 12,26f. (vgl. dazu U. Mell, Die „anderen" Winzer. Eine exegetische Studie zur Vollmacht Jesu Christi nach Markus 11,27–12,34 [WUNT 77], Tübingen 1994, 197–201.306–310) und das Auszugs-Geschehen gar nicht.

Lev, Dtn, Pss, XII, Jes), Passagen (Gen 1–2; Jes 29; 40; Dan 2) und Stellen (Gen 2,24; Ex 20,13–15 / Dtn 5,17–19; Dtn 6,4f.; Ps 109[110],1 samt 8,7),
- einen Beleg für die bei beiden, aber auch andernorts greifbare Einwirkung der Jesusüberlieferung (Zitation von Lev 19,18 als Zusammenfassung der Thora für den zwischenmenschlichen Bereich),
- zwei Anhaltspunkte für die Annahme, dass beide durch eine bestimmte frühchristliche Umgangsweise mit der Schrift geprägt worden sind, die sie dann unabhängig voneinander weiterentwickelt haben (allgemeiner Schriftbezug bei der Osterbotschaft; ähnliche Verteilung der Schriftbezüge auf Thora, Propheten und Psalmen – mit Vorrang für das Jesajabuch).

2.2 Zur Textgestalt der Zitate und zitatähnlichen Anspielungen

Die Erforschung des paulinischen Schriftgebrauchs hat hinsichtlich des Wortlauts seiner Zitate mittlerweile zu einer weitgehend konsensuellen Beurteilung des Befundes geführt[40]: (1) Paulus hat Schriftworte generell nach griechischen Textfassungen aus der Septuaginta-Überlieferung angeführt[41], und zwar häufig (das gilt für Jesaja und den Pentateuch) anhand der alexandrinischen Tradition; dabei verwendete er bisweilen Manuskripte, in denen die griechische Version nach dem hebräischen Text rezensiert worden war[42]. (2) Wie er bei Paraphrasen und Anspielungen naturgemäß bestimmte Textelemente betonte, so griff er auch bei Zitaten öfter in den Wortlaut ein, um ihre argumentative Kraft innerhalb seiner Gedankengänge zu stärken und seine Deutung der zitierten Sätze herauszustellen; solche Eingriffe erfolgten in Form von Umstellungen, grammatischen Änderungen, Auslassungen, Einfügungen und Umformulierungen (Letztere meist in Aufnahme verwandter Schriftworte – bis hin zu Mischzitaten). Gelegentlich, etwa in 1Kor 1,31 und 2,9, zitierte der Apostel sogar „geflügelte Worte", die auf der Basis von

---

40 Vgl. zum Folgenden D.-A. Koch, Schrift, 48–88.102–198; Chr.D. Stanley, Paul and the language of Scripture. Citation technique in the Pauline Epistles and contemporary literature (MSSNTS 74), Cambridge 1992, passim, ferner (speziell zu Jesajazitaten) F. Wilk, Bedeutung, 17–59 u.ö.; J.R. Wagner, Heralds, *passim*.
41 Den Nachweis führte bereits E.F. Kautzsch, De Veteris Testamenti locis a Paulo Apostolo allegatis, Leipzig 1869. Kritik an dieser Einschätzung brachten in jüngerer Zeit u.a. T.H. Lim, Holy Scripture in the Qumran Commentaries and Pauline Letters, Oxford 1997, und H.-J. Inkelaar, Conflict over Wisdom. The Theme of 1 Corinthians 1–4 Rooted in Scripture (CBET 63), Leuven 2011, 151–158.308–310 u.ö., vor.
42 Diese Rezensionsarbeit ist in der Zwölfprophetenrolle aus Naḥal Ḥever (8ḤevXII gr, verfasst noch im 1. Jh. v.Chr.) klar dokumentiert; vgl. dazu grundlegend D. Barthélemy, Les devanciers d'Aquila. Première publication intégrale du texte des fragments du Dodécapropheton, trouvés dans le désert de Juda (VT.S 10), Leiden 1963.

Schriftworten entstanden waren⁴³. Wo Zitationsformeln fehlen, war der Freiraum für Modifikationen noch größer; das zeigen insbesondere drei Stellen, an denen er aus mehreren Schriftworten und in Anlehnung an exegetische Traditionen palästinischer Provenienz Worte Gottes oder der Glaubensgerechtigkeit neu gebildet hat⁴⁴.

Vor-paulinische Änderungen am überlieferten LXX-Text und Modifikationen, die Paulus an seiner Textvorlage vorgenommen hat, dienten also je anderen Zwecken. Das wird dort besonders deutlich, wo der Wortlaut eines paulinischen Zitats dem hebräischen Original näher kommt als der LXX-Version, die Abweichung von dieser aber in Spannung zur Zitierabsicht des Apostels steht⁴⁵. Demgemäß lassen sich beide Sorten von Varianten zur LXX-Überlieferung bei Zitaten und dann auch bei zitatähnlichen, syntaktisch selbständigen Anspielungen gut unterscheiden⁴⁶. Wo Paulus – oder ein anderer Autor – ein Schriftwort weitergehend in die eigenen Ausführungen integriert hat, ist solch eine Unterscheidung freilich kaum noch möglich. Daher bleiben Paraphrasen und weitere Anspielungen im Folgenden unberücksichtigt.

Blickt man nun auf die Textgestalt der Zitate und zitatähnlichen Anspielungen im Markusevangelium⁴⁷, so zeigt sich ein ähnlich facettenreiches Bild:

---

43 Vgl. D.-A. Koch, Schrift, 35 f. (zu 1Kor 1,31), und F. Wilk, Jesajanische Prophetie im Spiegel exegetischer Tradition. Zu Hintergrund und Sinngehalt des Schriftzitats in 1Kor 2,9, in: Die Septuaginta – Entstehung, Sprache, Geschichte, hg. von S. Kreuzer/M. Meiser/M. Sigismund (WUNT 286), Tübingen 2012, 480–504.
44 Vgl. F. Wilk, Gottes Wort und Gottes Verheißungen. Zur Eigenart der Schriftverwendung in 2Kor 6,14–7,1, in: Die Septuaginta – Texte, Kontexte, Lebenswelten, hg. von M. Karrer/W. Kraus (WUNT 219), Tübingen 2008, 674–696 (zu 2Kor 6,16–18 und 4,6); W. Reinbold, Das Ziel des Gesetzes nach Röm 10,4–13, in: Judaistik und neutestamentliche Wissenschaft. Standorte – Grenzen – Beziehungen, hg. von L. Doering/H.-G. Waubke/F. Wilk (FRLANT 226), Göttingen 2008, 297–312, hier 302–304 (zu Röm 10,6–8).
45 Vgl. etwa die Jesajazitate in Röm 9,27f.; 11,26f. und dazu F. Wilk, Bedeutung, 37–40.
46 Zur Methodik vgl. F. Wilk, The Letters of Paul as Witnesses to and for the Septuagint Text, in: Septuagint Research. Issues and Challenges in the Study of the Greek Jewish Scriptures, eds. W. Kraus/R.G. Wooden (SBL.SCSt 53), Atlanta 2006, 253–271. – Wie P.T. Egan, Did Peter Change Scripture? The Manuscript Tradition of Greek Psalms 33–34 and 1 Peter 3:10–12, in: Die Septuaginta – Entstehung, Sprache, Geschichte, hg. von S. Kreuzer/M. Meiser/M. Sigismund (WUNT 286), Tübingen 2012, 505–528, exemplarisch (an 1Petr 3,10–12) demonstriert, setzt ein diesbezügliches Urteil allerdings in jedem Einzelfall die Prüfung der differenzierten handschriftlichen Überlieferung des Quelltextes voraus.
47 Viele wichtige Beobachtungen dazu sind zusammengestellt bei M. Meiser, Die Funktion der Septuaginta-Zitate im Markusevangelium, in: Die Septuaginta – Text, Wirkung, Rezeption, hg. von W. Kraus/S. Kreuzer (WUNT), Tübingen 2014, 517–544 [im Druck].

Grundlage der *Zitate* ist durchweg die Septuaginta. Evident ist dies zunächst für diejenigen Anführungen, bei denen der älteste Text des Markusevangeliums zumindest den meisten und wichtigsten Septuaginta-Handschriften entspricht: für Mk 7,10b (Dtn 5,16a)[48]; 11,17b (Jes 56,7c)[49]; 12,10 f. (Ps 117[118],22 f.) und 12,31 (Lev 19,18). Andernorts lassen sich vorhandene Abweichungen am besten als Modifikationen im Sinne der Zitierabsicht des Markus – so in 1,3 (Jes 40,3) – oder seiner Tradition – so vielleicht in 12,26 (Ex 3,6) – verstehen:

– In Mk 1,3 bringt das Pronomen αὐτοῦ (anstelle von τοῦ θεοῦ ἡμῶν) am Versende die Identität sowohl des κύριος als auch des „Rufenden" in die Schwebe – wie es der Funktion des Zitats in seinem markinischen Zusammenhang entspricht[50].

– In 12,26 könnte das Verb εἰμί fehlen, weil die Selbstaussage ἐγώ εἰμι bei Markus christologisch besetzt ist (vgl. 6,50; 13,6; 14,62). Die Auslassung der Wortfolge τοῦ πατρός σου, [ὁ] θεός (hinter ὁ θεός) aber entspricht dem Sachverhalt, dass das Gotteswort in 12,26, wie V. 27 zeigt, ganz auf die Beziehung Gottes zu den Erzvätern ausgerichtet ist, sodass deren Verhältnis zu Mose übergangen werden kann; die (textkritisch freilich unsichere) Ergänzung der Artikel vor θεός Ἰσαάκ und θεός Ἰακώβ betont daraufhin die Identität Gottes im Verhältnis zu jedem der drei Erzväter[51].

Ähnliches gilt für das Mischzitat in Mk 12,36 (Ps 109[110],1 und 8,7b)[52].

---

[48] In den meisten Handschriften zu Ex 20,12a fehlt das Personalpronomen hinter μητέρα.
[49] Das Fehlen der Konjunktion γάρ ergibt sich aus der Verwendung des Jesajaworts als selbständiger Aussage und ist daher nicht im eigentlichen Sinne als Auslassung zu werten.
[50] Vgl. dazu (sowie zur Textkritik bei Quell- und Folgetext) F. Wilk, Weg, 203–205.208.
[51] R. Pesch, Das Markusevangelium. II. Teil: Kommentar zu Kap. 8,27–16,20 (HThK II/2), Freiburg ⁴1991, 234, schließt aus dem hebräischen Psalm in Sir 51 sowie aus Pr. Man. 1; AssMos 3,9; Jub 45,3, dass eine freie Zitation von Ex 3,6 seinerzeit üblich war. Die Stellen belegen jedoch nur, dass man Gott im Gebet gerne als Gott Abrahams etc. anrief.
[52] Die Wendung ὑποκάτω τῶν ποδῶν σου (statt ὑποπόδιον τῶν ποδῶν σου) aus Ps 8,7 verknüpft die Unterwerfung der Feinde Christi mit der in kosmischen Dimensionen gedachten Parusie des Menschensohns (vgl. einerseits V. 4–7, andererseits Mk 14,62 und dazu 13,24–27). Ob der Artikel vor κύριος schon in der Vorlage fehlte (wie Hs. R) oder von Markus getilgt wurde (der sonst zwischen κύριος als Titel Gottes [vgl. 12,29; 13,20; anders 2,28, wo das Wort Prädikatsnomen ist] und ὁ κύριος als Bezeichnung Jesu [vgl. 5,19; 11,3; anders 12,9; 13,35 mit folgendem Genitiv im Rahmen von Gleichnissen] differenziert), muss offen bleiben.

In Mk 7,6 (Jes 29,13f.); 7,10d (Ex 21,16[17]) und 14,27 (Sach 13,7) ist sodann jeweils der Wortlaut der alexandrinischen Text-Überlieferung aufgenommen[53] und dem Verwendungszusammenhang gemäß bearbeitet worden:
- Der polemischen Anwendung von Jes 29,13 auf Pharisäer und Schriftgelehrte (vgl. Mk7,5) entspricht zum einen die Tilgung des einleitenden ἐγγίζει μοι – woraufhin das Demonstrativpronomen an den Satzanfang gerückt (vgl. dazu 9,29; 15,39) und das folgende Verb in den Singular gesetzt wurde –, zum andern die auf die „Überlieferung" (7,5.8 f.13) jener Leute zielende Formulierung διδασκαλίας ἐντάλματα ἀνθρώπων („*als* Lehren: Menschengebote") am Versende[54].
- In 7,10d lag die zweimalige Auslassung des Personalpronomens αὐτοῦ nach dem Dekalogzitat in V. 10b aus stilistischen Gründen nahe.
- In 14,27 passt die Form πατάξω[55] (statt πατάξατε oder πάταξον) zur Deutung des Zitats auf die nach Gottes Willen geschehende (vgl. V.36) Passion Jesu.

In Mk 1,2 wiederum liegt ein Mischzitat aus Mal 3,1 und Ex 23,20 vor, bei dem das erstgenannte Schriftwort aus einer dem hebräischen Text angenäherten Septuagintafassung stammen dürfte[56].

Zwei Zitate schließlich enthalten Abweichungen von der Septuaginta-Überlieferung, die weder auf eine „rehebraisierende" Rezension noch unmittelbar auf die Hand des Markus zurückzuführen sind: In Mk 10,19 ist die Liste der Gebote aus Ex 20,13–16*init.* mit negiertem Konjunktiv Aorist formuliert, durch eine Weisung aus Sir 4,1 ergänzt und dann mit Ex 20,12a abgeschlossen worden[57]; in Mk 12,29f.

---

[53] Vgl. das Fehlen der Phrase [ἐν] τῷ στόματι αὐτοῦ καὶ [ἐν] in der ersten Zitatzeile in Mk 7,6, den Ausdruck θανάτῳ τελευτάτω in 7,10d sowie die Formen τὸν ποιμένα und διασκορπισθήσονται in 14,27.

[54] Mit ihr spitzt Markus die Rede vom „leeren Gottesdienst" auf subtile Weise zu; vgl. J.R. Donahue/D.J. Harrington, The Gospel of Mark (Sacra Pagina Series 2), Collegeville 2002, 222. – In der LXX-Überlieferung findet sich diese Formulierung nur in wenigen, recht jungen Handschriften (106, V, 566, 233; ähnlich 301 und 88, 130–311, 410); sie dürfte daher dort sekundär sein. Das Zitat in 1 Clem 15,2 wiederum ist wohl (ähnlich wie die Zitate in 34,8 [dazu vgl. F. Wilk, Prophetie, 491f.] oder 36,3) neutestamentlich beeinflusst; vgl. die weiteren Anklänge zumal an matthäische Texte in 7,7; 13,2; 24,5; 27,5; 46,8; 48,5.

[55] Auch deren Bezeugung in LXX-Handschriften (V-538, 46–86ᶜ-711ᶜ, 106, 233–710) ist zu schwach, um auf einen alten Text schließen zu lassen.

[56] Vgl. F. Wilk, Weg, 205–208. – Beim Dodekapropheton-Zitat in Mk 14,27 rezipiert Markus übrigens ebenfalls eine Textfassung (s.o. Anm. 53), die dem hebräischen Original wesentlich näher steht als die vermutlich älteste LXX-Version.

[57] Da in Mk 10,19, anders als in 7,10, das zweite σου im Eltern-Gebot fehlt (s.o. Anm. 48), liegt hier der Exodus-Text zugrunde; vgl. A.Y. Collins, Mark. A Commentary (Hermeneia), Minneapolis 2007, 479. Zur Abfolge der drei erstgenannten Verbote s.o. Anm. 24.

erscheint die dreigliedrige Reihe von Dimensionen des Menschenlebens aus Dtn 6,4 f. durch eine vierte erweitert und am Ende begrifflich verändert. Vermutlich führt der Evangelist hier wie dort eine katechetische Fortschreibung des jeweiligen Septuagintatextes an, mit der er Jesus als weisheitlich geprägten Thoralehrer präsentieren kann.

Dass dem Zitat in Mk 10,19 eine LXX-Fassung des Dekalogs zugrunde liegt, zeigt sich an der wörtlichen Kongruenz in V. 19 g und der übereinstimmenden Begrifflichkeit in V. 19b–e[58]. Auch der Zusatz in V. 19 f entspricht dem Sprachgebrauch der LXX; Wortwahl und Formulierung erinnern dabei freilich primär an das Sirachbuch[59]. Dort und in den Sprüchen ist nun auch der paränetische Gebrauch des negierten Konjunktiv Aorist der 2. Person Singular besonders verbreitet[60]. So erweist sich die mit V. 19 f–g auf die soziale Verantwortung des Hörers zugespitzte[61] Kette von Geboten als weisheitlich konnotierte Adaption des LXX-Dekalogs[62].

Das Zitat in Mk 12,29 f. wiederum folgt bis auf die beiden oben genannten Differenzen präzise dem durch A und die Mehrheit der Handschriften bezeugten LXX-Text von Dtn 6,4 f.[63] Die Ersetzung von δύναμις durch ἰσχύς aber entspricht einer späteren, hellenistisch beeinflussten Tendenz, „Kraft" im Kontext der Gottesverehrung als innere Stärke zu verstehen[64]; und der zusätzliche Verweis auf διάνοια erweitert die Liste aus 6,5 um ein Vermögen, das nicht nur, aber gerade auch in Weisheits-Schriften als Ort der Treue zu dem einen Gott sowie der Kenntnis des Gesetzes gilt[65] und deshalb gerne mit Herz oder Seele verknüpft oder parallelisiert wird, ja, in der Textüberlieferung der Septuaginta wiederholt als Äqui-

---

58 Diesbezüglich ist zumal das sehr seltene Wort ψευδομαρτυρέω beweiskräftig; biblisch ist es außerhalb des Dekalogs und seiner Rezeptionen nur noch in SusTh 61 (nach A, Q etc.) sowie Mk 14,56 f. belegt.
59 Vgl. zum Ersten Dtn 24,14 (in dem von A und vielen anderen Handschriften gebotenen Wortlaut); Ex 21,10; Mal 3,5, zum Zweiten Sir 4,1 – die einzige exakte Parallele zu Mk 10,19 f – sowie Sir 29,6[8].7[10]; 31[34],25.27 (Rahlfs: 34,21.22). Auf Sir 4,1 und Dtn 24,14 verweist auch J. Gnilka, Das Evangelium nach Markus. 2. Teilband: Mk 8,27–16,20 (EKK II/2), Zürich/Neukirchen-Vluyn ⁵1999, 87.
60 Vgl. Sir 1,28[36] u.v.ö.; Spr 1,8 u.v.ö., ferner Dtn 12,30; Jos 1,9; Tob 4,3 u.ö.
61 Vgl. dazu K. Berger, Gesetzesauslegung, 418–421.
62 Auf ähnliche Weise wird Dtn 5,17 f. im Kontext von Jak 2,1–13 aufgenommen; vgl. V. 11.
63 B und andere Handschriften bieten allerdings in der ersten ἐξ-ὅλης-Wendung διανοίας anstelle von καρδίας; vgl. dazu J.W. Wevers, Notes on the Greek Text of Deuteronomy (SCSt 39), Atlanta 1995, 115.
64 Vgl. die Verknüpfung von Herz, Seele und Stärke in 4Regn[2Kön] 23,25 / 2Chr 35,19b (im Blick auf Josija) und Sir 5,2, ferner die Rede von der „Stärke des Herzens" in Hi 36,5.
65 Vgl. Dtn 4,39; 29,18[17] und Spr 9,10a; 13,15.

valent zum Herzen erscheint⁶⁶ – und dessen Nennung zudem den Anschluss des Nächstenliebegebotes in Mk 12,31 erleichtert⁶⁷.

Bei den *zitatähnlichen Anspielungen* ist die Sachlage noch komplexer. Unter ihnen finden sich nicht nur Beispiele für
- die wörtliche Übernahme, partielle Übernahme oder weitreichende Bearbeitung eines mehrheitlich bezeugten Septuaginta-Textes⁶⁸,
- die zurückhaltende Bearbeitung eines Septuaginta-Textes aus der alexandrinischen Tradition (so in 9,48 [Jes 66,24]) und
- die partielle Übernahme, zurückhaltende Bearbeitung oder umfassende Bearbeitung einer dem hebräischen Text angenäherten Septuaginta-Version⁶⁹,

sondern auch für
- die Korrektur des mehrheitlich bezeugten Septuaginta-Textes anhand einer aramäischen Version des Schriftwortes (so in 15,34 [Ps 21{22},2]) sowie
- die umfassende Bearbeitung eines Septuaginta-Textes in Anlehnung an eine im Targum bezeugte Auslegungstradition (so in 4,12 [Jes 6,9f.])⁷⁰.

Natürlich steht zu vermuten, dass – wie manche Zitate – jedenfalls einige dieser Anspielungen in der jetzt vorliegenden Form bereits im vor-markinischen Traditionsstoff enthalten waren; man kann also in solchen Fällen Markus selbst kaum für die Gestaltung des Wortlauts verantwortlich machen. Andererseits sah er dann

---

66 Vgl. zum Ersten Sir 22,17 (sowie 1Chr 29,18; Bar 1,22) und Jes 57,11; Jer 38[31],33 (sowie Jdt 8,14; Hi 36,28), für die Seele Jos 22,5; Spr 2,10, zum Zweiten Ex 35,9[10]; Num 32,7; Dtn 6,5; 28,47; Jos 14,8; 22,5; Hi 1,5; Spr 4,4; 27,19; Jes 14,13; Jer 38[31],33.
67 Vgl. die Kontrastaussage zu Lev 19,18b in V. 17a: „Du sollst deinen Bruder nicht hassen in deinem Denken (τῇ διανοίᾳ σου)". – Zur hellenistischen Prägung von Mk 12,28–34 insgesamt vgl. G. Bornkamm, Das Doppelgebot der Liebe, in: G. Bornkamm, Geschichte und Glaube. Erster Teil, Gesammelte Aufsätze, Bd. 3 (BEvTh 48), München 1968, 37–45.
68 Vgl. a) Mk 10,6 (Gen 1,27) sowie die Paraphrase 12,1b (Jes 5,2 – hier ist nur das Hapaxlegomenon προλήνιον durch das geläufigere ὑπολήνιον ersetzt), b) 10,7f. (Gen 2,24; zur Ursprünglichkeit des Kurztextes in Mk 10,7 vgl. M. Meiser, Funktion, 530) und c) 15,24 (Ps 21[22],19).
69 Vgl. a) Mk 11,9 (Ps 117[118]25f.), b) 8,18 (Jer 5,21) und 13,24 (Jes 13,10) sowie c) 13,25 (Jes 34,4).
70 Vgl. dazu V.A. Lehnert, Die Provokation Israels. Die paradoxe Funktion von Jes 6,9–10 bei Markus und Lukas. Ein textpragmatischer Versuch im Kontext gegenwärtiger Rezeptionsästhetik und Lesetheorie (Neukirchener Dissertationen und Habilitationen 25), Neukirchen-Vluyn 1999, 149f. – Dass Markus selbst an den beiden letztgenannten Stellen Schriftworte nach ihrem aramäischen (und andernorts nach dem hebräischen) Wortlaut anführe (so C.A. Evans, Beginning, 85), lässt sich m. E. nicht aufzeigen.

offenbar keinen Anlass, den Wortlaut an die ihm vertraute Textfassung anzupassen[71] – und dies ist seinerseits bemerkenswert.

Markus und Paulus teilen demnach (1) die grundlegende Orientierung an der Septuaginta[72], (2) die Abhängigkeit zumal von alexandrinischen Texttraditionen zu Pentateuch und Prophetenbüchern, (3) die wiederholte Nutzung von Textfassungen, die anhand des hebräischen Originals rezensiert worden waren, (4) die Freiheit, den Wortlaut von Zitaten (und erst recht zitatähnlichen Anspielungen) nach Bedarf der jeweiligen Zitierabsicht gemäß zu modifizieren, (5) die Fähigkeit, Mischzitate zu bilden, und (6) die gelegentliche Verarbeitung palästinisch-exegetischer Traditionen. Überdies haben beide je einmal Wendungen aus dem Sirachbuch in eine weisheitliche Fortschreibung eines Schriftwortes integriert[73]. Fast alle dieser Phänomene sind, für sich genommen, auch in anderen antik-jüdischen oder frühchristlichen Werken zu beobachten. Das beschriebene Ausmaß an Konvergenz lässt sich jedoch am besten durch die Annahme eines genetischen Zusammenhangs erklären. Allerdings liegt wohl kein direkter Einfluss in die eine oder andere Richtung vor; denn gerade bei solchen Schriftworten, die sowohl im Markusevangelium als auch bei Paulus (im 1. Korintherbrief) angeführt sind, weichen die Textfassungen signifikant voneinander ab[74]. Vielmehr dürften beide Autoren – wie bei der Auswahl, so auch – bei der Rezeption und Gestaltung des Wortlauts ihrer Schriftbezüge durch eine gemeinsame „Schule" geprägt worden sein.

2.3 Zum Verständnis der Schrift

In seiner Jesuserzählung gibt Markus selbst keine explizite Auskunft über seine Hermeneutik. Diese kann man in ihren Grundzügen jedoch schon aus seiner Darstellung Jesu als eines Interpreten der Schriften ableiten. Zumal in Streitgesprächen lässt der Evangelist ihn ja als denjenigen auftreten, der den ursprünglichen, in der Schöpfung verwurzelten Willen Gottes von der Schrift her zur Gel-

---

71 Genau dies hat Matthäus bei markinischen Zitaten und Anspielungen mehrfach – wenn auch nicht konsequent – getan; vgl. Mt 13,14f.; 19,4f.18f.; 22,32.37; 24,29; 26,31; 27,46.
72 So auch H.C. Kee, Function, 173f.180.
73 Vgl. Mk 10,19 (Sir 4,1; s.o. Anm. 59); 1Kor 2,9 (Sir 1,10; vgl. F. Wilk, Prophetie, 500f.).
74 Zu Ex 20,13–15 / Dtn 5,17–19 in Mk 10,19 und Röm 13,9 s.o. bei und in Anm. 24.58–62. Für Ps 109[110],1 und 8,7 bietet Paulus in 1Kor 15,25–27 ἄχρι οὗ ... ὑπὸ τοὺς πόδας statt ἕως ἂν ... ὑποπόδιον bzw. ὑποκάτω τῶν ποδῶν wie Mk 12,36 (ferner s.o. Anm. 35.52).

tung bringt und damit die Positionen seiner Gegner als unhaltbar entlarvt[75]. Demnach erscheint sie an wesentlichen Punkten als das Fundament der Lehre Jesu – und diese als der Schlüssel zum rechten Verständnis der Schrift[76].

Der wechselseitige Zusammenhang lässt sich exemplarisch an Mk 10,17–22 aufzeigen: Als „guter Lehrer" (10,17) erweist sich Jesus im Gespräch mit einem Reichen, der nach dem ewigen Leben trachtet, gerade dadurch, dass er, erstens, ihm zunächst das erste Gebot und dann die zweite Tafel des Dekalogs vorhält (V. 18 f.), zweitens deren Gebote auf die aus ihnen erwachsende soziale Fürsorgepflicht hin zuspitzt (V. 19 f–g) und dann drittens jenen Mann auf den Weg der besitzlosen, zum himmlischen Schatz führenden Nachfolge ruft (V. 21), in der sich das Tun der Gebote und damit des Willens Gottes (vgl. 3,35) vollendet[77]. Darin also soll der Reiche „den Gehorsam gegen Gott bewähren, daß er erkennt, wie dieser in Jesus auf ihn zukommt"[78].

Diese Auslegung und Inanspruchnahme der Schrift verknüpft sich nun mit der Einsicht, dass jetzt – im Kontext des Auftretens Jesu, der als Gottessohn durch Wort und Tat das Gottesreich vergegenwärtigt (vgl. Mk 1,9–15; 4,10 f.) – ihr eigentlicher Sinn erkennbar wird[79]. So identifiziert Jesus seine Kritiker als die „Heuchler", über die „Jesaja trefflich prophezeit hat" (7,6)[80], und seine Passion als das Geschehen, durch das „die Schriften erfüllt werden" (14,49). Ja, nach Markus ist der ganze Weg Jesu in der Schrift vorgezeichnet: seine Einsetzung zum Gottessohn (1,11), sein Wunderwirken (7,37), die Umstände seines Sterbens (9,12; 14,21; 15,24.34), sein Tod samt anschließender Flucht der Jünger (14,27), seine Erhöhung zur Rechten Gottes (12,36), die Umstände und Folgen seiner Parusie (14,62; 13,24–27). Entsprechendes gilt dann für geschichtliche Vorgänge, die mit diesem Weg

---

75 Vgl. zumal Mk 2,23–28 und 10,2–12 und dazu F. Wilk, Jesus, 75–77. S. Moyise, The Old Testament in the New. An Introduction, London 2001, 24, spricht treffend von einer „authoritative interpretation of the law"; gegen S. Schulz, Markus und das Alte Testament, in: ZThK 58 (1961), 184–197, hier 193 f.: Bei Markus sei eine „Ablehnung der alttestamentlichen Tora" erkennbar und demgemäß eine „Forderung (sc. des Gesetzes) an den Christen" nicht vorhanden.
76 Vgl. M.D. Hooker, Mark, in: It is Written: Scripture Citing Scripture. Essays in Honour of Barnabas Lindars, eds. D.A. Carson/H.G.M. Williamson, Cambridge 1988, 220–230, hier 224: Jesu Lehre stimme mit der des Mose überein, doch seine Autorität gehe über die des Mose hinaus.
77 Vgl. dazu K. Berger, Gesetzesauslegung, 412 f.
78 E. Schweizer, Das Evangelium nach Markus (NTD 1), Göttingen ¹⁵1978, 114.
79 Vgl. J. Marcus, The Way of the Lord. Christological Exegesis of the Old Testament in the Gospel of Mark, Edinburgh 1992, 202 f. – Nach C.A. Evans, Beginning, 86–103, richtet sich Markus hiermit gegen die Inanspruchnahme jüdischer Prophetie durch den römischen Kaiser Vespasian. Zu dieser Kontextualisierung generell vgl. M. Ebner, Markusevangelium, 175–180.
80 R.T. France, The Gospel of Mark. A Commentary on the Greek Text (NIGTC), Grand Rapids 2002, 284, spricht hier zu Recht von einem „‚contemporising' use of OT texts".

wesentlich verknüpft sind: das Wirken und das Geschick des Täufers als des verheißenen Elija (9,13), das Unverständnis, dem Jesus begegnet (4,12; 8,18), die Errichtung des nicht mit Händen gebauten „Gebetshauses für alle Völker" auf der Basis seines Todes und seiner Auferstehung (11,17; 12,10 f., vgl. 14,58), die Entweihung des Jerusalemer Tempels (13,14) im Kontext endzeitlicher Schrecken (13,7.12.19), schließlich die herrliche Zukunft des weltumspannenden Gottesreiches (4,32)[81]. Demgemäß stellt der Evangelist seiner Jesuserzählung ein Schriftzitat voran (1,2 f.), das als Leseanweisung dient und infolge seines schillernden Sinns dazu nötigt und befähigt, immer tiefer in den Zusammenhang sukzessiver Wegbereitungen einzudringen, der sich vom Auftreten des Täufers über die Wirksamkeit Jesu und das Leben seiner Nachfolger bis hin zur universalen Realisierung der Gottesherrschaft erstreckt[82]. Insgesamt präsentiert Markus damit die heilige Schrift als Urkunde, die – gelesen und gedeutet im Licht des „Evangeliums", das zunächst Jesus selbst (1,14 f.) und sodann seine Jünger (13,10; 14,9) verkündigt haben beziehungsweise verkündigen – den umstrittenen Weg Jesu zu verstehen und das Leben in seiner Nachfolge zu gestalten lehrt[83].

Mit diesem Schriftverständnis folgte der Evangelist zum Teil einer Bahn, die bereits in frühchristlichen Traditionen angelegt war. Wie deren Aufnahme durch Paulus erkennen lässt, bezeugen sie ihrerseits ein Interpretationsverfahren, bei dem die Schrift als Quelle der Bekräftigung und Mittel der Explikation des Christusglaubens aufgefasst und genutzt wurde, weil man das Christusgeschehen als den Zielpunkt ihrer Verheißungen identifiziert hatte[84]. Paulus selbst machte dann freilich im Anschluss daran deutlich, dass diese Verheißungen – in Christus bekräftigt (2Kor 1,20) – auch die geschichtlichen Erfahrungen derer umgreifen, die

---

[81] Zur Ausrichtung auf die Zukunft und zur Betonung der Notwendigkeit des Leidens als Merkmalen der markinischen Schriftinterpretation vgl. H. Anderson, Testament, 290–297.
[82] Vgl. dazu F. Wilk, Weg, 216–218, zur „Wiederholung" des Weges Jesu durch die Leser des Markusevangeliums auch J. Marcus, Way, 46 f. H.C. Kee, Function, 177, spricht insofern zu Recht von „Mark's concern ... to demonstrate by appeal to scripture that in Jesus the divinely determined plan of redemption is in the process of accomplishment".
[83] Bei S. Schulz, Markus (vgl. 188: „allein vom Kyrios-Kerygma ... bekommt er ... das Alte Testament in den Blickpunkt"), A. Suhl, Die Funktion der alttestamentlichen Zitate und Anspielungen im Markusevangelium, Gütersloh 1965 (vgl. 169: „Markus benutzt das AT als qualifizierte Sprache zur Interpretation."), und W.S. Vorster, The Function of the Use of the Old Testament in Mark, in: Neotest. 14 (1980), 62–72 (vgl. 69: „Mark uses ... the Old Testament material to tell his story of the life and work of Jesus."), wird dieser Befund nur verkürzt wahrgenommen. M. Meiser, Funktion, 543, betont demgegenüber mit Recht den „Bezug auf die Autorität Jesu", den er schwerpunktmäßig durch „Apologetik und Polemik" charakterisiert sieht.
[84] Vgl. 1Kor 15,3 f.; 11,25; Röm 3,25 f.; 4,25 etc. und dazu (sowie zu den antik-jüdischen Grundlagen solcher Schriftauslegung) F. Wilk, Schriftbezüge, 480–482.

sich an das Evangelium von Jesus Christus halten[85]; und diese Einsicht kommt, wie gezeigt, im markinischen Schriftgebrauch ebenfalls zur Geltung. Einander verwandt sind darüber hinaus die jeweiligen Zugänge zum Gesetz im Rahmen ethischer Reflexionen: Bringt Markus zufolge Jesus selbst durch seine Lehre und seinen Nachfolgeruf die Gebote Gottes als Weisung zum Leben zur Geltung (Mk 10,17–22; 12,28–34), so leistet dies nach paulinischer Darstellung der Geist, der in den Christusgläubigen wohnt[86].

Dieser Befund lässt wiederum einen genetischen Zusammenhang zwischen der markinischen und der paulinischen Schriftverwendung vermuten. Es fällt freilich auf, dass Jesus als Thoralehrer für Paulus praktisch keine Rolle spielt[87]; eine Einwirkung vor-markinischer Traditionen auf sein Schriftverständnis ist daher unwahrscheinlich. Umgekehrt fehlen im Markusevangelium alle Hinweise auf eine Vertrautheit mit den Charakteristika der paulinischen Hermeneutik: dass nämlich, erstens, die Schrift „um unsertwillen … geschrieben" sei, wie Paulus in 1Kor 9,10 bezüglich der Apostel, in Röm 4,23f. bezüglich der Christusgläubigen formuliert, also auch „zu unserer Zurechtweisung" (1Kor 10,11) oder „zu unserer Belehrung" (Röm 15,4)[88]; und dass, zweitens, erst vom Christusgeschehen her der heilsgeschichtliche Sinn des Gesetzes erkennbar wird[89]. Daher legt sich auch in dieser Hinsicht die Annahme nahe, dass Markus und Paulus ihr jeweiliges Schriftverständnis unabhängig voneinander, aber im Anschluss an eine gemeinsame Tradition ausgebildet haben.

---

[85] Vgl. dazu F. Wilk, Rühmen und Seufzen. Zur paulinischen Deutung geschichtlicher Prozesse und Erfahrungen im Horizont des Bekenntnisses zu dem einen Gott, in: Der eine Gott und die Geschichte der Völker. Studien zur Inklusion und Exklusion im biblischen Monotheismus, hg. von U. Mell (BThSt 123), Neukirchen-Vluyn 2011, 127–148, hier: 133–145.

[86] Vgl. Röm 8,2–4.9 im Rückbezug auf 7,10 (und dazu F. Wilk, Schriftbezüge, 489), ferner Gal 5,13–26. Zur Konvergenz beider Autoren in der Orientierung am Nächstenliebegebot s.o. nach Anm. 18 sowie die folgende Anm.

[87] Bei den expliziten Verweisen auf die Lehre Jesu in 1Kor 7,10f. und 9,14 werden die – sachlich durchaus vorhandenen – Bezüge auf die Thora nicht expliziert; und dort, wo Paulus das Nächstenliebegebot als Mittelpunkt des Gesetzes vorstellt (Röm 13,8–10; Gal 5,13–15), ist von Jesus keine Rede.

[88] Dazu vgl. F. Wilk, „Zu unserer Belehrung geschrieben…"

[89] Vgl. Röm 3,9–20; 4,15; 5,13.20; 7,1–8,11; 10,3–8; 2Kor 3; Gal 3,10–25 und dazu F. Wilk, Schriftbezüge, 487–490.

3 Schluss

Die Verwendung der heiligen Schrift im Markusevangelium weist bei der Auswahl der Quelltexte, bei der Textgestalt der Zitate und zitatähnlichen Anspielungen sowie beim Verständnis der Schrift spezifische Berührungspunkte mit dem paulinischen Schriftgebrauch auf, die die Annahme eines genetischen Zusammenhangs nahe legen: Beide Autoren dürften durch *eine* bestimmte Umgangsweise mit biblischen Texten geprägt worden sein, die sie unabhängig voneinander weiterentwickelten. Die materialen und hermeneutischen Aspekte jenes Zusammenhangs deuten auf eine frühchristliche Tradition als prägende Größe hin. Solch eine Tradition aber, die auf Markus und auf Paulus eingewirkt hat, lässt sich am ehesten in Syrien lokalisieren[90].

---

[90] Gegen R.E. Watts, Exodus, 387, der seine Auffassung von der inhaltlichen Eigenart der markinischen Schriftdeutung als „additional support for a Roman provenance for Mark" wertet.

Literatur

Anderson, H., The Old Testament in Mark's Gospel, in: The Use of the Old Testament in the New and Other Essays. Studies in Honor of William Franklin Stinespring, ed. J.M. Efird, Durham 1972, 280–306.

Barthélemy, D., Les devanciers d'Aquila. Première publication intégrale du texte des fragments du Dodécapropheton, trouvés dans le désert de Juda (VT.S 10), Leiden 1963.

Bauer, W., Griechisch-deutsches Wörterbuch zu den Schriften des Neuen Testaments und der übrigen urchristlichen Literatur, Berlin [5]1971.

Berger, K., Die Gesetzesauslegung Jesu. Ihr historischer Hintergrund im Judentum und im Alten Testament. Teil I: Markus und Parallelen (WMANT 40), Neukirchen-Vluyn 1972.

(Strack, H.L., und) Billerbeck, P., Das Evangelium nach Markus, Lukas und Johannes und die Apostelgeschichte, Kommentar zum Neuen Testament aus Talmud und Midrasch, Bd. 2, München [2]1956.

Blass, F./ Debrunner, A., Grammatik des neutestamentlichen Griechisch. Bearbeitet von Friedrich Rehkopf, Göttingen [15]1979.

Bornkamm, G., Das Doppelgebot der Liebe, in: G. Bornkamm, Geschichte und Glaube. Erster Teil, Gesammelte Aufsätze Bd. 3, (BEvTh 48), München 1968, 37–45.

Bovon, F., Das Evangelium nach Lukas. 2. Teilband: Lk 9,51–14,35 (EKK III/2), Zürich/Neukirchen-Vluyn 1996.

Broer, I., Einleitung in das Neue Testament. Studienausgabe, Würzburg 2006.

Burchard, Chr., Die Summe der Gebote (Röm 13,7–10), das ganze Gesetz (Gal 5,13–15) und das Christusgesetz (Gal 6,2; Röm 15,1–6; 1 Kor 9,21), in: Chr. Burchard, Studien zur Theologie, Sprache und Umwelt des Neuen Testaments, hg. von D. Sänger (WUNT 107), Tübingen 1998, 151–183.

Collins, A. Yarbro, Mark. A Commentary (Hermeneia), Minneapolis 2007.

Dautzenberg, G., Φεύγετε τὴν πορνείαν. Eine Fallstudie zur paulinischen Sexualethik in ihrem Verhältnis zur Sexualethik des Frühjudentums, in: G. Dautzenberg, Studien zur paulinischen Theologie und zur frühchristlichen Rezeption des Alten Testaments, hg. von D. Sänger (Gießener Schriften zur Theologie und Religionspädagogik 13), Gießen 1999, 142–168.

Donahue, J.R./Harrington, D.J., The Gospel of Mark (Sacra Pagina Series 2), Collegeville 2002.

Dunn, J.D.G., Jesus Remembered. Christianity in the Making, Vol. 1, Grand Rapids 2003.

Ebner, M., Das Markusevangelium, in: Einleitung in das Neue Testament, hg. von M. Ebner/ S. Schreiber, Stuttgart 2008, 154–183.

Eckey, W., Das Markusevangelium. Orientierung am Weg Jesu. Ein Kommentar, Neukirchen-Vluyn 1998.

Egan, P.T., Did Peter Change Scripture? The Manuscript Tradition of Greek Psalms 33–34 and 1 Peter 3:10–12, in: Die Septuaginta – Entstehung, Sprache, Geschichte, hg. von S. Kreuzer/M. Meiser/M. Sigismund (WUNT 286), Tübingen 2012, 505–528.

Evans, C.A., The Beginning of the Good News and the Fulfillment of Scripture in the Gospel of Mark, in: Hearing the Old Testament in the New Testament, ed. S.E. Porter (McMaster New Testament Studies), Grand Rapids 2006, 83–103.

France, R.T., The Gospel of Mark. A Commentary on the Greek Text (NIGTC), Grand Rapids 2002.

Frankemölle, H., Der Brief des Jakobus. Kapitel 2–5 (ÖTBK 17/2), Gütersloh/Würzburg 1994.

Gnilka, J., Das Evangelium nach Markus. 2. Teilband: Mk 8,27–16,20 (EKK II/2), Zürich/Neukirchen-Vluyn ⁵1999.
Hatina, Th.R., In Search of a Context. The Function of Scripture in Mark's Narrative (JSNT.S 232), Sheffield 2002.
Hay, D.M., Glory at the Right Hand. Psalm 110 in Early Christianity (SBL.MS 18), Nashville 1973.
Hooker, M.D., Isaiah in Mark's Gospel, in: Isaiah in the New Testament, eds. S. Moyise/ M.J.J. Menken, London 2005, 35–49.
—, Mark, in: It is Written: Scripture Citing Scripture. Essays in Honour of Barnabas Lindars, eds. D.A. Carson/H.G.M. Williamson, Cambridge 1988, 220–230.
Inkelaar, H.-J., Conflict over Wisdom. The Theme of 1 Corinthians 1–4 Rooted in Scripture (CBET 63), Leuven 2011.
Karrer, M./Sigismund, M./Schmid, U., Textgeschichtliche Beobachtungen zu den Zusätzen in den Septuaginta-Psalmen, in: Die Septuaginta – Texte, Theologien, Einflüsse, hg. von W. Kraus/M. Karrer (WUNT 252), Tübingen 2010, 140–161.
Kautzsch, E.F., De Veteris Testamenti locis a Paulo Apostolo allegatis, Leipzig 1869.
Kee, H.C., The Function of Scriptural Quotations and Allusions in Mark 11–16, in: Jesus und Paulus. Festschrift für Werner Georg Kümmel zum 70. Geburtstag, hg. von E.E. Ellis/ E. Gräßer, Göttingen 1975, 165–188.
Koch, D.-A., Die Schrift als Zeuge des Evangeliums. Untersuchungen zur Verwendung und zum Verständnis der Schrift bei Paulus (BHTh 69), Tübingen 1986.
Lehnert, V.A., Die Provokation Israels. Die paradoxe Funktion von Jes 6,9–10 bei Markus und Lukas. Ein textpragmatischer Versuch im Kontext gegenwärtiger Rezeptionsästhetik und Lesetheorie (Neukirchener Dissertationen und Habilitationen 25), Neukirchen-Vluyn 1999.
Lichtenberger, H., Schöpfung und Ehe in Texten aus Qumran sowie Essenerberichten und die Bedeutung für das Neue Testament, in: Judaistik und neutestamentliche Wissenschaft. Standorte – Grenzen – Beziehungen, hg. von L. Doering/H.-G. Waubke/F. Wilk (FRLANT 226), Göttingen 2008, 279–288.
Liddell, H.G./Scott, R., A Greek-English Lexicon. Revised and augmented throughout by H.S. Jones, Oxford 1982 (Nachdruck der 9. Auflage von 1940 samt Supplement von 1968).
Lim, T.H., Holy Scripture in the Qumran Commentaries and Pauline Letters, Oxford 1997.
Marcus, J., The Way of the Lord. Christological Exegesis of the Old Testament in the Gospel of Mark, Edinburgh 1992.
Meiser, M., Die Funktion der Septuaginta-Zitate im Markusevangelium, in: Die Septuaginta – Text, Wirkung, Rezeption, hg. von W. Kraus/S. Kreuzer (WUNT), Tübingen 2014, 517–544 [im Druck].
Mell, U., Die „anderen" Winzer. Eine exegetische Studie zur Vollmacht Jesu Christi nach Markus 11,27–12,34 (WUNT 77), Tübingen 1994.
Menken, M.J.J., Matthew's Bible. The Old Testament Text of the Evangelist (BEThL 173), Leuven 2004.
Merklein, H., Die Jesusgeschichte – synoptisch gelesen (SBS 156), Stuttgart 1994.
Moyise, S., The Old Testament in the New. An Introduction, London 2001.
Müller, K., Anmerkungen zum Verhältnis von Tora und Halacha im Frühjudentum, in: Die Tora als Kanon für Juden und Christen, hg. von E. Zenger (HBS 10), Freiburg 1996, 257–291.
Pesch, R., Das Markusevangelium. II. Teil: Kommentar zu Kap. 8,27–16,20 (HThK II/2), Freiburg ⁴1991.

Reinbold, W., Das Ziel des Gesetzes nach Röm 10,4–13, in: Judaistik und neutestamentliche Wissenschaft. Standorte – Grenzen – Beziehungen, hg. von L. Doering/H.-G. Waubke/ F. Wilk (FRLANT 226), Göttingen 2008, 297–312.
Roloff, J., Einführung in das Neue Testament, Stuttgart 1995.
Rusam, D., Das Alte Testament bei Lukas (BZNW 112), Berlin 2003.
Schaller, J.B., Gen.1.2 im antiken Judentum. Untersuchungen über Verwendung und Deutung der Schöpfungsaussagen von Gen.1.2 im antiken Judentum, Diss. theol. Göttingen 1961.
Schnelle, U., Paulus. Leben und Denken, Berlin 2003.
Schreiber, S., Chronologie: Lebensdaten des Paulus, in: Einleitung in das Neue Testament, hg. von M. Ebner/S. Schreiber, Stuttgart 2008, 265–276.
Schulz, S., Markus und das Alte Testament, in: ZThK 58 (1961), 184–197.
Schweizer, E., Das Evangelium nach Markus (NTD 1), Göttingen ^{15}1978.
Stanley, Chr.D., Paul and the language of Scripture. Citation technique in the Pauline Epistles and contemporary literature (MSSNTS 74), Cambridge 1992.
Steichele, H.-J., Der leidende Sohn Gottes. Eine Untersuchung einiger alttestamentlicher Motive in der Christologie des Markusevangeliums (BU 14), Regensburg 1980.
Suhl, A., Die Funktion der alttestamentlichen Zitate und Anspielungen im Markusevangelium, Gütersloh 1965.
Theißen, G., Die Entstehung des Neuen Testaments als literaturgeschichtliches Problem (SHAW.PH 40), Heidelberg 2007.
VanderKam, J.C., Einführung in die Qumranforschung. Geschichte und Bedeutung der Schriften vom Toten Meer, übers. v. M. Müller, Göttingen 1998.
Vorster, W.S., The Function of the Use of the Old Testament in Mark, in: Neotest. 14 (1980), 62–72.
Wagner, J.R., Heralds of the Good News. Isaiah and Paul „In Concert" in the Letter to the Romans (NT.S 101), Leiden 2002.
Washburn, D.L., A Catalog of Biblical Passages in the Dead Sea Scrolls (Text-critical Studies 2), Atlanta 2002.
Watts, R.E., Isaiah's New Exodus and Mark (WUNT II/88), Tübingen 1997.
Wevers, J.W., Notes on the Greek Text of Deuteronomy (SCSt 39), Atlanta 1995.
Wilk, F., Die Bedeutung des Jesajabuches für Paulus (FRLANT 179), Göttingen 1998.
—, „Zu unserer Belehrung geschrieben ..." (Römer 15,4). Die Septuaginta als „Lehrbuch" für Paulus, in: Die Septuaginta – Text, Wirkung, Rezeption, hg. von W. Kraus/S.Kreuzer (WUNT 325), Tübingen 2014, 560–579 [im Druck].
—, Jesus und die Völker in der Sicht der Synoptiker (BZNW 109), Berlin 2002.
—, The Letters of Paul as Witnesses to and for the Septuagint Text, in: Septuagint Research. Issues and Challenges in the Study of the Greek Jewish Scriptures, eds. W. Kraus/ R.G. Wooden (SBL.SCSt 53), Atlanta 2006, 253–271.
—, Paulus als Interpret der prophetischen Schriften, in: KuD 45 (1999), 284–306.
—, Jesajanische Prophetie im Spiegel exegetischer Tradition. Zu Hintergrund und Sinngehalt des Schriftzitats in 1Kor 2,9, in: Die Septuaginta – Entstehung, Sprache, Geschichte, hg. von S. Kreuzer/M. Meiser/M. Sigismund (WUNT 286), Tübingen 2012, 480–504.
—, Rühmen und Seufzen. Zur paulinischen Deutung geschichtlicher Prozesse und Erfahrungen im Horizont des Bekenntnisses zu dem einen Gott, in: Der eine Gott und die Geschichte der Völker. Studien zur Inklusion und Exklusion im biblischen Monotheismus, hg. von U. Mell (BThSt 123), Neukirchen-Vluyn 2011, 127–148.

—, Schriftbezüge im Werk des Paulus, in: Paulus Handbuch, hg. von F.W. Horn, Tübingen 2013, 479–490.
—, Wer bereitet wem den Weg? Überlegungen eines Neutestamentlers zum Verhältnis zwischen Septuaginta und Neuem Testament anhand von Mk 1,2f., in: Die Göttinger Septuaginta – ein editorisches Jahrhundertprojekt, hg. von R.G. Kratz/B. Neuschäfer (AAWG. Neue Folge 22), Berlin 2013, 185–223.
—, Gottes Wort und Gottes Verheißungen. Zur Eigenart der Schriftverwendung in 2Kor 6,14–7,1, in: Die Septuaginta – Texte, Kontexte, Lebenswelten, hg. von M. Karrer/W. Kraus (WUNT 219), Tübingen 2008, 674–696.

Anhang 1: Liste der paulinischen Schriftzitate, -paraphrasen u. ä.

Quelltext bei atl. Zitaten / neu gebildeten Worten	Zusatztext bei Mischzitaten	Quelltext bei atl. Paraphrasen/Verweisen	Paulus-Text
Gen 1,3	Jes 9,1		2Kor 4,6
Gen 2,7b			1Kor 15,45
		Gen 2,18.21–23	1Kor 11,8–12
Gen 2,24b			1Kor 6,16
		Gen 3,1–6.13	2Kor 11,3
		Gen 3,17–19, vgl. 2,17	Röm 5,12
		Gen 3,17–19, vgl. 2,17	1Kor 15,21
		Gen 1,11–27	1Kor 15,38–41
Gen 12,3c	Gen 18,18		Gal 3,8
Gen 13,15 / 17,8 / 24,7			Gal 3,16
Gen 15,5d		Gen 15,6; 17,17; 18,19	Röm 4,18–21
Gen 15,6			Röm 4,3
Gen 15,6			Gal 3,6
Gen 15,6b			Röm 4,22 f.
		Gen 15,6; 17,10–14	Röm 4,9–11
		Gen 16; 17,16; 21,1 f.	Gal 4,22–23
Gen 17,5c			Röm 4,17
Gen 18,14b–c	Gen 18,10		Röm 9,9
Gen 21,10		Gen 21,9	Gal 4,29–30
Gen 21,12f			Röm 9,7
Gen 25,23e		Gen 25,21 f.	Röm 9,10–12
Ex 9,16			Röm 9,17
		Ex 13,21 f.	1Kor 10,1
		Ex 14,22.29	1Kor 10,1
		Ex 16; Ps 77[78],24 f.	1Kor 10,3
Ex 16,18a–b			2Kor 8,15
		Ex 17,5 f.; Num 20,7–11	1Kor 10,4
		Ex 32,5 f.	1Kor 10,18
Ex 32,6b			1Kor 10,7
Ex 33,19c			Röm 9,15
		Ex 34,29 f.	2Kor 3,7
		Ex 34,33–35	2Kor 3,13
Ex 34,34a–b			2Kor 3,16
Lev 18,5b			Röm 10,5
Lev 18,5b			Gal 3,12
Lev 19,18b			Röm 13,9 g
Lev 19,18b			Gal 5,14
Lev 26,11–12	(Jub 1,17)		2Kor 6,16
		Num 11,4.34	1Kor 10,6
		Num 14,2.12.34; Ex 16,2 f.	1Kor 10,10

Quelltext bei atl. Zitaten / neu gebildeten Worten	Zusatztext bei Mischzitaten	Quelltext bei atl. Paraphrasen/Verweisen	Paulus-Text
		Num 14,16 u.ö.	1Kor 10,5
		Num 21,5f.; Ex 17,2	1Kor 10,9
		Num 25,1.9; 26,62	1Kor 10,8
Dtn 5,17–19.21a			Röm 13,9a–d
Dtn 5,21a / Ex 20,17a			Röm 7,7
Dtn 21,23c			Gal 3,13
Dtn 25,4			1Kor 9,9
Dtn 27,26a–b	Dtn 30,10		Gal 3,10
Dtn 29,3	Jes 29,10		Röm 11,8
Dtn 30,12a–b	*Dtn 8,17/9,4*		*Röm 10,6*
Dtn 30,13a–b	*Ps 106[107],26*		*Röm 10,7*
Dtn 30,14			Röm 10,8
Dtn 32,21c–d			Röm 10,19
Dtn 32,35a			Röm 12,19
Dtn 32,43c[a]			Röm 15,10
2Sam 7,14a–b.8/ 1Chr 17,13.7	Jes 43,6		2Kor 6,18
1Kön 19,10/14			Röm 11,3
1Kön 19,18			Röm 11,4
Ps 13[14],1–3	Pred 7,20		Röm 3,10–18
Ps 17[18],50			Röm 15,9
Ps 31[32],1–2			Röm 4,7–8
Ps 43[44],23			Röm 8,36
Ps 50[51],6b			Röm 4,4
Ps 68[69],10b			Röm 15,3
Ps 68[69],23–24			Röm 11,9–10
Ps 93[94],11			1Kor 3,20
Ps 111[112],9a–c			2Kor 9,9
Ps 115,1 [116,10] a–b			2Kor 4,13
Ps 116[117],1			Röm 15,11
Hi 5,13a			1Kor 3,19
Hos 2,23[25]; 1,10 [2,1]			Röm 9,25–26
Hos 13,14b–e			1Kor 15,55
Hab 2,4			Röm 1,17
Mal 1,2f–3a			Röm 9,13
Jes 1,9			Röm 9,29
Jes 10,22–23	Hos 1,10/2,23		Röm 9,27–28
Jes 11,10a–b			Röm 15,12
Jes 25,8a			1Kor 15,54
Jes 28,11–12			1Kor 14,21
Jes 28,16	Jes 8,14		Röm 9,33
Jes 28,16c			Röm 10,11
Jes 29,14b	(Ps 32[33],10)		1Kor 1,19
Jes 43,5c			*2Kor 6,17d*
Jes 45,23c	(Jes 49,18)		Röm 14,11

Quelltext bei atl. Zitaten / neu gebildeten Worten	Zusatztext bei Mischzitaten	Quelltext bei atl. Paraphrasen/Verweisen	Paulus-Text
Jes 49,8b			2Kor 6,2
Jes 52,5f			Röm 2,24
Jes 52,7a–c			Röm 10,15
Jes 52,11b–d			*2Kor 6,17–c*
Jes 52,15c–f			Röm 15,21
Jes 53,1a–b			Röm 10,16
Jes 54,1a–e			Gal 4,27
Jes 59,20–21	Jes 27,9		Röm 11,26–27
Jes 64,4[3]	(Sir 1,10)		1Kor 2,9
Jes 65,1a–b			Röm 10,20
Jes 65,2a			Röm 10,21
Jer 9,24[23]			1Kor 1,31

Anhang 2: Liste der paulinischen Schriftanspielungen

Quelltext bei atl. Anspielungen	Zusatztext(e) bei vermischten Anspielungen	alternativer Quelltext	Paulus-Text
Gen 1,27a–b			1Kor 11,7a
Gen 2,7*init.*			1Kor 15,47a
Gen 17,10–14			Phil 3,5a
Ex 12,40.43 u. ö.			Gal 3,17b
Ex 31,18c / 32,15c		Dtn 9,10	2Kor 3,3b–c
Num 15,20–21			Röm 11,16a–b
Num 18,8.31		Dtn 18,1–3	1Kor 9,13a
Dtn 6,4e–5a			1Kor 8,3a.4b.6
Dtn 10,17c	(Sir 32[35],16 [Ra: 35,13])		Gal 2,6c
Dtn 17,7c			1Kor 5,13b
Dtn 19,15c			2Kor 13,1b
Dtn 20,6a–b			1Kor 9,7b
Dtn 32,17a			1Kor 10,20b
Ps 8,7b			1Kor 15,27a
Ps 18[19],5a			Röm 10,18d
Ps 23[24],1c			1Kor 10,26
Ps 30[31],25a–b			1Kor 16,13c–d
Ps 61[62],13		Spr 24,12d	Röm 2,6
Ps 64[65],5d			1Kor 3,17c
Ps 93[94],14a		1Sam 12,22a	Röm 11,2a
Ps 105[106],20			Röm 1,23
Ps 109[110],1d			1Kor 15,25
Ps 142[143],2b	Gen 6,12		Röm 3,20a
Ps 142[143],2b	Gen 6,12		Gal 2,16c
Spr 3,4			Röm 12,17b
Spr 3,4			2Kor 8,21
Spr 3,7a			Röm 12,16c
Spr 22,8 A			2Kor 9,7c
Spr 25,21–22a			Röm 12,20
Hi 1,1 g.8d			1Thess 5,22
Hi 13,16a			Phil 1,19
Hi 27,6b			1Kor 4,4a
Hos 10,12a.d			2Kor 9,10*fin.*
Joel 2,32[3,5]a–c			Röm 10,13
Hab 2,4c			Gal 3,11b
Jes 1,3			Röm 10,19b[90]
Jes 19,12a	Jes 33,18b–d		1Kor 1,20a–c
Jes 22,13b–c			1Kor 15,32d–e
Jes 26,19a			1Thess 4,16c[90]
Jes 29,16b–c	Jes 45,9c–d		Röm 9,20c–d

Quelltext bei atl. Anspielungen	Zusatztext(e) bei vermischten Anspielungen	alternativer Quelltext	Paulus-Text
Jes 40,7b–8			Röm 9,6a[90]
Jes 40,13a–b			Röm 11,34
Jes 40,13a.c			1Kor 2,16a–b
Jes 43,18–19b	Jes 42,9a–b; 48,3.6–7a		2Kor 5,(16.)17c–d
Jes 45,17a.25			Röm 11,26a[90]
Jes 45,23c			Phil 2,10–11
Jes 49,1.5	Jes 42,6		Gal 1,15
Jes 49,4b			Phil 2,16c
Jes 49,13e			2Kor 7,6
Jes 50,8–9b			Röm 8,33–34b
Jes 51,1b			Röm 9,30b.31[90]
Jes 52,10a			Gal 1,16a–b[90]
Jes 53,6c			Röm 8,32a[90]
Jes 53,12d			Röm 4,25
Jes 55,10c			2Kor 9,10*init.*
Jes 56,1d			Röm 13,11c[90]
Jes 59,17			1Thess 5,8
Jes 59,19b–20			1Thess 1,10c[90]
Jes 61,1c			1Kor 1,17a[91]
Jer 6,14a–b			1Thess 5,3a–b
Jer 9,24[23]			2Kor 10,17
Ez 36,25–27		Ez 11,19f.	1Thess 4,(7.)8*fin.*
Dan 2,46–47a	Jes 45,14d–f		1Kor 14,25b

---

[91] Zu diesen Anspielungen vgl. Wilk, Bedeutung, 285f.299–301.311–316. 326–330.

Elizabeth V. Dowling
"Do this in Remembrance":
Last Supper Traditions in Paul and Mark

Little of the narrative of the Gospel of Mark has a direct counterpart in the content of Paul's letters. Descriptions of a ritual performed by Jesus at his Last Supper, however, do appear in both writings (1Cor 11:23-26; Mark 14:22-25). Some attention to these accounts will therefore be an important element in this volume which is comparing Mark with Paul. This study will begin by highlighting some of the debated issues regarding the Last Supper tradition. It will then explore the context and content of the Pauline and Marcan Last Supper rituals before identifying a connection between the Pauline account and another Marcan text, namely that of the story of the woman anointing Jesus in Mark 14:3-9. The study will argue that the connection between these accounts suggests that Mark is familiar with a similar Last Supper tradition to that described by Paul.

1 Some Debated Matters

Opinions vary as to whether or not the Last Supper ritual as described in the New Testament is based on the actions of the historical Jesus on the night before he died. Justin Taylor, for instance, considers that the origin of this ritual was not within the context of the Last Supper. He argues, furthermore, that Jesus and his disciples regularly performed a ritual of breaking bread.[1] While Raymond F. Collins acknowledges that the Pauline account (1Cor 11:23-26) is the result of community practice shaping the original tradition,[2] he insists on "the basic historicity of the narrative that Paul has recounted for the Corinthians."[3]

Dennis E. Smith, on the other hand, maintains that the tradition "provides a highly developed and ritualized interpretation" of the death of Jesus. He considers it more likely that such an interpretation developed after Jesus' death than prior to it.[4] Noting the variations between the New Testament versions, Albert

---

1 Justin Taylor, "Bread that is Broken – and Unbroken." In *A Wandering Galilean: Essays in Honour of Seán Freyne*, eds. Zuleika Rodgers with Margaret Daly-Denton and Anne Fitzpatrick McKinley, JSJSup 132 (Leiden: Brill, 2009), 525-37 at 527.
2 Raymond F. Collins, *First Corinthians*, SP 7 (Collegeville, Pa.: Liturgical Press, 1999), 426-27.
3 Collins, *First Corinthians*, 430.
4 Dennis E. Smith, *From Symposium to Eucharist: The Banquet in the Early Christian World* (Minneapolis, Minn.: Fortress Press, 2003), 226.

Eichhorn contends that they do not develop from an historical account but are rather the product of the early church's theological interpretation of Jesus' death and its ritual celebration.⁵ Andrea Bieler and Luise Schottroff seriously challenge the issue of historicity; "It is simply inappropriate to ask of the New Testament text whether the historical Jesus could have spoken of his death and the new covenant in these interpretive words...Likewise, the Last Supper accounts in the Gospels speak from the perspective of early Christian Eucharistic practice."⁶ Bieler and Schottroff also challenge the use of the term "words of institution" to refer to the words of the Last Supper ritual since the absence of these words in the *Didache* indicates that they were not common across all Eucharist rituals in the early church.⁷ Andrew B. McGowan goes further to query whether the Last Supper ritual has a basis in liturgical practice since the words are absent from second century descriptions of Eucharist in both the *Didache* and Justin Martyr. The extant evidence does not include the so-called words of institution in prayers until the third century.⁸

Within the Synoptic Gospels, Jesus' Last Supper is set in the context of a Passover meal (Mark 14:12; Matt 26:17; Luke 22:8). Such a setting is not specified in the Pauline text, however. Moreover, Smith considers that the Marcan account, other than in the introductory Marcan setting (Mark 14:12-16), has little to align it with a Passover meal.⁹ Others, such as Peter-Ben Smit, argue that the Last Supper reflects the liturgy of a common meal rather than that of a Passover meal.¹⁰ Thus, there is no scholarly consensus that the Last Supper was a Passover meal.

The fluidity of the tradition regarding the Last Supper ritual is also suggested by variations amongst the accounts. Even within 1Corinthians itself there are some differences. Exhorting the Corinthians to avoid the worship of idols (1Cor 10:14), Paul writes; "The cup of blessing that we bless, is it not a sharing in the blood of Christ? The bread that we break, is it not a sharing in the body of

---

5 Albert Eichhorn, *The Lord's Supper in the New Testament*, trans. Jeffrey F. Cayzer (Leiden: Brill, 2008), 68, 75.
6 Andrea Bieler and Luise Schottroff, *The Eucharist: Bodies, Bread, and Resurrection* (Minneapolis, Minn.: Fortress Press, 2007), 59.
7 Bieler and Schottroff, *The Eucharist*, 8.
8 Andrew B. McGowan, "'Is there a Liturgical Text in this Gospel?': The Institution Narratives and their Early Interpretive Communities." *JBL* 118 (1999): 73-87 at 75.
9 Smith, *From Symposium to Eucharist*, 225. Against this, see Ben Witherington, *Making a Meal of it: Rethinking the Theology of the Lord's Supper* (Waco, Tex.: Baylor University Press, 2007), 26, 61.
10 Peter-Ben Smit, *Fellowship and Food in the Kingdom*, WUNT 2.234 (Tübingen: Mohr Siebeck, 2008), 98.

Christ?" (1Cor 10:16).[11] This reference to the Eucharistic ritual refers to the cup before the bread which is different from the order presented by Paul in 1Cor 11:23-26. The cup is mentioned before the bread, however, in the *Didache* 9.2-3.[12] Noting the variations in the New Testament accounts, Taylor suggests that they are "the traces of different narrative traditions and liturgical customs. That the cup should be mentioned, first before, then after the bread in 1Cor within a page or two, strongly suggests that its place was not fixed, and so that the two did not necessarily or always go together."[13]

Differences between the Last Supper accounts lead to a widespread conclusion that they reflect two separate versions of the ritual, one evidenced in Mark and Matthew and the other evidenced in Paul and Luke.[14] An alternative understanding is presented by Eduard Schweizer who argues that though Mark's account is not sourced directly from Paul, the Marcan and Pauline accounts are both based on an earlier tradition.[15] Yet another view is expressed by Paul N. Tarazi who focuses on the similarities rather than the differences between the Marcan and Pauline accounts.[16] He claims a direct link between Mark and Paul, with Mark "part of Paul's entourage during the apostle's last days."[17] Since this claim from Tarazi is particularly pertinent to the contents of this volume, it needs further examination here. Tarazi's claim is based on his understanding that "with few exceptions the New Testament is a unitary production in the sense that it does not present us with discordant voices or 'differing points of view' as is often claimed...[I]t is Paul and his disciples who authored the writings that came to be known as the New Testament."[18] For Tarazi, then, the Gospel of Mark is one of many New Testament texts which emerged from a Pauline school of thought.

Tarazi's argument is that the death of Paul triggered the decision to write a Gospel in order to support the situation of the Gentile Churches. The aim of the writing was to convince Peter (or his following) of the Gentile cause for which

---

11 Unless otherwise indicated, Biblical quotes are from the NRSV text.
12 See Taylor, "Bread that is Broken," 527-28; and Collins, *First Corinthians*, 375.
13 Taylor, "Bread that is Broken," 529.
14 Paul F. Bradshaw, *Eucharistic Origins* (Oxford: Oxford University Press, 2004), 3. For the understanding of two different versions, see also Dennis E. Smith and Hal E. Taussig, *Many Tables: The Eucharist in the New Testament and Liturgy Today* (London: SCM, 1990), 38-40.
15 Eduard Schweizer, *The Lord's Supper According to the New Testament* (Philadelphia, Pa.: Fortress Press, 1967), 17.
16 Paul N. Tarazi, *The New Testament: An Introduction;* Volume 1: *Paul and Mark* (Crestwood, N.Y.: St Vladimir's Seminary Press, 1999), 216-17.
17 Tarazi, *Paul and Mark*, 120.
18 Tarazi, *Paul and Mark*, xi.

Paul had been the primary advocate.[19] Tarazi understands Mark to have been part of Paul's following (Phlm 23-24; Col 4:10; Acts 12:25; 15:37), as well as having connections to Peter (1Pet 5:13; Acts 12:12). This leads to the conclusion that Mark is a "natural bridge" between the Pauline and Petrine groups.[20] While Tarazi considers that this Mark to whom he refers may well be the author of the Gospel of Mark, he also considers it possible that the Gospel was written by another of the Pauline following, though the Gospel was named after Mark. Tarazi goes so far as to raise the possibility that the author of Luke-Acts may also have been the author of the Gospel of Mark, though he does not explore this in any depth.[21]

Tarazi's claim of Mark being the link between the Pauline and Petrine groups is based on a few assumptions. The first of these assumptions is that the various references to Mark in the New Testament are referring to the same person.[22] Given that Mark was a common name in the first century Roman world, this may not be the case. As Morna Hooker notes; "It would be no surprise if there were two men with this name in the early Christian community."[23]

This first assumption leads to a second assumption, namely that Mark is the John Mark of Acts (Acts 12:12.25; 15:37-9). This is a disputed identification amongst scholars, however. Many are loath to identify the author of the Gospel as John Mark.[24] While Joel Marcus would agree with Tarazi that Mark's theology is in line with Pauline thought,[25] he does not confirm that the author of Mark's Gospel is John Mark. After a comprehensive examination of the internal and external evidence pertaining to the issue, Marcus concludes that the hypothesis of John Marcan authorship of the Gospel is possible but not able to be proved.[26]

---

19 Tarazi, *Paul and Mark*, 120.
20 Tarazi, *Paul and Mark*, 120-21.
21 The main reasons that Tarazi gives to support this suggestion are Luke's high level of skill in Greek language, as well as Luke's use of the Gospel of Mark in writing the Gospel of Luke. Tarazi adds that if Luke did write "Mark," he would have been supervised by both Timothy and Mark; Tarazi, *Paul and Mark*, 121-22.
22 Joel Marcus considers it likely that the references to Mark do refer to the same person. See Joel Marcus, *Mark 1-8: A New Translation with Introduction and Commentary*, AB 27 (New York, N. Y.: Doubleday, 1999), 18.
23 Morna D. Hooker, *The Gospel According to Saint Mark* (Peabody, Mass.: Hendrickson, 1991), 6. See also William R. Telford, *Mark* (Sheffield: Sheffield Academic Press, 1995), 17.
24 See, for instance, Telford, *Mark*, 20; and Douglas R. A. Hare, *Mark* (Louisville, Ky.: Westminster John Knox Press, 1996), 4-5.
25 See Joel Marcus, "Mark – Interpreter of Paul," *NTS* 46 (2000): 473-87.
26 Marcus, *Mark 1-8*, 17-24. It is clear, however, that Marcus is at least sympathetic towards the hypothesis.

Of course, Tarazi leaves open the possibility that Mark is not the author of the Gospel. His suggestion of Luke as possible author is highly questionable, however. Adela Yarbro Collins considers the portrait of John Mark in Acts 13 and 15 and concludes that "the book of Acts presents a fairly negative portrait of Mark as a backslider or reluctant missionary to the Gentiles. Since the author of Acts also wrote the Gospel according to Luke, it could be that this critical portrait was intended to undercut the authority of the second Gospel."[27] From this it follows that Collins would not support the idea of Luke as the author of the Gospel of Mark. Tarazi's understanding is that Mark's portrayal in the New Testament is significant; "Mark was someone who actually shifted allegiance from Barnabas (and Peter) to Paul, i.e. he himself had done what was about to be asked of Peter or his successors."[28] Ultimately, however, Tarazi's justification is unconvincing and the suggestion of Lucan authorship of the Gospel of Mark has not been picked up in mainstream scholarship. Rather than assume a connection between Mark and Paul, therefore, this study will explore the texts themselves to see if a connection can be established.

From the above discussion, it is clear that several aspects of the Last Supper tradition are debated. This study will contribute to this debate, in particular by drawing on elements from the Marcan narrative of the woman anointing Jesus (Mark 14:3-9) to compare with the Last Supper accounts. While there are significant differences between the Pauline and Marcan Last Supper rituals, the study will argue that the Marcan account of the woman anointing Jesus suggests a closer connection between the Pauline and Marcan traditions than is immediately evident. First, however, it will be necessary to undertake an exploration of the Pauline and Marcan Last Supper rituals.

2 The Pauline Last Supper Ritual

Paul's reference to the ritual performed by Jesus at a meal on the night of his betrayal (1Cor 11:23-26) occurs within the context of Paul's address to the church in Corinth, in particular responding to issues of concern within the community. In 1Cor 11:17-22 he condemns the church's practices when they gather to eat the "Lord's supper" (κυριακὸν δεῖπνον). Paul's concern here is that there should not be divisions within the community nor distinctions between those with resources

---

[27] Adela Yarbro Collins, *Mark: A Commentary*, Hermeneia (Minneapolis, Minn.: Fortress Press, 2007), 5.
[28] Tarazi, *Paul and Mark*, 121.

and those with nothing.²⁹ This image of unity is again stressed in 1Cor 12:12-31 where Paul uses the image of the one body having many members who are each necessary to the body. For Paul, a Eucharistic meal requires a unified community for it to be authentic. The context which surrounds Paul's description of the Eucharistic ritual in 1Cor 11:23-26, then, is the struggle of the community at Corinth. Divisions are affecting the way the community lives out its church practices and Paul exhorts them to live as one, in Christ.

The ritual described in 1Cor 11:23-26 is part of Paul's teaching to bring them to act in this way; "It simultaneously refers to the origin of Christian eucharistic practices and provides a basis for reflection on the Corinthians' actual practice."³⁰ The first point which Paul stresses here is that he has received this tradition from the risen Jesus. What Paul intends to convey by this is debated. While Hyam Maccoby argues that Paul has received the tradition via a personal revelation,³¹ Panayotis Coutsoumpos counters; "It is more likely that a tradition has been given to him, as from the Lord."³² What is clear is that the use of the title "Lord" (κύριος; 1Cor 11:23.26) emphasises the authority which is imparted to this tradition. At the same time, "Lord" suggests a post-resurrectional context rather than an "historical memory."³³ Paul also states that he has handed on to the Corinthians this tradition that he received (1Cor 11:23), reinforcing that they can trust what he has told them.

Paul's description of the Last Supper lacks the passion narrative context of the Gospels. The temporal setting of the "night when he was betrayed" (1Cor 11:23), however, serves to connect Paul's account to the story of the passion. In the Pauline version of the Last Supper, Jesus takes the bread first (in contrast to the order in 1Cor 10:16), gives thanks, breaks the bread, and says "This is my body that is for you. Do this in remembrance of me" (1Cor 11:23-24). The Lucan account has clear parallels to this section of the Pauline text with the same verbs used, although once in a different form, for Jesus taking, giving thanks and breaking, as well as an "in remembrance" statement (Luke 22:19).

---

29 The reference in 1Cor 11:22 relates to those with no honour or status, not only those with no money. See Rachel M. McRae, "Eating with Honor: The Corinthian Lord's Supper in Light of Voluntary Association Meal Practices." *JBL* 130 (2011): 165-81 at 176.
30 Collins, *First Corinthians*, 425.
31 Hyam Maccoby, "Paul and the Eucharist," *NTS* 37 (1991): 247-67.
32 Panayotis Coutsoumpos, *Paul and the Lord's Supper: A Socio-Historical Investigation* (New York: Peter Lang, 2005), 117. Coutsoumpos proposes that Paul may have interpreted and adapted the tradition that he received (119).
33 Smith, *From Symposium to Eucharist*, 225.

1Cor 11:23-26	Luke 22:19-20
11:23 For I received from the Lord what I also handed on to you, that the Lord Jesus on the night when he was betrayed took (ἔλαβεν) a loaf of bread, 11:24 and when he had given thanks (εὐχαριστήσας), he broke (ἔκλασεν) it and said, "This is my body that is for you. Do this in remembrance (ἀνάμνησιν) of me." 11:25 In the same way he took the cup (ποτήριον) also, after supper, saying, "This cup is the new covenant in my blood. Do this, as often as you drink it, in remembrance (ἀνάμνησιν) of me." 11:26 For as often as you eat this bread and drink the cup, you proclaim the Lord's death until he comes.	22:19 Then he took (λαβὼν) a loaf of bread, and when he had given thanks (εὐχαριστήσας), he broke (ἔκλασεν) it and gave (ἔδωκεν) it to them, saying, "This is my body, which is given (διδόμενον) for you. Do this in remembrance (ἀνάμνησιν) of me." 22:20 And he did the same with the cup (ποτήριον) after supper, saying, "This cup that is poured out for you is the new covenant in my blood."

As the above table demonstrates, the words of Jesus, particularly those over the bread, are very similar in the two versions. Luke, though, includes two forms of the verb δίδωμι here which are not in Paul's account. In Luke, Jesus explicitly gives the bread to those with him before he speaks to them about the bread, and his words are "This is my body, which is given for you. Do this in remembrance of me" (Luke 22:19).[34]

The Pauline version portrays Jesus with the cup (ποτήριον) after supper and saying "This cup is the new covenant in my blood. Do this, as often as you drink it, in remembrance of me" (1Cor 11:25). Jesus' actions concerning the cup are prefaced by "in the same way," linking his actions with the cup to his actions with the bread. For the second time, the remembrance motif is present. Placing the call to remember in the words of Jesus gives it particular authority.[35] In this second occurrence, the inclusion of "as often as you drink it" suggests that this is to be an oft repeated practice.[36] This understanding is further reinforced in 1Cor 11:26 which connects the ritual to a proclamation of Jesus' death and culminates in an expectation of the second coming; "For as often as you eat this bread

---

34 One of the textual variants for the words of Jesus in 1Cor 11:24 includes the same participle (διδόμενον) which is in the Lucan version but the textual evidence indicates this is a later addition. See Bruce M. Metzger, *A Textual Commentary on the Greek New Testament* (Stuttgart: Deutsche Bibelgesellschaft, 2nd edn 1994), 496.
35 Ellen Bradshaw Aitken, *Jesus' Death in Early Christian Memory: The Poetics of the Passion*, NTOA 53 (Göttingen: Vandenhoeck & Ruprecht, 2004), 51.
36 Eichhorn, *The Lord's Supper*, 77.

and drink the cup, you proclaim the Lord's death until he comes." This verse "signals that the community is constituted as having an eschatological future."[37]

The Lucan account has a similar saying by Jesus about the cup (ποτήριον), describing it as "the new covenant in my blood" (Luke 22:20). Luke also includes the phrase "poured out (ἐκχυννόμενον) for you," which is absent from the Pauline version. The second remembrance statement is missing from the Lucan account, however. Furthermore, Luke has another statement about the cup which occurs prior to his taking the bread and cup as outlined above. In this other Lucan cup sequence, Jesus takes the cup, gives thanks, and says "Take this and divide it among yourselves; for I tell you that from now on I will not drink of the fruit of the vine until the kingdom of God comes" (Luke 22:17-18). While this cup sequence is not part of Paul's ritual, it does have links with the Marcan version as we shall see below.

The common elements of the Pauline and Lucan Last Supper narratives suggest that they may be linked in some way. Perhaps Luke used Paul's outline directly and made some adaptations to suit his own theological agenda. It is also possible that both versions resulted from an earlier tradition upon which each has drawn. For Collins, "There is no evidence that Luke was dependent on Paul; most probably both Luke and Paul represent different versions of a like tradition."[38]

3 The Marcan Last Supper Ritual

Unlike the Pauline account of the ritual of the Last Supper, the Marcan version (Mark 14:22-25) is set within the context of a passion narrative, though it may not have been part of an earlier passion account used by Mark, as will be discussed below. The Marcan passion narrative begins with a so-called Marcan sandwich in Mark 14:1-11, comprising the conspiracy against Jesus (Mark 14:1-2.10-11) framing the anointing of Jesus by an unnamed woman (Mark 14:3-9).[39] Following this introduction, the narrative focuses on the preparations for a meal which Jesus is to eat with his disciples (Mark 14:12-16) and then on the meal itself (Mark 14:17-25). The narrative build-up focuses the reader's attention upon the ritual of Mark 14:22-25, highlighting its significance.

---

37 Bradshaw Aitken, *Jesus' Death*, 52.
38 Collins, *First Corinthians*, 430.
39 This story of the anointing will be explored below as it has links with the Last Supper ritual, as already indicated.

The context of Passover is first introduced in Mark 14:1 where the temporal setting of two days before Passover and the festival of Unleavened Bread is provided. This context is developed further in Mark 14:12-16 where it is clearly articulated that the meal which Jesus will share with his disciples is a Passover meal. The Passover context is not evident in the content of the ritual of the meal (14:22-25), however. The ritual does not reflect the same interest in the Passover as the preparations might suggest.[40] It may be that the Passover context is used by Mark to enkindle notions of salvation, and to associate salvation with the events to follow in the passion narrative.

Collins also points out that there is nothing to link the bread and cup to a Passover meal and this forms part of her argument that the ritual in Mark 14:22-25 is unlikely to have been part of an earlier passion source used by Mark because it does not flow easily on from the preceding narrative in Mark 14:12-21. To expound her argument, she notes that the setting of "while they were eating" is restated in Mark 14:22a when this had previously been indicated in Mark 14:17-21,[41] specifically in Mark 14:18. Commenting on the two pericopes, Mark 14:17-21 and Mark 14:22-25, she states; "These two units appear to be independent stories or units of tradition placed one after the other, rather than two parts of the same narrative describing the same meal."[42] From a detailed exploration of the composition of the Marcan passion narrative, Collins concludes that Mark did use a pre-Marcan passion source, but that Mark 14:1-31 was not part of the source, being comprised instead of individual stories within the tradition.[43] The two pericopes, Mark 14:17-21 and Mark 14:22-25, can be considered two such independent stories.

When considering the Marcan Last Supper ritual of Mark 14:22-25, it is clear that there are points of similarity but also points of considerable difference from the Pauline ritual of 1Cor 11:23-26. The two versions are listed in the table below:

Mark 14:22-25	1Cor 11:23-26
	11:23 For I received from the Lord what I also handed on to you, that the Lord Jesus on the night when he was betrayed
14:22 While they were eating,	

---

40 Smit, *Fellowship and Food in the Kingdom*, 98.
41 Collins, *Mark*, 653-54.
42 Collins, *Mark*, 654.
43 Collins, *Mark*, 625-26. Marcus claims that Mark has used a tradition for his Last Supper ritual because of its parallel with 1Cor 11:23-26. See Marcus, "Mark – Interpreter of Paul," 485.

Mark 14:22-25	1Cor 11:23-26
he took (λαβὼν) a loaf of bread, and after blessing (εὐλογήσας) it	took (ἔλαβεν) a loaf of bread, 11:24 and when he had given thanks (εὐχαριστήσας), he broke (ἔκλασεν) it and said,
he broke (ἔκλασεν) it, gave (ἔδωκεν) it to them, and said, "Take; this is my body."	"This is my body that is for you. Do this in remembrance (ἀνάμνησιν) of me."
14:23 Then he took a cup (ποτήριον), and after giving thanks (εὐχαριστήσας) he gave (ἔδωκεν) it to them, and all of them drank from it. 14:24 He said to them, "This is my blood (αἷμά) of the covenant (διαθήκης), which is poured out (ἐκχυννόμενον) for many.	11:25 In the same way he took the cup (ποτήριον) also, after supper, saying, "This cup (ποτήριον) is the new covenant (καινὴ διαθήκη) in my blood (αἵματι). Do this, as often as you drink it, in remembrance (ἀνάμνησιν) of me."
14:25 Truly I tell you, I will never again drink of the fruit of the vine until that day when I drink it new in the kingdom of God."	
	11:26 For as often as you eat this bread and drink the cup, you proclaim the Lord's death until he comes.

In both versions, Jesus takes and breaks bread. While Paul uses a different form of the verb λαμβάνω here, the participle λαβὼν in Mark 14:22 is also the form of the verb which is used by Luke (Luke 22:19). In Mark, Jesus blesses the bread before breaking it, whereas in 1Corinthians, Jesus gives thanks before breaking (Mark 14:22; 1Cor 11:23-24). In Mark, Jesus explicitly gives the bread to the disciples (Mark 14:22), an action which is not recorded in the Pauline text, although it is in the Lucan text (Luke 22:19). In both the Pauline and Marcan versions, Jesus says "this is my body." In Mark, this is preceded by the imperative "take" (Mark 14:22), while Paul instead includes additional words after the statement; "This is my body that is for you. Do this in remembrance of me" (1Cor 11:24). The call to remembrance is not a part of the Marcan Last Supper ritual. Whether or not this is because Mark was unaware of the remembrance theme is an issue which will be discussed further below.

In relation to the cup in the two versions, only in Mark does Jesus give thanks and then explicitly give the cup to the disciples (Mark 14:23). While the Pauline text implies that the disciples will continue the practice of drinking from the cup (1Cor 11:25-26), the Marcan text states that "all of them drank from it" (Mark 14:23). This is a feature that does not occur in any of the other Gospel accounts of the Last Supper. In an earlier Marcan passage concerned with the demands of discipleship, Jesus asks James and John if they are able to drink the cup that he drinks and then goes on to say that they will drink it (Mark 10:38-39). At the Marcan Last Supper, James and John would be included in the larger group of disciples who all drank from the cup; "By accepting Jesus' invitation to drink from the cup, Jesus' disciples accept the suffering that befalls them as a consequence of following him and living the gospel."[44] This Marcan inclusion at the Last Supper therefore is also concerned with the demands of discipleship.

While there are links between the words said over the cup by Jesus in Mark 14:24 and 1Cor 11:25, there are also significant differences in the order of the words. Each refers to covenant and blood. As Coutsoumpos notes, however, blood is used to explain covenant in Paul, while covenant explains blood in Mark.[45] In the Pauline version, Jesus does not identify the cup as his blood but rather states that the cup is the new covenant.[46] In the Marcan version, Jesus refers to the cup when he says "This is my blood of the covenant" (Mark 14:24).[47] The words here of "blood of the covenant" evoke imagery from the ritual of ratification of a covenant between God and Israel from the Hebrew Scriptures (Exod 24:8). The use of "new covenant" in the Pauline version also evokes the imagery of a new covenant in the Hebrew Scriptures (Jer 31:31).[48] The words of Jesus over the cup in 1Cor 11:25a are closer to the words in the Lucan version than the Marcan version. As outlined in the earlier table, Luke includes similar words to Paul but with the inclusion of the words "that is poured out (ἐκχυννόμενον) for you" (Luke 22:20). Mark, on the other hand, has the phrase "poured out (ἐκχυννόμενον) for many" (Mark 14:22). The second Pauline reference to remembrance is missing from both the Marcan and Lucan versions.

The final words of Jesus in the Marcan ritual, "Truly I tell you, I will never again drink of the fruit of the vine until that day when I drink it new in the kingdom of God" (Mark 14:25), are significantly different from Paul's words of 1Cor 11:26. As noted previously, there is a closer connection between the Marcan and Lucan versions here (cf. Luke 22:18), although the closest parallel is with the Matthean account (Matt 26:29). In Mark, Jesus' statement in 14:25 should

---

44 Barbara E. Reid, *Taking Up the Cross: New Testament Interpretations Through Latina and Feminist Eyes* (Minneapolis, Minn.: Fortress Press, 2007), 45.
45 Coutsoumpos, *Paul and the Lord's Supper*, 122.
46 Eichhorn, *The Lord's Supper*, 76.
47 Bieler and Schottroff, *The Eucharist*, 59.
48 Bieler and Schottroff, *The Eucharist*, 59.

not be considered to be "a vow of abstinence," rather it signifies "his expectation of his impending...death and future vindication in the kingdom of God."[49]

The Matthean version of the Last Supper (Matt 26:26-29) is very closely paralleled with the Marcan account. Identical wording in several parts suggests that Matthew has simply used the Marcan version and adapted it slightly. The relationship between the Marcan and Matthean stories appears less complex than the relationship between the Marcan and Lucan stories which is complicated by Luke's close association in places with the Pauline account. A table comparing the Last Supper accounts in Matthew, Mark and Luke is presented below:

Matt 26:26-29	Mark 14:22-25	Luke 22:19-20
26:26 While they were eating, Jesus took (λαβὼν) a loaf of bread, and after blessing (εὐλογήσας) it	14:22 While they were eating, he took (λαβὼν) a loaf of bread, and after blessing (εὐλογήσας) it	22:19 Then he took (λαβὼν) a loaf of bread, and when he had given thanks (εὐχαριστήσας),
he broke (ἔκλασεν) it, gave (δοὺς) it to the disciples, and said, "Take, eat; this is my body."	he broke (ἔκλασεν) it, gave (ἔδωκεν) it to them, and said, "Take; this is my body."	he broke (ἔκλασεν) it and gave (ἔδωκεν) it to them, saying, "This is my body, which is given (διδόμενον) for you. Do this in remembrance (ἀνάμνησιν) of me." 22:20 And he did the same with the cup (ποτήριον) after supper,
26:27 Then he took a cup (ποτήριον), and after giving thanks (εὐχαριστήσας) he gave (ἔδωκεν) it to them, saying, "Drink from it, all of you; 26:28 for this is my blood (αἷμά) of the covenant, (διαθήκης) which is poured out (ἐκχυννόμενον) for many for the forgiveness of sins. 26:29 I tell you, I will never again drink of this fruit of the vine until that day when I drink it new with you in my Father's kingdom."	14:23 Then he took a cup (ποτήριον), and after giving thanks (εὐχαριστήσας) he gave (ἔδωκεν) it to them, and all of them drank from it. 14:24 He said to them, "This is my blood (αἷμά) of the covenant (διαθήκης), which is poured out (ἐκχυννόμενον) for many. 14:25 Truly I tell you, I will never again drink of the fruit of the vine until that day when I drink it new in the kingdom of God."	saying, "This cup that is poured (ἐκχυννόμενον) out for you is the new covenant (καινὴ διαθήκη), in my blood (αἵματί)."

---

49 Smit, *Fellowship and Food in the Kingdom*, 102.

As the table demonstrates, Matthew makes few changes to the Marcan account. The main inclusion by Matthew is "for the forgiveness of sins" (Matt 26:28), providing a reason for the blood being "poured out for many." Matthew also includes explicit instructions given by Jesus to the disciples to eat (Matt 26:26) and drink (Matt 26:27). While Mark does not have these explicit instructions, he does state that "all of them drank from it" (Mark 14:23). Despite the few variations, the closeness between the Matthean and Marcan versions of the Last Supper highlights Matthew's reliance on the Marcan account.

Links between the Lucan and Pauline Last Supper accounts have been discussed previously. In particular, both share a call to remembrance with very similar wording (Luke 22:19; 1Cor 11:24) and this remembrance motif is not included in the Marcan story of the Last Supper. At the same time, there are common elements in the Marcan and Lucan accounts that are not in the Pauline version. As identified earlier, the Lucan statement – "Take this and divide it among yourselves; for I tell you that from now on I will not drink of the fruit of the vine until the kingdom of God comes" (Luke 22:17-18) – is not part of the Pauline account but it has a strong parallel with Mark 14:25. Furthermore, Luke includes other features of Mark which are not in Paul, such as Jesus giving the bread to the disciples (Mark 14:22; Luke 22:19) and speaking of his blood or the cup "poured out" (Mark 14:25; Luke 22:18). This suggests that Luke has used Mark as a source, but the Lucan parallels with the Pauline text indicate that Luke has relied on more than simply the Marcan version.

Instead of focusing on the differences between the Pauline and Marcan versions, Tarazi demonstrates that several of the themes in Mark 14:22-26 are also present in Paul's letter. For example, Jesus acts as host offering food (cf. 1Cor 11:20); Jesus is also portrayed as the food (cf. 1Cor 11:24-25).[50] Does this indicate that Mark has used Paul's ritual to shape his own? The differences in the wording of the two rituals at the Last Supper raise a challenge in this regard. Luke's wording is closer to Paul's in places. This suggests that, while Luke has used Mark as a source, Luke may also have used Paul or an earlier tradition about the Last Supper used by both Luke and Paul.

But what of the Last Supper accounts in Mark and Paul? It is clear that both versions have an overlap of themes and language. It is also evident, however, that there are enough differences to raise questions about whether or not Mark is directly dependent on Paul. This is especially so since the Lucan version more closely parallels the Pauline account than does the Marcan version. Furthermore, the key aspect of "in remembrance" which is evident twice in Paul's

---

50 Tarazi, *Paul and Mark*, 217.

account and once in Luke's is not in the Marcan Last Supper story. So does Mark know and use Paul's account directly? Or does he use a different earlier version from that used by Paul? Or do they both use the same earlier version and adapt it differently? Before drawing conclusions on this issue, it will be important to consider another Marcan story (Mark 14:3-9) to see if it can shed any light on the situation.

4 The Woman Anointing Jesus (Mark 14:3-9)

As discussed previously, twice within the Pauline account, Jesus commands those at table with him to repeat his actions in remembrance (ἀνάμνησιν) of him (1Cor 11:24-25). The absence of the remembrance statements from the Marcan Last Supper ritual leads some scholars to assume that these statements must not have been known to Mark.[51] In another Marcan setting, however, Jesus does speak of remembrance. Describing the actions of the woman who anoints Jesus (Mark 14:3), he tells those at table with him that what she has done will be told in remembrance (μνημόσυνον) of her (Mark 14:9). The equivalence of ἀνάμνησις and μνημόσυνον can be seen by the fact that both words are used in the LXX to translate the Hebrew root zkr[52] (for example in Num 10:10 and Exod 12:14). Since Mark 14:9 is the only occurrence of the "in remembrance" motif in the Gospel of Mark, it is worth taking a closer look at the Marcan anointing narrative in Mark 14:3-9 to see if there are any other associations with the Last Supper tradition.[53]

Comparing Mark 14:3-9 with Mark 14:22-25, we see that both narratives take place within the context of a meal. A similar description of Jesus and/or the disciples reclining (κατακειμένου, Mark 14:3; ἀνακειμένων, Mark 14:18) links the settings of the two stories and gives formality to the meals. A further connection is found in the frames surrounding the stories. Mark 14:3-9 is framed by the plot to kill Jesus and his betrayal by Judas (Mark 14:1-2.10-11), and Mark 14:22-25 is framed by Jesus' announcements about one of the disciples betraying him and

---

[51] See Coutsoumpos, *Paul and the Lord's Supper*, 123; also Schweizer, *The Lord's Supper*, 17 n. 46.
[52] See Bieler and Schottroff, *The Eucharist*, 222 n. 10. They describe the two words ἀνάμνησις and μνημόσυνον as "in substance no different."
[53] These associations are explored in Elizabeth Dowling and Veronica Lawson, "Women, Eucharist, and Good News to All Creation in Mark." In *Reinterpreting the Eucharist: Explorations in Feminist Theology and Ethics*, eds. Anne Elvey, Carol Hogan, Kim Power and Claire Renkin (Sheffield: Equinox Publishing, forthcoming).

another denying him (Mark 14:17-21.26-31).⁵⁴ Actions of breaking and pouring (Mark 14:3.22.24) forge a further link between the two Marcan stories.

Within the Marcan anointing story, the woman broke (συντρίψασα) the jar and poured out (κατέχεεν) the ointment (Mark 14:3). These actions of the woman foreshadow the actions of Jesus at the Last Supper, later in the same chapter in Mark, where Jesus broke (ἔκλασεν) the bread and talked about the pouring out (ἐκχυννόμενον) of his blood (Mark 14:22.24).⁵⁵ The two verbs for "pouring out," καταχέω and ἐκχέω, are connected. The two stories use two different verbs for "breaking," συντρίβω and κλάω. The use of συντρίβω will be further discussed below. Mark's placement of the anointing story within the passion narrative, close to the story of the Last Supper, facilitates a comparison between the two stories and accentuates their common elements. Thus it would seem that Mark encourages the reader to see connections between the anointing story and the Last Supper story.

The woman breaks open the alabaster jar (ἀλάβαστρον) and pours the ointment on Jesus' head (Mark 14:3). This action of breaking the jar is unique amongst the Gospels to the Marcan version of the anointing story. As in the Last Supper stories, Matthew's anointing story (Matt 26:6-13) is closely paralleled to the Marcan version but even Matthew does not include the breaking action in his account.⁵⁶ The verb used here, συντρίβω, can be understood as "break," "shatter" or "smash."⁵⁷ As Marianne Sawicki demonstrates, it was not usual to smash an ἀλάβαστρος (or ἀλάβαστρον, as she refers to it) in order to open it.⁵⁸ This may well be why Matthew does not include this feature in his version. The use of συντρίβω here in Mark, therefore, is an interesting feature of the story. Drawing on the understanding of συντρίβω in the LXX, Sawicki considers that its use in Mark 14:3 is deliberate and significant; "The term is theologically loaded to connote dramatic divine agency. This word does more than lend Mark's text a Biblical resonance: it suggests that the woman's gesture enacts something

---

54 Dowling and Lawson, "Women, Eucharist, and Good News."
55 See Marie Noonan Sabin, *The Gospel According to Mark* (Collegeville, Pa.: Liturgical Press, 2006), 123-24; and Dowling and Lawson, "Women, Eucharist, and Good News."
56 Dowling and Lawson, "Women, Eucharist, and Good News."
57 See Walter Bauer, William F. Arndt, F. Wilbur Gingrich and Frederick W. Danker, *A Greek-English Lexicon of the New Testament and Other Early Christian Literature* (Chicago, Ill.: University of Chicago Press, 2nd edn 1979), 793.
58 Marianne Sawicki, "Making Jesus." In *A Feminist Companion to Mark*, eds. Amy-Jill Levine with Marianne Blickenstaff (Sheffield: Sheffield Academic Press, 2001), 136-170 at 156-57. See also Collins, *Mark*, 641.

divinely authorized."⁵⁹ Has Mark then specifically chosen this word, representing a breaking action, to include in his narrative of the anointing?

Collins contends that Mark 14:3-9 was not a part of a passion narrative source used by Mark. Since the anointing in Luke (Luke 7:36-50) is not set within a passion narrative context, she deems it likely that an anointing was "an originally independent story that circulated in at least two variant forms."⁶⁰ In Mark, the anointing story (Mark 14:3-9) is framed by the conspiracy and plot to kill Jesus (Mark 14:1-2.10-11). Such a contrived frame is evidence of Marcan editing.⁶¹ Mark has used the anointing story for his own purposes. It is very possible that Mark has similarly adapted and included elements within his anointing narrative to further his theological agenda. The feature of the woman breaking the jar which only occurs in the Marcan version could be one such added element.

Why might Mark have placed the anointing within a passion context and adapted some elements? While it is impossible to answer that with any certainty, it is possible to make some observations and suggestions. Collins understands the Marcan anointing story as countering an early tradition that Jesus was buried dishonourably, that is, unanointed.⁶² Mark's placement of the story within the passion narrative thus gives honour to Jesus at a time close to his death. As the Marcan Jesus says of the woman's action; "she has anointed my body beforehand for its burial" (Mark 14:8). This may account for the placement of the anointing story within the context of the passion. The use of συντρίβω in this context could also suggest that the granting of such honour to Jesus is divinely authorised. The inclusion of an action of breaking in the Marcan anointing narrative also connects this story to the Last Supper by the actions of "breaking" and "pouring out," as demonstrated above. While the two verbs for breaking are different in the two stories, συντρίβω and κλάω, the use of συντρίβω in the anointing story may have been a deliberate choice by Mark to include the overtones of divine authorisation.

Having compared the Marcan anointing story with the Marcan Last Supper, it is now necessary to compare it with the Pauline Last Supper tradition. In both, there is a breaking action. As in the Marcan Last Supper story, Paul uses κλάω to describe Jesus breaking the bread (1Cor 11:24) while in the anointing story the verb used is συντρίβω for the woman breaking the jar (Mark 14:3). Unlike the Marcan anointing and Last Supper stories, Paul does not include a "pouring out" action. As noted above, however, a significant link between the Pauline

---

59 Sawicki, "Making Jesus," 156.
60 Collins, *Mark*, 640.
61 Collins, *Mark*, 640.
62 Collins, *Mark*, 643.

story and the Marcan anointing story is the inclusion of an "in remembrance" theme in both (Mark 14:9; 1Cor 11:24-25). While the subject to be remembered is different in the two stories, the anointing story is the only Marcan account to include such a theme. This leads Marie Noonan Sabin to claim that Mark is here intentionally using the remembrance theme "to link this woman's gestures to the Eucharist."[63]

With the "breaking" and "pouring out" actions and the "in remembrance" theme, the Marcan anointing story has connections with both the Marcan and Pauline Last Supper stories. This finding raises several questions, of course. Why might this be the case? Has Mark deliberately adapted the anointing story to link it to the Last Supper traditions? Has Mark used Paul's story directly? What other possibilities are there? In the following section I will attempt to summarise the findings of this study and make some suggestions towards addressing these questions.

5 Summary and Conclusions

This study has shown that the Marcan and Pauline Last Supper stories (Mark 14:22-25; 1Cor 11:23-26) reveal aspects of a common tradition about Jesus at a final meal with his disciples at which he takes and breaks bread and then takes a cup. Words attributed to Jesus at the meal include "this is my body" in relation to the bread, and a saying over the cup connecting covenant and blood. As has been demonstrated, around these core elements there is quite a deal of variation between the two stories, however. Moreover, aspects of the Pauline story are paralleled more closely in words and detail with the Lucan version (Luke 22:19-20) than with Mark's story. In particular, both Paul and Luke include a theme of remembrance that is not included in the Marcan Last Supper story. At the same time, Luke includes several features of Mark which are not in Paul, in particular, the saying of Luke 22:18 (cf. Mark 14:25). Other features include Jesus giving the bread to the disciples (Mark 14:22; Luke 22:19) and speaking of his blood or the cup "poured out" (Mark 14:25; Luke 22:18). Assuming that Luke has used Mark as a source, these parallels are not unexpected. On the other hand, the Pauline elements which are in Luke but not Mark require a different explanation.

To complicate matters even further, it would seem that Mark deliberately forges links between his Last Supper story and the story of a woman anointing Jesus (Mark 14:3-9) which occurs earlier in the same chapter. Common literary settings and meal

---

63 Noonan Sabin, *The Gospel According to Mark*, 125.

contexts combine with common actions of "breaking" and "pouring out" to ensure that the Marcan reader/hearer makes connections between the two stories. While the "in remembrance" theme is not part of the Marcan Last Supper, it does feature in the Pauline and Lucan Last Supper accounts. Significantly, the "in remembrance" theme also occurs in the Marcan anointing story (Mark 14:3-9) in relation to the significance of the woman's actions. This establishes a further link between the Marcan anointing story and the Last Supper traditions.

The variation in the words of the Last Supper ritual in Mark in comparison with Paul tends to suggest that Mark has not used Paul directly. Luke is more likely to have used Paul, given the closer parallels between these two, but this is still debatable. It may be that Mark draws on a different version of the Last Supper tradition from that used by Paul. On the other hand, it would seem that Mark is aware of an "in remembrance" theme, although he incorporates it into his anointing story rather than into the Last Supper story. This suggests a closer alignment between Mark and Paul than is immediately evident. Perhaps Mark has not used Paul directly but is aware of a similar tradition to that used by Paul. Have they both used the same earlier tradition but adapted it differently to suit their own theological purposes? Or is there enough of a variation in language to suggest that they are adapting different versions of the tradition? The fluidity of the early tradition in regard to the Last Supper rituals, outlined at the beginning of this discussion, supports the idea that Mark and Paul have used traditions with similar elements but also with variations.

The reasons for Mark's apparently deliberate links between his anointing story and both his and the Pauline Last Supper accounts are impossible to know with any certainty. The result, however, is that the unnamed woman's actions become aligned with and foreshadow the actions of Jesus at the Last Supper, actions which the disciples are instructed to continue. This is in line with the portrayal of other Marcan women as models of faith and discipleship (Mark 5:25-34; 7:24-30; 12:41-44; 15:40-41).

The woman suffering from prolonged haemorrhaging (Mark 5:25-34), whom Jesus heals, is praised by Jesus for her faith (Mark 5:34). She models the faith found to be lacking within the disciples in the previous chapter (Mark 4:40). The Syrophoenician woman (Mark 7:24-30) is the only person to match, if not better, Jesus' words in the Gospel of Mark (Mark 7:27-28). Interestingly, bread (ἄρτος) features in this story, just as it does in the Last Supper tradition. Resulting from her response to Jesus, the Syrophoenician woman acquires access to "the children's bread" (Mark 7:27-29), an outcome with Eucharistic overtones.[64]

---

64 See Dowling and Lawson, "Women, Eucharist, and Good News."

The example of another Marcan woman, the widow contributing the two coins (Mark 12:41-44), is also pertinent here. While the story can be seen to function as a lament of the actions of the scribes who "devour widows' houses" (Mark 12:38-40), there is also another dimension to the story. Jesus says that the woman "has put in everything she had, all she had to live on" (Mark 12:44). The Greek words ὅλον τὸν βίον αὐτῆς can also be understood as the woman contributing the whole of her life. This foreshadows what Jesus will do in the passion narrative.[65] The women watching on at the crucifixion (Mark 15:40-41) are identified as having journeyed with Jesus to Jerusalem. We also learn that they have followed and served Jesus, characteristics which Jesus expects of his disciples (Mark 1:17; 2:14; 8:34; 9:35; 10:43-44).

Thus, the actions of the Marcan anointing woman can be seen to continue a Marcan motif in relation to the portrayal of women. Her actions foreshadow the actions of Jesus and model the required behaviour of disciples, just as other Marcan women have done. Finding links between the story of the anointing woman and the Last Supper tradition should perhaps not be a great surprise given such a motif in the Gospel of Mark. Since some women hosted house churches in the early Christian communities,[66] perhaps Mark has shaped his anointing story and his other stories of women so that they speak more closely to the experience of the Marcan community breaking bread together.

While this study cannot confidently draw the conclusion that Mark has directly used the Pauline Last Supper ritual in the creation of his own Gospel, it does highlight that there are closer links between Mark and Paul in this regard than are first thought. In particular, details in the Marcan story of the anointing woman suggest that Mark makes deliberate connections between this story and the Last Supper traditions and that he is familiar with a "remembrance" theme. While the differences between the two Last Supper rituals raise doubts about Mark's direct use of Paul, it would seem that Mark is at least familiar with a similar Last Supper tradition to that used by Paul. Enough of the Pauline content and themes in relation to the Last Supper resonate with the Marcan Gospel's material that this link cannot be ignored. The Marcan and Pauline traditions do overlap in significant elements of the Last Supper ritual, despite also displaying variation.

---

65 See Barbara E. Reid, *Choosing the Better Part? Women in the Gospel of Luke* (Collegeville, Minn.: Liturgical Press, 1996), 195-96. While Reid's comments relate to the Lucan version of the story (Luke 21:1-4), they are also applicable to the Marcan version.
66 See, for example, Rom 16:3-5; Col 4:15.

Bibliography

Bauer, Walter, William F. Arndt, F. Wilbur Gingrich and Frederick W. Danker. *A Greek-English Lexicon of the New Testament and Other Early Christian Literature.* Chicago, Ill.: University of Chicago Press, 2nd edn 1979.

Bieler, Andrea, and Luise Schottroff. *The Eucharist: Bodies, Bread, and Resurrection.* Minneapolis, Minn.: Fortress Press, 2007.

Bradshaw, Paul F. *Eucharistic Origins.* Oxford: Oxford University Press, 2004.

Bradshaw Aitken, Ellen. *Jesus' Death in Early Christian Memory: The Poetics of the Passion.* NTOA 53. Göttingen: Vandenhoeck & Ruprecht, 2004.

Collins, Adela Yarbro. *Mark: A Commentary.* Hermeneia. Minneapolis, Minn.: Fortress Press, 2007.

Collins, Raymond F. *First Corinthians.* SP 7; Collegeville, Pa.: Liturgical Press, 1999.

Coutsoumpos, Panayotis. *Paul and the Lord's Supper: A Socio-Historical Investigation.* New York: Peter Lang, 2005.

Dowling, Elizabeth, and Veronica Lawson, "Women, Eucharist, and Good News to All Creation in Mark," in: *Reinterpreting the Eucharist: Explorations in Feminist Theology and Ethics,* eds. Anne Elvey, Carol Hogan, Kim Power and Claire Renkin. Sheffield: Equinox Publishing, forthcoming.

Eichhorn, Albert. *The Lord's Supper in the New Testament,* trans. J. F. Cayzer. Leiden: Brill, 2008.

Hare, Douglas R. A. *Mark.* Louisville, Ky.: Westminster John Knox Press, 1996.

Hooker, Morna D. *The Gospel According to Saint Mark.* Peabody, Mass.: Hendrickson, 1991.

Maccoby, Hyam. "Paul and the Eucharist." *NTS* 37 (1991): 247-67.

Marcus, Joel. *Mark 1-8: A New Translation with Introduction and Commentary.* AB 27. New York, N.Y.: Doubleday, 1999.

—, "Mark – Interpreter of Paul." *NTS* 46 (2000): 473-87.

McRae, Rachel M. "Eating with Honor: The Corinthian Lord's Supper in Light of Voluntary Association Meal Practices." *JBL* 130 (2011): 165-81.

McGowan, Andrew B. "'Is there a Liturgical Text in this Gospel?': The Institution Narratives and their Early Interpretive Communities." *JBL* 118 (1999): 73-87.

Metzger, Bruce M. *A Textual Commentary on the Greek New Testament.* Stuttgart: Deutsche Bibelgesellschaft, 2nd edn 1994.

Noonan Sabin, Marie. *The Gospel According to Mark.* Collegeville, Pa.: Liturgical Press, 2006.

Reid, Barbara E. *Taking Up the Cross: New Testament Interpretations Through Latina and Feminist Eyes.* Minneapolis, Minn.: Fortress Press, 2007.

—, *Choosing the Better Part? Women in the Gospel of Luke.* Collegeville, Pa.: Liturgical Press, 1996.

Sawicki, Marianne. "Making Jesus," in: *A Feminist Companion to Mark,* eds. Amy-Jill Levine with Marianne Blickenstaff, 136-70. Sheffield: Sheffield Academic Press, 2001.

Schweizer, Eduard. *The Lord's Supper According to the New Testament.* Philadelphia, Pa.: Fortress Press, 1967.

Smit, Peter-Ben. *Fellowship and Food in the Kingdom.* WUNT 2.234. Tübingen: Mohr Siebeck, 2008.

Smith, Dennis E. *From Symposium to Eucharist: The Banquet in the Early Christian World.* Minneapolis, Minn.: Fortress Press, 2003.

Smith, Dennis E., and Hal E. Taussig. *Many Tables: The Eucharist in the New Testament and Liturgy Today*. London: SCM, 1990.

Tarazi, Paul N. *The New Testament: An Introduction;* Volume 1: *Paul and Mark*. Crestwood, N.Y.: St Vladimir's Seminary Press, 1999.

Taylor, Justin. "Bread that is Broken – and Unbroken," in: *A Wandering Galilean: Essays in Honour of Seán Freyne*, eds. Zuleika Rodgers with M. Daly-Denton and A. Fitzpatrick McKinley, 525-37. JSJSup132. Leiden: Brill, 2009.

Telford, William R. *Mark*. Sheffield: Sheffield Academic Press, 1995.

Witherington, Ben. *Making a Meal of it: Rethinking the Theology of the Lord's Supper*. Waco, Tex.: Baylor University Press, 2007.

Michael Theobald
Die Passion Jesu bei Paulus und Markus

Die Erinnerung an Jesu Passion bei Paulus und Markus jeweils für sich zu analysieren, ist gewiss ein spannendes Unterfangen, das alle Anstrengung lohnt und Exegeten und Theologen auch immer wieder neu in seinen Bann zieht. Paulus und das älteste Evangelium im Blick auf ihre Theologie des Kreuzes miteinander zu vergleichen, verspricht indes Erkenntnisgewinn, der über ihre getrennte Betrachtung möglicherweise noch hinausgeht[1]. Wer einen solchen Vergleich wagt, sieht sich freilich rasch mit der skeptischen Frage konfrontiert, wie weit er denn zu tragen vermöchte und ob er überhaupt konkrete Einsichten erwarten lasse[2]. Sollte er nur ideengeschichtliche Parallelen oder Strukturanalogien zu Tage fördern, ohne dass ein historischer Zusammenhang zwischen den verglichenen Autoren und ihrer Weise der Erinnerung an Jesus ersichtlich würde – sei es ein räumliches und zeitliches Kontinuum, in dem sich beide bewegen, seien es motivgeschicht-

---

[1] Während die Literatur zur Theologie des Todes Jesu jeweils bei einem der beiden Autoren Legion ist, sind Vergleiche beider in dieser Hinsicht eher selten; im Nachgang zur grundlegenden Studie von M. Werner, Der Einfluss paulinischer Theologie im Markusevangelium. Eine Studie zur neutestamentlichen Theologie (BZNW 1), Gießen 1923, 60–72 („Der Tod des Christus"), sind hierzu aus jüngerer Zeit vor allem folgende Autoren zu nennen, die freilich zum Thema „Passion/Kreuz Jesu bei Paulus und Markus" teils oft nur im Vorübergehen Stellung beziehen: A. Lindemann, Paulus im ältesten Christentum (BHTh 58), Tübingen 1979, 151–154 (153: „Mk hat unabhängig von Paulus das christliche Bekenntnis zur Auferweckung des Gekreuzigten prinzipiell ebenso wie der Apostel interpretiert"); K. Berger, Theologiegeschichte des Urchristentums. Theologie des Neuen Testaments, Tübingen/Basel 1994, 317–323 („Paulus und Markus"); C.C. Black, Christ Crucified in Paul and in Mark. Reflections on an Intracanonical Conversation, in: E.H. Lovering/J.L. Sumney (eds.), Theology and Ethics in Paul and His Interpreters (Essays in Honor of Victor Paul Furnish), Nashville 1996, 80–104; J. Marcus, Mark – Interpreter of Paul, in: NTS 46 (2000), 473–487 (gemessen an seiner „Theologie des Kreuzes" sei Markus ein „Paulinist": „both portray the death of Jesus in similarly overlapping ways" [486]); D. C. Allison, Constructing Jesus. Memory, Imagination, and History, Grand Rapids/Michigan 2010, 387–433, vor allem 392–423 („Death and Memory: The Passion of Jesus"). – Eine knappe Darstellung der älteren Forschung bietet K. Romaniuk, Le Problème des Paulinismes dans l'Évangile de Marc, in: NTS 23 (1967/77), 266–274, weitere Hinweise bei W. Schenk, Sekundäre Jesuanisierungen von primären Paulus-Aussagen bei Markus, in: F. van Segbroeck u.a. (ed.), The Four Gospels 1992, Vol. II., FS Frans Neirynck (BEThL 100), Leuven 1992, 877–904, hier 879–882.
[2] C.C. Black, Christ, 186: „In short, if some conjunction of Paul and Mark once appeared to open up a *Hauptstrasse* [highway] for exegetical traffic, now more than ever their intersection looks like a *Sackgasse* [dead end]"; er selbst bietet einen kanonischen Vergleich von 1Kor 1,18–2,16 und Mk 15,16–41, ohne den Versuch zu unternehmen, den Evangelisten und den Apostel historisch einander zuzuordnen.

liche oder überlieferungsgeschichtliche Überschneidungen in ihrem Reden vom Tod Jesu –, bliebe ihr Vergleich weitgehend eine Sache subjektiven Ermessens ohne *fundamentum in re*.

Schwierigkeiten tun sich einem solchen Unterfangen schon bei der *zeitlichen* und *örtlichen* Verhältnisbestimmung der Quellen auf: Ist die Entstehung der Paulusbriefe im Raum der Ägäis zwischen 50 und 60 n. Chr. Allgemeingut der Forschung[3], so lässt sich Vergleichbares von der verbreiteten Annahme, das Markusevangelium sei bald nach 70 n. Chr. in Rom entstanden[4], also dort, wo wenige Jahre zuvor der Apostel das Martyrium erlitten hat, nicht sagen. Sie konkurriert mit der alternativen Verortung des Evangeliums in Syrien[5], die sich vor allem auf seine besondere Nähe zum „vor- und nebenpaulinischen Heidenchristentum" berufen kann[6]. Ohne den Wettstreit der beiden Hypothesen hier

---

[3] Vgl. O. Wischmeyer (Hg.), Paulus. Leben – Umwelt – Werk – Briefe, Tübingen ²2012.
[4] M. Ebner, Das Markusevangelium, in: M. Ebner/St. Schreiber (Hgg.), Einleitung in das Neue Testament (KStTh 6), Stuttgart 2008, 154–183, hier 171f.
[5] I. Broer in Verbindung mit H.-U. Weidemann, Einleitung in das Neue Testament, Würzburg ³2010: „Massiv gegen Rom spricht m.E. [...] der Umstand, dass Markus der erste ist, der in großem Umfang das mündlich in den Gemeinden umlaufende Material sammelt [...] und in den Zusammenhang eines Lebens Jesu bringt. Dafür war er auf eine gewisse Nähe zum Ursprung und zum Zentrum der Jesusbewegung angewiesen". Er merkt an: „Die Ambivalenz der Argumente wird im übrigen schön deutlich, wenn man sieht, wie Ebner in seiner Einleitung (171) in Mk 12,42 mit der Erwähnung der kleinsten römischen Münze, des Quadrans, das entscheidende Argument für eine Abfassung in Rom findet, während Theißen (Entstehung, 79) gerade unter Verweis auf diese Stelle gegen Rom plädiert"; vgl. G. Theißen, Die Entstehung des Neuen Testaments als literaturgeschichtliches Problem (Schriften der Philosophisch-historischen Klasse der Heidelberger Akademie der Wissenschaften Bd. 40), Heidelberg 2007. – Syrien als Abfassungsort des Mk nennen bereits W.G. Kümmel, Einleitung in das Neue Testament, Heidelberg ¹⁸1976, 70; P. Vielhauer, Geschichte der urchristlichen Literatur. Einleitung in das Neue Testament, die Apokryphen und die Apostolischen Väter, Berlin/New York 1975, 347; A. Lindemann, Paulus, 153; vgl. auch W. Schmithals, Das Evangelium nach Markus. Kapitel 1–9,1 (ÖTK 2/1), Gütersloh/Würzburg 1979, 61: „Am ehesten wird man den Abfassungsort des Mk nicht weit von dem Entstehungsort der GS [= Grundschrift] im Osten des Reiches suchen".
[6] G. Theißen, Entstehung, 79: Der Evangelist teile „Traditionen des syrischen vor- und nebenpaulinischen Heidenchristentums: den Begriff ‚Evangelium' (εὐαγγέλιον), die Abendmahlsüberlieferung und die Gattung des Lasterkatalogs (Mk 7,21–23), alles Traditionen und Formen, die auch bei Paulus als vorgegebene Tradition begegnen und die Paulus von seinen syrischen Heimatgemeinden (etwa in Damaskus und Antiochien) übernommen habe". A. Lindemann, Paulus, 154, gibt zu dem von ihm erhobenen Befund, dass Mk „von Paulus und paulinischer Tradition nicht beeinflusst" sei, zu bedenken, „dass Syrien nicht zum unmittelbaren Missionsgebiet des Paulus gehört" habe; „der erste sichere Zeuge dafür, dass paulinische Briefe in Syrien, genauer: in Antiochia bekannt waren, ist Ignatius (um 110). Zur Zeit der Abfassung des Mk stand die syrische Kirche vermutlich überhaupt nicht unter paulinischem Einfluss [...] Anders verhielte es sich, wenn Mk [...] in Rom verfasst worden wäre. Dann wäre paulinischer

entscheiden zu müssen, verdient das genannte Argument zugunsten Syriens im Kontext unserer Fragestellung doch besondere Beachtung.

Der *zeitliche* Ansatz des Markusevangeliums bald nach der Zerstörung des Jerusalemer Tempels scheint weithin konsensfähig zu sein[7]. Allerdings ist das Gefälle von Paulus zu Markus[8] insofern komplexer, als mit einem Großteil der Forschung davon ausgegangen werden darf, dass der Evangelist eine Passions- und Ostererzählung in sein Buch integriert hat, die wesentlich älter ist und deren Vorform vielleicht sogar schon aus dem Jerusalem der 40er Jahre stammt[9]. Fraglich ist, auf welchem Weg diese Erzählung ihren Weg durch die früheste Geschichte der christlichen Gemeinden genommen und welche Verbreitung sie in ihnen gefunden hat. Kannte Paulus sie?[10] Interessierte er sich überhaupt für sie,

---

Einfluss naheliegend – und sein Fehlen schwerwiegend. Aber für die Rom-Hypothese spricht so gut wie nichts" (153f.).

7 Anders noch M. Hengel, Entstehungszeit und Situation des Markusevangeliums (1984), in: M. Hengel, Jesus und die Evangelien. Kleine Schriften V, hg. von C.-J. Thornton (WUNT 211), Tübingen 2007, 478–525, hier 522f.: Mk „entstand vermutlich in der politisch brisanten Zeit nach der Ermordung Neros und Galbas und vor der Erneuerung des Jüdischen Krieges durch Titus, das heißt etwa zwischen dem Winter 68/69 und dem Winter 69/70 n.Chr."; auch L. Schenke, Das Markusevangelium (UB 205), Stuttgart 1988, 35–39, plädiert für einen Zeitpunkt kurz vor dem Fall Jerusalems mit dem Hinweis darauf, dass die Zerstörung des Tempels selbst in 12,9; 13,2.14–20; 15,38 nicht vorausgesetzt sei; aber genau dies ist umstritten.

8 Die zeitliche Nachordnung von Markus eröffnet theoretisch die Möglichkeit, dass der älteste Evangelist unter dem Einfluss des Paulus stand, eine Möglichkeit, die M. Werner in seiner oben Anm. 1 genannten Studie mit guten Gründen, wie ich meine, verworfen hat; zuletzt wurde sie wieder von W. Schenk, Jesuanisierungen, J. Marcus, Mark und anderen (ebd. 474 Anm. 5) erneut ins Gespräch gebracht.

9 So G. Theißen, Lokalkolorit und Zeitgeschichte in den Evangelien. Ein Beitrag zur Geschichte der synoptischen Tradition, Freiburg i. d. Schweiz/Göttingen ²1992 (Studienausgabe der ersten Auflage 1989 = NTOA 8), 177–211; auch E. Lohse, Die Geschichte des Leidens und Sterbens Jesu Christi, Gütersloh 1964, 9–25, hier 13, rechnet mit einer Herkunft der ältesten Form der Passionserzählung schon aus Jerusalem.

10 Die Frage bejahen R. Pesch, Das Markusevangelium, II. Teil: Kommentar zu Kap. 8,27–16,20 (HThKNT II/2), Freiburg 1977, 21; P. Stuhlmacher, Achtzehn Thesen zur paulinischen Kreuzestheologie, in: P. Stuhlmacher, Versöhnung, Gesetz und Gerechtigkeit. Aufsätze zur biblischen Theologie, Göttingen 1981, 192–208, hier 204f.; vgl. ders., Biblische Theologie des Neuen Testaments, Bd. I: Grundlegung: Von Jesus zu Paulus, Göttingen ²1997, 304f.: „Von Gal 3,1; 1Kor 1,23–24; 2,8; 11,23–25; 15,1–11 und 2Kor 13,4 her ist unverkennbar, dass der Apostel auch im Gemeindeunterricht sein christologisches Hauptaugenmerk auf Jesu Passion, Kreuzigung und Auferweckung gerichtet hat [...]"; K. Berger, Theologiegeschichte, 317: „Da Paulus lt. Abendmahlsbericht in 1Kor 11 mit der synoptischen oder einer sehr ähnlichen Passionstradition vertraut war, kann man annehmen, dass er auch den entscheidenden Impuls für seine Kreuzestheologie aus der in den Synoptikern übereinstimmenden Darstellung der Kreuzigung Jesu selbst gewonnen (und dann weitergebildet) hat"; D.C. Allison, Constructing, 404f. – M. Hengel,

wo die Forschung ihm doch ein genaueres Interesse am irdischen Weg Jesu bis heute abspricht?[11] Richtig ist, dass sowohl der Apostel wie auch der Autor unseres ältesten Evangeliums – nach der Tradition Markus genannt – keine Augenzeugen der letzten Jerusalemer Tage Jesu waren. Aber davon abgesehen, scheint ihr gegenseitiges Verhältnis insgesamt von *Asymmetrie* bestimmt zu sein, was auch mit den von ihnen benutzten unterschiedlichen Gattungen – Evangelium und Briefen – zusammenhängt[12]. Verständigen wir uns im Folgenden zuerst kurz über die frühchristliche Genese der Memoria der Passion Jesu, bevor wir einen Vergleich von Paulus und Markus ins Auge fassen. Dass ein solcher Vergleich nur hypothetischer Natur sein kann (wobei es gegebenenfalls schon viel wäre, gewohnte Sicherheiten zu erschüttern), sei vorweg noch einmal eigens betont.

Die beschämende Hinrichtung des Nazareners am Kreuz durch die Römer war die erste Krise seiner Anhängerschaft, die sich traumatisch in ihr Gedächtnis einbrannte[13]. Sie bestimmte die Erinnerung an sein Leben, die sich unter dem Vorzeichen ihres Osterglaubens bald formieren sollte, auch wenn dies nicht in jeder einzelnen ihrer Erinnerungsgestalten, die der eigenen Identitätsfindung

---

Das Mahl in der Nacht, „in der Jesus ausgeliefert wurde" (1Kor 11,23) (2004), in: M. Hengel, Studien zur Christologie. Kleine Schriften IV, hg. von C.-J. Thornton (WUNT 201), Tübingen 2006, 451–495, hier 465, scheint die Frage weniger auf der literarischen als vielmehr auf der mündlichen Ebene anzusiedeln, wenn er von einem „*Erzählen* der Passionsgeschichte durch Paulus bei der Gemeindegründung" in Korinth spricht (Hervorh. von mir); „Paulus und die Korinther" haben nach seiner Einschätzung „die Passionsgeschichte bis in Details hinein gekannt". – W. Schrage, Der erste Brief an die Korinther, 3.Teilband: 1Kor 11,17–14,40 (EKK VII/3), Zürich/Neukirchen-Vluyn 1999, 32, mahnt zur Vorsicht: „Wie weit die geschichtliche Kenntnis vom Passionsgeschehen bei Paulus oder gar den Korinthern reicht, lässt sich nicht sagen" (mit Anm. 472).
11 Vgl. F. Holzbrecher, Paulus und der historische Jesus. Darstellung und Analyse der bisherigen Forschungsgeschichte (TANZ 48), Tübingen 2007.
12 Evangelium und Briefe überschneiden sich freilich markant in ihrer Verwendung der Auferweckungsformel: vgl. einerseits 1Kor 15,4 etc., andererseits Mk 16,6 (vgl. Mk 9,9). Im einzelnen siehe unten!
13 C. Keith/T. Thatcher, The Scar of the Cross: The Violence Ratio and the Earliest Christian Memories of Jesus, in: T. Thatcher (ed.), Jesus, the Voice, and the Text: Beyond the Oral and the Written Gospel, Waco TX 2008, 197–214, hier 204: „Violent events, like Jesus' crucifixion, traumatize group memory to such an extent that memorialization is necessary almost immediately, and the development of commemorative narratives is a typical mnemonic strategy for the maintenance of group identity. Simply put, the followers of Jesus could not continue as a coherent group without a strategy for moderating and rationalizing the trauma of his death, and it seems that the development of a passion narrative keyed to major themes from Jewish Scripture and tradition would be a likely means of accomplishing that goal".

dienten, unmittelbaren sprachlichen Ausdruck fand[14]. Diese sind pluriform: Neben den Passions- und Ostererzählungen[15] stehen Glaubensformeln, die den Heilstod Jesu und seine Auferweckung thematisieren[16], neben Jesusworten, die nach seinem Tod auf sein Sterben bezogen wurden[17], auch solche, die neu gebildet und ihm in den Mund gelegt wurden und sein Geschick jetzt wie in einem Brennglas rückblickend bündeln[18]. Die Schriften Israels, in denen die frühen Jesus-Bekenner von ihrer jüdischen Verwurzelung her schon immer lebten, bildeten den Humus, auf dem sich ihre Erinnerung an die Passion Jesu formte, nicht erst in der Weise expliziter „Schriftbeweise", sondern schon viel unmittelbarer bei deren erster Versprachlichung[19].

Bei all diesen Segmenten gepflegter Erinnerung lässt sich nun fragen, ob Paulus und Markus bzw. ihre Überlieferungen sich in dem einen oder anderen Punkt berühren oder sich fern stehen, und wenn sie sich berühren, wieweit die Berührungen reichen und wie sie sich erklären[20]. Eindimensionale Antworten sind

---

[14] So etwa nicht im Spruchevangelium Q, das die Kreuzigung Jesu bekanntlich nicht direkt thematisiert, aber mittels des Topos vom Prophetenmord doch anvisiert: vgl. Q 13,34f.; Q11,47 und 11,49f..
[15] Zu ihnen vgl. bereits die erhellenden Ausführungen von C. Keith/T. Thatcher in Anm. 13.
[16] Vgl. 1Thess 4,14; 5,10; Röm 4,24f. etc. (im Einzelnen siehe unten Punkt 2). – K. Wengst, Christologische Formeln und Lieder des Urchristentums (StNT 7), Gütersloh 1972, 27–129.
[17] Ein schönes Beispiel bietet Mk 2,19–20, im Munde Jesu ein einfaches Bildwort („Können etwa die Söhne des Brautgemachs fasten?"), im Markusevangelium schließlich eine verdeckte Prophetie seines Todes; vgl. J. Gnilka, Das Evangelium nach Markus (Mk 1–8,26) (EKK II/1), Zürich/Neukirchen-Vluyn 1978, 114f.
[18] Dazu dürften etwa die drei Ansagen vom Sterben und Auferstehen des Menschensohns Mk 8,31; 9,31 und 10,33f. gehören. – Hinzu kommen mancherlei Motive und Deutungsmuster, die um die Deutung seines Todes kreisen wie etwa das vom „Lamm Gottes" (Joh 1,29.36; 1Petr 1,19), vom „Paschalamm" (1Kor 5,7) oder vom „Sühnort" (Röm 3,25: ἱλαστήριον) etc. oder auch die vielfach verwendete „Blutformel" (Röm 5,9; 1Kor 11,25 etc.).
[19] Das betont jüngst wieder E.B. Aitken, Jesus' Death in Early Christian Memory. The Poetics of the Passion (NTOA 53), Göttingen/Fribourg 2004, 22, im Gespräch mit J.D. Crossan: „Although [...] I am in fundamental agreement with Crossan that the story of Jesus' passion arises out of the scriptures of Israel, I question his dependence on scribal exegesis as the vehicle for the formation of this story. Instead, I locate the development of such a narrative in relation to the cultic practice of various early Christian communities. That is, instead of speaking of ‚prophecy historicized,' I would rather speak of the reactualization of scripture in the context of its performance in ritual [...]".
[20] An das Ergebnis der Studie von M. Werner, Einfluss, 209, lässt sich anknüpfen: „Wo Markus mit Paulus übereinstimmt, handelt es sich immer um allgemein-urchristliche Anschauungen", ebd. 69 auf die „Sühnetodlehre" bezogen, in der beide zusammentreffen: „[...] da ergibt sich denn ohne weiteres, dass dieses Zusammentreffen niemals als Beeinflussung des Markus durch paulinische Theologie erwiesen werden kann. Weiß Markus nichts von der dem Paulus ‚eigen-

angesichts solcher Vielschichtigkeit nicht möglich: Wie beim Markusevangelium zwischen seiner Gesamtkonzeption und seinen Überlieferungen (soweit erkenntlich) zu unterscheiden ist, so gilt Analoges auch für Paulus: Das von ihm ausdrücklich übernommene Glaubensbekenntnis 1Kor 15,3–5a verlangt z.B. eine andere Gewichtung als der Schriftdiskurs zum Tod Jesu in Gal 3,13f., der auf ihn selbst zurückgeht.

Ausgangspunkt der folgenden Überlegungen sind Thesen zur Genese der Passions- und Ostererzählung, von der wir annehmen dürfen, dass sie auf zwei Säulen ruht: dem Bekenntnis zur Auferweckung Jesu und der christologischen Lektüre der Schriften Israels (unter 1.). Daran kann ein Vergleich mit Paulus anschließen – in Orientierung sowohl an der von ihm rezipierten Bekenntnistradition, insbesondere 1Kor 15,3b–5a (unter 2.), als auch an seinem Schriftgebrauch aus der Perspektive von Kreuz und Auferstehung Jesu mit Blick auf das Markusevangelium (unter 3.). Danach sind weitere mögliche Weisen der Erinnerung an die Passion Jesu beim Apostel zu besprechen (unter 4.), bevor aus den gesammelten Beobachtungen ein Resümee gezogen werden kann.

1 Zur Genese der Passions- und Ostererzählungen

Die Überlieferung der Passions- und Ostererzählung ist bekanntlich im Rahmen des frühchristlichen Überlieferungsguts ein Sonderfall: Zum einen stellt sie im Unterschied zur sonstigen Perikopen-Überlieferung einen fest gefügten größeren Erzählzusammenhang dar, der wahrscheinlich schon schriftlich fixiert war, bevor er Eingang in das älteste Evangelium fand[21]; zum anderen lässt sich dieser Erzählzusammenhang in mindestens zwei, womöglich sogar drei voneinander un-

---

tümlichen' Deutung des Todes Jesu als Überwindung der Geistermächte dieses Äons [siehe dazu unten Anm. 93], trifft er aber sogleich da mit Paulus zusammen, wo dieser in seiner Beurteilung des Todes Jesu aus der urchristlichen Tradition schöpft, dann ist doch der Schlussfolgerung gar nicht zu entgehen, auch Markus gebe 10,45 und 14,24 völlig unabhängig gemeinurchristliche Überzeugung wieder". Zu Mk 10,45 notiert M. Werner, Einfluss, 69f., zu Recht, dass der Terminus λύτρον in den echten Paulusbriefen gar nicht vorkomme, in den Pastoralbriefen nur als Kompositum ἀντίλυτρον (1Tim 2,6) und in der medialen Form λυτροῦσθαι (Tit 2,14). Eine Verwandtschaft bestünde mit (ἐξ-) ἀγοράζειν (vgl. 1Kor 6,20; 7,23; Gal 3,13; 4,5), wobei aber der in Gal charakteristische Zusammenhang des Gedankens vom „Loskauf" mit dem Gesetz bei Markus gerade fehle: „Mit dem Gesetz hat bei Markus der Tod Jesu überhaupt nicht das Geringste zu schaffen. Fest steht also jedenfalls, dass Markus den Ausdruck λύτρον nicht von Paulus hat", auch nicht die Rede von „Vielen", die in den Genuss des „Loskaufs" kommen.
21 Vgl. etwa F. Schleritt, Der vorjohanneische Passionsbericht. Eine historisch-kritische und theologische Untersuchung zu Joh 2,13–22; 11,47–14,31 und 18,1–20,29 (BZNW 154), Berlin 2007.

abhängigen vor-evangeliaren Fassungen nachweisen: der vor-markinischen, vor-johanneischen[22] und – mit dieser zweiten verwandt – auch in einer vor-lukanischen Fassung[23]. Diese Pluriformität, die durch die lokale Verzweigung des (Jerusalemer) Archetyps bedingt sein dürfte, verlangt nach einer näheren Erklärung.

Wahrscheinlich war die ursprünglich eigenständige Passions- und Ostererzählung nicht einfach nur ein Stück mündlicher Überlieferung oder Kleinliteratur, sie bot auch nicht (wie Martin Dibelius meinte) die historische Basis für das Kerygma – die Predigt[24] –, sondern war selbst schon eine auf rituelle Wiederholung angelegte Erzählung, die nach „performance" rief. Der Grund hierfür war wohl der, dass es sich bei ihr um eine Art Gründungserzählung der frühen Gemeinden mit „liturgischem" Sitz im Leben („myth and ritus") handelte[25]. Ihre Varianz bei konstanter Grundstruktur erklärt sich so am besten.

Offen ist die Frage, *welches* ihr „Sitz im Leben" war[26]. Plausibel ist die Annahme, dass es ein jährliches Paschafest war, das die an den Messias Jesus glaubenden jüdischen Gemeinschaften weiter begingen, jetzt allerdings als jährliches Gedenken an sein Sterben und Auferstehen. Das lag deshalb nahe, weil ja Jesus (wenigstens nach der johanneischen Chronologie, die historisch plausi-

---

22 Vgl. D.C. Allison, Constructing, 404, der mit „a pre-Markan passion narrative" rechnet – „one reason being that I judge John to be mostly independent of the Synoptics". Anders noch F. Neirynck, Jean et les Synoptiques. Examen critique de l' exégèse de M.-É. Boismard (BETL 49), Leuven 1979 etc., und seine Schüler.
23 Hierzu vgl. besonders die Studie von H. Klein, Zur Frage einer Lukas und Johannes zu Grunde liegenden Passions- und Ostererüberlieferung, in: H. Klein, Lukasstudien (FRLANT 209), Göttingen 2005, 65–84.
24 M. Dibelius, Die Formgeschichte des Evangeliums (Nachdruck der dritten Auflage mit einem erweiterten Nachtrag von G. Iber, hg. von G. Bornkamm), Tübingen ⁶1971, 21f.
25 E.B. Aitken, Death, 11, meint zu Recht: „the formation of the story of Jesus' suffering and death, prior to the written gospels, has never received an adequate explanation". Sie selbst verweist im Anschluss an die Studien von G. Nagy, Pindar's Homer. The Lyric Possession of an Epic Past, Baltimore/London 1990, und G. Nagy, Poetry as Performance. Homer and Beyond, Cambridge 1996, auf die gegenseitige Bezogenheit von „ritual and narrative" (15): „I test the hypothesis that the story of Jesus' suffering and death developed as part of the cultic practice of various early Christian communities"; darin spielen für sie die Schriften Israels – „as available in the cultic life of the community" – die entscheidende Rolle. Ihre Hypothese überprüft die Autorin freilich nicht an den Passionserzählungen selbst, sondern – entsprechend dem Untertitel ihrer Studie „The Poetics of the Passion" – an Texten wie 1Kor 15,3–5; 1Petr 2,22–24 („A Hymn"); Hebr 5,7–10 etc. und dem Barnabasbrief.
26 E.B. Aitken, Death, 170f.: „We may speculate that the first generative moment of this reenactment happened in the course of ritual meals, perhaps in response to an appearance of the risen Jesus" (Letzteres ist allerdings sehr spekulativ); ältere Überlegungen bei G. Schille, Das Leiden des Herrn. Die evangelische Passionstradition und ihr ‚Sitz im Leben', in: ZThK 52 (1955), 161–205.

bler erscheint als die synoptische) am Vorabend des Festes hingerichtet worden war, sein Tod aber in jedem Fall mit diesem Wallfahrtsfest ursächlich im Zusammenhang stand[27]. Auch wenn die ersten eindeutigen Belege für ein christliches Osterfest – die quartodezimanische Feier – erst ungefähr aus der Mitte des 2. Jh.s stammen[28], wurde es nicht erst zu dieser Zeit eingeführt, sondern setzte eine längst bestehende Tradition fort, die aus frühester Zeit stammen muss[29]. Darauf deuten Indizien in den neutestamentlichen Schriften selbst hin[30]. Im Einzelnen bedürfte diese These zwar weiterer hier nicht zu leistender Vertiefung, für unser Vorhaben genügt aber schon die grundsätzliche Einsicht, dass die Frage, ob Paulus die Passions- und Ostererzählung in irgendeiner Gestalt gekannt hat, keine Frage nur nach der Möglichkeit ihrer *literarischen* Verbreitung ist, es vielmehr zugleich darum geht, ob sie ihm nicht in irgendeiner Form über ein Paschafest im Gedenken an den Tod Jesu (zum Beispiel in Antiochien, wo er mehrere Jahre verbrachte[31]) bekannt geworden sein könnte. Diese Möglichkeit lässt sich nicht ausschließen, so wenig sie sich mangels Quellen beweisen lässt.

Um das Gewicht der alten Passions- und Ostererzählung richtig einschätzen zu können, sind drei Thesen (im Anschluss vor allem an ihre vor-markinische Fassung) von Bedeutung:

1.1 Der axiomatische Einsatzpunkt der Passions- und Ostererzählung

Entgegen der Ansicht, schon der Archetyp der Passionserzählung hätte mit der Episode der Grablegung Jesu geendet[32], ist daran festzuhalten, dass es wohl nie

---

[27] Jesus ist ja dem Zeugnis aller vier Evangelien zufolge zum Pesach-Fest nach Jerusalem hinaufgezogen, um hier – im Herzen Israels – seine Basileia-Botschaft auszurichten.
[28] Zu nennen sind vor allem: Meliton von Sardes, Peri Pascha; Epistula Apostolorum 15 (26).
[29] Vgl. G. Rouwhorst, Christlicher Gottesdienst und der Gottesdienst Israels. Forschungsgeschichte, historische Interaktionen, Theologie, in: M. Klöckener/A.A. Häußling/R. Messner (Hgg.), Theologie des Gottesdienstes Bd. 2 (GDK 2), Regensburg 2008, 493–572, hier 539–545.
[30] J. Jeremias, Art. πάσχα, in: ThWNT V (1954), 895–903, hier 900 mit Anm. 44: „Die ältesten Nachrichten über eine christliche Passafeier führen in die apostolische Zeit". Siehe auch unten Anm. 84.
[31] Nach J. Becker, Paulus. Der Apostel der Völker, Tübingen 1989, 32 („Lebensdaten des Paulus"), „ab 36/37 (?)" bis 49 n.Chr.
[32] So etwa W. Bousset, Kyrios Christos. Geschichte des Christusglaubens von den Anfängen des Christentums bis Irenäus. Unveränderter dritter Abdruck der zweiten, umgearbeiteten Auflage, Göttingen ⁵1965, 64; R. Bultmann, Die Geschichte der synoptischen Tradition, 308; E. Lohse,

eine Fassung ohne die Erzählung von der Verkündigung der Auferweckung im leeren Grab gegeben hat[33]. Der Grund dafür ist nicht nur allgemein darin zu sehen, dass von der Passion Jesu zu erzählen allein unter der Voraussetzung des Glaubens an seine Auferweckung Sinn machte, sondern vor allem in der literarischen Gestalt, welche die Botschaft des jungen Mannes im leeren Grab (Mk 16,6) besitzt. Ein näherer Blick zeigt nämlich, dass sie den axiomatischen Einsatzpunkt der Passionsüberlieferung enthält, von dem aus diese konstruiert worden ist[34]:

6 a Er aber [sc. der junge Mann] spricht zu ihnen [sc. den Frauen]:
  b Entsetzt euch nicht!
  c Jesus sucht ihr,
  d den Nazarener,
  e den Gekreuzigten (τὸν ἐσταυρωμένον):
  f Er ist auferweckt worden (ἠγέρθη),
  g er ist nicht hier.
  h Seht da der Ort,
  i wo sie ihn hinlegten.

Mit V.6f greift der Erzähler das frühchristliche Kernbekenntnis auf, nicht in dessen mutmaßlich ältester Form mit Gott als Subjekt eines Aussagesatzes („Gott hat ihn von den Toten auferweckt"), sondern in der passivischen Form: „Er ist auferweckt worden". Dieser Satz – im Munde des jungen Mannes jetzt kein Bekenntnis mehr, sondern eine Offenbarung aus der himmlischen Welt – bezieht sich auf den vorangehenden Satz, der lautet: „Jesus sucht ihr, den Nazarener, den Gekreuzigten". Auffällig ist die hier vorgenommene doppelte Qualifizierung Jesu. Rudolf Pesch begreift diese so: „Die sorgfältige Kennzeichnung Jesu als des Nazareners" und „des Gekreuzigten" dient „der Identifikation des Auferstandenen. Ver-

---

Geschichte, 24; auch W. Reinbold, Der Prozess Jesu, Göttingen 2006, 69, zufolge gehört die Erzählung Mk 16,1-8* nicht zum „Urgestein der Tradition".
33 T.A. Mohr, Markus- und Johannespassion. Redaktions- und traditionsgeschichtliche Untersuchung der Markinischen und Johanneischen Passionstradition (AThANT 70), Zürich 1982, 402 (auch mit Hinweis auf die von Mk unabhängige vorjoh. Passionserzählung); ebenso J. Becker, Die Auferstehung Jesu Christi nach dem Neuen Testament. Ostererfahrung und Osterverständnis im Urchristentum, Tübingen 2007, 15–17.
34 Voraussetzung dieser These ist die weithin anerkannte Annahme, dass Mk 16,6 zu der dem Evangelisten vorgegebenen Überlieferung, ja zu deren Urgestein gehört. In Joh 20,13 ist die Rede der himmlischen Boten zugunsten der Worte des unmittelbar danach erscheinenden Jesus zwar gekürzt, aber es gibt doch auch bei Joh Spuren, die auf die älteste Fassung verweisen: Mit γύναι, τί κλαίεις (Joh 20,13b = 20,15b) vgl. Mk 16,6b, mit dem anschließenden τίνα ζητεῖς Joh 20,15c vgl. Mk 16,6c: Ἰησοῦν ζητεῖτε; die Rede vom „Gekreuzigten" hat ihr Echo in der johanneischen Rede vom „Aufsteigen" Jesu zum Vater (vgl. Joh 20,17).

wechslungen werden ausgeschlossen"³⁵. Doch die beiden Appositionen könnten mehr besagen. Die Frage lautet, wie die Rede vom „Gekreuzigten" als *Klimax* des Satzes zu gewichten ist? Heinz-Wolfgang Kuhn hielt es für bemerkenswert, „dass weder in der zu vermutenden ältesten Passionserzählung [...] noch in der Markus vorliegenden Passion [...] noch in den Passionsgeschichten unserer synoptischen Evangelien Jesu Tod speziell am Kreuz, also die tatsächliche Weise seiner Tötung, theologisch bedacht wird. Eine Ausnahme macht nur Mk 16,6 (und die Parallele bei Matthäus)", schreibt er, „wo sich Gott in der Ostergeschichte gerade zu dem Gekreuzigten bekennt und Jesus nicht mit dem Aorist abgeschlossener Vergangenheit, sondern mit dem Perfekt gültiger Dauer als der ἐσταυρωμένος, der dies auch für die gegenwärtige Gemeinde bleibt, bezeichnet wird (noch dreimal bei Paulus wird Jesus [...] ‚der Gekreuzigte' genannt – immer wie bei Markus im Perfekt)"³⁶. Dahinter könnte (über die Beobachtung von Heinz-Wolfgang Kuhn und anderer hinaus) ein Einwand vonseiten der ersten Gegner der nachösterlichen Verkündigung Jesu in Jerusalem stehen, die sich auf Dtn 21,23 beriefen, um ihn mit Verweis auf seinen Tod am Schandpfahl als „Verfluchten" Gottes hinzustellen und so unter Berufung auf die Tora seiner Proklamation als Messias Israels entgegenzuwirken³⁷. Nimmt in Mk 16,6 schon die erste Kennzeichnung Jesu als „Na-

---

35 R. Pesch, Mk II, 533; ebd. 171 zu Mk 10,47: „Ἰησοῦς ὁ Ναζαρηνός (vgl. 14,67 [„und auch du warst mit dem Nazarener, dem Jesus": μετὰ τοῦ Ναζαρηνοῦ ... τοῦ Ἰησοῦ]; 16,6) ist Identifizierung des Trägers des verbreiteten Namens Jesus durch die Herkunftsbezeichnung: aus Nazaret. Sie kommt (abgesehen von der wortspielartig-christologischen Verwendung in 1,24) im Mk-Ev nur innerhalb der Passionsgeschichte vor, also in nichtgaliläischen Traditionen. Wahrscheinlich handelt es sich zunächst um eine ‚Außenbezeichnung' bzw. eine Auskunft zur Identifizierung Jesu für Außenstehende". Die alternative Bezeichnung Nazoräer (Ναζωραῖος) ist im NT, vor allem Lk und Joh, weitaus häufiger belegt.
36 H.-W. Kuhn, Jesus als Gekreuzigter in der frühchristlichen Verkündigung bis zur Mitte des 2. Jahrhunderts, in: ZThK 72 (1975), 1–46, hier 21; er verweist auf W. Schrage, Das Verständnis des Todes Jesu Christi im Neuen Testament, in: E. Bizer u.a. (Hg.), Das Kreuz Jesu Christi als Grund des Heils (STAEKU), Gütersloh 1967, 49–90, hier 66 Anm. 46: auf „die auffallende Perfektform in 16,6, wo man eigentlich den Aorist erwartet", habe bereits J. Schniewind (ThR 1930, 185) hingewiesen; vgl. ebd. 68 Anm. 51; außerdem J. Marcus, Mark, 480: „the continuing reality of Jesus' crucifixion for both Paul and Mark is expressed in a shared grammatical feature: both use the perfect passive participle ἐσταυρωμένον to remind their readers that the Risen Jesus continues to be the Crucified One"; W. Schenk, Jesuanisierungen, 901, will hier einen „Rückgriff auf Paulus" erkennen. Zu ihm vgl. 1Kor 1,23; 2,2; Gal 3,1 (in unmittelbarer Nähe zu 3,13 = Dtn 21,23!). Vgl. auch Apg 5,30; 10,39; 13,29 im Rahmen des Kontrastschemas: dazu siehe unten! In der markinischen Passionserzählung begegnet σταυρόω – abgesehen von Mk 16,6 – nur als beschreibendes Tätigkeitsverb, ohne jeden theologischen Beiklang (Mk 15,13.14.15.20.24.25.27).
37 Zu Recht erinnert U.B. Müller, Die Entstehung des Glaubens an die Auferstehung Jesu. Historische Aspekte und Bedingungen (SBS 172), Stuttgart 1998, 10, daran, dass Dtn 21,23 (rezipiert in 11 QT 64,6-13 und dort indirekt auf die Kreuzigung bezogen) nicht „verallgemeinert

zarener" eine Außenperspektive ein³⁸, so könnte Gleiches also auch von der pointiert am Ende der ganzen Passionserzählung stehenden Rede vom „Gekreuzigten" gelten, die damit deren ursprünglichen *Ort* im Kontext Jerusalems zu erkennen gibt³⁹. Die Antwort auf das mit der Tora begründete Verdikt wäre dann einerseits das Bekenntnis „*Er ist auferweckt worden*", das in diesem Zusammenhang besagt: Gott hat ihn gegen den Anschein, ein „Verfluchter" zu sein, rehabilitiert, andererseits die Passionserzählung selbst: Gespeist aus den Schriften Israels, konkret deren Bild vom ungerecht Leidenden, der in Gottes Hand ist, würde sie das Geschick Jesu sozusagen *mit* der Schrift *gegen* die Schrift (Dtn 21,23) deutend vergegenwärtigen. Es wird sich zeigen, dass Paulus mit derselben Problemlage vertraut war, aber einen anderen, eigenständigen Lösungsansatz bietet.

1.2 Die eucharistische „Kultätiologie" als Einlage in die Passions- und Osterzählung

Mit Rudolf Bultmann ist davon auszugehen, dass die von ihm „Kultuslegende" genannte Tradition Mk 14,22–25 kein genuiner Bestandteil der alten Passionser-

---

werden (darf), als gelte die Tatsache der Kreuzigung an sich als Verfluchung". „Für die Tempelrolle gilt nur der Volksverräter, der lebendig ans Holz gehängt wird, als Verfluchter Gottes oder einer, der ein Kapitalverbrechen begangen hat, der zu den Völkern flieht und das eigene jüdische Volk verflucht" (ebd. weitere Hinweise). Deshalb berechtige auch nichts „zu der Schlussfolgerung, dass die aufgezeigte theologische Wertung der Kreuzigung für die Jünger Jesu zwangsläufiger Anlass war, eine von Gott vollzogene Widerlegung von Jesu legitimem Sendungsanspruch anzunehmen und so die Sache Jesu aufzugeben". Vgl. auch U.B. Müller, Auferweckt und erhöht. Zur Genese des Osterglaubens, in: NTS 54 (2008), 201–220, hier 202. – Anders könnte sich freilich die Sachlage bei den Gegnern der nachösterlichen Jesusverkündigung darstellen: Sie hatten gewiss gute Gründe, Dtn 21,23 auf den gekreuzigten Jesus zu beziehen, was auch Paulus wohl getan hat (siehe unten!). Ein Indiz für den Einfluss von Dtn 21,23 auf die Gesamtkonstruktion der Passions- und Ostererzählung bietet möglicherweise auch die Grablegungserzählung, die dem Toratext genau entspricht: „[...] *darf sein Leichnam nicht über Nacht am Pfahl hängen bleiben, sondern du musst ihn noch am selben Tag begraben. Denn ein Gehängter ist von Gott verflucht* [...]." In Apg 13,29 wird der Zusammenhang von Dtn 21,23 und Grablegung deutlicher: „Und als sie alles vollendet hatten, was von ihm geschrieben steht, nahmen sie ihn vom *Holz* und legten ihn in ein Grab". – Zur Auslegung von Dtn 21,23 vgl. T. Veijola, Fluch des Totengeistes ist der Aufgehängte (Dtn 21,23), in: UF 32 (2000), 69–80.
38 Vgl. oben Anm. 35; es ist in jedem Fall die nicht-galiläische Perspektive, wohl eine Jerusalemer, die damit auch einen Hinweis auf die dortige Entstehung der Passionserzählung bieten könnte.
39 Vgl. dazu auch die Ausführungen von F. Schleritt, Passionsbericht, 539–542 („Der gekreuzigte Christus").

zählung war⁴⁰, sondern wohl erst vom Autor des Markusevangeliums in ihren neuen Kontext eingepflanzt wurde⁴¹. Gegen Bultmann wird man sie aber auf V.22–24 begrenzen und den eschatologischen Ausblick V.25 der Szene vom letzten Mahl Jesu mit den Seinen belassen, der im Unterschied zur „Kultätiologie" immer schon fest in der alten Passionserzählung verankert war⁴². Zugunsten dieser Annahme spricht nicht nur der johanneische Befund mit einer alten Passionserzählung ohne „Herrenmahl"-Szene, sondern auch die Beobachtung, dass Paulus seine Abendmahlsüberlieferung 1Kor 11,23b–25 als *eigenständige* Überlieferung zitiert. Mit ihr hat er nicht *per se* auch eine der alten Fassungen der Passions- und Ostererzählungen kennen gelernt.

1.3 Die Passions- und Ostererzählung als Nukleus des Markusevangeliums

Wer die Entstehung des Markusevangeliums erklären will, hat bei der vormarkinischen Passions- und Osterzählung als der ersten Phase einer Literarisierung der christlichen Gründungserzählung einzusetzen. Sie ist der Nukleus des Buches, damit auch der Kern dessen, was Markus in der Überschrift das „Evangelium Jesu Christi" nennt. Mehrfach durch Prolepsen seit Beginn des Buches angekündigt⁴³,

---

40 R. Bultmann, Geschichte, 285–287; ebenso E. Lohse, Geschichte, 24.
41 Das freilich ist umstritten; J. Gnilka, Das Evangelium nach Markus (Mk 8,27–16,20) (EKK II/2), Zürich/Neukirchen-Vluyn 1979, 240, geht davon aus, dass die Einfügung einem „vormarkinischen Redaktor zuzuschreiben" sei; Gründe zugunsten der Annahme, dass sie auf den Evangelisten zurückgeht, siehe in M. Theobald, Vom Sinai über den Berg der Verklärung zum Abendmahlssaal. Zur kontextuellen Einbindung des markinischen Becherworts (Mk 14,24), in: F. Bruckmann/R. Dausner (Hgg.), Im Angesicht der Anderen. Gespräche zwischen christlicher Theologie und jüdischem Denken (FS J. Wohlmuth), Paderborn 2013, 463-494, hier 485–490; vgl. auch H.-U. Weidemann, „Dies ist mein Bundesblut" (Mk 14,24). Die markinische Abendmahlserzählung als Beispiel für liturgisch beeinflusste Transformationsprozesse, in: W. Eisele/C. Schaefer/ders. (Hgg.), Aneignung durch Transformation (FS M. Theobald) (HBS 74), Freiburg 2013, 56-98.
42 Vgl. dazu M. Theobald, Eucharist and Passover: The Two ‚Loci' of the Liturgical Commemoration of the Last Supper in Early Church, in: T. Thatcher/C. Williams (Hgg.), Engaging with C.H. Dodd on the Gospel of John. Sixty Years of Tradition and Interpretation, Cambridge 2013, 231-254.
43 Vgl. etwa die Passionssummarien Mk 8,31; 9,31 und 10,33f. oder den ersten Todesbeschluss bereits in Mk 3,6. Doch wäre es zu wenig, nur auf diese spezifischen Analepsen zu achten. Die Passionserzählung strahlt z.B. auch auf die Zeichnung der Jünger-Figur aus, die vom markinischen Jesus immer wieder über die Kreuzesnachfolge und ihre Konsequenzen belehrt werden; dazu vgl. M. Ebner, Kreuzestheologie im Markusevangelium, in: A. Dettwiler/J. Zumstein (Hgg.), Kreuzestheologie im Neuen Testament (WUNT 151), Tübingen 2002, 151–168, der besonders auf

ist Jesu Sterben in dessen ellipsenförmiger Konzeption der eine Brennpunkt, der mit dem anderen – der Proklamation des Anbruchs der Königsherrschaft Gottes durch Jesus – in einer fruchtbaren Spannung steht. Die Faktoren, die zur Erweiterung der Passions- und Ostererzählung durch gezielte Rezeption von Jesusüberlieferung geführt haben, sind hier nicht zu erörtern. Bemerkenswert ist lediglich der Umstand, dass der älteste Evangelist die ihm vorgegebene Passions- und Ostererzählung als Fundament des „Evangeliums Jesu Christi" ansieht – wie analog dazu Paulus das von ihm in 1Kor 15,3b–5a rezipierte Glaubensbekenntnis als den sprachlichen Niederschlag des von ihm proklamierten Evangeliums begreift. Schon das Bekenntnis Mk 16,6 legt es deshalb nahe, das Verhältnis der Passions- und Ostererzählung zu der von Paulus rezipierten Bekenntnistradition näher zu betrachten.

2 Die Bekenntnistradition bei Paulus und Markus

Paulus hat Zugang zu einer breiten Tradition von Glaubenssätzen, die den Tod und die Auferstehung Jesu thematisieren, sowohl in voneinander getrennten Sätzen je für sich, als auch in Doppelaussagen, die beide Heilsdaten miteinander kombinieren. Die erste Form findet sich etwa in 1Kor 8,11[44], Gal 1,4 und Röm 8,32[45] bzw. Röm 3,25[46] sowie Röm 4,24 und 10,9[47], die zweite in 1Thess 4,14[48] und Röm 4,25[49]

---

den Kontrast des gemeindlichen Lebensstils im Namen Jesu zum gewöhnlichen Ringen um Macht und erste Plätze in der umgebenden römischen-hellenistischen Gesellschaft abhebt.
44 1Kor 8,11: „der Bruder, für den *Christus* gestorben ist (δι ὃν Χριστὸς ἀπέθανεν)"; vgl. Röm 14,15: „dein Bruder [...], für den *Christus* starb (ὑπὲρ οὗ Χριστὸς ἀπέθανεν)". M. Hengel, Mahl, 130f.: „Wenn er (sc. Paulus) in den ‚Sterbeformeln' gerne den *Christus*namen mit Aussagen über sein Sterben für uns (o.ä.) verbindet [vgl. Röm 5,6.8ff.; 6,9; 8,34; 14,9.15; 1Kor 8,11; 15,3; Gal 2,21], so mag, das zeigt vor allem die alte Formel 1Kor 15,3, das Wissen dahinterstehen, dass Jesus als *messianischer Prätendent* hingerichtet wurde".
45 Es sind zwei Formeln, die den Dahingabe-Gedanken variieren: Gal 1,4: „der sich selbst für unsere Sünden *dahingegeben* hat, um uns aus der gegenwärtigen bösen Welt zu erretten [...]"; Röm 8,32: „der seinen eigenen Sohn nicht verschont, sondern ihn für uns alle *dahingegeben* hat"; vgl. auch Röm 4,25 (s. Anm. 49).
46 Röm 3,25: „den Gott hingestellt hat als Sühnort durch den Glauben in seinem Blut [...]".
47 Zwei Belege für die Selbständigkeit der Auferweckungsformel: Röm 4,24: „denen, die glauben an den, der Jesus, unseren Herrn, von den Toten auferweckt hat"; Röm 10,9: „Gott hat ihn von den Toten auferweckt"; vgl. auch 2Kor 4,14: „wissend, dass derjenige, der den Herrn Jesus auferweckt hat, auch uns mit Jesus auferwecken und uns zusammen mit euch (vor sich) hinstellen wird".
48 1Thess 4,14: „Wenn wir glauben (πιστεύομεν): *Jesus* ist gestorben und auferstanden (ἀπέθανεν καὶ ἀνέστη), so wird Gott auch die Entschlafenen durch *Jesus* mit ihm führen".

und 8,34⁵⁰. Die Varianz ist erstaunlich. Wollen wir näher erfahren, wie Paulus die interne Logik dieser Sätze verstanden hat, lässt er uns in der Regel allein. Er selbst entfaltet sie nämlich nur selten, da er die Sätze gerne zur Begründung übergeordneter, zumeist soteriologisch relevanter Zusammenhänge als bekannte Argumentationsinstanzen verwendet. Obwohl die Tradition dieser Sätze in der frühen Christenheit eine breite Spur auch neben Paulus hinterlassen hat⁵¹, sucht man sie im Markusevangelium beinahe vergebens. Hängt dies mit der spezifischen Gattung des Erzählwerks zusammen, so fällt die schon erwähnte Rezeption der Auferweckungsformel in Mk 16,6 umso mehr ins Gewicht. Dabei reichen die Bezüge zum urchristlichen Bekenntnis im markinischen Kontext über diese Formel noch hinaus. Nimmt man das ausgebaute Credo 1Kor 15,3b–5a zum Maßstab, lassen sich dessen Etappen: *gestorben – begraben – auferweckt – erschienen* auch bei Markus wieder finden⁵². Das letzte Glied samt seinen beiden Dativen – „er erschien dem Kephas, dann den Zwölf" (ὤφθη Κηφᾷ εἶτα τοῖς δώδεκα) – könnte sich hinter dem Auftrag des jungen Mannes von Mk 16,7 verbergen: „Geht, sagt seinen *Jüngern* und *dem Petrus*: Er geht euch voraus nach Galiläa, dort *werdet ihr ihn sehen*"⁵³. Nicht wenige finden deshalb in diesem Credo gleichsam den Grundriss der alten Passions- und Ostererzählung wieder, der von ihr aufgegriffen und narrativ ausgestaltet worden sei. Auch die Alternative, dass das Credo eine nachträgliche formelhafte Verdichtung der Passions- und Ostererzählung sei, hat ihre Befürworter⁵⁴. Vielleicht handelt es sich aber auch nur um ein gemeinsames Muster – und beide Gestalten urchristlicher Verkündigung sind unabhängig voneinander zu denken. Ein genauer Vergleich von beidem bringt Licht in die Sache.

Der Text 1Kor 15,1–7 (ohne die Paulus selbst betreffenden Aussagen) lautet:

1 a Ich tue euch aber kund, Brüder, *das Evangelium*,
  b das ich euch verkündet habe,
  c das ihr auch angenommen habt,
  d in dem ihr auch steht,

---

49 Röm 4,25: „der *hingegeben* wurde (παρεδόθη) um unserer Verfehlungen wegen und *auferweckt* wurde (ἠγέρθη) um unserer Rechtfertigung willen".
50 Röm 8,34: „Wer will verdammen? *Christus* Jesus, der gestorben ist, ja vielmehr, der auch auferweckt wurde, der auch ist zur Rechten Gottes, der auch für uns eintritt".
51 Vgl. Apg 2,32f.; 3,15; 4,10; 1Petr 1,3.21 etc. – K. Wengst, Formeln.
52 Vgl. O. Schwankl, Auf der Suche nach dem Anfang des Evangeliums. Von 1Kor 15,3–5 zum Johannes-Prolog, in: BZ 40 (1996), 39–60, hier 46–48.
53 *Kephas* im NT nur Joh 1,42 sowie in 1Kor 1,12; 3,22 etc. und in Gal 1,18; 2,9.11.14.
54 Ein Beispiel hierfür gibt es: Apg 13,29–31 bietet eine derartiges Kondensat einer vorgegebenen Erzählung, nämlich der Lukaspassion, in Gestalt eines Summariums.

2 a durch das ihr auch gerettet werdet,
  b wenn ihr an dem Wortlaut festhaltet,
  c den ich euch verkündet habe,
  d es sei denn, ihr wäret umsonst zum Glauben gekommen.
3 a Ich habe euch nämlich in erster Linie weitergegeben,
  b was ich auch übernommen habe:
  c Dass Christus gestorben ist für unsere Sünden (ὑπὲρ τῶν ἁμαρτιῶν)
    gemäß den Schriften
4 a und dass er begraben worden ist (ἐτάφη),
  b und dass er auferweckt ist (ἐγήγερται) am dritten Tage
    gemäß den Schriften
5 a und dass er erschienen ist dem Kephas,
  b dann (εἶτα) den Zwölf.
6 a Danach (ἔπειτα) ist er erschienen mehr als fünfhundert ‚Brüdern' auf einmal,
  b von denen die meisten am Leben sind bis jetzt,
  c einige aber sind entschlafen.
7 a Danach (ἔπειτα) ist er erschienen dem Jakobus,
  b dann (εἶτα) den Aposteln allen.

Die Paulus vorgegebene Formel[55] – er „zitiert" sie „als eine im Wortlaut feststehende formelhafte (Kurz-)Fassung der von ihm verkündigten guten Nachricht"[56] – besitzt eine narrative Struktur, die durch das wiederholte „und" sowie die temporalen Konjunktionen „dann" und „danach" noch verstärkt wird[57]. Die erzählte „Geschichte" „Christi"[58], die von seinem Sterben bis hin zu seinen österlichen Erscheinungen reicht, scheint sie auf den ersten Blick der Passions- und Ostererzählung an die Seite zu stellen. Allerdings ist ihre vorrangige Intention nicht die, eine „Geschichte" zu erzählen, sondern sie zu deuten. Das zeigt sich schon an der näheren Bestimmung der Sterbensaussage mittels der Formel „*für unsere Sünden*". Auch die Markuspassion verwendet das ἀπέθανεν, aber nicht-theologisch (Mk 15,44). Vor allem übergeht das Credo – wie überhaupt die Sterbensformeln – die konkret-historische Todesart, die zu nennen für die Passionserzählung selbst-

---

[55] Sie umfasste ursprünglich wohl nur V.3c-5a. Danach wechselt der Stil; auch hat V.5b (im Unterschied zu V.5a) in der ersten Hälfte der Formel keine Entsprechung. Mit V.4b.5a vgl. zudem Lk 24,34: ὄντως ἠγέρθη ὁ κύριος καὶ ὤφθη Σίμωνι.
[56] A. Lindemann, Der Erste Korintherbrief (HNT 9/I), Tübingen 2000, 330. „Über den Sitz im Leben" lässt sich nichts sagen, insbesondere ist ein Zusammenhang mit der Taufe nicht erkennbar".
[57] Dass die so aufgereihten Aussagen eine Geschichte ergeben, betont F. Mußner, Zur stilistischen und semantischen Struktur der Formel von 1Kor 15,3-5 (1977), in: F. Mußner, Jesus von Nazareth im Umfeld Israels und der Urkirche. Gesammelte Aufsätze, hg. von M. Theobald (WUNT 111), Tübingen 1999, 190-200; er spricht von einer „enumerativen Redeweise".
[58] A. Lindemann, 1Kor, 330: „Χριστός wird als Name behandelt, wie das Fehlen des Art. zeigt (der Sprachgebrauch ist bei Paulus uneinheitlich)".

verständlich ist. Es spricht nicht vom „Skandalon des Kreuzes" (Gal 5,11; vgl. 1Kor 1,23), sondern deutet den Tod Jesu als ein „unsere Sünden" hinwegnehmendes heilvolles Sterben. Die beigesellte zweite Aussage *„und dass er begraben wurde"* wird deshalb auch keine historisch interessierte Aussage treffen[59], sondern unter Aufnahme der üblichen Sitte des Begräbnisses nur die Todesaussage bestätigen[60]: Im Blick auf die anschließende Auferweckungsaussage soll die Gewissheit des Todes Christi festgestellt werden. Dass die Glaubensformel genauere Kenntnis über die Vorgänge bei der Grablegung Jesu voraussetzt oder Paulus selbst sie besaß, lässt sich ihr nicht entnehmen[61]. Dagegen spricht auch ihre neutrale Terminologie, die von den konkreten Termini der Grablegungserzählungen markant abweicht[62].

Beachtliche Differenzen ergeben sich auch beim zweiten Aussagenpaar V.4a. b. „Das ganz ungewöhnliche Perf." ἐγήγερται[63] verweist „auf die andauernde Wirkung". „Betont wird nicht der einmal geschehene Vorgang, sondern es wird von dem gesprochen, der jetzt der Auferweckte ist und also als der gegenwärtig Lebendige bekannt wird"[64]. Damit scheint sich die temporale Angabe „am dritten

---

59 Da die Todesstrafe für Majestätsverbrechen (*crimen maiestatis*) meist über den Tod hinaus reichte – den Hingerichteten wurde die Totenehrung, das Begräbnis, in aller Regel rechtlich versagt (vgl. Dig. 48,24,1 [Ulpianus 9, De officiis Proconsulis: „Hodie autem eorum, in quos animadvertitur, corpora non aliter sepeliuntur, quam si fuerit petitum et permissum, et nonnumquam non permittitur, maxime maiestatis causa damnatorum"]), könnte V.4a genau dem entgegensteuern: Jesus wurde ehrenvoll bestattet!
60 Darin ist sie strukturell mit der vierten Aussage vergleichbar, die analog zum ersten Aussagenpaar die vorangehende dritte bekräftigt.
61 So aber M. Hengel, Das Begräbnis Jesu bei Paulus und leibliche Auferstehung aus dem Grabe (2001), in: M. Hengel, Kleine Schriften IV, 386–450; zutreffend A. Lindemann, 1Kor, 331.
62 ἐτάφη: Die Verben θάπτω, τάφος, ταφή begegnen kaum in den alten Überlieferungen vom Begräbnis Jesu, erst in späteren redaktionellen Aussagen: τάφος: Mt 27,61.64.66; EvPetr 24.31; ἐνταφιάζειν: Joh 19,40; θάπτω: EvPetr 5.23; ταφή: EvPetr 3. Dafür dominieren (auch in der mkn. Erzählung von der „Auffindung des leeren Grabes") μνῆμα: Mk 15,46; Lk 23,53; EvPetr 30.31.32 und μνημεῖον: Mk 15,46; 16,2.3.8; Mt 27,60; Lk 23,55; Joh 19,41f.; EvPetr 34. – Die Termini μνῆμα (W. Bauer, Griechisch-deutsches Wörterbuch zu den Schriften des Neuen Testaments und der frühchristlichen Literatur, Berlin/New York ⁶1988, 1061: „eigtl. *das Erinnerungszeichen* bes. für Verstorbene ..., dann allg. d. G r a b a n l a g e, d. G r a b") und μνημεῖον („eigtl. *das Gedächtnismal*", „d. D e n k m a l", „d. G r a b k a m m e r, d. G r a b") werden in der Passionserzählung deshalb bevorzugt gebraucht, um damit die Art des Grabes = Grabkammer zu bezeichnen (vgl. auch Mk 16,6: „seht der Ort, wo sie hin hingelegt haben"); vgl. auch M. Theobald, Angefochtener Osterglaube – im Neuen Testament und heute, in: ThQ 193 (2013) 4-31, hier 24-27.
63 Mk hat die Aoristform, wie Lk 24,34: ἠγέρθη.
64 A. Lindemann, 1Kor, 331; eine Perfektform in der Auferweckungsformel sonst nur noch 2Tim 2,8, dann auch in der Auslegung unseres Credos in V.12–20.

Tag" zu reiben, die aber auch nicht in erster Linie eine chronologische, sondern eine theologische Zeitansage trifft, entsprechend dem nachgestellten Hinweis „gemäß den Schriften": Hos 6,2 (wie auch anderen Aussagen der Schrift und der Tradition) zufolge ist es Gottes Art, nach kurzer Frist (= nach zwei Tagen) rettend einzugreifen. In der vormarkinischen Passions- und Ostererzählung ist diese theologische Aussage narrativ in die tatsächliche Abfolge dreier Tage umgesetzt[65], ohne dass die Zahl „drei" eine Erwähnung findet[66]. In jedem Fall ist diese chronologische Veranschaulichung gegenüber der theo-logischen Aussage entstehungsgeschichtlich sekundär. Sprachlich anders gefasst ist auch die Erscheinungsaussage V.5, die den aramäischen, nicht den griechischen Namen des behaupteten Erstzeugen (wie Mk 16,7) benutzt und von den „Zwölf" spricht, nicht (wie in Mk 16,7) unspezifisch von den „Jüngern"[67]. Zu berücksichtigen ist bei einer Verhältnisbestimmung von vorpaulinischem Credo und vormarkinischer Passions- und Ostererzählung auch die Möglichkeit, dass die Rede des jungen Mannes ursprünglich nur Mk 16,6 enthielt, nicht aber V.7, den dann der Evangelist aus seinem anderweitig vermittelten Wissen von einer Ersterscheinung des Auferweckten vor Petrus und den anderen Jüngern redaktionell nachgetragen hätte.[68]

Für eine Gesamtbeurteilung des Vergleichs, der nicht nur sprachliche, sondern auch konzeptionelle Differenzen zwischen dem Credo 1Kor 15,3b–5a und der alten Passionserzählung zu Tage befördert, ist natürlich auch noch einmal an deren oben schon genannten Angelpunkt bei Dtn 21,23 zu erinnern. Während die Erzählung vom „Skandalon des Kreuzes" ausgeht, das das messianische Bekenntnis zu Jesus zu vereiteln scheint, gründet das Credo in einer soteriologischen Deutung seines gewaltsamen Todes, die diesen – unabhängig von seiner anstö-

---

65 Fortan formen die drei Tage – Todestag Jesu, Sabbat, Ostermorgen – eine Art *mythische Urzeit* des christlichen Glaubens, die ihn über die Begehung der liturgischen Erinnerung zutiefst prägen sollte.
66 Vgl. aber Mk 8,31; 9,31; 10,34: „nach drei Tagen". Apg 10,40: „diesen hat Gott am dritten Tag erweckt und hat ihn erscheinen lassen [...]". Zum Motiv des „dritten Tags" vgl. W. Schrage, Der erste Brief an die Korinther, 4. Teilband: 1Kor 15,1–16,24 (EKK VII/4), Zürich/Neukirchen-Vluyn 2001, 41–43.
67 Einen weiteren Aspekt nennt K. Berger, Theologiegeschichte, 634: Das MkEv „gründet [...] die Passions- und Osterüberlieferung auf das Zeugnis der Frauen, insbesondere der Maria Magdalena. Damit wird ein Trägerkreis erschlossen, der auch in der Osterüberlieferung (vgl. 1Kor 15,1–9) bisher keine Rolle spielte".
68 So für viele D. Lührmann, Das Markusevangelium (HNT 3), Tübingen 1987, 270; anders F. Schleritt, Der Jüngling im Grab als Epigone des Auferstandenen. Zum Verhältnis der Geschichte vom Grabbesuch der Frauen zur Überlieferung von der Erscheinung Jesu vor Maria Magdalena, in: M. Janßen (Hg.), Frühes Christentum und Religionsgeschichtliche Schule (NTOA 95), Göttingen 2011, 83-95, hier 88.

ßigen historischen Gestalt – in die Dialektik von Sterben und Auferstehen, Tod und Leben hineinstellt. Damit spricht es ein weiteres Publikum an, gerade auch ein hellenistisches, das Bescheid weiß über sterbende und wieder zum Leben kommende göttliche Gestalten.

Kurzum: Weder scheint das Credo die Basis der Passions- und Ostererzählung noch umgekehrt deren nachträgliche Zusammenfassung gewesen zu sein, sondern es ist eher von einem „common pattern" auszugehen, das in beiden Verkündigungsformen eine jeweils sehr eigenständige Ausprägung erhalten hat: als Bekenntnis und als Gründungserzählung des Glaubens[69].

3 Die Schriften Israels als Ferment der Passionserinnerung bei Paulus und Markus

Das vorpaulinische Bekenntnis 1Kor 15,3b–5a verweist zweimal, in V. 3c und 4b, pauschal auf die „Schriften"[70]. Auch die Markuspassion tut dies an markanter Stelle: „*aber damit die Schriften erfüllt würden*" (Mk 14,49). Entfaltet werden diese Hinweise nicht. Sie signalisieren, dass sowohl das Sterben Jesu wie sein Auferstehen dem Heilswillen Gottes entsprechen, wie ihn die Schriften Israels, in denen sich die frühen Anhänger Jesu wie selbstverständlich bewegen, dokumentieren.

Aber bereits vor diesem expliziten Hinweis auf die „Schriften" lebt die Passions- und Ostererzählung aus der Schrift, ja diese ist gleichsam ihre Matrix, greifbar nicht nur an zahlreichen Zitaten, Anspielungen und biblischen Motiven, sondern auch an Grundmustern wie dem der *passio iusti*[71]. Vor allem folgende Schrifttexte sind von Bedeutung: Ps 22; 41; 42/43; 51; 69; Sach 12,10; 13,7; Jes 53,7.

Wer nach möglichen Überschneidungen im passionstheologischen Gebrauch dieser und weiterer alttestamentlicher Texte zwischen der Evangelientradition

---

[69] D.C. Allison, Resurrecting Jesus. The earliest Christian Tradition and its Interpreters, New York/London 2005, 239: „Amid all the diversity, we seem to have variations upon a common pattern. Paul is perhaps not so far removed from the Gospel traditions as sometimes implied".
[70] Vgl. hierzu E.B. Aitken, Death, 32, zur Sterbensformel: „if we move away from the perspective that sees the scriptures of Israel functioning as proofs or testimonies within the early stages of speaking of Jesus' death, then we can locate Isaiah 53 among other songs and stories that provide the language and patterns for the new story about Jesus".
[71] Auch formal scheinen diese Texte die alte Passionserzählung geprägt zu haben. Zu denken ist hier vor allem an das Stilmittel der Selbstmonologe der Frevler in Weish 2,10–20; 5,4; Ps 22,9; 35,21.25; 36,2 u.ö., das dazu dient, die Feindschaft der Frevler gegen den Gerechten gleichsam literarisch zu „inszenieren". Das tut auf ihre Weise auch die alte Passionserzählung: vgl. Mk 14,2; 15,29f.31c.32a.b.

und Paulus fragt, wird vom Ergebnis seiner Recherche enttäuscht sein: „Das einzige Schriftzitat des Paulus [...], das sich auf das Geschehen der Passion bezieht", ist Ps 69,10bLXX in Röm 15,2f.⁷². Dort heißt es: „Jeder von uns soll seinem Nächsten gefallen zum Guten, zum Aufbau. Denn auch Christus hat nicht sich selbst gefallen, sondern wie es in der Schrift heißt: *Die Schmähungen derer, die dich schmähen* (οἱ ὀνειδισμοὶ τῶν ὀνειδιζόντων σε), *sind auf mich gefallen*". Leider gibt das Zitat samt seiner kontextuellen Einbettung, zu der auch die schrifthermeneutische Erklärung V.4 gehört, nicht eindeutig zu erkennen, ob die passionstheologische Lesart des Psalms Paulus schon vorgegeben war⁷³ oder auf ihn selbst zurückgeht⁷⁴. Ersteres ist nicht auszuschließen, da Ps 69 auch in der alten Passionsüberlieferung der Evangelien eine wichtige Rolle spielt⁷⁵. Ob das mit Dale C.

---

72 D.-A. Koch, Die Schrift als Zeuge des Evangeliums. Untersuchungen zur Verwendung und zum Verständnis der Schrift bei Paulus (BHTh 69), Tübingen 1986, 324.
73 So R.B. Hays, Christ Prays the Psalms. Israel's Psalter as Matrix of Early Christology, in: R.B. Hays, The Conversion of the Imagination. Paul as Interpreter of Israel's Scripture, Grand Rapids 2005, 101–118; Paulus begründe das Verständnis des Psalms als eines Gebets Christi nicht eigens, sondern setze es stillschweigend voraus. Ebenso K.T. Kleinknecht, Der leidende Gerechtfertigte. Die alttestamentlich-jüdische Tradition vom ‚leidenden Gerechten' und ihre Rezeption bei Paulus (WUNT II/13), Tübingen ²1988, 367: „Die Art und Weise der Verwendung des Psalmzitats (es steht nicht in einem christologischen Lehrstück, sondern dient in einer Gemeindeparänese als christologisches Argument!) zeigt deutlich, dass diese Deutung der Passion nicht von Paulus ad hoc neu entworfen, sondern sowohl für ihn als auch für die römische Gemeinde (bei der das Argument ja wirken soll) eine geläufige Denkfigur darstellt".
74 D.-A. Koch, Schrift, 325, bezweifelt wegen der „ausdrückliche(n) Begründung der christologischen Verwendung von Ψ 68,10b" in V.4, „dass eine passionstheologische Interpretation von Ψ 68 insgesamt z. Zt. des Pls bereits selbstverständlich war". Zum Verständnis des Psalmworts durch Paulus führt er ebd. 326 aus, dass er es „zum einen als Verweis auf die Passion überhaupt" anführe, „und zum anderen als Interpretation der Passion im Sinne des οὐκ ἑαυτῷ ἀρέσκειν", nicht aber im Sinne des „Sühneleidens Christi" (so U. Wilckens) oder des „Erleidens rebellischer Lästerungen [...], das Jesu irdische Geschichte im ganzen bestimmte" (so E. Käsemann, An die Römer [HNT 8a], Tübingen ²1974, 366).
75 Wichtig ist die Anspielung auf Ps 69,22 („sie geben mir Galle zu essen und Essig zu trinken für meinen Durst") in Mk 15,23; Mt 27,34 (hier verdeutlicht) und Mk 15,36; vgl. Mt 27,48; Lk 23,36; Joh 19,28; EvPetr 5,16. Der intertextuelle Bezug zu Ps 69 dürfte schon zum Urgestein der Passionserzählung gehören. Beachtlich ist auch die Beobachtung von D.C. Allison, Constructing, 408: „Given the previous two allusions, one wonders whether the use of ὀνειδίζω (‚to reproach') in Mark 15:32 (‚Those who were crucified with him also taunted him') and in its Matthean parallel (27:44) might echo Ps 69, where (in the LXX) ὀνειδίζω occurs (68:10) and the related noun ὀνειδισμός (‚reproach') appears repeatedly (vv. 8,10,11,20,21 [it appears no more than once in any other psalm])". – Später kommt es zu regelrechten Zitationen: von Ps 69,5 in Joh 15,25 (LXX), von Ps 69,10a („der Eifer um dein Haus hat mich gefressen") in Joh 2,17, von Ps 69,26 in Apg 1,20 (Judas) und Ps 69,31–33 in 1Clem 52,2. Doch vgl. schon Röm 11,9f. mit dem Zitat von Ps 69,23f. – Zur Rolle des Psalms in der Passionsüberlieferung vgl. E. Flessman-van Leer, Die

Allison als Indiz dafür gewertet werden kann, dass Paulus eine ihrer Fassungen gekannt hat[76], lässt sich meines Erachtens nicht entscheiden.

Ansonsten blickt Paulus in seinem „leidenstheologischen" Gebrauch der Schrift nicht spezifisch auf Christus, sondern auf die christliche Existenz überhaupt. So etwa in Röm 8,36 (= Ps 43,23LXX), wo er fragt: „Wer wird uns trennen von der Liebe Christi? Bedrängnis oder Angst oder Verfolgung oder Hunger oder Blöße oder Gefahr oder Schwert? Wie geschrieben steht: *Um deinetwillen werden wir getötet den ganzen Tag; wir sind geachtet wie Schlachtschafe*"[77].

Insgesamt lässt sich mit Dietrich-Alex Koch festhalten: „[D]er Impuls, den das christologische Formelgut für eine christologische Schriftinterpretation hätte liefern können, wird von Paulus nicht aufgenommen. Nirgends sieht sich Paulus veranlasst, das doppelte κατὰ τὰς γραφάς von 1Kor 15,3b–5 in seinen Briefen durch die Anführung einzelner Zitate zu konkretisieren. Die Schriftgemäßheit von Christi Tod und Auferstehung ist für Paulus selbstverständlich gegeben, wie aus einigen christologisch verstandenen Zitaten indirekt hervorgeht, aber ihr Aufweis ist nie selbst der Zweck seiner Schriftanführung"[78].

Interpretation der Passionsgeschichte vom Alten Testament aus, in: F. Viering (Hg.), Zur Bedeutung des Todes Jesu. Exegetische Beiträge, Gütersloh 1967, 79–96, hier 91–94.

76 D.C. Allison, Constructing, 408: „if Paul uses ὀνειδισμός und ὀνειδίζω, the latter appears likewise in Mark 15:32, of the thieves reproaching Jesus (cf. Matt 27:44). Maybe, then, when Paul penned Rom 15:3, he had in mind what most of his subsequent readers have had in mind, namely, something like the tableau in Mark 15 and parallels"; ebd. 409 Anm. 79: „Perhaps one should note Paul's introduction to his citation of Ps 69: ‚ὁ χριστός did not please himself.' In Mark 15:32, Jesus is mockingly reproached as ‚ὁ χριστός, the king of Israel.' Is this a coincidence? Perhaps one should also note that, in Rom 15:1, Paul employs βαστάζω (‚bear the failings of the weak'), and that Luke 14:27 and John 19:17 use this of carrying a cross (cf. Chariton, *Chaereas and Callirhoë* 4.2.7; 3.10; Artemidorus, *Onir.* 2.56). In Aquila Isa 53:11, moreover, the suffering servant is the subject of this verb (cf. Matt 8:17). So some early Christians might have divined in βαστάζω an echo of Jesus' passion. The same verb reappears in Gal 6:17, where Paul ‚bears' the ‚stigmata' of Jesus".

77 Vgl. auch 2Kor 4,13 mit Ps 115,1LXX; zuweilen trifft man auf die Ansicht, „Paulus beziehe sich nicht nur auf den isolierten Psalmvers, sondern auf den ganzen Psalm, der von Leiden, Rettung und Dank handelt. Sicher ist das nicht": T. Schmeller, Der zweite Brief an die Korinther (2Kor 1,1–7,4) (EKK VIII/1), Neukirchen-Vluyn/Ostfildern 2010, 265; ebd. 358f. zu 2Kor 6,9, wo Paulus auf Ps 117,17f.LXX anspielt. Zur Thematik insgesamt vgl. auch K.T. Kleinknecht, Gerechtfertigte, 193–376; ferner C. Dietzfelbinger, Der Sohn. Skizzen zur Christologie und Anthropologie des Paulus (BThSt 118), Neukirchen-Vluyn 2011, 320f.

78 D.-A. Koch, Schrift, 286.

4 Weitere Gestalten der Erinnerung an die Passion Jesu bei Paulus

Seit geraumer Zeit meint man in einzelnen Passagen der Briefe des Paulus Indizien dafür erkennen zu können, dass er von den letzten Tagen Jesu mehr wusste, als gemeinhin angenommen wird. Sollten die beanspruchten Indizien belastbar sein, stellt sich die Frage nach der Herkunft seines Wissens: Bezog er es konkret aus der vor-evangeliaren Passionsüberlieferung oder sonst wie aus dem frühchristlichen Gedächtnis[79]? Die fraglichen Passagen werden unter (1) kurz vorgestellt und diskutiert. Zwei Deutungsmuster des Todes Jesu, die gleichfalls mit der vor-evangeliaren Passionserzählung indirekt zusammenhängen könnten (2), werden anschließend besprochen.

4.1 Passions-Memoria bei Paulus?

Entsprechend der mutmaßlichen Sequenz der Erinnerungsfragmente in der Passionsmemoria beginnen wir mit der Abendmahlsparadosis und schließen mit Angaben zur Kreuzigung Jesu.

(1) „In der Nacht, in der er ausgeliefert wurde". Zu 1Kor 11,23

In 1Kor 11,23–25 zitiert bekanntlich Paulus die Abendmahlsparadosis „als Norm für die Gestaltung des Herrenmahls"[80]. Sie beginnt mit der narrativen Notiz: „Der Herr Jesus nahm *in der Nacht, in der er ausgeliefert wurde*, Brot und sagte Dank [...]". Gewiss hebt die Zeitangabe „das Traditionsstück von mythischen Kultlegenden ab"[81], aber sie ist mehr als nur eine reine Datumsangabe. Zweierlei ist zu bedenken.

Zum einen resümiert sie, *was* in jener Nacht geschah: die „Dahingabe" des Herrn. Der Terminus der „Dahingabe" ist traditionsgeschichtlich zu sehr gefüllt, als dass er in erster Linie oder gar ausschließlich den Verrat Jesu durch Judas bezeichnen könnte. An Judas hängt „kein Interesse, da sein Name sonst genannt wäre. Auch wird nicht vermerkt, an wen Jesus ausgeliefert wurde". „Vermutlich soll das Geschehen der Dahingabe als solches (vgl. das Imperfekt) ausgesagt

---

[79] Immerhin war ja Paulus drei Jahre nach seiner Berufung fünfzehn Tage bei Kephas in Jerusalem und wird dort auch manches über Jesus selbst und dessen letzte Tage gehört haben: vgl. Gal 1,18.
[80] C. Wolff, Der erste Brief des Paulus an die Korinther. Zweiter Teil: Auslegung der Kapitel 8–16 (ThHK VII/2), Berlin ³1990, 83.
[81] Ebd.; ebenso W. Schrage, 1Kor III, 31; ihm zufolge ist diese Einleitungswendung „nach den meisten schon der Tradition zuzuschreiben".

werden"[82]. Dabei wird Paulus vor allem an das Handeln Gottes gedacht haben (vgl. Röm 4,25; 8,32).

Zum anderen ist das *Wann* der „Dahingabe" von Belang, nicht im Sinne einer „historisch-chronologischen" Angabe[83], sondern einer liturgischen – der Gattung des Traditionsstücks als „Kultätiologie" gemäß, deren Funktion darin bestand, die Mahlfeier zu normieren. Um welche Mahlfeier es dabei ging, lässt sich nur vermuten; ursprünglich vielleicht um das Mahl im Rahmen der jährlichen „judenchristlichen" Paschafeier, da die einleitende Wendung „in der Nacht (ἐν τῇ νυκτί), in der er ausgeliefert wurde" an Ex 12,12 gemahnt[84]. Damit wäre freilich vorrangig etwas über den ursprünglichen „Sitz im Leben" der „Kultätiologie" gesagt (bevor sie dann – auch Paulus zufolge – die Feier des „Herrenmahls" am „ersten Tag der Woche" normierte), aber noch nichts über den Charakter des historischen Abschiedsmahls Jesu selbst[85]. Vielmehr würde die Rede von der „Nacht" die Stunden in Erinnerung rufen, in denen Gott heilvoll handelte, einst beim Exodus, dann in der „Dahingabe" Jesu, die jetzt in der Feier des Gedenkens an ihn gegenwärtig wird.

Fragen wir zuletzt, was die „Kultätiologie" an *historischer* Passions-Memoria weitertransportiert – ganz abgesehen von der hier nicht zu behandelnden Frage nach dem jesuanischen Kern der eucharistischen Gabe-Worte –, sind die Ant-

---

[82] Ebd. 84, mit Verweis auf W. Popkes, Christus traditus (AThANT 49), Zürich/Stuttgart 1967, 205–211: „Ob der Akzent dabei auf dem göttlichen oder dem menschlichen Handeln liegt, kann nicht mehr erschlossen werden" (210). Vgl. auch die Texte oben in Anm. 45.49 sowie Apg 3,13.
[83] Von einer solchen spricht aber C. Wolff, 1Kor, 83, und meint, dass aus ihr hervorgehe, „dass das Traditionsstück die wesentlichen Ereignisse der Passion Jesu als bekannt voraussetzt (vgl. dazu das Imperfekt παρεδίδετο, das den Verlauf der Handlung ausdrückt)".
[84] Ex 12,12: ἐν τῇ νυκτὶ ταύτῃ; vgl. auch V.29f.42: ἐκείνη ἡ νύξ. – Aufschlussreich ist Apg 12, 6: „in jener Nacht (τῇ νυκτὶ ἐκείνῃ)": Gemeint ist sehr wahrscheinlich die Pascha-Nacht, in der die Jerusalemer Gemeinde im Gedenken an Jesus versammelt war (die synoptischen Abendmahltexte sprechen übrigens nicht von der Nacht, sondern vom „Abend" als der traditionellen Zeit des Pascha-Mahls: vgl. Mk 14,17 par. Mt 26,20; offener Lk 22,14: „als die Stunde gekommen war"). Ein weiteres Indiz für die ursprüngliche Verbindung der Überlieferung vom Herrenmahl mit einer „judenchristlichen" nächtlichen Paschafeier bietet der (zweifache) Erinnerungsbefehl 1Kor 11,24f., der „an die Memoria-Funktion des Passafestes" anknüpfen dürfte, „das in Ex 12,14 als ein μνημόσυνον ‚Erinnerungsmittel' (hebr.: לְזִכָּרוֹן ‚zur Erinnerung') bezeichnet wird; vgl. darüber hinaus Ex 13,2–10; Dtn 16,3 (‚damit ihr euch erinnert [ἵνα μνησθῆτε] an den Tag eures Auszugs aus Ägyptenland alle Tage eures Lebens'); Jub 49,6f.; Philo, De specialibus legibus 2,146): M. Wolter, Das Lukasevangelium (HNT 5), Tübingen 2008, 706; M. Theobald, Paschamahl und Eucharistiefeier. Zur heilsgeschichtlichen Relevanz der Abendmahlsszenerie bei Lukas (Lk 22,14–38), in: M. Theobald/R. Hoppe (Hgg.), „Für alle Zeiten zur Erinnerung" (Jos 4,7). Beiträge zu einer biblischen Gedächtniskultur (SBS 209), Stuttgart 2006, 133–180, hier 168–170.
[85] Nach wie vor spricht vieles für die johanneische Chronologie der Passionsgeschehnisse, so dass das letzte Mahl Jesu mit den Seinen kein Pesachmahl gewesen sein dürfte.

worten der Forschung äußerst kontrovers: Während etwa Wolfgang Schrage im παραδιδόναι „eine auf ein einziges Wort verdichtete Kurzformel für die ganze Passion Jesu" erblickt mit der Konsequenz, dass „sich nicht sagen" lässt, „wie weit die geschichtliche Kenntnis vom Passionsgeschehen bei Paulus oder gar den Korinthern reicht"[86], schließt Martin Hengel aus allgemeinen historischen Erwägungen, aber auch aus dem von ihm als „Abendmahls*bericht*" behandelten Stück, dass „Paulus und die Korinther die Passionsgeschichte bis in Details hinein gekannt haben"[87]. Wer indes das mangelnde Interesse der Tradenten an einer genauen Bestimmung des Charakters des letzten Mahls in Rechnung stellt, wird gegenüber dieser historischen Auslegung doch eher zurückhaltend bleiben.

(2) Das dreimalige Bittgebet des Paulus und Gethsemani

Das gilt erst recht bei einer passionshistorischen Auswertung von 2Kor 12,7–9: „Deshalb, damit ich mich nicht überhebe, wurde mir ein Stachel für das Fleisch gegeben, ein Satansengel, damit er mich mit der Faust schlage (κολαφίζῃ), damit ich mich nicht überhebe. Seinetwegen *bat ich dreimal den Herrn* (τρὶς τὸν κύριον παρεκάλεσα), dass er von mir ablasse. Und er hat zu mir gesagt: ‚Es reicht dir meine Gnade; denn die Kraft wird in Schwachheit vollendet'". Die dreimalige Bitte des Paulus um Befreiung von den Schlägen des Satans erinnert die Ausleger seit langem an das dreimalige Gebet Jesu in Gethsemani (Mk 14,25–41 par. Mt 26,39–44)[88]. Dale C. Allison geht noch einen Schritt weiter und behauptet, aufgrund der Parallelen läge es nahe, dass Paulus auf die Gethsemani-Episode *anspiele*[89]. Doch schon Hans Windisch erklärte mit Hinweis darauf, dass das dreimalige Bitten ein „geläufiger Brauch" gewesen sei, „dem er ebenso wie Jesus (bzw. der Evangelist, der die Perikope ausgestaltete) folgte": „Dass P(aulus) Jesu Beten in Gethsemane sich zum Vorbild genommen haben sollte, ist wenig wahrscheinlich"[90]. Auch die

---

[86] W. Schrage, 1Kor III, 31f.
[87] M. Hengel, Mahl, 468.
[88] Genannt seien nur J.A. Bengel, Gnomon Novi Testamenti. Secundum editionem tertiam (1773), Berlin 1860, 462: „*ter*, ut ipse Dominus in monte oliveti"; H. Windisch, Paulus und Christus (UNT 24), Leipzig 1934, 235; ders., Der zweite Korintherbrief (Neudruck der Auflage 1924), hg. von G. Strecker (KEK 6), Göttingen 1970, 390f.; C. Wolff, Der zweite Brief des Paulus an die Korinther (ThHK VIII), Berlin 1989, 248. Weitere Literatur nennt D.C. Allison, Constructing, 415 Anm. 102.
[89] D.C. Allison, Constructing, 415–423; 416: „Although such considerations hardly establish beyond reasonable doubt that 2 Cor 12:7–9 betrays acquaintance with the episode of Jesus in Gethsemane, they do move one to wonder"; ebenso T. Heckel, Kraft in Schwachheit. Untersuchungen zu 2Kor 10–13 (WUNT 2/56), Tübingen 1993, 85 Anm. 154.
[90] H. Windisch, 2Kor, 389; mit zahlreichen Belegen aus dem Judentum (z.B. Ber 32b: „wenn ein Mensch sieht, dass er betet, ohne erhört zu werden, so bete er immer aufs neue"), der griechischen Religion (z.B. Euripides, Hippolytus, 46: μηδὲν μάταιον *εἰς τρὶς εὔξασθαι*) und zur

verstreuten sprachlichen Hinweise, die Allison aus anderen paulinischen Texten zusammenträgt, machen seine Annahme nicht wahrscheinlicher.

(3) Die Verantwortung der Jerusalemer Autoritäten für den Tod Jesu

Im 1. Thessalonicherbrief vergleicht Paulus die Nachstellungen, die seine Adressaten von ihren Landsleuten erleiden, mit denen, die die Gemeinden in Judäa von den ihrigen erleiden, das heißt: von den „Juden, *die den Herrn Jesus getötet haben* und die Propheten", und fügt hinzu: „und die uns verfolgten und Gott nicht gefallen und allen Menschen Feind sind, indem sie uns wehren, den Heiden zu predigen, damit diese gerettet werden, womit sie das Maß ihrer Sünden unablässig voll machen. Es ist aber das Gericht über sie gänzlich hereingebrochen" (1Thess 2,15f.). Geht der Trend der Forschung inzwischen wieder dahin, diese Verse nicht als sekundär interpoliert auszuscheiden, sondern Paulus zu belassen, so steht andererseits fest, dass er sich hier eines Topos bedient – des Topos des Prophetenmords –, den er nicht nur um seine eigenen Erfahrungen ergänzt, sondern auch auf die Tötung Jesu bezieht[91]. Er spricht nicht von dessen Kreuzigung – das hätte die Verantwortlichkeit der *Römer* assoziiert –, sondern von seiner „Tötung", die er der Verantwortung „der *Juden*" auflastet. Auch wenn man das τῶν Ἰουδαίων auf der Linie des vorangehenden Hinweises auf die „Gemeinden Gottes, die *in Judäa* sind", auf dessen Einwohner – die Judäer – bezieht, bleibt es doch eine polemische Pauschalisierung. Paulus gibt zu erkennen, dass ihm die mutmaßliche Verantwortung der Jerusalemer Autoritäten am Verfahren gegen Jesus, die auch schon der Archetyp der Passions- und Ostererzählung behauptet, bekannt war[92] – aus der Passionserzählung selbst oder aus mündlicher Überlieferung (vgl. Gal 1,18), muss offen bleiben.

Dreizahl (Num 6,24ff.: dreimaliger Segen; Gen 9,25ff.: dreimaliger Fluch; Mt 7,7: dreimalige Aufforderung zum Bitten; Apg 10,16; Joh 21,17 etc.). – D.C. Allison, Constructing, 415, zitiert nur die jüdische Sitte des dreimal täglichen Gebets, um sie als Parallele zu Recht zu verwerfen.

91 O.H. Steck, Israel und das gewaltsame Geschick der Propheten. Untersuchungen zur Überlieferung des deuteronomistischen Geschichtsbildes im Alten Testament (WMANT 23), Neukirchen-Vluyn 1967, 274–278. – Ausdrücklich von der *Kreuzigung* Jesu spricht Paulus *nicht* im Brief (vgl. noch 1Thess 4,14; 5,1), vielleicht deshalb nicht, weil das Thema Konfliktpotential mit den Römern enthielt (vgl. auch unten Anm. 104). – Der Einbezug der Tötung Jesu in den Topos vom Prophetenmord begegnet schon im Spruchevangelium: vgl. oben Anm. 14. Zu 1Thess 2,14-16 vgl. zuletzt R. Kampling, Und so kam Paulus unter die Antisemiten. Transformation des Verstehens in der Auslegung von 1Thess 2,14-16 im 19. Jahrhundert, in: W. Eisele/C. Schaefer/H.-U. Weidemann (Hgg.), Aneignung durch Transformation (FS M. Theobald) (HBS 74), Freiburg 2013, 358–374.

92 So auch C. Dietzfelbinger, Sohn: Auch wenn „von einem gerichtlichen Verfahren gegen Jesus, sei es vor dem Synhedrium, sei es vor Pilatus, bei ihm [s.c. Paulus] nicht die Rede" ist (155), ist doch deutlich, „dass er von den ‚Juden', genauer von den Juden in Gestalt ihrer obersten Behörde als der treibenden Kraft bei Verurteilung und Tod Jesu wusste" (158).

(4) Die römische Verantwortung für den Tod Jesu

Eine weitere Spur des Prozesses gegen Jesus findet sich möglicherweise in 1Kor 2,6–8. Der Text lautet: „Weisheit aber reden wir unter den Vollkommenen, jedoch Weisheit nicht dieser Welt noch der Herrscher dieser Welt (τῶν ἀρχόντων τοῦ αἰῶνος τούτου), die zunichte werden, sondern wir verkündigen Gottes Weisheit im Geheimnis, die verborgen ist, die Gott vorherbestimmt hat vor aller Zeit zu unserer Verherrlichung, die keiner von den Herrschern dieser Welt (οὐδεὶς τῶν ἀρχόντων τοῦ αἰῶνος τούτου) erkannt hat. Denn wenn sie sie erkannt hätten, hätten sie den Herrn der Herrlichkeit nicht gekreuzigt". Umstritten ist, ob mit den ἄρχοντες τοῦ αἰῶνος τούτου dämonische Mächte[93] oder staatliche Machthaber[94] gemeint sind. Für die zweite Auffassung spricht nicht nur der Terminus ἄρχοντες[95], sondern vor allem die Rede von Jesu Kreuzigung durch sie. Paulus würde dann nicht nur an Pilatus als Repräsentanten des römischen Imperium denken[96], sondern auch an die jüdischen Autoritäten Jerusalems, das Synhedrium[97]. „[D]ass

---

93 M. Werner, Einfluss, 67: „Ein wesentliches Moment der in Frage stehenden, dem Paulus ‚eigentümlichen' Anschauung besteht darin, dass es eigentlich die Geistermächte, die über diese Welt herrschen, gewesen sind, die den ‚Herrn der Herrlichkeit' gekreuzigt haben (1Kor 2,8). Wenn Paulus 1Thess 2,15 hier ein Verbrechen der Juden sieht, [...] so kommen sie eben als die willigen Werkzeuge der hinter der Szene bleibenden Archonten in Betracht".
94 A. Lindemann, 1Kor, 63.
95 Nach M. Hengel, Mahl, 130, ist die Wendung „wohl" von Ps 2,2 beeinflusst (παρέστησαν οἱ βασιλεῖς τῆς γῆς, καὶ οἱ ἄρχοντες συνήχθησαν ἐπὶ τὸ αὐτὸ κατὰ τοῦ κυρίου καὶ τοῦ χριστοῦ αὐτοῦ); H. Hübner, Vetus Testamentum in Novo, Bd II: Corpus Paulinum, Göttingen 1997, 235, zieht Bar 3,16 heran: ποῦ εἰσιν οἱ ἄρχοντες τῶν ἐθνῶν καὶ οἱ κυριεύοντες τῶν θηρίων τῶν ἐπὶ τῆς γῆς. οἱ ἄρχοντες = Inhaber irdischer Macht: Apg 3,17; 4,5.8.26 (= Ps 2,2LXX); 13,27. Für dämonische Mächte ist der Terminus ἀρχαί gebräuchlich; ἄρχων im dämonologischen Sinn: Joh 12,31 (ὁ ἄρχων τοῦ κόσμου τούτου); 14,30 (ὁ τοῦ κόσμου ἄρχων); Eph 2,2 (κατὰ τὸν ἄρχοντα τῆς ἐξουσίας τοῦ ἀέρος). D.C. Allison, Constructing, dem zufolge die Deutung von ἄρχοντες = *hostile spirits* auf Markion und Origenes zurückgeht (Anm. 40), bietet ebd. 396–398 eine ganze Reihe von Argumenten zugunsten der alternativen Deutung.
96 D.C. Allison, Constructing, 398: „the empire appears to be implicated in Jesus' execution".
97 So A. Lindemann, 1Kor, 64: „Wenn, wie wahrscheinlich [...], die ἄρχονες die politischen Machthaber sind, dann wirkt V.8b fast wie eine knappe Bezugnahme auf Jesu Passion – die ἄρχονες wären geradezu das Synedrium und Pilatus"; ebenso M. Hengel, Mahl, 130; Anm. 60: „Bestenfalls ist denkbar, dass Paulus in 1Kor 2,6.8 irdische und dämonische ‚Weltherrscher' zusammenfasst. Die irdischen wären dann Werkzeuge Satans und seiner Dämonen"; auch W. Schrage, Der erste Brief an die Korinther, 1.Teilband: 1Kor 1,1–6,11 (EKK VII/1), Zürich/Neukirchen-Vluyn 1991, 250.253f., verbindet beide Auslegungen miteinander, zieht für V.6 aber die dämonologische Deutung vor.

Jesu Kreuzigung von menschlichen Machthabern befohlen wurde, dürfte für ihn keine Frage gewesen sein"[98], wobei wieder offen bleiben muss, woher er es weiß.

Exkurs: Passionstradition im Corpus Pastorale?

Die einzige Stelle im Neuen Testament, an der – abgesehen von den Passionserzählungen der Evangelien – der Prokurator Pontius Pilatus Erwähnung findet, ist 1Tim 6,13. Dort erteilt Pseudo-Paulus seinem Schüler Timotheus die Weisung: „Ich gebiete dir vor Gott, der alles lebendig macht, und vor *Christus Jesus, der vor Pontius Pilatus* (ἐπὶ Ποντίου Πιλάτου)[99] *das gute Bekenntnis bezeugt hat*, den Auftrag makellos und ohne Tadel zu bewahren bis zur Erscheinung unseres Herrn Jesus Christus" (V.13f.). Dass der Autor an Pontius Pilatus erinnert, hat mit der bislang kaum wirklich beachteten Präsenz des *Römischen Imperium* im Corpus Pastorale zu tun: Das Imperium bietet *dem weltweiten Auftreten des Völkerapostels* gleichsam *die Bühne*, weshalb die Brieftrilogie auch mit dem 2. Timotheusbrief, dem „Testament" des Apostels aus Rom, enden muss, wo sich „durch ihn die Verkündigung vollendet und alle Heiden sie hören" (vgl. 2Tim 4,17)[100]. In 1Tim 6,13 erscheint Jesus Christus sozusagen „als *der urbildhaft Bekennende*"[101] – hier dem Timotheus als Vorbild für die Erfüllung seines Ordinationsauftrags vor Augen gestellt. Wahrscheinlich blickt der Autor auf Jesu „Wortzeugnis", das er vor Pontius Pilatus, also „in einer forensischen Situation" abgelegt hat. „Um dessen Inhalt zu erfassen", meint Jürgen Roloff einschränkend, bedarf es allerdings „schwerlich der Rückschlüsse auf Einzelheiten des Passionsberichtes, etwa auf Mk 15,2 oder Joh 18,33–37". Es könnte „ganz allgemein darum gegangen sein, dass Jesus angesichts der durch Pilatus verkörperten feindlichen Macht die ihm aufgetragene Wahrheit Gottes bezeugt und sich so in prototypischer Weise als Zeuge [...] Gottes erwiesen hat. Dieses sein Zeugnis wurde Modell und zugleich Motivation für die Christen, die in feindlicher Umgebung bzw. vor heidnischen Tribunalen die ihnen aufgetragene Wahrheit Gottes und seinen Herrschaftsanspruch zu bezeugen hatten (vgl. Offb 2,13; 11,3; 17,6)"[102]. Die Kenntnis eines unserer Evangelien durch den Autor der Pastoralbriefe, an dessen Pilatus-Szene er dann gedacht haben könnte, lässt sich nicht nachweisen[103].

---

98 A. Lindemann, 1Kor (s. Anm. 56), ebd.: „Paulus kennt die Passionsüberlieferung im einzelnen wohl nicht", meint er.

99 Zur Übersetzung des ἐπί mit „vor" vgl. 1Kor 6,1.6; Apg 23,30; 24,19; 25,9f.; außerdem Apg 3,13; vgl. J. Roloff, Der erste Brief an Timotheus (EKK XV), Zürich/Neukirchen-Vluyn 1988, 344 mit Anm. 77. Zur Alternativübersetzung mit „unter", „zur Zeit von Pontius Pilatus" tendiert L. Oberlinner, Erster Timotheusbrief (HThK XI 2/1), Freiburg 1994, 295.

100 Dazu vgl. M. Theobald, Israel- und Jerusalem-Vergessenheit im Corpus Pastorale? Zur Rezeption des Römerbriefs im Titus- sowie im 1. und 2. Timotheusbrief, in: T. Nicklas u.a. (Hgg.), Perspectives, 317-412, und zwar näherhin den Exkurs: „Das römische Imperium – die Bühne des Apostels im Corpus Pastorale", 376-379.

101 J. Roloff, 1Tim, 351.

102 J. Roloff, 1Tim, 344f. Ein solches forensische Verständnis von 1Tim 6,13 liegt näher als eine christologische Deutung, die hier ganz allgemein das Zeugnis Jesu thematisiert sieht, wobei der geschichtliche Hinweis auf Pontius Pilatus „antignostisch" zu verstehen wäre; vgl. L. Oberlinner, 1Tim, 295.

103 Vgl. die Diskussion in den Kommentaren zu 1Tim 5,18b: „Denn die Schrift sagt: ‚Du sollst dem Ochsen zum Dreschen keinen Maulkorb anlegen'. Und: ‚Der Arbeiter ist seines Lohnes

(5) Die Umstände der Kreuzigung Jesu

Vom Kreuz Jesu spricht Paulus des Öfteren in christologischer Deutung, dabei immer so, dass das „Skandalon des Kreuzes" (Gal 5,11) – Jesus unter dem Fluch des Gesetzes, von dem sein Tod zugleich befreit – in seiner ganzen Härte bewusst bleibt, auch die mit dieser Hinrichtungsart verbundene Entehrung nicht abgeblendet wird[104]. Allerdings spricht er nur abgekürzt vom Kreuz: Er benennt nicht seine Umstände und verschweigt die Täter (auch wenn das Stichwort σταυροῦν keinen Zweifel über sie zulässt). Solch verknappende Rede hängt gewiss mit seinem theologischen Deutungswillen zusammen. Dennoch, so meint Dale C. Allison, verrieten seine Briefe, dass er über historisches Detailwissen verfüge habe, konkret: dass Jesus ans Kreuz *angenagelt* worden sei[105], dass andere *mit ihm gekreuzigt* worden seien[106], dass es einen *titulus crucis* mit der Angabe seines Hinrichtungsgrundes gegeben habe, der Paulus bekannt gewesen sei[107], und dieser im

---

wert'" (vgl. Lk 10,7). – Zu den Hingabe-Formeln Tit 2,14; 1Tim 2,6 als Echo von Mk 10,45 siehe die von D.C. Allison, Constructing, 407 Anm. 72, angegebene Lit.

104 Das Substantiv σταυρός in Gal 5,11; 6;12.14; Phil 2,8; 3,18, das Verb σταυρόω in 1Kor 1,13.23; 2,2.8; 2Kor 13,4; Gal 3,1; 5,24; 6,14. – Vom Kreuz spricht Paulus vor allem im Kontext „innerkirchlicher" Richtungskämpfe und Auseinandersetzungen mit Gegnern. Im Römerbrief, seiner großen theologischen Rechenschaftsablage, begegnet die Rede vom Kreuz Jesu auffälligerweise nicht (abgesehen von der Anspielung in Röm 6,6). Ob Paulus sie dort vermeidet, wo er jeden Anstoß zu einer Auseinandersetzung mit der römischen Gesellschaft vermeiden will?

105 Dies entnimmt D.C. Allison, Constructing, 392–395, den zahlreichen Aussagen vom „Blut Jesu" (Röm 3,25 etc.) („Although these texts make theological points, not historical observations, they do assume that Jesus' execution was not bloodless, which it might have been were ropes alone employed"), vor allem aber Gal 6,17 („ich trage nämlich die *Malzeichen Jesu* [τὰ στίγματα τοῦ Ἰησοῦ] an meinem Leib") und Kol 2,13f. (mit Fragezeichen; eine Anspielung auf den *titulus crucis* zieht er vor; siehe die übernächste Anm.); EV 13 (20,24–27): „Jesus zeigte sich. Er bekleidete sich mit jenem Buche. *Man nagelte ihn an ein Holz.* Er veröffentlichte den Befehl des Vaters an dem Kreuz" (Antike christliche Apokryphen in deutscher Übersetzung I/2 [2012], 1250) spiele auf Kol 2,13f. an (Kol hält Allison für einen genuinen Paulusbrief). M. Hengel, Mahl, 467, sieht in Gal 6,1 eine „Anspielung auf die Geißelung Jesu" und deutet die στίγματα „als Narben", „die der Apostel bei der dreimaligen Auspeitschung und der fünffachen synagogalen Prügelstrafe erhalten hat".

106 Hierzu verweist D.C. Allison, Constructing, 411f., darauf, dass das sehr seltene Kompositum συ-σταυρόω nur bei Paulus (Röm 6,6; Gal 2,19) und in den Erzählungen von der Kreuzigung Jesu (Mt 27,44; Mk 15,32; Joh 19,32) begegnet. „συσταυρόω appeared first in an early account of the passion, coined for the occasion. From there it entered the Synoptic tradition and the Johannine tradition; and from such an account Paul picked it up and then redeployed it for his own purposes" (412).

107 Ebd. 413f. mit Hinweis auf Kol 2,13f. (προσηλώσας αὐτὸ τῷ σταυρῷ); „nowhere else in ancient literature – apart from Paul, the canonical gospels, and later writings familiar with them – do we read of a declaration or document being displayed on a cross. This is reason enough for at least asking whether we should connect Col 2:13–14 with what we find in the Gospels". Einige

Anspruch Jesu auf die Königsherrschaft bestanden habe[108]. Die Beobachtungen, die Allison sammelt, sind scharfsinnig, doch von unterschiedlicher Überzeugungskraft. Paulus *konnte* von alldem wissen und *hat* in den aufgeführten Punkten wohl auch mehr gewusst, als er sich ausdrücklich zu sagen in den konkreten Briefsituationen genötigt sah. Ein solches Detailwissen anhand der Briefaussagen nachzuweisen, will freilich nicht gelingen.

4.2 Deutungen des Todes Jesu bei Paulus

Während Paulus das erste Deutungsmuster (1) aus der Tradition vor ihm bezogen hat, hat er das zweite selbst entwickelt (2).

(1) „Unser Paschalamm Christus" (1Kor 5,7)

Das Bild vom „Paschalamm Christus" ist bei Paulus „einzigartig"[109]. Es ist veranlasst durch den vorangehenden Grundsatz V.6, um dessen Bedeutung seine Adressaten wohl gewusst haben[110]. Die ethische Weisung V.7a.b, die Paulus aus ihm ableitet, stützt er mit der indikativischen Zusage V.7c: „wie ihr ja (tatsächlich) ungesäuert seid"[111], die ihrerseits zur sie begründenden Rede vom „Paschalamm

---

Kommentatoren rechnen mit einer Anspielung auf die Kreuzinschrift: vgl. E. Schweizer, Der Brief an die Kolosser (EKK 12), Zürich/Neukirchen-Vluyn 1976, 115 mit Anm. 363. – Zur Frage der Historizität des *titulus crucis* vgl. zuletzt I. Broer, Der Kreuzestitulus (Mk 15,26 parr.), in: U. Busse/M. Reichhardt/M. Theobald (Hgg.), Erinnerung an Jesus. Kontinuität und Diskontinuität in der neutestamentlichen Überlieferung (BBB 166), Göttingen 2011, 267–283.

108 D.C. Allison, Constructing, 398: „Paul nowhere says why Jesus found himself on a cross. Yet we would, without any of the Gospel materials, not be wholly in the dark. Paul reports three relevant items about Jesus: (a) he was said to be descended from David (Rom 1:3), progenitor of the Israelite kings; (b) he was known as ‚(the) Christ' (e.g., Rom 1:4; 9:5; 1 Cor 15:3), a title with royal associations in Jewish literature; (c) he was thought of as reigning and having a kingdom, which means that some reckoned him a king (Rom 15:12; 1 Cor 15:24–25; Col 1:13; 2:10). All this matters because crucifixion was standard punishment for political rebels".

109 M. Hengel, Mahl, 463; vgl. ansonsten 1Petr 1,19; Offb 5,6.12; 13,8; zum Text vgl. auch C. Schlund, Deutungen des Todes Jesu im Rahmen der Pesach-Tradition, in: J. Frey/J. Schröter (Hgg.), Deutungen des Todes Jesu im Neuen Testament (WUNT 181), Tübingen 2005, 397–411, hier 404f.

110 „Wisst ihr nicht!" – so leitet Paulus den Satz ein, der, wie die nachfolgende Weisung insgesamt, nur von jüdischen Voraussetzungen her verständlich ist. Die Adressaten werden gewusst haben, „dass am Rüsttage zum Passafest, bevor die Lämmer geschlachtet werden, alter Sauerteig aus dem Hause geschafft werden muss, damit man dem Gesetz gemäß das Passamahl mit ungesäuertem Brot feiern kann", so M. Hengel, Mahl, 462f. Anm. 48: „Der Satz 1Kor 5,6b [= c] findet sich wörtlich gleichlautend in Gal 5,9. D.h., Paulus scheint auch in Galatien über Passabräuche gesprochen zu haben".

111 Paulus spielt auf die *mazzot*, die ungesäuerten Brote an.

Christus" führt: Ihr seid schon in einer Heilssituation, weil Christus am Kreuz für euch als Paschalamm geopfert wurde.

6 a Nicht gut ist euer Ruhm.
  b Wisst ihr nicht,
  c dass ein wenig Sauerteig den ganzen Teig durchsäuert?
7 a Schafft den alten Sauerteig weg,
  b damit ihr neuer Teig seid,
  c wie ihr ja (tatsächlich) ungesäuert seid.
  d Denn es ist ja unser Pesachlamm geopfert worden,
  e Christus.
8 Lasst uns also das Fest nicht mit dem alten Sauerteig feiern, auch nicht mit dem Sauerteig der Schlechtigkeit und Bosheit, sondern mit dem Ungesäuerten der Lauterkeit und Wahrheit.

Ob diese ethische Weisung über ihre interne Bild-Logik hinaus auch eine konkrete Veranlassung in den Zeitumständen des Briefes besaß, lässt sich nur vermuten[112]. „Sicher würde [aber] Paulus nicht von Christus als dem geopferten Passalamm sprechen und zur *rechten* Feier auffordern, *wenn Christus nicht in der Zeit des Festes in Jerusalem hingerichtet worden wäre.* [...]. Die ‚Nacht der Auslieferung' und der darauffolgende Tod Jesu lagen in der Passazeit und geschahen in Jerusalem, denn nur dort durften die Pesachlämmer im Tempel als Opfer geschlachtet werden"[113]. Hiervon kann Paulus über eine alte Passions- und Ostererzählung sein Wissen erhalten haben, muss es aber nicht.

---

112 C.K. Barrett, A Commentary on the First Epistle to the Corinthians (BNTC), London ²1971, 129f.; M. Hengel, Mahl, 463 Anm. 48: „Nach 1Kor 16,8 ist ja das Passfest wohl zeitlich nicht mehr allzu weit entfernt"; ebd. 128: „Die darauf [sc. V.7] gründende Aufforderung ὥστε ἑορτάζωμεν μὴ ἐν ζύμῃ παλαιᾷ ... lässt vermuten, dass das Passafest in der Gemeinde in Korinth in einer ‚verchristlichten' Form gefeiert wurde und dass Paulus dieselbe [,] während seines ca. 18 Monate dauernden Aufenthaltes in der Hauptstadt der Provinz Achaia dort eingeführt hat". Anders A. Lindemann, 1Kor, 129: „dass in der Gemeinde von Korinth das Passafest gefeiert wurde, ist nach der Aussage von V.7 sehr unwahrscheinlich"; „eine Anspielung auf ein tatsächlich zu feierndes Fest [würde] voraussetzen, dass der Brief zu dem betreffenden Zeitpunkt bei den Adressaten eingetroffen sein müsste".
113 M. Hengel, Mahl, 464f. H. Löhr, Das Abendmahl als Pesach-Mahl. Überlegungen aus exegetischer Sicht aufgrund der synoptischen Tradition und des frühjüdischen Quellenbefunds, in: BThZ 25 (2008), 99–116, hier 99: „Wollte man diese Notiz für die Passions-Chronologie auswerten – was freilich keineswegs zwingend ist! –[,] so müsste man annehmen, Paulus stimme mit der johanneischen Chronologie überein"; ebenso H. Koester, Jesus' Presence in the Early Church, in: CrSt 15 (1994), 541–557, hier 553f.: „This statement may imply that Christ died on the day of the slaughtering of the Passover lambs, thus revealing that Paul followed the same dating of Jesus death as the Gospel of John" (ebd. eine Auseinandersetzung mit Conzelmann zur Stelle). Anders D.C. Allison, Constructing, 423: „This, however, probably reads too much into Paul's

(2) „Christus hat uns vom Fluch des Gesetzes freigekauft [...]" (Gal 3,13f.)

Die einzige Stelle im Neuen Testament, an der Dtn 21,23 in der Form: „*Verflucht ist jeder, der am Holz hängt* (ἐπικατάρατος πᾶς ὁ κρεμάμενος ἐπὶ ξύλου)" ausdrücklich zitiert wird, ist Gal 3,13[114]. Ob Paulus den Vers von sich aus für seinen exegetischen Diskurs herangezogen hat oder ihm seine Anwendung auf die Kreuzigung Jesu bereits bekannt war, ist schwer zu sagen. Sollte letzteres der Fall sein, bleiben theoretisch zwei Möglichkeiten: Entweder waren Jesus-Gläubige schon vor ihm von Dtn 21,23 beunruhigt worden oder es waren die Gegner der nachösterlichen Verkündigung des Gekreuzigten in Jerusalem, die den Text zuerst gegen Jesus-Gläubige ins Feld führten[115]. Von daher erscheint es auch denkbar, dass Paulus seine Anwendung auf den gekreuzigten Jesus bereits aus seiner vor-„christlichen" Zeit kannte[116].

Zugunsten der Annahme, dass er in Gal 3 auf Dtn 21,23 eigenständig zurückgreift, könnte der Kontext sprechen, in dem ihm der Vers als Argument in einem Beweisgang dient, in dem es um die Frage geht, ob ein Mensch bei Gott durch die Tora gerechtfertigt wird oder nicht (Gal 3,11)[117]. Dtn 21,23 in diesem Kontext heranzuziehen, gab ihm die hermeneutische Regel der *gezera schawa* den Anstoß, der zufolge zwei Schriftstellen sich gegenseitig erläutern, wenn sie in einem wichtigen Stichwort übereinstimmen[118]. Das ist bei Dtn 21,23 und dem vorgeordneten Zitat Dtn 27,26 (= Gal 3,10) der Fall: „*Verflucht* (ἐπικατάρατος) ist jeder, der nicht bleibt bei allem, was im Buch der Tora geschrieben steht, um es zu tun"[119]. Weil nun kein Mensch den Weisungen der Tora in seinem tatsächlichen Tun entspricht, stehen sie alle unter dem von ihr ausgesprochenen Fluch, von dem

---

words. In any case, since Mark sets Jesus' crucifixion during the week of Passover, one could hardly make much of the difference".

[114] Paulus führt das Zitat mit einem ὅτι γέγραπται ein; von der LXX-Fassung weicht es leicht ab. Diese lautet: „jeder, der am Holz hängt, ist von Gott verflucht (κεκατηραμένος ὑπὸ θεοῦ πᾶς κρεμάμενος ἐπὶ ξύλου)". Wahrscheinlich hat Paulus das Zitat an das vorangehende aus Dtn 27,26 (ἐπικατάρατος) angeglichen, vgl. unten Anm. 119.

[115] Vgl. oben 1.1 mit Anm. 37: nach U.B. Müller ist die erste Alternative, nach der die Jünger nach der Kreuzigung Jesu durch Dtn 21,23 in eine Krise gestürzt wurden, unwahrscheinlich.

[116] Vgl. P. Stuhlmacher, Thesen, 194f.205: „Die Verbindung zwischen Paulus und der Jerusalemer Passionsüberlieferung wird noch dadurch verstärkt, dass der Apostel mit seiner apologetisch-gesetzeskritischen Deutung von Dtn 21,23 in Gal 3,13 in die von Jerusalem ausgehende, urchristlich-jüdische Kontroverse um das rechte Verständnis des Todes Jesu eingreift".

[117] Zur Logik des Textes vgl. M. Theobald, „Verflucht ist jeder, der am Holz hängt". Die Deutung des Todes Jesu nach Gal 3,6–14, in: BiKi 64 (2009), 158–165, sowie C. Dietzfelbinger, Sohn, 142–152.

[118] Vgl. G. Stemberger, Der Talmud. Einführung – Texte – Erläuterungen, München 1982, 57f.

[119] Auch hier weicht die Textform, die Paulus bietet, leicht vom LXX-Standardtext ab; dieser lautet: Ἐπικατάρατος πᾶς ἄνθρωπος, ὃς οὐκ ἐμμενεῖ ἐν πᾶσιν τοῖς λόγοις τοῦ νόμου τούτου τοῦ ποιῆσαι αὐτούς.

allein Christus sie befreien kann. Er tat dies Gal 3,13f. zufolge, indem er gemäß Dtn 21,23 selbst „für sie" am Kreuz zum „Fluch" wurde. Paulus meint, dass Christus den „Fluch" der Tora am eigenen Leib *stellvertretend* für alle Sünder erlitt und ihn dadurch von ihnen abzog. Den Kern dieses Gedankens hat er schon früher durchdacht[120]. Hier bringt er ihn im Kontext der Frage nach der Rechtfertigung in die Form eines Schriftbeweises, der es ihm erlaubt, die ungeheure Provokation, die in einer Anwendung von Dtn 21,23 auf Jesus liegt – der gekreuzigte Messias ein von Gott Verfluchter! – nicht einfach brüsk zurückzuweisen, sondern in bemerkenswerter Dialektik aufzugreifen und zugleich ins Heilvolle umzuwenden: Der Fluch, der tatsächlich auf dem Gekreuzigten lag – es war der Fluch, der eigentlich die Übertreter der Tora hätte treffen sollen!

Dtn 21,23 stellt aber auch noch in seiner „positiven" Anwendung auf den gekreuzigten Christus eine ungeheure Provokation dar. Als Schriftargument gegen seine Proklamation als Messias musste sich die Stelle Juden, die diese Proklamation ablehnten, geradezu aufdrängen. Deshalb legt es sich nahe, dass sie es auch waren, die Dtn 21,23 als erste im Kontext der Kreuzigung Jesu heranzogen. Ein Indiz dafür bieten auch die Anspielungen auf Dtn 21,23 in unterschiedlichen Reden der Apostelgeschichte, und zwar in denen, die *Petrus* (mitsamt den Aposteln) in Jerusalem (Apg 5,29–32) und alleine in Caesarea hält (Apg 10,34–43), sowie in einer Rede des *Paulus* im pisidischen Antiochien (Apg 13,16–41). Die entsprechenden Passagen lauten:

	Apg 5,30	Apg 10,39	Apg 13,29
	Der Gott unserer Väter hat Jesus auferweckt,		
„Karfreitag" [Dtn 21,22f.]	an den *ihr* Hand angelegt habt, indem *ihr* ihn ans Holz gehängt habt (κρεμάσαντες ἐπὶ ξύλου).	[...] den haben *sie* aus dem Weg geschafft, indem *sie* ihn ans Holz gehängt haben (κρεμάσαντες ἐπὶ ξύλου).	[...] nachdem *sie* ihn vom Holz genommen hatten (καθελόντες ἀπὸ τοῦ ξύλου), legten sie ihn in ein Grab.
„Ostern"	Diesen hat *Gott* als Anführer und Retter zu seiner Rechten erhöht [...]	Diesen hat *Gott* am dritten Tag auferweckt [...]	*Gott* aber hat ihn von den Toten auferweckt.

---

120 Vgl. 1Kor 15,56f.; 2Kor 5,20.

Der Rahmen, in dem diese Anspielungen auf Dtn 21,22f.[121] begegnen, ist jeweils derselbe. Es geht um das sog. „Kontrastschema"[122]: Der Redner stellt dem Tun der *Menschen* die Antwort *Gottes* entgegen. Dabei mag zunächst überraschen, dass nicht die Römer für die Kreuzigung Jesu verantwortlich gemacht werden, sondern in allen drei Reden die Juden: in 5,30 der „Hohe Rat", in 10,39 ein unbestimmtes „sie" und in 13,29 „die Einwohner von Jerusalem und ihre Führer (ἄρχοντες)". Hier wird deren Tun sogar noch als Erfüllung der Schrift ausgegeben: „*Als sie alles vollendet hatten, was über ihn geschrieben steht*, nahmen sie ihn vom Holz und legten ihn in ein Grab". Das darf als Hinweis darauf gelten, dass die Anspielungen auf Dtn 21,23 hier sehr gezielt eingesetzt werden und auch der Kontext der Weisung V.22f. mitsamt dem Wort vom Gehängten als Verfluchten Gottes präsent ist[123]. Von daher erklärt es sich vielleicht auch, warum es Juden sind, von denen gesagt wird, sie hätten Jesus „ans Holz gehängt". *Sie* waren es, aber die Antwort *Gottes* sah anders aus. Sollte der Einsatz von Dtn 21,23 also genau das abwehren, was die Verwendung des Zitats durch jüdische Gegner so attraktiv machte: die Annahme, die Hinrichtung Jesu am Kreuz könne als Beweis seines Von-Gott-Verflucht-Seins gelten? Dann wäre die fast stereotyp zu nennende Verwendung der Rede vom „Ans-Holz-Hängen" im Kontext jüdischer Verantwortlichkeit am Tod Jesu ein Indiz für die Bedeutung des Zitats in der frühen Kontroverse mit den Anhängern Jesu schon in Jerusalem. Später ist es Justin, der in seinem Dialog mit Tryphon Dtn 21,23 als Einwand gegen den christlichen Anspruch dem jüdischen Gesprächspartner mehrfach in den Mund legt, was belegt, dass der Vers in der jüdisch-christlichen Kontroverse tatsächlich eine wichtige Rolle spielte[124]. Ob schon in den anfängli-

---

121 In Dtn 21,22LXX begegnet die Wendung gleichfalls in der 2. Person Plural: κρεμάσητε αὐτὸν ἐπὶ ξύλου.
122 Den Terminus hat J. Roloff, Die Apostelgeschichte (NTD 5), Göttingen 1981, 50f., geprägt.
123 Vgl. oben Anm. 37.
124 Justinus, Dialogus cum Tryphone Judaeo, 32,1: „Da ich in meiner Rede einhielt, nahm Tryphon das Wort: ‚Mein Herr, die erwähnten Schriften und ähnliche veranlassen uns, dass wir den, der als Menschensohn von dem Bejahrten die ewige Herrschaft erhält, in Herrlichkeit und Größe erwarten. Dieser euer sogenannter Christus aber ist ohne Ehre und Herrlichkeit gewesen, so dass er sogar dem schlimmsten Fluch verfiel, den das Gesetz Gottes verhängt: er ist nämlich gekreuzigt worden"; 89,1f.: „Tryphon entgegnete: ‚Wisse wohl: unser ganzes Volk wartet auf den Christus, auch geben wir zu, dass alle Schriftstellen, welche du erwähntest, auf ihn gesagt sind [...]. Aber daran zweifeln wir, ob es notwendig war, dass Christus in so schmachvoller Weise am Kreuze starb; denn verflucht ist nach dem Gesetz, wer gekreuzigt wird. Dies ist also noch eine Lehre, von der ich mich momentan nicht überzeugen kann"; vgl. auch noch 90,1; 93,4; 94,5; 95,2; 96,1; 111,1; 131,2. – H.-W. Kuhn, Gekreuzigter, 34, bemerkt zu 11QT 64,6–13 (vgl. auch 4QpNah I 6–8): dieser Text mache „es noch unwahrscheinlicher, dass man es bei dem entsprechenden Argument in Justins Dialog mit dem Juden Tryphon nur mit einer christlich erfundenen, d.h. aus Paulus erschlossenen Überlegung zu tun habe". – In der Literatur des 2. Jh.s spielt die Metapher

chen Auseinandersetzungen in Jerusalem, wie hier angenommen, lässt sich nicht erweisen, scheint aber doch plausibel zu sein.

Kommen wir wieder auf die anfänglichen Überlegungen zum archimedischen Punkt der Passions- und Ostererzählung zurück, dann lässt sich zwischen Paulus und Markus bzw. Paulus und dem Archetyp der markinischen Passions- und Ostererzählung der folgende – freilich hypothetische – Vergleich anstellen: Paulus wie die Autoren der alten Passions- und Ostererzählung wussten um die anti-jesuanische Verwendung von Dtn 21,23 und reagierten darauf. Die Autoren der Passions- und Ostererzählung taten dies in der Weise, dass sie mit dem vor allem aus den Psalmen geschöpften Muster der *passio iusti* gegen Dtn 21,23 den Weg Jesu zum Kreuz als von Gott gewollt darstellten, also *mit* der Schrift *gegen* sie argumentierten, während Paulus die Anwendung von Dtn 21,23 auf den Gekreuzigten nicht einfach zurückwies, sondern im Gegenteil dieses Schriftzeugnis im Licht des christologischen Deutungsmusters von der sühnenden Stellvertretung auf seine tiefere Wahrheit hin befragte. Der Ausgangspunkt beider Traditionslinien – die Provokation durch Dtn 21,23 – wäre dann derselbe, die jeweils eingeschlagenen Lösungswege aber unterschieden sich[125]. Damit sind wir soweit, aus den zusammengetragenen Beobachtungen und Überlegungen ein kleines Resümee zu ziehen.

---

vom „Holz" weiter eine wichtige Rolle, scheint aber ihre kontroverse Bedeutung von Dtn 21,23 her eingebüßt zu haben. Z.B. erklärt Barn 8,5, „dass die Herrschaft Jesu auf dem Holze gründe (ὅτι ἡ βασιλεία Ἰησοῦ ἐπὶ ξύλου) und die auf ihn Hoffenden in Ewigkeit leben werden"; Justin (1 Apologia 1,14,1; Dialogus cum Tryphone Judaeo 73,1) hat das Motiv in Ps 95,10LXX eingepflanzt: „Der Herr hat seine Herrschaft *vom Kreuzesholz aus* (ἀπὸ τοῦ ξύλου) angetreten"; vgl. auch Tertullian, Adversus Marcionem 3,19,1: „Dominus regnavit a ligno"; M. Hengel, Reich Christi, Reich Gottes und Weltreich im Johannesevangelium (1991), in: M. Hengel, Jesus und die Evangelien. Kleine Schriften V (WUNT 211), Tübingen 2007, 408–429, hier 412 Anm. 17, hält dies für einen Satz, der „vermutlich aus einer christlichen Testimoniensammlung" stammt.

125 H.-W. Kuhn, Gekreuzigter, 22: „Für das Markusevangelium ist statt von einer theologia crucis sachgemäßer von einer ‚Passionstheologie' zu sprechen. Die drei markinischen Leidens- und Auferstehungsvoraussagen (8,31; 9,31; 10,32-34) nennen nicht einmal die spezielle Hinrichtungsart Jesu!"; vgl. auch A. Lindemann, Paulus, 152f. Anders K. Berger, Theologiegeschichte, 317: Paulus und Markus verfolgten „zu den Stichworten ‚Kreuz' und ‚Zeichen' auch ein übereinstimmendes theologisches Darstellungsziel": nach Mk 15,29–32 wird Jesus „geschmäht, weil er sich nicht selbst retten kann. Diese Unfähigkeit wird den dabeistehenden Juden de facto zum Ärgernis. Ausdrücklich ist vom Nicht-Können die Rede (V.31 gr.: *ou dynatai*)"; auch „nach 1Kor 1,22f. steht die Verkündigung des gekreuzigten Christus der Erwartung von Zeichen (Juden) und Weisheit (Griechen) entgegen. Weil die Botschaft darin Juden enttäuscht, bedeutet sie für sie ein Ärgernis. Paulus stellt dagegen, dass er Christus gleichwohl als Gottes Kraft (gr.: *dynamis*) verkündigt".

5 Resümee

Es wäre schön, wenn wir sagen könnten: Paulus kannte eine der Vorformen unserer Passions- und Ostererzählungen, denn dann ließe sich sein Verhältnis zu Markus *in puncto* Passion Jesu als ein *indirekt vermitteltes* beschreiben. Die Ausgangslage der beiden wäre, wie eben angedeutet, gleich, ihre Lösungswege aber nicht. Nach allem, was wir oben zusammentragen konnten, lässt sich ein Beweis für diese These nicht erbringen, so suggestiv die vielen Beobachtungen, die Dale C. Allison aufbietet, auch insgesamt sein mögen. Daraus folgt nicht, dass die These selbst unwahrscheinlich oder gar falsch wäre[126], wohl aber, dass wir uns, was die Einsicht in mögliche literarische und historische Zusammenhänge zwischen Paulus und der vor-markinischen Passions- und Ostererzählung bzw. ihrem mutmaßlichen Archetyp angeht, bescheiden müssen. Zur Behauptung solcher Zusammenhänge gehört auch – wenigstens das sollte weiterführend deutlich werden – die Wahrscheinlichkeit, dass es bei ihnen immer auch um Kontinuitäten praktischer Lebensäußerungen in den Gemeinden geht, in unserem Fall um die Möglichkeit einer „judenchristlichen" Paschafeier, die als „Sitz im Leben" lebendiger Passions- und Osterüberlieferung an unterschiedlichen Orten der frühen Kirche in Frage kommt. Es ist nicht einzusehen, dass die im Judentum verwurzelten ersten Anhänger des Gekreuzigten das Fest aufgegeben haben sollten, anstatt es im Gedenken an seinen Tod und Übergang ins Leben als Grund aller Hoffnung in neuer und anderer Weise zu begehen[127]. Wichtig ist überdies die Einsicht, dass die ursprüngliche Zugehörigkeit der Abendmahlsparadosis zur alten Passions- und Ostererzählung keineswegs unhinterfragte Voraussetzung unserer Fragestellung sein kann. Wenn im Gegenteil mit einer zunächst *getrennt* verlaufenden Überlieferungsgeschichte der beiden Größen zu rechnen ist, bevor sie literarisch vereint wurden, hat das Konsequenzen auch für die Frage nach dem Verhältnis von Paulus und Markus. Unbeschadet der Annahme, dass die Abendmahls-„Kultätiologie" ihre Formung gleichfalls im Kontext einer „judenchristlichen" Paschafeier erfahren hat, ist doch deutlich, dass Paulus sie aus-

---

126 Grundsätzlich skeptisch ist E.B. Aitken, Death, 11: „[A]lthough it is clear that Paul is familiar with a story of Jesus' death, there is no evidence that Paul knew a text that we would recognize as one of the passion narratives in the gospels. Thus, the formation of the story of Jesus' suffering and death, prior the written gospels, has never received an adequate explanation". Ebd. 21 mit Anm. 41 geht sie davon aus, dass es keinen Archetyp der verschiedenen Passionserzählungen gegeben habe (Frontstellung gegen J.D. Crossan).
127 Paulus, der mehrere Jahre in der Gemeinde von Antiochien verbrachte, könnte ein solches „judenchristliches" Pascha dort gut und gerne kennen gelernt und mitgefeiert haben; vgl. bereits oben Anm. 30.

weislich von 1Kor 11 als theologische Norm für die Gestaltung auch des (wöchentlichen) „Herrenmahls" einsetzt. An ihre Deutung des Todes Jesu vom Stellvertretungsgedanken her konnte er eher anknüpfen als an das *passio-iusti*-Modell der alten Passions- und Ostererzählung.

Grundsätzlich bieten die hier gebotenen Überlegungen ein Lehrstück für die Frage, wie sich die *narrative* Überlieferung und die der *Glaubensformeln* samt ihrer theologischen Entfaltung – zwei recht unterschiedliche Gestalten frühchristlicher Traditionsbildung – zueinander verhalten. Dass die Passions- und Ostererzählung das „Credo" von 1Kor 15,3b–5a nicht einfach narrativ entfaltet, sollte hier deutlich geworden sein. Was Paulus selbst angeht, so dürfte er – wenn wir seine Brief-Argumentationen zum Maßstab nehmen (über die Inhalte seiner Missionsverkündigung wissen wir kaum etwas) – vor allem an der Frage interessiert gewesen sein, was Jesu Lebenshingabe für diejenigen, die an ihn glauben, *bedeutet*. Er spricht zwar oft von der Niedrigkeit Jesu und seiner Schwachheit (Röm 15,1–3; 1Kor 10,33–11,1; 2Kor 10,1; 8,9; Phil 2,7f. und öfter), zeigt dabei aber nirgends Ansätze, dies unter Rückgriff auf die Passionserzählung zu *veranschaulichen*[128]. Ihm liegt alles daran, dass Jesu Weg in den Tod in seiner Bedeutung für das Verständnis christlicher Existenz transparent wird, damit an ihm ablesbar wird, was es heißt, „in Christus" zu sein. Ein Desinteresse am irdischen Jesus kommt darin nicht zum Ausdruck, wohl aber der Wille zu einer Konzentration auf das Wesentliche, wie Phil 2,4f. zu zeigen vermag: Lebt „nicht so, dass ihr jeder nur das Eigene, sondern so, dass ihr alle immer auch das der Anderen im Blick habt. Habt jeder eine solche Gesinnung in euch, wie auch Jesus Christus sie in sich trug"[129].

---

[128] So benutzt er z.B. nirgends die *konkreten* Bezeichnungen der Handlungsträger der Passionserzählung („die Jünger", „die Zwölf" [nur einmal in 1Kor 15,5], „das Synhedrium", „Hohepriester, Älteste und Schriftgelehrten"; Pilatus). Die für den Tod Jesu verantwortlichen Autoritäten nennt er ganz allgemein „die Archonten".
[129] Zu dieser Übersetzung vgl. N. Walter, Der Brief an die Philipper (NTD 8/2), Göttingen 1998, 51.55f.

Literatur

Aitken, E.B., Jesus' Death in Early Christian Memory. The Poetics of the Passion (NTOA 53), Göttingen/Fribourg 2004.
Allison, D.C., Constructing Jesus. Memory, Imagination, and History, Grand Rapids/Michigan 2010.
—, Resurrecting Jesus. The earliest Christian Tradition and its Interpreters, New York/London 2005.
Barrett, C.K., A Commentary on the First Epistle to the Corinthians (BNTC), London ²1971.
Bauer, W., Griechisch-deutsches Wörterbuch zu den Schriften des Neuen Testaments und der frühchristlichen Literatur, Berlin/New York ⁶1988.
Becker, J., Die Auferstehung Jesu Christi nach dem Neuen Testament. Ostererfahrung und Osterverständnis im Urchristentum, Tübingen 2007.
—, Paulus. Der Apostel der Völker, Tübingen 1989.
Bengel, J.A., Gnomon Novi Testamenti. Secundum editionem tertiam (1773), Berlin 1860.
Berger, K., Theologiegeschichte des Urchristentums. Theologie des Neuen Testaments, Tübingen/Basel 1994.
Black, C.C., Christ Crucified in Paul and in Mark. Reflections on an Intracanonical Conversation, in: E.H. Lovering/J.L. Sumney (eds.), Theology and Ethics in Paul and His Interpreters (Essays in Honor of Victor Paul Furnish), Nashville 1996, 80–104.
Bousset, W., Kyrios Christos. Geschichte des Christusglaubens von den Anfängen des Christentums bis Irenäus. Unveränderter dritter Abdruck der zweiten, umgearbeiteten Auflage, Göttingen ⁵1965.
Broer, I., Der Kreuzestitulus (Mk 15,26 parr.), in: U. Busse/M. Reichhardt/M. Theobald (Hgg.), Erinnerung an Jesus. Kontinuität und Diskontinuität in der neutestamentlichen Überlieferung (BBB 166), Göttingen 2011, 267–283.
Broer, I./Weidemann, H.-U., Einleitung in das Neue Testament, Würzburg ³2010.
Bultmann, R., Die Geschichte der synoptischen Tradition, Göttingen ⁸1970.
Dibelius, M., Die Formgeschichte des Evangeliums (Nachdruck der dritten Auflage mit einem erweiterten Nachtrag von G. Iber, hg. von G. Bornkamm), Tübingen ⁶1971.
Dietzfelbinger, C., Der Sohn. Skizzen zur Christologie und Anthropologie des Paulus (BThSt 118), Neukirchen-Vluyn 2011.
Ebner, M., Das Markusevangelium, in: M. Ebner/St. Schreiber (Hgg.), Einleitung in das Neue Testament (KStTh 6), Stuttgart 2008, 154–183.
—, Kreuzestheologie im Markusevangelium, in: A. Dettwiler/J. Zumstein (Hgg.), Kreuzestheologie im Neuen Testament (WUNT 151), Tübingen 2002, 151–168.
Flessman-van Leer, E., Die Interpretation der Passionsgeschichte vom Alten Testament aus, in: F. Viering (Hg.), Zur Bedeutung des Todes Jesu. Exegetische Beiträge, Gütersloh 1967, 79–96.
Gnilka, J., Das Evangelium nach Markus (Mk 1–8,26) (EKK II/1), Zürich/Neukirchen-Vluyn 1978.
—, Das Evangelium nach Markus (Mk 8,27–16,20) (EKK II/2), Zürich/Neukirchen-Vluyn 1979.
Hays, R.B., Christ Prays the Psalms. Israel's Psalter as Matrix of Early Christology, in: R.B. Hays, The Conversion of the Imagination. Paul as Interpreter of Israel's Scripture, Grand Rapids 2005, 101–118.
Heckel, T., Kraft in Schwachheit. Untersuchungen zu 2Kor 10–13 (WUNT 2/56), Tübingen 1993.

Hengel, M., Das Begräbnis Jesu bei Paulus und leibliche Auferstehung aus dem Grabe (2001), in: M. Hengel, Studien zur Christologie. Kleine Schriften IV, hg. von C.-J. Thornton (WUNT 201), Tübingen 2006, 386–450.
—, Das Mahl in der Nacht, „in der Jesus ausgeliefert wurde" (1Kor 11,23) (2004), in: M. Hengel, Studien zur Christologie. Kleine Schriften IV, hg. von C.-J. Thornton (WUNT 201), Tübingen 2006, 451–495.
—, Entstehungszeit und Situation des Markusevangeliums (1984), in: M. Hengel, Jesus und die Evangelien. Kleine Schriften V, hg. von C.-J. Thornton (WUNT 211), Tübingen 2007, 478–525.
—, Reich Christi, Reich Gottes und Weltreich im Johannesevangelium (1991), in: M. Hengel, Jesus und die Evangelien. Kleine Schriften V, hg. von C.-J. Thornton (WUNT 211), Tübingen 2007, 408–429.
Holzbrecher, F., Paulus und der historische Jesus. Darstellung und Analyse der bisherigen Forschungsgeschichte (TANZ 48), Tübingen 2007.
Hübner, H., Vetus Testamentum in Novo, Bd II: Corpus Paulinum, Göttingen 1997.
Jeremias, J., Art. πάσχα, in: ThWNT V (1954), 895–903.
Käsemann, E., An die Römer (HNT 8a), Tübingen ²1974.
Kampling, R., Und so kam Paulus unter die Antisemiten. Transformation des Verstehens in der Auslegung von 1Thess 2,14-16 im 19. Jahrhundert, in: W. Eisele/C. Schaefer/H.-U. Weidemann (Hgg.), Aneignung durch Transformation (FS M. Theobald) (HBS 74), Freiburg 2013, 358-374.
Keith, C./Thatcher, T., The Scar of the Cross: The Violence Ratio and the Earliest Christian Memories of Jesus, in: T. Thatcher (ed.), Jesus, the Voice, and the Text: Beyond the Oral and the Written Gospel, Waco TX 2008, 197–214.
Klein, H., Zur Frage einer Lukas und Johannes zu Grunde liegenden Passions- und Ostererüberlieferung, in: H. Klein, Lukasstudien (FRLANT 209), Göttingen 2005, 65–84.
Kleinknecht, K.T., Der leidende Gerechtfertigte. Die alttestamentlich-jüdische Tradition vom ‚leidenden Gerechten' und ihre Rezeption bei Paulus (WUNT II/13), Tübingen ²1988.
Koch, D.-A., Die Schrift als Zeuge des Evangeliums. Untersuchungen zur Verwendung und zum Verständnis der Schrift bei Paulus (BHTh 69), Tübingen 1986.
Koester, H., Jesus' Presence in the Early Church, in: CrSt 15 (1994), 541–557.
Kuhn, H.-W., Jesus als Gekreuzigter in der frühchristlichen Verkündigung bis zur Mitte des 2. Jahrhunderts, in: ZThK 72 (1975), 1–46.
Kümmel, W.G., Einleitung in das Neue Testament, Heidelberg [18]1976.
Lindemann, A., Der Erste Korintherbrief (HNT 9/I), Tübingen 2000.
—, Paulus im ältesten Christentum (BHTh 58), Tübingen 1979.
Löhr, L., Das Abendmahl als Pesach-Mahl. Überlegungen aus exegetischer Sicht aufgrund der synoptischen Tradition und des frühjüdischen Quellenbefunds, in: BThZ 25 (2008), 99–116.
Lohse, E., Die Geschichte des Leidens und Sterbens Jesu Christi, Gütersloh 1964.
Lührmann, D., Das Markusevangelium (HNT 3), Tübingen 1987.
Marcus, J., Mark – Interpreter of Paul, in: NTS 46 (2000), 473–487.
Markschies, C./Schröter, J. (Hgg.), Antike christliche Apokryphen in deutscher Übersetzung, Bd. I/2, Tübingen 2012.
Mohr, T.A., Markus- und Johannespassion. Redaktions- und traditionsgeschichtliche Untersuchung der Markinischen und Johanneischen Passionstradition (AThANT 70), Zürich 1982.

Müller, U.B., Auferweckt und erhöht. Zur Genese des Osterglaubens, in: NTS 54 (2008), 201–220.
—, Die Entstehung des Glaubens an die Auferstehung Jesu. Historische Aspekte und Bedingungen (SBS 172), Stuttgart 1998.
Mußner, F., Zur stilistischen und semantischen Struktur der Formel von 1Kor 15,3–5 (1977), in: F. Mußner, Jesus von Nazareth im Umfeld Israels und der Urkirche. Gesammelte Aufsätze, hg. von M. Theobald (WUNT 111), Tübingen 1999, 190–200.
Nagy, G., Pindar's Homer. The Lyric Possession of an Epic Past, Baltimore/London 1990.
—, Poetry as Performance. Homer and Beyond, Cambridge 1996.
Neirynck, F., Jean et les Synoptiques. Examen critique de l' exégèse de M.-É. Boismard (BETL 49), Leuven 1979.
Oberlinner, L., Erster Timotheusbrief (HThK XI 2/1), Freiburg 1994.
Pesch, R., Das Markusevangelium, II. Teil: Kommentar zu Kap. 8,27–16,20 (HThKNT II/2), Freiburg 1977.
Popkes, W., Christus traditus (AThANT 49), Zürich/Stuttgart 1967.
Reinbold, W., Der Prozess Jesu, Göttingen 2006.
Roloff, J., Der erste Brief an Timotheus (EKK XV), Zürich/Neukirchen-Vluyn 1988.
—, Die Apostelgeschichte (NTD 5), Göttingen 1981.
Romaniuk, K., Le Problème des Paulinismes dans l'Évangile de Marc, in: NTS 23 (1967/77), 266–274.
Rouwhorst, G., Christlicher Gottesdienst und der Gottesdienst Israels. Forschungsgeschichte, historische Interaktionen, Theologie, in: M. Klöckener/A.A. Häußling/R. Messner (Hgg.), Theologie des Gottesdienstes Bd. 2 (GDK 2), Regensburg 2008, 493–572.
Schenk, W., Sekundäre Jesuanisierungen von primären Paulus-Aussagen bei Markus, in: F. van Segbroeck u.a. (ed.), The Four Gospels 1992, Vol. II (FS Frans Neirynck) (BEThL 100), Leuven 1992, 877–904.
Schenke, L., Das Markusevangelium (UB 205), Stuttgart 1988.
Schille, G., Das Leiden des Herrn. Die evangelische Passionstradition und ihr ‚Sitz im Leben', in: ZThK 52 (1955), 161–205.
Schleritt, F., Der vorjohanneische Passionsbericht. Eine historisch-kritische und theologische Untersuchung zu Joh 2,13–22; 11,47–14,31 und 18,1–20,29 (BZNW 154), Berlin 2007.
Schlund, C., Deutungen des Todes Jesu im Rahmen der Pesach-Tradition, in: J. Frey/J. Schröter (Hgg.), Deutungen des Todes Jesu im Neuen Testament (WUNT 181), Tübingen 2005, 397–411.
Schmeller, T., Der zweite Brief an die Korinther (2Kor 1,1–7,4) (EKK VIII/1), Neukirchen-Vluyn/Ostfildern 2010.
Schmithals, W., Das Evangelium nach Markus. Kapitel 1–9,1 (ÖTK 2/1), Gütersloh/Würzburg 1979.
Schrage, W., Das Verständnis des Todes Jesu Christi im Neuen Testament, in: E. Bizer u.a. (Hgg.), Das Kreuz Jesu Christi als Grund des Heils (STAEKU), Gütersloh 1967, 49–90.
—, Der erste Brief an die Korinther, 1.Teilband: 1Kor 1,1–6,11 (EKK VII/1), Zürich/Neukirchen-Vluyn 1991.
—, Der erste Brief an die Korinther, 3. Teilband: 1Kor 11,17–14,40 (EKK VII/3), Zürich/Neukirchen-Vluyn 1999.
—, Der erste Brief an die Korinther, 4. Teilband: 1Kor 15,1–16,24 (EKK VII/4), Zürich/Neukirchen-Vluyn 2001.

Schwankl, O., Auf der Suche nach dem Anfang des Evangeliums. Von 1Kor 15,3–5 zum Johannes-Prolog, in: BZ 40 (1996), 39–60.
Schweizer, E., Der Brief an die Kolosser (EKK 12), Zürich/Neukirchen-Vluyn 1976.
Steck, O.H., Israel und das gewaltsame Geschick der Propheten. Untersuchungen zur Überlieferung des deuteronomistischen Geschichtsbildes im Alten Testament (WMANT 23), Neukirchen-Vluyn 1967.
Stemberger, G., Der Talmud. Einführung – Texte – Erläuterungen, München 1982.
Stuhlmacher, P., Achtzehn Thesen zur paulinischen Kreuzestheologie, in: P. Stuhlmacher, Versöhnung, Gesetz und Gerechtigkeit. Aufsätze zur biblischen Theologie, Göttingen 1981, 192–208.
—, Biblische Theologie des Neuen Testaments, Bd. I: Grundlegung: Von Jesus zu Paulus, Göttingen ²1997.
Theißen, G., Die Entstehung des Neuen Testaments als literaturgeschichtliches Problem (Schriften der Philosophisch-historischen Klasse der Heidelberger Akademie der Wissenschaften Bd. 40), Heidelberg 2007.
—, Lokalkolorit und Zeitgeschichte in den Evangelien. Ein Beitrag zur Geschichte der synoptischen Tradition, Freiburg i. d. Schweiz/Göttingen ²1992 (Studienausgabe der ersten Auflage 1989 = NTOA 8).
Theobald, M., Angefochtener Osterglaube – im Neuen Testament und heute, in: ThQ 193 (2013) 4-31, hier 24-27
—, „Verflucht ist jeder, der am Holz hängt". Die Deutung des Todes Jesu nach Gal 3,6–14, in: BiKi 64 (2009), 158–165.
—, Eucharist and Passover: The Two ‚Loci' of the Liturgical Commemoration of the Last Supper in Early Church, in: T. Thatcher/C. Williams (Hgg.), Engaging with C.H. Dodd on the Gospel of John. Sixty Years of Tradition and Interpretation, Cambridge 2013, 231-254.
—, Israel- und Jerusalem-Vergessenheit im Corpus Pastorale? Zur Rezeption des Römerbriefs im Titus- sowie im 1. und 2. Timotheusbrief, in: T. Nicklas/A. Merkt/J. Verheyden (Hgg.), Ancient Perspectives on Paul (NTOA/StUNT 102), Göttingen 2013, 317-412.
—, Paschamahl und Eucharistiefeier. Zur heilsgeschichtlichen Relevanz der Abendmahlsszenerie bei Lukas (Lk 22,14–38), in: M. Theobald/R. Hoppe (Hgg.), „Für alle Zeiten zur Erinnerung" (Jos 4,7). Beiträge zu einer biblischen Gedächtniskultur (SBS 209), Stuttgart 2006, 133–180.
—, Vom Sinai über den Berg der Verklärung zum Abendmahlssaal. Zur kontextuellen Einbindung des markinischen Becherworts (Mk 14,24), in: F. Bruckmann/R. Dausner (Hgg.), Im Angesicht der Anderen. Gespräche zwischen christlicher Theologie und jüdischem Denken (FS J. Wohlmuth) (Studien zu Judentum und Christentum, Bd. 25), Paderborn 2013, 463-494.
Veijola, T., „Fluch des Totengeistes ist der Aufgehängte" (Dtn 21,23), in: UF 32 (2000), 69–80.
Vielhauer, P., Geschichte der urchristlichen Literatur. Einleitung in das Neue Testament, die Apokryphen und die Apostolischen Väter, Berlin/New York 1975.
Walter, N., Der Brief an die Philipper, in: NTD 8/2, Göttingen 1998.
Weidemann, H.-U., „Dies ist mein Bundesblut" (Mk 14,24). Die markinische Abendmahlserzählung als Beispiel für liturgisch beeinflusste Transformationsprozesse, in: W. Eisele/C. Schaefer/ders. (Hgg.), Aneignung durch Transformation (FS M. Theobald) (HBS 74), Freiburg 2013, 56-98
Wengst, K., Christologische Formeln und Lieder des Urchristentums (StNT 7), Gütersloh 1972.

Werner, M., Der Einfluß paulinischer Theologie im Markusevangelium. Eine Studie zur neutestamentlichen Theologie (BZNW 1), Gießen 1923.
Windisch, H., Der zweite Korintherbrief (Neudruck der Auflage 1924), hg. von G. Strecker (KEK 6), Göttingen 1970.
—, Paulus und Christus (UNT 24), Leipzig 1934.
Wischmeyer, O., (Hg.), Paulus. Leben – Umwelt – Werk – Briefe, Tübingen ²2012.
Wolff, C., Der erste Brief des Paulus an die Korinther. Zweiter Teil: Auslegung der Kapitel 8–16 (ThHK VII/2), Berlin ³1990.
—, Der zweite Brief des Paulus an die Korinther (ThHK VIII), Berlin 1989.
Wolter, M., Das Lukasevangelium (HNT 5), Tübingen 2008.

Udo Schnelle
Paulinische und markinische Christologie im Vergleich

1 Einleitung

Der Einfluss paulinischer Theologie auf das Markusevangelium war in der Wende vom 19. zum 20. Jahrhundert ein gewichtiges Thema neutestamentlicher Forschung. Heinrich Julius Holtzmann sieht bemerkenswerte Verbindungen zwischen beiden und stellt zu Mk 1,1 fest: „Demnach erklärt sich auch die Ueberschrift des Ganzen – bedeute sie nun ‚Anfang des von Jesus verkündigten Evglms' oder ‚Anfang des Evglms von Jesus Christus (ἀρχὴ εὐαγγελίου Ἰησοῦ Χριστοῦ) – einfach aus der paulin. Ausdrucksweise ... und wenn der hinzugefügte ‚Gottessohn' (υἱοῦ θεοῦ) textkritisch bestehen bleibt, so ist dies nur abermals ein paulin. Ausdruck"[1]. Johannes Weiß bemerkt zum Jüngerunverständnis im Markusevangelium: „Ihr Unverständnis ist die Folie für die beseligende Erkenntnis, die der Evangelist den Seinen predigt: das Kreuz ist der eigentliche Inhalt seines Lebens. Hier zeigt sich der Evangelist als ein Bekenner des paulinischen Evangeliums, und mit einiger Geringschätzung blickt er auf die Zwölf herab, die sich so gar nicht in diesen einzig wahren Sinn des Evangeliums finden konnten, weil sie menschliche aber nicht göttliche Gedanken hatten".[2] Diese Debatte kam mit der 1923 erschienenen Studie von Martin Werner ‚Der Einfluß paulinischer Theologie im Markusevangelium'[3] zu einem ersten Ende. Nach einer Analyse aller relevanten möglichen Berührungspunkte stellt er fest: „1. Wo Markus mit Paulus übereinstimmt, handelt es sich immer um allgemein-urchristliche Anschauungen. 2. Wo in den Briefen über diese gemeinsame Basis hinaus besondere, charakteristisch paulinische Anschauungen zutage treten, da fehlen entweder bei Markus die Parallelen vollständig, oder Markus vertritt geradezu entgegengesetzte Standpunkte. 3. Von einem Einfluß paulinischer Theologie im Markusevangelium kann daher nicht im geringsten die Rede sein".[4] Seitdem wird das Thema Paulus – Markus nur noch am Rande oder gar nicht mehr thematisiert[5].

---

[1] H.J. Holtzmann, Lehrbuch der neutestamentlichen Theologie I, Tübingen ²1911, 496f.
[2] J. Weiß, Das Urchristentum, Göttingen 1917, 541.
[3] M. Werner, Der Einfluß paulinischer Theologie im Markusevangelium. Eine Studie zur neutestamentlichen Theologie (BZNW 1), Gießen 1923.
[4] M. Werner, Einfluß, 209.

Ein Vergleich zwischen paulinischer und markinischer Christologie legt sich aber aus mehreren Gründen nahe:

(1) Paulus und Markus liegen zeitlich nicht weit auseinander; Paulus starb wahrscheinlich um 64 n. Chr. in Rom[6], das Markusevangelium könnte kurz nach 70 n. Chr. in Rom abgefasst worden sein[7]. Bei der überragenden Bedeutung des Völkerapostels (vgl. Röm 11,13; 15,16) in der Geschichte des frühen Christentums stellt sich natürlich die Frage, ob Markus in irgendeiner Form um Paulus und seine Theologie wusste und davon beeinflusst war. Auf jeden Fall setzt er den entscheidenden historischen und theologischen Ertrag des paulinischen Wirkens voraus: die Beschneidungsfreiheit für die Christen aus den Völkern. Das Fehlen des Substantivs περιτομή („Beschneidung")[8] bei Markus (und in der Logienquelle und den anderen Synoptikern) ist kein Zufall, sondern dokumentiert den theologischen Standort des Evangeliums außerhalb des Judentums, denn ohne Beschneidung kann es kein Judentum und auch keinen ernsthaften innerjüdischen Dialog geben![9]

(2) Paulus und Markus sind gewissermaßen literarische und theologische Pioniere, sie stehen jeweils am Anfang einer bedeutsamen Epoche. Die selbständige paulinische Mission im Anschluss an den Apostelkonvent leitete die entscheidende Expansion der Bewegung unter die Völker ein, die von Paulus energisch betrieben und theologisch durchdacht wurde. Markus verfasste mit der neuen Literaturgattung Evangelium die erste ausführliche Jesus-Christus-Geschichte. Dadurch bewahrte er nicht nur zahlreiche Jesus-Traditionen vor dem Verschwinden im Dunkel der Geschichte, sondern er formte durch seine narrative Präsentation und seine theologischen Einsichten wesentlich das Jesus-Christus-Bild des frühen Christentums.

---

5 Zur Markusforschung vgl. zuletzt E.-M. Becker, Das Markus-Evangelium im Rahmen antiker Historiographie (WUNT 194), Tübingen 2006, 7–36.

6 Vgl. U. Schnelle, Paulus, Leben und Denken, Berlin 2003, 425–431.

7 Vgl. U. Schnelle, Einleitung in das Neue Testament, Göttingen [7]2011, 238–260. Ich votiere für eine Entstehung kurz nach 70, weil die Gegenüberstellung des auf der Erzählebene gegenwärtig noch existierenden und des in Zukunft vollständig zerstörten Tempels in Mk 13,2 die eingetretene Zerstörung voraussetzt. Eine Eroberung Jerusalems und des Tempels durch die Römer war vorhersehbar, nicht aber die vollständige Zerstörung des Tempels!

8 Das Verb περιτέμνειν („beschneiden") ist nur in Lk 1,59; 2,21 belegt (Beschneidung des Jesuskindes).

9 Vgl. nur Gen 17,7.13, wo die Beschneidung gleichermaßen Zeichen des ewigen Bundes mit Abraham und mit ganz Israel ist; wer die Beschneidung unterlässt, bricht den Bund und muss ausgeschlossen werden (Gen 17,14).

(3) Paulus und Markus bilden jeweils den Anfangspunkt einer historischen und theologischen Entwicklung, wie ihre Rezeption in den Deuteropaulinen bzw. den anderen Evangelien zeigten.

Allerdings hat ein Vergleich auch seine Grenzen, denn Paulus und Markus befanden sich in grundlegend verschiedenen Situationen: Was Markus voraussetzt, musste von Paulus erst mühselig erkämpft werden: die beschneidungsfreie Mission unter den Völkern. Paulus war in ganz anderer Weise als Markus in die Identitäts- und Formierungsprozesse des frühen Christentums eingebunden bzw. verwickelt. Zwar finden sich auch im Evangelium Hinweise auf Falschlehrer (vgl. Mk 13,21f.), was jedoch in keiner Weise mit den paulinischen Kämpfen vergleichbar ist (Korinth, Galatien, Jerusalem). Schon aus diesem Grund ist es nicht zu erwarten, dass Paulus und Markus bruchlos zu vergleichen sind. Zudem sind wir über das Leben und Werk des Paulus in – für antike Verhältnisse – einzigartiger Weise informiert (Paulusbriefe, Apostelgeschichte), demgegenüber verbirgt sich Markus in und hinter seinem Evangelium[10]. Damit verbindet sich ein dritter grundlegender Unterschied: die Gattung. Markus schuf mit der neuen Literaturgattung Evangelium die erste ausführliche Jesus-Christus-Geschichte und bestimmte durch die Präsentation der Ereignisse/Charaktere, durch den geographisch/chronologischen Rahmen, den Geschehensverlauf, die Erzählperspektive und seine theologischen Einsichten wesentlich das Jesus-Christus-Bild des frühen Christentums. Paulus war ein meisterhafter Briefschreiber; neben seinen Gemeindeaufenthalten und den Besuchen der Mitarbeiter dienten Paulus vor allem Briefe zur Kommunikation mit seinen Gemeinden[11]. Die Form des Briefes hat seit Epikur[12] ihren festen Platz in der philosophisch-theologischen Unterweisung, die auf Erkenntnis, Selbsterkenntnis und Verhaltensänderung abzielt. Die Paulusbriefe wurden von Anfang an in den Gemeinden vorgelesen (vgl. 1Thess 5,27; Röm 16,16), und die Empfänger bekamen das Original unmittelbar zu Gesicht (vgl. Gal 6,11). Die Überzeugungskraft der Paulusbriefe wurde nach 2Kor 10,10f. auch von

---

[10] Zum Autor des Markusevangeliums vgl. U. Schnelle, Einleitung, 240–242; eine andere Position vertritt M. Hengel, Der umstrittene Petrus, Tübingen 2006, 162–166.167–179.

[11] Vgl. zum antiken und paulinischen Brief: O. Roller, Das Formular der paulinischen Briefe (BWANT 4.6), Stuttgart 1933; H. Koskenniemi, Studien zu Idee und Phraseologie des griechischen Briefes bis 400 n.Chr. (AASF B 102,2), Helsinki 1956; W.G. Doty, Letters in Primitive Christianity, Philadelphia 1973; S.K. Stowers, Letter Writing in Greco-Roman Antiquity, Philadelphia 1986; F. Schnider/W. Stenger, Studien zum neutestamentlichen Briefformular (NTTS XI), Leiden 1987; H.-J. Klauck, Die antike Briefliteratur und das Neue Testament, Paderborn 1998; Th.J. Bauer, Paulus und die kaiserzeitliche Epistolographie (WUNT 276), Tübingen 2011.

[12] Vgl. hier besonders den Brief an Menoikeus als Sachparallele; zu den beachtlichen Parallelen zwischen Epikur und Paulus vgl. P. Eckstein, Gemeinde, Brief und Heilsbotschaft. Ein phänomenologischer Vergleich zwischen Paulus und Epikur (HBS 42), Freiburg 2004.

den Gegnern gerühmt („*denn die Briefe, so sagt man, sind gewichtig und schwer*").
Aus der Vielzahl möglicher antiker Briefgattungen kommen den paulinischen Briefen der Freundschaftsbrief und der philosophische Brief am nächsten.

Trotz dieser Unterschiede gilt: Paulus und Markus repräsentieren die christliche Anfangsliteratur und sind gerade für die Christologie entscheidende Impulsgeber. *Christologie ist die Art und Weise, wie ein neutestamentlicher Autor das Wesen und die Bedeutung des Jesus von Nazareth als Messias für Israel und die Völker begrifflich und erzählerisch formt und umsetzt.* Von hieraus ist die Fragestellung zu präzisieren: Ein Vergleich paulinischer und markinischer Christologie muss zunächst mit der erzählerischen Präsentation des Jesus Christus bei den beiden Autoren einsetzen und sich dann zentralen Einzelaspekten zuwenden: Evangeliumsbegriff, christologische Titel, Glaubensverständnis, Gesetz, Kreuzestheologie und Auferstehung.

2 Die Jesus-Christus-Geschichte bei Paulus und Markus

Obwohl die Erzählgattung Evangelium und die vorwiegend argumentativ ausgerichtete Gattung Brief sich stark unterscheiden, gibt es vergleichbare Aspekte. Auch Paulus erzählt eine Jesus-Christus-Geschichte; seine Briefe sind mit narrativen Elementen und Bezugnahmen durchzogen, die gleichermaßen die Geschichte des irdischen Jesus wie seine Auferstehung und Parusie thematisieren[13]. So enthalten die Herrenmahlsparadosis 1Kor 11,23b–25[14] und die Bekenntnistradition 1Kor 15,3b–5 als narrative Abbreviaturen[15] in geformter Sprache die entscheidenden Grunddaten der Jesus-Christus-Geschichte, indem sie die Proexistenz des irdischen Jesus

---

13 Vgl. E. Reinmuth, Narratio und argumentatio – zur Auslegung der Jesus-Christus-Geschichte im Ersten Korintherbrief, in: ZThK 92 (1995), 21, wonach Paulus nicht eine abstrakte Geschichte des historischen Jesus, sondern die Jesus-Christus-Geschichte erzählt, so wie er „sie kennt und verkündet – die Jesus-Christus-Geschichte also, die die Geschichte des irdischen Jesus ebenso umgreift wie Präexistenz und künftige Parusie." Vgl. ferner A.J.M. Wedderburn, Paul and the Story of Jesus, in: Paul and Jesus, ed. A.J.M. Wedderburn (JSNT.S 37), Sheffield 1989, 161–189.
14 Vgl. dazu den Beitrag von E. Dowling im vorliegenden Band.
15 Vgl. J. Straub, Geschichten erzählen, Geschichte bilden, in: Erzählung, Identität und historisches Bewusstsein, hg. von J. Straub, Frankfurt 1998, 123: „Narrative Abbreviaturen enthalten Geschichten oder verweisen auf Geschichten, ohne selbst Geschichten zu sein. Narrative Abbreviaturen lassen sich nur im Rekurs auf die Geschichten, auf die sie anspielen oder hinweisen, hermeneutisch auslegen."

direkt thematisieren und in seiner theologischen Bedeutung reflektieren[16]: Seine bewusste Hingabe für die Seinen in der Nacht der Auslieferung, sein Tod, sein Begräbnis, seine Auferstehung am dritten Tag sowie seine Erscheinungen. Der irdische Jesus wird von Paulus nicht ausgeblendet, sondern von Ostern her interpretiert. Das Kreuz als zentrale narrative Abbreviatur ist weitaus mehr als eine kerygmatische Bestimmung; es bleibt immer auch historischer Ort und grausame Tötungsart, selbst dort, wo Paulus es in mythologische Erzählungen integriert (Phil 2,6–11)[17]. Wo das Kreuz bei Paulus erscheint, umfasst es immer die gesamte Jesus-Christus-Geschichte, die in 1Kor 1,18 als „Wort vom Kreuz" auf den Begriff gebracht wird. Das Kreuz ist vergangenes Ereignis und bleibendes Heilsgeschehen zugleich, denn in seiner wahren Bedeutung kann es nur vom Handeln Gottes an Jesus Christus begriffen werden[18].

Die sachliche Einheit des Irdischen mit dem Auferweckten zeigt sich auch überall dort, wo die geschichtlichen Dimensionen des Lebens Jesu in den Blick kommen. Sie sind jeweils theologisch determiniert, markieren aber zugleich den unverzichtbaren historischen Rückbezug. Als die Zeit erfüllt war, wurde Jesus von Nazareth von einer Frau geboren und unter das Gesetz getan (Gal 4,4). Paulus verbindet die Fakten einer natürlichen Geburt Jesu und seine kulturgeschichtliche Einordnung in das Judentum mit dem Erfüllungsgedanken und der Sohn-Gottes-Vorstellung. Gott sandte seinen Sohn in die ‚Gleichgestalt des sündigen Fleisches' (Röm 8,3); er kommt aus dem Stamm Davids (Röm 1,3), der Jude Jesus ist der Gesalbte (Röm 9,5) und hatte zumindest zwei Brüder (1Kor 9,5; Gal 1,19). Jesus lebte nicht für sich selbst, sondern nahm (lud) die Schmähung anderer auf sich (Röm 15,3). Er entäußerte sich seiner Gottgleichheit, nahm Knechtsgestalt an, wurde Mensch, war gehorsam bis zum Tod am Kreuz (Phil 2,7f.; Gal 3,1) und wurde begraben (1Kor 15,4; Röm 6,4). Obwohl er reich war, wurde er um unsertwillen arm, um uns reich zu machen (2Kor 8,9). Er wusste von keiner Sünde, wurde aber für uns zur Sünde gemacht, damit wir in ihm zur Gerechtigkeit Gottes würden in ihm (2Kor 5,21). Gekreuzigt wurde er in Schwachheit, jetzt aber lebt er durch die Kraft Gottes (2Kor 13,4). Paulus will nichts anderes als den Gekreuzigten verkünden (1Kor 2,2), der für unsere Sünden gestorben ist (1Kor 15,3; Gal 1,4) und nun von Gott erhöht wurde (Phil 2,9–11). Auch die paulinische Nachfolge-Forderung (vgl. 1Thess 1,6; 2,14; 1Kor 4,6;

---

16 Vgl. K. Scholtissek, „Geboren aus einer Frau, geboren unter das Gesetz" (Gal 4,4). Die christologisch-soteriologische Bedeutung des irdischen Jesus bei Paulus, in: Paulinische Christologie (FS H. Hübner), hg. von U. Schnelle/Th. Söding/M. Labahn, Göttingen 2000, 211f.
17 Vgl. K. Scholtissek, „Geboren aus einer Frau, geboren unter das Gesetz", 209f.
18 Vgl. E. Reinmuth, Jesus-Christus-Geschichte, 24f.

11,1; Phil 2,5; 3,17) verweist auf den irdischen Jesus[19], denn die Gemeinden sollen sich an der Sanftmut und Güte Jesu Christi orientieren (vgl. 2Kor 10,1; Röm 15,5; Phil 1,8).

Paulus setzt somit in seinen Briefen eine Kenntnis der Jesus-Christus-Geschichte durch die Gemeinden voraus und nimmt durchgehend auf sie Bezug[20]. Daher vermeidet er die historisch wie sachlich unangemessene Alternative zwischen einer Faktengeschichte des irdischen Jesus und einer davon abgelösten abstrakten Kerygma-Christologie. Vielmehr kommt bei ihm die Geschichte des irdischen Jesus aus der Perspektive der durch den Auferstandenen geschaffenen gegenwärtigen Heilswirklichkeit in den Blick (vgl. Gal 1,3f.). Jesu Bedeutsamkeit erschließt sich nicht als Summe einzelner bedeutender Worte oder Handlungen, sondern allein von der durch Gott in Jesus Christus vollzogenen Geschichte, die Jesus Christus als den endzeitlichen und endgültigen Heilsbringer qualifiziert. Innerhalb dieser Jesus-Christus-Geschichte bilden der Irdische und der Auferweckte und damit die Person Jesu Christi eine Einheit, die sich nicht in die eine oder andere Richtung auflösen lässt. Indem auch Paulus vom Handeln Gottes in Jesus Christus erzählt, vermeidet er die falsche Alternative von Faktizität und Interpretation und wahrt so das Ganze der Jesus-Christus-Geschichte[21].

Wie und warum präsentiert Markus seine Jesus-Christus-Geschichte in der neuen Literaturgattung Evangelium[22]? Die Logienquelle und Lk 1,1 lassen Vor-

---

19 Anders O. Merk, Nachahmung Christi, in: Neues Testament. FS R. Schnackenburg, hg. von H. Merklein, Freiburg 1989, 172–206.
20 Vgl. E. Reinmuth, Jesus-Christus-Geschichte, 22f: „Diese Jesus-Christus-Geschichte ist als Inhalt auch der mündlichen Verkündigung des Paulus vorauszusetzen."
21 Treffend J. Blank, Paulus und Jesus (StANT 18), München 1968, 183: „Die Urkirche hat letzten Endes nicht trotz Ostern am Kreuz Jesu und an der Jesus-Geschichte festgehalten, sondern gerade wegen Ostern und aufgrund von Ostern."
22 Zur Erzähltextanalyse des Markusevangeliums vgl. D. Rhoads/D. Michie, Mark as Story: An Introduction to the Narrative of a Gospel, Philadelphia 1982; F. Hahn (Hg.), Der Erzähler des Evangeliums. Methodische Neuansätze in der Markusforschung (SBS 118/119), Stuttgart 1985; N. R. Petersen, „Literarkritik", the New Literary Criticism and the Gospel according to Mark, in: F. van Segbroeck u.a. (ed.), The Four Gospels II (FS F. Neirynck), Leuven 1992, 935–948; C. Breytenbach, Das Markusevangelium als traditionsgebundene Erzählung?, in: The Synoptic Gospels, hg. von C. Focant (BETL CX), Leuven 1993, 77–110; Th. Söding (Hg.), Der Evangelist als Theologe. Studien zum Markusevangelium (SBS 163), Stuttgart 1995. Zur Methodik vgl. M.A. Powell, What is Narrative Criticism? A New Approach to the Bible, Minneapolis 1990; G. Genette, Die Erzählung, München ²1998; E. S. Malbon, Mark's Jesus. Characterization as Narrative Christology, Waco 2009. Malbon unterscheidet zwischen dem, was der Erzähler und andere Charaktere innerhalb des Evangeliums über Jesus sagen („projected Christology"), wie und was Jesus daraufhin antwortet („deflected Christology"), was Jesus demgegenüber über sich und Gott sagt („refracted Christology"), was Jesus tut („enacted Christology") und wie das Agieren anderer Akteure mit dem verbunden ist, was Jesus sagt und tut („reflected Christology").

formen von Evangelien und wahrscheinlich auch verlorene Evangelien vermuten, so dass Markus für das frühe Christentum eine entscheidende Leistung vollbringt: Er bewahrt sehr verschiedene Jesustraditionen vor dem Vergessen, verbindet sie erzählerisch und präsentiert Jesus von Nazareth als Verkündiger und Verkündigten. Markus ist der Erste innerhalb des frühen Christentums, der die geschichtliche Dimension des Auftretens Jesu umfassend in den Mittelpunkt stellt und so eine Enthistorisierung der Jesus-Christus-Geschichte verhindert, wie sie später z. B. im Thomas-Evangelium vorgenommen wird. Mit seinem Evangelium schuf Markus somit einen zentralen Baustein zum kulturellen Gedächtnis des frühen Christentums.

Markus setzt den Glauben an die Messianität Jesu Christi voraus (Mk 1,1), entfaltet dieses Bekenntnis durch seine erzählerische Linienführung und stellt in seinem Evangelium dar, in welchem Sinn Jesus Christus immer schon der Sohn Gottes ist und es zugleich innerhalb der Erzählung wird[23]. Für Markus ist der irdische Weg Jesu zugleich der Weg des Gottessohnes, Jesus Christus steht gleichermaßen mit Himmel und Erde in Verbindung, und deshalb ist seine Geschichte eine himmlische und irdische. Dieser fundamentale Zusammenhang wird durch die Erzählung von der Taufe Jesu (Mk 1,9–11), der Verklärungsgeschichte (Mk 9,2–9) und dem Bekenntnis des Centurio unter dem Kreuz (Mk 15,39) verdeutlicht[24]. Jesu Sein und Wesen stehen von Anfang an fest, er ist Gottes Sohn und verändert sein Wesen nicht. Aber für die Menschen wird er erst Gottes Sohn, denn sie brauchen einen Erkenntnisprozess[25]. Dieser Prozess ist die vita Jesu, so wie Markus sie in der neuen Literaturgattung Evangelium darstellt. Zum Ziel gelangt dieser Erkenntnisprozess erst am Ende des Evangeliums, am Kreuz, erst hier ist es ein Mensch und nicht Gott, der Jesus als υἱὸς θεοῦ erkennt (Mk 15,39). Zuvor wissen dies nur Gott (Mk 1,11; 9,7), die Dämonen (Mk 3,11; 5,7) und der Sohn selbst (Mk 12,6; 13,32). Der Mensch muss erst den ganzen Weg Jesu von der Taufe bis zum Kreuz durchschreiten, um zu einer angemessenen Erkenntnis der Gottessohnschaft Jesu Christi zu gelangen. Indem die Literaturgattung Evangelium diesen Weg des Gottessohnes darstellt und zur rechten Erkenntnis seiner Person führen will, ist sie nichts anderes als der literarische Ausdruck der theologischen Erkenntnis, dass der gekreuzigte Jesus von Nazareth von Anfang an seinen Weg als

---

23 Vgl. F.J. Matera, New Testament Christology, Louisville 1999, 24: „The Christiology of Mark's Gospel is in the story it tells."
24 Grundlegend bleibt hier Ph. Vielhauer, Erwägungen zur Christologie des Markusevangeliums, in: Aufsätze zum Neuen Testament, hg. von Ph. Vielhauer (TB 31), München 1965, 199–214.
25 Vgl. R. Weber, Christologie und ‚Messiasgeheimnis': ihr Zusammenhang und Stellenwert in den Darstellungsintentionen des Markus, in: EvTh 43 (1983), 108–125, hier 115f.

Gottessohn ging[26]. Die Literaturgattung Evangelium ist somit eine Form sui generis[27], sie verdankt sich der theologischen Einsicht, dass in der einmaligen und unverwechselbaren Geschichte des Jesus von Nazareth Gott selbst handelte. Eine Spannung zwischen vor- und nachösterlich, Geschichte und Kerygma oder textinterner und textexterner Ebene besteht dabei für Markus nicht, sondern seine theologische Leistung besteht gerade darin, beides jeweils entschieden als Einheit verstanden und dargestellt zu haben[28]. Indem Markus historiographisch-biographischen Erzähltext und kerygmatische Anrede fest verbindet und Jesu Weg zum Kreuz als dramatisches Geschehen darstellt, wahrt er die Einheit des Irdischen mit dem Erhöhten. Er nimmt damit eine bereits in 1Kor 15,3b–5 erkennbare Tendenz auf: Das Bekenntnis zum gekreuzigten und auferstandenen Jesus Christus ist ohne die elementare Bindung an den Weg des irdischen Jesus nicht möglich[29].

Hinzu kommt ein zweiter entscheidender Punkt: Die Geheimnistheorie als weitere zentrale christologische Erzählstrategie wahrt die grundlegende Einheit von Hoheit und Niedrigkeit in der Person Jesu Christi. Die Einzelelemente der markinischen Geheimnistheorie entspringen nicht einem historischen Interesse, sondern sie zielen auf den Leser und wollen ihn zu einer umfassenden Erkenntnis Jesu Christi führen. Zugleich ermöglicht die Geheimnistheorie dem Evangelisten Markus, die Jesustraditionen der vormarkinischen Wundergeschichten und die Passionstraditionen im Rahmen der neuen Literaturgattung Evangelium zu verbinden, zu einer neuen Einheit zu verschmelzen und so seine Jesus-Christus-Geschichte als ganze inhaltlich und erzählerisch zu profilieren[30]. Mk 9,9 ver-

---

26 Grundsätzlich zutreffend ist deshalb immer noch das Votum von H. Conzelmann, Gegenwart und Zukunft in der synoptischen Tradition, in: Theologie als Schriftauslegung, hg. von H. Conzelmann (BEvTh 65), München 1974, 60, zum markinischen Messiasgeheimnis: „Die Geheimnistheorie ist die hermeneutische Voraussetzung der Gattung ‚Evangelium'."
27 Zur Literaturgattung Evangelium vgl. zuletzt R.A. Burridge, What are the Gospels?, Grand Rapids ²2004; D. Frickenschmidt, Evangelium als Biographie (TANZ 22), Tübingen 1997; D. Dormeyer, Das Markusevangelium als Idealbiographie von Jesus Christus, dem Nazarener (SBB 43), Stuttgart 1999; D. Wördemann, Das Charakterbild des bios nach Plutarch und das Christusbild im Evangelium nach Markus, Paderborn 2002; G. Theißen, Die Entstehung des Neuen Testaments als literaturgeschichtliches Problem, Heidelberg 2007, 71–92.
28 Vgl. hierzu H.-F. Weiß, Kerygma und Geschichte, Berlin 1983.
29 Vgl. M. Hengel, Das Begräbnis Jesu bei Paulus und die leibliche Auferstehung aus dem Grabe, in: Auferstehung, hg. von F. Avemarie/H. Lichtenberger (WUNT 135), Tübingen 2001, 127: „das Evangelium als Erzählung des Heilsgeschehens stand von Anfang an in notwendiger Parallelität zum Evangelium als Kerygma".
30 Eine pragmatische Funktion gibt G. Theißen, Evangelienschreibung und Gemeindeleitung: Pragmatische Motive bei der Abfassung des Markusevangeliums, in: Antikes Judentum und Frühes Christentum (FS H. Stegemann), hg. von B. Kollmann/W. Reinbold/A. Steudel (BZNW 97), Berlin 1999, 389–414, dem Geheimnismotiv: Aus der Parallelität zwischen der Textwelt des

deutlicht zudem, dass die Geheimnistheorie als eine Form der markinischen Kreuzestheologie begriffen werden muss[31]. Der Gottessohn Jesus Christus bleibt derselbe in seinem Leiden und in seinem vollmächtigen Wirken. Markus zeigt, wie Jesus sein Volk im Zeichen der Gottesherrschaft durch sein vollmächtiges Wort, sein heilendes Wirken und seine Bereitschaft zur stellvertretenden Lebenshingabe sammeln will. Dabei nimmt der Evangelist den zentralen Gedanken der paulinischen Theologie auf und machte ihn zum Zentrum seiner dramatischen Erzählung: Der gekreuzigte Jesus von Nazareth ist der Sohn Gottes.

Paulus und Markus sind sich in ihrer christologischen Grundperspektive sehr nahe: Die Einheit des irdischen, gekreuzigten und auferstandenen Gottessohnes Jesus Christus ist die Basis ihrer Christologie. Die narrative Entfaltung dieser Grundeinsicht stellt sich in den verschiedenen Gattungen sehr unterschiedlich dar[32], bildet aber inhaltlich kein wirklich trennendes Element.

3 Zentrale Motive paulinischer und markinischer Christologie

3.1 Evangelium

Paulus und Markus sind die Träger des Begriffes εὐαγγέλιον („Evangelium")[33] und prägen ihn inhaltlich. Sie greifen damit einen religiös-politisch konnotierten Begriff

---

Evangeliums und der realen Welt der Leser/Hörer kann geschlossen werden, dass die sukzessive Enthüllung des Geheimnisses und die damit wachsende Gefährdung Jesu in der sozialen Welt der markinischen Gemeinde eine reale Entsprechung hat.
31 W. Wrede, Das Messiasgeheimnis in den Evangelien, Göttingen ⁴1969 = 1901, 145 u. ö., führte das Messiasgeheimnis nicht auf den Evangelisten Markus zurück, sondern sah in ihm das Werk der nachösterlichen, aber vormarkinischen Gemeinde. Es entstand aus der Notwendigkeit eines Ausgleiches zwischen dem unmessianischen Leben Jesu und dem nachösterlichen Gemeindeglauben. Im Verlauf der Forschungsgeschichte hatten sowohl die These unmessianischer Jesustraditionen als auch die Annahme eines vormarkinischen Ursprunges des Messiasgeheimnisses keinen Bestand. Speziell die Arbeiten von Eduard Schweizer zeigten, dass Markus als Urheber der Geheimnistheorie anzusehen ist (vgl. E. Schweizer, Zur Frage nach dem Messiasgeheimnis bei Markus, in: Beiträge zur Theologie des Neuen Testaments, hg. von E. Schweizer, Zürich 1970, 11–20).
32 Was M.E. Boring, Mark (NTL), Louisville 2006, 248, treffend zu Markus sagt, trifft grundsätzlich auch für Paulus zu: „Jesus is the central and primary charakter, and he appears in almost every scene."
33 εὐαγγέλιον: 76mal im NT; 48mal Protopaulinen; 8mal Markus; 4mal Matthäus; 0mal Lukas- und Johannesevangelium. Das Verb εὐαγγελίζω (54mal im NT) findet sich 19mal bei Paulus, 25mal

auf und machen ihn zu einem theologischen und – bei Markus – auch literarischen Schlüsselbegriff.

Das Verb εὐαγγελίζεσθαι verweist auf einen überwiegend atl.-jüdischen Hintergrund[34]. Es erscheint sowohl in der LXX als auch in Schriften des antiken Judentums und muss mit ‚das eschatologische Heil ansagen' übersetzt werden. Auch im hellenistischen Schrifttum ist εὐαγγελίζεσθαι im religiösen Sinn belegt (vgl. Philostratus, *Vita Apollonii*, I 28; vgl. ferner Philo, *Legatio ad Gajum*, 18.231). Das Substantiv εὐαγγέλια wird in der LXX ohne erkennbare theologische Füllung gebraucht[35], hingegen spielt es eine zentrale Rolle in der Herrscherverehrung. So wird in der Inschrift von Priene (9 v. Chr.) der Geburtstag des Augustus so glorifiziert: „Der Geburtstag des Gottes war aber für die Welt die erste der von ihm ausgehenden Freudenbotschaften (εὐαγγελίων)"[36]. Josephus verbindet die Erhebung Vespasians zum Kaiser mit Opfern und dem εὐαγγέλια-Begriff: „Schneller als der Flug des Gedankens verkündigten die Gerüchte die Botschaft vom neuen Herrscher über den Osten, und jede Stadt feierte die gute Nachricht (εὐαγγέλια) und brachte zu seinen Gunsten Opfer dar."[37] Die Himmelfahrt der Drusilla und des Claudius als Auftakt ihrer Vergöttlichung wird von Seneca ironisch als ‚gute Nachricht' bezeichnet[38]. Innerhalb der zeitgenössischen Enzyklopädie war der Terminus εὐαγγέλιον/εὐαγγέλια auch mit der Herrscherverehrung verbunden und hatte damit eine politisch-religiöse Konnotation. Die frühen Gemeinden nahmen mit dem Evangeliums-Begriff offenbar sehr bewusst Vorstellungen ihres kulturellen Umfeldes auf, zugleich unterschieden sie sich durch den Singular εὐαγγέλιον grundlegend von den εὐαγγέλια der Umwelt. Auch der paulinische Gebrauch von εὐαγγέλιον lässt sich in diese Anknüpfungs- und Überbietungsstrategie einordnen: Die wahre und exklusive gute Nachricht ist die Botschaft von Kreuz und Auferstehung. Nicht das Erscheinen des Kaisers rettet, sondern der vom Himmel kommende Gottessohn (vgl. 1Thess 1,9f.).

---

bei Lukas (Ev/Apg), 1mal bei Matthäus und 0mal bei Markus. – Vgl. dazu den Beitrag von Andreas Lindemann im vorliegenden Band.

34 Die atl.-jüdische Vorgeschichte von εὐαγγέλιον bzw. εὐαγγελίζεσθαι wird dargestellt von P. Stuhlmacher, Das paulinische Evangelium I. Vorgeschichte (FRLANT 95), Göttingen 1968.

35 Der Singular εὐαγγέλιον findet sich nicht in der LXX, der Plural εὐαγγέλια ist nur in 2Sam 4,10 belegt; vgl. ferner ἡ εὐαγγελία in 2Sam 18,20.22.25.27; 2Kön 7,9. Treffend G. Friedrich, Art. εὐαγγέλιον, in: ThWNT 2 (1935), 722: „LXX ist nicht der Ursprungsort des nt.lichen εὐαγγέλιον."

36 Vgl. G. Strecker/U. Schnelle (Hgg.), Neuer Wettstein II/1, Berlin 1996, 6–9.

37 Vgl. Josephus, *Bellum Iudaicum*, 4,618; ferner *Bellum Iudaicum*, 4,656 (= Neuer Wettstein II/1, 9f.).

38 Vgl. Seneca minor, *Divi Claudii apocolocyntosis*, 1,3.

Für Paulus vollzieht sich Gottes Offenbarung im εὐαγγέλιον[39], das seinem Ursprung und seiner Autorität nach das εὐαγγέλιον τοῦ θεοῦ ist („Evangelium Gottes"; vgl. 1Thess 2,2.8.9; 2Kor 11,7; Röm 1,1; 15,16). Deshalb umfasst εὐαγγέλιον weitaus mehr als eine ‚frohe Botschaft'; es ist wirksame Heilsmitteilung, ein Glauben schaffendes Geschehen und eine Glauben wirkende Macht, die von Gott ausgeht und durch die Kraft des Geistes auf das Heil der Menschen zielt (vgl. 1Thess 1,5; 1Kor 4,20; Röm 1,16f.). Das Evangelium erreichte Paulus nicht durch menschliche Vermittlung, es wurde ihm unmittelbar von Gott durch die Erscheinung Jesu Christi offenbart (vgl. Gal 1,11ff.; 2Kor 4,1-6; Röm 1,1-5). Paulus darf und muss dem Evangelium dienen, es steht nicht zu seiner Disposition (vgl. Röm 15,16). Das Evangelium wird zwar durch das menschliche Wort des Apostels dargeboten, geht darin aber keineswegs auf, vielmehr begegnet es den Hörern als Wort Gottes (vgl. 1Thess 2,13; 2Kor 4,4-6; 5,20). Für Paulus ist somit die Einsetzung des Evangeliums ein Heilserweis Gottes, der dem Glauben und der Heilserkenntnis der Gemeinde Jesu Christi vorangeht[40].

Seinem Inhalt nach ist das Evangelium das εὐαγγέλιον τοῦ Χριστοῦ („Evangelium Christi"; vgl. 1Thess 3,2; 1Kor 9,12; 2Kor 2,12; 9,13; 10,14; Gal 1,7; Röm 15,19; Phil 1,27). Dieses Evangelium hat eine ganz bestimmte Gestalt und einen eindeutig bestimmbaren Inhalt; deshalb bekämpft Paulus all jene, die ein anderes Evangelium verkünden, und stellt sie unter einen Fluch (vgl. Gal 1,7-9). Der Inhalt des Evangeliums (vgl. 1Thess 1,9f.; 1Kor 15,3-5; 2Kor 4,4; Röm 1,3b-4a) lässt sich nach Paulus so beschreiben: Von Uranfang an wollte Gott die Welt in und durch Christus retten (vgl. 1Kor 2,7; Röm 16,25), diese Heilsabsicht ließ er durch die Propheten verkünden (vgl. Röm 1,2; 16,26) und von der Schrift bezeugen (vgl. 1Kor 15,3.4; Gal 3,8)[41]. Als die Zeit erfüllt war, sandte Gott seinen Sohn, der durch den Tod am Kreuz und seine Auferstehung das Heil der Welt und der Menschen bewirkte (vgl. Gal 4,4f.; Röm 1,3f.; 15,8; 2Kor 1,20). Bis zur Sendung des Sohnes Gottes lebten Juden und Heiden gleichermaßen in Unkenntnis des wahren Willens Gottes, jetzt wird er im Evangelium durch den berufenen Heidenapostel Paulus verkündigt. Im Evangelium fasst sich somit für Paulus der endgültige Heilswille Gottes in Jesus Christus zusammen, es ist die Botschaft von dem gekreuzigten

---

39 Vgl. dazu G. Strecker, Das Evangelium Jesu Christi, in: Eschaton und Historie, hg. von G. Strecker, Göttingen 1979, 183-228; P. Stuhlmacher, Biblische Theologie I, Göttingen 1992, 311-348; H. Merklein, Zum Verständnis des paulinischen Begriffs „Evangelium", in: Studien zu Jesus und Paulus, hg. von H. Merklein (WUNT 43), Tübingen 1987, 279-295; J.D.G. Dunn, The Theology of Paul the Apostle, Grand Rapids 1998, 163-181; D.-A. Koch, Die Schrift als Zeuge des Evangeliums (BHTh 69), Tübingen 1986, 322-353.
40 Vgl. P. Stuhlmacher, Biblische Theologie I, 315.
41 Vgl. dazu J.D.G. Dunn, Theology of Paul, 169-173.

Gottessohn (vgl. 1Kor 1,17)⁴². Weil das Evangelium Heilsbotschaft ist, können weder seine Annahme noch seine Ablehnung folgenlos bleiben. Deshalb erscheint Jesus Christus im Evangelium nicht nur als Retter, sondern auch als Richter. Zugleich ist aber deutlich, dass für Paulus das Evangelium zuallererst eine δύναμις θεοῦ („Macht Gottes") ist, die jene rettet, die die Heilsbotschaft vom gekreuzigten und auferstandenen Jesus Christus im Glauben annehmen (vgl. Röm 1,16.17).

In Kontinuität zu Paulus gebraucht auch Markus εὐαγγέλιον als zentralen Verkündigungsbegriff und ist darüber hinaus Schöpfer der neuen Literaturgattung ‚Evangelium'. Alle sieben εὐαγγέλιον-Belege (vgl. Mk 1,1.14f.; 8,35; 10,29; 13,10; 14,9) gehen auf den Evangelisten zurück⁴³. Wurde *vor* Markus εὐαγγέλιον immer als Verkündigung von Jesus Christus verstanden, wobei ein genitivus objectivus Ἰησοῦ Χριστοῦ zu ergänzen war, zeigt sich nun eine grundlegende Veränderung. In Mk 1,1 ist Jesus Christus Verkünder und zugleich Inhalt des Evangeliums⁴⁴, der Genitiv Ἰησοῦ Χριστοῦ bezeichnet das Subjekt und das Objekt des Evangeliums⁴⁵. Die Korrespondenz zwischen Mk 1,1 und Mk 1,14f. verdeutlicht zudem, dass für Markus der im Evangelium verkündigte Jesus Christus zugleich der Verkünder des Evangeliums Gottes ist⁴⁶, ohne dass für Markus die *theo*-logische Verkündigung Jesu und das christologische Bekenntnis der Gemeinde einen Gegensatz darstellen⁴⁷.

Die Taten und Worte Jesu Christi sind Inhalte des Evangeliums, zugleich ist aber Jesus Christus für Markus nicht nur eine Gestalt der Geschichte, sondern der gekreuzigte und auferstandene Gottessohn und darum auch Subjekt des Evangeliums⁴⁸. Die Repräsentanz des Evangeliums durch Jesus und die Repräsentanz

---

42 Vgl. H. Merklein, Zum Verständnis des paulinischen Begriffs „Evangelium", 291–293.
43 Nachweis bei G. Strecker, Literarkritische Überlegungen zum εὐαγγέλιον-Begriff im Markusevangelium, in: Eschaton und Historie, hg. von G. Strecker, Göttingen 1979, 76–89.
44 Vgl. M. Feneberg, Der Markusprolog (StANT 36), München 1974, 118, wonach die Genitivverbindung einen vieldimensionalen Bedeutungsgehalt hat: „Anfang des Evangeliums, das Jesus Christus, der Sohn Gottes, bringt, dessen Urheber er ist (gen. auct.), das von ihm handelt (gen. obj.), das er selbst ist (gen. epexegeticus)." Gegen H. Weder, ‚Evangelium Jesu Christi' (Mk 1,1) und ‚Evangelium Gottes' (Mk 1,14), in: Die Mitte des Neuen Testaments. FS E. Schweizer, hg. v. U. Luz / H. Weder, Göttingen 1983, 402, der Mk 1,1 nur als genitivus objectivus auflösen will.
45 Vgl. J. Gnilka, Das Evangelium nach Markus (EKK II/2), Neukirchen 1979, 43.
46 Diesen Aspekt betont nachdrücklich J. Dechow, Gottessohn und Herrschaft Gottes (WMANT 86), Neukirchen 2000, 274–280.
47 Angesichts der theologischen und christologischen Füllung von Mk 1,1–15 erscheint mir eine Alternative unangemessen, wie sie J. Dechow, Gottessohn und Herrschaft Gottes, 42, formuliert: „Markus geht es in erster Linie darum, die Lesenden mit der eschatologischen Botschaft Jesu zu konfrontieren; die hoheitliche Identität des Botschafters spielt demgegenüber eine untergeordnete Rolle."
48 Vgl. dazu umfassend Th. Söding, Glaube bei Markus (SBB 12), Stuttgart ²1987, 198–251.

Jesu im Evangelium unterstreicht Markus nachdrücklich durch die Anfügung von „um des Evangeliums willen" an „um meinetwillen" in Mk 8,35; 10,29 (vgl. die universale Evangeliumsverkündigung in Mk 13,10; 14,9). Damit verbindet der Evangelist das vergangenheitliche und gegenwärtige Wirken Jesu Christi untrennbar mit dem Evangelium als Verkündigungsbotschaft und Literaturgattung. Zugleich verschränken sich hier die für die Gattung Evangelium konstitutive textinterne und textexterne Ebene. Der auf der textinternen Ebene von Jesus gesprochene Entscheidungsruf zielt auf textexterner Ebene auf die markinische Gemeinde, für die Jesus Christus im Evangelium zugänglich und gegenwärtig ist. Indem Markus in seinem Evangelium den irdischen Weg des Gottessohnes Jesus Christus darstellt, nimmt er eine bereits in 1Kor 15,3b–5 erkennbare Tendenz auf: Das Bekenntnis zum gekreuzigten und auferstandenen Jesus Christus ist ohne die elementare Bindung an den Weg des irdischen Jesus nicht möglich[49]. Gott selbst machte Jesus zu seinem Sohn (Mk 1,9–11) und beauftragte ihn mit der Verkündigung des Evangeliums, so dass die historiographische Darstellung des Weges Jesu, die christologischen Implikationen und die theologische Grundlegung einander immer bedingen und Ostern dabei keine Zäsur darstellt.

Markus nimmt den für Paulus zentralen εὐαγγέλιον-Begriff auf und profiliert ihn literarisch und theologisch: Jesus Christus ist nun innerhalb der narrativen Welt des Evangeliums Verkünder und Inhalt des Evangeliums zugleich.

3.2 Christologische Hoheitstitel

Jesu Stellung als Auferstandener und seine Funktion als endzeitlicher Retter und Befreier werden bei Paulus mit den christologischen Hoheitstiteln auf den Begriff gebracht. Die Hoheitstitel gehören zu den zentralen Interpretamenten des Christusgeschehens; sie sagen aus, wer und was Jesus von Nazareth für die glaubende Gemeinde ist[50]. In konzentrierter Form enthalten die Hoheitstitel die Grundgedanken paulinischer Christologie. So finden sich von den 531 Χριστός- bzw. Ἰησοῦς Χριστός-Belegen im Neuen Testament allein 270 in den Protopaulinen (1Thess: 10mal; 1Kor: 64; 2Kor: 47; Gal: 38; Röm: 66; Phil: 37; Phlm: 8)[51]. Κύριος ist

---

[49] Vgl. M. Hengel, Das Begräbnis Jesu bei Paulus und die leibliche Auferstehung aus dem Grabe, 127: „das Evangelium als Erzählung des Heilsgeschehens stand von Anfang an in notwendiger Parallelität zum Evangelium als Kerygma".
[50] Einen Überblick verschafft Ch. Böttrich, „Gott und Retter". Gottesprädikationen in christologischen Titeln, in: NZSTh 42 (2000), 217–236.
[51] Zählung nach K. Aland (Hg.), Vollständige Konkordanz zum griechischen Neuen Testament, Bd. II: Spezialübersichten, Berlin 1978, 300f.

im Neuen Testament insgesamt 719mal, bei Paulus 189mal belegt, d.h. mehr als ein Viertel aller Stellen entfallen auf Paulus (1Thess: 24mal; 1Kor: 66; 2Kor: 29; Gal: 6; Röm: 44; Phil: 15; Phlm: 5)[52]. Der Titel υἱὸς (τοῦ) θεοῦ erscheint zwar bei Paulus relativ selten (15mal), allerdings an sehr exponierten Stellen, so dass auch er für die paulinische Christologie von grundlegender Bedeutung ist. Von den einzelnen Titeln sind für den Vergleich mit Markus vor allem der Χριστός-Titel und der υἱὸς θεοῦ-Titel relevant.

Die zentrale Hoheitsbezeichnung innerhalb der Protopaulinen ist Χριστός bzw. Ἰησοῦς Χριστός[53]. Χριστός haftet bei Paulus an den ältesten Bekenntnistraditionen (vgl. 1Kor 15,3b–5; 2Kor 5,15), damit verbunden sind Aussagen über Tod und Auferstehung Jesu, die das gesamte Heilsgeschehen umfassen (vgl. als Basistext 1Kor 15,3b–5). Auch Aussagen über die Kreuzigung (1Kor 1,21; 2,2; Gal 3,1.13), den Tod (Röm 5,6.8; 14,15; 15,3; 1Kor 8,11; Gal 2,19.21), die Auferweckung (Röm 6,9; 8,11; 10,7; 1Kor 15,12–17.20.23), die Präexistenz (1Kor 10,4; 11,3a.b) und die irdische Existenz Jesu (Röm 9,5; 2Kor 5,16) verbinden sich mit Χριστός. Von der auf das gesamte Heilsgeschehen bezogenen Grundaussage verzweigen sich die Χριστός-Aussagen dann in vielfältige Bereiche. So spricht Paulus vom πιστεύειν εἰς Χριστόν (Gal 2,16: „glauben an Christus"; vgl. Gal 3,22; Phil 1,29), vom εὐαγγέλιον τοῦ Χριστοῦ („Evangelium Christi", vgl. 1Thess 3,2; 1Kor 9,12; 2Kor 2,12; 9,13; 10,14; Gal 1,7; Röm 15,19; Phil 1,27) und versteht sich selbst als Apostel Christi (vgl. 1Thess 2,7; 2Kor 11,13: ἀπόστολος Χριστοῦ).

Der selbstverständliche Gebrauch von Χριστός in Briefen an überwiegend heidenchristliche Gemeinden ist kein Zufall, denn die Adressaten konnten von ihrem kulturgeschichtlichen Hintergrund Χριστός im Kontext antiker Salbungsriten rezipieren. Die im gesamten Mittelmeerraum verbreiteten Salbungsriten zeugen von einem gemeinantiken Sprachgebrauch, wonach gilt: „wer/was gesalbt ist, ist heilig, Gott nah, Gott übergeben"[54]. Sowohl Judenchristen als auch Heidenchristen konnten Χριστός als Prädikat für die einzigartige Gottnähe und Heiligkeit Jesu verstehen, so dass Χριστός (bzw. Ἰησοῦς Χριστός) gerade bei Paulus als *Titelname* zum idealen Missionsbegriff wurde.

---

[52] Vgl. K. Aland (Hg.), Vollständige Konkordanz, 166f.
[53] Vgl. zu Χριστός bes. W. Kramer, Christos Kyrios Gottessohn (AThANT 44), Zürich 1963, 15–60.131–148; F. Hahn, Christologische Hoheitstitel, Göttingen ⁵1995, 133–225.466–472; G. Vermes, Jesus der Jude, Neukirchen 1993, 115–143; M. Karrer, Der Gesalbte. Die Grundlagen des Christustitels (FRLANT 151), Göttingen 1990; D. Zeller, Art. Messias/Christus, in: NBL 3 (1995), 782–786; M. de Jonge, Art. Christ, in: DDD (²1999), 192–200.
[54] M. Karrer, Der Gesalbte, 211.

Bei Markus erscheint der Χριστός-Titel an zwei hermeneutischen und theologischen Schlüsselstellen des Evangeliums[55]: Mk 1,1 und 8,29 (ferner 9,41; 12,35; 13,21; 14,61; 15,32). Mk 1,1 qualifiziert die markinische Verkündigung nicht nur als Evangelium von Jesus Christus, sondern Jesus ist als der Χριστός gleichermaßen Inhalt und Verkünder des Evangeliums. Was für den Sohnes-Titel gilt, trifft auch bei Χριστός zu: Jesus ist schon immer das, was er innerhalb der Erzählung *wird*. Dies verdeutlicht Mk 8,29, wo durch Petrus die einzige ausdrückliche Christusprädikation ausgesprochen wird: „Du bist der Christus" (σὺ εἶ ὁ Χριστός). Indem Markus sie unter ein Schweigegebot stellt (8,30), die erste Leidensweissagung anfügt (8,31) und das Ansinnen des Petrus, Jesus solle dem Leiden ausweichen, scharf zurückweist (8,32f), bringt der Evangelist literarisch und theologisch sein Verständnis von Χριστός zum Ausdruck: Petrus hat prinzipiell richtig erkannt, dass Jesus der Messias ist; zugleich gilt es festzuhalten, in welcher Weise er es wird. Der leidende Menschensohn und der hoheitliche Christus sind ein und derselbe, es gibt die Hoheit nicht jenseits der Niedrigkeit und umgekehrt. Damit stellt Markus den Χριστός-Titel keineswegs unter einen Vorbehalt[56], sondern wahrt das paradoxe Personengeheimnis Jesu Christi, das sich nicht aus der schriftgelehrten Reflexion ableiten lässt.

Der Titel υἱὸς (τοῦ) θεοῦ findet sich nur 15mal bei Paulus[57]. Der Apostel übernahm ihn aus der Tradition (vgl. 1Thess 1,9f.; Röm 1,3b–4a), religionsgeschichtlich dürften bei der Ausformung der Sohnes-Christologie alttestamentliche Vorstellungen vorherrschend gewesen sein (vgl. Ps 2,7; 2Sam 7,11f.14). Die zentrale Bedeutung des Sohnestitels bezeugt 2Kor 1,19, wo der Sohn Gottes als der Inhalt der Verkündigung des Apostels erscheint: „der Sohn Gottes, Christus Jesus, der durch uns unter euch verkündigt wurde". Die soteriologische Dimension des Sohnes-Titels unterstreicht Gal 1,16; der Sohn Gottes ist Inhalt der Berufungsvision bei Damaskus. Für die Glaubenden gab sich der Sohn Gottes dahin (vgl. Gal 2,20; Röm 8,32). In Gal 4,4; Röm 8,3 verbindet sich mit der Sendung des Sohnes die Präexistenzvorstellung (Gal 4,4). Die bleibende Bedeutsamkeit dieses Heilsgeschehens benennt Gal 4,6; durch die Gegenwart des Geistes des Sohnes dürften sich die Glaubenden selbst als Söhne verstehen. Im Sohn engagiert sich Gott für

---

55 Zum markinischen Titelgebrauch vgl. auch M.E. Boring, Mark, 249–257.
56 Anders F. Hahn, Theologie des Neuen Testaments I, Tübingen 2002, 501: „Der Messiastitel wird als im Blick auf den irdischen Jesus proleptisch verwendet und ist ebenso wie ‚Davidssohn' im Sinn des Messias designatus zu verstehen."
57 Das relevante Material wird besprochen bei M. Hengel, Der Sohn Gottes, Tübingen ²1977, 35–39.67–89; zu Qumran (vgl. neben 4QFlor I 11–13; 1QSa II 11 bes. 4Q 246) vgl. J.A. Fitzmyer, The „Son of God" Document from Qumran, in: Bib 74 (1993), 153–174; J. Zimmermann, Messianische Texte aus Qumran (WUNT 2.104), Tübingen 1998, 128–170.

das Heil und die Sohnschaft der ganzen Menschheit. Das spärliche Vorkommen des Gottessohn-Titels besagt nur wenig über seine inhaltliche Bedeutung für die paulinische Theologie[58]. Die besondere Platzierung von υἱός innerhalb der paulinischen Argumentationsgänge lässt vielmehr erkennen, dass er diesem Titel eine hohe theologische Bedeutung zumaß. Der Sohnes-Titel bringt sowohl die enge Verbindung Jesu Christi mit dem Vater als auch seine Funktion als Heilsmittler zwischen Gott und den Menschen zum Ausdruck.

Dem υἱὸς θεοῦ-Titel kommt innerhalb des Aufbaus des Markusevangeliums eine ganz besondere Bedeutung zu, denn er strukturiert nicht nur die Erzählung (vgl. Mk 1,1; 1,11; 3,11; 9,7; 12,6; 14,61; 15,39), sondern beantwortet prägnant die Leitfrage der markinischen Christologie: „Wer ist dieser?" (vgl. Mk 1,27; 4,41; 6,2f.14–16; 8,27ff.; 9,7; 10,47f.; 14,61f.; 15,39). Die bevorzugte Verwendung von υἱὸς θεοῦ ist kein Zufall, denn dieser Titel war sowohl für Juden als auch für Menschen griechisch-römischer Religiosität rezipierbar[59]. Durch die Wendung ὁ υἱὸς μου ὁ ἀγαπητός (1,11; 9,7: „mein geliebter Sohn") bzw. υἱὸς ἀγαπητός (12,6: „geliebter Sohn") werden die Erzählung von der Taufe Jesu (Mk 1,9–11), die Verklärungsgeschichte (Mk 9,2–9) und die Winzerallegorie (Mk 12,1–12) terminologisch verbunden und zu Leittexten. Sie formieren eine christologische Erkenntnislinie, insofern hier durch Gottes Stimme Himmel- und Erdenwelt zusammentreten und zur Bezeichnung der Gottzugehörigkeit Jesu jeweils der Titel υἱός gebraucht wird. Während Taufe und Verklärung Jesu Würde formulieren und präsentieren, präludiert die Winzerallegorie die Passion, so dass alle drei Texte auf das Bekenntnis des Centurio unter dem Kreuz (Mk 15,39) zulaufen. Im kompositorischen Gerüst des Evangeliums sind Taufe, Verklärung, Verwerfung und Bekenntnis unter dem Kreuz die Grundpfeiler, um die herum Markus seine Traditionen in Form einer vita Jesu gruppiert[60]. Der Titel υἱός markiert dabei die inhaltliche Mitte, denn er vermag Jesu göttliches Wesen und sein Leidens- und Todesgeschick gleichermaßen zu umfassen.

Die Verwendung christologischer Titel bei Paulus und Markus lässt einen begrenzten Vergleich zu: Paulus und Markus stimmen in der kreuzestheologischen Prägung des Χριστός-Titels überein, auch wenn Paulus diesen Titel umfassender gebraucht. Der Sohn-Gottes-Titel wiederum steht im Zentrum der markinischen Christologie, bei Paulus ist er zentral, aber weniger verbreitet.

---

[58] Gegen W. Kramer, Christos Kyrios Gottessohn, 189, der behauptet, der Gottessohntitel sei für Paulus „nur von untergeordneter Bedeutung".
[59] Vgl. dazu A. Yarbro Collins, Mark and His Readers: The Son of God among Jews, in: HThR 92 (1999), 393–408; dies., The Son of God among Greeks and Romans, in: HThR 93 (2000), 85–100.
[60] Vgl. R. Weber, Christologie und ‚Messiasgeheimnis', 108–125.

3.3 Der Glaube/glauben

Neben Johannes[61] sind Paulus und Markus im Frühen Christentum die Träger der Glaubensvorstellung als zentraler Aneignungsform des Heilsgeschehens. Paulus nimmt einerseits den Sprachgebrauch im hellenistischen Judentum[62] und paganen Hellenismus auf [63], andererseits geht er darüber hinaus, indem nun πίστις/πιστεύειν („Glaube"/„glauben"[64]) zur exklusiven Bezeichnung für das Gottesverhältnis und damit auch zum zentralen Identitätsmerkmal werden[65]. Eine zweite Besonderheit zeigt sich in der Ausrichtung des Glaubens auf Jesus Christus. Für Paulus ist der Glaube immer Glaube an den Gott, der Jesus Christus von den Toten auferweckte (vgl. Röm 4,17.24; 8,11). Jesus Christus ist gleichermaßen der Auslöser und der Inhalt des Glaubens. Zentrum des Glaubens ist somit nicht der Glaubende, sondern der Geglaubte. Der Glaube ist für Paulus eine Neuqualifikation des Ich, denn im Glauben eröffnet sich für den Menschen Gottes Zuwendung zur Welt. Grundlage und Ermöglichung des Glaubens ist Gottes Heilsinitiative in Jesus Christus. Der Glaube ruht nicht in einem Entschluss des Menschen, sondern er ist eine Gnadengabe Gottes (vgl. Röm 4,16; Phil 1,29)[66]. Der Glaube ist ein Werk des Geistes, denn: „Niemand kann sagen: ‚Herr ist Christus!' außer im Heiligen Geist" (1Kor 12,3b)[67]. Der Glaube zählt zu den Früchten des Geistes (vgl. 1Kor 12,9; Gal 5,22). Im Glauben eröffnet sich somit eine neue Beziehung zu Gott, die der Mensch nur dankbar annehmen kann. Der Geschenkcharakter von πίστις/πιστεύειν bestimmt auch die enge Verbindung von Glauben und Verkündigung bei Paulus. Der Glaube entzündet sich am Evangelium, das eine Macht Gottes ist (Röm 1,16). Gott gefiel es, „durch die Torheit der Verkündigung die zu retten, die glauben" (1Kor 1,21). Früh verbreitet sich über den Apostel die Kunde: „Der uns früher verfolgte, verkündigt jetzt den Glauben" (Gal 1,23). Der Glaube erwächst aus der Verkündigung, die ihrerseits auf das Wort Christi zurückgeht (Röm 10,17). Somit

---

61 Zum Glaubensverständnis bei Johannes vgl. U. Schnelle, Theologie des Neuen Testaments, Göttingen 2007, 677–682.
62 Vgl. umfassend D. Lührmann, Pistis im Judentum, in: ZNW 64 (1973), 19–38.
63 Die zentralen Belege sind angeführt und interpretiert bei G. Schunack, Glaube in griechischer Religiosität, in: Antikes Judentum und Frühes Christentum (FS H. Stegemann), hg. von B. Kollmann/W. Reinbold/A. Steudel (BZNW 97), Berlin 1999, 299–317.
64 Vgl. dazu den Beitrag von William Loader im vorliegenden Band.
65 Vgl. G. Barth, Art. πίστις, in: EWNT 3 (1983), 216–231, hier 220.
66 Vgl. dazu die grundlegenden Überlegungen von G. Friedrich, Glaube und Verkündigung bei Paulus, in: Glaube im Neuen Testament (FS H. Binder), hg. von F. Hahn/H. Klein (BThSt 7), Neukirchen 1982, 100ff.
67 Gegen R. Bultmann, Theologie des Neuen Testaments, Tübingen ⁷1977, 331, der behauptet, „daß Pls die πίστις nicht als inspiriert bezeichnet, sie nicht auf das πνεῦμα zurückführt."

handelt Christus selbst im Wort der Verkündigung. In 1Kor 15,11b schließt Paulus seine grundlegende Unterweisung mit den Worten ab: „So haben wir verkündigt und so habt ihr geglaubt." Der Glaube ist nicht Voraussetzung/Bedingung des Heilsgeschehens, sondern ein Teil desselben! Gott ist es, der das Wollen und das Vollbringen wirkt (Phil 2,13). Der Glaube entsteht aus der Heilsinitiative Gottes, der Menschen in den Dienst der Evangeliumsverkündigung ruft.

Bei Markus erscheinen die Wörter πίστις/πιστεύειν fast ausschließlich im Mund Jesu[68], d.h. der Glaube in all seinen Ausprägungen ist durchgängig auf die Person Jesu Christi bezogen. Die programmatische Glaubens-Forderung in Mk 1,15 verdeutlicht, dass es dabei gleichermaßen der irdische und der auferstandene Gottessohn ist, der Glauben fordert, erweckt und ermöglicht[69]. Glaube ist das Vertrauen, dass Gottes Herrschaft in seinem Sohn nahe gekommen ist und sich vollenden wird. Was der Glaube bedeutet und wie Menschen zum Glauben geführt werden, erläutert Markus an Heilungsgeschichten, in denen die grenzüberwindende Kraft des Glaubens sichtbar wird und Menschen Erfahrungen mit Jesus machen, die sie zum Glauben befähigen[70]. Der Glaube überwindet Mauern (Mk 2,1–12), er lässt sich nicht abdrängen (Mk 5,21–43) und sucht trotz Behinderungen die Nähe Jesu (Mk 10,46–52). Menschen wie Bartimäus, die Syrophönizierin (Mk 7,24–30), der namenlose Taubstumme (Mk 7,31–37) oder der verzweifelte Vater in Mk 9,14–29 erfahren, dass Jesus der Gottessohn ist, der die Gottesherrschaft an Leib und Seele nahebringt und dabei Angst, Verzweiflung und Unglauben überwindet. Sie werden so zu Gestalten des Glaubens, deren Vertrauen in Jesus die Gemeinde ermuntert und auffordert, wie Bartimäus den rettenden Glauben zu ergreifen und zu handeln (Mk 10,52). Der Weg des Glaubens wird von Markus auch an den Jüngern illustriert, die sich für Jesus begeistern (Mk 1,16–20; 6,6b–13), ihn bekennen (Mk 8,27–30) und verleugnen (Mk 14,50.66–72), aber dennoch von Jesus angenommen werden (Mk 14,28; 16,7). Gestalten des Glaubens sind aber auch die zahlreichen namenlosen Helfer der Kranken, die Kinder als Vorbilder reinen Glaubens (Mk 10,13–16), der reiche Jüngling mit seiner Traurigkeit (Mk 10,17–22), der verständige Schriftgelehrte (Mk 12,28–34), die arme Witwe mit ihrer Bereitschaft zum Geben (Mk 12,41–44), die Frau, die Jesus salbt (Mk 14,3–9), Josef von Arimathäa (Mk 15,43) und die Frauen unter dem Kreuz, beim Begräbnis und leeren Grab (Mk 15,40–16,8). Im Vertrauen auf Gottes Nähe in Jesus Christus findet der Glaube im Gebet seine Sprache (Mk 11,22–25), er erhofft alles und weiß, dass er in der Leidensnachfolge seine Vollendung findet (Mk 8,34–38).

---

68 Vgl. Mk 1,15; 4,40; 5,34.40; 9,19.23.42; 10,52; 11,22–25; 13,21; Ausnahmen: Mk 9,24; 15,32.
69 Vgl. Th. Söding, Glaube bei Markus, 522ff.
70 Zur ausführlichen Analyse vgl. Th. Söding, Glaube bei Markus, 385–511.

3.4 Das Gesetz

In der Gesetzesfrage[71] unterscheiden sich Paulus und Markus einerseits massiv aufgrund ihrer unterschiedlichen historischen Situation, andererseits sind sie aber sachlich bei dieser Frage sehr nah beieinander.

Paulus konzentriert in seinem ausgereiften Gesetzesverständnis des Galater- und Römerbriefes den positiven Gehalt des Gesetzes auf das Liebesgebot[72]. Zunächst demontiert er im Galaterbrief die Tora, indem er sie zeitlich (Gal 3,17) und sachlich (Gal 3,19f.) als sekundär einstuft. Ihr kam innerhalb der Geschichte lediglich die Aufgabe zu, die Menschen zu beaufsichtigen (vgl. Gal 3,24). Diese Zeit der Unfreiheit ist nun in Christus zu ihrem Ende gekommen, der die Menschen zur Freiheit des Glaubens befreite (Gal 5,1). Die Glaubenden aus dem Judentum und den Völkern sind jenseits der Beschneidung und der Tora die legitimen Erben der Verheißungen an Abraham (vgl. Gal 3,29). Paulus hebt im Galaterbrief die hamartiologische Sonderstellung der Juden und Judenchristen auf (Gal 2,16) und ordnet sie nun vollständig in die von der Sünde bestimmte Menschheitsgeschichte ein (vgl. Gal 3,22). Beschneidung und Tora gehören nicht zur soteriologischen Selbstdefinition des Christentums, weil sich Gott unmittelbar in Jesus Christus offenbarte und die Getauften und Glaubenden in der Geistgabe an diesem Heilsereignis partizipieren. Positiv findet das Gesetz in der Liebe seine Erfüllung, was Gal 5,14 und 6,2 zeigen. Vor allem Gal 6,2 (und Röm 3,27; 8,2) verdeutlicht, dass sich Paulus und seine Gemeinden trotz der Kritik an der Tora und der Feststellung ihrer soteriologischen Insuffizienz keineswegs als ‚gesetzlos' verstanden.

Der Römerbrief führt zum einen die eminent torakritische Argumentation des Gal weiter, denn die Tora ist sowohl sachlich (Röm 6,14b) als auch zeitlich defizitär (Röm 5,20a; Röm 7,1–3) gegenüber der in Jesus Christus erfüllten Verheißung. Die Tora steht in einem Gegensatz zur Verheißung (Röm 4,13; vgl. Gal 3,16–18) und zur Gerechtigkeit (Röm 3,28; 4,16; vgl. Gal 2,16; 3,11.21; 5,4), ihr kommt nun die Funktion der Sündenerkenntnis zu[73] (Röm 3,20.21a; Röm 4,15b). Deshalb gilt, dass Christus als alleiniger Ort der Gerechtigkeit und des Lebens das ‚Ende' des Gesetzes/der Tora ist (Röm 10,4). Zugleich geht Paulus im Röm über diese negativen Aussagen hinaus, indem er gegenüber dem Galaterbrief auf mehreren Ebenen substantielle Veränderungen vornimmt[74]: (1) Er führt δικαιοσύνη θεοῦ („Gerech-

---

71 Vgl. dazu den Beitrag von Jesper Svartvig im vorliegenden Band.
72 Vgl. dazu U. Schnelle, Paulus, 579–598.
73 Vgl. dazu Ps 19,13; 32; 51; 119.
74 Keineswegs handelt es sich nur um „Vertiefungen", wie J. Becker, Paulus. Der Apostel der Völker, Tübingen 1989, 419, meint. Auch der Einwand, der geringe zeitliche Abstand zwischen Gal und Röm spräche gegen Veränderungen (so J.D.G. Dunn, The Theology of Paul, 131) über-

tigkeit Gottes") als theologischen Leitbegriff ein, um damit den theologischen Grundertrag der Argumentation des Galaterbriefes zu sichern (vgl. Röm 3,21: δικαιοσύνη θεοῦ χωρὶς νόμου; ferner Röm 6,14b; 10,1–4). (2) Dies ermöglicht ihm eine partielle Neubewertung des Gesetzes/der Tora (vgl. Röm 3,31; 7,7.12); das Gesetz/die Tora wird nicht mehr als solches kritisiert, es ist nun zuallererst Opfer der Sündenmacht. Die Konzentration des gesamten Gesetzes auf das Liebesgebot ist auch im Röm das Ziel der Argumentation. Die These von Röm 13,8–10[75], die Liebe sei die Erfüllung des Gesetzes/der Tora (Röm 13,10: πλήρωμα οὖν νόμου ἡ ἀγάπη), sichert die paulinische Argumentation in vierfacher Hinsicht ab: a) Sie erlaubt die Behauptung, das Gesetz/die Tora in seinem innersten Wesen voll zur Geltung zu bringen und zu erfüllen, ohne ihm eine wie auch immer geartete soteriologische Funktion zuzubilligen. b) Zugleich ermöglicht diese Vorstellung im Hinblick auf die beschneidungsfreie Mission unter den Völkern die notwendige Reduktion des Gesetzes/der Tora. c) Paulus steht sowohl mit seiner Konzentration des Gesetzes/der Tora auf ein Gebot bzw. wenige ethische Grundnormen[76] als auch mit seiner Wesensbestimmung als Liebe in der Tradition des hellenistischen Judentums. Dort herrschte die Tendenz vor, die Toragebote mit einer vernunftgemäßen Tugendlehre zu identifizieren[77], um sie so zugleich zu öffnen und zu bewahren. d) Aber auch im griechisch-römischen Kulturbereich galt die Überzeugung, dass Güte und Liebe die eigentliche Form der Gerechtigkeit und der Erfüllung der Gesetze sind (vgl. Cicero, *De officiis*, III 5,21.23.27; Cicero, *De re publica*, 22; Dio Chrysostomus, *Orationes*, 80,5).

Das Fehlen des Wortes νόμος im Markus-Evangelium dürfte kein Zufall sein, sondern Markus setzt den entscheidenden Ertrag der paulinischen Gesetzesdebatte voraus: die beschneidungsfreie Völkermission, die dem Gesetz keine soteriologische, sondern ausschließlich eine ethische Bedeutung zumisst[78]. In den

---

zeugt nicht, denn sowohl der Textbefund in beiden Briefen als auch die veränderte historische Situation des Apostels weisen darauf hin, dass Paulus seine Position weiterentwickelt hat.
75 Vgl. hierzu O. Wischmeyer, Das Gebot der Nächstenliebe bei Paulus, in: BZ 30 (1986), 153–187.
76 Vgl. Aristeasbrief 131; 168; TestDan 5,1–3; TestIssa 5,2; Philo, *De specialibus legibus*, I 260; II 61–63; Philo, *De decalogo*, 154ff.; Josephus, *Contra Apionem*, 2,154; Josephus, *Antiquitates Iudaicae*, 18,117. Anders als bei Paulus wurden aber durch die Hochschätzung einzelner Gebote die anderen Gebote nicht außer Kraft gesetzt; vgl. dazu zuletzt R. Weber, Das Gesetz im hellenistischen Judentum (ARGU 10), Frankfurt 2000, 236–239.
77 Vgl. R. Weber, Das Gesetz im hellenistischen Judentum, 320: „So ist der Nomos im Grunde eine Form der Tugendlehre, denn die Tugend zielt auf Lebensgestalt."
78 Zum markinischen Gesetzesverständnis vgl. mit unterschiedlichen Akzenten H. Sariola, Markus und das Gesetz (AASF 56), Helsinki 1990; R. Kampling, Das Gesetz im Markusevangelium, in: Der Evangelist als Theologe. Studien zum Markusevangelium, hg. von Th. Söding (SBS 163), Stuttgart 1995, 119–150.

Streitgesprächen Mk 2,1–3,6 wird der Vorrang des einzelnen Menschen gegenüber äußeren religiösen Ansprüchen von Jesus selbst begründet. Seine Tischgemeinschaft mit Zöllnern und Sündern orientiert sich nicht an Ritualvorschriften, denn: „Nicht die Gesunden brauchen einen Arzt, sondern die Kranken" (Mk 2,17a). Eine programmatische Dimension erhält die Position des Evangelisten in Mk 7,1–23, indem Jesu Wirken unter den Heiden mit der Außerkraftsetzung jüdischer Ritualvorschriften beginnt (Mk 7,1–23)[79]. Die Heilungen einer Heidin (Mk 7,24–30), eines Taubstummen (Mk 7,31–37) und die Speisung der 4000 (Mk 8,1–10) müssen als Illustrationen der in Mk 7,1–23 grundsätzlich erfolgten Aufhebung der Fundamentalunterscheidung ‚rein-unrein' begriffen werden. In dem von Paulus und Markus gleichermaßen überlieferten Jesuswort über die wahre Unreinheit aus dem Inneren des Menschen (Mk 7,15/Röm 14,14)[80] zeigt sich eine bemerkenswerte inhaltliche Übereinstimmung: Die für das jüdische Religionssystem konstitutive Unterscheidung zwischen ‚rein' und ‚unrein' gilt nicht mehr, womit die ideologische Grundvoraussetzung der Tora außer Kraft gesetzt wird. Nicht zufällig werden mit der Aufforderung Gottes in Mk 9,7 (‚Hört auf ihn!') auch Mose und Elia und mit ihnen das Gesetz und die Propheten dem Willen Jesu untergeordnet. Die Akklamation in Mk 7,37 wird nach der markinischen Textfolge von Heiden gesprochen. Bildet die Speisung der 5000 (Mk 6,30–44) den Abschluss des Wirkens Jesu unter den Juden, so beschließt die Speisung der 4000 Jesu Wirken unter den Heiden. Die eucharistischen Anklänge in Mk 8,6 verdeutlichen aus markinischer Sicht zudem, dass Jesus auch mit Heiden Tischgemeinschaft hatte und sie nun in der Eucharistie fortsetzt. Markus votiert für eine neue, aus der Vollmacht Jesu abgeleitete Praxis des Zusammenlebens von Christen jüdischer und griechisch-römischer Religiosität. Die Tischgemeinschaft in der christlichen Gemeinde umfasst beide Gruppen (Mk 2,15f.; 7,24f.), denn im Zentrum des von Gott Gewollten steht der Mensch (Mk 2,23–28; 3,1–6). Deshalb gilt uneingeschränkt das Doppelgebot der Liebe (Mk 12,28–34), das den Dekalog aufnimmt (Mk 10,18f.), neue Prioritäten setzt und auf den Glauben als Grundlage des Verhältnisses des Menschen zu Gott verweist. Wie

---

[79] Zu beachten ist Mk 7,19c: καθαρίζων πάντα τὰ βρώματα („er erklärte alle Speisen für rein"). Markus verbindet in 7,17.18 die Gesetzesthematik in dreifacher Weise mit seiner Geheimnistheorie: 1) Rückzugsmotiv; 2) Jüngerunverständnis; 3) Parabeltheorie. Jesu Stellung zum Gesetz bewirkt bei den Gegnern den Vernichtungsbeschluss (vgl. Mk 3,6; 7,1) und bei den Jüngern Unverständnis! – Zu diesem Text vgl. auch den Beitrag von Lorenzo Scornaienchi im vorliegenden Band.
[80] H. Räisänen, Jesus and the Food Laws, in: JNST 16 (1982), 89ff., sieht hinter Mk 7,15 nicht den irdischen Jesus, sondern „an ‚emancipated' Jewish Christian group engaged in Gentile mission" (90).

bei Paulus hat auch bei Markus das Gesetz/die Tora keine soteriologische Funktion mehr und findet im Liebesgebot[81] sein Ziel.

3.5 Kreuz und Auferstehung

Die wohl bedeutendste Übereinstimmung zwischen Paulus und Markus besteht in der Kreuzestheologie[82]. Beide stimmen in der zentralen Heilsbotschaft überein, sie verkünden Jesus Christus, den *Gekreuzigten* (1Kor 1,23; Mk 16,6: ἐσταυρομένον).

Während der militante Pharisäer Paulus die Verkündigung über einen gekreuzigten Messias nur als Provokation verstehen konnte (vgl. 1Kor 15,9; Gal 1,13), führte ihn die Damaskuserfahrung zu der Einsicht, dass dem Kreuz unerwartetes Sinnpotential innewohnt[83]. Paulus erkennt, dass der am Holz Verfluchte Gottes Sohn ist, d.h. im Licht der Auferstehung wird das Kreuz vom Ort des Fluches zum Ort des Heils. Deshalb kann Paulus den Korinthern zurufen: „Wir aber verkündigen Christus als Gekreuzigten, für Juden ein Anstoß, für Heiden eine Torheit" (1Kor 1,23). Die Heilsbedeutung der Auferstehung wirft ein neues Licht auf den Tod Jesu, für Paulus ist der Auferstandene bleibend der Gekreuzigte (2Kor 13,4: „Denn er wurde aus Schwachheit gekreuzigt, aber er lebt aus Gottes Kraft"). Es gibt bei Paulus eine Wechselwirkung zwischen Tod und Auferstehung: Die Auferstehung begründet sachlich die Heilsbedeutung des Todes, zugleich gewinnt das Auferstehungskerygma in der paulinischen Hermeneutik des Kreuzes eine letzte Zuspitzung. Auch nach der Auferstehung bleibt Jesus der Gekreuzigte (Ptz. Perf. Pass. ἐσταυρωμένος 1Kor 1,23; 2,2; Gal 3,1)[84]. „Der Auferstandene trägt die Nägelmale des Kreuzes."[85] Eine biographische Erfahrung gewinnt somit bei Paulus eine theologische Qualität.

In den Briefen des Paulus erscheint das Kreuz (1) als historischer Ort, denn Paulus löst es nicht von der Geschichte, sondern der Ausgangspunkt ist immer das Kreuz als Ort des Todes des Jesus von Nazareth. Mit der Wendung σκάνδαλον τοῦ σταυροῦ (1Kor 1,25; Gal 5,11: „Anstoß des Kreuzes") nimmt der Apostel Bezug auf die konkrete, entehrende Hinrichtungsart der Kreuzigung, die einen Menschen als

---

81 Vgl. dazu auch den Beitrag von Thomas Söding im vorliegenden Band.
82 Vgl. dazu auch den Beitrag von Michael Theobald im vorliegenden Band.
83 Vgl. Th. Söding, Das Geheimnis Gottes im Kreuz Jesu, in: Das Wort vom Kreuz, hg. von Th. Söding (WUNT 93), Tübingen 1997, 71–92.
84 Vgl. F. Blass/A. Debrunner/F. Rehkopf, Grammatik des neutestamentlichen Griechisch, Göttingen ¹⁶1984, §340: das Perfekt drückt „die Dauer des Vollendeten" aus.
85 G. Friedrich, Die Verkündigung des Todes Jesu im Neuen Testament (BThSt 6), Neukirchen 1982, 137.

Verbrecher, nicht aber als Gottessohn ausweist. Einen Gekreuzigten als Gottessohn zu verehren, erschien den Juden als theologischer Anstoß[86] und der griechisch-römischen Welt als Verrücktheit[87]. Mit der zentralen Stellung eines Gekreuzigten in der paulinischen Sinnwelt wird jede geläufige kulturelle Plausibilität auf den Kopf gestellt, indem nun das Kreuz als signum göttlicher Weisheit erscheint. Das Kreuz ist (2) ein argumentativ-theologischer Topos, den Paulus vor allem in der Diskussion mit der korinthischen Gemeinde einsetzt. Die Weisheit des Kreuzes verträgt sich nicht mit der Weisheit der Welt (vgl. 1Kor 1,18ff.). Das Kreuz ist die radikale Infragestellung jeglicher menschlicher Selbstbehauptung und individualistischen Heilsstrebens, weil es in die Ohnmacht und nicht in die Macht, in die Klage und nicht in den Jubel, in die Schande und nicht in den Ruhm, in die Verlorenheit des Todes und nicht in die Glorie vollständig gegenwärtigen Heils führt. Diese Torheit des Kreuzes lässt sich weder ideologisch noch philosophisch vereinnahmen, sie entzieht sich jeder Instrumentalisierung, weil sie allein in Gottes Liebe gründet. Schließlich ist das Kreuz (3) ein theologisches Symbol. Es hat Verweischarakter und präsentiert zugleich durch die Kraft des Geistes das Vergangene als Gegenwärtiges. Als Ort des einmaligen Transfers Jesu Christi in das neue Sein prägt das Kreuz auch die gegenwärtige Existenz der Christusgläubigen. Es benennt jeweils die Statusüberschreitung vom Tod zum Leben und gewinnt in einem rituellen Kontext seine Aktualität: In der Taufe erfolgt die Einbeziehung in die anhaltende Wirklichkeit von Kreuz und Auferstehung, indem die Macht des Todes und der Sünde überwunden und durch den Geist der Status des neuen Seins verliehen wird (vgl. Gal 2,19; Röm 6,5.6).

Bei Markus ist das Kreuz der Fluchtpunkt seiner Evangelienkomposition[88]. Dies zeigt sich auf drei kompositionellen Ebenen: (1) Die bereits erwähnte Verbindung von Mk 1,11; 9,7 („mein geliebter Sohn") bzw. Mk 12,6 („geliebter Sohn") wird in Mk 15,39 zum Ziel geführt. Erst unter dem Kreuz erkennt, enthüllt und bezeugt ein Mensch, der römische Hauptmann, das Geheimnis der Person Jesu Christi: „Dieser war wahrhaftig Gottes Sohn". Die Vergangenheitsform ἦν signalisiert, dass für Markus der irdische Jesus der Gottessohn war. Am Ende dieses Weges provoziert die Akklamation des römischen Hauptmanns unter dem Kreuz unwillkürlich auch einen Vergleich mit dem imperialen Kult, denn die höchste

---

[86] Zur Übersetzung von σκάνδαλον mit „Anstoß" vgl. H.W. Kuhn, Jesus als Gekreuzigter in der frühchristlichen Verkündigung bis zur Mitte des 2. Jahrhunderts, in: ZThK 72 (1975), 36f.
[87] Vgl. Cicero, *Pro C. Rabirio*, 5,16; Plinius, *Epistulae*, X 96,8: „verworrener wüster Aberglaube".
[88] Vgl. M. Ebner, Kreuzestheologie im Markusevangelium, in: Kreuzestheologie im Neuen Testament, hg. von A. Dettwiler/J. Zumstein (WUNT 151), Tübingen 2002, 151–168.

Macht auf Erden steht nicht dem als Gottessohn/Gott verehrten Kaiser[89], sondern dem Gottessohn Jesus Christus zu. (2) Als leidender Menschensohn tritt Jesus Christus im Mittelteil des Evangeliums ‚auf dem Weg' nach Jerusalem (Mk 8,27–10,52) in den Vordergrund. Auf das Messiasbekenntnis des Petrus (Mk 8,27–30) folgt eine parallele Dreifachkomposition (a: Leidensankündigungen Mk 8,31; 9,31; 10,32–34; b: Jüngerunverständnis Mk 8,32b.33; 9,32–34; 10,35–40; c: Jüngerbelehrungen Mk 8,34–9,1; 9,35–37; 10,41–45), die nachdrücklich das Kreuz als Signatur des Weges Jesu und christlicher Existenz insgesamt erscheinen lässt. Die Rahmung des Mittelteils durch zwei Blindenheilungen (Mk 8,22–26; 10,46–52) verstärkt diese Perspektive: Den Jüngern und mit ihnen der markinischen Gemeinde sollen die Augen geöffnet werden, wer dieser Jesus von Nazareth ist: Der leidende Menschensohn, der in die Leidensnachfolge ruft. Seit Mk 8,27 gilt uneingeschränkt, dass Jesus auf das Kreuz zugeht und Markus vom Kreuz her denkt; d.h. die Rede vom leidenden Menschensohn ist eine Form mk. Kreuzestheologie. (3) Die markinische Geheimnistheorie insgesamt zielt, wie schon dargestellt, darauf ab, das Wirken des Gottessohnes Jesus Christus auf das Kreuz hin auszurichten und vom Kreuz her zu verstehen.

Bei Paulus sind die Auferstehung Jesu Christi von den Toten und die Erscheinungen des Auferstandenen unzweifelhaft die Basis seiner Theologie (vgl. nur 1Kor 15,1–11). Auch für Markus erschließt sich die Gottessohnschaft Jesu Christi aus der Auferstehung (vgl. Mk 9,9; 14,28; 16,6). Mit Mk 14,28 und 16,7 lenkt Markus wieder den Blick nach Galiläa zurück, wo die Geschichte Jesu anfing, d.h. das gesamte Evangelium will von der Ankündigung der Erscheinungen in Galiläa gelesen werden, die die Existenz der markinischen Gemeinde begründen[90]. Ob die Erscheinungen des Auferstandenen dann bewusst von Markus nicht erzählt wurden oder der ursprüngliche Markusschluss verloren ging, lässt sich nur schwer entscheiden. Markus könnte absichtlich Erscheinungsgeschichten weggelassen haben, um so eine theologia gloriae abzuwehren, bei der Jesu Leiden und sein Kreuzestod nur als Durchgangserscheinungen zur Herrlichkeit des Auferstandenen verstanden wurden[91]. Das Schweigen der Frauen und das Verschweigen der Erscheinungsberichte würden dann an die Stelle des Schweigegebotes im Rahmen des markinischen Messiasgeheimnisses treten. Damit ließe sich eine weitere Profilierung der Kreuzestheologie verbinden: Der Verzicht auf die erzählerische

---

89 Zum Kaiser als ‚Sohn Gottes' vgl. die Texte in: U. Schnelle (Hg.), Neuer Wettstein I/1.1, Berlin 2008 zu Mk 15,39; zum Kaiser als Gottheit vgl. M. Clauss, Kaiser und Gott, Stuttgart/Leipzig 1999, 217–419.
90 Vgl. K. Backhaus, „Dort werdet ihr ihn sehen" (Mk 16,7). Die redaktionelle Schlussnotiz des zweiten Evangeliums als dessen christologische Summe, in: ThGl 76 (1986), 277–294.
91 So z.B. A. Lindemann, Die Osterbotschaft des Markus, in: NTS 26 (1979/80), 298–317.

Umsetzung der Auferstehungswirklichkeit lässt das Kreuz umso stärker als Ort des Heils hervortreten. In andere Zusammenhänge führt die Vermutung, in Mk 16,1–8 werde die Apotheose Jesu angedeutet, „womit die apokalyptisch geprägte Auferweckungsvorstellung in die römische Welt hinein übersetzt wird. Jesu Knochen können nicht gefunden werden: ‚Nicht ist er hier' (Mk 16,6) – nach dem mythisch prägenden Modell des Herakles, dessen Knochen nach seiner Selbstverbrennung nicht gefunden werden können, das entscheidende Signal für die erfolgte Aufnahme des Verstorbenen unter die Götter."[92] Schließlich könnte mit der ‚Abwesenheit' Jesu ein theologisches Programm verbunden sein, das primär am irdischen Jesus und nicht am Auferstandenen orientiert ist[93].

Andererseits wird die Auferstehungswirklichkeit als Basis der markinischen Christologie und Soteriologie durch die Erzählung vom leeren Grab (Mk 16,1–8), das Streitgespräch mit den Sadduzäern über die Auferstehung der Toten (Mk 12,18–27), die Vorstellung vom kommenden Menschensohn in Herrlichkeit (Mk 13,24–27) und die redaktionellen Verweise Mk 14,28/16,7 theologisch vorausgesetzt[94], aber in der vorliegenden Gestalt des Evangeliums nicht erzählerisch umgesetzt. Konnte Markus theologisch hinter Paulus zurückfallen, für den die berichteten Erscheinungen des Auferstandenen das Fundament seiner Theologie sind (vgl. 1Kor 15,5–8)? Dachten der Evangelist und seine Hörer/Leser in den Kategorien moderner Erzähltheorien? Beides ist unwahrscheinlich; vermutlich ging der ursprüngliche Schluss des Evangeliums verloren[95], denn Mk 9,2–8 als Prolepse von Erscheinungsberichten und ἠγέρθη (Aor. Pass.: „er wurde auferweckt") in Mk 16,6 lassen deutlich erkennen, dass Markus die Auferstehung als ein Handeln Gottes an Jesus verstand und der Verweis sich ursprünglich mit der Erzählung von Erscheinungen verband.

---

92 M. Ebner, Kreuzestheologie im Markusevangelium, 166; vgl. als Parallele Plutarch, *Vita Numae*, 22.
93 Vgl. D. du Toit, Der abwesende Herr. Strategien im Markusevangelium zur Bewältigung der Abwesenheit des Auferstandenen (WMANT 111), Neukirchen 2006, 444f., wonach Markus die Frage nach dem abwesenden Jesus radikal mit dem Verweis auf den irdischen Jesus beantwortet: „Dazu entwickelte er das Konzept vom Evangelium als Ersatz Jesu, das angesichts der Abwesenheit des Herrn darauf zielt, diese zu kompensieren, indem es nach Ostern dem irdischen Jesus bei den Seinen und in der Welt Gehör verschafft bzw. seine Botschaft vergegenwärtigt."
94 Der redaktionelle Charakter von Mk 14,28; 16,7 lässt sich kaum bestreiten, vgl. z. B. J. Gnilka, Markus II, 252–338.
95 Vgl. dazu U. Schnelle, Einleitung, 248f.

4 Folgerungen

Gegenüber der weitverbreiteten Skepsis bzw. Nichtbehandlung des Verhältnisses Paulus – Markus ist zu betonen: Markus steht deutlich erkennbar in einer theologiegeschichtlichen Kontinuität zu Paulus, indem er die beschneidungsfreie Völkermission des Apostels selbstverständlich voraussetzt. Innerhalb der Christologie erzählen beide naturgemäß ihre Jesus-Christus-Geschichte perspektivisch im Blick auf ihre Gemeinden, dennoch zeigen sich beachtliche inhaltliche Übereinstimmungen:

(1) Paulus und Markus weisen eine vergleichbare christologische Grundperspektive auf: die Einheit des irdischen, gekreuzigten und auferstandenen Gottessohnes Jesus Christus.

(2) Paulus und Markus sind *die* Träger des urchristlichen Evangeliumsbegriffes und prägen ihn inhaltlich.

(3) Paulus und Markus sind (neben Johannes) im Neuen Testament *die* Vertreter einer dezidierten Kreuzestheologie, was vor allem ein Vergleich mit Matthäus und Lukas verdeutlicht.

(4) Der Glaube steht bei Paulus und Markus im Mittelpunkt der Anthropologie.

(5) Dem Gesetz kommt bei Paulus und Markus keine wie auch immer geartete soteriologische Qualität zu.

Auch wenn eine direkte Bezugnahme auf paulinische Briefe durch Markus nicht nachzuweisen ist, legt sich aus den genannten Übereinstimmungen eine Kenntnis und eigenständige Verarbeitung paulinischer Gedanken durch den ältesten Evangelisten nahe. Sie könnte in Rom erfolgt sein, wo beide mit einem nicht allzu großen zeitlichen Abstand wirkten und Markus seine Kenntnis paulinischer Theologie wahrscheinlich erwarb.

Literatur

Backhaus, K., „Dort werdet ihr ihn sehen" (Mk 16,7). Die redaktionelle Schlussnotiz des zweiten Evangeliums als dessen christologische Summe, in: ThGl 76 (1986), 277–294.
Barth, G., Art. πίστις, in: EWNT 3 (1983), 216–231.
Bauer, Th.J., Paulus und die kaiserzeitliche Epistolographie (WUNT 276), Tübingen 2011.
Becker, E.-M., Das Markus-Evangelium im Rahmen antiker Historiographie (WUNT 194), Tübingen 2006.
Becker, J., Paulus. Der Apostel der Völker, Tübingen 1989.
Blank, J., Paulus und Jesus (StANT 18), München 1968.
Blass, F./Debrunner, A./Rehkopf, F., Grammatik des neutestamentlichen Griechisch, Göttingen ^{16}1984.
Boring, M.E., Mark (NTL), Louisville 2006.
Böttrich, Ch., „Gott und Retter". Gottesprädikationen in christologischen Titeln, in: NZSTh 42 (2000), 217–236.
Breytenbach, C., Das Markusevangelium als traditionsgebundene Erzählung?, in: The Synoptic Gospels (BETL CX), hg. von C. Focant, Leuven 1993, 77–110.
Bultmann, R., Theologie des Neuen Testaments, Tübingen ^{7}1977.
Burridge, R.A., What are the Gospels?, Grand Rapids ^{2}2004.
Clauss, M., Kaiser und Gott, Stuttgart/Leipzig 1999.
Collins, A. Yarbro, Mark and His Readers: The Son of God among Jews, in: HThR 92 (1999), 393–408.
—, The Son of God among Greeks and Romans, in: HThR 93 (2000), 85–100.
Conzelmann, H., Gegenwart und Zukunft in der synoptischen Tradition, in: Theologie als Schriftauslegung, hg. von H. Conzelmann (BEvTh 65), München 1974, 42–61.
Dechow, J., Gottessohn und Herrschaft Gottes (WMANT 86), Neukirchen 2000.
Dormeyer, D., Das Markusevangelium als Idealbiographie von Jesus Christus, dem Nazarener (SBB 43), Stuttgart 1999.
Doty, W.G., Letters in Primitive Christianity, Philadelphia 1973.
Dunn, J.D.G., The Theology of Paul the Apostle, Grand Rapids 1998.
Ebner, M., Kreuzestheologie im Markusevangelium, in: Kreuzestheologie im Neuen Testament, hg. von A. Dettwiler/J. Zumstein (WUNT 151), Tübingen 2002, 151–168.
Eckstein, P., Gemeinde, Brief und Heilsbotschaft. Ein phänomenologischer Vergleich zwischen Paulus und Epikur (HBS 42), Freiburg 2004.
Feneberg, M., Der Markusprolog (StANT 36), München 1974.
Fitzmyer, J.A., The „Son of God" Document from Qumran, in: Bib 74 (1993), 153–174.
Frickenschmidt, D., Evangelium als Biographie (TANZ 22), Tübingen 1997.
Friedrich, G., Die Verkündigung des Todes Jesu im Neuen Testament (BThSt 6), Neukirchen 1982.
—, Glaube und Verkündigung bei Paulus, in: Glaube im Neuen Testament (FS H. Binder), hg. von F. Hahn/H. Klein (BThSt 7), Neukirchen 1982, 93–113.
Genette, G., Die Erzählung, München ^{2}1998.
Gnilka, J., Das Evangelium nach Markus (EKK II/2), Neukirchen 1978.
Hahn, F. (Hg.), Der Erzähler des Evangeliums. Methodische Neuansätze in der Markusforschung (SBS 118/119), Stuttgart 1985.
—, Christologische Hoheitstitel, Göttingen ^{5}1995.

—, Theologie des Neuen Testaments I, Tübingen 2002.
Hengel, M., Das Begräbnis Jesu bei Paulus und die leibliche Auferstehung aus dem Grabe, in: Auferstehung, hg. von F. Avemarie/H. Lichtenberger (WUNT 135), Tübingen 2001, 119–183.
—, Der Sohn Gottes, Tübingen ²1977.
—, Der umstrittene Petrus, Tübingen 2006.
Holtzmann, H.J., Lehrbuch der neutestamentlichen Theologie I, Tübingen ²1911.
Jonge, M. de, Art. Christ, in: DDD (²1999), 192–200.
Kampling, R., Das Gesetz im Markusevangelium, in: Der Evangelist als Theologe. Studien zum Markusevangelium, hg. von Th. Söding (SBS 163), Stuttgart 1995, 119–150.
Karrer, M., Der Gesalbte. Die Grundlagen des Christustitels (FRLANT 151), Göttingen 1990.
Klauck, H.-J., Die antike Briefliteratur und das Neue Testament, Paderborn 1998.
Koch, D.-A., Die Schrift als Zeuge des Evangeliums (BHTh 69), Tübingen 1986.
Koskenniemi, H., Studien zu Idee und Phraseologie des griechischen Briefes bis 400 n.Chr. (AASF B 102,2), Helsinki 1956.
Kramer, W., Christos Kyrios Gottessohn (AThANT 44), Zürich 1963.
Kuhn, H.W., Jesus als Gekreuzigter in der frühchristlichen Verkündigung bis zur Mitte des 2. Jahrhunderts, in: ZThK 72 (1975), 1–46.
Lindemann, A., Die Osterbotschaft des Markus, in: NTS 26 (1979/80), 298–317.
Lührmann, D., Pistis im Judentum, in: ZNW 64 (1973), 19–38.
Malbon, E. Struthers, Mark's Jesus. Characterization as Narrative Christology, Waco 2009.
Merk, O., Nachahmung Christi, in: Neues Testament (FS R. Schnackenburg), hg. von H. Merklein, Freiburg 1989, 172–206.
Merklein, H., Zum Verständnis des paulinischen Begriffs „Evangelium", in: Studien zu Jesus und Paulus, ed. H. Merklein (WUNT 43), Tübingen 1987, 279–295.
Petersen, N.R., „Literarkritik", the New Literary Criticism and the Gospel according to Mark, in: The Four Gospels II (FS F. Neirynck), ed. F. van Segbroeck u.a., Leuven 1992, 935–948.
Powell, M.A., What is Narrative Criticism? A New Approach to the Bible, Minneapolis 1990.
Räisänen, H., Jesus and the Food Laws, in: JNST 16 (1982), 79–100.
Reinmuth, E., Narratio und argumentatio – zur Auslegung der Jesus-Christus-Geschichte im Ersten Korintherbrief, in: ZThK 92 (1995), 13–27.
Rhoads, D./ Michie, D., Mark as Story: An Introduction to the Narrative of a Gospel, Philadelphia 1982.
Roller, O., Das Formular der paulinischen Briefe (BWANT 4.6), Stuttgart 1933.
Sariola, H., Markus und das Gesetz (AASF 56), Helsinki 1990.
Schnelle, U. (Hg.), Neuer Wettstein I/1.1, Berlin 2008.
—, Einleitung in das Neue Testament, Göttingen ⁷2011.
—, Paulus, Leben und Denken, Berlin 2003.
—, Theologie des Neuen Testaments, Göttingen 2007.
Schnider, F./ Stenger, W., Studien zum neutestamentlichen Briefformular (NTTS XI), Leiden 1987.
Scholtissek, K., „Geboren aus einer Frau, geboren unter das Gesetz" (Gal 4,4). Die christologisch-soteriologische Bedeutung des irdischen Jesus bei Paulus, in: Paulinische Christologie (FS H. Hübner), hg. von U. Schnelle/Th. Söding/M. Labahn, Göttingen 2000, 194–219.
Schunack, G., Glaube in griechischer Religiosität, in: Antikes Judentum und Frühes Christentum (FS H. Stegemann), hg. von B. Kollmann/W. Reinbold/A. Steudel (BZNW 97), Berlin 1999, 296–326.299–317.

Schweizer, E., Zur Frage nach dem Messiasgeheimnis bei Markus, in: Beiträge zur Theologie des Neuen Testaments, hg. von E. Schweizer, Zürich 1970, 11–20.
Söding, Th. (Hg.), Der Evangelist als Theologe. Studien zum Markusevangelium (SBS 163), Stuttgart 1995.
—, Das Geheimnis Gottes im Kreuz Jesu, in: Das Wort vom Kreuz, hg. von Th. Söding (WUNT 93), Tübingen 1997, 71–92.
—, Glaube bei Markus (SBB 12), Stuttgart ²1987.
Stowers, S.K., Letter Writing in Greco-Roman Antiquity, Philadelphia 1986.
Straub, J., Geschichten erzählen, Geschichte bilden, in: Erzählung, Identität und historisches Bewusstsein, hg. von J. Straub, Frankfurt 1998, 81–169.
Strecker, G., Das Evangelium Jesu Christi, in: Eschaton und Historie, hg. von G. Strecker, Göttingen 1979, 183–228.
—, Literarkritische Überlegungen zum εὐαγγέλιον-Begriff im Markusevangelium, in: Eschaton und Historie, hg. von G. Strecker, Göttingen 1979, 76–89.
Strecker, G./Schnelle, U. (Hgg.), Neuer Wettstein II/1, Berlin 1996.
Stuhlmacher, P., Biblische Theologie I, Göttingen 1992.
—, Das paulinische Evangelium I. Vorgeschichte (FRLANT 95), Göttingen 1968.
Theißen, G., Die Entstehung des Neuen Testaments als literaturgeschichtliches Problem, Heidelberg 2007.
—, Evangelienschreibung und Gemeindeleitung: Pragmatische Motive bei der Abfassung des Markusevangeliums, in: Antikes Judentum und Frühes Christentum (FS H. Stegemann), hg. von B. Kollmann/W. Reinbold/A. Steudel (BZNW 97), Berlin 1999, 389–414.
Toit, D. du, Der abwesende Herr. Strategien im Markusevangelium zur Bewältigung der Abwesenheit des Auferstandenen (WMANT 111), Neukirchen 2006.
Vermes, G., Jesus der Jude, Neukirchen 1993.
Vielhauer, Ph., Erwägungen zur Christologie des Markusevangeliums, in: Aufsätze zum Neuen Testament, hg. von Ph. Vielhauer (TB 31), München 1965, 199–214.
Weber, R., Christologie und ‚Messiasgeheimnis': ihr Zusammenhang und Stellenwert in den Darstellungsintentionen des Markus, in: EvTh 43 (1983), 108–125.
—, Das Gesetz im hellenistischen Judentum (ARGU 10), Frankfurt 2000.
Wedderburn, A.J.M., Paul and the Story of Jesus, in: Paul and Jesus, ed. A.J.M. Wedderburn (JSNT.S 37), Sheffield 1989, 161–189.
Weder, H., ‚Evangelium Jesu Christi' (Mk 1,1) und ‚Evangelium Gottes' (Mk 1,14), in: Die Mitte des Neuen Testaments (FS E. Schweizer), hg. von U. Luz/H. Weder, Göttingen 1983, 399–411.
Weiß, H.-F., Kerygma und Geschichte, Berlin 1983.
Weiß, J., Das Urchristentum, Göttingen 1917.
Werner, M., Der Einfluß paulinischer Theologie im Markusevangelium. Eine Studie zur neutestamentlichen Theologie (BZNW 1), Gießen 1923.
Wischmeyer, O., Das Gebot der Nächstenliebe bei Paulus, in: BZ 30 (1986), 153–187.
Wördemann, D., Das Charakterbild des bios nach Plutarch und das Christusbild im Evangelium nach Markus, Paderborn 2002.
Wrede, W., Das Messiasgeheimnis in den Evangelien, Göttingen ⁴1969 = 1901.
Zeller, D., Art. Messias/Christus, in: NBL 3 (1995), 782–786.
Zimmermann, J., Messianische Texte aus Qumran (WUNT 2.R. 104), Tübingen 1998.

Andreas Lindemann
Das Evangelium bei Paulus und im Markusevangelium

Der folgende Beitrag fragt nach dem Gebrauch des Wortes εὐαγγέλιον bei Paulus und im Markusevangelium (MkEv); es geht also nicht darum, die Theologie des Apostels Paulus und des Evangelisten Markus als „Evangelium" zu beschreiben, womöglich im Gegenüber zum „Gesetz", sondern gefragt wird, welche Aussagen sich bei Paulus und Markus mit der Vokabel εὐαγγέλιον verbinden. Das Wort εὐαγγέλιον ist im Neuen Testament 75mal belegt, ausschließlich im Singular. Es begegnet, mit Ausnahme von Apk 14,6[1], nur in den Paulusbriefen sowie deren weiterem Umfeld und im MkEv[2], davon abhängig auch im MtEv; Lukas verwendet es lediglich zweimal in der Apg[3]. Angesichts dieses Befundes ist ein Vergleich zwischen Paulus und dem MkEv hinsichtlich des Gebrauchs und des Verständnisses von εὐαγγέλιον angemessen und sinnvoll[4]. Zuvor soll die Verwendung des Wortes in der griechischen Bibel (LXX) sowie in außerchristlicher Literatur der hellenistisch-römischen Zeit untersucht werden, weil in der Exegese häufig mit einem starken Einfluss des dortigen Sprachgebrauchs auf die neutestamentlichen Texte gerechnet wird[5].

---

1 P. Stuhlmacher, Das paulinische Evangelium. I. Vorgeschichte (FRLANT 95), Göttingen 1968, 210–218 sieht in Apk 14,6 „die traditionsgeschichtlich älteste Verwendung von εὐαγγέλιον im urchristlichen Bereich", wobei der Seher mit dem Ausdruck εὐαγγέλιον αἰώνιον von „der ewig gültigen Botschaft von Gottes Kommen zum Weltgericht" spreche (213). Ähnlich schon W. Bousset, Die Offenbarung Johannis (KEK XVI), Göttingen ⁶1906, 383f. unter Hinweis auf das Fehlen des Artikels: „Ein ewig (geltendes) Evangelium ist der schon in 10,7 den Engeln Gottes verkündete Ratschluß in Beziehung auf das baldige Ende, der im folgenden nun noch einmal wie dort den Propheten so hier aller Welt verkündet wird." Dass ein anderes Verständnis von Evangelium vorliegt als etwa bei Paulus, liegt auf der Hand; dass dieser späte Text die „traditionsgeschichtlich älteste Verwendung" des Begriffs zeigt, ist wenig wahrscheinlich.
2 In Mk 1,1–16,8 gibt es sieben Belege; der sekundäre Mk-Schluss verwendet den Begriff τὸ εὐαγγέλιον in 16,15 (s.u.).
3 S. dazu unten S. 324.
4 E.K.C. Wong, Evangelien im Dialog mit Paulus. Eine intertextuelle Studie zu den Synoptikern (NTOA/StUNT 89), Göttingen 2012, 62f. vergleicht neben dem Gebrauch des Begriffs εὐαγγέλιον auch die Einsetzungsworte zum Abendmahl sowie das Schema, dass die Botschaft zuerst Juden und erst dann Heiden gilt (63 unter Hinweis auf Mk 7,27).
5 Zu der schon mit Homer einsetzenden Geschichte der Verwendung des Wortes s. immer noch G. Friedrich, Art. εὐαγγελίζομαι κτλ., in: ThWNT II (1935), 718–722.

1 εὐαγγέλιον in vor- und außerchristlicher Literatur

1.1 Septuaginta

In der LXX sind die Substantive εὐαγγέλιον und εὐαγγελία insgesamt sechsmal belegt; sie begegnen in einem sehr schmalen textlichen Umfeld, durchweg für hebräisch בשרה[6]. Dabei bezeichnet das nur im Plural vorkommende Wort εὐαγγέλιον den Lohn, den ein Bote für eine Nachricht erhält bzw. hätte erhalten müssen.

In 2Reg 4,10 sagt David: „Der mir gemeldet hatte (ὁ ἀπαγγείλας μοι), dass Saul tot war – und er war wie einer, der (eine Freudenbotschaft) verkündigt (αὐτὸς ἦν ὡς εὐαγγελιζόμενος, כמבשר) vor mir – ihn habe ich gefangen genommen und getötet in Sekelag, dem ich hätte Botenlohn geben müssen (δοῦναι εὐαγγέλια, בשרה)."[7]

In 2Reg 18,20–27 wird im Zusammenhang der Mitteilung vom Tod Absaloms von εὐαγγέλια bzw. εὐαγγελία als einer „guten Botschaft" gesprochen, als Joab zu Achimaaz sagt (V.20): „Du bist nicht der Mann für eine gute Nachricht (οὐκ ἀνὴρ εὐαγγελίας σύ, איש בשרה) an diesem Tag. An einem anderen Tag magst du (eine gute Nachricht) verkünden (εὐαγγελιῇ), an diesem Tag jedoch wirst du keine (gute Nachricht) verkünden (οὐκ εὐαγγελιῇ), denn der Sohn des Königs ist tot." In V.22 sagt Joab dann: „Warum läufst du dazu los, Kind? Es wird für dich keine gute Nachricht sein (οὐκ ἔστιν σοι εὐαγγελία, אין בשרה מצאת), die dir nützt, wenn du gehst."[8] Als dem König David das Kommen eines Boten gemeldet wird, sagt er (V.25): „Wenn er allein läuft, ist eine gute Botschaft in seinem Munde (εὐαγγελία, בשרה, ἐν τῷ στόματι αὐτοῦ)." Und als der Bote näher kommt, sagt David (V.27): „Ein guter Mann ist dieser, dafür (dass er) gute Nachrichten bringen wird (εἰς εὐαγγελίαν ἀγαθὴν ἐλεύσεται, ואל בשרה טובה יבוא)."

In 4Reg 7,9 entdecken Männer ein reichhaltiges feindliches Warenlager und verstecken es; doch dann stellen sie selbstkritisch fest: „Dieser Tag ist ein Tag der Frohbotschaft (ἡμέρα εὐαγγελίας ἐστίν, היום הז יום בשרה הוא), und wir schweigen und bleiben hier bis zum Licht der Frühe? Wir laden uns ein Unrecht auf ..."

---

[6] Das Verb εὐαγγελίζειν als Wiedergabe von בשר begegnet sehr viel häufiger.
[7] Die deutsche Übersetzung folgt der Septuaginta Deutsch. Der hebr. Text spricht vom „Geben des Botenlohns" in ironischer Weise: „Der mir berichtet hat: Sieh, Saul ist tot!, und der in seinen eigenen Augen ein Freudenbote war, den habe ich gegriffen und in Ziklag umgebracht, und so habe ich ihm den Botenlohn gegeben" (לתתי־לו בשרה).
[8] Hier könnte statt εὐαγγελία auch εὐαγγέλια gelesen werden.

Die Worte εὐαγγέλια (Plural von εὐαγγέλιον) bzw. εὐαγγελία bezeichnen in der LXX also eine für den Empfänger erfreuliche Information; über diesen allgemeinen Sinn geht die Bedeutung des Wortes nicht hinaus.

Das Verb εὐαγγελίζειν bzw. εὐαγγελίζεσθαι (für hebr. בשר) meint in der Regel „Gutes melden", bisweilen ausdrücklich mit dem entsprechenden Akkusativobjekt verbunden (... καὶ ἀγαθὰ εὐαγγέλισαι, so 3Reg 1,42 entsprechend hebr. וטוב תבשר)[9]. In Jes 52,7 heißt es: „Wie Frühling auf den Bergen, wie die Füße eines, der frohe Botschaft bringt (ὡς ὡραῖοι οἱ πόδες εὐαγγελιζομένου ἀγαθά, רגלי מבשר), Kunde vom Frieden (ἀκοὴν εἰρήνης), wie einer, der frohe Botschaft von Gutem bringt (ὡς εὐαγγελιζόμενος ἀγαθά, מבשר טוב), weil ich deine Rettung hörbar machen werde, indem ich zu Sion sage: Als König wird dein Gott herrschen (βασιλεύσει σου ὁ θεός)." εὐαγγελιζόμενος ist „einer, der eine (gute) Botschaft bringt"; um einen festen Begriff handelt es sich offenbar nicht, denn zum einen folgt das Objekt ἀγαθά, und zum andern zeigt der Kontext, um was für eine Botschaft es sich handelt – die ἀκοὴ εἰρήνης. Der Bote ist „wie einer, der Gutes meldet" (ὡς εὐαγγελιζόμενος ἀγαθά), wobei die partizipiale Wendung (ὁ) εὐαγγελιζόμενος (מבשר) nicht schon für sich genommen „*den* Freudenboten" bezeichnet[10].

Gerhard Friedrich folgert daraus: „Die Vorgeschichte des nt.-lichen Begriffes ist nicht in der LXX zu suchen"[11], denn dort meint εὐαγγέλιον / εὐαγγέλια bzw. εὐαγγελία entweder „Botenlohn" oder „eine erfreuliche Nachricht".[12] Aus der LXX-Verwendung des Verbs εὐαγγελίζεσθαι kann der neutestamentliche Gebrauch des Substantivs εὐαγγέλιον nicht abgeleitet werden.

1.2 Hellenistisch-römische Literatur

In außerchristlicher Literatur in hellenistisch-römischer Zeit ist εὐαγγέλιον „das, was zu einem εὐάγγελος gehört", woraus sich der Doppelsinn ergibt: „Für den, zu dem ein εὐάγγελος kommt, ist das, was zu einem εὐάγγελος gehört, eine frohe Botschaft, für den εὐάγγελος selbst ist εὐαγγέλιον Botenlohn." „Die Bedeutung

---

9 Vgl. Jes 40,9; 60,6; 61,1; Jer 20,15.
10 Anders P. Stuhlmacher, Evangelium, 162. Zu Jes 52,9 vgl. Nahum 1,15 (2,1); εὐαγγελιζόμενος begegnet außerdem in Jes 40,9, aber in keinem Fall liegt „technischer" Sprachgebrauch („*der* Freudenbote") vor.
11 G. Friedrich, Art. εὐαγγελίζομαι, 723 (im Orig. gesperrt).
12 In 2Reg 18,27 heißt es sogar ausdrücklich εἰς εὐαγγελίαν ἀγαθήν.

frohe Botschaft", so stellt Friedrich fest, „ist erst seit Cicero Att II 3,1 nachweisbar"[13].

Die Belege für εὐαγγέλιον bei Cicero[14] zeigen allerdings einen eher banalen Gebrauch des Wortes. In *Epistulae ad Atticum* II 3,1 heißt es: ‚Primum, ut opinor, εὐαγγέλια: Valerius absolutus est Hortensio defendente' („Zuerst eine, wie ich meine, gute Nachricht: Valerius ist, von Hortensius verteidigt, freigesprochen worden"). Ähnlich schreibt er in *Epistulae ad Atticum* II 10(12),1: ‚O suaves epistulas tuas uno tempore mihi datas duas! quibus εὐαγγέλια quae reddam, nescio.' („Wie reizend deine beiden Briefe, die ich gleichzeitig erhielt! Ich weiß nicht, mit welcher Freudenbotschaft ich sie Dir lohnen sollte")[15]. In *Epistulae ad Atticum*, XIII 49(40),1 fragt Cicero rhetorisch: ‚Itane? Nuntiat Brutus ilum ad bonos viros? εὐαγγέλια.' Die Übersetzung von Helmut Kasten („Ist's möglich! Brutus bringt die Nachricht mit, ER (Caesar) wolle zu den Optimaten abschwenken? Das wäre etwas!") zeigt, dass εὐαγγέλια im lateinischen Text geradezu ein „Slang-Ausdruck" ist, vergleichbar einem „okay" in einem ansonsten gut ausgeformten Brief in deutscher Sprache. Cicero hat in seine Privatbriefe relativ häufig griechische Worte eingestreut, nicht nur im Zusammenhang von Zitaten aus griechischer Literatur; mit dem Wort εὐαγγέλια zeigt er nur an, dass er eine Nachricht als erfreulich einstuft.

1.3 Kaiserkult

Besitzt das Wort εὐαγγέλιον eine besondere Bedeutung im Zusammenhang des römischen Kaiserkults? Aus dieser Annahme werden nicht selten weitreichende Konsequenzen für Herleitung und Interpretation von εὐαγγέλιον im Neuen Testament gezogen.

(1) Als wichtigster Beleg gilt eine in der kleinasiatischen Stadt Priene gefundene umfangreiche Inschrift aus dem Jahre 9 v. Chr., in der es heißt (Zeile 40 f.): ... ἦρξεν δὲ τῶι κόσμωι τῶν δι' εὐαγγελί[ων ἡ γενέθλιος ἡμέ]ρα τοῦ θεοῦ ... („... da schließlich für die Welt der Geburtstag des Gottes der Anfang der durch ihn ver-

---

13 G. Friedrich, Art. εὐαγγελίζομαι, 719. Der Hinweis auf diese Cicero-Stelle wird in neuerer Literatur durchgängig aufgenommen.
14 Text und deutsche Übersetzung nach: Marcus Tullius Cicero. Atticus-Briefe. Lateinisch-deutsch, hg. von H. Kasten, München ²1976.
15 Hier könnte entgegen der Übersetzung von H. Kasten die Bedeutung „Botenlohn" sogar näher liegen.

ursachten Freudenbotschaften war ...")¹⁶. „Am Schluss des komplizierten Satzgefüges, das noch weiterläuft, ist sinngemäß zu ergänzen: ... deshalb wird der Vorschlag des Prokonsuls, Augustus in der angegebenen Weise zu ehren, angenommen", d. h. der Beginn des neuen Jahres wird auf den Geburtstag des Augustus gelegt¹⁷. Claudio Ettl verweist darauf, dass „Vertreter einer Rückführung des Begriffs εὐαγγέλιον auf den Kontext der hellenistisch-römischen Religionsgeschichte, näherhin des hellenistischen Herrscher- und römischen Kaiserkults" diese Inschrift „als ‚Kronzeugen'" heranziehen¹⁸. Nach Georg Strecker sind in diesem Text „εὐαγγέλια sowohl Ankündigungen des mit dem Erscheinen des Kaisers heraufziehenden Heils (Z. 37f) als auch die Freudenbotschaften als Heilsereignis (Z. 40f)."¹⁹ Udo Schnelle folgert, das Substantiv εὐαγγέλια spiele

---

16 Inschrift Nr. 105. Der Text ist zitiert nach St. Schreiber, Weihnachtspolitik, 122–126. Übersetzung nach H.-J. Klauck, Die religiöse Umwelt des Urchristentums II. Herrscher- und Kaiserkult, Philosophie, Gnosis (KStTh 9,2), Stuttgart 1996, 51. Vgl. auch C. Ettl, Der „Anfang der ... Evangelien". Die Kalenderinschrift von Priene und ihre Relevanz für die Geschichte des Begriffs εὐαγγέλιον. Mit einer Anmerkung zur Frage nach der Gattung der Logienquelle, in: St.H. Brandenburger/Th. Hieke (Hgg.), Wenn drei das Gleiche sagen – Studien zu den ersten drei Evangelien. Mit einer Werkstattübersetzung des Q-Textes (Theologie 14), Münster 1998, 121–151, hier 138.
17 H.-J. Klauck, Umwelt, 51.
18 C. Ettl, „Anfang der ... Evangelien", 138. Die von Ettl genannten Positionen sind auf der einen Seite Deißmann, auf der anderen Seite Stuhlmacher. Ettl selber hält eine „einseitige traditionsgeschichtliche Rückführung" für unangemessen, man werde „auch weiterhin von einer multikausalen Entstehungsgeschichte und einem mehrschichtigen Bedeutungsinhalt ausgehen müssen. Als „Fazit" notiert er: „Der Begriff ‚Evangelium' meint im Kontext des hellenistisch-römischen Herrscher- und Kaiserkultes eine mit der Person des Kaisers verbundene ‚gute Nachricht'." Das Lexem begegne „in den epigraphischen und sonstigen literarischen Quellen meist im Plural", „was für den neutestamentlichen Sprachgebrauch vor vorschnellen Interpretationen bewahren sollte", aber der Singular bei Josephus könnte „darauf hindeuten, daß auch im hellenistisch-römischen Sprachbereich ein Transformationsprozeß festzustellen ist: Die εὐαγγέλια, die von der Person des Kaisers berichtet werden (Mündigkeitserklärung, Thronbesteigung etc.), können auch komprimiert bzw. personal zentriert werden zu einem εὐαγγέλιον" (138f.). „Eine direkte Einwirkung auf die neutestamentliche Begriffsgeschichte läßt sich anhand des vorhandenen Materials nicht belegen." Doch wer das Wort im zeitgenössischen Kontext hörte, konnte „durchaus auch einen spezifisch römische-griechischen Wortsinn assoziieren, und dies um so leichter, als in einem profan-politischen Umfeld das Lexem εὐαγγέλιον bereits ansatzweise mit der Biographie einer Persönlichkeit (z.B. mit der Geburt des Kaisers) in Verbindung gebracht werden konnte." In der Priene-Inschrift erhalte „der Begriff εὐαγγέλιον eine (zumindest rudimentäre) narrative Ausfaltung", doch konnten auch andere Ereignisse als εὐαγγέλια bezeichnet werden (139).
19 G. Strecker, Das Evangelium Jesu Christi, in: G. Strecker, Eschaton und Historie. Aufsätze, Göttingen 1979, 183–228, hier 190 unter Verweis auf A. Deißmann (Licht vom Osten. Das Neue Testament und die neuentdeckten Texte der hellenistisch-römischen Welt, Tübingen ⁴1923, 313f.:

„eine zentrale Rolle in der *Herrscherverehrung*", denn in der Priene-Inschrift werde „der Geburtstag des Augustus folgendermaßen glorifiziert: ‚Der Geburtstag des Gottes war aber für die Welt die erste von ihm ausgehende Freudenbotschaft (εὐαγγελίων)".[20] Thomas Witulski betont jedoch, der in dieser Inschrift festgehaltene Beschluss des Landtags (Koinon) von Kleinasien belege nur, dass die Beschlüsse „ursprünglich darauf zielten, den amtierenden Kaiser griechisch-hellenistischer Tradition entsprechend als θεός zu verehren, ohne die *Dea Roma* an diesem Kult zu beteiligen und die römische Tradition der erst mit der *consecratio* erfolgten Divinisierung des Herrschers zu berücksichtigen".[21] Das kleinasiatische Koinon treffe die Feststellung, „daß Augustus als σωτήρ den Krieg beendet hat und den Frieden einrichten wird. Im Wesentlichen diese *pax Augusta* und die daraus für die Provinz *Asia* und den gesamten κόσμος resultierenden, außerordentlich positiven Folgen begreifen die Delegierten als εὐαγγέλια und als bis zu diesem Zeitpunkt unvergleichliche Wohltaten, die auch in Zukunft kein anderer jemals wird übertreffen können."[22] Dass Augustus „wie selbstverständlich die θεός-Prädikation" erhält, deute darauf hin, „daß die Bezeichnung des amtierenden römischen Machthabers als θεός in der griechisch-hellenistischen Welt offensichtlich durchaus üblich und keinesfalls außergewöhnlich gewesen ist".[23] In der Inschrift von Priene ist die göttliche Verehrung des Kaisers vorausgesetzt; sie wird mit dem Begriff εὐαγγέλιον verbunden, aber nicht exklusiv und nicht im Singular. Die den Geburtstag des Kaisers betreffende Mitteilung gilt als *eine* der guten Nachrichten (εὐαγγέλια), aber nicht als *die* gute Nachricht, und es wären weitere εὐαγγέλια offenbar weitere „erfreuliche Nachrichten". Die Inschrift ist deshalb kein Beleg dafür, dass εὐαγγέλιον ein spezifischer Begriff des Kaiserkults ist[24].

„Es war aber [der Geburtstag] des Gottes für die Welt der Anfang der Dinge, die um seinetwillen Freudenbotschaft[en] sind").
20 U. Schnelle, Paulus. Leben und Denken, Berlin 2003, 456f. Ähnlich E.-M. Becker, Art. Evangelium/Evangelienliteratur. I. Neutestamentlich, in: LBH (2009), 164: Cicero gebrauchte den Begriff „erstmals für ‚frohe Botschaft/gute Nachrichten'. Im paganen Gebrauch steht der Begriff für kaiserliche Befehle oder für Kaiserproklamationen" (unter Verweis auf Josephus, Bellum Iudaicum, IV 656). Er „kann im Kaiserkult, etwa für Nachrichten aus dem Herrscherhaus, verwendet werden (Inschrift von Priene 105,40)".
21 Th. Witulski, Kaiserkult in Kleinasien. Die Entwicklung der kultisch-religiösen Kaiserverehrung in der römischen Provinz Asia von Augustus bis Antoninus Pius (NTOA/StUNT 63), Göttingen/Fribourg ²2010, 17.
22 Th. Witulski, Kaiserkult, 30.
23 Th. Witulski, Kaiserkult, 32f.
24 Vermutlich ist die Inschrift als solche überhaupt kein Zeugnis für den Kaiser*kult*. Vgl. H. Cancik, Art. Evangelium/Evangelienliteratur. I. Altphilologisch, in: LBH (2009), 166: „Als *ter-*

(2) Nach Georg Strecker belegt auch der Sprachgebrauch bei Philo und Josephus, dass sich das Wort εὐαγγέλιον auf „die Kaiserproklamation, Mündigkeitserklärung, Thronbesteigung o.a." bezieht²⁵. Aber bei Philo von Alexandria²⁶ ist das Nomen εὐαγγέλιον gar nicht belegt, wohl aber verwendet er das Verb εὐαγγελίζω im Zusammenhang der Erwähnung erfreulicher Nachrichten.²⁷ In *Legatio ad Gajum* 18 erwähnt Philo, die frohe Nachricht über die Genesung des Caligula (παντελὴ ῥῶσις εὐηγγελίσθη) sei mit großer Freude aufgenommen worden. Gemäß *Legatio ad Gajum* 99 müssen gute Nachrichten schnell mitgeteilt werden (τὰ λυσιτελῆ φθάνοντας εὐαγγελίζεσθαι προσήκει)²⁸. Und in *Legatio ad Gajum* 231 heißt es, dass sich die freudige Nachricht (εὐαγγελιουμένη) über die Thronbesteigung Caligulas von Jerusalem aus rasch in die anderen Städte ausgebreitet habe²⁹. Philo setzt in seiner Schrift *Legatio ad Gajum* die gottgleiche Verehrung Caligulas voraus (und ironisiert sie), aber dabei findet das Wort εὐαγγέλιον keine Verwendung.

(3) Verbindet Flavius Josephus, wie Schnelle meint, „die Erhebung Vespasians zum Kaiser mit Opfern und dem εὐαγγέλια-Begriff"?³⁰ Die Belege für εὐαγγέλιον bei Josephus sind in dieser Hinsicht unspezifisch³¹. In *Bellum Iudaicum*, IV 618

---

minus technicus wird in der griechischen Opfersprache εὐαγγέλια (Opfer für gute Botschaften) gebraucht". In der Priene-Inschrift hat „der Geburtstag des Gottes ... für die Welt den Anfang der durch ihn bewirkten Freudenbotschaft (εὐαγγέλιον) gemacht"; das Wort Evangelium „ist jedoch kein *terminus technicus* der Herrscherverehrung". Vgl. schon J. Schniewind, Euangelion. Ursprung und erste Gestalt des Begriffs Evangelium. Untersuchungen. Erster Teil, Gütersloh 1927, 92f.: „Das εὐαγγελ- des Neuen Testaments entsteht unabhängig vom Sprachgebrauch des Kaiserkults, und inhaltlich steht es in jäher Antithese zum kaiserkultischen εὐαγγέλιον".
25 G. Strecker, Evangelium, 190. Auch nach U. Schnelle, Art. Euangelion, in: DNP 4 (1998), 205, bezeugen Philo und Josephus die Verwendung von εὐαγγέλιον „im Kontext hell[enistischer] Herrscherverehrung". Beleg für die Aussage, die Kundgabe der Thronbesteigung des Kaisers sei als εὐαγγέλιον bezeichnet worden, ist offenbar nur die entsprechende Nachricht zu Caius Iulius Verus (Regierungsantritt 238 n.Chr.); Text bei A. Deißmann, Licht, 313f.
26 Philonis Alexandrini Opera quae supersunt. Vol. VI, hg. von L. Cohn/S. Reiter, Berlin 1915. Philo von Alexandria. Die Werke in deutscher Übersetzung, hg. von L. Cohn/I. Heinemann/M. Adler/W. Theiler. Band VII, Berlin 1964.
27 Vgl. J. Schniewind, Euangelion, 81–94.
28 Dazu J. Schniewind, Euangelion, 85f.
29 J. Schniewind, Euangelion, 87–92 sieht hier eine starke Nähe zu der im Kaiserkult verwendeten Terminologie; m.E. hebt er nicht deutlich genug heraus, dass das Nomen εὐαγγέλιον dabei nicht begegnet.
30 U. Schnelle, Paulus, 456f. Er folgert: „Innerhalb der zeitgenössischen Enzyklopädie war der Terminus εὐαγγέλιον / εὐαγγέλια auch mit der Herrscherverehrung verbunden und hatte damit eine politisch-religiöse und faktisch anti-imperiale Konnotation."
31 J. Schniewind, Euangelion, 95: Bei Josephus „kommt einmal ἡ εὐαγγελία vor, einmal τὸ εὐαγγέλιον, einmal τὰ εὐαγγέλια (im Sinn von ‚gute Botschaft') einmal ἑορτάζειν εὐαγγέλια,

schreibt Josephus, die Botschaft vom Herrschaftsantritt Vespasians habe sich rasch verbreitet, „und jede Stadt feierte die gute Nachricht und brachte zu seinen Gunsten Opfer dar" (πᾶσα μὲν πόλις ἑώρταζεν εὐαγγέλια δὲ καὶ θυσίας ὑπὲρ αὐτοῦ ἐπετέλει). Ähnlich heißt es in *Bellum Iudaicum*, IV 656: Als Vespasian in Alexandria ankam, „trafen gerade die frohen Nachrichten aus Rom (τὰ ἀπὸ τῆς Ῥώμης εὐαγγέλια) ein". An beiden Stellen sind die εὐαγγέλια einfach „gute Nachrichten" (good news), auch wenn sie den Kaiser betreffen[32]. Das bestätigen zwei Belege, die in ganz anderen Zusammenhängen stehen: In *Bellum Iudaicum*, II 420 berichtet Josephus, der römische Statthalter Florus habe Krieg gegen das jüdische Volk angestrebt, und als er von dem Wunsch der Vornehmen des Volkes hörte, er solle den beginnenden Aufstand niederschlagen, sei das für ihn „eine ausgemachte Freudenbotschaft" (δεινὸν εὐαγγέλιον) gewesen. Nach *Antiquitates Iudaicae*, XVIII 229 sagte Agrippa dem Boten, der ihm den Tod des Tiberius meldete, Dank für die gute Nachricht (ἐπὶ τῷδε εὐαγγελίας χάριτες ...).

Ein spezifischer Bezug von εὐαγγέλιον bzw. εὐαγγελία zum Kaiserkult[33] liegt in den Formulierungen des Josephus offenbar nicht vor; der Begriff sagt lediglich, dass eine Nachricht von den Empfängern als erfreulich eingeschätzt wird[34].

(4) Philostrat verwendet in seiner *Vita Apollonii* das Wort εὐαγγέλιον durchweg im Plural. In *Vita Apollonii* V 8 berichtet er, ein Eilbote habe verkündet, dass man ein Opfer darbringen solle wegen „guter Nachrichten" über den dreifachen Olympiasieg des Nero ... (κελεύοντος εὐαγγέλια θύειν τρισολυμπιονίκην Νέρωνα). Nach *Vita Apollonii*, VIII 27 sah Apollonius von Ephesus aus die Ermordung des Domitian in Rom, und „während man der Sache noch mißtraute, trafen Eilboten mit den guten Nachrichten ein" (... ἦλθον οἱ τῶν εὐαγγελίων δρόμοι). Dass Philostrat das Wort εὐαγγέλιον möglicherweise ironisch verwendet, also in bewusster Umkehrung eines für den Kaiserkult charakteristischen Sprachgebrauchs, ist nicht unmöglich; aber es ist angesichts fehlender positiver Belege für eine spezifische Verwendung von εὐαγγέλιον im Kaiserkult jedenfalls nicht nachweisbar.

---

achtmal εὐαγγελίζεσθαι"; das Verb begegne mehrfach in der Reproduktion der biblischen Geschichte.

32 J. Schniewind, Euangelion, 104 f. sieht hier den Zusammenhang mit dem Kaiserkult: „εὐαγγέλιον ist technischer Ausdruck für Kaiserproklamation", obwohl er zunächst m.R. feststellt: „Im strengen Sinn freilich steht der Terminus εὐαγγέλιον auch in unsrer Josephusstelle nicht."

33 Zur Problematik des Begriffs „Kaiserkult" s.u.

34 In Antiquitates Iudaicae, XVIII 229 handelt es sich sogar um die vom Empfänger als erfreulich verstandene Information über einen Tod.

1.4 Ergebnis

Georg Strecker kommt zu dem Ergebnis, „daß εὐαγγέλια Heilsereignisse kennzeichnen, welche die Bewohner des Imperiums in ihrer Existenz betreffen". Das Wort εὐαγγέλιον habe „also in diesem Zusammenhang eine sakrale, Heil schaffende Funktion, unabhängig von der weitergehenden Frage, ob bzw. inwieweit jeweils ein technischer Sprachgebrauch nachzuweisen ist".[35] Die Tatsache, dass im Kaiserkult nur der plurale Gebrauch, im Neuen Testament dagegen nur der singularische Gebrauch belegt ist, könne aber dafür sprechen, dass – allenfalls abgesehen von der Johannesoffenbarung – keine polemische Abgrenzung vorliegt. Jedenfalls dürfte „der primäre traditionsgeschichtliche Urgrund des neutestamentlichen εὐαγγέλιον … im Umkreis der hellenistischen Herrscherverehrung zu suchen sein, welche die Sprache auch des Kaiserkultes geprägt hat". Der Kaiserkult konnte auf allgemeines Verstehen rechnen, und so kann hier „die εὐαγγέλιον-Terminologie vorgeprägt worden sein, in der urchristliche Missionare das Christusgeschehen ihren griechischsprachigen Hörern verständlich machten". Der spezifisch neutestamentliche Gebrauch von εὐαγγέλιον im Singular „charakterisiert die Botschaft vom Christusgeschehen bzw. dieses selbst als ein eschatologisches Ereignis", neben dem andere εὐαγγέλια keinen Bestand haben[36].

Nach Udo Schnelle war der Terminus εὐαγγέλιον „innerhalb der zeitgenössischen Enzyklopädie … auch mit der Herrscherverehrung verbunden", und er hatte „damit eine politisch-religiöse und faktisch anti-imperiale Konnotation"; das gelte für die christlichen Gemeinden ebenso wie für Paulus: „Nicht das Erscheinen des Kaisers rettet, sondern der vom Himmel kommende Gottessohn (vgl. 1Thess 1,9 f). Paulus verwendet bewusst eine *politisch*-religiöse Semantik, um diese Wirklichkeit zu beschreiben."[37] Demgegenüber fordert Michael Wolter, man solle „mit einseitigen Festlegungen zurückhaltend sein"; denn „dass der Begriff ‚Evangelium' in der hellenistischen Herrscherverehrung eine ‚zentrale Rolle' spielte und Paulus mit ihm ‚bewusst eine *politisch*-religiöse Semantik (verwendet)', kann man getrost ausschließen". Da Paulus aber auch „nicht nur die Septuaginta-Semantik des Verbs assoziiert" habe, reiche es aus, „die allgemeine Verwendung von εὐαγγέλιον im Sinne von ‚gute Nachricht' oder ‚Frohbotschaft' als Grundlage für die paulinische Verwendung vorauszusetzen".[38]

---

35 G. Strecker, Evangelium, 190 Anm. 41.
36 G. Strecker, Evangelium, 192.
37 U. Schnelle, Paulus 457.
38 M. Wolter, Paulus, Ein Grundriss seiner Theologie, Neukirchen-Vluyn 2011, 53. Ähnlich schon H. Merklein, Zum Verständnis des paulinischen Begriffs „Evangelium", in: H. Merklein, Studien zu Jesus und Paulus (WUNT 43), Tübingen 1987, 279–295, hier 283.

Tatsächlich ist die Herleitung der Verwendung des Begriffs εὐαγγέλιον aus einem bestimmten religiösen oder gar politischen Umfeld offensichtlich nicht möglich[39]. Die Textbasis für die Annahme eines spezifisch auf den Kaiserkult verweisenden Hintergrunds der Verwendung des Wortes εὐαγγέλιον ist schmal[40], der für die urchristlichen Schriften kennzeichnende singularische Gebrauch von εὐαγγέλιον ist gar nicht belegt. Für die Frage nach der Bedeutung des Wortes εὐαγγέλιον bei Paulus und im MkEv genügt als sprachgeschichtliche Voraussetzung die allgemeine Bedeutung „gute Nachricht"[41]; alle weiteren Aspekte ergeben sich erst aus der jeweiligen Verwendung des Wortes im jeweiligen Kontext.

2 εὐαγγέλιον und εὐαγγελίζεσθαι bei Paulus

2.1 Sprachgebrauch von εὐαγγέλιον

Das Nomen εὐαγγέλιον ist in sämtlichen uns erhaltenen Paulusbriefen[42] (und bis auf Tit auch in allen pseudopaulinischen Briefen im NT[43]) belegt. Paulus verwendet es ausschließlich im Singular[44], sehr häufig absolut „*die* gute Nachricht, *das* Evangelium".[45] Nach Rudolf Bultmann gilt: „In strengem Sinne terminus technicus ist εὐαγγέλιον (bzw. εὐαγγελίζεσθαι) nur dann, wenn es absolut, d. h. ohne Angabe eines sachlichen Objekts gebraucht wird, um die inhaltlich bestimmte christliche Botschaft zu bezeichnen. Dieser bei Paulus und nach ihm ganz geläufige Gebrauch ist ohne jede Analogie sowohl im AT und im Judentum wie im

---

39 So schon R. Bultmann, Theologie des Neuen Testaments, hg. von O. Merk, Tübingen ⁹1984, 89 (s. unten bei Anm. 46).
40 Es ist problematisch, wenn H.-J. Klauck, Umwelt, 51 unter Hinweis auf die Inschrift von Priene feststellt, der Begriff εὐαγγέλια (Plural) sei „auch im Kaiserkult zu Hause" und werde dort „auf Geburtstag, Volljährigkeit, Thronbesteigung und Genesung von Krankheit angewandt".
41 Der Einfachheit halber wird im Folgenden εὐαγγέλιον in christlichen Texten mit „Evangelium" wiedergegeben, obwohl das natürlich keine Übersetzung im eigentlichen Sinne ist.
42 Röm 1,1.9.16; 2,16; 10,16; 11,28; 15,16.19; (16,25); 1Kor 4,15; 9,12.14 (2x).18 (2x).23; 15,1; 2Kor 2,12; 4,3f.; 8,18; 9,13; 10,14; 11,4.7; Gal 1,6f.11; 2,2.5.7.14; Phil 1,5.7.12.16.27 (2x); 2,22; 4,3; 4,15; 1Thess 1,5; 2,2.4.8.9; 3,2; Phlm 13.
43 Kol 1,5.23; Eph 1,13; 3,6; 6,15.19; 2Thess 1,8; 2,14; 1Tim 1,11; 2Tim 1,8.10; 2,8; vgl. 1Petr 4,17.
44 M. Wolter, Paulus, 54: Die vereinzelten Genitivverbindungen mit εὐαγγέλια außerhalb des NT verweisen auf Ereignisse der Vergangenheit, „während es sich in den neutestamentlichen Texten um Abstraktnomina handelt, die das *eine* Evangelium charakterisieren. Darum steht hier auch immer der Singular und dort immer der Plural."
45 Röm 1,16; 10,16; 11,28; 1Kor 4,15; 9,14.18.23; 15,1; 2Kor 4,3; 8,18; 11,7; Gal 1,6.11; 2,2.5.14; Phil 1,5.7.12.16.27; 2,22; 4,3.15; 1Thess 2,4; Phlm 13.

heidnischen Hellenismus, und die viel verbreitete Ansicht, daß εὐαγγέλιον ein sakraler Terminus des Kaiserkults gewesen sei, läßt sich nicht halten."[46]

εὐαγγέλιον kann bei Paulus mit einem Genitivattribut verbunden sein, häufig sind „Gott"[47] und „Christus".[48] Dabei kann die Funktion des Attributs entsprechend den unterschiedlichen Funktionen des Genitivs unterschiedlich sein: In dem Syntagma τὸ εὐαγγέλιον τοῦ θεοῦ ist Gott der Inhalt des εὐαγγέλιον (gen. obj.), doch könnte in Röm 1,1 der dann folgende Verweis auf die prophetische Verheißung darauf hindeuten, dass Gott auch als der Autor des εὐαγγέλιον gedacht ist[49]. Die Wendung τὸ εὐαγγέλιον τοῦ Χριστοῦ bezeichnet Christus bzw. das Christusgeschehen als den Inhalt der verkündigten Botschaft[50], bisweilen auch als nomen actionis im Sinne des Vollzugs der Verkündigung[51]; in keinem Falle meint τὸ εὐαγγέλιον τοῦ Χριστοῦ bei Paulus das von Jesus Christus selber verkündigte Evangelium. In 2Kor 4,3 meint τὸ εὐαγγέλιον ἡμῶν das von Paulus verkündigte Evangelium[52].

εὐαγγέλιον kann seinerseits auch als Genitivobjekt begegnen, wenn Paulus davon spricht, dass das Evangelium in einer bestimmten Beziehung steht[53]. εὐαγγέλιον kann Akkusativobjekt sein zu den verba dicendi λαλεῖν[54], κηρύσσειν[55] und καταγγέλλειν[56], aber auch zu εὐαγγελίζειν bzw. εὐαγγελίζεσθαι[57]. In Gal 1,7

---

46 R. Bultmann, Theologie des NT, 89. Vgl. H. Koester, Ancient Christian Gospels. Their History and Development, Cambridge/Mass. 1990, 5: „In the early Christian usage the word refers exclusively to the one and only saving message of Christ".
47 Paulus spricht sechsmal vom „Evangelium Gottes": 1Thess 2,2.8.9; 2Kor 11,7 (τὸ τοῦ θεοῦ εὐαγγέλιον); Röm 15,16.
48 Neunmal, spricht Paulus vom „Evangelium Christi": 1Thess 3,2; Phil 1,27; Gal 1,7 (hier im Kontrast zu einem in Galatien propagierten ἕτερον εὐαγγέλιον); 1Kor 9,12.
49 In Röm 1,1 fehlt bei beiden Substantiven der Artikel (ἀφωρισμένος εἰς εὐαγγέλιον θεοῦ), aber Paulus gibt eine heilsgeschichtliche Erläuterung (ὃ προεπηγγείλατο διὰ τῶν προφητῶν αὐτοῦ ἐν γραφαῖς ἁγίαις ...). Vgl. dazu B-D-R § 163.2.
50 In Röm 1,9 spricht Paulus im Kontext der Rede von Gott vom „Evangelium seines Sohnes".
51 2Kor 2,12; 9,13; 10,14; Röm 15,19.
52 In Röm 2,16 und 16,25 (κατὰ τὸ εὐαγγέλιόν μου) dürften spätere Glossen vorliegen (s.u.).
53 Phil 1,7 (Paulus hat Gnade empfangen ἔν τε τοῖς δεσμοῖς μου καὶ ἐν τῇ ἀπολογίᾳ καὶ βεβαιώσει τοῦ εὐαγγελίου); Phil 1,12 (εἰς προκοπὴν τοῦ εὐαγγελίου); Phil 1,16 (εἰς ἀπολογίαν τοῦ εὐαγγελίου κεῖμαι); in Phil 4,15 bezieht sich die Wendung ἐν ἀρχῇ τοῦ εὐαγγελίου auf die Anfangsphase der Verkündigung. In Gal 2,5.14 spricht Paulus von der ἀλήθεια τοῦ εὐαγγελίου, in 2Kor 4,4 vom φωτισμὸς τοῦ εὐαγγελίου τῆς δόξης τοῦ Χριστοῦ.
54 1Thess 2,2 (... λαλῆσαι πρὸς ὑμᾶς τὸ εὐαγγέλιον τοῦ θεοῦ ἐν πολλῷ ἀγῶνι).
55 1Thess 2,9 (ἐκηρύξαμεν εἰς ὑμᾶς τὸ εὐαγγέλιον τοῦ θεοῦ); Gal 2,2 (ἀνεθέμην αὐτοῖς τὸ εὐαγγέλιον ὃ κηρύσσω ἐν τοῖς ἔθνεσιν). κηρύσσειν ist offenbar spezifischer als λαλεῖν.
56 1Kor 9,14: οὕτως καὶ ὁ κύριος διέταξεν τοῖς τὸ εὐαγγέλιον καταγγέλλουσιν ἐκ τοῦ εὐαγγελίου ζῆν. Die Wendung ἐκ τοῦ εὐαγγελίου ζῆν ist ohne Parallele.

wirft Paulus „Irrlehrern" in Galatien (οἱ ταράσσοντες ὑμᾶς) vor, sie wollten das Evangelium Christi in sein Gegenteil verkehren (...καὶ θέλοντες μεταστρέψαι τὸ εὐαγγέλιον τοῦ Χριστοῦ)[58]. Ganz ungewöhnlich sind die Genitivverbindungen in Gal 2,7, wo Paulus, möglicherweise in Anknüpfung an einen vorgegebenen Sprachgebrauch, schreibt, ihm sei anvertraut worden (πεπίστευμαι) „das Evangelium der Vorhaut" (τὸ εὐαγγέλιον τῆς ἀκροβυστίας) so wie dem Petrus das der Beschneidung (καθὼς Πέτρος τῆς περιτομῆς).

Paulus wendet sich in seinen Briefen an Jesusgläubige („Christen"); dabei setzt er durchweg voraus, dass diese den Sinn des Wortes εὐαγγέλιον kennen und verstehen[59]. Dass er das Wort in der missionarischen Verkündigung Außenstehenden gegenüber verwendet hat, lässt sich nicht belegen[60].

Das entspricht grundsätzlich dem Sprachgebrauch in der Apostelgeschichte. Dort begegnet εὐαγγέλιον nicht in „Missionsreden", sondern in Reden des Petrus bzw. des Paulus, deren Adressaten Christen sind. In Apg 15,7 spricht Petrus beim „Apostelkonzil" von dem ihm anvertrauten λόγος τοῦ εὐαγγελίου, also von der durch das Wort weitergegebenen Botschaft. Paulus bezeichnet in 20,24 in seiner Abschiedsrede in Milet den Dienst, den er vom κύριος Ἰησοῦς empfing, als διαμαρτύρασθαι τὸ εὐαγγέλιον τῆς χάριτος τοῦ θεοῦ; hier ist εὐαγγέλιον der Inhalt der (mündlich bezeugten) Botschaft von der Gnade Gottes.

2.2 Sprachgebrauch von εὐαγγελίζεσθαι

Das Verb εὐαγγελίζω verwendet Paulus im Allgemeinen im Medium (εὐαγγελίζομαι); es begegnet terminologisch präzise als „(das Evangelium) verkündigen"[61],

---

[57] Passivisch in Gal 1,11 in der figura etymologica τὸ εὐαγγέλιον τὸ εὐαγγελισθὲν ὑπ' ἐμοῦ, im Medium in 1Kor 15,1 (τὸ εὐαγγέλιον ὃ εὐηγγελισάμην ὑμῖν) und in 2Kor 11,7 (τὸ τοῦ θεοῦ εὐαγγέλιον εὐηγγελισάμην ὑμῖν).
[58] Vgl. auf der anderen Seite 1Thess 2,8: εὐδοκοῦμεν μεταδοῦναι ὑμῖν οὐ μόνον τὸ εὐαγγέλιον τοῦ θεοῦ ἀλλὰ καὶ τὰς ἑαυτῶν ψυχάς.
[59] M. Wolter, Paulus, 52: Paulus verwendet εὐαγγέλιον und εὐαγγελίζεσθαι „niemals mit Bezug auf den Inhalt und die Intention seiner Briefe"; das Evangelium geht den Briefen immer voraus. Eine in gewisser Weise definitorische Rede vom εὐαγγέλιον findet sich nur in Röm 1; das ist vermutlich kein Zufall, denn der Röm ist der einzige Paulusbrief an ihm unbekannte Adressaten.
[60] Anders, aber m. E. nicht wirklich begründet, H. Merklein, Verständnis, 287: „Insbesondere ‚Evangelium Gottes' ist deutlich der monotheistischen *Missionspredigt* verhaftet."
[61] Röm 1,15 (...καὶ ὑμῖν τοῖς ἐν Ῥώμῃ εὐαγγελίσασθαι); 15,20; ferner 1Kor 1,17 (οὐ γὰρ ἀπέστειλέν με Χριστὸς βαπτίζειν ἀλλὰ εὐαγγελίζεσθαι); 9,16; Gal 4,13.

aber auch eher profan als Hinweis auf eine erfreuliche Nachricht[62]. εὐαγγελίζομαι kann ein Akkusativobjekt bei sich haben[63], darunter auch das Substantiv εὐαγγέλιον[64]. In Gal 1,11 wird εὐαγγελίζω passivisch verwendet (τὸ εὐαγγέλιον τὸ εὐαγγελισθὲν ὑπ' ἐμοῦ ...), im Aktiv ist εὐαγγελίζω bei Paulus nicht belegt.

2.3 Zum Verständnis von εὐαγγέλιον und εὐαγγελίζομαι in den Paulusbriefen[65]

(1) Im 1. Thessalonicherbrief [66] erinnert Paulus schon im Proömium (1Thess 1,4.5) an „unsere Verkündigung" in Thessaloniki (τὸ εὐαγγέλιον ἡμῶν)[67], wobei die Formulierung τὸ εὐαγγέλιον ... ἐγενήθη zeigt, dass die Botschaft nicht nur gehört, sondern durch das damit verbundene Geschehen auch leibhaftig erfahren wurde. Man weiß in Makedonien und in Achaja vom Auftreten (εἴσοδος) der Missionare in Thessaloniki (V.8.9a), und das erläutert Paulus durch die Erinnerung an die damals erfolgte Hinwendung der Adressaten zu Gott, weg von den εἴδωλα (V.9b.10). Er bietet damit eine kurze Zusammenfassung des Glaubens- und Hoffnungsin-

---

62 1Thess 3,6: Timotheus hat „uns (erfreulicherweise) informiert über euren Glauben und eure Liebe" (... εὐαγγελισαμένου ἡμῖν τὴν πίστιν καὶ τὴν ἀγάπην ὑμῶν).
63 Röm 10,15: ἀγαθά (im Zitat aus Jes 52,7; s. o.); 1Kor 15,1 (τὸ εὐαγγέλιον ὃ εὐηγγελισάμην ὑμῖν), ebenso 2Kor 11,7 (... δωρεὰν τὸ τοῦ θεοῦ εὐαγγέλιον εὐηγγελισάμην ὑμῖν;). In Gal 1,16 ist Christus das Objekt (... ἵνα εὐαγγελίζωμαι αὐτὸν ἐν τοῖς ἔθνεσιν), in Gal 1,23 ist es der Glaube (νῦν εὐαγγελίζεται τὴν πίστιν ἥν ποτε ἐπόρθει).
64 1Kor 15,1; Gal 1,11; in Röm 1,15 f.; 10,15 f.; 15,19 f.; 1Kor 9,14.16; Gal 1,7 f. stehen das Verb und das Subst. jedenfalls nahe beieinander.
65 Im Folgenden wird die von mir vermutete chronologische Abfolge der Abfassung der Paulusbriefe zugrundegelegt; es geht dabei nicht um die Wahrnehmung einer möglichen „Entwicklung" des paulinischen Sprachgebrauchs, sondern darum, ob sich ein adressatenspezifischer Gebrauch beobachten lässt.
66 Präskript und Proömium des 1Thess sind ungewöhnlich; das spricht nach M. Crüsemann, Die pseudepigraphen Briefe an die Gemeinde in Thessaloniki. Studien zu ihrer Abfassung und zur jüdisch-christlichen Sozialgeschichte (BWANT 191), Stuttgart 2010, für eine nichtpaulinische Autorschaft. Erstaunlich sei schon die Adresse τῇ ἐκκλησίᾳ Θεσσαλονικέων (1,1), mit der ein geradezu politischer, gegen Rom gerichteter Anspruch auf (ganz) Thessaloniki erhoben werde (a.a.O., 235– 240). M.E. ist aber eher anzunehmen, dass Paulus im 1Thess das epistolographische Muster noch nicht fest entwickelt hat; die ἐκκλησία Θεσσαλονικέων wird im übrigen durch die Angabe ἐν θεῷ πατρὶ καὶ κυρίῳ Ἰησοῦ Χριστῷ von der politischen Größe deutlich unterschieden. Vgl. die Besprechung durch Chr. vom Brocke, Rez. M. Crüsemann (s. o.), in: ThLZ 137 (2012), 44–47.
67 Der Plural ἡμῶν kann sich durchaus auf die Gruppe der an der missionarischen Arbeit beteiligten Personen beziehen. Paulus ist aber alleiniger Autor des Briefes (2,18; 3,5; 5,27).

halts, ohne jedoch das Wort εὐαγγέλιον zu verwenden[68] und ohne dass von einem formulierten „Bekenntnis" zu sprechen ist[69].

In 2,1f. knüpft Paulus an den in 1,9a begonnenen Gedanken an: Die εἴσοδος war nicht vergeblich; vielmehr waren die Missionare nach ihren anders gearteten Erfahrungen in Philippi dazu ermutigt worden, in Thessaloniki das „Evangelium Gottes" zu predigen (... λαλῆσαι πρὸς ὑμᾶς τὸ εὐαγγέλιον τοῦ θεοῦ)[70]. In 2,3 betont Paulus seine Lauterkeit und begründet sie (V.4) mit seinem Auftrag zum εὐαγγέλιον; die ungewöhnliche Wendung ὑπὸ τοῦ θεοῦ πιστευθῆναι τὸ εὐαγγέλιον besagt, dass sich dieser Verkündigungsauftrag unmittelbar Gott verdankt[71]. Danach handeln Paulus und die anderen Missionare (οὕτως λαλοῦμεν).

In 2,5–7 unterstreicht Paulus den in V.3 ausgesprochenen Gedanken der Lauterkeit seines Wirkens noch einmal. Dann äußert er (V.8) den Wunsch, wieder nach Thessaloniki zu reisen, weil er die dortigen Gläubigen nicht nur am Evangelium, sondern auch an seiner eigenen ψυχή teilhaben lassen will. Die Wendung εὐδοκοῦμεν μεταδοῦναι ὑμῖν οὐ μόνον τὸ εὐαγγέλιον τοῦ θεοῦ ἀλλὰ ... nimmt den Aspekt auf, dass das Evangelium bei den Adressaten wirklich „angekommen" ist, und Paulus möchte nun, dass dies auch für die ψυχαί gilt[72]. Abschließend erinnert er die Adressaten daran (2,9), dass er ihnen während seines Aufenthalts in Thessaloniki finanziell nicht zur Last fiel, sondern ihnen „Tag und Nacht arbeitend"[73] das Evangelium Gottes verkündigte (ἐκηρύξαμεν εἰς ὑμᾶς τὸ εὐαγγέλιον τοῦ θεοῦ).

Paulus verwendet in 1Thess 2,2–9 das Syntagma τὸ εὐαγγέλιον τοῦ θεοῦ dreimal, ohne diese Wortverbindung näher zu erläutern. Bezieht man die Wendung auf das in 1,9f. Gesagte, wo freilich das Nomen εὐαγγέλιον nicht begegnet, so wird deutlich, dass in der in Thessaloniki verkündigten Botschaft die Rede von Gott offenbar im Mittelpunkt stand[74]: Gott ist Thema und Inhalt, aber auch Ur-

---

[68] In der Auslegung von 1Thess 1,9f. wird das Fehlen des Begriffs εὐαγγέλιον bisweilen übersehen (vgl. etwa H. Merklein, Verständnis, 284f.).
[69] Vgl. dazu M. Zugmann, Missionspredigt in nuce. Studien zu 1Thess 1,9b–10, Linz o.J. (2011), 7–42.
[70] Die Verbindung von τὸ εὐαγγέλιον mit dem Verb λαλεῖν ist bei Paulus nur hier belegt (vgl. aber 2,4), die Genitivverbindung „Evangelium Gottes" verwendet Paulus im ganzen sechsmal.
[71] Diese Wendung begegnet ähnlich auch in Gal 2,7 (s.u.).
[72] Vgl. T. Holtz, Der erste Brief an die Thessalonicher (EKK XIII), Zürich/Neukirchen-Vluyn, 1986, 83: „Μεταδοῦναι τὰς ἑαυτῶν ψυχάς meint nicht das Aufgeben des eigenen Lebens, sondern eine Übergabe in dem Sinne, daß es ganz in den Dienst des anderen gestellt wird."
[73] Das Verb ἐργάζεσθαι bezieht sich auf die Arbeit mit den Händen.
[74] Vgl. P.-G. Klumbies, Die Rede von Gott bei Paulus in ihrem zeitgeschichtlichen Kontext (FRLANT 155), Göttingen 1992, 137–148.

heber des εὐαγγέλιον, wie vor allem 2,4 zeigt[75]. Der Christusbezug ist davon abgeleitet (vgl. 1,10), er enthält aber zugleich die soteriologische Substanz der Aussage (... Ἰησοῦν τὸν ῥυόμενον ἡμᾶς ἐκ τῆς ὀργῆς τῆς ἐρχομένης).

In 3,2 wird „unser Bruder Timotheus" als συνεργὸς τοῦ θεοῦ ἐν τῷ εὐαγγελίῳ τοῦ Χριστοῦ bezeichnet; hier meint εὐαγγέλιον offenbar den Vollzug der Verkündigung, deren Inhalt Christus ist. Dass zwischen dem „Evangelium Gottes" (2,2–9) und dem „Evangelium Christi" (3,2) eine Differenz besteht, ist nicht erkennbar; vielleicht soll einfach die Doppelung des Genitivobjekts τοῦ θεοῦ (direkt nach συνεργὸς τοῦ θεοῦ) vermieden werden[76].

(2) Im Philipperbrief[77] dankt Paulus für die κοινωνία ὑμῶν εἰς τὸ εὐαγγέλιον (Phil 1,5), womit er sich auf die einst erfolgte und nun fortdauernde Annahme der Evangeliumsbotschaft in Philippi bezieht[78]; die Wendung εἰς τὸ εὐαγγέλιον[79] scheint hier geradezu eine Richtung „hin zum Evangelium" anzudeuten[80]. Der absolute Gebrauch des Wortes (τὸ εὐαγγέλιον, ohne Genitivattribut) spricht für die Annahme, dass den Adressaten in der römischen ‚colonia' Philippi der spezifische Bezug von εὐαγγέλιον bekannt ist und keine Gefahr der Verwechslung mit einem anderen εὐαγγέλιον besteht[81].

Wenn Paulus in 1,7 seine Gefangenschaft zur Verteidigung und Bekräftigung des Evangeliums erwähnt, bezeichnet εὐαγγέλιον gleichermaßen den Inhalt wie

---

[75] Im Galaterbrief wird dies später klarer gesagt werden (s.u.).
[76] Vgl. T. Holtz, Erster Thessalonicher, 126: „Timotheus wird der Gemeinde gegenüber als einer bezeichnet, der am Werk Gottes mitarbeitet, indem er dem Evangelium Christi in der Welt Raum schafft und Gemeinde bildet." AaO., Anm. 611: „Χριστοῦ ist Gen.obj.; er wird dadurch freilich – von der Sache her – zugleich zum Gen.auct."
[77] M.E. ist der literarisch einheitliche Phil in Ephesus verfasst worden, während einer Gefangenschaft, die mit den in Apg 19,23–40 geschilderten Ereignissen in Verbindung stand; vgl. 1Kor 15,32; 2Kor 1,8. Dazu D.-A. Koch, Geschichte des Urchristentums. Ein Lehrbuch, Göttingen 2013, 305f.
[78] Das wird durch die Zeitangabe ἀπὸ τῆς πρώτης ἡμέρας ἄχρι τοῦ νῦν deutlich.
[79] In Phil 2,22 schreibt Paulus über Timotheus, dieser habe wie ein Kind dem Vater mit Paulus zusammen dem Evangelium gedient (ἐδούλευσεν εἰς τὸ εὐαγγέλιον).
[80] Nach E. Lohmeyer, Die Briefe an die Philipper, an die Kolosser und an Philemon (KEK IX), Göttingen 1956, 17 Anm. 3 soll die „merkwürdige" sprachliche Wendung „wohl nur das Evangelium als Ziel jeder urchristlichen Gemeinschaft bezeichnen"; die Funktion von εἰς sei freilich „nicht mehr scharf empfunden" worden.
[81] Am Briefende in 4,15 erinnert Paulus an den Beginn seiner Verkündigungstätigkeit (ἐν ἀρχῇ τοῦ εὐαγγελίου); solch absoluter Gebrauch spricht gegen die Annahme, der Gebrauch des Wortes εὐαγγέλιον enthalte eine Beziehung und damit indirekt eine Polemik gegen den Kaiserkult.

auch den Vollzug der Verkündigung⁸². In 1,12 informiert er die Adressaten darüber, „wie es um mich steht" (τὰ κατ' ἐμέ); die Aussage, seine Gefangenschaft geschehe μᾶλλον εἰς προκοπὴν τοῦ εὐαγγελίου⁸³, bezieht sich auf seine Verkündigungstätigkeit ἐν Χριστῷ (1,13).

Nach den Ausführungen über die unterschiedlichen Motive für die Verkündigung (1,15–17) und den Hinweisen auf seine gegenwärtige lebensbedrohliche Situation (1,18–26) mahnt Paulus (V.27) die Adressaten, sie sollten dem Evangelium Christi entsprechend leben (ἀξίως τοῦ εὐαγγελίου τοῦ Χριστοῦ πολιτεύεσθε) und eines Sinnes kämpfen (μιᾷ ψυχῇ συναθλοῦντες)⁸⁴ für die πίστις τοῦ εὐαγγελίου, ohne sich einschüchtern zu lassen⁸⁵. Die bei Paulus nur hier begegnende Wortverbindung ἡ πίστις τοῦ εὐαγγελίου meint den „Glauben an das Evangelium".⁸⁶ Die Redeweise vom „Kampf für das Evangelium" wird in Phil 4,3 wieder aufgenommen: Euodia und Syntyche haben „mit mir zusammen gekämpft ἐν τῷ εὐαγγελίῳ".⁸⁷

(3) Im Philemonbrief schreibt Paulus in V.13, dass er den Onesimus gern bei sich behalten hätte, damit dieser ihm diene ἐν τοῖς δεσμοῖς τοῦ εὐαγγελίου, also in der Gefangenschaft, die er „um des Evangeliums willen" erduldet. Hier meint εὐαγγέλιον die Verkündigung *und* zugleich auch deren Inhalt. Auch hier ist vorausgesetzt, dass Philemon den Sinn des Wortes εὐαγγέλιον sofort versteht.

---

82 E. Lohmeyer, Philipperbrief, 25 hebt hervor, es sei ein Zeichen der hier zum Ausdruck gebrachten „objektiven Anschauung", dass „keinem dieser drei Nomina ein persönliches Pronomen hinzugefügt ist".

83 Vgl. 1,16, wo Paulus von der Verteidigung des Inhalts des Evangeliums spricht, um dessentwillen er ein Gefangener ist (εἰδότες ὅτι εἰς ἀπολογίαν τοῦ εὐαγγελίου κεῖμαι).

84 Zu der Wendung μιᾷ ψυχῇ συναθλοῦντες τῇ πίστει τοῦ εὐαγγελίου vgl. J. Ernst, Die Briefe an die Philipper, an Philemon, an die Kolosser, an die Epheser (RNT), Regensburg 1974, 61: Es bestehen zwei Deutungsmöglichkeiten, „1. Kämpfen für das Evangelium und den Glauben. 2. Kämpfen in dem durch das Evangelium hervorgerufenen oder vor dem Evangelium immer aufs neue zu bewährenden Glauben."

85 Vgl. 1Kor 9,12: ... ἀλλὰ πάντα στέγομεν ἵνα μή τινα ἐγκοπὴν δῶμεν τῷ εὐαγγελίῳ τοῦ Χριστοῦ.

86 Die Wendung „glauben an das Evangelium" (πιστεύειν εἰς τὸ εὐαγγέλιον) begegnet bei Paulus gar nicht, aber in 2Kor 9,13 spricht er vom Bekenntnis der Adressaten zum Evangelium Christi (... ἐπὶ τῇ ὑποταγῇ τῆς ὁμολογίας ὑμῶν εἰς τὸ εὐαγγέλιον τοῦ Χριστοῦ), womit das „von Christus sprechende Evangelium" gemeint ist. E. Lohmeyer, Philipperbrief, 76 deutet die Wendung πίστις τοῦ εὐαγγελίου dahin, „daß der Glaube der eigentliche Streiter im Kampf gegen die Widersacher ist, dem die Gläubigen sich verbunden wissen"; das entspreche der Märtyreranschauung des Paulus, „die den Märtyrer zu dem gleichsam willenlosen Werkzeug macht, durch das eine göttliche Macht, eben ‚der Glaube' wider alle weltlichen Widerstände kämpft".

87 Die Wendung ἐν τῷ εὐαγγελίῳ wird nicht bedeuten, dass die namentlich genannten Frauen „im Evangelium" gekämpft haben; denn was sollte damit gemeint sein?

(4) Besonderes Gewicht besitzt die Wortgruppe εὐαγγελ- im Galaterbrief. Im Exordium bringt Paulus in Gal 1,6, eingeleitet mit der Wendung θαυμάζω, sein Erstaunen darüber zum Ausdruck, dass sich die Adressaten abgewandt haben von dem sie in der Gnade Christi berufenden Gott (ἀπὸ τοῦ καλέσαντος ὑμᾶς ἐν χάριτι Χριστοῦ)[88] hin zu einem „anderen Evangelium" – das es jedoch, wie er hinzufügt, gar nicht gibt (V.7a): „Ein ‚Evangelium', das ‚nicht Evangelium Gottes' und ‚Evangelium Christi' ist, kann es darum nicht geben, weil es in diesem Fall kein Evangelium wäre."[89] Die in Galatien agierenden „Irrlehrer" (οἱ ταράσσοντες ὑμᾶς), die τὸ εὐαγγέλιον bewusst in sein Gegenteil verkehren[90] wollen (θέλοντες), verwerfen also die Botschaft, die von Christus spricht und deren Inhalt Christus ist. Insofern richtet sich der Widerspruch des Paulus gegen ein ἕτερον εὐαγγέλιον nicht gegen eine bestimmte Auslegung des Evangeliums, für die er einen Ausschließlichkeitsanspruch erhebt[91], sondern aus seiner Sicht geht es um das εὐαγγέλιον als solches. In der weiteren Argumentation (V.8f.) verwendet Paulus dann das Verb εὐαγγελίζομαι: Jeder Verkündigung, die im Widerspruch steht zu dem Evangelium, das Paulus den Galatern gepredigt hatte (εὐηγγελισάμεθα ὑμῖν) und das von ihnen angenommen worden war (παρελάβετε), gilt der Fluch (ἀνάθεμα ἔστω). Paulus hatte schon sofort in V.6 mit dem Hinweis auf Gottes berufendes Handeln ἐν χάριτι gesagt, wodurch das εὐαγγέλιον inhaltlich bestimmt ist; ein ἕτερον εὐαγγέλιον steht demgemäß im Widerspruch zur Gnade Gottes und ist eben deshalb gar kein εὐαγγέλιον[92].

Mit den in 1,10a gestellten rhetorischen Fragen und der in V.10b gegebenen Antwort betont Paulus das Gegenüber von Gott und Mensch: Würde er nach menschlicher Interessenlage und nach menschlichen Vorstellungen predigen, so

---

88 Vgl. F. Vouga, An die Galater (HNT 10), Tübingen 1998, 22: „Ἐν χάριτι meint entweder das Mittel der Berufung ... oder das Ziel, wohin Gott gerufen hat: In die Gnade und unter die Gnade".
89 M. Wolter, Paulus, 60.
90 Das Verb μεταστρέφω ist bei Paulus nur hier belegt; vgl. aber μετασχηματίζω in 2Kor 11,13 – 15.
91 So F.W. Horn, Wollte Paulus „kanonisch" wirken?, in: E.-M. Becker/St. Scholz (Hgg.), Kanon in Konstruktion und Dekonstruktion. Kanonisierungsprozesse religiöser Texte von der Antike bis zur Gegenwart. Ein Handbuch, Berlin 2012, 400–422, hier 411. Paulus erhebe den Anspruch, „dass exklusiv die von ihm verkündete Botschaft als εὐαγγέλιον zu fassen ist", und damit „reklamiert Paulus seine Verkündigung als allein akzeptable Interpretation des Evangeliums, und er verwirft die von ihr abweichende Form als in der Sache substanzlos, weil es kein anderes gibt".
92 F. Vouga, Galaterbrief, 22: ἕτερος „disqualifiziert ... und setzt eine Alternative voraus: Die Darstellung impliziert die Notwendigkeit einer Entscheidung."

wäre er nicht Diener Christi. Als Erläuterung (γάρ) betont Paulus in V.11[93], dass das von ihm verkündigte εὐαγγέλιον[94] nicht κατὰ ἄνθρωπον ist, ein Reden wie das in V. 10a polemisch beschriebene wäre dagegen bloß ein Reden nach Menschenart[95]. Das wird in V.12 erläutert (γάρ): Paulus hat das Evangelium weder παρὰ ἀνθρώπου empfangen noch wurde er darüber belehrt, sondern dies geschah δι' ἀποκαλύψεως Ἰησοῦ Χριστοῦ. Das wiederum erläutert er (γάρ) in V.13 durch den Hinweis auf sein früheres Leben (ἀναστροφή) im „Judaismus" (ἐν τῷ Ἰουδαϊσμῷ)[96], womit er geradezu den „Beweis" führt, dass er für das Evangelium keinerlei Voraussetzungen mitbrachte[97]. Der Hinweis auf die „väterlichen Überlieferungen" (V.14)[98] signalisiert die Bindung des Paulus an den Pharisäismus, die er freilich von vornherein als Vergangenheit kennzeichnet (ποτε)[99].

In 1,15.16a knüpft Paulus an V.12 an: Die auf Gottes souveräne Erwählung zurückgehende Offenbarung wurde ihm zuteil, damit er Christus verkündige bei den Völkern (V.16b: ἵνα εὐαγγελίζωμαι αὐτὸν ἐν τοῖς ἔθνεσιν). Das eigentliche Ziel der Aussage steht in V.16c.17: Paulus fragte niemanden um Rat (εὐθέως οὐ προσανεθέμην σαρκὶ καὶ αἵματι) und ging insbesondere auch nicht nach Jerusalem,

---

93 Das Verb γνωρίζω in 1,11 muss nicht bedeuten, dass den Adressaten jetzt etwas bislang ganz Unbekanntes mitgeteilt wird; vgl. 1Kor 15,1.
94 Paulus formuliert offenbar bewusst sehr genau: τὸ εὐαγγέλιον τὸ εὐαγγελισθὲν ὑπ' ἐμοῦ, er schreibt nicht einfach: τὸ εὐαγγέλιον μου.
95 Vgl. schon 1Thess 2,4: οὕτως λαλοῦμεν, οὐχ ὡς ἀνθρώποις ἀρέσκοντες ἀλλὰ θεῷ τῷ δοκιμάζοντι τὰς καρδίας ἡμῶν.
96 Vgl. F. Vouga, Galaterbrief, 31: Gemeint ist nicht „das Judentum" womöglich im Unterschied zum „Christentum", sondern „die konfessionelle und praktische Betonung der jüdischen Identität durch die Abgrenzung gegen den Hellenismus und international-liberale Tendenzen des Judentums". Freilich war dieser Judaismus unmittelbar verbunden mit dem Versuch einer Zerstörung der (jetzt von Paulus so bezeichneten) ἐκκλησία τοῦ θεοῦ. Vgl. M. Öhler, Essen, Ethnos, Identität – der antiochenische Zwischenfall (Gal 2,11–14), in: W. Weiß (Hg.), Der eine Gott und das gemeinschaftliche Mahl (BThSt 113), Neukirchen-Vluyn 2011, 158–199, hier 172–177: Gal 1,13f. ist nach 2Makk 14,38 der erste Beleg für den Begriff Ἰουδαϊσμός in der antiken Literatur. Ob man, wie Öhler vorschlägt, „von ‚judäischer Lebensweise' oder ‚judäischer Kultur' sprechen" sollte (177), ist eine andere Frage.
97 Die einleitende Wendung ἠκούσατε zeigt, dass Paulus die Adressaten an etwas ihnen Bekanntes erinnert; das bedeutet aber vermutlich nicht, dass sie sämtliche im Folgenden genannten Einzelheiten kennen. Auf wen die Informationen zurückgehen, sagt Paulus nicht; entweder hatte er selber bei der gemeindegründenden Predigt davon gesprochen, oder die Informationen kamen von den in Galatien aktiven Gegnern des Paulus.
98 M. Wolter, Paulus, 57 meint, mit V. 11f. und V. 14 kontrastiere Paulus bewusst das Evangelium den „väterlichen Überlieferungen".
99 Vgl. A. Lindemann, Paulus – Pharisäer und Apostel, in: A. Lindemann, Glauben, Handeln, Verstehen. Studien zur Auslegung des Neuen Testaments. Band II (WUNT 282), Tübingen 2011, 33–72, hier 47–50.

sondern nach „Arabien" und dann zurück nach Damaskus; damit sagt er zumindest indirekt, er habe den ihm erteilten Auftrag zum εὐαγγελίζεσθαι ἐν τοῖς ἔθνεσιν sofort zu erfüllen begonnen. Im Anschluss an seinen später dann folgenden Besuch in Jerusalem (V.18–20) ging er, sicherlich missionierend, nach Syrien und Kilikien (V.21), und zugleich hörten die christlichen ἐκκλησίαι in Judäa, der einstige Verfolger verkündige jetzt den Glauben, den er zuvor zu vernichten versucht hatte (... νῦν εὐαγγελίζεται τὴν πίστιν ἥν ποτε ἐπόρθει, V.23). Der Bericht des Paulus über die Anfangsphase seiner Verkündigungstätigkeit ist also von der Aussage bestimmt, dass seine Aufgabe immer schon die Verkündigung des εὐαγγέλιον war, von dem die Christen in Galatien sich jetzt erstaunlicherweise (θαυμάζω, 1,6) abwenden.

Später beim „Apostelkonzil" (2,1–10) legte Paulus „ihnen"[100] das Evangelium dar (ἀνεθέμην), das er bei den Völkern predigt (V.2 τὸ εὐαγγέλιον ὃ κηρύσσω ἐν τοῖς ἔθνεσιν), d.h. er berichtete von der Ausführung des ihm von Gott übertragenen Auftrags zur Völkermission (vgl. 1,16), wobei er in seinem Referat darüber anstelle des Verbs εὐαγγελίζομαι (1,16.23) jetzt das Substantiv verwendet (τὸ εὐαγγέλιον ὃ κηρύσσω). Paulus sprach damals und er schreibt jetzt nicht von einem inhaltlich speziell für die ἔθνη bestimmten und an sie gerichteten εὐαγγέλιον, sondern es geht um das *eine* Evangelium, zu dem es – wie er in 1,7–9 gesagt hatte – gar keine Alternative gibt.

In mehrfacher Hinsicht auffällig ist die einen Anakoluth enthaltende Aussage in 2,4f.[101]. „Wir"[102] haben den „eingedrungenen Falschbrüdern" nicht nachgegeben, damit „die Wahrheit des Evangeliums für euch bewahrt bleibe".[103] ἡ ἀλήθεια τοῦ εὐαγγελίου meint nicht eine besondere Eigenschaft des εὐαγγέλιον, sondern es wäre das Evangelium selber gefährdet gewesen, wenn Paulus (und seine Begleiter?) den ψευδαδελφοί nachgegeben hätten; damit wird indirekt gesagt, dass die galatischen ἐκκλησίαι dank der Agitation der ταράσσοντες ὑμᾶς jetzt dabei sind, „genau den Fehler zu machen, den Paulus in Jerusalem vermieden hatte".[104] Als die δοκοῦντες „sehen", dass Paulus mit der Völkermission (τὸ

---

100 In V. 2a unterscheidet Paulus: Die Adressaten seiner Rede in Jerusalem bleiben zunächst ganz unbestimmt (ἀνεθέμην αὐτοῖς τὸ εὐαγγέλιον); zu den δοκοῦντες sprach er κατ' ἰδίαν (V. 2b), aber das mitgeteilte εὐαγγέλιον ist offenbar dasselbe.
101 Vgl. dazu F. Vouga, Galaterbrief, 45.
102 Die im Plural formulierte Wendung οὐδὲ πρὸς ὥραν εἴξαμεν τῇ ὑποταγῇ könnte sich auf Paulus allein beziehen; wahrscheinlich aber sind Barnabas und Titus eingeschlossen, doch die Aussage in 2,4f. ist insoweit nicht völlig klar.
103 Die Wendung διαμείνῃ πρὸς ὑμᾶς ist in gewisser Weise natürlich anachronistisch, denn Paulus wusste zu jenem Zeitpunkt noch nichts von einer Mission in Galatien.
104 H.D. Betz, Der Galaterbrief. Ein Kommentar zum Brief des Apostels Paulus an die Gemeinden in Galatien, München 1988, 177.

εὐαγγέλιον τῆς ἀκροβυστίας) beauftragt ist (πεπίστευμαι) so wie Petrus mit der Judenmission ([sc. τὸ εὐαγγέλιον] τῆς περιτομῆς, 2,7), kommt es zu der in V.9.10a zitierten bzw. referierten Vereinbarung. Die Genitivverbindungen τὸ εὐαγγέλιον τῆς … beziehen sich natürlich nicht auf zwei verschiedene Evangelien, sondern die Attribute bezeichnen jeweils die Adressaten, denen das *eine* Evangelium verkündigt wird[105].

Friedrich Wilhelm Horn sieht eine Spannung zwischen 2,7 und den Ausführungen in 1,8–10. Entgegen der dort aufgestellten Behauptung von der exklusiven („kanonischen") Geltung der paulinischen Interpretation des εὐαγγέλιον seien beim Apostelkonvent „zwei Formen der Evangeliumsverkündigung anerkannt worden: τὸ εὐαγγέλιον τῆς ἀκροβυστίας, also das Evangelium für die Heiden, sowie τὸ εὐαγγέλιον τῆς περιτομῆς, also das Evangelium für die Juden". Zwar bestehe kein absoluter Gegensatz zwischen beiden Aussagen, insofern „die galatische Gemeinde einen heidnischen Hintergrund hat und also nicht mit einem εὐαγγέλιον τῆς περιτομῆς, d. h. mit Inhalten jüdischen Glaubens konfrontiert werden darf"; aber „es geht auch nicht, die beiden εὐαγγέλια in Gal 2,7 f. einfach zu identifizieren". Da Paulus „üblicherweise von dem einen εὐαγγέλιον τοῦ Χριστοῦ" spreche, gehe die in 2,7 f. „gewählte Differenzierung" wohl auf Tradition zurück[106]. Auf dem Konvent seien „nicht zwei unterschiedliche Evangelien angedacht worden, sondern ein einziges Evangelium mit zwei unterschiedlichen missionarischen Ausrichtungen, die sowohl lokale als auch inhaltliche Aspekte implizieren".[107] Horn meint, die Vereinbarung habe „die Anerkennung einer die Inhalte jüdischer Existenz bewahrenden Einstellung gleichwie die Aufteilung der Missionsbereiche" umfasst; möglicherweise seien nicht nur die fremden Missionare in Galatien, sondern auch Paulus „einen deutlichen Schritt über die Gesprächslage des Apostelkonvents" hinausgegangen, da Paulus „nun eben ein εὐαγγέλιον τῆς περιτομῆς, das eine durch das Gesetz vermittelte Sonderstellung

---

105 Die schwierige Formulierung in V. 6 (ἀπὸ δὲ τῶν δοκούντων εἶναί τι – ὁποῖοί ποτε ἦσαν οὐδέν μοι διαφέρει·πρόσωπον ὁ θεὸς ἀνθρώπου οὐ λαμβάνει – ἐμοὶ γὰρ οἱ δοκοῦντες οὐδὲν προσανέθεντο) bedarf hier keiner näheren Interpretation; wichtig ist, dass die Wendung οὐδὲν προσανέθεντο vom Kontext her gelesen wird, denn hier wird offensichtlich 2,2 (ἀνεθέμην) wieder aufgenommen: Dem Evangelium, das Paulus ἐν τοῖς ἔθνεσιν verkündigt, wurde seitens der δοκοῦντες nichts hinzugefügt.
106 F.W. Horn, Wollte Paulus „kanonisch" wirken?, 411. Er bezieht sich auf H. Betz, Galaterbrief, 184, der unter Berufung auf E. Dinkler, Der Brief an die Galater. Zum Kommentar von Heinrich Schlier (1955), in: E. Dinkler, Signum Crucis. Aufsätze zum Neuen Testament und zur Christlichen Archäologie, Tübingen 1967, 270–282, hier 282 den nichtpaulinischen Charakter der in 2,7 verwendeten Begriffe hervorhebt. Von einem „absoluten Gegensatz" zu 1,6–7 sprechen freilich weder Dinkler noch Betz.
107 F.W. Horn, Wollte Paulus „kanonisch" wirken?, 411.

der Juden aufrecht erhält, ausschlägt und daher im Exordium ausschließlich das von ihm verkündete Evangelium als legitim erachtet".[108] Aber in Gal 2,7 ist nicht von zwei inhaltlich unterschiedlichen εὐαγγέλια die Rede, die Genitivattribute zu τὸ εὐαγγέλιον benennen vielmehr die unterschiedlichen Adressaten der Verkündigung des *einen* εὐαγγέλιον. Andernfalls müsste man annehmen, Paulus habe den Widerspruch zwischen 1,6–10 und 2,7 nicht bemerkt oder aber gehofft, die Adressaten in Galatien würden ihn nicht bemerken; das ist wenig wahrscheinlich. Auch 2,5 (ἡ ἀλήθεια τοῦ εὐαγγελίου) spricht dafür, dass Paulus nicht zwei „Wahrheiten des Evangeliums" für denkbar gehalten hat.

Im Bericht über den Konflikt mit Petrus in Antiochia schreibt Paulus, er habe Kephas scharf widersprochen (2,11), weil er und die übrigen Ἰουδαῖοι nach der Ankunft von τινες ἀπὸ Ἰακώβου die zunächst gepflegte Tischgemeinschaft mit den ἔθνη aufkündigten (2,12f.) und so die „Wahrheit des Evangeliums" verfehlten (2,14: οὐκ ὀρθοποδοῦσιν πρὸς τὴν ἀλήθειαν τοῦ εὐαγγελίου). Ebenso wie in 2,5 ist ἡ ἀλήθεια τοῦ εὐαγγελίου nicht ein Teilaspekt des Evangeliums, sondern das Evangelium als ganzes, das Petrus und die anderen antiochenischen (Juden-) Christen aus der Sicht des Paulus durch ihr verändertes Verhalten preisgegeben hatten[109]. Für Paulus hatten sie damit die Wahrheit des *einen* εὐαγγέλιον und die Einheit der Gemeinde zerstört. Ob er mit seiner Argumentation in Antiochia Erfolg hatte, schreibt Paulus nicht[110].

Obwohl Paulus im Fortgang des Briefes den Begriff εὐαγγέλιον nicht nochmals aufnimmt[111], kann der Galaterbrief im ganzen als ein Text gelesen werden, in dem der Apostel einerseits „die Wahrheit des Evangeliums", also das Evangelium verteidigt und in dem er zugleich aktiv dafür kämpft, dass die galatischen

---

108 F.W. Horn, Wollte Paulus „kanonisch" wirken?, 412.
109 Die an Petrus gerichtete rhetorische Frage in 2,14b bedeutet wohl nicht, dass die ἔθνη zum Zeitpunkt des Konflikts das ἰουδαΐζειν tatsächlich bereits praktizierten (so M. Öhler, ‚Essen, Ethnos, Identität', 164); dagegen spricht der im Präsens formulierte Vorwurf ἀναγκάζεις, d. h. das Verhalten des Petrus und der übrigen Ἰουδαῖοι hatte zum Ziel, dass die ἔθνη ihre bisherige Lebensweise aufgeben sollten, wenn sie an der Einheit der Gemeinde in Antiochia festhalten wollten. Dass dies bereits geschehen war, als Paulus seine fundamentale Kritik äußerte, ist nicht zu erkennen.
110 H.D. Betz, Galaterbrief, 209f. verweist aber zu Recht darauf, dass das Bild des Paulus in der Apg und bei Ignatius „schwer zu verstehen" wäre, wenn es in Antiochia zu einem Ausschluss des Paulus aus der Gemeinde gekommen wäre.
111 In 4,13f. erinnert er die Adressaten an seine zunächst δι' ἀσθένειαν τῆς σαρκός erfolgte Verkündigung (εὐηγγελισάμην ὑμῖν), und dann schreibt er, die Galater hätten ihn damals aufgenommen „wie einen Boten Gottes, ja, wie Christus Jesus". Mit der Wendung ὡς ἄγγελον θεοῦ ἐδέξασθέ με erinnert Paulus die Adressaten offenbar daran, dass er ihnen das εὐαγγέλιον gepredigt hatte.

ἐκκλησίαι sich entgegen den aktuellen Tendenzen dieser Deutung dessen, was εὐαγγέλιον heißt, anschließen.

(5) In den im 1. Korintherbrief erörterten innergemeindlichen Konflikten steht die Wahrheit des Evangeliums offenbar nicht auf dem Spiel. Paulus schreibt in 1Kor 1,17 im Zusammenhang der möglicherweise mit der Taufpraxis verbundenen korinthischen ἔριδες, Christus habe ihn nicht gesandt, damit er taufe, sondern damit er (das Evangelium) verkündige (... εὐαγγελίζεσθαι); damit bezieht er sich auf seinen ihm von Christus zugewiesenen Auftrag (vgl. Gal 1,16)[112]. Das Nomen εὐαγγέλιον begegnet erstmals in 4,15: Paulus sieht sich als der „Vater" der korinthischen Christen, da er sie in Christus Jesus durch das Evangelium „gezeugt" hat (ἐν γὰρ Χριστῷ Ἰησοῦ διὰ τοῦ εὐαγγελίου ἐγὼ ὑμᾶς ἐγέννησα), und er kann sie deshalb mahnend als seine τέκνα anreden. Er setzt voraus, dass die Adressaten in Korinth den absolut gebrauchten Begriff τὸ εὐαγγέλιον verstehen.

Im Zusammenhang seiner Ausführungen zum Unterhalt für die Verkündiger (9,3–18) schreibt Paulus, er habe von der entsprechenden im Gesetz des Mose formulierten Weisung (V.9.10a) keinen Gebrauch gemacht, um dem Evangelium Christi kein Hindernis in den Weg zu legen (V.12). Offenbar meint τὸ εὐαγγέλιον τοῦ Χριστοῦ hier den Vollzug der Verkündigung von Christus, der durch solche Zahlungen womöglich behindert werden könnte. Oder will Paulus sagen, eine solche Praxis könne zum Inhalt des Evangeliums im Widerspruch stehen? Die weitere Argumentation (V.13.14) spricht eher für die erste Annahme: Wer am Altar arbeitet, hat an den (Opfer-)Gaben Anteil; und dementsprechend hat auch der κύριος angeordnet[113], dass diejenigen, die das Evangelium verkündigen, vom Evangelium leben sollen (οὕτως καὶ ὁ κύριος διέταξεν τοῖς τὸ εὐαγγέλιον καταγγέλλουσιν ἐκ τοῦ εὐαγγελίου ζῆν). Auch hier meint εὐαγγέλιον die Verkündigungstätigkeit. In 9,18 betont Paulus dann nochmals, sein „Lohn" bestehe darin, dass er (sc. in Korinth) das Evangelium unentgeltlich predigt (εὐαγγελιζόμενος ἀδάπανον θήσω τὸ εὐαγγέλιον) und dass er von seiner ἐξουσία ἐν τῷ εὐαγγελίῳ keinen Gebrauch macht.

In 9,19–22 schildert Paulus die unterschiedlichen Kontexte, in denen sich seine Verkündigung vollzieht. Bedeutet dies, dass die in Gal 2,8.9 erwähnte Vereinbarung nicht (mehr) praktiziert wird? Jedenfalls predigt Paulus sowohl Juden

---

[112] Paulus setzt voraus, dass die Adressaten in Korinth das besondere Gewicht des Wortes εὐαγγελίζεσθαι richtig einzuschätzen wissen.
[113] Nach D. Zeller, Der erste Brief an die Korinther (KEK 5), Göttingen 2010, 308 hat der Kyrios „nur ein Recht auf Lebensunterhalt", aber „keine Pflicht establiert", und deshalb „kann Paulus keinen Gebrauch davon machen, ohne ihm ungehorsam zu werden". Aber Paulus zitiert die Aussage des κύριος mit dem Verb διέταξεν.

wie auch Nichtjuden (V.20–22)¹¹⁴, und er tut dies, wie er in V.23 abschließend schreibt, διὰ τὸ εὐαγγέλιον, um daran (sc. am Evangelium) Anteil zu bekommen. Hier meint εὐαγγέλιον den Inhalt der Verkündigung, freilich auch unter der Perspektive, dass dieser Inhalt durch die Predigt allen Menschen weitergegeben werden soll¹¹⁵.

Für das paulinische Verständnis von εὐαγγέλιον spielt 1Kor 15,1 eine besondere Rolle. Paulus eröffnet den ausführlichen Gedankengang, dessen Thema „Auferstehung der Toten" erst in V.12 explizit genannt wird, in V.1.2 mit der Erinnerung an „das Evangelium", das er den Adressaten verkündigt hatte (τὸ εὐαγγέλιον ὃ εὐηγγελισάμην ὑμῖν), das sie angenommen hatten (ὃ καὶ παρελάβετε), in dem sie „stehen" (ἐν ᾧ καὶ ἐστήκατε), und durch das sie gerettet werden, wenn sie daran festhalten (δι' οὗ καὶ σῴζεσθε ... εἰ κατέχετε). Als ihm überkommene Tradition (V.3a) zitiert Paulus dann in V. 3b–5 die Aussage, Christus sei gestorben ὑπὲρ τῶν ἁμαρτιῶν ἡμῶν κατὰ τὰς γραφάς und er sei auferweckt worden τῇ ἡμέρᾳ τῇ τρίτῃ κατὰ τὰς γραφάς. Ist die in V.2b vorangehende Wendung (τίνι λόγῳ εὐηγγελισάμην ὑμῖν) ein Indiz dafür, dass Paulus bei der gemeindegründenden Predigt in Korinth einen festen Wortlaut des Evangeliums weitergegeben hatte oder dass er zumindest jetzt einen solchen Text wörtlich zitiert¹¹⁶, und besteht hier dann womöglich ein Gegensatz zu Gal 1,11f.? Michael Wolter betont, in Gal 1,11f. grenze Paulus „das ihm von Gott geoffenbarte *Evangelium* von der ihm durch Menschen überlieferten *Tora* ab", in 1Kor 15,3a identifiziere er als Voraussetzung für die Auseinandersetzung mit den korinthischen Auferstehungsleugnern „einen bestimmten *Text* als von ihm übernommene *christliche* Basisüberlieferung".¹¹⁷ Die Wendung τίνι λόγῳ beziehe sich nicht auf den überlieferten Wortlaut des Evangeliums, sondern sei mit „aus welchem Grund" wiederzugeben; aber die von Wolter genannten Paralleltexte¹¹⁸ vermögen m. E. diese Argumen-

---

114 Dieser Hinweis wird in V. 19 eingeleitet mit dem Hinweis des Paulus auf seine Freiheit: ἐλεύθερος γὰρ ὢν ἐκ πάντων πᾶσιν ἐμαυτὸν ἐδούλωσα, ἵνα τοὺς πλείονας κερδήσω.
115 D. Zeller, Erster Korintherbrief, 320 betont m.R.: „Nicht das Evangelium wird angepasst, sondern sein Verkünder richtet sich in seiner Lebensweise nach seinen Adressaten".
116 D. Zeller, Erster Korintherbrief, 461: „Λόγος meint die verbale Gestalt der Verkündigung, den ,Wortlaut', wenn das nicht zu pedantisch genommen wird."
117 M. Wolter, Paulus, 57 Anm. 15.
118 M. Wolter, Paulus, 56 Anm. 12. Das entspreche der Übersetzung in der Vulgata (,per quod et salvamini qua ratione praedicaverim vobis'). Beleg für die Interpretation von τίνι λόγῳ im Sinne von *qua ratione* sei Apg 10,29, wo Petrus von Cornelius und seinen Leuten erfahren will, „aus welchem Grund" sie ihn hatten nach Caesarea kommen lassen. Aber dort bezeichnet λόγος vermutlich nicht abstrakt die Ursache, sondern tatsächlich das „Wort", das ihnen gesagt worden war (nach 10,3–6 hatte ein Engel Gottes mit Cornelius gesprochen und ihm den Auftrag gegeben, Simon Petrus herbeizurufen). In 10,21 hatte Petrus die von Cornelius nach Joppe ge-

tation nicht zu tragen. Der Gedankengang in V.1–3a.3b–5 spricht dafür, dass Paulus eine ihm überkommene Überlieferung im Wesentlichen wörtlich genau wiedergibt. Wolter betont m.R., dass in 15,1.2 beide Bedeutungen von εὐαγγέλιον nebeneinander stehen – Inhalt der Botschaft wie auch deren Verkündigung; darin finde „ein für die paulinische Theologie des Evangeliums zentraler Gedanke seinen Ausdruck: dass das von ihm verkündigte Evangelium nicht nur über ein Heilsgeschehen informiert, sondern dass es selbst Heil bewirkt".[119] Ein Widerspruch zu Gal 1 besteht nicht; denn dort hatte Paulus in der Aussage, er habe das Evangelium nicht von Menschen empfangen, vom Inhalt des Evangeliums gesprochen, während er hier eine Formulierung weitergibt, die sich selbstverständlich menschlichem Denken verdankt. Dass das die Tradition kennzeichnende Wort εὐαγγέλιον selber Bestandteil der Überlieferung war, ist unwahrscheinlich; vermutlich verwendet Paulus den Begriff, um die dann zitierte Überlieferung inhaltlich zu charakterisieren.

Wolter meint, mit der V.1 einleitenden Wendung γνωρίζω δὲ ὑμῖν, ἀδελφοί mache Paulus deutlich, dass er den Korinthern den *Wortlaut* der Überlieferung zum ersten Mal mitteilt, auch wenn ihnen der Sachgehalt natürlich nicht neu sei[120]. Aber γνωρίζω braucht hier ebenso wie in Gal 1,11 nicht zu bedeuten, dass eine im strikten Sinne „neue Information" vermittelt wird[121]; den Korinthern wird nicht etwas ihnen bisher Unbekanntes angekündigt, sondern sie werden an eine ihnen bekannte Aussage erinnert, die nun freilich im Zuge des im folgenden erörterten Themas besondere Bedeutung erhält.

---

schickten Männer nach der „Ursache" ihres Kommens gefragt (τίς ἡ αἰτία δι' ἣν πάρεστε; Vulgata: ‚quae causa est propter quam venistis'). Überdies wird durch τίνι λόγῳ, anders als in 1Kor 15,1f., in Apg 10,29 eine Frage eingeleitet. Das Lexem λόγος hat in der Apg unterschiedliche Bedeutungen und wird in der Vulgata auch unterschiedlich übersetzt. In 10,29 lautet der Vulgatatext: ‚interrogo ergo quam ob causam accersistis me'. In 8,21 sagt Petrus zu Simon Magus: οὐκ ἔστιν σοι μερὶς οὐδὲ κλῆρος ἐν τῷ λόγῳ τούτῳ, womit gesagt ist, dass Simon Magus am „Sachverhalt" der Verkündigung und der Gabe des Geistes keinen Anteil hat. Die Vulgata gibt λόγος hier mit ‚sermo' wieder: ‚non est tibi pars neque sors in sermone isto'. In 15,6 wird der Bericht über das „Apostelkonzil" eingeleitet mit der Bemerkung, die Apostel und Presbyter seien zusammengekommen „... um über diese Abgelegenheit zu beraten" (ἰδεῖν περὶ τοῦ λόγου τούτου, hier übersetzt die Vulgata: ‚videre de verbo hoc'). In 15,27 könnte λόγος geradezu die „Weisung" sein: Die Aussage ἀπεστάλκαμεν οὖν Ἰούδαν καὶ Σιλᾶν καὶ αὐτοὺς διὰ λόγου ἀπαγγέλλοντας τὰ αὐτά leitet das „Apostrldekret" ein (Vulgata: ‚misimus ergo Iudam et Silam qui et ipsi vobis verbis referent eadem'), und dessen „Wort" gilt als verbindlich. In 19,40 heißt ἀποδοῦναι λόγον „Rechenschaft geben" (Vulgata: ‚reddere rationem').
119 M. Wolter, Paulus, 56.
120 M. Wolter, Paulus, 66.
121 Vgl. D. Zeller, Erster Korintherbrief, 460: Als „Hinweis auf eigentlich Bekanntes" sei γνωρίζειν „ungewöhnlich", doch Zeller verweist selber auf Gal 1,11.

Paulus setzt in 1Kor 15 wie in dem ganzen Brief voraus, dass das εὐαγγέλιον als solches in Korinth nicht in Frage gestellt wird. Wohl aber zeigt 15,12, dass es unter den korinthischen Christen τινες gab, die aus dem auch von ihnen anerkannten εὐαγγέλιον eine nach dem Urteil des Paulus falsche Konsequenz zogen, indem sie sagten ὅτι ἀνάστασις νεκρῶν οὐκ ἔστιν. 1Kor 15 ist angesichts dessen ein besonders klares Beispiel dafür, wie das von Tod und Auferstehung Christi sprechende εὐαγγέλιον Fundament für eine umfassende theologische Argumentation sein kann.

(6) Im 2. Korintherbrief [122] schreibt Paulus, er sei nach Troas gekommen εἰς τὸ εὐαγγέλιον τοῦ Χριστοῦ (2Kor 2,12). Er habe für die Verkündigung des Evangeliums große Chancen gesehen (καὶ θύρας μοι ἀνεῳγμένης ἐν κυρίῳ), doch als er Titus nicht antraf, sei er nach Makedonien weitergereist; die in 2,12 angedeutete Perspektive wird in dem Text nicht weiter verfolgt[123]. Innerhalb des oft als „Apologie" bezeichneten Briefes, dessen Text jetzt als 2Kor 2,14–6,13; 7,2.3 überliefert ist, heißt es in 4,3, denen, die verloren gehen, sei „unser Evangelium" verborgen[124]; τὸ εὐαγγέλιον ἡμῶν meint hier nicht die Verkündigung, als werde diese von den ἀπολλύμενοι nicht wahrgenommen, sondern es ist der Inhalt des εὐαγγέλιον, der nicht akzeptiert wird. „Der Gott dieses Aion" hat den Verstand der ἄπιστοι verfinstert, damit sie „das Aufstrahlen des Evangeliums von der Herrlichkeit Christi" nicht sehen (εἰς τὸ μὴ αὐγάσαι τὸν φωτισμὸν τοῦ εὐαγγελίου τῆς δόξης τοῦ Χριστοῦ). Auch hier bezieht sich εὐαγγέλιον auf den Inhalt der Botschaft; das Syntagma ὁ φωτισμὸς τοῦ εὐαγγελίου zeigt aber an, dass jetzt an die mit dem Evangelium verbundene oder von ihm ausgehende „Erleuchtung" gedacht ist. εὐαγγέλιον meint den Vorgang der Verkündigung, deren Inhalt die δόξα Christi ist[125].

---

122 Der uns vorliegende 2Kor verdankt sich m. E. einer frühen nachpaulinischen, im Zusammenhang der Paulusbriefsammlung erfolgten Redaktion; vgl. A. Lindemann, „... an die Kirche in Korinth samt allen Heiligen in ganz Achaja". Zu Entstehung und Redaktion des „Zweiten Korintherbriefes", in: D. Sänger (Hg.), Der zweite Korintherbrief. Literarische Gestalt – historische Situation – theologische Argumentation. Festschrift zum 70. Geburtstag von Dietrich-Alex Koch (FRLANT 250), Göttingen 2012, 131–159.
123 M.E. liegt hier die Einleitung desjenigen Briefes innerhalb des 2Kor vor, in dem Paulus von Mazedonien aus nach der Rückkehr des Titus aus Korinth die Beilegung des Konflikts bestätigt (2,12.13 und 7,4–16).
124 Die Wendung εἰ δὲ καὶ ἔστιν κεκαλυμμένον τὸ εὐαγγέλιον ἡμῶν, ἐν τοῖς ἀπολλυμένοις ἐστὶν κεκαλυμμένον nimmt V. 2 auf: Die Verkündigung macht die Wahrheit „offenbar", und wo das Evangelium „verhüllt" zu sein scheint, da gilt das ausschließlich für die ἀπολλύμενοι (vgl. 1Kor 1,18).
125 M. Wolter, Paulus, 55: Ähnlich wie in Gal 2,5.14 geht es um „Eigenschaften des Evangeliums".

In dem „Kollektenbrief" 2Kor 8 erwähnt Paulus in V.18 „den Bruder", dessen ἔπαινος ἐν τῷ εὐαγγελίῳ in allen Kirchen bekannt sei; in diesem Lob meint εὐαγγέλιον das erfolgreiche Predigen des namentlich nicht genannten ἀδελφός. In dem anderen, offenbar nach Achaja gerichteten Kollektenbrief 2Kor 9 spricht Paulus in V.13 vom „Gehorsam eures Bekenntnisses zum Evangelium Christi" (... ἐπὶ τῇ ὑποταγῇ τῆς ὁμολογίας ὑμῶν εἰς τὸ εὐαγγέλιον τοῦ Χριστοῦ) und von der ἁπλότης, mit der sie „an allen Anteil nehmen". So unterstreicht Paulus das theologische Fundament für die Bereitschaft der Adressaten, zur Kollekte für Jerusalem beizutragen[126].

Im „Kampfbrief" (2Kor 10–13) spricht Paulus in 10,14 davon, dass er mit seiner Verkündigungstätigkeit bis nach Korinth gelangt ist (...ἄχρι γὰρ καὶ ὑμῶν ἐφθάσαμεν ἐν τῷ εὐαγγελίῳ τοῦ Χριστοῦ); die Wendung τὸ εὐαγγέλιον τοῦ Χριστοῦ zeigt zugleich, dass diese Verkündigung einen bestimmten Inhalt hat, nämlich Christus. Paulus sieht bei der Abfassung von 2Kor 10–13 in Korinth, ähnlich wie zuvor in Galatien, das Evangelium als solches in Gefahr, wie sich in 11,4–7 zeigt, wo er in der Vorbereitung zur „Narrenrede" ironisch schreibt (V.4): Wenn jemand kommt (ὁ ἐρχόμενος) und einen „anderen Jesus" verkündigt oder ein „anderes πνεῦμα" oder ein „anderes εὐαγγέλιον", so wird er von den Korinthern gern akzeptiert. Jesus, das πνεῦμα und das εὐαγγέλιον stehen nicht als drei verschiedene Größen nebeneinander, sondern in dem Begriff εὐαγγέλιον ist offenbar die Botschaft als ganze zusammengefasst[127]. Jedenfalls fragt Paulus in V.7 rhetorisch, ob er falsch gehandelt habe, als er „euch" das Evangelium von Gott kostenlos verkündigte (... ὅτι δωρεὰν τὸ τοῦ θεοῦ εὐαγγέλιον εὐηγγελισάμην ὑμῖν;). Mit der Verbindung des Syntagmas τὸ τοῦ θεοῦ εὐαγγέλιον mit dem Verb εὐαγγελίζεσθαι betont Paulus gleichermaßen den Vollzug der Predigt des Evangeliums und dessen Inhalt.

Die m. E. zeitlich später als der „Kampfbrief" verfassten Briefe nach Korinth[128] lassen nicht erkennen, dass das Thema εὐαγγέλιον weiterhin Gegenstand eines

---

126 Nach H.D. Betz, 2. Korinther 8 und 9. Ein Kommentar zu zwei Verwaltungsbriefen des Apostels Paulus, Gütersloh 1993, 222 sind die Worte des Paulus zweideutig; in Jerusalem mochte man die eigene Überordnung daraus ableiten, doch eine „Unterordnung unter das Evangelium hieß nicht Unterordnung unter Jerusalem, sondern die Unterordnung aller Christen unter das Evangelium Christi".
127 Es fällt auf, dass die Formulierungen offenbar bewusst variieren: Im Blick auf Jesus wird vom Verkündigen gesprochen (ἄλλον Ἰησοῦν κηρύσσει ὃν οὐκ ἐκηρύξαμεν), im Blick auf den Geist vom „Empfangen" (ἢ πνεῦμα ἕτερον λαμβάνετε ὃ οὐκ ἐλάβετε), im Blick auf das Evangelium vom „Annehmen" (ἢ εὐαγγέλιον ἕτερον ὃ οὐκ ἐδέξασθε), und alles wird in Korinth „gern akzeptiert" (καλῶς ἀνέχεσθε).
128 Das sind m.E. 2Kor 1,3–2,11 („Tränenbrief", vgl. 2,3f.) und der die Korrespondenz abschließende „Versöhnungsbrief" (2,12f.; 7,4–16).

Konflikts innerhalb der Gemeinde oder in der Beziehung zwischen Paulus und der Gemeinde war. Das könnte aber darauf zurückzuführen sein, dass es Paulus in diesen Briefen primär um die Versöhnung nach der vorangegangenen Auseinandersetzung ging und nicht so sehr um die Durchsetzung einer theologischen Position.

(7) Im Römerbrief finden sich theologisch fundamentale Aussagen zum Verständnis von εὐαγγέλιον, wobei auffällt, dass der Begriff in dem sehr umfangreichen Brief selten vorkommt. In Röm 1,1f., wo sich Paulus den ihm persönlich unbekannten Adressaten[129] als δοῦλος Χριστοῦ Ἰησοῦ vorstellt, erläutert er das durch die Apposition κλητὸς ἀπόστολος, die ergänzt wird durch die Aussage ἀφωρισμένος εἰς εὐαγγέλιον θεοῦ: Paulus ist „ausgesondert" für die Verkündigung des Evangeliums, das von Gott spricht. In V.2 wird deutlich, dass Gott in gewisser Weise auch Autor des εὐαγγέλιον ist, insofern dieses zuvor angesagt worden war durch seine Propheten in den Heiligen Schriften (... εὐαγγέλιον θεοῦ, ὃ προεπηγγείλατο διὰ τῶν προφητῶν αὐτοῦ ἐν γραφαῖς ἁγίαις)[130]. Da Paulus hier anders als im Gal keinen „Bekehrungsbericht" schreibt, sondern eine briefliche Selbstvorstellung gibt, liegt der Ton nicht „auf der Seite der *Herkunft* des Evangeliums, sondern auf der Seite seines *Inhalts* und seiner *Verkündigung*".[131]

Eric K. C. Wong folgert aus Senecas ironischer Schilderung der Apotheose des Claudius, „dass die Botschaft von der Einsetzung von Kaisern zu ‚Söhnen' Gottes damals auf Skepsis stieß". Vor diesem Hintergrund sage Paulus in Röm 1,3f., Christus stamme nicht aus dem julisch-claudischen Hause, sondern aus Davids Geschlecht, und sei nicht fiktiv durch Senatsbeschluss, sondern wirklich durch Gott zum Sohn Gottes eingesetzt worden: „Das Evangelium wäre dann bei Paulus auch zur Gegenbotschaft zu einem anderen Evangelium geworden: zum Kaiserkult."[132] Aber weder in 1,1–4 noch sonst im Röm ist zu erkennen, dass sich Paulus mit seinem Gebrauch des Wortes εὐαγγέλιον gegen ein „politisches" bzw. auf den Kaiserkult bezogenes Verständnis von εὐαγγέλιον wendet.

In 1,9 nimmt Paulus das zuvor im Präskript Gesagte wieder auf: λατρεύω (sc. Gott) ἐν τῷ πνεύματί μου ἐν τῷ εὐαγγελίῳ τοῦ υἱοῦ αὐτοῦ. Das Evangelium, dem Paulus dient, spricht vom Sohn Gottes (vgl. V.3), wobei Paulus voraussetzt, dass die Adressaten den Begriff εὐαγγέλιον in Verbindung mit Gott und mit Christus inhaltlich zu füllen vermögen.

---

[129] Das schließt nicht aus, dass es zu einigen der Jesusgläubigen in Rom Beziehungen gibt, an die die Grußliste in Röm 16 anknüpft.
[130] In V. 3–4 wird das christologisch näher ausgeführt; vgl. D.-A. Koch, Schrift, 328f. 342.
[131] M. Wolter, Paulus, 59.
[132] E. Wong, Evangelien im Dialog mit Paulus, 69.

In 1,13–15 erwähnt Paulus seine Reisepläne; er schließt mit dem Hinweis, da er zu den ἔθνη gesandt sei, wolle er „auch euch in Rom" das Evangelium predigen (εὐαγγελίσασθαι)[133]. Unmittelbar darauf folgt in V.16 die erläuternde Bemerkung (γάρ), er „schäme" sich des εὐαγγέλιον nicht[134], denn (γάρ) es sei Gottes δύναμις zur σωτηρία für jeden Glaubenden, Jude wie Grieche[135]. Hier ist deutlich, dass das εὐαγγέλιον nicht nur von der σωτηρία spricht, sondern dass es selber δύναμις θεοῦ zum Heil ist[136], also diese σωτηρία bewirkt; das wird dann in V.17 programmatisch weitergeführt. Helmut Merklein folgert aus 1,16 f., Paulus verstehe Evangelium als „Endgeschehen", und daher kommt ihm *„entscheidende, scheidende Funktion"* zu; das Evangelium „stellt vor die Entscheidung und scheidet zwischen Glaubenden und Ungläubigen, zwischen denen, die gerettet werden, und denen, die verlorengehen".[137] Aber 1,16 f. zufolge zeigt sich die Wirksamkeit des εὐαγγέλιον allein als σωτηρία, die ὀργὴ θεοῦ dagegen ergeht ἀπ' οὐρανοῦ (1,18)[138].

Nach 2,14 f. ist den ἔθνη, die das Gesetz nicht haben, gleichwohl τὸ ἔργον τοῦ νόμου ins Herz geschrieben, wie ihr Gewissen bezeuge. Dies werde, so heißt es in V. 16, sichtbar werden an dem Tag, da Gott richten wird τὰ κρυπτὰ τῶν ἀνθρώπων κατὰ τὸ εὐαγγέλιόν μου διὰ Ἰησοῦ Χριστοῦ. Udo Schnelle folgert aus 2,16, Heil und Gericht seien bei Paulus nicht zu trennen. „Deshalb erscheint Jesus Christus im Evangelium nicht nur als Retter, sondern auch als Richter."[139] Aber εὐαγγέλιον hat sonst bei Paulus nirgends einen Bezug zum (eschatologischen) Gericht. Die unpaulinische Wendung κατὰ τὸ εὐαγγέλιόν μου begegnet wieder im Revelations-

---

[133] Hier bezieht sich εὐαγγελίζεσθαι offensichtlich nicht auf die Missionspredigt, denn Paulus hatte die Adressaten in 1,7 ja als ἀγαπητοὶ θεοῦ und als κλητοὶ ἅγιοι angesprochen.
[134] Vgl. dazu E. Lohse, Der Brief an die Römer (KEK 4), Göttingen 2003, 76, der unter Verweis auf 2Tim 2,8; Mk 8,38 parr meint, dass οὐκ ἐπαισχύνομαι eine „Bekenntnisaussage" einleitet.
[135] Möglicherweise ist aus V.16b zu schließen, dass der Begriff ἔθνη in V.13 nicht allein die „Heiden" meinte, sondern allgemein „die Völker". Spätestens aus 11,14 geht hervor, dass Paulus bei seiner Mission auch Angehörige seines eigenen Volkes Israel zumindest mit im Blick hatte.
[136] Mit δύναμις bezeichnet Paulus die Wirksamkeit, die das Evangelium von Gott her besitzt. Ob man in der deutschen Übersetzung „Kraft" sagt oder aber „Macht", ist nebensächlich.
[137] H. Merklein, Verständnis, 290.
[138] Etwas widersprüchlich schreibt H. Merklein, Verständnis, 291: Evangelium ist „für Paulus *Gerichtsgeschehen*, scheidendes und wirksames Geschehen, das Tod und Leben verbreitet", aber dann gilt doch: „Das ‚Evangelium' ist vielmehr wirksame, be-wirkende, zur Wirklichkeit rufende Kraft Gottes, darauf ausgerichtet, eine allenthalben und ausnahmslos unter die Sünde versklavte Welt zum Heil zu führen."
[139] U. Schnelle, Paulus, 456. Er fährt fort, es sei zugleich „deutlich, dass für Paulus das Evangelium zuallererst eine δύναμις θεοῦ (‚Macht Gottes') ist, die jene rettet, die die Heilsbotschaft vom gekreuzigten und auferstandenen Jesus Christus im Glauben annehmen". Aber eine solche Relativierung („zuallererst") findet sich bei Paulus in diesem Zusammenhang nicht.

schema in dem Nachtrag 16,25–27, dort ohne eschatologischen Bezug[140]. In 2,16 liegt ebenso wie in 16,25(–27) ein unpaulinischer Sprachgebrauch vor, es handelt sich vermutlich um nachträgliche Interpolationen[141].

In dem die δικαιοσύνη θεοῦ explizierenden umfangreichen Abschnitt 3,21– 8,39 verwendet Paulus weder das Substantiv εὐαγγέλιον noch das entsprechende Verb. Das Nomen εὐαγγέλιον begegnet erst wieder in 10,16. Paulus spricht in 10,14–16 von denen, die zum κηρύσσειν ausgesandt sind (V.14.15a), und dazu beruft er sich in V. 15b auf die Schrift (καθὼς γέγραπται), und zwar auf Jes 52,7 LXX: ὡς ὡραῖοι οἱ πόδες τῶν εὐαγγελιζομένων τὰ ἀγαθά. Dann erörtert er die ihn seit 9,1 bewegende Frage, warum Israel (in seiner Mehrheit) die Botschaft nicht annimmt. Er antwortet darauf in V.16a mit der Feststellung: οὐ πάντες ὑπήκουσαν τῷ εὐαγγελίῳ, und dazu folgt (V.16b) als Schriftbeleg die in Jes 53,1 LXX gestellte rhetorische Frage: κύριε, τίς ἐπίστευσεν τῇ ἀκοῇ ἡμῶν; die mit „niemand" bzw. mit „nur wenige"zu beantworten ist. εὐαγγέλιον meint in V.16a natürlich den Inhalt der Verkündigung, dessen Annahme die Hörer verweigerten.

In 11,25–32 unternimmt Paulus den Versuch einer Erklärung der gegebenen Situation: Das μυστήριον, das er den Adressaten mitteilt, sagt, ein Teil Israels sei „verstockt" worden[142], bis τὸ πλήρωμα τῶν ἐθνῶν[143] „hinzugekommen" sein werde; so (οὕτως) werde dann πᾶς Ἰσραήλ gerettet werden, und dazu fügt Paulus einen Schriftbeleg an (V.26b.27)[144]. Zu der aus Jes 59,21 gewonnenen Erkenntnis, dass Gott an seiner διαθήκη festhält (V.27a) und dass er „ihnen" die Sünden vergibt (V.27b entsprechend Jes 27,9), fügt Paulus in V.28 übergangslos die Feststellung hinzu, sie, d. h. die nicht an Christus glaubenden Israeliten, seien „hinsichtlich des Evangeliums um euretwillen Feinde, hinsichtlich der Erwählung aber Geliebte um der Väter willen" (κατὰ μὲν τὸ εὐαγγέλιον ἐχθροὶ δι' ὑμᾶς, κατὰ δὲ τὴν ἐκλογὴν ἀγαπητοὶ διὰ τοὺς πατέρας). Die Begriffe ἐχθροί und ἀγαπητοί haben die Gottesbeziehung Israels im Blick, aber Gott selbst hält ungeachtet der gegenwärtigen Situation an der ursprünglichen Beziehung zu Israel fest (V.29). Der Begriff

---

140 Vgl. D. Lührmann, Das Offenbarungsverständnis bei Paulus und in paulinischen Gemeinden (WMANT 16), Neukirchen-Vluyn 1965, 122–124.
141 Vgl. R. Bultmann, Glossen im Römerbrief, in: R. Bultmann, Exegetica. Aufsätze zur Erforschung des Neuen Testaments, hg. von E. Dinkler, Tübingen 1967, 278–285, hier 282f.
142 Damit wird implizit der „Restgedanke" aufgenommen, der in 11,1–12 breit ausgeführt worden war. Vgl. dazu A. Lindemann, Paulus und Elia. Zur Argumentation in Röm 11,1–12, in: V. A. Lehnert/U. Rüsen-Weinhold (Hgg.), Logos-Logik-Lyrik. Engagierte exegetische Studien zum biblischen Reden Gottes. Festschrift für Klaus Haacker (ABG 27), Leipzig 2007, 201–218.
143 Diese „Vollzahl" kennt nur Gott.
144 Vermutlich bezieht sich Paulus mit dem Begriff ὁ ῥυόμενος auf Christus bei der Parusie (vgl. 1Thess 1,10). Zum besonderen Charakter des aus zwei Jes-Texten bestehenden Zitats s. D.-A. Koch, Schrift, 175–178.

εὐαγγέλιον markiert in V. 28 die gegenwärtig von Israel (von seiner Mehrheit) zurückgewiesene Botschaft; dadurch besteht gegenwärtig Feindschaft, aber diese ist zeitlich befristet[145].

In 15,14–21, wo er auf den nahezu abgeschlossenen Brief zurückblickt (V.14 f.), schreibt Paulus, er erfülle den Auftrag, als λειτουργὸς Χριστοῦ Ἰησοῦ εἰς τὰ ἔθνη das Evangelium als heilige Handlung zu vollziehen (ἱερουργοῦντα τὸ εὐαγγέλιον τοῦ θεοῦ), damit die Opfergabe der Völker Gott wohlgefällig sei (ἵνα γένηται ἡ προσφορὰ τῶν ἐθνῶν εὐπρόσδεκτος, V.17), sowohl λόγῳ καὶ ἔργῳ als auch ἐν δυνάμει σημείων καὶ τεράτων ἐν δυνάμει πνεύματος θεοῦ (V. 18b.19a)[146]; auf dieser Grundlage habe er „von Jerusalem bis Illyrien" τὸ εὐαγγέλιον τοῦ Χριστοῦ vollendet. Paulus schreibt hier also, dass er die Botschaft von Christus vollständig und „überall" ausgerichtet hat, und er gibt damit „der unauflösbaren Verschränkung von Gott und Christus in dem von ihm verkündigten Evangelium einen Ausdruck, der sich wie eine Transformation von Röm 1,1–5 in kultische Metaphorik liest, ansonsten aber dasselbe sagt".[147] Warum verwendet Paulus (nur!) an dieser Stelle kultische Begrifflichkeit, um seine Verkündigung zu charakterisieren? Sieht er sich als „Priester", der die ἔθνη gleichsam als Opfer für Gott darzubringen hat – und bedeutet dies implizit, dass Israel auf diesen „priesterlichen" Dienst nicht angewiesen ist, dass es des Evangeliums nicht bedarf? Das wäre nach der in Röm 9,1–11,36 vorangegangenen Argumentation ein jedenfalls sehr überraschender Gedanke, zumal Paulus nach 11,13 f. ja hofft, er könne durch seine Völkermission zumindest „einige" aus seinem Volk Israel für Christus gewinnen. Da Paulus niemals sonst seinen Verkündigungsdienst „priesterlich" versteht, dürfte die in 15,16 verwendete kultische Sprache metaphorisch zu verstehen sein[148].

Zusammenfassung: Paulus bietet im Römerbrief in 1,16 f. eine programmatische Definition des von ihm schon in 1,1 und dann nochmals in 1,9 verwendeten Begriffs εὐαγγέλιον; dadurch unterscheidet sich dieser Brief grundlegend von allen anderen uns erhaltenen Paulustexten. Paulus setzt voraus, dass die ihm

---

145 Vgl. E. Lohse, Römerbrief, 322: „Israels Ungehorsam hat zur Folge, daß das Evangelium zu den Heiden gelangte (δι' ὑμᾶς). Gleichwohl aber bleibt Gottes einst gesprochenes Wort in Gültigkeit ... Die den Vätern gegebene ἐκλογή gilt weiterhin, weil Gott selbst – und kein anderer – die Erwählung vollzogen hat".
146 Ob das Genitivattribut θεοῦ hier zu lesen ist oder nicht, lässt sich kaum sagen. Vgl. B.M. Metzger, A Textual Commentary on the Greek New Testament, Stuttgart ²1994, 473.
147 M. Wolter, Paulus, 63.
148 Vgl. E. Lohse, Römerbrief, 394: „Wurden bereits im hellenistischen Judentum des öfteren kultische Begriffe in ethischer Bedeutung gebraucht, so werden auch hier die Wörter, die priesterlichen Dienst beschreiben, in übertragenem Sinn verstanden ... Damit ist nicht an ein besonderes priesterliches Amt gedacht, sondern es soll die unvergleichliche Aufgabe charakterisiert werden, die Paulus als dem Apostel der Völker gestellt ist".

unbekannten Adressaten in Rom das Wort εὐαγγέλιον (auch) als christlichen Begriff kennen, aber er sieht sich veranlasst, ihnen schon im Proömium des Briefes darzulegen, was genau nach seinem theologischen Urteil mit diesem Wort bezeichnet ist – nämlich die Einsicht in das den glaubenden Menschen rechtfertigende Handeln Gottes. Nachdem Paulus dies in 1,1–17 expliziert hat, spielt der Begriff εὐαγγέλιον im übrigen Brief eine vergleichsweise geringe Rolle; anders als vor allem im Galaterbrief setzt Paulus voraus, dass in seiner Kommunikation das Evangelium nicht Gegenstand einer theologischen Kontroverse ist. Möglicherweise aber will er den ganzen Brief nach Rom *als* εὐαγγέλιον verstanden wissen, und eben deshalb hält er an den (wenigen) Stellen, wo er explizit vom εὐαγγέλιον spricht, eine inhaltliche Ausführung nicht für erforderlich.

2.4 εὐαγγέλιον als gute Botschaft

Dietrich-Alex Koch folgert aus der intensiven Verwendung biblischer Texte bei Paulus, dass „die Schrift" für den Apostel „Zeuge des εὐαγγέλιον" ist[149]. Das ist theologisch natürlich grundsätzlich richtig; aber es fällt doch auf, dass Paulus den *Begriff* εὐαγγέλιον mit der einen Ausnahme Röm 1,16f. niemals explizit mit einem Schriftzitat verbindet[150]. Ferdinand Hahn meint, „der von Paulus verwendete und explizierte Evangeliumsbegriff" sei „Grundlage für seine Verkündigung und Theologie", und dabei gehe es um „die Proklamation des schon im Alten Testament angekündigten und in der Gegenwart sich erfüllenden Heils. Nicht zufällig hat der von Paulus verwendete Begriff seine Wurzeln in der alttestamentlich-jüdischen Tradition."[151] Aber gerade dies lässt sich nicht belegen, und so ist das paulinische Verständnis von εὐαγγέλιον ist keinesfalls aus biblischer Tradition abzuleiten. Das Verständnis dessen, was εὐαγγέλιον bei Paulus meint, ist allein aus dem paulinischen Gebrauch des Wortes selber zu gewinnen.

εὐαγγέλιον meint bei Paulus im Wortsinn „gute Botschaft"; vom Machtcharakter des εὐαγγέλιον, so betont Michael Wolter, spricht Paulus nur mit Blick auf den Glauben, d. h. er nimmt die Bedeutung der Vorsilbe εὐ- ernst. „Demgegenüber sagt Paulus nie, dass das Evangelium in gleicher Weise auch das Unheil wirkt" – eine „indirekte Unheilswirkung" entsteht nur dort, wo die Adressaten die An-

---

[149] D.-A. Koch, Schrift, vor allem 322–353.
[150] In Röm 10,15 belegt das Zitat nicht den Inhalt des εὐαγγέλιον als schriftgemäß, sondern Jes 52,7 beweist nur, dass die Verkündigung tatsächlich geschieht.
[151] F. Hahn, Theologie des Neuen Testaments. Band I. Die Vielfalt des Neuen Testaments. Theologiegeschichte des Urchristentums, Tübingen 2002, 190.

nahme der Botschaft verweigern (2Kor 4,3 – 4)¹⁵². Das Wort εὐαγγέλιον meint meist den *Inhalt* der Botschaft; es ist deshalb oft verbunden mit einem Genitivattribut – „Evangelium von Gott" oder „Evangelium von Christus" (1Thess 2,2; 3,2 und öfter). Auch wo Paulus εὐαγγέλιον absolut gebraucht, setzt er voraus, dass die Adressaten den Sinn und den Inhalt dessen kennen, was das Wort εὐαγγέλιον bezeichnet (1Kor 15,1; Gal 2,5.14). Paulus verwendet das Wort εὐαγγέλιον aber auch als nomen actionis, um den *Vollzug* der Vermittlung der „guten Botschaft" zu benennen, also als Bezeichnung für die mündliche Verkündigung (so Röm 1,1.9; 1Thess 1,5). So kann εὐαγγέλιον gleichermaßen den *Vollzug* und den *Inhalt* der Botschaft bezeichnen, so in Röm 1,16 und im Philipperbrief (vgl. Phil 1,5.27; 4,3.15). Paulus hat den Begriff εὐαγγέλιον zwar wohl nicht schon in der unmittelbaren Missionspredigt verwendet, aber er gebrauchte ihn dann in der gemeindlichen Verkündigung als terminus technicus. Deshalb ist es offenbar kein Zufall, dass Paulus in dem einzigen Brief, in dem er sich an ihm unbekannte Leser wendet, gleich zu Beginn eine Interpretation dessen gibt, was εὐαγγέλιον bedeutet (Röm 1,16 f.)¹⁵³.

3 εὐαγγέλιον im Markusevangelium

Das Nomen εὐαγγέλιον ist im MkEv siebenmal belegt, überwiegend absolut (τὸ εὐαγγέλιον); aber gerade bei der ersten Verwendung in 1,1 und 1,14 ist es mit einem Genitivattribut verbunden, so dass das markinische Verständnis des Wortes zunächst einmal von dorther zu deuten ist[154]. Das Verb εὐαγγελίζειν bzw. εὐαγγελίζεσθαι fehlt im MkEv.

Im MtEv ist εὐαγγέλιον nur viermal belegt[155] – außer in 26,13 (entsprechend Mk 14,9) stets in der Genitivverbindung τὸ εὐαγγέλιον τῆς βασιλείας (Mt 4,23; 9,35;

---

152 M. Wolter, Paulus, 71.
153 Vgl. E. Lohse, Εὐαγγέλιον Θεοῦ. Paul's Interpretation of the Gospel in His Epistle to the Romans, in: E. Lohse, Das Neue Testament als Urkunde des Evangeliums. Exegetische Studien zur Theologie des Neuen Testaments III (FRLANT 192), Göttingen 2000, 89 – 103, hier: Präskript.
154 J. Dechow, Gottessohn und Herrschaft Gottes. Der Theozentrismus des Markusevangeliums (WMANT 86), Neukirchen-Vluyn 2000, 274 f. betont mit Recht, dass es um der „Erzähllogik" des MkEv willen geboten ist, bei der Analyse der Verwendung des Wortes εὐαγγέλιον in 1,1.14 f. einzusetzen und nicht von hinteren Belegstellen auszugehen [zu W. Marxsen, Der Evangelist Markus. Studien zur Redaktionsgeschichte des Evangeliums (FRLANT 67), Göttingen ²1959, 84]. Vgl. zum Folgenden J. Dechow a.a.O., 274 – 288.
155 In 4,23b verbindet Mt den direkten Paralleltext Mk 1,39 mit Mk 1,14b; in Mt 9,35 wird die Formulierung aus 4,23 ohne Mk-Parallele wieder aufgenommen; Mt 24,14 entspricht Mk 13,10, Mt

24,14)[156]. Im LkEv begegnet εὐαγγέλιον gar nicht, in der Apg nur zweimal[157]. Offensichtlich haben Matthäus und vor allem Lukas in ihren Jesuserzählungen weitgehend bzw. vollständig auf die Übernahme des im MkEv vergleichsweise oft gebrauchten Wortes εὐαγγέλιον verzichtet[158].

3.1 Mk 1,1–15

In Mk 1,1 (ἀρχὴ τοῦ εὐαγγελίου Ἰησοῦ Χριστοῦ, möglicherweise ergänzt durch die weitere Apposition υἱοῦ θεοῦ[159]) ist εὐαγγέλιον nicht Bezeichnung für eine literarische Gattung; offenbar ist aber das folgende umfangreiche Buch als von Jesus erzählendes εὐαγγέλιον zu verstehen, und so konnte εὐαγγέλιον im 2. Jahrhundert zur Bezeichnung einer literarischen (Erzähl-)Gattung werden[160]. Ob sich 1,1 und insbesondere das Wort ἀρχή auf das in V.2f. folgende Schriftzitat bezieht oder auf das durch das Zitat eingeleitete Auftreten Johannes des Täufers (V.4–8) oder auf

---

26,13 entspricht Mk 14,9. Ob die Annahme zutrifft, dass Mt die für ihn typischen Redekomplexe als „Evangelium" verstand (so W. Marxsen, Evangelist, 82) kann hier offen bleiben.

156 Das Verb εὐαγγελίζομαι begegnet bei Mt einmal (Mt 11,5/Lk 7,22 Q), sehr häufig dagegen im lukanischen Doppelwerk. H. Merklein, Verständnis, 282 folgert aus Mt 11,5 Q, es sei „sehr wahrscheinlich, daß bereits im palästinischen Judenchristentum die Ansage der ‚Gottesherrschaft' als ‚bᵉśôrāh' = ‚Freudenbotschaft' bezeichnet wurde". Aber aus der Verwendung des Verbs ist nicht auf den Gebrauch des Substantivs zu schließen.

157 Für das Verb εὐαγγελίζομαι gibt es im LkEv 10 Belege, in der Apg 15 Belege.

158 H. Koester, Gospels, 12f. hält es für möglich, dass der Begriff εὐαγγέλιον „had been inserted into a number of Markan passages by a later redactor"; Indiz dafür sei, dass es zu Mk 8,35; 10,29 und 1,15, wo εὐαγγέλιον ohne Genitivattribut gebraucht ist, keine Parallele im MtEv gibt, und auch bei 1,1 sei es „quite possible that a later scribe added this phrase", um den Beginn des Buches anzuzeigen. Aber für eine solche Praxis fehlen Analogien in anderen Werken.

159 Zum textkritischen Befund vgl. die ausführliche Darstellung bei H. Greeven/E. Güting, Textkritik des Markusevangeliums (Theologie. Forschung und Wissenschaft 11), Münster 2005, 41–46. Greeven liest den Kurztext, da ihm eine Streichung der Apposition „im ganzen als schwerer vorstellbar erschien als eine Einfügung" (43). So auch A.Y. Collins, Mark. A Commentary (Hermeneia), Minneapolis 2007, 130f. Anders D. Lührmann, Das Markusevangelium (HNT 3), Tübingen 1987, 33: Die kürzere Lesart könnte „entstanden sein unter Einfluß des vor allem aus Paulus vertrauten Sprachgebrauchs".

160 Vgl. den Exkurs bei D. Lührmann, Markusevangelium, 42–44. Das Wort εὐαγγέλιον als Bezeichnung für eine literarische Gattung begegnet bei Justin, der in Apologia I 66,3 schreibt, die ἀπομνημονεύματα der Apostel würden als εὐαγγέλια bezeichnet. In der Didache scheint εὐαγγέλιον mit dem MtEv verbunden zu sein: vgl. J.A. Kelhoffer, ‚How Soon a Book' Revisited: ΕΥΑΓΓΕΛΙΟΝ as a Reference to ‚Gospel' Materials in the First Half of the Second Century, in: ZNW 95 (2004), 1–34, hier 16–29.

die bis 1,13 oder bis 1,15 reichende Einleitung[161] oder auf das Buch als Ganzes, lässt sich nicht sicher sagen; der Verfasser setzt voraus, dass den impliziten Lesern die Bedeutung des Wortes εὐαγγέλιον grundsätzlich bekannt ist[162]. Wer das Werk liest, lernt darin den „Anfang des Evangeliums von Jesus Christus" kennen. Durch die Genitivverbindung ist Jesus Christus sowohl Inhalt als auch Urheber bzw. Verkündiger des εὐαγγέλιον[163]: „Gerade weil die markinische Erzählung die Geschichte der Verkündigung Jesu erzählt, erhebt sie den Anspruch, diese Verkündigung fortzusetzen."[164]

Stefan Schreiber meint, Markus eröffne sein Buch „mit Signalworten aus der politischen Rhetorik seiner Zeit": Indem Jesus Christus als „Bote und Inhalt des Evangeliums erscheint", erhalte Jesu Wirken „eine politische Dimension, die durch die Bestimmung als υἱὸς θεοῦ, als Sohn eines Gottes, noch verstärkt wird"; die Formulierung erinnere an den Kaisertitel ‚divi filius', auch wenn Markus im Folgenden sofort auf die prophetische Tradition Israels hinweise[165]. Diese Deutung

---

161 G. Guttenberger, Die Gottesvorstellung im Markusevangelium (BZNW 123), Berlin 2004, 56–74 bietet eine sorgfältige Analyse von Mk 1,1–15. Sie meint, V. 14.15 seien vom eigentlichen Prolog abzuheben, und dies könne „darauf hindeuten, dass der erste Satz des Prologs [sc. V. 1–3] ebenfalls von diesem abgehoben und ihm dennoch zugehörig sein könnte. Der durch das Wort εὐαγγέλιον erzielten Inclusio steht damit eine stilistische zur Seite" (62f.).
162 Vgl. dazu H. Baarlink, Anfängliches Evangelium. Ein Beitrag zur näheren Bestimmung der theologischen Motive im Markusevangelium, Kampen 1977, 57–60. E.-M. Becker, Das Markus-Evangelium im Rahmen antiker Historiographie (WUNT 194), Tübingen 2006, 111–116: Der Begriff ἀρχή zeige die „prinzipielle *Geschichts*orientierung" des MkEv (115). A.Y. Collins, Mark, 130 f.: „On the one hand, the author took up the familiar meaning of the term εὐαγγέλιον (‚good news') as the oral announcement and explanation of the salvific significance of the life and work and Jesus, especially his death and resurrection. On the other, he used the word in a new way, to refer to the content of a written work, in particular a narrative closely related to historical events of an eschatological nature".
163 E. Wong, Evangelien, 77: Der Genitiv Ἰησοῦ Χριστοῦ kann als gen. objectivus verstanden werden, und dann bezieht sich ἀρχή „auf das ganze Wirken und Geschick Jesu als Anfang des erlösenden Handelns Gottes"; oder es handelt sich um einen gen. subjectivus, und dann geht es um „den Anfang des Wirkens Jesu in Galiläa. In beiden Fällen umfasst ἀρχή aber das Wirken des irdischen Jesus, sei es nur den Anfang oder das Ganze."
164 D.S. du Toit, Der abwesende Herr. Strategien im Markusevangelium zur Bewältigung der Abwesenheit des Auferstandenen (WMANT 111), Neukirchen-Vluyn 2006, 284. Von dieser Verkündigung des Evangeliums werde dann in 13,10; 14,9 gesprochen.
165 St. Schreiber, Weihnachtspolitik. Lukas 1–2 und das Goldene Zeitalter (NTOA/StUNT 82), Göttingen 2009, 122–126, hier 81. Als Beleg verweist Schreiber auf Josephus Bellum Iudaicum IV 618. 656; er meint im Blick auf Mk 1,1 unter Berufung auf die erwähnten Stellen aus Josephus, εὐαγγέλιον sei verwendet worden, „um dem Regierungsantritt des römischen Kaisers Vespasian heilbringende Bedeutung zuzuschreiben". Diese politische Kritik sei von Lukas „durchaus verstanden" worden, er gestalte sie aber neu. Darauf, dass im LkEv das Wort εὐαγγέλιον vermieden

von Mk 1,1 würde von vornherein scheitern, wenn dort der Kurztext ohne υἱοῦ θεοῦ zu lesen ist; aber auch ein Leser des Langtextes wird kaum annehmen, dass Jesus Christus als „ein Sohn eines Gottes" in die Erzählung eingeführt wird[166].

Markus verwendet das Wort εὐαγγέλιον zweimal programmatisch bei der Einführung Jesu in die von ihm erzählende eigentliche Handlung: Nach der Gefangennahme des Täufers kam Jesus nach Galiläa, κηρύσσων τὸ εὐαγγέλιον τοῦ θεοῦ (1,14), und dann folgt diesem referierenden Hinweis in wörtlicher Rede Jesu Aufruf: μετανοεῖτε καὶ πιστεύετε ἐν τῷ εὐαγγελίῳ (1,15). Das εὐαγγέλιον Ἰησοῦ Χριστοῦ (1,1) beginnt auf der Ebene der erzählten Welt also damit, dass Jesus nach seiner Taufe, in der er als ὁ υἱός μου ὁ ἀγαπητός angesprochen worden war[167], und nach der Versuchung durch den Satan, nun in Galiläa das „Evangelium von Gott" verkündigt.

Die partizipiale Wendung κηρύσσων knüpft an die Aussage über den Täufer an (V.7a: καὶ ἐκήρυσσεν λέγων), doch der Inhalt des κηρύσσειν ist jetzt ein anderer: Hatte der Täufer das Kommen des Stärkeren „verkündigt", als der sich sogleich Jesus erweist[168], so verkündigt Jesus jetzt τὸ εὐαγγέλιον τοῦ θεοῦ als die (gute) Botschaft von Gott. Das in V.15 in wörtlicher Rede[169] zitierte εὐαγγέλιον τοῦ θεοῦ verkündet die verwirklichte Erfüllung der Zeit (πεπλήρωται ὁ καιρός)[170] und die Nähe der Herrschaft Gottes (ἤγγικεν ἡ βασιλεία τοῦ θεοῦ). Mit der sich anschließenden Aufforderung: μετανοεῖτε nimmt der markinische Jesus einen Aspekt jener Täuferbotschaft auf (1,4: κηρύσσων βάπτισμα μετανοίας), die mit der Vergebung der in der Taufe bekannten Sünden verbunden war (εἰς ἄφεσιν

---

wird, geht Schreiber in diesem Zusammenhang nicht ein. Ähnlich wie Schreiber auch E. Wong, Evangelien, 76: Mk hatte „den irdischen Aufstieg des Vespasian vom Feldherrn zum Kaiser vor Augen und hat damit den paradoxen Aufstieg Jesu zu seiner Würde als gekreuzigter ‚König der Juden' kontrastiert".

166 Anders verhält es sich mit 15,39: Der römische Hauptmann legt mit seiner Aussage ἀληθῶς οὗτος ὁ ἄνθρωπος υἱὸς θεοῦ ἦν kein Bekenntnis ab, sondern er spricht – wie ἦν zeigt – von Jesu Vergangenheit.

167 Es fällt auf, dass gesagt wird φωνὴ ἐγένετο ἐκ τῶν οὐρανῶν, nicht etwa „Gott sprach"; aber natürlich ist als Sprecher dieser Himmelsstimme Gott vorgestellt.

168 Mk 1,7: ἔρχεται ὁ ἰσχυρότερός μου ὀπίσω μου ..., 1,9: ἦλθεν Ἰησοῦς ... Ob der „historische" Täufer von Jesus (bzw. vom Messias) sprach oder nicht eher von Gott als dem zum Gericht Kommenden, spielt für den Mk-Text keine Rolle. Für Mk ist jedenfalls Jesus „der kommende Stärkere". ἦλθεν in 1,14 nimmt nochmals das ἔρχεται von 1,7 auf.

169 Die Struktur der Darstellung entspricht derjenigen der Täuferpredigt: Dem Referat (1,7a) folgte die wörtliche Rede (1,7b.8).

170 Nach W. Marxsen, Evangelist, 89 klingt hier Gal 4,4 an (ὅτε δὲ ἦλθεν τὸ πλήρωμα τοῦ χρόνου), doch sei die eschatologische Perspektive eine andere.

ἁμαρτιῶν, vgl. V.5: ἐξομολογούμενοι τὰς ἁμαρτίας αὐτῶν)[171]. Aber die in 1,14 als εὐαγγέλιον τοῦ θεοῦ eingeführte Botschaft Jesu lautet, dass sich die Adressaten dieser Botschaft auf die unmittelbare Nähe der Gottesherrschaft in der Gegenwart glaubend einlassen sollen[172]. Diese Nähe der βασιλεία τοῦ θεοῦ wird mit dem Wort εὐαγγέλιον charakterisiert, es geht hier also um die heilvolle Nähe Gottes; Jesus spricht nicht „neutral" vom erreichten Ziel der Geschichte oder vom bevorstehenden Gericht. Die Wendung πιστεύετε ἐν τῷ εὐαγγελίῳ (1,15b) ist im Neuen Testament ohne Parallele[173]; dennoch scheint gemeint zu sein, dass die Adressaten der Verkündigung Jesu „an das Evangelium" oder „dem Evangelium"[174] glauben, die Botschaft Jesu also im Glauben annehmen sollen[175]. Das gilt für die Hörer Jesu auf der Ebene der erzählten Welt, aber zugleich wendet sich die Botschaft auch an diejenigen, für die das Markusevangelium geschrieben wurde und die es jetzt lesen[176]. Dass in 1,14 τὸ εὐαγγέλιον τοῦ θεοῦ gesagt wird, in 1,15b aber absolut von τὸ εὐαγγέλιον die Rede ist, verweist nicht auf unterschiedliche Traditionsstufen[177]; diese Differenz bedarf gar keiner Erklärung, denn die Wendung πιστεύετε ἐν τῷ εὐαγγελίῳ in V.15b besagt im Anschluss an V.14 einfach, dass die Adressaten an das (soeben erwähnte) εὐαγγέλιον glauben sollen.

1,14.15 kann als sachliche Einleitung des ganzen folgenden Buches gelesen werden: Indem das MkEv vom κηρύσσειν Jesu erzählt, zeigt es, was τὸ εὐαγγέλιον

---

171 A.Y. Collins, Mark, 155: μετανοεῖτε beziehe sich nicht auf „a penitential discipline or primarily a human decision that begins a process of moral reform", sondern „it signifies a turning away from one's previous way of life ... and a turning to and acceptance of the new divine initiative through the agency of Jesus".

172 D. Lührmann, Markusevangelium, 41: Das Perfekt in V. 15a „ist zu verstehen aus der Gegenwart der Nähe des Reiches Gottes, nach Mk im Wort Jesu, wie sie im εὐαγγέλιον verkündet wird". Eine „erstaunlich nahe Parallele" finde sich in Gal 4,4, „wo Paulus die Zeit des Gesetzes als in der Sendung des Sohnes erfüllt bezeichnet".

173 Die Wortverbindung πιστεύειν εἰς bzw. πίστις εἰς ist im NT allerdings mehrfach belegt, aber niemals mit εὐαγγέλιον als Objekt.

174 In einigen Handschriften fehlt ἐν.

175 Vgl. D. Lührmann, Markusevangelium, 42: „Die Verbindung πιστεύειν ἐν entspricht der LXX-Wiedergabe von האמין ב; die typisch ntliche Verbindung πιστεύειν εἰς fehlt bei Mk". Siehe dazu B-D-R § 187,2.

176 D. Lührmann, Markusevangelium, 42: „Angesprochen sind in 15 vor allem die Hörer und Leser des Markusevangeliums, denen der Heilsruf 15a gilt und die in 15b aufgefordert werden, diesem εὐαγγέλιον zu vertrauen, dessen Inhalt die Nähe der Herrschaft Gottes in Jesu Wort ist". Marxsen, Evangelist Markus, 89 meint, der Evangelist stelle das Wort in 1,15 „nicht an den Anfang der Verkündigung des historischen Jesus, sondern an den Anfang der Verkündigung des Auferstandenen. Diese Verkündigung richtet sich also nicht an die Zeitgenossen Jesu, sondern an die Gemeinden ‚in Galiläa'." Aber das ist in der markinischen Darstellung offenbar keine Alternative.

177 So mit Recht P. Stuhlmacher, Evangelium, 236.

τοῦ θεοῦ bedeutet; alle weiteren Aussagen über Jesu κηρύσσειν und διδάσκειν bzw. über seine διδαχή sind von 1,14f. her inhaltlich zu füllen, als Explikation des durch Jesus verkündigten von Gott sprechenden εὐαγγέλιον[178]. Das umfasst auch Jesu Wirken – schon die in 1,21–28 erzählte Szene zeigt, dass Jesu Handeln und Jesu Lehren nicht voneinander zu trennen sind, und im Zusammenhang wunderbarer Taten Jesu wird mehrfach gesagt, dass Jesu Handeln auf Gott verweist[179].

3.2 Mk 8

Die weiteren Belege für εὐαγγέλιον stehen erst in dem mit 8,27 beginnenden zweiten Teil des MkEv nach der ersten der drei Leidens- und Auferstehungsansagen. Im Rahmen der Nachfolgesprüche (8,34–9,1) sagt Jesus in 8,35, wer seine ψυχή retten wolle, werde sie verlieren, und wer seine ψυχή verliere ἕνεκεν ἐμοῦ καὶ τοῦ εὐαγγελίου, werde sie retten (σώσει αὐτήν)[180]. Ist das καί additiv zu verstehen, gehören Jesus und τὸ εὐαγγέλιον also von vornherein zusammen, oder soll gerade zwischen Gegenwart (ἕνεκεν ἐμοῦ) und Zukunft (ἕνεκεν ... τοῦ εὐαγγελίου) unterschieden werden?[181] Tatsächlich können diejenigen, die auf der Ebene der erzählten Welt Jesus nachfolgen (8,34), ihr Leben verlieren „um Jesu willen" (ἕνεκεν ἐμοῦ); aber in der Gegenwart der Leser des MkEv gibt es eine solche unmittelbare

---

[178] Vgl. D.S. du Toit, Herr, 274f.: „Wie eine Überschrift bzw. Inhaltsangabe überschreibt Mk 1,14f. das in Mk 1–13 dargestellte Wirken Jesu und charakterisiert es als Verkündigung des Evangeliums Gottes ... Wenn also in Mk 1–13 von der Verkündigung oder Lehre Jesu die Rede ist, handelt es sich um die Verkündigung des in 1,14 erwähnten Evangeliums Gottes".
[179] Vgl. Mk 2,12; ähnlich 5,19; 7,37. Nach H. Koester, Gospels, 13 ergibt sich aus dem Zusammenhang von Mk 1,1 und 1,14f. „the somewhat odd consequence that Jesus here is the one who proclaims that gospel which has as its content his own death and resurrection". Aber das gilt in gleicher Weise auch für die Leidens- und Auferstehungsansagen und etwa für das Gleichnis 12,1–12.
[180] R. Bultmann, Die Geschichte der synoptischen Tradition (FRLANT 29), Göttingen [10]1995, 110 meint, das „von der Energie des Bußrufs" getragene Wort könne wohl Jesus zugeschrieben werden; aber die Worte ἕνεκεν ἐμοῦ καὶ τοῦ εὐαγγελίου seien „sicher sekundär" (116), so dass das Wort ursprünglich keine Beziehung zur Person Jesu gehabt hätte. Vgl. D. Lührmann, Markusevangelium, 152: „Das Evangelium (vgl. 1,14) ist die Vergegenwärtigung des Wortes Jesu". Nach D.S. du Toit, Herr, 286 besteht die Möglichkeit, dass εὐαγγέλιον in 8,35 (und auch in 10,29, s.u.) „nicht auf Jesu Verkündigung zu beschränken ist, sondern auf die Verkündigung des Evangeliums nach Ostern auszudehnen sein dürfte".
[181] D.S. du Toit, Herr, 286: Ein Zeitpunkt wird nicht explizit genannt. Vgl. E. Wong, Evangelien, 78: Das καί kann „auch qualitativ und epexegetisch gedeutet werden"; dann könne das Evangelium auch Jesus zum Inhalt haben, was dem paulinischen Verständnis von εὐαγγέλιον entspräche.

Beziehung zu Jesus nicht, und so scheint nun „das Evangelium" an Jesu Stelle getreten zu sein[182]. „Das Evangelium" repräsentiert die fortdauernde Gegenwart Jesu vor dem Hintergrund seiner realen Abwesenheit[183].

3.3 Mk 10

In 10,29f. in der Fortsetzung der Erzählung vom Reichen, dessen Berufung an seinem Besitz scheitert (10,17–27), reagiert Jesus auf den Hinweis des Petrus, die Jünger hätten „alles verlassen" (V.28), mit der Aussage, wer seine sozialen Bindungen aufgegeben habe ἕνεκεν ἐμοῦ καὶ ἕνεκεν τοῦ εὐαγγελίου, werde in der gegenwärtigen Zeit hundertfach Ersatz bekommen unter Verfolgungen und im kommenden Äon das ewige Leben. Hier ist die Ebene der erzählten Welt Jesu und der Jünger offenbar gar nicht im Blick; denn zwar haben die Jünger, wie Petrus sagt, „alles verlassen" (V.28), aber sie haben (noch) keines der „hundertfach" verheißenen Güter erhalten. Der gegenwärtige καιρός, von dem Jesus spricht, ist also nicht die Zeit des irdischen Jesus und seiner Jünger, sondern gemeint ist im eschatologischen Sinn die geschichtliche Gegenwart, auf die ὁ αἰὼν ὁ ἐρχόμενος, also die eschatologische Zukunft folgen wird. In der Gegenwart, die (auch) die Zeit des Autors und der Leser des MkEv ist[184], geben Menschen „um des Evangeliums willen" ihre sozialen Bindungen preis, indem sie durch ihre Annahme der Botschaft Jesu von ihrer bisherigen Welt getrennt werden[185]. Das Evangelium „vertritt" Jesus nicht im vollen Umfang, es „*kompensiert* vielmehr die Abwesenheit Jesu, indem es teilweise als funktionaler Ersatz an die Stelle des Irdischen tritt"[186].

---

[182] Nach W. Marxsen, Evangelist, 79 hat der Zusatz καὶ τοῦ εὐαγγελίου „in der Markus vorliegenden Tradition gefehlt", ist also jedenfalls redaktionell. Freilich ist das Fehlen bei den Seitenreferenten dafür kein Argument.
[183] Vgl. D.S. du Toit, Herr, 288f. und 298–302.
[184] D.S. du Toit, Herr, 287 Anm. 96 folgert aus der Angabe μετὰ διωγμῶν, dass es sich „wohl um eine Zusage für die Zeit nach Ostern" handelt: „Die Nachfolge Jesu zieht Lohn nach sich, der sich allerdings erst in der Zeit nach Ostern in vollem Umfang erfüllt." Aber inwiefern erhalten die Nachfolger auch schon in der Gegenwart Jesu „Lohn"?
[185] D.S. du Toit, Herr, 295: Die Zusage hundertfacher Ersatzgüter ergeht *sowohl* an diejenigen, „die vor Ostern um Jesu willen (ἕνεκεν ἐμοῦ) alles verlassen haben (VV. 28f.), *als auch* an diejenigen, die künftig nach Ostern um des Evangeliums willen (ἕνεκεν τοῦ εὐαγγελίου) alles verlassen werden". Damit werde eine Neudefinition „der Identität der Jünger" vorgenommen. Nach W. Marxsen, Evangelist, 85 ist das καί epexegtisch zu verstehen.
[186] D.S. du Toit, Herr, 302.

3.4 Mk 13

In der Endzeitrede Mk 13 kündigt Jesus an, dass „ihr" – also auf der Ebene der erzählten Welt: die Jünger – vor Gericht gebracht werdet ἕνεκεν ἐμοῦ (V.9). Auf der Ebene der Leser des MkEv ist diese Wendung, wie der Nachsatz εἰς μαρτύριον αὐτοῖς zeigt, offenbar bedeutungsgleich mit der hier allerdings fehlenden Wendung „um des Evangeliums willen": Die Adressaten der Rede Jesu werden in den geschilderten Gerichtsszenen vor den Anklägern ihr Christuszeugnis ablegen. Bevor dieser Gedankengang in V.11 fortgesetzt wird, sagt Jesus in V.10, es müsse zuerst allen Völkern das Evangelium gepredigt werden (καὶ εἰς πάντα τὰ ἔθνη πρῶτον δεῖ κηρυχθῆναι τὸ εὐαγγέλιον)[187]; damit wird zum ersten Mal im MkEv explizit „eine Verbindung zwischen Evangelium und der nachösterlichen Zeit der Abwesenheit Jesu" hergestellt[188]. Durch wen die Verkündigung des Evangeliums geschieht (κηρυχθῆναι), wird nicht gesagt; aber es ist jedenfalls an die Missionspredigt zu denken und nicht an einen Vorgang wie den in Apk 14,6 geschilderten. Meint die Wendung πρῶτον δεῖ κηρυχθῆναι, dass die Predigt εἰς πάντα τὰ ἔθνη ergehen muss, *bevor* die Verfolgungs- und Gerichtssituation eintritt, oder geschieht beides zur selben Zeit?[189] Jedenfalls spricht Jesus von dem künftig verkündigten Evangelium, das sich an „alle Völker" wenden wird; Adressaten sind, wie die Wendung πάντα τὰ ἔθνη zeigt (vgl. 11,17), „alle Völker", nicht etwa nur „die (Heiden-)Völker". Jesu Aussage bezieht sich auf der Ebene der erzählten Welt auf die nahe Zukunft, für den Autor und die Adressaten des MkEv ist dies bereits gegenwärtige Realität, denn die Verkündigung εἰς πάντα τὰ ἔθνη geschieht bereits[190]. V.10 steht im Kontext der apokalyptischen Rede; gleichwohl meint τὸ εὐαγγέλιον nicht anders als in 1,14 f. und in den anderen Mk-Texten explizit die

---

[187] Das δεῖ entspricht der ersten Leidensankündigung (8,31, vgl. 14,31) und der „Notwendigkeit" des Kommens des Elia (9,11); es gehört in den eschatologisch-apokalyptischen Kontext (13,7).
[188] D.S. du Toit, Herr, 277.
[189] A. Collins, Mark, 606 f.: „The point seems to be that, during the period of political, social, and economic upheaval, the task of the followers of Jesus is to be the proclamation of the good news ... Only after this task is accomplished will the divine intervention occur, and only those who do not succumb to the opposition involved will experience that intervention as blessing".
[190] D. Lührmann, Markusevangelium, 220: „Die Gegenwart ist nicht nur Zeit der Abwesenheit des Menschensohnes bis zu seinem Kommen (26), sondern Zeit der Nähe des Gottesreiches im Evangelium". D.S. du Toit, Herr, 278: „Die Zeit zwischen Tod bzw. Auferstehung Jesu und dem Kommen des Menschensohnes ist also eine Zeit der Verkündigung des Evangeliums, d.h. der Weitergabe der Verkündigung Jesu". G. Guttenberger, Gottesvorstellung, 76 meint, in V.10 werde die im Rahmentext erwähnte Verfolgungssituation „als Gelegenheit für die Verkündigung des Evangeliums" gedeutet; aber der Begriff „Gelegenheit" ist vielleicht doch zu schwach.

gute, heilvolle Botschaft und impliziert nicht etwa zusätzlich einen Gerichtsgedanken. Darüber, wie πάντα τὰ ἔθνη auf das εὐαγγέλιον reagieren, spricht der Text nicht.

3.5 Mk 14

Am Ende der Salbungserzählung in 14,3–9 kündigt Jesus in V.9 an, dort wo „das Evangelium" (τὸ εὐαγγέλιον) künftig verkündigt werde εἰς ὅλον τὸν κόσμον, werde man von dem, was die Frau an ihm getan hatte, ebenfalls sprechen „zu ihrem Gedächtnis" (λαληθήσεται εἰς μνημόσυνον αὐτῆς). Die Wendung ὅπου ἐὰν κηρυχθῇ τὸ εὐαγγέλιον εἰς ὅλον τὸν κόσμον knüpft deutlich an 13,10 an (... εἰς πάντα τὰ ἔθνη πρῶτον δεῖ κηρυχθῆναι τὸ εὐαγγέλιον), auch wenn jetzt der eschatologische Aspekt fehlt.[191] τὸ εὐαγγέλιον ohne Genitivattribut bezeichnet die von Jesus predigende Botschaft: „Mk 14,9 unterstreicht in besonderem Maße, dass nachösterlich das Evangelium dort verkündigt wird, wo die *geschichtliche* Verkündigung des irdischen Jesus erneut zu Wort kommt."[192] Ist in der Wendung λαληθήσεται κτλ. impliziert, man werde von dem besonderen Handeln jener Frau auch *lesen* können?[193] Dann wäre in 14,9, dem letzten Beleg für εὐαγγέλιον im MkEv, der in 1,1.14 f. enthaltene Aspekt nochmals aufgenommen, dass das εὐαγγέλιον nicht nur die Botschaft Jesu, sondern zugleich auch die erzählte und geschriebene Verkündigung an die Adressaten des Buches ist[194].

---

191 Anders D.S. du Toit, Herr, 282f., der meint, „dass künftig die Evangeliumsverkündigung hinsichtlich des Handelns der Frau gewissermaßen die Funktion eines virtuellen apokalyptischen Himmelsbuches übernehmen wird"; vgl. am angegebenen Ort, 84. Du Toit beruft sich dazu auf E. Lohmeyer, Das Evangelium des Markus (KEK II), Göttingen ¹⁶1963, 295f., der schreibt, εἰς μνημόσυνον αὐτῆς meine „nicht den heiligen Ruhm, den die Gläubigen aller Zeiten preisen werden – denn an keiner Stelle blickt das Mk-Evangelium auf die unabsehbare Folge kommender Geschlechter –, sondern den Ruhm, dessen Gott ‚gedenkt', wenn Er Sich der Frommen gnädig annimmt". Aber das MkEv denkt durchaus an eine geschichtliche Zukunft, in der sich die Evangeliumsverkündigung ereignen wird, und dabei wird von dem gesprochen werden, was diese Frau getan hat. Der Gedanke ist ein anderer als in Apg 10,4, wo der Engel dem Cornelius sagt, seine Gebete seien hinaufgegangen εἰς μνημόσυνον ἔμπροσθεν θεοῦ.
192 D.S. du Toit, Herr, 282.
193 A. Collins, Mark, 644: „It seems likely, then, that here the author of Mark refers to his own work as a ‚gospel'", nicht im Sinne einer neuen literarischen Gattung, sondern um zu zeigen „that no great distinction was made by this author, and probably his audiences, between an oral summary of the gospel and a written Gospel".
194 D. Lührmann, Markusevangelium, 233: Mk stellt „hier am Beginn der Passionsgeschichte wie in 1,14 f. am Beginn des ganzen Evangeliums noch einmal heraus, daß auch das, was nun in der Passion Jesu geschieht, Teil des Evangeliums als der Nähe des Reiches Gottes im Wort Jesu

3.6 Der sekundäre Markusschluss

Der Autor des sekundären Mk-Schlusses 16,9–20 nimmt in V.15 den Missions- und Taufbefehl von Mt 28,18–20 auf; anders als im gesamten übrigen Text orientiert er sich hier deutlich an der markinischen Terminologie: Die Wendung πορευθέντες εἰς τὸν κόσμον ἅπαντα knüpft an 14,9 an (εἰς ὅλον τὸν κόσμον), und vor allem sagt der auferstandene Jesus den Jüngern dann, dass sie „das Evangelium" verkündigen sollen (κηρύξατε τὸ εὐαγγέλιον)[195], wobei das Dativobjekt πάσῃ τῇ κτίσει an 10,6; 13,19 erinnert[196]. Die in V.16 folgende Gerichtsansage (ὁ πιστεύσας καὶ βαπτισθεὶς σωθήσεται, ὁ δὲ ἀπιστήσας κατακριθήσεται) lässt aber erkennen, dass der Autor des sekundären Mk-Schlusses das markinische Verständnis von εὐαγγέλιον nicht übernommen hat.

3.7 Auswertung

Der Gebrauch des Wortes εὐαγγέλιον im MkEv geht vermutlich durchweg auf die redaktionelle Arbeit des Evangelisten zurück. Dass hier eine deutliche Nähe zu den paulinischen Briefen besteht, ist unübersehbar, aber eine direkte literarische Abhängigkeit lässt sich nicht zeigen.

Eric K. Ch. Wong nimmt an, „dass Markus mit Paulus durch gemeinsame Traditionen in Berührung gekommen ist"[197]; „die allgemeine Nähe zur paulinischen Theologie" ergebe sich „aus der Verwendung des Begriffs ‚Evangelium' zur Bezeichnung der zentralen christlichen Botschaft".[198] Indiz dafür sei, dass das Wort „jeweils zwei Mal kurz nacheinander begegnet", am Anfang in der Genitivverbindung εὐαγγέλιον + Genitiv (1,1 und 1,14), dann in der Wendung ἕνεκεν

---

ist". Auch in 14,9 ist εὐαγγέλιον nicht als literarische Gattung zu verstehen. Aber unabhängig von der traditionsgeschichtlichen Herkunft der Wendung ὁ ἀναγινώσκων νοείτω in 13,14 ist klar, dass das MkEv (auch) ein zu lesender Text ist.
195 Nach J.A. Kelhoffer, Miracle and Mission. The Authentication of Missionaries and Their Message in the Longer Ending of Mark (WUNT II/112), Tübingen 2000, 100, „κηρύξατε τὸ εὐαγγέλιον are the only words of verse 15 that reflect the language and style of Mark". Vgl. Y.-I. Kim, Die Erscheinung Jesu. Eine rezeptionsorientierte Untersuchung der Erscheinungserzählungen in den synoptischen Evangelien (EHS XXIII/922), Frankfurt am Main u.a. 2011, 74f. zur Bedeutung von εὐαγγέλιον und Taufe im längeren Mk-Schluss.
196 J.A. Kelhoffer, ebd. betont den unmarkinischen Charakter dieser Terminologie; aber immerhin ist das Wort κτίσις in den Evangelien nur bei Mk belegt.
197 E. Wong, Evangelien, 64. Er sieht weitere Berührungspunkte zwischen Röm 14,1–23 und Mk 7,1–23 sowie zwischen 1Kor 7,1–40 und Mk 10,2–12.
198 E. Wong, Evangelien, 105. „Beide erheben damit einen öffentlichen Anspruch."

ἐμοῦ καὶ [ἕνεκεν] τοῦ εὐαγγελίου in 8,35 und 10,29 und dann in Verbindung mit κηρύσσειν (13,10 und 14,9). „Der Evangeliumsbegriff ist beim ersten Auftreten immer paulinisch gefärbt, wird aber beim zweiten Vorkommen jedes Mal markinisch abgewandelt."[199] Die Wendung ἀρχὴ τοῦ εὐαγγελίου begegne schon bei Paulus (Phil 4,15), doch verleihe Markus „dieser (traditionellen) Wendung von vornherein einen tieferen Klang", zumal sich in 1,1 eine starke Berührung mit der Priene-Inschrift zeige: „Eine neue Weltepoche hat begonnen."[200]

Nach Martin Ebner ist das ganze MkEv ein „Kontrast-Entwurf" – dass der Evangelist seine Jesus-Geschichte ein „Evangelium" nannte, habe „in den Ohren seiner Zeit provokativ klingen" müssen[201]. Aber die These, εὐαγγέλιον sei terminus technicus des „Kaiserkults" gewesen und insofern habe Markus „ein Anti-Evangelium geschrieben"[202], wird durch den oben dargestellten antiken Sprachgebrauch nicht bestätigt[203]. Der zugespitzten Behauptung Ebners, dass Markus für sein Evangelium „sicher keine kaiserliche Genehmigung bekommen" hätte, weil es „ein subversives Kontrastprogramm zur herrschenden religiösen, politischen und gesellschaftlichen Kultur" war[204], widerspricht schon allein die Tatsache, dass das Buch ja keineswegs geheim blieb, sondern alsbald Textvorlage für das LkEv und für das MtEv wurde[205].

τὸ εὐαγγέλιον ist im MkEv als nomen actionis Bezeichnung für den *Vollzug* der Weitergabe der „guten Botschaft". Dieses Verständnis gilt schon für die „Überschrift" des Buches (1,1), und dabei wird zugleich deutlich, dass Markus sein literarisches Werk unmittelbar als „Verkündigung" verstanden wissen will. Auch in 13,10 und in 14,9 ist das εὐαγγέλιον die Verkündigung, die im Auftreten Jesu ihren Anfang genommen hatte und die auch in der Zeit nach Jesu irdischem Wirken ihre Fortsetzung findet[206].

εὐαγγέλιον bezieht sich auch auf den *Inhalt* der Botschaft: In der Durchführung des Programms, die Jesuserzählung *als* εὐαγγέλιον Ἰησοῦ Χριστοῦ zu bieten, sagt Markus in 1,14, dass Jesus τὸ εὐαγγέλιον τοῦ θεοῦ, also „die frohe

---

199 E. Wong, Evangelien, 78f. (Zitat 79).
200 E. Wong, Evangelien, 80. Am angegebenen Ort, 81: „Das Evangelium von Jesus wird den Evangelien entgegengesetzt, die der Propaganda der damaligen römischen Kaiser dienten ... Nicht die Flavier werden die Welt retten, sondern Jesus von Nazareth".
201 M. Ebner, Evangelium contra Evangelium. Das Markusevangelium und der Aufstieg der Flavier, in: BN 116 (2003), 28–42, hier 32.
202 So M. Ebner, Evangelium, 33.
203 S.o. S. 316–322.
204 M. Ebner, Evangelium, 41.
205 Die Frage, ob das MkEv unabhängig von der Verwendung des Wortes εὐαγγέλιον politische, anti-römische Implikationen hat, kann hier offen bleiben.
206 Vgl. dazu D.S. du Toit, Herr, 276–278.

Botschaft von Gott" verkündigte, die nach 1,15a in der Ansage der Nähe der βασιλεία τοῦ θεοῦ besteht. In 1,15b ruft Jesus die Hörer (Leser) dazu auf, dem in 1,14 eingeführten εὐαγγέλιον Glauben zu schenken[207].

Absolut gebraucht bezeichnet das Wort εὐαγγέλιον gleichermaßen den *Vollzug* wie den *Inhalt* der Botschaft. In 8,35; 10,29 sowie 13,10; 14,9 spricht Markus von dem Evangelium, das in der Zeit von Jesu Abwesenheit gepredigt, gehört und angenommen wird. Versteht man in 8,35; 10,29 in der Wendung ἕνεκεν ἐμοῦ καὶ τοῦ εὐαγγελίου das καί explikativ, so könnte das bedeuten, dass Jesus selber zum Inhalt des εὐαγγέλιον wird; aber das würde jedenfalls erst und allein für die nachösterliche Zeit gelten – der irdische Jesus macht im MkEv sich selber niemals zum Gegenstand des εὐαγγέλιον[208]. Der Gebrauch des Wortes εὐαγγέλιον erweist sich gerade auch in der Vielfalt der Bedeutungen als *das* Charakteristikum des MkEv[209].

4 εὐαγγέλιον bei Paulus und im Markusevangelium

(1) Das Wort εὐαγγέλιον bezeichnet eine „gute Nachricht", εὐαγγέλια sind Informationen, die vom Absender und nach dessen Einschätzung auch vom Adressaten als erfreulich eingestuft werden. Der betonte Sprachgebrauch τὸ εὐαγγέλιον im Sinne der einen, inhaltlich eindeutig definierten „guten Botschaft" ist möglicherweise schon früh in der sich entwickelnden „christlichen Sprache" entstanden[210], aber literarisch greifbar wird dieser Sprachgebrauch erstmals bei Paulus im 1. Thessalonicherbrief, und dann begegnet er in allen uns erhaltenen paulinischen Briefen. In die synoptische Tradition wurde das Wort εὐαγγέλιον offensichtlich erst vom Verfasser des MkEv eingeführt[211]. Dass er dabei von Paulus direkt abhängig ist, lässt sich nicht zeigen; aber zweifellos weist auch das MkEv den bei Paulus belegten Gebrauch des Wortes als „*die* frohe Botschaft" auf.

---

207 Dazu D.S. du Toit, Herr, 275.
208 S. dazu D.S. du Toit, Herr, 278.
209 W. Marxsen, Evangelist, 83: „Das Substantiv εὐαγγέλιον ist offenbar ein Lieblingsausdruck des Markus".
210 Nach E. Wong, Evangelien, 65f. zeigt 1Kor 15,1, dass Paulus und Markus nicht die ersten Christen waren, die diesen Begriff übernahmen. Aber aus 1Kor 15,1–5 geht nicht hervor, dass die Verwendung des Begriffs εὐαγγέλιον Bestandteil der von Paulus übernommenen Tradition ist.
211 W. Marxsen, Evangelist, 83. Ebenso E. Wong, Evangelien, 80, freilich mit der betonten These, in Mk 1,1; 8,35; 13,10 sei „die paulinische Prägung" noch zu erkennen.

(2) Der Vergleich zwischen Paulus und dem MkEv muss berücksichtigen, dass das MkEv eine geschlossene literarische Jesuserzählung darstellt; der Autor kann annehmen, dass die Leser den Gebrauch des Wortes εὐαγγέλιον an den verschiedenen Stellen systematisch aufeinander zu beziehen vermögen. Grundsätzlich hat das Wort im MkEv stets dieselbe Bedeutung: Gemeint ist die Botschaft, die Jesus in Galiläa zu verkündigen begann und die in nachösterlicher Zeit die fortdauernde Gegenwart des Auferstandenen bezeugt; deshalb kann Markus die Geschichte Jesu als ἀρχὴ τοῦ εὐαγγελίου Ἰησοῦ Χριστοῦ erzählen, in der Jesus Christus gleichermaßen „Autor" wie Inhalt des εὐαγγέλιον ist. Paulus wendet sich in seinen Briefen an unterschiedliche Adressaten. Aber auch er kann grundsätzlich voraussetzen, dass εὐαγγέλιον immer als „die gute Botschaft" verstanden wird, deren Inhalt Jesus Christus bzw. Gottes Handeln in Christus ist; das gilt insbesondere auch dort, wo er absolut τὸ εὐαγγέλιον sagt[212].

Anders als in Mk 1,14, wo Jesus selber als Verkündiger des εὐαγγέλιον τοῦ θεοῦ eingeführt wird, ist bei Paulus die Genitivverbindung εὐαγγέλιον τοῦ Χριστοῦ niemals als gen. auctoris zu verstehen, als wäre Jesus selber Verkündiger des εὐαγγέλιον. Umgekehrt deutet Markus nur in 1,1 indirekt an, dass er selber das Evangelium verkündigt; τὸ εὐαγγέλιον ist, anders als bei Paulus, im MkEv niemals nomen actionis.

Weder bei Paulus noch bei Markus lässt der Sprachgebrauch erkennen, dass sie sich explizit von anderen εὐαγγέλια absetzen wollen, die sich auf ein anderes Gegenüber beziehen[213]. Sie verstehen τὸ εὐαγγέλιον auch nicht so, als werde darin Heil und Gericht angesagt; vielmehr ist für beide das Evangelium *die* gute, heilvolle und Heil schaffende Botschaft, die von den Hörern angenommen werden soll.

---

[212] Oft wird das auch durch den unmittelbaren Kontext verdeutlicht. So heißt es in 1Thess 1,5 zunächst τὸ εὐαγγέλιον ἡμῶν, aber dann sagt Paulus durchweg τὸ εὐαγγέλιον τοῦ θεοῦ (2,2.8.9). Im Phil heißt es zunächst τὸ εὐαγγέλιον (1,5.7.12.16), dann aber in 1,27a τὸ εὐαγγέλιον Χριστοῦ, woran 1,27b anknüpft (... συναθλοῦντες τῇ πίστει τοῦ εὐαγγελίου), ohne dass eine Differenz vorliegt. Im Röm heißt es in 1,1 εὐαγγέλιον θεοῦ, in 1,9 spricht Paulus vom εὐαγγέλιον τοῦ υἱοῦ αὐτοῦ, in 1,16 sagt er absolut τὸ εὐαγγέλιον.
[213] Selbst wenn es Zufall sein sollte, dass εὐαγγέλιον in jenen Texten, die bisweilen mit dem „Kaiserkult" in Verbindung gebracht werden, nicht im Singular belegt ist, so ist jedenfalls der charakteristische Sprachgebrauch bei Paulus und im MkEv nicht von dorther zu erklären. Die pauluskritischen Missionare in Galatien verkündeten ihr ἕτερον εὐαγγέλιον sicherlich als τὸ εὐαγγέλιον τοῦ Χριστοῦ (1,7); der Widerspruch des Paulus liegt darin, dass er den Charakter dieser Botschaft als εὐαγγέλιον bestreitet.

Literatur

Baarlink, H., Anfängliches Evangelium. Ein Beitrag zur näheren Bestimmung der theologischen Motive im Markusevangelium, Kampen 1977.
Becker, E.-M., Art. Evangelium/Evangelienliteratur. I. Neutestamentlich, in: LBH (2009), 164.
—, Das Markus-Evangelium im Rahmen antiker Historiographie (WUNT 194), Tübingen 2006.
Betz, H.D., 2. Korinther 8 und 9. Ein Kommentar zu zwei Verwaltungsbriefen des Apostels Paulus, Gütersloh 1993.
—, Der Galaterbrief. Ein Kommentar zum Brief des Apostels Paulus an die Gemeinden in Galatien, München 1988.
Bousset, W., Die Offenbarung Johannis (KEK XVI), Göttingen ⁶1906.
Brocke, Chr. vom, Rez. M. Crüsemann, Die pseudepigraphen Briefe an die Gemeinde in Thessaloniki. Studien zu ihrer Abfassung und zur jüdisch-christlichen Sozialgeschichte, in: ThLZ 137 (2012), 44–47.
Bultmann, R., Die Geschichte der synoptischen Tradition (FRLANT 29), Göttingen ¹⁰1995.
—, Glossen im Römerbrief, in: R. Bultmann, Exegetica. Aufsätze zur Erforschung des Neuen Testaments, hg. von E. Dinkler, Tübingen 1967, 278–285.
—, Theologie des Neuen Testaments, hg. von O. Merk, Tübingen ⁹1984.
Cancik, H., Art. Evangelium/Evangelienliteratur. I. Altphilologisch, in: LBH (2009), 166.
Collins, A. Yarbro, Mark. A Commentary (Hermeneia), Minneapolis 2007.
Crüsemann, M., Die pseudepigraphen Briefe an die Gemeinde in Thessaloniki. Studien zu ihrer Abfassung und zur jüdisch-christlichen Sozialgeschichte (BWANT 191), Stuttgart 2010.
Dechow, J., Gottessohn und Herrschaft Gottes. Der Theozentrismus des Markusevangeliums (WMANT 86), Neukirchen-Vluyn 2000.
Deißmann, A., Licht vom Osten. Das Neue Testament und die neuentdeckten Texte der hellenistisch-römischen Welt, Tübingen ⁴1923.
Dinkler, E., Der Brief an die Galater. Zum Kommentar von Heinrich Schlier (1955), in: E. Dinkler, Signum Crucis. Aufsätze zum Neuen Testament und zur Christlichen Archäologie, Tübingen 1967, 270–282.
Du Toit, D.S., Der abwesende Herr. Strategien im Markusevangelium zur Bewältigung der Abwesenheit des Auferstandenen (WMANT 111), Neukirchen-Vluyn 2006.
Ebner, M., Evangelium contra Evangelium. Das Markusevangelium und der Aufstieg der Flavier, in: BN 116 (2003), 28–42.
Ernst, J., Die Briefe an die Philipper, an Philemon, an die Kolosser, an die Epheser (RNT), Regensburg 1974.
Ettl, C., Der „Anfang der ... Evangelien". Die Kalenderinschrift von Priene und ihre Relevanz für die Geschichte des Begriffs εὐαγγέλιον. Mit einer Anmerkung zur Frage nach der Gattung der Logienquelle, in: St.H. Brandenburger/Th. Hieke (Hgg.), Wenn drei das Gleiche sagen – Studien zu den ersten drei Evangelien. Mit einer Werkstattübersetzung des Q-Textes (Theologie 14), Münster 1998, 121–151.
Friedrich, G., Art. εὐαγγελίζομαι κτλ., in: ThWNT II (1935), 718–722.
Greeven H./Güting, E. Textkritik des Markusevangeliums (Theologie. Forschung und Wissenschaft 11), Münster 2005.
Guttenberger, G., Die Gottesvorstellung im Markusevangelium (BZNW 123), Berlin 2004.
Hahn, F., Theologie des Neuen Testaments. Band I. Die Vielfalt des Neuen Testaments. Theologiegeschichte des Urchristentums, Tübingen 2002.

Holtz, T., Der erste Brief an die Thessalonicher (EKK XIII), Zürich/Neukirchen-Vluyn 1986.
Horn, F.W., Wollte Paulus „kanonisch" wirken?, in: E.-M. Becker/St. Scholz (Hgg.), Kanon in Konstruktion und Dekonstruktion. Kanonisierungsprozesse religiöser Texte von der Antike bis zur Gegenwart. Ein Handbuch, Berlin 2012, 400–422.
Kelhoffer, J.A., ‚How Soon a Book' Revisited: εὐαγγέλιον as a Reference to ‚Gospel' Materials in the First Half of the Second Century, in: ZNW 95 (2004), 1–34.
—, Miracle and Mission. The Authentication of Missionaries and Their Message in the Longer Ending of Mark (WUNT II/112), Tübingen 2000.
Kim, Y.-I., Die Erscheinung Jesu. Eine rezeptionsorientierte Untersuchung der Erscheinungserzählungen in den synoptischen Evangelien (EHS XXIII/922), Frankfurt am Main u. a. 2011.
Klauck, H.-J., Die religiöse Umwelt des Urchristentums II. Herrscher- und Kaiserkult, Philosophie, Gnosis (KStTh 9,2), Stuttgart 1996.
Klumbies, P.-G., Die Rede von Gott bei Paulus in ihrem zeitgeschichtlichen Kontext (FRLANT 155), Göttingen 1992.
Koch, D.-A., Die Schrift als Zeuge des Evangeliums. Untersuchungen zur Verwendung und zum Verständnis der Schrift bei Paulus (BHTh 69), Tübingen 1986.
—, Geschichte des Urchristentums. Ein Lehrbuch, Göttingen 2013.
Koester, H., Ancient Christian Gospels. Their History and Development, Cambridge/Mass. 1990.
Lindemann, A., „… an die Kirche in Korinth samt allen Heiligen in ganz Achaja". Zu Entstehung und Redaktion des „Zweiten Korintherbriefes", in: D. Sänger (Hg.), Der zweite Korintherbrief. Literarische Gestalt – historische Situation – theologische Argumentation. Festschrift zum 70. Geburtstag von Dietrich-Alex Koch (FRLANT 250), Göttingen 2012, 131–159.
—, Paulus – Pharisäer und Apostel, in: A. Lindemann, Glauben, Handeln, Verstehen. Studien zur Auslegung des Neuen Testaments. Band II (WUNT 282), Tübingen 2011, 33–72.
—, Paulus und Elia. Zur Argumentation in Röm 11,1–12, in: V.A. Lehnert/U. Rüsen-Weinhold (Hgg.), Logos-Logik-Lyrik. Engagierte exegetische Studien zum biblischen Reden Gottes. Festschrift für Klaus Haacker (ABG 27), Leipzig 2007, 201–218.
Lohmeyer, E., Das Evangelium des Markus (KEK II), Göttingen ^{16}1963.
—, Die Briefe an die Philipper, an die Kolosser und an Philemon (KEK IX), Göttingen 1956.
Lohse, E., Das Präskript des Römerbriefes als theologisches Programm, in: E. Lohse, Das Neue Testament als Urkunde des Evangeliums. Exegetische Studien zur Theologie des Neuen Testaments III (FRLANT 192), Göttingen 2000, 104–116.
—, Der Brief an die Römer (KEK 4), Göttingen 2003.
—, Εὐαγγέλιον Θεοῦ. Paul's Interpretation of the Gospel in His Epistle to the Romans, in: E. Lohse, Das Neue Testament als Urkunde des Evangeliums. Exegetische Studien zur Theologie des Neuen Testaments III (FRLANT 192), Göttingen 2000, 89–103.
Lührmann, D., Das Markusevangelium (HNT 3), Tübingen 1987.
—, Das Offenbarungsverständnis bei Paulus und in paulinischen Gemeinden (WMANT 16), Neukirchen-Vluyn 1965.
Marxsen, W., Der Evangelist Markus. Studien zur Redaktionsgeschichte des Evangeliums (FRLANT 67), Göttingen ^{2}1959.
Merklein, H., Zum Verständnis des paulinischen Begriffs „Evangelium", in: H. Merklein, Studien zu Jesus und Paulus (WUNT 43), Tübingen 1987, 279–295.
Metzger, B.M., A Textual Commentary on the Greek New Testament, Stuttgart ^{2}1994.

Öhler, M., Essen, Ethnos, Identität – der antiochenische Zwischenfall (Gal 2,11–14), in: W. Weiß (Hg.), Der eine Gott und das gemeinschaftliche Mahl (BThSt 113), Neukirchen-Vluyn 2011, 158–199.

Schnelle, U., Art. Euangelion, in: DNP 4 (1998), 205.

—, Paulus. Leben und Denken, Berlin 2003.

Schniewind, J., Euangelion. Ursprung und erste Gestalt des Begriffs Evangelium. Untersuchungen. Erster Teil, Gütersloh 1927.

Schreiber, St., Weihnachtspolitik. Lukas 1–2 und das Goldene Zeitalter (NTOA/StUNT 82), Göttingen 2009, 122–126.

Strecker, G., Das Evangelium Jesu Christi, in: G. Strecker, Eschaton und Historie. Aufsätze, Göttingen 1979, 183–228.

Stuhlmacher, P., Das paulinische Evangelium. I. Vorgeschichte (FRLANT 95), Göttingen 1968.

Vouga, F., An die Galater (HNT 10), Tübingen 1998.

Witulski, Th., Kaiserkult in Kleinasien. Die Entwicklung der kultisch-religiösen Kaiserverehrung in der römischen Provinz Asia von Augustus bis Antoninus Pius (NTOA/StUNT 63), Göttingen/Fribourg ²2010.

Wolter, M., Paulus, Ein Grundriss seiner Theologie, Neukirchen-Vluyn 2011.

Wong, E.K.C., Evangelien im Dialog mit Paulus. Eine intertextuelle Studie zu den Synoptikern (NTOA/StUNT 89), Göttingen 2012.

Zeller, D., Der erste Brief an die Korinther (KEK 5), Göttingen 2010.

Zugmann, M., Missionspredigt in nuce. Studien zu 1 Thess 1,9b–10, Linz o.J. (2011).

Oda Wischmeyer
Konzepte von Zeit bei Paulus und im Markusevangelium

Weder Paulus noch der Verfasser des Markusevangeliums thematisieren die *Zeit* im theoretisch-philosophischen oder physikalischen Sinn[1]. Anders als das Matthäusevangelium und das lukanische Doppelwerk wird Zeit im Markusevangelium auch nicht als Ordnungsgröße in der Form von Genealogien und datierenden Synchronismen in Anspruch genommen. Die Sorge um Kalenderfragen, in den Hochkulturen der Alten Welt ein Rückgrat der Konzeptionierung von Zeit[2] und auch in den frühen christlichen Gemeinden offensichtlich ein Bedürfnis, wird von Paulus als Rückfall in pagane oder jüdische Religion verstanden und brüsk zurückgewiesen[3]. Zeit wird in den neutestamentlichen Schriften auch nicht zur deutlichen eigenen Begrifflichkeit erhoben[4], sie stellt weder bei Paulus noch im Markusevangelium ein eigenes theologisches Thema dar und begegnet weder in den gegenwärtigen Darstellungen der paulinischen noch der markinischen Theologie[5]. Zeit gehört daher auch nicht zu den bekannten und bevorzugten Themenstellungen, mit denen die Paulus- und Markusexegese arbeiten.

---

1 Vgl. J. Assmann, M. Theunissen, H. Westermann, H.Ch. Schmitt, P. Porro, Y. Schwartz, G. Böwering, E. Kessler, H. Hühn/H.-J. Waschkies, R. Beuthan/M. Sandbothe, Art. Zeit I-VI, in: HWPh 12 (2004), 1186–1244; J. Frey, Art. Zeit/Zeitvorstellungen II.2, in: RGG⁴ 8, 2005, 1804 f.
2 Vgl. z. B. J. Assmann, Zeit und Ewigkeit im Alten Ägypten. Ein Beitrag zur Geschichte der Ewigkeit (HAW phil.-hist. Kl. 1975,1), Heidelberg 1975; ders., Zeitkonstruktion, Vergangenheitsbezug und Geschichtsbewußtsein im alten Ägypten, in: J. Assmann/K.E. Müller (Hgg.), Der Ursprung der Geschichte, Stuttgart 2005, 112–214; J. Rüpke, Kalender und Öffentlichkeit: Die Geschichte der Repräsentation und religiösen Qualifikation von Zeit in Rom (RGVV 40), Berlin 1995; W. Geerlings, Der Kalender. Aspekte einer Geschichte, Paderborn/München 2002; E. Arens (Hg.), Zeit denken. Eschatologie im interdisziplinären Diskurs (QD 234), Freiburg/Basel/Wien 2010.
3 Gal 4,10; Röm 14,5 f. Die Stigmatisierung des Themas durch Paulus wird von den Schriftstellern der deuteropaulinischen Briefe aufgenommen: Kol 2,16. Zur religiösen Dimension der antiken Kalender vgl. Art. Calendars in: ABD I, 810–820 (J.C. Vanderkam). Zum jüdischen Kalender vgl. auch Art. Calendars, in: Eerdmans Dictionary of Early Judaism, 457–460 (J. Ben-Dov). G. Delling kommt zu dem wichtigen allgemeinen Urteil: „Das Urchristentum...als ganzes... hat den jüdischen Festkalender offenbar nicht übernommen...es hat offenbar auch keinen eigenen gottesdienstlichen Kalender entwickelt" (G. Delling, Zeit und Endzeit. Zwei Vorlesungen zur Theologie des Neuen Testaments [BSt 58], Neukirchen-Vluyn 1970, 40).
4 Zum Vokabular s.u.
5 Dazu s.u.

Und doch trifft zu, was Ernst von Dobschütz in einem Aufsatz über „Zeit und Raum im Denken des Urchristentums"[6] geschrieben hat: „Man wird ... feststellen dürfen, wie stark die Zeitidee das Denken des Urchristentums bestimmt". Zeit ist an den entscheidenden Punkten bei Paulus und Markus ganz offensichtlich im Spiel:

> Als die Fülle/Erfüllung der Zeit (χρόνος) kam, sandte Gott seinen Sohn (Gal 4,4).
>
> Siehe, jetzt ist der gute Zeitpunkt (καιρός), siehe, jetzt ist der Tag des Heils (2Kor 6,2).
>
> ...Jesus kam nach Galiläa, verkündigte das Evangelium von Gott und sprach: „Erfüllt hat sich die Zeit (καιρός), und nahegekommen ist die Herrschaft Gottes" (Mk 1,14f.).

Paulus und Markus haben sehr eigene Konzeptionen von Zeit im Zusammenhang mit ihrer jeweiligen Darstellung des Evangeliums[7]. Diese Konzeptionen werden einerseits zu der doppelten Grundlage für die theologische Weiterentwicklung der frühchristlichen Evangeliumsverkündigung in den Briefen und Evangelienschriften der zweiten und dritten frühchristlichen Generation, andererseits stellen sie bereits selbst einen entscheidenden Beitrag zu einem neuen Verständnis von Zeit dar, das die jüdische Zeitkonzeption hinter sich lassen und im Lauf der Spätantike auch die paganen philosophischen und kulturellen Zeitkonzeptionen überlagern wird[8]. *Zeit* ist daher zusammen mit εὐαγγέλιον und neben Glauben und Liebe eines jener *Konzepte*, mit denen die Paulusbriefe und das Markusevangelium im Vergleich erschlossen werden können.

Im Folgenden werde ich beide Konzeptionen darstellen. Das *Ergebnis* sei thetisch vorweggenommen: Entscheidend ist ihre unterschiedliche Interpretation der Jesuszeit. *Paulus* versteht die Zeit der Evangeliumspredigt als die Zeit seit Jesu Auferstehung von den Toten: „Wenn aber Christus verkündigt wird, dass er von den Toten auferstanden ist..." (1Kor 15,12). Damit beginnt die Predigt der Apostel vom Heil. Erst der Autor des *Markusevangeliums* erschließt die Zeit des öffentlichen Wirkens Jesu bis zu seinem Tod als Heilszeit. In Mk 1,15 stellt Jesus selbst seine Mission der Ankündigung der Gottesherrschaft unter das Stichwort Evangelium. Seine Reden und Taten sind Bestandteil der Heilszeit. Aus diesen unterschiedlichen Zeitkonzeptionen ergeben sich die unterschiedliche Anteilnahme an

---

6 In: JBL 41 (1922), 212–223. Zitat: 220.
7 Vgl. dazu den Beitrag von A. Lindemann im vorliegenden Band.
8 Vgl. R. Feldmeier, Gott und die Zeit, in: Heil und Geschichte. Die Geschichtsbezogenheit des Heils und das Problem der Heilsgeschichte in der biblischen Tradition und der theologischen Deutung, hg. von J. Frey/St. Krauter/H. Lichtenberger (WUNT 248), Tübingen 2009, 287–305, 288f. zu dem jüdisch grundierten Zeitbegriff von Hans Jonas und der Veränderung des Zeitbegriffs in der christlichen Interpretation.

den Überlieferungen des Lebens Jesu von Nazareth sowie die unterschiedlichen literarischen Genera, in denen beide Autoren, Paulus und Markus, tätig werden.

1 Forschungsstand

Die Zeit gehört – wie schon gesagt – nicht zum Kernbestand traditioneller neutestamentlicher theologischer Themen, da sie lediglich als Element des großen, theologisch konzipierten Themas der Eschatologie verstanden wird[9]. Das Thema der Zeit wurde daher nur selten Gegenstand eigener neutestamentlicher Untersuchungen unabhängig von dem Rahmenthema der Eschatologie: Oscar Cullmann[10] und Gerhard Delling[11] haben hier sehr unterschiedliche Akzente gesetzt[12].

---

9 Die Eschatologie wird entweder als eigenes theologisches Thema verstanden (vgl. dazu zuletzt den Sammelband: Eschatologie – Eschatology. The Sixth Durham-Tübingen Research Symposium: Eschatology in Old Testament, Ancient Judaism and Early Christianity (Tübingen, September 2009), hg. von H.J. Eckstein, C. Landmesser und H. Lichtenberger (WUNT 272), Tübingen 2011) oder im Rahmen der ‚Theologie des Neuen Testaments' dargestellt. Vgl. dazu allgemein den Sammelband: Aufgabe und Durchführung einer Theologie des Neuen Testaments, hg. von C. Breytenbach/J. Frey (WUNT 205), Tübingen 2007. Jörg Frey führt umsichtig und gründlich in das Thema ein: Zum Problem der Aufgabe und Durchführung einer Theologie des Neuen Testaments, 3 – 55. Besonders widmet er sich in der Auseinandersetzung mit F. Hahn dem Vergleich der „historische(n) und systematische(n) Darstellung" (38 – 42). Was Frey *nicht* erörtert und was häufig auch bei der historischen Analyse selbst undiskutiert bleibt, ist die *unterschiedliche Heuristik* zwischen der historischen und der theologischen Darstellung. Unterschiedlich sind aber nicht nur die Fragestellungen und die aus ihnen resultierenden Methoden, sondern vor allem die Themen und Begriffe. Was die theologische Heuristik unter „Eschatologie" untersucht, handelt die historisch-interpretierende Heuristik unter „Zeitkonzept" ab. Sie hält einen gewissen Abstand zu dem theologischen Grundvokabular und kann damit zu neuen Interpretationen der neutestamentlichen Texte beitragen. – Das Thema wird in dem Sammelband: Zeit und Ewigkeit als Raum göttlichen Handelns. Religionsgeschichtliche, theologische und philosophische Perspektiven, hg. von R.G. Kratz/H. Spieckermann (BZAW 390), Berlin/New York 2009, aufgegriffen.
10 O. Cullmann, Christus und die Zeit, Zollikon/Zürich, 1945; ³1962.
11 G. Delling, Das Zeitverständnis des Neuen Testaments, Gütersloh 1940; ders., Zeit und Endzeit, hier die ältere Literatur. Die Bibliographie zeigt den Einfluss Bultmanns, aber auch die Themen, die Thorleif Boman mit seiner Monographie: Das hebräische Denken im Vergleich mit dem griechischen, Göttingen ⁴1965, gesetzt hatte.
12 Vgl. dazu F. Avemarie, Heilsgeschichte und Lebensgeschichte bei Paulus, in: Heil und Geschichte, 357– 383, zu Cullmann S. 357 mit Anm. 3. Avemarie setzt sich sorgfältig mit der älteren Literatur auseinander. Mit dem Thema *Zeit* beschäftigt sich auch S. Vollenweider in dem substantiellen Beitrag: Zeit und Gesetz. Erwägungen zur Bedeutung apokalyptischer Denkformen bei Paulus, in: ders., Horizonte neutestamentlicher Christologie. Studien zu Paulus und zur frühchristlichen Theologie (WUNT 144), Tübingen 2002, 143 – 162. Vor dem apokalyptischen

Ebenfalls zu berücksichtigen sind die eher religionsgeschichtlich orientierten Fragestellungen zu den neutestamentlichen Endzeitvorstellungen, die unter den Stichworten von Apokalyptik und Parusieverzögerung stehen[13]. Der umfangreiche Sammelband „Heil und Geschichte", der auf ein Kolloquium zu Martin Hengels 80. Geburtstag zurückgeht[14], hat nun vor einigen Jahren die Frage nach der Zeit als theologischer Kategorie wieder neu aufgeworfen. Reinhard Feldmeier[15] und Friedrich Avemarie[16] machen in ihren Beiträgen die Zeit selbst in eindringlicher Weise zum Thema neutestamentlich-theologischer Überlegungen. Friedrich Avemarie gibt im Zusammenhang des Themas von Geschichte und Heilsgeschichte eine umfassende Analyse der paulinischen Aussagen zur Zeit im Kontext von Geschichte, Heilsgeschichte und Eschaton. Er arbeitet heraus, „wie Paulus soteriologische Aussagen zeitlich strukturiert", und zeichnet den Zusammenhang nach, „den er [Paulus] zwischen dem geschichtlichen Heilshandeln Gottes und dem individuellen Lebensgeschick der Glaubenden sieht"[17].

Reinhard Feldmeier liest das Zeitkonzept des Markusevangeliums theologisch und interpretiert es als heilsgeschichtliches Konzept. Er stellt es in den doppelten Zusammenhang der Christologie und der Evangeliumskonzeption[18]. Besonders wichtig ist bei seiner Interpretation, dass es sich zunächst um ein „Stück vergangene Geschichte" bzw. ein „Stück menschlicher Geschichte"[19] handelt – also jener Geschichte Jesu von Nazareth, die im Markusevangelium erzählt wird, die den Bedingungen des Ablaufs von Zeit unterworfen und damit schlicht ‚vergangen' ist. Eben diese Geschichte wird als Heilszeit interpretiert.

Im Zusammenhang seiner Überlegungen zum Thema „Gott und die Zeit" hat Reinhard Feldmeier auch Paulus in den Blick genommen und schreibt zur paulinischen Christologie: „Paulus, der erste große Denker des Christentums, hat die Konsequenzen dieses Selbstweises Gottes als Vater im Sohn auch im Blick auf

---

Hintergrund entwirft Vollenweider das Zeitverständnis des Paulus als „christologisch fundierte Konfiguration von Gegenwart und Zukunft" (152).

13 Vgl. vor allem K. Erlemann, Naherwartung und Parusieverzögerung im Neuen Testament, Tübingen 1995.
14 S.o. Anm. 8. Zur Konzeption des Bandes vgl. die „Einführung" der Herausgeber (XI-XXIII). Die Herausgeber verzichten gemäß dieser integrativen Konzeption auf eine differenzierende Definition von Zeit und Geschichte sowie auf den Versuch, Zeit und Geschichte zunächst als nicht-theologische Konzepte zu verstehen, die von den neutestamentlichen (und späteren christlichen!) Autoren in unterschiedlicher Weise theologisch gedeutet werden konnten.
15 S.o. Anm. 8.
16 F. Avemarie, Heilsgeschichte.
17 F. Avemarie, Heilsgeschichte, 359 f.
18 R. Feldmeier, Gott und die Zeit.
19 A.a.O., 296.

den Zeitaspekt, im Blick auf Endlichkeit und Ewigkeit noch intensiver thematisiert...Die Metapher von der ἀπαρχὴ τῶν κεκοιμημένων deutet schon an, dass die in Christus bereits geschehene Zeitenwende die Zukunft aller Glaubenden vorwegnimmt, wie Paulus durchweg betont (1Thess 4,12; 1Kor 15,22; Röm 8,11 und öfter). Deshalb kann der Apostel ähnlich wie das Evangelium von der ‚Fülle der Zeit' sprechen, die sich im Kommen des Sohnes ereignet"[20].

Anders als Avemarie und Feldmeier nähert sich Giorgio Agamben[21] dem paulinischen Zeitverständnis. Agamben macht mit der Vorstellung ernst, dass Paulus ein eigenes Zeitkonzept habe. In seiner Interpretation von Röm 1,1 arbeitet er zwar mit den religionsgeschichtlichen Begriffen von Apokalyptik und messianischer Zeit, vermeidet aber theologische Interpretamente wie Heilsgeschichte und Christologie. Er findet in den paulinischen Aussagen zur Zeit, zum Zeitpunkt, zum Jetzt, zur kommenden Vollendung etc. ein komplexes Zeitkonzept, das er von dem chronologischen und dem apokalyptischen Zeitkonzept unterscheidet und als einen herausragenden Beitrag zum allgemeinen Zeitverständnis würdigt.

Vor dem Hintergrund der genannten Beiträge wird deutlich, was eine neue vergleichende Studie zur Konzeption von Zeit bei Paulus und Markus thematisieren muss. Die Zeit kann weder einseitig auf ihre gegenwärtige noch auf ihre zukünftige, eschatologische Dimension reduziert werden. Es ist daher nicht ausreichend, die Zeit entweder existenztheologisch als Element gegenwärtig verstandener Eschatologie, wie es Rudolf Bultmanns Ansatz war, oder religionsgeschichtlich als Funktion apokalyptischer Vorstellungen zu verstehen. Ebenso wenig reicht es, Zeit mit dem Verlauf von Geschehnissen und mit Geschichte gleichzusetzen, sondern Zeit ist als eigene Größe in ihren sehr unterschiedlich gewichteten Erscheinungsformen von Vergangenheit, Gegenwart und Zukunft sowie ihren komplexen Zusammenhängen mit chronologischer Zeit, Vorzeit, Geschichte (Israels), Zeit Jesu, Zeit Jesu Christi, Zeit der Gemeinden und Endzeit, d.h. apokalyptischen Zukunftsbildern wahrzunehmen.

---

20 A.a.O., 298. Feldmeier zitiert Gal 4,4.
21 Eine eigene Möglichkeit, neutestamentliche Texte zum Thema Zeit *außerhalb* des Rahmens christlicher Theologie zu lesen, haben Philosophen wie G. Agamben (Die Zeit, die bleibt [Edition Suhrkamp 2453], Frankfurt 2006) gewählt. Vgl. dazu u.a. einführend E. Kaufman, The Saturday of Messianic Time (Agamben and Badiou on the Apostle Paul), in: South Atlantic Quarterly 107 (2008), 37–54; E.St.T. Ostovich, Pauline Eschatology: Thinking and Acting in the Time that Remains, in: J.A.Parker/P.A. Harris/Ch. Steineck (eds.), Time: Limits and Constraints, Leiden 2010, 307–327.

2 Die Sprache der Zeit

Tabelle (1) Temporal verwendete Lexeme bei Paulus und im Markusevangelium

αἰών[22]	Röm 1,25; 9,5; 11,36; 1Kor 2,7; 8,13; 10,11; 2Kor; 9,9; 11,31; Gal 1,5; Phil 4,20. Mk 3,29; 11,14.
und die Verbindungen αἰὼν οὗτος, αἰὼν ἐκεῖνος, ὁ νῦν αἰών, ὁ μέλλων αἰών, ὁ ἐνεστὼς αἰών, ὁ ἐρχόμενος αἰών, ἡ συντέλεια τοῦ αἰῶνος bzw. τῶν αἰώνων	Röm 12,1; 13,12; 1Kor 1,20; 2,6–8; 3,18; 2Kor 4,4; Gal 1,4. Mk 4,19; 10,30.
ἀρχή	Phil 4,15. Mk 1,1; 10,6; 13,8.19
ἐγγύς und ἐγγίζω[23]	Röm 13,11; Phil 4,5. Mk 1,15; 13,28f.
τὰ ἐνεστῶτα	Röm 8,38; 1Kor 3,22; 7,26; Gal 1,4. Mkev: fehlt.
ἔσχατος	1Kor 15,26.45.52[24]. Mkev: fehlt in der zukünftigen Bedeutung.
ἔτος	Röm 15,23; 2 Kor 12,2; Gal 1,18. Mkev: die Kategorie eines Jahres fehlt.
ἤδη	Röm 13,11; Phil 3,12. Mkev: fehlt in der eschatologisch gefärbten Bedeutung.
ἡμέρα[25] und die Verbindungen ἔρχεται ἡμέρα (κυρίου bzw. ὀργῆς) bzw. κύριος bzw. πίστις bzw. τὸ τέλειον	Röm 2,5.16; 13,12; 1Kor 1,8; 4,5; 5,5; 13,10; 2Kor 1,14; 6,2; Gal 3,23–25; Phil 1,6.10; 2,16; 1Thess 1,10; 2,19; 3,13;5,2. Mk 2,20[26]; 13,17.19.20.24.32;14,25.
καινός[27] und καινὴ κτίσις	2Kor 5,17; Gal 6,15. Mk 1,27[28]; 2,21f.[29].

---

22 Vgl. die instruktive Tabelle zur temporalen Lexiomatik der Septuaginta bei G. Delling, Zeitverständnis, 50f. Delling erfasst χρόνος, καιρός, αἰών, ὥρα, ἀρχή, τέλος, ἡμέρα, ἔσχατος.
23 Im temporalen Sinn.
24 Im futurischen Sinn.
25 Im theologisch qualifizierten Sinn.
26 Im bildlichen Zusammenhang.
27 Im temporalen Sinn.
28 Sowohl temporal als qualitativ gesetzt.
29 Im bildlichen Zusammenhang.

und καινὴ διαθήκη	1Kor 11,25; 2Kor 3,6.
	Mk 14,25.
καιρός und ὁ νῦν καιρός	Röm 3,26; 5,6; 8,18; 11,5; 13,11; 1Kor 4,5;
	7,5.29; 2Kor 6,2; 8,14; Gal 4,10; 6,9f.; 1Thess 5,1.
	Mk 1,15; 10,30; 11,13³⁰; 12,2³¹; 13,33.
ἤμελλον, τὸ μέλλον,	Röm 5,14; 8,18.38; 1Kor 3,22; 1Thess 3,4.
τὰ μέλλοντα	Mk 10,32; 13,4.
νέος³²	1Kor 5,7³³.
	Mk 2,22³⁴; 10,20.
νῦν³⁵	Röm 5.9.11; 6,21; 8,22; 13,11; 2Kor 5,16; 6,2;
	Gal 2,20; 3,3; 4,9.25.29; Phil 1,5.20. Phlm 9.
	Mk 13,19.
(ὁ νῦν καιρός s. o. unter καιρός)	
παρουσία κυρίου	1Thess 2,19; 3,13; 4,15; 5,23; 1Kor 15,23.
	Mkev: fehlt.
πληροῦν³⁶	Paulus: fehlt.
	Mk 1,15³⁷; 14,49; [15,28].
πλήρωμα τοῦ χρόνου	Gal 4,4.
	Mkev: fehlt.
τέλος³⁸	Röm 10,4; 1Kor 10,11; 15,24; 1Thess 2,16.
	Mk 13,7.13.
χρόνος	Röm 7,1; 1Kor 7,39; 16,7; Gal 4,1.4; 1Thess 5,1.
	Mk 2,19; 9,21.
ὥρα (und ἐκείνη ὥρα)	Röm 13,11; 1Kor 4,11; 15,30; 2Kor 7,8; Gal 2,5;
	1Thess 2,17; Phlm 15.
	Mk 6,35; 11,11;13,11.32; 14,35.37.41; 15,25.33 f.

Paulus und Markus haben ein reiches temporales Vokabular. Einerseits verwenden sie die geläufigen griechischen Lexeme wie χρόνος, καιρός und αἰών durchaus in einem unspezifischen Alltagssinn, andererseits legen sie geläufigen temporalen Lexemen wie Tag, Stunde, Jahr, kommen, nahesein, bevorstehen, eintreffen, Jetzt

---

30 Im bildlichen Zusammenhang.
31 Im bildlichen Zusammenhang.
32 Im temporalen Sinn.
33 Im bildlichen Zusammenhang.
34 Im bildlichen Zusammenhang.
35 Auswahl von Belegen im eindeutig temporalen, nicht logischen und sachlich qualifizierten Sinn. Uneindeutige Stellen wie Röm 8,1 oder 1Kor 13,13; 15,20 können hier nicht diskutiert werden. Auch Belege, die einfach die ‚Gegenwart' bezeichnen, sind nicht eigens aufgeführt (z. B. Gal 1,23; 4,25; 1Thess 3,8 oder Mk 15,32).
36 Im Sinne von zeitlicher Erfüllung.
37 Keine synoptische Parallele.
38 Im temporalen Sinn. Belege wie Röm 10,4 sind temporal und sachlich zugleich.

und Dann, Anfang und Ende, und anderen Temporalbestimmungen oft spezifische Bedeutungen bei, die mehrheitlich apokalyptischen Zeitvorstellungen zugehören. Χρόνος, die Zeit, und καιρός, der Zeitpunkt, werden schon seit den Vorsokratikern semantisch unterschieden[39]. Bei Paulus und Markus spielt weniger χρόνος als vielmehr καιρός eine wichtige Rolle[40], teils christologisch akzentuiert (Röm 3,26; Mk 1,15[41]), teils zur Bezeichnung der Heilszeit selbst gesetzt (2Kor 6,2). Καιρός kann auch zusammen mit ἡμέρα (κυρίου), παρουσία (κυρίου) und ὥρα (ἐκείνη) sowie dem temporalen Gebrauch des Verbums ἔρχεσθαι bzw. μέλλειν im apokalyptischen Zusammenhang verwendet werden und meint dann den Zeitpunkt bzw. Moment des Einbrechens der Endereignisse und der Ankunft des Kyrios. Ἐγγύς[42] wird in Mk 13,28f. sowie in Röm 13,11 und Phil 4,5 zur Bezeichnung der eschatologischen Naherwartung gesetzt, ebenso ἔσχατος dreimal in 1Kor 15 im Zusammenhang mit dem zukünftige Ende. Τέλος korrespondiert ἀρχή, dem Schöpfungsbeginn, und wird vor allem in Mk 13 im strikt eschatologischen Sinne gebraucht: das Ende des Kosmos. Den positiven Aspekt des Endes bezeichnen die πληρο-Verbindungen. Die zahlreichen αἰών-Verbindungen werden weniger zur Bezeichnung der atemporalen Ewigkeit verwendet[43], sondern gelten häufiger der zugleich kosmisch und temporal vorgestellten Dualität der jetzigen und der kommenden Weltepoche von Schöpfung und Neuschöpfung, gegenwärtigem und zukünftigem αἰών, die ebenfalls aus der apokalyptischen Literatur bekannt ist. Νῦν als Zeitangabe[44] wird besonders von Paulus im Zusammenhang seiner eigenen Existenz gesetzt:

> Ich lebe, aber nicht ich, es lebt aber in mir Christus. Was ich jetzt (νῦν) im Fleisch lebe, lebe ich im Glauben an den Sohn Gottes (Gal 2,20).

---

39 H. Westermann weist in seinem Artikel Zeitkonzeptionen, in: DNP 12/2 (2002), 709–717, besonders auf die Semantik hin, die schon bei den Vorsokratikern ausdifferenziert ist (710): „Auf Aristoteles weisen verschiedene Aspekte voraus, so die Unterscheidung zw[ischen] χρόνος (chrónos) als Zeit*dauer* und καιρός (kairós) als günstigem Zeitpunkt". „Für die aristotelische Z[eitkonzeption] ist das Verhältnis von Zeitdauer (chrónos) und Zeitpunkt (ta nyn)" zentral. Dies Verhältnis bildet den Spannungsbogen des aristotelischen Zeitverständnisses (712). Die Stoa spricht nur der Gegenwart, nicht der Vergangenheit und Zukunft reale Existenz zu. Bei Paulus ist der Unterschied nicht immer deutlich: vgl. 1Thess 5,1.
40 So schon in Septuaginta, vgl. G. Delling, Zeitverständnis, Tabelle S. 50f.
41 Codex D setzt den Plural und nähert sich sachlich damit Gal 4,4.
42 Vgl. Offb 1,3: ὁ γὰρ καιρὸς ἐγγύς. Hier liegt apokalyptische Sprache vor. Die Nähe zu Paulus und zum Mkev ist deutlich.
43 So aber vor allem in den formelhaften Wendungen εἰς τὸν αἰῶνα u. ä.
44 Substantiviert als ‚Gegenwart' Mk 13,19.

Die verschiedenen Lexeme für das Neue (καινότης bzw. καινός und νέος) können ebenfalls in temporalen Zusammenhängen verwendet werden und entweder auf die neu qualifizierte Gegenwart oder auf die eschatologische Zukunft bezogen sein. Die Dynamik der ‚letzten Zeit' wird nicht nur durch die Verben ἐγγίζειν, ἔρχεσθαι und μέλλειν, sondern auch durch Temporalbestimmungen wie ἐγγύς und ἤδη ausgedrückt. Zusammengefasst: die temporalen Bestimmungen werden vielfach theologisch aufgeladen, sei es im Zusammenhang der Schöpfung, der Jetztzeit oder der Zukunft. Die zukunftsbezogenen Bestimmungen sind häufig apokalyptisch gefärbt.

3 Texte zur Zeit

Tabelle (2) Paulus- und Markustexte, die zur Entwicklung von Zeitkonzepten beitragen

1Thess[45] 4,13 – 5,11	Endzeitszenario.
Gal 1,13 – 2,13	Autobiographischer Rückblick.
Gal 3,6 – 4,5	Christologisch zentrierte Heilsgeschichte von Abraham bis zur Gegenwart der Briefadressaten.
Gal 4,4f.	*Christologische Zeitaussage*[46].
1Kor 2,7 – 9	Gottes geheime Geschichte mit den Menschen.
1Kor 3,13 – 15	Endzeitszenario: Gerichtsperspektive.
1Kor 4,4f.	Endzeitszenario: Gerichtsperspektive.
1Kor 6,2f.	Endzeitszenario: Gerichtsperspektive.
1Kor 7,29 – 31	*Zeitansage* (καιρός), verbunden mit einer Ausführung über „diesen Kosmos (κόσμος)".
1Kor 10,1 – 13 (bes. V. 11)	Geschichte Israels aus gegenwärtiger christologischer Perspektive (typologisch) und *gegenwärtige Zeitaussage*.
1Kor 11,23 – 26	Verweis auf Jesu Einsetzung des Herrenmahles.
1Kor 13,8 – 13	Endzeitszenario.
1Kor 15,1 – 8	Verweis auf Jesu Tod, seine Auferstehung und die Zeugen.
1Kor 15,20 – 28	Endzeitszenario.
1Kor 15,35 – 49	Adam-Christus-Epochen.
1Kor 15,51 – 55	Endzeitszenario.
2Kor 3,4 – 18	Rückblick auf Mose aus gegenwärtiger christologischer Perspektive (antithetisch: alt V. 14 *versus* Geist V. 17).
2Kor 4,18	*Zeitaussage* (πρόσκαιρα *versus* αἰώνια).
2Kor 5,1 – 10	Endzeitszenario. Gerichtsperspektive in V.10.
2Kor 5,17	*Zeitansage* (antithetisch: alt *versus* neu).

---

[45] Die Tabelle beansprucht keine Vollständigkeit. Zusammen mit Tabelle (1) stellt sie aber die Basis für die folgenden Ausführungen dar.
[46] Die Zeitaussagen im engeren Sinn sind kursiv gesetzt.

2Kor 6,2	*Zeitansage* (νῦν καιρὸς εὐπρόσδεκτος).
2Kor 11,23–31	Autobiographischer Rückblick (1).
2Kor 12,1–10	Autobiographischer Rückblick (2).
Röm 1,2	Rückblick auf die Propheten.
Röm 1,20	Rückblick auf die Schöpfung.
Röm 3,26	Gegenüberstellung der beiden Zeitepochen des Verhaltens Gottes gegenüber den Menschen (ἀνοχή und ὁ νῦν καιρός).
Röm 4	Rückblick auf Abraham aus der gegenwärtigen Perspektive (δι' ἡμᾶς).
Röm 5,12–21	Rückblick auf Adam und Mose aus der gegenwärtigen Perspektive.
Röm 6	*Zeitansage.*
Röm 7,7–11	Adamitische Biographie.
Röm 8,3	Rückblick auf Gottes Heilshandeln in Jesus Christus.
Röm 8,18–25	Endzeitszenario.
Röm 8,38	Ansage der Entmächtigung der Zeit (ἐνεστῶτα οὔτε μέλλοντα).
Röm 9,6–13	Rückblick auf Gottes Ratschluss in der Vätergeschichte (V. 11 πρόθεσις).
Röm 11,1–5	Rückblick auf die Geschichte Israels aus der gegenwärtigen Perspektive (ἐν τῷ νῦν καιρῷ).
Röm 11,25f.	Heilsgeschichtliches Gesamtkonzept für die Menschheit aus Juden und Nichtjuden.
Röm 13,11f.	*Zeitansage* (καιρός, ὥρα ἤδη, νῦν, ἐγγύς).
Röm 14,10–12	Endzeitszenario: Gerichtsperspektive.
Phil 3,12–14	Persönliche Existenz zwischen Schon und Noch nicht.
Phil 4,5	*Zeitansage* (ὁ κύριος ἐγγύς).
Mk[47] 1,15	*Zeitansage:* Erfüllung der Zeit als Inhalt der Evangeliumsbotschaft.
Mk 2,18–22	Metaphorische Rede Jesu über Alt und Neu mit aktueller Zeitansage (ὁ νύμφιος μετ' αὐτῶν).
Mk 13,9–27	Gemeindebezogenes und allgemeines Endzeitszenario.
Mk 13,30–33	*Zeitansage:* οὐκ οἴδατε γὰρ πότε ὁ καιρός ἐστιν.
Mk 14,25.28.62	Persönliche Endzeit- und Zukunftsaussagen Jesu.

---

47 Das narrative Zeitkonzept unterliegt dem gesamten Text. Die entsprechenden Lexeme werden in dieser Tabelle nicht eigens berücksichtigt.

4 Zeitkonzepte

4.1 Paulus

Die Zusammenstellung der Texte zeigt, dass sich in den Briefen des Paulus zahlreiche, teilweise sehr pointiert formulierte explizite Zeit*ansagen* und *-aussagen* finden[48]. Paulus hat eine eigene, qualifizierte Terminologie, die sich stellenweise mit stoischem und jüdisch-religiösem Sprachgebrauch deckt, sich aber als Ganze am besten unabhängig von theologischen und philosophischen Begriffen mit einer thematischen Ordnung erschließen lässt, die den Texten entnommen wird und eigenen Kriterien des Paulus folgt.

Paulus unterscheidet zwischen Vergangenheit einerseits, Gegenwärtigem und Zukünftigem andererseits[49]. Die Vergangenheit kann er einfach als Vergangenes verstehen[50], im Rahmen der typologischen Interpretation der Geschichte Israels erscheint sie aber auch als Vorläufer der Gegenwart, unter Umständen rückt er sie ganz nahe an die Gegenwart heran[51]. Die Zukunft ist für Paulus hauptsächlich Endzeit. Auch hier ist die Nähe zur Gegenwart so evident, dass sich die Gegenwart von vornherein als Zentrum im Verhältnis zu den beiden anderen zeitlichen Dimensionen darstellt. Die Zukunft tritt gerade im 1. Korintherbrief deutlich von der Gerichtsperspektive her in den Blick[52]. Daneben ist Paulus im 1. Korintherbrief mit Fragen beschäftigt, die das zukünftige Schicksal der Christusgläubigen betreffen[53]. In Röm 8,18–30 verbindet er diese Thematik mit dem zukünftigen Schicksal der gesamten Schöpfung (κτίσις). Auf der anderen Seite weitet Paulus die zeitliche Perspektive rückwärts bis zur anfänglichen Schaffung des κόσμος aus: κτίσις bzw. κόσμος[54] sind nicht ewig und der Zeit entzogen, sondern Paulus denkt beide

---

48 1Kor 7,29–31; 2Kor 4,18; 5,17; 6,2; Röm 6; 8,31–39; 13,11f.; Phil 3,12–14; 4,5.
49 Vgl. dazu die Einteilung der Zeit in Röm 8,38: „Gegenwärtiges oder Zukünftiges".
50 2Kor 5,17.
51 1Kor 10,6. In Röm 5,16 reicht diese Perspektive bis in die Schöpfung zurück und bindet diese gleichzeitig an die Christus-Gegenwart. Vgl. dazu jetzt J.D. Worthington, Creation in Paul and Philo. The Beginning and Before (WUNT 2.R. 317), Tübingen 2011.
52 1 Thess 4,13–5,11; 1Kor 3,13–15; 4,4f.; 6,2f.; 2Kor 5,10; Röm 14,11f.
53 1 Kor 13,8–12; 15,35–49. 51–55; 2Kor 5,1–10.
54 Das schwierige Verhältnis von κόσμος und κτίσις kann hier nicht untersucht werden. Vgl. dazu O. Wischmeyer, Kosmos und Kosmologie bei Paulus, in: P. Gemeinhardt/A. Zgoll (Hgg.), Weltkonstruktionen. Religiöse Weltdeutung zwischen Chaos und Kosmos vom Alten Orient bis zum Islam (ORA 5), Tübingen 2010, 87–102; weiter den Sammelband Cosmology and New Testament Theology, ed. by J.T. Pennington/S.M. McDonough (LNTS 355), London/New York 2008, darin besonders die Beiträge von M.F. Bird, Tearing the Heavens and Shaking the Heavenlies: Mark's Cosmology in its Apocalyptic Context, 45–59, und J. White, Paul's Cosmology:

Größen zeitlich, epochengegliedert und prozesshaft. Auch κτίσις und κόσμος haben Vergangenheit, Gegenwart und Zukunft im Sinne einer Entstehungs-, Vergänglichkeits- und Erlösungsgeschichte: Röm 1,20 und 8,18–22[55].

Diese weiteste zeitliche Perspektive, die von der Schöpfung und von Gottes Ratschluss vor der Entstehung der Zeit[56] bis zur endgültigen zukünftigen Einheit Gottes mit sich selbst (1Kor 15,28) reicht, kann Paulus unterschiedlich darstellen. Eine *erste* Möglichkeit ist die Abfolge zweier Schöpfungen: der ersten Schöpfung, deren Prototyp der erste Adam ist, und der zweiten, neuen Schöpfung, die ihren Anfang bereits in dem letzten Adam, Christus, genommen hat[57], deren Erfüllung aber noch aussteht. Von hieraus ergibt sich das zeitliche Schema einer Vergangenheit, die bis zum Beginn der Schöpfung zurück- und bis zu ihrem zukünftigen Ende vorreicht, wobei die Gegenwart in diese Zukunft hinein offen oder bereits deren Anfang ist. Die zwei Schöpfungen werden durch ihre ersten Geschöpfe, Adam und Christus, gekennzeichnet. Eine *zweite*, streng theo-logisch zentrierte Möglichkeit der Rückbeziehung auf die Vergangenheit im Sinne einer Epoche wählt Paulus in Röm 3,25 f., wenn er von der ἀνοχὴ θεοῦ als von einem Verhalten Gottes in der Vergangenheit spricht, die von der Jetztzeit (ὁ νῦν καιρός) abgelöst worden ist: der Zeit, die durch den Aufweis von Gottes Gerechtigkeit gekennzeichnet ist[58]. Hier sind zwei Epochen vorgestellt: eine von der Schöpfung bis zu Jesu Tod, d. h. bis in die Gegenwart des Apostels, die zweite eröffnet sich seit Christi Tod und der Gegenwart des Apostels, so dass dieser am Schnittpunkt beider Epochen und am Beginn der neuen Epoche lebt. Paulus spricht in diesem Zusammenhang nicht von den zwei Äonen[59], wie er überhaupt αἰών eher allgemein als „Zeit" verwendet, so besonders in der Zeitansage in 1Kor 10,11:

> Dies widerfuhr jenen paradigmatisch, es ist aber uns zur Weisung aufgeschrieben, uns, auf die das Ende der Zeiten (τὰ τέλη τῶν αἰώνων) gekommen ist.

The Witness of Romans, 1 and 2 Corinthians, and Galatians, 90–106. Vgl. weiter die gründliche neue Untersuchung von T.R. Jackson, New Creation in Paul's Letters (WUNT 2.R. 272), Tübingen 2010. Jacksons Ergebnis ist für die vorliegende Untersuchung über die Zeit bei Paulus bedeutungsvoll: „Romans 8 makes abundantly clear that Paul's cosmology and anthropology are inextricably linked" (167). Zu Philon: Ch.A. Anderson, Philo of Alexandria's Views of the Physical World (WUNT 2.R. 309), Tübingen 2011.

55 Hier wird besonders deutlich, dass die enge Verbindung zwischen Zeit und Kosmologie, die die griechische Philosophie prägt, in überarbeiteter Form auch bei Paulus besteht.
56 1Kor 2,7 (πρὸ τῶν αἰώνων).
57 Röm 5,14; 1Kor 15,22.45.
58 Zu den unterschiedlichen Möglichkeiten, heilsgeschichtliche Epochen zu bilden, vgl. genauer F. Avemarie, Heilsgeschichte, 363 f. (mit Lit.). Avemarie spricht von „konzise(n) Strukturbildungen statt umfassende(r) Synthese" (363).
59 So z. B. Mt 12,32.

Grundsätzlich gilt für die drei Erscheinungsformen der Zeit dasselbe: Paulus versteht die Zeiträume von Vergangenheit, Gegenwart und Zukunft von Gottes Handeln an der Welt und an den Menschen her. Zeit ist nicht einfach leerer Zeitraum, der in irgendeiner Weise gefüllt werden kann, sondern kosmologisch und anthropologisch bereits qualifizierter Raum und Bezugsgröße, Raum der Unfreiheit auf der einen und der Errettung auf der anderen Seite. Zeit ist damit stets theo-logisch qualifiziert, oder anders gesagt: Zeit ist immer Gottes Zeit mit den Menschen und mit der Schöpfung. Das gilt für Vergangenheit, Gegenwart und Zukunft, besonders aber, wie schon gesagt, für die Gegenwart, die Paulus als eigene, nach vorn offene Zeitspanne versteht und in Röm 8,24 f.[60] als die Zeit der Geistbegabung und der Hoffnung charakterisiert. Der νῦν καιρός ist die innere Achse, um die sich seine zahlreichen Aussagen zur Zeit drehen. Mit dem Kommen Jesu (Gal 4,4) hat die Heilszeit begonnen, die Paulus als christologische Zeitepoche versteht. Diese Epoche ist in höherem Maße als die Vergangenheit dynamisch vorgestellt. Sie eilt auf die Zukunft und letztlich auf ihr Ende hin. Zweimal spricht Paulus diesen Umstand in einer existentiellen Engführung aus. Im Römerbrief bezieht er die Gemeinde ein:

> Und dies tut, weil ihr den Zeitpunkt kennt, dass schon für euch die Stunde da ist, vom Schlaf aufzustehen, denn jetzt ist unsere Rettung näher als (zu dem Zeitpunkt), als wir gläubig wurden (Röm 13,11).

Im Philipperbrief schreibt er aus seiner persönlichen autobiographischen Perspektive:

> Nicht dass ich es schon ergriffen hätte oder schon vollendet wäre, ich jage ihm aber nach, ob ich es ergreifen könnte, weil ich auch von Christus Jesus ergriffen bin. Brüder, ich schätze mich selbst nicht so ein, dass ich (es) ergriffen hätte. Eins aber (sage ich): Das Rückwärtige lasse ich hinter mir, strecke mich aber aus (ἐπεκτεινόμενος[61]) nach dem vor mir (Phil 3,12).

Von dieser Zukunft kann Paulus in apokalyptischen Bildern sprechen, die sich aber nie verselbständigen, da Christus der Herr der Endereignisse ist. Die christologische Zeit und die apokalyptischen Bilder, die ebenfalls christologisch interpretiert sind, bleiben Dimensionen der Zeit Gottes zwischen der Schöpfung und ihrem Ende, wenn „auch der Sohn dem unterworfen sein wird, der ihm das All unterworfen hat, damit Gott alles in allem sei" (1Kor 15,28). Gottes Überzeitlichkeit

---

60 Vgl. Röm 8,19; 1Kor 1,7; Gal 5,5; Phil 3,20.
61 Hap.leg. im NT.

umschließt die Zeit. Die Zeit ist der Raum des Handelns Gottes an der Schöpfung und der Menschheit in ihrer Heillosigkeit und ihrer Errettung durch Jesus Christus.

Im Rahmen dieser allgemeinen und umfassenden theologisch-christologischen Zeitkonzeption mit ihren beiden Epochen: der Epoche der Nachsicht Gottes und der Epoche des Heils oder des ersten und zweiten Adam, markiert Paulus drei zeitlich begrenzte Bereiche mit eigenem Gewicht. Den *ersten* Bereich stellt die Geschichte Israels dar – für Paulus als Juden stets Teil seiner Kultur und seines Weltverständnisses und selbstverständlicher Gegenstand des Stolzes (Röm 11,1): Die Israeliten haben die „Väter" (Röm 9,5). Diese Dimension der Zeit begegnet immer wieder im Römerbrief, bezogen auf die Propheten (1,2), auf Abraham (Röm 4; 9,6–13 und Gal 3) und auf Mose (Röm 5, 14 und 1Kor 10,2[62]; 2Kor 3,4–18). Paulus versteht diesen Bereich aber nicht als Entfaltung der Geschichte Israels, vor allem nicht seiner politischen Geschichte, die als solche auch keinen Eigenwert für ihn hat. Wenn er die Wüstenwanderung Israels typologisch auf „uns", d. h. auf die Christus-gläubigen Gemeinden deutet (1Kor 10,4), verengt sich die Geschichte Israels auf ihre Vorbildfunktion für die Christus-gläubigen Zeitgenossen des Paulus und verliert ihre historische Eigendimension. Paulus betrachtet Israels Geschichte aus der Perspektive der gegenwärtigen Heilszeit: ἐν τῷ νῦν καιρῷ (Röm 11,5). Genauer: sein Blick auf die Zeit der Geschichte Israels ist durch und durch theologisch-soteriologisch, weder historisch[63] noch politisch[64]. Und er vertraut vor allem darauf, dass Israel vor Gott eine Zukunft hat: καὶ οὕτως πᾶς Ἰσραὴλ σωθήσεται (Röm 11,26)[65].

Der *zweite* Bereich umfasst die Geschichte Jesu[66], der *dritte* Bereich seine eigene Biographie[67]. Beides gehört der aktuellen Zeitgeschichte des Paulus an. Paulus hat eine eigene Lebensgeschichte, auf die er in seinen Gemeindebriefen immer wieder zurückkommt. Und Jesus hat eine eigene Lebensgeschichte gehabt,

---

62 Vgl. 10,1–13 insgesamt.

63 Daher beschäftigt er sich auch nur mit Abraham und Mose, nicht aber mit den Königen Israels. Vgl. F. Avemarie, Heilsgeschichte, 363–365.

64 Der aktuelle politische Blick auf das Imperium Romanum, den wir bei Philon (*Legatio ad Gaium!*) und Josephus finden, fehlt in den Briefen des Paulus gänzlich. Das belastet alle Versuche, Paulus politisch zu interpretieren. Vgl. auch F. Avemarie, Heilsgeschichte, 363: „... spielt das politische Tagesgeschehen für sein Geschichtsverständnis keine Rolle".

65 Eine zeitnahe politische Vision für Israel kann ich nicht erkennen. Gal 4,24–31 scheint sie eher auszuschließen.

66 Besonders beachtenswert ist die zeitlich genau strukturierte Textpassage in 1Kor 15,1–7, vgl. dazu den Beitrag von M. Theobald im vorliegenden Band.

67 Gal 1,13–2,13; 2Kor 11,23–31 und 12,1–10. Röm 7,7–11 ist eine adamitische autobiographische Skizze, die die Verstrickung des Menschen vor Christus in die Welt von Tod, Sünde und Gesetz exemplifiziert. – Vgl. allgemein den Beitrag von E.-M. Becker im vorliegenden Band.

die Paulus in der Herrenmahlsparadosis (1Kor 11,23 – 26) und in der Paradosis von Jesu Tod, Auferstehung und den Erscheinungen, deren letzter Zeuge Paulus selbst ist (1Kor 15,1 – 8), rekapituliert, so dass in diesem zentralen Text beide Aspekte, die Geschichte des Paulus und die Geschichte Jesu eine enge Verbindung eingehen[68].

4.2 Das Markusevangelium

Anders als bei Paulus ist die Situation im Markusevangelium. Hier findet sich nur *ein* Text, der sich als allgemeine Aussage über Zeit lesen lässt: Mk 1,15. Jesus selbst proklamiert seine Gegenwart als „erfüllte Zeit (καιρός)". Mk 1,15 ist damit der zentrale Text für die Interpretation der Zeitkonzepte des Markusevangeliums. In Spannung dazu steht Jesu Warnung in 13,30 – 33: „Ihr wisst nicht, wann der Zeitpunkt (καιρός) des Beginns der Endereignisse kommt". Im Übrigen liegt das Zeitkonzept des Evangelisten in der Strukturierung der Erzählung. Die verschiedenen Zeitkonzepte des Markusevangeliums und ihr Verhältnis zueinander können erst nach der narrativen Analyse des Textes dargestellt werden.

(1) Das Markusevangelium ist ein literarisches, nicht-fiktionales Erzählwerk[69]. Als solches basiert es auf einem durchgehenden *narrativen Zeitkonzept*[70]. Erzählt wird die kurze Epoche des öffentlichen Wirkens Jesu aus Nazareth. Die Erzählung betrifft historische Personen[71] und ein historisches Geschehen[72]. Die erzählte Zeit ist der Zeitraum des öffentlichen Wirkens Jesu von Nazareth, eröffnet mit dem jüdischen Propheten Johannes dem Täufer und abgeschlossen mit Jesu Hinrich-

---

[68] Vgl. dazu den Beitrag von M. Theobald im vorliegenden Band.
[69] Darauf weist besonders D.S. du Toit hin: D.S. du Toit, Der abwesende Herr. Strategien im Markusevangelium zur Bewältigung der Abwesenheit des Auferstandenen (WMANT 111), Neukirchen-Vluyn 2006, 8 – 14. Du Toit arbeitet auch den historischen Anspruch des Markusevangeliums heraus: „Das Markusevangelium als Geschichtsdarstellung" (14 – 22). Damit ergänzen sich du Toits Ansatz und der gleichzeitige Ansatz von E.-M. Becker, Das Markus-Evangelium im Rahmen antiker Historiographie (WUNT 194), Tübingen 2006. Vgl. auch C. Breytenbach, Current Research on the Gospel according to Mark: A Report on Monographs Published from 2000 – 2009, in: Mark and Matthew I. Comparative Readings: Understanding the Earliest Gospels in their First-Century Settings, ed. by E.-M. Becker/A. Runesson (WUNT 271), Tübingen 2011, 13 – 32.
[70] Zum Erzählkonzept: D. Rhoads/J. Dewey/D. Michie, Mark as Story: An Introduction to the Narrative of a Gospel, Minneapolis 2nd edition 1999. Dazu jetzt: K.R. Iverson/Ch.W. Skinner (eds.), Mark as Story: Retrospect and Prospect (SBL.RBS 65), Atlanta 2011; darin besonders nützlich der forschungsgeschichtliche Überblick von Ch.W. Skinner, Telling the Story: The Appearance and Impact of *Mark as Story*, 1 – 16. – Im vorliegenden Beitrag geht es nicht um das narrative Konzept selbst, sondern um den Umgang mit Zeit in der Erzählung.
[71] Das trifft auch für Jesus selbst zu.
[72] Vgl. dazu den Beitrag von E.-M. Becker im vorliegenden Band.

tung unter dem römischen Präfekten Pontius Pilatus. Das Zeitkonzept der Erzählung ist das einer historischen Erzählung: linear[73], personenzentriert[74] und episodisch[75]. Dabei stehen Reden und Handeln der Hauptperson ganz im Vordergrund. Die Erzählung ist in kurze Erzählepisoden gegliedert, die häufig nur durch die Kopula καί miteinander verbunden sind. Zeit ist hier historische Zeit; wird aber nicht im Sinne der datierten Zeit, sondern als Ereigniszeit einer Person wahrgenommen[76]. Die Zeitangaben selbst sind unpräzise und erfüllen lediglich die Aufgabe, die Episoden der Erzählung zusammenzuhalten, indem sie ihnen eine temporale Richtung geben. Jesus wird mit der Wendung „Und es geschah in jenen Tagen" (Mk 1,9) eingeführt. Damit wird sein Wirken zeitlich ebenso direkt wie ausschließlich an das Auftreten des Täufers angeschlossen[77].

Jesu öffentliche Taten und Reden sind in ein integriertes Raum-Zeit-Schema eingebettet, das ihn von Galiläa nach Jerusalem führt und nicht mehr als ein Jahr zu umfassen scheint, ohne dass dies expliziert würde. Der Erzähler arbeitet mit Wendungen wie „und dann", „und sogleich", „und wiederum", „und es geschah", selten einmal mit Angaben zu Tagen[78], Tages-[79] oder Jahreszeiten[80] und Festen. Neben diesen temporalen Wendungen sind es die Bewegungsverben wie „er ging", „sie kamen", „er ging weg", „sie fuhren im Boot", die zusammen mit bestimmten[81]

---

73 Das gilt trotz der Vor- und Rückblicke.
74 Zu dem Begriff vgl. E.-M. Becker, Das Markusevangelium, 191–194 u.ö.
75 Dabei spielt es keine Rolle, ob damit die Vorgänge im Leben Jesu von Nazareth im Einzelnen historisch richtig abgebildet sind. Zum Episodenstil und zum Erzählstil des Markusevangeliums vgl. nach wie vor C. Breytenbach, Das Markusevangelium als episodische Erzählung. Mit Überlegungen zum „Aufbau" des zweiten Evangeliums, in: F. Hahn (Hg.), Der Erzähler des Evangeliums: methodische Neuansätze in der Markusforschung (SBS 118/119), Stuttgart 1985, 137–169. C. Breytenbach nahm auf die 1. Auflage von Rhoads/Dewey/Michie (s.o. Anm. 69) Bezug: D. Rhoads/D. Michie, Mark as Story. An Introduction to the Narrative of a Gospel, Philadelphia 1982. Vgl. auch: Mark and Matthew: New Approaches in Biblical Studies, ed. by J.C. Anderson/St.D. Moore, Minneapolis 2nd ed. 2008.
76 Zu dem Begriff ‚Ereigniszeit' vgl. R. Levine, Eine Landkarte der Zeit, München 1999, 122–144.
77 Zu der Rückbindung der Jesusgeschichte an die Propheten Israels in Mk 1,1–4 vgl. O. Wischmeyer, Rom 1:1–7 and Mark 1:1–3 in Comparison. Two Opening Texts at the Beginning of Early Christian Literature, in: Mark and Paul. Comparative Essays Part II: For and Against Pauline Influence on Mark, eds. E.-M. Becker/T. Engberg-Pedersen/ M. Müller (BZNW 199), Berlin/Boston 2014, 121–146. Mk 1,14 ist neben der Hinrichtung unter Pontius Pilatus die wichtigste historische Datierung des gesamten Narrativs: Jesus beginnt seine öffentliche Wirksamkeit, „nachdem Johannes überantwortet worden war".
78 Z.B. 2,23.
79 Z.B. 1,32.35.
80 Z.B. 11,13.
81 Es werden bestimmte Orte genannt wie Kapernaum etc.

oder topischen[82] wechselnden Ortsangaben die Geschichte Jesu und seiner Begleitung in ihrer zeitlichen Erstreckung vorantreiben. Der Erzähler erzeugt den Eindruck einer dauernden zeitlichen Dynamik, die sachlich und topographisch zielgerichtet auf den Tod Jesu in Jerusalem hinführt. Nirgends außer in Jerusalem verweilt die Erzählung[83].

Die Dynamik der Erzählung nimmt im letzten Drittel des Evangeliums zu. Beginnend mit der neuen Ortsangabe in 10,1[84], findet in den Kapiteln 11–14 stufenweise eine Verdichtung des Narrativs statt, indem der Zeitraum der Erzählung stark komprimiert wird und sich gleichzeitig die personenbezogenen, topographischen und zeitlichen Angaben häufen. In Kap. 11–13 herrscht noch der episodische „und er tat"-„und er sagte"-Stil vor. Allerdings sind schon in diesem Erzählabschnitt die topographischen Angaben viel dichter und präziser, und durch den knappen „und"-Stil wird ein gewisser schneller Fluss der Episoden angedeutet. Aber erst in 14,1 beginnt die eigentliche zusammenhängende Erzählung der letzten Tage Jesu, die genaue Zeit- und Ortsangaben mit präzisen Personenangaben kombiniert[85]. Das Erzählkonzept geht bis zum Schluss durchgehend linear vor. Es beruht auf der Abfolge von einzelnen Vorgängen in der jeweiligen Gegenwart, blickt manchmal in die Vergangenheit zurück[86], manchmal in die Zukunft voraus[87] und erzählt die Abläufe des letzten Lebensjahres Jesu der Reihe nach in kurzen Episoden. Auch die Erscheinung des Jünglings ist noch Teil dieses Jesus-zentrierten Erzählkonzepts. Das zeigt sich in Mk 16,8: Die Erzählung schließt mit der „Furcht" der Frauen und endet im Schweigen[88]. Soweit wir wissen, war der Verfasser des Markusevangeliums der Erste, der aus den verschiedenen Spruch- und Erzähltraditionen, die die Jesusanhänger überlieferten, weitergaben

---

82 Z.B. Haus, See, Synagoge, Berg.
83 So beanspruchen z.B. die Gleichnisreden Jesu am See in Kap. 4 ausdrücklich nicht mehr als einen Tag (4,35).
84 Das Weg-Motiv (10,1) ist eng mit dem Zeitmotiv verbunden: 10,32.
85 Wie viel hier erzählende Tradition aus der sog. synoptischen Passionsgeschichte ist und wie viel auf den Verfasser des Markusevangeliums zurückgeht, kann hier unerörtert bleiben. Vgl. den Beitrag von M. Theobald im vorliegenden Band (bes. zu den Fragen des Zeitpunktes des letzten Mahles).
86 So in Mk 6,17–29. Dieser Rückblick ist offensichtlich durch 6,16 ausgelöst. Zu den Rück- und Zukunftsverweisen vgl. C. Breytenbach, Das Markusevangelium als episodische Erzählung, 126–132.
87 Zu den Vorwegnahmen der Zukunft in Worten Jesu vgl. unten.
88 Damit wird der personenzentriert-historisch-biographische Rahmen nicht überschritten. Zu den Deutungen des Markusschlusses vgl. A. Yarbro Collins, Mark. A Commentary, Minneapolis 2007, 797–801.

und ausweiteten, ein Gesamtnarrativ machte: die Jesus-Erzählung[89]. Das narrative Konzept des Evangelisten gliedert die Jesus-Erzählung episodisch zeitlich-linear.

(2) Unterstützung, Kohärenz und Sinngebung zugleich erhält das narrative Konzept durch die Vorhersagen und frühen erzählend-kommentierenden Hinweise auf die späteren Ereignisse. Eckpunkte dieser Kommentierung des narrativen Zeitkonzepts sind einerseits Mk 3,6, andererseits die drei Leidensweissagungen in 8,31; 9,31; 10,33 f. Damit gibt Markus seiner Jesus-Erzählung eine eigene interpretierende Zeitkonzeption, die in seinem Bekenntnis zu Jesus, dem Messias, dem Sohn Gottes (Mk 1,1), also in seiner Christologie[90], begründet ist. Ich nenne sie daher *christologische Zeitkonzeption*. Diese zweite Konzeption von Zeit ist aufs Engste mit dem Jesus-Narrativ verbunden, denn sie hat ihren Mittelpunkt im Leben und Sterben Jesu. Das Narrativ von Leben und Sterben Jesu wird durch eine übergeordnete Bestimmtheit, das δεῖ γενέσθαι, zusammengehalten, konzentriert[91] und mit Sinn erfüllt. Die Jesus-Erzählung mit ihren Episoden wird so als ganze zum εὐαγγέλιον (besonders 14,3–9).

In diesem zweiten Konzept lassen sich ein innerer und ein äußerer Zeitrahmen unterscheiden. Der innere Rahmen ist ganz an die Erzählung von Jesu Todesschicksal gebunden und begegnet das erste Mal in 3,6. Von da an bewegt sich für die Leser bzw. Hörer das gesamte Narrativ auf Jesu Tod zu. In den drei Leidensankündigungen[92] wird Jesus dann selbst zum prophetischen Interpreten seines Todesschicksals. Zugleich wird schon in den Leidensweissagungen dieser innere Rahmen durch den Hinweis auf die Auferstehung aufgebrochen. Das εὐαγγέλιον selbst kommt ins Spiel. Damit sind wir beim äußeren, weiteren Rahmen, der sich von 1,1 bis zu 14,9 und 16,6 spannt. Der Evangelist macht mit 1,1 das εὐαγγέλιον thematisch zum Horizont der folgenden Jesus-Erzählung. Das Syntagma ἀρχὴ τοῦ εὐαγγελίου hat zugleich eine temporale, eine zitierende und eine christologische Konnotation. Zunächst leitet 1,1 die Jesus-Erzählung ein und ist dem narrativ-temporalen Konzept zugeordnet. Der Verfasser nimmt Kontakt mit der Hörer- bzw. Leserschaft auf und eröffnet die Erzählung. Andererseits spielt der Verfasser auf Gen 1 und auf Hos 1,2 an und öffnet damit die Erzählung von Beginn an für die dem historischen Narrativ unterliegende jüdische prophetische Geschichts- und Zeitdeutung. Mit Mk 1,1–3 verweist der Verfasser aber nicht so sehr auf die Geschichte

---

[89] Er konnte dabei auf die Passionserzählung zurückgreifen. Vgl. die Einführung bei A. Collins, Mark, 620–639.
[90] Vgl. dazu den Beitrag von U. Schnelle im vorliegenden Band.
[91] Ein weiteres literarisches Mittel zur Konzentration der episodischen Jesus-Erzählung stellen die Summarien dar. Vgl. dazu die Analyse von E.-M. Becker, Die markinischen Summarien – ein literarischer und theologischer Schlüssel zu Mk 1–6, in: NTS 56 (2010), 452–474.
[92] Mk 8,31; 9,31; 10,33 f.

Gottes mit Israel[93], sondern setzt diese sogleich zur Unterstützung seiner grundlegenden These ein, die das historische Narrativ trägt: Die Erzählung von Jesu Wirken und Sterben ist nicht die Biographie eines leidenden Propheten oder eines scheiternden jüdischen Messiasprätendenten[94], sondern εὐαγγέλιον Ἰησοῦ Χριστοῦ.

Das gilt zunächst für die einzelnen Episoden von Jesu Wirken, die auf seinen Tod und seine Auferstehung ausgerichtet sind[95]. So sagt Jesus über die Frau, die ihn salbt:

> Sie hat meinen Leib im voraus gesalbt für mein Begräbnis. Wahrlich, ich sage euch, wo auch immer das εὐαγγέλιον gepredigt wird in aller Welt, da wird man auch das sagen zu ihrem Gedächtnis, was sie getan hat (Mk 14,9)[96].

Es gilt weiter über Jesu Tod hinaus, wie die Erzählung von Jesu letztem Mahl mit den Jüngern deutlich macht:

> Wahrlich ich sage euch, dass ich nicht mehr trinken werde von dem Gewächs des Weinstocks bis zu jenem Tag, an dem ich aufs Neue (καινόν) davon trinke im Reich Gottes (Mk 14,25).

Es gilt aber nach Mk 1,1 nicht nur für die genannten Texte, sondern für die gesamte Jesuserzählung, d. h. für die Gesamtheit von Jesu Taten und Worten in ihrem Verlauf, wie das Markusevangelium sie berichtet, da *alle* Worte und Taten Jesu unter seinem Todesschicksal stehen. Dadurch wird die Zeit des öffentlichen Wirkens Jesu von Anfang an zur Heilszeit. Die historische Zeit des Narrativs und die christologische Zeitdeutung fallen sachlich zusammen:

> Nachdem Johannes überantwortet war, kam Jesus nach Galiläa, verkündete das εὐαγγέλιον θεοῦ und sprach: Erfüllt ist der καιρός, und herbeigekommen ist die Gottesherrschaft. Kehrt um und glaubt dem εὐαγγέλιον (Mk 1,14f.).

Das christologische Zeitkonzept deutet die Jesus-Geschichte bzw. ihre Erzählung zentripetal. Das sich zeitlich vom Auftreten Johannes des Täufers bis zu Jesu Grab

---

[93] So die Genealogien im Matthäus- und Lukasevangelium.
[94] Dies wären Möglichkeiten einer biographisch gerichteten antiken Erzählung. Die Erzählung vom Tod Johannes des Täufers gehört in diesen Zusammenhang. Vgl. J.W. van Henten/F. Avemarie, Martyrdom and Noble Death: Selected Texts from Greco-Roman, Jewish and Christian Antiquity, London 2002.
[95] Vgl. 8,35; 10,29; 13,10. Hier ist der Hinweis auf die Verkündigung des Evangeliums jeweils mit Jesu Todesschicksal verbunden.
[96] Nicht zu erklären ist, dass gerade diese Frau namenlos bleibt (im Johannesevangelium ‚korrigiert': 12,13: Maria aus Bethanien).

erstreckende Narrativ stellt sich von hier aus als Einheit dar, zeitlich als καιρός beschrieben, theologisch im εὐαγγέλιον konzentriert[97].

(3) Nun arbeiten beide Entwürfe, das narrative und das christologische Konzept, mit *temporalen Vorstellungen, die besonders in der frühjüdischen Apokalyptik ausgearbeitet wurden*. Die Alt-Neu-Konfrontation (1,27; 2,18 – 22; 14,25), die Naherwartung (9,1; 13,4.24 – 37[98]; 14,25.62; 16,7), die detaillierte Ansage der „letzten Ereignisse" (Kapitel 13), die Periodisierung der Weltzeit in Äonen (9,11 – 13[99]; 10,30), die Abfolge von gegenwärtiger und zukünftiger Welt entstammen dem apokalyptischen Zeitverständnis. Johannes der Täufer kann als Elias redivivus bezeichnet werden[100], und Jesus spricht vom kommenden Menschensohn[101]. Von der Schöpfung des Kosmos bis zum Weltende (13,19) erstreckt sich Gottes Handeln[102], in dem Jesus die entscheidende Rolle hat. Jesus selbst ist es, der sein eigenes Schicksal und die nahen Endereignisse ansagt[103], und er wird es sein, der am Ende dieser Ereignisse „mit großer Kraft und Herrlichkeit" kommen wird (13,26). Der Evangelist zeichnet Jesus als Träger besonderen apokalyptischen Wissens: Kapitel 13 ist die längste zusammenhängende Rede Jesu im Markusevangelium. Sie steht unter der apokalyptischen Schlüsselfrage der Jünger:

> Wann wird das geschehen, und was wird das Zeichen sein, wenn das alles vollendet werden soll? (Mk 13,4)

---

97 Vgl. A. Lindemanns Beitrag im vorliegenden Band, bes. Anm. 179.
98 Wichtig 13,4 die typische apokalyptische Frage nach dem „Wann", in 13,20 das „Verkürzen" der Zeit der Drangsale, in 13,24 die Zeitangabe „in jenen Tagen" und V. 29 das Stichwort ἐγγύς (dazu gehört schon der καιρός in 11,13), außerdem das „Kommen" (vgl. auch 9,11 f. von Elia und dem Menschensohn und 14,62 von dem Menschensohn) und die Gliederung der Plagen. – Zu Kap. 3 vgl. E.E. Shively, Apocalyptic Imagination in the Gospel of Mark: The Literary and Theological Role of Mark 3:22 – 30 (BZNW 189), Berlin/Boston 2012, 20 – 38.
99 Vgl. dazu A. Collins, Mark, 483.
100 9,11 – 13. Dazu A. Collins, Mark, 428 – 432.
101 Mk 8,38; 13,26; 14,62. Mk 8,31; 9,9: der auferstehende Menschensohn.
102 Hierzu gehört das Bewusstsein von der Geschichte Gottes mit dem Volk Israel, das von 1,2 f. an jederzeit angesprochen werden kann, z. B. Mk 2,25 (David); 6,15; 8,28 (Elia). Die Geschichte Israels wird auch als „Schrift" durch die Diskussionen mit den Schriftgelehrten stets lebendig gehalten, z. B. 7,6 – 12; 10,2 – 12 und Kap. 12. Vgl. dazu den Beitrag von F. Wilk im vorliegenden Band. – Andererseits sind Mose und Elia auch gegenwärtige Gestalten (9,2 – 8). Vgl. dazu auch 11,10: „die *kommende* Königsherrschaft unseres Vaters David". Die Geschichte Israels wird insgesamt merkwürdig wenig im Markusevangelium thematisiert. Zu den Geschichtskonzeptionen bei Paulus und im Markusevangelium vgl. den Beitrag von E.-M. Becker im vorliegenden Band.
103 In den Leidensweissagungen; 14,28.

Jesu Rede über das Ende ist vom Evangelisten in die Zeit von Jesu Aufenthalt in Jerusalem gesetzt. Sie ist als Jüngerbelehrung gestaltet. Auslösender Faktor ist Jesu Wort über die bevorstehende Tempelzerstörung. Markus hat die Endzeitrede mit der Passionserzählung durch das Motiv der Tempelzerstörung verbunden: Ein Anti-Tempelwort Jesu steht im Zentrum der falschen Anklagen im Verhör vor dem Synhedrium (14,58). Jesu Todesschicksal ist dadurch direkt mit seiner apokalyptischen Rede verbunden. Ebenso gilt: Das Kommen der Endereignisse wird durch Jesu Todesschicksal vorangetrieben. Jesu Tod ist eine entscheidende Station im apokalyptisch vorgestellten Endzeitszenario. Dazu gehören auch die Leidensweissagungen.

Das Ende steht in Kürze bevor, wie besonders 9,1 für den Evangelisten deutlich macht. Aber es gibt den Raum der Zwischenzeit. David S. du Toit hat nachdrücklich auf diesen Zeitraum hingewiesen, der sich zwischen die Lebenszeit Jesu und die Endzeit schiebt: die Gegenwart des Evangelisten und seiner Leserschaft, die der Evangelist besonders deutlich in Kapitel 4,13 – 20; 7; 8,34 – 9,1; 10,2 – 12.28 – 31.35 – 45; 11,20 – 25 und 13 im Blick hat. Du Toit macht auf die Zeitstruktur von Anwesenheit, Abwesenheit und Wiederkehr Jesu aufmerksam, die im Gleichnis von dem abwesenden Hausherrn (13,33 – 37) abgebildet ist[104] und den Zeiträumen des Lebens Jesu, seiner Auferstehung und seiner Wiederkunft entspricht. Die Zeit der Abwesenheit, die vor der Wiederkehr Christi liegt, wird nach du Toit vom Erzähler dreifach charakterisiert: als „Zeit des Unbeteiligtseins Jesu"[105], als „Fasten- bzw. Trauerzeit"[106] und als „Zeit akuter Gefährdung"[107] sowie „drohenden Heilsverlustes"[108]. Dadurch, dass Jesus selbst in seiner Endzeitrede diesen Zeitraum – und sein Ende – beschreibt, rückt er die Zeit der κατάλυσις (13,2) direkt an seine Gegenwart heran: Die „Wehen" (13,8) werden zu Lebzeiten der Jünger beginnen, gleichzeitig wird das Evangelium „allen Völkern" verkündet werden: Diese Gegenwart ist die Zeit der Verkündigung. Hier kann man du Toit weiterdenken. Der Evangelist tut, was in seiner Gegenwart getan werden muss: Er erzählt das ‚Evangelium Jesu Christi, des Sohnes Gottes' in schriftlicher Form, als Jesus-Buch. In dieser Form kann das Evangelium ‚allen Völkern' verkündet werden. Der Evangelist richtet mit seinem Jesus-*Buch* *literarisch* dasselbe aus, was Paulus mit seiner Jesus-*Verkündigung* ‚von Jerusalem bis Rom bzw. Spanien' *missionarisch*

---

104 Vgl. dazu auch du Toit, Der abwesende Herr, 113–149.
105 A.a.O., 117.
106 A.a.O., 130.
107 A.a.O., 133.
108 A.a.O., 140.

unternommen hat[109]. Mk 13,10 macht deutlich, dass der Evangelist das Ende noch zu seinen eigenen Lebzeiten erwartet[110]. Der Zeitraum des abwesenden Herrn ist zugleich der Beginn der Endzeit und Teil des apokalyptischen Zeitkonzepts.

Zusammengefasst: Das apokalyptische Zeitkonzept des Evangelisten fungiert als großer zeitlicher Rahmen des narrativen und des christologischen Konzepts.

(4) Hier muss weiter gefragt werden. Das Markusevangelium verbindet drei Zeitkonzeptionen: ein narratives Zeitkonzept, ein christologisches Zeitkonzept und ein apokalyptisches Zeitkonzept. Damit stellt sich die Frage: Wie verhalten sich die drei verschiedenen Zeitkonzepte des Näheren zueinander, und wie verbindet sie der Evangelist? Zusammengehalten werden sie von der *einen* zentralen Aussage des εὐαγγέλιον: Christus ist gekreuzigt worden und gestorben, er wurde begraben und ist auferstanden. Die Auferstehungsvorstellung und -hoffnung entstand in verschiedenen religiösen und literarischen Milieus im Judentum des 2. und 1. Jahrhunderts v. Chr.[111] und war mit den apokalyptischen Szenarien kompatibel[112]. Das Markusevangelium setzt voraus, dass Jesus diese Hoffnung nicht nur teilte (10,30; 12,18–27), sondern auf sein eigenes Schicksal bezog[113], während sie den Jüngern zunächst mindestens unklar, wenn nicht fremd war (9,10)[114]. Im christologischen Zeitkonzept des Evangelisten wird Jesu Auferstehung in das apokalyptische Zeitkonzept integriert und zu seinem wesentlichsten Bestandteil. Jesu Auferstehung, die im narrativen Zeitkonzept nicht berichtet wird, kann im Rahmen des apokalyptischen Zeitkonzeptes angekündigt werden und öffnet damit das historische Narrativ für seine christologische Zeitdimension. Die Zeit der historischen Erzählung wird dadurch zum erfüllten καιρός. 1,14f. und 2,18–22 sind

---

109 Dies ist der Hintergrund meines Votums *für* die These von R. J. Bauckham, „For Whom Were Gospels Written?", in: The Gospels for All Christians: Rethinking the Gospel Audiences, ed. by R. J. Bauckham, Grand Rapids 1998, 9–48. Vgl. O. Wischmeyer, Forming Identity Through Literature. The Impact of Mark for the Building of Christ-Believing Communities in the Second Half of the First Century C.E., in: Mark and Matthew I, 355–378.

110 Im Jahre 70 n. Chr. leben noch Jünger Jesu, so dass Jesu Wort noch plausibel ist. Allerdings hat sich der Zeitraum der ‚Abwesenheit des Herrn' schon vergrößert, und das Anliegen des Markusevangeliums gilt nicht nur der Ansage der Nähe des Endes (Kap. 13), sondern ebenso der Sammlung und Sicherung der Jesustraditionen in einem ersten Evangelienbuch. Endzeitansage und Traditionssammlung lassen sich für das Markusevangelium nicht gegeneinander ausspielen.

111 Vgl. die ausgezeichnete Einführung bei A. Collins, Mark, 782–794.

112 Das zeigt sich bei dem früheren Pharisäer Paulus, der auch an apokalyptischen Vorstellungen partizipiert: s.u.

113 Vgl. die Leidensweissagungen.

114 Die Unklarheit bei den Jüngern ist allerdings offensichtlich Teil des sog. Jüngerunverständnisses, das mit dem Zug nach Jerusalem zunimmt.

die beiden Texte, in denen der Evangelist diesen Grundgedanken formuliert: Jesu Lebenszeit ist Heilszeit. Theologisch dominiert das christologische Zeitkonzept.

Als Ergebnis lässt sich festhalten: Das *narrativ-episodische Zeitkonzept* ist das Gerüst der Jesus-Erzählung. Hier spricht der Autor als Erzähler. Das *christologisch-konzentrierte Zeitkonzept* drückt die Überzeugung des Evangelisten aus, die Zeitspanne des öffentlichen Wirkens Jesu bis zu seinem Tod sei erfüllte Zeit und als solche εὐαγγέλιον. Hier spricht der Autor als Christus-bekennender Interpret der Erzählung von Jesus von Nazareth. Er deutet seine eigene Erzählung christologisch im Sinne seines Eröffnungssatzes. Für ihn fallen die Zeit von Jesu Wirken und Sterben und die erfüllte Zeit zusammen. Das *apokalyptische Zeitkonzept* ermöglicht die Verbindung der Jesuserzählung mit dem kosmischen und geschichtlichen Handeln Gottes an den Menschen „seit Anbeginn der Schöpfung" bis zu ihrem Ende[115]. Hier spricht der Autor als jüdischer[116] Theologe.

Die entscheidende literarische und theologische Leistung des Evangelisten liegt in der Verbindung der narrativen und der christologischen Zeitkonzeption in der Gestalt der Jesuserzählung, die εὐαγγέλιον Ἰησοῦ Χριστοῦ υἱοῦ θεοῦ ist. In Mk 1,15 wird Jesus selbst zum Verkünder der Zeitkonzeption des Evangelisten:

[Jesus sprach:] Erfüllt ist der καιρός, und nahe herbeigekommen ist die Gottesherrschaft[117].

5 Die Zeit des Apostolos Jesu Christi und die Zeit Jesu als Zentrum der Zeit: ein Vergleich

Nachdem deutlich geworden ist, welche Bedeutung das Thema *Zeit* für Paulus und für den Markusevangelisten hat und welche Zeitkonzeptionen die beiden Autoren am Beginn des Christentums entwerfen, soll nun in aller Kürze ein Vergleich versucht werden. Der Vergleich kann auf verschiedenen Ebenen durchgeführt werden. Ich beginne (1) mit der Frage nach strukturellen Parallelen und Differenzen beider Zeitkonzepte, um die Frage nach der theologischen Bedeutung der beiden Zeitkonzepte zu beantworten. Schwierig gestaltet sich (2) die historische Frage nach möglichen Traditionen, Einflüssen, Entwicklungen und Reaktionen

---

115 Vgl. Vollenweiders Hinweis auf die ungeheuren Dimensionen des apokalyptischen Zeitkonzepts (s.o. Anm. 12).
116 Dies Urteil impliziert nicht notwendig, dass der Verfasser des Markusevangeliums selbst Jude gewesen sei. Er hat aber mit Sicherheit grundlegende theologische Erklärungsmodelle aus der jüdischen Theologie übernommen.
117 Dieser Satz erfüllt in der markinischen Erzählung dieselbe Leistung wie Röm 1,16f. im Römerbrief. Es handelt sich jeweils um die *propositio generalis*, die dem εὐαγγέλιον gilt.

zwischen Paulus und dem Markusevangelium. Den Schluss bildet (3) eine methodische Reflexion zu der Bedeutung der Ergebnisse für die übergeordnete Fragestellung nach ‚Paulus und Markus'.

(1) Die strukturellen *Parallelen* zwischen beiden Konzepten sind evident. Sowohl Paulus als auch der Markusevangelist verstehen ihre eigene Zeit als erfüllte Zeit, als Zentrum der Zeit, als Heilszeit bzw. als Zeit des Evangeliums. Mit dem Kommen Jesu[118] ist die Heilszeit angebrochen. Zwischen der Lebenszeit Jesu und den Ereignissen der Endzeit, an denen Jesus Christus seine universale Herrschaft erweisen wird[119], liegt die kurze Zeitspanne der Gegenwart des Apostels bzw. des Evangelisten[120]. Diese Zeit ist nicht nur bei Paulus[121] Zeit der Verkündigung, der Freude, der Verfolgung, des Leidens, der Sehnsucht, der Wachsamkeit, der Bewährung, der Liebe und der Unterstützung durch den Geist, sondern diese Motive sind ebenso im Markusevangelium vorhanden[122]. Es ist die Zeitspanne der Wirksamkeit des Paulus in der Verkündigung des Evangeliums, aber eben auch die Zeit der Gemeinden und die Zeit der eigenen literarischen Arbeit des Evangelisten. Die Zukunft ist für Paulus und den Evangelisten gleichermaßen durch die Wiederkehr Christi als des endzeitlichen Richters und Herrschers über die kosmischen Mächte geprägt. Die Vorstellung von der Vergangenheit reicht bei beiden bis zur Schöpfung zurück[123] und ist durch die Geschichte Gottes mit Israel ausgefüllt, die aber dennoch bei beiden Autoren nicht zum eigenen Thema wird.

Die Zeit Jesu ist nicht erst im Markusevangelium, sondern grundsätzlich auch schon bei Paulus Heilszeit, wie Gal 4,4 unmissverständlich deutlich macht. Und doch liegt gerade hier die entscheidende *Differenz* in den zu vergleichenden Zeitkonzepten. Während Paulus in heilsgeschichtlichen Epochen, d. h. in unterschiedlichen Zeitabschnitten von Gottes Verhältnis zu den Menschen, denkt und Jesu irdisches Leben[124] – in Phil 2,7 f. beschränkt er sich auf die allgemeine For-

---

[118] Mk 1,14 f. und Gal 4,4.
[119] Mk 13,24–27 und 1Kor 15,24–26.
[120] Mk 13, bes. V. 14 und 2Kor 6,2. Es ist historisch nicht unwichtig, sich die zeitliche Nähe zwischen den Briefen des Paulus und dem wohl kurz nach 70 n.Chr. entstandenen ersten Evangelium vor Augen zu halten. Der Unterschied liegt in dem Sachverhalt, dass Paulus den Jüdischen Krieg und die Zerstörung des Tempels nicht mehr erlebt hat. Vgl. dazu den Beitrag von E.-M. Becker im vorliegenden Band.
[121] S.o.
[122] Du Toit benennt lediglich die negativen Aspekte dieser Zwischenzeit. Hinzuzufügen sind: (1) Sehnsucht: 13,21 f.; (2) Geist: 13,11; (3) ethische Bewährung (besonders ἀγάπη).
[123] Mk 10,6.
[124] Die Frage nach Jesus-Logien bei Paulus steht hier ebenso wenig zur Diskussion wie die Frage, wie viel Paulus von Jesus gewusst habe. Zur Fragestellung vgl. F. Holzbrecher, Paulus und der historische Jesus. Darstellung und Analyse der bisherigen Forschungsgeschichte (TANZ 48),

mulierung „in menschlicher Gestalt"[125], während in Gal 4,4[126] Jesu Menschsein durch den Hinweis auf seine natürliche Geburt und sein Jude-Sein dargestellt wird – lediglich von seinem „Kommen" und seinem Kreuzestod[127] her thematisiert, entwickelt der Verfasser des Markusevangeliums wie dargestellt die gesamte Geschichte des öffentlichen Wirkens Jesu mit ihren unterschiedlichen Facetten von Lehre, Wundertaten und Heilungen sowie der Passion als Heilszeit. Jesu öffentliches Auftreten beginnt mit der Zeitansage von Mk 1,15:

> Erfüllt ist der καιρός, und nahegekommen ist die Herrschaft Gottes. Tut Buße und glaubt an das Evangelium.

Sein Auftreten *ist* der Beginn der Heilszeit Gottes, und seine Botschaft *ist* diese Zeitansage, *ist* das Evangelium. Daher entwirft der Evangelist die literarische Form der umfangreichen Jesus-Erzählung, deren narrative Logik streng auf Jesu öffentliches Wirken beschränkt bleibt und weder seine Kindheit und Jugend noch seine Begegnungen mit den Jüngern und Frauen nach seiner Auferstehung umfasst[128]. Paulus ist – nur – am „Gekommensein Jesu" interessiert[129]. Jesu Leben ist für ihn mit der Kreuzes- und Erlösungstheologie verbunden[130] und theologisch gesehen auf die Soteriologie fokussiert bzw. beschränkt. Demgegenüber öffnet das Markusevangelium die christologische Zeitkonzeption für den Zeitraum des öffentlichen Wirkens Jesu und integriert Jesu Wirken in Wort und Tat in diese Konzeption. In diesem Konzept wird erstens Jesu eigener Botschaft – in tradierter

---

Tübingen 2007; vgl. die knappe Zusammenstellung bei J. Schröter, Jesus Christus als Zentrum des Denkens. Das Verhältnis zum irdischen Jesus und zur Jesusüberlieferung, in: Paulus Handbuch. Herausgegeben von F.W. Horn, Tübingen 2013, 279–285. Vgl. auch die Beiträge von U. Schnelle und I. Elmer im vorliegenden Band.
125 Vgl. Röm 8,3, dort auf „sündiges Fleisch" fokussiert.
126 Zu Gal 4 vgl. K. Scholtissek, „Geboren aus einer Frau, geboren unter das Gesetz" (Gal 4,4). Die christologisch-soteriologische Bedeutung des irdischen Jesus bei Paulus, in: Paulinische Christologie (FS H. Hübner), hg. von U. Schnelle/Th. Söding/M. Labahn, Göttingen 2000, 194–219. Scholtissek formuliert mit Bezug auf J. Blank, Paulus und Jesus. Eine theologische Grundlegung, (StANT 18), München 1968, 324, richtig: „Paulus ist nicht an einem isoliert verstandenen irdischen Jesus von Nazaret interessiert, wohl aber an dem Menschsein Jesu in einem heilsgeschichtlichen bzw. soteriologischen Sinn" (218).
127 Vgl. dazu den Beitrag von M. Theobald im vorliegenden Band.
128 Dass dieser Aspekt in den Leidensweissagungen angesprochen wird, wurde dargestellt. Außerdem wird in dem sog. Messiasgeheimnis auf Jesus als Gottessohn verwiesen (vgl. dazu den Beitrag von U. Schnelle im vorliegenden Band).
129 Vgl. ein Detail wie Gal 4,4, wo der Name der Mutter Jesu nicht genannt wird!
130 Vgl. dazu die Beiträge von M. Theobald und U. Schnelle im vorliegenden Band.

und überarbeiteter Form[131] – eine Stimme innerhalb des εὐαγγέλιον gegeben und werden zweitens Jesu Taten zu Zeichen der christologisch bestimmten neuen Zeit. Jesus tritt als Person am Beginn der Heilszeit (ἀρχὴ τοῦ εὐαγγελίου) in Erscheinung. Damit wird die Basis der Evangeliumsverkündigung, der Theologie und der Ethik des entstehenden Christentums, die von Paulus gelegt worden ist, durch das markinische Zeitkonzept verbreitet. Dies erweiterte Zeitkonzept führt zu einer grundsätzlichen Aufwertung der *dicta* und *facta* Jesu für die Gemeinden. Jetzt ist Jesus der Lehrer mit ἐξουσία, d. h. mit Autorität, der die Gemeinden lehrt. Aus der zeitlichen Perspektive gesehen heißt das: Die autoritative Lehre ist bereits durch Jesus formuliert worden. Für die Autorität des Paulus bedeutet das Markusevangelium daher faktisch eine Abwertung oder mindestens Begrenzung. Der *Herr* hat bereits gesprochen, und die Inhalte des Evangeliums sind bereits von Jesus selbst formuliert worden.

Ein Beispiel soll dies illustrieren: In 1Kor 15 entwickelt *Paulus* mit großer intellektueller Anstrengung eine erste christologisch fundierte[132] Argumentation, die in verschiedenen Anläufen die Auferstehung der Toten vorstellbar und plausibel machen soll. Paulus betritt hier theologisches Neuland und ist der souveräne Lehrer der korinthischen Gemeinde. In Mk 12,18–27 belehrt *Jesus* selbst in einem kurzen, autoritativen Text („Ihr irrt sehr") die Sadduzäer über die Auferstehung. Es ist in diesem Fall selbstverständlich, dass Jesu Lehre eine ungleich größere Autorität als die des Paulus haben wird, da Jesus derjenige ist, der auferstehen wird und auf dessen Schicksal Paulus seine Argumentation erst gründet. Weitere Beispiele stellen die Streitgespräche in Mk 12 dar, die Jesus als vollmächtigen Lehrer in den zentralen Fragen, mit denen es die ersten christlichen Gemeinden zu tun haben, ausweisen. Es geht um Themen, mit denen sich schon Paulus beschäftigt hat: das Verhältnis zur römischen Verwaltung[133], die Auferstehung der Toten – wie schon gesagt –, das höchste Gebot[134], den Messias und die Schriftauslegung. Nimmt man die Thematik der Ehescheidung in Mk 10,2–12[135] und der Reinheitsfrage in Mk 7,1–23[136] hinzu, so wird deutlich, dass die Lehre Jesu im Markusevangelium sachlich mit wesentlichen Teilen der Lehre des Paulus konkurriert

---

[131] Vielleicht der entscheidende Unterschied zwischen Paulus und ‚Markus' liegt im *Verzicht* des Paulus auf die Jesustradition, die er selbstverständlich in erheblichem Umfang gekannt hat. Entscheidend ist hier nicht, was Paulus aus der Jesustradition zitiert, sondern dass er so gut wie Alles unerwähnt lässt.
[132] Die jüdische Vorstellung von der Totenauferstehung kam ohne diese Begründung aus.
[133] Vgl. Röm 13,1–7.
[134] Vgl. Röm 13,8–10 u. ö.
[135] Vgl. 1Kor 7.
[136] Vgl. 1Kor 8 und 10,23–33 sowie Röm 14.

und diese, was die Autorität der Lehre betrifft, grundsätzlich überbietet. Paulus muss stets christologisch argumentieren. Der Jesus des Markusevangeliums *ist* der Christus (Mk 1,1). 1Kor 7,10 zeigt schlaglichtartig, dass Paulus selbst die Tendenz schon erkennt, zu der die Jesustradition führt: Er zitiert ein Jesuslogion[137], an dem er offensichtlich nicht vorbeikommt und auch nicht vorbeikommen will, bei dem er aber auch nicht stehen bleibt. Dabei benutzt er korrekter Weise für seine eigenen Vorschriften das einfache λέγω, für den Herrn aber das autoritative παραγγέλλω. Andererseits gibt das argumentative Gefälle der eigenen Lehre die wichtigere Position, während das Herrnwort gleichsam quer zur Argumentation eingefügt wird und erratisch im Gesamtzusammenhang mit seiner geschmeidigen und differenzierten Argumentation steht, die Paulus selbst für die Situation der korinthischen Gemeinde entwirft. V.12 macht besonders deutlich, wie sich Paulus für seine eigene ethische Weisung Raum verschafft[138].

Zusammengefasst: Paulus und das Markusevangelium füllen die Zeit der öffentlichen Wirksamkeit Jesu unterschiedlich. Für Paulus ist sie lediglich Teil des „Gekommenseins" oder „Gesendetseins" Jesu, das sich in Jesu Tod am Kreuz und in seiner Auferstehung als Gottes Heil für die Menschen erfüllt. Es ist die Aufgabe des Apostels, dies Evangelium zu verkünden. Für das Markusevangelium ist die Zeit des Wirkens Jesu bereits Zeit des Evangeliums, und Jesu Worte sind Teil des Evangeliums. *Er selbst* verkündet bereits das Evangelium. Der Evangelist ist derjenige, der die Zeit Jesu und seiner Worte und Taten erzählt und damit literarisch festhält. Damit verlagert sich der Akzent von der Zeit des Apostolos des Kyrios Jesus Christus auf die Zeit Jesu zurück, die seit Markus als Zeit des Kyrios verstanden wird, und die Worte Jesu entwickeln mehr Autorität als die Worte des Apostels, auch wenn dieser „den Herrn Jesus gesehen hat" (1Kor 9,1) und der Kyrios selbst zu ihm gesprochen hat (2Kor 12,9).

---

137 Vgl. dazu die ausführliche Studie von F. Neirynck, Paul and the Sayings of Jesus, in: A. Vanhoye (ed.), L'Apôtre Paul. Personnalité, style et conception du ministère (BETL LXXIII), Leuven 1986, 265–321; ders., The Sayings of Jesus in 1 Corinthians, in: R. Bieringer (ed.), The Corinthian Correspondence (BETL CXXV), Leuven 1996, 141–176. Neirynck erkennt nur zwei „Herrnworte" an: 1Kor 7,10f. (Mk 10,11) und 1Kor 9,14 (aus Q). Sein Fazit zu 1Kor 7,10: „This command of the Lord is still in Paul's mind when he formulates his own instructions on mixed marriages. The possibility of divorce is envisaged by Paul (v. 11a) without giving up the inspiration of the dominical logion. This involves a notion of divorce-separation, unattested I think in the gospel sayings and probably unknown in the pre-Pauline Jesus tradition" (176). A. Lindemann, Der Erste Korintherbrief (HNT 9/1), Tübingen 2000, 162–164, kommentiert sehr nüchtern: Paulus weist „einfach auf den Sachverhalt hin, daß die Quelle seiner Weisung Christus ist, auch wenn konkret jetzt er selber dies den Korinthern vermittelt" (164).
138 Vgl. auch 7,25.

(2) Haben wir erkennbare Hinweise auf historische Zusammenhänge zwischen beiden Konzeptionen, die über gemeinsame frühjüdische und frühchristliche Grundansichten zur Zeit hinausgehen? Wenn wir mit der großen Mehrheit der Exegeten davon ausgehen, dass Paulus bereits hingerichtet war, als Markus sein Evangelium verfasste, und wenn wir im Evangelium naturgemäß keine Spur eines Verweises auf Paulus, der nicht zu den Jüngern Jesu gehörte, finden, dann müssen wir die historische Frage offenlassen oder zunächst negativ beantworten. Die traditionsgeschichtliche Perspektive kann – anders als zum Beispiel bei der Abendmahlsparadosis – ebenfalls kaum zu eindeutigen Ergebnissen führen. Der Vergleich mehrerer theologischer Positionen, Grundbegriffe und Methoden – das Liebesgebot, der Glaube, das Evangelium, die Reinheitsdiskussion, christologische Titel, der Umgang mit der Schrift, besonders mit Jesaja, und auch die apokalyptischen und christologischen Grundzüge der Zeitkonzeption – mag auf direkte oder indirekte, vermittelte Beziehungen zwischen dem Verfasser des Markusevangeliums und den Paulusbriefen oder sogar der Person des Paulus hinweisen[139]. Für die Zeitkonzeptionen selbst gilt das aber gerade nicht. Sie sind zwar einem gemeinsamen frühjüdisch-frühchristlichen apokalyptisch und christologisch geprägten theologischen Milieu verpflichtet, zeigen aber keine direkten Abhängigkeits- oder Benutzungsverhältnisse, sondern eher einen strukturell-theologischen Gegensatz.

Allgemein mag gelten: Wenn man das Markusevangelium in Antiochia, der ersten wichtigen Gemeinde, in der und von der aus Paulus wirkte, situieren und mit der dortigen Petrustradition verknüpfen würde[140], könnte sich ein historischer Zusammenhang ergeben. Aber dasselbe würde ja auch auf Rom zutreffen[141] – eine Koinzidenz, die jede derartige geographisch-theologie- bzw. gemeindegeschichtliche Zuordnung äußerst fragwürdig werden oder mindestens ihren Nutzen in Zweifel ziehen lässt[142]. Es ist zugleich bescheidener und wissenschaftlich vertretbarer, unsere Unkenntnis über den Entstehungsort des Markusevangeliums und über seine Traditionsgaranten – Petrus (?) – zu bekennen und damit die

---

139 F. Wilk verweist in seinem Beitrag in diesem Band auf die syrischen Gemeinden.
140 Dass der 1. Korintherbrief der einzige Brief ist, in dem Paulus Jesuslogien anführt und auf die jesuanischen Einsetzungsworte des Herrnmahls verweist, könnte mit dem – möglichen – Aufenthalt des Petrus in Korinth und einer – möglicherweise – dort bestehenden Petruspartei, die über Jesustradition verfügt, zusammenhängen. Daraus lassen sich aber keine sicheren Schlüsse auf eine mögliche Reaktion des Paulus auf das Eindringen von petrinischer Jesustradition und -autorität nach Korinth ziehen, die für das Thema des Zeitkonzepts von Bedeutung wären.
141 So U. Schnelle in seinem Beitrag in diesem Band.
142 Vgl. dazu einführend A. Collins, Mark, 7–10; auch O. Wischmeyer, Forming Identity Through Literature, 362–365.

historische Frage nach dem Verhältnis von Paulus und dem Markusevangelium offen zu lassen. Jedenfalls lässt sich aus dem Vergleich der Zeitkonzepte keine Beeinflussung oder Abhängigkeit ableiten, die über gemeinsame frühchristliche Grundüberzeugungen hinausginge[143].

(3) Methodisch gesehen macht der Vergleich des paulinischen und markinischen Zeitkonzepts deutlich, dass dort, wo historische Fragestellungen und besonders Benutzungs-, Abhängigkeits- und Einflussmodelle keine klaren Ergebnisse bringen, doch *Strukturvergleiche* wichtige Einsichten vermitteln können. Das Ergebnis des hier angestellten Strukturvergleichs, nämlich *die Verlagerung des Fokus von der Zeit des Kyrios und seines Apostels auf die Zeit Jesu und seiner Jünger*, führt nicht nur zu einem besseren Verständnis des Markusevangeliums, sondern beleuchtet ebenfalls die selbständige und innovative Rolle des Paulus am Anfang des Christentums und ihre spätere Begrenzung durch den Jesus des Markusevangeliums. Die Tendenz geht nicht – wie oft angenommen – von der ‚einfachen' Verkündigung Jesu zur Christologie des Paulus, sondern umgekehrt von *Paulus*, dem Apostel Jesu Christi, und seiner Verkündigung des Evangeliums von Jesus Christus zu *Jesus* selbst, der der Jesus des Markusevangeliums ist, der Sohn Gottes, und dessen Worte und Taten das Evangelium sind. Durch den hier vorgenommenen strukturellen Vergleich zwischen der Konzeption von Zeit bei Paulus und im Markusevangelium wird deutlich, dass die Vorstellung, die Christologie des Paulus sei theologisch entwickelter – und damit zugleich problematischer – als die markinische Jesuserzählung, den markinischen Jesus mit Jesus von Nazareth verwechselt. Das Gegenteil trifft zu: Der markinische Jesus ist der Sohn Gottes. Der Verfasser des Markusevangeliums integriert die unterschiedlichen Jesustraditionen in seine Sohn-Gottes-Christologie und weitet damit den Bereich der Christologie zeitlich und sachlich aus[144].

---

[143] Vgl. das Ergebnis von J.G. Crossley, Mark, Paul and the Question of Influence, in: Paul and the Gospels: Christologies, Conflicts and Convergences, ed. by M.F. Bird/J. Willitts (LNTS 411), London/New York 2011, 10–29. Crossley ist vorsichtig gegenüber allen genaueren historischen Zuordnungen und erkennt nur gemeinsames frühchristliches theologisches Milieu. Anders votiert M.F. Bird, Mark: Interpreter of Peter and Disciple of Paul, in: Paul and the Gospels, 30–61. Seine These: „The Gospel of Mark points to an early synthesis of Peter and Paul: Petrine testimony shaped into an evangelical narrative conducive to Pauline proclamation" (32).
[144] Vgl. dazu den Beitrag von U. Schnelle im vorliegenden Band.

Bibliographie

Agamben, G., Die Zeit, die bleibt (Edition Suhrkamp 2453), Frankfurt 2006.
Anderson, Ch.A., Philo of Alexandria's Views of the Physical World (WUNT 2.R. 309), Tübingen 2011.
Anderson, J.C./Moore, St.D. (eds.), Mark and Matthew: New Approaches in Biblical Studies, Minneapolis 2nd edn. 2008.
Arens, E. (Hg.), Zeit denken. Eschatologie im interdisziplinären Diskurs (QD 234), Freiburg/Basel/Wien 2010.
Assmann, J., M. Theunissen, H. Westermann, H.Ch. Schmitt, P. Porro, Y. Schwartz, G. Böwering, E. Kessler, H. Hühn/H.-J. Waschkies, R. Beuthan/M. Sandbothe, Art. Zeit I-VI, in: HWPh 12 (2004), 1186–1244.
Assmann, J., Zeit und Ewigkeit im Alten Ägypten. Ein Beitrag zur Geschichte der Ewigkeit (HAW phil.-hist. Kl. 1975,1), Heidelberg 1975.
—, Zeitkonstruktion, Vergangenheitsbezug und Geschichtsbewußtsein im alten Ägypten, in: J. Assmann/K.E. Müller (Hgg.), Der Ursprung der Geschichte, Stuttgart 2005, 112–214.
Avemarie, F., Heilsgeschichte und Lebensgeschichte bei Paulus, in: Heil und Geschichte. Die Geschichtsbezogenheit des Heils und das Problem der Heilsgeschichte in der biblischen Tradition und der theologischen Deutung, hg. von J. Frey/St. Krauter/H. Lichtenberger (WUNT 248), Tübingen 2009, 357–383.
Bauckham, R.J., „For Whom Were Gospels Written?" in: The Gospels for All Christians: Rethinking the Gospel Audiences, ed. R.J. Bauckham, Grand Rapids 1998, 9–48.
Becker, E.-M., Das Markus-Evangelium im Rahmen antiker Historiographie (WUNT 194), Tübingen 2006.
—, Die markinischen Summarien – ein literarischer und theologischer Schlüssel zu Mk 1–6, in: NTS 56 (2010), 452–474.
Becker, E.-M./Runesson, A. (eds.), Mark and Matthew I. Comparative Readings: Understanding the Earliest Gospels in their First-Century Settings (WUNT 271), Tübingen 2011.
Ben-Dov, J., Art. Calendars, in: Eerdmans Dictionary of Early Judaism, 2010, 457–460.
Bird, M.F., Tearing the Heavens and Shaking the Heavenlies: Mark's Cosmology in its Apocalyptic Context, in: Cosmology and New Testament Theology, ed. by J.T. Pennington/S.M. McDonough (LNTS 355), London/New York 2008, 45–59.
—, Mark: Interpreter of Peter and Disciple of Paul, in: Paul and the Gospels. Christologies, Conflicts and Convergences, ed. by M.F. Bird/J. Willitts (LNTS 411), London/New York 2011, 30–61.
Blank, J., Paulus und Jesus. Eine theologische Grundlegung (StANT 18), München 1968.
Boman, T., Das hebräische Denken im Vergleich mit dem griechischen, Göttingen ⁴1965.
Breytenbach, C., Das Markusevangelium als episodische Erzählung. Mit Überlegungen zum „Aufbau" des zweiten Evangeliums, in: F. Hahn (Hg.), Der Erzähler des Evangeliums: methodische Neuansätze in der Markusforschung (SBS 118/119), Stuttgart 1985, 137–169.
—, Current Research on the Gospel according to Mark: A Report on Monographs Published from 2000–2009, in: Mark and Matthew I. Comparative Readings: Understanding the Earliest Gospels in their First-Century Settings, ed. by E.-M. Becker/A. Runesson (WUNT 271), Tübingen 2011, 13–32.
Collins, A. Yarbro, Mark. A Commentary (Hermeneia), Minneapolis 2007.

Crossley, J.G., Mark, Paul and the Question of Influence, in: Paul and the Gospels: Christologies, Conflicts and Convergences, ed. by M.F. Bird/J. Willitts (LNTS 411), London/New York 2011, 10–29.
Cullmann, O., Christus und die Zeit, Zollikon/Zürich 1945; ³1962.
Delling, G., Das Zeitverständnis des Neuen Testaments, Gütersloh 1940.
—, Zeit und Endzeit. Zwei Vorlesungen zur Theologie des Neuen Testaments (BSt 58), Neukirchen-Vluyn 1970.
Dobschütz, E. von, Zeit und Raum im Denken des Urchristentums, in: JBL 41 (1922), 212–223.
Dodewaard, J.A.E. van, Die sprachliche Übereinstimmung von Markus – Paulus und Markus – Petrus, in: Bib. 30 (1949), 91–108 und 218–238.
Du Toit, D.S., Der abwesende Herr. Strategien im Markusevangelium zur Bewältigung der Abwesenheit des Auferstandenen (WMANT 111), Neukirchen-Vluyn 2006.
Eckstein, H.J./C. Landmesser/H. Lichtenberger (eds.), Eschatologie – Eschatology. The Sixth Durham-Tübingen Research Symposium: Eschatology in Old Testament, Ancient Judaism and Early Christianity (Tübingen, September 2009), (WUNT 272), Tübingen 2011.
Erlemann, K., Naherwartung und Parusieverzögerung im Neuen Testament, Tübingen 1995.
Feldmeier, R., Gott und die Zeit, in: Heil und Geschichte. Die Geschichtsbezogenheit des Heils und das Problem der Heilsgeschichte in der biblischen Tradition und der theologischen Deutung, hg. von J. Frey/St. Krauter/H. Lichtenberger (WUNT 248), Tübingen 2009, 287–305.
Frey, J., Art. Zeit/Zeitvorstellungen II.2, in: RGG⁴ 8 (2005), 1804f.
—, Zum Problem der Aufgabe und Durchführung einer Theologie des Neuen Testaments, in: Aufgabe und Durchführung einer Theologie des Neuen Testaments, hg. von C. Breytenbach/J. Frey (WUNT 205), Tübingen 2007, 3–55.
Geerlings, W., Der Kalender. Aspekte einer Geschichte, Paderborn/München 2002.
Henten, J.W. van/Avemarie, F., Martyrdom and Noble Death: Selected Texts from Greco-Roman, Jewish and Christian Antiquity, London 2002.
Holzbrecher, F., Paulus und der historische Jesus. Darstellung und Analyse der bisherigen Forschungsgeschichte (TANZ 48), Tübingen 2007.
Iverson, K.R./Skinner, Ch.W. (eds.), Mark as Story: Retrospect and Prospect (SBL.RBS 65), Atlanta 2011.
Jackson, T. R., New Creation in Paul's Letters (WUNT 2.R. 272), Tübingen 2010.
Kaufman, E., The Saturday of Messianic Time (Agamben and Badiou on the Apostle Paul), in: South Atlantic Quarterly 107 (2008), 37–54.
Kratz, R.G./Spieckermann, H. (Hgg.), Zeit und Ewigkeit als Raum göttlichen Handelns. Religionsgeschichtliche, theologische und philosophische Perspektiven (BZAW 390), Berlin/New York 2009.
Levine, R., Eine Landkarte der Zeit, München 1999.
Lindemann, A., Der Erste Korintherbrief (HNT 9/1), Tübingen 2000.
Neirynck, F., Paul and the Sayings of Jesus, in: A. Vanhoye (ed.), L'Apôtre Paul. Personnalité, style et conception du ministère (BETL LXXIII), Leuven 1986, 265–321.
—, The Sayings of Jesus in 1 Corinthians, in: R. Bieringer (ed.), The Corinthian Correspondence (BETL CXXV), Leuven 1996, 141–176.
Ostovich, E.St.T., Pauline Eschatology: Thinking and Acting in the Time that Remains, in: J. Alyson Parker/P.A. Harris/Ch. Steineck (eds.), Time: Limits and Constraints, Leiden 2010, 307–327.

Rhoads, D./Dewey, J./Michie, D., Mark as Story, An Introduction to the Narrative of a Gospel, Minneapolis, 2nd edition, 1999, 3d edition 2012.

Rüpke, J., Kalender und Öffentlichkeit: Die Geschichte der Repräsentation und religiösen Qualifikation von Zeit in Rom (RGVV 40), Berlin 1995.

Scholtissek, K., „Geboren aus einer Frau, geboren unter das Gesetz" (Gal 4,4). Die christologisch-soteriologische Bedeutung des irdischen Jesus bei Paulus, in: Paulinische Christologie (FS H. Hübner), hg. von U. Schnelle/Th. Söding/M. Labahn, Göttingen 2000, 194–219.

Schröter, J., Jesus Christus als Zentrum des Denkens. Das Verhältnis zum irdischen Jesus und zur Jesusüberlieferung, in: Paulus Handbuch, hg. von F.W. Horn, Tübingen 2013, 279–285.

Shively, E.E., Apocalyptic Imagination in the Gospel of Mark: The Literary and Theological Role of Mark 3:22–30 (BZNW 189), Berlin/Boston 2012.

Skinner, Ch.W., Telling the Story: The Appearance and Impact of Mark as Story, in: K.R. Iverson/Ch.W. Skinner (eds.), Mark as Story: Retrospect and Prospect (SBL.RBS 65), Atlanta 2011, 1–16.

Vanderkam, J.C., Art. Calendars, in: ABD I (1992), 810–820.

Vollenweider, S., Horizonte neutestamentlicher Christologie. Studien zu Paulus und zur frühchristlichen Theologie (WUNT 144), Tübingen 2002, 143–162.

Westermann, H., Art. Zeitkonzeptionen, in: DNP 12/2 (2002), 709–717.

White, J., Paul's Cosmology: The Witness of Romans, 1 and 2 Corinthians, and Galatians, in: Cosmology and New Testament Theology, ed. by J.T. Pennington/S.M. McDonough (LNTS 355), London/New York 2008, 90–106.

Wischmeyer, O., Kosmos und Kosmologie bei Paulus, in: P. Gemeinhardt/A. Zgoll (Hgg.), Weltkonstruktionen. Religiöse Weltdeutung zwischen Chaos und Kosmos vom Alten Orient bis zum Islam (ORA 5), Tübingen 2010, 87–102.

—, Forming Identity Through Literature. The Impact of Mark for the Building of Christ-Believing Communities in the Second Half of the First Century C.E., in: Mark and Matthew I. Comparative Readings: Understanding the Earliest Gospels in their First-Century Settings, ed. by E.-M. Becker/A. Runesson (WUNT 271), Tübingen 2011, 355–378.

—, Rom 1:1–7 and Mark 1:1–3 in Comparison. Two Opening Texts at the Beginning of Early Christian literature, in: Mark and Paul. Comparative Essays Part II: For and Against Pauline Influence on Mark, ed. by E.-M. Becker/T. Engberg-Pedersen/M. Müller (BZNW 199), Berlin/Boston 2014, 121–146.

Wong, E.K.C., Evangelien im Dialog mit Paulus. Eine intertextuelle Studie zu den Synoptikern (NTOA/SUNT 89), Göttingen/Oakville CT, 2012.

Worthington, J.D., Creation in Paul and Philo. The Beginning and Before (WUNT 2.R. 317), Tübingen 2011.

Eve-Marie Becker
Die Konstruktion von ‚Geschichte'. Paulus und Markus im Vergleich*

‚Geschichte' wird zuerst und zuletzt dadurch konstruiert, dass sie *geschrieben* und narrativ entfaltet wird. Spätestens seit *Johann Gustav Droysen, Theodor Mommsen* und *Hayden V. White* wissen wir: Geschichtsschreibung, also Historiographie, ist der eigentliche literarische und hermeneutische Rahmen, in dem sich die Konstruktion und Deutung von Geschichte ereignet.

Im frühesten Christentum ist Lukas der einzige Schriftsteller und Theologe, der historiographische Erzählformen wählt, mit Hilfe derer er Zeit strukturiert (z. B. Lk 16,16) und ‚Geschichte' konstruiert[1]. Weder der Briefeschreiber Paulus noch der Verfasser des Markus-Evangeliums reichen literarisch oder konzeptionell in dieser Hinsicht an Lukas heran. Und doch – so werde ich im Folgenden argumentieren – sind Paulus und Markus in einem bestimmten Sinne *mehr* als historische Vorläufer des ‚lukanischen Geschichtswerks'. Beide Autoren schaffen nämlich in ihrer je eigenen Weise prä-historiographische Erzählungen, in denen sie zeitliche Abläufe ordnen und literarisch wie theologisch deutend konstruieren[2].

Bei *Paulus* kommt es vor allem bei der autobiographischen Darstellung des eigenen Wirkens, bei der Rückerinnerung an die Missions- und Gemeindegeschichte sowie im Zusammenhang heilsgeschichtlicher Deutung zu so etwas wie der Konstruktion einer Geschichte. Im *Markus-Evangelium* entstehen prä-histo-

---

* Der folgende Beitrag knüpft an Überlegungen zu den Anfängen des frühchristlichen Geschichtsdenkens an (vgl. E.-M. Becker, Patterns of Early Christian Thinking and Writing of History. Paul – Mark – Acts, in: Thinking, Recording, and Writing History in the Ancient World, ed. by K.A. Raaflaub, Hoboken 2014, 276–296 und vertieft einzelne Aspekte zur paulinischen Konstruktion von Geschichte, die in meiner Monographie: „*Memoria – tempus – historia*: The earliest Christian shape of history-writing" (New Haven 2014 [im Druck]) nur angedeutet werden können. Im Kontext des Paulus-Markus-Projektes soll in diesem Beitrag zudem die mögliche literarische und theologische Nähe der beiden Initiatoren frühchristlicher ‚Anfangsliteratur' diskutiert werden.
1 „Acts is a history", R.I. Pervo, Acts. A Commentary (Hermeneia), Minneapolis 2009, 15.
2 Diese Perspektive wird in den vorliegenden Darstellungen zur Konstruktion von Geschichte oder Geschichtsauffassung neutestamentlicher Autoren zumeist nicht gewählt – vgl. z.B. C. Rowland, Art. Geschichte/Geschichtsauffassung V. Neues Testament, in: RGG⁴ 3 (2000), 783–789. Sie stellt ein Desiderat dar, das gerade vor dem Hintergrund der gewachsenen Bedeutung der Narratologie bearbeitet werden muss. – Zur Zeit vgl. den Beitrag von O. Wischmeyer im vorliegenden Band.

riographische Erzählzusammenhänge besonders dadurch, dass der Evangelienschreiber seine ereignisgeschichtliche Darstellung chronologisch, geographisch und logisch ordnet und in ein narratives Gesamtkonzept einordnet, das der Erzählung über die ‚Anfänge des Evangeliums' dient (Mk 1,1; vgl. auch Phil 4,15). Wieweit Markus, der Initiator der Evangelienerzählung, dabei seinerseits in Kontinuität zu dem Briefeschreiber Paulus steht, soll abschließend diskutiert werden.

Die Ansätze und Grenzen einer Konstruktion von Geschichte bei Paulus und Markus werden und bleiben zugleich greifbar, wenn wir uns vor Augen führen, an welche grundlegenden historiographischen Formen die Konstruktion von Geschichte im lukanischen Doppelwerk gebunden ist.

1 Historiographische Geschichtskonstruktion bei Lukas

Was den Verfasser des lukanischen Doppelwerkes wohl am Ende des 1. Jahrhunderts zu einem historiographischen Autor, zu einem ‚Geschichtsschreiber' macht[3], ist vor allem sein Interesse daran, die Geschichte des Lebens und Wirkens Jesu im Evangelium (Lk) und die Geschichte der wesentlich durch Paulus beförderten Ausbreitung der ersten nachösterlichen Gemeinden in der Apostelgeschichte (Apg) nicht nur in einem literarischen Doppelwerk zu verbinden, sondern dabei zugleich auch jeweils mit der Zeit- und Weltgeschichte zu synchronisieren[4]. Die ineinander greifenden Ereignisse in Galiläa und Jerusalem[5] und die Geschichte des Wirkens der Osterzeugen finden in und unter den zeitlichen und räumlichen Bedingungen des *Imperium Romanum* statt (z. B. Lk 2,1; 3,1). Sie sind zugleich untrennbar mit der Geschichte Israels verbunden[6]. Mit Hilfe dieses historiographischen *framing* gelingt es dem Verfasser des Doppelwerkes, den allgemeinen Wirkungsanspruch des Evangeliums räumlich wie zeitlich[7] herauszustellen. Es

---

3 Vgl. J. Roloff, Die Apostelgeschichte (NTD 5), Göttingen/Zürich² 1988, 9. – „Für die Historiographie sind entscheidend: ein Vorwort, die Synchronisierung, Reden und Briefe", J. Jervell, Die Apostelgeschichte (KEK 3), Göttingen 1998, 77.
4 Das Phänomen der lukanischen Synchronismen ist in der Kommentar-Literatur immer wieder herausgestellt worden, vgl. z. B.: J. Fitzmyer, The Gospel According to Luke (I–IX) (AncB 28), Garden City 1981, 172–179.
5 Lk 24,50–53; Apg 1,9–14.
6 M. Wolter, Das Lukasevangelium (HNT 5), Tübingen 2008, 26–33 spricht daher bei Lukas von einer „Epochengeschichte".
7 S. die mit der Augustus-Verehrung einhergehenden Friedenserwartungen.

geht aber – wie schon *Ernst Haenchen* betont hatte[8] – dem *auctor ad Theophilum* bei diesem Zugriff auf die Ereignisgeschichte primär nicht darum, Geschichte zu dokumentieren, sondern sie narrativ zu erfassen und unter den Bedingungen seiner Zeit zu deuten. Damit nimmt Lukas die grundsätzlich deutende Aufgabe eines antiken Historiographen wie *Tacitus* oder *Josephus* wahr.

Dass Lukas bei seiner in einem Doppelwerk dargelegten Konzeption von Ereignisgeschichte über die Evangelien des Markus und Matthäus weit hinausgeht und sich auch in literarischer und historischer Hinsicht als faktisch einziger frühchristlicher Autor in die Nähe der hellenistisch-römischen Geschichtsschreibung im engeren Sinne begibt, ist seit der älteren literaturgeschichtlichen Forschung (vgl. neben *Franz Overbeck* und *Eduard Meyer* auch *Eduard Norden*)[9] bis in die gegenwärtige Acta-Forschung (z. B. *Eckhard Plümacher*)[10] gern und häufig konstatiert worden. Die diegetische Darstellung des Lukas umfasst in der Tat Quellenstudium, literarische *aemulatio*, also Wettbewerb mit Vorgängerwerken und Zeitgenossen, sowie eine geschichtlich strukturierte und zeitgeschichtlich geordnete Darstellung des auf ihn gekommenen Überlieferungsmaterials (Lk 1,1 ff.; Apg 1,1 f.). Der vergleichsweise hohe Selbstanspruch des Autors, der in den Proömien zum Ausdruck kommt, korrespondiert überdies mit dem historischen und literarischen Programm seiner Darstellung.

Im Vergleich dazu bleiben Paulus und Markus – die Initiatoren der epistolographischen und der narrativen frühchristlichen Schriftstellerei[11], deren Schriften damit auch unmittelbar oder mittelbar zu den literarischen Quellen des Lukas im Evangelium und der Apg gezählt haben dürfen – blass. Ihr Interesse an der Konstruktion von Welt-Geschichte ist – gemessen an der lukanischen Kon-

---

[8] Vgl. E. Haenchen, Tradition und Komposition in der Apostelgeschichte, in: ders., Gott und Mensch. Gesammelte Aufsätze, Tübingen 1965, 206–226.
[9] So z. B. E. Norden, Antike Kunstprosa. Vom VI. Jahrhundert v. Chr. bis in die Zeit der Renaissance, Bd. 2, Darmstadt ⁵1958, 480 ff.
[10] Vgl. E. Plümacher, Geschichte und Geschichten. Aufsätze zur Apostelgeschichte und zu den Johannesakten, hg. von J. Schröter/R. Brucker (WUNT 170), Tübingen 2004; ders., Lukas als griechischer Historiker, in: RE.S 14 (1974), 235–264. – Vgl. insgesamt auch die verschiedenen Beiträge, in: J. Frey et al. (Hgg.), Die Apostelgeschichte im Kontext antiker und frühchristlicher Historiographie (BZNW 162), Berlin/New York 2009. S. auch den Forschungsüberblick bei K. Backhaus, Die Apostelgeschichte im Kontext der hellenistisch-römischen Kultur, in: ThLZ 137 (2012), 887–900, der allerdings in dieser Hinsicht eher unvertieft bleibt.
[11] „Paulus und der Markus-Evangelist sind somit die entscheidenden Gestalten der ersten Phase der urchristlichen Literatur. Beide schufen eine personenbezogene Literatur, die in den Evangelien auf Jesus, in den Briefen auf Paulus konzentriert war", G. Theißen, Die Entstehung des Neuen Testaments als literaturgeschichtliches Problem. Vorgetragen am 27.11.2004 (Schriften der Philosophisch-historischen Klasse der Heidelberger Akademie der Wissenschaften 40), Heidelberg 2007, 135.

zeption – äußerst begrenzt. Gleichwohl finden sich bei Markus, sogar schon bei Paulus, prä-historiographische Elemente und Erzählformen, die zur Konstruktion *frühchristlicher Geschichte*[12] und damit auch zur Identitätsfindung frühchristlicher Gemeinden beitragen. Um eine vergleichende Zusammenstellung dieser prä-historiographischen Elemente, die dann auch bei Paulus und Markus in verschiedener Form zur Konstruktion von ‚Geschichte' führen, soll es im Folgenden gehen.

2 Prä-historiographische Geschichtskonstruktionen bei Paulus und Markus

2.1 Historische Bezüge und Synchronismen

Im Vergleich zur lukanischen Geschichtskonstruktion ist der Bezug auf Welt- und Zeitgeschichte in den paulinischen Briefen, aber auch in der frühesten Evangelienschrift marginal. Er lässt sich mit wenigen Federstrichen zeichnen. Wir finden lediglich an einer Stelle die Erwähnung einer zeitgeschichtlich bedeutenden politischen Person, nämlich des in Damaskus regierenden Nabatäer-Königs Aretas (2 Kor 11,32: ... ὁ ἐθνάρχης Ἀρέτα τοῦ βασιλέως ...)[13]. Zeit- oder weltgeschichtliche Referenzen zu Orten oder Institutionen, die mit dem *Imperium Romanum* verbunden sind, begegnen höchst unspezifisch, und zwar einerseits im Zusammenhang mit eher unpräzisen Hinweisen zum Gefangenschaftsort des Paulus (Phil 1,13) und andererseits in einer formalisierten Rede von der von Rom ausgehenden politischen Herrschaft (Röm 13,1ff.: ἐξουσία)[14]. Es zeigt sich, dass his-

---

[12] Es lässt sich sogar sagen, dass die vier, von C. Markschies (Art. Geschichte/Geschichtsauffassung VI. Kirchengeschichte, in: RGG⁴ 3 [2000], 789–791) benannten „Grundprobleme" christlicher Geschichtskonstruktion bereits bei Paulus und Markus begegnen: die Darstellung aus einer „Innenperspektive", das Spannungsfeld zwischen „zeitgenössischer Historiographie... und syst(ematischer) Theologie", „Selektion" sowie die Konstruktion und Rekonstruktion von Geschichte „aufgrund einer kleinen Zahl relativ einfacher Modelle" (alle Zitate im Original kursiv).

[13] Der Hinweis des Paulus hat seinerseits allgemein historischen Wert, vgl. E. Schürer, Geschichte des jüdischen Volkes im Zeitalter Jesu Christi, Bd. 1, Hildesheim/New York 1970 (Nachdruck der Ausgabe Leipzig 1901), 736–739; M. Hengel/A.M. Schwemer, Paulus zwischen Damaskus und Antiochien. Die unbekannten Jahre des Apostels, mit einem Beitrag von E.A. Knauf (WUNT 108), Tübingen 1998, 174–194.

[14] Zum Begriff im Sinne der Verwaltungsterminologie vgl. die Hinweise bei R. Jewett, Romans. A Commentary (Hermeneia), Minneapolis 2007, 787f. (Lit.!).

torische Referenzen bei Paulus – wenn sie überhaupt festzustellen sind – in erster Linie in autobiographischem Erzählzusammenhang begegnen[15]. An der Bezugnahme auf politische Personen der Zeitgeschichte zeigt Paulus insgesamt kein Interesse. Er selbst erwähnt keinen der Namen aus der römischen Verwaltung, die wir aus der Apostelgeschichte kennen[16].

Bei Markus kommt es in Kapitel 6 zu einem umfassenderen Verweis auf Herodes Antipas, der einerseits die breite gesellschaftliche Wirkung der Mission Jesu widerspiegeln soll (6,14–16), also eine konstatierende Funktion hat, andererseits an eben dieser Stelle (s. 1,14; 2,18–22) oder aber in einem *flashback* die gesellschaftspolitisch begründeten Todesumstände des Täufers eher legendarisch darstellt (6,17–29)[17]. In der markinischen Passionsgeschichte schließlich wird neben dem Aufrührer Barabbas (Mk 15,7)[18] lediglich Pilatus als politische Autorität, die die Verurteilung Jesu zu verantworten hat, namentlich angeführt (Mk 15,1ff.)[19]. Die mehrfache Erwähnung der Hohenpriester (bes. Mk 14,1.43.53ff.; 15,1), die zusammen mit dem Täufer zu den politisch-religiös relevanten Personen der Zeitgeschichte zählen, bleibt unspezifisch. Immerhin lässt sich die Hinrichtung Jesu in Jerusalem damit zeitgeschichtlich fassen und kontextualisieren: Sie findet *nicht* außerhalb der Zeit- und Weltgeschichte statt, sondern ist an die Nennung politischer und administrativer Handlungsträger gebunden[20].

Die einzigen weiteren Elemente, die bei Markus die erzählte Ereignisgeschichte mit Ereignissen oder Daten verknüpfen, begegnen in 1,14 (μετὰ δὲ ... ἦλθεν) und in 14,1 (... μετὰ δύο ἡμέρας): Es handelt sich hierbei freilich nicht wie bei Lukas um Verknüpfungen der erzählten Ereignisgeschichte mit der Weltgeschichte, sondern vielmehr um eine Darstellungsweise, die eine – wenn auch eher lose – Synchronie mit innerjüdischen bzw. inner-palästinischen Daten wie dem Beginn des Passah-Festes oder teils auch politisch relevanten Ereignissen wie der auch von *Josephus* berichteten Gefangennahme des Täufers[21] herstellt. Auch

---

15 Die Bedeutung der Biographie und Autobiographie des/bei Paulus also ist auch hinsichtlich der Frage nach der Konstruktion von Geschichte kaum überzubewerten.
16 Das gilt auch für Nero Phil 4,22, vgl. M. Frenschkowski, Art. Nero in: RAC Lieferung 199, 2013, 839–878, 871.
17 Vgl. dazu auch E.-M. Becker, Das Markus-Evangelium im Rahmen antiker Historiographie (WUNT 194), Tübingen 2006, bes. 230–237.
18 Die historisch kaum weiter zu identifizierende Person des Barabbas wird im Passionsbericht – durchaus im historiographischen Sinne – zu einem ‚Antitypen' zu Jesus konstruiert: Vgl. D. Dormeyer, Art. Barabbas, in: RGG⁴ 1 (1998), 1105.
19 Bei Paulus fehlt auch dieser politische Bezug!
20 Die hinter Markus liegenden Quellen und Traditionen weisen damit ihrerseits sog. ‚Lokalkolorit' (G. Theißen) auf.
21 Antiquitates Iudaicae 18,116–119.

verknüpft Markus die von ihm erzählte Ereignisgeschichte nicht direkt mit der Welt- und Zeitgeschichte. Nur in zwei Erzählzusammenhängen bietet er überhaupt historische Bezüge: im Blick auf die Hinrichtung des Täufers (6,17 ff.) und im Blick auf die Passion Jesu (14–15). Dass allein der gewaltsame Tod des Täufers und die Hinrichtung Jesu unter Bezugnahme auf die politische Zeitgeschichte erzählt werden, ist sicher nicht zufällig, sondern macht wahrscheinlich, dass *exitus*-Erzählungen zum historischen wie literarischen Quellenbestand des Markus-Evangelisten gezählt haben[22]. Im Unterschied dazu sind die lukanischen Synchronismen breiter angelegt und bewusst gestaltet. Sie dienen nicht nur der zeitlichen Kontextualisierung der Todesschicksale, sondern betonen von vornherein den Beginn der Wirksamkeit Jesu (Lk 2–3). Außerdem sind sie über die bloß zeitlich eher lose Einbettung der Ereignisgeschichte selbst Teil der historiographischen Konstruktion ihres Verfassers. So schafft Lukas explizit mit dem literarischen Mittel des Synchronismus weltgeschichtliche Zusammenhänge.

Dagegen bleiben Paulus und Markus alles in allem äußerst sparsam, ja dürftig mit ihren Referenzen auf die Zeit- und Weltgeschichte – die Zusammenschau von Ereignisgeschichte und Weltgeschichte ist für ihre ‚Erzählstrategie' offenbar weitgehend irrelevant. Die Konstruktion von Geschichte liegt bei Paulus und Markus eher implizit vor. Sie geschieht allein auf der Ebene der Konstruktion einer ‚Ereignisgeschichte'. Paulus und Markus nämlich nehmen durchaus die geschichtliche Zeit als vergangen und gleichzeitig die Gegenwart beeinflussend wahr. Sie gestalten die Erzählung über das Vergangene von dieser Wahrnehmung her. So ist nicht erst Lukas – wie vielfach in der Forschung behauptet wurde[23] – gleichsam der ‚Erfinder' einer frühchristlichen Geschichtskonstruktion. Vielmehr knüpft der ‚erste christliche Historiker' Lukas in seiner historiographischen Arbeit grundlegend an Paulus und Markus an.

Bevor ich im Folgenden die einzelnen Elemente der paulinischen und der markinischen Geschichtskonstruktion näher in den Blick nehme, frage ich nach den historischen Kontexten, in denen sich beide Verfasser bewegen und die ihren Zugriff auf ‚Geschichte' prägen. Dabei wird auch zu überlegen sein, ob und inwieweit sich die Wahrnehmung und Deutung von Geschichte von Paulus zu Markus hin bereits signifikant verändert hat.

---

22 Vgl. ausführlicher dazu: E.-M. Becker, Markus-Evangelium, bes. 376–382.
23 Vgl. vor allem: R. Bultmann; E. Dinkler; H. Conzelmann; zuletzt auch: M. Bauspieß, Geschichte und Erkenntnis im lukanischen Geschichtswerk. Eine exegetische Untersuchung zu einer christlichen Perspektive auf Geschichte, Leipzig 2012.

2.2 Historische Standortbestimmungen

Paulus und Markus äußern sich in unterschiedlicher Weise zum *Jerusalemer Tempel*. Das Thema hat exemplarische Bedeutung für die Frage, wie beide Autoren ihre Beziehung zur Zeitgeschichte in Hinsicht auf politische oder religiöse Institutionen gestalten und wieweit der ‚historische Standort‘, von dem aus sie Geschichte wahrnehmen, auf ihre Konstruktion von Geschichte eingewirkt hat. Beide Autoren erwähnen den Jerusalemer Tempel mehrfach und deuten übereinstimmend auf eine Denk- und Erzählwelt hin (‚erzählte Zeit‘), die von der Situation *ante eventum* 70 n.Chr. geprägt ist. Bei Paulus dient der Tempel als vitale Metapher (z. B. 1 Kor 3,16 f.; 6,19), die über die οἰκοδομή der Gemeinde hinaus ein umfassendes semantisches Inventar generiert[24]. Bei Markus fungiert der Tempel als betriebsamer Austragungsort für Jesu Streitgespräche in Jerusalem (Mk 11,27 ff.) analog den Synagogen in Galiläa (Mk 1,39; 3,1)[25].

Anders als Paulus, der zu Beginn der flavischen Dynastie, und d.h. auf dem Höhepunkt des ersten jüdisch-römischen Krieges und der damit einhergehenden Tempelzerstörung nicht mehr am Leben war, hat Markus, der als Evangelist einige Jahre später tätig wurde, bei seiner Sicht auf den Tempel (‚Erzählzeit‘) das Wissen um dessen Gefährdung und Zerstörung in seine Erzählung durchaus einfließen lassen – wenn freilich auch hier wieder nur implizit: Das jesuanische Tempelwort (Mk 13,1 f.) und das Tempel-Prodigium im Augenblick des Todes Jesu (Mk 15,38) erlauben aber wertvolle Einsichten in die markinische Sicht auf die Bedeutung des Tempels und seine historiographische Funktion bei der Deutung und Bewältigung des Schicksals Jesu kurz nach 70 n.Chr.[26]

Gerade im Blick darauf, welche geschichtsdeutende Funktion dem Jerusalemer Tempel beigemessen wird, lässt sich an diesem Punkt eine signifikante

---

24 Vgl. z.B. A.L.A. Hogeterp, Paul and God's Temple. A Historical Interpretation of Cultic Imagery in the Corinthian Correspondence (Biblical Tools and Studies 2), Leuven/Paris/Dudley 2006; C. Böttrich, „Ihr seid der Tempel Gottes". Tempelmetaphorik und Gemeinde bei Paulus, in: Gemeinde ohne Tempel. Zur Substituierung und Transformation des Jerusalemer Tempels und seines Kults im Alten Testament, antiken Judentum und frühen Christentum, hg. von B. Ego et al. (WUNT 118), Tübingen 1999, 411–425.
25 Ob für die ‚erzählte Zeit‘ überhaupt schon Synagogen in Galiläa zu vermuten sind, ist in der Forschung bis heute umstritten: Synagogen im 1. Jh. n.Chr. sind bisher nur an folgenden Orten in Palästina überhaupt nachweisbar: Jerusalem (vgl. sog. Theodotus-Inschrift), Gamla, evtl. Kapernaum (eher umstritten), herodianisches Jericho und Masada sowie evtl. Qiryat Sefer (nördlich von Jerusalem), Modi'in (nordwestlich von Jerusalem), vgl. J.F. Strange, Art. Synagogue, in: Encyclopedia of the Historical Jesus, ed. by C.A. Evans, New York/London 2008, 612–616.
26 Vgl. noch einmal: E.-M. Becker, Markus-Evangelium, 77–102 und 316–340.

Entwicklung von Paulus zu Markus hin feststellen: Der innere geschichtliche Zusammenhang zwischen dem gewaltsamen Tod Jesu und der endzeitlich vorgestellten Zerstörung des Tempels, wie er bei Markus hergestellt wird (Mk 13.15), hat sich für Paulus *noch nicht* abgezeichnet. Der briefeschreibende Apostel beschränkt sich lediglich darauf, Jesus Christus als ἱλαστήριον zu bezeichnen (Röm 3,25)[27], wenn er seine Tempelmetaphorik soteriologisch und auf Christus bezogen in seiner Argumentation einsetzt. Paulus deutet den Tod Jesu vor dem Hintergrund des jüdischen Kultus – die Wahrnehmung der Zeitgeschichte und der Bezug auf sie erweisen sich dabei nicht als relevant. Anders Markus: von der Passion und dem Sterben Jesu lässt sich aus seiner Sicht nur berichten, wenn zugleich auch auf das Schicksal des Jerusalemer Tempels Bezug genommen wird[28]. Der markinische Zugriff auf ‚Geschichte' ist daher erkennbar von einer Perspektive *post eventum* 70 n. Chr. geprägt[29].

2.3 ‚Erinnerung' und Zukunftsorientierung

Trotz dieser differierenden historischen Standorte teilen die paulinische und die markinische Konstruktion von Geschichte zwei Dimensionen: die Vermittlung geschichtlichen Wissens (‚Erinnerung') und die Erwartung vom Ende der Geschichte (Zukunftsorientierung). Beide Autoren propagieren *einerseits* die Rück-Erinnerung an den „Anfang des Evangeliums" (Phil 4,15; Mk 1,1) und das Handeln seiner Protagonisten (z. B. Mk 14,1 ff.) als Medium der Überlieferung von Ereignisgeschichte. Bei Paulus spielen in diesem Zusammenhang die Konstruktion der eigenen Biographie[30] und der Missions- und Gemeindegeschichte eine besondere Rolle. *Andererseits* richten beide Autoren ihre Deutung von Geschichte und Gegenwart an der Erwartung der Nähe der Parusie (z. B. 1 Thess 4,13 – 18) bzw. des Einbruchs der Gottesherrschaft (Mk 13,24 ff.; 1,15) aus. Beide Autoren nehmen Zeit

---

27 Vgl. zur Semantik z. B. R. Jewett, Romans, 284 – 290 (Lit.!).
28 Das gilt unabhängig von der Frage, ob das sog. Tempelwort Jesu (vgl. Mk 13,2; 14,58; 15,29 und parr.) einen authentischen Kern hat.
29 Das gilt für Markus und Matthäus – einzig Lukas arbeitet die Bezüge zum jüdisch-römischen Krieg noch deutlicher heraus (Lk 19,41 – 44). Vgl. zuletzt auch: E.-M. Becker, Dating Mark and Matthew as Ancient Literature, in: Mark and Matthew I, Comparative Readings. Understanding the Earliest Gospels in their First-Century Setting, eds. E.-M. Becker/A. Runesson (WUNT 271), Tübingen 2011, 123 – 143.
30 Vgl. dazu auch: F. Avemarie, Heilsgeschichte und Lebensgeschichte bei Paulus, in: Heil und Geschichte: Die Geschichtsbezogenheit des Heils und das Problem der Heilsgeschichte in der biblischen Tradition und in der theologischen Deutung, hg. von J. Frey et al. (WUNT 248), Tübingen 2009, 357 – 383.

und Geschichte aus der eschatologischen Perspektive wahr und deuten sie von hier her.

Zugleich aber greifen die Dimensionen der Erinnerung und Zukunftsorientierung bei Paulus und Markus ineinander: Bei Paulus wird die eschatologische Heilszeit in der jetzigen Geschichte durch den Akt der Akklamation („Maranatha": 1 Kor 16,22) oder der Konfession des Glaubens (Röm 10,9) präsent. An die hier zugrunde liegenden Traditionen (*paradosis*) muss Paulus wiederum teilweise in formelhafter Sprache[31] rückerinnern (z. B. 1 Kor 15,1ff.), was nicht zuletzt auch der eigenen Autorisierung als Apostel und Gemeindeleiter dienen soll (1 Kor 15,8f.). Bei Markus realisiert sich die eschatologische Zeit in der Jetztzeit durch die Proklamation des Evangeliums (Mk 1,1; 1,14f.), die ihrerseits polyvalent entfaltet wird. Teils wird sie im Blick auf das Handeln Jesu als in der Vergangenheit liegend erzählt; teils wird eine bestimmte Textpragmatik erzeugt: Mittels Rückerinnerung nämlich vollzieht sich der Anbruch der Gottesherrschaft im aktuellen Lesevorgang sowie im rechten Verstehen der apokalyptischen Botschaft Jesu[32]. Der Begriff „Evangelium" selbst spiegelt diese Polyvalenz, indem er die in der Vergangenheit liegende Verkündigung Jesu mit der literarischen Erzählung, die wiederum selbst im Akt der Proklamation wirken kann, verknüpft.

Gerade dies Ineinandergreifen der zeitlichen Dimensionen von Geschichte, Gegenwart und eschatologischer Zeit macht deutlich, dass wir es bei Paulus und Markus mit religiös geprägter Prosa-Literatur – Epistolographie und personenzentrierter Geschichtserzählung – zu tun haben. Ihren „Sitz im Leben" hat diese Literatur bei den Anhängern des Evangeliums von Jesus Christus. Die Interdependenz von Erinnerung, gegenwartsbezogener Proklamation des Evangeliums und Zukunftsorientierung führt schließlich dazu, dass das paulinische und das markinische Geschichtsdenken weder zyklisch noch im eigentlichen Sinne linear noch gar chaotisch konzipiert ist[33], sondern sich – wie schon *Bultmann* zu recht betont hatte[34] – eschatologisch, zugleich aber heilsgeschichtlich orientiert.

Doch auch wenn das geschichtliche Denken des Paulus in erster Linie als heilsgeschichtlich und eschatologisch zu bestimmen ist, lässt sich daraus nicht folgern, dass die „*Geschichtsanschauung des Paulus*... ganz von der Eschatologie

---

31 Z.B.: λέγω δὲ ὑμῖν, Παῦλος ἀπόστολος, οἴδατε ...
32 Sog. Leseappell in Mk 13,14.
33 Zur Übersicht über die geschichtsphilosophischen Modelle vgl. zuletzt auch B.M. Sheppard, The Craft of History and the Study of the New Testament, Atlanta 2012, bes. 32–34.
34 Vgl. R. Bultmann, Das Verständnis der Geschichte unter dem Einfluß der Eschatologie, in: ders., Geschichte und Eschatologie, Tübingen ³1979, 24–43.

bestimmt" wäre[35]. Vielmehr konstruiert bereits Paulus Zeit und Geschichte mit genuinen sprachlichen und literarischen, teils narrativen[36] Mitteln zum Zwecke der Vergegenwärtigung des Vergangenen[37]. Dies gilt verstärkt für Markus, der die *narratio* über die ‚Anfänge des Evangeliums' (Mk 1,1 ff.) zum Gegenstand einer überwiegend in Vergangenheitstempora abgefassten Prosa-Erzählung gemacht hat, in welcher Narrativität und Verkündigung an einander gebunden sind. Indem aber das ereignis- und heilsgeschichtliche Denken narrativ entfaltet wird, tritt es allmählich in die Strukturen linearen Geschichtsdenkens ein. Die ‚Geschichte' ist dann nicht mehr nur als in Auflösung begriffen verstanden, sondern sie wird, wie wir nun sehen, narrativ strukturiert und somit auf- und fortgeschrieben.

2.4 Chronologisierung und Narrativität

Als Prosa-Schriftsteller, die Vergangenheitstempora zum Zwecke der Erzählung verwenden, strukturieren Paulus wie Markus ihre Darstellung chronologisch. Der Gegenstandsbereich variiert freilich. Paulus konstruiert im Wesentlichen neben seiner Autobiographie in Ansätzen Missionsgeschichte und zudem auch Heilsgeschichte. Markus konstruiert eine Ereignisgeschichte, die die Anfänge der Evangeliumsverkündigung (Mk 1,1) in Kontinuität zur Geschichte Israels (Mk 1,2f.) nachzeichnet. Es empfiehlt sich, die paulinische und die markinische Konstruktion von Zeit und Geschichte zunächst je für sich zu betrachten.

---

35 So R. Bultmann, Das Problem der Eschatologie A. Die Historisierung und die Neutralisierung der Eschatologie im Urchristentum, in: ders., Geschichte und Eschatologie, Tübingen ³1979, 44– 64, hier: 46: „Die Geschichte, auf die Paulus zurückblickt, ist keineswegs die Geschichte Israels, also Volksgeschichte, sondern die Geschichte der Menschheit" (ebd.).
36 Vgl. insgesamt zur Diskussion über die Narrativität des Paulus: R. B. Hays, „Is Paul's Gospel Narratable?", in: JSNT 27 (2004), 217–239.
37 Vgl. dazu etwa auch H.D. Betz, Der Galaterbrief. Ein Kommentar zum Brief des Apostels Paulus an die Gemeinden in Galatien. Aus dem Amerikanischen übersetzt und für die deutsche Ausgabe redaktionell bearbeitet von S. Ann, München 1988, 71 im Blick auf die Funktion des Galater-Briefes: „... Gleichzeitig dient er (= Gal) als *Erinnerung* an die Geschichte der Galater. Sie werden nicht nur über Ereignisse der Vergangenheit informiert, sondern wenn sie den Brief gelesen haben, sehen sie sich selbst zurückversetzt zu dem Augenblick, als sie dem Evangelium zuerst begegneten...". – Dass bereits Paulus an der Konstruktion von Geschichte Interesse zeigt, wird in der Paulus-Forschung gemeinhin gerne übersehen, vgl. zuletzt auch: F. W. Horn (Hg.), Paulus Handbuch, Tübingen 2013, wo ein entsprechender Beitrag zum Geschichtsverständnis des Paulus nicht begegnet.

2.4.1 Paulus

Insgesamt lassen sich drei sachliche Ebenen unterscheiden, auf denen wir das Zeit- und Geschichtsverständnis des Paulus erkennen können: auf der Ebene der Autobiographie, der Missions- und Gemeindegeschichte sowie der ‚Heilsgeschichte'.

(1) In autobiographischen Zusammenhängen[38] konstruiert Paulus seine eigene Biographie im Spannungsfeld seiner Herkunft aus dem pharisäisch geprägten Judentum (Gal 1–2; Phil 3) und seiner gegenwärtigen konflikt- und entbehrungsreichen Missions- und Gemeindeleitertätigkeit als ‚Apostel Jesu Christi'[39]. Die umfangreichste autobiographische *narratio* begegnet in Gal 1,11–2,14. Sie erweist sich für die Analyse der paulinischen Geschichtskonstruktion in besonderer Weise als aufschlussreich und soll daher exegetisch etwas ausführlicher betrachtet werden.

In diesem Textabschnitt, in dem Paulus auf sein ‚früheres' Leben im Judentum, seine Beauftragung zum Apostel Jesu Christi sowie die Anfänge seines apostolischen Wirkens in chronologischer Folge zu sprechen kommt, fällt die sorgfältige sprachliche und literarische Gestaltung der Darstellung auf. Das gilt besonders für die temporale Strukturierung des Textes. So leitet Paulus den Bericht über zwei ‚Ereignisse' mit der temporalen Konjunktion ὅτε ein (Gal 1,15; 2,11 f.): Das *erste* ‚Ereignis' besteht in der göttlichen Beauftragung, die zwar im Sinne prophetischer Berufung bereits vor seiner Geburt erfolgt ist, aber erst durch die Offenbarung des Gottes-Sohnes ἐν ἐμοί vollzogen wird. Das Ziel der Beauftragung (ἵνα) benennt Paulus in Gal 1,16b in einer parallel angelegten Syntagmatik: So wie der Gottes-Sohn an Paulus offenbar gemacht wurde (Gal 1,16a), soll der Apostel ihn ‚unter den Heiden' (ἐν τοῖς ἔθνεσιν) bekannt machen. Dem entspricht die ‚Unverzüglichkeit' der paulinischen Reaktion (Gal 1,16c: εὐθέως) – Paulus beschließt, zunächst in die Arabia, dann nach Damaskus zu gehen (Gal 1,17b).

Dieser Entschluss ist – wie sich nun zeigt – folgenreich. Es schließt sich eine dreimalige ἔπειτα-Struktur an (Gal 1,18.21; 2,1). Mit Hilfe dieses temporalen Adverbs stellt Paulus mit mehr oder weniger genauen Zeitangaben im Folgenden die chronologischen Zusammenhänge seines frühen apostolischen Wirkens dar[40].

---

38 Vgl. allgemein: E.-M. Becker, Autobiographisches bei Paulus. Aspekte und Aufgaben, in: Biographie und Persönlichkeit des Paulus, hg. von E.-M. Becker/P. Pilhofer (WUNT 187), Tübingen 2005/2009, 67–87.
39 Z.B. 2 Kor 1,10–12; bes.: Peristasenkataloge.
40 Nur am Rande sei hier vermerkt, dass diese Chronologie gemeinhin vor allem in historischer Hinsicht als zentraler Ausgangspunkt der relativen Chronologisierung der paulinischen Bio-

Nach drei Jahren (Gal 1,18) kommt Paulus nach Jerusalem, um sich mit Kephas zu besprechen (ἱστορῆσαι): Ein Lexem vom Stamm ἱστορ-, dem Grundbegriff historiographischer Terminologie in der Gräzität[41], begegnet innerhalb der neutestamentlichen Schriften allein hier. Das ist kaum zufällig. Mit der Wahl dieses Lexems unterstreicht Paulus nämlich, dass ihm hier eine *authentische* Kontaktaufnahme mit dem Jerusalemer Kreis der Christus-Zeugen, also eine Art der Autopsie, möglich war[42]. Damit tritt Paulus selbst in die Zeugenkette (ἵστωρ) ein.

Paulus bleibt bei seinem ersten Besuch seit seiner Beauftragung vierzehn Tage bei Petrus in Jerusalem (Gal 1,18b). Nur lose fügt er in seiner Darstellung nun die nächste Etappe seines Wirkens mit dem zweiten ἔπειτα in V. 21 an: Paulus kommt ‚danach' nach Syrien und Kilikien. Die dritte Verwendung von ἔπειτα in Gal 2,1 hingegen ist wiederum mit einer genaueren Zeitangabe verknüpft: Vierzehn Jahre später kommt Paulus wieder (πάλιν) nach Jerusalem, nun in Begleitung von Barnabas und Timotheus. Mit dieser Formulierung leitet Paulus seine Darstellung des sog. Apostelkonzils in Jerusalem ein (vgl. dazu Apg 15,1–29), das er in Gal 2,9b–10 in die Einigung auf die Aufteilung des Missionsgebietes – unter ‚Heiden' und unter die ‚Beschneidung' – münden lässt. Die Kollektensammlung für die ‚Armen' in Jerusalem wird als einzige Auflage genannt (Gal 2,10). Paulus kommt, wie er betont, dieser Aufgabe seither[43], äußerst engagiert nach[44].

Mit dem Beschluss des Apostelkonzils zur Aufteilung der Missionsgebiete wird gleichsam ‚nachvollzogen', was aus der Sicht des Paulus bereits Inhalt seiner Beauftragung durch Gott selbst war[45]. So ergibt sich syntaktisch folgerichtig erst hier die Notwendigkeit, die Erzählung über das *zweite ‚Ereignis'*, das die Geschichte des paulinischen Wirkens und damit die Vorgeschichte des Schreibens an

---

graphie dient – vgl. etwa J. Becker, Paulus. Der Apostel der Völker, Tübingen 1989, 6–33; E. Ebel, Das Leben des Paulus, in: Paulus. Leben – Umwelt – Werk – Briefe, hg. von O. Wischmeyer (UTB 2767), Tübingen/Basel ²2012, 105–118. – Mir geht es im Folgenden jedoch darum, den geschichtskonstruierenden Charakter dieser autobiographischen Rede in den Blick zu nehmen. – H.D. Betz, Galaterbrief, 151 gliedert dann auch auf der Basis der ἔπειτα-Struktur die narratio in Gal 1,12–2,14.

41 Vgl. dazu auch: E.-M. Becker, Art. Geschichte/Geschichtlichkeit II. Neutestamentlich, in: LBH (2009/2013), 206–207. – Übersicht auch bei: O. Hofius, Gal 1,18 ἱστορῆσαι Κηφᾶν, in: Ders., Paulusstudien (WUNT 51), Tübingen 1989, 255–267.

42 H. Schlier, Der Brief an die Galater (KEK 7), Göttingen ⁴1965, 60 formuliert zurückhaltender: „Ἱστορῆσαι Κηφᾶν ist mit Bedacht gesagt. Denn ἱστορῆσαι bezeichnet im hellenistischen Griechisch den Besuch zum Zwecke des Kennenlernens..." – mit Verweis auf z.B. Epiktet, Diss 2,14,28; 3,7,1; Josephus, Antiquitates Iudaicae 1,203; 7,46 etc.

43 ἐσπούδασα als ingressiver Aorist.

44 S. auch bes. 1 Kor 16; 2 Kor 8–9; Röm 15,25ff.

45 S.o. zu Gal 1,16b.

die Galater prägt, mit einer entsprechenden ὅτε-Konstruktion einsetzen zu lassen. Und umgekehrt reicht der narrative Spannungsbogen, der in Gal 1,15 eingeleitet wird, bis Gal 2,10. Im zweiten Spannungsbogen (Gal 2,11–14) berichtet Paulus über den sog. antiochenischen Zwischenfall (Gal 2,11–14). Die Frage, wieweit die Darstellung des Paulus über das Apostelkonzil und den Zwischenfall in Antiochia historisch zuverlässig sei[46], ist in unserem Zusammenhang von untergeordneter Bedeutung. Entscheidend ist vielmehr nachzuzeichnen, wie Paulus seine Autobiographie konstruiert und dabei frühchristliche ‚Ereignisgeschichte' deutend schafft.

Aus den genannten narrativen Spannungsbögen, die syntaktisch strukturiert sind, ergibt sich nämlich, dass Paulus das ‚Ereignis' der Berufung mit dem antiochenischen Zwischenfall zusammendenkt. In der Konsequenz misst er dem – aus seiner Sicht – provokativen Verhalten des Petrus in Antiochia (Gal 2,11–14) dieselbe ereignishafte Bedeutung bei wie seiner göttlichen Beauftragung zum ‚Heidenapostel' – jedenfalls gilt dies im Rahmen seines aktuellen Briefeschreibens an die Gemeinde(n) in Galatien. Die beiden narrativen Spannungsbögen lassen sich daher zutreffend unter den Stichworten: die ‚Richtigkeit der paulinischen Beauftragung' und die ‚Heuchelei des Petrus' zusammenfassen. Textpragmatisch zielt die Erzählung in Gal 1–2 also vor allem darauf, die Authentizität und Legitimität des paulinischen Apostolates herzuleiten und zu verteidigen. ‚Geschichte' wird nicht um ihrer selbst willen erzählt, sondern dient der aktuellen Begründung und Verteidigung des paulinischen Wirkens sowie der Rückerinnerung der Gemeinde an das ‚rechte Evangelium' (Gal 1,9). Es soll dabei gleichsam bei den Adressaten zu einer ‚Horizontverschmelzung' von Jetztzeit und der früheren Zeit des Erstkontakts mit dem Evangelium kommen[47].

Umgekehrt aber gilt: Paulus konstruiert durchaus Geschichte. Er gestaltet die Apologie seines Apostolates mit rhetorischen und literarischen Mitteln, indem er gehäuft die Form der autobiographischen *narratio* wählt – teils tut er dies mit eher geschichtlicher (Gal 1–2), teils mit eher apokalyptischer Perspektivierung (2 Kor 12). Im Sinne der epistolographischen Schreibstrategie dient die narrative Selbstkonstruktion nicht zuletzt auch der Repräsentation der Person[48]. Geschichtliche Konstruktionen haben bei Paulus immer Gegenwartsbezug.

---

46 Die Frage nach der historischen Rekonstruktion der paulinischen Biographie ist z.B. grundlegender Gegenstand der Darstellung in: M. Hengel/A. M. Schwemer, Paulus.
47 Vgl. H.D. Betz, Galater, 71 (s.o.), der so weit geht, den Paulus-Brief in der Konsequenz in die Nähe eines ‚himmlischen Briefes' zu rücken.
48 Vgl. dazu zuletzt auch: E.-M. Becker, Art. Person des Paulus, in: Paulus Handbuch, hg. von F. W. Horn, Tübingen 2013, 128–134.

Doch worin liegt – so könnten wir zu Abschluss dieser ausführlichen Textbetrachtung fragen – der ‚geschichtskonstruierende Überschuss', den der autobiographische Rückblick in Gal 1–2 freisetzt? Bei seiner Konstruktion der autobiographischen *narratio* legt Paulus insgesamt besonderen Wert darauf, einerseits die Dialektik zwischen dem ‚einstigen' Leben und der ‚jetzigen' Aufgabe als von Gott selbst beauftragter Apostel aufzuzeigen. Nicht zufällig werden in Gal 1,23 in der Mitte des Satzes die Partikel πότε und das Adverb νῦν antithetisch kontrastiert. Andererseits gibt Paulus mit der syntaktischen Strukturierung des Textabschnitts sowie der Wahl temporaler Semantik zu erkennen, dass es ihm um eine präzise Darstellung seiner Autobiographie geht, die zugleich der Rückerinnerung an und der Rückbesinnung auf das ‚rechte Evangelium' dienen soll (Gal 1,9–11). Die Wendung πρὸς ὥραν in Gal 2,5 expliziert diesen Gedanken *pars pro toto*: Die ‚Geschichte' seines Wirkens wird auf ‚die Stunde hin' genau bedacht und kann so vor den Adressaten (Gal 1,11.13.20) sowie vor Gott selbst (Gal 1,20) verantwortet werden. Die Konstruktion von ‚Geschichte' ist Teil eines kommunikativen Geschehens, das durch die ‚Person' des Paulus verantwortet und so auch authentifiziert ist. Damit versteht Paulus sich selbst als Protagonisten des Evangeliums und schreibt sich in diese neue Geschichte ein. Hier liegt die Voraussetzung für den Paulus-Teil der Apostelgeschichte: Die Geschichte der Entstehung der kleinasiatischen und griechischen Missionsgemeinden wird als Geschichte der missionarischen Tätigkeit des Paulus dargestellt.

(2) Im Rückblick auf seine missionshistorischen Anfänge in Thessaloniki oder Philippi (1 Thess 1 f.; Phil 4) entwirft Paulus *zweitens* eine ‚*collective memory*', die in der Folge dazu beiträgt, dass sich die frühchristlichen Gemeinden ihrer je eigenen ‚Gründungsgeschichte' und damit im Blick auf ihre Herkunft auch ihrer Identität bewusst werden können. Die paulinischen Ansätze zur Konstruktion einer Gemeindegeschichte sind literarisch folgenreich. Unabhängig davon, ob wir *Hubert Cancik* folgen und die Apostelgeschichte speziell als ‚Institutionsgeschichte' begreifen[49], hat Lukas mit seinen *Acta* etwa vierzig Jahre nach den Anfängen der paulinischen Korrespondenz *einen weiteren* Impuls aufgenommen, den der Apostel selbst in seinen Briefen gegeben hat[50]. Schon bald nach seinem Gründungsaufenthalt in Thessaloniki hatte Paulus nämlich die Notwendigkeit erkannt, die ‚Geschichte' seiner Missionstätigkeit festzuhalten und den brieflichen Adressaten mit dem Ziel der Rückerinnerung und -versicherung mitzuteilen.

---

49 Vgl. H. Cancik, Das Geschichtswerk des Lukas als Institutionsgeschichte. Die Vorbereitung des zweiten Logos im ersten, in: Die Apostelgeschichte im Kontext antiker und frühchristlicher Historiographie, hg. von J. Frey et al. (BZNW 162), Berlin/New York 2009, 519–538.
50 M. Hengel/A.M. Schwemer, Paulus, 31 haben daher Gal 1 f. als „„Apostelgeschichte in nuce"" bezeichnet.

In gewisser Weise setzt sich die Konstruktion von Gemeindegeschichte auch in den anderen Paulus-Briefen fort. In den Korinther-Briefen geht Paulus noch einen Schritt weiter. Denn hier wird die ‚Geschichte der brieflichen Korrespondenz', die wir uns als regen Austausch von Briefen zwischen der Gemeinde und Paulus vorstellen dürfen (z. B. 1 Kor 5,9; 7,1), selbst zu einem eigenständigen Thema des Briefeschreibens (vgl. 2 Kor 1,12–14; 2; 7; 10)[51]. Sogar im Römerbrief, der dem Erstbesuch des Apostels noch vorausgeht, lassen sich geschichtskonstruierende Elemente finden. In Röm 15,15 reflektiert Paulus das aktuelle Ziel seines Briefs an die ihm bisher weitgehend unbekannte Gemeinde in Rom. Auch hier geht es ihm um Rückerinnerung (ἐπαναμιμνῄσκειν)[52] und die Legitimierung seines Heidenapostolats (Röm 15,16: ... εἰς τὰ ἔθνη)[53]. Doch bereits das verhältnismäßig lange Präskript des Römerbriefes hat geschichtskonstruierende Züge. In der ausgedehnten *superscriptio* (V. 1–6) erläutert Paulus in geschichtlicher Perspektivierung wichtige ‚Grundbegriffe' seiner Mission und seines Apostolats. Er begründet *erstens* die Herkunft des ‚Evangeliums' (V. 2–3), verweist *zweitens* auf den Status des Gottes-Sohnes (V. 4) und *drittens* die legitimierende Bedeutung der Kyrios-Würde für den apostolischen Dienst unter den ‚Heiden' (V. 5). *Viertens* schließt Paulus seine Adressaten in Rom (V. 7) in diese Zielgruppe – ἐν πᾶσιν τοῖς ἔθνεσιν – explizit ein (V. 6). Das Präskript dient also nicht nur der Vorstellung und Empfehlung des Apostels, sondern konstruiert gleichermaßen die ‚Vorgeschichte' der paulinischen Evangeliumsverkündigung[54]. Die Geschichtskonstruktion geschieht hier zum Zwecke der Vorbereitung einer Reise, die Paulus nach Spanien führen (Röm 15,22 ff.) und so dem Abschluss seiner Heidenmission näherbringen soll[55]. In den verschiedenen Paulus-Briefen lässt sich beobachten, wie die jeweilige Form der Geschichtskonstruktion und der literarische Charakter des Briefes gegenseitig auf einander einwirken. Im Römer-Brief erschließt sich die dahinter liegende missionsstrategische Ambition aber auch vor dem Hintergrund apokalyptischer Sprach- und Denkwelt (Röm 11,25). So entspricht die geschichtliche Zeit der Mission der Zeit der ‚Verstockung' Israels. Erst wenn die ‚Fülle der Heiden' in den

---

51 Vgl. dazu: E.-M. Becker, Schreiben und Verstehen. Paulinische Briefhermeneutik im Zweiten Korintherbrief (NET 4), Tübingen/Basel 2002.
52 Ein Hapaxlegomenon bei Paulus und im Neuen Testament.
53 Wird allerdings im Codex B (Vaticanus) ausgelasssen.
54 Vgl. zur vergleichenden Analyse von Röm 1 und Mk 1 auch O. Wischmeyer, Romans 1:1–7 and Mark 1:1–3 in Comparison. Two Opening Texts at the Beginning of Early Christian Literature, in: Mark and Paul. Comparative Essays II. For and Against Pauline Influence on Mark, ed. by E.-M. Becker et al. (BZNW 199), Berlin/Boston 2014, 121–146.
55 O. Wischmeyer, Römerbrief, in: dies. (Hg.), Paulus. Leben – Umwelt – Werk – Briefe (UTB 2767), Tübingen/Basel ²2012, 281–314, hier: 292f. meint allerdings, dass Röm 15,14 ff. in gattungstypologischer Hinsicht besser nur als ein ‚Teilbrief' zu verstehen ist.

Ölbaum eingepfropft ist, wird ‚ganz Israel gerettet' (Röm 11,25–26; 11,17–24). Das geschichtliche Denken des Paulus bleibt also von der apokalyptischen Vorstellungswelt gerahmt und wird immer wieder durch sie gebrochen.

Fassen wir die bisherigen Beobachtungen kurz zusammen: Beide Aspekte, die Anfänge der paulinischen Konstruktion einer apostolischen ‚Selbstgeschichte' *und* die einer Gemeindegeschichte, sind in der Missionsgeschichte sachlich miteinander verbunden. Es ist die missionarische Tätigkeit mit den dabei entstehenden Konflikten in den Gemeinden und/oder mit den dort auftretenden Gegnern, die Paulus dazu bringt, seine ‚Selbstgeschichte' sowie die Geschichte der Gemeindegründungen nicht nur zu reflektieren, sondern auch zu konstruieren und damit seinen Adressaten narrativ zu vergegenwärtigen. In beiden Konstruktionszusammenhängen kommt es dabei gelegentlich auch zur Überhöhung oder besser: zur Außerkraftsetzung des geschichtlichen Denkens. Im Blick auf die autobiographische Selbstinszenierung etwa kann Paulus im Gestus der prophetischen Rede davon sprechen, bereits vor seiner Geburt zur Evangeliumsverkündigung berufen bzw. ausgesondert worden zu sein (Gal 1,15: ἀφορίζειν). Damit verlässt er die Ebene immanenter Geschichtsbetrachtung. Auch in Hinsicht auf die Gestaltung der Missionsgeschichte ‚ent-zeitlicht' die Metapher vom ‚Leib Christi' (z. B. 1 Kor 12) in gewisser Weise die Frage nach der geschichtlichen Herkunft und Stellung der Gemeinde. Der ent-zeitlichte Blick auf die Ekklesiologie wiederum ist christologisch bedingt, denn die paulinische Christologie tendiert zu einer außer- oder übergeschichtlichen Betrachtung Jesu (Gal 4,4). Erste Andeutungen zu einer Präexistenz-Christologie (evtl. Phil 2,6)[56] werden vor diesem Hintergrund verständlich. Insgesamt erschließt sich das paulinische Denken in den Kategorien von Zeit und Geschichte gerade erst in dieser dialektischen Spannung von geschichtlicher und außer- bzw. über-geschichtlicher Betrachtung, die auch apokalyptisch geprägt ist.

(3) Die beiden bisher genannten Aspekte der Anfänge der paulinischen Konstruktion einer ‚Selbst'- und einer Gemeindegeschichte sind gerade im Blick auf ihre literarisch-narrative Rezeption bei Lukas in den *Acta* folgenreich[57]. Eine *dritte* Dimension der paulinischen Reflexion und Konstruktion von Geschichte tritt hinzu, nämlich die Heilsgeschichte. In seiner brieflichen Argumentation bemüht sich Paulus darum, das εὐαγγέλιον in der Spannung von heilsgeschichtlicher

---

[56] Für J. Gnilka, Der Philipperbrief (HThK X/3), Freiburg u.a. ⁴1987, 146 f. liegt hier „sehr wahrscheinlich... die älteste ntl. Aussage von der Präexistenz" vor. Vgl. insgesamt auch: B. Byrne, Art. Präexistenz Christi, in: RGG⁴ 6 (2003), 1538–1539.
[57] Vgl. E.-M. Becker, Patterns.

Erwartung und Erfüllung zu charakterisieren (z. B. Röm 1,16 f.)[58]. Hierbei ist er grundlegend an der Geschichte Israels interessiert, und zwar sowohl als einer sich fortsetzenden ‚Parallelgeschichte' zur christlichen Missionsgeschichte, bis die ‚Fülle der Heiden' in den Ölbaum eingepfropft wird (Röm 11,25), als auch als Vorgeschichte des Christuskerygmas (vgl. 1 Kor 15,3b–5). So argumentiert Paulus in Gal 3 durchaus ‚geschichtlich', wenn er auf die Vorläufigkeit des durch Mose vermittelten νόμος hinweist und die an Abraham ergangene Verheißung für älter und damit auch ursprünglicher erklärt. Der νόμος hingegen ist nachträglich (Gal 3,19) und lediglich befristet hinzugekommen. Er fungiert als ‚Erzieher auf Christus hin' (Gal 3,24). Christus aber repräsentiert den ‚Loskauf vom Fluch des Gesetzes' (Gal 3,13). Insofern findet die Geschichte ihren eigentlichen Fluchtpunkt in Christus. Mit seiner Sendung ist die ‚Zeit erfüllt' (Gal 4,4).

Auch hier wird die dialektische Spannung von Geschichtlichkeit und Über-Geschichtlichkeit nicht aufgehoben, sie ist vielmehr gerade ein produktives Element bei der Konstruktion von Zeit und Geschichte. So kann und muss Paulus notwendigerweise in heilsgeschichtlichen Kategorien denken und sich damit auch für die Geschichte Israels interessieren: Denn die Schrift selbst hat ‚vorausgesehen', dass ‚Gott aus Glauben heraus die Heiden gerecht (macht)' (Gal 3,8). Entsprechend hat *Dietrich-Alex Koch* seinerzeit herausgearbeitet, wie das paulinische Zeitverständnis besonders auf der Verwendung der Schrift basiert und durch die Verwendung der Schrift zum Ausdruck kommt: „Die Schrift bringt ein vergangenes Handeln Gottes zur Sprache, das heutiges Verstehen ermöglicht... Die Schrift bringt ein vergangenes Handeln Gottes zur Sprache, das für die gegenwärtige Gemeinde begründende Funktion hat"[59]. Mit dem Verweis auf die Schrift referiert Paulus also auf das in der Vergangenheit Liegende, das für die Gegenwart Bedeutung hat. Und damit wird das Vergangene im Kern als ‚Geschichte' verstanden und konstruiert.

Die Beobachtungen zur *geschichtlichen Konstruktion* heilsgeschichtlichen Denkens bei Paulus haben in verschiedener Hinsicht semantische Evidenz. Zum einen weisen theologische Grundbegriffe bei Paulus wie ἐλπίς auf den konstitutiven Zusammenhang einer in die Zukunft gerichteten Hoffnung (Röm 8,20 ff.) und der darin implizierten geschichtlichen Begründung hin: Die Hoffnung nämlich äußert sich in einem gegenwärtigen Warten auf Künftiges (Röm 12,12; 15,4), das auf

---

58 Zur Problematik des Konzepts der ‚Heilsgeschichte' vgl.: H.-J. Kraus, Die Biblische Theologie. Ihre Geschichte und Problematik, Neukirchen-Vluyn 1970, 352 ff.
59 D.-A. Koch, Die Schrift als Zeuge des Evangeliums. Untersuchungen zur Verwendung und zum Verständnis der Schrift bei Paulus (BHTh 69), Tübingen 1986, 302 und 307.

dem vorhergehenden soteriologischen Handeln Christi basiert (Röm 5,1f.)[60]. Zum anderen finden sich bei Paulus spezifische Komposita[61] oder Präfix-Verbindungen, die der Geschichtskonstruktion dienen. In Gal 3,8 begegnet nicht zufällig an entscheidender Stelle zweimal das Präfix προ-: Die Schrift hat ‚vorausgesehen' (προ-ιδεῖν), und darum ist dem Abraham, der an anderer Stelle auch als προπάτωρ bezeichnet werden kann (Röm 4,1), die Segnung der Heiden ‚vorausverkündet worden' (προ-ευαγγελίζεσθαι). Damit erkennt Paulus der Schrift prophetische Qualität zu und konstatiert zugleich die Kontinuität der Verheißungen Gottes. Und doch impliziert die breite Verwendung des Präfixes προ- weit mehr. Mit Hilfe dieser Präfix-Form erbringt Paulus nämlich nicht nur den Beweis für die Integrität der Schrift und den Aufweis der damit einhergehenden geschichtlichen Kontinuität im Handeln Gottes. Vielmehr blickt Paulus mit Hilfe dieses Präfixes in vielfältiger Weise zeitlich zurück. Mit anderen Worten: Er verweist in unterschiedlichen Zusammenhängen auf das Vergangene als Voraus-liegendes.

Besonders in heilsgeschichtlicher Hinsicht versucht Paulus die vorausliegende Zeit und Geschichte genealogisch zu erfassen[62] sowie die ‚alte' und die ‚neue Zeit' in einem soteriologischen Kontrast einander gegenüberzustellen[63], damit aber auch in einen Zusammenhang zu stellen. Das in der Vergangenheit liegende Handeln Gottes interpretiert Paulus mit einer Vielzahl an Lexemen im Sinne der Providenz und der Determinierung der Geschichte[64]. Auch hiermit unterstreicht Paulus ein weiteres Mal die Aspekte der geschichtlichen Kohärenz und der Kontinuität göttlichen Handelns.

So strukturiert Paulus nicht zuletzt mit Hilfe der Präfix-Form προ- die Zeit[65], und zwar weitgehend in den Textabschnitten, in denen er nicht unmittelbar an der Konstruktion einer Selbst- oder Gemeindegeschichte Interesse zeigt (z.B. 2 Kor 8–9).

Die Strukturierung von zeitlichen Abläufen prägt das paulinische Denken. Doch auch hierbei bleiben die ‚Konstruktion von Zeit und Geschichte' und die

---

60 Die Anregung zu dieser Überlegung verdanke ich stud. theol. Marie Sigaard Andersen (Aarhus) und ihrer BA-thesis zur „Hoffnung bei Paulus". Vgl. dazu auch: R. Bultmann, Art. ἐλπίς D. und E.: ThWNT 2 (1935), 525–530.
61 Vgl. zu einer ähnlichen Untersuchung zu Komposita: G. Delling, Zum steigernden Gebrauch von Komposita mit ὑπέρ bei Paulus, in: NT 11 (1969), 127–153.
62 Abraham als προπάτωρ: Röm 4,1.
63 Προγινέσθαι in Röm 3,25 referiert auf die Sünden, die in der früheren Zeit begangen wurden – versus dem νῦν καιρός.
64 Προγινώσκειν: Röm 8,29; 11,2; προετοιμάζειν: Röm 9,23; προέχεσθαι: Röm 3,9; πρόθεσις: Röm 8,28; 9,11; προθεσμία: Gal 4,2; προκυροῦν: Gal 3,17; προορίζειν: 1 Kor 2,7; Röm 8,29f.
65 Vgl. ausführlicher: E.-M. Becker, Det pauliniske προ-. Et semantisk aspekt af hedningeapostelens tids- og historieforståelse, in: Præeksistens: Forum for Bibelsk Eksegese 18, hg. von K. Mejrup et al., Kopenhagen 2014, 269–278.

‚Auflösung der Zeit und Geschichte' – entweder im Sinne der ‚erfüllten Zeit' oder im Blick auf verschiedene Vorstellungen von präexistenter oder eschatologischer Zeit – dauerhaft in einer dialektischen Spannung (z. B. Röm 3,25).

Mit der Konstruktion von Zeit und Geschichte verfolgt Paulus eine doppelte Absicht: Nicht nur geht es ihm darum, die geschichtliche Kontinuität im Handeln Gottes zu erweisen. Vielmehr zielt er auch darauf, den Christus-Glaubenden selbst, die im Anbruch des neuen Äons leben, eine existentielle Orientierung zu geben. Die Ansage des Heils fungiert als Zeitansage[66], die erst vor dem Hintergrund der Reflexion der ‚früheren Zeit' an eigentlicher Aktualität erfährt. Christus begegnet dabei in verschiedenen Zusammenhängen typologisch: Wenn Paulus die Metapher vom ‚alten' und ‚neuen Bund' verwendet, stellt er deren Repräsentanten – Mose und Christus – einander gegenüber (2 Kor 3). Denkt Paulus dagegen im Urzeit-Endzeit-Schema (Röm 5,12ff.), so werden Adam als der Mensch, durch den die Sünde in die Welt kam (Röm 5,12), und Christus als derjenige, der die Welt mit Gott versöhnte (Röm 5,15), miteinander kontrastiert.

So richtet Paulus die existentielle Orientierung des Menschen immer an Christus aus. Sein Handeln und Wirken hat dementsprechend zugleich eine mythische und eine geschichtliche Dimension. In Phil 2,1–11 macht Paulus im Stile einer Beispielerzählung (2,6–11) deutlich[67], dass Christus zwar auf einen gottgleichen, mythisch zu denkenden Status verzichtet hat, dass dieser Statusverzicht aber geschichtlich, d. h. unter den Bedingungen der Zeit, geleistet wird (V. 8, bes.: σταυρός) und als Ethos der ‚Demut' (ταπεινοφροσύνη) so auch für die Christus-Glaubenden in der Gemeinde vorbildhaft werden kann (2,1–5). Der geschichtliche Rückverweis auf Christus hat also über Phil 2 hinaus weitreichende ethische Folgen, die sogar im praktischen Sinne, so etwa, wenn es um die Kollektensammlung geht (2 Kor 8,9), relevant werden können. Die Bereitschaft derer, die sich an Christus orientieren, wird zuletzt dann auch geschichtlich beispielhaft für andere[68], die sich in der Gemeinschaft der Christus-Glaubenden befinden.

Die genannten drei Dimensionen – Selbstgeschichte, Missionsgeschichte, Heilsgeschichte –, unter denen sich die paulinische Konstruktion von ‚Geschichte' wahrnehmen und bündeln lässt, sind in literarischer Hinsicht durch die Formen von ‚Erzählung' und Schriftauslegung, beides im Prosa-Stil, gekennzeichnet. Der dahinter stehende Autor, der Briefschreiber Paulus, bleibt in der Person des

---

66 Z.B. 2 Kor 6,2; Röm 8,18.
67 Vgl. dazu: E.-M. Becker, Mimetische Ethik im Philipperbrief, in: Formen der Ethikbegründung im frühen Christentum: Metaphorische, narrative, mimetische und doxologische Ethik, hg. von U. Volp et al. (Kontexte und Normen der neutestamentlichen Ethik 5), Tübingen 2014 (im Druck).
68 2 Kor 9,2; vgl. aber auch Phil 2,19–30.

Missionars, Apostels und Schriftinterpreten immer greifbar. Die Geschichtskonstruktion des Paulus also ist grundlegend an die historische und literarische Person des Briefeschreibers gebunden.

Hier liegt der eigentliche Unterschied zur markinischen Geschichtskonstruktion. Auch wenn sie wichtige sachliche Aspekte im Umgang mit Zeit und Geschichte mit Paulus teilt, so etwa die Verknüpfung von Mythos und Historie, Eschatologie, apokalyptische Sprach- und Denkformen und Heilsgeschichte, verändern sich doch der Gegenstandsbereich der Darstellung, vor allem aber die Rolle des Autors. Bei ‚Markus', dem uns nicht näher bekannten Verfasser des frühesten Evangeliums, werden daher auch – anders als bei Paulus – Fragen der Quellenkenntnis und -verwendung relevant.

2.4.2 Markus

Im Markus-Evangelium dienen Chronologisierung und Narrativität der zusammenhängenden ereignisgeschichtlichen Darstellung der Anfänge der Evangeliums-Verkündigung (Mk 1,1)[69]. Aus markinischer Sicht reichen sie über das Wirken des Täufers (Mk 1,4 ff.) bis zur Prophetie Jesajas (Mk 1,2) zurück. Das markinische *incipit* und das Präskript des Römerbriefs sind im Blick auf den geschichtlichen Rückverweis auf Prophetie einander also strukturell ähnlich. Wie aber lässt sich der ereignisgeschichtliche Zugriff auf die Geschichte im Markus-Evangelium literarisch und theologisch näher charakterisieren?

Markus wählt bereits zu Beginn seines Evangeliums (Mk 1,4; 1,9)[70] die Semantik der geschichtlichen Darstellung, indem er von dem erzählt, was in der Vergangenheit geschehen ist (ἐγένετο = Aorist), nicht aber von dem, was geschehen sollte oder könnte (z. B. δεῖ γενέσθαι ἐν τάχει, Apk 1,1). Es liegen keine Indizien vor, dass Autor und Erzähler im Markus-Evangelium *nicht* identisch seien. Demnach handelt es sich um eine faktuale Erzählung[71]. Diese Erzählung ist nicht

---

[69] Zum Begriff der ‚Ereignisgeschichte' vgl. bereits: F. Braudel, Die Ereignisgeschichte, in: ders., Geschichte als Schlüssel zur Welt. Vorlesungen in deutscher Kriegsgefangenschaft 1941, hg. von P. Schöttler, Stuttgart 2013, 25–36.

[70] Vgl. dazu E.-M. Becker, Mk 1:1 and the Debate on a ‚Markan Prologue', in: Filologia Neotestamentaria 22 (2009), 91–106.

[71] Aus Sicht der Narratologie ist zwischen ‚faktualem' und ‚fiktionalem' Erzählen zu unterscheiden: Vgl. dazu G. Genette, Fiktion und Diktion, München 1992, 65 ff. Diese Unterscheidung geht bekanntlich bereits auf die aristotelische Beschreibung dessen, was der ἱστορικός und der ποιητής zu tun haben, zurück: Der Historiker schreibt über das Geschehene (... τὰ γενόμενα λέγειν ...) und der Dichter über das, was geschehen könnte (... οἷα ἂν γένοιτο..., poetica 9,1451b). *Aristoteles* wollte mit dieser Unterscheidung „die Geschichtsschreibung nicht abwerten, sondern

auto-referentiell, also als autonomes literarisches Kunstwerk oder als ein – wie bei Paulus – auf die eigene Person bezogener Text zu lesen, sondern ist hetero-referentiell angelegt, d. h., sie bleibt auf die Sichtung der Überlieferungen durch den Autor verwiesen[72]. Im Unterschied zu *Herodot*, Lukas (Lk 1,1–4) oder *Tacitus*[73] macht Markus diese Hetero-Referentialität allerdings nicht explizit, er verweist also nicht eigens auf die Identität von ‚Historiker' und Erzähler. Auch wird im Markus-Evangelium der Erzähler überhaupt nur sporadisch erkennbar (bes. Mk 7,11.19b)[74]. So kommt Markus nicht über den Status eines prä-historiographischen Autors hinaus.

Die überlieferungsgeschichtliche Frage, ob der Autor ‚Markus' selbst direkt Zugriff auf Augenzeugenberichte hatte[75] oder ob seine Darstellung auf der Verwendung von schriftlichen und mündlichen Quellen und/oder Überlieferungen beruht, ist im Blick auf die Konzeption der markinischen Evangelienschrift als Gesamttext letztlich unerheblich: In beiden Fällen nämlich konstruiert der Verfasser ‚Geschichte' nicht vollkommen selbständig, sondern greift auf Überlieferungen zurück, bei denen die Darstellung der Geschehnisse bereits vor Markus einen Deutungsprozess durchlaufen hat. Demnach sind der markinischen Er-

---

zum Ausdruck bringen, dass die für die Tragödie geforderte Einheit der Handlung in der Geschichte nicht einfach vorzufinden ist, sondern aus der Fülle von Taten und Erlebnissen Vieler allererst hergestellt werden muss", H. Flashar, Aristoteles. Lehrer des Abendlandes, München 2013, 169.

[72] Als Historiograph ist der Erzähler an die Referentialität seiner Augenzeugenschaft bzw. seines Quellenstudiums gebunden. So kann das literarische Produkt seiner Arbeit, das historiographische Werk, in dem Sinne nicht als ‚literarisches Kunstwerk' betrachtet werden, als etwa nach Jakobson der literarische Text „autonom" ist, d. h. „um seiner selbst willen gelesen werden soll", so P. V. Zima, Art. Literaturtheorie, in: Fischer Lexikon Literatur Bd. 2, hg. von U. Ricklefs, Frankfurt 1996, 1118–1155, hier: 1127. Historiographische Texte hingegen sind als faktuale Erzählungen nicht auto-referentiell, sondern referentiell, besser: hetero-referentiell, d. h. in erster Linie an die Referentialität des Autors als ‚Historiker' gebunden. Die Referentialität des Autors schließt den „Wirklichkeitsbezug" mit ein, vgl. anders: J. Süßmann, Art. Erzählung, in: Lexikon Geschichtswissenschaft. Hundert Grundbegriffe, hg. von S. Jordan, Stuttgart 2002, 85–87, hier: 87, der den Wirklichkeitsbezug der Geschichtsschreibung unabhängig vom Historiker darstellt.

[73] Leser von römischer Historiographie neigen nicht dazu, „(to) distinguish the voice that narrates the text from the voice of the person who produced it", D. Sailor, Writing and Empire in Tacitus, Cambridge 2008, 7.

[74] Vgl. dazu die Übersicht in: E.-M. Becker, Text und Hermeneutik am Beispiel einer textinternen Hermeneutik, in: Die Bibel als Text. Beiträge zu einer textbezogenen Bibelhermeneutik, hg. von O. Wischmeyer/S. Scholz (NET 14), Tübingen/Basel 2008, 193–215, hier: 206f.

[75] S. Papias-Notiz. Vgl. besonders: Eusebius, historia ecclesiastica 3,39,15.

zählung die einzelnen ‚geschichtlichen Ereignisse' in ihren Kausalzusammenhängen bereits weitgehend (anders Mk 13) vorgegeben[76].

Und doch ist Markus *mehr* als ein Sammler und Tradent von auf ihn gekommenen Überlieferungen. Er erweist sich vielmehr gerade dadurch als ein prähistoriographischer Autor, dass er einen kohärenten Erzählzusammenhang schafft und zur Deutung einer ‚Gesamtgeschichte' beiträgt, die über die Erzählung szenenhafter Einzelereignisse in Galiläa oder Jerusalem hinausreicht. *Zum einen* besteht die historiographische Leistung des Schriftstellers Markus darin, die ihm vorliegenden heterogenen Überlieferungsbereiche – die pluriformen Galiläa-Überlieferungen und die verschiedenen Jerusalem-Überlieferungen – miteinander zu verknüpfen und daraus eine zusammenhängende Ereignisgeschichte zu konstruieren. Die historiographische Leistung hat eine geschichtliche und eine literarische Dimension: Die geschichtliche Dimension wird in der chronologisch sinnvollen Zusammenordnung der Überlieferungen evident, die literarische Dimension an der chronologischen (*story*) und kausalen (*plot*) Verknüpfung und Deutung der Ereignisfolgen.

Zum anderen verbindet Markus die Erzählfolgen nicht nur parataktisch, sondern deutet sie zu einer kausal verwobenen Ereignisgeschichte aus. Mit sog. redaktionellen Notizen (z. B. Mk 3,6) stellt er das ‚Ereignis' der souveränen galiläischen Lehrtätigkeit Jesu mit den Passionsereignissen in Mk 14 ff. in einen logischen Zusammenhang. Die sog. Leidensweissagungen (Mk 8,31 u. ö.) dienen nicht nur dazu, die Kausalitäten in der Ereignisfolge zu betonen, sondern haben

---

[76] Aus dem Bereich galiläischer Überlieferungen sind z. B. Auszüge aus Jesu Lehre, die bereits apophthegmatisch gefasst, d. h. narrativ geformt, sind (z. B. Mk 2–3), oder Berichte über Jesu Wunderwirken (z. B. Mk 1 oder 5) zu nennen. Die ‚Ereignisse' hinter diesen Einzelüberlieferungen beruhen zunächst auf singulären Begebenheiten. Doch verändern beide Typen von Jesus-Überlieferungen – die Streitgespräche und die Wundergeschichten – dann in ihrer jeweiligen Summe ihren ‚Ereignis'-Charakter: Denn die mehrmalige Überlegenheit Jesu in Streitgesprächen mit den jüdischen Autoritäten und die mehrmalige Konstatierung von Jesu Macht über Dämonen, Krankheiten, Wind und Meer generalisieren das in den Einzelepisoden erzählte Geschehen: So generiert die Sammlung von Streitgesprächen nun das ‚Ereignis', dass Jesus sich als besserer jüdischer Lehrer ausweist, und die Sammlung von Wundergeschichten macht Jesu erfolgreiches Wunderwirken und damit die persönliche Autorität Jesu zu einem ‚Ereignis'. Mit der Summarien-Form schließlich entwickelt Markus diese Generalisierung von Einzel-‚Ereignissen' eigenständig weiter. Aus dem Bereich der Jerusalemer Überlieferungen könnten die apokalyptische Rede (Mk 13) sowie die Passionsgeschichte (Mk 14–16) stammen. Während das ‚Ereignis' der Kreuzigung Jesu in seiner Geschehensfolge Markus weitgehend schon vorliegt, ist es wohl erst Markus selbst, der die Wortüberlieferung hinter Mk 13 narrativ einbettet und ihr damit einen ‚Ereignis'-Charakter gibt: Jesu Ansage der Tempelzerstörung (Mk 13,1–3) und Jesu Erwartung von Endzeit und Parusie (Mk 13,4bff.) stehen nicht nur in zeitlicher Nähe zu einander, sondern sind letztlich identisch.

darüber hinaus eine strukturgebende Funktion. Mit den sog. Summarien (z. B. Mk 1,32–34) präsentiert Markus das ‚Ereignis' des Wunderwirkens Jesu in konzentrierter Form und bietet zugleich ein *emplotment* innerhalb von Mk 1–6 an[77]. Das *emplotment* ist überhaupt ein wichtiges Kennzeichen für die vom Autor ausgehende deutende Konstruktion seiner Geschichte, die zugleich die ‚Repräsentation der Vergangenheit' beim Leser ermöglicht oder erleichtert.

Markus wählt für seine Erzählung eine ‚personenzentrierte Darstellungsweise'. Die Geschichte der Evangeliumsverkündigung ist an einzelne Handlungsträger wie den Täufer, in erster Linie aber an Jesus von Nazaret gebunden. Diese Personenzentrierung wird nicht zuletzt deswegen möglich und nötig, weil Markus – anders als der Briefeschreiber Paulus – nicht im Sinne der Selbst-Referentialität seine eigene Person als narratives Scharnier oder auch als autorisierenden Referenzpunkt seiner Darstellung anführen kann. Im lukanischen Doppelwerk ändert sich die narrative Bedeutung der Personenzentrierung wiederum. Indem Lukas nämlich in beiden Werken eingangs die Hetero-Referentialität seiner Erzählung explizit macht, ermöglicht er dem Leser, die Handlungsträger der Darstellung, also vor allem Jesus, Petrus und Paulus, deutlicher von der Rolle des erzählenden Historikers abzugrenzen. Damit variiert auch der geschichtliche Raum, dem sich der einzelne Autor narrativ zuwenden kann: Während Paulus faktisch nur über den von ihm selbst erlebten Zeitraum sprechen und Markus lediglich die zeitliche Periode, die an das Wirken seiner Handlungsträger gebunden ist, in den Blick nehmen kann, dehnt Lukas den zeitlichen Rahmen seiner Darstellung nach vorne und hinten erheblich aus: Die ereignisgeschichtliche Darstellung kann dort beginnen, wo der Historiker und Erzähler – für seine Leser erkennbar – seinen Quellen folgt[78]. *So kann erst die Explikation der Hetero-Refe-*

---

[77] Ein emplotment ist eine „Erklärung durch formale Schlußfolgerung und Erklärung durch ideologische Implikation", M. Martinez/M. Scheffel, Einführung in die Erzähltheorie, München ⁴2003, 157. Als ein solches emplotment hatte Hayden White die narrative Strategie innerhalb von historiographischen Werken definiert, die die erzählte Geschichte mit Sinn (meaning) versehen soll, vgl. H. White, The Content of the Form. Narrative Discourse and Historical Representation, Baltimore/London 1987, 52: „.... in telling a story, the historian necessarily reveals a plot" – hier mit Hinweis auf Paul Ricœur. – „Providing the ‚meaning' of a story by identifying the *kind of story* that has been told is called explanation by emplotment", H. White, Metahistory. The Historical Imagination in Nineteenth-Century Europe, Baltimore/London 1973, 7. White folgt hier (7 ff.) N. Fryes (Anatomy of Criticism. Four Essays, Pinceton 1971) vier ‚modes of emplotment' (romance, Satire, Komödie, Tragödie), vgl. auch M. Martinez/M. Scheffel, Einführung, 157 f. Vgl. auch: L. Volkmann, Art. Emplotment, in: Grundbegriffe der Literaturtheorie, hg. von A. Nünning, Stuttgart/Weimar 2004, 41–42; insgesamt: E.-M. Becker, Die markinischen Summarien – ein literarischer und theologischer Schlüssel zu Mk 1–6, in: NTS 56 (2010), 452–474.
[78] S. besonders: Lk 1–2; 24; Apg 1.

rentialität zur zeitlichen Ausdehnung der ereignisgeschichtlichen Darstellung führen.

Es verwundert kaum, dass Markus die gesamte ‚Ereignis'-Folge nicht als *historia* oder Diegese (Lk 1,1), sondern als ‚Evangelium' deutet. Diese Klassifizierung ist keine Verlegenheitslösung. Vielmehr schafft Markus – womöglich in Anknüpfung an Paulus – ein neues *genre*, das im Blick auf seine konzeptionelle Leistung und Funktion für die Entwicklung frühchristlicher Geschichtsschreibung grundlegend wird: Lukas übernimmt die Erzählform von Markus. Doch Markus bleibt ein Vorläufer des Lukas – das gilt, wie gerade gesehen, im defizienten, aber auch im innovativen Sinne. Sein Umgang mit Zeit- und Geschichtsvorstellungen macht dies besonders deutlich. Die markinische Erzählform ist nicht nur zufällig durch *brevitas* bestimmt[79]. Vielmehr bringt die gehäufte Verwendung des Adverbs εὐθύς die Schnelligkeit der Erzählung zum Ausdruck, die dem eschatologischen Konzept ihres Verfassers entspricht[80]. Im Unterschied zu Lukas (z. B. 16,16) bietet Markus weder ausgedehnte Erzähleinheiten (bes. Lk 9,51 ff.) noch weiterführende Reflexionen über den Verlauf oder die Periodisierung von Zeit und Geschichte.

Zusammenfassend lassen sich vier Texte nennen, in denen die markinische Geschichtsauffassung implizit greifbar wird:

(1) Wenn Markus in 1,1 auf den ‚Anfang des Evangeliums' rekurriert, so ist er – so wie Paulus (Phil 4,15) – um die retrospektive Erinnerung an die Ursprünge des Evangeliums bemüht. Die Frage nach dem ‚Anfang' (ἀρχή) hat dabei eine geschichtliche *und* eine autorisierende Funktion im Blick auf die gegenwärtige Bedeutung der Evangeliumsverkündigung.

(2) Wenn Markus in dem sachlich nicht ganz korrekten sog. Mischzitat in 1,2 f. den Beginn seiner Darstellung von der jesajanischen Prophetie herleitet, so verweist er – wie Paulus in Röm 1,2 – auf den heilsgeschichtlichen Zusammenhang von prophetischer Voraussage und endzeitlicher Erfüllung.

(3) Die epitomehafte Bündelung der Jesus-Verkündigung in Mk 1,14 f. macht deutlich, warum Markus als Erzähler auf eine weitergehende Konstruktion von Zeit und Geschichte verzichten kann. Jesus von Nazaret selbst tritt mit einer Zeitansage auf. Das Konzept von der ‚erfüllten Zeit' ist vor Markus bereits bei Paulus belegt (Gal 4,4). Die jesuanische Ansage von der mit dem Wirken Jesu anbrechenden zeitlichen Nähe (ἐγγύς) der βασιλεία, welche bei den Seitenreferenten zwar auf-

---

[79] Vgl. allgemein: C. Kallendorf (übers. v. L. Gondos), Art. Brevitas, in: Historisches Wörterbuch der Rhetorik 2 (1994), 53–60; A. Dziuba, Brevitas as a Stylistic Feature in Roman Historiography, in: The Children of Herodotus. Greek and Roman Historiography and Related Genres, ed. by J. Pigón, Newcastle 2008, 317–328.
[80] Vgl. auch A. Yarbro Collins, Mark. A Commentary (Hermeneia), Minneapolis 2007, 42, die das Markus-Evangelium als „eschatological historical monograph" bezeichnet.

genommen (Mt 4,17), aber auch entscheidend modifiziert wird – Lukas lässt sie erst in der apokalyptischen Rede aufscheinen (Lk 21,30 f.; vgl. auch Mt 24,32 f.) –, macht die eschatologische Perspektivierung der Evangelien-Erzählung zum Gegenstand der Jesus-Verkündigung und verleiht ihr damit zusätzliche Autorität.

(4) Die Ermahnung zur ‚Wachsamkeit' in der apokalyptischen Rede (Mk 13,23.33 ff.) knüpft hier an: Die Parusie des Menschensohns steht nahe bevor (Mk 13,28 f.). Spekulationen über Zeit und Geschichte erweisen sich aber als wenig sinnvoll, denn die zeitlichen Umstände der Parusie sind – was Paulus ähnlich betont (1 Thess 5,1 ff.) – niemandem außer Gott selbst bekannt (Mk 13,32; vgl. auch Mt 24,36). Die Nähe der Parusie lässt sich also kaum erkennen (anders: Lk 21,31) oder beobachten, sondern nur wachsam erwarten und verkündigen.

Das zeitliche Konzept im Markus-Evangelium ist also – ähnlich Paulus[81] – von fortgesetzter Naherwartung geprägt (so auch Mk 9,1). Mit dem Auftreten Jesu ist die ‚Zeit erfüllt' (Mk 1,15). Der Abschluss der Endzeit steht indes mit der Parusie des Menschensohnes in ungewisser zeitlicher Nähe aus (Mk 13,24 ff.). Markus stellt einen zeitlichen Zusammenhang zwischen den Ereignissen des jüdisch-römischen Krieges (Mk 13,1–14a: ὅταν...) und dem Abschluss der Endzeit (Mk 13,14b: ...τότε) her[82]. So verweist er auf die Jetztzeit, in der sich Autor und Adressat befinden, und gibt als Erzähler Orientierung über den geschichtlichen ‚Standort' im endzeitlichen Geschehen. Markus spiegelt damit eine frühchristliche Erfahrung, die schon Paulus in Ansätzen in seiner eigenen Missionsgeschichte gemacht hatte: Die eschatologische Zeit wird von der Geschichte aufgehalten. Es ist indes gerade diese Einsicht in die Unterwerfung der eschatologischen Erwartung unter die geschichtliche Erfahrung, die Markus zum prä-historiographischen Erzähler über den Anbruch der Endzeit und später dann Lukas zum frühchristlichen Historiographen werden lässt.

3 Kurzer Ausblick: Von Paulus zu Markus

Die vorhergehenden Beobachtungen haben Paulus und Markus hinsichtlich ihrer Konstruktion von Zeit und Geschichte in Nähe und Differenz gezeigt. Historisch gesehen scheint es insgesamt unwahrscheinlich, Markus ganz unabhängig von Paulus zu denken[83]. Zugleich können wir davon ausgehen, dass Paulus mit be-

---

81 1 Thess 4,13–18; auch Phil 4,5.
82 Vgl. E.-M. Becker, Markus 13 re-visited, in: Apokalyptik als Herausforderung neutestamentlicher Theologie, hg. von M. Becker/M. Öhler (WUNT 2.214), Tübingen 2006, 95–124.
83 Auch G. Strecker bezweifelt in literaturgeschichtlicher Hinsicht die Annahme „zweier unabhängiger Strömungen im frühen Christentum": „einer Paulus-Linie und einer Jesus-Linie".

stimmten synoptischen Traditionen vertraut war, die wiederum auch Eingang in das Markus-Evangelium fanden (so 1 Kor 11,23–25 und Mk 14,22–26; 2 Kor 3,14.18 und Mk 9,2–8)[84]. Die Wechselwirkungen zwischen Paulus und Markus sind im Einzelnen komplex[85]. Ich möchte nur fünf Aspekte herausgreifen, die mir bei der vergleichenden Darstellung der paulinischen und der markinischen Geschichtskonstruktion als wesentlich erscheinen:

(1) Für Paulus und Markus ist der Begriff des ‚Evangeliums' literarisch wie theologisch grundlegend[86]. Damit sind beiden Autoren – dem Briefeschreiber wie dem Evangelienschreiber – sachliche Spannungen vorgegeben, in denen sich ihr Umgang mit der geschichtlichen Vergangenheit bewegt: zum einen die Spannung von geschichtlicher Überlieferung und deutender Verkündigung oder Erzählung, zum anderen die Spannung von geschichtlichem ‚Beginn' (Mk 1,1–3) und endzeitlicher Erfüllung. Der Evangelien-Begriff ist weder allein eschatologisch noch allein geschichtlich zu denken. Er entfaltet sich erst in der produktiven Spannung von geschichtlicher Explikation und eschatologischer Verkündigung. Nicht zufällig hebt Lukas diese Spannung auf, indem er das Wortfeld εὐαγγελ- in seiner Bedeutung dadurch stark minimiert, dass er es auf die Verkündigungsdimension beschränkt (s. auch Lk 16,16) und damit gerade nicht zum Gegenstand geschichtsbezogener Reflexionen macht[87].

(2) Die paulinische und die markinische Geschichtskonstruktion unterscheiden sich im Blick auf den Gegenstandsbereich und die Personenbindung der Erzählung. Paulus konstruiert Geschichte in autobiographischem, missionsgeschichtlichem und heilsgeschichtlichem Zusammenhang. Die Interaktion von Apostel und Gemeinde ist dabei konstitutiv. Markus erzählt über die Anfänge der Evangeliumsverkündigung – der Leserkreis wird nicht näher definiert (nur: Mk 13,14). Das paulinische Schreiben bleibt auto-referentiell, während Markus in Grundzügen Hetero-Referentialität herstellt. Da er diese aber im Unterschied zu

---

„Die Briefform erweist sich gegenüber der Aufnahme von Evangelienstoff als nicht günstig", G. Strecker, Literaturgeschichte des Neuen Testaments (UTB 1682), Göttingen 1992, 120 f.

84 Vgl. dazu E.-M. Becker, 2 Corinthians 3:14, 18 as Pauline Allusions to a Narrative Jesus Tradition, in: „What Does the Scripture Say?" Studies in the Function of Scripture in Early Judaism and Christianity, eds. C.A. Evans/H.D. Zacharias (LNTS 470), London/New York 2012, 121–133.

85 S. dazu die Vielzahl der Beiträge im vorliegenden Band sowie in: E.-M. Becker/T. Engberg-Pedersen/M. Müller (eds.), Mark and Paul Comparative Essays II: For and Against Pauline Influence on Mark (BZNW 199), Berlin/Boston 2014. Vgl. zuletzt auch: E. K.C. Wong, Evangelien im Dialog mit Paulus. Eine intertextuelle Studie zu den Synoptikern (NTOA 89), Göttingen 2012.

86 Vgl. dazu A. Lindemanns Beitrag im vorliegenden Band.

87 J. Fitzmyer, Gospel, 173 diskutiert, ob der lukanische Verzicht auf den Evangeliums-Begriff im Evangelium eine Reaktion „against the Marcan usage of it" war.

Lukas nicht explizit macht, gelangt er noch nicht zu einem literarischen Selbstverständnis als Autor, das etwa Historiographen eigen ist. Dabei versteht Markus die Evangeliumsverkündigung Jesu bereits in Ansätzen im Sinne einer historischen Ereignisfolge und Jesus als den Protagonisten dieser Geschichte.

(3) Paulus und Markus stimmen darin überein, dass sie über Vergangenes deutend erzählen. Es kommt im Akt der Proklamation oder Paränese gleichsam zu einer Verschmelzung von ‚früherer Zeit', der Vergangenheit, und ‚Jetztzeit'. Dennoch setzt Geschichtskonstruktion bereits da ein, wo das, was in der Vergangenheit geschehen ist, mit dem Anspruch von Gegenwartsbedeutung nicht nur überliefert und aktualisiert, sondern im Erzählzusammenhang interpretierend dargelegt und entfaltet wird. Mit dem Aufkommen von Literarizität und Narrativität – schon bei Paulus – wird also im frühesten Christentum in Grundzügen ‚Geschichte' konstruiert.

(4) Paulus konstruiert seine eigene Person als Protagonisten der Geschichte des Evangeliums – unter Umständen in Kontakt zu oder in Auseinandersetzung mit Petrus und Jakobus, die damit bereits bei Paulus so etwas wie eigene Protagonisten, aber auch Konkurrenten der Missionsgeschichte werden – und schafft so die Grundlage für die personenzentrierte Missions- und Gemeindegeschichte, die Lukas schreiben wird. Markus führt Jesus als historischen Protagonisten des Evangeliums ein. Die Jünger, vor allem Petrus, erhalten in dieser Geschichtserzählung einen Platz als Jesu Begleiter. Damit steigt ihre ‚historische' Bedeutung im Sinne der ἀρχή des Evangeliums.

(5) Paulus und Markus sind beide in ihrer je eigenen Weise Vorläufer des Lukas. Im Evangelium greift Lukas auf Markus zurück, in den *Acta* nimmt er den paulinischen Impuls der Missions- und Gemeindegeschichte auf. Im Blick auf die Konstruktion von Geschichte sind Paulus und Markus Wegbereiter des Lukas. Die komparative Sicht auf die Konstruktion von Zeit und Geschichte bei Paulus und Markus kommt daher erst dann zu ihrem eigentlichen Abschluss, wenn sie auch Lukas vergleichend miteinbezogen hat.

Bibliographie

Avemarie, F., Heilsgeschichte und Lebensgeschichte bei Paulus, in: Heil und Geschichte: Die Geschichtsbezogenheit des Heils und das Problem der Heilsgeschichte in der biblischen Tradition und in der theologischen Deutung, eds. J. Frey et al. (WUNT 248), Tübingen 2009, 357–383.

Backhaus, K., Die Apostelgeschichte im Kontext der hellenistisch-römischen Kultur, in: ThLZ 137 (2012), 887–900.

Bauspieß, M., Geschichte und Erkenntnis im lukanischen Geschichtswerk. Eine exegetische Untersuchung zu einer christlichen Perspektive auf Geschichte, Leipzig 2012.

Becker, E.-M./Engberg-Pedersen, T./Müller, M. (eds.), Mark and Paul. Comparative Essays II. For and Against Pauline Influence on Mark (BZNW 199), Berlin/Boston 2014.

—, Mimetische Ethik im Philipperbrief, in: Formen der Ethikbegründung im frühen Christentum: Metaphorische, narrative, mimetische und doxologische Ethik, hg. von U. Volp et al. (Kontexte und Normen der neutestamentlichen Ethik 5), Tübingen 2014 (im Druck).

—, Patterns of Early Christian Thinking and Writing of History. Paul – Mark – Acts, in: Thinking, Recording, and Writing History in the Ancient World, ed. by K. A. Raaflaub, Hoboken 2014, 276–296.

—, Art. Person des Paulus, in: Paulus Handbuch, hg. von F. W. Horn, Tübingen 2013, 128–134.

—, Det pauliniske προ-. Et semantisk aspekt af hedningeapostelens tids- og historieforståelse, in: Præeksistens: Forum for Bibelsk Eksegese 18, hg. von K. Mejrup et al., Kopenhagen 2014, 269–278.

—, 2 Corinthians 3:14, 18 as Pauline Allusions to a Narrative Jesus Tradition, in: „What Does the Scripture Say?" Studies in the Function of Scripture in Early Judaism and Christianity, eds. C. A. Evans/H. D. Zacharias (LNTS 470), London/New York 2012, 121–133.

—, Dating Mark and Matthew as Ancient Literature, in: Mark and Matthew I, Comparative Readings. Understanding the Earliest Gospels in their First-Century Setting, eds. E.-M. Becker/A. Runesson (WUNT 271), Tübingen 2011, 123–143.

—, Die markinischen Summarien – ein literarischer und theologischer Schlüssel zu Mk 1–6, in: NTS 56 (2010), 452–474.

—, Mk 1:1 and the Debate on a ‚Markan Prologue', in: Filologia Neotestamentaria 22 (2009), 91–106.

—, Art. Geschichte/Geschichtlichkeit II. Neutestamentlich, in: LBH (2009/2013), 206–207.

—, Text und Hermeneutik am Beispiel einer *textinternen* Hermeneutik, in: Die Bibel als Text. Beiträge zu einer textbezogenen Bibelhermeneutik, hg. von O. Wischmeyer/S. Scholz (NET 14), Tübingen/Basel 2008, 193–215.

—, Das Markus-Evangelium im Rahmen antiker Historiographie (WUNT 194), Tübingen 2006.

—, Markus 13 re-visited, in: Apokalyptik als Herausforderung neutestamentlicher Theologie, hg. von M. Becker/M. Öhler (WUNT 2.214), Tübingen 2006, 95–124.

—, Autobiographisches bei Paulus. Aspekte und Aufgaben, in: Biographie und Persönlichkeit des Paulus, hg. von E.-M. Becker/P. Pilhofer (WUNT 187), Tübingen 2005/2009, 67–87.

—, Schreiben und Verstehen. Paulinische Briefhermeneutik im Zweiten Korintherbrief (NET 4), Tübingen/Basel 2002.

Becker, J., Paulus. Der Apostel der Völker, Tübingen 1989.

Betz, H.D., Der Galaterbrief. Ein Kommentar zum Brief des Apostels Paulus an die Gemeinden in Galatien. Aus dem Amerikanischen übersetzt und für die deutsche Ausgabe redaktionell bearbeitet von S. Ann, München 1988.
Böttrich, C., „Ihr seid der Tempel Gottes". Tempelmetaphorik und Gemeinde bei Paulus: Gemeinde ohne Tempel. Zur Substituierung und Transformation des Jerusalemer Tempels und seines Kults im Alten Testament, antiken Judentum und frühen Christentum, hg. von B. Ego et al. (WUNT 118), Tübingen 1999, 411–425.
Braudel, F., Die Ereignisgeschichte, in: ders., Geschichte als Schlüssel zur Welt. Vorlesungen in deutscher Kriegsgefangenschaft 1941, hg. von P. Schöttler, Stuttgart 2013, 25–36.
Bultmann, R., Das Verständnis der Geschichte unter dem Einfluß der Eschatologie, in: ders., Geschichte und Eschatologie, Tübingen ³1979, 24–43.
—, Das Problem der Eschatologie A. Die Historisierung und die Neutralisierung der Eschatologie im Urchristentum, in: ders., Geschichte und Eschatologie, Tübingen ³1979, 44–64.
—, Art. ἐλπίς D. und E., in: ThWNT 2 (1935), 525–530.
Byrne, B., Art. Präexistenz Christi, in: RGG⁴ 6 (2003), 1538–1539.
Cancik, H., Das Geschichtswerk des Lukas als Institutionsgeschichte. Die Vorbereitung des zweiten Logos im ersten, in: Die Apostelgeschichte im Kontext antiker und frühchristlicher Historiographie, hg. von J. Frey et al. (BZNW 162), Berlin/New York 2009, 519–538.
Collins, A. Yarbro, Mark. A Commentary (Hermeneia), Minneapolis 2007.
Delling, G., Zum steigernden Gebrauch von Komposita mit ὑπέρ bei Paulus, in: NT 11 (1969), 127–153.
Dormeyer, D., Art. Barabbas, in: RGG⁴ 1 (1998), 1105.
Dziuba, A., *Brevitas* as a Stylistic Feature in Roman Historiography, in: The Children of Herodotus. Greek and Roman Historiography and Related Genres, ed. by J. Pigón, Newcastle 2008, 317–328.
Ebel, E., Das Leben des Paulus, in: Paulus. Leben – Umwelt – Werk – Briefe, hg. von O. Wischmeyer (UTB 2767), Tübingen/Basel ²2012, 105–118.
Fitzmyer, J., The Gospel According to Luke (I–IX) (AncB 28), Garden City 1981.
Flashar, H., Aristoteles. Lehrer des Abendlandes, München 2013.
Frenschkowski, M., Art. Nero in: RAC Lieferung 199, 2013, 839–878.
Frey, J. et al. (Hgg.), Die Apostelgeschichte im Kontext antiker und frühchristlicher Historiographie (BZNW 162), Berlin/New York 2009.
Genette, G., Fiktion und Diktion, München 1992.
Gnilka, J., Der Philipperbrief (HThK X/3), Freiburg u. a. ⁴1987.
Haenchen, E., Tradition und Komposition in der Apostelgeschichte, in: ders., Gott und Mensch. Gesammelte Aufsätze, Tübingen 1965, 206–226.
Hays, R.B., „Is Paul's Gospel Narratable?", in: JSNT 27 (2004), 217–239.
Hengel, M./Schwemer, A.M., Paulus zwischen Damaskus und Antiochien. Die unbekannten Jahre des Apostels, mit einem Beitrag von E.A. Knauf (WUNT 108), Tübingen 1998.
Hofius, O., Gal 1,18, ἱστορῆσαι Κηφᾶν, in: Ders., Paulusstudien (WUNT 51), Tübingen 1989, 255–267.
Hogeterp, A.L.A., Paul and God's Temple. A Historical Interpretation of Cultic Imagery in the Corinthian Correspondence (Biblical Tools and Studies 2), Leuven/Paris/Dudley 2006.
Jervell, J., Die Apostelgeschichte (KEK 3), Göttingen 1998.
Jewett, R., Romans. A Commentary (Hermeneia), Minneapolis 2007.

Kallendorf C. (übers. v. L. Gondos), Art. Brevitas, in: Historisches Wörterbuch der Rhetorik 2 (1994), 53–60.
Koch, D.-A., Die Schrift als Zeuge des Evangeliums. Untersuchungen zur Verwendung und zum Verständnis der Schrift bei Paulus (BHTh 69), Tübingen 1986.
Kraus, H.-J., Die Biblische Theologie. Ihre Geschichte und Problematik, Neukirchen-Vluyn 1970.
Markschies, C., Art. Geschichte/Geschichtsauffassung VI. Kirchengeschichte, in: RGG⁴ 3 (2000), 789–791.
Martinez, M./Scheffel, M., Einführung in die Erzähltheorie, München ⁴2003.
Norden, E., Antike Kunstprosa. Vom VI. Jahrhundert v. Chr. bis in die Zeit der Renaissance, Bd. 2, Darmstadt ⁵1958.
Pervo, R.I., Acts. A Commentary (Hermeneia), Minneapolis 2009.
Plümacher, E., Geschichte und Geschichten. Aufsätze zur Apostelgeschichte und zu den Johannesakten (WUNT 170), hg. von J. Schröter/R. Brucker, Tübingen 2004.
—, Lukas als griechischer Historiker, in: RE.S 14 (1974), 235–264.
Roloff, J., Die Apostelgeschichte (NTD 5), Göttingen/Zürich² 1988.
Rowland, C., Art. Geschichte/Geschichtsauffassung V. Neues Testament, in: RGG⁴ 3 (2000), 783–789.
Sailor, D., Writing and Empire in Tacitus, Cambridge 2008.
Schlier, H., Der Brief an die Galater (KEK 7), Göttingen ⁴1965.
Schürer, E., Geschichte des jüdischen Volkes im Zeitalter Jesu Christi, Bd. 1, Hildesheim/New York 1970 (Nachdruck der Ausgabe Leipzig 1901).
Sheppard, B.M., The Craft of History and the Study of the New Testament, Atlanta 2012.
Strange, J.F., Art. Synagogue, in: Encyclopedia of the Historical Jesus, ed. by C. A. Evans, New York/London 2008, 612–616.
Strecker, G., Literaturgeschichte des Neuen Testaments (UTB 1682), Göttingen 1992.
Süßmann, J., Art. Erzählung, in: Lexikon Geschichtswissenschaft. Hundert Grundbegriffe, hg. von S. Jordan, Stuttgart 2002, 85–87.
Theißen, G., Die Entstehung des Neuen Testaments als literaturgeschichtliches Problem. Vorgetragen am 27.11.2004 (Schriften der Philosophisch-historischen Klasse der Heidelberger Akademie der Wissenschaften 40), Heidelberg 2007.
Volkmann, L., Art. Emplotment, in: Grundbegriffe der Literaturtheorie, hg. von A. Nünning, Stuttgart/Weimar 2004, 41–42.
White, H., The Content of the Form. Narrative Discourse and Historical Representation, Baltimore/London 1987.
—, Metahistory. The Historical Imagination in Nineteenth-Century Europe, Baltimore/London 1973.
Wischmeyer, O., Romans 1:1–7 and Mark 1:1–3 in Comparison. Two Opening Texts at the Beginning of Early Christian Literature, in: Mark and Paul. Comparative Essays II. For and Against Pauline Influence on Mark, ed. by E.-M. Becker et al. (BZNW 199), Berlin/Boston 2014, 121–146.
—, Römerbrief, in: dies. (Hg.), Paulus. Leben – Umwelt – Werk – Briefe (UTB 2767), Tübingen/Basel ²2012, 281–314.
Wolter, M., Das Lukasevangelium (HNT 5), Tübingen 2008.
Wong, E.K.C., Evangelien im Dialog mit Paulus. Eine intertextuelle Studie zu den Synoptikern (NTOA 89), Göttingen 2012.
Zima, P. V., Art. Literaturtheorie, in: Fischer Lexikon Literatur Bd. 2, hg. von U. Ricklefs, Frankfurt 1996, 1118–1155.

William Loader
The Concept of Faith in Paul and Mark

Faith is a central concept in both Mark and Paul's undisputed letters and serves as a useful basis for comparison between the two. There have been few attempts to compare faith in Mark and Paul, most focusing on what is believed rather than the nature of faith itself.[1] The following discussion understands faith as the expected or hoped for response by human beings to God, especially as expressed in response to the good news set forth in word and action. It includes therefore much more than a word study of the πιστ –stem, not least because sometimes faith's response is depicted not by such words but by narrative description. It necessarily includes beliefs, which are addressed more directly in other contributions to this volume. In this chapter they cannot be ignored, because how faith responds has much to do with what faith believes, but they will be dealt with only in overview. The chapter first explores faith in Mark (understood as the earliest Gospel) and Paul (the undisputed letters) before turning to compare the two and reflect on the implications of the comparison.

---

[1] Thus Joel Marcus, "Mark – Interpreter of Paul," *NTS* 46 (2000): 473-87, notes the following similarities: use of εὐαγγέλιον; the crucifixion as apocalyptic turning point; victory over demonic powers; fulfilment of prophecy; Jesus as the new Adam; faith in God and Jesus; the dualism of election and universal choice; atoning death; the sequence, first Jews, then Gentiles; change to the Law, including abrogation of food laws. See also Joel Marcus, *Mark*, AB 27 and 27A (2 vols; New Haven, Conn.: Yale University Press, 1999, 2009), 74-75. Similarly William R. Telford, *The Theology of the Gospel of Mark* (Cambridge: Cambridge University Press, 1999), who also includes the eucharistic tradition; attitude towards the state; preference for Son of God over Son of David; language of mystery; tensions with the Jerusalem church (164-69). See also John R. Donahue and Daniel J. Harrington, *The Gospel of Mark*, SP 2 (Collegeville, Pa.: Liturgical Press, 2002), who list also common vice lists; Rufus (Mark 15:21; Rom 16:13); and church houses (40). For a critical assessment of such claims and their significance see most recently James G. Crossley, "Mark, Paul and the Question of Influence." In *Paul and the Gospels: Christologies, Conflicts and Controversies*, eds. Michael F. Bird and Joel Willitts, LNTS 411 (London: T & T Clark International, 2011), 10-29, who argues that many are not limited to Mark and Paul, but reflect common tradition, some contain significant differences (such as on Israel's ultimate salvation), and others are wrongly conceived (disputing Mark's alleged abrogation of food laws). Marcus is deliberately challenging the arguments by Martin Werner, *Der Einfluss paulinischer Theologie im Markusevangelium. Eine Studie zur neutestamentlichen Theologie* (Giessen: Töpelmann, 1923), who disputed such influence. Werner's exposition is unmatched in detail and precision by the dissenting responses and so remains fundamental to the discussion.

1 Reading for Faith in Mark

The discussion of faith in Mark must delineate two levels of meaning, that of the narrative world of Mark, and that of Mark and his hearers. The extent to which they overlap is in itself an important question. For instance, while within the narrative faith in Jesus as the Christ rarely appears, from Mark's perspective his narrative is the good news of Jesus the Christ and to be believed as such.

1.1 Setting the Parameters of Faith in 1:1-20

At the level of the narrative and its participants, John's call for faith (1:4) entails μετάνοια, changing one's ways in the context of the promise of forgiveness, which John offers freely to all through baptism (1:5). That response was called for as part of preparing the way of the Lord (1:2-3), which John's listeners hear as promising someone greater than himself, who would baptise with the Spirit (1:7-8). No reference is made to their witnessing Jesus' baptism. The narrative implies that some probably did, though not its secret communications which only Jesus sees and hears. The people of the narrative next appear as those now called to faith by Jesus (1:14-15), again a call to change, but without mention of forgiveness, which was surely implied, or baptism, yet similarly in the light of God's action in the future and as belonging to the end of time, namely the kingdom of God. Their faith response was to turn around and embrace the good news which Jesus announced. Within the narrative we are not told immediately how they would have understood that hope or what their response of faith would look like. Mark's continuing narrative will shed light on this.

At the level of Mark's hearers much more information is to hand. The issue of faith confronts them in the opening words of the Gospel according to Mark, because it declares itself to be reporting "good news/gospel," which is clearly something to be believed and welcomed (1:1). The opening words find their echo within what is portrayed as the summary of Jesus' message: "repent and believe in the good news" (1:15). At the level of Mark this believing assent has as its substantial focus "the good news," which one can rightly identify as the whole of the document,[2] but, within it, also as particular "good news." The ambiguity of the genitive in "good news of Jesus Christ" (1:1) might be resolved as a

---

[2] Thomas Söding, *Glaube bei Markus. Glaube an das Evangelium. Gebetsglaube und Wunderglaube im Kontext der markinischen Basileiatheologie und Christologie*, SBB 12 (Stuttgart, Katholisches Bibelwerk, 1987), 277.

subjective genitive in the light of 1:15, but it certainly applies also objectively, whether intended or not, in the way the prologue proceeds, for it is also *about* Jesus.[3] Ultimately, as the summary of 1:14 puts it, it is about "the good news of God," which Jesus brings on God's behalf and has as its focus God's coming reign.

They are to believe that the good news fulfils Biblical prophecy, in the mixed citation of 1:2-3, and Biblical patterns, in portraying John in prophetic style (1:6) and portraying both John and later Jesus as entering the wilderness, the place of preparation and promise (1:4. 12). This is also implied in Jesus' proclamation in 1:15 which begins with the words; "The time is fulfilled."

We may assume that Mark intends John's call to faith, namely that his hearers change and be baptised to receive forgiveness of sins (1:4-5), also to have relevance for Mark's hearers. Their faith also entailed radical change and almost certainly baptism, but in the name of Christ, which they may have recognised as prefigured in Jesus' baptism (1:9-11). They might have associated forgiveness now primarily with Christ's death (cf. 14:24). While significant, however, forgiveness was not the primary focus, but treated as preliminary in preparation for what God was going to do. It is not even mentioned in Jesus' call to change, though it is surely implied. Jesus' proclamation continues: "The kingdom of God is at hand" (1:15). Faith's focus is the coming kingdom of God.

By the time Mark's listeners hear this call, however, they have far more information and a much better idea of what that future will be about. For unlike the participants in Mark's narrative world, they will mostly already know the whole story, and here have had the privilege of being reminded who Jesus is, Jesus the Christ (1:1), one whose coming both Scripture (1:2-3) and John as forerunner had announced (1:7-8) and who is about to embark on a ministry of baptising with the Spirit. Above all, they have been made privy to secrets in Jesus' baptism (1:9-11). For its symbolic narrative has God tear open the sky to enable Jesus alone to see the Spirit's descent and hear God's affirmation of his unique relation of sonship (a relation not further defined) (1:9-11; cf. Isa 64:1; 42:1; Ps 2:7). The wilderness scene has given some profile to what this Spirit-bearing and Spirit-baptising means: it enables Jesus to confront Satan and by implication the demonic powers (1:12-13). When therefore Mark's listeners hear Jesus' call to change and believe the good news that God's reign is at hand in 1:15, they know whose authority is speaking, what equipment he has, and at least part of what that en-

---

3 Söding, *Glaube*, notes that the genitive is best seen as encompassing both (223).

tails: deposing the rule of Satan and his spirits, as the exorcisms will show.[4] Belief in the gospel is therefore both belief in God's kingdom and inextricably at the same time belief in Jesus as the Son of God, its agent, and his story.[5]

Mark adds a further component to what faith meant and means: it meant for some in the narrative that they followed Jesus to be engaged in his ministry, which included bringing others to faith (1:16-20). For Mark's hearers it implies that a faith response may entail a special calling to such leadership and that people in such leadership are to be recognised and respected, though as Mark will also point out they are also fallible and can themselves fail when it comes to faith.

The opening 20 verses of Mark thus set important parameters for Mark's understanding of faith, which remain visible in the remainder of the Gospel.[6] Reduced to a summary one might say that for Mark faith means welcoming the good news in a way that is transformative and includes appropriation of forgiveness of sins. It means believing claims about Jesus which set him in continuity with God's engagement with Israel in the past (in prediction and pattern), give him a unique status before God as God's Son, and portray him as the bearer of God's Spirit to bring about God's reign and to dethrone the powers of Satan. It also means acknowledging other human beings as enlisted to be part of this action.

1.2 Exorcisms and Faith

Mark is writing primarily to evince and sustain faith among his hearers. It is therefore noteworthy how he chooses to begin his depiction of Jesus' ministry. He begins with an exorcism which is depicted as a sign of Jesus' teaching authority (1:21-28). This opens up a number of issues relating to Mark's understanding of faith.

---

[4] Werner, *Einfluss*, observes: "Überaus charakteristisch ist es auch, dass für Markus das erste Werk des Messias in der Überwindung einer satanischen Versuchung besteht" (52).
[5] So rightly Söding, *Glaube*, who writes: "Der Glaube an das Evangeium, von Jesus im Programmwort seiner Basileiaverkündigung gefordert (1,15), ist für Markus Glaube an Jesus Christus (den vollmächtig wirkenden, den leidenden und den auferstandenen Gottessohn) *und* – grundlegend – Glaube an Gott" (547). See also 250, 276, 278, 293, 517.
[6] Christopher D. Marshall, *Faith as a Theme in Mark's Narrative*, SNTSMS 64 (Cambridge: Cambridge University Press, 1989), rightly notes that 1:15 is to be heard throughout the narrative which follows (38-39).

Here in 1:21-28, in the accounts of summary healings and exorcisms (1:32-34 and 3:7-12), and in the dramatic exorcism at Gerasa (5:1-20), demons, who belong to the spiritual world and should know, recognise who Jesus is, but resist him. As James wrote, the demons believe and shudder (2:19). They illustrate right belief, but wrong response. Mark is also using these accounts both as arguments for the truth of who he claims Jesus to be and as indications of the power he can exercise. Other indications of the latter are the report of his exorcisms throughout Galilee (1:39), the exorcism of the Syrophoenician's daughter at a distance (7:24-30), of the boy (9:14-29), and of the storm (4:35-41). For Mark, as we have seen in 1:12-13, Jesus' equipment with the Spirit enables him to confront the demonic world. Mark carries this through consistently, so that in defending the integrity of Jesus' exorcisms against criticism that he performs them with the help of Beelzebul (3:22-30), he has Jesus declare that they are a work of the Spirit and so warns against blaspheming not himself but the Spirit (3:28-30).[7]

While one could read Mark's account as operating only at the level of propaganda, that is, reinforcing (or evoking) faith (as hearing and hearkening) on the basis of what he claims Jesus could do – and that is surely part of it – it seems likely that the depiction of Jesus as exorcist speaks to faith in other ways as well. One clue to this is in the sending out of the disciples in 6:6-13, where exorcism remains among their tasks. While the few statements about the future actions of disciples in the post-Easter period, such as we find in Mark 13, do not include exorcisms, it seems likely that they still occur in Mark's time. That would make sense of the exchange between Jesus and his disciples in 9:29 about their failure to exorcise the boy. While one might argue that it serves simply to underline Jesus' exorcistic power, it most likely also addresses a problem of contemporary relevance for Mark's hearers: why they sometimes fail as exorcists.[8] Some exorcisms will work only by prayer (9:29). The earlier comment by Jesus in that context, "If you are able – all things can be done for the one who believes" (9:23),[9] and the saying about the prayer of faith being able to move mountains (11:23-24), even though related immediately to cursing fig trees and God's judgement on the

---

[7] "Sein Christus ist nicht der δοῦλος, sondern vielmehr der Bezwinger der Geistermächte: in der Wüste bezwingt er die Anschläge des Satans und die Dämonen, die unreinen Geister, müssen seinem Befehlswort gehorchen; sie erkennen ihn als den, der gekommen sei ἀπολέσαι ἡμᾶς (1 24)." So Werner, *Einfluss*, 60.

[8] On Mark's addressing the post-Easter community in the depiction of instruction about prayer and faith here and in 11:22-24, see Söding, *Glaube*, 526-30.

[9] Best understood as including a self-reference. Cf. Sharyn Dowd, *Prayer, Power, and the Problem of Suffering: Mark 11:22-25 in the Context of Markan Theology*, SBLDS 105 (Atlanta Ga.: Scholars Press, 1988), who believes it is left deliberately ambiguous (111).

temple,[10] would imply that the issue is both prayer and faith and remains current for Mark and his hearers.[11] "Have faith in God" (11:22) is as central for Mark as "Believe in the gospel" (1:15).[12] Mark may well intend that his hearers make a connection between Jesus' withdrawal for prayer and the power he can employ, a juxtaposition present in 1:12-13 before 1:21-28; 1:35 before 1:39; 6:46 before 6:47-52; and 9:2-8 before 9:14-29.[13]

Exorcisms require the Spirit's power in the exorcism and faith, that is, belief in what the Spirit can do. The account in 9:14-29 has Jesus issue the rebuke; "You faithless generation, how much longer must I be among you? How much longer must I put up with you? Bring him to me" (9:19). It follows someone in the crowd explaining the boy's condition, but is addressed to "them," probably meaning not the crowd to which the man belonged but the disciples.[14] Their faith was inadequate for them to be able to perform the exorcism. In conversation with the father, Jesus then makes the statement cited above about faith (9:23), to which the father famously responds; "I believe; help my unbelief" (9:24). Mark does not explain why Jesus requires belief on the part of the father, except at least to imply that it should include believing that Jesus can help and so bringing the child to him.

Mark makes no reference to faith being required in the victims of demon possession, though their exorcism can be depicted as persuading them and those seeing the exorcism to believe (5:19-20). Thus exorcisms fall into the category of occasional divine intervention through the exorcist. Belief that this is possible would cohere with Mark's belief that the kingdom of God will come not only in such occasional acts, as the Q saying explicitly notes (Matt 12:28; Luke 11:20), but

---

10 One might take it as a reference to Zion, subverting the hope of elevating Zion (Mic 4:1; Isa 2:2), as does William Telford, *The Barren Temple and the Withered Tree*, JSNTSup 1 (Sheffield: JSOT Press, 1980), 59; or as an allusion to making mountains low in Isa 40:3-5; 49:11; 54:10; cf. Mark 1:2-3, as does Ferdinand Hahn, "Das Verständnis des Glaubens im Markusevangelium." In *Glaube im Neuen Testament. Festschrift für Hans Binder*, eds. Ferdinand Hahn and Hans Klein (Neukirchen: Neukirchener Verlag, 1982) 43-67 at 51; or as an allusion to the moving of the Mount of Olives in Zech 14:4, as does Mary Ann Beavis, "Mark's Teaching on Faith," *BTB* 16 (1986): 139-42. Allusions to Zechariah in the wider context favour the latter. All would be more applicable to Jesus' faith than to that of the disciples, whose faith is the focus in what immediately follows. But then we need to see Mark portraying the praying community as the temple's replacement, thus making sense of the focus here on prayer within the context of the narrative of judgement on temple, which was meant to be a house of prayer for all peoples (11:17).
11 On faith as believing that God can do the impossible as a feature of Hellenistic thought, see Dowd, *Prayer*, 96-102.
12 Söding, *Glaube*, 516-17.
13 See also Dowd, *Prayer*, 119.
14 Marcus, *Mark*, 653.

also in the final intervention of God's reign at the climax of history. That could be seen as a great exorcism, which would, among other things, disempower Rome.[15] Belief both that Jesus performed exorcisms and that disciples still could would contribute to such hope. Mark does not, however, make the connection explicit. A central aspect of faith, nonetheless, remains belief in hope, even in the face of what might seem hopeless, as depicted in the parables of the sower (4:3-9), the growing seed (4:26-29), and the mustard seed (4:30-32; cf. Matt 17:20; Luke 17:6). Mark's Jesus, speaking to the disciples about the future, promises the coming of the Son of Man and the gathering of the elect within a generation 13:26-27, as he had with a similar time-frame promised the coming of the kingdom in power (9:1).

1.3 Miracles and Faith

Similar issues arise in relation to miracles of healing, which fill out the rest of Mark's account of the first day of Jesus' ministry (1:29-45). We turn to them before returning to the issue of authority and teaching in 1:21-28.

Within Mark's narrative world people flock to Jesus because they believe he can heal, either themselves or others (1:32-34). In a number of instances a response of faith is expressed by the victim before healing, such as with the leper (1:40-45), the man with the withered hand, at least in stretching out his hand (3:1-6),[16] the woman who touches Jesus' garment (5:25-34), and Bartimaeus, whose cry reflects both correct belief and confidence in Jesus' power to heal (10:46-52). The words, "Your faith has made you well," there (10:52) and in 5:34, are not commending the power of auto-suggestion, nor identifying what earned the healing response, but indicating that coming to Jesus in the belief that he could heal was the basis for the achievement. The use in both instances of σῴζειν suggests that more than simply bodily healing is being described. At the very least they are experiencing the blessing promised for the end time in the prophets.[17]

In many other instances no preliminary faith is required on the part of the victim, but the faith of accompanying persons is noted. Thus no preliminary re-

---

[15] On the potential relevance of Mark's christological claims as contrasting with claims made of the emperors in imperial propaganda, see Craig A. Evans, *Mark 8:27-16:20*, WBC 34B (Nashville, Tenn.: Nelson, 2001), lxxx-xciii.
[16] One might with Marshall, *Faith*, add the paralysed man, who at least has to respond to Jesus' instruction to get up (87).
[17] So Hahn, "Verständnis des Glaubens," 56; and Marshall, *Faith*, 96.

sponse of faith is required on the part of Simon's mother-in-law (1:29-31), though her son-in-law Simon and friends believe, nor of the paralytic, though his friends' faith is noted, who demonstrate it by cutting a hole in the roof (2:1-12), nor of Jairus' daughter (who has, of course, died), though Jairus believes (5:21-24.35-43), nor of the Syrophoenician woman's daughter, effectively an exorcism by distance (7:24-30), though her mother's like the paralytic's friends' faith is exemplary, nor of the exorcism of the boy, though his father asserts his belief (9:14-29). Nor is faith required of the deaf and dumb man in the Decapolis (7:31-37), nor of the blind man at Bethsaida, except at the level of consultation about the effects (8:22-26). Negatively, Mark notes of Jesus' hometown (kin and house) that with a few exceptions, Jesus "could do no deed of power there" (6:5), clearly because they typically reflected the behaviour of people not honouring one of their own as a prophet despite the astonishing reports, but demonstrating unbelief (6:1-6).

The role of faith on the part of accompanying persons is best taken not as something which Jesus counts as earning a reward or deserving a response, nor psychologically as a kind of transference of auto-suggestivity without which the miracle cannot work, but simply as Jesus noting with approval their belief in his power to heal and so their calling on him to act.[18] Where response to healings is mentioned, it includes responses of faith (5:19-20), the increased popularity of Jesus (1:32-34; 3:7-8; 7:36-37) and praising God (2:12).

For Mark and Mark's hearers such stories, like the exorcisms and also the nature miracles, serve as propaganda. They "prove" the authority of Jesus and the Christian gospel. Mark is aware that "signs and wonders" belong also to the propaganda of others, as the warnings about false messiahs and prophets in 13:22 show. Does faith within Mark's community still include belief that healings can happen? Again, as with exorcisms, the sending of the disciples (6:6b-13) may well imply that this is so.[19] There seems no reason to suggest that what Mark portrays in Jesus' world was not applicable in his. Thus acts of healing would promote faith and faith would lead people to access healing.

---

[18] So Donahue and Harrington, *Mark*, who write that faith is not a precondition for healing; "rather it dramatizes the willingness of suffering people to break through physical and social boundaries in order to approach Jesus" (98). Similarly Robert A. Guelich, *Mark 1-8:26*, WBC 34A (Waco, Tex.: Word Books, 1989), who writes that faith "involves actions that transcend human obstacles or limitations and cross social boundaries (crowds – 2:4 and 10:48; futility and shame – 5:26-27.33; death – 5:35). And in each case faith is seen in the actions taken to receive Jesus' help rather than in any specific Christological content" (85). Similarly Werner, *Einfluss*, 108.
[19] So Söding, *Glaube*, 292.

The so-called nature miracles, the stilling of the storm (4:35-41), walking on water (6:45-52), and the miraculous feedings (6:30-44; 8:1-10), will have served propaganda purposes and were probably not seen by Mark as foreshadowing similar achievements in his day, unlike the healings and exorcisms. For Mark's hearers they served two further roles. Typological correspondences with acts of God, Moses, Elijah and Elisha, would serve propaganda arguments or faith sustenance for those steeped in Jewish tradition. In addition Mark uses them in a sophisticated way to serve as symbols, especially the feedings, of the inclusion of both Jews and Gentiles (8:14-21), as he does also some of the healings, such as of the blind in contrast to the faith blindness of the disciples (8:22-26; cf. 8:27-31; 10:46-52; cf. 10:32-45).

The account of the transfiguration (9:2-9) also fits broadly within the category of the miraculous. Within the narrative world of the text it draws a positive but inappropriate faith response from the disciples, a regular theme to which we return below. The appropriate response is to listen to him, particularly telling as he confronts their values and declares God's will in what follows through to chapter 10. For Mark's hearers the scene functions similarly to the symbolic narrative of Jesus' baptism with which the gospel began. Thus it reinforces that faith is to believe that Jesus is God's Son, though again without further explication.

The appearance of Elijah with Moses would most likely have intimated to them that this is a foreshadowing of history's climax when these two figures were to reappear and to which Mark had already alluded in 8:27 and to which he would return in the account of the discussion on the way down the mountain, identifying John in Elijah's role (9:11-13), and in the passion narrative where some misunderstand Jesus as having called for Elijah (15:35-36). The immediately preceding verses, 8:38-39 and 9:1 pointed them already to the eschatological theme.

For faith, then, the account of the transfiguration reinforced belief that Jesus is God's Son and that he would indeed appear at the climax of history. The other figures may well have also reinforced their belief that Jesus stood in continuity with Israel's faith, a secondary emphasis, as some have subsequently seen it, with Moses representing the Law and Elijah the prophets.[20] Certainly the notion of continuity with Israel's past through typological allusion and reuse of scriptural motifs, not least from Zechariah and the Psalms, finds reinforcement in the passion narrative.

The resurrection clearly serves Mark's hearers as a fundamental proof of Jesus' legitimacy and of the promise of future hope. Within the narrative world of the text, however, despite the young man's interpretation of the event as evi-

---

[20] So already Origen, *Commentary on Matthew*, 12.38.

dence that Christ has been raised from the dead (16:5-7), we seem to be left with the prospect of a fearful silence (16:8). This provocatively enigmatic ending may well be a literary ploy to invite hearers to fill the apparent void. They may have seen their own fears before their eyes in 16:8, but they know that the story went on, as Mark's Jesus had already clearly intimated in Mark 13.

One peculiar element in the stories of exorcism and healing is that sometimes Jesus urges the event not be reported and sometimes allows it. The leper's failure to keep silent (1:44-45) made it difficult for Jesus to enter towns, but one wonders how credible that is after already the mass success reported in 1:32-34 (similarly 3:12), where thronging the door already happened before it happened again in 2:1 after the leper's disobedience. It may make better sense as something Mark included to impress his hearers about Jesus' impact and to serve his story line, which will have Jesus needing to escape to a boat (3:9; 4:1). The silencing of Jairus and friends (5:43) similarly strains credibility within the narrative, as does the silencing of those who saw the deaf man healed (7:36).[21] The blind man is not to enter the town of Bethsaida (8:26). Within the narrative world, these may relate to Jesus' fears, perhaps of too much publicity, of distraction (cf. 1:36-37), perhaps of danger to himself through being acclaimed messiah or as a powerful figure. The latter appears as a motive in John 6:12-13, but not specifically in Mark.[22] Some might see fear of Rome determining the clarification about taxes in 12:13-17, either in the world of the narrative or in Mark's world, or possibly both.

For Mark and his hearers such inconsistencies about silencing or not silencing responses may simply serve to enhance the propaganda value; Jesus was so popular. Even when he tried to silence people his popularity was irrepressible. Did they also sense some dangers for themselves through such activities, especially when associated with proclaiming Jesus as messiah and God's kingdom/empire? One can only speculate. The suggestion that the silencing serves polemical purposes against a miracle-based christology[23] might be more convincing if

---

[21] "Viewed historically, the injunctions to secrecy are quite implausible" – so Telford, *Theology of Mark*, 45.

[22] Cf. Telford, *Theology of Mark*, who connects the demoting of the title, "Son of David" in 12:35-37 to a wider concern to reject nationalistic messianism (41, 50-54), following Joseph B. Tyson, "The Blindness of the Disciples in Mark." In *The Messianic Secret*, ed. Christopher Tuckett (Philadelphia, Pa.: Fortress Press, 1983), 35-43, but it is not clear to me that this implies that Mark embraces a Hellenistic thaumaturgical model. See the discussion in Crossley, "Mark, Paul," 22-24.

[23] Cf. Theodore J. Weeden, "The Heresy that Necessitated Mark's Gospel." In *The Interpretation of Mark*, ed. William Telford (Edinburgh: T & T Clark, 1995), 89-104. On this see Telford, *Theology of Mark*, 49-50; Marshall, *Faith*, 45-58; and Jesper Svartvik, "Matthew and Mark." In *Matthew and*

the silencing were consistent and Mark showed no propensity to use miracles for propaganda himself, but the opposite is the case. It makes no sense to depict Mark carefully making a case with miracles for the in-breaking of the kingdom in the first eight chapters only to have him reverse his theology in what follows. Mark appears to have been able to hold together belief in Jesus' miraculous power and belief in his vulnerability to political powers, perhaps a reflection of his community's own experience.

Faith in Mark's world appears then to embrace belief in the ability which Jesus had, and some of them had, to perform exorcisms and healing miracles and that this was both useful for propaganda and indicative of the gospel they proclaimed, namely that it was about liberation and would one day be comprehensive when God's empire/kingdom would be established.[24] In this sense the understanding of the gospel within Mark's narrative world coheres with Mark's own understanding of the gospel and so, therefore, does its understanding of faith.

1.4 Teaching and Faith

If we return to the opening scene of Jesus' ministry, Mark juxtaposes statements about Jesus' authority as a teacher with an exorcism (1:21-28); "They were astounded at his teaching, for he taught them as one having authority, and not as the scribes…'What is this? A new teaching – with authority! He commands even the unclean spirits, and they obey him'" (1:22.27). In part the connection is at the level of propaganda: anyone who can perform exorcisms deserves to be listened to. But it is more than that. Mark refers to Jesus' teaching, but fails to mention what he taught. The hearer has to supply this from the context. The relevant immediate context is the message of the nearness of God's kingdom (1:14-15), which follows immediately after the account of Jesus' defeat of Satan (1:12-13) and his empowerment through the Spirit to baptise people with the Spi-

---

his *Christian Contemporaries*, LNTS 333, eds. David C. Sim and Boris Repschinski (London: T & T Clark International, 2008) 27-49 at 32-33.

24 Marshall, *Faith*, writes of miracles in Mark as "dramatic parables which refer beyond themselves to the manifestation of God's kingly power in Jesus and its radical implications for those who respond to its demands" (64). Similarly Werner, *Einfluss*, 107.

rit's liberating power (1:8-11). So the teaching is about the coming of the kingdom as divine exorcism. The exorcism then illustrates the substance of the teaching.[25]

In the narrative world admiration for Jesus' authoritative teaching and admiration for his exorcisms and miracles go hand in hand, as the further references to teaching, healing, and exorcism illustrate (1:39; 4:1; 6:2.6b.34).Mark gives special emphasis to Jesus' teaching for his hearers in the chapter which follows. Thus teaching with authority and not as the scribes (1:22) comes to be illustrated first in any detail in 2:1-3:6, where we find the first scene (2:1-12) returning to the motif of authority as authority to forgive sins (2:10), and the centrepiece of the fivefold structure (2:18-22) talking about the "new" (2:21-22; cf. 1:27). Faith in the narrative world of Mark means accepting Jesus' approach to Scripture, rather than that of the scribes (1:22) and this is clearly also what Mark understands faith to entail in his world.

The first conflict has Jesus claim authority to declare God's forgiveness (2:10), as had John before him (1:4-5), over against criticism which misses the point by alleging blasphemy as though Jesus claimed to do on his own right what only God can do (2:7). Probably at the level of Mark's hearers this, like the Jewish trial which it foreshadows (14:53-65), mirrors accusations they faced from Jews of their day (cf. 13:9-13). Conflict over claims for Jesus echoes in the claims that he makes to "have come" (2:17b), and to be "Lord also of the Sabbath" (2:28; cf. 2:10), but the stories also show Jesus advocating an approach to Biblical Law which puts response to human need ahead of demarcation disputes about forgiveness (2:9), concern about bad company (2:17a) and about Sabbath (2:27; 3:4). The stance of Jesus in these disputes informs the way Mark gives profile to faith.

The next major dispute (7:1-23), which begins over ritual hand washing (7:1-5), leads to the declaration that nothing from outside can make a person unclean (7:15). That is not just a statement about clean food being declared clean under all circumstances,[26] but about all food, as the argument of the context indicates (7:17-19), and on the basis of which Mark's Jesus shows such food laws to

---

[25] While it is true that teaching in the form of collections of sayings is confined in Mark to Mark 4 and 13, it is not true as alleged by Svartvik, "Matthew and Mark," that Mark is like Paul in showing "an astounding lack of interest in the teaching of Jesus" (31).

[26] So Crossley, "Mark, Paul," who reads Mark 7:19 as declaring that reads it as "all foods permitted in the Law are clean" (14). Cf. also Michael F. Bird, "Mark: Interpreter of Peter and Disciple of Paul." In Bird and Willitts, *Paul and the Gospels*, 30-61 at 49-51, who wonders why Matthew would then need to omit it (51).

be therefore invalid (καθαρίζων πάντα τὰ βρώματα) (7:19c).²⁷ At the level of Mark's composition this then serves to indicate the removal of what had apparently made the belonging of Gentiles along with Jews in the people of God problematic. Such belonging had to override the food laws. Mark's argument is not that such provisions now no longer apply, but that they never made sense, because food is external and simply goes into the stomach and then the toilet. Only what comes from within matters in relation to purity (7:21-23). Espousing central values of Scripture can, however, also lead in the opposite direction: not setting laws aside but making them stricter, as the discussion of divorce illustrates (10:2-12), and understanding the commandments to imply radical concern for the poor shows (10:17-22).

Faith, especially for Mark, entails therefore a differentiating stance towards Scripture in the light of what Mark has Jesus defend as scriptural values. It includes setting food laws aside, as it probably included setting the requirement of circumcision aside, of which however Mark makes no mention. It also included replacing the temple with the community of faith (11:12-25; 12:10; 14:58; 15:29-30.38).²⁸

For Mark, however, faith's response did not abandon Scripture. In response to the scribe's question Mark has Jesus affirm the two great commandments, understood as a setting of priorities rather than as a mandate to observe everything without discrimination (12:28-34). Within the framework of his selective hermeneutic Mark portrays faith as doing the will of God. This comes through most clearly in the response of Jesus to the rich man's quest for eternal life (10:17-22). Jesus' response of requiring that he keep the commandments, which Jesus loosely summarises, was not deliberately false or inadequate, but real.²⁹ The problem lay not with Jesus' answer, nor with the man's claim to have done just that, but that he failed to do so in the way that Jesus taught the command-

---

27 Boris Repschinski, *Nicht aufzulösen sondern zu erfüllen. Das jüdische Gesetz in den synoptischen Jesuserzählungen*, FzB 120 (Würzburg: Echter, 2009), describes Mark as pushing the argument to its "sarkastischen Höhepunkt" (180; cf. Also 183-86, 212). Even if we read καθαρίζον with some later uncials (Κ Γ 33), the import is the same, a dismissal of food laws. See also William Loader, "Attitudes to Judaism and the Law and Synoptic Relations." In *Studies in the Synoptic Problem: Oxford Conference, April 2008*, eds. Andrew Gregory, Paul Foster, John S. Kloppenborg and Joseph Verheyden, BETL 239 (Leuven: Peeters, 2011), 347-69 at 348-53.
28 On this see further William Loader, *Jesus' Attitude Towards the Law: A Study of the Gospels*, WUNT 2.128 (Tübingen: Mohr Siebeck, 1997), 65-85, 122-36; Repschinski, *Nicht aufzulösen*, 213. Cf. Werner, *Einfluss*, who notes Mark's foregrounding of the ethical (87), but argues that Mark espouses full Torah observance and the setting aside only of oral law (81, 84).
29 Werner, *Einfluss*, 92.

ments.³⁰ For if he had, the demand that he give to the poor and follow Jesus would not have been so problematic.

For Mark, then, faith means doing the commandments as Jesus teaches them, thus following Jesus, whether that entailed leaving behind possessions and joining him like the itinerant disciples or staying at home. Heard in the context of Mark's world, the challenge of faith in Jesus included commitment to keep the commandments as Jesus interpreted them. It meant to "listen to him" (9:7). It coheres with this emphasis that in speaking of his new fictive family of believers Jesus declares as his brothers and sisters those "do the will of God" (3:31-35). That, therefore, included following his teaching about marriage (10:2-12), but also his teaching about greed, which the sequel to the conversation with the rich man (10:23-31), the parable of the sower (4:19) and the judgement on temple leaders (12:8-40) identify as a chief concern.

While Mark cites a tradition which speaks of little ones who believe (9:42), depicts the scribes as challenged to believe Jesus if they believed John (11:31), has the scribes make belief in Jesus conditional on his descent from the cross (15:32), and warns people about believing false prophets (13:21), Mark's usual way of expressing commitment to Jesus is to speak of following him, not to speak of believing in him.³¹ Where faith is directed towards Jesus it is fundamentally understood as belief that in Jesus God's reign is being exercised. It is believing that good news, as in 1:15, and so is less focused on his person than on his power.³² It is faith in God. In the four instances cited above, it relates to believing in his legitimacy.³³ They are not, however, to be seen as a separate category, but

---

30 Werner, *Einfluss*, notes that 10:17-22 is "von entscheidender Bedeutung" for understanding Mark's attitude towards the Law (91).
31 Hahn, "Verständis des Glaubens," notes: "Es bleibt auffällig, dass dieser Sprachgebrauch bei Markus nicht häufiger auftritt, wie das bei Johannes oder bei Paulus der Fall ist" (62-63).
32 Thus in relation to 5:35 Hahn, "Verständis des Glaubens," writes: "Hier geht es nicht um das Vertrauen auf irgendeine menschliche Macht, aber auch nicht auf Jesu Person und Wunderkraft, an den sich der Vater ja bereits hilfesuchend gewandt hat, sondern um ein uneingeschränktes μόνον Sich-verlassen auf den Gott, der Tote wieder lebendig machen kann" (55; similarly 60). Similarly Werner, *Einfluss*, who notes that the focus in Mark is on faith in God, and response to the kingdom of God, not faith in Jesus as messiah (107-108). For someone responding he writes; "Es steht ihm frei, Jesus einfach für einen wundertätigen Gottesmann und Propheten von der Art eines Elia oder Elisa zu halten, und das mag ihm als Stütze für seinen Glauben genügen" (109; similarly 111).
33 So Hahn, "Verständis des Glaubens," 61-62. "Aber Markus folgt, abgesehen von Mk 9,42, der ihm vorgegebenen Jesus Tradition, die πιστεύειν/πίστις im Zusammenhang mit dem Vertrauen auf die Heilsmacht Gottes verwendet und die unmittelbare Bindung an Jesu Person nicht mit dem Begriff des Glaubens, sondern mit der Vorstellung der Nachfolge zum Ausdruck bringt.

rather reflect the complex interconnection in Mark between faith in God and faith in Jesus, especially as seen from the perspective of Mark and his hearers.[34] Always theocentric, even to the extent of sometimes having no explicitly christological link, as in instruction on prayer, Mark's various references to faith must be seen as integrated with belief in who Jesus is. His acclamation as Son of God by God in the baptism and transfiguration and by the centurion at the cross is central, and confessing him is made the criterion of judgement (8:38).[35] The call to believe in Jesus, rarely expressed, though widely assumed as central, in Mark, reflects the understanding of faith in Mark's day and comes closer to the direct notion of faith in Christ found in Paul. In Mark such faith means believing that Jesus is the Son of God, authorised to announce and enact God's reign, in exorcism and healing, in bearing forgiveness including through his death, in teaching, including instruction about prayer and faith in God, and in calling to discipleship.

1.5 Failure and Faith

Mark's account also addresses potential problems with faith. It will be with an eye to his own day that Mark presents the exposition of the parable of the sower (4:13-20). Besides affirming the certainty of a harvest and depicting it as coming about despite setbacks, surely an encouragement for Mark's hearers facing adversity, Mark has Jesus explain why faith sometimes fails. Faith sometimes fails to get a start; Satan taking away the seed (4:15). Sometimes it fails in face of adversity or because of greed (4:16-19). Endurance in faith facing adversity is a theme in the predictions of the future in Mark 13:13b.33-37 and by implication in the Gethsemane scene (14:32-42). Jesus becomes its model in the passion narrative and the disciples, Peter, and Judas, in particular, of failure, though except for the latter not hopelessly so. Mark rationalises failure by drawing on Isa 6:9, which suggests that God blocks people from responding in faith (4:12), explaining the use of parables as designed to produce this effect.[36] The obverse is that those who believe are elected by God, from which they can take assurance and so strengthen their resolve to remain faithful. Typical of the literature of the time Mark does not take this to its logical conclusion which would make faith so pre-

---

Glaube ist hier noch nicht umfassende Beschreibung der christlichen Existenz, sondern Bezeichnung für ein wesentliches Element christlichen Verhaltens" (63).
34 Söding, *Glaube*, 518-26, 551.
35 So Söding, *Glaube*, 251, 276, 376-77, 381.
36 So already Werner, *Einfluss*, 188.

determined as to become meaningless. It was a common way of trying to come to terms with failure and finding consolation in being special.

From the Caesarea Philippi episode on (8:27-9:1) faith faces a crisis. Already exposed for not grasping Jesus' teaching (4:13), not believing in Jesus' power (4:40), and not reading the symbolic message of the feedings, a failure making sense only at the level of Mark and his hearers (8:14-21), they now find their faith in Jesus as the Christ flawed. The crisis is over correct belief about Jesus and ultimately about God and plays itself out among Jesus' closest followers (8:27-33; 9:30-37; 10:32-45). For Mark's community that might be a reflection on leaders known to them with connections to the disciples,[37] but they could just serve a provocative educational strategy to show that even Jesus' closest followers could get it wrong.[38] Peter's sincere faith and devotion has no place for a Christ who as Son of Man suffers and dies instead of succeeding (8:27-33). Success and power, as opposed to a path of suffering, inform both the dispute among the disciples about who is the greatest (9:30-37) and the hope of James and John to be Jesus' vice-regents (10:32-45).

Pitted against these ambitions, which they have for themselves and project onto Jesus, are the images of Jesus as Son of Man going to Jerusalem to his death and the values of lowly service. Ultimately, the issue of faith is depicted as theological, that is, a matter of what they believed were God's priorities, expressed in the rebuke given to Peter; "you are setting your mind not on divine things but on human things" (8:33). There is, accordingly, a coherence between Mark's approach to Scripture and Mark's depiction of the belief about God which Jesus represents and which is Jesus' own belief; it rests on his understanding of God's priorities. Mark's passion narrative continues the theme of subverting the disciples' values by depicting Jesus as the Christ, the king, but crowned with thorns on a cross. It also coheres with these values that Mark portrays the lowly and powerless as the ones who truly understand Jesus,[39] including the women.[40]

Within the passion narrative is the account of Jesus' last meal with his disciples (14:22-25). It includes reference to his own death. In giving the bread, he simply states; "This is my body;" but in relation to the cup, declares: "This

---

[37] Marcus, "Mark – Interpreter of Paul," 475; and Telford, *Theology of Mark*, 164.
[38] Bird, "Mark," writes: "The misunderstanding and failure of the disciples are narrative devices in Mark about epistemology and discipleship – knowing and following Jesus – and attempts to freight them with internecine Christian polemics are blandly overstated" (34).
[39] Marshall, *Faith*, who illustrates this in detail (75-133).
[40] On women in Mark see Mary Ann Beavis, "Women as Models of Faith in Mark," *BTB* 18 (1988): 3-9.

blood is the new covenant in my blood poured out for many." The only other reference of this kind speaks of his giving his life as a "ransom for many" (10:45). An allusion to Isa 53:12 is likely in 14:24 and probable in 10:45.[41] Both sayings interpret Jesus' death as on behalf of or in the interests of others. This must be an allusion to the widespread tradition which saw Christ's death as "for us," "for our sins." One could conclude that these two references indicate that faith for Mark now sees Christ's death as the salvific moment which brought forgiveness of sins, so that this should be seen as the unexpressed assumption wherever Mark speaks of the gospel and intends it to apply to his own day.

The problem with such a conclusion is the paucity of references to it in Mark and especially in the passion narrative where Mark could easily have included comment and citation making this clear. He does, after all, edit the passion narrative to develop key themes, such as his threefold reference to Jesus in relation to the temple (14:58; 15:29-30; 15:38) and as messiah, Son of God (14:61; 15:32.39),[42] and his depicting Jesus as a model for those facing similar trials and adversity. That he did not do so in relation to his death as vicarious does not indicate that the two logia, which he probably inherited from tradition, are mere relics or reluctant concessions.[43] But equally it strains credibility to claim that Christ's death as vicarious was just as central as in Paul; it is just

---

[41] So Adela Yarbro Collins, *Mark*, Hermeneia (Minneapolis, Minn.: Fortress Press, 2007), 81, 83; and Marcus, *Mark*, 756-57, 966-67.

[42] The threefold structure makes clear that Mark's primary allusion in the tearing of the curtain (15:38) is to judgement on the temple which the previous two verses mention, the charge and the mockery, reinforced by the similar structure of the charge, the mockery and the confession of Jesus as Son of God. As many have noted the verb σχίζω which is natural enough here, is a striking parallel to its use to describe the rending of the heavens in 1:10 at the baptism, but there it derives from the allusion to Isa 64:1 (though not LXX), so should not be oppressed. Brendan Byrne, "*Paul and Mark before the Cross: Common Echoes of the Day of Atonement Ritual.*" In Transcending Boundaries: Contemporary Readings of the New Testament: In Honour of Professor Francis Moloney, S.D.B., eds. Rekha M. Chennattu and Mary L. Coloe (Rome: LAS Publications, 2005), 217-30, has speculated that with the rending of the curtain (15:38) Mark reflects atonement day typology, like Paul in Rom 3:25. This is far from secure, given the primary reference, and even then one would have to ask, as with 14:25, how Mark would then have understood this in the light of already acclaiming universal forgiveness through John and Jesus during his ministry. For Mark its primary reference, a symbolic fulfilment of God's judgement, foreshadowing the temple's destruction, this is more than negative, since it relates to the promise that the new community will function as a temple and so be a bearer of the good news of atonement. If in some ways this may sound Pauline, it is because of the common tradition which each uses with significantly different weight.

[43] Cf. David Seeley, "Rulership and Service in Mark 10:41-45." *NovT* 35 (1993): 234-50 at 249. So rightly Bird, "Mark," 46.

that Mark failed to make much of it.⁴⁴ For Mark indicates that universal forgiveness was already an aspect of both John's and Jesus' teaching during his ministry (1:4-5; 2:10).⁴⁵ Clearly for Mark, Jesus' ministry was already bringing liberation and future liberation was at the heart of the message of the kingdom. Mark may well have seen Jesus' death as reinforcing the promise of forgiveness, but for Mark the gospel is about much more. For Mark forgiveness of sins is simply an element of the promised liberation.

For the figures within Mark's narrative world, faith means primarily believing Jesus' claim to be bringing the kingdom of God and therefore his ability through the Spirit to heal and exorcise. Beyond that, a faith response means both believing what he teaches and living accordingly by doing God's will as expounded by Jesus, which has particular application to wealth but also the ethical commandments generally, being alert and prepared to endure persecution and not be deceived in the future by false claims, and, for some, following Jesus in his tours of ministry and sharing in his activity.

For Mark and his hearers faith means the same, except that it now includes believing the whole story as narrated by Mark,⁴⁶ which includes, in addition, his death and resurrection, and an understanding of his death as vicarious, though it appears that this does not assume central or sole significance, since the Gospel remains focused primarily on the liberation which God's reign brings and will bring. Faith is strongly focused on hope but also on endurance, for which Jesus' own arrest, trial, passion and resurrection serve as a comforting model.

While the narrative distinguishes between those who respond by following and those who respond by remaining where they are, there is some indication that following is being used metaphorically in a broader sense to apply to all, especially in the saying about denying self and taking up the cross (8:34-37). Faith is such following. It is nowhere itself made the focus of rival understand-

---

44 Werner, *Einfluss*, writes: "Diese Lehre von der Notwendigkeit der stellvertretenden Selbstopferung des Messias erscheint freilich bei Markus nicht zu strenger, prinzipieller Allgemeingültigkeit erhoben" (64).
45 So already Werner, *Einfluss*, 118-19.
46 Marshall, *Faith*, rightly observes: "Just as the disciples' present role is an extension of the ministry of Jesus set out in 1:14f, so is their predicted future role. They are given the same essential message and the same sphere of action that Jesus adopts at the beginning. In 13:10, Jesus entrusts his followers with the proclamation (κηρύσσειν) of the εὐαγγέλιον to all nations as a prelude to the End (cf. 14:9). Within the logic of the narrative, '*the* gospel' can be none other than that first announced by Jesus, although now enriched with additional content supplied in the intervening material" (40). Bird, "Mark," writes: "Jesus' gospel is dissimilar to the early church in that his announcement is theocentric and focused on the kingdom with no reference to atonement theology" (44), a message entirely conceivable within the Judaism of the time (44).

ings, though clearly Mark strongly affirms that faith believes that both Jews and Gentiles, in that order (7:27), are to be seen as recipients of the gospel and that whatever is believed to prevent that, including Biblical laws, is to be set aside. Failure on the part of disciples includes not understanding this as they fail to understand Jesus' mission (8:16-21), but nowhere does this appear to reflect seriously rival notions of faith, such as in Paul. Similarly doing the will of God is determined not by a process in relationship whereby the Spirit bears fruit, but by obedience to Jesus' teaching of God's will, in attitude and action. The Spirit's role remains primarily as the power to enable manifestation of the kingdom in the present, not to generate ethics.

2 Faith in Paul

As with Mark, to understand faith in Paul's writings we need to look at more than just the occurrence of the individual words for faith and believing. We need to examine both elements of what was believed, though we can do this only in overview, and what was deemed as appropriate response to such believing. Unlike Mark, who offers us narrative which includes accounts of people coming to believe and continuing to believe, Paul's undisputed letters are largely occasional, in which particular issues are addressed, and in which faith's belief and response is to some degree incidental, except where matters of belief become central or where Paul's understanding of the response of faith is set in contrast to that of others. The different nature of the material thus determines to some degree what is said about faith.

2.1 Faith and Eschatology

There is an important cognitive component to Paul's understanding of faith. It includes, uncontroversially, belief that a day of judgement is soon coming associated also with the coming of Christ (1Thess 2:19-20; 3:13; 5:9-10.24; 1Cor 16:22; 2Cor 1:14; 2:14-16; 5:9-10; 11:2; Phil 1:6.10; 3:20; 4:5; Rom 2:3.5-16; 5:9) and that human beings need to be delivered from the prospect of divine anger on that day. It is typically represented in 1Thess 1:9-10 ("how you turned to God from idols, to serve a living and true God, and to wait for his Son from heaven, whom he raised from the dead – Jesus, who rescues us from the wrath that is coming") (similarly 1Cor 5:5.13; 6:2-3; 10:33). This is a consistent feature, sufficient to describe it as an axiom of Paul's belief system, like the belief in one God (cf. also 1Cor 8:1-6; 10:14-22). It comes in many variations, including traditional language of the kingdom of God (1Thess 2:12; 1Cor 6:9-11; 15:50), as in Mark.[47] Paul uses Hab 2:4 to link the promise of future "life," which justification guarantees, with the response of faith (Gal 3:11; Rom 1:17), in contrast, again, to judgement and God's wrath from which one can be rescued (Rom 1:18; 2:3.5-16; 5:9).

2.2 Faith in Christ's Redemptive Death

Though absent from 1Thessalonians, a second core element in Paul's belief system and preaching is that God has taken an initiative to rescue people from future judgement by offering right standing, justification, having made it possible by Christ's dying for us. The issue at stake in being right with God is sin and God's action through Christ's death dealt with sin, bringing forgiveness and thus making restoration to a right relationship possible, most fully expounded in Romans (1:16-17; 3:23-26; 5:1.12-21; 9:30-32; 10:6; cf. also Gal 5:5) and rooted in the tradition of Christ's death for our sins (1Cor 15:3-5). Christ's status and role in this and in the future, variously expressed, is a core element in faith's belief, as is his resurrection, which plays a key role in demonstrating God's power and assuring the believers that they, too, will be raised to life at the judgement (1Cor 15:1-28; Rom 4:25; 10:9; 1Thess 4:14;5:24). That belief entails an understanding of resurrected life as being of a spiritual transformed state not a physical resuscitation (1Cor 15:35-57; 2Cor 5:1-5). A consistent element in such belief is also a claim that what it believes fulfils God's intent as predicted and foreshadowed in Israel's Scriptures (Rom 1:2.17; 3:21).

2.3 Faith and Faithfulness

Faith includes believing in the hope and in what made it possible, Christ's redemptive death, and responding both by acceptance of the offer of a restored right relationship with God and by living out the consequences of that relationship, a life pleasing to God. Sometimes Paul speaks of faith to refer to the moment of coming to faith, to the initial act of believing (1Thess 1:3.8; Gal 2:16; [ἐξ ἀκοῆς πίστεως] 3:2.14; Rom 1:8.16-17; 3:22.25.28.30; 5:1; 10:17; 1Cor 15:11). Sometimes he uses it to refer to a believer's ongoing faith (1Thess 3:2.5-7.10; Rom 1:12;

---

[47] Like Mark, Paul also preserves sayings which refer to the kingdom of God as in part a present reality manifest in miracles.When Paul then announces his intent to visit, he focuses not on spoken word, but on power as characteristic of "the kingdom of God" (οὐ γὰρ ἐν λόγῳ ἡ βασιλεία τοῦ θεοῦ ἀλλ' ἐν δυνάμει, 1Cor 4:20). Cf. also Rom 14:17.

15:13; 1Cor 2:5; 16:13; 2Cor 1:24; 5:7; 10:15; 13:5; Gal 5:6; Phil 1:25; Phlm 5-6). Always Paul assumes that faith is to be something which continues.[48] Paul writes of his calling as to bring about ὑπακοὴν πίστεως (Rom 1:5), a double expression indicating that he understand faith as both belief and acting in accordance with belief in submitting to its claims (Rom 10:3; 10:16; cf. Rom 15:18; 16:19.[26]; 2Cor 10:5).[49] Paul accordingly uses ἄπιστος as a term to describe unbelievers (1Cor 6:6; 7:13-15; 10:27; 14:22-24; 2Cor 4:4; 6:14-15), as he does πίστος and πιστεύω for believers (e.g. 1Cor 14:22; 2Cor 6:15; 1Thess 1:7; 2:10), and ἀπιστία and ἀπίστησαν to depict the act of unbelief and the continuing refusal to believe (Rom 3:3; 11:20.23). Sometimes he speaks of "the faith," to refer to the new possibility offered in the gospel (Gal 1:23; 3:23.25) and speaks of the body of believers as the household of faith (Gal 6:10; cf. also Phil 1:27).

To ongoing faith as the basis of the relationship with God in Christ belongs also the quality of faithfulness. It can be thus separately identified as a virtue or fruit as in Gal 5:22 (as it can be as a charism related to miracles as in 1Cor 12:9; 13:2 to which we return below) and is sometimes used of Paul's faithful colleagues (1Cor 4:2.17; 7:25). More significantly Paul can use it of God to underline God's utter dependability: "God is faithful, who..." (1Cor 1:9; 10:13; similarly 2Cor 1:18 and Rom 3:3). God also entrusts, treats as faithful, people deemed reliable, like Paul himself (1Thess 2:4; 1Cor 9:17; Gal 2:7; Rom 3:2). In Paul faith regularly comes to expression as ongoing faithfulness, especially in the face of adversity, including mortal danger (2Cor 1:3-8; 4:7-12; Phil 1:27-29; cf. also 1Thess: 1:3.5-6; 2:1-12). What grounds that faithfulness is faith's belief in hope, based on belief in what Christ has done, and assurance through the resurrection that it will be realised and soon (2Cor 1:9-11.14-18). Paul uses Christ's suffering, death, and resurrection as the basis for claiming that his suffering also will bring life (2Cor 4:7-18). Holding onto the unseen hope of the future is fundamental to Paul's faith (2Cor 5:7-10) and confidence in his ministry (2Cor 5:11-20).

There has been debate in recent years as to whether some expressions translated traditionally as "faith in Christ" (διὰ πίστεως Ἰησοῦ Χριστοῦ, Gal 2:16; similarly 2:17.20; Rom 3:26; Phil 3:9) should to be read as referring to Christ's faithfulness in acting as God's agent.[50] One can then also read the matching double

---

[48] James D. G. Dunn, *The Theology of Paul the Apostle* (Grand Rapids, Mich.: Eerdmans, 1998) 635.
[49] See the discussion in Andrie du Toit, "Faith and Obedience in Paul." In *Focusing on Paul. Persuasion and Theological Design in Romans and Galatians*, BZNW 151, eds. Cilliers Breytenbach and David S. du Toit (Berlin: de Gruyter, 2007) 117-27; and Dunn, *Theology*, 635.
[50] See the most recent discussions in Michael F. Bird and Preston M. Sprinkle, eds., *The Faith of Jesus Christ: Exegetical, Biblical, and Theological Studies* (Peabody, Mass.: Hendrickson, 2009).

expressions in Rom 1:17 (ἐκ πίστεως εἰς πίστιν) and Rom 3:22 (δικαιοσύνη δὲ θεοῦ διὰ πίστεως Ἰησοῦ Χριστου εἰς πάντας τοὺς πιστεύοντας) as referring first to Christ's faithfulness and then to the believer's response to that of faith, although the proximity in 1:17 of ἐκ πίστεωςin the citation of Hab 2:5 meaning the believer's faith makes this less likely, at least there.[51]

Abraham serves not as an example of faithfulness as elsewhere in his willingness to sacrifice Isaac (Jas 2:21-23; 1Macc 2:52), but of belief in God's promise, given in Gen 12:3, 15:1-5, and 18:18 (Gal 3:8), and being willing to act on it, which God, as Paul argues, counted as righteousness (Gen 15:6), right standing with himself. He is thus the forerunner of all who by believing in God's promise in Christ and embracing it are similarly therewith brought into right relationship with God (Rom 4:1-25; cf. also Gal 3:6-9).[52] Paul exploits the story to build the parallels, including both the important cognitive element, that God can do the impossible, bring life from the dead, something out of nothing (4:17.19.24-25), and the responsive element, acting on his belief by engaging in sexual relations with Sarah despite their age to become the father of many nations (4:19-20).

2.4 Faith and the Law

In most of Paul's letters he shows himself in conflict with other Christians who differed from him over what faith should entail. His defence of his understanding of faith must be seen in the light of these conflicts, because they have clearly

---

James D. G. Dunn, in the "Forward" observes that the notion of Christ's faithfulness is not dependent on reading the genitive as subjective (xvi-xvii). Some of the concern with arguing for a subjective genitive appears to relate to the fear of otherwise seeing faith as a work, as, for instance, in Mark A. Seifrid, "The Faith of Christ." In Bird and Sprinkle, *The Faith of Jesus Christ*, 129-46 at 146, but this is not necessary. It may be, as suggested by Richard H. Bell, "Faith in Christ: Some Exegetical and Theological Reflections on Philippians 3:9 and Ephesians 3:12." In Bird and Sprinkle, *The Faith of Jesus Christ*, 111-25, that the idea of Christ's faithfulness in Hebrews is read into the Pauline texts (124). See also the discussion in Moisés Silva, "Faith Versus Works of Law in Galatians." In *Justification and Variegated Nomism*. Volume II. The Paradoxes of Paul, eds. Donald A. Carson, Peter T. O'Brien, and Mark A. Seifrid, WUNT 2.181 (Tübingen: Mohr Siebeck, 2004), 217-48, who argues that the weight of linguistic evidence, such as the use of the verb, suggests that the genitive is objective (233).

51 So rightly Francis Watson, "By Faith (of Christ): An Exegetical Dilemma and its Scriptural Solution." In Bird and Sprinkle, *The Faith of Jesus Christ*, 147-63, who concludes; "In Galatians as also in Romans, Paul's prepositional faith-formulations all derive from the ἐκ πίστεως of Habakkuk 2:4 which also occurs in variant and extended forms" (162).

52 On Paul's creative linking of Gen 15:6 not with Genesis 22 as commonly occurred (e.g. Jas 2:21-23; 1Macc 2:52; 4QMMT) but Gen 15:5; 17:5, see Dunn, *Theology*, 376-78.

shaped his approach. In Galatians he confronts an alternative view which required of Gentiles that their response of faith include circumcision and observance of Torah, much as would have been expected of anyone converting to Judaism as a proselyte (1:6-9; 4:1-4; 5:11-12; 6:12-13). In many ways that alternative view was the normal view and still is. We may suspect that what will have in part motivated Paul and others in the movement to drop the scriptural requirement of circumcision was at one level basic human kindness in not requiring that Gentile men undergo that ordeal (Acts 15:10.19). This is possibly what evoked the charge that Paul was seriously compromising God's Law in the interests of making it easier for Gentiles, that he was as he puts it in Gal 1:10 trying to please Gentiles by watering down the requirements.

Paul defends his stance towards faith, however, not by an appeal for sympathy for those who might have to undergo circumcision, but by a range of arguments, mostly theological in character. In Galatians he appeals to his stance in not requiring circumcision as an agreed stance which had the support of the leading apostles, Peter, James, and John (Gal 2:1-10; cf. Acts 15). But even before that, he had been engaging in mission to Gentiles without that requirement (Gal 1:22-24; 2:1-2). His experience may have been similar to that of Peter, namely seeing signs of God's acceptance of Gentiles before and without their being circumcised (Acts 10:44-48; 11:1-18; cf. Gal 3:1-5). Perhaps it had been one of the reasons for his earlier passionate attacks on the Christian movement (Gal 1:23). However he reached this conclusion, he defended it vigorously.

Paul argues that the free offer of a right relationship with God comes with no pre-requisites (Rom 1:16-17; 3:21-26; Gal 2:16; Phil 3:9). Faith is simply to believe in the offer and to accept it, thus entailing both a cognitive and a responsive component. Accordingly, he denies that Torah observance is the basis for both entering right standing with God and, as we shall see, sustaining that relationship, both getting in (Gal 3:2, 5) and staying in (Gal 2:16.19). To demand Torah observance, including circumcision, is to contradict what he believes God has now made possible through Christ's death (Gal 2:18-19). He thus dismisses what others would doubtless have described as an essential element of faith's response, because he sees it being in conflict with faith as he understands it and with the gospel itself. In his view such a view of faith is therefore not a tolerable variation in belief, as he can treat different views about whether to eat meat (e.g. Rom 14:13-23), but a position hostile to the gospel which can even be deemed a work of Satan (2Cor 11:3-15; cf. 12:7) and as equivalent to calling people back to serve false gods (Gal 4:8-11). Its perpetrators should be dismissed like Hagar and Ishmael in his allegory (Gal 4:28-31).

Paul opposes the approach of requiring Torah observance on grounds that it discriminates against Gentiles and leads to Jews claiming a superiority which is unwarranted, and which is also divisive (Rom 3:27-30; Gal 2:11-14; 6:12-13). That set him at loggerheads, however, not only with those demanding circumcision, but also with others who still required observance of other parts of Torah, including food laws, including some, like James and his people, who saw Torah observance requiring separation between Jews and Gentiles at meals (Gal 2:11-14). In Galatians Paul correlates the three alternatives he identifies, those promoting circumcision (1:6-9; 5:2-12; 6:12-15), those promoting separation (2:12), and those persuaded by the latter (2:11-14), as denying the gospel that required only faith and not the works of the Law, with which he especially singles out what he sees as the divisive requirements (2:16; 3:2.5.10; Rom 3:19-20), but refers thereby not just to them[53] but to Law observance as a whole (Rom 3:19-20; 9:30-32; 10:2-3; 11:7).[54]

His defence of his understanding of faith includes arguing that it is to be seen as what counted for Abraham before God, long before there was a Law (Gal 3:15-18), and before he was circumcised (Rom 4:1-12), that the fact that Gentiles received the Spirit before they did anything like becoming Jews confirms that it has God's approval (the argument used by Peter in relation to the descent of the Spirit on Cornelius and friends in Acts) (Gal 3:2-5; Acts 10:44-48; 11:1-18), and that if observance is to count, it should be total, and no one achieves this, so observance cannot suffice, thus levelling Jews and Gentiles as people needing rescue by a gift of God's grace (Gal 3:10-14; Rom 3:9-20.23). Paul uses Lev 18:5 to secure his argument that Torah observance must be total (Gal 3:12; Rom 10:5). This then has implications not only for the faith response of Gentiles, but also for that of Jews, who, Paul argues, must now accept the gift of life offered through God's new initiative, and so are no longer required to observe

---

53 A view propounded initially, for instance by James D. G. Dunn, "The Justice of God," *JTS* 43 (1992): 1-22 at 11-12, but then significantly modified as the following comment shows. "Thus we can recognize the criterion by which Paul judged the relevance of the law as a whole and in any of its particulars. Whatever commandment directed or channelled that reliance on God or helped bring that reliance to expression in daily living was the law still expressive of God's will. Conversely whatever law required more than faith...could not be lived out as an expression of such trust in God alone, whatever ruling hindered or prevented such faith, that was the law now left behind by the coming of Christ;" Dunn, *Theology*, 641. Bird, "Mark," opines that "Paul's 'Law-free gospel' is really a 'proselytism-free gospel' since his antithetical remarks about the Law pertain primarily to instances where Gentile believers are compelled to be circumcised and to a adopt a Jewish way of life (e.g. Gal. 2.11-21)" (48), but goes on to note that a change of epochs means that believers have died to the Law, which is fundamentally terminated and has only a "*consultative* role" (48).

54 So Silva, "Faith Versus Works of Law," 221-26. He writes that "the works of the law" "*includes* those ceremonial elements of the Mosaic law that served to highlight the distinction between Jew and Gentile. But we have no good reason to infer that this phrase overshadows – much less that it excludes – the requirements of the Sinaitic covenant more generally" (222).

Torah, but have died to the Law (Gal 3:16-19; Rom 7:1-6; 1Cor 9:20). That releases them, accordingly, also from behaviour which Paul sees as discriminatory, such as in the incident at Antioch which he reports (Gal 2:11-14).

As Paul faced controversy about what faith should entail, so Paul's own stance has been a source of controversy. While the outline above depicts the danger of boasting as something done over against Gentiles (Rom 3:27), an important strand of Pauline interpretation tracing itself at least back to Luther and still with many exponents today argues that Paul's concern is boasting before God (Rom 3:19-20; cf. also Eph 2:8-9;[55] Tit 3:5). Accordingly, they see faith set in contrast to an approach to God which seeks to make a claim on God on the basis of good works that a person deserves right standing.[56] While some texts can be read in that way, and Paul's stance warrants the conclusion that making claims on God, self-justification by human achievement, is wrong, a profound observation on the human condition, this is not Paul's primary focus.

In dismissing Torah observance as an element of faith's response and as inadequate Paul must counter a number of criticisms, including whether he is calling God's covenant faithfulness to Israel and its election into question, whether he is disparaging the Law, and whether not requiring Torah observance by implication promotes lawlessness and sin. His answers to these all inform his understanding of faith.

Paul refutes the suggestion that he questions God's keeping faith (Rom 3:1-8), resorting ultimately to a claim that somehow God will eventually bring Israel to faith, even though in the interim he had hardened all but a remnant of Israel into unbelief (Rom 9-11). In a tortuous argument Paul defends God's right to make selections, explains why Israel failed by not embracing the offer of a right relationship by faith and instead seeking it on the basis of Law observance (9:30-33; 10:2-3), rationalises it as opening the offer to Gentiles, whose response he believes will prompt Israel to change (11:11-24), but ultimately affirms his belief that all Israel will be saved (11:25-36).

---

[55] Though there, too, the focus of the broader context is unity between Jews and Gentiles, which must be seen as the context of the concern about boasting.

[56] Ed Parish Sanders, *Paul and Palestinian Judaism* (London: SCM, 1977), most notably challenged the assumption that Judaism was a legalistic religion obsessed with self-righteousness. For a defence of the notion that Paul's issue about justification by faith was about more than relations with Gentiles, against Sanders, Dunn, and Wright, see Peter T. O'Brien, "Was Paul a Covenantal Nomist?" In Carson, O'Brien and Seifrid, *Justification and Variegated Nomism*, 249-96; and Stephen Westerholm, *Perspectives Old and New on Paul: The "Lutheran" Paul and His Critics* (Grand Rapids, Mich.: Eerdmans, 2004).

He resolves the status of the Law, partly by giving it a lower status as something given only indirectly by God through lesser beings (angels) (Gal 3:19-20), partly by arguing that God had assigned it a temporary role as the means for establishing the need for the gift that now God offers through Christ (Gal 3:21-25; Rom 4:15; 5:20), and partly by describing its psychological effects as counterproductive in terms of trying to effect right behaviour (Rom 7:7-24). It is consistent with this latter argument, which is most developed in Romans 7, that Paul also addresses the criticism that in dismissing the Law, except as predicting the gospel, he promotes lawlessness (Rom 6:1-23). For he argues that when believers respond in faith to the gospel, they are raised to a new life made possible by the Spirit and as long as they remain open to the Spirit, produce behaviour which more than fulfils what he still values in the Law, namely ethical attitudes and behaviour, at the heart of which is love (Rom 8:1-4; similarly 8:5-17).

This, in turn, enables Paul to argue that far from disparaging or doing away with the Law (which is "good" Rom 7:7.12), he upholds it (Rom 3:31).[57] But he can make this claim only by an approach to the Law which argues from its core intent (Rom 3:27),[58] readily sets aside aspects which he sees as divisive, and sees it fulfilled not by keeping commandments but by living out the fruit of the Spirit, which he argues is the best way to end up doing and doing more than the commandments require (Rom 8:4). Observing the Law has become for Paul not a necessity, but a strategy to be engaged in as appropriate to the context for the sake of not giving offence and promoting good relations (1Cor 9:19-23; 10:23-11:1; Rom 14:13-15:13). In Rom 15:7-12 Paul may be suggesting that Jesus "became a servant of the circumcised" in the same strategic spirit. For Paul the believer has died to the Law and is no longer under the Law (Gal 2:19; 5:16; Rom 7:1-4; 3:21).

---

[57] νόμος here may mean principle or approach. So, for instance, Ed Parish Sanders, *Paul, The Law, and the Jewish People* (London: SCM, 1982), 33. But here and in 9:30-33 it could refer to the Law treated in two different ways, as possibly in 3:27-31 since Gerhard Friedrich, "Das Gesetz des Glaubens Römer 3,27," *ThZ* 10 (1954): 409-11. Cf. Dunn, *Theology*, 638.

[58] One approach to Torah emphasises the need to keep it in full (διὰ ποίου νόμου τῶν ἔργων), while the other focuses on adhering to its deeper values as seen by faith (διὰ νόμου πίστεως) (3:27) and so is prepared to set some things aside. Accordingly Israel was pursuing the law of righteousness the wrong way. So Dunn, *Theology*, 639-40. See also Francis Watson, *Paul and the Hermeneutics of Faith* (London: T & T Clark, 2004), who has mounted a case that in fact Paul stands within a legitimate stream of interpretation of Scripture in his approach towards the Law: "Paul's controversy with 'Judaism' (Christian or otherwise) is in fact a conflict about interpretation of Torah" (528).

2.5 Faith and Ethics

Love is a fruit of the Spirit (Gal 5:22-23). Paul consistently derives his ethics, both in terms of positive behaviours and of warnings against sin, not from Biblical commandments of Torah, but from insights and implications drawn from the new relationship of the believer with God through the Spirit (1Thess 2:12; 3:13; 4:3.7-8.9-12; 1Cor 6:12-20; 12-14; Gal 5:1.13-25; Rom 6:1-23; 8:4-17; 12:1-21). This new relationship, Paul argues, sets the believer free from the fruitless bind of seeking to observe the Law produces (Rom 8:3-4; 7:1-6), and so faith means both believing in what God has offered and remaining faithful and submissive to the dynamics which that new life in the Spirit makes possible.

Paul can also, however, point out that by walking in the Spirit and bearing the fruit of love one thereby meets the requirements of the commandments, clearly having the ethical ones in mind. Thus he explains that "the one who loves another has fulfilled the Law" (Rom 13:8) and that loving one another sums up the requirements of the second table of the Decalogue (13:9-10; similarly Gal 5:13-15). Paul's exhortation is neither to observe these commandments in order to receive eternal life nor to do so in order to retain it, but to walk in the Spirit (Gal 5:16). This does not hinder Paul sometimes using Biblical Law to reinforce his ethical concerns (e.g. 1Cor 9:8-9), but the primary driver of faith's ongoing response is not the commandments but the relationship with Christ through the Spirit and the way it leads to Christ's and ultimately God's behaviour reproducing itself in the believer. In Galatians he describes this as "faith working through love" (5:6),[59] fulfilling the "law of Christ" (6:2; similarly 1Cor 9:21), and a "new creation" (6:15). Faith thus serves the expression of love: "And now faith, hope, and love abide, these three; and the greatest of these is love" (1Cor 13:13; cf. also 16:14; Rom 8:31-39).

Clearly faith's response, however, entails something more than the spontaneity which might result from such freedom in the Spirit. It also needs instruction and focusing, as Paul's many ethical instructions illustrate, but the underlying assumption is that Paul is telling people how faith should work, how fruit should be born, and making the connections between the new freedom in finding God's goodness and the impact it should be allowed to have on daily life (1Thess 2:12 walk worthily in the interim). In this the corporate dimension of faith's response is a regular feature, because for Paul love has relational impli-

---

[59] Dunn, *Theology*, writes of "faith operating effectively through love" (637): "It is precisely faith as complete reliance on and openness to God's grace which (inevitably) comes to expression in love" (638).

cations which embrace not only the individual's relation to God but also common life (1Cor 12-14; Rom 12; Gal 6:1-10). This includes what Paul sees as good order, with women taking their ordered place and behaving accordingly (1Cor 11:2-16; 14:33-36), marriage being upheld, except where Paul's preferred option of celibate singleness in the light of the nearness of the end and non-sexual character of the age to come is adopted, and for periods of prayer when entering the holy requires such abstinence (1Cor 7:1-6).

Faith's response may entail compromise, where one acts contrary to one's own beliefs in order not to create problems for those within the believing community who take a different stance within the range of acceptable beliefs (1Cor 10:14-11:1; Rom 14-15). In such contexts the word πίστις can refer to one's choice within such a range of beliefs, which Paul designates strong and weak (Rom 14:2.22-23). He clearly places himself on the side of the strong; "I know and am persuaded in the Lord Jesus that nothing is unclean in itself; but it is unclean for anyone who thinks it unclean" (14:14). Interestingly, in stating his opinion, Paul, on the one hand, does not impose it but relates it to conscience (as 14:5): to act against one's conviction is sin (14:23). This expresses a degree of tolerance. His statement, "For the kingdom of God is not food and drink but righteousness and peace and joy in the Holy Spirit" (14:17), serves the appeal to the strong like himself, that unity in the community of the kingdom of God is a higher priority than exercising their freedom to eat anything and so offend the weak, even though as Paul restates in 14:20; "Everything is indeed clean" (πάντα μὲν καθαρά). On the other hand, he claims that he has been persuaded of his view "in the Lord Jesus," but offers no further explanation.

Faith's response also includes concern for the poor within the community of faith, which at one level expresses itself in Paul's making a collection for the poor believers in Jerusalem (Gal 2:10; 1 Cor 16:1; 2 Cor 8-9; Rom 15:15.25-27). Christ's generosity serves as a model (2Cor 8:9). Similarly Paul reminds Philemon of their shared faith and so responsibility as he confronts the Corinthians about neglect of their poorer members and about disorder (1Cor 11:17-34).

Sometimes Paul uses faith to speak of confidence or assurance, in the face not only of adversity but also of conflict and of the need to exercise authoritative leadership (Gal 1:10-12; 2Cor 4:13; Rom 1:5-7). Faith for Paul entails both believing the goodness and submission to what it offers, which includes, to Paul's mind, submission also to the one who offers it (2Cor 2:9.16-17; 7:15; 9:13; 10:5-6; 12:20-13:2; 13:6-10; 1Thess 5:12-13). This is not a claim to power in itself, but a claim that inasmuch as someone is truly authorised to represent the gospel, submission to the gospel ought to include submission to that person's authority. Sometimes Paul simply assumes that faith would understand this; at other times he must defend the claim against those who dismiss his having such status (2Cor 10:1-12:13; Phil 3:2-6.17-19; 1Cor 9:1-23; Gal 1:10-24).

Paul can also use faith to describe the particular roles to which people are called and equipped to exercise as part of their response of faith (Rom 12:3.6; cf. 1Cor 12:9). These are often associated with the Spirit, which is seen as enabling such roles, and may also be described as gifts of the Spirit (1Cor 12:9; 13:2). Paul uses the word χάρις to describe his own role as apostle to the Gentiles. Within the range of such roles exercised as one's response of faith under the impact of the Spirit Paul also includes charismatic phenomena, including speaking in tongues and miracles. Paul notes that he exercises the first (1Cor 14:18), and on a few occasions mentions signs and wonders as accompanying his apostolic ministry, presumably acts of healing (1Thess 1:5; 1Cor 2:4; 4:20; 2Cor 12:12; Gal 3:5; Rom 15:18-19), described also as manifestation of the kingdom of God in the present (1Cor 4:20). As in Mark, these appear to have a legitimising function, a tool of propaganda to evoke faith. Sometimes Paul uses faith in the sense of belief being sufficient to effect miracles, sharing with Mark the formulation, faith to move mountains, probably as in Mark linked to prayer for power to do miracles (1Cor 13:2; cf. Mark 11:22-24).

3 Key Aspects of Faith in Mark and Paul Compared

3.1 Hermeneutics: Faith and the Law

Both Paul and Mark share as part of their faith the belief that Christ's coming fulfilled Scripture. Typically, therefore, Paul commences his letter to the Romans with reference to fulfilment of Scripture (1:2), and Mark does the same (1:2). The latter inherits typologically rich anecdotes which connect Jesus to God's actions through Moses, Elijah, Elisha, and Jonah, and in his own way Paul alludes typologically to Moses and allegorically to Abraham. Mark has Jesus argue for priorities in Scripture, Genesis over Deuteronomy on divorce, an argument about theological intent, and Paul argues similarly in relation to Abraham and the Mosaic Law. Both shared such prioritising with others in the Christian movement.

(1) Removing Barriers Created by the Law

Paul's statements about the Law relate closely to conflict over incorporation of Gentiles into the people of God, their acceptance before God. Mark also engages the Law in the context of affirming that the nourishment represented in the bread of the feedings is given to both Jews and Gentiles. This is important common ground.⁶⁰ Both also assume God's offer has been first to Israel and then to the Gentiles (Mark 7:27; Rom 1:16), a sequence hardly unique to the two.⁶¹ This is the context for Paul's reflection on hardening, though he concludes that all Israel will be saved. Mark's comments on hardening, also using Isa 6:9, are not directed to this theme in particular nor does he indicate belief in Israel's ultimate salvation.⁶² Indeed Mark explains the process of hardening as effected through the use of parables.⁶³ Dealing with rejection and also belonging by using notions of election and hardening or predestination was a common strategy, not peculiar to these two authors.⁶⁴

(2) Mark's Stance on Law

Mark has Jesus address those issues of Law which he assumed created barriers to the admission of Gentiles. They related not to circumcision, but to food laws. He employs a logion of Jesus which asserted that not so much what entered a person made them unclean but what came out of them, actions stemming from evil attitudes, and used it to make an absolute claim that what enters a person cannot by its very nature make them unclean, no longer a relativisation of purity laws in relation to food, but a dismissal of such categories altogether as making no sense, and so removing also what he sensed was a barrier, laws about unclean foods.

(3) Paul's Stance on Law

The later Paulinist author of Ephesians re-presents Paul's stance, when declaring that God had removed the barrier, the enmity between Jew and Gentile, namely the law of commandments (Eph 2:15). Paul's own stance was to remove the Law from its absolute position and so dismiss its continuing validity, both for Gentiles who joined the people of God and for Jews. Its observance for him is now just a matter of mission strategy depending on the circumstances or of sensitivity to living with the weak, who are still observant. Paul's statements in Romans that he believes that nothing is unclean in itself (14:14), that everything is clean (14:20) and that "the kingdom of God is not food and drink but righteous-

---

60 This inspires, for instance, Jesper Svartvik, *Mark and Mission: Mk 7:1-23 in its Narrative and Historical Contexts*, CBNTS 32 (Stockholm: Almqvist & Wiksell, 2000) to claim that Mark is "a narrative presentation of the Pauline gospel" (2). See also, Svartvik, "Matthew and Mark," 33.
61 Crossley, "Mark, Paul," points out that already Gal 2:15 shows that Paul assumes it is also Peter's view (18-19). Cf. Marcus, "Mark-Interpreter of Paul," 475.
62 So Werner, *Einfluss*, 193-94; Crossley, "Mark, Paul," 12, rejecting the argument of Benamin W. Bacon, *Is Mark a Roman Gospel?* (Cambridge: Cambridge University Press, 1919), 263. Cf. also Marcus, "Mark – Interpreter of Paul," 475; and Telford, *Theology of Mark*, 164, 168.
63 Werner, *Einfluss*, 188, 192.
64 So already Werner, *Einfluss*, 196, who notes that Mark writes of the hardening of the disciples, a most unlikely move had he known of the special usage in Paul (195).

ness and peace and joy in the Holy Spirit" are close to Mark's view, especially Mark's editorial comment, that Jesus was making all foods clean (7:19), but lacks the disparagement present in Mark's discussion. If there is connection between the two here, it is scarcely from Mark to Paul, but could be from Paul to Mark if Mark's formulation καθαρίζων πάντα τὰ βρώματα in some way stands under the influence of Paul's πάντα μὲν καθαρά (Rom 14:20), though the parallels are not precise. Paul, on the other hand, may have stood under the influence of a Jesus logion like that preserved in Mark 7:15, especially in Rom 14:14, but on that one can only speculate.[65] But these are not the only authors to deal with food laws as an issue, as Acts 10 shows.[66]

(4) Mark is More Radical than Paul

While Paul can employ the contrast between literal circumcision and circumcision of the heart, external and internal, earlier and later (Rom 1:25-29), and even argue that the letter kills (2Cor 3:6) and the Law though good does not work (Rom 7:5.8.10-13; 8:3-4),[67] he never goes so far as Mark to dismiss aspects of the Law as making no sense. On this Mark is more radical.

(5) Paul more Radical than Mark

On the other hand, Paul is more radical than Mark in consistently basing ethics not on the commandments, but on what flows from one's relation to Christ and what constitutes the fruit of the Spirit. He argues that he upholds the Law in the sense that the gospel he preaches produces as an outcome behaviours which more than satisfy the Law's demands. In such contexts he can cite the ethical commandments of the Decalogue as evidence that this is so and even loving one's neighbour as summarising the Law. One gains eternal life through faith in Christ, however, not by keeping the Biblical commandments.

(6) Mark and the Commandments

Mark is clearly different. Mark would not embrace the notion that believers had died to the Law, nor that it was impossible to keep it, let alone that Christ's death brought its end.[68] His Jesus tells the rich man that the way to inherit eternal life is by keeping such commandments, as elsewhere he identifies the criterion for being his fictive family as doing the will of God and affirms the need to

---

65 Bird, "Mark," who argues that Paul could have said such a thing without dominical authority and suggests that ἐνκυ΄ριῳ Ἰησοῦ ὅτι may reflect this (50-51).
66 So Crossley, "Mark, Paul," 13.
67 Werner, *Einfluss*, notes that Mark gives no indication that the Law as summarised in 12:29-31 cannot be fulfilled, unlike Paul (96). On the contrary Mark sees the Law as able to be fulfilled.
68 So Werner, *Einfluss*, 89. He writes: "ein ganz besonderes Gewicht kommt aber der Tatsache zu, dass die Heilsbedeutung des Kreuzestodes wie Markus sie fasst, nicht in Gegensatz tritt zu der Grundanschauung über die Heilsbedeutung des Gesetzes" (92).

keep the greatest commandments. Doing the will of God also includes believing in Jesus, but Mark's understanding is that following Jesus includes following his understanding of the commandments, which the test question to the rich man exposed him as unwilling to do. Mark's faith addresses greed and poverty generally. While Paul's shares concern for the poor, his focus is on the poor among believers, "the saints" (1Cor 16:1; 2Cor 9:1; Rom 15:26; cf. also Gal 2:10).[69]

(7) Significant Differences in Attitude Towards the Law

If Paul's approach to Scripture is one which gives priority to the gospel as ancient promise and dismisses the Law as no longer in force, Mark's approach is to dismiss aspects of the Law as never having been valid, but affirm that keeping, above all, its ethical commandment is essential to faith's response.[70] These are thus significant variations, but overall Mark and Paul share a willingness to set parts of Torah aside in the interests of inclusion of Gentiles in contrast to Matthew and Luke. On the other hand, both Mark and Paul hold firmly to commands attributed to Jesus, including on divorce and remarriage and support of people on mission. Both use Gen 2:24 similarly to argue permanence, Jesus, the permanence of marriage, Paul, the permanence of severing oneself from Christ when joining oneself in sex to an illicit partner.

3.2 Soteriology

(1) Soteriology in Mark

The different responses of faith cohere with a difference in soteriology. Mark's Jesus promises hope, but already during his ministry brings the transforming reign of God through healing, exorcism, and the call to change, offering forgiveness and belonging in God's people to all. Faith is to believe who Jesus is and what he offers and to respond by heeding his teaching, which includes the message about what God requires: to do God's will as described above. The message of hope promises change in the future. Faith in Mark as in Paul means believing the coming day of judgement and the appearance of Christ and the hope

---

69 See William Loader, "What Happened to 'Good News for the Poor'? On the Trail of Hope Beyond Jesus." In *Reflections on Early Christian History and Religion*, eds. Cilliers Breytenbach and Jörg Frey, AJEC 81 (Leiden: Brill, 2012), 233-66 at 256-59.
70 Crossley, "Mark, Paul," concedes this when he writes: "Even if Mark was aware of non-observance, he shows no serious indication of such a phenomenon and no indication of a Pauline view that the Law is a thing of the past or a Pauline view that the Law has no role in salvation and justification" (21). Repschinski, *Nicht aufzulösen*, writes of Mark's stance towards the law as a "kuriose Mischung aus Kontinuität und Diskontinuität" (209).

of being with him rather than suffering divine judgement. Both use the term εὐαγγέλιον, though Mark with a much wider application. Though also a term used in imperial propaganda, it most likely derives from use of Isaianic LXX texts (61:1; 57:6),[71] the former of which is attested elsewhere, rather than indicating a dependence of Mark on Paul or Pauline tradition,[72] though at least the latter is one possible option among others.[73]

In Mark the promise of the kingdom seems to exist in itself with faith needing to believe that Jesus is indeed God's agent to announce it and to achieve it. It is the good news and constitutes Mark's soteriology. Neither within Mark's narrative world, which depicts the time before Jesus' death, nor in projections beyond it, is there clear evidence that the cross as effecting atonement has become the main focus of the good news, as it is in Paul, according to whom only on that basis can freedom from divine judgement be possible. Had this been so also for Mark, one would expect to see traces of it at least in the passion narrative, where Mark has been actively engaged in highlighting other key values. Mark's message in Jesus' ministry is already about belonging and already included forgiveness, offered to all, as it was already in the call to change by John.

Mark also knows the tradition about Christ's death as redemptive, to which he alludes in the ransom saying and the words over the wine. They could now serve simply refer to Jesus' self-giving throughout his life and even to death in order to bring the benefit of the good news to all and so be saving in that sense.Mark is here drawing on tradition, just as Paul had earlier, for whom Christ's redemptive death formed the heart of his gospel. The two allusions in Mark are scarcely derived from Paul, who uses neither λύτρον nor "for many;" nor is his account of the last meal where the latter reference occurs derived from Paul's tradition as does Luke's. While for Paul it is the saving event *par excellence*, in the light of which Jesus' prior ministry is largely without significance, this is not the case with Mark.[74] For, while sharing with Paul the common eschatological meaning of being saved from the judgement, Mark's understanding of salvation is not just about sin and redemption, but about liberation and healing,

---

71 Crossley, "Mark, Paul," 20. Werner, *Einfluss*, argues on the basis of Gal 1:6-9 that Paul inherited use of the term from tradition (103).
72 Cf. Marcus, "Mark – Interpreter of Paul," 475; and Telford, *Theology of Mark*, 168.
73 Cf. Bird, "Mark," who writes: "the language and perspective in Mk 13.10 is undoubtedly Christian and, more specifically, Pauline" (47). "This suggests that the Pauline mission to the nations is the social context of Mark's Gospel" (47).
74 I find the argument of Marcus, "Mark – Interpreter of Paul," 479-81, that the emphasis of each is on the cross needs significant qualification. The commonality lies in both in very different ways highlighting the path of suffering, but not in the weight given the cross's soteriological significance, which is so much more in Paul.

which he finds already coming to expression in Jesus' ministry, to which forgiveness belongs but only as one element.[75] As we have seen, it is also highly unlikely that Mark saw Jesus' ministry as expressing a different understanding of salvation from what Mark would now preach in his own time.[76] He did after all write a Gospel, to indicate not only what *was* good news but what *is* good news. Its balance and proportions, including the place of atonement theology, are likely to indicate the nature of Mark's own theology and understanding of the Christian message. Thus Mark shows that he knows the motif which for Paul was so central, but weights it very differently.

(2) Soteriology in Paul

Paul's soteriology is, indeed, very different. He says little of Jesus' ministry. Rather the focus is his death, about which he has a range of traditions, all of which signify that this was the event in which God dealt with human sin by having Christ die. Christ died for us. Christ died for our sins. That made forgiveness and reconciliation possible. That was the act of a righteous God, setting about to set people in right relationship with himself, as a result of which they would then live rightly. The soteriology is directly related to the ethics. Righteousness gives birth to righteousness, otherwise described as the fruit of the Spirit, generated in the new life which through Christ's death has died and through his resurrection has risen to new life and new beginnings. Paul enables us to see how transformative all this is for the individual who embraces it in faith. This is a sophisticated theology in which faith's response is entry into an ongoing relationship which through the Spirit generates goodness in response to goodness, righteousness in response to righteousness.

This is not Mark's theology, though one can argue that what Paul identifies as happening in Christ's death, an act of reconciliation and justification, Mark demonstrates indirectly as occurring in Jesus' ministry. Mark's account of Jesus' baptism find echoes in Paul's notion of baptism and the receiving of the Spirit as the moment when the believer is adopted as a child of God, but Mark sees fictive kinship differently: Jesus' family are those who do the will of God, though surely Mark's community also saw baptism as part of the process

---

75 So Werner, *Einfluss*, 62, 118-19.
76 Werner, *Einfluss*, astutely relates the different soteriology to the different stance towards the Law: "In Wahrheit stossen wir hier einfach auf die Konsequenz der positiven soteriologischen Wertung des Gesetzes, wie Markus sie vertritt: wo es sich um die Bedingung zur Erlangung der ζωὴ αἰωνίος handelt, eben da erscheint bei Markus nicht die Forderung des Glaubens an den Messias Jesus, sondern da heisst es einfach: 'Du kennst die Gebote' (10:19). Hier muss also in der Tat der Grund für das auffallende Zurücktreten der Forderung des Glaubens an Jesus als den Christus liegen" (111-12).

of joining the believing community. Mark shows no awareness of the response of faith as engagement in a relationship which by the Spirit engenders ethical fruit. Ethics mean keeping the commandments and following Jesus. The Spirit enables miracles.

3.3 Common Eschatology

Despite the very different soteriology and significantly different approach to the Law, both Mark and Paul share a common eschatology. Both use kingdom of God to refer to the future hope, associated with the return of Christ, sometimes expressed in similar terms (coming in clouds and accompanied by holy ones). Both speak of a future judgement, a surprisingly constant and frequently neglected feature in Paul's thought. If, as appears to be the case, Mark understands the transfiguration scene as a foreshadowing of the return of Christ, then both share an understanding of resurrected existence as transfigured into something spiritual, not a physical resuscitation. Both assumes a sexless age to come, though, unlike Paul, Mark shows no signs of knowing people who want to impose this on the present. Both have an expectation that the coming of Christ and the kingdom will occur within a generation. The common eschatology is best explained as derived from common early tradition.[77]

3.4 Christology

Mark also shares with Paul the belief in Jesus' unique relation to God, though without specifically identifying pre-existence as an element of his christology or drawing on wisdom christology. Paul lacks the title Son of Man,[78] but otherwise shares a similar apocalyptic eschatology. Both affirm Christ's resurrection, including the appearance to Peter. The major differences in christology between Paul and Mark are the absence of reference to Christ's pre-existence in Mark and the absence in Paul of references to the significance of Jesus' ministry. Both

---

[77] Werner, *Einfluss*, while noting common traditions (144) also points to significant differences including Mark's reference to signs before the end, unlike Paul (147-48), different understandings of future resurrection and the fate of unbelievers, and the absence in Mark of the notion an interim reign of Christ (153-55, 161-77).
[78] On attempts to find commonality between Son of Man and last Adam see Telford, *Theology of Mark*, 166. Marcus, "Mark – Interpreter of Paul," sees the commonality in Adam tradition in Mark's wilderness scene (475).

share an emphasis on Christ's suffering, Paul, as an interpretation and defence of his own frailty and suffering, Mark, apparently in presenting Jesus as a model for believers of his day, perhaps even to the extent of having the Jewish trial sound more like a trial of Christians in his day than an historical event of forty years earlier. Mark has nothing equivalent to what many read in Paul as a reference to the faith or faithfulness of Christ, not surprisingly since it occurs in Paul's statements about Christ's death for our sins, not an emphasis in Mark. On the other hand, Mark's narrative of the passion does illustrate Christ's faithfulness. Mark's christology does not show signs of having derived from Paul's, which is more developed.

3.5 Misdirected Faith

It is equally interesting that both deal with what they deem is misdirected faith. For Paul that entails confronting the Corinthians whose powerful charismatic experiences threaten both the unity of the community and its integrity. A significant element is also that it appears to fuel disparagement of Paul's authority as an apostle. Against these trends Paul asserts love and mutual responsibility, both in caring for one another and in recognising different kinds of gifts. In his own defence he aligns his apparent unimpressiveness with Christ's suffering and death, arguing for the cross as a symbol God's way of love which is superior to powerful miracles and powerful wisdom.

While Mark does not appear to be confronted with lofty claims to wisdom, his gospel challenges what it depicts as the obsession of the leading disciples with positions of power. Peter does not want a suffering messiah. The disciples argue about who will be the greatest. James and John want the top positions beside Jesus in the kingdom. Mark's messiah is then depicted as a crucified king, crowned on a cross with thorns. Nothing indicates a direct relation to Paul's arguments, but there is a common emphasis.[79] Such issues of appropriate faith are, however, by no means peculiar to Paul and Mark. Dealing with faith overly focused on signs and wonders was apparently a widespread problem, evident in the closing sections of Matthew's Sermon on the Mount (7:15-23), and in the depiction of those who on the basis of miracles trusted in Jesus' name in John 2:23–

---

[79] Crossley, "Mark, Paul," writes: "Certainly, we can say that issues of authority and/or suffering are tied in with terms such as 'son of God' and 'son of man' and the general issue of a theology of the cross is no doubt a clear similarity between the two" (27).

3:5, and in whom Jesus could not bring himself to trust, but who required new birth if they were to see the kingdom.

Miracles served both Mark's account and Paul as corroboration of God's presence in people, but assume much greater significance in Mark as signs of the kingdom. Both know the image of faith moving mountains. Such use of signs and wonders as propaganda was not unproblematic, as our discussion has shown, but, for all its dangers, remains in both a component which serves to enhance faith. This was probably something they shared in common with others in the movement.

3.6 Pneumatology

For Mark the Spirit is primarily the power of God in Jesus which enables him to perform exorcisms and healings and at most is promised as a helper of believers facing trials, a motif developed into the Paraclete in the Johannine final discourses. It also inspired David to write Ps 110:1. Faith's focus in relation to the Spirit is thus primarily on the miraculous, not the ethical. In Paul, by contrast, the Spirit is manifest primarily in the fruit of the Spirit, especially love, which is the measure for assessing all other expressions or claims to the Spirit's activity. So while Paul, too, shares the primitive notion that the Spirit empowered miracles of healing and exorcisms, he has gone far beyond such notions along paths clearly unknown to Mark.[80]

3.7 Authority and Leadership

In both Mark and Paul faith entails for some a special calling, to share Jesus' ministry and represent him. Paul's difficult manoeuvrings reflect dispute about his status as apostle and indicate conflict with Peter, whose leadership of the in-

---

[80] So Werner, *Einfluss*, 126-27. Maureen W. Yeung, *Faith in Jesus and Paul: A Comparison with Special Reference to 'Faith Can Remove Mountains' and 'Your Faith Has Healed/Saved You'* , WUNT 2.147 (Tübingen: Mohr Siebeck, 2002), develops the argument that Paul in fact developed the approach of the historical Jesus towards faith, which she portrays as faith in his ability and in his person, leading both to healing and to salvation, as acceptance into the kingdom, illustrated by the statement that faith saved the woman with the bleeding (in relation to impurity) (175-79) and Bartimaeus (in relation to no longer being seen as a sinner) (183). On the basis of use of Hab 2:4 and Gen 15:6 she argues that Paul takes "Jesus' miracle-salvation faith a step forward" (281), indeed, much further forward as he develops a different soteriology based on Christ's death.

itial group is assumed in Mark, and with the subsequent leader in Jerusalem, James, brother of Jesus, who barely features in Mark. One might speculate that Mark's depiction of the disciple's dullness and failure to understand is replaying Paul's earlier conflicts or perhaps continuing the fight with the conservatives and moderates. That is speculation.[81] For Mark's final words affirm Peter's priority as witness to Christ's appearance in Galilee without any hint of denigration.[82] Mark reflects the tradition according to which the twelve disciples are apostles (6:30), possibly exclusively so, unlike in Paul,[83] who also never used "disciples" of them.[84] The poor performance of the disciples in Mark probably has less to do with history, including the history of Paul's conflict with some of them or Mark's conflict with their influence in his day, than with Mark's pedagogical agenda which challenges all to an informed faith. One might at least conclude that Mark is not in a context where to say such things would have offended anyone to whom he or his community is beholden. On the other hand, Mark's stance would certainly put him and his community offside with the Law observant Christians. That doesn't make him Pauline, any more than John's one-upmanship of the beloved disciple over Peter, while respecting the latter's legitimacy as leader. Paul's conflicts with these leaders was over Law; Mark's depiction of their weakness relates not to Law, but to their failure to understand the way of lowly suffering. Both Paul and Mark advise respect for secular authorities, including payment of taxes,[85] though differently (Mark 12:13-17; Rom 13:1-7), but are not alone in this.

---

[81] Crossley, "Mark, Paul," notes that "the disputes with family and the disciples in Mark do not, in sharp contrast to Paul, directly involve the Law and its validity and Jesus even defends his disciples on the issue of plucking grain on the Sabbath, which, as we saw, is the kind of interpretative dispute known in early Judaism" (23); cf. Marcus, "Mark – Interpreter of Paul," 475; and Telford, *Theology of Mark*, 164. According to Werner, *Einfluss*, Mark has a high view of the twelve despite their lack of understanding (179-80), since they are privileged throughout. Their failure to understand the need for Jesus' suffering and death is not the same as their role in Paul where they oppose the true gospel and that the cross sets Law aside (unlike in Mark) (181-82). Mark's disciples are not legalistic but free as 2:1-3:6 and 7:1-23 show (182).

[82] For an attempt to reclaim the second century tradition of Mark's dependence on Peter, see Bird, "Mark," 30-61. I still find the comment by Fenton, "Paul and Mark," more apposite: "The extant evidence points as much to Mark's companionship with Paul as to Mark's companionship with Peter" (111).

[83] Werner, *Einfluss*, 178-79.

[84] Werner, *Einfluss*, attributes this to his different understanding of the relationship with Jesus.

[85] Telford, *Theology of Mark*, 166.

4 Conclusions

What brings Mark and Paul together is the common interest in dealing with the inclusion of Gentiles by redefining the place of Law in a way that sets them apart from Matthew and Luke, who show by their reworking of Mark, that they disagree with Mark, though Paul and Mark still differ on the Law's status. What sets Mark and Paul apart also is the very different soteriology, pneumatology, and basis for ethics, such that it would be hard to place Mark in a Pauline trajectory, such as we find in Colossians, Ephesians, or the Pastoral epistles.[86] These differences have major implications for the understanding of faith in each, which accordingly is significantly different. In Paul it means believing and embracing the gift of reconciliation made possible through Christ's death which guarantees escape from the wrath to come and through the Spirit living out that relationship in ways that more than fulfil the Law's demands. In Mark it means believing and embracing the promise of the kingdom, including the promise now of forgiveness and belonging, and following Jesus by doing God's will, including a selective keeping of the Law based on priorities set by Jesus.[87] It is hard to get from Paul to Mark in the light of such difference.

Mark and Paul share enough, however, for us to say that Mark will have been written in a community which has needed to affirm Gentile participation, and so is probably predominantly Gentile, though with a sufficiently well-educated constituency of Jews and possibly proselytes for the many subtle allusions to Scripture in Mark not to be lost on them. This makes it likely that Mark's radical approach to the Law draws its inspiration not from non-Jewish or anti-Jewish circles, but from the fringes of Judaism where Paul had been at home and whose thought could address the issues of Gentile belonging so radically. Given levels of communication in their world, it is surely possible that Mark

---

[86] Marcus, *Mark*, concludes: "The most reasonable conclusion would seem to be that Mark writes in the Pauline sphere of activity and shows some sort of Pauline influence on his thought, although he is not a member of the Pauline 'school' in the same sense that the authors of Colossians-Ephesians and the Pastorals are; unlike them, he has not studied, internalized, and imitated Paul's letters" (75).

[87] Werner, *Einfluss*, writes: "Der Gottesglaube des Markus zeigt praktisch-religiöse Art: er ist die ungeteilte Zuversicht, dass Gott Bitten, wie sie des Lebens Notdurft Tag für Tag dem Menschen auf die Lippen zwingt, erhören wird (Mc 11 24). Der Gottesglaube des Paulus ist mehr theologisch-theoretisch: er ist die Zuversicht, dass Gott in Erfüllung gehen lässt, was er im heiligen Buch vor Zeiten dem auserwählten Volk versprochen hat. Hinter dem Gottesglauben des Markus steht die Vorstellung von Gott als Vater, der das einzelne Individuum kennt und sich seiner in den Sorgen der Erde annimmt; hinter dem Glauben des Paulus steht der Gott der Heilsgeschichte" (113).

would have known of Paul and known of Pauline traditions, though these are difficult to trace.

Mark's theology has most in common with what is probably Paul's earlier extant letter, 1Thessalonians. Both share a focus on the eschaton (kingdom, judgement, coming of Christ), on faith as enduring adversity, some ethical implications as appropriate for life in the interim, a corporate dimension, including respect for leaders, and use of Spirit-generated miracles (and the resurrection) to enhance credibility of the message; and nothing about Christ's death as salvific.

The different soteriology and pneumatology, and so the difference in the understanding of what are to be faith's beliefs and faith's response, suggest that Mark cannot be seen as simply a more radical Paulinist. The common ground suggests a Christian group within the diverse mix of evolving Christian communities, which had also needed to deal with inclusion of Gentiles by addressing issues of Law, but in its self-understanding and primitive concept of faith was much more closely aligned with what appears to have been the message and mission of the historical Jesus, which it therefore seeks to re-present.

Bibliography

Bacon, Benjamin W. *Is Mark a Roman Gospel?* Cambridge: Cambridge University Press, 1919.
Beavis, Mary Ann. "Mark's Teaching on Faith," *BTB* 16 (1986): 139-42.
—, "Women as Models of Faith in Mark," *BTB* 18 (1988): 3-9.
Bell, Richard H. "Faith in Christ: Some Exegetical and Theological Reflections on Philippians 3:9 and Ephesians 3:12," in: *The Faith of Jesus Christ: Exegetical, Biblical, and Theological Studies*, eds. Michael F. Bird and Preston M. Sprinkle, 111-25. Peabody, Mass.: Hendrickson, 2009.
Bird, Michael F. "Mark: Interpreter of Peter and Disciple of Paul," in: *Paul and the Gospels: Christologies, Conflicts and Controversies*, eds. Michael F. Bird and Joel Willitts, 30-61. LNTS 411. London: T & T Clark International, 2011.
Byrne, Brendan. "Paul and Mark before the Cross: Common Echoes of the Day of Atonement Ritual," in: *Transcending Boundaries: Contemporary Readings of the New Testament: In Honour of Professor Francis Moloney, S.D.B.*, eds. Rekha M. Chennattu and Mary L. Coloe, 217-30. Rome: LAS Publications, 2005.
Collins, Adela Yarbro. *Mark: A Commentary.* Hermeneia. Minneapolis, Minn.: Fortress Press, 2007.
Crossley, James G. "Mark, Paul and the Question of Influence," in: *Paul and the Gospels: Christologies, Conflicts and Controversies*, eds. Michael F. Bird and Joel Willitts, 10-29. LNTS 411. London: T & T Clark International, 2011.
Donahue, John R. and Daniel J. Harrington. *The Gospel of Mark.* SP 2. Collegeville, Pa.: Liturgical Press, 2002.
Dowd, Sharyn. *Prayer, Power, and the Problem of Suffering: Mark 11:22-25 in the Context of Markan Theology.* SBLDS105. Atlanta, Ga.: Scholars Press, 1988.
du Toit, Andrie. "Faith and Obedience in Paul," in: *Focusing on Paul. Persuasion and Theological Design in Romans and Galatians*, eds. Cilliers Breytenbach, and David S. du Toit, 117-27. BZNW 151. Berlin: de Gruyter, 2007.
Dunn, James D. G. "The Justice of God," *JTS* 43 (1992): 1-22.
—, *The Theology of Paul the Apostle.* Grand Rapids, Mich.: Eerdmans, 1998.
—, "Forward," in: *The Faith of Jesus Christ: Exegetical, Biblical, and Theological Studies*, eds. Michael F. Bird, and Preston M. Sprinkle, xv-xix. Peabody, Mass.: Hendrickson, 2009.
Evans, Craig A. *Mark 8:27-16:20.* WBC 34B. Nashville, Tenn.: Nelson, 2001.
Fenton, John C. "Paul and Mark," in: *Studies in the Gospels: Essays in Memory of R. H. Lightfoot*, ed. Dennis E. Nineham, 89-112. Oxford: Blackwell, 1955.
Friedrich, Gerhard. "Das Gesetz des Glaubens Römer 3,27," *ThZ* 10 (1954): 409-11
Guelich, Robert A. *Mark 1-8:26.* WBC 34A. Waco, Tex.: Word Books, 1989.
Hahn, Ferdinand. "Das Verständnis des Glaubens im Markusevangelium," in: *Glaube im Neuen Testament. Festschrift für Hans Binder*, eds. Ferdinand Hahn and Hans Klein, 43-67. Neukirchen: Neukirchener Verlag, 1982.
Loader, William. *Jesus' Attitude Towards the Law: A Study of the Gospels.* WUNT 2.128. Tübingen: Mohr Siebeck, 1997.
—, "Attitudes to Judaism and the Law and Synoptic Relations," in: *Studies in the Synoptic Problem: Oxford Conference, April 2008*, eds. Andrew Gregory, Paul Foster, John S. Kloppenborg and Joseph Verheyden, 347-69. BETL 23. Leuven, Peeters, 2011.

—, "What Happened to 'Good News for the Poor'? On the Trail of Hope Beyond Jesus," in: *Reflections on Early Christian History and Religion*, AJEC 81, eds. Cilliers Breytenbach and Jörg Frey, 233-66. Leiden: Brill, 2012.
Marcus, Joel. "Mark – Interpreter of Paul," *NTS* 46 (2000): 473-87.
—, *Mark*. 2 vols. AB 27and 27A. New Haven, Conn.: Yale University Press, 1999, 2009.
Marshall,Christopher D. *Faith as a Theme in Mark's Narrative*. SNTSMS 64. Cambridge: Cambridge University Press, 1989.
O'Brien, Peter T. "Was Paul a Covenantal Nomist?," in: *Justification and Variegated Nomism. Volume II. The Paradoxes of Paul*, eds. Donald A. Carson, Peter T. O'Brien and Mark A. Seifrid, 249-96.WUNT 2.181. Tübingen: Mohr Siebeck, 2004.
Repschinski, Boris. *Nicht aufzulösen sondern zu erfüllen. Das jüdische Gesetz in den synoptischen Jesus Erzählungen*. FzB 120.Würzburg: Echter, 2009.
Sanders, Ed Parish. *Paul and Palestinian Judaism*. London: SCM, 1977.
—, *Paul, The Law, and the Jewish People*. London: SCM, 1982.
Seeley, David. "Rulership and Service in Mark 10:41-45," *NovT* 35 (1993): 234-50.
Seifrid, Mark A. "The Faith of Christ," in: *The Faith of Jesus Christ: Exegetical, Biblical, and Theological Studies*, eds. Michael F. Bird, and Preston M. Sprinkle, 29-46. Peabody, Mass.: Hendrickson, 2009.
Silva, Moisés. "Faith Versus Works of Law in Galatians," in: *Justification and Variegated Nomism. Volume II. The Paradoxes of Paul*, eds. Donald A. Carson, Peter T. O'Brien, and Mark A. Seifrid, 217-48. WUNT 2.181. Tübingen: Mohr Siebeck, 2004.
Söding, Thomas. *Glaube bei Markus. Glaube an das Evangelium. Gebetsglaube und Wunderglaube im Kontext der markinischen Basileiatheologie und Christologie*. SBB 12. Stuttgart, Katholisches Bibelwerk, 1987.
Svartvik, Jesper. *Mark and Mission: Mk 7:1-23 in its Narrative and Historical Contexts*. CBNTS 32. Stockholm: Almqvist & Wiksell, 2000.
—, "Matthew and Mark," in: *Matthew and his Christian Contemporaries*, eds David C. Sim and Boris Repschinski, 27-49. LNTS 333. London: T&T Clark International, 2008.
Telford, William. *The Barren Temple and the Withered Tree*. JSNTSup 1. Sheffield: JSOT Press, 1980.
—, *The Theology of the Gospel of Mark* (Cambridge: Cambridge University Press, 1999).
Tyson, Joseph B. "The Blindness of the Disciples in Mark," in: *The Messianic Secret*, ed. Christopher Tuckett, 35-43. Philadelphia: Fortress Press, 1983.
Watson, Francis. "By Faith (of Christ): An Exegetical Dilemma and its Scriptural Solution," in: *The Faith of Jesus Christ: Exegetical, Biblical, and Theological Studies*, eds. Michael F. Bird, and Preston M. Sprinkle, 147-63. Peabody, Mass.: Hendrickson, 2009.
—, *Paul and the Hermeneutics of Faith*. London: T & T Clark, 2004.
Weeden, Theodore J. "The Heresy that Necessitated Mark's Gospel," in: *The Interpretation of Mark*, ed. William Telford, 89-104. Edinburgh: T& T Clark, 1995.
Werner, Martin. *Der Einfluss paulinischer Theologie im Markusevangelium: eine Studie zur neutestamentlichen Theologie*. Giessen: Töpelmann, 1923.
Westerholm, Stephen. *Perspectives Old and New on Paul: The "Lutheran" Paul and His Critics*. Grand Rapids, Mich.: Eerdmans, 2004.
Yeung, Maureen W. *Faith in Jesus and Paul: A Comparison with Special Reference to 'Faith Can Remove Mountains' and 'Your Faith Has Healed/Saved You'*. WUNT 2.147. Tübingen: Mohr Siebeck, 2002.

Thomas Söding
Das Liebesgebot bei Markus und Paulus. Ein literarischer und theologischer Vergleich

1 Fragestellung

Das Gebot der Nächstenliebe aus dem Heiligkeitsgesetz (Lev 19,18)[1] hat im Neuen Testament ein starkes Echo ausgelöst[2]. Die ältesten Zeugnisse stehen bei Markus und Paulus.

Im Markusevangelium bildet das Gebot der Nächstenliebe[3] eine Einheit mit dem Doppelgebot Jesu; es bildet einen starken Akkord in den Jerusalemer Debatten, mit denen sein öffentliches Wirken endet[4]. Es führt ausnahmsweise zu einer Verständigung, anders als nach den Seitenreferenten. Die Nächstenliebe in ihrer Einheit mit der Gottesliebe ist – nicht erst für Matthäus, der es explizit (Mt 22,40), sondern auch schon – für Markus die entscheidende Stellungnahme Jesu zur Geltung des Gesetzes. Sie bildet das Koordinatensystem, an dem sich das Glaubensleben in der Nachfolge Jesu orientiert.

---

[1] Vgl. H.-P. Mathys, Liebe deinen Nächsten wie dich selbst. Untersuchungen zum alttestamentlichen Gebot der Nächstenliebe (OBO 71), Freiburg i.d. Schweiz/Göttingen, 1986; B. Becking, Love thy neighbour ... Exegetical remarks on Leviticus 19:18,34, in: „Gerechtigkeit und Recht zu üben" (Gen 18,19). Studien zur altorientalischen und biblischen Rechtsgeschichte, zur Religionsgeschichte Israels und zur Religionssoziologie. FS für Eckart Otto zum 65. Geburtstag, hg. von R. Achenbach/M. Arneth (BZAR 13), Wiesbaden 2009, 182–187.
[2] L.S. Navarro, El cumplimiento del amor. Derás neotestamentario de LV 19,18B, in: EstB 66 (2008), 499–529. C. Gionotto, Amerai il prossimo tuo come te stesso. Alcune osservazioni sull'interpretazione di Lv 19,18 nell'antica letteratura cristiana, in: Nuovo Testamento. Teologie in dialogo culturale. Scritti in onore di Romano Penna nel suo 70 compleanno, ed. by G.P.N. Ciola (RevBib.S 60), Bologna 2008, 479–489; W. Reinbold, Die Nächstenliebe (Lev 19,18), in: Die Verheißung des Neuen Bundes. Wie alttestamentliche Texte im Neuen Testament fortwirken, hg. von B. Kollmann (BTSP 35), Göttingen 2010, 115–127.
[3] Vgl. M. Ebersohn, Das Nächstenliebegebot in der synoptischen Tradition (MThSt 37), Marburg 1993.
[4] Vgl. W. Weiss, „Eine neue Lehre in Vollmacht". Die Streit- und Schulgespräche des Markus-Evangeliums (BZNW 52), Berlin 1989; K. Huber, Jesus in Auseinandersetzung. Exegetische Untersuchungen zu den sogenannten Jerusalemer Streitgesprächen des Markusevangeliums im Blick auf ihre christologischen Implikationen (FzB 75), Würzburg 1995.

Paulus zitiert Lev 19,18 zweimal (Gal 5,13 f.; Röm 13,8 ff.)[5]. Beide Stellen stehen in Briefen, die auf das Thema der Rechtfertigung konzentriert sind. Beide führen an die Schnittstelle von Soteriologie und Ethik. Beide sprechen – in leicht unterschiedlicher Weise – von der Erfüllung des Gesetzes; beide setzen deshalb einen Kontrapunkt zur Kritik der „Gesetzeswerke", die zur Rechtfertigung nicht beitragen. Beide sollen die Ethik des Glaubens organisieren. Beide kennen keine direkte Verbindung mit dem Hauptgebot der Gottesliebe (Dtn 6,4 f.), stehen aber in einem explizit theologischen Kontext, der durch die rechtfertigende Wirkung des Glaubens bestimmt wird.

Der Galater- und der Römerbrief sind deutlich vor dem Markusevangelium geschrieben worden. Deshalb gibt es die Debatte, ob Markus – direkt oder indirekt – von Paulus (oder den urchristlichen Ethik-Traditionen, die er repräsentiert) beeinflusst worden ist[6]. Da Markus aber eine Jesustradition aufnimmt, gibt es auch die umgekehrte These, dass Paulus direkt oder indirekt von ihr beeinflusst worden ist[7]. In jedem Fall stellt sich die Frage, ob es eine direkte oder indirekte Traditionslinie zwischen den beiden frühesten Zeugnissen des Liebesgebotes im Neuen Testament gibt. Diese Diskussion kann nicht geführt werden, ohne dass die Rezeptionsgeschichte des Liebesgebotes im frühen Judentum vor Augen steht.

Wesentlich ist allerdings auch der theologische Vergleich: Wie ist bei Markus und Paulus vom Gesetz die Rede? Was heißt bei ihnen Nächstenliebe? Wie ist das Gebot begründet? Welchen Stellenwert hat es? Wie wird es konkretisiert? Welche theologischen und anthropologischen Dimensionen öffnet das Liebesgebot?[8] Diese Diskussion kann nicht geführt werden, ohne dass die theologische Bedeutung der Ethik vor Augen steht.

2 Das Liebesgebot bei Markus

In den theologischen Statements, mit denen Jesus nach Markus in Jerusalem seine Positionen abschließend markiert, sticht das Doppelgebot der Gottes- und

---

5 Vgl. Th. Söding, Das Liebesgebot bei Paulus. Die Mahnung zur Agape im Rahmen der paulinischen Ethik (NTA 26), Münster 1995.
6 Grundlegend: M. Werner, Der Einfluß paulinischer Theologie im Markusevangelium. Eine Studie zur neutestamentlichen Theologie (BZNW 1), Gießen 1923. Von einer starken theologischen Beeinflussung des Markusevangeliums durch Paulus ist Udo Schnelle überzeugt: Theologie des Neuen Testaments, Göttingen 2007, 398.
7 Vgl. D. Wenham, Paul. Follower of Jesus or Founder of Christianity, Grand Rapids 1995.
8 Für die exegetische und interdisziplinäre Diskussion anregend ist H. Meisinger, Liebesgebot und Altruismusforschung. Ein exegetischer Beitrag zum Dialog zwischen Theologie und Naturwissenschaft (NTOA 33), Freiburg i.d. Schweiz/Göttingen 1996.

Nächstenliebe heraus (Mk 12,38 – 34). Durchweg geht es um die Ehre, das Recht, die Macht und den Willen Gottes: schon in der Antwort auf die Frage, mit welcher Legitimation Jesus seine Revolution der Heiligkeit im Tempel angezettelt habe (Mk 11,28 – 12,12), dann explizit auch in der Frage nach den Steuern (Mk 12,13 – 17) und der Auferstehung (Mk 12,18 – 27), indirekt ebenso in der Diskussion über die Davidssohnschaft des Messias (Mk 12,35ff.), in der Kritik an der Heuchelei der Schriftgelehrten (Mk 12,37 – 40) und beim Gegenbeispiel mit dem Opfer der armen Witwe (Mk 12,41 – 44).

Das Gespräch über das größte Gebot sticht heraus (Mk 12,28 – 34). Es kombiniert zwei Tora-Gebote. Es arbeitet mit Wiederholung und Übereinstimmung. Es ist kein Konflikt-, sondern ein Konsensgespräch. Es zeigt von Anfang bis Ende die Alternative zur Verfolgung Jesu durch die Hohenpriester und Schriftgelehrten: ein theologisches Agreement auf der Basis der Tora und einer Konzentration auf die Liebe, das die Nähe der Gottesherrschaft offenhält, ohne dass vom Glauben an das Evangelium, von Jüngerschaft und Nachfolge explizit die Rede wäre[9].

2.1 Die Verbindung von Gottes- und Nächstenliebe

Jesus wird nach Mk 12,28 von einem Schriftgelehrten, der Zeuge der vorangegangenen Streitgespräche geworden und von Jesus überzeugt worden war, gefragt: „Welches ist das größte Gebot von allen?" Die Frage ist ebenso präzis wie voraussetzungsreich gestellt. Vorausgesetzt wird zum einen die fundamentale Bedeutung des Gesetzes[10], zum anderen eine Hierarchie der Gebote, die Unterscheidungen erlaubt. In den jüdischen Debatten über die Geltung des Gesetzes, die zeitgenössisch geführt worden sind[11], ordnet sich das Gespräch deshalb von vornherein bei denjenigen Exegeten und Juristen ein, die aus pädagogischen und theologischen Gründen zwischen leichteren und schwereren Geboten unterscheiden, ohne deshalb die Einheit des Gesetzes und die Verbindlichkeit, die ihm

---

9 Vgl. F. Prast, Ein Appell zur Besinnung auf das Juden wie Christen gemeinsame Erbe im Munde Jesu. Das Anliegen einer alten vormarkinischen Tradition (Mk 12,28 – 34), in: Gottesverächter und Menschenfeinde? Juden zwischen Jesus und frühchristlicher Kirche, hg. von H. Goldstein, Düsseldorf 1979, 79 – 88.
10 Joachim Gnilka ist der Meinung, der Schriftgelehrte frage nicht speziell nach dem Gesetz, sondern nach dem größten Gebot „von allem" (Das Evangelium nach Markus II [EKK I/2], Zürich u. a./Neukirchen-Vluyn 1979 [2000], 164.)
11 Aus den Quellen erschlossen und breit aufgearbeitet von K. Berger, Die Gesetzesauslegung Jesu. Teil I: Markus und Parallelen (WMANT 40), Neukirchen-Vluyn 1972.

insgesamt zukommt, aufzulösen[12]. Die Zustimmung, die Jesus beim Schriftgelehrten erfährt, rührt in der erzählten Welt des Markusevangeliums anscheinend daher, dass Jesus sich in den Auseinandersetzungen um seine Autorität und den Willen Gottes konsequent auf den Boden des Gesetzes stellt, aber ihm eine Auslegung gibt, die für die Prophetie und Weisheit, damit aber für ein theologisches *aggiornamento* geöffnet ist.

Die Präzision der Frage liegt zum einen daran, dass der Schriftgelehrte das Gesetz als Verbindung verschiedener Gebote betrachtet, die mehr bedeutet als die Summe einzelner Vorschriften; sie liegt zum anderen darin, dass der Schlüssel zum Verständnis der Tora als ganzer nicht außerhalb, sondern innerhalb des Gesetzes gesucht wird. Damit setzt sich das Gespräch von solchen Positionen der frühjüdischen Debatte ab, die auf allgemeine ethische Maximen abheben[13], und führt an die Seite derjenigen, die darauf setzten, die Tora mit der Tora auszulegen und in ihrem Grundcharakter als Gebot zu konkretisieren[14].

So wie Markus die Episode erzählt, ist Jesus mit dieser Gesprächseröffnung einverstanden. Sie entspricht seiner eigenen Intention. Das gute Ende ist von Anfang an vorgezeichnet. Jesus sprengt jedoch in seiner Antwort den Horizont der Frage. Denn strenggenommen führt er nicht ein Gebot, sondern zwei Gebote an. Diese Doppelung ist aber gerade die Pointe. Das Hauptgebot zu nennen, wäre zu erwarten gewesen. Das Liebesgebot ist gleichfalls ein Kandidat. Die Verbindung ist das Typische; sie hat jüdische Parallelen, ist aber – deshalb – für Jesus charak-

---

[12] Die Differenzierung klingt in Mt 22,36 („Welches Gebot ist groß im Gesetz?") deutlich nach; vgl. Mt 5,19.

[13] Rabbi Hillel soll die Goldene Regel genannt haben (Schab 31a), nicht unähnlich Mt 7,12; eine ähnliche kritierielle Funktion erhält sie in LibAnt XI 10.13; vgl. Tob 4,15; EpAr 207; TestNaph (hebr) 1; Hen (slaw) 61,1; Philo, Hypothetica (bei Eusebius, Praeparatio Evangelica, 8,7); AbRN 15.16; TargJerusch I Lev 19,18. Ab 1,18 sind Wahrheit, Recht und Frieden genannt.

[14] Starke Akzentuierungen des Liebesgebotes finden sich in den Patriarchentestamenten: TestRub 6,9; TestIss 7,6; Dan 5,1ff. (Schlusspointe) sowie TestSim 4,7, TestSeb 8,5; TestBenj 3,1 (Eingangsweisung) und TestGad 6,1.3; 7,7 (Rahmen), vor allem TestJos 17,1f. (Zusammenfassung); vgl. Th. Söding, Solidarität in der Diaspora. Das Liebesgebot nach den Testamenten der Zwölf Patriarchen im Vergleich mit dem Neuen Testament, in: Kairos 36/37 (1994/95), 1–19; M. Konradt, Menschen- und Bruderliebe? Beobachtungen zum Liebesgebot in den Testamenten der Zwölf Patriarchen, in: ZNW 88 (1997), 296–310. Weniger stark sind die Akzente in 1QS 1,2–11; 1QS 9 und CD 19,15–18; vgl. Th. Söding, Feindeshaß und Bruderliebe. Beobachtungen zur essenischen Ethik, in: RdQ 17 (1995), 601–619. Beachtenswert sind auch die schwer zu datierenden Belege für die Wertschätzung von Lev 19,18 in der rabbinischen Literatur. AbRN (A) 16 (32b): „in einer großen Stunde gesagt" (Rabbi Schimon ben Elazar,), AbRN (B) 26 (27a) „ein Wort, an dem die ganze Welt hängt" (Priestervorsteher Chananja); SifraLev 19,18 (89b): „großer Hauptsatz der Tora" (Rabbi Akiba). Andere Texte nennen die Gottesebenbildlichkeit (SifraLev 19,18 [89b]), den Glauben (mit Hab 2,4 TanchB § 10 [16b]), die Torah, Liturgie und Caritas (Ab 1,2).

teristisch und theologisch signifikant[15]. Mit dem Doppelgebot findet Jesus, dem weiteren Gesprächsverlauf zufolge, die Zustimmung des Schriftgelehrten. Auf diese Weise wird von Markus der Primat des Lehrens Jesu ebenso sublim wie nachhaltig zum Ausdruck gebracht.

Beide Gebote werden aber nicht addiert, sondern auf präzise Weise kombiniert. Deshalb weicht Jesus der klar gestellten Frage nicht aus, sondern gibt eine klare, eindeutige Antwort. Die Kombination, die er vornimmt, ist eine Strukturierung: „Das erste ist: ... Das zweite ist: ..." (Mk 12,29.31). Der Weg der Antwort führt zuerst zur Gottesliebe, dann zur Nächstenliebe. Dazu gibt es Parallelen im hellenistischen Frühjudentum[16]. Die Nächstenliebe muss unter dem Vorzeichen der Gottesliebe verstanden werden, so wie umgekehrt die Gottesliebe nicht ohne die Nächstenliebe gedacht werden kann. Jesus gibt nach Mk 12,28–34 weder für die Rangfolge noch für die Verbindung eine Begründung. Die Zustimmung des Schriftgelehrten, von der Markus erzählt, unterstreicht aber die Plausibilität, die das Doppelgebot für den Evangelisten im jüdisch-christlichen Dialog seiner Zeit gewinnen kann. Die Einheit kann aus dem Kontext, den alttestamentlichen Vorgaben, dem religionsgeschichtlichen Umfeld und dem theologischen Grundsinn der Gottes- wie der Nächstenliebe erschlossen werden.

In seiner Repetition gibt der Schriftgelehrte durch eine kleine Variation einen wichtigen Hinweis, den seinerseits Jesus nicht als Fehler ansieht, sondern als sinnvolle Ergänzung wertet. Der Schriftgelehrte rekurriert auf die Opferhandlungen, die man in Israel vielfach zuerst nennen würde, wenn nach den wesentlichen religiösen Pflichten gefragt wird, und erklärt, Gottes- und Nächstenliebe seien „sehr viel mehr", heißt: qualitativ besser. Dadurch wird das Doppelgebot auf die Kult- und Opferkritik der Propheten bezogen, die zwar nicht auf eine Abschaffung der Riten, aber auf ihre Purifizierung und Transformation zielen. Vor dem Hintergrund der Tempelaktion Jesu und seines Plädoyers für den bergeversetzenden Glauben macht diese Zuspitzung einen besonders guten Sinn.

Im Alten Testament sind die beiden Gebote der Gottes- und der Nächstenliebe nicht direkt verbunden. Aber ihr Verhältnis lässt sich prinzipiell ähnlich wie das der beiden Tafeln des Dekaloges bestimmen: Die Verehrung Gottes ist pure Heuchelei, wenn sie nicht durch Moralität gedeckt wird, weil Gott selbst in seinen Geboten zur Unterstützung des Nächsten anhält; umgekehrt kann der Nächste nur

---

15 Vgl. G. Theißen, Das Doppelgebot der Liebe. Jüdische Ethik bei Jesus, in: G. Theißen, Jesus als historische Gestalt. Beiträge zur Jesusforschung, hg. von A. Merz (FRLANT 202), Göttingen 2003, 57–72.
16 Ps-Phokylides nennt zuerst die Ehre Gottes, dann das Gebot, die Eltern zu ehren, gemäß der Akolouthie des Dekalogs. Den Primat der Gottesliebe, Gottesfurcht und Gottesverehrung markieren auch EpAr 132; Josephus, Contra Apionem, 2,190; Philo, De decalogo 65.

dann als er selbst geliebt werden, wenn er als Kind Gottes bejaht wird; das aber leuchtet nur in der Liebe zu Gott ein (vgl. Dtn 10,12–19). Dort, wo es im Frühjudentum Parallelen zum Doppelgebot gibt[17], wird diese Struktur konkretisiert: Zur Gottesliebe gehört – nicht formaler, sondern von Herzen kommender – Gebotsgehorsam, also auch Zustimmung zu der Liebe, mit der Gott den Nächsten liebt; Nächstenliebe folgt aus der Gottesliebe; denn nur durch die Bejahung des Gebotes kann die horizontale Ebene der Ethik mit der vertikalen der Liebe Gottes verknüpft werden, die der Nächstenliebe Format und Gewicht verleiht. Die jesuanische Tradition ist in dieser Perspektive zu verstehen. Sie bricht nicht aus einer breiten (wenngleich nicht unumstrittenen) Tradition aus. Allerdings gibt es Besonderheiten: Die Akzentuierung ist auffällig stark; der Stellenwert auffällig groß, die sprachliche Fassung auffällig präzis, der Rekurs auf die Tora auffällig programmatisch. Mehr noch: Durch die Person und die Verkündigung Jesu werden die Dimensionen der Gottes- wie der Nächstenliebe soteriologisch fundiert und eschatologisch geweitet. Das Doppelgebot gehört in den Kontext der Reich-Gottes-Verkündigung (vgl. Mk 12,34): nicht als Bedingung, sondern als Konsequenz jener Heilszusage, die in Gott nicht nur den Schöpfer, sondern auch den Erlöser, und zwar als Vater Jesu erkennt, und im Nächsten nicht nur das Geschöpf, sondern auch den Bruder und die Schwester Jesu, die zur eschatologischen Rettung bestimmt sind und sie gegenwärtig bereits im Glauben erfahren können.

Beide Gebote werden in Mk 12,28–34 von allen anderen noch einmal abgesetzt und dadurch zusammengeschlossen: „Größer als diese ist kein Gebot" (Mk 12,31). Damit stellt sich die hermeneutische Aufgabe, mit Jesus, wie er von Markus in seinem Evangelium dargestellt wird, die hermeneutische Schlüsselbedeutung des Doppelgebotes zu entdecken. Das verlangt eine Verbindung mit der erzählten Gesetzesauslegung Jesu und deren Ortsbestimmung in der ethischen Konkretisierung der Evangeliumsverkündigung.

2.2 Der Hintergrund der Gesetzestheologie

Jesus setzt sich nach dem Markusevangelium mehrfach und eingehend mit dem Gesetz auseinander[18]. Seine grundlegende Geltung steht nie zur Debatte; durch-

---

17 Wichtig sind die Testamente der Zwölf Patriarchen (Iss 5,1f; Dan 5,1ff sowie Iss 7,6 f; Benj 3,1–5 und Benj 3,3.4; vgl. Jos 11,1 [Gottesfurcht und Nächstenliebe]). Weitere Belege: Jub 36,7 (Gottesfurcht und Bruderliebe); ferner Ab 6 sowie SifreDtn 32,29 § 323 (138b) (Furcht des Himmels – Werke der Barmherzigkeit); Midr. Leolam 7 (Liebe zum Frieden – Liebe des Heiligen); Schab 88a (Liebe zu Gott – Überwindung der Vergeltung).
18 Vgl. C. Focant, Le rapport à la loi dans l'évangile de Marc, in: RThL 27 (1996), 281–308.

weg geht es um seine Auslegung und seinen theologischen Stellenwert. Markus betont die Konflikte Jesu mit Pharisäern und Schriftgelehrten, weil er das Interesse hat, das Spezifikum der Gesetzestheologie Jesu durch die Konfrontation mit alternativen Positionen zu profilieren. Von grundlegender Bedeutung sind die Zehn Gebote – wie prinzipiell für das Judentum auch. Freilich begegnen sie in spezifischer Akzentuierung, die auf das Evangelium der Gottesherrschaft abgestimmt ist, mit dem Doppelgebot konkludiert und die Nächstenliebe konkretisiert.

Im Hintergrund der galiläischen Streitgespräche (Mk 2,1–3,6)[19] stehen – wenigstens – beim Thema des Sabbats (Mk 2,23–28; 3,1–6)[20] explizite Fragen der Gesetzesgeltung, während es bei der Heilung des Gelähmten prinzipiell um die Vollmachtsfrage, beim Zöllnermahl grundsätzlich um die Einstellung zu Sündern und beim Fasten praktisch um eine Frömmigkeitsübung geht. Im Streit um das Ährenraufen[21] zitiert Jesus nach Markus die Schrift (Mk 2,25 f. – 1Sam 21,2–7); im Streit um die Heilung eines Mannes mit verdorrter Hand[22] wird erzählt, dass Jesus genau beobachtet wird, damit man eine Anklage begründen kann (Mk 3,3). Beides unterstreicht die Brisanz des Konflikts: Die Geltung eines zentralen Gebotes steht auf dem Prüfstand. Beide Episoden lassen auch die Art und Weise erkennen, wie Jesus nach Markus zum Gesetz steht. „Der Sabbat ist um des Menschen willen, nicht der Mensch für den Sabbat" (Mk 2,27), ist ein Plädoyer, das den Sabbat nicht abschaffen, sondern reformieren, heißt: auf den ursprünglichen Sinn zurückführen will, und zwar auf jene Version des Dekaloges abgestimmt, die den sozialen Zweck unterstreicht (Dtn 5,12–15)[23]. Die rhetorische Frage Jesu in der Synagoge: „Ist es erlaubt, am Sabbat Gutes zu tun oder Böses zu tun? Leben zu retten oder zu

---

[19] Vgl. C. Focant, Les implications du nouveau dans le permis (Mc 2,1–3,6), in: Ouvrir les Écritures. FS Paul Beauchamp, ed. by P. Bovati (LeDiv 162), Paris 1995, 201–223.
[20] Vgl. A.J. Haas, „Geschenk aus Gottes Schatzkammer" (bSchab 10b). Jesus und der Sabbat im Spiegel der neutestamentlichen Schriften (NTA 43), Münster 2003, 136–258 (die eher die Autorität Jesu als die Transformation des Sabbats betont).
[21] Vgl. J.A. Filho, Colhendo espigas no sábado. Um estudo de Marcos 2,23–28, in: EstB 84 (2004), 58–69.
[22] Vgl. A. Lindemann, Jesus und der Sabbat. Zum literarischen Charakter der Erzählung Mk 3,1–6, in: Text und Geschichte. FS Dieter Lührmann, hg. von S. Maser/E. Schlarb (MThSt 50), Marburg 1999, 122–135 (der meint, die Abweichung von der pharisäischen Praxis solle gerechtfertigt werden); A. Maggi, ‚Il sabato è per l'uomo e non l'uomo per il sabato' (Mc 2,27), in: A partire dai cocci rotti. Problema divorziati; riflessioni, ricerca, prospettive, eds. N. Trentacoste/G. Cereti, Assisi 2001, 42–56; vgl. zur Einzelexegese auch S.J. Stasiak, Controversia in Galilea e guarigione dell'uomo con la mano inaridita. Analisi sincronica di Mc 3,1–6, in: Antonianum 77 (2002), 617–647.
[23] Vgl. P.L. Vasconcellos, Guardar o sábado: como? Anotações sobre Mc 2,27, in: EstB 51 (1996), 50–57.

töten?" (Mk 3,4) spitzt die Frage seiner Kritiker zu, weil die Heilung[24] in den größeren Zusammenhang der Reich-Gottes-Verkündigung gestellt wird. Beide Pointen sind kongruent. Sie passen genau mit dem Doppelgebot zusammen. Sie gehen von der Voraussetzung praktizierter Gottesliebe aus und akzentuieren dann die Notwendigkeit einer möglichst intensiven Verbindung mit praktizierter Nächstenliebe, die zum Kriterium der Gesetzesauslegung am Sabbat wird. Am Beispiel des Sabbats zeigt sich ebenso wie im Umgang Jesu mit Sündern, dass seine Grundorientierung am Doppelgebot dazu führt, die Tora nicht auf die sozialgeschichtliche Funktion zu reduzieren, eine Grenze zwischen dem Volk Gottes und den Heiden und innerhalb Israels zwischen den Gerechten und den Sündern, gegebenfalls auch zwischen Gesunden und Kranken zu ziehen; in der Perspektive Jesu aber wird die Tora so präsentiert, dass sie das Volk für die Völker öffnet, so dass alle im Gotteslob zusammenkommen (Mk 11,15–19 – Jes 56,7), die Gerechten für die Sünder, so dass Vergebung real wird, und die Gesunden für die Kranken, so dass Heilung geschieht.

Von grundsätzlicher Bedeutung ist das Streitgespräch über Reinheit und Unreinheit in Mk 7,1–23[25]. Die Reinheitsgebote[26] sind für die jüdische Identität in einer paganen Umgebung von größter Wichtigkeit[27]; sie sind aber auch innerhalb Israels, propagiert von den Pharisäern, Ausdruck der religiösen Grundüberzeugung, dass der Übergang aus der Sphäre der Produktion in die der Konsumtion rituell gestaltet werden muss, um Gott die Ehre zu geben. Jesus hingegen bezieht nach Markus eine grundsätzlich andere Position[28]: Vom rituellen Händewaschen kommt er auf die Reinheitsvorschriften. Jesus setzt sich für eine radikale Moralisierung oder Personalisierung von Reinheit und Unreinheit ein[29]. Dem Volk sagt Jesus: „Nichts, was von außen in den Menschen hineinkommt, kann ihn unrein machen, sondern was aus dem Menschen herauskommt, kann ihn unrein ma-

---

[24] Eine Allegorese der Intertextualität mit dem Exodus riskiert K. Queller, ‚Stretch out your hand!' Echo and metalepsis in Mark's sabbath healing controversy, in: JBL 129 (2010), 737–758.
[25] Vgl. dazu auch den Beitrag von L. Scornaienchi im vorliegenden Band.
[26] Vgl. B.J. Schwartz (ed.), Perspectives on purity and purification in the Bible (Library of Hebrew Bible, Old Testament studies 474), New York/London 2008.
[27] Vgl. E. Ottenheim, Impurity between Intention and Deed. Purity Disputes in First Century Judaism and in the New Testament, in: Purity and Holiness. The Heritage of Leviticus, eds. M.J.H. M. Poorthuis/J. Schwarz (JCPS 2), Leiden u. a. 2000, 129–147.
[28] Vgl. I.M. Blecker, Rituelle Reinheit vor und nach der Zerstörung des Zweiten Tempels. Essenische, pharisäische und jesuanische Reinheitsvorstellungen im Vergleich, in: Fremde Zeichen. Neutestamentliche Texte in der Konfrontation der Kulturen. FS Karl Löning, hg. von A. Leinhäupl-Wilke/S. Lücking (Theologie 15), Münster 1998, 25–40.
[29] Eine Relativierung sieht hingegen J.D.G. Dunn, Jesus and purity. An ongoing debate, in: NTS 48 (2002), 449–467.

chen" (Mk 7,15; vgl. 7,18.20.23). Das scheint an die archaische Vorstellung anzuknüpfen, dass die körperlichen Ausscheidungen unrein sind, wird aber in der anschließenden Jüngerbelehrung gerade gegenteilig (Mk 7,19) auf Laster gedeutet, die im Herzen nisten (Mk 7,21f.). Die revolutionäre Bedeutung notiert Markus lakonisch: „... womit er alle Speisen für rein erklärte" (Mk 7,19). Damit weist er die Leserschaft auf die wichtigste praktische Konsequenz hin. Sie entspricht im Ergebnis der paulinischen Position (Röm 14,14), ist aber nicht soteriologisch begründet wie in Gal 2,11–16 oder schöpfungstheologisch wie in 1Kor 10,26 mit Ps 24,1, sondern anthropologisch, weil es nicht auf den Bauch, sondern nur auf das Herz ankomme. Diese Betonung des Herzens aber konvergiert bei Markus mit dem Doppelgebot: Die Nächstenliebe ist das Kriterium der Gottesliebe. Der Lasterkatalog zeigt, was der Nächstenliebe widerspricht. Das Herz, mit dem Gott geliebt werden soll, ist das, an dem sich moraltheologisch Reinheit oder Unreinheit entscheiden.

Die Verbindung ist aber noch enger. Markus hat, bevor er Jesus zur Reinheitsfrage das Wort gibt, durch die Pharisäer und Schriftgelehrten ein theologisches Schlüsselwort der Gesetzeshermeneutik einführen lassen: die „Überlieferung der Alten" (Mk 7,5). Wie sie die Tora verstehen, hat der Evangelist durch die Beschreibung der rituellen Reinigungspraktiken in Mk 7,3f. veranschaulicht[30]. Die kritische Frage an Jesus bezüglich der Laxheit seiner Jünger geht von der Einheit zwischen dem Gesetz Gottes und der Überlieferung der Alten aus. Jesus hingegen deckt nach Markus einen Widerspruch zwischen „Gottes Gebot" und der „Überlieferung von Menschen" auf (Mk 7,8). Die Dimensionen dieses Widerspruchs zeigt er mit Rekurs auf Jes 29,13 (Mk 7,6f.); sie sind ungeheuerlich, weil sie ein reines Lippenbekenntnis seien, ohne das Herz des Menschen zu berühren. Etwas später variiert er: „Ihr hebt Gottes Wort durch eure Überlieferung auf" (Mk 7,13; vgl. 7,9). Der Grund ist die Herzlosigkeit der Überlieferung.

Als Beispiel dient die Korban-Praxis (Mk 7,9–13). Sie meint eine Weihe von materiellen Gütern für den Tempel. In der Tora gibt es keine direkte Bestimmung, sondern nur die allgemeine Maßgabe, dass Gelübde einzuhalten sind (Num 30,3; Dtn 23,24); wohl aber hat es eine frühjüdische Tradition gegeben, die später kodifiziert worden ist (Ned 1,1). Jesus sagt nicht, die Korban-Praxis an sich sei unsittlich. Er kritisiert aber, dass im Interesse des Tempels toleriert, vielleicht sogar propagiert werde, diese Weihe auch dann vorzunehmen, wenn mit den Gütern

---

30 Vgl. M. Meiser, Reinheitsfragen und Begräbnissitten. Der Evangelist Markus als Zeuge der jüdischen Alltagskultur, in: Neues Testament und hellenistisch-jüdische Alltagskultur. Wechselseitige Wahrnehmungen. III. Internationales Symposium zum Corpus Judaeo-Hellenisticum Novi Testamenti, hg. von R. Deines/J. Herzer/K.-W. Niebuhr (WUNT 274), Tübingen 2011, 443–446.

eigentlich die Eltern unterstützt werden müssten. Diese Fürsorge aber wird durch das Vierte Gebot vorgeschrieben (Ex 20,12; Dtn 5,16). Im Zweifel steht sie vor der Korban-Praxis, nicht umgekehrt, ohne dass vorausgesetzt zu werden brauchte, die Weihe an den Tempel sei nur versteckter Eigennutz. Die Vorrangstellung des Dekaloges vor anderen Gesetzesvorschriften ist im Judentum der Zeit weit verbreitet; sie gewinnt bei Jesus ihre innere Logik durch das Doppelgebot: Er will in jedem Fall verhindern, dass Gottesliebe auf Kosten der Nächstenliebe praktiziert wird, und nimmt deshalb mit den Eltern die Nächsten der Nächsten als Beispiel. Jesus versteht das Vierte Gebote wie seine Zeitgenossen in erster Linie als soziale Verpflichtung wirtschaftlich stärkerer Kinder ihren bedürftiger werdenden Eltern gegenüber. Sein Votum zielt nicht unbedingt auf die Abschaffung der Korban-Praxis, aber auf ihre Regelung unter dem Vorzeichen des Vierten Gebotes. Das ist eine für Jesus typische, im Judentum tief verwurzelte[31] Position.

Dann aber zeigt sich, dass die Korban-Thematik kein Exkurs, sondern ein Beitrag zur Sache ist. Er klärt die Paradigmatik der Stellungnahme Jesu zu den Reinheitsvorgaben und konkretisiert seine Gesetzeshermeneutik. Mit seiner Stellungnahme zu Reinheit und Unreinheit löst Jesus nach Markus die Tora-Bestimmungen nicht auf, sondern gibt ihnen ihren ureigenen Sinn, so wie er sich aus der nahekommenden Gottesherrschaft ergibt. Das Problem, das Jesus dem Markusevangelium zufolge bei den Pharisäern und Schriftgelehrten aufdeckt, ist nicht ihr Engagement für die Reinheit, sondern ihre Fixierung auf die traditionellen Reinigungsriten, die vom entscheidenden ablenken: von dem, was das Herz spricht.

In der Ehescheidungsfrage (Mk 10,2–12)[32] kritisiert Jesus seine pharisäischen Gesprächspartner, die auf seine Frage hin, was Mose zur Sache gesagt habe (Mk 10,3), nur die Regel nennen (Mk 10.4), der Mann solle einen Scheidungsbrief ausstellen (Dtn 24,1–4). Diese Regel aber deutet Jesus als Konzession an die „Herzenshärte" (oder „Herzensverkalkung") der Israeliten (Mk 10,5). Er begründet diese Deutung und damit seine Kritik an den Pharisäern wiederum mit der Tora (Mk 10,7f.), deren traditioneller Autor Mose ist, nämlich mit dem ursprünglichen Schöpfungsakt (Gen 1,26f.) und Schöpfwerwillen Gottes (Gen 2,24), dass Mann und Frau eins sind[33]. Daraus leitet er das Verbot der Ehescheidung ab (Mk 10,9), das er

---

31 Vgl. R. Kieffer, Traditions juives selon Mc 7,1–23, in: Texts and contexts. Biblical texts in their textual and situational context. FS Lars Hartmann, ed. by T. Fornberg, Oslo 1995, 675–688.
32 Vgl. H. Frankemölle, Ehescheidung und Wiederverheiratung im Neuen Testament, in: Geschieden – Wiederverheiratet – Abgewiesen? Antworten der Theologie (QD 157), hg. von Th. Schneider, Freiburg/Basel/Wien 1995, 28–50; J. Kremer, Jesu Wort zur Ehescheidung, ebd. 51–67.
33 Vgl. M. Tiwald, ΑΠΟ ΔΕ ΑΡΧΗΣ ΚΤΙΣΕΩΣ ... (Mk 10,36): Die Entsprechung von Protologie und Eschatologie als Schlüssel für das Tora-Verständnis Jesu, in: Erinnerung an Jesus. Kontinuität

seinen Jüngern eigens erläutert (Mk 10,10 ff.). Grund und Motiv für die Regelung sind strittig. Vor allem werden Frauen profitiert haben. Aber war das der Zweck?[34] Geht es darum, die Heiligkeit Gottes durchzusetzen? Oder ist vielleicht doch eine Liebe zwischen den Eheleuten zu erschließen. Unterstrichen wird zweierlei: dass konsequente Gebotserfüllung das ewige Leben (nicht verdient, sondern) gewinnt und dass die Zehn Gebote die wichtigsten Gesetze sind. Beides bleibt im Rahmen ambitionierter jüdischer Gesetzestheologie. Er wird durch die Fortführung des Gespräches nicht gesprengt, aber ausgefüllt. Jesus weist den Weg der Vollkommenheit in seiner Nachfolge (Mk 10,21); zu ihr gehört es, dass der Reiche seinen Besitz verkauft und den Armen spendet. Beides ist kein Gebot, das erfüllen muss, wer ins Reich Gottes eingehen willen, aber eine Konsequenz der Ambition, die aus der Frage und der Zwischenantwort des Mannes (Mk 10,20) spricht. Die sozialethische Akzentuierung der Nachfolge zeigt paradigmatisch, wie Jesus das Doppelgebot konkretisiert[35].

Im Kontext des gesamten Evangeliums betrachtet, zeigt sich, dass das Doppelgebot nicht allein steht, sondern die Programmatik der jesuanischen Gesetzestheologie, wie Markus sie verstanden und dargestellt hat, auf den Punkt bringt. Entscheidend ist zweierlei: die positive Grundbestimmung des Gesetzes und die klare Hierarchisierung durch das Doppelgebot, auch wenn es nicht zitiert oder reflektiert wird. Sowohl das Verständnis zentraler Themen wie der Reinheit und der Ehe als auch die Praxis des Sabbats sind von diesem Ansatz geprägt. Sie dienen durchweg der Verbindung von Gottes- und Nächstenliebe.

2.3 Das Verständnis der Nächstenliebe

Bei Markus fehlt eine Diskussion der Frage: „Wer ist denn mein Nächster", wie Lukas sie dokumentiert (Lk 10,29), um die Antwort Jesu mit dem Samaritergleichnis zu positionieren (Lk 10,30 – 35). Markus kennt auch nicht die programmatische Ausweitung und Konkretisierung der Nächstenliebe als Feindesliebe, wie sie Matthäus aus der Redenquelle (vgl. Lk 6,27– 36) in der Bergpredigt vornimmt (Mt 5,43 – 48). Der Radius und der Gehalt der Nächstenliebe lassen sich aber indirekt aus dem Gang des Evangeliums erschließen.

---

und Diskontinuität in der neutestamentlichen Überlieferung. FS Rudolf Hoppe, hg. von U. Busse (BBB 166), Göttingen 2011, 367– 380.
34 So P. Hoffmann, Das Recht der Frau oder „Wider die legalisierte Willkür des Mannes" (1975), in: ders., Studien zur Frühgeschichte der Jesus-Bewegung (SBAB 17), Stuttgart 1994, 95 – 117.
35 Vgl. D. Sänger, Recht und Gerechtigkeit in der Verkündigung Jesu. Erwägungen zu Mk 10,17– 22 und 12,28 – 34, in: BZ 36 (1992), 179 – 184.

Im Heiligkeitsgesetz[36] ist der Nächste das Mitglied des Gottesvolkes (Lev 19,17 f.)[37]. Allerdings wird das Liebesgebot auf die „Fremden" ausgeweitet (Lev 19,34). Beides erklärt sich aus der Theologie des Volkes Gottes. Die Konzentration auf die Nächsten aus Israel vollzieht die Erwählung und die Heiligung durch Gott nach, die Öffnung für die „Fremden" die Schutzfunktion, die von den Vollmitgliedern aufgrund der heilsgeschichtlichen Sendung des Gottesvolkes für die Gastmitglieder ausgeübt werden soll, weil Israel in Ägypten selbst fremd gewesen ist. Die Nächstenliebe bewährt sich nach Lev 19,18, dem Kontext zufolge, vor allem in der Überwindung von Streit und Schuld. Das ist der Theologie der Einheit Israels geschuldet. Überwindung des eigenen Grolls, Verzicht auf Rache und konstruktive Kritik sind paradigmatische Konkretionen. Die Fortschreibungen und Aktualisierungen in der frühjüdischen Ethik, sei es in Palästina, sei es in der Diaspora, forcieren den Zusammenhalt der Judenschaft oder einer Bewegung mit besonders starken Ambitionen und verleihen ihm moralische Qualität.

Das Verständnis der Nächstenliebe bei Markus (und in der gesamten synoptischen Tradition) bewegt sich auf dieser Linie, gewinnt aber durch die Reich-Gottes-Botschaft an Kraft und Weite. Der Bezug auf das Gottesvolk wird nicht aufgegeben, aber die Grenzen des Gottesvolkes werden geweitet; die Konkretion durch die Überwindung von Schuld bleibt, wird aber auf die Basis der Heilssendung Jesu wie seiner Jünger gestellt und gewinnt dadurch qualitativ neue Möglichkeiten.

Wesentlich ist die Praxis Jesu selbst. Durch seine Heilungen und Exorzismen öffnet er den Kreis derjenigen, die zum Gottesvolk der Nächstenliebe gehören[38]. Insbesondere bei der Heilung von Aussatz (Mk 1,40 – 45) und Blutung (Mk 5,25 – 34)[39] wird anschaulich, dass Krankheiten aufgrund sakralrechtlicher Bestimmungen von der aktiven Teilnahme am Leben des Gottesvolkes, insbesondere dem Kult, ausschließen. Diese Bestimmungen werden mit keiner Silbe unter moralischen Generalverdacht gestellt; Jesus hat nur die Vollmacht, die Krankheit zu heilen und dadurch die Integration zu bewirken. Die Angst, die Unreinheit würde auf ihn und durch ihn übertragen, ist unbegründet, weil er im Gegenteil mit seiner

---

36 Vgl. K. Grünwaldt, Das Heiligkeitsgesetz Leviticus 17– 26. Ursprüngliche Gestalt, Tradition und Theologie (BZAW 271), Berlin 1999.
37 Vgl. J.S. Kaminsky, Loving one's (Israelite) neighbor. Election and commandment in Leviticus 19, in: Interpretation 62 (2008), 123 – 132.
38 Vgl. zum folgenden Th. Söding, Jesus und die Kirche. Was sagt das Neue Testament?, Freiburg/Basel/Wien 2007.
39 Vgl. zur Gender-Perspektive M.R. D'Angelo, Gender and Power in the Gospel of Mark: The Daughter of Jairus and the Woman with the Flow of Blood, in: Miracles in Jewish and Christian Antiquity. Imagining Truth, ed. by J. Cavadini, Notre Dame 1999, 83 – 109.

Reinheit und Heiligkeit ansteckt. Nicht anders bei den Exorzismen (Mk 1,20 – 28; 9,14 – 29[40]): Es gibt keinen gesetzlichen Ausschluss der Besessenen aus Israel, aber eine faktische Befreiung durch Jesus, die zur aktiven Partizipation befähigt. Auf derselben Ebene liegen die Sündenvergebung (Mk 2,1–12), die Berufung eines notorischen Sünders in die Nachfolge und das Gastmahl mit Sündern (Mk 2,13 – 17). Durch die Kritik, die Jesus entgegengehalten wird, werden zwei Aspekte beleuchtet: die Vollmacht, die nur als Wahrnehmung der Vollmacht Gottes selbst gedeutet werden kann, und die Grenze zwischen Sündern und Gerechten, die von Jesus, so Markus, nicht eingerissen wird, damit die Sünde, sondern damit die Gerechtigkeit sich ausbreitet. Jesus ist nach Mk 2,17 der „Arzt", der die Kranken heilt, an Leib und Seele. Dieser Dienst ist pure Nächstenliebe. Sie richtet sich auf diejenigen, die im Verdacht stehen könnten, nicht mehr zu den „Nächsten" zu gehören. Er hat die Fähigkeit, ihnen wirksam zu helfen; er macht sie zu „Nächsten" oder zeigt, dass sie nie etwas anderes gewesen sind, auch wenn ihnen anscheinend auf Erden nicht zu helfen war. Die Tatsache, dass die Heilungen – nicht stereotyp, aber signifikant – auf den Glauben zurückgeführt werden[41], zeigt, dass die Geheilten nicht nur Objekte des Heilshandelns Gottes *in persona Christi* sind, sondern Subjekte, die in Freiheit zu Jesus stehen und dadurch ihre Zugehörigkeit zum Gottesvolk eschatologisch neu realisieren.

Die Jünger werden von Jesus beauftragt, in derselben Weise wie er dasselbe Evangelium wie er zu verkünden (Mk 3,14 f.; 6,7.13). Sie brauchen keine Angst vor Dämonen und Krankheiten zu haben, weil sie der Vollmacht Jesu teilhaftig geworden sind; sie müssen aber die ihnen gegebenen Möglichkeiten nutzen, um die vollmächtige Nächstenliebe wirklich real werden zu lassen. Das geschieht, der Aussendungsrede (Mk 6,6b–13) gemäß, dadurch, dass sie tatsächlich losziehen, um wie Jesus nicht nur die Botschaft und den Glauben zu verbreiten, sondern dadurch auch die Vitalität Israels zu steigern. Die Jünger stehen mit ihrer Gewaltlosigkeit und Armut in der Nachfolge Jesu. Indem die Jünger – wie Jesus[42] – sich von der Gastfreundschaft derer abhängig machen, denen sie das Evangelium

---

40 Vgl. M. Grilli, Die heilende Schwachheit Gottes. Lektüre von Mk 9,14 – 29 in ihrem Kontext, in: Jesus als Bote des Heils. Heilserfahrung und Heilsverkündigung in frühchristlicher Zeit. FS Detlev Dormeyer, hg. von L. Hauser/F.R. Prostmeier/Ch.G. Zöller, Stuttgart 2008, 56 – 71; J. Marcus, ‚I believe – help my unbelief!' Human Faith and Divine Faithfulness in Mark 9.14 – 29, in: Paul, Grace and Freedom. FS John K. Riches, eds. P. Middleton/A. Paddison/K. Wenell, London/ New York 2009, 39 – 49.
41 Vgl. Th. Söding, Heilsamer Glaube. Die synoptische Tradition, in: Gottvertrauen. Die ökumenische Diskussion um die Fiducia, hg. von I.U. Dalferth/S. Peng-Keller (QD 250), Freiburg/ Basel/Wien 2012, 48 – 79.
42 Vgl. zur Parallele G. Hotze, Jesus als Gast. Studien zu einem christologischen Leitmotiv im Lukasevangelium (FzB 111), Würzburg 2007.

bringen, geben sie ihnen Gelegenheit, Nächstenliebe zu erweisen, und unterlaufen dadurch, ganz im Sinne des Dienens, das Jesus ihnen ans Herz legt (Mk 10,42ff.), das Gegenüber von Geben und Nehmen, das in einer klassischen Konstellation ethisch unvermeidbar ist. Wiewohl die Aussendungsrede als Teil des Evangeliums in erster Linie die Erinnerung an Jesus schärft, wohnt ihr eine Vergegenwärtigung des nachösterlichen Missionsauftrages inne, der bei Markus allerdings nur indirekt zum Ausdruck kommt.

Jesus nutzt seinen Heilungsdienst nach Markus aber auch, um bereits vorösterlich gezielt über die Grenzen des klassischen Israel hinauszugehen. Er wirkt als Exorzist (Mk 5,1–20) und Therapeut (Mk 7,31–37) auch in der Dekapolis; er heilt die Tochter einer Syrophönizierin (Mk 7,24–30). Diese Samariterdienste folgen der Dynamik der nahekommenden Gottesherrschaft; sie weiten die Mitgliedschaft im Gottesvolk aus; sie vergrößern den Radius der praktizierten Nächstenliebe.

Markus erzählt aber nicht nur die Erfolgsgeschichten der Evangeliumsverkündigung; er lässt auch den Widerspruch, den Jesus findet, plastisch werden: innerhalb Israels bei den Pharisäern und Schriftgelehrten, vor allem jedoch den Hohenpriestern, außerhalb am Ende bei den Römern. Bei Markus fehlt eine Bitte Jesu um Vergebung für die Henker wie bei Lukas (Lk 23,34) ebenso wie die explizite Forderung der Feindesliebe. Aber in seiner radikalen Bereitschaft zum Dienen, die sich auch auf diejenigen erstreckt, die ihn kleinmachen (Mk 10,42–45), ist das Ethos der Feindesliebe angelegt.

Die Jünger sollen sich nach Markus von Jesus belehren lassen, in der Nachfolge den Glauben so zu leben, dass die Einheit von Gottes- und Nächstenliebe verwirklicht wird. Das Wort vom bergeversetzenden Glauben ist mit einer Mahnung zur wechselseitigen Vergebung verbunden (Mk 11,23–25), die der Bergpredigt (Mt 5,21–26) mit dem Vaterunser (Mt 6,9–13) an die Seite zu stellen ist[43]. Die Schule des Gebetes, die Jesus nach der Tempelaktion öffnet, um die Verheißung, das Heiligtum werde ein „Haus des Gebetes für alle Völker" sein (Jes 56,7), Wirklichkeit werden zu lassen, ist eine genaue Entsprechung zum Doppelgebot.

Es gewinnt – seiner Struktur nach – in der Unterweisung Jesu aber auch eine kritische Note. Die Jünger sind doppelt gefährdet: aus Sorge um Jesus und die Heiligkeit Gottes die Grenzen zu eng zu ziehen und aus dem Eifer des Glaubens heraus die Sache Gottes mit den eigenen Interessen zu identifizieren. Sie müssen sich deshalb mehrfach von Jesus belehren lassen, weiter zu denken und offener zu werden, nicht aus Gleichgültigkeit, sondern aus Glaubensüberzeugung, aber auch

---

43 Vgl. F. Vouga, ‚Habt Glauben an Gott!' Der Theozentrismus der Verkündigung des Evangeliums und des christlichen Glaubens im Markusevangelium, in: FS Lars Hartmann (s. Anm. 31), 93–109.

selbstkritischer und demütiger zu werden, nicht aus Glaubenszweifel, sondern aus dem Engagement für das Evangelium.

Die Kritik an der inneren Einstellung der Jünger wird bei Markus regelmäßig im Anschluss an die Leidens- und Auferstehungsprophetien Jesu (Mk 8,31; 9,31; 10,32 ff.)[44] laut. Der Evangelist hat den Kontrast gesucht, um die Hauptschwierigkeit des Christusglaubens auch in ihren ethischen Dimensionen aufzuzeigen. Während Jesus nach Markus auf seinem Weg Gottes- und Nächstenliebe vereint, weil er um Gottes Willen „für viele" (Mk 10,45; 14,24) stirbt, und durch seinen Dienst die ethischen Dimensionen der Heilsvermittlung begründet, brechen seine Jünger regelmäßig aus der Kreuzesnachfolge (Mk 8,34–38) aus, schon bevor sie zum Ernstfall wird. Ihr moralisches Hauptproblem ist ekklesiologisch sensibel: Sie suchen nach Größe vor anderen (Mk 9,34) und nach den besten Plätzen im Reich Gottes (Mk 10,37). Damit verraten sie das Prinzip des Glaubens in seiner ethischen Essenz: „Wer Erster sein will, sei der Letzte von allen und aller Diener" (Mk 9,35; vgl. 10,43). Diese Maxime widerspricht nicht der Selbstliebe als Maß der Nächstenliebe, weil Hingabe nach Markus zur Selbstverwirklichung gehört; aber sie begründet eine Nachahmung Jesu in der Einheit von Gottes- und Nächstenliebe, die den Heilsdienst Jesu nicht ersetzt oder ergänzt, sondern umsetzt und erfahrbar macht.

Die Kritik an der Glaubensenge der Jünger ist mit der Kritik ihres Hochmutes verbunden. Markus nennt zwei Beispiele: den fremden Exorzisten, dem die Jünger am liebsten in den Arm fallen würden, weil er nicht zur Nachfolgegemeinschaft gehört (Mk 9,38–41)[45], und Kinder, deren Mütter die Jünger abhalten wollen, zu Jesus zu kommen (Mk 10,13–16; vgl. Mk 9,36 f.)[46]. Im ersten Fall sagt er: „Wer nicht gegen uns ist, ist für uns" (Mk 9,40)[47], und öffnet die Augen seiner Jünger für all diejenigen, die ihnen einen noch so kleinen Dienst der Nächstenliebe erweisen (Mk 9,41). Im zweiten Fall segnet er die Kinder, die er zuvor in die Mitte der Jünger

---

44 Vgl. A. Weihs, Die Deutung des Todes Jesu im Markusevangelium. Eine exegetische Studie zu den Leidens- und Auferstehungsansagen (FzB 99), Würzburg 2003.
45 Vgl. J. Schlosser, L' exorciste étranger (Mc 9,38–39), in: RevSR 56 (1982), 229–239; E.A. Russell, A plea for tolerance (Mark 9.38–40), in: IBSt 8 (1986), 154–160; X. Pikaza, Exorcismo, poder y evangelio. Trasfondo histórico y eclesial de Mc 9,38–40, in: EstB 57 (1999), 539–564.
46 Die Sozialkritik akzentuiert M. Ebner, ‚Kinderevangelium' oder markinische Sozialkritik. Mk 10,13–16 im Kontext, in: JBTh 17 (2002), 315–336.
47 Vgl. A. de la Fuente, A favor o en contra de Jesús. El logion de Mc 9,40 y sus paralelos, in: EstB 53 (1995), 449–459; J. Schlosser, Q 11,23 et la christologie, in: Von Jesus zum Christus. Christologische Studien. FS Paul Hoffmann, hg. von R. Hoppe/U. Busse (BZNW 93), Berlin 1998, 217–224; J.S. Gellar, Matthew 12:30; Mark 9:40; Luke 9:50; 11:23 – ‚with and for' or ‚against'?, in: Lutheran Theological Review 14 (2001/2002), 10–26.

gestellt hatte (Mk 9,36f.): „Ihrer ist das Reich Gottes" (Mk 10,15). Sie werden zu Vorbildern für die Jünger (Mk 9,37; 10,16)[48].

2.4 Auswertung

Die hermeneutische Schlüsselstellung des Doppelgebotes zeigt sich im Kontext des gesamten Evangeliums. Wie es einer Erzählung mit historiographischen[49] und biographischen[50] Zügen gemäß ist, wird diese Schlüsselbedeutung nicht theoretisch reflektiert, sondern in einzelnen Episoden und narrativen Konstruktionen paradigmatisch veranschaulicht. Markus nutzt die Form des Evangeliums, um zu zeigen, dass Jesus selbst die Einheit von Gottes- und Nächstenliebe nicht nur fordert, sondern lebt; sie ist der Nerv seiner Heilssendung; sie zeigt sich in seinem Beten ebenso wie in seinen Machttaten, die durchweg Hilfeleistungen sind. Die Nächstenliebe ist deshalb auch nicht nur Forderung, sondern in ihrem wesentlichen Zusammenhang mit der Gottesliebe Erschließung eines Erfahrungs- und Handlungsraumes, in dem sich die Nähe der Gottesherrschaft realisiert (Mk 12,34). Die Begründung und die Reichweite der Nächstenliebe werden durch das Kommen der Gottesherrschaft geliefert. Die Nächstenliebe wird in ihrer Intensität und in ihren Dimensionen der Zuwendung durch Jesu Evangeliumsverkündigung möglich und notwendig. Ihr Radius wird ausgeweitet, aber sie bleibt immer konkret. Sie verwirklicht sich als Dienst und Hingabe, aber gewinnt in der Jesusnachfolge die Freiheit zur Selbstverwirklichung, weil sie in Gottes Nähe geschieht.

Im Kontext des gesamten Evangeliums ergibt sich eine wechselseitige Erschließung. Einerseits zeigen die vielen anderen direkten Mahnungen und Weisungen, Einladungen und Ermutigungen Jesu, wie sich die Nächstenliebe auf eine Fülle von Lebensfeldern konkretisiert: vor allem in der Familie und dem Haus, aber auch in der politischen und religiösen Öffentlichkeit. Anderseits werden durch das Doppelgebot, das Jesus sich bei Markus für den Schluss aufbewahrt, die Einzelgebote auf ihre Mitte und ihren Zusammenhalt zurückgeführt: Nur als Ausdruck der Liebe haben sie theologischen Wert.

Im Kontext des gesamten Evangeliums ergibt sich auch der theologische Zusammenhang, in dem das Liebesgebot und der durch das Liebesgebot erschlossen wird. Entscheidend ist nach Markus der Bezug auf die Tora. Sie wird

---

[48] Vgl. G. van Oyen, Marcus 10:13–16: als was men een kind, in: NedThT 57 (2003), 177–192.
[49] Vgl. E.-M. Becker, Das Markusevangelium im Rahmen antiker Historiographie (WUNT 194), Tübingen 2006.
[50] Vgl. D. Dormeyer, Das Markusevangelium als Idealbiographie von Jesus Christus, dem Nazarener (SBS 143), Stuttgart 2001.

durch das Doppelgebot nicht exkludiert, aber transzendiert und nicht marginalisiert, aber hierarchisiert. Die Tora bleibt gültig, indem sie vom Doppelgebot erschlossen wird; das Doppelgebot ergibt sich gerade im Zusammenhang des Gesetzes mit all seinen Geboten. Das Doppelgebot lässt sich aber der Liebe wegen nicht in feste Regeln fassen; es verweist auf ein Jenseits des Gesetzes, von dem her es sich versteht: den Heilswillen Gottes, den Jesus in eschatologischer Klarheit verkündet und verwirklicht.

Durch das Liebesgebot wird der Zusammenhalt der Jünger gefestigt, aber nicht gegen andere, sondern für sie, die durch die Nachfolgegemeinschaft ihrerseits in Kontakt mit der Gottesherrschaft kommen sollen und können. Das ist in der Sendung Jesu vorgezeichnet.

Signifikant ist die essentielle Verbindung der Nächsten- mit der Gottesliebe. Strukturell im Alten Testament vorgegeben und im Frühjudentum vorbereitet, gewinnt sie durch die Reich-Gottes-Verkündigung Jesu an Dramatik und Perspektive, weil ohne jede Relativierung der Schöpfung und der Heilsgeschichte der „Kairos" göttlicher Nähe (Mk 1,15) gefüllt und die Vollendung des Reiches Gottes nicht nur verheißen, sondern auch antizipiert wird. Weshalb Gottesliebe Nächstenliebe fordert und welche Tiefe die Nächstenliebe durch die Gottesliebe gewinnen kann, lässt sich durch Jesu Evangelium im Glauben entdecken.

3 Das Liebesgebot bei Paulus

Paulus kennt eine ausgeprägte Theologie der Liebe[51]. Er preist die Liebe Gottes und Jesu Christi (Röm 5,1–11; 8,31–38 u. ö.). Er hat das „Hohelied" der Liebe 1Kor 13 geschrieben, das die Liebe Gottes in der Liebe von Menschen feiert[52]. Er redet von der Liebe zu Gott, die hören und sehen lässt, wo anderen Hören und Sehen vergeht (1Kor 2,9 u. ö.)[53]. Er stellt vom 1. Thessalonicherbrief an[54] seine Ethik auf die Agape ab. Er hat aber die Rechtfertigungstheologie des Galater- und des Römerbriefes genutzt, um das Liebesgebot Lev 19,18 zu zitieren, auf das Gesetz zu beziehen, als

---

51 Eine Skizze habe ich angefertigt in: Art. Liebe, in: TBLNT 2 (2000), 1318–1326.1329–1331.
52 Vgl. O. Wischmeyer, Der höchste Weg. Das 13. Kapitel des 1. Korintherbriefes (StNT 13), Gütersloh 1981; P.G. Kirchschläger, Die eschatologische Dimension von Liebe. 1 Kor 13 und der ‚andere Weg', in: BiLi 85 (2012), 61–72.
53 Vgl. Th. Söding, Gottesliebe bei Paulus, in: ders., Das Wort vom Kreuz. Studien zur paulinischen Theologie (WUNT 93), Tübingen 1997, 303–326.
54 Vgl. (von einer anderen Seite aus) M. Konradt, Gericht und Gemeinde. Eine Studie zur Bedeutung und Funktion der Gerichtsaussagen im Rahmen der paulinischen Ekklesiologie und Ethik im 1Thess und 1Kor (BZNW 117), Berlin 2003.

theologische Mitte der Ethik zu markieren und mit der Heilsverkündigung zu verbinden[55]. Hier kann eine historische und theologische Interpretation anknüpfen, um den Stellenwert und Gehalt des Liebesgebotes bei Paulus zu bestimmen.

3.1 Der Ort des Liebesgebotes in der paulinischen Theologie

Die beiden expliziten Zitate von Lev 19,18 bei Paulus (Gal 5,13f.; Röm 13,8ff.) erklären sich im Kontext der Rechtfertigungslehre; denn der Apostel sieht sich genötigt, angesichts seiner Kritik am Heilsvertrauen auf „Werke des Gesetzes" (Gal 2,16; Röm 3,28 u. ö.) und seiner starken Betonung der Gnade Gottes die ethische Substanz des Evangeliums im Verhältnis zur Tora zu bestimmen. Wie der Blick in seine anderen Briefe zeigt, ist es Paulus aber auch von sich aus ein Anliegen, den „Aufbau" der Kirche (1Kor 14) nicht nur durch eine gute Katechese, sondern auch durch eine motivierende Paraklese zu fördern. Das geschieht im Galater- wie im Römerbrief auf prinzipiell analoge, im einzelnen aber unterschiedliche Weise.

Beide Briefe führen die Ethik nicht als sekundäres, sondern primäres Thema in die Argumentation ein, lange bevor die Schlusskapitel, in denen sich die Zitate von Lev 19,18 finden, auf moraltheologische Themen konzentriert werden. Der Galaterbrief arbeitet bei der ersten Begründung der Rechtfertigungsthese (Gal 2,16) den Einwand (der Paulus-Gegner?) auf, Christus werde zum „Diener der Sünde" herabgewürdigt, wenn die Rechtfertigung nicht an Werken des Gesetzes, sondern am Glauben festgemacht werde (Gal 2,17)[56]; Paulus hält dagegen, dass der Kyrios zwar ein „Diener" ist (vgl. Röm 15,8; Phil 2,6ff.) und dass sein Dienst den Sündern zugutekommt, aber die Sünde nicht groß macht, sondern besiegt; auf das Dass und Wie dieses Sieges konzentriert Paulus sich in Gal 2,17–21, wenn er die Partizipation an Jesu Kreuz und Auferstehung als Glaubensidentität beschreibt.

Im Römerbrief hat Paulus den ersten Argumentationsschritt (Röm 1,18–3,20) so gestaltet, dass die Katastrophe der Sünde als Ungerechtigkeit identifiziert und an Übertretungen des Gesetzes wie an Verstößen gegen die Stimme des Gewissens,

---

55 Vgl. Th. Söding, Glaube, der durch Liebe wirkt. Rechtfertigung und Ethik im Galaterbrief, in: Umstrittener Galaterbrief. Studien zur Situierung der Theologie des Paulusschreibens, hg. von B. Kollmann/M. Bachmann (BThSt 106), Neukirchen-Vluyn 2010, 165–206.
56 Der Vers ist allerdings seit der Antike bis in die Syntax hinein strittig. Dass ein Realis vorliegt, der eine rhetorische Frage einleitet, begründet H. Schlier, Der Brief an die Galater (KEK VII), Göttingen [15]1989 [[10]1949]), 58f.; anders jedoch R. Bultmann, Zur Auslegung von Gal 2,15–18 (1952), in: R. Bultmann, Exegetica. Aufsätze zur Erforschung des Neuen Testaments, hg. von E. Dinkler, Tübingen 1967, 394–399.

mithin als ethisches Versagen exemplifiziert wird. Bei der theologischen Begründung der Rechtfertigungsthese (Röm 3,21–31) kommt von Anfang an die Ethik ins Spiel – jedenfalls dann, wenn die Rechtfertigung nicht nur als Freispruch für diejenigen betrachtet wird, die Sünder bleiben, weil ihnen Gottes Gnade immer fremd bleibt, sondern als Gerechtmachung derer, die durch Gottes Gnade zu neuen Menschen geworden sind (vgl. Röm 7,1–5; Gal 6,15)[57]. Paulus begründet nicht nur die Heilseffektivität des Glaubens, für die Abraham steht (Röm 4), sondern beschreibt ebenso den „Frieden mit Gott" (Röm 5,1) und den „Zugang zur Gnade" (Röm 5,2), die sich aus der Liebe Gottes ergeben (Röm 5,1–11). Beides hat nicht nur die Gottesbeziehung der Gläubigen nachhaltig verändert, sondern auch ihr Verhältnis zu den anderen Menschen. In Röm 5,12–21 konzentriert sich Paulus auf den Gegensatz zwischen dem Ungehorsam Adams mit all seinen desaströsen Folgen für die Menschen, die seine Sünde, die Übertretung des göttlichen Gebotes, wiederholen, und dem Gehorsam Jesu Christi, der Gottes Heilswillen erfüllt. Die ethischen Implikationen werden in Röm 5,21 angedeutet („Die Gnade herrsche durch Gerechtigkeit") und in Röm 6 ausgeführt. Gegen den gespielten oder realen, jedenfalls absurden Einwand, das Vertrauen auf Gottes Gnade lade zum Sündigen ein (Röm 6,1.15), stellt Paulus die Teilhabe an der Gerechtigkeit Jesu Christi selbst als Wirkung des Glaubens wie der Taufe dar. Diese Gerechtigkeit ist zwar transmoralisch, weil Jesus Christus mit ihr das eschatologische Heil bringt, das den Gläubigen zugeeignet wird; aber sie unterläuft die Ethik nicht, sondern justiert sie.

So wie einerseits die theologische Bedeutung der Ethik in der Rechtfertigungstheologie des Galater- wie des Römerbriefes von langer Hand vorbereitet ist, ist andererseits die Paraklese der Agape selbst in beiden Briefen theologisch substantiell. Im Galaterbrief steht dafür das Stichwort der Freiheit. Im Sara-Hagar-Midrasch (Gal 4,21–31) ekklesiologisch vorbereitet, wird „Freiheit" an der Schwelle zur brieflichen Paraklese zum soteriologischen Schlüsselwort mit ethischen Implikationen[58]. Gal 5,1 („Zur Freiheit hat uns Christus befreit") öffnet den Raum einer Zukunft, die durch engagierten Glauben gestaltet, aber nicht durch einen Rückfall in das System der Gesetzeswerke irritiert werden soll; Gal 5,13 („Ihr seid zur Freiheit berufen") nimmt diesen Impetus auf, verbindet ihn aber mit einer Warnung („... nur nicht die Freiheit zum Einfallstor für das Fleisch") und kündigt

---

[57] Das hat Ernst Käsemann mit breiter ökumenischer Wirkung in der Paulusexegese stark gemacht: Gottesgerechtigkeit bei Paulus (1961), in: E. Käsemann, Exegetische Versuche und Besinnungen II, Göttingen 1964, 181–193.
[58] Vgl. Th. Söding, Die Freiheit des Glaubens. Konkretionen der Soteriologie nach dem Galaterbrief, in: Frühjudentum und Neues Testament im Horizont Biblischer Theologie, hg. von W. Kraus/K.-W. Niebuhr (WUNT 192), Tübingen 2003, 113–134; ders., Zur Freiheit befreit. Paulus und die Kritik der Autonomie, in: Communio 37 (2008), 92–112.

damit einen Passus an, der die moralische Verantwortung der geschenkten Freiheit stark macht[59]. Dadurch gelangt die Ethik auf die volle theologische Höhe der Soteriologie. Die Rechtfertigungslehre wäre ohne die Ethik der Agape nur die halbe Wahrheit.

Im Römerbrief ist es nicht anders. Die Schlüsselstelle ist Röm 12,1f., die programmatische Eröffnung der Paraklese[60]. Sie klärt, dass sich das „Erbarmen Gottes" nicht nur in den Mahnungen des Apostels ausspricht, sondern auch im Ethos des Glaubens auswirkt. Im unmittelbaren Kontext des Liebesgebotes (Röm 13,8 ff.) vergegenwärtigt Paulus die eschatologische Wende, die durch Jesus Christus herbeigeführt worden ist und mit Macht auf die Vollendung drängt (Röm 13,11–14). Sie fordert Nüchternheit und Wachsamkeit; sie drängt zur Konformität mit Jesus Christus, auch im Lebensstil[61].

Ist der theologische Ort der Ethik bei Paulus aus der Dynamik der Heilsvermittlung, aus der Gerechtigkeit Gottes und dem Ethos Jesu selbst entwickelt, ergibt sich die Fokussierung auf das Liebesgebot aus der Logik des Glaubens[62]. Beide Briefe sehen den rechtfertigenden Glauben nicht nur als Bekehrung und Vertrauen, als Erkenntnis und Bekenntnis, sondern eben deshalb auch als eine Form der Lebensführung, die sowohl in der Religiosität als auch in der Moralität das Bekenntnis bewahrheitet.

Im Galaterbrief hat Paulus das Ich der Glaubenden an der Liebe Jesu Christi festgemacht: „Der ich nun im Fleisch lebe, lebe ich im Glauben an den, der mich geliebt und sich für mich hingegeben hat" (Gal 2,20)[63]. Die Liebe, die im Glauben erkannt und empfangen wird, muss aber im Glauben auch gelebt werden, wenn das Bekenntnis kein Lippenbekenntnis sein und die Erkenntnis Folgen haben soll.

Das ist für Paulus im Glaubensbegriff selbst gesichert. Deshalb kann er im Übergang von der Vergewisserung dessen, was Gott in Jesus Christus durch den Heiligen Geist für die Glaubenden getan hat, zur Eröffnung dessen, worin die Antwort bestehen soll, die durch Jesus Christus im Heiligen Geist die Gläubigen

---

[59] Vgl. M. Konradt, Die Christonomie der Freiheit. Zu Paulus' Entfaltung seines ethischen Ansatzes in Gal 5,13–6,10, in: Early Christianity 1 (2010), 60–81.
[60] Vgl. D. Jodoin, Rm 12,1–2 – une intrigue discursive. De l'offrande des membres à l'offrandre des corps, in: ETR 85 (2010), 499–512.
[61] Vgl. H. Giesen, Nächstenliebe und Heilsvollendung. Zu Röm 13,8–14, in: SNTU 33 (2008), 67–97.
[62] Vgl. A. von Dobbeler, Glaube als Teilhabe. Historische und semantische Grundlagen der paulinischen Theologie und Ekklesiologie des Glaubens (WUNT II/22), Tübingen 1987.
[63] Zur Position in der Argumentation vgl. S. Shauf, Galatians 2.20 in context, in: NTS 52 (2006), 86–101.

Gott geben sollen⁶⁴, den rechtfertigenden Glauben als „Glaube, der durch Liebe wirksam ist" kennzeichnen (Gal 5,6). Dieser Satz, der unglücklicherweise in die Mühlen der Kontroverstheologie geraten ist, spricht von der prägenden Kraft des Glaubens. Er stellt den Glauben in einen eschatologischen Horizont, weil er von der Hoffnung auf Gerechtigkeit spricht. Der Horizont der Hoffnung wird durch die Liebe gefüllt, durch die der Glaube seine Wirksamkeit entfaltet⁶⁵.

Die Wirksamkeit, die er vor Augen stellt, ist die der Rechtfertigung, die allerdings nicht nur als eine Art Initialzündung am Beginn des Glaubensweges verstanden wird, sondern als dauernde Kraft der Gnade Gottes. Die Liebe, die Gal 5,6 meint, ist die Nächstenliebe, von der im Kontext die Rede ist, aber unter dem Aspekt, dass sich in ihr die empfangene und angenommene Liebe Jesu Christi selbst auswirkt. Deshalb bleibt der Glaube Subjekt. Die Partizipialkonstruktion, die Paulus wählt, sichert den Primat der Gnade Gottes und deshalb die rechtfertigende Kraft des Glaubens, der keinerlei Sonderkonditionen kennt, macht aber die Gnade Gottes gerade dadurch groß, dass sie zeigt, wie und wo sie wirkt: in der Liebe. Die Agape setzt den Glauben voraus, weil sie aus dem vertrauensvollen Bekenntnis zur Liebe Jesu Christi selbst lebt; der Glaube entfaltet seine Kraft durch die Liebe, weil er Gehorsam gegenüber Gottes Wort ist, das auf das Liebesgebot zuläuft (Gal 5,13 f.), und sich von Jesus Christus bewegen lässt, der definitiv seine Liebe erwiesen hat (Gal 2,20).

Im Römerbrief hat Paulus den Zusammenhang zwischen Glaube und Liebe nicht so programmatisch konzentriert wie in Gal 5,6. Der Sache nach ist er aber ähnlich angelegt. Eine Schlüsselpassage ist Röm 5,1–11⁶⁶. Paulus führt die Rechtfertigung der Glaubenden auf die Liebe Gottes selbst zurück, der seine Feinde zu seinen Freunden macht. Sie verwirklicht sich in der Lebenshingabe Jesu Christi (Röm 5,6 ff.); sie wird den Gläubigen ganz zu eigen durch den Heiligen Geist: „Die Liebe Gottes ist in unseren Herzen ausgegossen durch den Heiligen Geist" (Röm 5,5). Deshalb ist das Herz von dieser Liebe voll. Genau deshalb und auf diese Weise bestimmt sie auch das Handeln der Gläubigen. Der innere Zusammenhang zwischen Soteriologie und Ethik ist bei Paulus in der Liebe Gottes selbst begründet. Deshalb nimmt das Liebesgebot eine theologische Spitzenposition ein.

---

64 Vgl. V. Rabens, Power from in Between. The Relational Experience of the Holy Spirit and Spiritual Gifts in the Paul's Churches, in: The Spirit and Christ in the New Testament and Christian Theology. FS Max Turner, eds. I.H. Marshall/V. Rabens/C. Bennema, Grand Rapids/Cambridge 2012, 138–155.
65 Vgl. Th. Söding, Die Trias Glaube, Hoffnung, Liebe bei Paulus. Eine exegetische Studie (SBS 150), Stuttgart 1992, 145–162.
66 Vgl. S. Romanello, La condizione e il futuro dei credenti. Lo sguardo di Rm 5,1–11, in: Nuovo Testamento (s. Anm. 2), 233–247.

3.2 Der Hintergrund der Gesetzestheologie

Im Galater- wie im Römerbrief reflektiert Paulus, dass er mit dem Liebesgebot eine Weisung des Gesetzes zitiert. Er nutzt das Zitat, um den Stellenwert der Nächstenliebe in der Tora und in der Befolgung der Gebote durch die Glaubenden zu beschreiben. Diese Ortsbestimmung ist ein wichtiger Aspekt seiner Theologie des Gesetzes.

Im Galaterbrief formuliert Paulus: „Das ganze Gesetz ist in dem einen Wort erfüllt: Du sollst deinen Nächsten lieben wie dich selbst" (Gal 5,14). Die Gegenüberstellung des Ganzen und des Einen ist die Pointe. Paulus sieht das Gesetz, die Tora, als Einheit; sie bildet ein großes Ganzes. Es ist keine Frage, dass es viele Gebote hat, so dass es auch zu vielen Übertretungen kommt; aber mit dieser Vielfalt repräsentiert das Gesetz den einen, in sich kohärenten Willen Gottes. Das „eine" Wort des Liebesgebotes ist nicht nur eines von vielen Geboten, sondern der Schlüssel zum Ganzen. Paulus identifiziert nicht das „Ganze" mit dem „Einen"; dann würde er insinuieren, man könne auf alle anderen Gebote verzichten, oder meinen, das Liebesgebot enthielte alle anderen Gebote in sich. Paulus spricht vielmehr von Erfüllung. Die Kategorie der Erfüllung nutzt er, um die eschatologische Qualität der Gottesbegegnung in Jesus Christus zum Ausdruck zu bringen. Sie ist mit der Fülle und Überfülle der Gnade Gottes verbunden[67]. Wenn dies auch für Gal 5,14 gelten soll, werden die Einzelgebote durch das Liebesgebot nicht aufgehoben, sondern auf sich selbst zurück- und über sich selbst hinausgeführt: Sie werden auf den Heilswillen Gottes selbst bezogen, dessen ethischen Grundsinn das Liebesgebot beschreibt, nicht ohne den Raum der Moral für den umfassenden Raum der Heilsvermittlung immer schon geöffnet zu haben. Einerseits erfasst das Liebesgebot die Fülle dessen, was das Gesetz gebietet; andererseits gewinnt es seine theologische Bedeutung und ethische Orientierungsleistung nur im Kontext des ganzen Gesetzes.

Zur Erfüllung gehört die Praxis, aber zugleich die Anteilhabe an jener Gnade, die immer unendlich mehr bewirkt als die Lösung ethischer Fragen. In jedem einzelnen Gebot ist es die Liebe, und nur die Liebe, die Anspruch auf Gehorsam erhebt; aber die Liebe bleibt nicht abstrakt, sondern wird in der Erfüllung der Gebote konkret. Dass die Wichtigkeit des Liebesgebotes auch außerhalb des Christusglaubens einleuchtet und dass es außerhalb der Kirche intensive Erweise der Nächstenliebe gibt, würde Paulus nie und nimmer bestreiten, im Gegenteil gehört es zur Identität Gottes mit sich selbst, dass alles, was sein Heilswille fordert,

---

[67] Vgl. M. Theobald, Die überströmende Gnade. Studien zu einem paulinischen Motivfeld (FzB 22), Würzburg 1982.

bereits in der Tora steht und dass denjenigen, die das Gesetz nicht als Buch kennen, das Gebot ins Herz geschrieben ist, wie er – allerdings erst – im Römerbrief ausführen wird (Röm 2,15). Was im Glauben geschieht, ist nach dem Galaterbrief dreierlei: erstens die Einsicht, dass und weshalb das ganze Gesetz in diesem einen Wort erfüllt ist; zweitens die Motivation durch den Geist, aus dem inneren Zwiespalt der Sünde herauszufinden in die Freiheit der Kinder Gottes hinein; drittens eine Praxis, die Sinn und Geltung der Einzelgebote aus dem Zusammenhang des Ganzen heraus und deshalb nach dem Kriterium des Liebesgebotes bestimmt.

Von der Liebe her verstanden, zeigt sich also die konstruktive Verbindung zwischen dem rechtfertigenden Glauben und dem Anspruch des Gesetzes auch dort, wo Gerechtigkeit praktiziert werden soll. Gleichzeitig zeigt sich der Gegensatz zu den Paulusgegnern, die nach Gal 5,1–12 die Beschneidung[68] zum Schlüssel machen. Ob sie es wollen und sagen oder nicht, steuern sie auf eine Praxis vollständigen Gebotsgehorsams zu (Gal 5,3), die scheitern muss, weil sie auf die Logik von Befolgen und Übertreten festlegt; es fehlt ihnen das Denken von der Fülle her, das aber heißt: von der Liebe her. Wo die Liebe herrscht, wird das Gesetz nicht obsolet, sondern erfüllt.

Paulus hat diese Pointe im Galaterbrief genau vorbereitet. Er weist mit der Schrift selbst nach, dass das Gesetz nicht gegeben worden ist, um das ewige Leben zu schenken. Nach Gal 3,10 bringt es nicht Segen, sondern Fluch, weil es – seine heilige Pflicht – die Sünder bestraft. Dieser Strafe entgeht niemand, weil jede Übertretung sanktioniert wird (Dtn 27,26) und – so die im Galaterbrief unausgesprochene, erst im Römerbrief argumentativ eingeholte Voraussetzung – niemand sich von jeder Schuld freisprechen kann. Daraus folgt aber nicht, dass das „Gesetz wider die Verheißung" ist (Gal 3,21). Es fungiert vielmehr, „bevor der Glaube kam", wie eine Art Schutzhaft, aus der erst Jesus Christus befreit (Gal 3,23), und wie ein Pädagoge, der – sei es auch mit drakonischen Erziehungsmaßnahmen – auf die Entlassung und Resozialisierung vorbereitet (Gal 3,24). Die Paraklese geht den nächsten Schritt. Nachdem die Befreiung geschehen ist, kann das Gesetz auf seine positive Rolle konzentriert werden, den Weg des Glaubens als Weg der Gerechtigkeit zu weisen. Das Liebesgebot ist der Kompass.

Im Römerbrief bringt Paulus mit ähnlichen Formulierungen wie im Galaterbrief das Liebesgebot ein. Entscheidend ist erneut das Motiv der Erfüllung: „Wer den Nächsten liebt, hat das Gesetz erfüllt ... Also ist des Gesetzes Fülle die Liebe" (Röm 13,8.10). Der Aspekt ist nur leicht verschoben: vom „Wort" (Gal 5,14) zur

---

68 Vgl. A. Blaschke, Beschneidung. Zeugnisse der Bibel und verwandter Texte (TANZ 28), Heidelberg 1998.

Antwort, vom Gebot (das erfüllt werden soll) zur Praxis (die das Gebot erfüllt). Das Motiv der Fülle wird dadurch noch plausibler: Die Liebe erfüllt den Gesetzesgehorsam mit Leben; denn sie macht ihn zur Konformität mit der Liebe und Gerechtigkeit Jesu Christi selbst.

Paulus erläutert im Römerbrief allerdings auch, wie die Erfüllung zu verstehen ist. Dazu führt er einen *terminus technicus* frühjüdischer Gesetzeshermeneutik ein: „Denn das: ‚Du sollst nicht die Ehe brechen', ‚du sollst nicht töten', ‚du sollst nicht stehlen', ‚du sollst nicht begehren' und welches Gebot auch immer – in dem einen Wort gipfeln sie auf: ‚Du sollst deinen Nächsten lieben wie dich selbst'" (Röm 13,9)[69]. Die Kategorie der „Aufgipfelung" – oder, nach anderer Lesart, „Zusammenfassung" – ist in der schriftgelehrten Auseinandersetzung des frühen Judentums mit der Frage entwickelt worden, wie in der Fülle der – so wird traditionell gezählt – 613 Gebote und Verbote ein Prinzip, ein Spitzensatz oder auch nur ein guter Einstieg in das System der Vorschriften gefunden werden kann. Diesen „Gipfel" findet Paulus – ähnlich wie später Rabbi Akiba nach der ihm zugeschriebenen Tradition (Sifra Lev 19,18) und vergleichbar mit jüdisch-hellenistischen Akzenten der Ethik – im Liebesgebot. Gemeint ist, dass der Grundsinn des Gesetzes im Spitzensatz des Liebesgebotes am besten herauskommt, so dass jedes Gebot unter seinem Vorzeichen gelesen und verstanden, gewichtet und befolgt wird.

Um diese Pointe zu markieren, macht Paulus zwei stillschweigende Voraussetzungen, die aber zu plausibilisieren sind. Erstens hebt er den Dekalog hervor. Damit entspricht er einer breiten Strömung des frühen Judentums; im Vergleich zu den Zehn Geboten sind alle weiteren Gebote „andere". Sie sind vom ihm her zu verstehen und auszulegen. Die Akzentuierung durch das Liebesgebot geht nur einen Schritt weiter in dieser Hermeneutik. Zweitens konzentriert er sich auf die Zweite Tafel. Das ist im Kontext stimmig und wertet die Erste Tafel nicht ab, sondern berücksichtigt, dass die grundlegende Rolle des Glaubens, zu dem auch die Liebe zu Gott gehört, bereits intensiv bearbeitet worden ist.

Aus beiden Gründen gewinnt die Gesetzestheologie gegenüber dem Galaterbrief noch an Präzision. Einerseits fordert und fördert Paulus eine „Konzentration"[70]. Anderseits hat Paulus das Gesetz im Römerbrief an entscheidenden Stellen so gedeutet, dass plausibel wird, weshalb und wie die Tora nicht aufgelöst, sondern „aufgerichtet" (Röm 3,30) und nicht reduziert, sondern transformiert wird.

---

[69] Die Reihenfolge entspricht Dtn 5,17 ff. B; vgl. Philo, De decalogo, 36.51.121–137.168–171.
[70] Vgl. E. Lohse, Der Brief an die Römer (KEK IV), Göttingen 2003, 362.

Grundsätzlich entspricht die Gesetzestheologie des Römerbriefes derjenigen des Galaterbriefes. Es gibt keine tiefgreifende Veränderung[71], aber auch nicht nur situativ bedingte Varianten[72], sondern eine genauere Ausarbeitung, die neue Aspekte erschließt[73]. Es bleibt bei der Leitlinie, dass die „Werke des Gesetzes" nicht rechtfertigen können, weil das Gesetz zwar die Sünde kenntlich machen soll, aber nicht besiegen kann (Röm 3,20). Es bleibt auch dabei, dass Christus des Gesetzes „Ziel" oder „Ende" ist (Röm 10,4) und dass diese Teleologie des Gesetzes auf die soteriologische Dialektik zurückgeführt wird, dass es kein Heil ohne Gericht (Röm 2,1–11), das Gericht aber um des Heiles willen gibt (Röm 8,1)[74].

Allerdings hat Paulus an drei strittigen Stellen gezeigt, dass er die Erfüllung des Gesetzes auch in dem Sinn ernst nimmt, dass die Tora radikal bejaht wird[75]. *Die erste Stelle* betrifft den Kult und das Opfer. Nach Röm 3,24 ist Jesus der „Sühneort"; durch sein Kreuz und seine Auferstehung werden die Riten, die im Jerusalemer Heiligtum gefeiert werden, nicht abgetan, sondern zu ihrer eschatologischen Fülle geführt, so dass nun eine qualitativ neue Liturgie gefeiert werden kann[76]. *Die zweite Stelle* betrifft die Beschneidung; dass sie Heidenchristen nicht abverlangt werden darf, braucht Paulus im Römerbrief anscheinend nicht zu begründen. Dass sie – nur – dem „nützt", der das Gesetz hält, hat Paulus in Röm 2,25 vorausgesetzt. Dass es eine Art geistliche Beschneidung bei denen gibt, die Gottes Willen erfüllen, auch wenn sie äußerlich nicht beschnitten sind, hat er in Röm 2,26 ff. ausgeführt. Die Frage, worin dann der Nutzen der körperlichen Beschneidung bestehe, hat er in Röm 4,11 *en passant* beantwortet: Sie ist ein „Siegel der Glaubensgerechtigkeit"; sie ist die Unterschrift unter die Glaubensverheißung und die Ratifizierung der Glaubensgerechtigkeit, also immer ein Zeichen geborener Juden für die Universalität des Heiles, das durch den Messias verwirklicht wird. *Die dritte Stelle* betrifft die Reinheitsgebote und Speisevorschriften. Paulus muss sie in Röm 14 diskutieren, weil es über sie Streit zwischen „Starken" und „Schwachen" gibt, auch wenn die Konstellation nicht mit derjenigen des Galat-

---

71 Von Wandlungen spricht U. Schnelle, Paulus. Leben und Denken, Berlin 2003.
72 So F. Hahn, Theologie des Neuen Testaments I, Tübingen ³2011, 1801.
73 Von einer „Entwicklung" spricht U. Wilckens, Theologie des Neuen Testaments I/3, Neukirchen-Vluyn 2005, 25–266.
74 Vgl. H. Merklein, Gericht und Heil. Zur heilsamen Funktion des Gerichts bei Johannes dem Täufer, Jesus und Paulus (1990), in: H. Merklein, Studien zu Jesus und Paulus II (WUNT 105), Tübingen 1998, 60–81.
75 Vgl. K.-W. Niebuhr, Offene Fragen zur Gesetzespraxis bei Paulus und seinen Gemeinden (Sabbat, Speisegebote, Beschneidung), in: BThZ 25 (2008), 16–51.
76 Vgl. Th. Söding, Echtes Opfer. Gottesdienst bei Paulus, in: Objektive Feier und subjektiver Glaube? Beiträge zum Verhältnis von Liturgie und Spiritualität, hg. von S. Böntert (Studien zur Pastoraltheologie 32), Regensburg 2011, 9–34.

erbriefes identisch ist[77]. Paulus argumentiert nach eigenen Bekunden von einem theologischen Urteil aus, das er „im Herrn Jesus" gefällt hat; es kann offenbleiben, ob es sich für Paulus um eine Jesustradition handelt, die dann Mk 7,1–23 entsprechen könnte, oder um eine Deduktion aus der Rechtfertigungslehre, für die er sich auf Jesus beruft: „Nichts ist an sich unrein" (Röm 14,14). Aber der Apostel bleibt nicht bei dieser Position stehen, sondern bedenkt, was Reinheit und Unreinheit „für" andere bedeuten kann; darauf muss Rücksicht genommen werden (Röm 14,15–22). Wer das nicht tut, verkennt seine eigene Einsicht. Paulus ist an den pastoralen Problemen interessiert. Deshalb fehlt eine ähnliche Programmatik wie in Mk 7. Aber die Pointe ist kompatibel. Zum Schluss wird der Apostel grundsätzlich: „Alles, was nicht aus Glauben geschieht, ist Sünde" (Röm 14,23). Damit wird die Frage des Gesetzesgehorsams auf genau die Ebene verschoben, die von der Rechtfertigungslehre vermessen und von der Ethik der Agape kultiviert wird. Alle drei Transformationen verstehen sich als Konkretisierungen der Liebe: die Sühnetheologie durch die Hingabe Jesu, die Beschneidungsspiritualität durch die Öffnung für das Heil der Heiden und die Reinheitsidee durch die Sorge um die Gewissensnot des Nächsten.

3.3 Das Verständnis der Nächstenliebe

Im Galater- wie im Römerbrief zeigt Paulus paradigmatisch und prinzipiell, wie die Nächstenliebe zu verstehen ist. In beiden Briefen wird die Nächstenliebe ekklesiologisch verortet, weil sie die Glaubensgemeinschaft stärkt, aber im Ansatz über die Gemeindegrenzen hinaus für diejenigen geöffnet, die außerhalb der Gemeinde Kontakt mit den Gläubigen bekommen.

Der Galaterbrief formuliert das Prinzip am Ende der Paraklese: „Lasst uns, wie wir Zeit haben, allen Gutes tun, besonders aber den Hausgenossen des Glaubens" (Gal 6,10)[78]. Die Konzentration auf die Mitglieder der Kirchengemeinden ist ein Echtheitsbeweis der Nächstenliebe, weil die Nahbeziehung der moraltheologische Ernstfall ist. Aber die Öffnung für andere ergibt sich notwendig aus der Heilsuniversalität Gottes. Wenn sich die Existenz der Gemeinde ihr verdankt, muss sich in ihrem Gottesdienst und ihrem Glaubenszeugnis, aber auch in ihrer Ethik diese Offenheit realisieren.

---

[77] Weiter lässt ein Blick auf 1Kor 8–10 blicken; vgl. Th. Söding, Starke und Schwache. Der Götzenopferstreit in Korinth als ethisches Paradigma (1994), in: Th. Söding, Das Wort vom Kreuz (s. Anm. 57), 346–369.
[78] Vgl. K. Fretheim, Grums i Galaterbrevet. Om kristen etikk, Paulus og den prioriterte Andre, in: TTK 79 (2008), 113–129.

In Gal 5 konzentriert sich Paulus auf die innergemeindlichen Beziehungen. Dazu bestand angesichts der Konflikte aller Anlass (Gal 5,15). Paulus stellt aber keinen Verhaltenskatalog auf, sondern setzt auf die Dynamik des Geistes. Er, der Anteil an der Gottessohnschaft Jesu gibt und deshalb „Abba" beten lässt (Gal 4,6 ff.), treibt die Gläubigen auch an, ihre Liebe zu leben. Er ist einerseits in der Lage, das „Begehren des Fleisches" (Gal 5,16) zu besiegen, worunter Paulus nicht den Sexualtrieb versteht, sondern die Versuchung zum Bösen, die auch den Gläubigen nicht fremd ist[79]. Der lange Lasterkatalog Gal 5,19 ff. illustriert die verheerenden Folgen, die unbedingt vermieden werden müssen. Andererseits hält der Geist zum Guten an, wie der Tugendkatalog Gal 5,22 f. veranschaulicht. Diese positive Wirkung reflektiert Paulus durch einen doppelten Bezug auf das Gesetz. Zum einen: „Wenn ihr im Geist handelt, seid ihr nicht unter dem Gesetz" (Gal 5,18)[80]. Gemeint ist: Wer sich vom Geist führen lässt, setzt auf den Glauben (Gal 3,1–5), nicht jedoch auf die Beschneidung und all die anderen „Werke des Gesetzes", und steht deshalb nicht unter dem Fluch, mit dem das Gesetz alle Übertreter belegt, sondern unter dem Segen der Verheißung. Zum anderen: „Dagegen ist das Gesetz nicht!" (Gal 5,23), notiert Paulus lakonisch, nachdem er die Tugend als „Frucht des Geistes" (Gal 5,22) klassifiziert und exemplifiziert hat. Denn das Gesetz ist auch ethisch der Verheißung zugeordnet, formuliert es doch das Liebesgebot. Wer sich vom Geist führen lässt, erfüllt das Gesetz.

Besonders eng werden die Bezüge zu Lev 19,17 f. in Gal 6,1 f. Denn dort schärft Paulus die Pflicht zur wechselseitigen Vergebung ein. Er bleibt aber nicht bei der Forderung stehen, sondern deutet sie in eminenter Weise: „Einer trage des anderen Last, so werdet ihr das Gesetz Christi erfüllen." (Gal 6,2). Die „Last", die einer dem anderen abnehmen soll, ist, nach Gal 6,1 zu urteilen, die Schuld, die er auf sich geladen hat. Gemeint ist nicht nur die Bereitschaft zu Vergebung, sondern auch das solidarische Eintreten für die Folgen: die Hilfe bei der Aufarbeitung und Wiedergutmachung.

Das „Gesetz Christi" (Gal 6,2) ist weder ein Schlagwort der galatischen Nomisten[81] noch einfach eine Regel[82], sondern die Tora, die von Christus erfüllt

---

[79] Vgl. O. Hofius, Widerstreit zwischen Fleisch und Geist? Erwägungen zu Gal 5,17, in: Der Mensch vor Gott. Forschungen zum Menschenbild in Bibel, antikem Judentum und Koran. FS Hermann Lichtenberger, hg. von U. Mittmann-Richert, Neukirchen-Vluyn 2003, 147–159.
[80] Vgl. W.A. Todd, „Under Law" in Galatians. A Pauline theological abbreviation, in: JThS 56 (2005), 362–392.
[81] So H.D. Betz, Der Galaterbrief, München 1988 [engl. 1979], 510 f.
[82] So R. Bultmann, Theologie des Neuen Testaments (1948–1953), hg. von O. Merk, Tübingen ^{9}1984, 260. M. Winger (The Law of Christ, in: NTS 46 [2000], 537–546) meint, dass das ethische System des Christentums als Alternative zur Tora vorgestellt werde.

wird[83]. Sie ist das „Gesetz Christi", weil Jesus die Liebe, die es fordert, verwirklicht[84]. Weil dies die Hingabe seines Lebens umschließt (Gal 1,5; 3,13f.), ist die Vergebung der Sünden, zu der die Gläubigen aufgefordert werden, vom Heilstod Jesu begründet und gedeckt. Sie ist eine Konsequenz des Glaubens, ein Erweis der Liebe[85].

Im Römerbrief hat Paulus die Zitation des Liebesgebotes sorgfältig vorbereitet. Seine grundlegende Mahnung, Gott das Opfer der Hingabe im ganzen Leben zu machen (Röm 12,1f.), führt er zuerst durch eine parakletisch zugespitzte Variante des Leib-Christi-Gleichnisses weiter (Röm 12,4f.)[86]. Sie orientiert die Charismenlehre nicht nur katechetisch, sondern auch diakonisch: „Wer gibt – in Lauterkeit, ... wer sich erbarmt – in Freundlichkeit" (Röm 12,6).

Der folgende Passus (Röm 12,9–21) ist eine konzentrierte Darlegung paulinischer Agape-Ethik. Er ist genau strukturiert. Die Verse 9 und 21 bilden den Rahmen: Am Guten festzuhalten (Röm 12,9) und gar das Böse durch das Gute zu besiegen (Röm 12,21), erfordert die Praxis der Agape. Der positive Ansatz in Vers 9 leitet zum ersten Teil über, der die innergemeindliche Liebe charakterisiert (Röm 12,10–13; 12,16a). Sie ist ganz auf den Grundton der Achtsamkeit, Herzlichkeit und Freundlichkeit gestimmt. Dass es allen Anlass gibt, die innergemeindliche Solidarität einzufordern, ergibt sich erst aus Röm 14, wo Paulus den Streit zwischen „Starken" und „Schwachen" schlichten muss. Vers 13 weitet den Blick, indem er die Gastfreundschaft anspricht, auf die Paulus selbst bald bauen will und angewiesen sein wird. Der kritische Ansatz in Vers 21 ist durch den zweiten Teil der Agape-Paraklese vorbereitet (Röm 12,14–21). Hier geht es vor allem um das Verhältnis zu den Außenstehenden. Im Vordergrund steht der Umgang mit Verfolgung (Röm 12,14) und Bosheit, die erfahren wird (Röm 12,16). Die paulinischen Mahnungen stehen nahe an der Bergpredigt[87], lassen sich aber auch vor dem Hintergrund von Lev 19,17f. gut verstehen. Die Antwort auf Fluch soll Segen sein (Röm 12,14), die Antwort auf Gewalt nicht Gegengewalt (Röm 12,17), sondern Verzicht auf

---

83 So H. Schlier, Galater, 201f.
84 So H. Schürmann, Das ‚Gesetz des Christus' (Gal 6,2). Jesu Verhalten und Wort als letztgültige sittliche Norm nach Paulus (1974), in: H. Schürmann, Studien zur neutestamentlichen Ethik (SBAB 7), Stuttgart 1990, 53–76.
85 Claude Pigeon (‚La loi du Christ' en Galates 6,2, in: SR 29 [2000], 425–438) identifiziert das „Gesetz Christi" mit dem Doppelgebot. Das ist zu eng.
86 Vgl. M. Walter, Gemeinde als Leib Christi. Untersuchungen zum Corpus Paulinum und zu den „Apostolischen Vätern" (NTOA 49), Freiburg i.d. Schweiz/Göttingen 2001.
87 Vgl. E. Kamlah, Prophetie und Paränese. Ein Vergleich des Gebots der Feindesliebe in der Redenquelle mit der Ermahnung zu aufrichtiger Liebe in Römer 12,9ff., in: „Ich bin ein Hebräer". Gedenken an Otto Michel, hg. von H. Lindner, Gießen 2003, 288–298.

Rache – im Vertrauen auf Gottes Gerechtigkeit (Röm 12,19 f.)[88]. Paulus lässt die weisheitliche Maxime Spr 25,21 f. anklingen, um verstehen zu lassen, was praktizierte Liebe ist, die – wenn es gut geht – aus Feinden Nächste macht.

3.4 Auswertung

Der Galaterbrief und der Römerbrief sind thematisch verwandt, aber in der Situation ihrer Entstehung unterschiedlich. Im Galaterbrief kämpft Paulus gegen nomistische Konkurrenten[89] um seine Gemeinde; im Römerbrief will er hingegen die Gemeinde als Partnerin seiner ambitionierten Missionspläne für Spanien gewinnen[90]. Im Galaterbrief will er aber über den Konflikt hinaus die Basis einer Versöhnung legen, im Römerbrief die Unterstützung der Gemeinde nicht finden, ohne dass er dargelegt hat, wofür er theologisch – wirklich – steht. Deshalb entsteht eine starke Kongruenz zwischen dem Liebesgebot in beiden Schreiben, auch wenn es von unterschiedlichen Seiten her entwickelt wird.

Die Konzentration von Lev 19,18 ist in beiden Briefen eine Konsequenz der Christologie; deshalb wird durch das Liebesgebot die moraltheologische Dimension der Rechtfertigungslehre geöffnet. Paulus löst auch auf dem Gebiet der Ethik sein Postulat ein, dass er das Gesetz zu vollen Ehren bringt. Er behält die Freiheit, auch ohne die Beschneidung die Völker zu missionieren und die Einheit der Kirche ohne die Verpflichtung auf die Reinheitsgebote zu begründen (Gal 2,11–14). Er bestimmt den theologischen Status der Ethik in der geistgewirkten Partizipation an der Liebe Jesu Christi selbst. Er zeigt die prägende Kraft des Glaubens in der Lebensführung. Er zeigt, wie der Glaube im Kern als Gehorsam gegenüber Gottes Wort ernstgenommen wird. Er bindet umgekehrt den ethischen Ernst an die Freude des Glaubens zurück und das Engagement der Gläubigen an das Wirken der Gnade. Er konkretisiert das Liebesgebot so, dass sowohl die innergemeindlichen Bande gestärkt als auch die Beziehungen zu den Nicht-Christen im Geist der Versöhnung gestaltet werden. Im Galaterbrief zeigt er dadurch seinen Gegnern die theologische Substanz der Ethik wie die ethische Substanz der Soteriologie; gleichzeitig spricht er die Gemeinde, die gespalten und ihm abspenstig gemacht zu

---

[88] J.N. Day, ‚Coals of fire' in Romans 12:19–20, in: BS 160 (2003), 414–420.
[89] J.C. Hurd, Reflections concerning Paul's ‚Opponents' in Galatia, in: Paul and his Opponents, ed. by S.E. Porter (Pauline Studies 2), Leiden 2005, 129–148.
[90] Vgl. R. Vorholt, Alle Wege führen nach Rom. Die Hauptstadt im Blickfeld des Paulus, in: Das frühe Christentum und die Stadt, hg. von R. von Bendemann/M. Tiwald (BWANT 198), Stuttgart 2012, 204–237; M. J.C. Hurd, Reflections concerning Paul's ‚Opponents' in Galatia, in: Paul and his Opponents, ed. by S.E. Porter (Pauline Studies 2), Leiden 2005, 129–148.

werden droht, auf ihren sehnlichsten Wunsch an, zum Gottesvolk zu gehören, und zeigt ihnen mit Rekurs auf die Tora an, wie dieser Weg in der realen Welt verläuft und dass er aus dem Glauben folgt. Im Römerbrief kann er durch die Agape-Ethik auch noch die letzten Bedenken zerstreuen, dass seine Gnadentheologie verantwortungslos sei; er kann die Hauptstadtgemeinde innerlich einigen und sie nicht nur in ihrem Bekenntnis, sondern auch moralisch mit den Glaubenden in aller Welt verbinden.

4 Das Liebesgebot bei Paulus und Markus

4.1 Das literarische Verhältnis zwischen dem Liebesgebot bei Markus und Paulus

Im Markusevangelium und im Galater- wie im Römerbrief ist die theologische Prominenz des Liebesgebotes auffällig. Im Horizont frühjüdischer Ethik auf alttestamentlicher Grundlage ist diese Betonung verständlich, aber nicht selbstverständlich. So programmatisch wie bei Markus und Paulus ist das Liebesgebot nur noch in anderen neutestamentlichen und frühchristlichen Schriften betont. Deshalb reicht die Erklärung nicht aus, beide Schriften würden in ihrer Konzentration auf das Liebesgebot im Strom zeitgenössischer Ethik des Judentums mitschwimmen. Eher erklärt sich eine andere Intention: die christliche Ethik alttestamentlich zu verwurzeln. Markus hatte als Evangelist der Heidenchristen, als der er meist gesehen wird, daran starkes Interesse, was Matthäus ihm besonders gedankt hat; Paulus will im Galaterbrief die Gemeinden davon überzeugen, dass sie ihr Heil nicht im Nomismus zu suchen brauchen, wenn sie engeren Kontakt zur Tora haben wollen, und im Römerbrief diejenigen, die in der Gefahr stehen, sich über die Juden zu erheben (Röm 11,20–26), an die bleibende Geltung des Gesetzes erinnern (was sich später in der Auseinandersetzung mit Markion bewähren wird). Paulus schreibt im Galaterbrief, er knüpfe an seine frühere Verkündigung an; davon wird auch die Einschärfung des Liebesgebotes nicht auszunehmen sein. Im Römerbrief hingegen rechnet er damit, dass er auch eine ihm *bis dato* unbekannte Gemeinde mit Rekurs auf das Liebesgebot von der ethischen Substanz seiner Rechtfertigungslehre überzeugen kann. Das spricht für eine weite Verbreitung des Liebesgebotes im Urchristentum, wenigstens aber für die Annahme des Apostels, die Ethik der Agape könne auf einem guten Resonanzboden zum Klingen gebracht werden.

Allerdings ist auch eine direkte literarische Verbindung zwischen Markus und Paulus beim Liebesgebot nicht wahrscheinlich. Dass Markus theologische Voraussetzungen hat, die mit denen, die Paulus durch seine Briefe erkennen lässt und durch sein missionarisches Wirken mit geschaffen hat, kompatibel sind, braucht gar nicht in Abrede gestellt zu werden. Aber die literarischen Unterschiede sind zu groß: Für Markus ist das Doppelgebot charakteristisch, anders als für Paulus. Markus situiert das Liebesgebot sorgfältig in einer bestimmten (idealen) Situation des Lebens Jesu; dafür kann er von Paulus keinen Anstoß erhalten haben. Der Evangelist ist gewiss am katechetischen Nutzen für seine Adressaten interessiert; aber er bringt die Gesprächsszene, weil er sie als typisch jesuanisch betrachtet.

Andererseits rekurriert Paulus weder im Galater- noch im Römerbrief auf ein Wort Jesu oder ein Schriftzitat Jesu, obwohl für ihn die ethische Autorität Jesu über alles geht (1Kor 7) und er – gerade im Römerbrief – großes Interesse hat, Jesus als den zu kennzeichnen, der von der Heiligen Schrift nicht nur angekündigt wird (Röm 1,2ff. u. ö.), sondern auch beseelt ist (Röm 15,8–12). Er geht vielmehr programmatisch, wie durch die Rechtfertigungslehre begründet, auf die Schrift als solche zu. Er will die Ethik der Agape in der Tora begründen und zitiert deshalb das Liebesgebot.

Erklärungsbedürftig bleibt dann allerdings die auffällige Übereinstimmung in der Akzentuierung des Liebesgebotes. Paulus und Markus steht offensichtlich nicht nur das Einzelgebot der Nächstenliebe vor Augen, sondern auch sein Kontext. Sowohl im Galater- wie im Römerbrief ist in den Konkretionen der Nächstenliebe der Zusammenhang des Heiligkeitsgesetzes, besonders der engere Passus Lev 19,17 f. offensichtlich präsent. Bei Markus erschließen sich die Zusammenhänge eher von den Konkretionen der Nächstenliebe im Ganzen des Evangeliums her und in der Zuordnung der Nächsten- zur Gottesliebe.

Markus legt die Spur zurück zur Verkündigung Jesu selbst: zu seiner Liebe, seiner Gesetzestreue und seiner Glaubenstheologie. Paulus stellt seine Begründung auf zwei Säulen: die Lebenshingabe Jesu selbst und seine radikale Bejahung des Gesetzes, die auf seine Erfüllung aus ist. Beides zeigt, dass es eine falsche Alternative wäre, entweder Lev 19 und seine frühjüdische Rezeption oder die Ethik Jesu im Hintergrund zu erkennen. Beides gehört zusammen, weil Jesus die Verbindung hergestellt hat. Dann aber liegt die Schlussfolgerung nahe, dass es letztlich die Erfahrung der Liebe Gottes in der Person Jesu Christi gewesen ist, die bei Markus und Paulus, wie (mit anderen Zugängen und Akzenten) nicht nur bei Matthäus und Lukas, sondern auch bei Johannes und ebenso bei Jakobus, das Liebesgebot ins Zentrum hat rücken lassen.

Durch die große Übereinstimmung zwischen der paulinischen und der markinischen Ethik vertieft sich der Eindruck, dass das Neue Testament eine – in sich vielschichtige – Einheit darstellt. Mit dem Liebesgebot gewinnt es ein charakteristisches Profil der Ethik, nicht gegen das Alte Testament, sondern mit ihm und nicht im Unterschied zum Judentum der Zeit, sondern in Übereinstimmung sowohl mit der Verkündigung Jesu als auch dem Grundsinn seines Heilstodes und seiner Auferstehung. Durch die Komposition des Kanons entsteht der Eindruck, dass in der paulinischen Ethik dieselbe Spur wie in der Verkündigung Jesu verfolgt wird – auch wenn die historischen Verhältnisse erheblich differenzierter sind.

4.2 Das theologische Verhältnis zwischen dem Liebesgebot bei Markus und Paulus

Die markinische Perspektive auf das Liebesgebot ist klar von der paulinischen unterschieden. Für die Interpretation des Markustextes ist die Erinnerung an Jesus entscheidend. Jesus braucht die grundlegende Geltung des Gesetzes nach dem markinischen Text nicht zu begründen, weil sie nicht im Streit steht, gerade auch bei den Gegnern Jesu nicht. Er muss aber die aktuelle Bedeutung des Gesetzes erschließen, auch für seine Jünger. Hier gewinnt das Doppelgebot eine Schlüsselbedeutung. Durch die Verbindung der Nächsten- mit der Gottesliebe unterläuft Jesus den Blasphemie-Vorwurf und zeigt unter dem Vorzeichen der Ethik die Logik seiner Zuwendung zu den Kranken und Sündern. Vom Liebesgebot her erklärt sich die bleibende Verbindlichkeit des Gesetzes auch für die – mehrheitlich wohl heidenchristlichen – Gemeindemitglieder. Die hermeneutische Dominanz der Nächstenliebe erweist sich bei der Reform des Sabbats und der Reinheitsgebote, der Ehe und des Umgangs mit Besitz als produktiv. Der „Nächste", den es zu lieben gilt, ist im Rückblick auf Jesus jeder Mensch, aus Israel oder nicht, der den Weg Jesu kreuzt, weil die Nähe der Gottesherrschaft die Identität des Gottesvolkes nach innen und außen weitet. Das „Ich", das zur Nächstenliebe nach dem Maß der Selbstliebe gerufen wird, ist das Geschöpf Gottes, das Jesus in die Herrschaft Gottes einlädt und das sich deshalb in einer überraschenden Nähe zu all denen befindet, die ihrerseits sich von Jesus auf den Weg der Nachfolge haben rufen lassen oder noch auf die Begegnung mit dem Kyrios und seinem Wort warten. Sünder gehören dazu, sind doch die Jünger selbst schwach. In der Nächstenliebe können kraft der Vollmacht Jesu Sünden vergeben werden, so wie durch die Nächstenliebe klar wird, in welcher Richtung die Motivationspfeile des Glaubens verlaufen. Die Formulierung des Doppelgebotes ist flexibel genug, um auf den weiten nachösterlichen Missionsfeldern, die Markus abzustecken beginnt (Mk 13,10; 14,9), Räume ethischer Begegnung zu öffnen, die vom Glauben getragen werden oder zum Glauben einladen; sie ist präzis genug, um den Anspruch des Evangeliums nicht unverbindlich werden zu lassen, sondern die offene Gemeinschaft der Jünger so zu stärken, dass sie glaubwürdig das Evangelium verbreiten kann.

Paulus hingegen schaut auf gerade erst gegründete, stürmisch wachsende, aber krisenhaft erschütterte Gemeinden der ersten Generation, die ihre Identität noch finden müssen. Das Liebesgebot stärkt die Gemeinschaft zwischen Juden- und Heidenchristen, verankert das Evangelium im Gesetz und begründet eine – kritische – Partnerschaft mit denjenigen Juden, die nicht an Jesus glauben. Es liefert ein Grundverständnis des Gesetzes, das mit dem Grundverständnis des Heilshandelns Gottes konvergiert. Das Liebesgebot ist die Matrix für die Regelung innergemeindlicher Konflikte und die Stärkung des inneren Zusammenhalts. Es öffnet die Gemeinden für die Welt, ohne dass sie ihre theologischen Konturen verlieren. Aus theologischen Gründen sieht es den Nächsten in erster Linie als Mitglied der eigenen Glaubensfamilie, ohne dass andere ausgeschlossen würden. Es stößt die Suche nach Konkretisierungen an, die mit der Ethik Jesu – nicht nur des Markusevangeliums, auch der Bergpredigt – konvergieren. Das „Ich" der Nächstenliebe ist gerade jenes, das „mit" Jesus Christus gekreuzigt ist, so dass es „in" ihm lebt, der sein wahres Ich ausmacht (Gal 2,19 f.)[91].

Kennzeichnend ist für das Markusevangelium wie für Paulus die Theozentrik der Agape. Es geht nicht nur um eine formale Erfüllung dessen, was der Wille Gottes vorschreibt, sondern um eine innere Übereinstimmung mit dem, was Gott will und durch Jesus Christus durchsetzt. Im Markusevangelium ist die Theozentrik der Nächstenliebe dadurch eingeschrieben, dass sie aus der Gottesliebe folgt, die ihrerseits den Glauben an das Evangelium (Mk 1,15) realisiert. Paulus hat die Liebe zu Gott weniger, desto mehr aber den Glauben betont und in Gal 5,6 auch die gültige Formel für das Verhältnis gefunden.

Für das Markusevangelium wie für die Paulusbriefe ist der Bezug zum Gesetz für das theologische Profil des Liebesgebotes wesentlich. Allerdings zeigt bereits der Blick auf die jüdischen Parallelen, dass gerade das Liebesgebot geeignet ist, den Raum einer rein innerbiblischen Plausibilität zu überschreiten und an das humane Ethos anderer Kulturen anzuknüpfen. Deshalb gehört das Liebesgebot auch in die Geschichte der urchristlichen Mission. Es wächst aus dem Evangelium, das Gehör finden soll.

Literatur

Becker, E-M., Das Markusevangelium im Rahmen antiker Historiographie (WUNT 194), Tübingen 2006.

---

[91] Vgl. Th. Söding, ‚Ich lebe, aber nicht ich' (Gal 2,20). Die theologische Physiognomie des Paulus, in: Communio 38 (2009), 119 – 134. Zur systematischen Reflexion vgl, F. Nüssel, ‚Ich lebe, doch nun nicht ich, sondern Christus lebt in mir'. Dogmatische Überlegungen zur Rede vom Sein in Christus, in: ZThK 99 (2002), 480 – 502.

Becking, B., Love thy neighbour ... Exegetical remarks on Leviticus 19:18,34, in: „Gerechtigkeit und Recht zu üben" (Gen 18,19). Studien zur altorientalischen und biblischen Rechtsgeschichte, zur Religionsgeschichte Israels und zur Religionssoziologie. Festschrift für Eckart Otto zum 65. Geburtstag, hg. von R. Achenbach/M. Arneth (BZAR 13), Wiesbaden 2009, 182–187.

Berger, K., Die Gesetzesauslegung Jesu. Teil I: Markus und Parallelen (WMANT 40), Neukirchen-Vluyn 1972.

Betz, H.D., Der Galaterbrief, München 1988 (engl. 1979).

Blaschke, A., Beschneidung. Zeugnisse der Bibel und verwandter Texte (TANZ 28), Heidelberg 1998.

Blecker, I.M., Rituelle Reinheit vor und nach der Zerstörung des Zweiten Tempels. Essenische, pharisäische und jesuanische Reinheitsvorstellungen im Vergleich, in: Fremde Zeichen. Neutestamentliche Texte in der Konfrontation der Kulturen. FS Karl Löning, hg. von A. Leinhäupl-Wilke/S. Lücking (Theologie 15), Münster 1998, 25–40.

Bultmann, R., Theologie des Neuen Testaments (1948–1953), hg. von O. Merk, Tübingen ⁹1984.

—, Zur Auslegung von Gal 2,15–18 (1952), in: R. Bultmann, Exegetica. Aufsätze zur Erforschung des Neuen Testaments, hg. von E. Dinkler, Tübingen 1967, 394–399.

Burchard, Ch., Das doppelte Liebesgebot in der frühen christlichen Überlieferung, in: ders., Studien zur Theologie, Sprache und Umwelt des Neuen Testaments, hg. von D. Sänger (WUNT 107), Tübingen 1998, 3–26.

D'Angelo, M.R., Gender and Power in the Gospel of Mark: The Daughter of Jairus and the Woman with the Flow of Blood, in: Miracles in Jewish and Christian Antiquity. Imagining Truth, ed. by J. Cavadini, Notre Dame 1999, 83–109.

Day, J.N., ‚Coals of fire' in Romans 12:19–20, in: BS 160 (2003), 414–420.

Dobbeler, A. von, Glaube als Teilhabe. Historische und semantische Grundlagen der paulinischen Theologie und Ekklesiologie des Glaubens (WUNT II/22), Tübingen 1987.

Dormeyer, D., Das Markusevangelium als Idealbiographie von Jesus Christus, dem Nazarener (SBS 143), Stuttgart 2001.

Dunn, J.D.G., Jesus and purity. An ongoing debate, in: NTS 48 (2002), 449–467.

Ebersohn, M., Das Nächstenliebegebot in der synoptischen Tradition (MThSt 37), Marburg 1993.

Ebner, M., ‚Kinderevangelium' oder markinische Sozialkritik. Mk 10,13–16 im Kontext, in: JBTh 17 (2002), 315–336.

Filho, J.A., Colhendo espigas no sábado. Um estudo de Marcos 2,23–28, in: EstB 84 (2004), 58–69.

Focant, C., Le rapport à la loi dans l'évangile de Marc, in: RThL 27 (1996), 281–308.

—, Les implications du nouveau dans le permis (Mc 2,1–3,6), in: Ouvrir les Écritures. FS Paul Beauchamp, ed. by P. Bovati (LeDiv 162), Paris 1995, 201–223.

Frankemölle, H., Ehescheidung und Wiederverheiratung im Neuen Testament, in: Geschieden – Wiederverheiratet – Abgewiesen? Antworten der Theologie QD 157, hg. von Th. Schneider, Freiburg/Basel/Wien 1995, 28–50.

Fretheim, K., Grums i Galaterbrevet. Om kristen etikk, Paulus og den prioriterte Andre, in: TTK 79 (2008), 113–129.

Fuente, A., de la, A favor o en contra de Jesús. El logion de Mc 9,40 y sus paralelos, in: EstB 53 (1995), 449–459.

Gellar, J.S., Matthew 12:30; Mark 9:40; Luke 9:50; 11:23 – ‚with and for' or 'against'?, in: Lutheran Theological Review 14 (2001/2002), 10–26.
Giesen, H., Nächstenliebe und Heilsvollendung. Zu Röm 13,8–14, in: SNTU 33 (2008), 67–97.
Gionotto, C., Amerai il prossimo tuo come te stesso. Alcune osservazioni sull'interpretazione di Lv 19,18 nell'antica letteratura cristiana, in: Nuovo Testamento. Teologie in dialogo culturale. Scritti in onore di Romano Penna nel suo 70 compleanno, ed. by G.P.N. Ciola (RevBib.S 60), Bologna 2008, 479–489.
Gnilka, J., Das Evangelium nach Markus II (EKK I/2), Zürich u. a./Neukirchen-Vluyn 1979 [2000].
Grilli, M., Die heilende Schwachheit Gottes. Lektüre von Mk 9,14–29 in ihrem Kontext, in: Jesus als Bote des Heils. Heilserfahrung und Heilsverkündigung in frühchristlicher Zeit. FS Detlev Dormeyer, hg. von L. Hauser/F.R. Prostmeier/Ch.G. Zöller, Stuttgart 2008, 56–71.
Grünwaldt, K., Das Heiligkeitsgesetz Leviticus 17–26. Ursprüngliche Gestalt, Tradition und Theologie (BZAW 271), Berlin 1999.
Haas, A.J., „Geschenk aus Gottes Schatzkammer" (bSchab 10b). Jesus und der Sabbat im Spiegel der neutestamentlichen Schriften (NTA 43), Münster 2003.
Hahn, F., Theologie des Neuen Testaments I (UTB M3500), Tübingen ³2011.
Hoffmann, P., Das Recht der Frau oder „Wider die legalisierte Willkür des Mannes" (1975), in: P. Hoffmann, Studien zur Frühgeschichte der Jesus-Bewegung (SBAB 17), Stuttgart 1994, 95–117.
Hofius, O., Widerstreit zwischen Fleisch und Geist? Erwägungen zu Gal 5,17, in: Der Mensch vor Gott. Forschungen zum Menschenbild in Bibel, antikem Judentum und Koran. FS Hermann Lichtenberger, hg. von U. Mittmann-Richert, Neukirchen-Vluyn 2003, 147–159.
Hotze, G., Jesus als Gast Studien zu einem christologischen Leitmotiv im Lukasevangelium (FzB 111), Würzburg 2007.
Huber, K., Jesus in Auseinandersetzung. Exegetische Untersuchungen zu den sogenannten Jerusalemer Streitgesprächen des Markusevangeliums im Blick auf ihre christologischen Implikationen (FzB 75), Würzburg 1995.
Hurd, J.C., Reflections concerning Paul's ‚Opponents' in Galatia, in: Paul and his Opponents, ed. by S.E. Porter (Pauline Studies 2), Leiden 2005, 129–148.
Jodoin, D., Rm 12,1–2 – une intrigue discursive. De l'offrande des membres à l'offrandre des corps, in: ETR 85 (2010), 499–512.
Kaminsky, J.S., Loving one's (Israelite) neighbor. Election and commandment in Leviticus 19, in: Interpretation 62 (2008), 123–132.
Kamlah, E., Prophetie und Paränese. Ein Vergleich des Gebots der Feindesliebe in der Redenquelle mit der Ermahnung zu aufrichtiger Liebe in Römer 12,9 ff., in: „Ich bin ein Hebräer". Gedenken an Otto Michel, hg. von H. Lindner, Gießen 2003, 288–298.
Käsemann, E., Gottesgerechtigkeit bei Paulus (1961), in: E. Käsemann, Exegetische Versuche und Besinnungen II, Göttingen 1964, 181–193.
Kertelge, K., Das Doppelgebot der Liebe im Markusevangelium, in: TThZ 103 (1994), 48–55.
Kieffer, R., Traditions juives selon Mc 7,1–23, in : Texts and contexts. Biblical texts in their textual and situational context. FS Lars Hartmann, ed. by T. Fornberg, Oslo 1995, 675–688.
Kiilunen, J., Das Doppelgebot der Liebe in synoptischer Sicht. Ein redaktionskritischer Versuch über Mk 12,28–34 und die Parallelen (AASF.B 250), Helsinki 1989.
Kirchschläger, P.G., Die eschatologische Dimension von Liebe. 1 Kor 13 und der ‚andere Weg', in: BiLi 85 (2012), 61–72.

Konradt, M., Die Christonomie der Freiheit. Zu Paulus' Entfaltung seines ethischen Ansatzes in Gal 5,13–6,10, in: Early Christianity 1 (2010), 60–81.

—, Gericht und Gemeinde. Eine Studie zur Bedeutung und Funktion der Gerichtsaussagen im Rahmen der paulinischen Ekklesiologie und Ethik im 1Thess und 1Kor (BZNW 117), Berlin 2003.

—, Menschen- und Bruderliebe? Beobachtungen zum Liebesgebot in den Testamenten der Zwölf Patriarchen, in: ZNW 88 (1997), 296–310.

Kremer, J., Jesu Wort zur Ehescheidung, in: Geschieden – Wiederverheiratet – Abgewiesen? Antworten der Theologie QD 157, hg. von Th. Schneider, Freiburg/Basel/Wien 1995, 51–67.

Lindemann, A., Jesus und der Sabbat. Zum literarischen Charakter der Erzählung Mk 3,1–6, in: Text und Geschichte. FS Dieter Lührmann, hg. von S. Maser/E. Schlarb (MThSt 50), Marburg 1999, 122–135.

Lohse, E., Der Brief an die Römer (KEK IV), Göttingen 2003.

Maggi, A., ‚Il sabato è per l'uomo e non l'uomo per il sabato' (Mc 2,27), in: A partire dai cocci rotti. Problema divorziati; riflessioni, ricerca, prospettive, eds. N. Trentacoste/G. Cereti, Assisi 2001, 42–56.

Marcus, J., ‚I believe – help my unbelief!' Human Faith and Divine Faithfulness in Mark 9.14–29, in: Paul, Grace and Freedom. FS John K. Riches, eds. P. Middleton/A. Paddison/K. Wenell, London/New York 2009, 39–49.

Mathys, H.-P., Liebe deinen Nächsten wie dich selbst. Untersuchungen zum alttestamentlichen Gebot der Nächstenliebe (OBO 71), Freiburg i.d. Schweiz/Göttingen 1986.

Meiser, M., Reinheitsfragen und Begräbnissitten. Der Evangelist Markus als Zeuge der jüdischen Alltagskultur, in: Neues Testament und hellenistisch-jüdische Alltagskultur. Wechselseitige Wahrnehmungen. III. Internationales Symposium zum Corpus Judaeo-Hellenisticum Novi Testamenti, hg. von R. Deines/J. Herzer/K.-W. Niebuhr (WUNT 274), Tübingen 2011, 443–446.

Meisinger, H., Liebesgebot und Altruismusforschung. Ein exegetischer Beitrag zum Dialog zwischen Theologie und Naturwissenschaft (NTOA 33), Freiburg i.d. Schweiz/Göttingen 1996.

Merklein, H., Gericht und Heil. Zur heilsamen Funktion des Gerichts bei Johannes dem Täufer, Jesus und Paulus (1990), in: H. Merklein, Studien zu Jesus und Paulus II (WUNT 105), Tübingen 1998, 60–81.

Navarro, L.S., El cumplimiento del amor. Derás neotestamentario de LV 19,18B., in: EstB 66 (2008), 499–529.

Niebuhr, K.-W., Offene Fragen zur Gesetzespraxis bei Paulus und seinen Gemeinden (Sabbat, Speisegebote, Beschneidung), in: BThZ 25 (2008), 16–51.

Nüssel, F., ‚Ich lebe, doch nun nicht ich, sondern Christus lebt in mir'. Dogmatische Überlegungen zur Rede vom Sein in Christus, in: ZThK 99 (2002), 480–502.

Ottenheim, E., Impurity between Intention and Deed. Purity Disputes in First Century Judaism and in the New Testament, in: Purity and Holiness. The Heritage of Leviticus (JCPS 2), eds. M.J.H.M. Poorthuis/J. Schwarz, Leiden u.a. 2000, 129–147.

Oyen, G. van, Marcus 10:13–16: als was men een kind, in: NedThT 57 (2003), 177–192.

Pigeon, C., ‚La loi du Christ' en Galates 6,2 , in: SR 29 (2000), 425–438.

Pikaza, X., Exorcismo, poder y evangelio. Trasfondo histórico y eclesial de Mc 9,38–40, in: EstB 57 (1999), 539–564.

Prast, F., Ein Appell zur Besinnung auf das Juden wie Christen gemeinsame Erbe im Munde Jesu. Das Anliegen einer alten vormarkinischen Tradition (Mk 12,28–34), in: Gottesverächter und Menschenfeinde? Juden zwischen Jesus und frühchristlicher Kirche, hg. von H. Goldstein, Düsseldorf 1979, 79–88.

Queller, K., ‚Stretch out your hand!' Echo and metalepsis in Mark's sabbath healing controversy, in: JBL 129 (2010), 737–758.

Rabens, V., Power from in Between. The Relational Experience of the Holy Spirit and Spiritual Gifts in the Paul's Churches, in: The Spirit and Christ in the New Testament and Christian Theology. Festschrift Max Turner, eds. I.H. Marshall/V. Rabens/C. Bennema, Grand Rapids/Cambridge 2012, 138–155.

Reinbold, W., Die Nächstenliebe (Lev 19,18), in: Die Verheißung des Neuen Bundes. Wie alttestamentliche Texte im Neuen Testament fortwirken, hg. von B. Kollmann (BTSP 35), Göttingen 2010, 115–127.

Romanello, S., La condizione e il futuro dei credenti. Lo sguardo di Rm 5,1–11, in: Nuovo Testamento. Teologia in dialogo culturale. Scritti in onore di Romano Penna nel suo 70, Compleanno, ed. by N. Ciola (RevBib.S 60), Bologna 2008, 233–247.

Russell, E.A., A plea for tolerance (Mark 9.38–40), in: IBSt 8 (1986), 154–160.

Sänger, D., Recht und Gerechtigkeit in der Verkündigung Jesu. Erwägungen zu Mk 10,17–22 und 12,28–34, in: BZ 36 (1992), 179–184.

Schlier, H., Der Brief an die Galater (KEK VII), Göttingen ^{15}1989 (^{10}1949).

Schlosser, J., L' exorciste étranger (Mc 9,38–39), in: RevSR 56 (1982), 229–239.

—, Q 11,23 et la christologie, in: Von Jesus zum Christus. Christologische Studien. FS Paul Hoffmann, hg. von R. Hoppe/U. Busse (BZNW 93), Berlin 1998, 217–224.

Schnelle, U., Paulus. Leben und Denken, Berlin 2003.

—, Theologie des Neuen Testaments, Göttingen 2007.

Schürmann, H., Das ‚Gesetz des Christus' (Gal 6,2). Jesu Verhalten und Wort als letztgültige sittliche Norm nach Paulus (1974), in: H. Schürmann, Studien zur neutestamentlichen Ethik (SBAB 7), Stuttgart 1990, 53–76.

Schwartz, B.J. (ed.), Perspectives on purity and purification in the Bible (Library of Hebrew Bible, Old Testament studies 474), New York/London 2008.

Shauf, S., Galatians 2.20 in context, in: NTS 52 (2006), 86–101.

Söding, Th., ‚Ich lebe, aber nicht ich' (Gal 2,20). Die theologische Physiognomie des Paulus, in: Communio 38 (2009), 119–134.

—, Art. „Liebe", in: TBLNT 2 (2000), 1318–1326. 1329–1331.

—, Das Liebesgebot bei Paulus. Die Mahnung zur Agape im Rahmen der paulinischen Ethik (NTA 26), Münster 1995.

—, Die Freiheit des Glaubens. Konkretionen der Soteriologie nach dem Galaterbrief, in: Frühjudentum und Neues Testament im Horizont Biblischer Theologie, hg. von W. Kraus/K.-W. Niebuhr (WUNT 192),Tübingen 2003, 113–134.

—, Die Trias Glaube, Hoffnung, Liebe bei Paulus. Eine exegetische Studie (SBS 150), Stuttgart 1992.

—, Die Verkündigung Jesu – Ereignis und Erinnerung, Freiburg/Basel/Wien ^{2}2012 (2011).

—, Echtes Opfer. Gottesdienst bei Paulus, in: Objektive Feier und subjektiver Glaube? Beiträge zum Verhältnis von Liturgie und Spiritualität, hg. von S. Böntert (Studien zur Pastoraltheologie 32), Regensburg 2011, 9–34.

—, Feindeshaß und Bruderliebe. Beobachtungen zur essenischen Ethik, in: RdQ 17 (1995), 601–619.

—, Glaube, der durch Liebe wirkt. Rechtfertigung und Ethik im Galaterbrief, in: Umstrittener Galaterbrief. Studien zur Situierung der Theologie des Paulusschreibens, hg. von B. Kollmann/M. Bachmann (BThSt 106), Neukirchen-Vluyn 2010, 165–206.

—, Gottesliebe bei Paulus, in: Th. Söding, Das Wort vom Kreuz. Studien zur paulinischen Theologie (WUNT 93), Tübingen 1997, 303–326.

—, Heilsamer Glaube. Die synoptische Tradition, in: Gottvertrauen. Die ökumenische Diskussion um die Fiducia, hg. von I.U. Dalferth/S. Peng-Keller, QD 250, Freiburg/Basel/Wien 2012, 48–79.

—, Jesus und die Kirche. Was sagt das Neue Testament?, Freiburg/Basel/Wien 2007.

—, Solidarität in der Diaspora. Das Liebesgebot nach den Testamenten der Zwölf Patriarchen im Vergleich mit dem Neuen Testament, in: Kairos 36/37 (1994/95), 1–19.

—, Starke und Schwache. Der Götzenopferstreit in Korinth als ethisches Paradigma (1994), in: Th. Söding, Das Wort vom Kreuz. Studien zur paulinischen Theologie (WUNT 93), Tübingen 1997, 346–369.

—, Zur Freiheit befreit. Paulus und die Kritik der Autonomie, in: Communio 37 (2008), 92–112.

Stasiak, S.J., Controversia in Galilea e guarigione dell'uomo con la mano inaridita. Analisi sincronica di Mc 3,1–6, in: Antonianum 77 (2002), 617–647.

Theißen, G., Das Doppelgebot der Liebe. Jüdische Ethik bei Jesus, in: G. Theißen, Jesus als historische Gestalt. Beiträge zur Jesusforschung, hg. von A. Merz (FRLANT 202), Göttingen 2003, 57–72.

Theobald, M., Die überströmende Gnade. Studien zu einem paulinischen Motivfeld (FzB 22), Würzburg 1982.

Tiwald, M., ΑΠΟ ΔΕ ΑΡΧΗΣ ΚΤΙΣΕΩΣ … (Mk 10,36): Die Entsprechung von Protologie und Eschatologie als Schlüssel für das Tora-Verständnis Jesu, in: Erinnerung an Jesus. Kontinuität und Diskontinuität in der neutestamentlichen Überlieferung. FS Rudolf Hoppe, hg. von U. Busse (BBB 166), Göttingen 2011, 367–380.

Todd, W.A., „Under Law" in Galatians. A Pauline theological abbreviation, in: JThS 56 (2005), 362–392.

Vasconcellos, P.L., Guardar o sábado: como? Anotações sobre Mc 2,27., in: EstB 51 (1996), 50–57.

Vorholt, R., Alle Wege führen nach Rom. Die Hauptstadt im Blickfeld des Paulus, in: Das frühe Christentum und die Stadt, hg. von R. von Bendemann/M. Tiwald (BWANT 198), Stuttgart 2012, 204–237.

Vouga, F., ‚Habt Glauben an Gott!' Der Theozentrismus der Verkündigung des Evangeliums und des christlichen Glaubens im Markusevangelium, in: Texts and contexts. Biblical texts in their textual and situational context. FS Lars Hartmann, ed. by T. Fornberg, Oslo 1995, 93–109.

Walter, M., Gemeinde als Leib Christi. Untersuchungen zum Corpus Paulinum und zu den „Apostolischen Vätern" (NTOA 49), Freiburg i.d. Schweiz/Göttingen 2001.

Weihs, A., Die Deutung des Todes Jesu im Markusevangelium. Eine exegetische Studie zu den Leidens- und Auferstehungsansagen (FzB 99), Würzburg 2003.

Weiss, W., „Eine neue Lehre in Vollmacht". Die Streit- und Schulgespräche des Markus-Evangeliums (BZNW 52), Berlin 1989.

Wenham, D., Paul. Follower of Jesus or Founder of Christianity, Grand Rapids 1995.

Werner, M., Der Einfluß paulinischer Theologie im Markusevangelium. Eine Studie zur neutestamentlichen Theologie (BZNW 1), Gießen 1923.

Wilckens, U., Theologie des Neuen Testaments I/3, Neukirchen-Vluyn 2005.
Winger, M., The Law of Christ, in: NTS 46 (2000), 537–546.
Wischmeyer, O., Der höchste Weg. Das 13. Kapitel des 1. Korintherbriefes (StNT 13), Gütersloh 1981.
Wolter, M., Paulus. Ein Grundriss seiner Theologie, Neukirchen-Vluyn 2011.

Lorenzo Scornaienchi
Die Relativierung des Unreinen.
Der Einfluss des Paulus auf „Markus"
in Bezug auf die Reinheit

1 Markus und Paulus, zwei verwandte Gestalten

Das berühmte Diptychon von Albrecht Dürer „Die vier Apostel" von 1526 ist ein seltenes ikonographisches Beispiel für die gemeinsame Darstellung von Paulus und Markus. Das Gemälde besteht aus zwei Holztafeln, die je zwei Apostel abbilden: Petrus und Johannes auf einer Tafel, Paulus und Markus auf der anderen[1]. Die unübliche Zusammenstellung der vier Apostel beruht vielleicht auf der Annahme, dass der Evangelist Markus identisch mit jenem Johannes Markus, Mitarbeiter des Paulus, sei, von dem die Paulusbriefe sprechen[2]. Im Bild ist Paulus mit einem langen weißen Gewand bekleidet und steht im Profil im Vordergrund. Er trägt einen dicken Band, sein Briefcorpus, in der linken Hand und stützt sich mit der rechten Hand auf ein langes Schwert – Hinweis auf die Art seiner Hinrichtung[3]. Markus, der wesentlich jünger ist, ist dunkel gekleidet, steht hinter Paulus und schaut diesen wie ein treuer Schüler voller Ehrfurcht an. Er trägt eine Schriftrolle in der Hand, sein Evangelium. Paulus selbst schaut seitlich direkt dem Betrachter ins Auge.

Die hier im Bild alludierte These, Markus sei ein Schüler des *Paulus* gewesen, wird in der modernen Exegese von verschiedener Seite bekräftigt. Daneben steht

---

[1] Bayerische Staatsgemäldesammlungen – Alte Pinakothek München, Inv.-Nr. 545, 540. Kirchengeschichtlich grundlegend: K. Arndt/B. Moeller, Albrecht Dürers „Vier Apostel". Eine kirchen- und kunsthistorische Untersuchung (NAWG.PH 4/2003), Göttingen 2003.
[2] Apg 12,12; 12,25; 15,37-39; Kol 4,10; Phlm 24; 2Tim 4,11; 1Petr 5,13. Nach H.J. Holtzmann, Lehrbuch der historisch-kritischen Einleitung in das Neue Testament, Freiburg 1885, 372, ist die Verbindung des Johannes Markus zu Petrus allerdings stärker als zu Paulus. Johannes Markus stammt aus Jerusalem und ist seit Apg 12,12 mit Petrus befreundet. 1Petr 5,13 nennt ihn sogar Sohn des Petrus. Mit Paulus war er nur durch Barnabas in Kontakt, und er wendet sich schließlich auch von Paulus ab, als Barnabas sich von diesem entfremdet. Allerdings steht in Phlm 24 Johannes Markus noch in Verbindung zu Paulus. W. Kümmel, Einleitung in das Neue Testament, Heidelberg [17]1973, 69, widerlegt diese These einer Identifizierung des Evangelisten mit Johannes Markus mit folgenden Argumenten: Die schlechte Kenntnis der palästinischen Geographie und die polemische Ausrichtung passen nicht gut zu einem gebürtigen Jerusalemer.
[3] Vgl. S. Vollenweider, Art. Paulus, in: RGG[4] 5 (2003), 1035-1065, Sp. 1060. Das Schwert symbolisiert die Art der Hinrichtung und die Verkündigung des Evangeliums (Eph 6,17; Hebr 4,12).

aber die alte Annahme, dass Markus eher als Schüler des *Petrus* zu verstehen sei. Der Verfasser des zweiten Evangeliums sei der Dolmetscher des Petrus in Rom gewesen und habe uns schließlich die „Erinnerungen" des Petrus in seinem Evangelium überliefert[4]. Welche Bedeutung Dürer selbst dieser bildlichen Komposition zugeschrieben hat, ist nicht geklärt[5]. Aus der Beobachtung der Gesichter könnte die Auffassung abgeleitet werden, nach der die vier Gestalten die vier Temperamente (Choleriker, Melancholiker, Phlegmatiker und Sanguiniker) verkörpern sollen[6]. Die Absicht des Malers kann aber nicht nur die Darstellung der vier Temperamente gewesen sein. Die vier Gestalten des frühen Christentums sind für Dürer, der die Anfänge der Reformation mit großen Hoffnungen verfolgte, vielmehr vier autoritative Verfasser der neutestamentlichen Schriften, die in diesen Schriften klar Stellung gegen die falsche Prophetie bezogen haben. Zu diesem Zweck fügte Dürer den Bildtafeln Unterschriften mit Zitaten aus dem Markusevangelium, den Paulusbriefen, den Johannesbriefen und den Petrusbriefen bei, die sich gegen die falsche Prophetie richten und dem Rat der Stadt Nürnberg als Warnung dienen sollten[7]. Die vier Autoren („treffliche vier menner" steht auf der Tafel) sollten gemäß Dürer die Obrigkeit seiner Zeit belehren. Dabei war Dürer der Auffassung, dass *Paulus und Markus* als theologische Autoren zusammengehören.

Die Rolle des Markus[8] als Autor ist aber bis heute umstritten. Entweder wird er als der nicht originelle Schüler des Petrus oder jedenfalls als derjenige verstanden, der *ex post* die matthäische Fassung des Evangeliums epitomeartig zusammengefasst hat, oder aber als erster Sammler und Redaktor von Jesustraditionen. Aber auch die zweite Hypothese von der Markuspriorität, die die moderne Exegese

---

[4] Diese These vertreten die meisten Autoren der frühchristlichen Literatur. Eusebius geht auf das Zeugnis des Papias zurück, Historia ecclesiastica 39,15; Irenäus, Adversus haereses III 20–23 schreibt: „post vero horum excessum, Marcus discipulus et interpres Petri et ipse quae a Petro adnuntiata erant per scripta nobis tradidit".

[5] Die symbolische Bedeutung dieses Diptychons untersucht: V. Ritter, Die „vier Apostel" in beiden Darstellungen von Albrecht Dürer. Die verborgene Geometrie und die Echtheitsfrage, Kaufbeuren 2001.

[6] Diese Theorie wurde bereits seit 1547 in den „Nachrichten von Künstlern und Werkleuten" von Johann Neudörffer vertreten. Johannes sei der Sanguiniker, Petrus der Phlegmatiker, Markus der Choleriker und Paulus der Melancholiker (vgl. M. Schawe, Dürer, Albrecht: Vier Apostel, in: Historisches Lexikon Bayerns, URL: http://www.historisches-lexikon-bayerns.de/artikel/artikel_45639) (1.9.2010). Weiteres bei G. Pfeiffer, Die Vorbilder zu Albrecht Dürers „Vier Aposteln". Melanchthon und sein Nürnberger Freundeskreis, Nürnberg 1960, 3.

[7] Die Stellen sind 2Tim 3,1–7 und Mk 12,38–40 einerseits und 1Petr 2,1–3 und 1Joh 4,1–3 andererseits.

[8] Die Frage, ob der Verfasser Markus hieß, wird hier nicht diskutiert. ‚Markus' meint den Verfasser des Evangeliums nach Markus.

beherrscht, hat die Position des Markus nicht nachhaltig verbessert. Die Formgeschichte hat ihn als Sammler, nicht als Autor verstanden. Auch die Redaktionsgeschichte ließ das theologische und literarische Gewicht des Markus noch als eher gering erscheinen. Der folgende Vergleich des Paulus mit Markus versteht dagegen Markus als *Autor* und setzt voraus, dass Markus und Paulus *die* beiden innovativen Persönlichkeiten in den christlichen Gemeinden der ersten Jahrzehnte waren: Paulus als Urheber der Schriftlichkeit der christusbekennenden Gemeinden und des Gebrauchs der Briefform, Markus als Verfasser des ersten christlichen Buches, des Evangeliums[9].

2 Methodische Überlegung

Der theologische Vergleich von Markus und Paulus ist ein modernes Anliegen. Nachdem die historisch-kritische Exegese die patristischen Belege zur *biographischen* Identität des Markus in Frage gestellt hatte, legte es sich nahe, seine *theologische* Identität bzw. Individualität zu hinterfragen. Ob Markus mit Petrus oder mit Paulus in Zusammenhang stand, lässt sich nur im theologischen Vergleich dieser Autoren untersuchen, da explizite historische Hinweise auf Abhängigkeiten oder Einflüsse gänzlich fehlen. Der Vergleich wird jedoch durch die literarische und inhaltliche Heterogenität von Evangelium und Brief erschwert. Das Evangelium setzt als narrative Gattung andere Schwerpunkte als der Brief. Die Gestalt Jesu wird im Evangelium in seinen irdischen Aspekten dargestellt, während für Paulus die Beschreibung des Lebens Jesu gerade nicht interessant ist[10]. Die literarischen, historischen und inhaltlichen Unterschiede des ältesten Evangeliums zu den Briefen des Paulus könnten die beiden Werke als unvergleichbar erscheinen lassen. In der Fachliteratur findet man dennoch eine breite Palette an Möglichkeiten, wie sich ein allfälliger Einfluss des Paulus auf Markus definieren

---

9 Vgl. O. Wischmeyer, Forming Identity Through Literature: The Impact of Mark for the Building of Christ-Believing Communities in the Second Half of the First Century C.E., in: Mark and Matthew I. Comparative Readings. Understanding the Earliest Gospels in their First-Century Settings, eds. E.-M. Becker/A. Runesson (WUNT 271), Tübingen 2011, 355-378, S. 377.
10 J.C. Fenton, Paul and Mark, in: Studies in the Gospels: Essays in Memory of R.H. Lightfoot, ed. by D.E. Nineham, Oxford 1955, 89–112, hier: 89, betont diesen Unterschied der beiden Gattungen. Seine Meinung „the Epistles are easier than the Gospel", (ebenda), ist dagegen nicht plausibel.

lassen könnte[11]. Aus methodischer Perspektive sind vor allem zwei Ansätze zu unterscheiden.

Der erste Ansatz geht *apriorisch-deduktiv* vor. Vorausgesetzt wird, dass Paulus der wichtigste Theologe der frühchristlichen Kirche war, mit dem sich alle Autoren gemessen haben. Eine Abhängigkeit muss daher nicht bewiesen werden, sondern wird als gegeben angenommen. Diese Position vertritt vor allem die Tübinger Schule, durch die dieser Vergleich zum ersten Mal thematisiert wurde. F. Chr. Baur prägte den Begriff des „Paulinismus", um die besondere Richtung der paulinischen Theologie in der frühchristlichen Kirche zu benennen. Der Paulinismus koinzidiert mit der Theologie des Paulus und ist zugleich eine besondere Bewegung, die sich über die Wirkung des Paulus hinaus verbreitete. Paulinismus heißt nach Baur die Überwindung des auf dem Gesetz beruhenden jüdischen Partikularismus und der Durchbruch des christlichen Universalismus[12]. Gerade dieser Universalismus verursachte nach Baur die Reaktion des Judenchristentums, das den gesetzlich basierten jüdischen Partikularismus beibehalten wollte. Alle Briefe des Paulus dokumentieren nach Baur diesen Konflikt des Apostels mit dem Judenchristentum[13]. Baur beschreibt die Entwicklung der christlichen Theologie mithilfe der Hegelschen Dialektik, insbesondere mit der Abfolge von These, Antithese und Synthese. Paulinismus und Judenchristentum finden eine Synthese in der katholischen, bischöflichen Kirche, indem Paulus und Petrus, Rechtfertigung und Werke, *nebeneinander* und nicht mehr in Gegensatz zueinander gestellt werden[14]. In diesem Schema steht Markus dem Paulinismus näher, ohne sich allerdings von dem Einfluss des Matthäusevangeliums lösen zu können[15]. Nach diesem ersten Ansatz gilt der Kommentar von Gustav H.J.Ph. Volkmar, der die

---

11 J.C. Fenton, Paul and Mark, 91, listet die verschiedenen Varianten auf: a) das Evangelium ist paulinisch und rechtfertigt die paulinische Theologie, b) das Evangelium ist von der hellenistischen prä-paulinischen Christologie beeinflusst, c) das Evangelium bezieht keine besondere theologische Position, d) das Evangelium ist petrinisch geprägt.
12 F.Chr. Baur, Geschichte der christlichen Kirche, Bd. 1, Tübingen ³1863, 44: „Er war es somit auch, welcher den christlichen Universalismus in seinem principiellen Unterschied von jüdischen Particularismus nicht nur zuerst ausdrücklich in bestimmter Form aussprach, sondern auch von Anfang an sosehr zur Aufgabe und leitenden Norm seines apostolischen Wirkens machte, dass er in seinem christlichen Bewusstsein das Eine von dem Anderen nicht trennen konnte, die Berufung zum Apostelamt und die Bestimmung des Christentums zum allgemeinen Heilprincip aller Völker".
13 F. Chr. Baur, Die Tübinger Schule und ihre Stellung zur Gegenwart, Tübingen ²1860, 38: „... worin besteht denn noch der prinzipielle Gegensatz des Judenchristentums und des Paulinismus? Er kann nur in dem Universalismus des Einen und dem Particularismus des Anderen gesetzt werden".
14 Ebd. 39-40.
15 Vgl. dazu den Beitrag von Johannes Wischmeyer im vorliegenden Band.

Theorie der Tübinger Schule aufnimmt, als Meilenstein des Vergleichs von Markus und Paulus. Nach Volkmar ist Markus ein Pauliner, der seinen Stoff kunstvoll und vernünftig ordnet. Er „lässt eine Ahnung aufgehen von der ganzen, wunderbaren Größe des so viel höheren Meisters"[16]. Die Funktion des Markusevangeliums sei es gewesen, einen Angriff gegen die Judenchristen einzuleiten und die Apologie der paulinischen Theologie zu übernehmen[17].

Die jüngst erschienene monographische Untersuchung von Eric K.C. Wong[18] steht ebenfalls diesem älteren methodischen Ansatz nahe. Wong setzt eine überwiegende Prägung der frühchristlichen Literatur durch Paulus voraus. Er geht davon aus, dass Paulus als „die bedeutendste Gestalt am Anfang des Christentums"[19] alle synoptischen Evangelien, sogar das Matthäusevangelium, beeinflusst habe. Dieses Evangelium führe eine verdeckte Polemik gegen die Positionen des Paulus zum Gesetz[20]. Wong spricht von „Echos" des Paulus in den synoptischen Evangelien. Allerdings relativiert er die Bedeutung des paulinischen Einflusses insofern, als er sich vor allem auf diejenigen Logia Jesu konzentriert, die sowohl in den Briefen des Paulus als auch im Markusevangelium zitiert oder alludiert werden. Wong stellt ein komplexes Szenarium her, in dem Paulus und die Synoptiker aus einem gemeinsamen Traditionsgut schöpfen. In diesem neuen Versuch, einen apriorischen Einfluss des Paulus auf die neutestamentliche Evangelienliteratur zu belegen, fehlt aber eine historische Erklärung dafür, wie sich die theologischen Strömungen in den christlichen Gemeinden ausgewirkt haben. Anders als die von Hegel beeinflusste Tübinger Exegese bleibt die Intertextualitätstheorie, mit der Wong arbeitet, hier historisch ungenau.

Der zweite methodische Ansatz ist *induktiv* und versucht, die Mängel der apriorischen Methode zu beheben. Aus meiner Sicht kommt hier vor allem die gegenwärtige Abneigung gegen eine systemische Theorie zum Ausdruck. Die in-

---

16 G. Volkmar, Die Evangelien oder Marcus und die Synopsis der kanonischen und ausserkanonischen Evangelien: Nach dem ältesten Text mit historisch-exegetischem Commentar, Leipzig 1870, 301.
17 G. Volkmar sieht in Mk 9,38 eine „Philippica gegen Pauliner". Der Evangelist macht diesen Einwand zum Grund einer offenen Apologie für Paulus: Jesus lässt auch andere, die nicht seine direkten Nachfolger sind, als Jünger zu.
18 E.K.C. Wong, Evangelien im Dialog mit Paulus. Eine intertextuelle Studie zu den Synoptikern (NTOA 89), Göttingen 2011.
19 E.K.C. Wong, Evangelien im Dialog mit Paulus, 24.
20 E.K.C. Wong, Evangelien im Dialog mit Paulus, 107–130. Diese Hypothese einer verdeckten Polemik des Matthäus gegen Paulus vertritt auch G. Theißen, Kritik an Paulus im Matthäusevangelium? Von der verdeckten Polemik im Urchristentum, in: Polemik in der frühchristlichen Literatur. Texte und Kontexte, hg. von O. Wischmeyer/L. Scornaienchi (BZNW 170), Berlin/New York 2011, 465–490.

duktive Perspektive geht nicht mehr von einer allgemeinen Prägung der neutestamentlichen Schriften durch Paulus aus, sondern beschränkt dessen Einfluss auf wenige Themen oder Vorstellungen, die durch Vergleiche expliziert werden müssen. Diesem Ansatz folgt Martin Werner in seiner Monographie über den „Einfluß paulinischer Theologie auf das Markusevangelium". Werner will aber durch die induktive Methodik nicht nur die Konstruktion des Paulinismus[21], sondern mit William Wrede auch die zentrale Rolle der Rechtfertigungslehre für die Theologie des Paulus in Frage stellen[22]. Die angestellten Vergleiche betreffen einige wichtige Themen der paulinischen Theologie: Christologie, Gesetz und Evangelium, Glauben und Sünde, Sakramente, Eschatologie, Juden und Heiden. In all diesen Themen sieht Werner keine besondere paulinische Prägung, sondern die Übernahme von allgemeinen Positionen, die in den christlichen Gemeinden verbreitet waren. Am Schluss seiner Untersuchung fasst Werner seinen wissenschaftlichen Ertrag in Form von Thesen zusammen:

(1) Wo Markus mit Paulus übereinstimmt, handelt es sich immer um allgemein-christliche Anschauungen. (2) Wo in den Briefen über diese gemeinsame Basis hinaus besondere, charakteristische paulinische Anschauungen zutage treten, da fehlen entweder bei Markus die Parallelen vollständig, oder Markus vertritt geradezu entgegengesetzte Standpunkte. (3) Von einem Einfluss paulinischer Theologie im Markusevangelium kann daher nicht im Geringsten die Rede sein[23].

Was allerdings bei Werner nicht thematisiert wird, ist die Definition des Begriffs „Einfluss"[24]. Die intertextuelle Fragestellung lässt eine breite Vielfalt von Möglichkeiten, diesen Begriff zu verstehen, zu. Nach Werners Verständnis ist es nicht notwendig, dass eine Uniformität der Positionen vorliegt: Ein Schüler kann von seinem Meister beeinflusst werden und die übernommenen Ansichten trotzdem neu formulieren. Dabei scheint es mir wichtig, wiederum von theologischen Strömungen zu sprechen und das Besondere einer theologischen Richtung zu erkennen. Paulus und Markus beziehen sich gleichermaßen auf Jesus, um ihre Position zu den Reinheitsgesetzen zu bekräftigen. Das allein könnte bereits

---

[21] M. Werner, Der Einfluß paulinischer Theologie im Markusevangelium. Eine Studie zur neutestamentlichen Theologie (BZNW 1), Gießen 1923, 29–32.
[22] M. Werner, Der Einfluß paulinischer Theologie, 66.
[23] M. Werner, Der Einfluß paulinischer Theologie, 209.
[24] E.K.C. Wong, Evangelien im Dialog mit Paulus, 63, zieht dem Begriff „Einfluss" das Wort „Echo" vor: „Die Rede vom Einfluss des Paulus auf Markus ist ohnehin unangemessen" (ebenda).

ein Hinweis darauf sein, dass sich beide auf derselben theologischen Schiene bewegen[25].

Eine weitere Anwendung dieses Ansatzes findet man bei John C. Fenton, der ebenfalls keine klaren Hinweise auf einen paulinischen Charakter des Markusevangeliums findet. Die Themen, die er untersucht, sind: Erfüllung, Verborgenheit und Offenbarung, Niederlage und Sieg, Herrschaft Jesu, Glaube und Nachfolge und Zukunftserwartung. Er kommt zu dem Schluss, dass die Beweise für einen Einfluss des Paulus auf das Evangelium nicht eindeutig sind:

> „The extent evidence points as much to Mark's companionship with Paul as to Mark's companionship with Peter"[26].

Beide Ansätze, der deduktive und der induktive, können sich gegenseitig ergänzen. Paulus war mit seinen Briefen sicherlich eine prägende theologische Persönlichkeit in den frühen Gemeinden. Um eine theologische Priorität des Paulus nachzuweisen, sind jedoch vergleichende Analysen der verschiedenen Themen notwendig. Ein rein theologischer und terminologischer Vergleich mit der Suche nach einer perfekten Entsprechung der Aussagen, wie Werner ihn konzipiert, ist dabei von vornherein zum Scheitern verurteilt. Im Markusevangelium findet man immer wieder Abweichungen von und Kontinuitäten zur paulinischen Tradition.

Im Folgenden frage ich nach der *Reinheit* als Thema einer bestimmten Debatte oder eines prägenden Diskurses in den christlichen Gemeinden der ersten Generationen. Die Reinheit ist kein einfaches *Theologoumenon*, sondern ein fundamentales Thema, das eine religiöse und rituelle Positionierung in Theorie und Praxis erfordert. Je nachdem wie sie definiert wurde, bezogen die frühchristlichen Gemeinden und ihre Autoren eine Stellung, die eine theologische Richtung determinierte. Die markinische Position zu diesem Thema soll nun mit der paulinischen Auffassung verglichen werden, um festzustellen, ob sie sich als Entwicklung aus der Konzeption des Apostels verstehen lässt. Dabei können die Begriffe von Diskurs oder Debatte das Verhältnis zweier Autoren wie Paulus und Markus, bei denen Kontinuitäten und Variationen festzustellen sind, am besten beschreiben. Beide beteiligten sich an derselben Debatte und blieben einer gewissen Linie treu, ohne unbedingt dieselben Aussagen zu machen. Dies detailliert darzustellen ist das Ziel dieses Aufsatzes.

---

25 Dieser Aspekt des Bezuges von Markus und Paulus auf die Jesus-Tradition wird unten vertieft.
26 J.C. Fenton, Paul and Mark, 100.

3 Die Reinheit und der Begriff κοινός

Zunächst sind zwei Präzisierungen der Fragestellung notwendig.

Erstens: es geht in dieser Untersuchung um die Frage nach der Reinheit und der Unreinheit bei Paulus und bei Markus bezüglich des Gebrauchs des Terminus κοινός (und des Verbs κοινόω). Dazu sind einige Vorüberlegungen nötig. Die Konzeption von Reinheit ordnet die Beziehungen einer religiösen Gemeinschaft zur Außenwelt und fördert die Entwicklung eines Systems, das solche Beziehungen regelt. Das ist eine konstitutive Frage einer jeden Gemeinschaft, durch die sich diese gegen außen abgrenzt und nach innen eine Ordnung und eine gewisse Macht etabliert[27]. Für Israel darf allgemein gelten, was Hannah K. Harrington prägnant zusammenfasst:

> „Purity in early Jewish tradition usually refers to a state of ritual fitness necessary for the people of Israel to enjoy the holy presence and power of God. Impurity describes not only a lack of purity but a threatening force generated primarily by the human being. Less often, purity denotes physical cleanliness or the clarity of refined metals"[28].

H. Harrington weist weiter auf die doppelte Qualität von Reinheit/Unreinheit hin: Während im Pentateuch der rituelle Aspekt dominiert, liegt das Gewicht bei den übrigen Textgruppen auf dem ethischen Verständnis. Unreine Speisen stellen eine besondere Thematik im ersten Zusammenhang dar:

> „Impure, forbidden foods form an interesting juncture between ritual and moral impurity ... In the Second Temple period, the kosher diet became a sticking point among Jews under Hellenistic rule where pork was a food of choice"[29].

Zweitens: Die Studien von Mary Douglas haben dazu beigetragen, dass neben dieser religiösen auch die soziologische und anthropologische Relevanz der Reinheitsfrage und der Reinheitsgebote deutlich in den Blick kamen. Das Buch

---

[27] G. Theißen, Die Religion der ersten Christen. Eine Theorie des Urchristentums, Gütersloh ⁴2008, 156, betont vor allem diesen internen Aspekt der Reinheitsfrage. Die Unterscheidung heilig/unheilig sei daher ein Mittel zur Machtsicherung. Sie gehört zu den „Strategien zur Statussicherung, zur Abgrenzung von Laien, zur Sicherung von Privilegien". Die Abgrenzung innerhalb einer Gemeinschaft wird in den anthropologischen und soziologischen Studien selten behandelt. Da ist die Hauptfrage die Abgrenzung von der Welt.
[28] H.K. Harrington, Art. Purity and Impurity, in: The Eerdmans Dictionary of Early Judaism, Grand Rapids/Cambridge UK 2010, 1121–1123, hier: 1121.
[29] Ebd.

Leviticus wurde in dieser Hinsicht wissenschaftlich neu interessant[30]. Nach Douglas ist die Reinheit die Definition eines Systems, in dem eine gewisse Ordnung gegeben ist:

> „Dirt was created by the differentiating activity of mind, it was a by-product of the creation order"[31].

Die Befolgung der Reinheitsgebote diene dazu, die Schöpfung vor der Gefährdung durch das Chaos (Unreinheit) zu bewahren. Jerome H. Neyrey, der die These von M. Douglas als Neutestamentler rezipiert, unterscheidet verschiedene „maps", die diese Ordnung hierarchisch schützen: Orte (map of places), Menschen (map of people); Unreinheiten (map of impurities) und Zeiten (map of times)[32].

Eine *dritte* Überlegung gilt der Lexik und Semantik von „Reinheit". Meine Untersuchung konzentriert sich speziell auf den Gebrauch des Adjektivs κοινός und des Verbs κοινόω in Mk 7 und in Röm 14. Κοινός hat zunächst die allgemeine Bedeutung von „gemeinsam", „gemein", wird aber in der jüdisch-hellenistischen Literatur auch in der besonderen Bedeutung von „unrein" verwendet, eine semantische Konnotation, die sich vielleicht von der Vorstellung ableitet, dass das Gemeinsame/Gemeine gleichzeitig „ordinär" und daher „unrein" ist. Diese spezielle Bedeutung ist allerdings sprachlich nicht unmittelbar einsichtig und benötigt eine genaue Erklärung für Menschen, die diese Konnotation nicht kennen. Markus muss diesen Terminus also für seine nicht-jüdischen Leser erklären. Das geschieht in Mk 7,2–3, obwohl seine Erklärung nicht präzis ist: κοινός heißt tatsächlich etwas anderes als „ungewaschen".

Nun ziehen einige Exegeten die Bedeutung „unrein" für Mk 7 in Zweifel und versuchen, in dem markinischen Text eine andere Bedeutung zu finden, die der allgemeinen Bedeutung näher steht und nicht direkt mit „unrein" wiedergegeben werden kann. So vertritt Wolfgang Stegemann die Meinung, es handele sich bei κοινός nicht um einen *terminus technicus*: „Vielmehr bezeichnet er einen Zustand

---

[30] M. Douglas, Leviticus as Literature, Oxford/ New York 1999. Zur Auslegungsgeschichte von Lev vgl. M. Elliott, Engaging Leviticus: Reading Leviticus Theologically with Its Past Interpreters, Eugene 2012.
[31] M. Douglas, Purity and Danger. An Analysis of the Concept of Pollution and Taboo, London 1966, 161. Auf die Frage, warum das Schwein unrein sein soll, gebe es keine logische Antwort. Es sei nur aufgrund eines vorgegebenen Schemas so.
[32] J.H. Neyrey, The Idea of Purity in Mark's Gospel, in: Semeia 35 (1986), 91–128, hier: 94-98. Dieser soziologische Ansatz der Reinheitsgebote wird von der neuen alttestamentlichen Forschung in Frage gestellt, die die Unreinheit deutlicher mit der Sünde in Verbindung bringt und zu einer ethischen Interpretation neigt, vgl. J.S. Baden/C.R. Moss, The Origin and Interpretation of ṣāraʿat in Leviticus 13–14, in: JBL 130/4 (2011), 643–662.

der Alltäglichkeit bzw. des Allgemeinen, eben nicht einen aus dem Alltag herausgehobenen Zustand"[33]. Nach Christina Tuor-Kurth ist der Bezug auf die Gemeinschaft, κοινωνία, grundlegend für das Verständnis dieses besonderen Terminus[34]. Nach Clinton Wahlen ist der Terminus κοινός in der Vision des Petrus (Apg 10,14–15 und 11,8–9) eine Art dritter Begriff, der semantisch zwischen ἀκάθαρτον und καθαρός steht. Mit diesem Wort wurden gemäß Wahlen einige Speisen definiert, die rein sind, deren Reinheit aber nicht als gesichert gilt[35]. Die Heiden, die die jüdischen Reinheitsgebote akzeptiert hatten, konnten nicht in die Tischgemeinschaft aufgenommen werden, weil immer diese Unsicherheit bezüglich ihres Zustandes der Reinheit bestand. Das gebe eine neue Erklärung der Petrusvision: Gott sagt Petrus in Apg 10,15, er solle aufhören, Speisen als potentiell unrein (*potential* unclean) zu betrachten, die Gott für rein erklärt habe[36].

Betrachtet man aber die verschiedenen Belege in den Makkabäerbüchern, wird man doch κοινός als Synonym von „unrein" verstehen[37]. 1Makk 1,47 spricht von „Opfern von Schweinen und unreinen Tieren" als höchstem Grad der Unreinheit (ὕεια καὶ κτήνη κοινά). 1Makk 1,62 wendet dieses Adjektiv mit dem μὴ φαγεῖν κοινά auf die Speisen an. In 4Makk 7,6 wird der Priester Eleazar gelobt, denn er hat „seine heiligen Zähne nicht besudelt, seinen Magen, der Platz für

---

[33] W. Stegemann, Hat Jesus die Speisegesetze der Tora aufgehoben? Zur neuesten kontroversen Einschätzung der traditionellen Deutung des sog. „Reinheitslogion" von Mk 7,15, in: Jesus – Gestalt und Gestaltungen. Rezeptionen des Galiläers in Wissenschaft, Kirche und Gesellschaft. FS für G. Theißen, hg. von P. von Gemünden u.a. (NTOA 100), Göttingen 2013, 29–50, hier: 39. Um seine Auffassung zu erklären, erwähnt Stegemann das deutsche Wort „gemein", das eine breite Semantik hat (S. 40). Die Belege zeigen aber, dass es sich vielmehr gerade um einen terminus technicus handelt.
[34] C. Tuor-Kurth, Unreinheit und Gemeinschaft. Erwägungen zum neutestamentlichen Gebrauch von κοινός, in: ThZ 65/3 (2009), 229–245, hier: 232-233. E.K.C. Wong, Evangelien im Dialog mit Paulus, 89–90, vermutet auch einen Zusammenhang dieser Bedeutung „unrein" mit κοινωνία: „Aus der Gemeinschaft (mit Heiden) wurde im jüdischen Sprachgebrauch die Bedeutung „Befleckung" und „Verunreinigung"" (S. 90). Ich halte diese Vermutung für nicht korrekt. Die Erklärung könnte eher in der Vorstellung liegen, dass das Gemeinsame ordinär und nicht heilig ist. Im Tempelkult ist das Reine unzugänglich und vom Alltagsleben getrennt.
[35] C. Wahlen, Peter's Vision and Conflicting Definitions of Purity, in: NTS 51/4 (2005), 505–518, hier: 512: „The term κοινά is singularly appropriate to describe each doubtfully pure food, the acceptability of which could not be assured".
[36] C. Wahlen, Peter's Vision and Conflicting Definition of Purity, 515–516. Die Lösung von Wahlen würde ermöglichen, das neue Verständnis in Apg 10 und 11 zu relativieren. Die These ist aber philologisch nicht haltbar. Κοινός ist auch in Apg 10 ein Synonym von ἀκάθαρτος.
[37] E. Lohse, Der Brief an die Römer (KEK IV), Göttingen [15]2003, 377: „Das Adjektiv κοινός wurde im hellenistischen Judentum als Wiedergabe von hebräisch טמא gebraucht (vgl 1 Makk 1,47.62 u. ö.), um die von der Thora gebotene Unterscheidung von rein (καθαρός) und unrein (ἀκάθαρτος) zu bezeichnen".

Reinigung und Heiligkeit machte, nicht verunreinigt (κοινόω) mit schmutzigen Speisen"³⁸. Κοινός lässt sich daher im hellenistischen Judentum durchaus als Begriff für Unreinheit bezeichnen. Er ist ein Synonym von ἀκάθαρτος, wie man aus Apg 10,14 οὐδέποτε ἔφαγον πᾶν κοινὸν καὶ ἀκάθαρτον und in variierter Form in 11,8 μηδαμῶς, κύριε, ὅτι κοινὸν ἢ ἀκάθαρτον οὐδέποτε εἰσῆλθεν εἰς τὸ στόμα μου, entnehmen kann. Das Adjektiv ἀκάθαρτος benutzt Markus im Unterschied zu Lukas nur, um die Dämonen zu bezeichnen, von denen die Menschen besessen sein können, und nicht für rituell-gesetzliche Themen (Mk 1,23.26.27; 3,11.30; 5,2.8.13; 6,7; 7,25; 9,25). Das Substantiv καθαρισμός begegnet in 1,44, wo es die jüdischen Rituale für geheilte Leprakranke beschreibt, περὶ τοῦ καθαρισμοῦ σου ἃ προσέταξεν Μωϋσῆς. Im gleichen Zusammenhang findet sich zwei Mal das Verb καθαρίζειν für die Heilung von der Lepra. Eine weitere Stelle, in der das Verb vorkommt, ist Mk 7,19 mit einem klaren Bezug auf die Nahrungsgesetze. Jesus erklärt alle Speisen für rein. Paulus dagegen benutzt das Adjektiv ἀκάθαρτος nie, das Substantiv ἀκαθαρσία in einem allgemein ethischen Sinne meistens in Lasterkatalogen (Röm 1,24; 6,19; 2Kor 12,21; Gal 5,19). πάντα καθαρά setzt er in Röm 14,20 als Äquivalent zu οὐδὲν κοινόν.

Fazit: Paulus und Markus verwenden κοινός bzw. κοινόω für die rituelle Unreinheit von Speisen, wie es im jüdisch-hellenistischen Sprachgebrauch üblich war. Hier liegt die gemeinsame jüdisch-hellenistische terminologische Grundlage für Paulus und Markus.

4 Die Reinheit der Speisen in Röm 14,13–23

(1) Die Debatte über die Speisen in Röm 14 steht unter dem Vorzeichen der „Schwachen im Glauben". Sie erinnert semantisch und thematisch an die Opferfleischthematik in 1Kor 8 und 10. Die Unterscheidung von „Schwachen" und „Starken" zeigt, dass es weder in Korinth noch in Rom einfach um die Befolgung der *Speisegebote* geht, sondern um die *Kraft*, einen konsequenten freien Umgang mit Speisen zu praktizieren, die als problematisch galten³⁹. Unklar ist, ob die Begriffe „stark" und „schwach" eine soziale oder lediglich eine religiös-rituelle Konnotation haben, konkret, ob sie Menschen aus der Ober- bzw. Mittel- oder aus

---

38 So auch R. Jewett, Romans. A Commentary (Hermeneia), Minneapolis 2007, 859f.
39 U. Wilckens' Annahme, Der Brief an die Römer 3. (12–16) (EKK VI/3), Zürich u.a. 1982, 88, einer Ausbreitung der Auffassung der Starken in der römischen Gemeinde scheint mir unwahrscheinlich. Dabei handelt es sich vielmehr um eine typisch paulinische Terminologie, die er auch in einer unbekannten Situation wie der in Rom anwendet. Auch hier deutet Paulus an, dass er mit den Starken sympathisiert.

der Unterschicht meinen. Die Bezeichnungen scheinen jedenfalls aus der Auseinandersetzung in der korinthischen Gemeinde zu stammen, insbesondere aus dem Urteil einer Gruppe, die die anderen als Schwache disqualifizierte. Diese nahmen daran Anstoß, dass ein Teil der christlichen Gemeinde ohne Bedenken Opferfleisch aß. In Röm 14 nimmt Paulus die Terminologie der Korinther wieder auf, um die beiden möglichen Einstellungen zur Nahrung zu bezeichnen. Die Bezeichnung „stark" spiegelt eine bestimmte Perspektive: Sie beinhaltet eine Verurteilung jener, die gewisse Speisen ablehnen und daher als schwach im Glauben gelten.

Paulus vertritt in Röm 14 die Meinung, die *Überzeugung* des einzelnen Christen sei entscheidend. Wenn jemand eine religiöse Meinung vertritt, muss diese ernst genommen werden und darf nicht disqualifiziert werden. Paulus benutzt hier das Stichwort πίστις nicht primär als „Glauben" im theologischen Sinne (Glaube an Gott oder Glaube an Jesus Christus), sondern allgemein als „Überzeugung".[40] Paulus scheint in diesem Punkt mit der Semantik des Wortes zu spielen. Der Verzicht auf Fleisch allein ist kein „schwacher Glaube", sondern Ausdruck einer persönlichen Überzeugung, die nicht verurteilt werden darf. Diese Bedeutung von πίστις hält sich bis zum Ende des Kapitels (Rom 14,23) durch: „Alles, was nicht aus Überzeugung geschieht, ist Sünde"[41]. Paulus will auf keinen Fall, dass eine der

---

40 So auch J.A. Fitzmyer, Romans. A New Translation with Introduction and Commentary (AncB 33), New York u.a. 1993, 689. Gegen diese Interpretation vgl. B. Corsani, Hor tutto ciò che non è di fede, è peccato, in: Protestantesimo 34 (1979), 65–81, hier: 76-80: „Mi sembra chiaro che qui Paolo non ragiona in termini di „convinzione" o „non-convinzione", ma in termini di servizio di Cristo o servizio di noi stessi; di unione con Cristo o di isolamento nel nostro egoismo" (S. 78).
41 Die Interpretation dieses Satzes und des Wortes πίστις ist umstritten. Die meisten Exegeten übersetzen mit „Glauben". U. Wilckens, Der Brief an die Römer, 97, betont: „Wie durchweg in unserem Abschnitt, so ist gerade auch in V23 πίστις im vollen und präzisen Sinn als der Christusglaube gemeint". Die Aussage betone daher die Freiheit des Glaubens. So paraphrasiert Wilckens: „Alles, was einer, wenn auch vielleicht im Namen des Glaubens, aber nicht *aus* Glauben, nämlich nicht aus der *Freiheit* des Glaubens heraus tut, ist Sünde". E. Lohse, Der Brief an die Römer, 382, übersetzt πίστις ebenfalls mit „Glauben". Er will damit das Wort „Glauben" im Sinne von Gal 5,6 mit der Liebe in Verbindung setzen, die es dem Starken ermöglicht, die Schwachen zu verstehen und ihre Meinung zu akzeptieren: „Der negativen Formulierung des letzten Satzes entspricht daher die positive Aufgabe, daß der Glaube in der Liebe tätig zu sein hat". Für diese Deutung plädiert auch J.D.G. Dunn, Romans II, WBC 38b, Dallas 1988, 829; E. Käsemann, An die Römer (HNT 8a), Tübingen ⁴1980, 366, ist prinzipiell für die Deutung πίστις als Glauben, er gibt aber zu, dass hier eine allgemeine Bedeutung vorliegt, die ein eindimensionales Verständnis dieses Begriffes widerlegt: „Man kann auch zugeben, dass πίστις sich hier besonders dem profanen Wortgebrauch „Überzeugung" nähert, und wie anderswo Gläubigkeit, Christlichkeit oder das Christentum selbst bezeichnet." R. Bultmann, Theologie des Neuen Testaments (hg. von O. Merk), Tübingen ⁹1984, 220, hält den Begriff für praktisch identisch mit Gewissen in 1 Kor 8,11 und plädiert daher für die Bedeutung „Überzeugung". – Paulus kon-

beiden Parteien auf ihre Überzeugung verzichten muss und die Meinung des anderen einfach (ohne daran zu glauben) übernimmt. Der Weg ist daher nicht die Überredung des Anderen, auch nicht die Durchsetzung einer starken Position gegenüber den Schwachen, sondern die Annahme des Anderen in christlicher Liebe[42]. Soviel sei zur Textpragmatik gesagt.

(2) Ich komme nun zur Thematik im engeren Sinn. Das Kapitel leistet einen Beitrag zu der in der Antike oft debattierten Frage, ob es besser sei, Fleisch zu essen, oder ob eine vegetarische Ernährung vorzuziehen sei: φαγεῖν πάντα oder λάχανα ἐσθίειν[43]. Welchen Diskursstrang dieser von verschiedenen Gruppen geführten Debatte hat Paulus im Blick? In Röm 14,5 lässt die ‚Observanz der Tage' eine Konfrontation mit der Heiligung des Sabbats und daher eine indirekte Auseinandersetzung mit jüdischen Positionen vermuten, obwohl die Terminologie des Paulus so allgemein gehalten ist, dass sie auch zu anderen religiösen oder kulturellen Vorstellungen passt[44]. Es scheint mir aber trotz der ganz allgemeinen

---

frontiert in diesem Text zwei Überzeugungen, die er aus seiner Perspektive als „stark" und „schwach" definiert. Wichtig ist für ihn, dass niemand auf seine Überzeugung verzichten muss. Er bittet nur die Starken, den Schwachen mit Liebe zu begegnen. Ich teile daher die Meinung der Exegeten, die den Begriff allgemein als „Überzeugung" verstehen. J.A. Fitzmyer, Romans, 699–700, sieht in dieser Interpretation die Betonung der Neutralität vieler menschlicher Taten. Es handle sich um „confidence that proceeds from Christian faith, which is distinct from it and manifests itself as liberty with regard to indifferent matters" (S. 700).

42 Die Diskussion über die Bedeutung des Wortes πίστις bei Paulus kann hier nicht weiter vertieft werden. Man kann m.E. sagen, dass der „Glaube" sich für Paulus ausschließlich auf die Lebenskraft Gottes stützt, die sich in der Auferstehung Jesu Christi erfüllt. Vgl. die neuen Studien zu diesem Begriff, wie z.B. T. Schumacher, Zur Entstehung christlicher Sprache. Eine Untersuchung der paulinischen Idiomatik und der Verwendung des Begriffs πίστις (BBB 168), Göttingen 2012. Ich kann aber Schumachers Meinung zur Bedeutung von πίστις in dieser Perikope nicht teilen: Hier sei πίστις im Sinne von Glauben zu verstehen, als „Maßstab ethischen Verhaltens. Damit wird zugleich auch deutlich, dass die geltenden Wertmaßstäbe in der Offenbarung Gottes und in seiner Zuwendung in Christus ihren Bezugspunkt finden" (S. 367).

43 Exemplarisch für die Diskussion über das Fleischessen scheint mir der Traktat des Plutarch *De esu carnium*. Plutarch verteidigt die Positionen der Vegetarier, die in der Antike von den Pythagoreern vertreten wurden. Die Hauptargumente sind: a) Der Mensch ist von Natur her kein Fleischesser. Er hat dazu keine geeigneten Fingernägel und Zähne, und seine Verdauung ist eher langsam (994 f) (Thema der ersten Rede). b) Der Mensch isst Fleisch nicht aus Not oder Bedürfnis, sondern aus Lust. Das Fleischessen unterstützt daher seine Begierde (997b) (Thema der zweiten Rede). Die beiden Reden sind aber nur fragmentarisch erhalten, und ihre Authentizität ist teilweise umstritten.

44 E. Lohse, Der Brief an die Römer, 371–373, plädiert für die Hypothese eines allgemeinen Verständnisses der Worte des Paulus. Er denke nicht speziell an Judaisten oder an die jüdischen Reinheitsgebote. – Zu der umstrittenen Frage des Anteils jüdischer Mitglieder der römischen Hausgemeinden vgl. die ausgewogene Darstellung bei R. Jewett, Romans, 70–72 (die römischen

Formulierung von 14,21 unwahrscheinlich, anzunehmen, dass Paulus in diesem Kapitel konkret andere philosophische Gruppen, die Vegetarier waren (z.B. die Pythagoreer), im Sinn hatte. Es liegt eher nahe, dass er auf indirekte Art jüdische Positionen ansprechen will, die seiner Vermutung nach einige aus dem Judentum stammende Gemeindemitglieder betreffen.

Im Mittelpunkt der paulinischen Argumentation steht die These in Röm 14,14, die Paulus in fester Überzeugung formuliert: οὐδὲν κοινὸν δ' ἑαυτοῦ „Nichts ist von sich aus unrein". Diese apodiktische Aussage wird nicht in ihrer allgemeinen Gültigkeit, wohl aber in ihrer Anwendbarkeit eingeschränkt im Fall, dass jemand der Meinung ist, etwas sei unrein. In dieser Situation *ist* es für diese Person wirklich unrein. Die Unreinheit der Speisen wird damit nicht von ihrer Substanz her verstanden, sondern von der subjektiven Überzeugung des einzelnen Gemeindegliedes abhängig gemacht und insoweit relativiert. Damit will Paulus nach Wong mögliche Konflikte zwischen Heiden- und Judenchristen in der römischen Gemeinde vermeiden.[45] Die Entscheidung für oder gegen eine Speise beruht nun nicht mehr auf dem Charakter der Speise und ihrer Beurteilung durch die Tora, sondern ist eine individuelle ethische Entscheidung, die von dem Gewissen des Einzelnen abhängig ist:

> „Das Reich Gottes besteht nicht aus Essen und Trinken, sondern aus Gerechtigkeit und Frieden und Freude im heiligen Geist" (Röm 14,17).

(3) Diese Aussage des Paulus hebt die Grenzen und die Gebote des Reinheitssystems der Tora in doppelter Hinsicht auf: *erstens* im Hinblick auf die grundsätzliche Relativierung des *rituellen* Reinheitsbegriffs und *zweitens* durch die Einführung einer neuen Instanz: der πίστις im Sinne der persönlichen Überzeugung. Die Einleitungsformel dieser Aussage betont dementsprechend die feste Überzeugung des Apostels (οἶδα καὶ πέπεισμαι) und die Autorität Jesu (ἐν κυρίῳ Ἰησοῦ). Die Beziehung auf den „Herrn Jesus" ist exegetisch umstritten. Man kann diese Frage in zwei Richtungen beantworten: Entweder handelt es sich hier um ein Jesus-Wort, das Paulus aus der Tradition übernimmt[46], oder aber um die Überzeugung des Paulus, die auf der Autorität des erhöhten Christus basiert. Die meisten Exegeten sehen in dieser Aussage einen Bezug auf den erhöhten Jesus:

Gemeinden sind mehrheitlich heidenchristlich, schließen aber eine judenchristliche Minderheit ein). – Wichtig ist der Hinweis bei R. Jewett, Romans, 835, dass in Rom auch Heiden aus einem asketischen Milieu Gemeindemitglieder sein könnten. Wichtig bleibt außerdem die Tatsache, dass Paulus hier die frühere religiöse Zugehörigkeit der ‚Schwachen' offenhält.
45 E.K.C. Wong, Evangelien im Dialog mit Paulus, 91.
46 So R. Jewett, Romans, 859 (Lit. in Anm. 56).

Wenn Paulus wirklich ein Wort Jesu in seinem Traditionsgut gehabt hätte, hätte er es im Streit mit den Jerusalemer Aposteln und den Judaisten über die Gültigkeit des Gesetzes verwendet[47]. Mir scheint eine mittlere Lösung die plausibelste zu sein: Es handelt sich um ein Logion Jesu, das aber in der christlichen Gemeinde nicht als eindeutig gegen die Reinheitsgebote gerichtet betrachtet wurde. Paulus gehört dann in eine Interpretationslinie der christlichen Gemeinde, die ein Jesus-Wort als Votum für die Aufhebung aller Reinheitsgesetze interpretierte. Diese Interpretationslinie verbindet unsere Stelle mit Mk 7,15, die sich vermutlich auf dasselbe Jesus-Wort bezieht. Auch der Evangelist interpretiert das Logion Jesu präziser. Diesen Punkt werde ich bei der Analyse von Mk 7 vertiefen. *Der Zusammenhang von Paulus und Markus bei der Reinheitsfrage besteht also in einer besonderen Auslegung eines Jesuswortes, d.h. der vorgegebenen Logientradition.* Beide berufen sich auf die Autorität Jesu, um die Lehre der Christen über die Reinheit zu klären. Durch diese Aussage Jesu werden für Paulus und den Verfasser des Markusevangeliums die religiöse und rituelle Bedeutung von Speisen und Reinheit relativiert. Das einzige Kriterium für Reinheit bleibt die individuelle Überzeugung, auf die die Gemeinschaft Rücksicht nehmen muss (οἰκοδομὴ τῆς εἰς ἀλλήλους, Röm 14,19). Das Urteilen, κρίνειν, im Sinne von ‚Verurteilen', das in der Perikope in verschiedenen Formen zum Ausdruck kommt, ist destruktiv[48] gegen die Gemeinschaft und vor allem gegen das Heilswerk[49] Gottes gerichtet. Jeder Christ wird durch Jesu Tod erlöst. Er wird damit zum Diener Gottes und darf daher nicht ‚beurteilt' werden (14,4: „Wer bist du, um den Diener eines anderen zu beurteilen?").

---

47 Die Betonung liegt vor allem auf dem hellenistischen Ursprung dieser Tradition: E. Käsemann, An die Römer, 362; U. Wilckens, Der Brief an die Römer, 9. O. Michel, Der Brief an die Römer (KEK IV), Göttingen ¹⁴1978, 431 Anm. 1, vermutet, dass es sich um einen Lehrsatz Jesu handelt, obwohl Paulus ihn nicht als Wort Jesu zitiert. E. Lohse, Der Brief an die Römer, 377, Anm. 1, schließt dagegen aus, dass Paulus hier ein Jesuswort benutzt: „Wo Paulus Herrenworte anführte, bediente er sich eindeutiger Hinweise wie 1 Thess 4,15; 1Kor 7,10.12 9,14".
48 Interessant sind hier die Verben, die diese Destruktivität des Urteilens ausdrücken: ἀπόλλυμι 14,15, καταλύω 14,20. Liebe und Rücksicht auf den anderen sind im Gegenteil konstruktive Verhaltensweisen (τὰ τῆς οἰκοδομῆς 14,19). Die Zentralität dieses Gegensatzes zwischen Konstruktivität und Destruktivität behandle ich in meiner Dissertation: L. Scornaienchi, Sarx und soma bei Paulus. Der Mensch zwischen Destruktivität und Konstruktivität (NTOA 67), Göttingen 2011, bes. S. 62-66.
49 U. Wilckens, Der Brief an die Römer, 89, betont die Verbindung von destruktivem Handeln und Bild der Konstruktion, indem er 14,20 folgendermaßen übersetzt: „Reiße nicht aus Speisegründen das (Bau-)werk Gottes ein!".

5 Jesus und die Reinheit in Mk 7,1–23

Die Frage nach der Reinheit wird im Markusevangelium in einem Streitgespräch zwischen Jesus und den Pharisäern und Schriftgelehrten in Mk 7,1–23 behandelt. J. Neyrey hebt zwar auch noch weitere Passagen der markinischen Erzählung hervor, in denen Jesus nicht den jüdischen Reinheitsnormen folgt, sondern eine neue Auffassung der Reinheit vertritt.[50] Das Streitgespräch ist aber die einzige Textstelle, in der die Reinheit *thematisch* behandelt wird. Wie viele andere Streitgespräche geht auch dieses von einem Vorwurf aus, den die Pharisäer gegen Jesus bzw. gegen seine Jünger erheben: Der Vorwurf lautet, seine Jünger äßen Brot mit unreinen Händen. Der Evangelist erklärt seinen Lesern die Bedeutung dieses Vorwurfs der Pharisäer im Rahmen der jüdischen Lebensweise, die durch eigene religiöse Vorschriften geprägt ist („wie alle Juden"). Die Perspektive ist *extern*, wie die Erklärung des Wortes κοινός und der Ausdruck οἱ Φαρισαῖοι καὶ πάντες οἱ Ἰουδαῖοι in Mk 7,3 zeigen.

(1) Die Frage, wie die *Unreinheit* hier zu verstehen sei, ist mit der Einschätzung des Verhältnisses von Tradition, Redaktion und eigener literarischer Gestaltung des Evangelisten verbunden. Es handelt sich bei Mk 7,1–23 um eine komplexe Perikope, die verschiedene Aspekte behandelt: die Handwaschung vor dem Essen – in diesem Zusammenhang fällt das Stichwort κοινός –, die pharisäische Tradition, den Korban, die Reinheit der Speisen und die ethische Reinheit, auch diese mit κοινόω bezeichnet (7,15).[51] Die formgeschichtlich arbeitende Exegese versuchte, das ursprüngliche Streitgespräch zu rekonstruieren, das Markus aus der synoptischen Tradition übernommen habe. Rudolf Bultmann unterscheidet drei Teile in der Perikope: 1–8 (den Hauptteil), 9–13 (einen polemischen Teil über den Brauch des Korban) und 7,15 sowie die Kommentare (18b–19). 7,20–23 sei von einem hellenistischen Redaktor verfasst worden und sei eine Diskussion über die Tradition[52]. Eine weitere Hypothese sieht in der Perikope eine ursprüngliche Debatte über die Reinheit, in der Mk 7,5 die Frage und Mk 7,15 die Antwort bilden[53].

---

50 J.H. Neyrey, The Idea of Purity in Mark's Gospel, 106–109. Er stellt sich nicht die Frage, ob diese Ereignisse der Jesus-Tradition fundiert sind.
51 Für die einzelnen Themen vgl. A. Yarbro Collins, Mark. A Commentary (Hermeneia), Minneapolis 2007, 339–363.
52 R. Bultmann, Geschichte der synoptischen Tradition (FRLANT 29), Göttingen ⁵1995, 15. Die gleiche These einer Debatte über die Tradition vertritt W. Weiß, Eine neue Rede in Vollmacht". Die Streit- und Schulgespräche des Markus-Evangeliums (BZNW 52), Berlin/New York 1989, 64.
53 Vgl. D. Lührmann, ...womit er alle Speisen für rein erklärte (Mk 7,19), in: WuD 16 (1981), 71–92, hier: 86, und K. Berger, Die Gesetzauslegung Jesu. Ihr historischer Hintergrund im Judentum und im Alten Testament, Neukirchen-Vluyn 1972, 463.

Ich bezweifle, dass die ursprüngliche Debatte rekonstruiert werden kann. Meine Hypothese ist, dass der Evangelist verschiedene Elemente aus der Tradition übernimmt und sie zu einer neuen thematischen Einheit zusammenfügt. Die beiden Teile des Kapitels 7,1–13 und 7,14–24 sind miteinander durch Stichworte verbunden: das Adjektiv κοινός bzw. das Verb κοινόω (Mk 7,2; 7,5; 7,15; 7,18; 7,23), die anthropologischen Termini χεῖλα/ καρδία 7,6 καρδία/ κοιλία 7,19.21 und Innen-Außen. Das Jesaja-Zitat bietet eine Art Synthese der Thematik des Kapitels. Es enthält die Gegensätze, die für den Text von wesentlicher Bedeutung sind: die Äußerlichkeit des Gottesdienstes und der Reinheitsgesetze, die Kritik der menschlichen Satzungen und der Tradition.

(2) Im Mittelpunkt der markinischen Komposition steht das Jesus-Logion in 7,15. Die Diskussion über die Authentizität dieses Jesuswortes ist kontrovers. Die Antwort auf die Authentizitätsfrage ist nicht nur für die Frage nach der Einstellung des historischen Jesus zum Gesetz und zu den Reinheitsgeboten relevant, sondern hat auch eine grundsätzliche Bedeutung für die Interpretation des Markustextes und muss daher kurz angesprochen werden. Die „dritte Frage" (third quest) nach dem historischen Jesus, die den jüdischen Charakter der Verkündigung des historischen Jesus in den Mittelpunkt stellt, vertritt eine theologische und rituelle Kontinuität zwischen Jesus und seinem jüdischen Kontext und votiert daher gegen die Authentizität.[54] Die ältere Jesusforschung, die das Differenzkriterium anwendete, hegte dagegen keinen Zweifel an der Echtheit des Logions[55]. Gerd Theißen nimmt hier eine mittlere Position ein, wenn er die Authentizität des Logions nach den neuen Kriterien der „Wirkungsplausibilität" im Christentum und der „Kontextplausibilität" im Judentum betont[56]. Der Kontext ist nach Theißen derjenige der Gruppe des Täufers, die die Frage nach der Reinheit stellte: Jesus

---

54 Vgl. J.G. Crossley, From Jesus Observing Food and Purity Laws to Some Christians not Bothering: A Socio-Historical Explanation, in: Jesus in Continuum, ed. by T. Holmén (WUNT 289), Tübingen 2012, 94-95: „There is no criticism of Jesus overriding food laws and there would have been outcry if he had done so, not just from Jews in general but at least from some of his disciples"; 95–96: „Contrary to much of recent scholarship, I do not think that Jesus overrode any biblical purtiy law, or at least in any way that was unparalleled in Judaism". Er erklärt die Kritik der Reinheitsgebote als ein Phänomen der ersten Gemeinde. Sie veränderte sich, weil so viele Heiden zu Mitgliedern wurden.
55 H. Merkel, Markus 7,15 – Das Jesuswort über die innere Verunreinigung, in: ZRGG 20 (1968), 340–366, hier: 355.
56 G. Theißen, Das Reinheitslogion Mk 7,15 und die Trennung von Juden und Christen, in: ders., Jesus als historische Gestalt. Beiträge zur Jesusforschung (hg. von A. Merz), Göttingen 2003, 57–72, hier: 88 „Unser Fazit ist daher: Das Reinheitslogion in Mk 7,15 passt ausgezeichnet in das Judentum des 1. Jh. n. Chr. Es dürfte von Jesus stammen. Jüdische Kontextplausibilität und christliche Wirkungsplausibilität machen es wahrscheinlich."

als „Schüler des Johannes" forderte die Umkehr ohne Taufritus. Die Wirkungsplausibilität bietet die Erklärung, dass dies Logion gut in die Tätigkeit der Tradenten der Jesus-Überlieferung, der Wandercharismatiker, passt. Diese konnten als Wanderer die Reinheitsgesetze nicht mehr befolgen, sondern mussten alles essen, was ihnen angeboten wurde[57]. Wie Röm 14,14 sei diese Aussage indikativisch formuliert (was für einen Spruch und nicht für eine Vorschrift spricht), und erst mit der Apostelgeschichte werde dann in der Vision der Petrus in Joppe (Apg 10,13) imperativisch formuliert.

Klaus Berger und Heikki Räisänen vertreten demgegenüber die These, Mk 7,15 sei nicht authentisch. Nach Berger ist der Spruch erst später in der christlichen Gemeinde entstanden: Er enthalte die hellenistische Vorstellung der Reinheit, die durch die allegorische Auslegung eine moralische Dimension annehme und ihre rituelle Relevanz verliere[58]. Räisänen betont die typisch markinische Sprache des Logions. Das wichtigste Argument für die Nicht-Authentizität ist nach Räisänen die Tatsache, dass Paulus diesen Spruch nicht in der Polemik gegen die Judaisten benutzt. Paulus übernehme den Spruch nicht aus der Tradition; es sei außerdem nicht möglich, einen Trägerkreis des Spruches in Antiochia zu finden. Räisänen versteht Mk 7,15 als eine Entwicklung von Röm 14,14.20:

> „It seems to me much more likely that Mark is influenced by the insights gained in the Gentile mission, expressed by Paul in Röm 14,14.20, than that Paul is dependent on Jesus"[59].

(3) Mir scheint demgegenüber die Erwähnung des „Herrn Jesus" in Röm 14,14 ein deutlicher Bezug auf die Jesus-Tradition zu sein. Paulus hat sich auf eine überlieferte Aussage Jesu bezogen, die dann mit dem griechischen Terminus κοινός – einem gängigen Wort für „unrein" – formuliert wurde.

Man kann vielleicht vermuten, dass der Spruch nicht eindeutig gegen die Reinheit der Speisen gerichtet war und dass Paulus als erster eine klare Deutung dieses Spruchs in diese Richtung lieferte[60]. Es lassen sich einige Ähnlichkeiten in der Ausdrucksform der beiden Texte finden, einmal die apodiktische Aussage: οὐδέν ἐστιν ἔξωθεν τοῦ ἀνθρώπου ὃ δύναται κοινῶσαι αὐτόν (Mk 7,15) / οὐδέν

---

57 G. Theißen, Das Reinheitslogion, 86–87.
58 K. Berger, Die Gesetzauslegung, 465–466. Als Beispiele des hellenistischen Judentums zitiert Berger die Auslegung von Num 19,22 bei Philo, De specialibus legibus, 3,208–209 und Ps. Phoklides 228 (S. 467).
59 H. Räisänen, Jesus and the Food Laws, 145.
60 R.P. Booth, Jesus and the Laws of Purity. Tradition History and Legal History in Mark 7 (JSNT. S 13), Sheffield 1986, 69–71, vermutet, dass nur der zweite Teil des Spruches authentisch sei. Eine Bestätigung könnte darin liegen, dass in EvThom 14,5 nur der zweite Teil des Spruches enthalten ist.

κοινόν δι' ἑαυτοῦ (Röm 14,14) und dann eine Einschränkung, die doch die Existenz der Unreinheit einräumt: ἀλλὰ τὰ ἐκ τοῦ ἀνθρώπου ἐκπορευόμενα / εἰ μὴ τῷ λογιζομένῳ τι κοινόν εἶναι. Es liegt nahe anzunehmen, dass Jesus die Bedeutung der Reinheit des Herzens über die rituelle Reinheit stellen wollte[61], d.h. dass der Spruch eine ethische Intention hatte. Paulus hätte dann das Jesus-Logion dahingehend interpretiert, dass Jesus damit *alles* für rein erklären wollte. Damit hätte das Jesus-Logion eine Anwendung bzw. Verengung in Richtung auf die Speisegesetzgebung bekommen. Ich vermute deshalb, dass Paulus *dieselbe Tradition* verwendet, die in Mk 7 dokumentiert ist, und dass er sie für die Aufhebung der Reinheitsgesetze in den christusgläubigen Missionsgemeinden einsetzt. Der Schlüsselsatz der paulinischen Interpretation ist Röm 14,20: πάντα μὲν καθαρά. Diese Deutung des Paulus beeinflusst dann die Interpretation des Markus, der eine ähnliche Schlussfolgerung zieht. Diese hat die Form einer redaktionellen Anmerkung in der Rede Jesu: καθαρίζων πάντα τὰ βρώματα (Mk 7,19)[62]. Jesus erklärt alle Speisen für rein. *Das ist die paulinische Deutung, die Markus in seinem Text übernimmt*, und das ist auch genau der Satz, den Matthäus *nicht* aus dem markinischen Text übernimmt, weil er in diesem Punkt eine andere Meinung vertritt: Er ist für das Beibehalten aller Gebote.

Markus komponiert dies Streitgespräch, indem er verschiedene Teile der Jesustradition verbindet. Die Kritik an der pharisäischen Tradition und ihren Satzungen betrifft die Sorge um das Äußerliche, das auch in den Reinheitsgeboten vorhanden ist. Dagegen betont der markinische Jesus die Reinheit des Herzens: Hier gewinnt die *ethische* Reinheitsvorstellung auf der ganzen Linie. Das Streitgespräch soll möglichen heidnischen Lesern des Evangeliums zeigen, dass Jesus zum Thema Reinheit keine rituell fokussierte Position vertritt, die gegen die Lebensweise der Heiden und gegen die römische Macht gerichtet ist. Im Gegenteil: er

---

61 Die Tatsache, dass das Logion keine deutliche Aussage gegen die Reinheitsgesetze enthält, wird oft als Beweis dafür genommen, dass Jesus die Tora nicht kritisiert habe. W. Stegemann, Hat Jesus die Speisegesetze der Tora aufgehoben?, 45–49, sieht in dem Streitgespräch eine Kritik Jesu an der pharisäischen Tradition und die Betonung der Reinheit des Herzens, aber ohne jede kritische Funktion gegen das Gesetz. Die Jesus-Überlieferung lässt m.E. aber klar erkennen, dass einige Verhaltensweisen Jesu eine Provokation oder sogar eine Kritik gegen die etablierte religiöse rituelle Reinheit darstellten (Anfassen der Lepra-Kranken, einer menstruierenden Frau, Umgang mit Fremden und Sündern).
62 Ich halte die weitere Interpretation dieses Partizipialsatzes, wonach Jesus damit die Reinigung der Speisen durch die Verdauung meinen soll, nicht für korrekt. Vgl. B.J. Malina, A Conflict Approach to Mark 7, in: Forum 4 (1988), 3–30, hier: 23; Jesus' Satz will „effect that once food is ingested and subsequently defecated, it is no longer unclean". Das sei von der Leseart καθαρίζον als Neutrum bezeugt. W. Stegemann, Hat Jesus die Speisegesetze der Tora aufgehoben?, 45–46, scheint diese These einer Reinigung durch Verdauung zu teilen.

hat von der inneren Reinheit des Herzens gesprochen. Dies Streitgespräch dient daher zusammen mit den anderen Streitgesprächen der markinischen Apologie der Gestalt Jesu und der Widerlegung aller Argumente, die ihn als antirömischen Rebellen oder als religiösen Blasphemiker darstellen wollen[63].

6 Markus als Pauliner?

Fährt Markus auf derselben theologischen Schiene wie Paulus? Diese kontroverse Frage kann hier nur aus einer sehr begrenzten Perspektive, nämlich aus derjenigen des Diskurses über die Reinheit, der die christlichen Gemeinden im ersten Jahrhundert n.Chr. sehr stark beschäftigte, beantwortet werden. Aus der Geometrie wissen wir, dass man, um eine Gerade zu ziehen, mindestens zwei Punkte braucht, die verbunden werden müssen. Ausgangspunkt ist die Position des Paulus nach Röm 14; ihr kann man als Endpunkt den Text in Tit 1,15 gegenüberstellen. Hier heißt es:

> πάντα καθαρὰ τοῖς καθαροῖς, τοῖς μεμιαμμένοις καὶ ἀπίστοις οὐδὲν καθαρόν, ἀλλὰ μεμίανται αὐτῶν καὶ ὁ νοῦς καὶ ἡ συνείδησις.

Dieser Text stellt eine Art Synthese der paulinischen Auffassung in 1Kor 8–10 und Röm 14 dar. Der Terminus κοινός wird im Titusbrief allerdings nicht mehr gebraucht, weil es eine sprachliche und semantische Weiterentwicklung gegeben hat. Die jüdischen Gebote werden hier als μῦθοι und ἐντολαὶ ἀνθρώπων angesehen. Ist dies ein Bezug auf die markinische Bemerkung über die pharisäische Tradition? Die Frage muss offen bleiben. Man kann aber wenigstens feststellen, dass die Position des Markus durchaus ihren Platz auf der Geraden zwischen Paulus und dem Autor des Titusbriefes, dessen späterem Schüler, findet.

---

[63] Diese Interpretation der Streitgespräche als eines wichtigen Bestandteils des Markusevangeliums und als Mittelpunkt der Apologie der Gestalt Jesu vertrete ich in meiner Erlanger Habilitationsschrift: „Jesus und seine Apologie. Die markinischen Streitgespräche" (masch. 2013).

Literatur

Arndt, K./ Moeller, B., Albrecht Dürers „Vier Apostel". Eine kirchen- und kunsthistorische Untersuchung (NAWG.PH 4/2003), Göttingen 2003.
Baden, J.S. / Moss, C.R., The Origin and Interpretation of ṣāraʿat in Leviticus 13–14, in: JBL 130/4 (2011), 643–662.
Baur, F. Chr., Geschichte der christlichen Kirche, Bd. 1, Tübingen ³1863.
—, Die Tübinger Schule und ihre Stellung zur Gegenwart, Tübingen ²1860.
Berger, K., Die Gesetzauslegung Jesu. Ihr historischer Hintergrund im Judentum und im Alten Testament, Neukirchen-Vluyn 1972.
Booth, R.P., Jesus and the Laws of Purity. Tradition History and Legal History in Mark 7 (JSNT.S 13), Sheffield 1986.
Bultmann, R., Geschichte der synoptischen Tradition (FRLANT 29), Göttingen ⁵1995.
—, Theologie des Neuen Testaments (hg. von O. Merk), Tübingen ⁹1984.
Collins, A. Yarbro, Mark. A Commentary (Hermeneia), Minneapolis 2007.
Corsani, B., Hor tutto ciò che non è di fede, è peccato, in: Protestantesimo 34 (1979), 65–81.
Crossley, J.G., From Jesus Observing Food and Purity Laws to Some Christians not Bothering: A Socio-Historical Explanation, in: Jesus in Continuum, ed. by T. Holmén (WUNT 289), Tübingen 2012.
Douglas, M., Leviticus as Literature, Oxford/ New York 1999.
—, Purity and Danger. An Analysis of the Concept of Pollution and Taboo, London 1966.
Dunn, J.D.G, Romans II, WBC 38b, Dallas 1988.
Elliott, M., Engaging Leviticus: Reading Leviticus Theologically with Its Past Interpreters, Eugene 2012.
Fenton, J.C., Paul and Mark, in: Studies in the Gospels: Essays in Memory of R.H. Lightfoot, ed. by D.E. Nineham, Oxford 1955, 89–112.
Fitzmyer, J.A., Romans. A New Translation with Introduction and Commentary (AncB 33), New York u.a. 1993.
Harrington, H.K., Art. Purity and Impurity, in: The Eerdmans Dictionary of Early Judaism, Grand Rapids/ Cambridge UK 2010, 1121–1123.
Holtzmann, H.J., Lehrbuch der historisch-kritischen Einleitung in das Neue Testament, Freiburg 1885.
Jewett, R., Romans. A Commentary (Hermeneia), Minneapolis 2007.
Käsemann, E., An die Römer (HNT 8a), Tübingen ⁴1980.
Kümmel, W., Einleitung in das Neue Testament, Heidelberg ¹⁷1973.
Lohse, E., Der Brief an die Römer (KEK IV), Göttingen ¹⁵2003.
Lührmann, D., ...womit er alle Speisen für rein erklärte (Mk 7,19), in: WuD 16 (1981), 71–92.
Malina, B.J., A Conflict Approach to Mark 7, in: Forum 4 (1988), 3–30.
Merkel, H., Markus 7,15 – Das Jesuswort über die innere Verunreinigung, in: ZRGG 20 (1968), 340–366.
Michel, O., Der Brief an die Römer (KEK IV), Göttingen ¹⁴1978.
Neyrey, J.H., The Idea of Purity in Mark's Gospel, in: Semeia 35 (1986), 91–128.
Pfeiffer, G., Die Vorbilder zu Albrecht Dürers „Vier Aposteln." Melanchthon und sein Nürnberger Freundeskreis, Nürnberg 1960.
Räisänen, H., Jesus and the Food Laws. Reflections on Mark 7,15, in: ders., Jesus, Paul and Torah. Collected Essays (JSNT SS 43) Sheffield 1992, 127-148.

Ritter, V., Die „vier Apostel" in beiden Darstellungen von Albrecht Dürer. Die verborgene Geometrie und die Echtheitsfrage, Kaufbeuren 2001.

Schawe, M., Dürer, Albrecht: Vier Apostel, in: Historisches Lexikon Bayerns, URL: http://www.historisches-lexikon-bayerns.de/artikel/artikel_45639) (1.9.2010).

Schumacher, T., Zur Entstehung christlicher Sprache. Eine Untersuchung der paulinischen Idiomatik und der Verwendung des Begriffs πίστις (BBB 168), Göttingen 2012.

Scornaienchi, L., Sarx und soma bei Paulus. Der Mensch zwischen Destruktivität und Konstruktivität (NTOA 67), Göttingen 2011.

Stegemann, W., Hat Jesus die Speisegesetze der Tora aufgehoben? Zur neuesten kontroversen Einschätzung der traditionellen Deutung des sog. „Reinheitslogion" von Mk 7,15, in: Jesus – Gestalt und Gestaltungen. Rezeptionen des Galiläers in Wissenschaft, Kirche und Gesellschaft. FS für G. Theißen, hg. von P. von Gemünden u.a. (NTOA 100), Göttingen 2013, 29–50.

Theißen, G., Das Reinheitslogion Mk 7,15 und die Trennung von Juden und Christen, in: ders., Jesus als historische Gestalt. Beiträge zur Jesusforschung (hg. von A. Merz), Göttingen 2003, 57–72.

—, Die Religion der ersten Christen. Eine Theorie des Urchristentums, Gütersloh [4]2008.

—, Kritik an Paulus im Matthäusevangelium? Von der verdeckten Polemik im Urchristentum, in: Polemik in der frühchristlichen Literatur. Texte und Kontexte, hg. von O. Wischmeyer/L. Scornaienchi (BZNW 170), Berlin/New York 2011, 465–490.

Tuor-Kurth, C., Unreinheit und Gemeinschaft. Erwägungen zum neutestamentlichen Gebrauch von κοινός, in: ThZ 65/3 (2009), 229–245.

Volkmar, G., Die Evangelien oder Marcus und die Synopsis der kanonischen und ausserkanonischen Evangelien: Nach dem ältesten Text mit historisch-exegetischem Commentar, Leipzig 1870.

Vollenweider, S., Art. Paulus, in: RGG[4] 5 (2003), 1035-1065.

Wahlen, C., Peter's Vision and Conflicting Definitions of Purity, in: NTS 51/4 (2005), 505–518.

Weiß, W., „Eine neue Rede in Vollmacht". Die Streit- und Schulgespräche des Markus-Evangeliums (BZNW 52), Berlin/ New York 1989.

Werner, M., Der Einfluß paulinischer Theologie im Markusevangelium. Eine Studie zur neutestamentlichen Theologie (BZNW 1), Gießen 1923.

Wilckens, U., Der Brief an die Römer. 3 (12–16) (EKK VI/3), Zürich u.a. 1982.

Wischmeyer, O., Forming Identity Through Literature: The Impact of Mark for the Building of Christ-Believing Communities in the Second Half of the First Century C.E., in: Mark and Matthew I. Comparative Readings. Understanding the Earliest Gospels in their First-Century Settings, eds. E.-M. Becker/ A. Runesson (WUNT 271), Tübingen 2011, 355–378.

Wischmeyer, O./ Scornaienchi, L. (Hgg.), Polemik in der frühchristlichen Literatur. Texte und Kontexte (BZNW 170), Berlin/ New York 2011.

Wong, E.K.C., Evangelien im Dialog mit Paulus. Eine intertextuelle Studie zu den Synoptikern (NTOA 89), Göttingen 2011.

John Painter
Mark and the Pauline Mission

In my 1997 commentary on Mark, I suggested that Mark is an expression of the Pauline mission, rather than a Petrine Gospel as claimed by Papias.[1] I argued that *Mark* is shaped by and provides a basis for the Pauline Law-free mission to the nations.[2] By Law-free I meant free from those ritual elements of Jewish Law, like circumcision and purity laws, that separated Jews from Gentiles. The argument for this hypothesis was further developed in my monograph on James.[3] Although the evidence of two missions is generally recognised (see Gal 2:7-8 in context), the complexity of divisions (factions) within the two missions is not. In 1998 Joel Marcus gave a paper entitled "Mark – Interpreter of Paul" at the Orlando SBL Meeting, which was published two years later.[4] While it is relevant to my study, I have a more limited objective, seeking only to show that Mark was both shaped by and provided a basis for the Pauline mission to the nations. Two recent books, whose conclusions are relevant to this position, can be used as a way into this discussion.[5]

1 James G. Crossley: Mark as Pre-Pauline

James Crossley sets out to show that the commonly accepted date for Mark (c. 70 CE) is not convincingly established. It is true that the evidence upon which the authorship and date of composition are to be identified is flimsy, not only for Mark, but for each of the four canonical Gospels. None of them identifies its author. Authorial names appear to have been added when the fourfold Gospel col-

---

1 Papias was Bishop of Hierapolis in the first half of the second century. Around 130 CE he wrote *Expositions of the Oracles of the Lord*, a work in "five books" now lost but known in fragments preserved in the works of others, especially by Eusebius the early fourth century bishop of Caesarea. See especially Eusebius, *H.E.* 2.15.2; 3.36.2; 3.39; and also Irenaeus (c. 180 CE) *Adv. Haer.* 5.33.4.
2 John Painter, *Mark's Gospel* (London: Routledge, 1997), i, 3-8, 24, 113, 168, 175, 213, 217.
3 John Painter, *Just James: The Brother of Jesus in History and Tradition* (Columbia, S.C.; University of South Carolina Press, 1997), 67-102.
4 Joel Marcus, "Mark – Interpreter of Paul." *NTS* 46 (2000): 473-87. See the revised version of this article in vol. II of "Mark and Paul".
5 James G. Crossley, *The Date of Mark's Gospel: Insight from the Law in Earliest Christianity*, JSNTSup 266 (London: T & T Clark International, 2004); and Michael F. Bird, *Jesus and the Origins of the Gentile Mission*, LNTS 331 (London: T & T Clark International, 2007).

lection was made and the title of each added. This collection was the first to be spoken of as "canon," and the individual parts of it were named in the added titles as: ΚΑΤΑ ΜΑΘΘΑΙΟΝ ΚΑΤΑ ΜΑΡΚΑΝ ΚΑΤΑ ΛΟΥΚΑΝ ΚΑΤΑ ΙΩΑΝΝΗΝ. These titles presuppose that each of them stands under the overarching title of ΕΥΑΓΓΕΛΙΟΝ.[6] For the identification of the author of each Gospel we cannot get further back than this. Whether the testimony of Papias to Mark and Matthew is related to the titles, or is of comparable age and value is debatable (see Eusebius, *H.E.* 3.39.15). Consequently there is no certainty about the identification of the authors.

When it comes to dating each of the Gospels, the evidence is not much better. Clement of Alexandria asserts that the Gospels with genealogies are earlier than those without and he (Eusebius *H.E.* 6.14.4b-7) and Irenaeus (*Adv. Haer.* 3.1.1 and cf. Eusebius *H.E.* 5.8.2-4) name John as the last of the four. As far as John is concerned, that agrees with the canonical order, which Augustine initially accepted as the chronological order, but later concluded that Mark was dependent on both Matthew and Luke, thus agreeing with Clement. But the dominant view today is that Mark was first and was used by Matthew and Luke, who also made use of another common source (Q).[7] At the same time, there is a growing tendency to stress the oral culture of the early Christian movement, for example, in the work of James D. G. Dunn, leading to a reduced stress on literary dependence to explain agreements, and appealing to variations in oral performance to explain differences.[8] His arguments in support of the early dominance of oral tradition tend not to support very early dates for the written Gospels. We may well ask about how soon written sources in Greek appeared, be-

---

[6] Around 320 CE, Eusebius (*H.E.* 6.25.3) refers to Origen (c. 185-251 CE), in his commentary on Matthew, defending the canon (κανών) of the church. This rare use of κανών describes Origen's defence of the four-Gospel canon. Origen was building on the clear defence of the four Gospels by Irenaeus (*Adv. Haer.* 3.11.8).

[7] Austin Farrer challenged the Q hypothesis in his revolutionary essay of 1955, "On Dispensing with Q." In *Studies in the Gospels*, ed. Dennis E. Nineham (Oxford: Blackwell, 1955), 55-88. Since then there has been a significant minority arguing that Luke made use of Mark and Matthew. Another "Two Gospel hypothesis" argues that Mark made use of Matthew and Luke (the so-called Griesbach hypothesis).

[8] See James D. G. Dunn, *Jesus Remembered* (Grand Rapids, Mich.: Eerdmans, 2003), and my review in RBL 06/2004. Dunn builds on his Presidential address to the 2002 Durham Meeting of SNTS entitled "Altering the Default Setting" dealing with early Christian tradition about the importance of oral tradition and twentieth century attempts to give an account of the place and importance of oral tradition in the earliest church. The growing focus on the role of oral tradition raises doubts about the rapid rise of written sources on the basis of which the Gospels were written.

cause the Synoptic evidence not only involves common content but the common use of the same Greek wording.

Crossley argues for a date for Mark between the mid-thirties and mid-forties (p. 208).[9] In support, he asserts that Mark is free of any sign of influence from the Pauline Law-free mission to the Gentiles. He uses this conclusion to argue in favour of dating Mark before the fifties, when Pauline influence became widespread. At the same time, he uses the early date to exclude a reading of Mark 7:19b as evidence of Pauline influence. His sub-title notes that the distinctive approach of his book is its focus on the Marcan use of Jewish legal material. He considers that his reading shows that Mark presupposes a date prior to the Pauline Law-free mission, arguing that the Marcan Jesus breaks no Biblical Law (p. 208-09) and that, as Mark shows "no signs of the biblical Torah being challenged, then a date for Mark sometime before the fifties could reasonably be suggested" (p. 125) which, as we have seen, is pushed back to between the mid-thirties and mid-forties (p. 208).[10] There is no early evidence for such a date, nor does anything in Mark suggest it, and arguments based on the role of oral tradition are against it. Crossley is not persuaded by traditions that identify John Mark as the author and dependent on the witness of Peter. While this deals with one basis for a later date, it does nothing to establish an earlier date. For this he attempts to date Mark on the basis of internal evidence, leaving any connection with John Mark and Peter undecided (17-18).[11] He regards Mark's presentation of Jesus as Law observant to be pre-Pauline, and so providing evidence of its early date.

2 Mark 7:1-23 and its Interpretation

Whether Jesus was Sabbath observant according to Mark is debatable. Much depends on the way Jesus justifies his actions on the Sabbath. In Mark and John his justification is related to Jesus' peculiar authority (Mark 2:27-28; John 5:16-18).[12]

---

9 See my review, RBL 01/2006.
10 Of all the Gospels, Matthew shows Jesus as Torah observant, and is aware and critical of a challenge to this position that might reflect the influence of Paul (Matt 5:19).
11 Given that the Petrine tradition assumes a later date for Mark than argued by Crossley, the Petrine hypothesis is hardly left open/undecided.
12 Only Mark has Jesus assert, "The Sabbath was made for man not man for the Sabbath," making this the basis (ὥστε) for the statement shared, with variations of word order, by all three Synoptic Gospels: "The Son of Man is Lord of the Sabbath." The words he alone attributes to Jesus might seem to reduce the authority implied by the shared statement, but the authoritative

But even if Jesus was Sabbath observant, Crossley is not justified in assuming that, a Law observant Jesus "can be expected of Mk 7:1-23" (p. 192). In the quest to find a Law observant *Marcan* Jesus, he allows the expectation to become an assumption that leads him to overlook the implications of the parabolic saying of 7:15 and to an unacceptable reading of Mark 7:19b; "making all foods clean." Thus, for him, "all foods" means, in this context, only all "permitted food." He rightly insists that the issue under discussion in Mark 7:1-23 is the requirement of hand-washing before eating, found in "the tradition of the elders." He is wrong to limit Mark's editorial conclusion to this meaning, and unjustified in arguing that Matt 15:20b correctly interprets Mark 7:19b. Rather, it seems, Matthew has recognised that Mark 7:19b is an unacceptable (to him) Marcan editorial comment, and replaces Marcan editorial with words attributed to Jesus; "but to eat with unwashed hands does not defile a person" (Matt 15:20b). Matthew's conclusion fits the context, whereas the Marcan conclusion opens up a new issue that is nevertheless implied by Jesus' parabolic saying in Mark 7:15 and his explanation in 7:18-19a.20-23.

Crossley argues that Mark's words (7:19b) only took on an unacceptable meaning for Matthew in the light of later (subsequent to Mark) Pauline influence. Prior to Paul's influence, he asserts, πάντα τὰ Βρώματα would have been understood in terms of foods defined as pure by the Jewish food laws. In that case, Mark 7:19b asserts only that such foods were not made unclean by unwashed hands, which is made clear by Matt 15:20b. This reading takes no account of Mark 7:15.18-19a.20-23, about which Matthew also evidences discomfort.

Crossley defends Matthew's reading of Mark, not as a correction, but as one that gets Mark right. His treatment of Mark 7:1-23 fails to take account of the radical nature of Jesus' parabolic response to his critics; "There is nothing from outside (οὐδέν ἐστιν ἔξωθεν) a person by going into him that is able (ὃ δύναται) to make him unclean; but the things coming out of a person are what defile a person" (7:15). The Marcan form of the parable does not specify the part of the person anything enters and exits. Given the discussion is about eating food, Matthew's clarification, naming the mouth as the point of entry and exit might seem obvious (Matt 15:11). As it turns out in the explanation, he was wrong. In Mark, only in Jesus' explanation does it become clear that what goes in is *into the belly* while what defiles comes *out of the heart* (7:19a.20-23). But even without the explanation, the implications of the parabolic saying can hardly be restricted

---

statement about the place and role of Sabbath law marks his authority. What is more, it is this view of the place and role of Sabbath law that guides the implied answer to the question of what is lawful on the Sabbath (Mark 3:4) in the next incident (Mark 3:1-6 par. Matt 12:9-14 and Luke 6:6-11).

to the hand-washing incident. It is *not what goes in*, but *what comes out* that defiles a person.

Matthew seeks to soften and limit possible implications by leaving out the highlighted words above and adding some interpretative changes; "It is not what goes into the *mouth* that defiles a person but what comes out of the *mouth* defiles a person" (Matt 15:11). The potential stark crudeness of the parable in Mark 7:15 was unacceptable to Matthew. In Mark the parabolic saying is capable of meaning; "it is not food going into a person that defiles, but human excreta coming out defiles a person." In Jesus' explanation in Mark what goes into the belly goes out as human excreta into the latrine. Hence the wording of the parable in Mark is open to this meaning. That this is not the meaning only becomes clear in the explanation of the parable, clarified by "what come out of the heart." In Matthew, the parable already excludes this crude possibility by changing the wording to say; "it is not what goes into the *mouth* but what comes out of the *mouth* that defiles" (Matt 15:11). This is a step in the direction of Jesus' explanation in Mark. But, while the common use of mouth for what goes in and out excludes any possible reference to human excreta, the mouth is hardly the source of "fornication, theft, murder, adultery, wickedness, deceit, licentiousness, envy…pride, folly," for which the Marcan use of *heart* is entirely appropriate. Though Jesus' explanation in Matthew makes a further adjustment, "what comes out of the mouth proceeds from the heart," most of the evil things are actions that do not proceed out of the heart *via the mouth*.

In Mark, the implications of Jesus' parabolic saying (7:15) are spelt out in his response (7:18-23) to the request of the disciples for clarification (7:17). The issue with which Matthew struggles, the abolition of the food laws, is inherent in Jesus' parabolic saying and explanation, not only the blatant statement of Mark's conclusion. As Jesus explains to the disciples; "nothing from outside entering into a person is able to defile him, because it does not enter into his heart but into the belly, and goes out into the latrine" (7:18-19a). The Marcan Jesus identifies the human heart as the source of defilement and evil (7:20-23) and in this he is followed, though less clearly, by Matthew (15:18-20a), who concludes; "These [what comes out of the mouth proceeding from the heart] are what defile a person, but to eat with unwashed hands does not defile" (15:20).

Editors of the Greek text and commentators rightly identify the words of Mark 7:19b as a Marcan editorial addition, not part of Jesus' explanation. Crossley struggles to make these words address the hand-washing incident, arguing that they are rightly interpreted in Matt 15:20b, which continues to report the words of Jesus; "but to eat with unwashed hands does not defile." Nevertheless, according to both Mark and Matthew, Jesus' parabolic saying still applies to anything eaten. Nothing eaten enters the heart, where defilement occurs. Everything eaten goes into the belly and from thence out into the latrine. What defiles *comes out of the heart!* Two simple distinctions are made. 1. It is not what goes *into* person, but what goes *out* of a person that defiles. 2. It is not what goes out of the *belly* but what goes out from the *heart* that defiles.

Even in Matthew, who seeks to limit the implications to hand-washing, Jesus' parable turns the focus from ritual defilement, from eating food defined as unclean by a legal authority, to focus on ethical issues. Although the Marcan conclusion appears to flow from this, Mark does not attribute his conclusion to Jesus. The parabolic saying of the Marcan Jesus (7:15) addresses the issue of hand-washing, but the logical implications are far broader, as Mark notes. Whether the historical Jesus anticipated Mark's conclusion or not is unclear.[13] It may be a Marcan insight in the light of later times and events. Jesus' parabolic saying and explanation may have been placed in the context of the hand-washing controversy by Mark.[14] Mark's conclusion is consistent with the view that the Marcan Gospel reflects the perspective of Paul's Law-free gospel. Matthew's modifications of Mark 7:1-23 struggle to neutralise this perspective but his conclusion limits the implications of Jesus' parable and explanation to the hand-washing incident.

Crossley repeats much of his argument in a more recent study.[15] He asserts, "Mk 7:19 is better understood as 'all foods permitted in the Law are clean'," arguing that "Matthew understood Mark correctly in his Mk 7:19 parallel where he wrote, 'but to eat with unwashed hands does not defile' (Mt 15:20)" (p. 14). But the Marcan form of Jesus' parable and his explanation of it do not support this reading. His case depends on a very early date for Mark and this needs much stronger evidence than Crossley provides in his book and subsequent chapter. We can date the career of Paul fairly accurately, but dating Mark is more problematic.

My argument so far could imply that the Marcan conclusion of 7:19b does not reflect the influence of the Pauline mission because Jesus' parabolic saying and interpretation already foreshadow it! If these verses contain authentic sayings of

---

[13] By "historical Jesus" I mean the Jesus reconstructed with some probability from surviving historical evidence. The complexity of this task should not be underestimated.
[14] See the discussion of Heikki Räisänen below.
[15] James G. Crossley, "Mark, Paul and the Question of Influences." In *Paul and the Gospels: Christologies, Conflicts and Convergences*, eds. Michael F. Bird and Joel Willitts, LNTS 411 (London: T & T Clark International, 2011), 10-29.

the historical Jesus, the Pauline mission to the nations was in continuity with the mission of Jesus. But there are objections to this conclusion.[16]

3 Indecision Concerning the Terms of the Pauline Mission in Acts

If the Pauline mission was a continuation of the mission of Jesus, the indecision and opposition of the Jerusalem Church, or sectors of it, to the Pauline mission is an inexplicable puzzle (see Acts 10; 15; 11:9; Gal 2:1-10. 11-14). Even if the Jesus tradition does not foreshadow the Pauline approach, Peter's experience with Cornelius, and the seeming acceptance of Peter's report by the Jerusalem church (Acts 11:1-18) make the incidents at Antioch more than perplexing (Acts 15:1.5; and Gal 2:11-14). The perplexity grows when a second incident at Antioch is seen to follow the Jerusalem assembly/"council."[17] Some scholars, who describe themselves as "conservative," situate the events of Gal 2 prior to the Jerusalem Council (Acts 15).[18] They identify the Jerusalem visit of Gal 2:1-10 with the so-called famine relief visit in Acts 11:27-30; 12:25.[19] The indecision about common meals in Gal 2:11-14 might seem to be lessened if this took place before the council. Two matters count against this move. First, Gal 2:1-10 makes no reference to the purpose of famine relief, which is the focus of Acts 11:27-30; 12:25 and looks much more like Paul's account of the events recorded in Acts 15.[20] Second, the Acts account of the council nowhere deals with the issue of Jewish and Gentile believers sharing common meals, so it is no less perplexing before than after the events of Acts 15. The requirements of the so-called "decree" are directed to the Gentile churches and deal with issues exclusively relevant to Gentiles, without implications for

---

16 Interestingly, Luke omits Mark 6:45-8:26, which contains the narrative of Jesus' detour into Gentile territory which might be seen as a precedent for a mission to the Gentiles.
17 Though this gathering of the Jerusalem church is not like later church councils, it functioned decisively like a council and this term is used in subsequent references.
18 For example, Fredrick F. Bruce, *The Book of the Acts* (Grand Rapids, Mich.: Eerdmans, new edn 1988), 231, 282-284; I. Howard Marshall, *Acts* (Grand Rapids, Mich.: Eerdmans, 1980), 204-05, 242-248; Ben Witherington, *The Acts of the Apostles: A Socio-Rhetorical Commentary* (Grand Rapids, Mich.: Eerdmans, 1998), 82-83, 90-97, 374-375.
19 In favour of this order is the harmonisation of the numbering of Paul's visits to Jerusalem according to Acts and Galatians.
20 Though the textual evidence in 12:25 does not clearly favour reference to the "return to Antioch," that is where they are in 13:1. Perhaps the Western reading (D) to a return ἀπὸ Ἰερουσαλήμ has a claim to originality (see the alternative ἐξ Ἰερουσαλήμ p^{74} A). Then Antioch would be the implied destination.

shared/common meals with Jewish believers. Thus, locating the events of Gal 2 prior to the council does nothing to alleviate the problem because, either way, they follow the incident of Peter and Cornelius and Peter's report to the Jerusalem church (Acts 10:1-11:18). Only in Jerusalem, with the accusation against Peter prior to his report to the Jerusalem church, is the problem of common meals between Jewish and Gentile believers raised prior to the events of Gal 2:11-14. Peter's report on Cornelius is his defence against the charge, "to having gone into the company of uncircumcised men and eaten with them" (Acts 11:2-3). His defence is not as a denial of the charge, but is a justification of the practice. He claims divine justification both in terms of his vision and also because of the giving of the Spirit to Gentiles who believed in the same way as the Spirit had been given to Jewish believers (Acts 11:5.16-17). His account to the Jerusalem church concludes with recognition and acclamation because God had given to the Gentiles repentance leading to life (11:18).

Following this event, the incident leading up to the Jerusalem council is a puzzle. The appearance in Antioch of some men from Judaea, who assert, "Unless you are circumcised according to the custom of Moses you cannot be saved," causes dissension and uncertainty (15:1). Paul, Barnabas, and some others took this matter to Jerusalem to be resolved. There the matter was restated with clarification; "It is necessary to circumcise them (Gentile believers) and to charge them to keep the Law of Moses" (15:5). In effect this maintains the Jewish character of the Jesus movement. It is a move away from seeing the blessings of a restored/renewed Israel overflowing to the nations. It is a step back from the recognition that God had bestowed his blessings on the household of the Gentile Centurion Cornelius and the practice of shared meals that apparently flowed from it.

Though the Jerusalem church accepted Peter's report that God had accepted Gentile believers (11:18), the Jerusalem council now faced the issue of whether Gentile believers must be circumcised and observe the Law of Moses. The council answered that question with a resounding "No!" Yet nothing in the accounts in Acts or Galatians raises the question of the equality of Gentile believers with their Jewish counterparts or the viability of common meals. These issues emerge subsequently in Antioch (Gal 2:11-14). In the light of the account of Peter's meeting with Cornelius and its aftermath, this is puzzling.

Apparently, prior to the Jerusalem council, no considered decision had been made as to whether Jewish and Gentile believers in Jesus would form one integrated movement or if there would be two semi-independent movements. The sharing of common meals, at first practised by Peter on the basis of his vision and the shared experience of the Spirit, stands in tension with the Jewish practice of circumcision and observance of the Law of Moses. When they become an issue (Acts 11:3; 15:1.5) they are deemed not to be required of Gentile believers, for whom only the four elements of the "decree" are applicable. But there is no indication whether or not keeping these made Jewish and Gentile believers equal and would make common meals possible. Apparently these issues were unforeseen and ignored at the Jerusalem council, though they seem to be already covered in the incident of Peter and Cornelius and accepted by the Jerusalem church. Does this cast some doubt on the credibility of the Acts account of the Cornelius incident in which Peter adopts a Pauline approach to the relationship between Jewish and Gentile believers? Or are we to think of Peter spontaneously acting in a way that would not be sustained when the implications were thought through? Against the latter is the affirmation given to Peter's approach by the Jerusalem church (Acts 11:18). The Pauline account of the outworking of the Jerusalem council involves the recognition of two missions: Cephas to the circumcision, and Paul to the nations (Gal 2:6-9). Though Paul probably did not foresee the implications of this, differing terms of mission are implicit, which seem to preclude an equality that included the sharing of common meals. If one mission was Law observant and the other was not, there would be points upon which they were irreconcilable. But for Paul this was an impossible outcome. Hence the scene depicted in Gal 2:11.

4 Mark 7:1-23 and the Pauline Mission

Either Mark 7:19b reflects the Pauline mission, or Mark 7:15.18-19a.20-23 imply that the historical Jesus foreshadowed a Law-free mission to the nations. The question this raises is, do these verses stand secure as sayings of the historical Jesus? Concerning Mark 7:15 Heikki Räisänen notes; "a broad consensus among NT scholars that this belongs to the bedrock of those *ipissima verba*, the authenticity of which is hardly open to serious doubt."[21] Given the stress on the Jewishness of Jesus in "the Third Quest", and the impact this emphasis has had on historical Jesus studies, I doubt that the broad consensus remains. As far as the authenticity of the saying of 7:15 is concerned, Räisänen considers the case to be inconclusive.[22] The saying of 7:15 may qualify as dissimilar from Judaism. It is hardly dissimilar from Paul (see Rom 14:14), especially when taken together

---

21 Heikki Räisänen "Jesus and the Food Laws: Reflections on Mk 7:15." In Heikki Räisänen, *Jesus, Paul and Torah: Collected Essays* (Sheffield: JSOT Press, 1992), 127-48 at 127. The chapter was first published in 1986.
22 Räisänen "Jesus and the Food Laws," 139.

with commentary.[23] Räisänen accepts the view that the saying of 7:15 was placed in its present context by Mark, perhaps with the secondary commentary already attached at the pre-Marcan stage. But the pattern of Jesus' explanation to the disciples alone at a later time is a Marcan characteristic. Even if the explanation (7:18-19a.20-23) was added to the parabolic saying (7:15) by Mark or at a pre-Marcan stage, the parable alone remains a critique of the food laws as well as hand-washing because, it is *not what goes in* but *what comes out* that defiles.

The implications of the parabolic saying of Jesus with his explanation (Mark 7:15.18-19a.20-23) go beyond the controversy over hand-washing. Mark's conclusion in 7:19b arises from the parabolic saying and expresses the Marcan editorial point of view. The Matthean view found in Matt 15:20 arises from the hand-washing incident rather than from the parabolic saying, even in its modified Matthean form, yet is expressed as the continuing words of Jesus. Indeed, Matt 15:17-20 modifies both the parabolic saying of Mark 7:15, and the explanation of it in 7:18-19a, not only the narrator's conclusion in 7:19b.

From the perspective of Marcan priority, Matthew has modified the Marcan conclusion and has tinkered with the parabolic saying and explanation in an attempt to refocus it on his own conclusion. Why has he done this? Is it because Matthew thinks Mark's conclusion is unjustified by the Jesus tradition? Or is it because of Matthew's own more conservative position? The Marcan conclusion flows naturally from Jesus' dramatic parabolic saying of 7:15 and his explanation in 7:18-19a.20-23, with which Matthew tinkers but largely retains.

Did Matthew change Mark's conclusion (7:19b) because it is expressed as Marcan editorial that goes beyond the scope of the hand-washing incident? Did he fail to change effectively the dramatic parable of Mark 7:15 with its explanation (7:18-19a. 20-23) because he accepted these as authentic Jesus tradition? Yet his minor tinkering reveals his discomfort with them, though it fails to safeguard them from a reading consistent with Mark's conclusion. It is likely that Matthew rejected Mark's editorial conclusion because it reflects Pauline influence. But, as we have seen, there is reason to doubt that the parabolic saying and explanation go back to Jesus in their present form. They, like the editorial conclusion of 7:19b, might reflect Pauline influence.

---

[23] See Dunn, *Jesus Remembered*, 573-77, especially 575 n. 139.

5 The Emergence of the Great Church

The Jerusalem church under James adopted the position described as the mission to the circumcision represented by Peter, which is distinct from the mission to the nations as represented by Paul (Gal 2:1-10). James evidently understood that this arrangement excluded Gentile believers from table fellowship with Jewish believers, while Paul opposed this discrimination (Gal 2:11-21). Even in the account of Acts 15, there is no suggestion that observance of the requirements of the "Jerusalem decree" would make Gentile believers equal to Jewish believers or make common meals possible. The recognition of two distinct missions seems to imply the observance of separate rules such as those that prevent common meals shared by Jewish and Gentile believers (see Gal 2:11-14). Paul might not have foreseen this, though James may have assumed it. In the Acts account, Paul was not a party to the formulation of the "decree" and was excluded from its circulation. Peter, Barnabas and other Jewish believers at Antioch fell into line when the message came from James and they withdrew from meals shared with Gentiles. Only Paul stood against that judgement.[24]

How, in a very short time, did a predominantly Gentile church emerge from a distinctively Jewish movement? This has long been a matter of contention between scholars of early Christianity.[25] The most likely answer is complex, and includes the following lines of evidence and argument. The success of the Pauline Law-free mission to the nations is one side of this. Another involves the destruction of the Jewish leadership of the Jerusalem church. This side is complex, involving the violent death of James, the brother of the Lord, in 62 CE. He had been the outstanding champion of the priority of the circumcision mission and the subordinate role of the mission to the nations. The impact of his death was magnified by the Jewish war that led to the destruction of the temple and much of Jerusalem in 70 CE, an event that led to the temporary dissolution of the Jerusalem church. When it was reconstituted under the leadership of Symeon, the cousin of Jesus and James (Eusebius, *H.E.* 3.11), it was with reduced influence. It continued to be a Jewish church until the end of the second Jewish revolt in 135 CE (Eusebius, *H.E.* 4.5). At that point the Jewish church in Jerusalem and its significant Jewish influence in the universal church ended. Jerusalem became a Gentile city with a Gentile church and Gentile leaders (Eusebius, *H.E.* 4.6). What emerged universally was the Law-free church of all nations. While other elements of the

---

24 On this complex issue see Painter *Just James*, 67-78, 83-102.
25 For example, see David Horrel, "'Becoming Christian': Solidifying Christian Identity and Content." In *Handbook of Early Christianity: Social Science Approaches*, eds Anthony J. Blasi, Jean Duhaime, and Paul-Andre´ Turcotte (New York, N.Y.: Alta Mira Press, 2002), 309-35 at 309.

Pauline gospel and mission fell from universal prominence, this aspect of his mission prevailed, and the distinctive form of Jewish Christianity represented by the early Jerusalem church shrank in significance and influence until eventually it disappeared. It is difficult to know whether this element of the Pauline mission would have triumphed so completely had the Jewish Jerusalem church survived, embedded within Judaism. But Judaism itself lost its central point of cohesion (Jerusalem and the temple), and became a phenomenon characterised by scattering, dispersion (*diaspora*). No significant Jewish church remained to balance or restrain the drive of burgeoning Gentile Christianity. To know what difference the survival of Judaean Judaism and the Jewish Jerusalem church might have made would be to rewrite history, a luxury that we do not have the resources to do with any degree of probability.

We are left with the suspicion that the parabolic saying attributed to Jesus in Mark 7:15 reflects Pauline influence along with the explanation of 7:17-19a.20-23, and with a stronger conviction that the editorial conclusion of Mark 7:19b does. Other aspects of Mark also suggest a post-Pauline perspective. Possibly Mark has organised his Gospel so that a Galilean mission is followed by a mission *into Gentile territories* (6:45-8:26), a section omitted by Luke. Because Luke does not provide any rationale for his omissions or inclusions, we are left guessing, and often without much to go on. The recognition of the omission builds on the recognition that Luke knew and used Mark as one of his sources. If that is true, Luke omitted the incident concerning hand-washing before eating, including the Pharisaic critique, Jesus' parabolic response, and Mark's startling conclusion. If Luke intentionally omitted Mark 6:45-8:26, the absence of this material might mean that Luke objects to an implied mission of Jesus to Gentiles.

A close look at the detail of Mark's account of Jesus' detour into Gentile territory (6:45-8:26) suggests that Jesus visited the scattered Jewish communities in this area, encountering Gentiles only by accident. Nevertheless, those accidents create precedents. They suggest that, although Jesus was focused on a mission to renew Israel, he did not turn his back on human need beyond the borders of Israel. He did not shun or refuse to touch people portrayed as the outcasts of society, the unclean, like lepers, or a woman with a bleeding problem, or those perceived to be demon possessed/possessed by unclean spirits. By bridging the gap separating outcasts, Jesus perhaps foreshadowed the bridging of the gap between Jews and Gentiles. But had Jesus enunciated a clear program of mission to the Gentiles, in which all discriminatory differences between Jews and Gentiles were abolished, the history of early Christianity would probably have followed a different course. Some detailed attention to the evidence of Acts and

Paul's letters may throw some light on this issue.²⁶ First there is an important incident in Mark that puts in question the existence of any explicit Gentile mission during the mission of Jesus.

6 Jesus' Mission and the Syrophoenician Woman, Mark 7:24-30

A highlight of the Marcan section omitted by Luke (6:45-8:26) is the incident with the Syrophoenician woman in a house in the region of Tyre (Mark 7:24-30; Tyre and Sidon according to Matt 15:21 and some variants of Mark 7:24). Tyre and Sidon mark the region of Syrophoenicians, in which Alexander the Great had established centres of Greek culture. Thus it is not surprising that the woman was Greek by culture/language. The surprise is her appearance inside the house, which Jesus entered in order to keep his presence a secret. This he was unable to do because the woman penetrated his cover (7:24). She is not portrayed as an invited guest but as an intruder who entered the house because of an emergency involving her daughter. She has come begging Jesus for help (7:26).²⁷

Nothing suggests that Jesus enters a Gentile house. Rather, Mark's indication that Jesus entered a house serves the secrecy motif, which is characteristic of Mark. Jesus withdraws into a house seeking (unsuccessfully) to keep his presence a secret. Characteristically, the secrecy is breached immediately by the unannounced presence in the house of a Greek speaking Syrophoenician woman. Without any preliminary action, Mark has her prostrate herself at Jesus' feet (προσέπεσεν πρὸς τοὺς πόδας αὐτοῦ) using a strong image of the suppliant (7:25).²⁸ Though Mark has already noted for the reader that the woman had a daughter with an *unclean spirit*, only now does she request Jesus to "cast out the demon from her daughter." Matthew narrates a repeated petition in abbreviated form, and now addressed to Jesus, "Lord/Sir, help me."

---

26 See Acts 10; 13-14; 15; 21; Gal 2:1-10.11-21 for evidence of the struggle to determine the conditions for Gentiles to join the Jesus movement and the struggle for equal status with Jewish followers.
27 See Painter, *Mark's Gospel*, 114-16. The woman is portrayed as a suppliant begging for help and the language used to describe her prostration at the feet of Jesus is comparable to that used of the demon possessed in 3:11 (cf. 5:6), and Jairus who falls at Jesus' feet in worshipful/petitionary attitude.
28 In Matthew also the woman adopts the posture of a suppliant (προσεκύνει), though less dramatically.

Only in Mark does Jesus say, "First (πρῶτον) permit the children to be satisfied," using graphic imagery to assert the *priority* of his mission to his own people. What follows is common to Matthew and Mark with very minor variations; "For (γάρ) it is not good (appropriate) to take the children's bread and throw it to the dogs" (Mark 7:27; Matt 15:26).[29]

In Mark (7:28) her response appears to correct Jesus' words; "Lord/Sir, even the dogs under table eat from the children's crumbs."[30] Her response may be encouraged by the "*First* (πρῶτον) permit the children to be satisfied," which implies a second. She however objects to the temporal distinction that implies the necessity to wait. Yet the crumbs falling to the dogs is a kind of secondary, overflow feeding. It is not temporally secondary, but is a consequence of the feeding of the children, thus secondary in this sense. Encouraged by the use of *first*, she responds, "Lord, even the dogs under the table eat from the children's crumbs" (7:28), and wins Jesus' approval. Jesus commends her response (7:29, "Because of this saying...") and grants the woman her request for her daughter. In other words, the benefits of his ministry to Israel overflow to a Gentile.

This story resonates with a strand of Biblical tradition that envisages God's blessings to Israel overflowing to the Gentiles.[31] Her saying is thus not merely a clever riposte; it goes to the heart of the implications of Jesus' mission to Israel. Yet this hardly breaks down the distinction between Jew and Gentile or removes the priority given to the Jews, as might be implied by the Marcan editorial conclusion of 7:19b. It is possible that the historical Jesus envisaged an overflow of the blessings of his mission to Israel to flow to Gentiles and that Mark has read this in the light of the Law-free gospel of the Pauline mission.

Eleven changes in Matt 15:21-28 modify the Marcan story: the *first* expands Mark's reference from the region of Tyre to Tyre and Sidon (15:21); the *second* refers to the suppliant as "a Canaanite woman" not "a Syrophoenician woman" of Greek culture; the *third* omits Mark's secrecy motif, and has the woman confront Jesus publicly in the street (15:22); the *fourth* describes the woman crying out loudly (ἔκραξεν), and publicly addressing Jesus and imploring, "Have mercy

---

[29] Having omitted the first part of the statement, Matthew also omits the connecting "for" (γάρ).

[30] The woman's response in Matthew has only minor variations from Mark but Jesus' saying about the priority of the children cannot provide a basis for her claim. Nevertheless, the woman finds a way to agree with Jesus while pressing her request; "*Yes* Lord/Sir, *for* even the dogs eat of the crumbs that fall from the table of their masters/Lords." (Matt15:27).

[31] See Isa 2:2-3; 42:1.4; 49:6; 60:1-4; Zech 8:20-23; Mic 4:1-2. There is also common reference to Gentiles worshipping God in all parts of the earth, Isa 45:6.22; 49:6.23; 56:6-8; 59:19; Zech 2:11; Mic 7:17; Mal 1:11, in a way consistent with the overflow of the blessings of God to the nations, perhaps also consistent with the promise to Abraham in Gen 12:1-3.

on me Lord, son of David;" in the *fifth* the woman concludes her public appeal with a statement of the plight of her daughter, "my daughter is severely demonised (δαιμονίζεται)" (15:22), not as "having an unclean spirit" as in Mark who continues the purity motif; the *sixth* has the disciples (not mentioned in Mark's account) intervene directing Jesus to "send her away because she is crying out after us" (15:23); the *seventh* inserts Jesus' response prior to meeting the woman, "I was not sent except for the lost sheep of the house of Israel" (15:24), which seems to be a response to the disciples because, only after this mission statement by Jesus does the woman approach Jesus. This statement echoes Jesus' commission of the disciples, limiting their mission to the lost sheep of the house of Israel (10:5-6), which is now shown to be consistent with Jesus' own mission. Together they confirm Matthew's view that Jesus' mission into Gentile territory was for lost/scattered (*diaspora*) Israelites/Jews; the *eighth* omits the first part of Jesus' response to the woman in Mark 7:27, "*First* allow the children to be fed." Apparently Jesus mission statement to the disciples (15:24) was thought to be more adequate than the priority asserted by the Marcan Jesus. As a full address and request has already been made loudly and publicly, the woman adopts the attitude of a suppliant, and simply requests, "Lord, help me." The woman in Mark responds to the double statement, "*First permit the children to be fed for* it is not fitting to take the children's bread and cast it to dogs;" whereas the woman in Matthew responds only to the latter; *ninth*, where the woman in Mark appears to object to the temporal priority, "Lord, even the dogs under the table eat from the children's crumbs," the woman in Matthew agrees with Jesus, "Yes Lord, *for* also the dogs eat from the crumbs that fall from their Lord's table;" *tenth*, the woman in Matthew changes the image of the "children's table" to "their Lord's table." This image change acknowledges the subservience of those who receive the crumbs; *eleventh*, in Mark, Jesus commends the woman for her astute word, "Because of this word, go, the demon has come out of your daughter." In Matthew, Jesus commends the woman for her faith, "O woman, great is your faith, let it be to you as you will." In each case the daughter was healed. Matthew provides a summary statement to that affect while Mark reports that when the woman "departed into her house she found child lying on the bed, the demon having come out [of her]" (Matt 15:28; cf. Mark 7:30).

In Matthew's account the woman's appeal to Jesus as "Son of David" acknowledges the Jewish roots of Jesus so that the woman appears more like a Godfearer than the Marcan woman. This aspect of Matthew's account is similar to Mark's account of Bartimaeus, who publicly confronted Jesus as he entered Jericho and began to cry out (ἤρατοκραξειν), "Jesus, Son of David, have mercy on me," and although there were many attempts to silence him, he continued to cry out (ἔκραξεν), "Son of David, have mercy on me" (Mark 10:47-48 and compare Matt 15:22-23). Matthew's account of the healing of the two unnamed blind men (20:29-34) retains these features, as does Luke in his account of the healing of an unnamed blind man (Luke 18:35-43). Luke twice reports the words of the blind man saying; "Son of David, have mercy on me" (18:38. 39). But only Matthew uses this form of address in the appeal of a Gentile to Jesus (15:22). Her public cry of appeal addressing Jesus as "Son of David" perhaps identifies her with Gentile suppliants who had come to one of Israel's prophets seeking healing/help from the God of Israel (cf. Elisha and Naaman, 2 Kgs 5). She now simply says, "Lord, help me."

For Matthew there is no mission of Jesus to the Gentiles on special terms, but as of old, the crumbs fall to Gentiles who come seeking help from the God of Israel. Such suppliants might be considered "Godfearers" or proselytes (like Cornelius in Acts 10). Matthew's account of the commission by the risen Lord in 28:16-20 presupposes a single Law-observant mission "to make disciples of all the nations...teaching them to observe all that I have commanded you," which is probably consistent with the commission of the disciples (10:5-6) and Jesus' view of his own mission (15:24).

A subservient relationship to "Israelites" is retained by the woman's reference to "the crumbs falling from their Lord's table." The woman in Mark penetrates the house where Jesus was staying and thereby adopts a more intimate relationship. From this Matthew has drawn back to a public encounter, a confession of faith mediated by Judaism, a clear statement of Jesus' mission restricted to Israel and without acknowledging any temporal space for an independent mission to the Gentiles such as is intimated in the saying; "First allow the children to be fed." Where the Jesus of Matthew emphasised the woman's great faith as the basis of her success, the Marcan Jesus attributes it to her perceptive response which saw the blessings overflowing directly to Gentiles.

7 Michael F. Bird: Jesus and the Gentile Mission

According to Michael Bird, Jesus established a Gentile mission. In developing his case he asks, "Did Jesus sanction or intimate a future Gentile mission?" (p. 3). There is ample evidence to show that the Gospels and Acts narrate such an intimation and even a commission (see Mark 13:10; Matt 28:16-20; Luke 24:47-49; John 17:18; 20:21-23; Acts 1:6-8). Mark sets Jesus' prediction of the universal proclamation in the context of his apocalyptic discourse on the eve of his arrest. Matthew, Luke, and John set the commission in the context of the appearances of the risen Jesus, as does Acts 1:6-8, which should be seen in relation to the

Lucan reference. However we judge the historical reliability of these accounts, they suggest that the historical Jesus conducted no programmatic mission to the nations/Gentiles. Had he done so, the future projection and post-resurrection commission would be redundant. The commission of the twelve in Mark 3:6-13 and Luke 9:1-6 looks like a mission to the surrounding Jewish villages and Matt 10:5-15 explicitly excludes going into the way of the Gentiles or Samaritans. Rather they are to go to "the lost sheep of the house of Israel" (Matt 10:5-6). While this may be no more than a clarification of Mark and Luke, it is probably rigidly more negative than Mark and Luke imply. Bird goes on; "The purpose of this monograph is to argue that Jesus' intention was to renew and to restore Israel, so that a restored Israel would extend God's salvation to the world" (p. 3). The implication seems to be that although the world was the goal, Jesus' historic mission was to renew and restore Israel. "First (πρῶτον) permit the children to be satisfied." However, Bird asserts that, as "this restoration was already being realized in Jesus' ministry" it was "possible for Gentiles to share in the benefits of Israel's restoration" (p. 3). This means that the followers of Jesus represent the restored Israel and provide continuity between the historical Jesus and the early Christian mission to the Gentiles (p. 5).

Bird has good grounds for seeing Jesus' mission to renew and restore Israel fulfilled in nuce in his disciples. The appointment of the twelve, symbolic of the twelve tribes of Israel, is inseparably linked to Jesus' commission of them, sending them out and thus extending his mission (see Mark 3:13-19; 6:6b-13 and parallels).

Matthew combines the naming of the twelve (10:1-4) and their commission to go out announcing the coming of the kingdom, healing the sick, cleansing lepers, and casting out demons (10:5-15), but they seem already to be a group of twelve (10:1). In Mark 3:13-19 at the choosing and appointment of the twelve the purpose is said to be "that they may be with him (Jesus) and that he may send them out to preach" (3:14). Thus, although they are not sent out to preach, cast out demons, anoint and heal until 6:7-13, the connection is established at their call/appointment. Like Mark, Luke separates the appointment of the twelve (Luke 6:12-16) from their commission (9:16). Unlike Mark, Luke does not make Jesus' purpose for them to extend his mission clear from the beginning, though in all three accounts they are called apostles.

Nothing suggests that their mission extended to Gentiles and Matthew explicitly excludes this. Rather their mission extended the scope of Jesus' mission to Israel. Bird contends that the future Gentile mission rests on the mission of the twelve, approximating to the role of Israel as "a light to the nations" (p. 3 and note Luke 2:32 and Isa 42:6; 46:13; 49:6). In Isaiah the light to the nations is identified with God's servant whose role is to raise up Israel and also fulfills the role of ideal Israel to be a light to the nations (see especially Luke 4:1.16-21; Isa 61:1-2a; cf. 60:1-7). This overlap provides a basis for a close connection between Jesus and his followers and the Gentile mission, even if neither Jesus nor the disciples actually entered into a mission to Gentiles during his lifetime. It leaves a somewhat blurred perception about whether Jesus instituted a mission to the Gentiles during his own historic mission and about the terms of relationship between Jewish and Gentile followers.

A view something like Bird's view of Jesus' historic mission to restore and renew Israel seems likely. It is unlikely that Jesus or his disciples undertook a specific mission to the nations/Gentiles. There is however a basis for acknowledging Jesus' vision of the blessings of the renewed Israel overflowing to the Gentiles, but without spelling out the terms of the relationship of Gentiles to the renewed Israel. Ekhard Schnabel seems to be on solid ground in suggesting the terms of mission were in dispute, not the mission *per se*.[32] On the one hand, Matthew reports his understanding of the nature of the mission commissioned by Jesus in 28:16-20. This mission is to the nations, but does not envisage the breaking down of the discriminatory differences between Jews and Gentiles. Matthew presupposes that, in becoming followers of Jesus, Gentiles will convert to the form of Judaism taught by Rabbi Jesus, being observant of the Law as taught by him. The commission is to "*make disciples* of all the nations, teaching them *to observe all that I have commanded you.*" But if Matthew reflects a single Law observant mission to the nations, Acts plots a different course.

8 Acts 10: Peter and Cornelius

After almost two thousand years it is hard to find a way back to Simon Peter and his place in the earliest church. In particular his relationship to a mission to the Gentiles is a puzzle. On the one hand Paul names him as the leading figure of the circumcision mission (Gal 2:1-11). Alternatively, on the basis of Acts 10, he is often seen as the leading initiator of the mission to the Gentiles/nations, which seems to be supported by his role at the Jerusalem Council. A close look at Luke's account of the incident with Cornelius tends to undermine this view, especially in the light of other evidence.

---

[32] Eckhard Schnabel, "Jesus and the Beginnings of the Misson to the Gentiles." In *Jesus of Nazareth Lord and Christ: Essays on the Historical Jesus and New Testament Christology*, eds. Joel B. Green and Max Turner (Grand Rapids, Mich.: Eerdmans, 1994), 37-58 at 41.

8.1 What is Said about Cornelius?

Acts first refers to Cornelius in terms of his his Roman credentials, as a Centurion of the Italian Cohort (Acts 10:1.22). Then, Acts 10:2.22 describe Cornelius as "a devout man who feared God (εὐσεβὴς καὶ φοβούμενος τὸν θεὸν) with all his household giving alms *to the people* and praying constantly to God (ἐλεημοσύνας πολλὰς τῷ λαῷ καὶ δεόμενος τοῦ θεοῦ διὰ παντός)" (10:2); "an upright/righteous and God-fearing man (ἀνὴρ δίκαιος καὶ φοβούμενος τὸν θεὸν) well spoken of by the whole Jewish nation" (10:22). These references overlap because, in 10:2 the narrator informs the reader about Cornelius, while, in 10:22 the servants sent by Cornelius inform Peter of the sender of the message. The overlap consists of the repetition of καὶ φοβούμενος τὸν θεὸν, describing Cornelius as a person who *fears God*. This language, here and elsewhere in Acts, is part of the evidence that led to the distinction between "Godfearers" and "proselytes." Proselytes were understood to be converts to Judaism who underwent circumcision and undertook full Law observance, while Godfearers were not circumcised but were otherwise broadly Law observant. Certainly Cornelius was sympathetic to and supportive of Judaism in material ways as an expression of his devotion to the God of Israel (10:3-4). This is made clear in the supportive language surrounding the overlapping common reference in 10:2.22. Reference to Cornelius as "a devout man" (εὐσεβὴς) and a "righteous man" (ἀνὴρ δίκαιος) probably affirm him as Law observant apart from circumcision. Prominently included are the weightier matters of the Law like the works of mercy for the people (ἐλεημοσύνας πολλὰς τῷ λαῷ).

8.2 Cornelius as a "Godfearer" and Acceptability to God

The narrative quickly establishes Cornelius as a man of rank and importance in the Roman world who has an existing relationship to Judaism. He, and all his household, are sincere worshippers of God. This is not an encounter between Peter and the paganism of the Gentile world, but because Cornelius was not circumcised and fully Law observant, Peter had reservations about his level of contact with Cornelius. In spite of the nature of Peter's vision, it seems that the issue at stake here was not eating food prohibited by the Jewish food laws. In all probability these laws were kept by Cornelius and his household. But Cornelius and his household were not Jewish, though they were sympathetic to Judaism. When Peter arrived in the house of Cornelius in Caesarea he said to those gathered; "You know how unlawful it is for a Jewish man to associate with or visit a person of another nation (ἀλλοφύλῳ)" (10:28).Yet this is what Peter does, and uses his vision in Joppa to justify his deviant actions; "but God has shown me that I should not call any man common or unclean (κἀμοὶ ὁ θεὸς ἔδειξεν μηδένα κοινὸν ἢ ἀκαθάρτον λέγειν ἄνθρωπον) (10:28)." Though the vision was about the abolition of the distinction between clean and unclean animals (food), the lesson Peter explicitly draws concerns the abolition of the distinction between clean and unclean people (see 10:12-14.16 and 10:28).[33] As a result Peter announces to those gathered in the house of Cornelius that God does not show partiality towards persons (οὐκ ἔστιν προσωπολήμπτης ὁ θεός). God does not discriminate on the basis of race and culture, but in every nation the person fearing God (ὁ φοβούμενος αὐτὸν) and working righteousness (ἐργαζόμενος δικαιοσύνην) is acceptable to God (10:34-35). Although there is no explicit indication that Peter shared meals with the household of Cornelius, either in the account of the event, or in Peter's report to the Jerusalem church, the opponents of Peter in Jerusalem accuse him of having done so (Acts 11:2-3). As he does not deny this, the implications of this incident pose questions for the actions of Peter and others in the incident described in Gal 2:11-14.

9 Galatians 2:11-14 and Acts 10 and 15

Assuming that the incident described in Gal 2:11-14 is subsequent, not only to the events of Acts 10, but also to the Jerusalem council described in Acts 15, what are we to make of Peter and other Jewish believers (apart from Paul) withdrawing from shared meals with Gentile believers in Antioch, having shared common meals prior to the arrival of the messengers from James? It could be argued that Peter, following the logic of his visionary experience and the associated events in the household of Cornelius, which had been reported to James and the Jerusalem church, assumed that common meals with Gentile believers were appropriate. The messengers from James called them back from this practice, which threatened the already precarious relationship of the Jerusalem church to the broader Jewish community (see Acts 21:17-26).

How could this state of affairs emerge after the agreement achieved by Barnabas and Paul, with the support of Peter and the agreement of James at the Jerusalem council of Acts 15? Just what was agreed at the council? Clearly it was decided that Gentile believers were not required to be circumcised or to keep

---

[33] Yet precisely this language (κοινὸν ἢ ἀκαθάρτον) is used in Mark 7:2.5.15.18.19.20.23 in relation to food that is or becomes unclean and defiles. But Mark asserts that Jesus declared all foods clean.

other distinctively Jewish elements of the Jewish Law. At the council the two main speakers, whose words are reported, are Peter and James. Between their speeches Acts notes only that "Barnabas and Paul recounted what signs and wonders God performed through them among the Gentiles" (15:12). In summing up James appealed to Peter's testimony concerning the way the gospel was first preached to the Gentiles by him, and James asserts that this is in harmony with the words of the prophet (Amos 9:11-12). On this basis he concludes; "Wherefore I judge (διὸ ἐγὼ κρίνω) that we should not trouble those of the Gentiles who turn to God, but should write to them to abstain from the pollution of idols and from unchastity, and from what is strangled and from blood" (15:19-20). James' considered judgement was not discussed but the gathered apostles, elders, and the whole church agreed to send their pastoral letter embodying the "decree" *formulated by James* to Antioch with Paul and Barnabas but *by the hand of* their trusted messengers, Silas and Judas/Barsabbas (15:22-29).

Though Acts finds a gracious way of explaining the role of the special messengers, the message is not entrusted to Barnabas and Paul, and Paul shows no evidence that he required his congregations to observe the four demands of the decree. Further, nothing in the account of the council, or in the letter embodying the decree, suggests that the question of shared meals between Jewish and Gentile believers was envisaged or discussed. The focus of the council was the question of whether circumcision and observance of the Law of Moses were to be required of Gentile believers, Acts 15:1.5. The clear answer to this question was "No!" All that is asked beyond the response to the gospel was observance of the four requirement set out by James and confirmed by the Jerusalem church (Acts 15:19-21.24-29).

Thus, even after the Jerusalem council it remains unclear whether Jewish believers could fraternise with Gentile believers, sharing meals with them (see 10:28). Peter may have believed that this was now possible, joining other Jewish believers at the common meals in Antioch. Only when messengers came from James calling on Jewish believers to withdraw from common meals did the controversy concerning the variant practice of the two missions become apparent. Of the Jewish believers, only Paul withstood this demand. This difference with Barnabas who, with the other Jewish believers, complied with James' demand, was probably a factor leading to their decision to go their separate ways, each choosing new partners in their missionary activities (see Gal 2:13 and Acts 15:36-41).

10 Barnabas and Saul/Paul

The partnership between Barnabas and Saul began when, after his Damascus road experience, Saul came to Jerusalem. Because of his reputation he was held in suspicion by the apostles until Barnabas introduced him to them as a new convert (Acts 9:26-28). Later, when Barnabas was sent to Antioch to oversee the rapidly expanding mission there, he sought out Saul in Tarsus and brought him to Antioch to share the work (Acts 11:21-25). In all of this Saul is dependent on Barnabas as his assistant. Two things need to be noted. The first is the name of Saul, which is used initially. Second, his name appears in the subordinate place following that of Barnabas. This is repeated in Acts 13 where, in the list of prophets and teachers in Antioch, Barnabas is mentioned first and Saul last (13:1). In the commissioning of 13:2, the Holy Spirit commands "set apart for me Barnabas and Saul," so confirming the priority and leadership of Barnabas.

When they set out they sailed to Salamis in Cyprus, Barnabas being a native of that country (4:36 and cf. 9:26-28; 11:21-25). His choice of his cousin John Mark as an assistant (ὑπηρέτην), also bears out his leadership of the mission (13:5). That Mark leaves when the leadership and location of the mission change implies that there were some serious differences between Paul and Barnabas. The differences were perhaps evident to Mark, who departs, but perhaps only clear to Paul and Barnabas on return to Antioch after the council (see Gal 2:11-14 and Acts 15:36-41).

The transition of the use of the name from Saul to Paul in Acts coincides with the reversal of order from the priority of Barnabas to the priority of Paul; cf. the order of Barnabas and Saul in 11:24-26.29-30; 12:24-25; 13:1-3.7. The transition is explicitly marked by the explanation, "But Saul, who was also Paul, being filled with the Holy Spirit" (13:9-10.11-12). This rubric-like explanation by the narrator reflects the action of Paul in assuming the leading role. Thus when they leave Cyprus from Paphos, en-route to Perga of Pamphylia, it is "Paul and those with him," and John Mark separates himself from the party and returns to Jerusalem (13:13). It seems as if he came on a mission to Cyprus under Barnabas and left when the mission changed leadership and location. Paul continues to assume leadership in 13:14-16a.16b-41. Then the order is Paul and Barnabas (13:43.46.50), or Paul showing leadership (13:45; 14:8.9). Though Barnabas is mentioned first in 14:12, it is Paul who is "the chief speaker." The order is Paul and Barnabas twice in 15:2, but the order returns to Barnabas and Paul in Jerusalem, in recognition that Barnabas is the delegate of the Jerusalem church in Antioch 15:12.25. Once the transition from Saul to Paul is noted (13:9) there is no reversion to Saul, not even in Jerusalem with the return to the priority of Barnabas. Because there is no evidence of the use of Saul in

Paul's letters we may doubt Luke's use of this name, which serves as a thematic marker. In the same way the changing order of the names is significant, and returns to Paul and Barnabas in 15:22 and after the Jerusalem council in 15:35.36.

After the council, when Paul and Barnabas had returned to Antioch, and after the disagreement of Gal 2:11-14, Paul proposed a second mission, but there was disagreement between Paul and Barnabas (Acts 15:36-41). Barnabas wanted to return to Cyprus, where he began as the leader and with John Mark again. Paul therefore chose Silas and returned to the churches established in Pamphylia under his leadership. It is arguable that these two missionary enterprises adopted different policies concerning the relationship between Jewish and Gentile believers, Barnabas adopting the Jamesian view that the blessings of the mission to renew Israel overflowed to the Gentile believers, but the two remained separate communal developments. But Paul adopted the view that God did not discriminate in this way because οὐκ ἔστιν προσωπολήμπτης ὁ θεός but in every nation the person fearing God (ὁ φοβούμενος αὐτὸν) and working righteousness (ἐργαζόμενος δικαιοσύνην) is acceptable to God" (Acts 10:34-35 and cf. Rom 2:11; Jas 2:1.9).

The point of this discussion is to make clear the tangled and complex nature of the Acts narrative. This might be a result of an author who is more sympathetic of the Pauline perspective in his reading of the progression of the Jerusalem church towards the acceptance of the Gentile mission. There may be a reading of Peter's role in a somewhat Pauline light in the interest of a more harmonious progress to the church of all nations. This might account for a somewhat more Pauline outcome in Peter's dealing with Cornelius than fits the overall progress of the story in Acts. Alternatively, that unevenness might be a consequence of differences between Peter and James which lead Peter in a more Pauline direction until he is recalled by James.

11 Mark and the Pauline Mission

Mark has retained the perspective of the mission of the historical Jesus to Israel in a restoration and renewal movement. At the same time, there are aspects of the Marcan account that press in a direction that seems to lessen the shock of the Pauline Law-free mission to the nations. There is a focus on Sabbath and purity issues and the daring way Jesus deals with them.

It is notable that the first of Jesus' mighty works according to Mark occurred in a synagogue in Capernaum on a Sabbath where Jesus drove out an *unclean spirit* (πνεῦμα ἀκαθάρτον) from a man (1:23-27).[34] Then there is the cleansing (καθαρίσαι) of a leper (1:40-45), and the case of the woman with an issue of blood who touched Jesus to be made whole (5:24b-34) before the two issues involved in 7:1-30. These are followed immediately by the first of two healings, found only in Mark, in which Jesus uses spittle to heal. The first of these occurred in the Gentile region of the Decapolis where Jesus healed a deaf and dumb man by putting his fingers into to the man's ears, spat and touched his tongue (7:31-37). In the second, Jesus spat on the eyes of a blind man in Bethsaida and laid his hands on his eyes twice before he saw clearly (8:22-26). This use of bodily fluids was irregular, revealing Jesus pushing at the boundaries of the purity laws. Mark seems to stress these issues, which are treated in more detail in the two incidents in 7:1-30. Mark 7:1-30 is in a part of Mark with no Lucan parallel. It narrates two incidents that have a bearing on the relation of this Gospel to the historical Jesus and to Paul and his mission to the nations.

The first (7:1-23) is an intra-Jewish dispute about the authority of the tradition of the elders. In dealing with this dispute the Jesus of Mark answers his critics with a characteristic parabolic saying (a *mashal*), or riddle. Only in Jesus' explanation privately to the disciples is the hidden meaning made clear. The Marcan editorial conclusion, like the words of Peter in Acts 10:34-35, have a Pauline ring about them, as does the Petrine interpretation of the pouring out of the Spirit on Cornelius and his household (Acts 10:44-48).The Marcan conclusion declares all food to be clean/pure, removing a serious barrier separating Jews and Gentiles. Indeed, there is reason to suspect Pauline influence of the Marcan Jesus tradition at this point (7:15.18-19a.20-23) and not only the Marcan editorial conclusion (7:19b).

The second story is of Jesus' encounter with a Syro-Phoenician woman in Mark 7:24-30. The meeting is not a result of the initiative of Jesus, but is brought about by the initiative of the woman who frustrates Jesus' attempt to keep his presence a secret by penetrating the house in which he was staying. The woman is carefully identified as a Greek speaking/cultured Syrophoenician (7:26). She is a Gentile with no prior relationship to Judaism but aware of Jesus' reputation as a healer. The scene reported is privately between Jesus and the suppliant who prostrates herself at his feet to make her appeal to Jesus "that he cast the demon out of her daughter." Thus, though not planned

---

[34] Not found in Matthew. Is it irony that the unclean spirit is encountered in the synagogue and on the Sabbath? This healing on the Sabbath comes prior to the pronouncement of the Marcan Jesus, "The Sabbath was made for man, not man for the Sabbath" (2:27), thus building up to this saying. The Marcan Jesus presses the boundary of Jewish Law that separated Jew and Gentile.

by Jesus, this is an encounter with a Gentile woman without an existing relationship to Judaism.

Jesus' initial response to the woman in Mark 7:27 ("*First* permit the children to be satisfied") is of special importance for recognising the relationship of Mark to the Pauline mission (see Rom 1:16 and cf. Acts 13:45-46; 18:6; Rom 9-11). In Romans Paul describes the *priority* of the gospel to the Jew *first* and also to the Greeks (Gentiles), and Acts describes this practice in the Pauline mission. It involved going to the Jews first and turning to the Gentiles only in the face of Jewish rejection (Acts 13:45-46; 18:6). This practice is implied by Paul in the extended argument of Rom 9-11, though not quite in the manner illustrated in Acts. In Romans Paul seems to be responding to a charge that he as a Jew was a Jew hater, having rejected his own people in favour of Gentiles. In the face of this charge he argues that his purpose in turning to the Gentiles is to provoke the Jews to jealousy, who were enjoying the blessings intended for Israel and, that thus provoked, they would turn to the Lord. What is important here is that the Pauline principle of "to the Jew first" does not imply that the Gentiles must await the completion of the mission to Israel. Nor does it in Mark 7:27, because the woman was granted her request (7:29-30). It was granted without any conditions involving an existing relation to the God of Israel or of Law observant discipleship to Jesus. The woman acknowledged the secondary nature of the mission to the Gentiles, as implied by Jesus, and therefore *objected* to Jesus' reference to taking the children's bread. Instead she appealed to the crumbs falling from the table. It is an overflow of blessings rather than the taking from one to give to another. Here the woman has hit on a prophetic vision of the way the blessing of Israel flow to the nations. The Jesus of Mark commends the woman because of her perceptive word.

There is no evidence here that suggests that Jesus' mission sought to break down the distinction between Jew and Gentile. It is perhaps Paul who was persuaded that the abolition of discrimination was rooted in the character of God whose very being was antithetical to discrimination based on cultural difference (Rom 2:11). Certainly the evidence of Gal 2:11-14 suggests that he was deeply committed to the acceptance of all believers without discrimination; "For you are all sons of God through faith in Christ Jesus; for as many as were baptised into Christ have put on Christ. There is no longer Jew or Greek, slave or free, male or female; for you are all one in Christ Jesus. And if you are of Christ, you are Abraham's seed, heirs according to the promise" (Gal 3:28-29).

The language concerning purity and defilement used in Mark 7:1-23 recurs in the incident involving Peter and Cornelius in Acts 10, which specifically raises the question of clean and unclean animals (as food), of clean and unclean people, and being defiled or made common (Acts 10:14-15.28.34-35.44-48; 11:1-3). Here

Peter appears to accept the equality of Jew and Gentile on the basis of his vision and prior to the reception of the Spirit by these Gentiles in a way comparable to their own reception (10:34-35.44-48). Some of the language here suggests Pauline influence and Peter's report, and the reception of it by the Jerusalem church (Acts 11:1-18) prior to the mission of the Hellenists to Antioch (Acts 11:19-30), and the council of Jerusalem (Acts 15), poses problems. The council was precipitated by the Judaean/Jerusalem assertion that Gentiles believers must be circumcised and observe the Law of Moses (Acts 15:1.5). This position was rejected at the council and only the four requirements of the Jerusalem decree were demanded of Gentiles. The demand that came from James to Antioch that Jewish believers should withdraw from common meals with Gentile believers caused a crisis (Gal 2:11-14). This situation seems to be an improbable outcome following Peter's report to the Jerusalem church, which was also a response to the accusation brought against him in Jerusalem prior to his report (Acts 11:3). He was accused of sharing hospitality and meals with Gentiles, a charge which he answered by defending his practice. His defence was received at the time and referred to with approval at the council. But nothing in Acts 15 suggests that Jewish and Gentile believers were equals or shared common meals. The separation seems to be implied also by James' words to Paul on his return to Jerusalem in Act 21:17-26. In the light of this it seems likely that the author of Acts, who has focused on Peter in the first half of Acts and on Paul in the second, has a tendency to bring them into harmony. Historically it is probably true that Peter and Paul were closer than Paul and James, but Peter remained the figurehead of the circumcision mission and Paul of the mission to the nations.[35]

---

35 See Painter, *Just James*, 58-104.

Bibliography

Bird, Michael F. *Jesus and the Origins of the Gentile Mission*. LNTS 331. London: T & T Clark International, 2007.
Bruce, Fredrick F. *The Book of the Acts*. Grand Rapids, Mich.: Eerdmans, new edn 1988.
Crossley, James G. *The Date of Mark's Gospel: Insight from the Law in Earliest Christianity*. JSNTSup 266. London: T & T Clark International, 2004.
—, "Mark, Paul and the Question of Influences," in: *Paul and the Gospels: Christologies, Conflicts and Convergences*, eds. Michael F. Bird and Joel Willitts, 10-29. LNTS 411. London: T & T Clark International, 2011.
Dunn, James D. G., *Jesus Remembered*. Grand Rapids, Mich.: Eerdmans, 2003).
Farrer, Austin. "On Dispensing with Q," in: *Studies in the Gospels*, ed. Dennis E. Nineham, 55-88. Oxford: Blackwell, 1955.
Horrel, David. "'Becoming Christian': Solidifying Christian Identity and Content," in: *Handbook of Early Christianity: Social Science Approaches*, eds Anthony J. Blasi, Jean Duhaime, and Paul-André Turcotte, 309-35. New York, N.Y.: Alta Mira Press, 2002.
Marcus, Joel. "Mark – Interpreter of Paul." *NTS* 46 (2000): 473-87.
Marshall, I. Howard. *Acts*. Grand Rapids, Mich.: Eerdmans, 1980.
Painter, John. *Just James: The Brother of Jesus in History and Tradition*. Columbia, S.C.; University of South Carolina Press, 1997.
—, *Mark's Gospel*. London: Routledge, 1997.
—, Review of James D. G. Dunn, *Jesus Remembered*. Grand Rapids, Mich.: Eerdmans, 2003), RBL 06/2004.
—, Review of James G. Crossley, *The Date of Mark's Gospel: Insight from the Law in Earliest Christianity*. JSNTSup 266. London: T & T Clark International, 2004, RBL 01/2006.
Räisänen, Heikki. "Jesus and the Food Laws: Reflections on Mk 7:15," in: Heikki Räisänen, *Jesus, Paul and Torah: Collected Essays*, 127-48. Sheffield: JSOT Press, 1992.
Schnabel, Eckhard. "Jesus and the Beginnings of the Misson to the Gentiles," in: *Jesus of Nazareth Lord and Christ: Essays on the Historical Jesus and New Testament Christology*, eds. Joel B. Green and Max Turner, 37-58. Grand Rapids, Mich.: Eerdmans, 1994.
Witherington, Ben. *The Acts of the Apostles: A Socio-Rhetorical Commentary*. Grand Rapids, Mich.: Eerdmans, 1998.

Teil 4 / Part 4: **Rezeptionsgeschichte /
Reception-History**

Alan H. Cadwallader
The Struggle for Paul in the Context of Empire: Mark as a Deutero-Pauline Text

1 Introduction

It was one thing to be "a man born to trouble as the sparks fly upward"[1] during his lifetime. After Paul's death, reputedly at the instigation of the Roman emperor Nero,[2] that trouble only compounded. Those who were Paul's familiar opponents were supplemented by those who scrambled over his authority and influence, divided about the direction that his legacy should follow. It might be thought that Paul's voice was consistent in its address of Christian communities as to patterns of organisation and living that delineated the members from a Roman-shaped identity,[3] even if there was some confusion or dispute about what Paul's meaning was. Be that as it may, there was no univocal or unilinear succession. The reference to the growing authority of Paul's letters at the beginning of the second century in 2Pet 3:16 ought not mask the admission in the same verse that contentions over meaning and application were equally part of the Pauline trajectory of authority formation.[4]

Mark, as many essays in this volume (and beyond) argue, was not immune from engagement with Paul's ideas,[5] though the Gospel is a text that omits any identification of its author.[6] But the New Testament, let alone the corpus of extra-canonical writings, contains a number of works generally acknowledged

---

[1] Charles K. Barrett, *On Paul: Essays on His Life, Work and Influence in the Early Church* (London: T & T Clark, 2003), 155.
[2] *Acts of Paul* 11.2–6. See Wilhelm Schneemelcher, *New Testament Apocrypha*, trans. Robert McL. Wilson, 2 vols (Cambridge: James Clarke, 1992), 2:261–63. See generally, David L. Eastman, *Paul the Martyr: The Cult of the Apostle in the Latin West* (Atlanta, Ga.: SBL, 2011).
[3] See, for example, Warren Carter, *The Roman Empire and the New Testament: An Essential Guide* (Nashville, Tenn.: Abingdon Press, 2006), 83–92.
[4] See Gerd Lüdemann, *Opposition to Paul in Jewish Christianity* (Minneapolis, Minn.: Fortress Press, 1989); William S. Babcock, ed., *Paul and the Legacies of Paul* (Dallas, Tex.: Southern Methodist University Press, 1990).
[5] Eugene Boring, *Mark: A Commentary* (Louisville, Ky.: Westminster John Knox Press, 2006), 31; note also the recent work of Steve Mason, *Josephus, Judea and Christian Origins: Methods and Categories* (Peabody, Mass.: Hendrickson, 2009), 285–302.
[6] "Mark" is simply a convenient modern designation of the second evangelist, built as it may be on early Christian embellishment. Originally, all the canonical gospels were anonymous works.

as post-Pauline yet claiming his name for the composition of the texts. One Deutero-Pauline letter in particular, that to the Colossians,[7] is dated to approximately the same time as the dating assigned to the Gospel of Mark, that is, to around 70 CE.[8] This essay proposes to explore the contention about the appropriation of the Pauline legacy by two writers, one anonymous, one pseudonymous, drawing upon Paul's influence and authority, and to suggest one of the catalysts or accelerants to those appropriations.

2 The Pauline Legacy and the Household Code

Paul himself wrote within the context of the ubiquity of Roman imperial presence; so also his successors continued to be surrounded by imperial values. In this sense, these writers are negotiating two unavoidable realities: the death of Paul and the life of the empire. Indeed, the one had engineered the other, as surely as in the crucifixion of Jesus. Rome and death were the two unavoidable realities for the Christians of Paul's generation and of the generation after Paul. Whether these Christians were of Jewish ethnicity, they confronted the reality of Seneca's Neronian conceit; "I am the arbiter of life and death for the nations."[9]

---

[7] On the pseudonymity of the letter to the Colossians, see Mark Kiley, *Colossians as Pseudepigraphy* (Sheffield: JSOT Press, 1986); Hans-Dieter Betz, "Paul's 'Second Presence' in Colossians." In *Texts and Contexts: Biblical Texts in Their Textual and Situational Contexts*, eds. Tord Fornberg and David Hellholm (Oslo: Scandinavian University Press, 1995), 507–18; Angela Standhartinger, *Studien zur Entstehungsgeschichte und Intention des Kolosserbriefs* (Leiden: Brill, 1999); Outi Leppä, *The Making of Colossians: A Study in the Formation and Purpose of a Deutero-Pauline Letter* (Helsinki: Finnish Exegetical Society, 2003). My own sense of a pseudepigraphal Colossians has been strengthened in recent times by an analysis of Colossians 3:11. See Alan H. Cadwallader, "Greeks in Colossae: Shifting Allegiances in the Letter to the Colossians and its Context." In *Attitudes to Gentiles in Ancient Judaism and Early Christianity*, eds. David C. Sim and James S. McLaren (London: Bloomsbury T & T Clark, 2013), 224–41. Nicole Frank divides the proponents of the pseudonymity of Colossians into minimalist (e.g. Standhartinger, Kiley) and maximalist (e.g. Leppä) positions: see Nicole Frank, *Der Kolosserbrief im Kontext des Paulinischen Erbes*, WUNT 271 (Tübingen: Mohr Siebeck, 2009), 10–11.

[8] So Joachim Gnilka, *Der Kolosserbrief*, HTKNT 10 (Freiburg: Herder & Herder, 1980), 22–3; Petr Pokorný, *Colossians: A Commentary* (Peabody, Mass.: Hendrickson, 1991), 18; Udo Schnelle, *Einleitung in das Neue Testament* (Göttingen: Vandenhoeck & Ruprecht, 1994), 336–37; Leppä, *Making of Colossians*, 268; Frank, *Kolosserbrief im Kontext*, 38 ("not very long after Paul's missionary activity"); Helmut Koester, *Introduction to the New Testament* (Philadelphia, Pa.: Fortress Press, 1982), 266 ("generally before 80 C.E." and "relatively shortly after his [Paul's] death"); Margaret Y. MacDonald, *Colossians and Ephesians*, SP 17 (Collegeville, Pa.: Liturgical Press, 2000), 9–10.

[9] Seneca, *Clementia* 1.1.2.

The destruction of Jerusalem engineered by Vespasian and Titus is the expansive panorama of Roman execution for the early Jesus movement. It not only intrudes on the question of the dating of Mark and Colossians; it concentrates the issue of household organisation in the early Christian communities, and it chillingly warns of the need to negotiate Roman imperial values.

The conflict in the Pauline legacy becomes particularly apparent in a comparison of the modes of community and domestic organization in the two writings, commonly distilled as the "household code." Strictly, this "household code" is the classification of a literary form[10] that is applied to a paranetic section in Colossians (3:18–4:1), as also to parallels in further Deutero-Pauline texts (Eph 5:21–6:9; 1Tim 2:9–15, 6:1–2 cf. 1Pet 2:11–20).[11] The relevant section in Mark's Gospel has not traditionally been classified by this term. However, a suggestion made by Warren Carter that Matthew 19 should be called an "inverted household code" has found considerable support.[12] To my knowledge this line of analysis has not been turned towards Mark 10:1–31.[13] It does not require that Mark or Colossians knew the other directly, though this has been raised obliquely for the latter.[14] The fact that household codes do occur in a number of writings in the New Testament indicates a breadth of negotiations of this aspect of paranesis. Certainly, those who uncover the use of pre-Marcan material can-

---

[10] See David L. Balch, "Household Codes." In *Greco-Roman Literature and the New Testament*, ed. David E. Aune (Atlanta, Ga.: Scholars Press, 1988), 25–50; and James L. Bailey and Lyle D. Vander Broek, *Literary Forms in the New Testament: A Handbook* (Louisville, Ky.: Westminster John Knox Press, 1992), 68–71.

[11] On the question of the Petrine epistles as Pauline texts, see Winsome Munro, *Authority in Paul and Peter* (Cambridge: Cambridge University Press, 1983), 37–56; David G. Meade, *Pseudonymity and Canon: An Investigation into the Relationship of Authorship and Authority in Jewish and Early Christian Tradition* (Grand Rapids, Mich.: Eerdmans, 1987), 179–93.

[12] Warren Carter, *Households and Discipleship: A Study of Matthew 19–20*, JSNTSup 103 (Sheffield: Sheffield Academic Press, 1994), 216; William D. Davies and Dale C. Allison, *Matthew 19–28*, ICC (Edinburgh: T & T Clark, 1997), 1–2; Janice Capel Anderson and Stephen D. Moore, "Matthew and Masculinity." In *New Testament Masculinities*, eds. Janice Capel Anderson and Stephen D. Moore, Semeia Studies 45 (Atlanta, Ga.: SBL, 2003), 67–91 at 90–91.

[13] This essay has provided an opportunity to develop some ideas I raised in "The Markan/Marxist Struggle for the Household: Juliet Mitchell and the challenge to patriarchal/familial ideology." In *Marxist Feminist Criticism of the Bible*, eds. Roland Boer and Jorunn Økland (Sheffield: Sheffield Phoenix, 2008), 151–81.

[14] Outi Leppä suggests the author of Colossians may have been familiar with pre-Marcan traditions (*Making of Colossians*, 69, 70, 75, 103, 129, 152, 195, 260) but rejects this particular instance (179–80 n. 793).

vassing three (sometimes four) aspects of household management,[15] would seem to support the sense that the household code figures *in some way* in Mark's Gospel.

3 The Colossian Household Code and the Pauline Legacy

The usual (though not singular) arrangement of the household code is fitted to a tripartite segmentation. In Colossians, that three-fold arrangement is based on a set of pairs that have, as their anchor, the *paterfamilias* of a household, the one who variously acts as husband, father and master. Thus husbands are to love their wives and receive submission from their wives (3:18–19); fathers are not to provoke their children because of the threat of despondency and, similarly, are to receive obedience (20–21); masters are to treat their slaves well and, yet again, receive obedience (3:22–4:1). The extended treatment of the master-slave relationship has occasionally drawn comment, even the speculation that Paul's authentic letter to Philemon has bred some undesirable, perhaps unruly, behaviour amongst slaves (cf. Gal 4:7).[16] What matters for my purposes here, however, is to recognise that submission (ὑποτάσσω), obedience (ὑπακούω) – the two used in this passage as stylistic synonyms of a single imperative[17]– is the steely metal of the anchor of the ruling male of the household. William Walker argues that the use of this obedience language in the Deutero-Paulines is an

---

15 Heinz-Wolfgang Kuhn, *Ältere Sammlungen in Markusevangelium* (Göttingen: Vandenhoeck & Ruprecht, 1971), 146–91; and Ernest Best, *Disciples and Discipleship: Studies in the Gospel according to Mark* (Edinburgh: T & T Clark, 1986), 80–97.
16 This demands a reading of Philemon as Paul advocating either manumission for Onesimus or a much improved treatment, a reading that lacks credibility in my view. See Alan H. Cadwallader, "Name Punning and Social Stereotyping: Reinscribing Slavery in the Letter to Philemon."*ABR* 60 (2013): 18–31.
17 The Byzantine lexicographer, Hesychius, lists ὑπείκω, ὑποχωρέω (in the sense of "make way for"), ὑποακούω and ὑποτάσσομαι as synonyms (*Lexicon*, Upsilon, § 283). A similar list is found in a scholium (500) to the second century poet Oppian's *Halieutica*. Hippolytus in his *Commentary on Daniel* (1.8.1) uses the two words as synonyms as does an interpolation into Ignatius' *Letter to the Ephesians* (Epistle 11.5.4 in the long recension). Leppä (*Making of Colossians*, 181) overweights the difference between the active ὑπακούετε of children and slaves and the middle ὑποτάσσεσθε of wives in Col 3:18.20.22. Basil of Caesarea simply equates the terms in his combination of Luke 2:51 (where Jesus submits [ὑποτασσόμενος] to his parents) with Eph 6:1 (where children, in imitation of the child Jesus, are to obey [ὑπακούετε] their parents).

advance on Paul's much narrower usage.[18] Certainly, what are now subsidiary elements of the household parade in and out of the code as required in order to illustrate the naturalised, if not divinised, authority structure and how it might function well. As Margaret MacDonald notes; "the importance of the theme of 'ruling and being ruled' stands out sharply."[19] Accordingly, some have drawn the comparison with the Christ's subjection and authority over all things, suggesting that household management is a (if not *the*) mundane expression of that divine architecture.[20] The development in Eph 5:22–24 is therefore not a breach but a consolidation of this understanding. This should not be read as necessarily implying a radical or subversive conception,[21] at least in contradistinction to imperial values.

Equally, the household code should not necessarily be read as merely an expression of Paul's own understanding of the Christian household. For those who do not distinguish authentic and pseudepigraphal Pauline texts, at least as occurring in the canonical texts, this is not an issue.[22] However, as I have already suggested, Colossians represents *one* development of the Pauline tradition, which claims the authority and authoring of Paul for that development. That it is a development is clear from the observation that the household *topos* as found in Colossians, Ephesians and elsewhere is not to be found in Paul's authentic letters.[23] At the same time, it would be a mistake to consider the incorporation of the code into Pauline texts as having no foundation in Paul whatsoever.

Issues related to marriage and divorce, children and parents, slaves and masters do appear in the authentic Pauline writings (on marriage and divorce: 1Cor 7:1–16.25–40; 1Thess 4:3–5; on children and parents: 1Cor 7:14; 2Cor

---

18 William O. Walker, *Interpolations in the Pauline Letters* (Sheffield: Sheffield Academic Press, 2001), 79.
19 MacDonald, *Colossians and Ephesians*, 160.
20 Andrew T. Lincoln, "The Household Code and Wisdom Mode in Colossians." *JSNT* 74 (1999): 93–112; Margaret Y. MacDonald, *The Pauline Churches: A Socio-Historical Study of Institutionalization in the Pauline and Deutero-Pauline Writings*, SNTSMS 60 (Cambridge: Cambridge University Press, 1988), 154; and Mary Rose D'Angelo, "Colossians." In *Searching the Scriptures. Volume Two. A Feminist Commentary*, ed. E. Schüssler Fiorenza (New York, N.Y.: Crossroad, 1993), 314–15.
21 Contra Bailey and Vander Broek (*Literary Forms*, 70) who seem to assume that any Christianising of a pre-existent household *topos* represents a "liberating tendency." It could as readily represent a Christian ideological justification for imperial conformity. See further below.
22 John Barclay avoids the issue by leaving it up to the reader after a judicious survey of the evidence. See John M. G. Barclay, *Colossians and Philemon* (Edinburgh: T & T Clark, 1997), 35. Unfortunately this can leave interpretation of key parts of the letter, such as the *haustafel*, lacking in explanatory force.
23 So Bailey and Vander Broek, *Literary Forms*, 69.

12:14; on slaves and masters: 1Cor 7:21–22, Phlm 16). What does not appear is a delineated tripartite codification of these relationships; moreover, elements of Paul's concern – the privileging of celibacy, the use of marriage as a guard against porneia, divorce, widowhood – are absent from Colossians, where marriage is the norm.[24] More importantly, some of Paul's lines of argument about these issues are at least capable of alternate interpretations. There is no automatic requirement that they devolve into a household code. Paul himself frequently uses these relationships metaphorically of himself or in theological explication; for example, Gal 4:1–7 of the Galatians move from slaves to inheriting children (υἱοί), and Phil 2:22 and 1Cor 4:17 of the relationship between Paul and Timothy as father and child.[25]

Occasionally one can a sense of Paul's own views on family relationships even if he does use an instance in a metaphorical extension. Thus, in 2Cor 12:14, in picturing his connection with the Corinthians, he draws on the parent-child relationship. However, unlike the authoritative call of 1Cor 4:14–15 admonishing his Corinthian children, Paul in 2Corinthians speaks of his own sacrifice for the Corinthians. It places the children as the focus of attention, not the parent. One may be suspicious of Paul's rhetorical stance here but the enthymemic appeal constructs its decisive line as if it is a maxim; "children ought not to invest (θησαυρίζειν) for their parents but parents for their children."[26] Such a line is capable of an interpretation of the reinforcement of family duty, such as is found in the *Letter of Aristeas* 248.[27] But equally one needs to recognise that in Roman law, the responsibility was decreed in the opposite direction, viz. children were required to attend to the needs of their parents. Quintilian stated the law concisely; "Children shall support their parents under penalty of imprisonment."[28] Although not explicitly found in the Roman juridical foundation of the Twelve Tables, precedent saw Tables IV and XII as demanding filial support.[29]

---

[24] Gillian Beattie, *Women and Marriage in Paul and his Early Interpreters* (London: T & T Clark, 2005), 74; cf. Angela Standhartinger, "The Epistle to the Congregation in Colossae and the Invention of the 'Household Code'." In *A Feminist Companion to the Deutero-Pauline Epistles*, ed. Amy-Jill Levine (London: T & T Clark, 2003), 88–121 at 94.
[25] On the problem of drawing a connection between metaphor and explicit advice, see O. Larry Yarbrough, "Parents and Children in the Letters of Paul." In *The Social World of the First Christians*, eds. L. Michael White and O. Larry Yarbrough (Minneapolis, Minn.: Fortress Press, 1995), 126–41.
[26] As Yarbrough thinks; "Parents and Children," 131.
[27] See also Philo, *Moses* 2.245, Plutarch, *On the Love of Wealth* 526a.
[28] Quintilian, *Institutes* 7.6.5.
[29] The Fourth Table related to the rights of a father, notably the *patria potestas*, i.e. the right of deposition and disposition of a son (including life and death). In Roman law, because of the

Book 5 of the (Ps-)Quintilian *Declamatory Exercises* is devoted to exploring the potential convolutions of operation of this requirement.[30] Such an attitude is not absent from Jewish understanding either. Jesus ben Sirach held, for example, that "the Lord honours a father above his children" (3:2) – a curious extension of the fourth commandment. This warranted the flow of honour and care from child to parent (3:3 – 16) and not the reverse, or at least as superior to the reverse. Paul himself appears to make use of this understanding in 2Cor 6:13, so that, at least at the level of the foundations of Paul's metaphors, there is no singular teaching. Whilst one, as a consensual interpreter, could doubtless divide these requirements into the stages of life for different members of a family, the crucial point is that, especially with the blurring that occurs as one turns familial relationships into metaphor, there is no simple teaching from Paul that governs parent-child relationships.

We find the same in Paul's considerably more voluble treatment of the husband-wife relationship. Paul can freely advise in favour of marriage as a check against immorality (1Cor 7:2.9.36) and yet, in the same breath, allow divorce (though without remarriage during the former partner's lifetime) even as an exception to an apparently-known dominical teaching (1Cor 7:10 – 11). He can also privilege the single state above the married and advise against marriage (1Cor 7:7.28b.32–33.38.40). Yet for those within marriage, Paul adopts a remarkable equity of behaviours: in relation to sexual desire, "worldly matters," recommendations against divorce and mixed marriages (1Cor 7:3 – 4.10 – 11.12 – 14.32 – 34; cf. 11:11 – 12). One might be tempted to read a thoroughly democratic if not egalitarian Paul here were it not for the headship language of 1Cor 11:3 that provided a ready incentive for the development in Eph 5:22 – 24,[31] let alone Paul's own recommendations on worship clothing and practice in the Corinthian assemblies. Of course it may be argued that the whole of 1Cor 11:2 – 16 is a later interpolation along the lines of that which can be conclusively (in my opinion) demonstrated

---

conjoined entity of father and son, a son's wealth accumulation strictly belonged to the father. Only with the father's death, did the son (automatically) inherit. The Twelfth Table prevents the deposition of property to a sacred institution as a means of evading responsibilities (cf. Mark 7:10 – 13).

30 Jeffrey Walker argues that such domestic concerns go the very heart of the concerns of the Roman elite; see Jeffrey Walker, *Rhetoric and Poetics in Antiquity* (Oxford: Oxford University Press, 2000), 98.

31 The two passages are combined (with that of Colossians as well) by Clement of Alexandria as the demonstration of his assertion that "the ruling power is the head" (κεφαλὴ τοίνυν τὸ ἡ ἡγεμονικόν, *Stromata* 4.8.65).

for 1Cor 14:33b-36.³² However, I am not prepared to sacrifice 1Cor 11:2–16 just yet, especially as there is a danger of requiring a consistency in Paul in an egalitarian direction as much as the pastoralist endeavoured to develop a consistency in Paul in another direction. We must remember the *ad hoc* nature of Paul's epistolary output.

Direct instruction or tangential reference to children and marriage-divorce are clearly capable of divergent interpretations of Paul. It would seem from the analysis thus far, that Paul himself could take divergent approaches dependent on the issues at hand and the literary-rhetorical use that Paul placed upon his language. Accordingly one ought not expect thoroughgoing consistency in relation to the master-slave relationship either. What is striking, at least by comparison with the volume of verses given to slavery in Colossians, is how little attention Paul actually gives to the master-slave relationship, the letter to Philemon notwithstanding. By contrast, the metaphor of slavery figures prominently in Paul's own self-definition and in some of his constructions of the Christian life,³³ especially the accent on service. And this proves to be the case in a small cache of verses in 1Corinthians 7. Verses 20 to 21were seen by Winsome Munro to be so inconsistent that she could only explain them by the intervention of the pastoralist.³⁴ By contrast, Brad Braxton argued that Paul was being deliberately ambiguous, avoiding making any resolution about fixed slave status in the new movement.³⁵ Certainly the conclusion to v. 21 leaves the preferred state of life to pursue unclear (τῷ ἐλευθερίᾳ or τῷ δουλείᾳ could be supplied). Whether or not Paul was being deliberately ambiguous, what is apparent is that Paul's ideas were easily susceptible to multiple refractions. Indeed, the actual practice and network of relationships implied in the Greco-Roman institution of slavery does not receive concerted attention in the authentic letters of Paul making it even more possible (or rather predictable) that Paul's ideas could

---

32 So Munro, *Authority*, 67–80. On the interpolation in 1Cor 14, see Walker, *Interpolations*, 68–72, 78–90; Philip B. Payne, "Fuldensis, Sigla for Variants in Vaticanus, and 1 Cor 14.34–5." *NTS* 41 (1995): 240–62; Philip B. Payne and Paul Canart, "The Originality of Text-Critical Symbols in Codex Vaticanus." *NovT* 42 (2000): 105–13; and Shelly Li, "Imposing the Silence of Women: A Suggestion about the Date of the Interpolation in 1 Corinthians." In *Hermeneutics and the Authority of Scripture*, ed. Alan H. Cadwallader (Adelaide: ATF Press, 2011), 125–37.
33 See Dale B. Martin, *Slavery as Salvation: The Metaphor of Slavery in Pauline Christianity* (New Haven, Conn.: Yale University Press, 1990). Frank (*Kolosserbrief im Kontext*, 343, 351) sees in Colossians a literalising of Paul's metaphors, comparing Col 3:22 with Rom 6:16–17, 2Cor 5:11, Gal 1:10 and Phlm 16.
34 Munro, *Authority*, 80.
35 Brad R. Braxton, *The Tyranny of Resolution: 1 Corinthians 7:17–24* (Atlanta, Ga.: SBL, 2000), 228.

spin out with greater variability, however much Paul's general commitment that status carries no weight for inclusion in the body of Christ might remain intact. Even in the brief letter to Philemon, the dynamics appear to be more focused on Paul's authority in relation to Philemon and the Christian gathering that meets in his house, than on any decision about Onesimus' future status.[36] Thus, when Paul does mention slavery, there is at least one possible strand, probably inherited from his Jewish upbringing (cf. *Aristeas* 24), that appears to encourage moves towards manumission. But these verses are encased with an encouragement to accept the state of life one was in when one became a follower of Christ and so sanctifies an existing state by a Christian overlay.[37] Whilst for Munro these verses indicate the hand of the pastoralist keen that Christians not be seen as disruptive of social conventions, it is my view that the letter to Philemon indicates Paul's acceptance of slavery as a fact of life that nevertheless could be turned to advantage in the Christian mission and in the conduct of the Christian household.

Before we turn to the inverted household code in Mark, however, there are two further elements of authentic Pauline teaching that require notice. The first is the attention that Paul gives to wealth, especially in the context of that peculiar mark of Pauline authenticity – the collection for the poor of the Jerusalem church.[38] This is not the place for a detailed study of the collection.[39] But the general principles that Paul uses to imbue his plea[40] in 2Cor 8:3–5 – of promiscuous and free liberality as an expression of their Christian commitment – provide an indication of a disbursement of wealth that became a hallmark (though often idealised as in Acts) of Christian practice, and indeed Paul's own regimen

---

36 Allen D. Callahan, "Paul's Epistle to Philemon: Toward an Alternative *Argumentum*." *HTR* 86 (1993): 357–76; Chris Frilingos, "'For My child, Onesimos': Paul and Domestic Power in Philemon." *JBL* 119 (2000): 91–104.
37 So Jennifer A. Glancy, *Slavery in Early Christianity* (Oxford: Oxford University Press, 2002).
38 Kiley, *Pseudepigraphy*, 46–47.
39 See Dieter Georgi, *Remembering the Poor: The History of Paul's Collection for Jerusalem*, trans. Ingrid Racz (Nashville, Tenn.: Abingdon Press, 1992 [1965]); Keith F. Nickle, *The Collection: A Study in Paul's Strategy* (London; SCM, 1966); David J. Downs, *The Offering of the Gentiles: Paul's Collection for Jerusalem*, WUNT 248 (Tübingen: Mohr Siebeck, 2008); Bruce W. Longenecker, *Remember the Poor: Paul, Poverty and the Greco-Roman World* (Grand Rapids, Mich.: Eerdmans, 2010).
40 The more relevant as general principles if Gal 2:10 is not a reference to the collection but to general practice in the Pauline churches: so Bruce W. Longenecker, "Good News to the Poor: Jesus, Paul and Jerusalem." In *Jesus and Paul Reconnected: Fresh Pathways into an Old Debate*, ed. Todd D. Still (Grand Rapids, Mich.: Eerdmans, 2007), 37–65 at 58. See too Longenecker, *Remember the Poor*, 183.

(1Cor 9:8–18; 2Cor 11: 7–11, 1Thess 2:9, Phlm 18–19).⁴¹ It lies behind Paul's castigation of the inequities and inequalities in the Corinthian gatherings (1Cor 11:17–34; cf. 2Cor 8:12–15), features in his elaboration of gifts in Rom 12:8 (an indication that individual as well as corporate practice is in Paul's purview) and becomes a crucial lens for Christological understanding (2Cor 8:9).This element of care for the poor (as in Gal 2:10) – not just reference to "the collection" – is notably absent from the Deutero-Pauline codifications of the household, even though the management of one's property (which included slaves) is a well-known permutation of the code in Greco-Roman literature (see more on this below). Indeed the Deutero-Pauline letters are decidedly thin on instruction about care for the poor (cf. Eph 4:28, 2Thess 3:13), compared with the organisation of Christian gatherings and households. Dennis McDonald even suggests that care for the poor was sacrificed for maintenance of church hierarchy!⁴²

Secondly, even though Paul provides the elements that could be developed into or be deemed to provide warrant for a Christian form of the *haustafel*, there are other elements of the Christian household that mark Paul's commitment. The primary relationship of the Christian community is that of "brother," though one would not think so if one were to concentrate on Ephesians or Colossians.⁴³ This is to be understood as an inclusive reference (that is, "brothers and sisters"),⁴⁴ even though the specific term "sister" does occasionally occur (5 times) but always to confer recognition of the female.⁴⁵ The reference to ἀδελφοί in 1Cor 1:10 is immediately followed by mention of Chloe (v. 11) – which is hardly likely to exclude her from the sweep of the address in the preceding verse. Of the 106 uses of "brother(s)" in the authentic Paulines, only 18 to 22 clearly have a male in view.⁴⁶ And of these only 2 appear to indicate lines of sanguinity in the "brother" (1Cor 9:5; Gal 1:19; cf. Rom 9:3, 16:15). Blood relationships are definitely inconsequential to Paul. The fictive relationship, established in Christ, is what counts.

---

41 1Cor 9:14–15 is noteworthy in this regard for Paul's abstention from a dominical authorisation. Compare 2Thess 3:6–13 where Paul's practice is given an unexpected, sharp twist against "the idle."

42 Dennis R. MacDonald, *The Legend and the Apostle: The Battle for Paul in Story and Canon* (Philadelphia, Pa.: Westminster Press, 1983), 75.

43 Eph 6:23 (of Tychikos), Col 1:1 (of Timothy), Col 4:7 (of Tychikos), Col 4:9 (of Onesimos). See David G. Horrell, "From *adelphoi* to *oikostheou*: Social Transformation in Pauline Christianity." *JBL* 120 (2001): 293–331 at 304–06.

44 See Reidar Aasgaard, *My Beloved Brothers and Sisters: Christian Siblingship in Paul* (London: T & T Clark, 2004).

45 Rom 16:1 (of Phoebe), Rom. 16:15 (the sister of Nereas); 1Cor 7:15, 9:5; Phlm 2.

46 Rom 16:23; 1Cor 1:1, 7:12.14.15, 9:5, 16:12; 2Cor 1:1, 2:13, 8:18.22 [Apollos?]; Gal 1:19; Phil 2:25; 1Thess 3:2; Phlm 1.7.16.20; *quaere* 1Cor 6:1.5–6, 1Thess 4:6.

The numerical count for fictive kinship likewise far surpasses "neighbour" (πλησίον) even though the scriptural warrant for the exercise of love is well-known to Paul (Rom 13:9, Gal 5:14 drawing on Lev 19:18). But of particular significance here is the conjunction of "neighbour" with household (οἰκοδομή) in Rom 15:2. The latter term is often translated in terms of "edification" but this elides the architectural and, with it, the metaphorical associations. This is the Christian household, the household of God (1Cor 3:9), designed for the beloved (2Cor 12:19). This household is populated and characterised, in Paul above all, by the brotherhood/sisterhood, though occasionally it can include fictive mothers (e.g. Rom 16:13) and (slightly more often) fathers (1Cor 4:15, Phlm 10). The sibling relationship is affirmed above all markers (including ethnicity, gender and status) because believers are preeminently children of the same Father (Rom 8:15; Gal 4:5). While Paul may not be inventing the linguistic usage,[47] neither is he expunging consanguine relationships.[48] After all, he is frequently dependent on existing conventional social households for the cultivation of the extended relationships (such as the household of Stephanas or Chloe in 1Cor 1:11, 16). But what is clear is the privileging that he gives to the children and fellow-heirs of Christ (Rom 8:17).

All this confirms firstly that there is no formal household code in Paul. Further, in the elements that would find a cohesive formalisation in the Christian use of a household code after Paul, there is no requirement that it do so. Thirdly, Paul's decided emphasis is on the sibling relationship of believers and, lastly, the quality of this relationship is to express itself, *inter alia*, in care for the least of its members (cf. 1Cor 12:22–23), a care which is to be expressed materially.

---

47 So, Peter Arzt-Grabner, "'Brothers' and 'Sisters' in Documentary Papyri and in Early Christianity." *RivB* 50 (2002):185–204; Philip A. Harland, "Familial Dimensions of Group Identity: 'Brothers' (Ἀδελφοί) in Associations of the Greek East." *JBL* 124 (2005) 491–513. See also the helpful treatments by Peter Arzt-Grabner, *Philemon* (Göttingen: Vandenhoeck & Ruprecht, 2003), 145–56; id et al, *1. Korinther* (Göttingen: Vandenhoeck & Ruprecht, 2006), 39–40, 64–65. On the use of "mothers" and "fathers" in a fictive context, see *NDIEC* 1.18 (p.60); and Philip A. Harland, *Associations, Synagogues and Congregations: Claiming a Place in Ancient Mediterranean Society* (Minneapolis, Minn.: Fortress Press, 2003), 30–33.
48 Aasgaard, *Brothers and Sisters*, 311.

4 The Marcan Inverted Household Code and the Pauline Legacy

It has been the argument of this study so far that Paul's authentic writings bequeathed a legacy to the next generation that was neither unambiguous nor (consequentially) unilinear in the succession. The apocryphal *Acts of Thecla* makes it very clear that a social code that re-centres conventional household relationships as the fundamental practical expression of Christianity was not inevitable. There is no need to rehearse the story of Thecla. Suffice to note that when she is captivated by an ascetic rendition of Paul's preaching, she resolves to model her own life on that of Paul – clothing, hair-style, celibacy, preaching, baptising as an itinerant minister. For her, this demands a break with both consanguine and conventional social ties, from parent, husband-to-be, and servants. As the text brilliantly captures the three-fold dimensions of the *haustafel*, Thecla fractures the household, in devotion to and imitation of Paul;[49] "Then they wept heart-rendingly: Thamyris, that he had lost his wife; Theoclia, that she had lost her child; and the maids, that they had lost their mistress" (*Acts of Thecla* 10).

Mark 10 has sometimes been viewed as adopting a type of the pre-existing household code.[50] The distillation of the text into "marriage, children, possessions" is, however, no more than descriptive of a break-down of the sections (vv. 2–9.[11].13–16.17–23. [31]) even allowing for the use of a pre-existent form.[51] The question of course is *how* Mark's Gospel utilises the material and how this relates to the Pauline heritage. The answer to these questions is not helped by the general assumption of scholarship that Mark is delivering dominical (and therefore timeless and absolute) teaching. This merely extends the reach of the "pastoral stratum" uncritically into the Gospel.[52] Such scholarship tries to assert that this pastoral teaching is "radical,"[53] even though this line

---

[49] Cf. Reggie M. Kidd, *Wealth and Beneficence in the Pastoral Epistles*, SBLDS 122 (Atlanta, Ga.: Scholars Press, 1990), 81–82.
[50] Chad Myers, *Binding the Strong Man* (Maryknoll, N.Y.: Orbis, 1988), 266.
[51] Best, *Disciples and Discipleship*, 87.
[52] David Parker has shown that it is impossible to find the original teaching of Jesus, let alone a juridical pronouncement. See David Parker, *The Living Text of the Gospels* (Cambridge: Cambridge University Press, 1997), 91–93.
[53] See, for example, John R. Donahue and Daniel J. Harrington, *The Gospel of Mark*, SP 2 (Collegeville, Pa.: Liturgical Press, 2002), 295–98.

of interpretation could be seen as readily, even more rigorously, pursuing Augustan imperial ideals.[54]

The clue lies in the shock of the third section. As indicated already, the household code is not required to be a three-tiered formula (though this is the most common manifestation) nor are the elements, especially the last, required to be identical.[55] What is clear in the literary exposition of the household code within the Augustan realities of empire, is that property has become a crucial element. One of Augustus' poetic extollers, Horace, distilled the three tiers as "nuptiae…genus…domos," that is marriage, offspring, property.[56] The historian Velleius Paterculus credits Augustus Caesar's adoption of Tiberius as his son as securing "the perpetual security and eternal existence of the Roman empire" which was manifested in the key elements of the code: parents, marriage and owners of property.[57] Arius Didymus, the philosopher counselor to the emperor Augustus, reiterated the standard division of husband-wife, parents-children, master-slave but then summed it up with a quaternity of elements to which the man who is to rule his household needed to attend: "the arts of fatherhood, marriage, being a master and money-making."[58] Arius then gives the greatest expansion to the issue of money-making. Slavery, it appears, has been subsumed into the management of one's business, just as in Rev. 18:12–17.[59] Philodemos, a near-contemporary of Arius, agreed.[60] As David Balch concluded, "'money-making' is the most important topic in the discussion."[61]

It is hard to imagine a treatment of wealth as more counter-imperial than Mark's story and commentary on the rich man. Not only is wealth to be given over to the poor (v. 21) but the call impacts on the rendition of the Decalogue.

---

54 See Sharyn Dowd, *Reading Mark: A Literary and Theological Commentary on the Second Gospel* (Macon, Ga.: Smith & Helwys, 2000), 100–01. Note especially the extremely conservative Roman attitudes to divorce, at least in origin; Susan Tregiarri, *Roman Marriage: Iusti Coniuges from the Time of Cicero to the Time of Ulpian* (Oxford: Clarendon Press, 1991), 441–46.
55 Balch, "Household Codes," 45–47 *et passim*.
56 Horace, *Ode* 3.6.
57 Velleius Paterculus, *History of Rome* 2.103.5.
58 Arius Didymus *apud* Stobaeus 2.7.26 (p.149, ll.11–12 in the edition edited by Curt Wachsmuth and Otto Hense, *Stobaeus, Anthologium* [Berlin: Weidmann, 1958]; translation by David Balch "Household Codes," 42).
59 Cf. Josephus, *Jewish War* 2.372.
60 Philodemos, *Vices and Virtues*, Bk 9 (On Household Management), 38, 5–9, 17–19; cf. Josephus, *Against Apion*, 198–210.
61 Balch, "Household Codes," 45. However, Balch claims that the New Testament dropped this aspect of the discussion. Once Mark is restored to the discussion, even as an "inverted household code," an adjustment is needed to this claim.

Gone is the injunction against coveting (Exod 20:17; Deut 5.21), so important to Paul (Rom 7:7) but in its place comes a requirement that was never part of the social dimensions of the ten commandments, the call not to extort (μὴ ἀποστερήσῃς v. 19). Such a call fundamentally drives a wedge between wealth and morality, an ideological mystification that had already been named in the *Testament of Asher* (2.8; cf. Luke 16:14–15).[62] Indeed, as Richard Hicks has shown, this had already found its way into the finale to the prophetic tradition (Mal 3:5 LXX).[63] The rich man might parade an innocence and moral uprightness in Mark 10:20, but this is precisely the target of an accusation that Tacitus allows to a speech by the British chieftain, Calgacus; "to plunder, butcher, steal, these things they misname empire; they make a desolation and they call it peace."[64] The moral sheen claimed by the rich man is exposed as a blistered veneer precisely in the one thing that he refuses, to give his goods to the poor (v. 21). If a writer like Pliny the Elder, himself a wealthy landowner, can lament the concentration of landed wealth in the early empire (which he sees as contrary to Augustan values),[65] how much more evident must it have been to those at the bottom end of the social scale – the very audience Mark addresses.[66] This re-distribution of wealth to the poor we have seen to be part of Paul's message. Mark develops this Pauline teaching in a radical direction, first by working it into a subversion of a key tenet of the household code and second by connecting it inextricably with the other elements of that code.

Particularly significant is the exposition that Mark works into the story as an explanation for Jesus' disciples (vv. 24–31). The failure of the rich man is turned back to the familiar elements of the household (v. 29), but rather than endorse a valorisation of father, mother, children, property, these are expressly embroiled in the abdication that has been the call to the rich man. Little wonder then that the Marcan Jesus adds persecutions to the list of new connections for the disciples, for Jesus has just subverted one of the fundamentals of imperial expectation – the making of money. And, as I suggest, this is not the only element being subverted.

---

[62] See Cadwallader, "Struggle for the Household," 163–64.
[63] Richard Hicks, "Markan Discipleship according to Malachi: The Significance of μὴ ἀποστερήσῃς in the Story of the Rich Man (Mark 10:17–22)." *JBL* 132 (2013): 179–99 at 187–8, 191–2.
[64] Tacitus, *History* 3.3. The efforts to restore or make a claim to restore moral values is probably behind Tacitus' speech, an effort evident also in another imperial conservative, Pliny the Elder. See *Natural History* 25.4, 26.20.
[65] Pliny, *Natural History*, 18.35.
[66] See Alan H. Cadwallader, "The Peasant, the Farmer and the Gardener: Approaches to the Environment of the Mustard Seed." In *A Wild Ox Knows: Biblical Essays in Honour of Norman C. Habel*, ed. Alan H. Cadwallader (Sheffield: Sheffield Phoenix Press, 2013), 129–44.

Mark takes up the ambiguities of the Pauline use of familial terminology, wherein both consanguine and fictive kinship patterns have been found. But there has been a noticeable hardening in Mark's attitude. There is a distinct distrust of family relationships, even in Jesus' own kinship circle. It is not family relationships are removed or seen as irredeemably opposed to the way of Jesus. After all, it is important to Mark's community that Simon of Cyrene's sons, Alexander and Rufus, are mentioned (15:21) – almost certainly indicating a positive appreciation by Mark. But children are also capable of rising against their parents in the battles over the reign of God (13:12). Parents also might turn against their children (13:12a), even if only temporarily in the case of Mary (3:21.31–32; cf. 15:40.47.16:1). Accordingly, even though fathers and mothers gain scriptural notice in Mark,[67] the key arbiter is the will of God (3:35), the gospel itself (10:30).

The new fictive kinship is marked by familiar terms – the language of family – but with two distinctive accents. "Sisters" are noticeably added for specific and distinctive recognition in a number of instances – 3:35 (cf. 3:32 where they are not mentioned)[68] and in 10:30–31. Equally noticeable is the removal of "fathers" as part of the blessings of the new *basileia* community (10:30) even though Simon of Cyrene, Jairus and the epileptic's father (*quaere* Zebedee) figure as honourable parents (15:21; 5:21–24a.35–43; 9:21–24). Both these elements, a specificity of sisters and a muting of fathers, are present in the Pauline tradition, but they seem in Mark to have garnered an edge. The *abba* of Jesus (14:36) is the only acceptable father. Any and all other fathers devolve from that acknowledgment or they are dispelled from the way of Jesus, the community of disciples.

The inversion of the last tier of the household code therefore cautions against an assumption that the other two tiers, marriage and children, conform to the code as found in Colossians and elsewhere, even in its Christian costume. And this is where Mark's structural arrangement bolsters a sense that conventional values may well be under threat. The passage, as it is often interpreted by commentators, is delineated as 10:2–31.[69] But the frame is crucial. The pas-

---

67 Mark 7:10=Exod 20:12/Deut 5:16, 21:17/Lev 20:9; Mark 10:17=Gen 2:24; Mark 10:19=Exod 20:12/Deut 5:16.
68 The manuscript tradition is not uniform. Some manuscripts add "sisters" to the crowd's announcement but this is clearly a clumsy assimilation to Jesus' own words that follow in v. 35, possibly to protect Jesus' verbal accuracy. Verse 33, where Jesus takes up the crowd's report, is decisive, and corroborated by the parallels in Matt 12:47 (even if Matthew is itself an assimilation to Mark in this verse) and Luke 8.20.
69 So Robert H. Gundry, *Mark: A Commentary on His Apology for the Cross* (Grand Rapids, Mich.: Eerdmans, 1993), 529, 534–35; Dale C. Allison, *Jesus of Nazareth: Millenarian Prophet* (Min-

sage is clearly brought to an end by the third passion prediction (vv. 32–34), where the persecutions of v. 30 suddenly gain an impending and detailed focus, especially with the use of the first person plural that indicates that the pain of the Jerusalem goal would be felt by more than Jesus. And for the first time, "the Gentiles" are introduced as culpably implicated in that pain and death. This is followed shortly by a further reference to "the Gentiles" as those whose values and patterns of life are *not* to provide the pattern for the disciples of Jesus (v. 42). To improvise Margaret MacDonald's observation, ruling and being ruled are not the way of Jesus according to Mark.[70]

Accordingly, one can suspect any approbative use of the household code by Mark, given that the code was an integral part of imperial ideology and statecraft. This is where 10:1 becomes crucial. As frequently in Mark's Gospel, the topographical reference carries immense directive force[71] and helps to explain why the Pharisees' question (v. 2) is such a test.[72] The test (πειράζω) does not lie in a dispute over general divorce laws as is often argued, though without satisfactorily explaining how this could amount to a Satanic trial (cf. 1:13, again πειράζω).[73] After all, the Pharisees have already been circumscribed as hatching an execution plan for Jesus (3:6), both in the narrator's and Jesus' insight (3:6; 8:15). Death had stained the very territory into which Jesus venture, the region of Judea and the Transjordan, for this had been where John preached against the marriage of Herod Antipas and Herodias (1:5.9; 6:17) with its deathly consequences. The initiation of divorce by both parties in Jesus' explanation to the disciples (vv. 11–12) carries a direct reference to the use of marriage and divorce as instruments of elite power-mongering, moving far beyond the Pharisees' ques-

---

neapolis, Minn.: Fortress Press, 1998), 52; and Richard A. Horsley, *Hearing the Whole Story: The Politics of Plot in Mark's Gospel* (Louisville, Ky.: Westminster John Knox Press, 2001), 187–88. Even when v. 1 is included in the section, it has no bearing on the interpretation (especially of the "test"). See Francis J. Moloney, *The Gospel of Mark, A Commentary* (Peabody, Mass.: Hendrickson, 2002), 192–95. Cf. however William L. Lane, *The Gospel according to Mark* (Grand Rapids, Mich.: Eerdmans, 1974), 352–54.

70 Warren Carter also sees this passage (in the Matthean parallel) as crucial to the interpretation of the household code in this part of the Gospel tradition; Carter, *Households and Discipleship*, 161–92.

71 "the *site of a reading*...is decisive in Mark." So, Fernando Belo, *A Materialist Reading of the Gospel of Mark* (Maryknoll, N.Y.: Orbis, 1975), 4–5.

72 Contra Dowd, *Reading Mark*, 98.

73 Gundry (*Mark*, 529) for example admits, "Mark does not specify the difficulty which makes the question testing." Sharyn Dowd imagines that the text is addressing an infra-community debate: *Reading Mark*, 99.

tion and response (vv.2.4), as well as Jewish Law,[74] into the realm of Herodian and imperial political manoeuvring.[75] Marriage was, under Augustan legal prescription and in Herodian practice, a key instrument of state policy and manipulation.[76] The narrative context given to this instruction removes any atemporal absolute from Jesus' teaching just as surely as did Paul's "exception" in 1Cor 7:11.15. Similarly, the seeming balance in divorce initiative does not pander to egalitarian desires, even if it may mollify the extremes of patriarchal dissymmetry of marital relations – note the absence of a parallel to the "against her" of v. 11 in v. 12.[77] Rather, Jesus offers a critique of marriage and divorce as they, like the temple itself (11:15–18), have become abused by those in power. The "in the house" contrast is designed precisely to stand against the way in which the household code was beginning to influence the development of the early Christian communities. Mark clearly has something in view that has either not emerged or not gained attention in Paul's time. But both Mark and Paul allow that there is no absolute instruction to be given on marriage and divorce.

There is no requirement that the citation of Gen 2:24 be read as the reinforcement of dominical teaching about marriage by reference to creation edicts.[78] I have argued elsewhere, that in a conflictual context, the abrogation of creation language removes the ability of interested parties (whether religious or political) to claim nature and divine providence for their position.[79] Meg Warner has also demonstrated that the text of Gen 2:24 is not a prescriptive text in its origins but

---

[74] The ability of wife to initiate divorce proceedings in Jewish Law is heavily curtailed. Some Jewish women were using Roman legal practice for the purpose, but this availability was largely determined by class. See Tal Ilan, "Notes and Observations on a Newly Published Divorce Bill from the Judaean Desert." *HTR* 89 (1996): 195–202. Note however that Paul knows of the ability of women to initiate divorce in 1Cor 7:10.

[75] This may lie behind Luke's severance of the marriage and divorce logion but yet retaining a link with the Baptist (Luke 16:16–18). But even the transmission of the Marcan text appears to demonstrate knowledge that the Herods are in view. Some manuscripts invert vv. 11 and 12, with the woman's initiation of divorce coming first. J. Neville Birdsall thinks that memory of Herodias' action has wrought the change. See J. Neville Birdsall, "The Western Text in the Second Century." In *Gospel Traditions in the Second Century*, ed. William L. Peterson (Notre Dame, Ind.: University of Notre Dame Press, 1989), 3–18 at 15–16.

[76] See further below.

[77] Luke 16:18 removes the woman from the culpability of adultery altogether, even if the woman becomes merely a display for male honour.

[78] Even Warren Carter interprets the usage in prescriptive or purposive terms. See Warren Carter, "Matthean Christology in Roman Imperial Key: Matthew 1:1." In *The Gospel of Matthew in its Roman Imperial Context*, eds. John Riches and David C. Sim (London: T & T Clark International, 2005), 143–65 at 152.

[79] Cadwallader, "Struggle for the Household," 157.

an aetiological one.[80] After all, Jewish marital arrangements did not require the man to leave his father and mother; rather, just as in Greek practice, the woman left her filial home to become joined to the family of her husband (cf. Gen 24). Mark's text may in fact accent the leaving far above the joining: a number of important and distinct manuscripts omit καὶ προσκολληθήσεται πρὸς τὴν γυναῖκα αὐτοῦ. Of course this makes father and mother the immediate referent of the two becoming one flesh in v. 8. Most would see this as confusing the marriage question,[81] even if, as I think, Mark's Jesus is aligning himself with John the Baptist in his criticism of the Herodian divorce and re-marriage as an epitome of political intrigue. Jesus thereby indicates his willingness to face death as did John.[82] But this can be taken further. The leaving of father and mother is precisely what is promoted at the end of this subversion of the household code, even allowing that the word for leaving in v. 7 (καταλείπω) is different from that in vv. 28–29 (ἀφίημι). The semantic overlap of the two terms is clear in 12:19, and, for Paul, ἀφίημι (1Cor 7:11.13) does the work of ἀπολύω in Mark (10:11–12).[83] Both are also joined by the metaphorical use of χωρίζω (Mark 10:9; 1Cor 7:10). This would suggest that in the creative handling of scriptural texts that Jesus (and Mark) have already clearly demonstrated (cf. Mark 1:2–3), the accent on the radical call of the *basileia* is being seeded. For Paul, issues of marriage, separation, divorce and celibacy are primarily pastoral crises accompanying the beginnings of the Jesus movement (cf. 1Cor 7:1). For Mark, marriage has become tarnished by the apparatus of the state, threatening that movement now living post-Paul. This is not to say that marriage has no place in the Jesus' movement, but resurrection life that touches to the core of the believer's existence releases a person from the expectations and narrow vision of marriage, especially for the woman. Marriage has been made contingent, even marginalised, by the resurrection (Mark 12:24–25).[84] Where marriage does exist, it is not Caesar who guarantees its sanctity (as Velleius argued), but God (Mark 10:9).

---

[80] Megan Warner, "'Set in Tradition and History': Genesis 2:24 and the Marriage Debate." In *Pieces of Ease and Grace*, ed. Alan H. Cadwallader (Adelaide: ATF Press, 2013), 1–16.
[81] So Bruce M. Metzger, *A Textual Commentary on the Greek New Testament* (London: UBS, 1971), 104.
[82] A pattern that is discernible in Mark – note especially the only two instances of the use of πτῶμα (6:29, 15:45).
[83] Compare the use of χωρίζω in Mark 10:9 and 1Cor 7:10.
[84] Luke will push this further (Luke 20:35), prompting the comment that here we have the beginnings of ascetic Christianity. See Turid K. Seim, "Children of the Resurrection: Perspectives on Angelic Asceticism in Luke-Acts." In *Asceticism and the New Testament*, eds. Leif E. Vaage and Vincent L. Wimbush (New York, N.Y.: Routledge, 1999), 118.

When the second tier of the household code is introduced, any ambiguities about Mark's intent remaining from the section on marriage and divorce disappear, quite simply because there are no parents mentioned. Those who bring children to Jesus could not be more opaquely identified (προσέφερον v.13). There is no Jairus, no Simon, no Zebedee in whom a child is embedded.[85] Indeed, the rebuke from the disciples is likely to be directed to the children themselves, as the contrast between Jesus and the disciples is highlighted (αὐτῶν α ‛ψηται...ἐπιτίμησαν αὐτοῖς v. 13b.c). And it is not as if Jesus has become a substitute father for these children (cf. Herod in 6:22), though he may be modeling how the disciples are to behave in relation to such children;[86] rather he identifies with them (9:37) and makes them, in the household (the location granted by v. 10), *the basileia* sign. This section, says Halvor Moxnes, "represents a break with the traditional role of children within the family."[87] Paul's privileging of the position of children as calling for sacrifice by the parents (2Cor 12:14 cf. Mark 5:43b) has been radicalised, possibly beyond what he would have sanctioned, given his understanding that children represent a stage to be grown out of (1Cor 13:11 cf. 14:20).

Here then we have a quite different development of the Pauline tradition, one which, like the *Acts of Thecla* in the second century, would preserve the radical tendency in Paul's writings and mute those elements that might represent the wisdom of accommodation to the socio-political realities of the day. But, as was stated in the opening, there were two realities bearing in upon the Pauline inheritance – the death of Paul at the hands of Rome and Rome's continuing vibrancy. Colossians and Mark are two early Christian writings seeking to deal with these realities, and they do so taking quite different paths. Colossians retains an accent on the centrality of Christ but portrays Christ as head of the very realities that Rome was inculcating, evidenced in family structures. Mark likewise retains the centrality of Christ but does so in a more resistant stance against the impress of imperial Rome, including a specific subversion of conventional family structures.

---

[85] Andries van Aarde thinks these are street urchins; Andries van Aarde, *Fatherless in Galilee: Jesus as Child of God* (Harrisburg, Pa.: Trinity Press International, 2001), 139–48.
[86] So Peter Spitaler, "Welcoming a Child as a Metaphor for Welcoming God's Kingdom: A Close Reading of Mark 10:13–16." *JSNT* 31 (2009): 423–46. Spitaler's detailed analysis does not set the section into the wider passage however, most particularly failing to note that the very elements that he uses to characterise the children (fragility, domination and the like: p. 424) are precisely the elements that occur in the passion predictions as characterising Jesus' own experience. Cf. Carter, *Households and Discipleship*, 114.
[87] Halvor Moxnes, *Constructing Early Christian Families: Family as Social Reality and Metaphor* (London: Routledge, 1997), 34

This therefore raises one final issue. Most explorations of the *haustafel* in Colossians interact with textual affinities in other philosophical writings, usually beginning with Aristotle and moving through Hellenistic and Roman literary sources.[88] Occasionally such influences are denied, resulting either in a privileging of claimed Jewish progenitors[89] or a quarantining of Christian examples of *haustafeln* from non-Christian analogues.[90] This restriction of context or influence to *literary* parallels defies the realities of the lives bounded by the Roman empire, those in Christian communities no less than any other groups, associations or households. The visual, linguistic, legal, economic and political symbols of the Roman imperial ideology – its all-pervasive ubiquity – dominated the horizons of most of the population under the governance of Rome and its representatives in the various provinces, such as Asia and Syria.[91]

5 Cultivating the Ideology of Empire: The "Ara Pacis Augustae" and the Household

A foundational expression of this ideology is the "Ara Pacis Augustae."[92]The monument stands as one of the great legacies and symbols of the Augustan revolution in Rome's control of the Mediterranean basin.[93] The importance of the "Ara Pacis" is reinforced by another of Augustus' monuments, the "Res Gestae" (s. 12) which provides the linguistic intertextual support for the visual symbols of

---

[88] See for example, David L. Balch, *Let Wives be Submissive: The Domestic Code in 1 Peter* (Chico, Ca.: Scholars Press, 1981). Cf. also the rehearsal of this comparative material by Carter, *Households and Discipleship*, as a contrast to the Matthean argument.
[89] See, for example, Wolfgang Schrage, "Zur Ethik der neutestamentlichen Haustafeln." NTS 21 (1975–6): 1–22; James E. Crouch, *The Origin and Intention of the Colossian Haustafel*, FRLANT 109 (Göttingen: Vandenhoeck & Ruprecht, 1972).
[90] See, for example, James P. Hering, *The Colossian and Ephesian Haustafeln in Theological Context: An Analysis of their Origins, Relationship and Message* (New York, N.Y.: Peter Lang, 2007); cf. Ben Witherington, *The Living Word of God: Rethinking the Theology of the Bible* (Waco, Tex.: Baylor University Press, 2007), 99–106.
[91] The provenance of Mark's gospel has no impact on the arguments presented here, given the deliberate diffusion of imperial ideology throughout the empire.
[92] For access to photographs of the "Ara Pacis Augustae," see http://www.vroma.org/images/mcmanus_images/index15.html (last accessed June 2013).
[93] See generally, Andrew Wallace-Hadrill, *Rome's Cultural Revolution* (Cambridge: Cambridge University Press, 2008); Paul Zanker, *The Power of Images in the Age of Augustus* (Ann Arbor, Mich.: University of Michigan Press, 1990), 171–79 *et passim*.

the altar building.⁹⁴ Indeed, the bronze plates of the "Res Gestae" adorned the mausoleum of Augustus, the last of three grand constructions on the Campus Martius,⁹⁵ and copies were sent throughout the empire for display. The most complete extant version is found on the walls of the Roma Temple in Ankara,⁹⁶ but the recent discovery of a fragment of the "Res Gestae" at Sardis, to be added to the list of notices around the Mediterranean, demonstrates the imperial hold on the public ingestion of propaganda.⁹⁷ The altar itself was extolled by the poets, who recognised its symbolic power and assisted in its promotion through the glorificatory agency of language; "the guarantee of peace."⁹⁸ And it became configured into the calendrical reformulations of Augustus, many copies of which have survived.⁹⁹ It was reproduced in miniature on coins as well.¹⁰⁰ The "Ara Pacis" then was a localised configuration of a much larger, more widely disseminated message that yet by its saturation and extent of media presentations, was designed by such cross-referencing to reinforce a singular message. Of particular importance, then, is to explore the relation between the "Ara Pacis" and those measures that Augustus trumpeted as the restoration of ancestral traditions

---

94 "Ti. Nerone et P. Quintilio consulibus, aram Pacis Augustae senatus pro reditumeo consecrandam censuit ad campum Martium in qua magistratus et sacerdotes virgins que vestals sacrificium facere iussit:" in the consulship of Tiberius Nero and Publius Quintilius, the Senate voted in honour of my return the consecration of an altar to the Augustan Peace in the Campus Martius, and ordered the magistrates and priests and Vestal Virgins to make annual sacrifice upon it." See Giacomo D. Pietà, "Le Res Gestae Augusti e l'Ara Pacis." *Engramma* 58 (2007) http://www.engramma.it/engramma_revolution/58/058_saggi_dallapieta.html last accessed June, 2013.
95 The other was a giant sun-dial that deployed as its gnomon an obelisk brought from Egypt. Here, time, as much as material artefacts, were controlled by Rome.
96 The most recent editions are Alison E. Cooley, *Res Gestae Divi Augusti* (Cambridge: Cambridge University Press, 2009); Stephen Mitchell and David French (eds.), *The Greek and Latin Inscriptions of Ankara (Ancyra)*, Vol. 1: *From Augustus to the Third Century AD* (Munich: Beck, 2012), no. 1.
97 Peter Thonemann, "A Copy of Augustus' Res Gestae at Sardis." *Historia* 61 (2012): 282–88.
98 See, as one unrestrained example, Ovid, *Fasti* 1.709–22. Helmut Koester notes that the poets were the first to understand and express the beginning of the new age: "The Historical Jesus and the Historical Situation of the Quest: an Epilogue." In *Studying the Historical Jesus: Evaluations of the State of Current Research*, eds. Bruce Chilton and Craig A. Evans (Leiden: Brill, 1998), 535–45 at 535. It is clear however that they were encouraged, at least in the case of Augustus, in that expression.
99 For example, *CIL* 1².212, 229, 232; 2.244, 248; 6.2028b, 32347a.
100 Larry Kreitzer, *Striking New Images: Roman Imperial Coinage and the New Testament World* (Sheffield: Sheffield Academic Press, 1996), 120–21; Giacomo C. diRoccolino, "Ara Pacis Augustae: le fontinumismatiche." *Engramma* 58 (2007) http://www.engramma.it/engramma_revolution/58/058_saggi_calandra.html last accessed June, 2013.

and the establishment of worthy items to be universally imitated (s. 9). According to Suetonius, these measures touched those elements familiar in the household code.[101] The visual symbols of the "Ara Pacis," combined with the manifold representations in diverse media, are far closer to the great bulk of the people of the empire than the literature usually reviewed for an assessment of the household code. Early Christian communities were confronted by such representations constantly.[102]

The altar complex combined a multiplicity of ideas and allusions that communicated, in its friezes, its use and its position, how the empire was understood and how its subjects were to conceive of themselves and operate within the empire. It captures in its visual multivalency what have come to be known as the three settlements orchestrated by Augustus: the military, the political and, as recently argued, the moral.[103]

It is this last that is most important for my purposes, though they cannot of course be isolated from each other. There are two pilgrim friezes that adorn the longitudinal external faces of the construction – Janus-like conjunctions that were the regular sighted feature for passers-by.[104] In addition to the ordered procession of officials that lead towards the opening at the front of the construction – the altar of sacrifice – there is worked into the friezes, especially on the southern side, a marked innovation in artistic representation. Children are now foregrounded and prominent under the control of women and the preponderance of men in the procession.[105] Family connections are manifest. And there is the pres-

---

[101] Suetonius, *Augustus*, 34, 89.
[102] See the analysis of the Sebasteion at Aphrodisias for an example of how such large structures were designed to communicate imperial values. Cf. Harry O. Maier, "Reading Colossae in the Ruins: Roman Imperial Iconography, Moral Transformation, and the Construction of Christian Identity in the Lycus Valley." In: *Colossae in Space and Time: Linking to an Ancient City*, eds. Alan H. Cadwallader and Michael Trainor, NTOA 94 (Göttingen: Vandenhoeck & Ruprecht, 2011), 212–31.
[103] Beth Severy, *Augustus and the Family at the Birth of the Roman Empire* (London: Routledge, 2003), 45–56.
[104] The overt cultic usage of the altar seems to have been limited to an annual celebration, according to the "Res Gestae" 13. This meant that the constant communication of the "Ara Pacis" lay not in the festival but in the visual presence. The means of passage on the Via Flamina brought constant exposure, just as the horological time-piece drew regular attention to the area. See Peter Holliday, "Time, History and Ritual on the Ara Pacis Augustae." *Art Bulletin* 72 (1990): 542–57.
[105] Diane Conlin notes that children did appear in funerary reliefs prior to the "Ara Pacis" but they were in the background, fairly stereotyped and partial in bodily extent. The effect of the "Ara Pacis" reliefs was to be seen in mimetic reiteration thereafter in representations of children:

ence of the barbarian captive (S-31, N-35), a child now raised by paternalistic oversight into participation in the civilisation that empire brought.[106]

The family set that most clearly demonstrates this accent is the complex numbered S-36 to S-39 usually interpreted as the family of Antonia Minor and Drusus.[107] Counter to the flow of forward-looking faces in the procession, the wife's head is turned back towards her husband, who, in soldier's garb, yet attends to her, the military in support of domesticity. Two figures are between them: the child, Germanicus, and a veiled woman. The young boy's hand is held by his mother. Directly above the child, behind his mother's shoulder, the head of a veiled woman is cast in low relief, holding a finger to her lips (S-37).

This last feature has traditionally been interpreted as an injunction upon silence, the *favetelinguis* that was uttered by cultic officials to participants.[108] Certainly the phrase is well known.[109] But a number of factors qualify this understanding. Firstly, the injunction to silence, if that is what it is, is not equally distributed. The fact that the older woman is represented as behind the younger woman's shoulder, closer to Antonia Minor than to Drusus, suggests that this silence is something either for, or to be shared by, women – at least more than men. Secondly, the holding of the finger to the lips is not only an injunction to silence; it can be an imposition of silence on oneself, even if that then be taken as directive to others. Thus Juvenal writes; "when he comes near you, put your finger to your lip."[110] Thirdly, the standard interpretation pays no heed to the gender of the person in its impact upon the gesture, even though some efforts have been exercised to discern the identity of the old woman concerned.[111] The examples that are usually given for the cultic setting of *favetelinguis* (understood as "hold your tongue") have a male subject, either express or

---

see Diane A. Conlin, *The Artists of the Ara Pacis: The Process of Hellenization of Roman Art* (Chapel Hill, N.C.: University of North Carolina Press, 1997), 71.
106 Paul Rehak, "Women and Children on the Ara Pacis Augustae." Paper at Classical Association of the Middle West and South, 16th April, 2004.
107 Nero Claudius Drusus was the leader of the German campaigns of 12 BCE and 9 BCE. His presence in military gear probably indicates his absence in the second Germanic campaign, wherein he died shortly after the "Ara Pacis" was consecrated.
108 Steven J. Green, *Ovid Fasti 1: A commentary* (Leiden: Brill, 2004), 61; Paul Rehak, *Imperium and Cosmos: Augustus and the Northern Campus Martius* (Madison, Wisc.: University of Wisconsin Press, 2006), 97.
109 Cicero, *On Divination* 1.2, 83, 102; Horace, *Carmina* 2.3.2, 3.1.2; Pliny, *Natural History* 28.11
110 Juvenal, *Satire* 1.159.
111 Gaius Stern, "Women, Children and Senators on the Ara Pacis Augustae: A Study of Augustus' Vision of a New World Order in 13 BC." (Unpublished Ph.D Berkeley, 2006), 274.

implied.¹¹² Here it is a woman, just as, it seems, an older woman on the northern frieze also gestures silence, though in a slightly different fashion, having her hand covered with her palla (N-39). All this suggests that this is more than an innocuous domestic scene; it is didactic and expressive, directed towards the expected pattern of life under the empire: women turned towards their husbands, bearing children, maintaining appropriate silence in public settings, with husbands fulfilling public duties of benefit to the empire. All this is set into a cultic procession, making familial concord a religious duty.

A second featuring of a child on the south panel, comes under the hand of an austere male wearing a head covering, identified as Agrippa, Augustus' right hand man in the empire (S-31, S-28 respectively). The child, with thick curling locks slipping out from his head covering and wearing a short tunic rather than a toga, has been identified as a foreigner (similar to a yet younger one identified on the northern frieze, N-35) and probably a slave under the authority of Agrippa.¹¹³ A hand reaches out from an ill-defined background and is placed on the child's head. No other child on the southern frieze (four in all) is so configured. Children frequently clasp the robes of an adult but only this foreign child has a master's hand placed on his head. This is more than simple protection; it is the mark of the conferral of civilisation should it be accepted (cf. "Res Gestae" 3)

Here in the "Ara Pacis" was the visual representation of the intentions of the various laws regarding the family that Augustus had proposed and the Senate had ratified. The propaganda poets were similarly not slow in extolling this development in the imperial scheme. Horace wrote; "bring up our progeny and bring success to the edicts of the senate concerning the marrying of women and the matrimonial legislation which will be productive of new offspring,"¹¹⁴Augustus himself underscored the significance of this role as guardian of the law and customs ("Res Gestae" 6). Although sometimes understood to be a restoration of old family ideals,¹¹⁵ this was the familiar rhetorical semblance that governed many of the emperor's initiatives. The address of both men and women in the legislation was part of the imperial project: marriage, children were now the province of state interest for the reinforcement of the state, as surely as Augustus fashioned himself as the father of the nation, a title dutifully conferred by the Senate in 2 BCE.¹¹⁶ Just as the borders of the state had been secured

---

112 Horace, *Carmina* 3.1.2–4, *Ode* 1.5.2; Seneca, *Dialogue* 7.26, 27.
113 Charles B. Rose, "Princes and Barbarians on the Ara Pacis." *AJA* 94 (1990): 453–67.
114 Horace, *Carmina* 17–20.
115 Turid K. Seim, *Double Message: Patterns of Gender in Luke-Acts* (Edinburgh: T & T Clark, 1994), 192.
116 "Res Gestae" 35; Suetonius, *Augustus* 58.

by Augustus, so the borders of what was the fundamental institution of the state were similarly to be secured, not only against adultery but against sullying by confusion between classes. Although widowhood and singleness were not banned altogether, a combination of penalties and incentives were legislated to promote marriage and child-bearing, especially among the aristocratic classes.[117] One epitaph surviving from Colossae clearly indicates how this pro-family stance was received in one city of the province of Asia.[118] The inscription on this first century funerary stele records the deceased, one Tatianos son of Bartas.[119] However, there is no mention in the inscription of wife or son, the ususal expectation in funerary inscriptions (apart from the military). Rather his younger kinsfolk (συγγενικὸν νειώτερον) are responsible for the honour of a public burial.[120] However, the relief that dominates the record of Tatianos' life is the common-place family banquet scene with husband and wife and two children (possibly daughters).[121] Whatever dissonance exists between the relief and the inscription is resolved by the public, visual indication of Tatianos' commitment (at least as presented by his kin) to traditional family values as promoted in the Augustan imperial program and reiterated under succeeding emperors.[122] Onno van Nijf notes that the function of such presentations was the signal to others that the recorded are "bound by a morality similar to that of the polis community,"[123] or in this case, the polis community as shaping itself in the light of imperial realities.

---

117 See Severy, *Augustus and the Family*.
118 *MAMA* VI.48, *SEG* 29.1391
119 Jean and Louis Robert have suggested (*BE* 1979: 15) that the text is capable of an alternative translation: Tatianos, son of Tatianos, son of Artas, that is, with the letter *beta* being a numerical indicator.
120 συγγενικόν normally indicates a much wider arc than the immediate family: Isaeus 8.33. This most likely indicates that Tatianos was (at least for the purpose of burial) unmarried and childless, with the responsibility devolving on the wider relations. See Stephen C. Todd, *The Shape of Athenian Law* (Oxford: Clarendon Press, 1993), 207.
121 This identification is based on William Calder's notebook entry which was not published in the minimalist entry in *MAMA* VI.48: University of Aberdeen, Special Library, Calder Archives Ms 3286/4, "1933 Notebook," p. 43 #170.
122 This is not the place to discuss the various claims related to randomness in choice of a previously carved epitaphal relief.
123 Onno M. van Nijf, *The Civic World of Professional Associations in the Roman East* (Amsterdam: J. C. Gieben, 1997), 216–17; see also Keith Hopkins, *Death and Renewal* (Cambridge: Cambridge University Press, 1986), 17–18.

6 Conclusions

There were two fundamental issues confronting the early Christian congregations dotted around the Mediterranean: Paul was dead and the instrument of his execution, imperial Rome, was still very much alive. How the surviving Christian leaders were to negotiate this two-fold reality was not clear. One of the key arenas for this negotiation was the constituent members of those congregations, often families and households but not necessarily confined or confining themselves to such classifications. The legacy of the apostle, in the surviving letters and in the memories of succeeding generation, was not singular. There was a "proliferation of meaning,"[124] not only possible, but as in the analysis presented here, very much alive. Whether or not one or both of the conflicting renditions of the household code in Colossians and Mark had the other in mind is mute. What is clear is that the generation following Paul was divided in how to configure his teaching in regard to families and households within the context of Christian community. The shadow of Paul's death was a salutary warning that confrontation with the Empire was dangerous, threatening the survival of the Church. For the writer of Colossians, the inheritance of Paul was to be accommodated to those imperial realities, taking up the ubiquitous valorisation of the familial household that privileged the male head and addressed the relationships that he had within the household. This did not relinquish a commitment to Christ but it modeled that commitment on the imperial template of headship promoted by the propaganda machine of the Augustan revolution and legacy. Paul was the authority providing the resources for this Christian commitment just as the resulting formulation was designed to narrow the "proliferation of meaning" that was equally part of the legacy of Paul. For the second evangelist, the cost of such a rapprochement with the Roman empire was too great, a betrayal of the memory of Jesus and his greatest exponent (for Mark, that is), Paul. Both, after all, were executed by Rome. Both accented "the cross" as the mark of Christian discipleship. Mark could not extract the household code from its imperial hold. Accordingly Paul's references to community and his metaphorical use of familial language became, in the second Gospel, the warrant for a major critique of the household code, part of the apparatus of an empire against which the early followers of Jesus (and Paul) were pitted.

---

124 The evocative phrase of Michael Foucault, "What is an Author?" In *Modern Criticism and Theory: A Reader*, ed. David Lodge (London: Longman, 1988), 209, taken up by Beattie, *Women and Marriage*, 66.

Bibliography

Aasgaard, Reidar. *My Beloved Brothers and Sisters: Christian Siblingship in Paul.* London: T & T Clark, 2004.
Allison, Dale C. *Jesus of Nazareth: Millenarian Prophet.* Minneapolis, Minn.: Fortress Press, 1998.
Anderson, Janice Capel, and Stephen D. Moore, "Matthew and Masculinity," in: *New Testament Masculinities*, eds. Janice Capel Anderson and Stephen D. Moore, 67–91. Semeia Studies 45. Atlanta, Ga.: SBL, 2003.
Arzt-Grabner, P., "'Brothers' and 'Sisters' in Documentary Papyri and in Early Christianity." *RivB* 50 (2002):185–204.
—, *Philemon.* Göttingen: Vandenhoeck & Ruprecht, 2003.
Arzt-Grabner, Peter et al., *1. Korinther.* Göttingen: Vandenhoeck & Ruprecht, 2006.
Babcock, William S., ed. *Paul and the Legacies of Paul.* Dallas, Tex.: Southern Methodist University Press, 1990.
Bailey, James L., and Lyle D. Vander Broek. *Literary Forms in the New Testament: A Handbook.* Louisville, Ky.: Westminster John Knox Press, 1992.
Balch, David L. *Let Wives be Submissive: The Domestic Code in 1 Peter.* Chico, Ca.: Scholars Press, 1981.
—, "Household Codes," in: *Greco-Roman Literature and the New Testament*, ed. David E. Aune, 25–50. Atlanta, Ga.: Scholars Press, 1988.
Barclay, John M. G. *Colossians and Philemon.* Edinburgh: T & T Clark, 1997.
Barrett, Charles K. *On Paul: Essays on His Life, Work and Influence in the Early Church.* London: T & T Clark, 2003.
Beattie, Gillian. *Women and Marriage in Paul and His Early Interpreters.* London: T & T Clark, 2005.
Belo, Fernando. *A Materialist Reading of the Gospel of Mark.* Maryknoll, N.Y.: Orbis, 1975.
Best, Ernest. *Disciples and Discipleship: Studies in the Gospel according to Mark.* Edinburgh: T & T Clark, 1986.
Betz, Hans-Dieter. "Paul's 'Second Presence' in Colossians," in: *Texts and Contexts: Biblical Texts in Their Textual and Situational Contexts*, eds.Tord Fornberg and David Hellholm, 507–18. Oslo: Scandinavian University Press, 1995.
Birdsall, J. Neville. "The Western Text in the Second Century," in: *Gospel Traditions in the Second Century*, ed. William L. Peterson, 3–18. Notre Dame, Ind.: University of Notre Dame Press, 1989.
Boring, Eugene. *Mark: A Commentary.* Louisville, Ky.: Westminster John Knox Press, 2006.
Braxton, Brad R. *The Tyranny of Resolution: 1 Corinthians 7:17–24.* Atlanta, Ga.: SBL, 2000.
Cadwallader, Alan H. "The Markan/Marxist Struggle for the Household: Juliet Mitchell and the Challenge to patriarchal/familial ideology," in: *Marxist Feminist Criticism of the Bible*, eds. Roland Boer and Jorunn Øklund, 151–81. Sheffield: Sheffield Phoenix, 2008.
—, "Name Punning and Social Stereotyping: Reinscribing Slavery in the Letter to Philemon." *ABR* 60 (2013): 18–31.
—, "The Peasant, the Farmer and the Gardener: Approaches to the Environment of the Mustard Seed," in: *A Wild Ox Knows: Biblical Essays in Honour of Norman C. Habel*, ed. Alan H. Cadwallader, 129–44. Sheffield: Sheffield Phoenix Press, 2013.

—, "Greeks in Colossae: Shifting Allegiances in the Letter to the Colossians and its Context," in: *Attitudes to Gentiles in Ancient Judaism and Early Christianity*, eds. David C. Sim and James S. McLaren, 224–41. London: Bloomsbury T & T Clark, 2013.
Callahan, Allen. D. "Paul's Epistle to Philemon: Toward an Alternative Argumentum." *HTR* 86 (1993): 357–76.
Carter, Warren. *Households and Discipleship: A Study of Matthew 19–20*. JSNTSup 103. Sheffield: Sheffield Academic Press, 1994.
—, "Matthean Christology in Roman Imperial Key: Matthew 1:1," in: *The Gospel of Matthew in its Roman Imperial Context*, eds. John Riches and David C. Sim, 143–65. London: T & T Clark International, 2005.
—, *The Roman Empire and the New Testament: An Essential Guide*. Nashville, Tenn.: Abingdon Press, 2006.
Conlin, Diane A. *The Artists of the Ara Pacis: The Process of Hellenization of Roman Art*. Chapel Hill, N.C.: University of North Carolina Press, 1997.
Cooley, Alison. E. *Res Gestae Divi Augusti*. Cambridge: Cambridge University Press, 2009.
Crouch, James E. *The Origin and Intention of the Colossian Haustafel*. FRLANT 109. Göttingen: Vandenhoeck & Ruprecht, 1972.
D'Angelo, Mary Rose. "Colossians," in: *Searching the Scriptures. Volume Two. A Feminist Commentary*, ed. E. Schüssler Fiorenza, 313–24. New York, N.Y: Crossroad, 1993.
Davies, William D., and Dale C. Allison. *Matthew 19–28*. ICC. Edinburgh: T & T Clark, 1997.
diRoccolino, Giacomo C. "Ara Pacis Augustae: le fontinumismatiche." *Engramma* 58 (2007) http://www.engramma.it/engramma_revolution/58/058_saggi_calandra.html
Donahue, John R., and Daniel J. Harrington. *The Gospel of Mark*. SP 2. Collegeville, Minn.: Liturgical Press, 2002.
Dowd, Sharyn. *Reading Mark: A Literary and Theological Commentary on the Second Gospel*. Macon, Ga.: Smith & Helwys, 2000.
Downs, David J. *The Offering of the Gentiles: Paul's Collection for Jerusalem*. WUNT 248. Tübingen: Mohr Siebeck, 2008.
Eastman, David L. *Paul the Martyr: The Cult of the Apostle in the Latin West*. Atlanta, Ga.: SBL, 2011.
Foucault, M. "What is an Author?" in: *Modern Criticism and Theory: A Reader*, ed. David Lodge, 196–210. London: Longman, 1988.
Frank, Nicole. *Der Kolosserbrief im Kontext des Paulinischen Erbes*. WUNT 271. Tübingen: Mohr Siebeck, 2009.
Frilingos, Chris. "'For my child, Onesimos': Paul and Domestic Power in Philemon." *JBL* 119 (2000): 91–104.
Georgi, Dieter. *Remembering the Poor: The History of Paul's Collection for Jerusalem*, trans. I. Racz. Nashville, Tenn.: Abingdon Press, 1992 [1965].
Glancy, Jennifer A. *Slavery in Early Christianity*. Oxford: Oxford University Press, 2002.
Gnilka, Joachim. *Der Kolosserbrief*. HTKNT 10. Freiburg: Herder & Herder, 1980.
Green, Steven J. *Ovid Fasti 1: a commentary*. Leiden: Brill, 2004.
Gundry, Robert H. *Mark: A Commentary on His Apology for the Cross*. Grand Rapids, Mich.: Eerdmans, 1993.
Harland, Philip A. Associations, *Synagogues and Congregations: Claiming a Place in Ancient Mediterranean Society*. Minneapolis, Minn.: Fortress Press, 2003.
—, "Familial Dimensions of Group Identity: 'Brothers' (Ἀδελφοί) in Associations of the Greek East." *JBL* 124 (2005): 491–513.

Hicks, Richard. "Markan Discipleship according to Malachi: The Significance of μὴ ἀποστερήσῃς in the Story of the Rich Man (Mark 10:17–22)." *JBL* 132 (2013): 179–99.
Hering, James P. *The Colossian and Ephesian Haustafeln in Theological Context: An Analysis of their Origins, Relationship and Message*. New York, N.Y: Peter Lang, 2007.
Holliday, Peter. "Time, History and Ritual on the Ara Pacis Augustae." *Art Bulletin* 72 (1990): 542–57.
Hopkins, Keith. *Death and Renewal*. Cambridge: Cambridge University Press, 1986.
Horrell, David. G. "From adelphoi to oikostheou: Social Transformation in Pauline Christianity." *JBL* 120 (2001): 293–331.
Horsley, Richard A. *Hearing the Whole Story: The Politics of Plot in Mark's Gospel*. Louisville, Ky.: Westminster John Knox Press, 2001.
Ilan, Tal. "Notes and Observations on a Newly Published Divorce Bill from the Judaean Desert." *HTR* 89 (1996): 195–202.
Kidd, Reggie M. *Wealth and Beneficence in the Pastoral Epistles*. SBLDS 122. Atlanta, Ga.: Scholars Press, 1990.
Kiley, Mark. *Colossians as Pseudepigraphy*. Sheffield: JSOT Press, 1986.
Koester, Helmut. *Introduction to the New Testament*. Philadelphia, Pa.: Fortress Press, 1982.
—, "The Historical Jesus and the Historical Situation of the Quest: an Epilogue," in: *Studying the Historical Jesus: Evaluations of the State of Current Research*, eds. Bruce Chilton and Craig A. Evans, 535–45. Leiden: Brill, 1998.
Kreitzer, Larry. *Striking New Images: Roman Imperial Coinage and the New Testament World*. Sheffield: Sheffield Academic Press, 1996.
Kuhn, Heinz-Wolfgang. *Ältere Sammlungen im Markusevangelium*. Göttingen: Vandenhoeck & Ruprecht, 1971.
Lane, William L. *The Gospel according to Mark*. Grand Rapids, Mich: Eerdmans, 1974.
Leppä, Outi. *The Making of Colossians: A Study in the Formation and Purpose of a Deutero-Pauline Letter*. Helsinki: Finnish Exegetical Society, 2003.
Shelly, I. "Imposing the Silence of Women: A Suggestion about the Date of the Interpolation in 1 Corinthians," in: *Hermeneutics and the Authority of Scripture*, ed. Alan H. Cadwallader, 125–37. Adelaide: ATF Press, 2011.
Lincoln, Andrew T. "The Household Code and Wisdom Mode in Colossians." *JSNT* 74 (1999): 93–112.
Longenecker, Bruce W., "Good News to the Poor: Jesus, Paul and Jerusalem," in: *Jesus and Paul Reconnected: Fresh Pathways into an Old Debate*, ed. Todd D. Still, 37–65. Grand Rapids, Mich.: Eerdmans, 2007.
—, *Remember the Poor: Paul, Poverty and the Greco-Roman World*. Grand Rapids, Mich.: Eerdmans, 2010.
Lüdemann, Gerd. *Opposition to Paul in Jewish Christianity*. Minneapolis, Minn.: Fortress Press, 1989.
MacDonald, Dennis R. *The Legend and the Apostle: The Battle for Paul in Story and Canon*. Philadelphia, Pa.: Westminster Press, 1983.
MacDonald, Margaret Y. *The Pauline Churches: A Socio-Historical Study of Institutionalization in the Pauline and Deutero-Pauline Writings*. SNTSMS 60. Cambridge: Cambridge University Press, 1988.
—, *Colossians and Ephesians*. SP 17. Collegeville, Pa.: Liturgical Press, 2000.
Maier, Harry O. "Reading Colossae in the Ruins: Roman Imperial Iconography, Moral Transformation, and the Construction of Christian Identity in the Lycus Valley," in:

Colossae in Space and Time: Linking to an Ancient City, eds. Alan H. Cadwallader and Michael Trainor, 212–31. NTOA 94. Göttingen: Vandenhoeck & Ruprecht, 2011.

Martin, Dale B. *Slavery as Salvation: The Metaphor of Slavery in Pauline Christianity.* New Haven, Conn.: Yale University Press, 1990.

Mason, Steve. *Josephus, Judea and Christian Origins: Methods and Categories.* Peabody, Mass.: Hendrickson, 2009.

Meade, David G. *Pseudonymity and Canon: An Investigation into the Relationship of Authorship and Authority in Jewish and Early Christian Tradition.* Grand Rapids, Mich.: Eerdmans, 1987.

Metzger, Bruce M. *A Textual Commentary on the Greek New Testament.* London: UBS, 1971.

Mitchell, Stephen, and David French (eds), *The Greek and Latin Inscriptions of Ankara (Ancyra), Vol. 1: From Augustus to the Third Century AD.* Munich: Beck, 2012.

Moloney, Francis J. *The Gospel of Mark, A Commentary.* Peabody, Mass.: Hendrickson, 2002.

Moxnes, Halvor. *Constructing Early Christian Families: Family as Social Reality and Metaphor.* London: Routledge, 1997.

Munro, Winsome. *Authority in Paul and Peter.* Cambridge: Cambridge University Press, 1983.

Myers, Chad. *Binding the Strong Man.* Maryknoll, N.Y.: Orbis, 1988.

Nickle, Keith F. *The Collection: A Study in Paul's Strategy.* London: SCM, 1966.

Parker, David. *The Living Text of the Gospels.* Cambridge: Cambridge University Press, 1997.

Payne, Philip B., "Fuldensis, Sigla for Variants in Vaticanus, and 1 Cor 14.34–5." *NTS* 41 (1995): 240–62.

Payne, Philip B., and Paul Canart, "The Originality of Text-Critical Symbols in Codex Vaticanus." *NovT* 42 (2000): 105–13.

Pietà, Giacomo D. "Le Res Gestae Augusti e l'Ara Pacis." *Engramma* 58 (2007) http://www.engramma.it/engramma_revolution/58/058_saggi_dallapieta.html.

Pokorný, Petr. *Colossians: A Commentary.* Peabody, Mass.: Hendrickson, 1991.

Rehak, Paul. "Women and Children on the Ara Pacis Augustae." Paper at the Classical Association of the Middle West and South, 16thApril, 2004.

—, *Imperium and Cosmos: Augustus and the Northern Campus Martius.* Madison, Wins.: University of Wisconsin Press, 2006.

Rose, Charles B. "Princes and Barbarians on the Ara Pacis." *AJA* 94 (1990): 453–67.

Schneemelcher, Wilhelm. *New Testament Apocrypha*, trans. Robert McL. Wilson. 2 vols. Cambridge: James Clarke, 1992.

Schnelle, Udo. *Einleitung in das Neue Testament.* Göttingen: Vandenhoeck & Ruprecht, 1994.

Schrage, Wolfgang. "Zur Ethik der neutestamentlichen Haustafeln." *NTS* 21 (1975–6): 1–22.

Seim, Turid K., *Double Message: Patterns of Gender in Luke-Acts.* Edinburgh: T & T Clark, 1994.

—, "Children of the Resurrection: Perspectives on Angelic Asceticism in Luke-Acts," in: *Asceticism and the New Testament*, eds. Leif E. Vaage and Vincent L. Wimbush, 115–26. New York, N.Y.: Routledge, 1999.

Severy, Beth. *Augustus and the Family at the Birth of the Roman Empire.* London: Routledge, 2003.

Spitaler, Peter."Welcoming a Child as a Metaphor for Welcoming God's Kingdom: A Close Reading of Mark 10:13–16." *JSNT* 31 (2009): 423–46.

Standhartinger, Angela. *Studien zur Entstehungsgeschichte und Intention des Kolosserbriefs.* Leiden: Brill, 1999.

—, "The Epistle to the Congregation in Colossae and the Invention of the 'Household Code'," in: *A Feminist Companion to the Deutero-Pauline Epistles*, ed. Amy-Jill Levine, 88–121. London: T & T Clark, 2003.
Stern, Gaius. "Women, Children and Senators on the Ara Pacis Augustae: A Study of Augustus' Vision of a New World Order in 13 BC." Unpublished Ph.D Berkeley, 2006.
Thonemann, Peter."A Copy of Augustus' Res Gestae at Sardis." *Historia* 61 (2012): 282–88.
Todd, Stephen C. *The Shape of Athenian Law*. Oxford: Clarendon Press, 1993.
Tregiarri, Susan. *Roman Marriage: Iusti Coniuges from the Time of Cicero to the Time of Ulpian*. Oxford: Clarendon Press, 1991.
van Aarde, Andries. *Fatherless in Galilee: Jesus as Child of God*. Harrisburg, Pa.: Trinity Press International, 2001.
van Nijf, Onno M. *The Civic World of Professional Associations in the Roman East*. Amsterdam: J. C. Gieben, 1997.
Wachsmuth, Curt, and Otto Hense. *Stobaeus: Anthologium*. Berlin: Weidmann, 1958.
Walker, Jeffrey. *Rhetoric and Poetics in Antiquity*. Oxford: Oxford University Press, 2000.
Walker, William O. *Interpolations in the Pauline Letters*. London: Sheffield Academic Press, 2001.
Wallace-Hadrill, Andrew. *Rome's Cultural Revolution*. Cambridge: Cambridge University Press, 2008.
Warner, Megan. "'Set in Tradition and History': Genesis 2:24 and the Marriage Debate," in: *Pieces of Ease and Grace*, ed. Alan H. Cadwallader, 1–16. Adelaide: ATF Press, 2013.
Witherington, Ben. *The Living Word of God: Rethinking the Theology of the Bible*. Waco, Tex.: Baylor University Press, 2007.
Yarbrough, O. Larry. "Parents and Children in the Letters of Paul," in: *The Social World of the First Christians*, eds. L. Michael White and O. Larry Yarbrough, 126–41. Minneapolis, Minn.: Fortress Press, 1995.
Zanker, Paul. *The Power of Images in the Age of Augustus*. Ann Arbor, Mich.: University of Michigan Press, 1990.

David C. Sim
The Reception of Paul and Mark in the Gospel of Matthew

1 Introduction

The reception of Paul and Mark in the Gospel of Matthew raises many complex and interesting issues. First of all, to speak of the reception of a prior author or text presumes that the later writer knew the earlier documents in question. In the current study, the reception of Paul (or his letters) and the Gospel of Mark in the Gospel of Matthew assumes that that later evangelist was aware of and had read at least some of the Pauline literature and had access to the Marcan Gospel. Yet neither of these assumptions can be taken for granted. In the case of Paul and Matthew, many scholars would deny any direct link between the two. For most exegetes Matthew was clearly un-Pauline and represented a different strand of the Christian tradition, which suggests that the evangelist and his community were completely uninfluenced by the apostle, his theology and his epistles. The situation is in terms of Mark and Matthew is perhaps less problematic, but even so scholars have hardly reached a consensus. While most Matthean scholars accept Marcan priority and Matthew's dependence upon Mark, the majority view still continues to be challenged in a number of quarters. In short the reception of Paul and Mark in the Gospel of Matthew is not a straightforward proposition, even at the level that Matthew knew these earlier sources.

Secondly, even amongst those scholars who accept that Matthew knew some of Paul's epistles and/or the Gospel of Mark, there is little agreement over the manner in which the evangelist received, interpreted and treated these sources. In the case of Paul and Matthew, there is a minority of scholars who do accept that, despite the ambiguity of the evidence and the difficulty of establishing intertextual connections, there are clear points of contact between Paul and Matthew, and that the latter was familiar with some of the Pauline literature. But this agreement in terms of knowledge and reception soon gives way to divergent views over whether Matthew accepted the authority and theology of Paul or whether he opposed them. Matthew's attitude towards Paul and his reaction to the Pauline literature is currently a lively topic of debate. It might be thought that examining the relationship between Mark and Matthew is a much more simple proposition, given that most scholars accept the latter's dependence upon the former, but even here there is a measure of complexity and a host of unanswered and difficult questions. It is an oddity of Matthean scholarship that, even though most exegetes accept that Matthew had access to Mark, little thought has been given to Matthew's attitude towards his major source. Did he use Mark because he was favourable to it and/or that it had authority for him? If this were the case, then we would need to conclude that Matthew wrote to supplement his primary source. This has been the unstated dominant view in Matthean studies. But this thesis has recently been challenged, and it has been argued that Matthew was not favourably disposed towards Mark but in fact wrote his own account in order to replace Mark. In turn this particular hypothesis has been questioned, and the issue of Matthew's attitudes towards Mark is beginning to shape as a new 'storm centre' in Matthean scholarship.

In this study I wish to explore the relevant issues associated with the reception of Paul and Mark in the Gospel of Matthew. I will begin with the more contentious issue of the reception of Paul in the Gospel. It will be argued that Matthew knew of Paul himself and the Pauline tradition, and that it is probable that he reacted to certain Pauline texts in his Gospel narrative. Then I will move on to the reception of Mark in Matthew. The examination of that topic will establish that Matthew was dissatisfied with his primary source at a number of levels, especially its Pauline elements, so he decided to rewrite and correct Mark in order to produce an alternative narrative about Jesus that was designed to replace Mark. In this respect Matthew treats Paul and the Pauline Mark in an entirely consistent fashion.

2 Paul and Matthew

Over ten years ago I published an article that lamented that Matthean scholars had largely neglected the relationship between Paul and Matthew.[1] In that study I surveyed the few references to this topic in the scholarly literature over some five decades, and noted that most scholars at that time were content to note that Paul and Matthew stood in different Christians traditions. Matthew was un-Pauline or non-Pauline,[2] but few were prepared to go beyond that conclusion. Of the exceptions to the rule, both Michael D. Goulder and Thomas L. Brodie presented arguments that Paul was an authority for Matthew, and that the evangelist made use of at least one Pauline epistle in the composition of

---

[1] David C. Sim, "Matthew's Anti-Paulinism: A Neglected Feature of Matthean Studies. *HTS* 58 (2002): 767–83.
[2] Perhaps the most distinguished advocate of this position was Graham N. Stanton, *A Gospel for a New People: Studies in Matthew* (Edinburgh: T & T Clark, 1992), 314.

his Gospel.³ As the title of my article suggests, I held a rather different position. There seemed to me to be plenty of evidence in the Gospel that Matthew was neither pro-Pauline nor simply un-Pauline; rather, the evangelist was openly anti-Pauline.⁴

Of course such a proposal was not new. In the middle of the last century, Samuel G. F. Brandon mounted an argument that Matthew's very Jewish Gospel contained critiques of Paul and his "liberal" theology at certain points.⁵ Brandon's very meagre arguments were not especially persuasive, and were mercilessly attacked by William D. Davies in his magisterial monograph on the Sermon on the Mount.⁶ The critique of Davies was so devastating that the whole subject of Matthew's relationship with the Pauline tradition receded into the background for the next three decades or so. The next serious attempt to study the issue of possible anti-Pauline polemic in Matthew was that of Ulrich Luz in 1993.

Luz contends that Matthew contains no anti-Pauline polemic, despite the fact that he disagreed with the apostle over the validity of the Torah and over the issue of the relationship between the Christian tradition and Judaism. While Paul maintained that Judaism stood in sharp contrast to Christianity, Matthew saw no such opposition. In pinpointing the evangelist's Christian theological location, Luz claims that Matthew in fact stood closer to the "judaisers" who opposed Paul in Galatia than to the apostle himself, and Luz wryly remarks that had the two ever met they would not have been close friends.⁷ Yet Luz contends that we should resist the temptation to put Matthew and Paul at opposite ends of the early Christian theological spectrum because they share many areas of agree-

---

3 See Michael D. Goulder, *Midrash and Lection in Matthew* (London: SPCK, 1974), 156–70; and Thomas L. Brodie, *The Birthing of the New Testament: The Intertextual Development of the New Testament Writings* (Sheffield: Sheffield Phoenix, 2004), 218–35. For a brief critique of their theses, see David C. Sim, "Matthew and the Pauline Corpus: A Preliminary Intertextual Study." *JSNT* 31 (2009): 401–22 at 409–10.
4 Much of the following discussion is based upon an earlier study that also considers the relationship between Paul and Matthew; David C. Sim, "Conflict in the Canon: The Pauline Literature and the Gospel of Matthew." In *Religious Conflict from Early Christianity to the Rise of Islam*, eds. Wendy Mayer and Bronwen Neil. AKG 121 (Berlin: de Gruyter, 2013), 71–86 at 76–85.
5 Samuel G. F. Brandon, *The Fall of Jerusalem and the Christian Church* (London: SPCK, 2ⁿᵈ edn 1957), 232–37.
6 William D. Davies, *The Setting of the Sermon on the Mount* (Cambridge: Cambridge University Press, 1966) 334–40.
7 Ulrich Luz, *The Theology of the Gospel of Matthew* (Cambridge: Cambridge University Press, 1993), 147–48.

ment – the priority of grace, the theology of works, the interior dimensions of righteousness, love as the core of the Law, and the universality of faith in Christ.[8]

There is much to applaud in Luz's discussion. He is absolutely right to point out that Matthew and Paul agree with one another on a number of important points. This, however, is not surprising. Both were Christians, followers of Jesus of Nazareth, whom they jointly regarded as messiah and Lord, as crucified and vindicated, as the fulfiller of the ancient prophecies, and now residing in heaven with all power and authority until his triumphant return at the judgement. But we should not allow the many similarities between them to overshadow the issues that separated them. The major issue that divided Paul and Matthew, as Luz acknowledges, was the role of the Torah in the light of the Christ event, and this was clearly no minor matter. It was the single issue that underlay the apostolic council, the dispute between Peter and Paul in Antioch (Gal 2:11–14) and Paul's conflict in Galatia and probably elsewhere.[9] I have no doubt that Paul's Christian Jewish opponents in Galatia would have agreed with the apostle over all sorts of theological and christological questions, but they bitterly disputed his understanding of the place of the Torah for Gentile converts and sought to undermine his apostleship and authority because of it. For his part, Paul responds in Galatians with a bitter polemic of his own. The lesson to be learnt here is this. If the point of disagreement is fundamental and serious enough to both parties in a dispute, then it can easily outweigh the many other factors that they may share in common. For this reason, I think Luz's otherwise excellent discussion goes awry by highlighting the agreements between Matthew and Paul at the expense of the absolutely fundamental matter that separated them. If, as Luz correctly claims, Matthew stood theologically close to Paul's "judaising" opponents in Galatia, then it would seem to follow logically that Matthew would have responded to Paul in much the same way as they did. He would have overlooked their agreements and focused his attention on questioning Paul's gospel and his claims to authority and leadership.

Not long after Luz's important but limited contribution, I began my own quest to demonstrate that Matthew was indeed anti-Pauline. In my 1998 monograph on the history and social setting of the Matthean community, I argued that Matthew and Paul stood on different sides of the early Christian factional dispute and that the evangelist offered critiques of Paul and his Law-free theology.[10] Over

---

[8] Luz, *Theology of the Gospel of Matthew*, 150–52.
[9] See my chapter in this volume, "The Family of Jesus and the Disciples of Jesus in Paul and Mark: Taking Sides in the Early Church's Factional Dispute."
[10] David C. Sim, *The Gospel of Matthew and Christian Judaism: The History and Social Setting of the Matthean Community*, SNTW (Edinburgh: T & T Clark, 1998), 188–211.

the next decade and a half I have published a number of articles that have refined and expanded that initial work. Let me present a very brief summary of the cumulative argument. The triad of sayings in Matt 5:17–19, whereby Jesus dispels the notion that he has abolished the Torah and affirms that every part of the Law is to obeyed, is a clear refutation of the Pauline position that the Torah was only a temporary measure that has been brought to an end by Christ (cf. Gal 3:23–25; Rom 10:4).[11] The eschatological scenario in Matt 7:21–23, in which Jesus condemns those who call him Lord because of their lawlessness (ἀ νομία), is a strict condemnation of Law-free Christians and recalls Pauline passages such as Rom 10:9–10 and 1Cor 12:3.[12] Likewise, the material created by Matthew in 13:36–43 makes the point that the Law-free Christian tradition has its origin in Satan and its members will be punished in the fires of Gehenna.[13] The evangelist also confronts the issue of the leadership of the early Christian movement. While Mark presents the future leaders of the Jerusalem church, the disciples and the family of Jesus, in a very poor light, Matthew rehabilitates both groups.[14] In the heavily edited material in 16:17–19, Jesus proclaims the supremacy of Peter as the head of the church using the very language and motifs that Paul employs when referring to his own divine call and mission (Gal 1:12–17).[15] At the end of the Gospel the risen Christ commissions the disciples to lead and oversee both the Jewish and Gentile missions (28:16–20), which completely undercuts Paul's constant claim to have been appointed the apostle to the Gentiles (e.g. Rom 15:16; Gal 1:16).[16]

The point of these studies was not to show that Matthew simply differed from Paul. Rather, they attempted to demonstrate that in these heavily redacted passages (5:17–19; 7:21–23; 13:36–43; 16:17–19; 28:16–20) the evangelist was consciously responding to and criticising particular claims and theological positions that can be most easily identified with Paul. On the basis of parallels and intertextual echoes between certain Pauline and Matthean texts, aligned with

---

[11] Sim, *Matthew and Christian Judaism*, 207–09. For a more detailed statement on the very different stances regarding the Torah in both the Pauline and Matthean traditions, see David C. Sim, "Paul and Matthew on the Torah: Theory and Practice." In *Paul, Grace and Freedom: Essays in Honour of John K. Riches*, eds. Paul Middleton, Angus Paddison and Karen Wenell (London: T & T Clark, 2009), 50–64.
[12] David C. Sim, "Matthew 7.21–23: Further Evidence of Its Anti-Pauline Perspective." *NTS* 53 (2007): 325–43.
[13] Sim, *Matthew and Christian Judaism*, 203–07.
[14] Sim, *Matthew and Christian Judaism*, 188–99.
[15] Sim, "Matthew and the Pauline Corpus," 411–17.
[16] David C. Sim, "Matthew, Paul and the Origin and Nature of the Gentile Mission: The Great Commission in Matthew 28:16–20 as an Anti-Pauline Tradition." *HTS* 64 (2008): 377–92.

the fact that Paul's letters were widely available at the end of the first century, I made a case that the evangelist probably had access to some of the Pauline epistles.[17]

Yet in arguing in this fashion, I tried to keep the extent of Matthew's anti-Pauline polemic in perspective. The evangelist was motivated to write his story of Jesus by a number of factors and circumstances, and he used his narrative to discredit a number of opponents or contrary views. The most immediate threat to Matthew's community was that posed by nascent Formative Judaism, and for this reason the scribes and Pharisees receive the most polemical attention,[18] but it is also clear that at certain points in his Gospel Matthew took the opportunity to attack both Paul himself and his version of the gospel, as well as other Christians who held similar beliefs.[19] This polemical perspective against Paul should not be read into every pericope and it should not be overstated, but by the same token it should not be downplayed. Despite their common commitment to Jesus as the Christ, Matthew's Law-observant stance put him fundamentally at odds with the apostle, and it is true to say that the reception of Paul in Matthew was basically a hostile one.

While it was true in 2002 to state that the relationship between Paul and Matthew had been neglected in Matthean scholarship, that is not the case today. Indeed, there have been a number of studies in recent years devoted to this topic, and it is beginning to emerge as an important area of discussion and debate. Perhaps surprisingly, it has been German-language scholarship that has defended the thesis that Matthew does contain elements of anti-Pauline polemic. The work of Gerd Theissen is of special importance in this respect.[20] Theissen begins his analysis by stating his substantial agreement with my con-

---

[17] Sim, "Matthew and the Pauline Corpus," 402–11.
[18] See the definitive study by J. Andrew Overman, *Matthew's Gospel and Formative Judaism: The Social World of the Matthean Community* (Minneapolis, Minn.: Fortress Press, 1990). Cf. too Sim, *Matthew and Christian Judaism*, 109–63; and Boris Repschinski, *The Controversy Stories in the Gospel of Matthew: Their Redaction, Form and Relevance for the Relationship Between the Matthean Community and Formative Judaism*. FRLANT 189 (Göttingen: Vandenhoeck & Ruprecht, 2000).
[19] On measuring Matthew's perceived threats to his community by the level of his polemic, see David C. Sim, "Polemical Strategies in the Gospel of Matthew." In *Polemik in der frühchristlichen Literatur: Texte und Kontexte*, eds. Oda Wischmeyer and Lorenzo Scornaienchi, BZNW 170 (Berlin: de Gruyter, 2011), 491–515.
[20] Gerd Theissen, "Kritik an Paulus im Matthäusevangelium? Von der Kunst verdeckter Polemik im Urchristentum," in Wischmeyer and Scornaienchi, *Polemik in der frühchristlichen Literatur*, 465–90. Theissen had signaled his views in an earlier study; id, "Kirche oder Sekt? Über Einheit und Konflikt im frühen Urchristentum." *ThG* 48 (2005): 162–75.

tribution,²¹ but then moves the debate into other areas. He distinguishes between different types of polemic – anonymous polemic, figurative polemic, pseudonymous polemic and mythological polemic²² – and finds instances of these in the five major Matthean discourses (cf. Matt 5:19; 10:9; 13:25; 18:6; 23:15).²³ Not long after the appearance of Theissen's work, Eric K. Wong also wrote in defence of Matthew's anti-Paulinism. While some of his arguments are in some ways similar to those of Theissen, Wong's work is doubtless independent and the agreements coincidental. Wong argues that Matthew uses the term "gospel" (εὐαγγέλιον) quite differently from Paul's use and perhaps in contrast to it.²⁴ This is followed by a discussion of the parable of the tares and its interpretation (Matt 13:24– 30.36–43), where Wong (like Theissen) identifies the enemy who sows weeds among the wheat as Paul.²⁵ According to Wong, Matthew attacks other aspects of Paul's missionary endeavours. In Matt 10:9 there is a direct refutation of Paul's manner of conducting his mission by working to supplement his endeavours (so too Theissen),²⁶ and in 23:15 the evangelist has Paul the former Pharisee in mind (again Theissen as well).²⁷ Finally Wong considers the statements of the Matthean Jesus concerning the continuing validity of the Torah in Matt 5:17–20 as directed specifically against the more liberal stance of Paul.²⁸ Both Theissen and Wong have made considerable further contributions to the hypothesis that Matthew's reception of the Pauline tradition was not favourable.

English-language scholarship, however, has adopted the opposite point of view. In a general study of Paul and Matthew, Daniel J. Harrington generously concluded that while my hypothesis of Matthew's anti-Paulinism may not convince all, it does at least provide "a stimulus for us to rethink our largely canon-influenced tendency to harmonize Paul and Matthew."²⁹ Other scholars have been more openly critical. In the very same volume in a comparison of Matthew and James, Jürgen Zangenberg engaged very briefly with my work, and

---

21 Theissen, "Kritik an Paulus," 466–67.
22 Theissen, "Kritik an Paulus," 468–70.
23 Theissen, "Kritik an Paulus," 471–84.
24 Eric K. C. Wong, *Evangelien im Dialog mit Paulus*. NTOA 89 (Göttingen: Vandenhoeck & Ruprecht, 2011), 109–12.
25 Wong, *Evangelien*, 116–19.
26 Wong, *Evangelien*, 119–21.
27 Wong, *Evangelien*, 121–23.
28 Wong, *Evangelien*, 123–29.
29 Daniel J. Harrington, "Matthew and Paul." In *Matthew and His Christian Contemporaries*, eds. David C. Sim and Boris Repschinski, LNTS 333 (London: T & T Clark International, 2008), 11–26 at 25–26.

found it unconvincing.[30] The following year Joel Willitts published a response to my analysis of Matt 28:16–20 as an anti-Pauline tradition, though he made a number of more general observations as well.[31] More recently, in a collection of essays devoted to Paul and the Gospels there were no less than two discussions of the relationship between Matthew's Gospel and the apostle and his letters, and each was critical of my work in this area. One of these was by Joel Willitts, who expanded his earlier critique, and the other was by Paul Foster.[32] It is not possible here to analyse these important studies in detail, but I will highlight a number of their major points and respond briefly to these.

Both Willitts and Foster contend that it is impossible ever to be sure that Matthew was directly attacking Paul. In the view of Willitts any comparison between these two Christian authors is nigh on impossible because they wrote from different social contexts using different genres and different rhetorical strategies, and so on. These sorts of issues make it extremely problematic to attempt any comparison or contrast as I had attempted.[33] Foster goes even further by arguing that Matthew never refers to Paul and has no interest in the apostle, since the Gospel "is primarily written to tell the story of Jesus in order to commend faith in that person as God's Messiah."[34] I would respond to these points by referring to the work of Ulrich Luz, who has correctly reminded us that the evangelist has written his story of Jesus on two distinct levels; one is the story of Jesus of Nazareth, while the other concerns the history of the Matthean church. Matthew shapes his narrative about Jesus to be meaningful for his intended readers and to address the issues that were most pressing to them at the end of the first century.[35] Most scholars would agree that Matthew's depiction of the conflict between Jesus and the scribes and Pharisees tells us more about the dispute between Matthew's community and Formative Judaism than about Jesus and his scribal and Pharisaic opponents. In the same way we can interpret the sayings of the Matthean Jesus about true and false Christians as much more applicable

---

30 Jürgen Zangengerg, "Matthew and James," in Sim and Repschinski, *Matthew and His Christian Contemporaries*, 104–22 at 120.
31 Joel Willitts, "The Friendship of Matthew and Paul: A Response to a Recent Trend in the Interpretation of Matthew's Gospel." HTS 65 (2009): 150–58.
32 Joel Willitts, "Paul and Matthew: A Descriptive Approach from a Post-New Perspective Interpretive Framework." In *Paul and the Gospels: Christologies, Conflicts, Convergences*, eds. Michael F. Bird and Joel Willitts, LNTS 411 (London: T & T Clark International, 2011), 62–85; and Paul Foster, "Paul and Matthew: Two Strands of the Early Jesus Movement with Little Sign of Connection," in Bird and Willitts, *Paul and the Gospels*, 86–114.
33 Willitts, "Friendship of Matthew and Paul," 155–56; and id, "Paul and Matthew," 64–65.
34 Foster, "Paul and Matthew," 86.
35 Ulrich Luz, *Studies in Matthew* (Grand Rapids, Mich. Eerdmans, 2005), 27–28.

to the time of the evangelist than to the time of the historical Jesus. On these grounds at least, it is permissible to examine the Gospel for possible or potential references to Paul and his particular gospel.

But these critics have a further argument that is intended to kill stone dead any such possibility. It runs as follow. Matthew was produced in an environment where Paul and his gospel were either not known or little known. In the light of this, there would simply be no need or even no possibility to polemicise against Paul. We first find this line of argument in the work of Zangenberg. Writing in reference to Matthew and the epistle of James, Zangenberg accepts that both must be distinguished from the Pauline tradition and "that both have developed in a distinctly non-Pauline milieu."[36] This claim of course is not controversial, at least in terms of Matthew. Almost no Matthean scholar would argue that Matthew stood in or even near the camp of Paul; it is well accepted that he belonged to an alternative and independent tradition in the early Christian movement. But Zangenberg continues; "even if they (Matthew and James) came into contact with strange and suspicious theological positions they might or might not have known as 'Pauline,' they commented on them and rejected them on the basis of their own, independently grown convictions."[37] It is clear that for Zangenberg Matthew was written in a location where Paul was either not known or hardly known, and any contradictions between Matthew's theology and Paul's theology are simply coincidental and not deliberate on the evangelist's part.

At the beginning of his article Foster claims that 'it is not possible, due to the limitations of the evidence to postulate whether Matthew was aware of the Pauline mission and the teachings enshrined in his writings."[38] This view is echoed and expanded at the end of his study; "in fact from the available evidence one could not even infer that Matthew had significant awareness of Paul."[39] Noting that modern readers might be bemused by this contention, Foster believes that his claim can be explained in a number of ways: 1. Matthew was completely isolated theologically and had never heard of Paul 2. Paul was less significant in the time of Matthew so there was no need to mention him or 3. Matthew knew of Paul but thought he was irrelevant for his own theological project.[40] The approach of Willitts to this issue is slightly different and more concrete. Willitts makes the claim that my understanding of the Matthew/Paul relationship is nec-

---

36 Zangenberg, "Matthew and James," 120.
37 Zangenberg, "Matthew and James," 120.
38 Foster, "Paul and Matthew," 87.
39 Foster, "Paul and Matthew," 114.
40 Foster, "Paul and Matthew," 114.

essarily tied in with my view that the Gospel was written in Antioch,[41] and he attempts to undermine this by arguing, in agreement with some other scholars, that the Gospel was perhaps composed in Galilee where Pauline influence was minimal.[42]

How reasonable are these related arguments? Let me first address the issue of Matthew's knowledge of Paul. How plausible is the claim that Matthew was written in a location that had little or no knowledge of the apostle? One might be able to argue in this fashion if Matthew were written in the first century in Chinese for Chinese readers, or in some other faraway and exotic location. Were this the case, then Matthew must necessarily be placed in a remote location where we would not perhaps expect the Pauline tradition to have travelled. But the uncontested fact is that Matthew was written in Greek, the common language of the Roman empire, and it must be situated somewhere in that large geographical region. It is of course within the realms of possibility that Matthew was composed in some extremely remote outpost within the empire, but this is unlikely. Once we accept that a number of quite different Christian sources, namely the Gospel of Mark and Q, had made their way into the Matthean community, the most reasonable conclusion to draw is that the evangelist and his community must be located within the inner parameters of the empire. And if this is the case, then it is becomes almost impossible to accept that that Mark and Q reached Matthew but not the Pauline tradition. I note and largely accept the argument of Richard Bauckham that there was extensive communication and interaction between the various Christian communities in the first century,[43] and this makes it extremely difficult to find any part of the Greek-speaking Christian world (or even the Aramaic-speaking Christian world for that matter) that had no knowledge of Paul. This conclusion is confirmed by considering the following further points.

First of all, over his thirty year career as a Christian, Paul was active in a number of Christian centres – three years in the Damascus church (Gal 1:17–18) and some twelve years in the Antiochene church (Gal 1:21; 2:1). After leaving

---

[41] For my arguments favouring Antioch as the location for Matthew, see Sim, *Matthew and Christian Judaism*, 53–62.

[42] Willitts, "Paul and Matthew," 83–84.

[43] Richard Bauckham, "For Whom Were Gospels Written?" In *The Gospels for All Christians: Rethinking the Gospel Audiences*, ed. Richard Bauckham (Grand Rapids, Mich.: Eerdmans, 1998), 9–48. Accepting this aspect of Bauckham's argument does not entail agreement with his further hypothesis that the Gospels were written for all Christians and not for specific communities. See David C. Sim, "The Gospels for All Christians?: A Response to Richard Bauckham." *JSNT* 84 (2001): 3–27.

Antioch (c. 49 CE), Paul established churches in Asia Minor and Greece, staying for prolonged periods in Ephesus and Corinth. As a Christian Paul also travelled to Jerusalem three times (Gal 1:18–20; 2:1–10; Acts 21:17; cf. Rom 15:25–28). The much-travelled apostle probably knew personally more followers of Jesus, Jewish and Gentile, than any other Christian at that time. He was so well-known and so well-connected that he could write with some authority and offer advice to the members of the Roman church, even though he had not founded that church and had not previously visited it. Paul was thus known from Jerusalem to Rome and in all points in between.

Secondly, Paul was a participant at the so-called apostolic council (Gal 2:1–10; Acts 15:1–39). While it is extremely difficult to reconstruct what precisely happened at that meeting,[44] we should not undervalue the fact that the apostolic council took place and that Paul was one of the major players at that event. So far as we know, the apostolic council was the one and only meeting in the first century that was convened between different Christian traditions to iron out a significant difference between them. This meeting involved the major Christian churches in Jerusalem and Antioch, and was called to settle the issue of Law-observance for Gentile Christian converts. Paul and Acts provide two different accounts of this meeting and it is likely that Paul's opponents in Galatia circulated an entirely different version,[45] but these differences need not concern us. What is of immediate relevance is that the apostolic council deliberated upon the fundamental question of Law-observance of Gentile Christians, an issue that affected the general Christian community. It must be assumed, given the extreme importance of this meeting, that most or even all Christians, whatever their ethnicity or theology, had heard about the deliberations in Jerusalem and Paul's participation in it. Consequently, Paul would have been widely known in the Christian world for his part in this unique meeting, although whether he was cast as the villain or the hero would vary according to the different versions.

Thirdly, Paul was a very contentious and controversial figure. He claimed to have had an experience of the risen Christ that was the same as those experienced by Peter, James and others in the Jerusalem church (1Cor 15:3–8), but there were many who did not believe him and who thereby questioned his apostolic credentials.[46] He had a public conflict with Peter in Antioch in the aftermath

---

[44] See Sim, *Matthew and Christian Judaism*, 82–92; and Ian J. Elmer, *Paul, Jerusalem and the Judaisers: The Galatian Crisis in its Broadest Historical Context*, WUNT 2.258 (Tübingen: Mohr Siebeck, 2009), 90–104.
[45] See Elmer, *Paul*, 151–54.
[46] David C. Sim, "The Appearances of the Risen Christ to Paul: Identifying Their Implications and Complications." *ABR* 54 (2006): 1–12.

of the apostolic council (Gal 2:11–14), which led to him leaving Antioch and beginning new missions in Asia Minor and Greece. In those missions he was opposed by Christian Jews with links to Jerusalem who sought to impose the Torah on his Gentile converts. These people questioned Paul's apostolic status and the validity of his gospel.[47] Paul's notoriety would have ensured that he was a well-known and well-discussed figure throughout the early church.

More could be said on this issue, but the above points establish very firmly that Paul, his gospel and his various conflicts and battles must have been very widely known in the early Christian movement during his lifetime. It is reasonable to conclude that most Christians, whether supporters or critics of the apostle, must have known a good deal about his life, his version of the gospel and the fierce opposition he faced in the final phase of his long apostolic career. Moreover, there is every reason to think that Paul's influence and reputation did not diminish in the decades following his death.

By the end of the first century, Paul's letters were circulating around the Christian world as a distinct corpus[48] and in the early second century Ignatius of Antioch had access to an extensive Pauline collection.[49] Further, the fact that a number of pseudepigraphical letters were composed in the name of Paul towards the end of the first century testifies to the apostle's continuing and widespread influence. There would be little point writing in the name of the apostle if his name did not carry the utmost authority. In addition Luke wrote the Acts of the Apostles at this time, the second half of which is devoted almost exclusively to the missions of Paul. This hagiographical tradition testifies to the importance of Paul in this period. On the other side of the coin, we find in the epistle of James a probable critique, or at least a refinement, of Paul's theology in the same period.[50] This response by the author of James provides concrete evidence that Paul and his letters were well-known and influential at this time. If they were not, then there would be no need to criticise or refine his position.

The above evidence indicates strongly that in the latter part of the first century knowledge of Paul and his letters was widespread throughout the Christian

---

[47] See my chapter in this volume, "The Family of Jesus and the Disciples of Jesus in Paul and Mark: Taking Sides in the Early Church's Factional Dispute."

[48] See Ernest R. Richards, *Paul and First Century Letter Writing: Secretaries, Compositions and Collection* (Downers Grove, Ill.: InterVarsity Press, 2004), 156–61, 214–15, 218–19.

[49] Robert M. Grant contends that Ignatius had access to Romans, 1 and 2Corinthians, Galatians, Philippians, 1Thessalonians, Ephesians, Colossians, and 1 and 2Timothy. See Robert M. Grant, *The Apostolic Fathers*, vol. 1, *An Introduction* (London: Thomas Nelson and Sons, 1964), 57. For a detailed analysis of Pauline allusions in the Ignatian epistles, see Robert M. Grant, *The Apostolic Fathers*, vol. 4, *Ignatius of Antioch* (London: Thomas Nelson & Sons, 1966).

[50] See the discussion in Zangenberg, "Matthew and James," 117–20.

world and that the apostle was highly influential in many quarters but criticised in others. The claim that Matthew was written in a Greek-speaking milieu ignorant of Paul (or largely so) almost beggars belief and can be safely dismissed. Even the attempt by Willitts to follow an emerging trend that locates Matthew in Galilee does not affect this point. The so-called Galilean hypothesis is itself problematic,[51] but given the extensive communication between the various Christian churches in that time it is simply unlikely that Galilean Christians lived in a vacuum that sealed it off from any knowledge of the influential and controversial Paul. No matter where we situate Matthew and his home community, it has to be conceded that they must have known a good deal about Paul's life, gospel and theology.

But even if this is accepted, it could well be the case that Matthew was simply not interested in the apostle, a possibility raised by Foster. Standing in a different Christian tradition, the evangelist may have been completely indifferent to Paul, and saw no need to refer to the apostle or his theology in his own narrative about Jesus of Nazareth. This claim too seems to me to be rather implausible. Apart from the points made above, that Pauline influence was widespread and increasing its influence in the late first century, and that Paul was a highly contentious figure, Matthew's Gospel deals with issues that the apostle was very much involved with during his lifetime. These include the role of the Torah in the Christian community, the terms of the Gentile mission, and the question of leadership and authority of the early church. On *a priori* grounds we might expect that Matthew would have been extremely interested in Paul's position on these and other matters, and reacted to them in his Gospel narrative.

The arguments of Zangenberg, Willitts and Foster that Matthew either had not heard of Paul or was indifferent to him and his version of the gospel do not stand up to scrutiny. It must be concluded that the evangelist knew a good deal about Paul, certainly from oral traditions about him that were circulating in the late first century and perhaps even from his epistles which were widely distributed and available. Moreover, if Matthew stood theologically near the Christian Jewish tradition that so vehemently opposed Paul in Galatia, then we might expect that he would use his Gospel narrative to discredit the apostle and his understanding of the gospel.

---

51 See David C. Sim, "Reconstructing the Social and Religious Milieu of Matthew." In *Matthew, James and Didache: Three Related Documents in Their Jewish and Christian Settings*, eds. Huub van de Sandt and Jürgen Zangenberg, SBLSS 45 (Atlanta, Ga: SBL, 2008), 13–32 at 21–24. One of the major problems with this hypothesis is that Galilee was largely Aramaic-speaking, which renders it unlikely that the Greek Gospel of Matthew was written there.

A different tack on this whole question has been recently introduced by Kelly R. Iverson.[52] Iverson devotes a whole article to calling into question my view that Matthew probably had access to some of the Pauline letters and that in some redactional passages he may have been responding to certain Pauline texts. After an introductory section where he summarises my general view, Iverson examines the method of intertextuality itself, and notes that my use of this method has theoretical shortcomings., though he does concede the possibility that an intertextual relationship might have existed between the Pauline corpus and Matthew.[53] Next Iverson examines the one example I proffered for a plausible intertextual connection between the two, Matt 16:17–18 and Gal 1:12.16–17, whereby the evangelist counters Paul's claim to have been commissioned by divine revelation by having the Matthean Jesus proclaim Peter as the leader of the church on account of a divine revelation. In Iverson's judgement, my methodology is both selective and unsophisticated, especially when measured against the intertextual criteria of Manfred Pfister.[54] Finally, Iverson criticises my emphasis on Matthew's "readers," which ignores the interpretive oral context in which the Gospel was transmitted.[55]

There is no doubt that Iverson's critique makes an important contribution to the topic of the Pauline/Matthean relationship. Unfortunately, limitations of space do not permit a full-scale discussion of all his arguments, but a few points can be made in response. The sub-title of my article under review makes clear that the study in question was a *preliminary* investigation of an intertextual relationship between the Pauline corpus and the Gospel of Matthew. It was intended to introduce the subject to the world of Matthean scholarship and was never intended to be the last or final world on the topic. Later studies, either by me or by others, would be able to offer a more refined or sophisticated use of intertextuality than was possible in that initial article. Moreover, I selected only a single instance of a plausible intertextual connection between these two authors from a wide number of possibilities. If all of the possible intertextual references were to be gathered together and discussed, then the combined weight of the many examples would strengthen the overall hypothesis. This means that even if my one example does not stand up to scrutiny, and I am not conceding this, any final conclusion would depend upon an examination of all the relevant texts.

---

[52] Kelly R. Iverson, "An Enemy of the Gospel: Anti-Paulinisms and Intertextuality in the Gospel of Matthew." In *Unity and Diversity in the Gospels and Paul: Essays in Honour of Frank J. Matera*, eds. Christopher W. Skinner and Kelly R. Iverson (Atlanta, Ga: SBL, 2012), 7–32.
[53] Iverson, "An Enemy of the Gospel," 7–12.
[54] Iverson, "An Enemy of the Gospel," 12–23.
[55] Iverson, "An Enemy of the Gospel," 26–31.

Iverson's reference to the oral culture in which the Gospel was written raises another point. We can never know with absolute certainty that the evangelist had read the Pauline epistles. That must be conceded. But even if he had not, it is still completely plausible and perhaps even probable that he knew some parts of them in oral form. It is very likely that Matthew was in direct contact and conflict with contemporary followers of Paul (Matt 7:15–23; 24:11–12).[56] If that was the case, then we can well imagine that in the heat of the debate these Pauline opponents would have cited certain texts from the Pauline corpus to defend the apostle and his and their theological position. Paul's defence of his apostleship and his justification of his Law-free gospel would doubtless have been hot topics of debate, just as they were in the time of the apostle. Thus Matthew could have been very well versed, not simply in Paul's overall theological position, but also in explicit Pauline language, even if he had never read a single Pauline epistle. When responding to these points in his Gospel, Matthew would have been forced to rely on his own memory and even the accuracy of the Pauline citations by his opponents. This point too needs to be worked out in more detail, but it might explain why the evangelist's intertextual references to Paul are not so verbally extensive as some might expect them to be. On this scenario there is still a clear relationship between the letters of Paul and the Gospel, but one that was transmitted through the oral proclamation and citation of Paul's letters by later followers.

3 Mark and Matthew

The first point to be discussed in terms of the reception of Mark in Matthew is that concerning the dependent relationship between the two texts. This introduces the perennial issue of the Synoptic Problem, and the various hypotheses that have been produced to explain the interrelationships between the three Synoptic Gospels. Limitations of space preclude a detailed analysis of the evidence or the scholarly attempts to explain it, but a few points can and should be noted.

The thesis that Mark was the first Gospel to be written and was subsequently used as a major source by Matthew and Luke is still favoured by most scholars.[57]

---

[56] For full discussion, see Sim, *Matthew and Christian Judaism*, 211–12
[57] For a recent overview of Synoptic scholarship, see Christopher M. Tuckett, "The Current State of the Synoptic Problem." In *New Studies in the Synoptic Problem: Oxford Conference, April 2008. Essays in Honour of Christopher M. Tuckett*, eds. Paul Foster, Andrew Gregory, John S. Kloppenborg and Joseph Verheyden. BETL 239 (Leuven: Peeters, 2011), 9–50. This very large volume

The majority of these continue to support in some form the longstanding Two-Document hypothesis, which holds that Matthew and Luke combined Mark with the Sayings Source Q. An alternative view is the Farrer-Goulder hypothesis, whose proponents maintain that Matthew used Mark, and Luke both used of these, which effectively dispenses with Q.[58] While the differences between these two positions have significant implications for interpreting Matthew and especially Luke, these need not detain us here. What is important is that both theories accept the priority of Mark, and Matthew's use of that text as a major source. On either view, it is permissible to speak of the reception of Mark by Matthew.

Another explanation of Synoptic interrrelationships, which disagrees with Marcan priority, is the neo-Griesbach or Two-Gospel Hypothesis. This hypothesis argues that Matthew was written first and was used by Luke, and that Mark came last and both conflated and abbreviated his two Gospel sources.[59] If this theory is correct, then we cannot entertain Matthew's reception of Mark; rather, we should need to consider Mark's reception of Matthew. In my view the Two-Gospel Hypothesis contains some explanatory power and should not be dismissed as easily as it usually is,[60] but in the final analysis it faces major and perhaps insur-

---

of collected essays contains chapters from leading scholars on the Synoptic Problem, and is representative of the various hypotheses that have been proposed.

58 See Austin. M. Farrer, "On Dispensing with Q." In *Studies in the Gospels: Essays in Memory of R. H. Lightfoot*, ed. Dennis E. Nineham (Oxford: Blackwell, 1959), 55–88. Farrer's radical views were defended and extended in the many works of Michael D. Goulder. See especially Goulder, *Midrash and Lection in Matthew*; and id, *Luke: A New Paradigm*, 2 vols, JSNTSup 20 (Sheffield: JSOT Press, 1989). The main proponent of this thesis today is Mark Goodacre. Of Goodacre's many contributions, see in particular Mark Goodacre, *Goulder and the Gospels: An Examination of a New Paradigm*, JSNTSup 133 (Sheffield: Sheffield Academic Press, 1996); id, *The Synoptic Problem: A Way Through the Maze* (Sheffield: Sheffield Academic Press, 2001); and Mark Goodacre and Nicholas Perrin, eds., *Questioning Q* (London: SPCK, 2004).

59 This hypothesis was first proposed in the eighteenth century by Johann J. Griesbach, but it was resurrected in modern times in the works of William R. Farmer, *The Synoptic Problem: A Critical Analysis* (Dillboro, N.C.; West North Carolina Press, 2nd edn 1976); and id, *The Gospel of Jesus: The Pastoral Relevance of the Synoptic Problem* (Louisville, Ky.: Westminster John Knox Press, 1994). Farmer's views have been defended by a number of his former students in many works. See especially Alan J. McNicol, ed., with David L. Dungan and David. B . Peabody, *Beyond the Q Impasse: Luke's Use of Matthew* (Valley Forge, Pa.: Trinity Press International, 1996); and David B. Peabody, ed., with Lamar Cope and Alan J. McNicol, *One Gospel From Two: Mark's Use of Matthew and Luke* (Harrisburg, Pa: Trinity Press International, 2002).

60 See David C. Sim, "Matthew and the Synoptic Problem." In Foster et al, *New Studies in the Synoptic Problem*, 188–208.

mountable difficulties.⁶¹ Because of its serious shortcomings, the Two-Gospel has failed to attract much support. In this study I will assume the consensus view that Mark was the earliest Gospel and that Matthew wrote his own narrative using Mark as his major source. The reception of Mark by Matthew is therefore a legitimate question to explore.

I have dealt with the topic of Matthew's attitude towards Mark in some detail in a previous study,⁶² and the following discussion draws heavily upon that. Let us begin with an overview of Matthew's treatment of Mark. The first point to note is that Matthew was indebted to his Marcan source in a number of ways. He adopted the Gospel genre that Mark had seemingly created, based upon the genre of ancient Graeco-Roman biographies, and he followed the Marcan story-line of a Galilean mission preceding the climactic events in Jerusalem.⁶³ Further, Matthew mostly followed Mark's order of events. While it is true that he made some changes to the Marcan order in the first half of his narrative, he largely retains his source's chronology in the second half of his Gospel.⁶⁴ Matthew's debt to Mark is further evident from the fact that he included most of Mark's content in his own account of Jesus' mission. The precise percentage of material he took over is difficult to determine because of a number of ambiguous and subjective factors, but most scholars accept that Matthew reproduced some 90 % of Mark's content.⁶⁵ We may conclude from this brief analysis that Matthew was largely indebted to Mark in terms of genre, order and content.

But this provides only a partial piece of the picture. There is good evidence that, despite his acceptance of certain Marcan characteristics, Matthew was rather dissatisfied with his major source in a number of ways. Let us enumerate these briefly. First, Mark's language is often simplistic, ungrammatical and pleonastic,

---

[61] The definitive refutation of the Neo-Griesbach Hypothesis is still that of Christopher M. Tuckett, *The Revival of the Griesbach Hypothesis: Analysis and Appraisal*, SNTSMS 44 (Cambridge: Cambridge University Press, 1983). See his updated critique in Tuckett, "Synoptic Problem," 25–33.

[62] David C. Sim, "Matthew's Use of Mark: Did Matthew Intend to Supplement or to Replace His Primary Source." *NTS* 57 (2011): 176–92. In agreement with my view is Richard Last, "Communities that Write: Christ-Groups, Associations and Gospel Communities." *NTS* 58 (2012): 173–98 at 197.

[63] Richard C. Beaton, "Why Matthew Writes." In *The Written Gospel*, eds. Marcus Bockmuehl and Donald A. Hagner (Cambridge: Cambridge University Press, 2005) 116–34 at 120.

[64] See Willoughby C. Allen, *A Critical and Exegetical Commentary on the Gospel according to Saint Matthew*, ICC (Edinburgh: T & T Clark, 2nd edn 1907), xiii-xvii. Cf. too Beaton, "How Matthew Writes," 120 n. 26.

[65] This figure was first suggested by Burnett H. Streeter, *The Four Gospels: A Study of Origins* (London: Macmillan, 1924) and has been widely accepted.

and Matthew took considerable pains to rewrite and improve the Marcan text.[66] Secondly, Matthew obviously felt that Mark was too short, and lacked detail both in terms of narrative material and teaching material. He therefore inserted the genealogy and infancy narratives at the beginning of his narrative and the resurrection appearance traditions at the end, and he greatly supplemented the teaching of Jesus by incorporating traditions from Q and other sources. Thirdly, despite retaining the greater bulk of Mark, Matthew did omit a number of whole pericopes (e.g. 7:32–35; 8:22–26), and it must be assumed that he did so because he found these passages either irrelevant, unhelpful or offensive. Fourthly, even when Matthew did not omit sections of Mark, he often edited what he kept either to remove offence or to correct what he deemed to be unpalatable theological features in Mark's account. For example, in Mark 6:5 Jesus is unable to work miracles in Nazareth, but the Matthean parallel in Matt 13:58 states that he did not do many miracles there. Fifthly, it is seems clear that Matthew, writing some two or three decades after Mark, deemed his source to be sadly inadequate to meet the needs of his own community at the end of the first century. He therefore updated Mark's story of Jesus to make it more relevant to the situation of his intended readers and more helpful to meet their specific requirements.[67] A good example of this updating is the evangelist's tendency to intensify the opposition between Jesus and the scribes and Pharisees, which reflects his own community's conflict with Formative Judaism.[68]

What are the implications of all these disparate pieces of evidence? How can we account for Matthew's acceptance of certain parts of Mark's Gospel, and for his contrary tendencies to treat Mark in such a drastic fashion in terms of omissions, additions, editorial modifications and so on? Of those scholars who have attempted to engage with this question, the majority have argued that Matthew, despite his severe treatment of his Marcan source, viewed Mark as authoritative and largely stood in theological agreement with it. Let us provide some examples from prominent Matthean specialists.

John K. Riches remarks that Mark had considerable authority for Matthew because he treated it "with considerable respect and care, preserving the major-

---

[66] See the detailed discussion in Allen, *Matthew*, xix-xxxi. *According* to Streeter, *Four Gospels*, 159, Matthew's editing and abbreviating of Mark's cumbersome language resulted in him retaining only 51 % of Mark's wording. Other scholars using different criteria of measurement put the figure a little higher. For example, Beaton, "How Matthew Writes," 120 n. 25 suggests Matthew took over 73 % of Mark's words. The majority of scholars follow the percentage of Streeter.

[67] See Luz, *Studies in Matthew*, 19–28. Cf. too Beaton, "How Matthew Writes," 123–34.

[68] See n. 18 above.

ity of Mark's Gospel and incorporating even quite small snippets of Markan material into his narrative."[69] According to Donald A. Hagner; "Since Matthew takes over so much of Mark, we may expect that he shares Mark's theology."[70] In similar vein, Richard C. Beaton states "the implication is that when Matthew adopts Mark, even though adjustments are made, he embraces the Marcan tradition and theological commitments."[71] John P. Meier goes even further in his assessment. Meier contends that Mark's Gospel was influential early on in Matthew's community, and became *the Gospel* for liturgy, catachesis, apologetics and polemics before Matthew decided to subject it to revision and expansion."[72] This particular view is also supported by the great German commentator, Ulrich Luz. In the opinion of Luz, Matthew is "the heir of his theological fathers, Mark and Q,"[73] though he concedes that Mark is the more important of these two sources.[74]

The view that Mark was an authoritative text for Matthew and his community has more recently been championed by J. Andrew Doole in his monograph devoted to Matthew's attitude towards Mark,[75] and his important contribution needs to be stated. Doole accepts that since Matthew took over so much of Mark that he found his source congenial, which suggests both social and theological proximity.[76] Matthew develops what Mark had initiated,[77] but in a manner that is in continuity with his major source.[78] Doole follows the lead of earlier scholars in maintaining that Mark enjoyed considerable authority for Matthew and his community which explains Matthew's loyalty to the Marcan tradition.[79]

The views of the above-mentioned scholars are all conditioned to some extent by the fact that Matthew reproduces some 90 % of the Marcan text. It is assumed on the basis of this that Mark had considerable authority for Matthew, and that Matthew basically accepted Mark's theological positions. But this needs to be questioned, especially the contention that the two evangelists

---

[69] John K. Riches, *Conflicting Mythologies: Identity Formation in the Gospels of Mark and Matthew*, SNTW (Edinburgh: T & T Clark, 2000), 305. Cf. too David Hill, *The Gospel of Matthew* (Grand Rapids, Mich.: Eerdmans, 1972), 30.
[70] Donald A. Hagner, *Matthew 1–13*. WBC 33 A (Dallas: Tex.: Word Books, 1993), lx.
[71] Beaton, How Matthew Writes," 120.
[72] John P. Meier, "Antioch," in Raymond E. Brown and John P. Meier, *Antioch and Rome* (New York, N.Y.: Paulist Press, 1983), 12–86 at 51–52.
[73] Ulrich Luz, *Matthew 1–7*, Hermeneia (Minneapolis, Minn: Fortress Press, rev. edn 2007), 4
[74] Luz, *Studies in Matthew*, 24, 28.
[75] J. Andrew Doole, *What Was Mark for Matthew?* WUNT 2.344 (Tübingen: Mohr Siebeck, 2013).
[76] Doole, *What Was Mark for Matthew?*, 175–77.
[77] Doole, *What Was Mark for Matthew?*, 178–83.
[78] Doole, *What Was Mark for Matthew?*, 183–86.
[79] Doole, *What Was Mark for Matthew?*, 186–89.

stood in close theological proximity. As noted in my earlier chapter in this volume on the factional conflict in the early church, the primitive Christian community was deeply polarised, in particular on the topic of Law-observance. This was not a minor issue but one which almost split the church in two.[80] And when we examine the Gospels of Mark and Matthew, we find that they stand on either side of this factional divide.

It is well-known that the Marcan Jesus had a liberal attitude towards the Jewish Law,[81] which is well illustrated in the tradition concerning purity in Mark 7:1–23. Mark betrays his understanding of this tradition with his addition in 7:19b; "thus he declared all foods clean." Matthew's perspective was completely different. The Matthean Jesus spells out clearly and definitively in Matt 5:17–19 that all of the Mosaic Law, even the least of its commandments, was to be obeyed without exception until the *parousia*. Nor is it unexpected that Matthew consistently edits those Marcan sections dealing with the Law so that in his narrative Jesus always preserves the Torah.[82]

Matthew also omits or edits other Pauline themes that are found in Mark. Mark has famously been called a passion narrative with an extended introduction because he emphasises the sacrificial death of Jesus rather than his teachings. There are clear contacts here with the Pauline tradition which also highlights the death of Jesus and makes hardly any reference to the teachings of Jesus. Matthew corrects this imbalance by introducing a great deal of teaching material from Q (and other sources as well). Moreover, Mark depicts Jesus as engaged in a Gentile mission (with no Torah requirements), which precedes and so validates the later missionary activity of Paul.[83] Matthew completely overrules this and confines the mission of the historical Jesus to the Jews alone (Matt 15:24; cf. 10:5–6). As noted above, when the Gentile mission is commissioned by the risen Christ it is the disciples who are to be responsible for it, which totally undercuts the claims of Paul to be the apostle to the Gentiles. Mark supports the position of Paul who was opposed by the disciples and the family of Jesus, and

---

[80] This crucial point is severely underplayed by Doole, *What Was Mark for Matthew?*, 184.
[81] For detailed examinations of the Torah in Mark's Gospel, see William R. G. Loader, *Jesus' Attitude Towards the Law*, WUNT 2.97 (Tübingen: Mohr Siebeck, 1997), 9–136; and more recently, Boris Repschinski, *Nicht aufzulösen, sondern zu erfüllen: Das jüdische Gesetz in den synoptischen Jesuserzählungen*, FzB 120 (Würzburg: Echter, 2009), 143–216.
[82] See Loader, *Jesus' Attitude Towards the Law*, 137–232; and Repschinski, *Nicht aufzulösen*, 57–141.
[83] David C. Sim, "Matthew and Jesus of Nazareth." In Sim and Repschinski, *Matthew and His Christian Contemporaries*, 155–72 at 156–57.

in particular James and Peter, by depicting them in a very poor light.[84] For his part, Matthew extensively edits the relevant Marcan pericopes, and substantially rehabilitates the disciples and the family of Jesus.[85]

These few examples are sufficient for our purposes. Despite agreeing on many theological and Christological points because of their common Christian heritage,[86] Mark and Matthew stood in very different Christian theological traditions. The Marcan Jesus was very close theologically to Paul, and Matthew found cause to critique and correct that depiction of Jesus just as he had corrected what he saw as Paul's invalid theological position.

This brings us to a further point in our quest to determine the reception of Mark by Matthew. What did Matthew intend for Mark once he had written his own expanded and edited version of the original Gospel? This question has been quite neglected in Matthean scholarship, but it is emerging as an important issue. Ulrich Luz has argued that Matthew's intention was to supplement the Marcan account. Luz begins with the contention that Matthew has written a conservative new story of Jesus based upon the Marcan narrative. He continues; "In this way he makes clear that his story renarrates a *given story*. There are no indications that in Matthew Gospel...that he intended to replace the Markan Gospel with which...he assumed at least some of his readers to be familiar."[87] The logic of Luz's argument is not clear, but he seems to suggest that Matthew still envisaged a role for Mark in his own community because his intended readers were already familiar with it. Despite Luz's expertise and erudition, there is reason in this case to pause and question his conclusion.

The fundamental issue can be put very simply. What role could Mark have possibly played in Matthew's community once Matthew had published his own corrected, revised, enlarged, improved and updated edition of Mark? Since the evangelist was motivated to write and circulate his own story of Jesus to meet the specific needs of his post-70 Christian Jewish community, there would be no reason for his readers to continue to consult Mark when it so obviously failed to satisfy so many of their basic requirements. Surely they would have needed only Matthew's Gospel, especially as it reflected their own theology and Christology, and it directly addressed the circumstances they were facing. The complete lack of necessity for Mark comes into even sharper focus once we recall that Matthew reproduces some 90 % of Mark's content.

---

84 See my chapter in this volume, "The Family of Jesus and the Disciples of Jesus in Paul and Mark: Taking Sides in the Early Church's Factional Dispute."
85 Sim, *Matthew and Christian Judaism*, 190–92, 194–99.
86 For a list of these, see Sim, "Matthew's Use of Mark," 184.
87 Luz, *Studies in Matthew*, 35 (original emphasis).

After the publication of Matthew, Mark had very little distinctive material to offer. Why would the later evangelist want his readers to consult the earlier Gospel when his own text reproduced almost all of that source and often improved and corrected what he did retain?

The questions continue when we consider Matthew's omission and redaction of certain Marcan passages. Why would he want his community to read of the healing of the blind man of Bethsaida in Mark 8:22–26 when he himself had deemed it unworthy of inclusion? Why would he be content to have his readers learn that Jesus' power was limited in Mark 6:5 when he had rewritten that text in Matt 13:58 so as not to convey that impression? Why would he desire his intended readers to learn from Mark 3:19b-21 that the family of Jesus believed he was demon-possessed after he himself deemed it to be so offensive that he ensured that it did not appear in his parallel account? Why would Matthew think it beneficial for his community to read in Mark 7:19b that Jesus declared all foods clean when he clearly opposed this view and omitted the offending statement, and elsewhere took pains to depict Jesus as a Law-observant Jew? These questions could be multiplied without any difficulty, but they will suffice for our purposes. They demonstrate the implausibility of Luz's thesis that Matthew intended his Gospel narrative to supplement the earlier Marcan account that was known to his readers. Reading them together would simply have caused confusion because of their significant differences and contradictions.

A much plausible suggestion is to argue that Matthew's purpose was to replace Mark because of its serious deficiencies.[88] It lacked important narrative material concerning the birth of Jesus and his resurrection appearances, it was deficient in terms of teaching material, it contained offensive pericopes, it was stylistically crude and it did not meet the needs of Matthew's post-70 Christian Jewish readers. Furthermore, Matthew saw Mark for what it really was, a narrative account of the mission of Jesus that was designed, at least in part, to support the activity and the theology of Paul. Such a depiction of Jesus, for Matthew, was utterly wrong and perhaps even dangerous, since it contradicted the theology and praxis of the Jerusalem church and it probably misrepresented the teaching and activity of the historical Jesus on some fundamental points.[89] For all of these

---

88 So Richard Bauckham,"For Whom Were Gospels Written?," 13; and Graham, N. Stanton, "The Fourfold Gospel." *NTS* 43 (1997): 317–46 at 341. Yet neither Stanton nor Bauckham spells out his case in detail.
89 Sim, "Matthew's Use of Mark," 187–88. On Matthew and the historical Jesus, see Sim, "Matthew and Jesus of Nazareth," 155–72.

reasons Mark had to be substantially rewritten, corrected and ultimately replaced.[90]

It is interesting to note that the recent study of Doole also argues that Matthew wrote his own Gospel to replace Mark, despite the fact that the latter had a favourable view of the former and granted it much authority. For Doole "Matthew's new edition of Mark is…a justification and improvement of the Markan Gospel,"[91] and "Matthew's gospel replaces Mark in a spirit of respectful succession."[92] Even more pointedly, Doole writes; "Matthew has replaced Mark, the authoritative tradition with which he long been familiar, with a gospel which both agrees with Mark and develops Mark in the same direction that the Jesus story had been taking. Thus Matthew shared a common aim with Mark, and provided a gospel very much in agreement with Mark's portrayal of events."[93]

Doole thus argues that Matthew rewrote and improved Mark because he respected that source and wished to continue the earlier evangelist's aims. But this is hardly likely. Matthew's Gospel is not in alignment with Mark on a number of fundamental issues. These include the patently Pauline elements in Mark; the role of the Torah in the mission of Jesus and in the Christian church, the role and nature of the Gentile mission, and the treatment of those who eventually held positions of power in the Jerusalem church. In short Matthew does not continue Mark's trajectory but attempts to overturn it and to replace it with one that was more acceptable to him and his intended readers. His attempt to dispense with Mark is perfectly consistent with his attitude to critique the mission and theology of Paul.

4 Conclusions

The above discussion on the reception of Paul and Mark in Matthew has yielded the following conclusions. Matthew was not simply un-Pauline, as many scholars suggest; he was vehemently anti-Pauline. He stood with the Jerusalem church against the Pauline tradition in the early church's factional dispute, and used his narrative about the mission of Jesus to discredit, where possible, the mission and theology of the apostle. The opposing position that Matthew was ignorant of

---

[90] It is likely that in this respect Matthew was no different from Luke and John, both of whom also saw deficiencies in Mark and wrote their own Gospels to replace it. See Sim, "Matthew's Use of Mark," 188–92.
[91] Doole, *What Was Mark for Matthew?*, 176.
[92] Doole, *What Was Mark for Matthew?*, 193.
[93] Doole, *What Was Mark for Matthew?*, 193.

Paul and his theology and had no reason to criticise him, strains credulity and must be dismissed. Matthew must have known a good deal about Paul, who was well known in the early church and whose influence was increasing in the late first century, and it is perhaps only to be expected that the Law-observant evangelist would use his story of Jesus to respond and critique the Law-free theology of the apostle. As to whether Matthew had actually read the Pauline epistles is difficult to determine. The intertextual echoes that exist between certain Pauline and Matthean texts can be explained in a number of ways. Either Matthew knew the Pauline corpus directly or he knew it indirectly by engaging in debates with Pauline opponents. In either case, he saw fit to respond to particular Pauline claims and to correct or discredit them.

In the case of Mark, Matthew correctly identified the original Gospel as a Pauline-influenced account of Jesus' ministry. He therefore decided to write his own version of Jesus' life and mission that improved many aspects of Mark's inferior narrative, and which corrected Mark's pro-Pauline and anti-Jerusalem stance. Matthew's overall intention was to replace Mark with a Gospel that was grammatically superior, more detailed in terms of the teaching of Jesus, more politically acceptable in terms of Jesus' relationship with his family and disciples, and more theologically accurate in terms of Jesus' observance of the Torah. The contention of Doole that Matthew largely accepted Mark's theological position and replaced it with a more detailed account that promoted and expanded the Marcan agenda, is problematic to say the least. It is much more plausible that the later evangelist wished to replace Mark because he saw it as a theologically inaccurate and even as a dangerous text.

Matthew's reception of Paul and Mark is therefore characterised by mutual hostility towards these texts. Standing within the Christian Jewish and Law-observant tradition of the Jerusalem church, Matthew viewed the Pauline gospel and epistles and the Pauline-influenced Gospel of Mark, as requiring substantial correction and critique. The Gospel of Matthew therefore stands as a clearly anti-Pauline document, not simply criticising Paul and his errant theology but also critiquing and emending the original Gospel that was so closely tied in with Paul's Law-free theology.

Bibliography

Allen, Willoughby C. *A Critical and Exegetical Commentary on the Gospel according to Saint Matthew.* ICC. Edinburgh: T & T Clark, 2nd edn 1907.
Bauckham, Richard. "For Whom Were Gospels Written?" in: *The Gospels for All Christians: Rethinking the Gospel Audiences*, ed. Richard Bauckham, 9–48. Grand Rapids, Mich.: Eerdmans, 1998.
Beaton, Richard C. "Why Matthew Writes," in: *The Written Gospel*, eds. Marcus Bockmuehl and Donald A. Hagner, 116–34. Cambridge: Cambridge University Press, 2005.
Brandon, Samuel G. F. *The Fall of Jerusalem and the Christian Church.* London: SPCK, 2nd edn 1957).
Brodie, Thomas L. *The Birthing of the New Testament: The Intertextual Development of the New Testament Writings.* Sheffield: Sheffield Phoenix, 2004.
Davies, William D. *The Setting of the Sermon on the Mount.* Cambridge: Cambridge University Press, 1966.
Doole, J. Andrew. *What Was Mark for Matthew?.* WUNT 2.344. Tübingen: Mohr Siebeck, 2013.
Elmer, Ian J. *Paul, Jerusalem and the Judaisers: The Galatian Crisis in its Broadest Historical Context.* WUNT 2.258. Tübingen: Mohr Siebeck, 2009.
Farmer, William R. *The Synoptic Problem: A Critical Analysis.* Dillboro, N.C.; West North Carolina Press, 2nd edn 1976.
—, *The Gospel of Jesus: The Pastoral Relevance of the Synoptic Problem.* Louisville, Ky.: Westminster John Knox Press, 1994.
Farrer, Austin. M. "On Dispensing with Q." in: *Studies in the Gospels: Essays in Memory of R. H. Lightfoot*, ed. Dennis E. Nineham, 55–88. Oxford: Blackwell, 1959.
Foster, Paul. "Paul and Matthew: Two Strands of the Early Jesus Movement with Little Sign of Connection," in: *Paul and the Gospels: Christologies, Conflicts, Convergences*, eds. Michael F. Bird and Joel Willitts, 86–114. LNTS 411. London: T & T Clark International, 2011.
Goodacre, Mark. *Goulder and the Gospels: An Examination of a New Paradigm.* JSNTSup 133. Sheffield: Sheffield Academic Press, 1996.
—, *The Synoptic Problem: A Way Through the Maze.* Sheffield: Sheffield Academic Press, 2001.
Mark Goodacre, and Nicholas Perrin, eds., *Questioning Q.* London: SPCK, 2004.
Goulder, Michael D. *Midrash and Lection in Matthew.* London: SPCK, 1974.
—, *Luke: A New Paradigm.* 2 vols. JSNTSup 20. Sheffield: JSOT Press, 1989.
Grant, Robert M. *The Apostolic Fathers, vol. 1, An Introduction.* London: Thomas Nelson and Sons, 1964.
—, *The Apostolic Fathers, vol. 4, Ignatius of Antioch.* London: Thomas Nelson & Son, 1966.
Hagner, Donald A. *Matthew 1–13.* WBC 33 A. Dallas: Tex.: Word Books, 1993.
Harrington, Daniel J. "Matthew and Paul." in: *Matthew and His Christian Contemporaries*, eds. David C. Sim and Boris Repschinski, 11–26. LNTS 333. London: T & T Clark International, 2008.
Hill, David. *The Gospel of Matthew.* Grand Rapids, Mich.: Eerdmans, 1972.
Iverson, Kelly R. "An Enemy of the Gospel: Anti-Paulinisms and Intertextuality in the Gospel of Matthew," in: *Unity and Diversity in the Gospels and Paul: Essays in Honour of Frank*

J. Matera, eds. Christopher W. Skinner and Kelly R. Iverson, 7–32. Atlanta, Ga: SBL, 2012).

Last, Richard. "Communities that Write: Christ-Groups, Associations and Gospel Communities." *NTS* 58 (2012): 173–98.

Loader, William R. G. *Jesus' Attitude Towards the Law*. WUNT 2.97. Tübingen: Mohr Siebeck, 1997.

Luz, Ulrich. *The Theology of the Gospel of Matthew*. Cambridge: Cambridge University Press, 1993.

—, *Studies in Matthew*. Grand Rapids, Mich. Eerdmans, 2005.

—, *Matthew 1–7*. Hermeneia. Minneapolis, Minn.: Fortress Press, rev. edn 2007).

McNicol, Alan J., ed., with David L. Dungan and David. B . Peabody. *Beyond the Q Impasse: Luke's Use of Matthew*. Valley Forge, Pa.: Trinity Press International, 1996.

Meier, John P. "Antioch," in: Raymond E. Brown and John P. Meier, *Antioch and Rome*, 12–86. New York, N.Y.: Paulist Press, 1983.

Overman, J. Andrew. *Matthew's Gospel and Formative Judaism: The Social World of the Matthean Community*. Minneapolis, Minn.: Fortress Press, 1990.

Peabody, David B., ed., with Lamar Cope and Alan J. McNicol. *One Gospel From Two: Mark's Use of Matthew and Luke*. Harrisburg, Pa: Trinity Press International, 2002.

Repschinski, Boris. *The Controversy Stories in the Gospel of Matthew: Their Redaction, Form and Relevance for the Relationship Between the Matthean Community and Formative Judaism*. FRLANT 189. Göttingen: Vandenhoeck & Ruprecht, 2000.

—, *Nicht aufzulösen, sondern zu erfüllen: Das jüdische Gesetz in den synoptischen Jesuserzählungen*. FzB 120. Würzburg: Echter, 2009.

Riches, John K. *Conflicting Mythologies: Identity Formation in the Gospels of Mark and Matthew*. SNTW. Edinburgh: T & T Clark, 2000.

Richards, Ernest R. *Paul and First Century Letter Writing: Secretaries, Compositions and Collection*. Downers Grove, Ill.: InterVarsity Press, 2004.

Sim, David C. *The Gospel of Matthew and Christian Judaism: The History and Social Setting of the Matthean Community*. SNTW. Edinburgh: T & T Clark, 1998.

—, "The Gospels for All Christians?: A Response to Richard Bauckham." *JSNT* 84 (2001): 3–27.

—, "Matthew's Anti-Paulinism: A Neglected Feature of Matthean Studies." *HTS* 58 (2002): 767–83.

—, "The Appearances of the Risen Christ to Paul: Identifying Their Implications and Complications." *ABR* 54 (2006): 1–12.

—, "Matthew 7.21–23: Further Evidence of Its Anti-Pauline Perspective." *NTS* 53 (2007): 325–43.

—, "Matthew, Paul and the Origin and Nature of the Gentile Mission: The Great Commission in Matthew 28:16–20 as an Anti-Pauline Tradition." *HTS* 64 (2008): 377–92.

—, "Reconstructing the Social and Religious Milieu of Matthew," in: *Matthew, James and Didache: Three Related Documents in Their Jewish and Christian Settings*, eds. Huub van de Sandt and Jürgen Zangenberg, 13–32. SBLSS 45. Atlanta, Ga: SBL, 2008.

—, "Matthew and Jesus of Nazareth," in: *Matthew and His Christian Contemporaries*, eds. David C. Sim and Boris Repschinski, 155–72. LNTS 333. London: T & T Clark International, 2008.

—, "Matthew and the Pauline Corpus: A Preliminary Intertextual Study." *JSNT* 31 (2009): 401–22.

—, "Paul and Matthew on the Torah: Theory and Practice," in: *Paul, Grace and Freedom: Essays in Honour of John K. Riches*, eds. Paul Middleton, Angus Paddison and Karen Wenell, 50–64. London: T & T Clark, 2009.
—, "Polemical Strategies in the Gospel of Matthew," in: *Polemik in der frühchristlichen Literatur: Texte und Kontexte*, eds. Oda Wischmeyer and Lorenzo Scornaienchi, 491–515. BZNW 170. Berlin: de Gruyter, 2011.
—, "Matthew and the Synoptic Problem," in: *New Studies in the Synoptic Problem: Oxford Conference, April 2008. Essays in Honour of Christopher M. Tuckett*, eds. Paul Foster, Andrew Gregory, John S. Kloppenborg and Joseph Verheyden, 188–208. BETL 239. Leuven: Peeters, 2011.
—, "Matthew's Use of Mark: Did Matthew Intend to Supplement or to Replace His Primary Source." *NTS* 57 (2011): 176–92.
—, "Conflict in the Canon: The Pauline Literature and the Gospel of Matthew," in: *Religious Conflict from Early Christianity to the Rise of Islam*, eds. Wendy Mayer and Bronwen Neil. 71–86. AKG 121. Berlin: de Gruyter, 2013.
Stanton, Graham N. *A Gospel for a New People: Studies in Matthew*. Edinburgh: T & T Clark, 1992.
—, "The Fourfold Gospel." *NTS* 43 (1997): 317–46.
Streeter, Burnett H. *The Four Gospels: A Study of Origins*. London: Macmillan, 1924.
Theissen, Gerd. "Kirche oder Sekte? Über Einheit und Konflikt im frühen Urchristentum." *ThG* 48 (2005): 162–75.
—, "Kritik an Paulus im Matthäusevangelium? Von der Kunst verdeckter Polemik im Urchristentum," in: *Polemik in der frühchristlichen Literatur: Texte und Kontexte*, eds. Oda Wischmeyer and Lorenzo Scornaienchi, 465–90. BZNW 170. Berlin: de Gruyter, 2011.
Tuckett, Christopher M. *The Revival of the Griesbach Hypothesis: Analysis and Appraisal*. SNTSMS 44. Cambridge: Cambridge University Press, 1983.
—, "The Current State of the Synoptic Problem," in: *New Studies in the Synoptic Problem: Oxford Conference, April 2008. Essays in Honour of Christopher M. Tuckett*, eds. Paul Foster, Andrew Gregory, John S. Kloppenborg and Joseph Verheyden, 9–50. BETL 239. Leuven: Peeters, 2011.
Willitts, Joel. "The Friendship of Matthew and Paul: A Response to a Recent Trend in the Interpretation of Matthew's Gospel," *HTS* 65 (2009): 150–58.
—, "Paul and Matthew: A Descriptive Approach from a Post-New Perspective Interpretive Framework," in: *Paul and the Gospels: Christologies, Conflicts, Convergences*, eds. Michael F. Bird and Joel Willitts, 62–85. LNTS 411. London: T & T Clark International, 2011.
Wong, Eric K. C. *Evangelien im Dialog mit Paulus*, NTOA 89. Göttingen: Vandenhoeck & Ruprecht, 2011.
Zangenberg, Jürgen. "Matthew and James," in: *Matthew and His Christian Contemporaries*, eds. David C. Sim and Boris Repschinski, 104–22. LNTS 333. London: T & T Clark International, 2008.

Lukas Bormann
Die Paulusbriefe und das Markusevangelium in der Perspektive des Lukasevangeliums und der Apostelgeschichte

1 Lukas, Markus und Paulus in den altkirchlichen Zeugnissen

Über die Identität des Autors des lukanischen Doppelwerks äußern sich etwa 180 n. Ch. Irenäus von Lyon, circa 200 n. Ch. der Kanon Muratori, und in den Jahren nach 300 Eusebius von Caesarea[1]. Alle diese Quellen nennen als Verfasser einen „Lukas" und bringen ihn in unmittelbare Beziehung zu Paulus. Irenäus berichtet, Lukas habe das Evangelium, das Paulus gepredigt habe, veröffentlicht[2]. Er hält aber auch fest, dass dies erst nach dem Tod von Paulus und Petrus geschehen sei. Lukas habe dann das Evangelium des Paulus, Markus das des Petrus schriftlich niedergelegt. Der Kanon Muratori notiert, Paulus habe den „Arzt Lukas" („Lucas iste medicus") zu sich genommen, damit dieser ein Evangelium unter eigenem Namen („nomine suo"), aber aus der Sicht („ex opinione") des Paulus niederschreibe[3]. Paulus habe das so bestimmt, da er in Lukas einen „Kenner der Wis-

---

[1] F. Bovon, Das Evangelium nach Lukas, 4 Bde., Düsseldorf 1989–2009, Bd. 1, 22–24; J.A. Fitzmyer, The Gospel According to Luke. Introduction, Translation, and Notes, 2 Bde. (AncB 28–28 A), New York 1981/1985, 27–35; H. Klein, Das Lukasevangelium (KEK I/3), Göttingen 2006, 62–67; G. Schneider, Das Evangelium nach Lukas, 2 Bde. (ÖTK 3/1+2), Gütersloh ³1992, 32f.; M. Wolter, Das Lukasevangelium (HNT 5), Tübingen 2008, 4–6.
[2] Irenaeus, Adversus haereses, III 1,1: „Et Lucas autem sectator Pauli quod ab illo praedicabatur evangelium in libro condidit." – „Auch Lukas hat als Begleiter des Paulus, was von jenem als Evangelium verkündigt worden war, in ein Buch zusammengestellt."
[3] H. Lietzmann (Hg.), Kleine Texte für Vorlesungen und Übungen, Bd. 1: Das Muratorische Fragment und die monarchianischen Prologe zu den Evangelien, Berlin ²1933, 4: „Tertium evangelii librum secundum Lucam. Lucas iste medicus, post ascensum Christi, cum eum Paulus quasi litteris studiosum secum adsumpsisset, nomine suo ex opinione conscripsit." – „Das dritte Evangelium ist das Buch des Lukas. Dieser Arzt Lukas hat es nach der Himmelfahrt Christi, während ihn Paulus als einen gebildeten Mann zu sich genommen hatte, unter eigenem Namen aus der Sicht (des Paulus) verfasst."

senschaften" („studiosum litteris") gefunden habe[4]. Die ältesten Zeugnisse über die Evangelienverfasser stellen somit einen „Lukas" an die Seite des Paulus und in gleicher Weise einen „Markus" an die des Petrus. Dieser Lukas habe Paulus persönlich gekannt, wie auch Markus ein Schüler des Petrus gewesen sei. Über das Verhältnis des Lukas zu Markus erfahren wir nichts Näheres.

Eusebius von Caesarea ergänzt die kirchliche Traditionsbildung über die Evangelienautoren, indem er zusätzlich die Paulusbriefe auswertet[5]. Nach Euseb war die Beziehung des Paulus zu Lukas besonders eng[6]. Lukas habe als Reisebegleiter des Paulus die Apostelgeschichte verfasst und Paulus habe mit der Wendung „mein Evangelium" (z. B. Röm 2,16: τὸ εὐαγγέλιόν μου) jeweils auf das Evangelium des Lukas verwiesen[7]. Euseb verbindet zudem seine Informationen über den Evangelienverfasser gezielt mit den neutestamentlichen Texten, die einen „Lukas" erwähnen. Nach Euseb ist der in Phlm 24 genannte Lukas die gleiche Person, die in den Schlussgrüßen des Kolosserbriefes (4,14) als „Lukas, der geliebte Arzt" Erwähnung findet. Dieser sei zudem der gleiche Lukas gewesen, der bei der Abfassung des 2. Timotheus in Rom als einziger noch bei Paulus war (2Tim 4,11; vgl. 4,16). Schließlich stellt Kol 4,10 – 14 Lukas als Heidenchrist vor, da in 4,11 drei Personen, zu denen Lukas nicht gehört, ausdrücklich als die „(einzigen) aus der Beschneidung" bezeichnet werden. Euseb wertet den Sachverhalt aus, dass kein vermeintlicher Name eines anderen Evangelienautors in einer solchen Breite im Neuen Testament verankert ist.

Allerdings sind drei Einwände zu berücksichtigen: (1) In der Apostelgeschichte selbst wird kein Lukas erwähnt. (2) Es spricht einiges dafür, dass 2Tim 4,11 von Kol 4,14 und Phlm 24 abhängig ist, so dass sich die Anzahl der unabhängigen Nennungen eines Lukas im Neuen Testament auf zwei (Kol 4,14 und Phlm 24) reduziert[8]. (3) Schließlich ist noch zu beachten, dass die Bezeichnung als „geliebter Arzt" in Kol 4,14 als Unterscheidungsmerkmal zu gelten hat. Eine solche Näherbestimmung passt gut zum Stil des Kol, der auch einen „Markus" durch den Hinweis, dieser Markus sei ein Verwandter des Barnabas, vor Verwechslungen schützen möchte (Kol 4,10). Die Leser des Kol sollen also Lukas, den Arzt, von einem anderen Lukas unterscheiden können. In der ersten apostolischen Gene-

---

4 H. Lietzmann, Fragment, 5: zu „litteris studiosum": „der wissenschaftlich gebildete Mann erschien als geeigneter Secretär und Evangelist."
5 Eusebius, Historia ecclesiastica, 2.22.1.
6 Eusebius, Historia ecclesiastica, 3.24.15.
7 Eusebius, Historia ecclesiastica, 3.4.7.
8 A. Weiser, Der zweite Brief an Timotheus (EKK 16), Düsseldorf 2003, 314 – 316. Kol 4,14 scheint mir hingegen nicht von Phlm 24 abhängig zu sein: L. Bormann, Der Brief des Paulus an die Kolosser (ThHK 10/1), Leipzig 2012, 11 u. 196.

ration waren demnach zwei Personen mit dem Namen Lukas bekannt: der „Arzt" heidenchristlicher Herkunft und ein anderer, der vielleicht in Phlm 24 und 2Tim 4,11 gemeint ist.

Vor diesem Hintergrund ist es wahrscheinlich, dass erst die spätere Traditionsbildung das Doppelwerk ad Theophilum einer Person namens Lukas aus dem Umkreis der Apostel zugeschrieben hat. Aufgrund der Selbstvorstellung des Autors in Lk 1,1–4 und Apg 1,1f. schied die Zuweisung dieser Schriften an einen Jünger aus. Die sogenannten „Wir-Stücke" der Apostelgeschichte ließen an einen Reisebegleiter des Paulus denken[9], der wegen der Aussagen in Apg 28 Rom erreicht haben musste. 2Tim 4,11 bezeichnet Lukas als denjenigen, der als einziger während der Haft und des Gerichtsverfahrens des Paulus bei diesem geblieben sei. Die altkirchliche Tradition fand in diesen Aussagen über die Treue zum Apostel den Beleg für die Zuverlässigkeit, die sie von einem Evangelisten erwartete. Eine bessere namentliche Verbindung des Verfassers des Doppelwerks mit der apostolischen Zeit bot sich nicht an.

Irenäus nennt das Evangelium des Markus, das damit eigentlich ein Petrusevangelium ist, und das des Lukas, welches eine Art Paulusevangelium darstellt, in einem Atemzug. Dem apostolischen Paar, Petrus und Paulus, treten die Apostelschüler und Evangelisten Markus und Lukas an die Seite. Eine Konkurrenz dieser Schriften zueinander oder eine Spannung zwischen der Apostelgeschichte und den Paulusbriefen wird nicht angedeutet. Es müsste dann ja Unterschiede oder Differenzen zwischen dem Evangelium des Petrus und dem des Paulus gegeben haben, eine Vorstellung, die der kirchlichen Traditionsbildung allzu große Schwierigkeiten bereitet hätte, als dass man sie auch nur hätte in Erwägung ziehen mögen. Jedenfalls wählte man für die beiden Evangelien, die im Gegensatz zu jenen des Matthäus und des Johannes nicht auf einen Jünger Jesu zurückgeführt werden konnten, eine analog gestaltete Entstehungsgeschichte, die ganz ohne den Gedanken der Konkurrenz auskam. Die Vorstellung, der Verfasser des Lukasevangeliums habe mit seinem Evangelium das des Markus ersetzen oder gar mit der Apostelgeschichte die Paulusbriefe überflüssig machen wollen[10], ist doch eher modern gedacht. Charles K. Barrett hat die Vermutung angestellt, dass die Kombination von Evangelium und Apostelüberlieferung in manchen Gemeinden durch das Markusevangelium und eine Paulusbriefsammlung, in anderen durch das lukanische Doppelwerk repräsentiert gewesen sei. Man habe aber auf die eine wie auf die andere Weise am Zusammenhang von Jesusüberlieferung und apostoli-

---

9 Apg 16,10–17; 20,5–15; 21,1–18; 27,1–28,16. Dazu Eusebius, Historia ecclesiastica, 3.4.6.
10 R. von Bendemann, Zwischen doxa und stauros. Eine exegetische Untersuchung der Texte des sogenannten Reiseberichts im Lukasevangelium (BZNW 101), Berlin/New York 2001, 58.

scher Überlieferung festgehalten[11]. Tatsächlich ist die Petrustradition sowohl mit einem „Markus" (1Petr 5,13) als auch mit den Paulusbriefen verbunden (2Petr 3,15f.) und stellt also eine Brücke zwischen „Markus" bzw. Petrus und den Paulusbriefen her[12].

Nach Tertullian hatte Markion das Lukasevangelium als maßgebende Fassung der Jesusüberlieferung ausgewählt. Markion verschweige aber den Verfassernamen, um es als das Evangelium des Paulus ausgeben zu können[13]. Wenn diese Informationen einigermaßen zutreffend sind, dann zeigt die Entscheidung des Markion für ein anonymes Lukasevangelium und für die Paulusbriefe, dass nicht die Autoren dieser Schriften konkurrierende Evangelien verdrängten, sondern dass es die Rezipienten in der Hand hatten, einzelne Evangelien zu bevorzugen. Die Aufnahme der Paulusbriefe in den Kanon des Markion beinhaltete schließlich de facto auch die Ablehnung der Apostelgeschichte, eine Schrift, die auch für Markion erkennbar vom gleichen Autor wie das von ihm wiederum akzeptierte Lukasevangelium war.

Die Verhältnisbestimmung des lukanischen Doppelwerks zum Markusevangelium und zur Paulusbriefsammlung war durch den Autor dieser Schrift nicht in der Weise festgelegt, dass sich die beiden genannten Evangelien oder die Apostelgeschichte und die Paulusbriefe ausschließen mussten. Das zeigt letztlich auch die weitere Kanongeschichte, in der alle diese Schriften nebeneinander bestehen konnten. Das Lukas- und das Markusevangelium hatten aber als Schriften, die nicht wie das Johannes- und das Matthäusevangelium auf Jünger Jesu zurückgeführt werden konnten, einen erhöhten Rechtfertigungsbedarf. Die aus diesem Anlass entwickelte kirchliche Tradition stellte diese beiden Schriften als Evangelien des Petrus und des Paulus auf einer Stufe nebeneinander, aber doch auch eine Stufe unter die beiden anderen Evangelien des Kanons.

2 Lukas und Markus

Das Verhältnis des lukanischen Schrifttums zum Markusevangelium besteht in erster Linie in der Nutzung des Markusevangeliums als Quelle für die Abfassung

---

[11] Ch.K. Barrett, The First New Testament, in: NT 38 (1996), 94–104, bes. 102f.
[12] R. Feldmeier, Der erste Brief des Petrus (ThHK 15), Leipzig 2005, 19; vgl. J. Herzer, Petrus oder Paulus? Studien über das Verhältnis des ersten Petrusbriefes zur paulinischen Tradition (WUNT 103), Tübingen 1998, 261.
[13] Tertullianus, Adversus Marcionem, 4.2.

des Lukasevangeliums[14]. In der Apostelgeschichte hingegen gibt es nur wenige Texte, in denen das Markusevangelium eine Rolle spielt. Im Folgenden werden zunächst einige Überlegungen zum synoptischen Problem angestellt und dann die literarischen Beziehungen zwischen dem lukanischen Schrifttum und dem Markusevangelium untersucht.

Die meisten Theorien zum synoptischen Problem legen die Markuspriorität zugrunde[15]. Einige derjenigen Vorschläge, die die Existenz einer weiteren Quelle, der Spruchquelle Q, bestreiten, etwa die einflussreiche Theorie von Burnett H. Streeter, rechnen ebenfalls mit der Markuspriorität[16]. Auch Michael D. Goulder, der davon ausgeht, Lukas habe parallel zum Markusevangelium das Matthäusevangelium genutzt („combining Mark and Matthew") und damit auch Mk-Stoff aus Mt übernommen, hält an der Markuspriorität fest[17]. Letztlich lassen sich in vielen Einzelfällen die Fragen der literarischen Abhängigkeit und der redaktionellen Überarbeitung zur jeweiligen Stelle unter der Voraussetzung der Markuspriorität relativ unabhängig von komplexeren Quellentheorien analysieren. Diejenigen allerdings, die in Mk eine Kurzversion von Lk und Mt sehen (Griesbachsche Hypothese), werden die nachfolgenden Überlegungen nur teilweise als hilfreich empfinden[18].

Die Frage, wie Kürzungen und Auslassungen, Erweiterungen und sprachliche Überarbeitungen, terminologische und narrative Neuakzentuierungen, Umstellungen innerhalb der Gesamterzählung und Veränderungen in der Erzählstruktur, die Lukas im Mk-Stoff bzw. gegenüber dem Markusevangelium vornimmt, zu interpretieren sind, ist dann wiederum etwas stärker von übergreifenden Annahmen zur Quellennutzung, Redaktionstätigkeit und Kreativität des Autors abhängig. Allzu weitreichende Schlüsse aus dem Umgang mit dem Markusevangelium auf die Gesamtkonzeption des Lukasevangeliums verbieten sich aber angesichts der Einsicht, dass Lukas seine Stoffe tiefgreifend bearbeitet hat und zudem in einem bedeutenden Umfang Material verwendet, das sich weder auf Mk noch auf Mt bzw. Q zurückführen lässt. Die Theologie des Lukas ist in erheblichem Ausmaß von Stoffen bestimmt, die nur sein Evangelium bietet und welche als Sondergut be-

---

[14] T. Schramm, Der Markus-Stoff bei Lukas. Eine literarkritische und redaktionsgeschichtliche Untersuchung (SNTS.MS 14), Cambridge 1971, 5f.; R. von Bendemann, Doxa, 51–54; F. Bovon, Lukas 1, 19–22; J.A. Fitzmyer, Luke, 65–67; H. Klein, Lukasevangelium, 44–48; G. Schneider, Lukas, 26–28; M. Wolter, Lukasevangelium, 10–16.
[15] J.A. Fitzmyer, The Priority of Mark and the „Q" source in Luke, in: To Advance the Gospel. New Testament Studies, ed. by J.A. Fitzmyer, Grand Rapids ²1989, 3–40, esp. 3–16.
[16] B.H. Streeter, The Four Gospels, London ¹⁰1961.
[17] M.D. Goulder, Luke: A New Paradigm (JSNT.SS 20), Sheffield 1989, 22f.
[18] W.R. Farmer, The Synoptic Problem. A Critical Analysis, Dillsboro 1976, 211–220.

zeichnet werden[19]. Goulder etwa urteilt über die Sondergutgleichnisse: „Lucan thinking is so heavily stamped on the Lucan parables that if we removed it we should have nothing left but our Matthew"[20]. Diese Einschätzung ist sicherlich übertrieben, da sich die lukanische Theologie nicht nur im Sondergut, sondern auch in der Art und Weise wie sie die narrative Struktur der Jesuserzählung konzipiert, Ausdruck verleiht. Das lässt sich etwa an der sehr eigenständigen Gestaltung der Passions- und Auferstehungsberichte oder an der Aufnahme der lukanischen Jesuserzählung in den Reden der Apostelgeschichte zeigen. Diese narrative Gesamtkonzeption bliebe vom Ausschluss der Sondergutgleichnisse weitgehend unberührt. Es ist aber tatsächlich so, dass das Sondergut, das etwa circa 45 Prozent des Evangeliums ausmacht, die Theologie des Lukasevangeliums weit stärker als die aus Mk übernommenen Stoffe prägt[21]. Wie sehr sich Lukas vom markinischen Konzept löst, zeigen die Kapitel Lk 22–24. Manche Exegeten kommen zu dem Urteil, dass dieser Abschnitt auf einer von Mk unabhängigen vorlukanischen Passionsgeschichte beruht[22]. Selbst diejenigen, die auch in Lk 22–24 die markinische Passion im Hintergrund sehen[23], betonen in der Regel, wie tiefgreifend Lukas in die Markusvorlage eingegriffen habe[24].

Im Umgang des Lukas mit dem Markusstoff lassen sich die Prinzipien der quellenbezogenen Textkonstruktion des Evangelisten am klarsten analysieren und auswerten. Die Ergebnisse lassen sich zwar nicht einfach auf den Umgang des Evangelisten mit seinen anderen Quellen übertragen, sie können aber doch dazu in Beziehung gesetzt werden und ermöglichen einen methodisch abgesicherten Vergleich.

Lässt sich aber auch die Frage beantworten, wie Lukas das Markusevangelium gelesen und verstanden hat? Wie also wurde das Markusevangelium von einem höchst kompetenten Leser und Autor aufgefasst? Kann man im Umgang mit seiner Quelle erkennen, welche Stärken und Schwächen er im Markusevangelium ge-

---

[19] Es hat sich inzwischen durchgesetzt, die Sondergutstoffe in Lk 1+2, 3–19 und im Passionsbericht voneinander getrennt zu untersuchen. Manche beschränken sich sogar auf Lk 5–19, s. B. Pittner, Studien zum lukanischen Sondergut (EThSt 18), Leipzig 1991, 9–11; vgl. K. Paffenroth, The Story of Jesus According to L (JSNT.SS 147), Sheffield 1997, 27–30.
[20] M.D. Goulder, Luke, 88.
[21] R. Morgenthaler, Statistische Synopse, Zürich 1971, 89: 8887 Wörter von insgesamt 19448 des Lukasevangeliums seien lukanisches Sondergut, d. h. 45,7 %.
[22] F. Bovon, Lukas 4, 261: Lk verlässt mit Lk 22,14 Mk und ist „zu seiner zweiten Quelle, dem Sondergut, zurückgekehrt (ist)". Ähnlich: H. Klein, Lukasevangelium, 655f.
[23] J.M. Harrington, The Lukan Passion Narrative. The Markan Material in Luke 22,54–23,25 (NTTS 30), Leiden 2000, 802: „Indeed Mk has continued to guide Luke in the passion narrative."
[24] J.A. Fitzmyer, Luke, 1365–1372; G. Schneider, Lukas, 435–437; M. Wolter, Lukasevangelium, 688–692.

sehen hat? Hier sind sicherlich einige Schlussfolgerungen möglich. Es ist aber bei der Auswertung der Textbeobachtungen zu beachten, dass im jetzigen Lukasevangelium nur etwa 55 Prozent des Markusstoffes aufgenommen sind, das heißt nur circa 350 von 661 Versen des Markusevangeliums finden im Lukasevangelium ein gewisses Pendant.[25] Insbesondere die letztlich eher rätselhafte große Auslassung von Mk 6,45–8,26 spricht dafür, dass Lk ein anderes Markusevangelium vor sich hatte als das uns heute bekannte. Über Vermutungen zu einem „Urmarkus" oder einem „Deuteromarkus" kommt man in dieser Frage allerdings nicht hinaus.

2.1 Evangelium

Das Lukasevangelium enthält zahlreiche Abschnitte, die im Wortlaut und in der Erzählstruktur mit dem Markusevangelium übereinstimmen. Andererseits sind die Unterschiede zwischen diesen beiden Schriften, etwa durch divergierende syntaktische Konstruktionen, abweichende Wortwahl und veränderte erzählerische Gestaltung, ebenfalls überaus deutlich. Deswegen soll zunächst nach identischen Wortfolgen aus mindestens fünf Wörtern gesucht werden, da identische Wortfolgen, die sich nicht auf eine weitere Quelle zurückführen lassen, als deutlichster Hinweis auf eine direkte literarische Abhängigkeit gelten[26]. Die beiden längsten identischen Wortfolgen auf der Basis des Textes der 27. Auflage des NestleAland finden sich in Mk 10,14 f. = Lk 18,16 f. mit 29 (30) Wörtern und in Mk 1,24 f. = Lk 4,34 f. mit 26 Wörtern[27]. Besonders aussagekräftig ist zudem, dass die Übereinstimmungen in der Wortfolge in diesen Fällen mehrfach über Satzgrenzen hinausgehen. Daneben gibt es zahlreiche weitere identische Wortfolgen von einem Umfang zwischen 6 und 15 Wörtern[28]. Damit ist die literarische Abhängigkeit deutlich genug nachgewiesen. Etwas schwieriger ist die Frage zu beantworten, welche Textfassung des Mk dem Lukasevangelium zugrunde liegt, denn diese signifikanten Übereinstimmungen in der Wortfolge sind nicht dicht über den Stoff

---

25 J.A. Fitzmyer, Luke, 66.
26 Vgl. die Übereinstimmung im Zitat von Jes 40,3 in Mk 1,3 und Lk 3,4 in der Wortfolge aus 14 Wörtern und gegen LXX und MT (αὐτοῦ statt τοῦ θεοῦ ἡμῶν bzw. ולאלהינו).
27 Mk 10,14 f. = Lk 18,16 f.: μὴ κωλύετε αὐτά, τῶν γὰρ τοιούτων ἐστὶν ἡ βασιλεία τοῦ θεοῦ. ἀμὴν λέγω ὑμῖν, ὃς ἂν μὴ δέξηται τὴν βασιλείαν τοῦ θεοῦ ὡς παιδίον, οὐ μὴ εἰσέλθῃ εἰς αὐτήν. (καὶ ...). Mk 1,24 f. = Lk 4,34 f.: τί ἡμῖν καὶ σοί, Ἰησοῦ Ναζαρηνέ; ἦλθες ἀπολέσαι ἡμᾶς; οἶδά σε τίς εἶ, ὁ ἅγιος τοῦ θεοῦ. καὶ ἐπετίμησεν αὐτῷ ὁ Ἰησοῦς λέγων· φιμώθητι καὶ ἔξελθε.
28 Z. B.: Mk 1,4 = Lk 3,3; 1,7 = 3,16; 1,44 = 5,14; 2,8 f. = 5,22 f.; 6,41 = 9,16; 9,38 = 9,49; 10,18 f. = 18,19 f.; 12,38 f. = 20,46 f.; 12,40 = 20,47; 12,41 = 21,4; 13,30 = 21,32; 13,30 f. = 21,33 f.; 14,48 = 22,52; 15,2 = 23,3; 15,33 = 23,44.

verteilt, den Lukas und Markus gemeinsam haben. Zudem fällt auf, dass die Erzähltexte in Mk 6,45–8,26 gar nicht und der Abschnitt Mk 13,1–16,8 im Wortlaut kaum von Lukas aufgegriffen worden sind. Das von Lukas für seine eigene Textproduktion *benutzte* Markusevangelium umfasst vor allem 1,1–6,44 (Lk 3,1–9,17), 8,27–9,41 (Lk 9,18–50) und 10,13–13,37 (Lk 18,15–21,36). Die Verteilung der identischen Wortfolgen, die sich auch über Lk 22+23 erstrecken, und die Abfolge, in der die Stoffe bei Lukas zusammengestellt sind, zeigen, dass Lukas mindestens Mk 1,1–6,44 und 8,27–16,8 *gekannt* hat. Reinhard von Bendemann meint zudem, im Lukasevangelium Textbeziehungen („Markus-Reminiszenzen") zur großen Auslassung erkennen zu können, die seiner Ansicht nach den Schluss erlauben, Lukas habe auch diesen Teil des Mk „gekannt" und „gezielt genutzt"[29]. Tatsächlich aber sind die Belege, die von Bendemann für die *Nutzung* des von Lukas übergangenen Markus anführt, in ihrer Aussagekraft nicht eindeutig. Man kann aber bereits auf der Basis des sicheren Befundes sagen: Lukas *kannte* die literarische Konzeption des Markusevangeliums in einer Form, die die Gesamtaussage der narrativen Theologie des Markus erkennen ließ. Die wichtigen christologischen Texte (Mk 1,11; 9,7; 14,61f.; 15,39), das Messiasbekenntnis (Mk 8,27–30), die Leidensankündigungen (Mk 8,31; 9,31; 10,33f.), die Endzeitrede (Mk 13) und vermutlich auch die Passionsgeschichte (Mk 14–16,8) lagen ihm vor. In dem ihm bekannten Material konnte er die Motive Schweigegebot, Jüngerunverständnis, Parabeltheorie und esoterische Jüngerunterweisung ebenso identifizieren wie die Geschichtskonzeption der dualistisch-apokalyptisch geprägten Endzeitrede in Mk 13,5–37. Lukas hat die Bestandteile der narrativen Theologie des Markus, die in der heutigen Markusforschung im Mittelpunkt stehen, vor sich gehabt.

Konnte er aber auch die heute analysierte Gesamtkonzeption erkennen, nach der diese Schrift eine narrative Antwort auf die Frage „Wer ist dieser?" ist?[30] Um diese Frage zu beantworten, sollen zunächst einige aussagekräftige Textbeobachtungen benannt werden. Lukas lässt alle sieben Fälle, in denen Mk den Begriff

---

29 R. von Bendemann, Doxa, 52f.: z. B. Lk 11,37–39a zu Mk 7,1–6. Es handelt sich allerdings nur um eine thematische Beziehung (Speisegebote der pharisäischen Tora) und nicht um eine Textbeziehung. Von einer solchen kann man eher in Lk 11,16 zu Mk 8,11b sprechen, vgl. allerdings Mt 12,38.
30 H.-J. Klauck, Vorspiel im Himmel? Erzähltechnik und Theologie im Markusprolog, Neukirchen-Vluyn 1997, 111: „Das Markusevangelium ist kein systematischer Traktat, sondern eine Erzählung. Es entfaltet seine Christologie nicht begrifflich, sondern narrativ." Ähnlich: P. Müller, „Wer ist dieser?". Jesus im Markusevangelium (BThSt 27), Neukirchen-Vluyn 1995; O.I. Oko, „Who then is this?". A Narrative Study of the Role of the Question of the Identity of Jesus in the Plot of Mark's Gospel (BBB 148), Berlin 2004; Ch. Rose, Theologie als Erzählung im Markusevangelium. Eine narratologisch-rezeptionsästhetische Untersuchung zu Mk 1,1–15 (WUNT 2/236), Tübingen 2007.

„Evangelium" (εὐαγγέλιον) verwendet (Mk 1,1; 1,14f.; 8,35; 10,29; 13,10; 14,9, [16,15]), aus. Er selbst benutzt den Begriff nur in Apg 15,7 und 20,24. Für ihn selbst sind vielmehr Wendungen, die von der Verkündigung des Reiches Gottes sprechen, charakteristisch. Am deutlichsten ist das in Lk 18,29 zu fassen, ein Wort, das auf Mk 10,29 beruht. Aus „um meines und des Evangeliums willen" (ἕνεκεν ἐμοῦ καὶ ἕνεκεν τοῦ εὐαγγελίου) in Mk 10,29 wird in Lk 18,29 „um des Reiches Gottes willen" (ἕνεκεν τῆς βασιλείας τοῦ θεοῦ). Für Lukas besteht dieses Wissen um das „Reich Gottes" in der Einsicht in den Heilsplan Gottes und in den Stand seiner Verwirklichung[31]. Markus scheint unter „Evangelium" hingegen eher die Möglichkeit der Rettung angesichts des in apokalyptischen Vorstellungen entfalteten Endes zu verstehen (Mk 13,9–13). Das „Evangelium" unterstützt die Selbstbehauptung der Glaubenden in einer „verlassenen Welt"[32]. Die geschichtstheologische Konzeption in Lk 21 setzt deutlich andere Akzente. Die Verfolgung der Glaubenden wird in ein positives Licht gestellt. Das heißt, Lukas rechnet damit, dass die Christen vor Gericht und vor den Vertretern antiker Institutionen bestehen können (21,18f.)[33]. Die zukünftigen Ereignisse gelten dem Autor als historische Ereignisse, etwa die Eroberung Jerusalems durch Titus in der „Zeit der Heiden" (21,24)[34]. Lukas erfasste demnach die besondere apokalyptisch-paränetische Intention des Markusevangeliums, griff sie allerdings nicht auf[35]. Ebenso wenig folgt er der Christologie des Markus, die sich narrativ vom Ende in 16,6 her erschließt: „Ihr sucht Jesus von Nazareth, den Gekreuzigten (ἐσταυρωμένον). Er ist auferweckt worden, er ist nicht hier." Für die literarische Konzeption des Lukas ist hingegen seit Lk 1,32 klar, dass Jesus der Sohn Gottes und der von Gott beauftragte Mittler ist. Dies wird nicht zuletzt dadurch erzählerisch verdeutlicht, dass die Erzählfigur Jesus von Nazareth im Lukasevangelium als „der Herr" agiert (Lk 7,13; 10,1.39 und öfter: ὁ κύριος). Lukas versteht, worum es Markus theologisch geht, er folgt ihm aber weder in der literarischen Konzeption noch in der apokalyptischen Geschichtstheologie noch in der narrativ entfalteten Christologie, um nur diese drei Bereiche hervorzuheben. Lukas betrachtet das Markusevangelium vor allem

---

[31] A. Prieur, Die Verkündigung der Gottesherrschaft (WUNT 2/89), Tübingen 1996, 282. Vgl. die stärker christologische Akzentuierung bei: M. Wolter, „Reich Gottes" bei Lukas, in: NTS 41/4 (1995), 541–563.
[32] E. Brandenburger, Markus 13 und die Apokalyptik (FRLANT 134), Göttingen 1984, 135–147; D. S. du Toit, Der abwesende Herr. Strategien im Markusevangelium zur Bewältigung der Abwesenheit des Auferstandenen (WMANT 111), Neukirchen-Vluyn 2006, 443f.
[33] L. Bormann, Die Verrechtlichung der frühesten christlichen Überlieferung im lukanischen Schrifttum, in: Religious Propaganda and Missionary Competition in the New Testament World, eds. L. Bormann/K. Del Tredici/A. Standhartinger (NT.S 74), Leiden 1994, 283–311, bes. 299f.
[34] L. Bormann, Verrechtlichung, 283–300.
[35] L. Bormann, Verrechtlichung, 294.

als Stoff, das heißt als zu gestaltendes Material, das er seinen eigenen theologischen und literarischen Interessen dienstbar macht, ohne dabei die Intentionen der Vorlage aufzunehmen.

2.2 Apostelgeschichte

Richard I. Pervo führt unter den Quellen der Apostelgeschichte auch das Markusevangelium auf [36]. Das liegt insofern nahe, als Lukas bei der Abfassung des Evangeliums das Markusevangelium benutzt hat. Verwendet er Mk aber auch als Quelle für die Apg? Jedenfalls ist ein zentraler Unterschied im Umgang mit Mk in Lk und in der Apg deutlich: „Never does he quote"[37]. Hat er aber nicht doch auch Material aus dem Markusevangelium in der Apostelgeschichte genutzt? Oder noch präziser: Blieb ihm gelegentlich „aus Materialmangel nichts anderes übrig, als Material aus dem noch nicht benutzten Markusstoff zu nehmen"?[38]

So sicher es ist, dass Lk und Apg vom gleichen Verfasser stammen, so erstaunlich sind angesichts dieser Nähe die verbleibenden Differenzen. Morgenthaler beobachtet im Vokabular der beiden Schriften folgenden Sachverhalt: „Im Lukasevangelium, das etwas länger als die Apostelgeschichte ist, stehen überraschenderweise viel weniger Sondergutwörter als in dieser"[39]. Adelbert Denaux bestätigt die Beobachtung, dass sich die so genannten lukanischen Vorzugsvokabeln nicht über beide Schriften gleichermaßen verteilen: „When a word is characteristic of Acts (...), it does not automatically follow that it is also characteristic of Luke. Compare, for example the word μαρτυρέω (1/0/1+11, i.e. the frequency of Mt/Mk/Lk+Acts)"[40].

Angesichts dieser stilistischen Differenzen zwischen Lk und Apg und der Nähe von Lk zu Mk lassen sich in der Apostelgeschichte nur in sehr wenigen Fällen markinisches Vokabular und markinische Wendungen so klar fassen, dass sie nicht auch auf das Lukasevangelium zurückgeführt werden können. Immerhin werden einige wenige Vorschläge gemacht: (1) In Apg 20,31, der Miletrede des Paulus, begegnet der Wachsamkeitsruf „Wachet" (γρηγορεῖτε), der aus Mk 13,35.37 bekannt ist, im Lukasevangelium aber nicht vorkommt (vgl. Lk 12,37.39).

---

[36] R.I. Pervo, Acts. A Commentary (Hermeneia), Minneapolis 2009, 12.
[37] M.S. Enslin, Once Again, Luke and Paul, in: ZNW 61 (1970), 253–271, hier 268.
[38] L. Aejmelaeus, Die Rezeption der Paulusbriefe in der Miletrede (APG 20:18–35) (AASF B/232), Helsinki 1987, 143.
[39] R. Morgenthaler, Statistik des neutestamentlichen Wortschatzes, Zürich/Frankfurt 1958, 33.
[40] A. Denaux/R. Corstjens, The Vocabulary of Luke (Biblical Tools and Studies 10), Leuven 2009, XXV; vgl. B. Pittner, Studien, 9–11.

(2) Apg 23,8 nutzt für seine Aussage über die Haltung der Sadduzäer zur Auferstehung (μὴ εἶναι ἀνάστασιν μήτε ἄγγελον μήτε πνεῦμα) über die lukanische Fassung der Sadduzäerfrage (Lk 20,27–36) hinaus auch direkt Mk 12,18–25, da nur in Mk 12,25 wie in Apg 23,8 ausdrücklich von „Engeln" die Rede ist, während Lk 20,36 „engelsähnliche Kinder Gottes" (ἰσάγγελοι γάρ εἰσιν καὶ υἱοί εἰσιν θεοῦ) beziehungsweise „Kinder der Auferstehung" (τῆς ἀναστάσεως υἱοὶ ὄντες) nennt. (3) Apg 20,10 nutzt die Wendung „beunruhigt euch nicht!" (μὴ θορυβεῖσθε), die in der Fassung „was beunruhigt ihr euch?" (τί θορυβεῖσθε) in Mk 5,39 vorkommt, in Lk 8,52 aber übergangen wird. (4) Apg 24,24 (καὶ ἤκουσεν αὐτοῦ), Apg 25,22 (ἐβουλόμην καὶ αὐτὸς τοῦ ἀνθρώπου ἀκοῦσαι) und der Sonderguttext Lk 23,8 (θέλων ἰδεῖν αὐτὸν διὰ τὸ ἀκούειν περὶ αὐτοῦ) formulieren das Motiv, dass hochgestellte Persönlichkeiten Protagonisten der neutestamentlichen Erzählung „hören" (ἀκούειν) wollen, in Anknüpfung an Mk 6,20 (καὶ ἀκούσας αὐτοῦ πολλὰ ἠπόρει, καὶ ἡδέως αὐτοῦ ἤκουεν). (5) Die Aussage über den Täufer in Apg 13,25 beruht wie Lk 3,16 auf Mk 1,7 f. (6) Für Apg 20,29 f. scheint das Vorbild für die Warnung des Paulus vor „Männern" aus der Gemeinde, die die Verkündigung verdrehen und die „Jünger" zur Gefolgschaft verführen werden, in Mk 13,22 f. zu finden zu sein[41]. Die Aussage in Mk 13,22 f. über das Auftreten von falschen Christussen und Propheten, die die „Auserwählten" in die Irre führen werden, wird in Lk 21 übergangen, könnte aber auf die Miletrede des Paulus (Apg 20,18–35) eingewirkt haben. Allerdings gibt es hier keine terminologische, sondern nur thematische Übereinstimmungen. (7) Einige Passagen aus den Wundererzählungen der Apostelgeschichte stehen den markinischen Wundererzählungen, besonders den Heilungssummarien, terminologisch näher als den lukanischen Varianten, zum Beispiel Apg 5,15 f. zu Mk 6,56 f., Apg 8,7 zu Mk 1,26 f. und 5,7 f., Apg 9,40 zu Mk 5,40 f., Apg 16,17 zu Mk 1,24 und 5,7 f., Apg 19,11 f. zu Mk 6,56.

Die Aussagekraft dieser und weiterer möglicher Textbeobachtungen ist begrenzt. Der Autor der Apostelgeschichte mag in diesen Fällen Wendungen des Markusevangeliums im Sinn gehabt haben. Eine Quellennutzung im engeren Sinn, das heißt die Benutzung des Markustexts, ist aber nicht nachzuweisen, da keine identischen Wortfolgen oder prägnante markinische Syntagmata in der Apostelgeschichte vorliegen.

Zur theologischen Beziehung von Mk und dem lukanischem Schrifttum wird man unter Einbeziehung der Apg das oben Gesagte noch um die Unterschiede in der geschichtstheologischen Dimension ergänzen müssen. Ein Evangelium mit den apokalyptischen Vorstellungen von Mk 13, die zudem die Erwartung enthalten, dass zuerst das Evangelium allen Völkern verkündet werden muss (13,10), ist

---

[41] L. Aejmelaeus, Rezeption, 142–148.

mit der geschichtstheologischen Konzeption der Apostelgeschichte, die von der Verkündigung des Reiches Gottes um Israel willen spricht (Apg 28,20; vgl. Apg 1,6; 13,23; Lk 1,16.54.68; 2,25.32; 23,21), nicht vereinbar.

3 Lukas und Paulus

Obwohl der Autor des Lukasevangeliums in der Alten Kirche als Mitarbeiter und Schüler des Paulus und sein Evangelium als das Evangelium des Paulus verstanden worden ist, werden die meisten Exegeten der Feststellung von Joseph A. Fitzmyer zustimmen: „There is no evidence that Luke had ever read any of Paul's letters"[42]. Die Aussage, dass kein sicherer Beleg für die Benutzung der Paulusbriefe vorliegt, ist aber nicht zwingend mit der Schlussfolgerung Fitzmyers verbunden, Lukas habe die Paulusbriefe auch nicht *gelesen* und damit nicht *gekannt*[43], eine Annahme, für die tatsächlich immer wieder Exegeten plädieren[44]. Aus der Unterscheidung von Nutzung und Kenntnis ergeben sich aber weitere Aporien, und zwar genau drei: (1) Wenn Lukas die Paulusbriefe gekannt und nicht genutzt hat, stellt sich die Frage nach der Motivation eines Autors, der zweifelsohne ein positives Paulusbild entwirft, dabei aber ein wesentliches Merkmal seines „Helden", nämlich dessen briefliche Kommunikation, verschweigt. (2) Wenn er die Paulusbriefe gekannt und genutzt hat, ist zu klären, warum davon nur so wenige Spuren zu erkennen sind. (3) Wenn er sie nicht gekannt hat und deswegen nicht nutzen konnte, steht die Forschung vor dem Rätsel, dass ein geschulter Autor oder gar „Historiker" wie der Verfasser der Apostelgeschichte zwar das Markusevangelium, möglicherweise die Logienquelle, die Septuaginta und schließlich umfangreiches Sondergut zur Verfügung hatte, nicht aber die wichtigen und einflussreichen Paulusbriefe. Immerhin hält Paulus in 2Kor 10,10 eine selbst von seinen Gegnern geteilte Sichtweise fest: „Die Briefe [des Paulus] sind zwar gewichtig und kraftvoll, sagen sie [die Gegner], das persönliche Auftreten hingegen schwach und die Rede unbedeutend." Die Apostelgeschichte hingegen stellt die Reden des Paulus in den Mittelpunkt. Obwohl mehrmals Briefe anderer Personen erwähnt und einige sogar im Wortlaut zitiert werden (Apg 9,2; 15,23–31; 22,5; 23,25–30.33), schweigt die Apostelgeschichte über den Sachverhalt, dass Paulus solche wichtigen Dokumente abgefasst hat, und verzichtet vollständig auf Textübernahmen aus diesen. Theodor Zahn staunt über dieses „unglaubliche

---

42 J. A. Fitzmyer, Luke, 28.
43 Ch. K. Barrett, Acts and the Pauline Corpus, in: ET 88 (1976), 2–5.
44 R. I. Pervo, Acts, 12.

Nichtwissen des Lukas" und kommt zu dem Schluss: Dieser stand Paulus so nahe, dass er meinte, „auf ein Studium seiner Briefe zum Zweck der Bereicherung seiner Geschichtskenntnis verzichten zu können"[45]. Zahn unterstellt dem Autor des dritten Evangeliums eine nur oberflächliche Kenntnis der Briefe und einen naiven Verzicht auf deren Nutzung. Eine ähnliche Sicht vertritt Andreas Lindemann, der offensichtlich davon ausgeht, dass Lukas die Paulusbriefe *kannte*. Als Argument verweist er vor allem auf die Übereinstimmungen im Personeninventar und in den geographischen Angaben[46]. Der Verfasser der Apostelgeschichte habe die ihm bekannten Briefe „illustrieren" wollen[47]. Solch undramatische Lösungen des Problems, wie sie Zahn und Lindemann anbieten, werden allerdings sonst nur selten vertreten. Immer wieder wird vermutet, die Paulusbriefe seien zur Grundlage einer als häretisch empfundenen Paulusrezeption geworden[48]. Deren Vertreter/innen werden meist in einem „vormarkionitischen" Milieu vermutet. Lukas wollte Paulus gegen diese Vereinnahmung retten und verzichtete deswegen auf die Paulusbriefe, die ja tatsächlich auch im Neuen Testament bereits in 2Thess 2,2 und 2Petr 3,15 f. eine ambivalente Würdigung finden. Wie ein solches „Schweigen" des Lukas zu deuten ist, ist allerdings unklar. Es ist zumindest lesenswert, wie Morton S. Enslin die Nuancierungen des Verfassers der Apostelgeschichte im Wechsel von Betonung und Schweigen erläutert[49]. Allerdings lassen sich derartige Vermutungen weder beweisen noch widerlegen und bewegen sich jenseits einer methodisch reflektierten Exegese.

Angesichts der Spannung zwischen der historisch plausiblen Annahme, Lukas müsse die Paulusbriefe gekannt haben, und dem philologisch deutlichen Befund, dass er die Briefe nicht benutzt hat, stellt sich die Frage, bis zu welchem Grad eher indirekte sprachliche Beziehungen zwischen dem lukanischen Schrifttum und den Paulusbriefen zu identifizieren sind. Die Nähe zu Paulus könnte doch dazu geführt haben, dass bestimmte von Paulus bevorzugte schriftgestützte Argumentationen und bestimmte terminologische Verfestigungen im lukanischen Schrifttum begegnen. Im Folgenden werden deswegen die Schriftzitate und die terminologischen Beziehungen untersucht.

---

45 Th. Zahn, Einleitung in das Neue Testament, Wuppertal 1994, 414–420, Zitate 414 u. 419.
46 A. Lindemann, Paulus im ältesten Christentum (BHTh 58), Tübingen 1979, 161–173.
47 A. Lindemann, Paulus, 173.
48 J. Knox, Acts and the Pauline Letter Corpus, in: Studies in Luke-Acts. Essays Presented in Honor of Paul Schubert, eds. L.E. Keck/J.L. Martyn, London 1976, 279–287, hier 284–286; M.S. Enslin, Once Again, 270 f.; W. Schenk, Luke as Reader of Paul. Observations on his Reception, in: Intertextuality in Biblical Writings, ed. by S. Draisma, Kampen 1989, 127–139, hier 127 f.
49 M.S. Enslin, Emphases and Silences, in: HTR 73 (1980), 219–225.

3.1 Schriftzitate im lukanischen Schrifttum und in den Paulusbriefen

Sowohl das lukanische Schrifttum als auch die Paulusbriefe, zumindest der Römerbrief, die beiden Korintherbriefe und der Galaterbrief, zitieren häufig das griechische Alte Testament. Für die Paulusbriefe hat Dietrich-Alex Koch und für das lukanische Schrifttum Dietrich Rusam jeweils eine Liste der eindeutigen Schriftzitate vorgelegt[50]. Koch zählt in den Paulusbriefen 89 Zitate, Rusam im lukanischen Schrifttum 43, davon 17 im Evangelium und 26 in der Apostelgeschichte. Die Analyse der Schriftzitate zeigt, dass Paulus zu kürzeren Zitaten von Versen und Teilversen neigt, während Lukas immer wieder auch längere, fast perikopenartige Zitate bietet[51]. Die Anzahl der Übereinstimmungen im Schriftgebrauch ist außerordentlich gering. Das gilt auch, wenn man nicht nur die Zitate, sondern auch die Anspielungen berücksichtigt, die im Appendix III zu Nestle/Aland aufgelistet sind. Folgende Schriftzitate werden sowohl von Paulus als auch von Lukas verwendet: (1) Dtn 5,16–21 wird verkürzt in Lk 18,20 und in Röm 13,9 zitiert. Lk verzichtet auf die charakteristische Wendung „Du sollst nicht begehren" (οὐκ ἐπιθυμήσεις), die für Paulus als Zusammenfassung des Dekalogs gilt (vgl. Röm 7,7). Damit fehlt bei Lukas die paulinische Pointe, nach der ἐπιθυμία als „Wurzelsünde" zu gelten hat[52]. Lukas verwendet ἐπιθυμία nur in Lk 22,15 und zwar mit der Bedeutung „Sehnsucht". (2) Das Gebot der Nächstenliebe aus Lev 19,18 wird in Lk 10,27 und Röm 12,19; 13,9 und Gal 5,14 zitiert. Bei Lk ist es durch Mk 12,28–31 vorgegeben und wird mit dem Gottesgebot aus dem *Schema Israel* (Dtn 6,4f.) zum Doppelgebot der Liebe zusammengefasst. Paulus hingegen stellt das Liebesgebot in Beziehung zum Dekalog, ohne das *Schema* in diesem Zusammenhang heranzuziehen. In 1Kor 8,4 wird wiederum ausgerechnet die Wendung aus dem *Schema* aufgenommen (οὐδεὶς θεὸς εἰ μὴ εἷς), die Lk 10,27 auslässt. (3) Joel 3,1–5 wird in Apg 2,17–21 zitiert. Die Wendung „jeder, der den Namen des Herrn anruft, wird gerettet werden" (πᾶς ὃς ἂν ἐπικαλέσηται τὸ ὄνομα κυρίου σωθήσεται) aus Joel 3,5 findet sich auch in Röm 10,13. (4) Lev 18,5 wird in den gesetzeskritischen Passagen von Röm 10,5 und Gal 3,12 zitiert. Lk 10,28 spielt im Anschluss an die Ausführungen zur Perikope vom Doppelgebot der Liebe auf diese Wendung an: „tue sie und du wirst leben". (5) Das Motiv vom Töten der Propheten

---

50 D.-A. Koch, Die Schrift als Zeuge des Evangeliums (BHTh 69), Tübingen 1986, 21–23; D. Rusam, Das Alte Testament bei Lukas (BZNW 112), Berlin 2003, 2f.
51 Jes 40,3–5 in Lk 3,4–6; Ps 91,11f. in Lk 4,10f.; Jes 61,1f. in Lk 4,18f.; Ps 110,1 in Lk 20,42 und Apg 2,34f.; Joel 3,1–5 in Apg 2,17–21; Ps 15,8–11 in Apg 2,25–28; Am 5,25–27 in Apg 7,42f.; Jes 66,1f. in Apg 7,49f.; Jes 6,9f. in Apg 28,26f. u.ö.
52 M. Theobald, Studien zum Römerbrief (WUNT 136), Tübingen 2001, 268f.

aus 1Kön 19,10 wird sowohl in Apg 7,52 als auch in Röm 11,3 aufgenommen. (6) Ps 110,1, das im Neuen Testament am häufigsten zitierte und angespielte Schriftwort, wird von Koch gar nicht in der Liste der Schriftzitate bei Paulus aufgeführt, weil er im Gegensatz zu den meisten Exegeten in Röm 8,34 und 1Kor 15,25 keine Anspielung auf Ps 110,1 sieht[53]. Lukas zitiert den Psalm ausführlich in Lk 20,42f. und Apg 2,34f. Anspielungen finden sich in Lk 22,69 und in Apg 7,55.

Wertet man diese Übersicht rein quantitativ aus, dann sind von den 89 Schriftzitaten bei Paulus nur drei auch im lukanischen Schrifttum aufgenommen, nämlich die Dekalogparaphrase aus Dtn 5,16–21, das Gebot der Nächstenliebe aus Lev 19,18 und die Wendung über die Anrufung des Gottesnamens aus Joel 3,5. Darüber hinaus sind in beiden zu untersuchenden Schriftenkorpora Anspielungen auf Lev 18,5; 1Kön 19,10 und Ps 110,1 zu finden. Im Falle dieser wenigen Überschneidungen folgt der Gebrauch der Schriftzitate jeweils sehr unterschiedlichen, wenn nicht gar gegensätzlichen Argumentationszielen. Berücksichtigt man noch, dass für Paulus so wichtige Zitate wie Gen 15,6; Hab 2,4b; Jes 40,13 oder auch das eher floskelhafte Jer 9,22f. im lukanischen Schrifttum völlig unbeachtet bleiben, dann wird man zu dem Schluss kommen, dass die für Lukas relevanten Schriftbezüge sich so gut wie gar nicht mit denen des Paulus überschneiden. Zudem verwendet Lukas die Schrift unter völlig anderen Gesichtspunkten. Während Paulus sie nicht dazu nutzt, um seine Christologie biblisch zu verankern, sondern um die Schlussfolgerungen, die er aus seinen christologischen Überzeugungen zieht, zu begründen[54], setzt Lukas Schriftzitate und Verweise auf „die Schrift(en)" (Lk 4,21; 24,27.32.44f.) beständig christologisch ein, um die Übereinstimmung des Schicksals des Kyrios Jesus von Nazareth mit den von ihm prophetisch interpretierten Schriften zu belegen[55].

Die Analyse der Schriftzitate spricht deutlich dafür, dass Lukas die Briefe des Paulus nicht genutzt hat. Sie spricht zudem auch dagegen, dass er sie überhaupt gekannt hat. Die Schriftauslegungen des Paulus hätten es auch einem Autor, der bewusst auf die Nutzung der ihm bekannten Briefe verzichtet, erlaubt, die Argumentationsstrategien des Paulus eigenständig weiterzuführen und etwa in die

---

[53] D.-A. Koch (Schrift, 19f.) meint, dass Ps 110,1 nicht in Röm 8,34 angedeutet und ebenso wenig in 1Kor 15,25 zitiert ist. Dagegen erkennen in Röm 8,34 und 1Kor 15,25 Anspielungen auf Ps 110,1: A. Lindemann, Der Erste Korintherbrief (HNT 9/1), Tübingen 2000, 347; M. Hengel, Psalm 110 und die Erhöhung des Auferstandenen zur Rechten Gottes, in: Anfänge der Christologie, hg. von H. Paulsen/C. Breytenbach, Göttingen 1991, 43–73, hier 55.
[54] N. Walter, Alttestamentliche Bezüge in christologischen Ausführungen des Paulus, in: Paulinische Christologie, hg. von U. Schnelle/Th. Söding, Göttingen 2000, 246–271, bes. 262.
[55] D. Rusam, Schrift, 494; M. Meiser, Das Alte Testament im lukanischen Doppelwerk, in: Im Brennpunkt: die Septuaginta. Studien zur Entstehung und Bedeutung der Griechischen Bibel, hg. von H.-J. Fabry/U. Offerhaus (BWANT 153), Stuttgart 2001, 167–195, bes. 180–183.

Ausführungen von Apg 13,38 f. das Zitat von Gen 15,6 zu integrieren, wenn er es denn gewollt und gekonnt hätte.

Darüber hinaus wäre bei einer aktiven Auseinandersetzung mit der paulinischen Theologie damit zu rechnen, dass sich der Schrifttheologe Lukas, der sich immer wieder auf ein prophetisches und christologisches Schriftverständnis beruft, mit zentralen Schriftauslegungen des Paulus, etwa zur Abrahamskindschaft der Heidenchristen in Gal 3 und Röm 4, zur Schriftauslegung nach 2Kor 3 oder zur Stellung Israels nach Röm 9–11, befasst, unter Umständen eben auch kritisch, um sich davon abzugrenzen. Das ist jedoch nicht zu beobachten. Der Umgang mit der Schrift ist sowohl material (hinsichtlich der verwendeten Texte) als auch theologisch (hinsichtlich der mit der Schriftauslegung verbundenen Ziele) bei Lukas und Paulus sehr verschieden. Die Schnittmenge ist so gering, dass man dem lukanischen Schrifttum eine völlige Ignoranz des paulinischen Schriftgebrauchs attestieren kann. Die Analyse des Schriftgebrauchs bei Lukas und Paulus belegt zudem, dass die Tiefenstrukturen der theologischen Argumentationen beider Autoren so sehr voneinander isoliert sind, dass eine Vertrautheit mit den Paulusbriefen kaum vorstellbar ist.

3.2 Evangelium

Eric Wong kommt in seiner intertextuellen Studie über die Textbeziehungen zwischen den Synoptikern und Paulus zu dem Ergebnis, dass Lukas „die geringsten intertextuellen Bezüge zu Paulus in seinem Evangelium" hat[56]. Es sind nur wenige Texte in den Paulusbriefen, bei denen eine Nutzung im Lukasevangelium in Erwägung gezogen werden kann. Hier sind vor allem drei Texte zu nennen: die Abendmahlsüberlieferung in 1Kor 11,23–26 (vgl. Lk 22,15–20), der liturgische Abendmahlstext in 1Kor 10,16 (vgl. die Kurzfassung im Codex Bezae Lk 22,17 f.) und die Auferstehungsüberlieferung in 1Kor 15,1–7 (vgl. Lk 23,34).

(1) 1Kor 11,23–26 zu Lk 22,19 f.: Die große Ähnlichkeit und die enge Verwandtschaft der Texte sind offensichtlich. Die Wortfolge ist insgesamt weniger durch divergierende Terminologie als vielmehr durch die unterschiedliche Setzung von Possessivpronomen und Partikeln unterbrochen. Die längste identische Wortfolge ist dennoch signifikant für eine literarische Abhängigkeit. Sie umfasst 10 Wörter und überschreitet syntaktische Grenzen (Lk 22,20/1Kor 11,25): μετὰ τὸ δειπνῆσαι λέγων τοῦτο τὸ ποτήριον ἡ καινὴ διαθήκη. Kurz vor dieser identischen

---

[56] E.K.C. Wong, Evangelien im Dialog mit Paulus. Eine intertextuelle Studie zu den Synoptikern (NTOA/StUNT 89), Göttingen 2012, 173.

Wortfolge findet sich eine weitere, die sechs Wörter umfasst (Lk 22,19/1Kor 11,24): τοῦτο ποιεῖτε εἰς τὴν ἐμὴν ἀνάμνησιν. Die Bedeutung dieser Übereinstimmungen wird noch dadurch gestärkt, dass die neuere Exegese nicht mehr damit rechnet, dass es sich bei den Einsetzungsworten um liturgische Texte handelt[57]. Vielmehr geht man davon aus, dass es sich um erklärende Deutungen handelt, die eher als katechetische Texte zu verstehen sind. Das bedeutet dann auch, dass weder Lukas noch Paulus hier auf Texte ihrer aktuellen Abendmahlspraxis und damit auf „heilige Worte", die einem typischen Prozess der Verfestigung unterliegen, zurückgreifen, sondern auf reflexive Ausführungen, die der jeweiligen Kommunikationssituation angepasst werden konnten. Die katechetische Tradition der Einsetzungsworte, die Lukas und Paulus nutzen, wird in der Regel mit der Gemeinde in Antiochien in Verbindung gebracht[58]. Paulus verwendet diese Worte, um einen aktuellen Konflikt um die Mahlgemeinschaft zu klären, Lukas bindet sie, vermutlich inspiriert durch die Markuspassion, in seine Jesuserzählung ein. Im Vergleich mit der markinischen Fassung betont diese antiochenische Tradition die ekklesiologische Funktion des Abendmahls durch die Wendung „Blut des Bundes" und die heilsgeschichtliche Dimension durch die Aussage „zu meinem Gedächtnis". Die Unterschiede zwischen Paulus und Lukas wiederum sind ebenfalls klar zu bestimmen. Lukas verstärkt die bereits in der Markuspassion vorgegebene Verbindung zum Passahmahl, indem er über Markus hinaus das Passah in die Worte, die Jesus zum Mahl spricht, also in die Abendmahlsparadosis, integriert und eine Variante des Verzichtsworts auf das Passah bezieht (Lk 22,15 f.). Nach Lukas feiert Jesus mit seinen Jüngern die Erinnerung an den Auszug aus Ägypten und an die Befreiung Israels[59]. Im Passah wird ein Mahl gesehen, an dem Gott in besonderer Weise beteiligt ist, nämlich als geschichtlich an Israel, dem Gottesvolk, handelnder Gott. Das Mahl Jesu tritt an die Seite des Passahs und bleibt funktional auf das eschatologische Mahl, das auch als Passah vorgestellt wird, bezogen. Lukas sieht keinen Gegensatz zwischen Passah und Abendmahl. Der „Neue Bund" begründet eine Gemeinschaft, die das eschatologische Mahl als Passahmahl erwartet und die bis zum Eintritt dieses Ereignisses ihres „Herrn" im Abendmahl gedenkt. Das vorgestellte endzeitliche Mahl ist mit einem Gericht über die zwölf Stämme Israels (Lk 22,30, vgl. Lk 14,24) und der Wiederherstellung Israels im Horizont der Eliatradition verbunden (Lk 1,17). Paulus hingegen greift auf die Abendmahlsparadosis im Rahmen einer umfassenden Erörterung der Mahlprak-

---

57 D. Zeller, Der erste Brief an die Korinther (KEK 5), Göttingen 2010, 264–375; J. Schröter, Die Funktion der Herrenmahlsüberlieferungen im 1. Korintherbrief, in: ZNW 100 (2009), 78–100, bes. 90 f.
58 D. Zeller, Korinther, 375.
59 F. Bovon, Lukas 4, 236–248.

tiken der Korinthergemeinde zurück (1Kor 8–11). Im direkten Kontext von 1Kor 11,23–26 geht es um die Frage, wie sich Sättigungsmahl und symbolisches Mahl und damit auch die Besitzenden zu den Besitzlosen der Gemeinde verhalten. Die heilsgeschichtliche Dimension, die Lukas durch die Verbindung des Herrenmahls mit der Passahtradition erreicht, fehlt bei Paulus.

Die identische Wortfolge spricht zunächst für eine literarische Abhängigkeit des Lukasevangeliums von 1Kor. Die unterschiedlichen Verwendungsweisen der Abendmahlsparadosis und die divergierenden Sinnhorizonte, einerseits eschatologisches Passah bei Lukas (Lk 22,15f.) und andererseits Verkündigung des Todes und der Parusie bei Paulus (1Kor 11,26), verweisen aber auch darauf, dass Lukas den intentionalen Kontext von 1Kor 11,23–26 ignoriert. Es ist deswegen wahrscheinlicher, dass sich Lukas und Paulus unabhängig voneinander auf eine schriftliche Vorlage aus der antiochenischen Abendmahlsparänese beziehen.

(2) 1Kor 10,16 zu Lk 22,17f.: Das liturgische Wort zu Brot und Kelch stellt eine Abfolge der Abendmahlshandlung vor, nach der zuerst der Kelch und dann das Brot gereicht wird. Diese Reihenfolge, die auch in Did 9,2–4 belegt ist, stimmt mit derjenigen überein, die in der Kurzfassung der Einsetzungsworte aus Lk 22,17f. nach Codex Bezae (D=05) und einigen altlateinischen Zeugen enthalten ist[60]. Die Lesart der Kurzfassung wird allerdings mit guten Gründen nicht als die älteste erreichbare Textgestalt angesehen. Aber auch die lukanische Langfassung spricht zunächst von einem ersten Kelch mit Verzichtswort, dann vom Brot mit Deutewort und abschließend von einem zweiten Kelch mit Deutewort. Die Parallelen reflektieren eine Verbundenheit in der Tradition, aber keine literarische Abhängigkeit des Lukasevangeliums von 1Kor 10,16.

(3) 1Kor 15,5 zu Lk 24,34: Der Zusammenhang dieser beiden Worte ist immer wieder Gegenstand von exegetischen Überlegungen. Hier lohnt es sich, den Wortlaut zu vergegenwärtigen:

Lk 24,34: ὅτι ὄντως ἠγέρθη ὁ κύριος καὶ ὤφθη Σίμωνι.

1Kor 15,3–5: ὅτι Χριστὸς (...) ἐγήγερται τῇ ἡμέρᾳ τῇ τρίτῃ (...) καὶ ὅτι ὤφθη Κηφᾷ εἶτα τοῖς δώδεκα.

Enslin sieht in 1Kor 15,5 die Quelle für Lk 24,34[61]. Ulrich Wilckens hingegen denkt an gemeinsame Tradition. Er unterscheidet eine „Auferstehungsformel" (Der Herr ist wahrhaftig auferstanden!) und eine „Petrusformel" (Er ist dem Petrus er-

---

60 F. Bovon, Lukas 4, 239f.; H.-W. Bartsch, Codex Bezae versus Codex Sinaiticus im Lukasevangelium, Hildesheim 1984, 184–187.
61 M. S. Enslin, ‚Luke' and Paul, in: JAOS 58 (1938), 81–91, bes. 86f.: „source of Luke's own phrase". Ders., Once Again, 260f.

schienen!), die in der Traditionsentwicklung sekundär zusammengefügt worden seien[62]. Das lässt sich nun allerdings kaum methodisch abgesichert belegen. Die knappen, eher schlagwortartigen Übereinstimmungen erlauben es auch nicht, von einer literarischen Abhängigkeit zu sprechen. Die Auferstehungsaussage unterscheidet sich in der Terminologie („Herr" versus „Christus"), in der kontextuellen Einbindung und in der syntaktischen Gestaltung. Die Erscheinungsaussage ist hingegen weitgehend identisch, der Namenswechsel zwischen „Simon" in Lk 23,34 und „Kephas" ist wenig aussagekräftig, auch in Gal 2,6–9 wird zwischen dem griechischen Petrus und dem aramäischen Kephas innerhalb einer Satzkonstruktion gewechselt. Ein Zweiwortsatz ist wenig signifikant für die Klärung der Frage nach literarischer Abhängigkeit. Die Gemeinsamkeit zwischen Lukas und Paulus erklärt sich eher durch die gemeinsame antiochenische Gemeindetradition.

Die Abendmahls- und die Auferstehungsüberlieferung belegen, dass Lukas und Paulus an einer gemeinsamen Tradition partizipieren. Im Falle der Abendmahlsparadosis im engeren Sinn (1Kor 11,23–26; Lk 22,19f.) kann auch eine literarische Abhängigkeit des Lk vom 1Kor erwogen werden. Es würde sich dann aber um den einzigen Beleg für eine literarische Abhängigkeit handeln, der zudem durch keine weiteren textbezogenen Hinweise gestützt wird. Es verbietet sich demnach, daraus allzu weitgehende Schlussfolgerungen zu ziehen.

Angesichts dieser eher punktuellen Nähe stellt sich die Frage, ob es Belege für weitere sprachliche und religionsgeschichtliche Beziehungen gibt. In der älteren Forschung wird bisweilen damit gerechnet, dass Lukas an einigen Stellen recht komplexe Textkombinationen durchgeführt habe. So behauptet Lars Aejmelaeus, Lk 21,34–36 sei eine verkürzte Paraphrase von 1Thess 5,1–11, die gleichzeitig aber auch Mk 13,33–37, Jes 24 und 32, schließlich noch Lk 8,11–15; 12,22 und Eph 6 miteinander verbinde[63]. Eine solche Analyse kann allein schon wegen des quantitativen Missverhältnisses der Referenztexte, die sehr umfangreich sind, zu dem Ausgangstext, der nur aus drei Versen besteht, nicht überzeugen. Auf dieser Basis lassen sich Textbeziehungen nicht zuverlässig nachweisen beziehungsweise die Behauptung von Textbeziehungen wirkt fast willkürlich. Das Modell einer autorenzentrierten Textverwendung, das Aejmelaeus zugrunde legt, wird den Textbeziehungen nicht gerecht. Ein Abgleich der in den Paulusbriefen und im Lukasevangelium verwendeten Terminologie hingegen zeigt, dass es einige *fra-*

---

62 U. Wilckens, Die Missionsreden der Apostelgeschichte. Form- und traditionsgeschichtliche Untersuchungen (WMANT 5), Neukirchen-Vluyn 1974, 79.
63 L. Aejmelaeus, Wachen vor dem Ende. Die traditionsgeschichtlichen Wurzeln von 1. Thess 5:1–11 u. Luk 21:34–36 (Schriften der Finnischen Exegetischen Gesellschaft 44), Helsinki 1985, 130–136.

mes, Sprach- und Sachzusammenhänge, gibt, die in beiden Texten eine gewisse Rolle spielen. Ein erster Hinweis auf solche gemeinsamen *frames* sind terminologische Besonderheiten, die die Paulusbriefe und das Lukasevangelium gemeinsam haben, etwa das Wort „untadelig" (ἄμεμπτος), das in der synoptischen Tradition nur in Lk 1,6 verwendet wird, wiederum häufig bei Paulus begegnet, und zwar dort wie in Lk 1,6 (ἐν πάσαις ταῖς ἐντολαῖς καὶ δικαιώμασιν τοῦ κυρίου ἄμεμπτοι) auch im Zusammenhang mit Toraobservanz (Phil 3,6: κατὰ δικαιοσύνην τὴν ἐν νόμῳ γενόμενος ἄμεμπτος; vgl. Phil 2,15; 1Thess 2,10; 3,13; 5,23)[64]. Eine vollständige Analyse des gesamten Sachverhalts kann in diesem Zusammenhang nicht geleistet werden, aber eine erste methodische Sichtung und Strukturierung des Materials ist möglich.

(1) Toraorientierte Sitte und Frömmigkeit: die erzählte Welt in Lk 1 und 2 ist die Welt jüdischer Frömmigkeit[65]. Handlungsprinzip der Erzählfiguren ist die Tora im Sinne der religiös-ethnischen Überlieferung des Judentums. Damit sind Sprach- und Sachzusammenhänge verbunden, die sowohl im Lukasevangelium als auch in den Paulusbriefen terminologisch präsent sind. Neben dem bereits erörterten Begriff ἄμεμπτος und dem durch ihn repräsentierten *frame* Toraobservanz in Lk 1,6 und Phil 3,6 sind noch zu nennen: die Beschneidung am achten Tag (Lk 1,59/ Phil 3,5), die Darbietung vor dem Herrn (Lk 2,22/Röm 12,1), die Stellung des Menschen vor Gott (Lk 2,52/Röm 14,18), das Motiv der Versuchung (Lk 4,12f./1Kor 10,9), die Vergebung (Lk 7,42/Röm 8,23 und öfter), geduldiges gutes Wirken (Lk 8,15/Röm 2,7), die Würde des Arbeitslohns (Lk 10,7/Phil 4,18; 1Kor 9,4–14; vgl. Dtn 25,4), die Haushalter Gottes (Lk 12,42/1Kor 4,1f.), die Kenntnis des Willens Gottes (Lk 12,47/Röm 2,18), der Sauerteig, der am Passah hinausgeschafft wird (Lk 13,21/ 1Kor 5,6), Erhöhung und Erniedrigung (Lk 14,11/2Kor 11,7; Phil 2,8), (mit den Sündern) essen (Lk 15,2/Gal 2,12), im Gebet verharren (Lk 18,1/Röm 12,12), Laster (Lk 18,11/Röm 1,29), Heuchler (Lk 20,20/Gal 2,13), Opfergaben geben (Lk 21,3/2Kor 8,12), die Heiden (Lk 21,24/Röm 11,25), mit Christus (im Paradies) sein (Lk 23,43/ 2Kor 12,4; Phil 1,23), am ersten Tag nach dem Sabbat (Lk 24,1/1Kor 16,2).

(2) Gerechtigkeit: das Lukasevangelium reflektiert die Frage, unter welchen Bedingungen Menschen sich selbst vor Gott als „gerecht" erachten können (Lk 10,29; 16,15; 18,9.14; 20,20)[66]. Schenk interpretiert diesen Sachverhalt als den

---

64 A. Denaux, Vocabulary, 30.
65 L. Bormann, Das Lukasevangelium als tragische Geschichtserzählung vom Zusammenbruch der Rechtsgemeinschaft des Judentums in Galiläa und Judäa, in: Law and Narrative in the Bible and in Neighbouring Ancient Cultures, eds. K.-P. Adam/F. Avemarie/N. Wazana (FAT 2/54), Tübingen 2012, 299–325, bes. 308–10.
66 L. Bormann, Gerechtigkeit im Neuen Testament, in: Gerechtigkeit, hg. von M. Witte (ThTh 6), Tübingen 2012, 69–97, bes. 88–91.

Versuch des Lukas, die paulinische Theologie in seinem Evangelium zu verankern[67]. Diese These überzeugt nicht, da die Ausführungen zur Gerechtigkeit anders als bei Paulus im lukanischen Schrifttum nicht mit der Christologie verbunden werden[68]. Sie beruhen vielmehr auf der hellenistisch beeinflussten Vorstellung, dass in der Tora und ihrer Befolgung das Tugendideal Israels Ausdruck findet (Lk 1,75)[69]. Die Ausführungen über Gerechtigkeit im lukanischen Schrifttum stehen sachlich wie terminologisch der jüdischen Weisheitsliteratur näher (zum Beispiel Sir 7,5; 10,29; 18,2) als der paulinischen Vorstellung von der Glaubensgerechtigkeit (zum Beispiel Phil 3,9; Röm 3,21f.; 10,3f.). Lukas kennt anders als Paulus (Röm 2,13; 3,10) Menschen, die zweifelsfrei „gerecht" sind und bezeichnet sie auch unvoreingenommen als „Gerechte", zum Beispiel Zacharias und Elisabeth (Lk 1,6), Simeon (2,15), Joseph von Arimathäa (23,50) und Cornelius (Apg 10,22).

(3) Terminologie des Heils: François Bovon identifiziert mit Schwerpunkt auf Lk 1 und 2 und 24 eine Wortgruppe, die er als „Wortschatz des Heils" bezeichnet[70]. Die Begriffe (ἀπο-)λύτρωσις (Lk 1,68; 2,38; 21,28), λυτροῦσθαι (24,21), σωτήρ (1,47; 2,11), σωτηρία (1,69.71.77; 19,9) finden sich jeweils auch im Corpus Paulinum und stellen eine Gemeinsamkeit des lukanischen und des paulinischen Schrifttums dar, in der sich diese von den übrigen neutestamentlichen Schriften unterscheiden[71]. Die Interpretation dieses Befunds führt aber wie im Fall der Abendmahlsüberlieferung zu der Beobachtung, dass im lukanischen Schrifttum der Bezug des „Heils" auf Israel dominiert, bei Paulus hingegen die soteriologischen Vorstellungen universal ausgerichtet sind (Röm 1,14; 2,9–11; 3,23f.29).

(4) Mächte und Gewalten, Satan: der Gebrauch und die variierende Zusammenstellung der Begriffe ἀρχή, ἐξουσία und δύναμις zur Bezeichnung der Repräsentanten politisch-institutioneller und transzendenter Macht ist ebenfalls ein Sprach- und Sachzusammenhang, der das lukanische Schrifttum mit den Paulusbriefen, vor allem aber mit der Paulustradition verbindet. Das gilt besonders für die Wendung „Mächte und Gewalten" (Lk 12,11; 20,20/Eph 1,21; 6,12; Kol 1,6; 2,15), die aus der Verwaltungssprache stammt,[72] und für die Rede vom „Satan" (Lk 10,18;

---

67 W. Schenk, Luke, 133.
68 D. Lührmann, Art. Gerechtigkeit III: Neues Testament, in: TRE 12 (1984), 414–420, bes. 415.
69 H. Merkel, Das Gesetz im lukanischen Doppelwerk, in: Schrift und Tradition, hg. von K. Backhaus/F.G. Untergaßmair, Paderborn/München/Wien/Zürich 1996, 119–133, bes. 130.
70 F. Bovon, Lukas 4, 191; L. Bormann, Befreiung und Rettung. Das Politische in der lukanischen Vorgeschichte (Lk 1–2), in: Neues Testament und Politische Theorie. Interdisziplinäre Beiträge zur Zukunft des Politischen, hg. von E. Reinmuth (Religionskulturen 9), Stuttgart 2011, 98–113, bes. 108–111.
71 A. Denaux, Vocabulary, 72f., 381f., 592f.
72 L. Bormann, Verrechtlichung, 290f.

13,16; 22,3.31; Apg 26,18/1Kor 5,5; 7,5; 2Kor 2,11; 11,14; 12,7).⁷³ Die damit angesprochene Vorstellung, nach der Repräsentanten der weltlichen und der transzendenten Mächte auf analoge Weise Heil und Unheil zugleich repräsentieren, ist im antiken Judentum und im Neuen Testament allgemein verbreitet. Die meisten religiösen Schriften der hellenistisch-römischen Zeit neigen jedoch dazu, sich auf die transzendente Macht zu konzentrieren, während die Paulustradition und Lukas auf realistische und politisch reflektierte Weise die Bedeutung beider, der weltlichen und der himmlischen Macht, für die Gemeinde thematisieren.

(5) Gemeindepraxis: zwei Sachverhalte aus der Gemeindepraxis sind noch zu erwähnen. Der Terminus „Kuss" (φίλημα) zur Bezeichnung des Begrüßungs- und Gemeinderituals findet sich im Rahmen der synoptischen Überlieferung nur in Lk 7,45 („Sünderin") und 22,48 (Judas; vgl. Mk 14,44–46).⁷⁴ Paulus setzt den „heiligen Kuss" (Röm 16,16; 1Kor 16,20; 2Kor 13,12; 1Thess 5,26; vgl. 1Petr 5,14) als Gemeinderitual voraus. Lukas integriert damit in seine Evangelienerzählung ein Element der Gemeindewirklichkeit, die er mit Paulus, vermutlich vermittelt über die antiochenische Gemeinde, teilt. Das gilt auch für die Anweisung zum Essen im Rahmen der Gastfreundschaft, die in Lk 10,8 (ἐσθίετε τὰ παρατιθέμενα ὑμῖν) und 1Kor 10,27 (πᾶν τὸ παρατιθέμενον ὑμῖν ἐσθίετε) festgehalten ist.

3.3 Apostelgeschichte

Es wurde bereits erwähnt, dass die Apostelgeschichte die Paulusbriefe weder zitiert noch erwähnt. Es gibt aber einige wenige Texte der Apostelgeschichte, die zumindest eine gewisse terminologische und sachliche Nähe zu den Paulusbriefen erkennen lassen. Manche Exegeten deuten diese Nähe als Beleg für die Kenntnis oder sogar Nutzung der Paulusbriefe. Sie müssen sich dann aber mit dem weit offensichtlicheren Sachverhalt auseinandersetzen, dass die Apostelgeschichte biographische Informationen der Paulusbriefe übergeht, ja sogar höchst dramatische Ereignisse unerwähnt lässt, zum Beispiel den Aufenthalt in der Arabia (Gal 1,17), die Schiffbrüche und Folterungen (2Kor 11,24f.), die Kollekte für Jerusalem (1Kor 16,3; Röm 15,25–29) und die Reisepläne nach Spanien (Röm 15,24.28).⁷⁵ Darüber hinaus ist auch noch zu berücksichtigen, dass die Paulusbriefe und die Apostelgeschichte in ihren Aussagen über eine ganze Reihe von Ereignissen erheblich voneinander abweichen, etwa zum Apostelkonvent (Apg 15;

---

73 A. Denaux, Vocabulary, 82 u. 556.
74 A. Denaux, Vocabulary, 630.
75 J.A. Fitzmyer, Luke, 49.

Gal 2,1–10), dem Apostedekret (Apg 15,23–29; 21,25; 1Kor 8,8) oder zum Verhältnis von Paulus und Barnabas (Apg 15,39; Gal 2,13). Damit ist deutlich, dass der Autor der Apostelgeschichte die Paulusbriefe nicht als Quelle für seine Darstellung ausgewertet hat.

Die Texte, die an eine Vertrautheit des Verfassers der Apostelgeschichte mit den Paulusbriefen denken lassen, sind nicht zahlreich. Im Grunde sind hier nur drei zu nennen: (1) der Damaskusaufenthalt des Paulus nach Apg 9,24b–25 (vgl. 2Kor 11,32f.), (2) die Bemerkung zu Sündenvergebung, Rechtfertigung und Gesetz nach Apg 13,38f. (vgl. Röm 3,21–28), (3) Teile der Miletrede nach Apg 20,18–35 (vgl. 1Thess 2–4), bes. Apg 20,18.20 (vgl. 1Thess 2,1f.) und Apg 20,31f. (vgl. 1Thess 2,9–13).

2Kor 11,32f. berichtet davon, dass Paulus vor den Truppen des Ethnarchen Aretas geflohen sei. In Apg 9,24f. hingegen ist davon die Rede, Paulus sei vor „den Juden" geflohen. Die beiden Texte weichen damit bereits in der Sachverhaltsschilderung deutlich voneinander ab. Allerdings gibt es gewisse Übereinstimmungen in der Terminologie. Beide Texte benutzen die Wendungen „die Mauer hinab" (διὰ τοῦ τείχους) und „herablassen im" (χαλᾶν ἐν). Die Bezeichnung für das Behältnis, in dem Paulus herabgelassen wurde, weicht wiederum voneinander ab (σαργάνη bzw. σπυρίς). Immerhin wird also die Übereinstimmung in der Terminologie noch durch eine syntaktische Konstruktion mit dem gleichen Verb (χαλᾶν) und zwei identischen präpositionalen Bezügen (διά, ἐν) gestützt. Die historische und literarische Problematik dieser beiden Texte ist bereits mehrfach ausführlich untersucht worden[76]. Die auffälligen Übereinstimmungen in der Terminologie und in der syntaktischen Struktur sind aber vor dem Hintergrund der erheblichen terminologischen, syntaktischen und sachlichen Divergenzen eher durch eine variierende „Damaskustradition" als mit einer Benutzung von 2Kor 11,32f. durch den Autor der Apostelgeschichte zu erklären: „Apg 9,24b–25 beruht also nicht auf 2Kor 11,32f"[77].

Apg 13,38f. spricht in einer sonst im lukanischen Schrifttum außergewöhnlichen Weise von der Rechtfertigung „aus Glauben": „Von allen (Dingen), in denen ihr nicht durch das Gesetz des Moses gerecht gemacht werden konntet, wird durch diesen [den Auferweckten] jeder, der glaubt, gerecht gemacht" (ἀπὸ πάντων ὧν οὐκ ἠδυνήθητε ἐν νόμῳ Μωϋσέως δικαιωθῆναι ἐν τούτῳ πᾶς ὁ πιστεύων δικαιοῦται). Nur noch in Apg 15,11 ist eine ähnliche Wendung zu finden, die von der Rettung aus Gnade spricht: „sondern durch die Gnade des Herrn Jesus glauben wir

---

[76] Z. B. R. Riesner, Die Frühzeit des Apostels Paulus (WUNT 71), Tübingen 1994, 66–79; Ch. Burchard, Der dreizehnte Zeuge. Traditions- und kompositionsgeschichtliche Untersuchungen zu Lukas' Darstellung der Frühzeit des Paulus (FRLANT 103), Göttingen 1970, 155–158.
[77] Ch. Burchard, Zeuge, 158.

gerettet zu werden" (ἀλλὰ διὰ τῆς χάριτος τοῦ κυρίου Ἰησοῦ πιστεύομεν σωθῆναι). Natürlich erinnern Apg 13,38 f. an Röm 3,21 f.28 bzw. Gal 2,16 und Apg 15,11 an Röm 10,9 oder auch 3,24. Ernst Haenchen merkt zur Stelle an: „Daß Paulus von der Rechtfertigung aus dem Glauben gepredigt hat, weiß man zur Zeit des Lukas noch"[78]. Wong interpretiert die Textbeziehung als einen von Lukas intendierten Verweis auf die Theologie des Paulus, der seinen nächsten textlichen Anhalt in Gal 2,16 habe[79]. Theobald verweist aber zu Recht darauf, dass das Verb „gerecht machen" (δικαιοῦν) in Apg 13,38 f. nicht die „Gabe des Heils", und auch „glauben" (πιστεύειν) an den genannten Stellen nicht den Glauben im „vollen paulinischen Sinn" meint[80]. Vielmehr bleiben die lukanischen Überlegungen zur Gerechtmachung auf die Sündenvergebung beschränkt und zielen nicht auf einen neuen Status, der bei Paulus als neue Schöpfung, Rettung und Befreiung verstanden wird[81]. Es ist unwahrscheinlich, dass die lukanischen Wendungen literarisch von einem Paulusbrief abhängig sind.

Apg 20,18–35, die Abschiedsrede des Paulus in Milet, erscheint als die paulinischste der Reden in der Apostelgeschichte. Ebenso deutlich ist aber auch, dass sich in ihr Paulinisches und Unpaulinisches beständig abwechseln und letztlich die Rede auf den Verfasser Lukas zurückgeht[82]. Lassen sich im Text aber Hinweise auf die Benutzung der Paulusbriefe finden?[83] Aejmelaeus bejaht dies und nennt folgende Textbeobachtungen: 1Thess 2,1 f. in Apg 20,18.20 und 1Thess 2,9–13 in Apg 20,31 f. Die Atmosphäre der Erstmission, wie sie Paulus in seinem Schreiben an das makedonische Thessaloniki darstellt, wird in der Miletrede auf eine ähnliche Weise hinsichtlich der paulinischen Mission der Gemeinden Asiens geschildert. Lindemann rechnet hier mit einer Vermittlung über die Paulustradition, aus der auch die Information stammte, Paulus habe kein Geld angenommen und mit seinen „Händen" gearbeitet (Apg 20,33 f. zu 1Kor 4,12; 9,12 und 2Kor 7,2).[84] Da keine terminologischen oder idiomatischen Übereinstimmungen festzustellen sind und zudem die thematische Korrespondenz vage ist, ist eine Benutzung des 1Thess eher unwahrscheinlich.

---

78 E. Haenchen, Die Apostelgeschichte (KEK 3), Göttingen 1956, 361.
79 E.K.Ch. Wong, Evangelien, 147: „eine markierte intertextuelle Bezugnahme auf Paulus, die Lukas bewusst gestaltet hat".
80 M. Theobald, Der Kanon von der Rechtfertigung (Gal 2,16; Röm 3,28), in: Studien zum Römerbrief, hg. von M. Theobald (WUNT 136), Tübingen 2001, 164–225, bes. 196–207.
81 J. Jervell, Die Apostelgeschichte (KEK 3), Göttingen 1998, 360 f.
82 U. Wilckens, Missionsreden, 187; L. Aejmelaeus, Rezeption, 266 f.
83 Das sehen z. B. M.S. Enslin, Luke, 81; A. Lindemann, Paulus, 169.
84 A. Lindemann, Paulus, 169.

Schließlich sind noch punktuelle terminologische und sachliche Übereinstimmungen zu nennen, die auf die Vertrautheit des Lukas mit den Paulusbriefen hinweisen könnten. Einige Beispiele seien genannt: „Eiferer des Gesetzes", ζηλωταὶ τοῦ νόμου in Apg 21,20 setze die Kenntnis der paulinischen Haltung zum Gesetz voraus[85]. Die Wendung „Zelot sein", ζηλωτὴς ὑπάρχειν, verbinde Apg 21,20; 22,3 mit Gal 1,14. Der Begriff „Ausrotten", πορθεῖν in Apg 9,21 sei Gal 1,13 entliehen[86]. Ähnlich stichwortartige Verbindungen werden noch für „Engel" (Apg 7,53 zu Gal 3,19 f.) und das absolute „machen" (ποιεῖν in Apg 11,30 zu Gal 2,10) gesehen[87].

Diese wenigen Textbeziehungen erlauben es nicht, von einer lukanischen Rezeption der Theologie des Paulus zu sprechen. Die Beziehung der beiden Textgruppen zueinander ist bestenfalls jenseits der literarischen Abhängigkeit auf einer thematischen Ebene herzustellen. So hat etwa Ernst Käsemann vorgeschlagen, dass man trotz fehlender direkter Beziehungen die Ekklesiologie des Epheserbriefs als eine zur Apostelgeschichte parallele Entwicklung verstehen kann[88]. Das Interesse an der Kirche ist zumindest den Deuteropaulinen und der Apostelgeschichte gemeinsam.

4 Fazit

Die Alte Kirche rechtfertigte das Markus- und das Lukasevangelium dadurch, dass sie in ihnen eigentlich ein Petrus- und ein Paulusevangelium sah. Sie hatte zudem ein Interesse daran, die Evangelienüberlieferung und die apostolische Tradition miteinander zu verbinden. Das lukanische Schrifttum erfüllte diese Erwartung.

Im Evangelium benutzt Lukas das Markusevangelium, wählt aber aus den Stoffen aus und lässt das Markusevangelium immer wieder unberücksichtigt, wo er auf andere Quellen oder auf seine kreative Gestaltungskraft zurückgreifen kann. Die narrative Theologie des Markus und deren apokalyptischen Horizont nimmt Lukas nicht auf. In der Apostelgeschichte finden sich in den Wundersummarien Wendungen, die dem Markusevangelium nahe stehen. Insgesamt handelt es sich dabei um kleinste Spuren einer Nutzung des Markusevangeliums.

---

[85] A. Lindemann, Paulus, 169.
[86] M.S. Enslin, Once Again, 262. Vgl. aber 4Makk 4,23; 11,4; Josephus, Bellum Iudaicum, 4,405; Josephus, Antiquitates Iudaicae, 10,135.
[87] M.S. Enslin, Once Again, 262; weitere solche stichwortartige Berührungen bei W. Schenk, Luke, 133–137.
[88] E. Käsemann, Ephesians and Acts, in: Studies in Luke-Acts. Essays Presented in Honor of Paul Schubert, eds. L.E. Keck/J.L. Martyn, London 1976, 288–297, esp. 296 f.

Eine literarische Beziehung zu den Paulusbriefen ist wiederum nur in der Abendmahlsparadosis mit größerer Wahrscheinlichkeit zu belegen. Die wörtlichen Übereinstimmungen zwischen 1Kor 11,23–26 und Lk 22,19f. sind so zahlreich und umfangreich, dass die gemeinsame Nutzung einer schriftlichen Quelle wahrscheinlich ist. Allerdings wird diese eine Textbeobachtung durch keine weitere gestützt, so dass weitergehende Überlegungen, die auf diesem Sachverhalt aufbauen, nicht sinnvoll sind. Sehr viel aussagekräftiger sind die Divergenzen zwischen dem lukanischen Schrifttum und den Paulusbriefen. Von circa 89 Schriftzitaten bei Paulus und 43 im lukanischen Schrifttum werden nicht mehr als drei von beiden Autoren herangezogen (Dtn 5,16–21 in Teilen; Lev 19,18; Joel 3,5) und auch die Berücksichtigung von Anspielungen lässt die Zahl der gemeinsamen Schriftbezüge nur auf sechs steigen (Lev 18,5; 1Kön 19,10; Ps 110,1). Nimmt man dann noch die Divergenzen im Schriftverständnis hinzu, wird deutlich, dass der Autor des lukanischen Schrifttums auch in den Tiefenstrukturen seiner Theologie von den Paulusbriefen unabhängig ist.

Auch im Blick auf die Ekklesiologie sind die Unterschiede deutlich. Während Paulus die universale Heilsgemeinschaft aus Juden und Nichtjuden angesichts der Parusie und des endzeitlichen Gerichts als Mitte des Heilsgeschehens sieht, stellt sich Lukas die Gemeinschaft der Christusanhänger als eine Kirche auf Dauer einerseits in Nähe zu Israel und andererseits in Distanz zur heidnischen Welt vor. Das Interesse an der Kirche, das die Apostelgeschichte prägt, ist in dieser Weise bei Paulus nicht vorhanden. In ekklesiologischer Hinsicht steht das lukanische Schrifttum am ehesten dem Epheserbrief nahe.

Aus diesen eher negativen Ergebnissen sollte aber nicht geschlossen werden, dass Markus, Lukas und Paulus exegetisch als getrennte Welten zu behandeln sind. Die Konzentration auf einzelne Schriften geht zu weit, wenn zum Beispiel in einer Arbeit über die „Freude" im Lukasevangelium an keiner Stelle auf die Freudenterminologie im Philipperbrief und im Kolosserbrief eingegangen wird[89]. Gerade der Vergleich ist hermeneutisch fruchtbar, da er es ermöglicht, das jeweilige Profil deutlich nachzuzeichnen. So wird im Umgang des Lukas und des Paulus mit der Schrift und mit den durch *frames* repräsentierten gemeinsamen Themenfeldern wie Toraobservanz, Gerechtigkeit, Terminologie des Heils und Mächte und Gewalten deutlich, dass sich beide Autoren voneinander unabhängig auf eine sehr ähnliche Wahrnehmung des antiken Judentums beziehen, die womöglich durch eine gemeinsame antiochenische Perspektive geprägt ist. Sie

---

[89] A. Inselmann, Die Freude im Lukasevangelium. Ein Beitrag zur psychologischen Exegese (WUNT 2/322), Tübingen 2012. Vgl. im Gegensatz dazu die Arbeit von E.G. Gulin, Die Freude im Neuen Testament, 2 Bde. (AASF B 26,2/37,3), Helsinki 1932/1936.

kommen dabei aber zu unterschiedlichen theologischen Schlussfolgerungen, insbesondere was die Bedeutung Israels und seiner Heilserwartungen für die Kirche betrifft.

Die eindrücklichste Gemeinsamkeit in der Rezeption des Markusevangeliums und der Paulusbriefe durch Lukas besteht in der theologischen Unabhängigkeit, die Lukas unter Beweis stellt. Lukas nutzt das Markusevangelium vordringlich als Material und weist dessen Theologie deutlich zurück. Im Falle der Paulustradition konzentriert sich Lukas auf die schriftstellerische Verwertung der Biographie, lässt aber die Paulusbriefe, in denen dieser seine Theologie, sein dialektisches Gottesverständnis und seine universale Heilsperspektive entfaltet, völlig unbeachtet. Weder die narrative Theologie des Markusevangeliums noch die begrifflich dialektische Theologie des Paulus haben den Theologen Lukas erkennbar beeinflusst. Da Lukas aber wohl doch mit beiden vertraut war, wird man schließen können, dass ihn weder die Theologie des Markus noch die des Paulus überzeugen konnte.

Bibliographie

Aejmelaeus, L., Die Rezeption der Paulusbriefe in der Miletrede (APG 20:18–35) (AASF B/232), Helsiniki 1987.
—, Wachen vor dem Ende. Die traditionsgeschichtlichen Wurzeln von 1. Thess 5:1–11 u. Luk 21:34–36 (Schriften der Finnischen Exegetischen Gesellschaft 44), Helsinki 1985.
Barrett, Ch.K., Acts and the Pauline Corpus, in: ET 88 (1976), 2–5.
—, The First New Testament, in: NT 38 (1996), 94–104.
Bartsch, H.-W., Codex Bezae versus Codex Sinaiticus im Lukasevangelium, Hildesheim 1984.
Bendemann, R. von, Zwischen doxa und stauros. Eine exegetische Untersuchung der Texte des sogenannten Reiseberichts im Lukasevangelium (BZNW 101), Berlin/New York 2001.
Bormann, L., Befreiung und Rettung. Das Politische in der lukanischen Vorgeschichte (Lk 1–2), in: Neues Testament und Politische Theorie. Interdisziplinäre Beiträge zur Zukunft des Politischen, hg. von E. Reinmuth (Religionskulturen 9), Stuttgart 2011, 98–113.
—, Der Brief des Paulus an die Kolosser (ThHK 10/1), Leipzig 2012.
—, Gerechtigkeit im Neuen Testament, in: Gerechtigkeit, hg. von M. Witte (ThTh 6),Tübingen 2012, 69–97.
—, Das Lukasevangelium als tragische Geschichtserzählung vom Zusammenbruch der Rechtsgemeinschaft des Judentums in Galiläa und Judäa, in: Law and Narrative in the Bible and in Neighbouring Ancient Cultures, hg. von K.-P. Adam/F. Avemarie/N. Wazana (FAT 2/54), Tübingen 2012, 299–325.
—, Die Verrechtlichung der frühesten christlichen Überlieferung im lukanischen Schrifttum, in: Religious Propaganda and Missionary Competition in the New Testament World, hg. von L. Bormann/K. Del Tredici/A. Standhartinger (NT.S 74, 283–311), Leiden 1994.
Bovon, F., Das Evangelium nach Lukas, Bd. 1, Düsseldorf 1989–2009.
Brandenburger, E., Markus 13 und die Apokalyptik (FRLANT 134), Göttingen 1984.
Burchard, Ch., Der dreizehnte Zeuge. Traditions- und kompositionsgeschichtliche Untersuchungen zu Lukas' Darstellung der Frühzeit des Paulus (FRLANT 103), Göttingen 1970.
Denaux, A./Corstjens, R., The Vocabulary of Luke (Biblical Tools and Studies 10), Leuven 2009.
Du Toit, D.S., Der abwesende Herr. Strategien im Markusevangelium zur Bewältigung der Abwesenheit des Auferstandenen (WMANT 111), Neukirchen-Vluyn 2006.
Enslin, M.S., Emphases and Silences, in: HTR 73 (1980), 219–225.
—, ‚Luke' and Paul, in: JAOS 58 (1938), 81–91.
—, Once Again, Luke and Paul, in: ZNW 61 (1970), 253–271.
Farmer, W.R., The Synoptic Problem. A Critical Analysis, Dillsboro 1976.
Feldmeier, R., Der erste Brief des Petrus (ThHK 15), Leipzig 2005.
Fitzmyer, J.A., The Gospel According to Luke. Introduction, Translation, and Notes, 2 Bd. (AncB 28–28 A), New York 1981/1985.
—, The Priority of Mark and the „Q" source in Luke, in: To Advance the Gospel. New Testament Studies, ed. by J.A. Fitzmyer, Grand Rapids ²1989, 3–40.
Goulder, M.D., Luke: A New Paradigm (JSNT.SS 20), Sheffield 1989.
Gulin, E.G., Die Freude im Neuen Testament, 2 Bde. (AASF B 26,2/37,3), Helsinki 1932/1936.
Haenchen, E., Die Apostelgeschichte (KEK 3), Göttingen 1956.
Harrington, J.M., The Lukan Passion Narrative. The Markan Material in Luke 22,54–23,25 (NTTS 30), Leiden 2000.

Hengel, M., Psalm 110 und die Erhöhung des Auferstandenen zur Rechten Gottes, in: Anfänge der Christologie, hg. von H. Paulsen/C. Breytenbach, Göttingen 1991, 43–73.
Herzer, J., Petrus oder Paulus? Studien über das Verhältnis des ersten Petrusbriefes zur paulinischen Tradition (WUNT 103), Tübingen 1998.
Inselmann, A., Die Freude im Lukasevangelium. Ein Beitrag zur psychologischen Exegese (WUNT 2/322), Tübingen 2012.
Jervell, J., Die Apostelgeschichte (KEK 3), Göttingen 1998.
Käsemann, E., Ephesians and Acts, in: Studies in Luke-Acts. Essays Presented in Honor of Paul Schubert, eds. L.E. Keck/J.L. Martyn, London 1976, 288–297.
Klauck, H.-J., Vorspiel im Himmel? Erzähltechnik und Theologie im Markusprolog, Neukirchen-Vluyn 1997.
Klein, H., Das Lukasevangelium (KEK I/3), Göttingen 2006.
Knox, J., Acts and the Pauline Letter Corpus, in: Studies in Luke-Acts. Essays Presented in Honor of Paul Schubert, eds. L.E. Keck/J.L. Martyn, London 1976, 279–287.
Koch, D.-A., Die Schrift als Zeuge des Evangeliums (BHTh 69), Tübingen 1986.
Lietzmann, H. (Hg.), Kleine Texte für Vorlesungen und Übungen, Bd. 1, Das Muratorische Fragment und die monarchianischen Prologe zu den Evangelien, Berlin ²1933.
Lindemann, A., Der Erste Korintherbrief (HNT 9/1), Tübingen 2000.
—, Paulus im ältesten Christentum (BHTh 58), Tübingen 1979.
Lührmann, D., Art. Gerechtigkeit III: Neues Testament, in: TRE 12 (1984), 414–420.
Meiser, M., Das Alte Testament im lukanischen Doppelwerk, in: Im Brennpunkt: die Septuaginta. Studien zur Entstehung und Bedeutung der Griechischen Bibel, hg. von H.-J. Fabry/U. Offerhaus (BWANT 153), Stuttgart 2001, 167–195.
Merkel, H., Das Gesetz im lukanischen Doppelwerk, in: Schrift und Tradition, hg. von K. Backhaus/F.G. Untergaßmair, Paderborn/München/Wien/Zürich 1996, 119–133.
Morgenthaler, R., Statistik des neutestamentlichen Wortschatzes, Zürich/Frankfurt 1958.
—, Statistische Synopse, Zürich 1971.
Müller, P., „Wer ist dieser?". Jesus im Markusevangelium (BThSt 27), Neukirchen-Vluyn 1995.
Oko, O.I., „Who then is this?". A Narrative Study of the Role of the Question of the Identity of Jesus in the Plot of Mark's Gospel (BBB 148), Berlin 2004.
Paffenroth, K., The Story of Jesus According to L (JSNT.SS 147), Sheffield 1997.
Pervo, R.I., Acts. A Commentary (Hermeneia), Minneapolis 2009.
Pittner, B., Studien zum lukanischen Sondergut (EThSt 18), Leipzig 1991.
Prieur, A., Die Verkündigung der Gottesherrschaft (WUNT 2/89), Tübingen 1996.
Riesner, R., Die Frühzeit des Apostels Paulus (WUNT 71), Tübingen 1994.
Rose, Ch., Theologie als Erzählung im Markusevangelium. Eine narratologisch-rezeptionsästhetische Untersuchung zu Mk 1,1–15 (WUNT 2/236), Tübingen 2007.
Rusam, D., Das Alte Testament bei Lukas (BZNW 112), Berlin 2003.
Schenk, W., Luke as Reader of Paul. Observations on his Reception, in: Intertextuality in Biblical Writings, ed. by S. Draisma, Kampen 1989, 127–139.
Schneider, G., Das Evangelium nach Lukas, 2 Bd. (ÖTK 3/1+2), Gütersloh ³1992.
Schramm, T., Der Markus-Stoff bei Lukas. Eine literarkritische und redaktionsgeschichtliche Untersuchung (SNTS.MS 14), Cambridge 1971.
Schröter, J., Die Funktion der Herrenmahlsüberlieferungen im 1. Korintherbrief, in: ZNW 100 (2009), 78–100.
Streeter, B.H., The Four Gospels, London ¹⁰1961.

Theobald, M., Der Kanon von der Rechtfertigung (Gal 2,16; Röm 3,28), in: Studien zum Römerbrief, hg. von M. Theobald (WUNT 136), Tübingen 2001, 164–225.
—, Studien zum Römerbrief (WUNT 136), Tübingen 2001.
Walter, N., Alttestamentliche Bezüge in christologischen Ausführungen des Paulus, in: Paulinische Christologie, hg. von U. Schnelle/Th. Söding, Göttingen 2000, 246–271.
Weiser, A., Der zweite Brief an Timotheus (EKK 16), Düsseldorf 2003.
Wilckens, U., Die Missionsreden der Apostelgeschichte. Form- und traditionsgeschichtliche Untersuchungen (WMANT 5), Neukirchen-Vluyn 1974.
Wolter, M., Das Lukasevangelium (HNT 5), Tübingen 2008.
—, ‚Reich Gottes' bei Lukas, in: NTS 41/4 (1995), 541–563.
Wong, E.K.C., Evangelien im Dialog mit Paulus. Eine intertextuelle Studie zu den Synoptikern (NTOA/StUNT 89), Göttingen 2012.
Zahn, Th., Einleitung in das Neue Testament, Wuppertal 1994.
Zeller, D., Der erste Brief an die Korinther (KEK 5), Göttingen 2010.

Wilhelm Pratscher
Die Rezeption von Paulus und Markus bei Johannes

Traditioneller Weise wird die johanneische Literatur erst gegen Ende des 1. Jahrhunderts angesiedelt[1]. Als Entstehungsgebiete kommen Syrien und/oder das westliche Kleinasien in Frage. In beiden Gebieten ist auch die paulinische und synoptische Tradition lebendig. Der Bezug der johanneischen Schriften zu Paulus und den Synoptikern ist somit zeitlich und geographisch möglich. Aber wie sieht er genauerhin aus? Besteht nur eine allgemeine Verwandtschaft, basierend auf der gemeinsamen Teilhabe an der urchristlichen Verkündigung, oder liegen nähere traditionsgeschichtliche oder gar literarische Bezüge vor? Dazu ist es nötig, nach Gemeinsamkeiten und Differenzen zwischen den einzelnen Schriften(gruppen) zu suchen. Davor sind aber noch kurze methodologische Bemerkungen nötig.

1 Methodologische Vorbemerkungen

Aufgrund der unterschiedlichen Textsorten Brief und Evangelium wird der Bezug Paulus-Johannes bzw. Markus-Johannes differieren.

Bei ersterem geht es primär um die Suche nach gemeinsamen Themen bzw. Motiven (sowie den diesbezüglichen Differenzen). Übereinstimmende Terminologie, vielleicht auch gemeinsame Wortfelder, zeigen eine (zumindest) sachliche Nähe. Je genauer diese Parallelen sind, desto eher kann man auf traditionsgeschichtliche (oder wie bei manchen Exegeten: auch literarische) Beziehungen schließen. Wörtliche Übereinstimmungen sind nur in geringem Ausmaß zu erwarten.

In der Frage nach dem Bezug Markus-Johannes sieht es freilich anders aus. Zusätzlich ist hier nicht nur die gemeinsame Großgattung Evangelium zu nennen, sondern auch die Komposition im Ganzen wie in den einzelnen gemeinsamen Perikopen. Die Suche nach wörtlichen Übereinstimmungen (eventuell auch grammatikalischer Art) ist methodisch ganz analog zur Bestimmung des Verhältnisses zwischen den Synoptikern vorzunehmen – auch wenn die Gemeinsamkeiten ungleich geringer sind als dort. Dabei geht es im Wesentlichen um die synchrone Ebene, die Frage nach der Diachronie (Schichten) kann zwar nicht

---

[1] Die Frühansetzung, wie sie J.A.T. Robinson, Redating the New Testament, London 1976, 307, u. a. vornehmen, bewährt sich nicht (Trennung von der Synagoge; Doketismus u. dgl.).

prinzipiell ausgeblendet werden, die Thesenhaftigkeit der Ergebnisse erhöht sich in diesem Fall allerdings gravierend. Statistische Untersuchungen sind dabei durchaus hilfreich, auch wenn sie jeweils in den größeren thematischen Kontext eingeordnet werden müssen.

In der Frage, ob und gegebenenfalls welche Art von Abhängigkeit besteht, sind verschiedene Antworten möglich. In einer Großklassifizierung kann man unterscheiden: (1) literarische Unabhängigkeit bei a) bloßer sachlicher Verwandtschaft bzw. b) Benutzung spezifischer gemeinsamer Traditionen[2], (2) literarische Abhängigkeit im Sinn von a) sekundärer Oralität oder b) direkter literarischer Benutzung.

Um die Rezeption von Paulus und Markus bestimmen zu können, sind nicht nur die Gemeinsamkeiten, sondern auch die Differenzen in den parallelen Themen und Texten zu untersuchen bzw. auch die darüber hinausgehenden Differenzen. Das eigenständige Profil der jeweiligen Autoren kommt nur so (wenn auch nur im Rahmen des hier Möglichen) in den Blick. Dabei bestimmt das Ausmaß an Gemeinsamkeiten noch nicht den Grad an Rezeption, und ein gemeinsamer Topos deutet noch nicht eo ipso auf Abhängigkeit. Andererseits ist das Ausmaß an Differenzen umgekehrt proportional zur Bestimmung von Nähe: je mehr Differenzen, desto geringer die Nähe.

2 Das Verhältnis von Paulus und Johannes

Das Verhältnis des Paulus zu Johannes wurde in der liberalen Theologie als ein sehr enges verstanden[3]: bei Johannes komme Paulus zur Vollendung[4], er fuße auf Paulus[5] bzw. setze den Paulinismus voraus[6] und sei geradezu der Testamentsvollstrecker des Paulus[7]. Im Gegensatz dazu hat besonders Rudolf Bultmann aufgrund seiner religionsgeschichtlichen Einordnung der johanneischen Literatur in die werdende Gnosis und ihrer Lokalisierung in Syrien den Bezug zu Paulus

---

2 Die Grenze ist freilich nur schwer zu ziehen.
3 Zur Forschungsgeschichte vgl. U. Schnelle, Paulus und Johannes, in: EvTh 47 (1987), 212–228; Ch. Hoegen-Rohls, Johanneische Theologie im Kontext paulinischen Denkens? Eine forschungsgeschichtliche Skizze, in: Kontexte des Johannesevangliums. Das vierte Evangelium in religions- und traditionsgeschichtlicher Perspektive, hg. von J. Frey/U. Schnelle, Tübingen 2004, 593–612.
4 J. Weiß, Die Predigt Jesu vom Reiche Gottes, Göttingen ²1900, 61.
5 J. Wellhausen, Das Evangelium Johannis, Berlin 1908, 121.
6 A. Jülicher, Einleitung in das Neue Testament, Tübingen/Leipzig ³,⁴1901, 315.
7 H.J. Holtzmann, Lehrbuch der Neutestamentlichen Theologie II, Tübingen ²1911, 402.

minimalisiert. Zwar bestehe eine „tiefe sachliche Verwandtschaft"[8], aber Johannes gehöre nicht in die paulinische Schule und sei auch nicht von ihr beeinflusst. Beide Positionen unterscheiden sich nicht in der Beurteilung der sachlichen Nähe, wohl aber in der Frage der historischen Beziehungen. Rudolf Bultmann schließt sowohl eine literarische Abhängigkeit aus als auch eine traditionsgeschichtliche, und zwar nicht nur im Sinn der Kenntnis der von Paulus abhängigen Tradition, sondern auch im Sinn einer Johannes und Paulus gemeinsamen, also vorjohanneischen und vorpaulinischen Tradition. Die Ablehnung einer literarischen Abhängigkeit ist in der Folge mehr oder minder opinio communis[9]. Anders sieht das in der Frage einer traditionsgeschichtlichen Beziehung aus, die mehr ist als die Teilhabe an der allgemeinen urchristlichen Tradition. Im Folgenden soll an ausgewählten Beispielen der Bezug Paulus-Johannes untersucht und näher bestimmt werden[10].

2.1 Christologie/Soteriologie

Eine besondere Nähe zwischen Paulus und Johannes besteht in der Christologie und Soteriologie. Außer Hebr 1,8f (auch 2Petr 1,1) wird die Göttlichkeit Jesu nur von Paulus (Phil 2,6; vgl. Tit 2,13) und Johannes (1,1; 20,28) vertreten. Dementsprechend ist das prägende soteriologische Modell die Präexistenz- und Sen-

---

8 R. Bultmann, Theologie des Neuen Testaments, Tübingen [6]1968, 361.
9 Vgl. nur St.S. Smalley, The Christ-Christian Relationship in Paul and John, in: Pauline Studies. Essays presented to Professor F.F. Bruce on his 70th Birthday, eds. D.A. Hagner/M.J. Harris, Exeter/Grand Rapids 1980, 100; D. Zeller, Paulus und Johannes. Methodischer Vergleich im Interesse einer neutestamentlichen Theologie, in: BZ 27 (1983), 182; R. Schnackenburg, Ephesus: Entwicklung einer Gemeinde von Paulus zu Johannes, in: BZ 35 (1991), 60; U. Schnelle, Theologie als kreative Sinnbildung. Johannes als Weiterbildung von Paulus und Markus, in: Johannesevangelium – Mitte oder Rand des Kanons? Neue Standortbestimmungen, hg. von Th. Söding, Freiburg/Basel/Wien 2003, 142; M. Theobald, Das Evangelium nach Johannes. Kapitel 1–12, Regensburg 2009, 76. Anders z.B. M. Goulder, An Old Friend Incognito, in: SJTh 45 (1992), 487–513, der meint, Johannes habe 1Kor und Gal direkt benutzt. A. Lindemann, Paulus im ältesten Christentum. Das Bild des Apostels und die Rezeption der paulinischen Theologie in der frühchristlichen Literatur bis Marcion, Tübingen 1979, 158–160, diskutiert bei Joh 1,17; 8,34f. die Möglichkeit einer literarischen Abhängigkeit, lehnt sie aber ab.
10 Vgl. dazu insbesondere U. Schnelle, Paulus und Johannes, sowie J. Becker, Das Verhältnis des johanneischen Kreises zum Paulinismus. Anregungen zur Belebung einer Diskussion, in: Paulus und Johannes: Exegetische Studien zur paulinischen und johanneischen Theologie und Literatur, hg. von D. Sänger/U. Mell, Tübingen 2006, 473–495.

dungschristologie. Gal 4,4f. und Röm 8,3f.[11] stimmen mit 1Joh 4,9f.14 (auch Joh 3,16) in den entscheidenden Punkten überein: Sein bei Gott, Sendung und Heilswirken. Im Detail bestehen freilich Differenzen, auch innerhalb der paulinischen bzw. johanneischen Versionen. So nennt z.B. Gal 4,4 den eschatologischen Zeitpunkt der Sendung, Röm 8,3 stellt den Konnex zum Gesetz her, das diese Heilswirkung nicht erzielen konnte, 1Joh 4,9f. (vgl. Joh 3,16) nennt die Liebe Gottes als Voraussetzung der Sendung (auch Röm 5,8; 8,39 – Joh 3,16 redet nur von der Dahingabe in den Tod). Auch das Verb für senden variiert. Röm 8,3 verwendet πέμπειν, Gal 4,4 ἐξαποστέλλειν, 1Joh 4,9f.14 ἀποστέλλειν. Das Heilswirken hat beide Male universale Bedeutung; Gal 4,4f; Röm 8,7 implizit, Joh 3,17; 1Joh 4,9 explizit. Es erfolgt durch die stellvertretende Hingabe Jesu in den Tod (Gal 1,4; 2,20; Joh 10,11; 1 Joh 3,16 und öfter).

Die Aussagen zur Präexistenz- und Sendungschristologie (bzw. -soteriologie) sind in den Einzelaussagen so unterschiedlich, dass eine literarische Abhängigkeit des Johannes von Paulus nicht zu begründen ist. Beide partizipieren aber an der christologischen Explikation des frühjüdischen Sophia-Mythos. Die grundlegenden Themen sind vorgegeben, damit auch eine prinzipielle theologische Nähe. Auch eine traditionsgeschichtliche Abhängigkeit des Johannes von Paulus anzunehmen, ist nicht nötig.

Eine spezifische Nähe zwischen Paulus und Johannes liegt auch in der Betonung des Kreuzes vor, auch wenn in der Verwendung des Terms σταυρός wieder große Unterschiede bestehen. Bei Paulus erscheint das Kreuz „als historisches Grunddatum des Heilsgeschehens"[12]. Die Bedeutung des Todes Jesu ist grundlegend für das am Kerygma orientierte frühe Christentum. Nur in den Traditionen über den irdischen Jesus (Spruch- und Wundertradition) ist das nicht der Fall, allerdings sind diese auch durch Tradenten weitergetragen worden, die den Tod Jesu durch das Sehen des Auferstandenen neu verstanden hatten. Insofern ist es sachgemäß, dass Jesu Tod auch in den Evangelien entsprechend gewürdigt wird. In besonders reflektierter Form geschieht diese Reflexion bei Johannes (und vorher noch bei Paulus). Die paulinische Fokussierung des Todes Jesu auf das Kreuz ist deshalb folgerichtig, wie schon die vermutlich von ihm stammende Einfügung von σταυρός Phil 2,8 zeigt[13]. Auch Gal 3,1 betont Paulus den Galatern gegenüber, er habe ihnen Christus vor Augen gemalt – als Gekreuzigten. 3,13 ist der

---

11 Zum Präexistenzgedanken vgl. auch Phil 2,5–11; 1Kor 10,4 und nicht zuletzt die Leibmetaphorik, die Christus als präexistenten Megalanthropos voraussetzt.
12 U. Schnelle, Paulus und Johannes, 215.
13 Die paulinische Herkunft des Verweises auf den σταυρός ist zwar nicht unumstritten, aber doch wahrscheinlich: vgl. J. Gnilka, Der Philipperbrief, Freiburg/Basel/Wien 1968, 124 (unter Hinweis auf Ernst Lohmeyer).

Fluch des Gesetzes dadurch beseitigt, dass Christus für uns zum Fluch geworden ist – entsprechend dem Zitat aus Dtn 27,26 (Verflucht ist jeder, der am Holz hängt). Dass nicht der Tod an sich, sondern der schmähliche Tod am Kreuz das Hineingehen Gottes in die tiefsten Tiefen des Menschseins umfasst und dabei alle menschlichen Maßstäbe über Bord wirft, hat Paulus am eindrucksvollsten in den Korintherbriefen expliziert: In der Argumentation gegen das Parteiwesen in Korinth redet er betont vom Kreuz als dem entscheidenden Heilsgeschehen: Ist etwa Paulus für euch gekreuzigt? (1Kor 1,13). Die Predigt des Evangeliums darf nicht durch kluge Worte zunichte gemacht werden (1Kor 1,17). Der λόγος τοῦ σταυροῦ ist zwar für die, die verloren gehen, eine Torheit, für die, die gerettet werden, aber eine Kraft Gottes (1Kor 1,18; vgl. 2Kor 13,4). Deshalb predigt Paulus den gekreuzigten Christus (1Kor 1,23) und will unter den Korinthern nichts anderes wissen als Jesus Christus, den Gekreuzigten (1Kor 2,2). Das Kreuz zerstört allen menschlichen Selbstbehauptungswillen Gott gegenüber. Es steht gegen die Enthusiasten in Korinth ebenso wie gegen die Judaisten in Galatien oder Philippi (Gal 3,1; 5,11; Phil 3,18). Das Kreuz demonstriert wie nichts anderes die Paradoxie der christlichen Existenz: gerade im Niedrigsten ist Gott zu finden.

Eine Kreuzestheologie im Sinn der besonderen Betonung der Wortfamilie σταυρόω liegt zwar bei Johannes nicht vor[14], gegenüber der auch schon bei den Synoptikern vorliegenden Konzentration auf Leiden und Tod Jesu ist aber doch eine signifikante Akzentsetzung auffällig. Schon Joh 1,29.36 betonen mit dem Hoheitstitel ἀμνὸς τοῦ θεοῦ die Perspektive Richtung Kreuz, dasselbe gilt für die Hinweise auf seine Stunde (3,4; 8,20; 13,1 und öfter), die Bedeutung Jerusalems im Rahmen der wiederholten Reisen zu Festen (2,13.23; 5,1; 6,4 und öfter), die Sühnetodaussagen (10,11.15.17; 15,13), nicht zuletzt das letzte Wort Jesu am Kreuz: es ist vollbracht (19,30), wo das Wirken Jesu am Kreuz seinen letzten Ausdruck findet. Das Kreuz ist bei Johannes nicht Durchgangsstadium, sondern Ort der Erhöhung und Verherrlichung Jesu (3,14; 8,28; 12,23 und öfter). Es ist nicht ein, sondern der entscheidende Akt des Heilsgeschehens. Auf dem Hintergrund der Präexistenz- und Sendungschristologie verdichtet sich für Johannes das Heilsgeschehen im Kreuz. Die Herrlichkeit des Gottessohnes kommt gerade in der Niedrigkeit zum Ausdruck. In dieser theologischen Akzentuierung des Kreuzesgeschehens liegt somit eine enge Parallele zu Paulus vor.

Im Kontext von Christologie und Soteriologie ist ein kurzer Blick auf die Gesetzeslehre sinnvoll. Im Umfang und in der Differenziertheit der Detailaussagen liegen zwar durchaus beachtliche Differenzen vor, im Kernpunkt stimmen aber beide überein. Hier können nur die wichtigsten Aspekte der paulinischen Geset-

---

14 Vgl. E. Käsemann, Jesu letzter Wille nach Johannes 17, Tübingen ⁴1980, 111.

zeslehre kurz angedeutet werden. Dabei beschränke ich mich auf den Römerbrief[15]. Die Kernaussage von Röm 7,7–24[16] ist: Das Gesetz ist zwar Gottes Gesetz und damit heilig, gerecht, gut und zum Leben gegeben. Es hat aber nicht die Kraft, die Sünde zu beseitigen, sondern deckt sie nur auf, und führt (wider seine Intention) nur immer tiefer in sie hinein, so dass am Ende nur der Schrei der Verzweiflung bleibt. Die Intention und die faktische Wirkung des Gesetzes fallen auseinander. Die Ursache für das Versagen des Gesetzes in Bezug auf die Rettung sieht Paulus in der sarkischen Verfasstheit des Menschen (ante Christum). Die Sünde hat sich in der Sarx eingenistet und kann vom Gesetz nicht daraus vertrieben werden. Rettung ist nur möglich durch einen neuen Heilsakt Gottes, den Paulus (wie die urchristliche Tradition generell) im Heilshandeln Jesu Christi verwirklicht sieht.

Die soteriologische Insuffizienz des Gesetzes drückt auch Johannes 1,17 aus: Das Gesetz ist durch Moses gegeben worden, die Gnade und die Wahrheit sind durch Jesus Christus gekommen. Das Gesetz wird nur auf seine Herkunft von Moses hin betrachtet. Eine inhaltliche Bestimmung wird nicht direkt gegeben, wohl aber indirekt: Gnade und Wahrheit gehen von Christus aus. Gesetz auf der einen und Gnade und Wahrheit auf der anderen Seite stehen einander gegenüber. Johannes greift dabei das Begriffspaar χάρις und ἀλήθεια aus 1,14 auf. Es erscheint dort in christologischer Hinsicht: Am Inkarnierten ist die δόξα des himmlischen Gesandten erkennbar, die durch χάρις und ἀλήθεια näher interpretiert wird. Durch die Verbindung mit νόμος wird „der Joh sonst fremde, aus der paulinischen Schule stammende Gegensatz νόμος – χάρις eingebracht"[17]. Johannes redet sehr plakativ von νόμος und χάρις. Das Verhältnis Moses – Christus wird nicht näher expliziert. Der antithetische Parallelismus setzt aber voraus, dass Gnade und Wahrheit nicht durch das Gesetz vermittelt werden. Das Gesetz hat somit keine positive Heilsfunktion. Es wird als Schrift anerkannt (1,45; 8,17 und öfter), sogar als Bezeugung des Messias (8,34), auch als Norm für das Verhalten (7,19.23), seine Unkenntnis im

---

[15] Im Römerbrief argumentiert Paulus ohne die Affekte von Gal 2–4 und Phil 3. Eine gravierende sachliche Differenz besteht nicht. Von einer „Entwicklung" der paulinischen Gesetzeslehre (vgl. H. Hübner, Das Gesetz bei Paulus. Ein Beitrag zum Werden der paulinischen Theologie, Göttingen 1978, 9) zu reden, ist zumindest einseitig. Der entscheidende Grund für Differenzen zwischen dem Galater- und dem Römerbrief liegt nicht in einer Entwicklung der paulinischen Theologie, sondern in der anderen historischen Einbettung. Im Römerbrief polemisiert Paulus nicht gegen Gegner, sondern versucht, seine Position der fremden römischen Gemeinde verständlich zu machen.

[16] Paulus greift dabei auf Aussagen zurück, die er (ohne nähere Vermittlung) schon früher gemacht hatte: das Gesetz bewirkt Erkenntnis der Sünde (Röm 3,20); es ermöglicht die Anrechnung der Sünde (Röm 5,13) und es macht die Sünde über alle Maßen groß (Röm 5,20).

[17] R. Bultmann, Das Evangelium des Johannes, Göttingen [10]1941, 53.

Volk wird bedauert (7,49), aber mit ihm wird auch Jesus verurteilt und hingerichtet (18,31; 19,7). Es ist Gottes Gesetz, steht aber in keinem unmittelbaren Heilsbezug. Die Differenziertheit in der Gesetzesauffassung des Paulus fehlt zwar bei Johannes[18], eine grundsätzliche Übereinstimmung ist aber gleichwohl festzustellen.

2.2 Pneumatologie/Ekklesiologie

Die Erfahrung des Geistes ist neben dem Wirken Jesu und den Christophanien das dritte konstitutive Element des frühen Christentums. Dass der Geist in der Endzeit ganz Israel verheißen ist, prophezeit schon Joel 3,1–5 und wird Apg 2,16 auf die Gemeinde bezogen. Paulus wie Johannes stehen in dieser Tradition und versuchen, eine erste genauere Entfaltung der Pneumatologie vorzunehmen. Trotz aller Differenzen liegen beachtliche Gemeinsamkeiten vor.

Auf den Geist als Gabe Gottes für die Gemeinde der Endzeit kommt Paulus insbesondere Röm 8 zu sprechen, wo er das Sein in der σάρξ dem Sein im πνεῦμα gegenüberstellt. Κατὰ σάρκα bzw. κατὰ πνεῦμα charakterisieren 8,4f. das vorchristliche bzw. christliche Sein. Der Dualismus von σάρξ und πνεῦμα dient zur Herausarbeitung der christlichen Identität als Pneumatiker. Die Glaubenden leben ἐν πνεύματι, weil das πνεῦμα θεοῦ in ihnen wohnt (8,9). Es bestimmt als πνεῦμα τῆς πίστεως (2Kor 4,13) deren Sein. Die Glaubenden sind Tempel des Heiligen Geistes (1Kor 3,16). Dabei ist weniger die Vorstellung vom Geist als einer souveränen, überwältigenden Macht im Blick (Ri 3,10; 1Sam 10,6 und öfter), sondern der Aspekt des kontinuierlichen Erfüllt- und Bestimmtseins (Jes 11,2; Joel 3,1; Ps 51,12f. und öfter). Ἐν πνεύματι ist eine Parallelformel zu ἐν Χριστῷ[19], einer Formel, die im Rahmen der Partizipationsvorstellung größte Bedeutung in Soteriologie und Ekklesiologie hat, z. B. 2Kor 5,17: Ist jemand in Christus, so ist er ein neues Geschöpf[20]. Die Verbundenheit zwischen Christus und dem Glaubenden ist in dieser Formelsprache darin gegeben, dass das Sein in Christus und das Sein Christi bzw. des Geistes in den Glaubenden (Röm 8,9f; Gal 2,20; 4,19 und öfter) nebeneinanderstehen und sich gegenseitig interpretieren. Die Geisterfülltheit ist bei alledem nicht statischer Besitz, sondern dynamisch von Gott gegebene, je neue Ermögli-

---

18 Dahinter steht nicht zuletzt die andere geschichtliche Situation von Paulus und Johannes. Während ersterer noch um den Konnex Kirche-Synagoge ringt und (im Römerbrief) sehr differenziert urteilt, ist der Konnex z. Z. des Joh zerbrochen (vgl. nur das ἀποσυνάγωγος 9,22; 12,42; 16,2).
19 Vgl. auch die Parallelformel ἐν κυρίῳ Röm 16,8.10; 2Kor 2,12; Phil 4,2 u.ö.
20 Für die ekklesiologische Anwendung sind vor allem die Ausführungen im Rahmen der Leibmetaphorik Röm 12 und 1Kor 12 von Bedeutung.

chung der glaubenden Existenz. Am πνεῦμα haben alle Christen teil. Zwar gibt es, wie Paulus Röm 12; 1Kor 12–14 ausführt, verschiedene Charismen, aber jedes Gemeindeglied partizipiert an ihnen. Auch haben alle Charismen nur ihren Wert im Konnex mit dem Wohlergehen der Gemeinde.

Das πνεῦμα ist bei alledem noch nicht die sachgemäße Bestimmung der endgültigen eschatologischen Existenz, sondern nur deren Anfang (ἀπαρχή Röm 8,23) bzw. deren Anzahlung (ἀρραβών 2Kor 1,22; 5,5) – eine entscheidende Bestimmung der neuen Existenz in Abwehr eines falschen, weltverneinenden Enthusiasmus.

Der Kontrast von σάρξ und πνεῦμα ist auch die Basis der johanneischen Pneumatologie und Ekklesiologie. Der Dualismus kennzeichnet Johannes mindestens so stark wie Paulus. Die Geburt aus dem Geist (3,6; aus Gott 1,13 bzw. von oben 3,3.7) beschreibt das neue Sein der Glaubenden. Sie sind dem Bestimmtsein durch die σάρξ entnommen und dem Bereich des πνεῦμα eingegliedert. Bei allem Wissen um die zukünftige Vollendung (14,2f; 17,27) wird das präsentische Moment des neuen Seins noch stärker als bei Paulus betont. Das πνεῦμα ist die lebensspendende Macht Gottes, die den Menschen neu – und nun erst wirklich – ins Dasein ruft (6,63). Das ekstatische Moment im Geistverständnis, das Paulus nicht fremd ist, das er aber – soweit nötig – zurückdrängt[21], ist bei Johannes ganz an den Rand gedrängt. Der Geist bezeichnet bei Paulus wie bei Johannes die alle Christen auszeichnende und bestimmende Verbindung zu Gott bzw. Christus. Er wird ganz selbstverständlich mit der Taufe verbunden (1Kor 12,13; 2Kor 1,21 f. bzw. Joh 3,5 f.)[22], ohne seine Freiheit eingrenzen zu wollen. Die Partizipationsterminologie findet sich nicht nur bei Paulus, sondern auch bei Johannes: Nach 1Joh 4,13 erkennen wir an der Geistgabe, dass wir in Gott bleiben und er in uns (1Joh 3,16). Entsprechend kann Johannes auch von einem Sein in Christus bzw. Christi in uns sprechen (1Joh 3,24; Joh 6,56 bringt diesen Konnex in eucharistischem Zusammenhang zur Sprache, auch Joh 15,4–7; 1 Joh 2,6 und öfter). Zwischen Joh 7,39 und 1Joh 4,13 besteht insofern ein Unterschied, als an ersterer Stelle, auf der Erzählebene des Evangeliums, die Geistgabe erst durch den Auferstandenen erfolgen wird (20,22). Eine sachliche Differenz ist damit nicht gegeben. Insofern gilt die pneumatolo-

---

21 Die Stellungnahme zur Glossolalie zeigt das. Sie ist selbstverständlich eine Gnadengabe 1Kor 12,10.28, darf aber im Gottesdienst nur bei Übersetzung in verständliche Sprache geübt werden. Ihr Gegenstück ist die verständliche prophetische Rede. Wohl nicht zufällig fehlt sie im Charismenkatalog Röm 12,6–8, obwohl dort die Prophetie genannt wird.
22 Das gilt generell für das frühe Christentum: Die Apostelgeschichte setzt ein Zusammenwachsen beider Größen voraus: 2,1–13 ist allein von der Geistbegabung die Rede; 2,38 und 8,16 f. folgt dagegen die Geistbegabung auf die Taufe; 10,44–47 ist es umgekehrt.

gische Begründung der Gottes- bzw. Christusverbundenheit nicht nur für Paulus, sondern auch für Johannes[23].

Stärker noch als in ekklesiologischer Hinsicht kommt in theologischer, genauer „trinitätstheologischer" Hinsicht ein enges Verhältnis von Paulus und Johannes zum Ausdruck. Paulus stellt in einer Reihe von Aussagen Gott, Christus und den Geist eng zusammen: 2Kor 3,17a identifiziert er κύριος und πνεῦμα: ὁ δὲ κύριος τὸ πνεῦμά ἐστιν – eine Aussage, die den κύριος definiert, nicht umgekehrt – 3,17b redet unmittelbar danach vom πνεῦμα κυρίου, beschreibt somit ein Zuordnungsverhältnis. Wie schon ausgeführt, sind die Formeln ἐν Χριστῷ und ἐν πνεύματι austauschbar (Röm 8,1.9), ebenso die vom Sein Christi bzw. des Geistes in den Glaubenden (Röm 8,9f). Weiters steht Röm 8,9 πνεῦμα θεοῦ neben πνεῦμα Χριστοῦ. Nach Gal 4,6 sendet Gott den Geist seines Sohnes. Den vielen Geistesgaben entspricht 1Kor 12,4f. der eine Gott, der eine Christus, der eine Geist. Zu verweisen ist auch auf die triadische Formulierung 2Kor 13,13, die wenn schon nicht ein unreflektiertes, so doch ein unartikuliertes Nebeneinander von Gott, Christus und Geist voraussetzt. Schließlich ist auf das Gebet des Geistes Röm 8,26f. zu verweisen, das man gleichsam als ein innergöttliches Geschehen verstehen könnte. Alle diese Aussagen stellen noch keine explizite Trinitätslehre dar, nötigen aber, in diese Richtung zu gehen.

Stärker als bei Paulus – und erst recht im sonstigen Neuen Testament – ist der Geist bei Johannes personal verstanden. Er ist hypostasiert als ἄλλος παράκλητος[24], der nach Jesu Rückkehr zum Vater auf Dauer bei der Gemeinde bleibt (14,16). In fünf Parakletsprüchen kündigt Jesus das zukünftige Wirken des Geistes an, das in der Gegenwart bereits Wirklichkeit geworden ist (14,16f.26; 15,26; 16,7–11.13–15). Der Paraklet tritt dabei in mehrfacher Weise handelnd auf: Er lehrt die Jünger alles, nicht indem er eine neue Lehre präsentiert, sondern indem er an die Worte Jesu erinnert (14,26). Er führt sie in die ganze Wahrheit (16,13). Die Erinnerung an

---

23 Bei Paulus findet sich situationsbedingt auch die Verbindung von νόμος und πνεῦμα: Röm 8,2 führt der νόμος τοῦ πνεύματος zum Leben (vgl. νόμος πίστεως Röm 3,27 und νόμος τοῦ Χριστοῦ Gal 6,2). Es ist das in Christus eschatologisch zur Geltung gebrachte Gesetz, das ohne diesen Bezug als νόμος τῆς ἁμαρτίας καὶ τοῦ θανάτου fungiert (Röm 8,2; die genauere Explikation erfolgt Röm 7,7–24). Die stärkere Expliziertheit der paulinischen Rede vom πνεῦμα (vgl. auch die Thematik der Charismen oder die Rede von der Gemeinde als Tempel des Heiligen Geistes – dazu oben) ist aber kein Gegensatz zur prinzipiellen Übereinstimmung beider.
24 Das setzt voraus, dass auch Jesus als παράκλητος verstanden wurde, was zwar im Johannesevangelium nicht der Fall ist, wohl aber 1Joh 2,1, dort freilich auf das zukünftige Gericht bezogen. Ob daraus ein Argument für die zeitliche Priorität von 1Joh gegenüber Joh zu gewinnen ist, wie U. Schnelle, Einleitung in das Neue Testament, Göttingen ³1999, 469 meint, ist fraglich, da die sachliche Priorität noch keine zeitliche in Bezug auf die Entstehung von Schriften bedeutet.

die Worte Jesu setzt voraus, dass das Hineinführen in die ganze Wahrheit nicht die Ergänzung einer sachlich insuffizienten Verkündigung Jesu meint, sondern deren eschatologische In-Kraft-Setzung, da Jesus erst jetzt als Erhöhter erkennbar ist – als der, der er immer war und sein wird. Johannes hat so am konsequentesten im Neuen Testament den Geist mit dem in der Verkündigung präsenten Christus verbunden. Von beiden finden sich gleichlautende Aussagen: Sendung durch den Vater (14,24 bzw. 14,26), Lehre (7,14 bzw. 14,26), Zeugnisablegung (8,14 bzw. 15,26), Überführung des κόσμος in Bezug auf die Sünde (3,18–21 bzw. 16,8–11). Eine Identität zwischen dem Erhöhten und dem Parakleten liegt nicht vor, da ersterer letzteren sendet, nicht umgekehrt (15,26; 16,7; 20,22), ebenso wie das der Vater tut (14,16.26; 15,26). Der Paraklet macht die Geschichte Jesu in ihrem eigentlichen, eschatologischen Sinn verstehbar. Sie ist nicht Vergangenheit, sondern gegenwärtige Wirklichkeit. Der Paraklet führt die Geschichte Jesu nachösterlich fort. Er ist die adäquate Vergegenwärtigung des in den Himmel Zurückgekehrten. Von diesen Aussagen aus ist in der Folge die Entwicklung der Trinitätslehre besonders nötig. Paulus und Johannes stehen am Beginn dieser Entwicklung. Sie unterscheiden sich graduell in der Explikation, nicht aber in der prinzipiellen Notwendigkeit[25] derselben.

2.3 Ethik

Der sachlich enge Konnex zwischen Paulus und Johannes (bei gleichzeitiger geringerer Reflexion dieses Sachverhalts in anderen frühchristlichen Schriften) liegt auch in der Ethik vor, genauerhin: in der Begründung des erwünschten Handelns im Heilsgeschehen[26]. Schon in der Jesustradition ist dieser Konnex fest verankert, man denke nur an die Gleichnisse vom Suchen des Verlorenen (Lk 15) oder an Jesu generelle Zuwendung zu Diskriminierten jedweder Art. Bei Paulus und Johannes wird dieser Sachverhalt jedoch theologisch genauer durchdacht und gedanklich expliziert.

---

25 Eine prinzipielle Differenz besteht auch nicht zu anderen neutestamentlichen Schriften, vgl. nur Mt 28,16–20.
26 Auch hier liegt keine prinzipielle Differenz vor: dass Gottes Heilshandeln vor allem menschlichen Handeln steht und dieses ermöglicht, ist schon im Selbstverständnis Israels enthalten: Es weiß sich aus Ägypten befreit, in den Erzvätern erwählt und mit dem Bundesschluss am Sinai begnadet. Es weiß sich durch die Propheten je und je neu gerufen und selbst durch Katastrophen wie das Exil hindurch bewahrt. In den eschatologischen Prophetien und in der messianischen Erwartung weiß es sich in der Zukunft in letzter Konsequenz gehalten – eine Erwartung, die im Neuen Testament als gegenwärtige Wirklichkeit erlebt wird.

Bei Paulus formuliert das sog. Indikativ-Imperativ-Verhältnis die entscheidende Begründung des Handelns[27], im pneumatologischen Kontext heißt es Gal 5,25: Wenn wir im Geist leben, so lasst uns auch dem Geist entsprechend handeln. Im Kontext der Tauftheologie formuliert Paulus Röm 6,11f: Erkennt, dass ihr der Sünde abgestorben seid ... so soll nun die Sünde nicht mehr in euch herrschen. In der Metaphorik des Brotbackens heißt es 1Kor 5,7: Entfernt den alten Teig, damit ihr ein neuer Teig werdet – wie ihr ja ungesäuert seid. Dasselbe sagen (in Kombination) Gal 3,27 und Röm 13,14 mit der Gewandmetaphorik, Gal 5,24 und Röm 8,13 mit Bezug auf das Töten des Fleisches oder 1Kor 1,2 und 1Thess 4,3 in Bezug auf die Heiligung. Die beiden Schritte sind deutlich getrennt. Der Indikativ formuliert das Heilsgeschehen: Der Christ ist dadurch ein neuer Mensch geworden, lokalisiert in der Taufe und vermittelt durch den Geist[28]. Der Imperativ formuliert die Notwendigkeit, das geschenkte neue Sein umzusetzen in konkretes Handeln. Hier wird nur erwartet, was vorher schon geschenkt wurde. D.h., der Glaubende wird nicht erst durch sein Handeln zu einem neuen Menschen, er ist es schon. Im Grunde müsste der Imperativ gar nicht ausgesprochen werden. Er bezeichnet nur eine Selbstverständlichkeit. Ein neues Leben, das sich nicht als solches äußert, ist keines. Das „muss" oder „soll" des Imperativs setzt allerdings das (unter den Bedingungen dieses Äons) unausweichliche Defizit an Sinngestaltung voraus. Der Imperativ formuliert also nur eine Selbstverständlichkeit, die gleichwohl in persönlicher Verantwortung erst realisiert werden will. Bei alledem ist klar: Der Indikativ geht dem Imperativ voraus und begründet ihn. Das Verhältnis ist nicht umkehrbar[29].

Das Indikativ-Imperativ-Verhältnis findet sich in gleicher Eindrücklichkeit auch in der johanneischen Literatur. Besonders deutlich ist 1Joh 4,11: Wenn uns Gott so geliebt hat, sind auch wir verpflichtet, einander zu lieben; ebenso 1Joh 4,19: Wir (sollen) lieben, denn er hat uns zuerst geliebt[30]. Gleiches gilt für das Evangelium: Joh 13,34: Ein neues Gebot gebe ich euch, dass ihr einander lieben sollt, wie ich euch geliebt habe. Oder 15,9: Wie mich der Vater geliebt hat, habe auch ich euch geliebt. Bleibt in meiner Liebe! Auch hier liegt durchgehend die theologische bzw. christologische Begründung des Handelns vor. Voraussetzung

---

27 Vgl. W. Schrage, Ethik des Neuen Testaments, Göttingen ⁵1989, 170–175.
28 Die traditionelle Verbindung von Taufe und Geistbegabung kommt so auch in der ethischen Reflexion zum Ausdruck.
29 Das Ergebnis wäre sonst Gesetzlichkeit, d.h. der Erwerb des Heils aufgrund von Leistung – eine dauernd präsente Gefahr im christlichen Lebensvollzug.
30 Ἀγαπῶμεν ist als Indikativ oder als Kohortativ zu verstehen. Beide Male ist aber die göttliche Liebe die Voraussetzung. Die Differenz liegt nur darin, dass die christliche Liebe einmal vorausgesetzt, einmal gefordert wird.

ist das Bleiben, das verschieden formuliert sein kann: Bleiben beim Wort Jesu (Joh 8,31)[31] bzw. bei seiner Lehre (2Joh 9), Halten seiner Gebote (1Joh 3,24), Vermeidung der Sünde (1Joh 3,6), gleichsam zusammenfassend: Bleiben in der Liebe Jesu (Joh 15,9)[32]. Die Notwendigkeit zu diesem Bleiben schildert der Evangelist eindrücklich in der Bildrede vom Weinstock (15,1–27): Wie Weinreben nur dann wachsen und Frucht bringen können, wenn sie Teil des Weinstocks bleiben, so ist auch das Bleiben bei Jesus Voraussetzung der Jüngerexistenz.

Es zeigt sich auch in der Begründung der Ethik: In der reflektierten Zuordnung von Indikativ und Imperativ stehen Paulus und Johannes im Unterschied zum sonstigen frühen Christentum ganz eng beieinander. Die johanneische Ethik vertritt ganz sicher den Grundansatz paulinischer Ethik. Ob sie ihn aber von Paulus „übernommen" hat[33], ist freilich nicht so sicher. Denn das setzt eine Abhängigkeit von Paulus voraus, die erst erwiesen werden müsste.

Insgesamt gilt für das Verhältnis Paulus-Johannes: Die Übereinstimmung in wesentlichen Bereichen der Theologie ist erstaunlich groß: Das gilt (1) im Bereich von Christologie und Soteriologie von der Präexistenz- und Sendungstheologie an bis zur Betonung des Kreuzes und der Gesetzeslehre. Beide Male sind (2) Pneumatologie und Ekklesiologie eng miteinander verbunden: Das zeigen die dualistische Terminologie, die Partizipationsformeln, die Betonung der präsentischen Heilserfahrung im Geistbesitz bei gleichzeitigem Ausblick auf die zukünftige Vollendung, insbesondere auch die Hypostasierung des Geistes, die letzten Endes auf die Trinitätslehre zusteuert. All das sind signifikante Parallelen. Nicht zuletzt ist (3) die konstitutive Verankerung der Ethik im Heilsgeschehen und deren Artikulierung im Indikativ-Imperativ-Modell überaus auffällig.

Alles in allem ist die Nähe signifikant. Eine unmittelbare Übernahme paulinischer Texte durch Johannes liegt zwar nicht vor. Im Evangelium ist das ohnehin nicht zu erwarten. Und auch die Johannesbriefe atmen so sehr den Geist dieses Kreises, dass eine Intertextualität mit Paulus nicht unbedingt zu erwarten ist. Eine literarische Abhängigkeit ist auszuschließen, eine Abhängigkeit im Sinne einer sekundären Oralität ist dagegen möglich, wenn auch nicht stringent zu beweisen. Immerhin sind die meist nur motivlichen Parallelen[34] doch erstaunlich. Eine

---

31 Die wechselseitig ausgedrückte Partizipation, die Paulus voraussetzt (vgl. oben), kennt auch Johannes: dem Bleiben beim Wort (Joh 8,31) korrespondiert das Bleiben der Worte Jesu bei den Glaubenden (Joh 15,7).
32 Die Betonung der Liebe, speziell der Geschwisterliebe, ist keine Reduktion, sondern eine Konzentration ethischen Verhaltens.
33 U. Schnelle, Paulus und Johannes, 220.
34 Interessant ist die wortstatistische Untersuchung von M. Schmidl, Überlegungen zur Methode des Vergleichs, in: Pneuma und Gemeinde. Christsein in der Tradition des Paulus und

vielleicht noch größere Wahrscheinlichkeit besitzt die Annahme einer Paulus und Johannes gemeinsamen Tradition. Ansonsten müsste man annehmen, dass sämtliche Parallelen bloß unabhängige Entwicklungen im Rahmen der allgemeinen frühchristlichen Theologiegeschichte darstellen – was doch ein wenig merkwürdig wäre.

3 Das Verhältnis von Markus und Johannes

Wesentlich stärker als das Verhältnis von Paulus zu Johannes wird in der Literatur die Frage nach dem Verhältnis von Markus und den Synoptikern überhaupt zu Johannes diskutiert. Im Folgenden geht es freilich nicht um einen Forschungsbericht[35]. Während es in der Zeit der liberalen Theologie viele Fürsprecher der Abhängigkeitsthese gab[36], wurde Mitte des 20. Jahrhunderts, vor allem unter dem Einfluss von Percival Gardner-Smith und Rudolf Bultmann[37], die literarische Unabhängigkeit stark favorisiert. Diese Position wird auch in der jüngeren Vergangenheit vertreten[38]. Allerdings hat sich die Abhängigkeitsthese, vor allem unter

---

Johannes. Festschrift für Josef Hainz zum 65. Geburtstag, hg. von J. Eckert/M. Schmidl/H. Steichele, Düsseldorf 2001, 223–254. Schmidl nimmt einen paulinischen Einfluss auf die johanneischen Schriften, insbesondere die Johannesbriefe (und hier wiederum 1Joh 4) an. Die Listen der nur bei einem oder bei beiden Autoren (nicht) vorkommenden Wörter (vgl. S. 240) lassen freilich manche Unsicherheit in der Bewertung zurück.
35 Vgl. dazu I. Dunderberg, Johannes und die Synoptiker. Studien zu Joh 1–9, Helsinki 1994, 11–36; M. Lang, Johannes und die Synoptiker. Eine redaktionsgeschichtliche Analyse von Joh 18–20 vor dem markinischen und lukanischen Hintergrund, Göttingen 1999, 11–60; I.D. Mackay, John's Relationship with Mark: An Analysis of John 6 in the Light of Mark 6–8, Tübingen 2004, 9–54; M. Labahn/M. Lang, Johannes und die Synoptiker: Positionen und Impulse seit 1990, in: Kontexte des Johannesevangeliums, 443–515.
36 Signifikant ist das Urteil von Hans Windisch, die Annahme der Kenntnis der Synoptiker durch Johannes sei eine „Selbstverständlichkeit": H. Windisch, Johannes und die Synoptiker: Wollte der vierte Evangelist die älteren ergänzen und ersetzen?, Leipzig 1926, 43.
37 P. Gardner-Smith, Saint John and the Synoptic Gospels, Cambridge 1938, 92. Nach R. Bultmann, Theologie des Neuen Testaments, 355 kennt Johannes aber wohl die synoptische Tradition.
38 Ph. Vielhauer, Geschichte der urchristlichen Literatur: Einleitung in das Neue Testament, die Apokryphen und die Apostolischen Väter, Berlin/New York 1975, 420; R. Schnackenburg, Das Johannesevangelium I. Teil. Einleitung und Kommentar zu Kap 1–4, Freiburg/Basel/Wien [6]1986, 30; P. Borgen, John and the Synoptics: Can Paul offer Help, in: Tradition and Interpretation in the New Testament. Essays in Honor of E. Earle Ellis for His 60th Birthday, eds. G.F. Hawthorne/O. Betz, Grand Rapids/Tübingen 1987, 92. B. Witherington, III, John's Wisdom: A Commentary on the Fourth Gospel, Louisville 1995, 8; J. Becker, Das vierte Evangelium und die Frage nach seinen externen und internen Quellen, in: Fair Play: Diversity and Conflicts in Early Christianity. Essays

dem Einfluss der Löwener Schule[39], in der jüngeren Vergangenheit verstärkt Geltung verschafft und scheint derzeit eher im Vordergrund zu stehen[40]. Anhand von Überlegungen zur Textsorte und Komposition des Johannesevangeliums insgesamt sowie anhand ausgewählter Stellen und ihrer Parallelen bei Markus soll der Frage nach Abhängigkeit oder Unabhängigkeit etwas genauer nachgegangen werden. Dass die Ergebnisse nicht eindeutig sein werden, dürfte freilich schon auf Grund der disparaten Urteile in der Literatur anzunehmen sein.

3.1 Textsorte und Komposition

Was die beiden thematischen Argumente Textsorte und Komposition betrifft, argumentiert Udo Schnelle, „die Rezeption der Gattung Evangelium und die Kompositionsanalogien" sprächen „für eine Kenntnis der Synoptiker durch Johannes"[41]. Wäre das Johannesevangelium unabhängig von Markus entstanden, hätte „innerhalb des johanneischen Traditionskreises die Gattung Evangelium ein zweites Mal neu konstituiert" werden müssen[42]. Genau das behauptet aber Jürgen Becker: „Er war also ein zweiter Mk"[43]. Schnelle argumentiert mit dem zeitlichen Abstand. 30 Jahre nach der Schaffung der Gattung Evangelium durch Markus und

---

in Honour of Heikki Räisänen, eds. I. Dunderberg/Ch. Tuckett/K. Syreeni, Leiden/Boston/Köln 2002, 203–241, bes. 214–218; M. Theobald, Johannes, 81.
39 Frans Neirynck in zahlreichen Veröffentlichungen, vgl. nur: Evangelica. Gospel Studies – Etudes d'Evangile. Collected Essays, Leuven 1982; ders., Evangelica. II 1982–1991. Collected Essays, Leuven 1991; ders., John and the Synoptics 1975–1990, in: John and the Synoptics, ed. by A. Denaux, Leuven 1992, 3–62; ders., John and the Synoptics, ed. by A. Denaux, Leuven 1992; M. Sabbe, Studia neotestamentica. Collected Essays, Leuven 1991.
40 Vgl. H. Thyen, Das Johannesevangelium, Tübingen 2005, 4; ders., Johannes und die Synoptiker, in: H. Thyen, Studien zum Corpus Iohanneum, Tübingen 2007, 155–181; M. Labahn/M. Lang, Johannes, 510; M. Hengel, Die johanneische Frage. Ein Lösungsversuch, Tübingen 1993, 206; U. Schnelle, Einleitung, 506f.; U. Wilckens, Das Evangelium nach Johannes, Göttingen ²2000, 4; Ch. Dietzfelbinger, Das Evangelium nach Johannes. Teilband 1: Johannes 1–12, Zürich 2001, 11: Johannes kennt vielleicht alle drei, mindestens aber ein synoptisches Evangelium; J. Frey, Das Vierte Evangelium auf dem Hintergrund der älteren Evangelientradition: Zum Problem: Johannes und die Synoptiker, in: Johannesevangelium – Mitte oder Rand des Kanons? Neue Standortbestimmungen, hg. von Th. Söding, Freiburg/Basel/Wien 2003, 113; U. Schnelle, Sinnbildung, 143; Ders., Das Evangelium nach Johannes, Leipzig ³2004, 17; P. Pokorný/U. Heckel, Einleitung in das Neue Testament. Seine Literatur und Theologie im Überblick, Tübingen 2007, 548; U.C. von Wahlde, The Gospel and Letters of John. Volume 1: Introduction, Analysis and References, Grand Rapids/Cambridge 2010, 374.
41 U. Schnelle, Einleitung, 508f.
42 Ebd., 508.
43 J. Becker, Das Evangelium nach Johannes. Kapitel 1–10, Gütersloh/Würzburg ³1991, 47.

10–20 Jahre nach deren Rezeption durch Matthäus und Lukas sei es „sehr unwahrscheinlich", dass Johannes in Unkenntnis des Markusevangeliums dieselbe Gattung geschaffen habe[44]. Dass dabei „die Einzigartigkeit und Neuheit der Gattung Evangelium auf Markus als der einzig existierenden Vorlage für Johannes" weise[45], hat zwar das höhere Alter des Markus gegenüber Matthäus und Lukas hinter sich, aber die Schlussfolgerung auf einen größeren Bekanntheitsgrad des Markus ist damit noch nicht gesichert. Auch der Hinweis auf die Übernahme der beiden konstitutiven Elemente der Gattung Evangelium, Jesus als Protagonist und die Darstellung seines Wirkens mit Ausrichtung auf Kreuz und Auferstehung, spricht nicht nur für Markus. Johannes könnte – was die Gattung betrifft – mithin genauso gut von Matthäus oder Lukas abhängig sein. Die Abhängigkeit von der erstmals bei den Synoptikern vorliegenden Gattung scheint freilich einige Plausibilität für sich zu haben. Dass zudem die Parallelen zu den Synoptikern vor allem in Markus-, weniger in Q- oder Sondergut-Stoffen, bestehen, dürfte tatsächlich bei Annahme einer Rezeption von synoptischem Traditionsgut an Markus denken lassen. Die Schlussfolgerung von der Gattung her auf eine Abhängigkeit von Markus bleibt aber gleichwohl in hohem Maße ein Ermessensurteil[46].

Auch Kompositionsparallelen zwischen Markus (bzw. den Synoptikern) und Johannes spielen in der Frage der Abhängigkeit des letzteren eine Rolle[47]. Die Gesamtkomposition der beiden Evangelien ist bekanntermaßen sehr unterschiedlich: Die markinische Reihenfolge der Wirksamkeit Jesu (Galiläa – Reise nach Jerusalem – Ereignisse in Jerusalem bis zum Tod) fehlt bei Johannes, der von mehreren Jerusalemreisen weiß und bei dem dementsprechend die Dauer der Wirksamkeit Jesu wesentlich länger ist. Zusätzlich gibt es große Differenzen bezüglich des Vorkommens von Erzähleinheiten[48]. Verglichen mit den Synoptikern sind die Übereinstimmungen so gering, dass eine Kenntnis des Markus von der Gesamtkomposition her nicht zu begründen ist[49]. Wesentlich genauer sind die Parallelen in der Passionsgeschichte. Hier ist allerdings der Ablauf der Einzelereignisse im Großen und Ganzen vorgegeben, so dass auch in diesem Textbereich

---

44 U. Schnelle, Einleitung, 508.
45 U. Schnelle, Einleitung, 509.
46 Die Argumentation mit der Grundfassung oder einer Quelle des Johannesevangeliums bietet keine Stütze der These der Unabhängigkeit des Johannes von Markus (vgl. R.T. Fortna, The Fourth Gospel and Its Predecessor, Edinburgh 1989, 206), da die Entscheidung für oder gegen eine Abhängigkeit vom Grad der Übereinstimmungen mit Markus abhängt.
47 Vgl. dazu U. Schnelle, Johannes und die Synoptiker, in: The Four Gospels. Festschrift Frans Neirynck. III, ed. by F. van Segbroeck u.a., Leuven 1992, 1799–1814.
48 Vgl. dazu nur die entsprechenden Abschnitte in den Einleitungen in das Neue Testament; besonders übersichtlich: U. Schnelle, Einleitung, 506f.
49 Dazu genau unten in P.3.

Parallelen nur bedingt aussagekräftig sind. Immerhin finden sich mit Ausnahme der Einsetzung des Herrenmahls (Mk 14,22–25; vgl. Joh 6,51–59) alle wichtigen Einzelereignisse des Markus auch bei Johannes, wenn auch im Detail mitunter in stark veränderter Fassung. Bei der Annahme einer völligen Unkenntnis des Markus durch Johannes wäre diese Nähe aber doch ein nicht ganz unbeträchtliches Problem.

Die Frage der Abhängigkeit ist am ehesten beim Vergleich paralleler Texte zu lösen – soweit das überhaupt möglich ist. Deshalb sollen im Folgenden ausgewählte Texte jeweils in Bezug auf Inhalt, Komposition und Wortgebrauch untersucht werden[50].

3.2 Ausgewählte Parallelen

Eine Parallele zu Joh 5,1–11 liegt Mk 2,1–12 vor[51]. Das Heilungswort ist praktisch identisch: Joh 5,8 lautet es: ἔγειρε ἆρον τὸν κράβαττόν σου καὶ περιπάτει[52]. Derselbe Wortlaut mit Ausnahme eines zusätzlichen καί zwischen ἔγειρε und ἆρον findet sich Mk 2,9. V.11 wiederholt Markus ἔγειρε ἆρον τὸν κράβαττόν σου und setzt mit ὕπαγε εἰς τὸν οἶκόν σου fort. Die Erzählungen selbst sind freilich sehr verschieden. Sie differieren in Bezug auf den Ort der Heilung (Joh 5,1f: Jerusalem; Mk 2,1: Kafarnaum) und die Krankheit (Joh 5,5: ein Kranker; Mk 2,3: ein Gelähmter). Das Motiv der Sündenvergebung (Mk 2,5–10) fehlt bei Johannes, das des Sabbats (Joh 5,9) bei Markus. Überhaupt ist auch der Ablauf der Handlung ganz verschieden, und die nicht unbeträchtlichen redaktionellen Motive des Markus[53] fehlen bei Johannes. Eine Abhängigkeit von Markus ist nicht angezeigt, auch nicht im Sinne einer sekundären Oralität. Trotzdem fällt die frappante Übereinstimmung im Heilungswort auf. Wenn das nicht bloßer Zufall sein soll[54], könnte man am ehesten an eine gemeinsame Tradition denken[55]. Markus und Johannes hätten dann unabhängig voneinander eine Erzählung ausgebaut, deren Heilungswort so

---

50 Vgl. ausführlich zu Joh 1–9: I. Dunderberg, Johannes; zu Joh 6: D. Mackay, Relationship; zu Joh 18–20: M. Lang, Johannes.
51 Vgl. I. Dunderberg, Johannes, 108–115.
52 Der Text des Johannes ist näher bei Markus als bei Mt 9,5f. bzw. Lk 5,23f.
53 Vgl. I. Dunderberg, Johannes, 109–113. Z.B. wäre das markinische παραλυτικός (2,3) für Johannes sehr brauchbar gewesen.
54 Die Argumentation mit Zufällen ist in der Regel ein Eingeständnis, zu keiner befriedigenden Lösung gekommen zu sein.
55 Ch.K. Barrett, The Gospel according to St John: An Introduction with Commentary and Notes on the Greek Text, London ²1978, 249.

eindrücklich war, dass es in ganz unterschiedlichen neuen Textierungen erhalten blieb.

Eine wichtige Rolle in der Frage nach der Abhängigkeit des Johannes spielt Joh 6,1–15 im Verhältnis zu Mk 6,32–44. Die Struktur der Erzählungen ist im Wesentlichen identisch: Fahrt Jesu über den See Genezareth; Kommen einer großen Volksmenge; Erblicken des Volkes durch Jesus; Notwendigkeit der Besorgung von Brot, wobei allerdings die vorhandenen 200 Denare nicht reichen; Hinweis auf die vorhandenen fünf Brote und zwei Fische; Aufforderung an das Volk, sich auf dem Gras zu lagern; Dankgebet Jesu; Austeilen der Brote und der Fische; Sattwerden aller; Einsammlung der übrig gebliebenen zwölf Körbe voller Brotbrocken. Es handelt sich offensichtlich um dieselbe Geschichte, die z.T. auch in wörtlich identer Weise beschrieben wird: Joh 6,1; Mk 6,32: ἀπέρχεσθαι; – Joh 6,2.5; Mk 6,34: πολὺς ὄχλος; – Joh 6,5; Mk 6,36: ἀγοράζειν – φαγεῖν; – Joh 6,7; Mk 6,37: διακόσια δηνάρια; – Joh 6,9; Mk 6,38: πέντε ἄρτοι; – Joh 6,10; Mk 6,39: χόρτος; – Joh 6,10; Mk 6,40: ἀναπίπτειν; – Joh 6,11; Mk 6,44: πεντακισχίλιοι; – Joh 6,11; Mk 6,41: λαμβάνειν; – Joh 6,13; Mk 6,43: δώδεκα κοφίνους κλασμάτων (in leichter grammatikalischer Variation)[56]. Differenzen zwischen Markus und Johannes zeigen das spezifische Interesse des letzteren, so z.B. schneidet nach Johannes Jesus das Thema des Brotkaufens an, nicht die Jünger – Jesus wird aus christologischem Interesse stärker betont[57], zudem werden Joh 6,5.8 Philippus und Andreas genannt (Joh 1,40.43). Die Übereinstimmungen zwischen den Versionen des Markus und Johannes sind beachtlich. Die Frage ist, ob daraus eine Abhängigkeit von Markus gefolgert werden kann (als literarische Vorlage oder im Rahmen der sekundären Oralität) oder ob eher eine gemeinsame Vorlage anzunehmen ist. Möglicherweise (oder gar: vermutlich) liegt markinische Redaktion in Mk 6,32–44 (insbesondere 6,35–37) vor. Von den von Dunderberg[58] genannten Punkten hat der Hinweis auf die Wiederholung der späten Stunde (Mk 6,35) einiges Gewicht, doch kommt er bei Johannes nicht vor, die anderen fehlen ebenfalls. Eine direkte Benutzung des Markus ist deshalb nicht stringent zu erweisen, die vielfachen Berührungen in Struktur und Vokabular lassen aber eine Kenntnis des Markus durch Johannes im Sinne einer sekundären Oralität als durchaus gut möglich, vielleicht sogar als

---

56 Vgl. auch ἔφαγον ... καὶ ἐχορτάσθησαν Mk 6,42; 8,9 sowie der Rückbezug auf die Speisungsgeschichte Joh 6,26: ἐφάγετε ... καὶ ἐχορτάσθητε.
57 Auch das Motiv der Prüfung der Jünger Joh 6,6 weist in diese Richtung.
58 I. Dunderberg, Johannes, 143f. nennt u.a: die einsame Gegend, die Anwesenheit der Jünger und der Volksmenge, die Wiederholung des Hinweises auf die späte Stunde und das Motiv des Jüngerunverständnisses.

wahrscheinlich erscheinen[59]. Vor allem die (wenn auch nur punktuelle) Kombination beider Speisungsberichte Mk 6,32–44 und 8,1–9 sowie des Einsetzungsberichtes des Herrenmahls Mk 14,22–25[60] spricht für eine Kenntnis des Markus durch Johannes.

Im unmittelbaren Anschluss an die Speisung der Fünftausend berichten sowohl Markus (6,45–52) als auch Johannes (6,16–21) vom Seewandel Jesu. Die Akoluthie ist ein starkes Argument für die Zusammengehörigkeit beider Evangelien, auch wenn dadurch Abhängigkeit (literarisch oder als sekundäre Oralität) ebenso wenig eindeutig zu beweisen ist wie Benützung gemeinsamer Tradition. Die strukturelle Verbindung beider Versionen ist trotz inhaltlicher Vorgegebenheit auffällig: Fahrt der Jünger über den See; Seenot; Begegnung mit Jesus; Angst der Jünger; Trostwort Jesu; Entspannung der Situation. Es besteht kein Zweifel. Es handelt sich um dieselbe Geschichte. Auch in sprachlicher Hinsicht gibt es einige auffällige Gemeinsamkeiten, die freilich wiederum z.T. nahe liegend, aber gleichwohl nicht notwendig und deshalb auch nicht zufällig sind: Joh 6,17; Mk 6,45: ἐμβαίνειν εἰς πλοῖον; – ebd.: πέραν; – Joh 6,18; Mk 6,48: ἄνεμος; – Joh 6,19; Mk 6,49: περιπατεῖν ἐπὶ τῆς θαλάσσης[61]; – Joh 6,20; Mk 6,50: ἐγώ εἰμι· μὴ φοβεῖσθε; – Joh 6,21; Mk 6,51: εἰς τὸ πλοῖον. Wiederum sind die Differenzen (anders als bei der synoptischen Parallelversion Mt 14,22–33) so groß, dass eine unmittelbare literarische Abhängigkeit nicht möglich ist. Um nur einige zu nennen: Joh 6,16 geht die Initiative zur Fahrt von den Jüngern aus, Mk 6,45 von Jesus. Das Reiseziel ist Joh 6,17 Kafarnaum, Mk 5,45 Bethsaida. Das Volk wird nur Mk 6,45 erwähnt, ebenso Mk 6,46 Jesu Gebet. Als Zeit nennt Joh 6,17 die eingetretene Dunkelheit, Mk 6,47 den Abend. Die Notizen von der Mitte des Sees und den Schwierigkeiten beim Rudern finden sich nur Mk 6,47 f. Als Zeit der Begegnung mit Jesus nennt Joh 6,19 eine Stunde nach Fahrtantritt, Mk 6,48 die vierte Nachtwache, d.h. die Zeit zwischen drei und sechs Uhr morgens. Nach Joh 6,19 kommt Jesus nahe an das Boot heran, nach Mk 6,49 will er an den Jüngern vorbeigehen. Mk 6,49 erklärt die Furcht der Jünger mit der Meinung, sie sähen ein Gespenst; entsprechend schreien sie; nach Joh 6,21 wollen die Jünger Jesus ins Boot holen. Während Joh 6,21 kurz auf die

---

59 Vgl. das Urteil von D. Mackay, Relationship, 158: „The verbal parallels (particulary at Mark 6: 36–37 and John 6: 5–7 where common language encloses crucial strategic differences between the two accounts), too few to warrant a suggestion of direct use, and too many to exclude any contact at all, imply strong secondary influence." Ebd. und S. 293 redet Mackay auch von „echo".
60 Joh 6,11: Jesus nahm die Brote, dankte und gab sie denen, die sich gelagert hatten.
61 Die Wendung könnte markinische Redaktion sein (vgl. I. Dunderberg, Johannes, 161; dort weitere Stellen, die Dunderberg für Redaktion hält). Sollte das stimmen, wäre es ein ganz starkes Argument für die Kenntnis des Markus durch Johannes, auch wenn einzelne (und letzten Endes immer auch unsichere) redaktionelle Textteile des Markus bei Johannes noch nicht stringent dessen unmittelbare Kenntnis beweisen.

baldige Landung verweist, erzählt Mk 6,51 vom Einsteigen Jesu in das Boot sowie von der einsetzenden Windstille und erwähnt nochmals das Entsetzen der Jünger und deren Unverständigkeit. Verbietet sich deshalb wohl die Annahme einer literarischen Abhängigkeit des Johannes von Markus[62], so ist aufgrund der vielen Gemeinsamkeiten auch die Abhängigkeit von einer gemeinsamen Tradition unwahrscheinlich. Es bleibt als wahrscheinlichste Lösung die Annahme der Abhängigkeit im Sinne der sekundären Oralität.

Eine große Nähe (trotz aller Differenzen im Aufbau oder in der Darstellung einzelner Szenen) besteht in den Passionsberichten Mk 14 f. und Joh 11 (12)–19. Das ist in der Szenerie im Ganzen wie im Detail nahe gelegt, da der Ablauf der Ereignisse nicht beliebig variiert werden kann. Es ist gleichwohl auffällig, wie eng die Parallelität ist: Schon der Todesbeschluss, die Salbung in Bethanien, der erste Hinweis auf die Auslieferung durch Judas sowie deren Ankündigung stehen in engem Konnex, erst recht gilt das für die Ereignisse ab dem Gang nach Gethsemane: Gefangennahme, Verhör durch das Synedrion, Verleugnung durch Petrus, Übergabe an Pilatus, Ablehnung der Freilassung Jesu durch das Volk im Rahmen der Passa-Amnestie, Verurteilung, Verspottung, Kreuzigung zusammen mit zwei Zeloten, Zeugen unter dem Kreuz, Tod und Begräbnis. Bei völliger Unkenntnis des Markus durch Johannes ist eine derart genaue Parallelität schwerlich zu erwarten (trotz der notwendigen Akoluthie von Ereignissen[63]). Dass gravierende Differenzen bestehen, liegt in der Akzentsetzung durch Johannes: Er lässt z. B. die Vorbereitung und Durchführung des Passamahls (einschließlich der Einsetzung des Herrenmahls) beiseite, ebenso auch die Verspottung Jesu durch die zwei Mitgekreuzigten. Dafür bringt er den Bericht über die Fußwaschung ein und insbesondere die Abschiedsreden, in denen der Offenbarer abschließend zu den Jüngern spricht. Charakteristisch ist auch das freundlichere Pilatusbild und nicht zuletzt die Szene mit Jesu Mutter und dem Lieblingsjünger unter dem Kreuz. Hier kommen jeweils johanneische Sondertraditionen zum Ausdruck, die aber eine grundlegende Übereinstimmung der beiden Passionsberichte nicht aufheben.

Zwei Beispiele mögen Nähe und Distanz des markinischen und johanneischen Passionsberichts exemplifizieren:

Große Nähe zeigt die Erzählung von der Salbung Jesu Joh 12,1–8; Mk 14,3–9. Die Erzählsequenz ist im Wesentlichen dieselbe: Jesus wird in Bethanien von einer

---

62 I. Dunderberg, Johannes, 164 und D. Mackay, Relationship, 294 sprechen in dieser Hinsicht von einer Möglichkeit. Das dürfte doch eine etwas zu optimistische Bestimmung der Nähe beider Evangelien an dieser Stelle sein.

63 Über Ermessensurteile kommen wir (streng genommen) in der Frage der Relation von Markus und Johannes nicht hinaus. Solche Urteile sind aber nicht beliebig, sondern zeigen eine im Prinzip nachvollziehbare Argumentationslinie.

Frau gesalbt. Sie verwendet ein teures Öl im Wert von 300 Denaren. Das führt zur Kritik, man hätte das Geld besser für die Armen verwenden können. Jesus weist diese Kritik mit dem Hinweis zurück, Arme gäbe es immer, die Salbung sei jedoch als vorweggenommene Salbung seines Leichnams zu verstehen. Eine Reihe von Aussagen sind wörtlich ident (oder grammatikalisch bzw. vokabelmäßig nur leicht verschieden). Joh 12,1: εἰς Βηθανίαν, Mk 14,3: ἐν Βηθανίᾳ|; – Joh 12,3: μύρου νάρδου πιστικῆς πολυτίμου, Mk 14,3: μύρου νάρδου πιστικῆς πολυτελοῦς; – Joh 12,5: ἐπράθη τριακοσίων δηναρίων καὶ ἐδόθη πτωχοῖς, Mk 14,5: πραθῆναι ... δηναρίων τριακοσίων καὶ δοθῆναι ... πρωχοῖς; – Joh 12,7: εἶπεν ... ὁ Ἰησοῦς· ἄφες αὐτήν, Mk 14,6: ὁ ... Ἰησοῦς εἶπεν· ἄφετε αὐτήν; – Joh 12,7: εἰς τὴν ἡμέραν τοῦ ἐνταφιασμοῦ μου, Mk 14,8: εἰς τὸν ἐνταφιασμόν; – Joh 12,8: τοὺς πτωχοὺς γὰρ πάντοτε ἔχετε μεθ' ἑαυτῶν, ἐμὲ δὲ οὐ πάντοτε ἔχετε; Mk 14,7: πάντοτε γὰρ τοὺς πτωχοὺς ἔχετε μεθ' ἑαυτῶν ... ἐμὲ δὲ οὐ πάντοτε ἔχετε. Die Differenzen erklären sich aus dem Kontext bzw. dem christologischen Konzept des Johannes: Die Ersetzung Simons durch Lazarus ist von Joh 11 her angezeigt, damit verbunden liegt auch die Identifizierung der unbekannten Frau mit Maria nahe, die Salbung der Füße ist von Joh 13 her vorgeprägt, die Personifizierung der τινες, die Jesus kritisierten, mit Judas ist angesichts der immer negativer werdenden Beschreibung seiner Person auch verständlich (12,6; 13,2 und öfter). Angesichts der weitgehenden Übereinstimmung in der Erzählsequenz und der nicht unbeträchtlichen wörtlichen Übereinstimmungen ist ein Konnex Markus-Johannes mit größter Wahrscheinlichkeit vorauszusetzen. Eine direkte, unmittelbare literarische Abhängigkeit lässt sich freilich nicht beweisen und ist auch „nicht sehr wahrscheinlich"[64]. Die Nähe ist aber so groß, dass auch nicht bloß eine unabhängige Tradition hinter beiden Evangelien stehen dürfte. So legt sich am ehesten die Annahme der Abhängigkeit des Johannes von Markus im Sinne der sekundären Oralität nahe[65].

Als Beispiel für die Darstellung des Prozesses gegen Jesus sei auf Joh 18,39 f verwiesen (Parallele: Mk 15,6 f.9.11.13): die Passa-Amnestie. Die wesentlichen Punkte sind bei Markus und Johannes dieselben: Information über die Amnestie; Wahl zwischen Jesus und dem Zeloten Barabbas; Frage des Pilatus nach dem Freizulassenden; Bevorzugung des Barabbas durch das Volk infolge des Einflusses der Hohenpriester. Die Szene ist bei Johannes quantitativ stark ausgeweitet und stellt qualitativ vor allem Pilatus wesentlich freundlicher dar, der Jesu Unschuld

---

64 Vgl. das Urteil von P. Vielhauer, Geschichte, 419.
65 In diesem Sinn ist wohl auch P. Vielhauer, Geschichte, 419 zu verstehen, wenn er eine „traditionsgeschichtlich weitergebildete Fassung der Salbungsgeschichte" als Vorlage des Johannes annimmt. Vielhauer lehnt z.R. eine unmittelbare literarische Abhängigkeit ab, setzt aber doch die Kenntnis des Markus (wenn auch in weitergebildeter Form) voraus, d. h. mit a.W.: die Abhängigkeit von ihm im Sinne einer sekundären Oralität.

betont (Lk 23,22[66]). Als Ende des Prozesses Jesu vor Pilatus, der den Rahmen für das Motiv der Passa-Amnestie bildet, steht jedes Mal die Auslieferung Jesu zur Kreuzigung[67]. Der Teil über die Passa-Amnestie hat bei Markus und Johannes enge sprachliche Parallelen: Joh 18,39a: ἔστιν δὲ συνήθεια ὑμῖν ἵνα ἕνα ἀπολύσω ὑμῖν ἐν τῷ πάσχα. Die direkte Rede bei Johannes ist bei Markus als Bericht formuliert, sodass sprachliche (nicht sachliche) Differenzen entstehen, obwohl die entscheidenden Wörter ἕνα ἀπολύειν beide Male vorliegen; Joh 18,39b: βούλεσθε οὖν ἀπολύσω ὑμῖν τὸν βασιλέα τῶν Ἰουδαίων; Mk 15,9: θέλετε ἀπολύσω ὑμῖν τὸν βασιλέα τῶν Ἰουδαίων; Der Text ist hier fast völlig identisch. Eine größere Nähe besteht auch zwischen Joh 18,40: ἐκραύγασαν οὖν πάλιν und Mk 15,13: οἱ δὲ πάλιν ἔκραξαν. Κράζειν meint bei Johannes (7,28.37; 12,44) das prophetisch-vollmächtige Reden, deshalb hat Johannes vermutlich κραυγάζειν für das Geschrei des Pöbels verwendet[68]. Auch bei dieser Szene sind die Übereinstimmungen so groß, dass ein Konnex anzunehmen ist, und gleichzeitig ist die Selbstständigkeit der johanneischen Version so groß, dass Johannes Markus nicht schriftlich vor sich liegen gehabt haben wird[69]. Die Annahme der sekundären Oralität scheint wiederum die nächstliegende Lösung zu sein.

Für die These der literarischen Unabhängigkeit des Johannes von Markus hat in neuerer Zeit insbesondere Jürgen Becker votiert. Die entscheidenden Argumente: Auslassung von markinischem Stoff, Widersprüche zu Markus, Fehlen längerer identer Textpartien[70]. Verglichen mit Matthäus und Lukas ist die Rezeption des Markus durch Johannes tatsächlich minimal. Eine literarische Abhängigkeit wäre trotz dieser Defizite theoretisch möglich – Johannes hätte dann aufgrund einer eigenständigen Position eben nur wenig rezipiert. Faktisch spricht das Verhältnis von Gemeinsamkeiten und Differenzen aber gegen eine unmittelbare literarische Benützung. Die Gemeinsamkeiten sind aber doch so groß, dass die These einer bloßen Partizipation an der vorausliegenden, gemeinsamen frühchristlichen Tradition auch nicht ausreicht. Eine Kenntnis des Markus durch

---

66 M. Lang, Johannes, 159 meint deshalb, Joh 18,39f. sei von Mk 15,6–13 und Lk 23,16–20 abhängig. Ob Johannes Lukas tatsächlich kennt, kann (im vorliegenden Kontext) offen bleiben. Die deutlich positivere Darstellung des Präfekten fällt aber auf und zeigt vielleicht die Kenntnis der lukanischen Akzentuierung durch Johannes.
67 Die Wortwahl ist teilweise identisch: Joh 19,16 und Mk 15,15: παρέδωκεν ... ἵνα σταυρωθῇ.
68 Nach M. Lang, Johannes, 162 ist in Joh 18,40 das ἐκραύγασαν πάλιν dem markinischen πάλιν ἔκραξαν (15,13) nachgebildet.
69 J. Becker, Evangelium, bes. 215–225.
70 Ebd. 215f. 224. Details brauchen hier nicht genannt zu werden, da sie hinreichend bekannt sind. Die Differenzen gelten in hohem Maße auch für das Verhältnis zu Lukas und insbesondere zu Matthäus.

Johannes ist anzunehmen, übermittelt am ehesten auf dem Weg der sekundären Oralität.

Fazit: Zwischen Paulus und Markus einerseits und Johannes andererseits bestehen enge sachliche Parallelen. Die Relation von Gemeinsamkeiten und Differenziertheit ist aber dergestalt, dass eine literarische Benützung nicht nachweisbar ist. Die Beziehungen sind am ehesten durch die Annahme sekundärer Oralität zu erklären.

Literatur

Barrett, Ch.K., The Gospel according to St John. An Introduction with Commentary and Notes on the Greek Text, London ²1978.

Becker, J., Das Verhältnis des johanneischen Kreises zum Paulinismus. Anregungen zur Belebung einer Diskussion, in: Paulus und Johannes: Exegetische Studien zur paulinischen und johanneischen Theologie und Literatur, hg. von D. Sänger/U. Mell (WUNT 198), Tübingen 2006, 473–495.

—, Das vierte Evangelium und die Frage nach seinen externen und internen Quellen, in: Fair Play: Diversity and Conflicts in Early Christianity. Essays in Honour of Heikki Räisänen, eds. I. Dunderberg/Ch. Tuckett/K. Syreeni, (NT.S 103), Leiden/Boston/Köln 2002, 203–241.

—, Das Evangelium nach Johannes. Kapitel 1–10, Gütersloh/Würzburg (ÖTBK 4,1) ³1991.

Borgen, P., John and the Synoptics: Can Paul offer Help, in: Tradition and Interpretation in the New Testament. Essays in Honor of E. Earle Ellis for His 60th Birthday, eds. G.F. Hawthorne/O. Betz, Grand Rapids/Tübingen 1987, 80–94.

Bultmann, R., Das Evangelium des Johannes (KEK 2), Göttingen ¹⁰1941.

—, Theologie des Neuen Testaments, Tübingen ⁶1968.

Dietzfelbinger, Ch., Das Evangelium nach Johannes. Teilband 1: Johannes 1–12 (ZBKNT 4,1), Zürich 2001.

Dunderberg, I., Johannes und die Synoptiker. Studien zu Joh 1–9 (AASF.D 69), Helsinki 1994.

Fortna, R.T., The Fourth Gospel and Its Predecessor, Edinburgh 1989.

Frey, J., Das Vierte Evangelium auf dem Hintergrund der älteren Evangelientradition. Zum Problem: Johannes und die Synoptiker, in: Johannesevangelium – Mitte oder Rand des Kanons? Neue Standortbestimmungen, hg. von Th. Söding (QD 203), Freiburg/Basel/Wien 2003, 60–118.

Gardner-Smith, P., Saint John and the Synoptic Gospels, Cambridge 1938.

Gnilka, J., Der Philipperbrief (HThK X 3), Freiburg/Basel/Wien 1968.

Goulder, M., An Old Friend Incognito, in: SJTh 45 (1992), 487–513.

Hengel, M., Die johanneische Frage. Ein Lösungsversuch (WUNT 67), Tübingen 1993.

Hoegen-Rohls, Ch., Johanneische Theologie im Kontext paulinischen Denkens? Eine forschungsgeschichtliche Skizze, in: Kontexte des Johannesevangliums. Das vierte Evangelium in religions- und traditionsgeschichtlicher Perspektive, hg. von J. Frey/U. Schnelle (WUNT 175), Tübingen 2004, 593–612.

Holtzmann, H.J., Lehrbuch der Neutestamentlichen Theologie II, Tübingen ²1911.

Hübner, H., Das Gesetz bei Paulus. Ein Beitrag zum Werden der paulinischen Theologie (FRLANT 119), Göttingen 1978.

Jülicher, A., Einleitung in das Neue Testament, Tübingen/Leipzig ³,⁴1901.

Käsemann, E., Jesu letzter Wille nach Johannes 17, Tübingen ⁴1980.

Labahn, M./Lang, M., Johannes und die Synoptiker: Positionen und Impulse seit 1990, in: Kontexte des Johannesevangeliums. Das vierte Evangelium in traditionsgeschichtlicher Perspektive, hg. von J. Frey/U. Schnelle (WUNT 175), Tübingen 2004, 443–515.

Lang, M., Johannes und die Synoptiker: Eine redakationsgeschichtliche Analyse von Joh 18–20 vor dem markinischen und lukanischen Hintergrund (FRLANT 182), Göttingen 1999.

Lindemann, A., Paulus im ältesten Christentum. Das Bild des Apostels und die Rezeption der paulinischen Theologie in der frühchristlichen Literatur bis Marcion (BHTh 58), Tübingen 1979.

Mackay, I.D., John's Relationship with Mark: An Analysis of John 6 in the Light of Mark 6–8 (WUNT 2/182), Tübingen 2004.
Neirynck, F., John and the Synoptics 1975–1990, in: John and the Synoptics, ed. by A. Denaux (BETL 101), Leuven 1992, 3–62.
—, Evangelica. Gospel Studies – Etudes d'Evangile, ed. F. van Segbroeck (BETL 60), Leuven 1982.
—, John and the Synoptics, ed. by A. Denaux (BETL 101), Leuven 1992.
—, Evangelica. II 1982–1991. Collected Essays, ed. F. van Segbroeck (BETL 99), Leuven 1991.
Pokorný, P./Heckel, U., Einleitung in das Neue Testament. Seine Literatur und Theologie im Überblick (UTB 2798), Tübingen 2007.
Robinson, J.A.T., Redating the New Testament, London 1976.
Sabbe, M., Studia neotestamentica. Collected Essays (BETL 98), Leuven 1991.
Schmidl, M., Überlegungen zur Methode des Vergleichs, in: Pneuma und Gemeinde. Christsein in der Tradition des Paulus und Johannes. Festschrift für Josef Hainz zum 65. Geburtstag, hg. von J. Eckert/M. Schmidl/H. Steichele, Düsseldorf 2001, 223–254.
Schnackenburg, R., Ephesus: Entwicklung einer Gemeinde von Paulus zu Johannes, in: BZ 35 (1991), 41–64.
—, Das Johannesevangelium. I. Teil. Einleitung und Kommentar zu Kap 1–4 (HThK IV 1), Freiburg/Basel/Wien ^{6}1986.
Schnelle, U., Das Evangelium nach Johannes (ThHK 4), Leipzig ^{3}2004.
—, Johannes und die Synoptiker, in: The Four Gospels. Festschrift Frans Neirynck. III, ed. by F. van Segbroeck u. a. (BETL 100), Leuven 1992, 1799–1814.
—, Paulus und Johannes, in: EvTh 47 (1987), 212–228.
—, Theologie als kreative Sinnbildung: Johannes als Weiterbildung von Paulus und Markus, in: Johannesevangelium – Mitte oder Rand des Kanons? Neue Standortbestimmungen, hg. von Th. Söding (QD 203), Freiburg/Basel/Wien 2003, 119–145.
—, Einleitung in das Neue Testament (UTB 1830), Göttingen ^{3}1999.
Schrage, W., Ethik des Neuen Testaments (GNT 4), Göttingen ^{5}1989.
Smalley, St.S., The Christ-Christian Relationship in Paul and John, in: Pauline Studies. Essays presented to Professor F.F. Bruce on his 70th Birthday, eds. D.A. Hagner/M.J. Harris, Exeter/Grand Rapids 1980, 95–105.
Theobald, M., Das Evangelium nach Johannes. Kapitel 1–12 (RNT), Regensburg 2009.
Thyen, H., Johannes und die Synoptiker, in: H. Thyen, Studien zum Corpus Iohanneum (WUNT 214), Tübingen 2007, 155–181.
—, Das Johannesevangelium (HNT 6), Tübingen 2005.
Vielhauer, Ph., Geschichte der urchristlichen Literatur. Einleitung in das Neue Testament, die Apokryphen und die Apostolischen Väter, Berlin/New York 1975.
Wahlde, U.C. von, The Gospel and Letters of John. Volume 1: Introduction, Analysis and References (ECC), Grand Rapids/Cambridge 2010.
Weiß, J., Die Predigt Jesu vom Reiche Gottes, Göttingen ^{2}1900.
Wellhausen, J., Das Evangelium Johannis, Berlin 1908.
Wilckens, U., Das Evangelium nach Johannes (NTD 4), Göttingen ^{2}2000.
Windisch, H., Johannes und die Synoptiker. Wollte der vierte Evangelist die älteren ergänzen und ersetzen?, Leipzig 1926.
Witherington, B., III. John's Wisdom: A Commentary on the Fourth Gospel, Louisville 1995.
Zeller, D., Paulus und Johannes: Methodischer Vergleich im Interesse einer neutestamentlichen Theologie, in: BZ 27 (1983), 167–182.

Ian J. Elmer
Robbing Paul to Pay Peter: The Papias Notice on Mark

1 Introduction

A few commentators in the past have argued in favour of possible connections between Paul and Mark; but their views have failed to win widespread support.[1] More recently, as the essays in this volume demonstrate, New Testament scholars have become increasingly open to accepting Pauline influence on Mark's Gospel in general and, in particular, Mark's views on such things as the Law, the Gentile Mission, the passion of Jesus, the Lord's Supper, the theology of the cross, and Judaism, to name only a few. One of the most significant impediments to any argument for Pauline influence within the Second Gospel is the almost unanimous Patristic testimony yoking the evangelist to Peter. The more developed versions of this tradition identify the author with "John Mark" known elsewhere in the New Testament as a companion of both Paul and Peter (1Pet 5:13; Acts 12:12.25; 13:13; 15:37–39; Phlm 24; Col 4:10; 2Tim 4:11). Eusebius, however, preserves fragments of what appears to be the earliest stratum of this tradition in his *Historia Ecclesiastica* (3.39.15–16). Attributed to the second century bishop, Papias of Hierapolis (c. 70–140 CE), the tradition is presented as the product of an even earlier source, the "presbyter" (or "elder"). On the foundation of such oral testimony, Papias claimed that the evangelist was a follower and "interpreter" of Peter who wrote his Gospel as a compendium Peter's "anecdotes."

Although in this short chapter it is not possible to provide a comprehensive assessment of the value of the Papias' comments on Mark, it is necessary to make some pertinent comments about the nature of the Papias' fragments. Of

---

[1] Benjamin W. Bacon, *The Gospel of Mark: Its Composition and Date* (Oxford: Oxford University Press, 1925); John C. Fenton, "Paul and Mark." In *Studies in the Gospels: Essays in Memory of R. H. Lightfoot*, ed. Dennis E. Nineham (Oxford: Blackwell, 1955), 89–112; Michael D. Goulder, "Those Outside (Mk 4:10–12)." *NovT* 33 (1991): 289–302; and id, "Jesus, Resurrection and Christian Origins: A Response to N. T. Wright," *JSHS* 3 (2005): 187–95; William R. Telford, *The Theology of the Gospel of Mark* (Cambridge: Cambridge University Press, 1999), 164–69; Joel Marcus, "Mark – Interpreter of Paul." *NTS* 46 (2000): 473–87; id, *Mark 8–16: A New Translation with Introduction and Commentary*, AB 27 (New Haven, Conn.: Yale University Press, 2009), 73–75; and James G. Crossley, "Mark, Paul and the Question of Influences." In *Paul and the Gospels: Christologies, Conflicts and Convergences*, eds. Michael F. Bird and Joel Willitts, LNTS 411 (London: T & T Clark International, 2011), 10–29.

particular interest to this study are questions pertaining to the reliability and historicity of Papias. Is Papias' information about Mark's association with Peter trustworthy; and, if not, is it merely hagiography, or intentional misdirection? Many commentators have suggested that Papias created the link between Mark and Peter for apologetic or ideological reasons.² Commonly, commentators assume that Papias wanted to provide Mark with the very best apostolic credentials in the person of Peter, the chief apostle. All agree that the stature and authority of Mark's Gospel benefited from its association with Peter. But few consider the reverse: what did the memory and legacy of Peter gain by this association between the chief apostle and the second evangelist?³ Perhaps Papias wanted to provide Peter with a Gospel, so that he could join the other apostolic evangelists Matthew, John and, via the well-established association with Luke, Paul. Or, put otherwise, is Papias attempting to rob Paul to pay Peter, in terms of apportioning apostolic authority to the Gospels?

2 The Papias Notice

There is an old spoonerism that applies to the author of Mark's Gospel: "I remember your name perfectly, but I just can't think of your face!" Most commentators accept that the titular inscription, "the Gospel according to Mark," which has come down to us was not the product of the author himself. The title appears in two formats and is placed variously in different manuscripts at the beginning or the end of the work. The most likely explanation for these discrepancies is that the Gospel circulated for some time as an anonymous work and that the attribution to Mark was added by a later scribe to distinguish this work from other "Gospels" that emerged in its wake.⁴ Unfortunately, the title tells us very little about

---

2 See, for example, Kurt Niederwimmer, "Johannes Markus und die Frage Nach dem Verfasser des Zweiten Evangeliums." *ZNW* 58 (1969): 172–88; Benjamin W. Bacon, *Is Mark a Roman Gospel?* (Cambridge: Cambridge University Press, 1919), 9–11; Willi Marxsen, *Introduction to the New Testament: An Approach to Its Problems* (Philadelphia, Pa.: Fortress Press, 1973), 211–24; Jürgen Regul, *Die Antimarcionitischen Evangelienprologe* (Freiburg: Herder, 1969), 96; Theodore J. Weeden, "Polemics as a Case for Dissent: A Response to Richard Bauckham's *Jesus and the Eyewitnesses.*" *JSHJ* 6 (2008): 218–24; Hans Conzelmann, *History of Primitive Christianity* (Nashville, Tenn.: Abingdon Press, 1973), 153; and Pieter J. J. Botha, "The Historical Setting of Mark's Gospel: Problems and Possibilities." *JSNT* 16 (1993): 27–55 at 32.
3 The one exception here is C. Clifton Black, *Mark: Images of an Apostolic Interpreter* (Edinburgh: T & T Clark, 2001), 209.
4 While Martin Hengel, *Studies in the Gospel of Mark* (Philadelphia, Pa.: Fortress Press, 1985), 70, would be one of the few to argue otherwise, the majority of scholars argue for the late

the author, other than the name Mark (Marcus), which proves to be one of the most common in the first-century Greco-Roman world.[5]

The earliest, biographical statement that purports to deliver some of the lost pieces of the Marcan puzzle is the Papias notice preserved by Eusebius in his *Historia Ecclesiastica* (3.39.15–16):

And this is what the presbyter used to say, "Mark, who had indeed been Peter's interpreter (ἑρμηνευτὴς), accurately wrote as much as he remembered (ἐ μνημόνευσεν), yet not in order (τάξει), about that which was either said or done by the Lord." For he neither heard the Lord nor followed him, but later, as I said, Peter, who composed his teachings in anecdotes (χρείας) and not as a complete work (σύνταξιν) of the Lord's sayings (λογίων); so Mark did not fail by writing certain things as he recalled (ἀπεμνημόνευσεν). For he had but one purpose, not to omit what he heard or falsify them. Now this is reported by Papias about Mark, but about Matthew this was said, "Now Matthew compiled the reports in a Hebrew dialect but each interpreted them as he could."

This data connecting Peter and Mark is rehearsed later in the anti-Marcionite prologue (c. 169–80) that also denotes Mark as "stubby-fingered" (*colobodactylus*) and informs us that Mark wrote after the death, or possibly departure (*post excessionem*) of Peter, somewhere "in the regions of Italy" (*in Italiae partibus*). Irenaeus (*Adv. Haer.* 3.1.1), from approximately the same time period, also makes the Mark/Peter/Rome connection, although he includes mention of Paul's ministry in Rome. Nearer the end of the second century, Clement of Alexandria claims that Mark wrote his Gospel in Rome prior to Peter's death (Eusebius, *H.E.* 6.14.6–7). Later versions of this tradition identify the author with

---

addition of the title to the Gospel. So, Black, *Mark*, 4; Adela Yarbro Collins, *Mark: A Commentary*, Hermeneia (Minneapolis, Minn.: Fortress Press, 2007), 2–5; John R. Donahue and Daniel J. Harrington, *The Gospel of Mark*, SP 2 (Collegeville, Pa.: Liturgical Press, 2002), 38–39; Kelly R. Iverson, *Gentiles in the Gospel of Mark: "Even the Dogs under the Table Eat the Children's Crumbs"*, LNTS 339 (London: T & T Clark International, 2007), 17–18; Morna D. Hooker, *The Gospel According to St. Mark* (Peabody, Mass.: Hendrickson, 1993), 5–8; and Werner H. Kelber, *The Kingdom in Mark; A New Place and a New Time* (Philadelphia, Pa.: Fortress Press, 1974), 38–41. See also Rudolf Pesch, *Das Markusevangelium*, 2 vols., HTKNT (Freiburg: Herder, 1976, 1977), 1:5, who speculates that the designation "The Gospel according to Mark" most likely derives from the term Mark uses in the heading of his book, "The beginning of the gospel" (Mark 1:1). However, while this may be true, it does not explain how the name Mark came to be attached to this Gospel. Moreover, there are a sufficient number of variants of Mark 1:1 in the manuscripts to suggest that even this first line may be a later addition as well; see discussion in Josef Kürzinger, *Papias von Hierapolis und die Evangelien des Neuen Testaments: Gesammelte Aufsätze, Neuausgabe, und Übersetzung der Fragmente, Kommentierte Bibliographie* (Regensburg: Friedrich Pustet, 1983), 105–27.

5 Kelber, *The Kingdom in Mark*, 39; Collins, *Mark*, 5; and Donahue and Harrington, *Mark*, 39.

"John Mark" known in the New Testament as a resident of Jerusalem and a coworker in the Pauline and Petrine missions (1Pet 5:13; Acts 12:12, 25; 13:13; 15:37–39; Phlm 24; Col 4:10; 2Tim 4:11). All our sources, including our earliest sources, were familiar with 1Peter 5:13, which explicitly yokes together Peter, Mark and Rome (i.e. "Babylon").[6] Most commentaries on Mark assume that all our sources are dependent upon the earliest witness, Papias, which puts the weight of evidence on Papias.[7]

While the Papias notice does not appear to allege anything that is either inherently incredible or historically impossible, Papias' testimony does present the historian with a number of significant problems. Few commentators today are willing to accept the veracity of the later tradition linking the evangelist to John Mark of Jerusalem. It may even be possible that Papias or the presbyter have extrapolated their information about Mark based upon 1Pet 5.13. Although Silvanus is explicitly named as the one who wrote the letter (1Pet 5.12), he would have made a more likely candidate to be Peter's secretary. Hence, others are willing to argue strongly for a direct dependence of Mark upon traditions going back to Peter, primarily on the basis of the antiquity of the Papias' notice.[8] A few scholars have even argued that Papias' source, the presbyter, was none other than the apostle John.[9] But for the majority of commentators, Papias' information about Mark has proven problematic.

There are two significant considerations here. First, to draw on legal terminology, we must consider the "chain of custody" or what we would call the "transmission history." Do we have a true report of the evidence – in this case, Papias' allegation of a direct connection between Peter and Mark – and can it be unmistakably traced back to a reputable source (the presbyter)? Has the evidence been passed on accurately and without alteration? Second, we

---

[6] Black, *Mark*, 201–06, 25.
[7] E.g. Collins, *Mark*, 7; Black, *Mark*, 82, 99–100, 225; and Willard M. Swartley, *Violence Renounced: René Girard, Biblical Studies, and Peacemaking* (Telford, Pa.; Pandora Press, 2000), 5; Joachim Gnilka, *Das Evangelium Nach Markus*. 2 vols (Zurich: Benziger, 1978), 1:33; and Harold C. Kee, *Community of the New Age: Studies in Mark's Gospel* (Macon, Ga.: Mercer University Press, 1983), xxvi.
[8] In particular, I would draw attention to the arguments presented in Hengel, *Studies in the Gospel of Mark*, 1–30; Robert H. Gundry, *Matthew: A Commentary on His Literary and Theological Art* (Grand Rapids, Mich.: Eerdmans, 1982), 609–22; id, *Mark: A Commentary on His Apology for the Cross* (Grand Rapids, Mich.: Eerdmans, 1993), 1026–45; and Richard Bauckham, *Jesus and the Eyewitnesses: The Gospels as Eyewitness Testimony* (Grand Rapids, Mich.: Eerdmans, 2006), 155, 202–21.
[9] Probably nowhere more cogently argued than by Gundry, *Mark*, 1027–31.

need to examine the character and consistency of the witnesses. Is the information supplied by the presbyter *via* Papias, reliable and trustworthy?

3 Transmission History

In addressing the chain of custody issue, we observe that we do not have direct access to Papias' original work. Papias' material survives only in fragmentary form, most notably in Eusebius where the Bishop of Hierapolis is press-ganged into the service of Eusebius' grand project of charting the history of the church from its earliest beginnings. Hence, Eusebius quotes with approval Irenaeus' comments about Papias being an "ancient man" who was a "hearer of John and a companion of Polycarp" (*H.E.* 3.39.1, 13; cf. Irenaeus, *Adv. Haer.* 5.33.4; cf.). He also notes that Papias claims to have gleaned information about the apostolic age from the daughters of Philip the evangelist (Acts 21:8–9) who later settled in Hierapolis (*H.E.* 3.39.9). In the preface to his five-volume work, *Expositions of the Lord's Sayings*, Papias testifies to his enduring interest in "the living and abiding voice" of the "disciples of the Lord" as conveyed by their "followers," whose words Papias was always keen to hear and record (*H. E.* 3.39.3, 7). So, it would seem that Eusebius cites Papias because of his antiquity and his connections to the original disciples of Jesus.

Those scholars who want to grant credence to Papias' comments on Mark and Matthew are similarly impressed by Papias' antiquity and his apostolic connections. In the past, it was generally thought that the Papias' notice dated from around 130 CE during the reign of the Emperor Hadrian (117–138 CE), primarily on the basis of a statement in the *Epitome* of Philip of Side (c. 430 CE).[10] More recent scholarship has raised doubts about Philip's statement suggesting that while dependent upon Eusebius, who wrote a century earlier (c. 324 CE), Philip misread and distorted that data, possibly even confusing Eusebius' material on Papias with what Eusebius says of the apologist Quadratus of Athens (*H.E.* 4.3.1–3).[11]

Eusebius, by contrast, appears to consider Papias a contemporary of Polycarp and Ignatius of Antioch (*H.E.* 3.36.1–2). In his *Historia Ecclesiastica* Eusebius places his discussion of Papias between that of Clement of Rome who died at the turn of the first century and the Trajan persecution, which began around 110 CE (*H.E.* 3.39.1; 4.2). Similarly, in his *Chronicon*, Eusebius provides

---

10 Robert W. Yarbrough, "The Date of Papias: A Reassessment." *JETS* 26 (1982): 181–82.
11 Gundry, *Mark*, 1028.

a chronological list of such luminaries, placing Papias directly after the apostle John, which might derive from Irenaeus' comments about Papias being a "hearer of John" (*Adv. Haer.* 5.33.4; cf. Eusebius *H.E.* 3.39.1.13).[12] Papias is further quoted by Eusebius (*H.E.* 1.39.1–2) as saying that he was always keen to hear what the "presbyters" who had known "the Lord's disciples" had to report, signifying that he stood but once or twice removed from the original apostolic circle, depending on how one interprets the title "presbyter." As we shall see presently, some commentators posit that Papias uses the term "presbyter" to include members of Jesus' disciples, including his own sources Ariston and the "presbyter John." Others, however, would argue along with Eusebius that we must distinguish between the disciples and those who came after them, in this case, the presbyters or elders.[13]

The weight of evidence seems to go against Philip and in favour of Eusebius, suggesting a date for Papias within the first decade of the second century and amongst the second generation of Christian leadership.[14] However, Eusebius' comments are not devoid of possible misinformation or hagiographical interpolation. It may be true that Philip of Side, by virtue of his distance from Papias, is forced to work from secondary sources, which are open to misinterpretation. But the same challenges may have faced Eusebius also.

Eusebius may predate Philip by a century, but Papias predates Eusebius by two centuries; and we cannot even be sure that Eusebius possessed a complete copy of all Papias' works. Normally Eusebius is exacting and scrupulous in his quotations from original texts.[15] Eusebius' citations of Papias, by contrast, are atypically vague and fragmented.[16] What few quotations Eusebius does provide are supported by appeals to earlier testimony and qualified by reassurances of their veracity, which might suggest that he is dependent upon secondary sources

---

[12] Although A. C. Perumalil, "Are Not Papias and Irenaeus Competant to Report on the Gospels?" *ExpT* 91 (1980): 332–37 at 333–34 makes the point that Irenaeus does not explicitly name John as "John the disciple", he does so elsewhere (cf. *Adv. Haer.* 3.1.1; 5.18.2).

[13] For a thorough discussion of the identity of the presbyters, see Bauckham, *Jesus and the Eyewitnesses*, 21–38.

[14] Gundry, *Mark*, 1027–30, who follows Yarbrough, "The Date of Papias," 190–91. See also Bauckham, *Jesus and the Eyewitnesses*, 12–38.

[15] Bernt Gustafsson, "Eusebius' Principles in Handling His Sources, as Found in His Church History, Books I-VII." *Studia Patristica* 4 (1961): 429–41 at 430–32.

[16] Philip Sellew, "Eusebius and the Gospels." In *Eusebius, Christianity and Judaism*, eds. Harold W. Attridge and Gohei Hatta (Leiden: Brill, 1992), 110–38 at 113; and Charles E. Hill, "What Papias Said about John (and Luke): A 'New' Papian Fragment." *JTS* 49 (1998): 582–629 at 610–11.

for his quotations.[17] Much of what Eusebius knows of Papias is gleaned from earlier sources. So, for example, Eusebius tells us that "the writings of Papias in common circulation are five in number and these are called *Exposition of the Oracles of the Lord*;" however, he goes on to cite Irenaeus' knowledge of Papias' work as the source of his information about the extent of Papias' compositions (*H.E.* 3.39:1–7; cf. Irenaeus, *Adv. Haer.* 5.33.4). In other places he is forced to make assumptions about Papias' sources, in particular Ariston and the presbyter John. Eusebius conjectures that Papias knew both men personally based purely on Papias' frequent mention of their names – to which he appends the caveat; "These things we hope have not been uselessly adduced by us' (*H.E.* 3.39.7). Even more significantly, from the point of view of this chapter, Eusebius does not quote Papias in any systematic fashion, and his citations of Papias' information on the origins of the Gospels are secondary to his central concern – to chart the succession of the apostolic tradition through such luminaries as Clement of Rome, Ignatius, Polycarp and Papias (*H.E.* 3.36.1; 37.1.4; 38.1; 39.1). Hence, Eusebius quotes Papias' interesting story on the origins of Mark and a short reference to Matthew's genesis only as an addendum to, and an illustration of, his more salient information about Papias' apostolic links.[18] It may be that Eusebius quotes this information to substantiate Papias' credentials, which were not necessarily clear.

It should be noted that Eusebius' opinion of Papias is not entirely laudatory. In the course of his discussion of Papias' contributions to the history of the church, he impeaches his own witness by opining that Papias seems to be "a man of very limited intelligence." The context of the comment suggests that Eusebius was suspicious of Papias' millenarian views, knowledge of which he also derived in part for earlier sources, Irenaeus in particular (*H.E.* 3.39.1, 7–13; cf. Irenaeus, *Adv. Haer.* 5.33.3–4). Eusebius notes that Papias does pass on "some strange parables and teachings of the Saviour, and other more mythical things," which Eusebius surmises derived from a "misunderstanding of the apostolic accounts" (*H.E.* 3.39.11–13).[19]

In a similar vein, Eusebius' treatment of Papias' material raises questions about Papias' sources. Eusebius claims that Papias derived his traditions about Mark and Matthew from the "presbyter;" yet we cannot determine with

---

17 Black, *Mark*, 85, who follows Gustafsson, "Eusbius' Principles," 429–33.
18 Hill, "What Papias Said About John," 611–13.
19 See Tim Hegedus, "Midrash and Papias of Hierapolis." *BTB* 42 (2012): 30–35. Hegedus suggests that Eusebius' disparagement of Papias might reflect Eusebius' preference for Origen's spiritual readings of Biblical prophecy. He notes that "the Origenist tradition regarded those who took the Scriptures literally rather than spiritually as *simplicores*, a term which is not far removed from Eusebius' description of Papias as 'a man of very little intelligence'" (31).

any certainty either the identity of the "presbyter" or the manner in which Papias received his information from that source.[20] The context in which Eusebius places Papias' information about the Gospels suggests that the presbyter in question was named John, who was earlier associated with another, otherwise unknown tradent of apostolic traditions called Ariston (*H.E.* 3.39.1, 3–4). The passage in question is as follows; "If, then, any one came, who had been a follower of the presbyters, I questioned him in regard to the words of the presbyters; what Andrew or what Peter said, or what was said by Philip, or by Thomas, or by James, or by John, or by Matthew, or by any other of the disciples of the Lord, and what things Ariston and the presbyter John, the disciples of the Lord, say" (*H.E.* 3.39.4).

This citation from Papias' preface seems to imply that the presbyter John and the apostle John are one and the same. Most scholars argue, however, that Papias had in mind two distinct groups; otherwise he would have employed a single term to describe them – presbyters or disciples.[21] This distinction is common in the New Testament (e.g. Acts 15.2.4.6.22–23; 16:4; 1Peter 5.1), including in documents that Eusebius explicitly names as known to Papias (*H.E.* 3.39.6). Moreover it seems unlikely that any of Jesus' original disciples would have been alive in Papias' lifetime, even if we allow for a very early date in the first decade of the second century.[22] In any event, Eusebius explicitly denies that Papias claimed to have heard the disciples directly; "But Papias himself in the preface to his discourses by no means declares that he was himself a hearer and eyewitness of the holy apostles, but he shows by the words which he uses that he received the doctrines of the faith from those who were their friends" (3.39.1–2). We should also note that Papias is not even claiming to have any direct contact with the likes of Ariston and the presbyter John, only chance encounters with associates who came his way (*H.E.* 3.39.4). So while Papias may have been keen to hear "what Andrew or what Peter said, or what was said by Philip, or by Thomas, or by James, or by John, or by Matthew, or by any other of the disciples of the Lord, and what things Ariston and the presbyter John, the disciples of the Lord, say," it seems highly unlikely that he ever managed to hear them directly.

---

[20] A point made most forcefully by Vincent Taylor, *The Gospel According to St. Mark. The Greek Text with Introduction, Notes, and Indexes* (London: Macmillan, 1966), 13–15.

[21] David C. Sim, "The Gospel of Matthew, John the Elder and the Papias Tradition: A Response to R. H. Gundry." *HTS* 63 (2007): 283–99 at 292. See also Bauckham, *Jesus and the Eyewitnesses*, 31–33; and Hegedus, "Midrash and Papias of Hierapolis," 32.

[22] Ulrich H. J. Körtner, *Papias von Hierapolis: Ein Betrag zur Geschiche des Frühen Christentums*, FRLANT 133 (Göttingen: Vandenhoek & Ruprecht, 1983), 125–26.

Finally, it should be observed that the quotation from Papias as it stands in Eusebius does not admit of any clear distinction between what derives from John the presbyter and what derives from Papias. Some scholars limit John's material to a single sentence: "Mark, who had indeed been Peter's interpreter, accurately wrote as much as he remembered, yet not in order, about that which was either said or done by the Lord." The rest of the citation most likely represents Papias' own interpretation or extrapolations upon the tradition.[23] But we need not labour the point. It does not matter where the tradition from the presbyter ends and Papias' interpretations begin, even if we could delineate between the two with any accuracy. Regardless of how one reads the transmission history, what emerges from this exploration is the conclusion that we are dealing with a convoluted and complex chain of custody. The tradition linking Mark to Peter was read by Eusebius in Papias (or, perhaps, in a secondary source that quoted Papias), who in turn received it second-hand from some unknown person who by mere happenstance knew the presbyter John, to which both Papias and Eusebius have added their interpretations (the extent of which we can no longer determine).

None of the above discussion definitively negates the veracity of Papias' statements about Mark's origins, and particularly his claim that Mark was the "interpreter" of Peter and, by implication, that the second Gospel reports reminiscences of Peter's teachings – which is the kernel of the tradition. It does, however, raise questions about the antiquity and the integrity of the original message. First, on the matter of dating, it would seem unwise to place any confidence in Eusebius' claim that Papias was a contemporary of Polycarp and Ignatius. Given the somewhat fragmentary nature of Eusebius' citations of Papias and the questions surrounding his sources, we might wonder if Eusebius had any firm data relating to the provenance of Papias' material. His assignment of Papias as a contemporary of Ignatius and Polycarp may be no more than supposition. David C. Sim has suggested that Eusebius may have intentionally dated Papias early in his list of church fathers on account of Papias' millenarian beliefs so as to imply that his information was accurate – i.e. close proximity to the fountainhead guarantees the integrity of the flow of data.[24] Even if this were not so, and we can date Papias to the first decade of the second century, the incomplete character of Papias' material as it is preserved in Eusebius, replete with cautionary, editorial comments, raises serious doubts about the integrity of the chain of custody and the genuineness of the evidence. What Eusebius has pre-

---

23 Black, *Mark*, 90. For a more detailed discussion, see Bacon, *The Gospel of Mark*, 22–34.
24 Sim, "The Gospel of Matthew," 286, who follows Sellew, "Eusebius," 124.

served is torn from its original context and we cannot even be sure if Eusebius was in any better position to corroborate Papias' credentials as an early chronicler of genuine apostolic traditions.

4 The Reliability of Papias

The second issue we must address, albeit briefly, is that of the consistency and reliability of information supplied by Papias and his source, the presbyter. To begin with, we observe that some elements of Papias' statement are either implausible or, at best, inexplicable. Papias and, in this case, probably the presbyter, describe Mark as having "been Peter's interpreter (ἑρμηνευτὴς), [who] accurately wrote as much as he remembered (ἐμνημόνευσεν)." Scholars are undecided as to what exactly the term "interpreter" means in this case; it could denote a translator (e.g. from Aramaic to Greek), a secretary or scribe (e.g. working from notes) or, what is more likely in this context so full of semi-technical rhetorical language, the transmitter (middleman) of Peter's teaching to others.[25] Josef Kürzinger has written a number of articles in which he argued that Papias was indebted to the language of the rhetorical schools.[26] More precisely he argues that in his treatment of Mark, Papias is asserting that Mark's Gospel is an unordered collection of *chreiai* or anecdotes. In a very important sense, Papias is presenting Mark in terms very similar to his own role as a collector of the sayings of the Lord (*H.E.* 3.39.1–2). Both he and Mark are "interpreters" or "expositors" of Jesus' traditions.

Papias, in expanding upon the tradition he received from the presbyter, explicitly reasons that Mark recorded the instructions of "Peter, who composed his teachings in anecdotes and not as a complete work of the Lord's sayings." Papias presents this as an explanation of the presbyter's observation that Mark "wrote as much as he remembered, yet not in order." In this further reflection, Papias makes two value judgements about Mark's Gospel. First, Mark composed his Gospel without order. Second, Mark incorporated Peter's teachings accurately, carefully, and honestly. The latter comment is exactly what we would expect

---

[25] Robert A. Guelich, *Mark 1–8:26*, WBC 34 A (Waco, Tex.: Word Books, 1989), xxvii; and Black, *Mark*, 88–93.
[26] Josef Kürzinger, "Das Papiaszeugnis und die Erstgestalt des Matthäusevangeliums." *BZ* 4 (1960), 19–38; and id, "Die Aussage des Papias von Hierapolis zur Literarischen Form des Markusevangeliums." *BZ* 21 (1977), 245–64. These important articles have been brought together with a collection of Papias' fragments into a single volume: Kürzinger, *Papias von Hierapolis*.

in a preface to a Greco-Roman prologue.[27] One need only compare these comments to the prologue in Luke (1:1–4), which makes very similar claims as to the care and attention with which the author investigated his subject, as well as the comprehensiveness of his final record.

The first charge against Mark, that he wrote without order, seems less certain. Some scholars have suggested that the presbyter's comments refer to chronological order; and in this case it may be that the Papias is comparing Mark unfavourably with John on the basis of the duration of Jesus' public ministry.[28] By contrast, Kürzinger and others have suggested that τάξις must be understood as a technical and rhetorical reference to thematic arrangement or logical sequence.[29] The latter seems the most appropriate in view of the other rhetorical terminology employed by Papias, which implies that Mark wrote in a paratactic, anecdotal style. Once again, we might cite Luke's prologue, in which the author claims his intention to write "in order" or "in sequence" (καθεξῆς) (Luke 1.3). The word καθεξῆς, which is a cognate of τάξις, can refer to chronological, spatial, or logical sequence. When Luke uses it elsewhere in Acts (11.4) to describe the preaching of Peter, the term indicates logical sequence – i.e. the order of the account is determined by the internal logic of Peter's overall message. So in his prologue, Luke is claiming that his account is comprehensive for its purpose and, therefore, follows a logical sequence in accordance with his view of its overall message.[30] Returning to Papias it would seem that he, by contrast, is claiming that Mark composed his Gospel based explicitly his reminiscences of Peter's preaching, but *sans* any overall theme or according to any internal logic. The emphasis appears to be on Mark as an eyewitness to the teachings of Peter, which serves to explain the lack of order and the incompleteness of the record. Hence, Mark's Gospel is also comprehensive in as much as Mark's intention was to record "accurately" and without error all that he remembered of Peter's preaching. In this case, order was secondary to Mark's purpose.

The most obvious implication of this statement is that Papias is describing Mark's Gospel as a disordered anthology of disparate sayings. We will return to this subject presently. However, at this point in the discussion there are two issues that arise. First, it is difficult to avoid the conclusion that Papias may not be talking about canonical Mark. Although in the past, commentators tended

---

[27] Hengel, *Studies in the Gospel of Mark*, 49; and Guelich, *Mark 1–8:26*, xxvii.
[28] So, most notably, Hengel, *Studies in the Gospel of Mark*, 48–49.
[29] Kürzinger, "Die Aussage Des Papias," 252–53; Gundry, *Mark*, 1037–38; and David E. Aune, *The New Testament in Its Literary Environment* (Philadelphia, Pa.: Westminster Press, 1987), 67.
[30] François Bovon, *Luke 1: A Commentary on the Gospel of Luke 1:1–9:50*, Hermeneia (Minneapolis, Minn.: Fortress Press, 2002), 22.

to see Mark as a loose arrangement of traditional materials, recent scholarship has come to recognise that Mark is a complex and carefully constructed narrative. Mark's Gospel is anything but a collection of anecdotes derived from the reminiscences of a single editor. Most commentators assume that canonical Mark is the product of an evolutionary process drawing upon various traditional and liturgical materials, even if some of that material might go back to the apostle Peter. When Papias describes Mark as an anthology of anecdotes, one is left to wonder if he is referring to the extant, narrative Mark that now stands in the canon. What Papias describes sounds more like the sayings source Q or the Gnostic Gospel of Thomas. But, since he never quotes any of the passages of the Gospel, one cannot draw any firm conclusions about this issue.

A similar problem attends Papias' claim that Matthew compiled the sayings of the Lord in the "Hebrew dialect," which scholars variously understand to mean either in Aramaic or, perhaps, in the "Hebrew manner of speech."[31] Given that the Matthew we possess is most certainly based on Greek sources (primarily Mark), Papias cannot be referring to that work, if his information is founded upon a trustworthy tradition. But since it is impossible to doubt that at the time Papias wrote, Matthew's Gospel was not only in existence but already highly regarded through Christianity, it is correspondingly difficult to believe Papias is referring to anything other than our existing work.[32] The same can surely be said of Mark. Moreover, if such a theory were to be aggressively prosecuted, it would destroy the whole value of Papias' testimony, both with regard to Matthew *and* Mark. To quote Frederick Gast's colourful analogy, using Papias in this way "is an instance of eating one's cake and having it too;" for if there were earlier versions of Matthew and Mark, a collection of Hebrew sayings and a loosely composed record of Peter's teachings about Jesus, now lost, and Papias accurately describes these, than his testimony sheds no light whatsoever on the ones we do have.[33]

Let us assume, however, that Papias does have canonical Matthew and Mark in mind. In this case we still have a second problem with the link between Mark and Peter, and that relates to the fact that Mark's Gospel has a very peculiar view of Peter. Richard Bauckham would argue that one can detect the vestigial re-

---

31 See discussion of the translation of this key phrase in Gundry, *Matthew*, 617–20; Black, *Mark*, 89–91. Both Black and Gundry draw heavily on Kürzinger, "Das Papiaszeugnis," 30–36; and id, "Die Aussage des Papias," 260–64.
32 Taylor, *Mark*, 15.
33 Frederick Gast, "Synoptic Problem." In *The Jerome Biblical Commentary*, eds. Raymond E. Brown, Joseph A. Fitzmyer, and Roland A. Murphy (London: Geoffrey Chapman, 1968), 2–6 at 4.

mains of "Petrine perspective" in Mark.³⁴ As evidence of this "Petrine perspective," Bauckham cites the following: the significantly high instances in which Peter is cited or singled out in the Marcan narrative, especially in the passion narrative (e.g. Mark 14.33.37.54.66.67.70. 72); the Marcan use of the rhetorical *inclusio*, which frames the beginning and end of the Gospel with references to Peter (Mark 1.16; 16.7); and Mark's sympathetic portrayal of Peter. To these well-rehearsed arguments, Bauckham adds an additional literary consideration, Mark's "plural-to-singular narrative device." According to Bauckham this technique involves Mark using one or more third-person plural verbs with unspecified subjects to depict Jesus and his disciples. Bauckham contends that the third-person plural verbs of this device were originally first-person plural, which could only originate with one of Jesus' disciples.³⁵

By way of response, one might note that in comparison with Matthew, Peter is not particularly dominant in Mark. And the so called literary features identified by Bauckham do not *a priori* prove the existence of a direct connection between Peter and the second evangelist.³⁶ *A posteriori* one must observe that reading into the Marcan plural-to-singular technique the original voice of Peter by substituting the first person plural pronoun is founded entirely on the presumption that Peter stands behind Mark's Gospel. This literary evidence points only to the fact that a major focus of Mark's Gospel is Jesus' relationship with his disciples, of whom Peter is the most prominent. Given that a central theme of Mark's Gospel is discipleship, one might reasonably expect a major focus on the disciples. However, as Theodore Weeden points out, the Marcan perspective on Peter and the other disciples is far from positive – something which he has argued extensively elsewhere.³⁷

---

34 Bauckham, *Jesus and the Eyewitnesses*, 155–80, 202–21. Similar arguments are proffered by Gundry, *Mark*, 1030–33; Hengel, *Studies in the Gospel of Mark*, 1–30, 52–53; and Taylor, *Mark*, 1–3. For a recent response to Bauckham, see Weeden, "Polemics as a Case for Dissent," 218–24. A good summary of the arguments for and against possible Petrine elements in Mark is provided by Michael F. Bird, "Mark: Interpreter of Peter and Disciple of Paul." In Bird and Willitts, *Paul and the Gospels*, 30–61.
35 Bauckham, *Jesus and the Eyewitnesses*, 156–54.
36 Weeden, "Polemics as a Case for Dissent," 219.
37 Theodore Weeden, *Mark – Traditions in Conflict* (Philadelphia, Pa.: Fortress Press, 1979). The disciples have been the subject of many articles, dissertations and monographs. Of particular note are Ernest Best, *Following Jesus: Discipleship in the Gospel of Mark* (Sheffield: JSOT Press, 1981); id, *Disciples and Discipleship: Studies in the Gospel According to Mark* (Edinburgh: T & T Clark, 1986); C. Clifton Black, *The Disciples According to Mark: Markan Redaction in Current Debate* (Sheffield: JSOT Press, 1989); Jack D. Kingsbury, *Conflict in Mark: Jesus, Authorities, Disciples* (Minneapolis, Minn.: Fortress Press, 1989); Elizabeth Struthers Malbon, *In the Company*

Bauckham does accept that Mark's portrayal of Peter and the disciples is ambiguous; but prefers to characterise Mark's portrayal of Peter as "sympathetic." According to Bauckham, Mark presents Peter as "well-meaning" (Mark 8.29, 32–33) but ultimately confused (Mark 9.2–6) and weak (Mark 14.35–41); in other words, a fallible follower of Jesus like Mark's own hearers/readers.[38] However, a close reading of the Gospel suggests otherwise.

It is notable that in Mark's Gospel the more positive interactions with Jesus are typically displayed, not by the central players – most notably Peter and the twelve – but by characters living on society's margins: the leper (1.40–45); the paralytic (2.1–12); the deaf (7.31–37); the blind (8.22–26; 10.46–52); the widow (12.41–44); tax collectors and sinners (2.15). Many of these marginal people were women (5.25–34; 7.24–30; 12.41–44; 14.3–9; 15.40–41) and, according to Mark, "many" women formed part of Jesus' retinue (15.40–41).

To pursue this last point further, Mark's models of discipleship consistently subvert conventional assumptions about social status. As the Marcan Jesus explicitly demonstrates; "many who are first will be last, and the last (notably women, but also the sick, the poor, the lame, servants, slaves and even Gentile demoniacs) will be first" (9.35; cf. 5.19; 10.31.43–44). By way of example, those who one might assume to be among the "first in the kingdom," Peter and the disciples, are seen in Mark as bickering among themselves over their own importance (9.33), and clambering over each other to attain exalted positions (10.35–37). They disdain the meek and lowly, especially children (10.13–16). They try to terminate the ministry of a competing disciple because he is not one of them (9.34–41). During his final, fateful clash with the religious authorities in Jerusalem, Jesus is betrayed by one disciple, Judas (14.12), denied by another, Peter (14.66–71), and forsaken by the rest (14.50). Only the women remain to share his suffering (15.40–41), anoint his body (16:1) and, accordingly, are the "first" to be commissioned to proclaim the resurrection, while the promise of redemption for Peter and the twelve remains unfulfilled (16.7). If Mark had wanted to present a more sympathetic picture of Peter, surely he would have included an explicit reference to Peter as the first recipient of a post-resurrection Christophany; especially in the case of one who is credited as being the chief apostle's "interpreter" whose task it was to record *all* that he had heard from Peter.

By contrast, while the twelve do function in Matthew's Gospel as examples of discipleship – both positive and negative – the portrait of Peter in that gospel

---

of Jesus: Characters in Mark's Gospel (Louisville, Ky.: Westminster John Knox Press, 2000); and Suzanne Watts Henderson, *Christology and Discipleship in the Gospel of Mark*, SNTSMS 135 (Cambridge: Cambridge University Press, 2006).
38 Bauckham, *Jesus and the Eyewitnesses*, 176–77.

provides a personalised example of discipleship for Matthew's church. For the most part, Matthew presents the disciples as a nameless, faceless, collective unity; but Peter stands out in sharp relief against this backdrop of anonymity, being the only named disciple to become the focus of special attention. In Matthew, Peter is presented as both the "ecclesiastical overlord" and the "representative disciple" (e.g. Matt 10.2; 17.24).[39] If Papias or the presbyter John had suggested collaboration between Peter and the author of Matthew's Gospel, we might not have been surprised – although, as we have seen, what little Papias has to say of the origins of Matthew is not without serious difficulties.

The conundrum for us with regard to our specific enterprise, however, is that the tradition connects Peter to Mark's Gospel, the very Gospel which presents the most unsympathetic (some would same hostile) portrait of Peter and the twelve. This observation, and all of the foregoing discussion on the antiquity and accuracy of the Papias' notice, suggests that the presence of Peter in this tradition is secondary and, more likely, little more than hagiography.

Finally, we should note that there is an additional problem with taking Papias at his word when he indicates that Mark's Gospel is based on an eyewitness report of Peter: virtually everything else that Papias says is widely, and rightly, discounted by scholars as pious imagination rather than historical fact. We need only remind ourselves of the problems associated with Papias' material on Matthew. Similarly, we noted Eusebius' poor estimation of Papias' intelligence, most likely based upon Eusebius' knowledge of Papias' retailing of "strange parables and teachings of the Saviour, and other more mythical things" (*H.E.* 3.39.13). We do possess a number of fragments of Papias' collection of sayings, and there are indeed many that are clearly fictional. For example, Eusebius indicates that Papias heard stories about Justus, surnamed Barsabas, who drank poison but suffered no harm and another story *via* a daughter of Philip concerning the resurrection of a corpse (H.E. 3.39.9). There is also a very lurid and highly fanciful version of the death of Judas attributed to Papias and recorded by Apollinaris of Laodicea. According to Papias, Judas did not hang himself, as found in Matt 27:5; but experienced the torment of girth until he literally burst open (cf. Acts 1:18).[40]

Papias is clearly given to flights of fancy, and one gets the feeling that much of the positive scholarly analyses of the Papias' notice vis-à-vis the origins of Mark and Matthew can be attributed to cases of selective preference. All too

---

39 Gundry, *Matthew*, 9.
40 See full translation and recent discussion of this intriguing story in Christopher B. Zeichmann, "Papias as Rhetorician: Ekphrasis in the Bishop's Account of Judas' Death." *NTS* 56 (2010), 427–29.

often, commentators who want certain comments to be factual accept them as fact, even when there are other comments they are willing and eager to admit are fictitious. Of course, no one would deny that when it comes to the question of Mark's origins we have very little information, but the ambiguity of the little we do have is seldom acknowledged.[41] The complexities of our available historical evidence are often misjudged. As we have seen in the foregoing discussion, the fragments of Papias are particularly difficult to appraise; although one would hardly realise this while reading through much of the scholarly use of Papias. Nevertheless, despite these complexities, the foregoing discussion indicates that what Papias tells about Mark is probably no more accurate than what he tells us about the death of Judas or the daughters of Philip. Like those other, wildly fanciful stories, Papias' story about Mark being a follower and interpreter of Peter is little more than wishful thinking or, perhaps, wilful misdirection.[42]

5 Peter, Paul and Mark

There is one further question to do with motive that we have yet to explore: why Peter? We have seen that the link with Peter is most likely fictitious; but that conclusion does call for some explanation, albeit speculative.

Commentators have consistently argued that there is a polemical intent in the prologue of Papias' *Expositions of the Lord's Sayings* (H.E. 3.39.1–7). And, indeed, there does seem to be a sharp edge to the retort that Papias, "unlike the many…was not delighted with those who say many things, but with those who teach the truth, or with those who remember not the commandments of others but those given by the Lord to the faith and derived from truth itself" (H.E. 3.39.3). To this he adds the further remark that he "did not assume that whatever comes from books is as helpful to me as what comes from a living and lasting voice."

Unfortunately, it is not clear against whom Papias' criticism is directed. We do know whose "voice" and whose "commandments" he did value. Those "who teach the truth" are plainly identified with the "disciples of the Lord" and the "presbyters" who followed them; the former named as Andrew, Peter, Philip, Thomas, James, John and Matthew; of the latter we hear of Ariston and John. Those in the opposing camp who "say many things" and who, by implication,

---

41 Botha, "Historical Setting," 32; and Black, *Mark*, 84–85.
42 Niederwimmer, "Johannes Markus," 172–88; Bacon, *Is Mark a Roman Gospel?*, 9–11; Regul, *Die Antimarcionitischen Evangelienprologe*, 96; and Conzelmann, *History of Primitive Christianity*, 153.

put stock in strange "commandments" and "books," are not named. Speculation on the identity of these opponents range far and wide, with Marcionites and Gnostics being the two most popular; but the issue is seldom addressed today.[43] One reason for this lack of interest is the matter of Papias' dating which, as we have seen, is hard to determine with any accuracy. Arguments in favour of either Marcionite or Gnostic opponents would require a much later dating for Papias than is now generally assumed. Moreover, there is nothing in the fragments of Papias that would suggest that he addresses his comments to either group, and both Irenaeus and Eusebius are silent as to any such opposition. If there is any polemic intent in Papias, it is notably muted. Still, this need not mean that Papias' comments are without bias or criticism of an unnamed person or persons.

One surprising aspect of the Papias tradition is that Papias says nothing of Paul. Papias does know of several letters that would later enter the canon, 1John and 1Peter but apparently he never mentions any of Paul's letters or, for that matter, Luke-Acts (which tradition links to a companion of Paul). This does seem surprising in that Papias was Bishop of Hierapolis, a city in the Lycos Valley that was part of the Pauline mission (cf. Col 4.13). It would seem highly unlikely that Papias would not have known of Paul's letters or of churchmen and women who championed Pauline ideas. This silence has led to suggestions from various commentators going back to Ferdinand Christian Baur that Papias may have had Paul or Paulinists in mind when he spoke of "others" who retail strange commands that do not come from the Lord. Given that Papias was so enamoured of Jesus' traditions that derived from apostolic sources, this suggestion is at least plausible.[44] For Papias, the valid authorities were the disciples of Jesus, whose teachings had been transmitted *via* the presbyters. Following this view, we would expect Papias to omit Paul's letters, devalue Luke-Acts, and chide those who put their trust in such "books."

Charles Nielsen sharpened this proposal by pointing the finger at Polycarp, who was an early and ardent Paulinist and a close neighbour to Papias, as well as one who is also explicitly named by Irenaeus and Eusebius as a contemporary

---

43 Ralph P. Martin, *Mark, Evangelist and Theologian* (Grand Rapids, Mich.: Zondervan, 1973), 80–83. Martin posits a Marcionite background to Papias' comments. See Gundry, *Matthew*, 616 for further comment on Martin's theory. Further discussion of theories about Gnostic opponents can be found in Frederick C. Grant, *The Earliest Gospel: Studies of the Evangelistic Tradition at Its Point of Crystallization in Writing* (New York, N.Y.: Abingdon-Cokesbury, 1943), 34–36.
44 So, for example, Johannes Munck, "Presbyters and Disciples of the Lord in Papias." *HTR* 52 (1959): 223–44 at 230; and Rupert Annand, "Papias and the Four Gospels." *SJT* 9 (1956): 46–62 at 49.

of Papias.⁴⁵ Nielsen builds upon earlier scholarship that noted the differences between Polycarp and Papias. The first tended to ignore the Old Testament and to accept Paul's letters as "Scripture;" while the second reflected on the fulfilment of Old Testament promises and favours the likes of the more "Jewish" evangelists Matthew and John over Mark and Luke.⁴⁶

Admittedly, Nielsen's evidence is thin and his article is seldom referenced today. The uncertainty of Papias' dating raises real problems with suggesting Polycarp as the subject of Papias' criticism. However, commentators have proposed a Christian-Jewish context for Papias. For example, Tim Hegedus has detected evidence of midrash in the fragments of Papias suggesting that Papias and his sources may have been heavily influenced by Judaism, most probably *via* a connection to Johannine Christianity.⁴⁷ Others have noticed that Papias' millenarian views owe much to Jewish apocalyptic eschatology.⁴⁸ Given that later Christian Jewish texts were openly hostile towards Paul, we might reasonably expect something similar in Papias.

While Nielsen is aware of the dangers of making an argument from silence, he suggests that the absence of Paul's name from the list of Jesus' disciples and their presbyters might have some bearing on Papias' views on the origins of the Gospels. After all, Paul, even by his own admission was not an eyewitness to the Christ event (e.g. Gal 1.17; 1Cor 15.9). His relationship with the original disciples of Jesus was ambiguous, as I have argued more fully elsewhere.⁴⁹ Furthermore, it is noteworthy that the Biblical and extra-Biblical books with which Eusebius claims Papias was familiar are ones that we might traditionally ascribe to Christian Judaism – 1John; 1Peter; Matthew's Gospel; the Gospel to the Hebrews (*H.E.*

---

45 Charles M. Nielsen, "Papias: Polemicist against Whom?" *TS* 35 (1974): 529–34.
46 On the issue of Polycarp's view of Paul's letters as "Scripture," Nielson ("Papias," 532–33) explains; "In 12:1 of his epistle, Polycarp quotes Eph 4.26 and calls it Holy Scripture. While it is true that the first half of Eph 4.26 is also found in Ps 4:5, there is no reason to think that Polycarp knew this fact. It is clear from his letter that he was well versed in the Pauline epistles but hardly in the Old Testament. Why, then, would he think a verse from Eph 4.26 came from the Old Testament rather than from Ephesians itself? Moreover, the second part of Eph 4.26 is not found in the Psalms or in the Old Testament at all. Yet the entire verse is called Holy Scripture."
47 Hegedus, "Midrash and Papias of Hierapolis," 34; Charles E. Hill, "Papias of Hierapolis." *ExpT* 117 (2006): 309–15 at 314; and id, *The Johannine Corpus in the Early Church* (Oxford: Oxford University Press, 2004), 408–09.
48 Oskar Skarsaune, "Fragments of Jewish Christian Literature Quoted in Some Greek and Latin Fathers." In *Jewish Believers in Jesus*, eds. Oskar Skarsaune and Reidar Hvalvik (Peabody, Mass.: Hendrickson, 2007), 326–33.
49 Ian J. Elmer. *Paul, Jerusalem and the Judaisers: The Galatian Crisis in its Broadest Historical Context*. WUNT 2.258 (Tübingen: Mohr Siebeck, 2009).

3.39.16–17). Missing from that list are any texts from the Pauline corpus, which must suggest that the "books" that Papias disparaged were the letters of Paul.[50]

Alternatively, Papias may have omitted quotations from Paul because he treasured oral tradition ("a living and lasting voice") much more highly than material that could be gathered "from books." But this seems unlikely. If that were the case it would appear hypocritical, if not completely nonsensical, for Papias to denigrate book learning in the preface to a five-volume set of books. Moreover, given the content and intent of Papias' *Expositions of the Lord's Sayings*, it seems clear enough that Papias does not mean books in general; but, rather, "sacred writings."[51] And that being the case, it is improbable to suppose that a Christian-Jewish writer like Papias would be referring to either the books of the Old Testament or the Christian-Jewish texts known to him. He could be referring to Gnostic texts; but again we must contend with the absence of other anti-Gnostic polemic in either the Papias fragments or the later Patristic commentary on Papias. The only other set of "books" considered as Scripture by some Christians contemporaneous with Papias was the Pauline corpus.

There is sufficient evidence to conclude that by the end of the first century some of Paul's letters were being circulated and collected in various churches.[52] References and allusions to most of Paul's letters can be found in Ignatius of Antioch and Polycarp. Polycarp, in addition to his own collection, is aware of a similar collection in the Philippian church ("when absent he [Paul] wrote you letters that will enable you, if you study them carefully, to grow in the faith delivered to you," – *Phil* 3.2). Prior to Polycarp, the author of 2Peter (3.15–16) speaks of Paul's letters and warns against those who misconstrue their meaning, "as they do the other Scriptures" (τὰς λοιπὰς γραφὰς). Such a warning would be fulfilled spectacularly with the advent of Marcion, who Irenaeus attacked vociferously for "dismembering the letters of Paul" (*Adv. Haer.* 1.27.2). Neilsen is probably correct in suggesting that while Papias does not admit that the Pauline collection is Scripture, he may have taken unfavourable notice that other Christians did.[53]

---

50 Nielsen, "Papias," 533–34. See also Robert M. Grant, *The Formation of the New Testament* (London: Hutchinson, 1965), 62–107.
51 Nielsen, "Papias," 536.
52 David Trobisch, *The First Edition of the New Testament* (Oxford: Oxford University Press, 2000), 22–26; and id, *Paul's Letter Collection: Tracing the Origins* (Minneapolis, Minn.: Fortress Press, 1994), 48–54. Similar conclusions are offered by Günther Zunzt, *The Text of the Epistles: A Disquisition Upon the Corpus Paulinum* (Oxford: Oxford University Press, 1963), 14; and Frederick F. Bruce, *The Canon of Scripture* (Downers Grove, Ill.: Intervarsity Press, 1988), 130.
53 Nielsen, "Papias," 530.

We need to remember that in the early decades of the second century the size and extent of the Pauline corpus, as yet joined to the larger canon, looked much more impressive; especially with the addition of the Gospel of Luke. Pauline Christianity had continued to produce pseudonymous works in Paul's name, and a good number of these – the Pastoral epistles, as well as Ephesians and Colossians – would later find their way into the Christian canon. From these letters emerges, what Victor Furnish called, a "*Paulusbild;*" a new exalted "view" of Paul as apostle and martyr, whose sufferings "are said to have completed Christ's afflictions, and to have been, like Christ's own, on behalf of the whole church" (e.g. Col 1:23–25; 4:10; Eph 3:1; 4:1).[54] Similarly, the author of 1Clement (5:2–7) places Paul alongside Peter as one of two apostolic pillars of the church, whose "great example of endurance" won him a place in heaven (cf. Polycarp, *Phil.* 9:2). So regardless of the strength of Nielsen's argument, we must accept that from the perspective of Papias and others of his ilk, such as the author of 2Pet (3.15–16), Paul and the Pauline corpus must have dominated the emerging Christian literary landscape. It is against this background that we must read the Papias' notice linking Mark's Gospel to a companion of Peter.

We noted earlier that Papias and the presbyter characterised Mark as lacking order, which is probably best understood as logical sequence. What remains unclear from this statement is Papias' attitude towards Mark. Is Papias expressing a negative view of Mark for this lack of order, or is commending him? Richard Bauckham has argued for the former, suggesting that Papias favoured John's Gospel over that of Mark (and, possibly also Matthew) and, most likely, belonged to the Johannine School – despite the fact that Eusebius does not record Papias' comments on John's Gospel. Bauckhman argues that this is not surprising, given Eusebius' concerns about the Book of Revelation and his focus on the apostolic origin of the Gospels.[55]

Bauckham posits that Papias' purpose in writing on the Gospels is less about proving apostolic authorship than it was about explaining the lack of σύνταξις in Mark and Matthew. On this line of thinking, Papias is seen to stand with those in the early church who preferred the chronological structure and narrative style of

---

54 Victor Paul Furnish, "On Putting Paul in His Place." *JBL* 113 (1994): 3–17 at 5.
55 Bauckham, *Jesus and the Eyewitnesses*, 225–26. Bauckham supports his claim by arguing that Papias believed John the Elder was the author of the Fourth Gospel, despite Eusebius' claims to the contrary. But even a person who believed John the son of Zebedee wrote the Gospel and Papias' John the Elder wrote Revelation would no doubt concede that the Elder John was working in the so-called "Johannine school" and would have been familiar with the Fourth Gospel or early forms of what would become that work. The point is simply that however one breaks this down, Papias knew the Fourth Gospel.

John to that of the Synoptic Gospels. In Bauckham's view, Papias is not defending Mark, or Matthew for that matter; but is rather comparing the inadequacies of both to the only other Gospel he knew that was also the product of an eyewitness. Bauckham concludes that "[t]he only reason Papias could have had for thinking that the Gospels of Matthew and Mark both lacked the kind of order to be expected in a work deriving from an eyewitness is that he knew another Gospel, also of eyewitness origin, whose chronological sequence differed significantly from Mark's and Matthew's Gospels and whose 'order' Papias preferred."[56]

By contrast, Ralph P. Martin thought that Papias may have been defending Mark from Marcionite criticisms that viewed Mark as inferior to Luke's Gospel, the author of whom had traditionally been considered a companion of Paul (e.g. Irenaeus, *Adv. Haer.* 3.1.1; 3.14.1).[57] Luke (if by virtue of his preface alone) could be claimed by its supporters as being a proper rhetorical arrangement of a historical theme. Mark is being deemed inaccurate on the basis of his lack of historical completeness (e.g. the absence of infancy narratives and post-resurrection Christophanies). Martin hypothesises that Papias and the Marcionite critics of Mark have been influenced by the vocabulary of Luke's prologue, and it is the occurrence of cognates of τάξις as a key term in both Papias and Luke that he sees as his fundamental argument. Papias retails the tradition of the presbyter that links Mark with Peter to demonstrate that while Mark lacks the sort of chronological order proper to a historical work, this can be attributed to occasional and anecdotal manner of Peter's preaching. By appealing to Mark's role as Peter's "interpreter," Mark's accuracy is affirmed, even though his lack of order is conceded – indeed it is commended as demonstrative of an accurate record on Mark's part.

The propositions of both Bauckham and Martin are difficult to sustain. First, Bauckham's claim that Mark is being critiqued by someone who prefers John over Mark fails because there is no explicit reference to John or, indeed, any explicit attempt to compare Mark to another Gospel. The same is probably true for Martin's view of his Marciontes who prefer Luke to Mark. Second, Papias' supposed criticism of Mark is an implication that has been imposed upon the Papias' notice by commentators. Papias is quite clear in saying that Mark was careful; his recollection was accurate; and his account of Peter's teachings is comprehensive. It may be true that Papias is defending Mark against critics of

---

56 Bauckham, *Jesus and the Eyewitnesses*, 226.
57 Martin, *Mark, Evangelist and Theologian*, 80–83. See also Robert M. Grant, "Papias and the Gospels." *ATR* 25 (1943): 218–22.

Mark's order; but these are unlikely to be Marcionites. The point Papias is at pains to make is that Mark did nothing wrong, because the he was not writing a history or a biography; but compiling a collection of Peter's "anecdotes" and, as such one would not expect an "orderly" arrangement, chronological or otherwise.[58] Thus, as noted earlier, the introduction of the tradition linking Mark to Peter as his interpreter serves to explain why Mark wrote without order.

This brings us back to the question with which we began this section: why Peter? Why does Papias and his source link Mark to Peter? Why not Paul? If we are right in assuming that Papias differed ideologically from the Paulinists, it is unlikely that he would have ascribed Mark to the Pauline library, especially given that he may have already considered Paul to have said far too much already. But there may be more to Papias' motives for choosing Peter in particular.

Commentators assume that Mark's reputation benefited greatly by the link to Peter. By contrast, it is often assumed that the legacy of Paul was greatly enhanced by the tradition yoking Luke/Acts to the Pauline school. Is it not possible that the same is true of Peter? Would not the ascription of Mark to Peter provide a similar increase for the Petrine school? By reversing the conventional wisdom, we realise that there may be a degree of reciprocity between Peter and Mark inherent to the Papias' notice. [59]

Following our earlier discussion of the origins and veracity of the Papias' notice, we can probably conclude that the titles of the Gospels are earlier than the Papias tradition, which give grounds for associating the Gospel with someone called Mark quite independent of the Petrine tradition. The tradition identifying this Mark with John Mark of Jerusalem is undoubtedly even later again. Nevertheless, by the time Papias was writing, Mark's Gospel was well established and had attained an assured place within the nascent Christian orthodoxy of the second century, a movement that also increasingly embraced Peter as the key figure its underlying mythos. Like Paul, the hallmark of the apostle Peter was claimed for a variety of texts emerging during the Patristic period. But, unlike Paul, a majority of these texts were later deemed heretical with the two canonical letters, 1 and 2Peter, being the exceptions. Contrary to what we might normally assume, the figure of Peter was the source of some controversy in the latter part of the first, and during the early decades of the second, centuries.[60] Only

---

58 So, correctly, Kürzinger, "Die Aussage des Papias," 251–52.
59 Black, *Mark*, 209.
60 For a complete discussion, see Terence V. Smith, *Petrine Controversies in Early Christianity: Attitudes Towards Peter in Christian Writings of the First Two Centuries*, WUNT 15 (Tübingen: Mohr Siebeck, 1985).

later was Peter styled as the archetypical disciple and chief apostle much lauded by orthodox Christianity.

Conventionally, commentators on the Papias' notice about Mark conclude that the addition of Peter to the tradition was intended to provide a suspect Gospel with a patina of apostolic authority. Papias did make good use of the claim that Mark was Peter's "interpreter" to explain the apparent inadequacies of the second Gospel; and this may ultimately have provided Mark with additional credit to gain admission to the canon. However, the same cannot be said of other second-century Petrine texts, like the *Preaching of Peter* (c. 100–150), the *Apocalypse of Peter* (c. 135) and the *Gospel of Peter* (c. 150).[61] The mere ascription of Petrine authority to these apocryphal works was not a sufficient guarantee of their acceptance within the emerging orthodoxy. These works later failed to measure up to the *regula fidei* (Eusebius, *H.E.* 3.25.6–7), which Eusebius demonstrates by telling of Serapion's rejection of the use and reading of the *Gospel of Peter* in his churches (c. 195) according to just such a criterion (*H.E.* 6.12.1–6). Mark survived, prospered and was eventually canonised, therefore, not solely on the basis of the tradition linking it to Peter. It carried a certain gravitas of its own, despite lacking any apostolic credentials.

We have already noted that Papias' primary concern was to chart the transmission of the apostolic traditions. So it is entirely feasible that Peter's reputation in the first and second centuries might have enjoyed a "reciprocal confirmation" by claiming that the second Gospel was penned by Peter's interpreter Mark.[62] In the early decades of the second century when Peter's legacy was still ambiguous, the addition of such a well-established and long-recognised orthodox Gospel could only bolster Peter's status as the chief apostle. While Matthew's Gospel may have been the better choice, given its more positive portrait of Peter, it was already ascribed to an apostle. The same is true for John. Luke may have been an option; after all, Acts tells of Peter's pivotal role in the foundation of Christianity. But tradition had already yoked that Gospel to Paul. By placing Mark in the Petrine camp, Papias completes the set by ascribing all four Gospels to apostolic authors or to their companions. As a Christian Jew who may have been ideologically opposed to Paul and his disciples, Papias would have found the ascription of Mark to Peter a convenient conceit.

---

61 Black, *Mark*, 208–09.
62 Black, *Mark*, 209.

6 Conclusions

Papias and his source present Mark's relationship with Peter in much the same way as tradition understood Luke's role as companion and secretary to Paul. The earliest tradents of the tradition may have derived justification for this idea from 1Peter (5.13), where Mark is described as Peter's "son" and companion in Babylon (Rome). Unfortunately the fragmentary nature of the Papias notice makes it extremely difficult to draw any firm conclusions about the ultimate source of Papias' information. Despite Eusebius' testimony to the contrary, we cannot have any confidence in the chain of custody that might have provided some reassurance of reliability to the Papias notice. It would seem that his source was the presbyter John, who was a "follower" of the disciples; but we cannot now determine how Papias came by John's musings on Mark. We cannot even delineate from the Papias notice where the presbyter John's words end and Papias' extrapolations begin.

As we have demonstrated here, it must be remembered that Eusebius is citing Papias, and both the extent and the reliability of his citation cannot be verified – and the same is probably true of Papias' use of his source, the presbyter John. Eusebius probably not only changed his attitude towards Papias while quoting him, but also reproduced Papias with very specific aims in mind: Papias says only what Eusebius wants him to say. Within the context of Eusebius's *Historia Ecclesiastica*, Papias' remarks are part of the discussion about the acknowledged writings from earliest times (*H.E.* 3.3.3). For Eusebius, Papias' comments on Mark are incidental to his central concern and serve only to illustrate Papias' place in the transmission history of apostolic traditions. Similarly, Papias may have seen much to admire in Mark who, like himself, was a careful collector and accurate recorder of anecdotes about Jesus. Despite attempts to see in the Papias' notice an attack upon Mark, a closer reading of Papias' comments suggest otherwise. Papias is lauding Mark's Gospel because it bears the vestigial traces of its origins as a record of apostolic teachings. For Papias, and certainly for Eusebius too, the point at issue is apostolic succession (*H.E.* 1.1.1; 3.39.1.3.14), the unbroken chain securing the traditions of the apostles. About these things both Eusebius and Papias held strong opinions and a robust self-interest guided the results of both their enquiries. There are clear problems with the Papias notice, as there are with much else that has survived from the hand of Papias. Papias is far from being a trustworthy witness.

Many commentators have accordingly suggested that the association of Peter with the second evangelist is little more than hagiography. It has been widely assumed that Mark benefited greatly from its association with the chief apostle. However, the figure and stature of Peter also enjoyed an increase as a result of that claim. Moreover it seems possible that Papias may have been ideologically opposed to Paul and his heirs. The decades of the late first and early second centuries, saw a growing body of Pauline literature that must have loomed large for a Christian Jew like Papias. It is probable that the "books" that Papias disdained were the letters of Paul. In the light of these observations, the ascription of Mark to Peter served not only to defend Mark against accusation of inadequate order and inept style *via* an appeal to apostolic authority, but also to provide a literary bolster to the legacy of Peter as a bulwark against the increasingly dominant *Paulusbild* of the second century. This chapter and those others in this volume provide further support to the view that Mark may have more in common with Paul than with Peter. It may even be the case that Mark belonged to the library of texts originating in Pauline Christianity. If that proposition has any veracity, then, the Papias notice may be a simple case of robbing Paul to pay Peter.

Bibliography

Annand, Rupert. "Papias and the Four Gospels." *SJT* 9 (1956): 46–62.
Aune, David E. *The New Testament in Its Literary Environment.* Philadelphia, Pa.: Westminster Press, 1987.
Bacon, Benjamin W. *The Gospel of Mark: Its Composition and Date.* Oxford: Oxford University Press, 1925.
—, *Is Mark a Roman Gospel?* Cambridge: Cambridge University Press, 1919.
Bauckham, Richard. *Jesus and the Eyewitnesses: The Gospels as Eyewitness Testimony.* Grand Rapids, Mich.: Eerdmans, 2006.
Best, Ernest. *Following Jesus: Discipleship in the Gospel of Mark.* Sheffield: JSOT Press, 1981.
—, *Disciples and Discipleship: Studies in the Gospel According to Mark.* Edinburgh: T & T Clark, 1986.
Bird, Michael F. "Mark: Interpreter of Peter and Disciple of Paul," in: *Paul and the Gospels: Christologies, Conflicts and Convergences*, eds. Michael F. Bird and Joel Willitts. LNTS 411, 30–61. London: T & T Clark International, 2011.
Black, C. Clifton. *The Disciples According to Mark: Markan Redaction in Current Debate.* Sheffield: JSOT Press, 1989.
—, *Mark: Images of an Apostolic Interpreter.* Edinburgh: T & T Clark, 2001.
Botha, Pieter J. J. "The Historical Setting of Mark's Gospel: Problems and Possibilities." *JSNT* 16 (1993): 27–55.
Bovon, François. *Luke 1: A Commentary on the Gospel of Luke 1:1–9:50.* Hermeneia. Minneapolis, Minn.: Fortress Press, 2002.
Bruce, Frederick F. *The Canon of Scripture.* Downers Grove, Ill.: Intervarsity Press, 1988.
Collins, Adela Yarbro, *Mark: A Commentary.* Hermeneia. Minneapolis, Minn.: Fortress Press, 2007.
Conzelmann, Hans. *History of Primitive Christianity.* Nashville, Tenn.: Abingdon Press, 1973.
Crossley, James G. "Mark, Paul and the Question of Influences," in: *Paul and the Gospels: Christologies, Conflicts and Convergences*, eds. Michael F. Bird and Joel Willitts, 10–29. LNTS 411. London: T & T Clark International, 2011.
Donahue, John R., and Daniel J. Harrington. *The Gospel of Mark.* SP 2. Collegeville, Pa.: Liturgical Press, 2002.
Elmer, Ian J. *Paul, Jerusalem and the Judaisers: The Galatian Crisis in its Broadest Historical Context.* WUNT 2.258. Tübingen: Mohr Siebeck, 2009.
Fenton, John C. "Paul and Mark," in: *Studies in the Gospels: Essays in Memory of R. H. Lightfoot*, ed. Dennis E. Nineham, 89–112. Oxford: Blackwell, 1955.
Furnish, Victor Paul. "On Putting Paul in His Place." *JBL* 113 (1994): 3–17.
Gast, Frederick. "Synoptic Problem," in: *The Jerome Biblical Commentary*, eds. Raymond E. Brown, Joseph A. Fitzmyer and Roland A. Murphy, 2–6. London: Geoffrey Chapman, 1968.
Gnilka, Joachim. *Das Evangelium nach Markus.* 2 vols. Zurich: Benziger, 1978.
Goulder, Michael D. "Those Outside (Mk 4:10–12)." *NovT* 33 (1991): 289–302.
—, "Jesus, Resurrection and Christian Origins: A Response to N. T. Wright." *JSHS* 3 (2005): 187–95.
Grant, Frederick C. *The Earliest Gospel: Studies of the Evangelistic Tradition at Its Point of Crystallization in Writing.* New York, N.Y.: Abingdon-Cokesbury, 1943.

Grant, Robert M. *The Formation of the New Testament.* London: Hutchinson, 1965.
—, "Papias and the Gospels." *ATR* 25 (1943): 218–22.
Guelich, Robert A. *Mark 1–8:26.* WBC 34 A. Waco, Tex.: Word Books, 1989.
Gundry, Robert H. *Matthew: A Commentary on His Literary and Theological Art.* Grand Rapids, Mich.: Eerdmans, 1982.
—, *Mark: A Commentary on His Apology for the Cross.* Grand Rapids, Mich.: Eerdmans, 1993.
Gustafsson, Bernt, "Eusebius' Principles in Handling His Sources, as Found in His Church History, Books I-VII." *Studia Patristica* 4 (1961): 429–41.
Hegedus, Tim. "Midrash and Papias of Hierapolis." *BTB* 42 (2012): 30–35.
Henderson, Suzanne Watts. *Christology and Discipleship in the Gospel of Mark.* SNTSMS 135. Cambridge: Cambridge University Press, 2006.
Hengel, Martin. *Studies in the Gospel of Mark.* Philadelphia, Pa.: Fortress Press, 1985.
Hill, Charles E. *The Johannine Corpus in the Early Church.* Oxford: Oxford University Press, 2004.
—, "Papias of Hierapolis." *ExpT* 117 (2006): 309–15.
—, "What Papias Said About John (and Luke): A 'New' Papian Fragment." *JTS* 49 (1998): 582–629.
Hooker, Morna D. *The Gospel According to St. Mark.* Peabody, Mass.: Hendrickson, 1993.
Iverson, Kelly R. *Gentiles in the Gospel of Mark: "Even the Dogs under the Table Eat the Children's Crumbs".* LNTS 339. London: T & T Clark International, 2007.
Kee, Harold C. *Community of the New Age: Studies in Mark's Gospel.* Macon, Ga.: Mercer University Press, 1983.
Kelber, Werner H. *The Kingdom in Mark; a New Place and a New Time.* Philadelphia, Pa.: Fortress Press, 1974.
Kingsbury, Jack D. *Conflict in Mark: Jesus, Authorities, Disciples.* Minneapolis, Minn.: Fortress Press, 1989.
Körtner, Ulrich H. J. *Papias von Hierapolis: Ein Betrag zur Geschiche des Frühen Christentums.* FRLANT 133. Göttingen: Vandenhoek & Ruprecht, 1983.
Kürzinger, Josef. *Papias von Hierapolis und die Evangelien des Neuen Testaments: Gesammelte Aufsätze, Neuausgabe, und Übersetzung der Fragmente, Kommentierte Bibliographie.* Regensburg: Friedrich Pustet, 1983.
—, "Das Papiaszeugnis und die Erstgestalt des Matthäusevangeliums." *BZ* 4 (1960): 19–38.
—, "Die Aussage des Papias von Hierapolis zur Literarischen Form des Markusevangeliums." *BZ* 21 (1977): 245–64.
Malbon, Elizabeth Struthers. *In the Company of Jesus: Characters in Mark's Gospel.* Louisville, Ky.: Westminster John Knox Press, 2000.
Marcus, Joel. "Mark – Interpreter of Paul." *NTS* 46 (2000): 473–87.
—, *Mark 8–16: A New Translation with Introduction and Commentary.* AB 27. New Haven, Conn.: Yale University Press, 2009.
Martin, Ralph P. *Mark, Evangelist and Theologian.* Grand Rapids, Mich.: Zondervan, 1973.
Marxsen, Willi. *Introduction to the New Testament: An Approach to Its Problems.* Philadelphia, Pa.: Fortress Press, 1973.
Munck, Johannes. "Presbyters and Disciples of the Lord in Papias." *HTR* 52 (1959): 223–44.
Niederwimmer, Kurt. "Johannes Markus und die Frage Nach dem Verfasser des Zweiten Evangeliums." *ZNW* 58 (1969): 172–88.
Nielsen, Charles M. "Papias: Polemicist against Whom?" *TS* 35 (1974): 529–34.

Perumalil, A. C. "Are Not Papias and Irenaeus Competant to Report on the Gospels?" *ExpT* 91 (1980): 332–37.
Pesch, Rudolf. *Das Markusevangelium*. HTKNT. 2 vols. Freiburg: Herder, 1976, 1977.
Regul, Jürgen. *Die Antimarcionitischen Evangelienprologe*. Freiburg: Herder, 1969.
Sellew, Philip. "Eusebius and the Gospels," in: *Eusebius, Christianity and Judaism*, eds. Harold W. Attridge and Gohei Hatta. 110–38. Leiden: Brill, 1992.
Sim, David C. "The Gospel of Matthew, John the Elder and the Papias Tradition: A Response to R. H. Gundry." *HTS* 63 (2007): 283–99.
Skarsaune, Oskar. "Fragments of Jewish Christian Literature Quoted in Some Greek and Latin Fathers," in: *Jewish Believers in Jesus*, eds. Oskar Skarsaune and Reidar Hvalvik, 325–78. Peabody, Mass.: Hendrickson, 2007.
Smith, Terence V. *Petrine Controversies in Early Christianity: Attitudes Towards Peter in Christian Writings of the First Two Centuries*. WUNT 15. Tübingen: Mohr Siebeck, 1985.
Swartley, Willard M. *Violence Renounced: René Girard, Biblical Studies, and Peacemaking*. Telford, Pa.: Pandora Press, 2000.
Taylor, Vincent. *The Gospel According to St. Mark. The Greek Text with Introduction, Notes, and Indexes*. London: Macmillan, 1966.
Telford, William. R. *The Theology of the Gospel of Mark*. Cambridge: Cambridge University Press, 1999.
Trobisch, David. *Paul's Letter Collection: Tracing the Origins*. Minneapolis, Minn.: Fortress Press, 1994.
—, *The First Edition of the New Testament*. Oxford: Oxford University Press, 2000.
Weeden, Theodore J. *Mark – Traditions in Conflict*. Philadelphia, Pa.: Fortress Press, 1979.
—, "Polemics as a Case for Dissent: A Response to Richard Bauckham's *Jesus and the Eyewitnesses*." *JSHJ* 6 (2008): 211–24.
Yarbrough, Robert W. "The Date of Papias: A Reassessment." *JETS* 26 (1982): 181–91.
Zeichmann, Christopher B. "Papias as Rhetorician: Ekphrasis in the Bishop's Account of Judas' Death." *NTS* 56 (2010): 427–29.
Zuntz, Günther. *The Text of the Epistles: A Disquisition Upon the Corpus Paulinum*. Oxford: Oxford University Press, 1963.

Beiträger und Beiträgerinnen/
List of Contributors

Eve-Marie Becker ist Professorin für Neues Testament an der Universität Aarhus, Dänemark.

Lukas Bormann ist Professor für Neues Testament an der Universität Erlangen-Nürnberg, Deutschland.

Alan H. Cadwallader is a Senior Lecturer in the Faculty of Theology and Philosophy at the Canberra Campus of the Australian Catholic University.

Elizabeth V. Dowling is a Lecturer in the Faculty of Theology and Philosophy at the Ballarat Campus of the Australian Catholic University.

Ian J. Elmer is a Lecturer in the Faculty of Theology and Philosophy at the Brisbane Campus of the Australian Catholic University.

Nina Irrgang M.A. ist Studienrätin in München, Deutschland.

Andreas Lindemann ist em. Professor für Neues Testament an der Kirchlichen Hochschule Wuppertal-Bethel, Deutschland.

William Loader is Professor Emeritus of New Testament at Murdoch University, Perth, Australia, and External Research Collaborator, North-West University, South Africa.

John Painter is Professor of Theology at St Mark's National Theological Centre, Charles Sturt University, Canberra, Australia.

Wilhelm Pratscher ist em. Professor für Neues Testament an der Universität Wien, Österreich.

Udo Schnelle ist Professor für Neues Testament an der Universität Halle-Wittenberg, Deutschland.

Lornezo Scornaienchi ist Pfarrer an der Chiesa Evangelica der Waldenser in Zürich, Schweiz.

David C. Sim is an Associate Professor in the Faculty of Theology and Philosophy at the Melbourne Campus of the Australian Catholic University.

Thomas Söding ist Professor für Neues Testament an der Universität Bochum, Deutschland.

Jesper Svartvik is the Krister Stendahl Professor of Theology of Religions at the Centre for Theology and Religious Studies at Lund University, Sweden, and the Swedish Theological Institute in Jerusalem.

Michael Theobald ist em. Professor für Neues Testament an der Universität Tübingen, Deutschland.

Michael P. Theophilos is a Lecturer in the Faculty of Theology and Philosophy at the Melbourne Campus of the Australian Catholic University.

Florian Wilk ist Professor für Neues Testament an der Universität Göttingen, Deutschland.

Johannes Wischmeyer ist Vikar in Stuttgart, Deutschland.

Oda Wischmeyer ist em. Professorin für Neues Testament an der Universität Erlangen-Nürnberg.

Autorenregister/Index of Modern Authors

Aageson, J.W. 58. 68
Aejmelaeus, L. 635. 640
Agamben, G. 365
Aitken, E.B. 227. 228
Allen, W.C. 605. 606
Allison, D.C. 261f. 265f. 269f. 276. 559. 571. 581. 584
Anderson, J.C. 559. 583
Annand, R. 669. 698
Avemarie, F. 126. 364f.
Arzt-Grabner, P. 567. 583
Arndt, W.F. 235
Aune, D.E. 48. 68. 559. 583

Babcock, W.S. 557. 583
Bacon, B.W. 53. 59. 68. 452. 661. 672. 679. 686
Bailey, J.L. 557. 561. 583
Balch, D.L. 559. 569. 576. 583
Barclay, J.M.G. 561. 583
Barrett, C.K. 45. 68. 76. 77. 557. 583. 619
Bauckham, R. 598. 610. 672. 674. 676. 682–84. 690. 691
Bauer, B. 24
Bauer, W. 235
Baur, F.C. V.1. 3. 5. 10. 20–25. 29f. 33. 35. 39. 42. 47. 49. 68. 73. 508. 687
Beaton, R.C. 605. 606. 607
Beattie, G. 562. 582. 583
Beavis, M.A. 428. 438
Becker, E.-M. 8
Becker, J. 660. 667
Beer, J. 66. 68
Bell, R.H. 444
Belo, F. 572. 583
Bendemann, R. von 624
Berger, K. 522
Best, E. 92. 560. 568. 583. 683. 690. 696
Bieler, A. 222. 231. 234
Billerbeck, P. 161. 188
Bird, M.F. 57. 61. 63. 68. 434. 438. 440. 443. 446. 453. 455. 460. 526. 532. 542. 543. 553. 573. 583. 683. 688

Black, C.C. 45. 49. 51. 53. 68f. 92. 672–674. 677. 679f. 683. 693. 696
Blass, F. 50. 68
Bockmuehl, M. 56. 68
Boring, E. 557. 583
Bormann, L. 9f.
Bornkamm, G. 45. 46. 68
Botha, P.J.J. 672. 686. 696
Boyarin, D. 182. 657. 677
Bovon, F. 637. 681. 696
Bradshaw, P.F. 223
Brandon, S.G.F. 591
Braxton, B.R. 564. 583
Brodie, T.L. 591
Brown, R.E. 86. 87. 88. 89. 682. 696
Bultmann, R. 253f. 322. 365. 401. 520. 648f. 659
Byrne, B. 47. 64. 68. 439

Cadwallader, A. 9. 558. 564. 570. 574. 578. 583. 585f.
Callahan, A.D. 167. 186. 565. 584
Canart, P. 564. 586
Cancik, H. 406
Carter, W. 557. 559. 572f. 575f. 584
Clarke, G.W. 49. 65. 68. 557. 586
Claußen, C. 111
Collins, A. Yarbro 51. 55. 61. 68. 86. 132. 225. 229. 236. 439. 673. 696
Collins, R.F. 76. 77. 221. 223. 226. 228
Conlin, D.A. 578. 579. 582
Conzelmann, H. 672. 686. 696
Cooley, A.E. 577. 584.
Cope, L. 604
Coutsoumpos, P. 226. 231. 234
Cranfield, C.E.B. 48. 52. 55. 58. 60. 68
Crossan, J.D. 86. 88. 89. 90
Crossley, J.G. 57. 68. 423. 432. 434. 452–455. 458. 460. 526. 528. 530. 532. 553. 670. 696
Crouch, J.E. 576. 584
Cullmann, O. 363

D'Angelo, M.R. 561. 584

Danker, F.W. 235
Davies, W.D. 559. 584. 591
de Boer, M. 78. 81f.
Debrunner, A. 50. 68
Deissmann, A. 62. 68
Delling, G. 131. 363
Denaux, A. 626
Dibelius, M. 53. 69. 249
Dinter, P.E. 58. 69
DiRoccolino, G.C. 577. 584
Dobschütz, E. von 362
Douglas, M. 512f.
Dodd, C.H. 48. 69
Donahue, J.R. 53. 58. 84. 98. 423. 430.
 568. 584. 672. 698
Donfried, K.P. 46. 59. 86. 87. 88f
Doole, J.A. 607. 608. 611
Dowd, S. 427f. 569. 572. 584
Dowling, E. 7. 234f. 238
Downs, D.J. 83f. 565. 584
Droysen, J.G. 393
Dungan, D.L. 604
Dschulnigg, P. 51. 69
Dunn, J.D.G. 46. 57–59. 74. 78. 80–84.
 162. 186. 443f. 446. 448f. 528. 536. 553
Du Toit, A. 443
Du Toit, D.S. 381
Dunderberg, I. 663

Eastman, D.L. 557. 584
Ebner, M. 354
Edelstein, L. 61. 69
Edwards, J.R. 61. 69
Eichorn, A. 222. 227. 231
Eisenbaum, P. 161. 171. 186
Ellis, E.E. 58. 69. 557. 569. 669
Elmer, I.J. 9. 74. 78. 80–84. 569. 599. 688.
 696
Enslin, M.S. 629. 634
Esler, P.F. 78. 81f.
Ettl, C. 317
Evans, C.A. 58. 63. 69. 429. 577f.

Farmer, W.R. 604
Farrer, A.M. 604
Feine, P. 40f.
Feldmeier, R. 364f.

Fenton, J.C. 46. 53. 69. 70. 460. 682. 696
Fitzmyer, J.A. 46. 49. 56. 61. 76. 77. 628.
 682. 696
Forster, E.M. 175. 186
Foster, P. 596f.
Foucault, M. 582. 584
Fowler, R.M. 182. 186
Fredriksen, P. 157. 169f. 186
French, D. 577. 586
Frend, W.H.C. 65. 69
Friedrich, G. 315f. 448
Frilingos, C. 690. 696
Furnish, V.P. 565. 584

Gager, J. G. 157. 168. 172. 182. 186
Garner-Smith, P. 659
Gast, F. 682. 696
Genette, G. 146
Georgi, D. 45. 69. 565. 584
Gingrich, F.W. 235
Glancy, J. 167. 186. 565. 584
Gnilka, J. 52. 69. 558. 584. 674. 696
Goodacre, M. 604
Goulder, M.D. 53. 69. 74. 83. 90. 93. 591.
 604. 621f. 671. 697
Grant, R.M. 600. 613. 689. 691. 697
Green, S.J. 579. 584
Grundmann, W. 52. 69
Güder, E. 30
Guelich, R.A. 430. 680. 681. 697
Gundry, R.H. 88. 571f584. 674–678. 681.
 685. 697f.
Gustafsson, B. 676. 678. 697
Guttenberger, G. 135

Haacker, K. 139
Haenchen, E. 49. 69. 395. 640
Hagner, D.A. 607
Hahn, F. 343. 428f. 436
Hamerton-Kelly, R.G. 161. 186
Hare, D.R.A. 224
Harland, P.A. 567. 584
Harnack, A. von 35
Harrington, H.K. 512
Harrington, D.J. 56. 69. 423. 430. 568. 584.
 595. 673. 698
Harris, H. 73

Hays, R.   58. 69
Headlam, A.C.   61. 71
Hegedus, T.   677f. 688. 697
Henderson, S.W.   684. 697
Hengel, M.   50–52. 69. 265
Hense, O.   569. 587
Hicks, R.   570. 585
Hilgenfeld, A.   21f. 29–32
Hill, C.E.   676f. 688. 697
Hill, D.   607
Hitzig, F.   31
Hofius, O.   59. 69
Holliday, P.   578. 585
Holsten, K.   33–36. 39. 41
Holtzmann, H.J.   30–33. 35. 37. 39. 283
Hooker, M.D.   51. 56. 61. 64. 67. 224. 673. 671
Hopkins, K.   581. 585
Horn, F.W.   332
Horrell, D.   566. 585
Horsley, R.A.   64. 70. 573. 585
Hort, F.J.A.   46. 56. 70

Ilan, T.   573. 585
Incigneri, B.   51. 52. 64. 70
Irrgang, N.   6
Iverson, K.   55. 70. 94. 602. 673. 697

Jervis, L.A.   46–48. 64. 70
Jewett, R.   45. 47. 48. 69
Jospe, R.   157. 187
Jülicher, A.   40

Käsemann, E.   48. 70. 641
Keck, L.E.   57. 70
Kee, H.C.   674. 697
Keenan, J.G.   51. 70
Kelber, W.H.   176. 186. 673. 697
Kidd, R.M.   568. 585
Kiley, M.   558. 565. 585
Kingsbury, J.D.   683. 697
Kipling, R.   178. 181. 186
Koch, D.-A.   262. 343. 409. 630f.
Kloppenborg, J.   51. 70
Koester, H.   45. 50. 70. 558. 577. 585
Koperski, V.   167. 186
Körtner, U.H.J.   678. 697

Kreitzer, L.   577. 587
Kuhn, H.-W.   252. 560. 585
Kürzinger, J.   673. 680–682. 692. 697
Kuula, K.   46. 70

Lampe, P.   61. 70
Lane, W.L.   52. 70. 175f. 572. 585
Larsson, G   166. 186
Last, R.   605
Lawson, V.   234f238
Leppä, O.   558f. 585
Lincicum, D.   59. 70
Lincoln, A.T.   561. 585
Lindemann, A.   7. 629. 640
Loader, W.R.G.   8. 94. 435. 454. 608
Longenecker, B.W.   64. 70. 565. 585
Lüdemann, G.   74. 77. 80. 84. 557. 587
Luz, U.   591. 592. 596. 606f. 609

Majoros-Danowski, J.   122
McGowan, A.B.   222
McLaren, J.S.   66. 70. 558. 584
McNicol, A.   604
McRae, R.M.   226
Maccoby, H.   226
MacDonald, D.R.   566. 573. 586
MacDonald, M.Y.   558. 561. 586
Magness, J.   179. 186
Malbon, E. Struthers   94. 178. 186. 683. 697
Mann, C.S.   54. 70
Marcus, J.   53. 56f. 59. 61–63. 70. 75. 86–89. 157f. 186. 224. 229. 423. 428. 438f. 452. 455. 457. 460f. 672f. 691
Marshall, C.D.   426. 429. 433. 438. 440
Martin, D.B.   564. 586
Martin, R.P.   687. 691. 697
Martyn, J.L.   74. 78–82
Marxsen, W.   49. 54. 63. 70. 672. 697
Mason, S.   557. 586
Meade, D.G.   559. 586
Meier, J.P.   607
Merklein, H.   340
Metzger, B.M.   227. 574. 586
Meyer, E.   395
Meyer, M.   164. 168
Millard, A.   51. 70
Michie, D.   171. 178. 187

Mitchell, S.   577. 586
Moloney, F.J.   54. 70. 572. 584
Mommsen, Th.   393
Montefiore, C.G.   163. 187
Moore, S.D.   559. 583
Morgenthaler, R.   626
Moxnes, H.   575. 585
Munck, J.   58. 70. 687. 697
Munro, W.   559. 564f. 584
Murphy, R.A.   682. 696
Murphy-O'Connor, J.   80
Myers, C.   568. 585

Nanos, M.D.   157. 169–172. 187
Neyrey, J.H.   513. 520
Niebuhr, K.-W.   141
Niederwimmer, K.   672. 686. 697
Nielsen, C.M.   687–690. 697
Nickle, K.F.   565. 586
Nineham, D.E.   54. 70. 174. 181. 671. 696
Norden, E.   395
Nutton, V.   61. 69

O'Brien, P.T.   447
Outler, A.C.   45. 70
Overbeck, F.   395
Overman, J.A.   594

Painter, J.   8. 56. 71. 87–90. 93f. 157f. 527. 537. 552f.
Parker, D.   568. 586
Payne, P.B.   564. 586
Peabody, P.B.   604
Perkins, P.   93
Perrin, N.   604
Perumalil, A.C.   676. 698
Pervo, R.I.   626
Pesch, R.   251
Pfleiderer, O.   32. 35–37. 42
Pieta, G.D.   576. 586
Plevnik, J.   167. 187
Plümacher, E.   395
Pokorny, P.   558. 586
Powell, M.A.   179. 187
Pratscher, W.   9
Pritz, R.A.   177. 187

Quesnell, Q.   55. 71

Rad, G. von   58. 71
Räisänen, H.   53. 71. 522. 532. 535f. 553
Regul, J.   673. 687. 693. 698
Rehak, P.   579. 586
Rehkopf, F.   50. 68
Reid, B.E.   231. 239
Ritschl, A.   22. 35. 38
Repschinski, B.   94. 435. 454. 594. 608
Rhoads, D.   177f. 181
Richards, E.R.   600
Riches, J.K.   607
Robertson, A.T.   50. 71
Romaniuk, K.   57
Rose, C.B.   580. 584. 586
Rudolph, D.   56
Rusam, D.   630

Sabin, M.N.   235. 237
Sanday, W.   61
Sanders, E.P.   166. 447. 448
Sawicki, M.   235f.
Sawyer, J.F.A.   182
Schenk, W.   53. 636
Schmidt, T.E.   63
Schmithals, W.   139
Schneemelcher, W.   557
Schnelle, U.   7. 317. 319. 321. 340. 558. 660
Schottroff, L.   222. 231. 234
Schrage, W.   265. 576
Schreiber, S.   346
Schweizer, E.   52. 223. 234
Scornaienchi, L.   2. 8
Seeley, D.   53. 439
Segal, A.F.   161. 170. 172
Seifrid, M.A.   444
Seim, T.K.   580
Sellew, P.   676. 679
Senior, D.   64
Severy, B.   578. 582
Shelly, I.   564
Sherwood, Y.   180
Silva, M.   444. 446
Sim, D.C.   2. 6. 9. 74. 77. 80f. 85. 96. 156f. 188. 194. 558. 573. 584. 590–594. 598f. 601. 603–605. 608–611. 678f.

Skarsaune, O.   688
Smit, P.-B.   222. 229. 232
Smith, A.   167
Smith, D.E.   221. 223. 226
Smith, T.V.   692
Söding, Th.   8. 424–428. 430. 437
Soden, H. von   32
Solomon, N.   165
Sordie, M.   65
Spitaler, P.   575
Sprinkle, P.M .   443
Standhartinger, A.   558. 586
Stanton, G.N.   590. 610
Stegemann, W.   513
Stendahl, K.   160f164f. 187
Stern, D.   183
Stern, G.   157. 183. 187
Strack, H.L.   161
Strecker, G.   317. 319. 321
Streeter, B.H.   605f.
Svartvik, J.   6. 57. 157f. 169. 175f. 178. 180. 432. 434. 452
Swartley, W.   178. 183. 189
Swete, H.B.   50

Tannehill, R.   93. 176. 188
Tarazi, P.N.   223–233
Taussig, H.E.   223
Taylor, J.   221. 223
Taylor, V.   678. 681. 683
Telford, W.R.   53. 86. 93–224. 423. 428. 432. 438. 452. 455. 457. 460. 674
Theissen, G.   56. 521. 594. 595
Theobald, M.   7. 640
Theophilos, M.   6
Thielman, F.   64
Thonemann, P.   577
Todd, S.C.   567. 581
Tolbert, M.A.   178
Tomson, P.J.   162
Tregiarri, S.   569
Trobisch, D.   689
Trocmé, É.   86. 88f.
Tuckett, C.M.   603. 605
Tyson, J.B.   93. 432

Van Aarde, A.   575. 587

Vander Broeck, L.D.   559. 561. 583
Van Nijf, O.M.   581. 587
Volkmar, G.H.J.Ph.   23–33. 36. 39–41. 508f.

Wachsmuth, C.   569
Wahlen, C.   514
Walker, J.   564
Walker, W.O.   561. 563
Wallace-Hadrill, A.   576
Warner, M.   573f.
Watson, F.   81–83. 164. 444. 448
Watts, R.E.   57f. 71. 684
Weeden, T.J.   432. 672. 683
Wefald, E.   94
Weiß, J.   283
Weisse, Ch.H.   23
Weizsäcker, C.H.   32
Wenham, D.   672. 683
Werner, M.   V.1f. 5f. 10. 15. 45. 53. 59. 71. 177. 283. 510f.
Wernle, P.   38–40
Westerholm, S.   159. 188. 447
White, H.V.   393
Wilckens, U.   634
Wilk, F.   6
Wilke, Ch.G.   23
Willitts, J.   596. 598
Wilson, R.M.   557. 586
Winn, A.   51. 66
Wischmeyer, J.   5
Wischmeyer, O.   7. 137
Witherington, B.   222. 533. 553. 576
Witulski, Th.   318
Wolter, M.   321. 335f. 343
Wong, E.K.C.   339. 353. 509. 518. 595. 632. 640
Wrede, W.   39

Yarbrough, O.L.   562
Yarbrough, R.W.   676. 678
Yeung, M.W.   459

Zahn, Th.   628f.
Zangenberg, J.   596f. 600
Zanker, P.   576
Zeichmann, C.B.   673
Zuntz, G.   689

Sachregister

Apokalyptik/apokalyptisch 364f. 368f. 373. 380–383. 388
Apostelkonvent 284
Autobiographie/autobiographisch 393. 397. 402f. 405f. 408. 418

Bekenntnis/Glaubensbekenntnis/Glaubenssatz/Credo 248. 251. 253. 255–260. 277
Beschneidung/beschneidungsfrei 284f. 301f. 308
Brief/Freundschaftsbrief/philosophischer Brief 285f.

Christologie 364f. 378. 389. 625. 631. 637
Credo s. Bekenntnis

Doppelgebot 466. 469–475. 478. 480f. 495f.

Einfluss 505. 507–511
Erinnerung s. Memoria
Eschatologie 363. 365
Ethnos (ἔθνος)/ethnisch 104. 135. 137f. 140. 143f. 147f.
Ethos 109–112. 116. 136. 143
Evangelium/εὐαγγέλιον 4. 7. 25. 27. 32f. 283–286. 288–299. 300. 313–349. 351–356

Gegenwart 365. 369. 371–373. 375. 377. 381. 384
Geheimnistheorie 290f. 306
Gericht/richten/Gerichtsansage 340. 348. 351–353. 356
Geschichte/Geschichtlichkeit/Geschichtsbegriff/geschichtlich 19f. 24f. 364f. 369f. 371f. 374f. 377–379. 384f. 393–419
Geschichts- bzw. Weltdeutung 117f. 120. 127
Gesetz 286f. 301–304. 308. 465–468. 470–477. 481–484. 486–497. 650. 652f. 657

Glaube/πίστις/glauben 286. 289. 293. 297. 299–301. 303. 308. 325. 328. 331f. 340. 343. 348. 355. 510f. 515f. 518. 639. 640
Gottessohn 283. 289–292. 294f. 298. 300. 305f. 308

Heidenmission 21
Heilsgeschichte/heilsgeschichtlich 117f. 121. 131. 133. 142f. 148. 364f. 369
Historiographie 393
Historismus/historisch 20f. 23
Hoheitstitel 295

Identität(-smarker) 108f. 136f. 143
Indikativ-Imperativ 657f.
Israel 628. 630. 632f. 637. 642f.

Jesus-Wort/Logion 518f. 521–523
Jüngerschaft 467

Kaiserkult 316–318. 320–323. 339. 354
Konstruktion (von Geschichte) 393–396. 398–400. 402f. 405–412. 415–419
Kreuz/Kreuzigung/Gekreuzigter 246. 252f. 258f. 263. 266. 650f. 657. 661. 665. 667
Kreuz(estheologie) 283. 286f. 289–296. 298. 300. 304–306. 308

Liebesgebot 465–466. 468. 476. 481f. 484–488. 491–497
Literatur (christliche) 13f.

Markus 11–13
Memoria/Erinnerung 243. 246–248. 264
Mission/missionarisch/Missionare 321. 324–326. 331f. 342. 344. 351. 353

Nachfolgesprüche 349
Nächstenliebe 465–467. 469–481. 485–487. 490f. 495–497
Narrativität/narrativ/narratio 393–395. 402f. 405f. 408. 412. 415. 419

Opfer/Opfergabe 319 f. 334. 342
Oralität (sekundäre) 648. 657. 662–668

Paraklet 655 f.
Passion/Passion Jesu/Passionsüberlieferung 243. 246. 251. 254 f. 263. 275 f.
Passions- und Ostererzählung 245. 247. 250. 252–266. 257. 259 f. 266. 276
Paulinismus/Antipaulinismus 10. 21. 23. 29 f. 32. 35. 38 f. 41 f. 508. 510
Paulus 11–13
Personenzentrierte Darstellung 415

Rechtfertigung 639 f.
Reinheit/Unreinheit 505. 510–515. 518–524
Religionsgeschichtliche Schule 38–41
Schöpfung 368 f. 370 f. 372–374. 380. 383 f.
Schriftverständnis (bzw. -hermeneutik) 189. 191 f. 195 f. 207–210

Schriftverwendung 189–219
– Formen 189–198
– Frühchristliche Vorgaben 190 f. 195 f. 198. 200 f. 204. 206 f. 209 f.
– Textgestalt 201–207. 210
– Quelltexte 192–201. 210
Speisegebote 515
Starke/Schwache 515–517

Tendenzkritik/tendenzkritisch 21. 29 f. 33. 39. 41 f.
Theologie/theologische Konzepte 4. 12. 15
Tübinger Schule 20. 23 f. 31. 33. 35. 38. 40

Universalismus/universalistisch/universal 22. 31 f. 41. 637. 642. 643

Vergangenheit 365. 371–373. 377. 384

Zeit/-konzept 361–389
Zukunft 365. 369. 370–374. 377. 384

Index of Subjects

Anti-Paulinism 590–603
Apocalyptic 64. 542f. 543. 689
Apostles 47. 75–77. 533f. 694
Apostolic Council 80f
Authority 48. 557f. 561–65. 580. 590. 692–94. 695

Canon/Canonicity 527f. 557–59. 561. 681–83. 687. 690. 694
Christian Jews 543. 594. 688–89
Christology 59–61. 159. 457f.
Circumcision 78. 81. 169–71. 527. 534f. 538. 545–47
Collection, the 83–85
Cross, Theology of 59–63. 66. 179. 671f. 674
Commandments 60. 159–161. 166–169. 171. 184. 570. 608. 686–89

Dietary Laws 56f. 67. 177. 530f. 536. 545
Disciples (of Jesus) 90–94.
Discipleship 63–66. 568–70. 582. 682–84

Eschatology 46f. 441f. 457. 689. 693
Exorcisms 426–29

Family (of Jesus) 85–90
Faith 423–64

Gentile mission 94. 157. 170f. 175. 182f. 184. 542–49. 671
Gospel 47–50. 52f. 56. 160–62. 169–71. 173–75. 527–33. 538. 540. 671–673. 680–82

Household codes 569–76

Israel 57–59. 66. 164–168. 170–72. 182f. 534–36. 540–45. 551

Jerusalem Church 75–85
John Mark 224f. 630f. 648f. 672–74. 692
Judaism 159–61. 163f. 172. 538–42. 545–51. 671. 688
Justification 161. 166. 529. 534

Last Supper, the 221–41
Law 55–57. 60. 169–172. 176. 444–48,451–54. 529–32. 535–42. 544. 547–52. 572f. 580. 672. 686–87
Law-free Gospel/mission 79–80. 81. 90. 169–72. 527. 529–32. 538–40.

Miracles 429–33
Mission 48–56. 165–78. 524. 534–39. 542–44. 550–52. 675. 687

Purity 161. 166. 541f. 550–52. 529–34.

Slaves/Slavery 62. 160–162. 165f. 168f. 560. 566–568. 684
Soteriology 46. 55f. 453–57. 543. 560. 564. 565–67. 569

Theology 46. 59. 61f. 157–66. 168f. 171–74. 182f. 671
Tradition, Patristic 52f. 672–75. 678–80. 685f. 691–93
Transmission History 573. 675–80. 694
Tübingen School 73f.

Universalism 157. 164–69. 173

Women 169. 234–37. 238f. 563f. 573. 578–80. 684

www.ingramcontent.com/pod-product-compliance
Lightning Source LLC
Chambersburg PA
CBHW052008290426
44112CB00014B/2157